Twentieth-Century Literary Criticism

Guide to Gale Literary Criticism Series

When you need to review criticism of literary works, these are the Gale series to use:

If the author's death date is:	You should turn to:
After Dec. 31, 1959 (or author is still living)	**_CONTEMPORARY LITERARY CRITICISM_** for example: Jorge Luis Borges, Anthony Burgess, Ernest Hemingway, Iris Murdoch
1900 through 1959	**_TWENTIETH-CENTURY LITERARY CRITICISM_** for example: Willa Cather, F. Scott Fitzgerald, Henry James, Mark Twain, Virginia Woolf
1800 through 1899	**_NINETEENTH-CENTURY LITERATURE CRITICISM_** for example: Fyodor Dostoevsky, Nathaniel Hawthorne, George Sand, William Wordsworth
1400 through 1799	**_LITERATURE CRITICISM FROM 1400 TO 1800_** **_(excluding Shakespeare)_** for example: Anne Bradstreet, Alexander Pope, François Rabelais, Phillis Wheatley **_SHAKESPEAREAN CRITICISM_** Shakespeare's plays and poetry
Antiquity through 1399	**_CLASSICAL AND MEDIEVAL LITERATURE CRITICISM_** for example: Dante, Homer, Plato, Sophocles, Vergil

Gale also publishes related criticism series:

CHILDREN'S LITERATURE REVIEW

This series covers authors of all eras who have written for the preschool through high school audience.

SHORT STORY CRITICISM

This series covers the major short fiction writers of all nationalities and periods of literary history.

POETRY CRITICISM

This series covers poets of all nationalities, movements, and periods of literary history.

DRAMA CRITICISM

This series covers playwrights of all nationalities and periods of literary history.

BLACK LITERATURE CRITICISM

This three-volume set presents criticism of works by major black writers of the past two hundred years.

WORLD LITERATURE CRITICISM, 1500 TO THE PRESENT

This six-volume set provides excerpts from criticism on 225 authors from the Renaissance to the present.

ISSN 0276-8178

Volume 21

Twentieth-Century Literary Criticism

**Excerpts from Criticism of the
Works of Novelists, Poets, Playwrights,
Short Story Writers, and Other Creative Writers
Who Lived between 1900 and 1960,
from the First Published Critical
Appraisals to Current Evaluations**

**Dennis Poupard
Editor**

**Marie Lazzari
Thomas Ligotti
Associate Editors**

 Gale Research Inc. • *DETROIT* • *WASHINGTON, D.C.* • *LONDON*

Contents

Preface 7

Authors to Be Featured in *TCLC*, Volumes 22 and 23 11

Additional Authors to Appear in Future Volumes 13

Appendix 463

Preface

It is impossible to overvalue the importance of literature in the intellectual, emotional, and spiritual evolution of humanity. Literature is that which both lifts us out of everyday life and helps us to better understand it. Through the fictive lives of such characters as Anna Karenina, Jay Gatsby, or Leopold Bloom, our perceptions of the human condition are enlarged, and we are enriched.

Literary criticism can also give us insight into the human condition, as well as into the specific moral and intellectual atmosphere of an era, for the criteria by which a work of art is judged reflects contemporary philosophical and social attitudes. Literary criticism takes many forms: the traditional essay, the book or play review, even the parodic poem. Criticism can also be of several types: normative, descriptive, interpretive, textual, appreciative, generic. Collectively, the range of critical response helps us to understand a work of art, an author, an era.

Scope of the Series

Twentieth-Century Literary Criticism (TCLC) is designed to serve as an introduction for the student of twentieth-century literature to the authors of the period 1900 to 1960 and to the most significant commentators on these authors. The great poets, novelists, short story writers, playwrights, and philosophers of this period are by far the most popular writers for study in high school and college literature courses. Since a vast amount of relevant critical material confronts the student, *TCLC* presents significant passages from the most important published criticism to aid students in the location and selection of commentaries on authors who died between 1900 and 1960.

The need for *TCLC* was suggested by the usefulness of the Gale series *Contemporary Literary Criticism (CLC)*, which excerpts criticism on current writing. Because of the difference in time span under consideration (*CLC* considers authors who were still living after 1959), there is no duplication of material between *CLC* and *TCLC*. For further information about *CLC* and Gale's other criticism series, users should consult the Guide to Gale Literary Criticism Series preceding the title page in this volume.

Each volume of *TCLC* is carefully compiled to include authors who represent a variety of genres and nationalities and who are currently regarded as the most important writers of this era. In addition to major authors, *TCLC* also presents criticism on lesser-known writers whose significant contributions to literary history are important to the study of twentieth-century literature.

Each author entry in *TCLC* is intended to provide an overview of major criticism on an author. Therefore, the editors include fifteen to twenty authors in each 600-page volume (compared with approximately fifty authors in a *CLC* volume of similar size) so that more attention may be given to an author. Each author entry represents a historical survey of the critical response to that author's work: some early criticism is presented to indicate initial reactions, later criticism is selected to represent any rise or decline in the author's reputation, and current retrospective analyses provide students with a modern view. The length of an author entry is intended to reflect the amount of critical attention the author has received from critics writing in English, and from foreign criticism in translation. Critical articles and books that have not been translated into English are excluded. Every attempt has been made to identify and include excerpts from the seminal essays on each author's work.

An author may appear more than once in the series because of the great quantity of critical material available, or because of a resurgence of criticism generated by events such as an author's centennial or anniversary celebration, the republication or posthumous publication of an author's works, or the publication of a newly translated work. Generally, a few author entries in each volume of *TCLC* feature criticism on single works by major authors who have appeared previously in the series. Only those individual works that have been the subjects of vast amounts of criticism and are widely studied in literature classes are selected for this in-depth treatment. Thomas Mann's *Der Zauberberg (The Magic Mountain)* and Bernard Shaw's *Man and Superman* are examples of such entries in *TCLC*, Volume 21.

Organization of the Book

An author entry consists of the following elements: author heading, biographical and critical introduction, principal works, excerpts of criticism (each followed by a bibliographical citation), and an additional bibliography for further reading.

- The *author heading* consists of the author's full name, followed by birth and death dates. The unbracketed portion of the name denotes the form under which the author most commonly wrote. If an author wrote consistently under a pseudonym, the pseudonym will be listed in the author heading and the real name given in parentheses on the first line of the biographical and critical introduction. Also located at the beginning of the introduction to the author entry are any name variations under which an author wrote, including transliterated forms for authors whose languages use nonroman alphabets. Uncertainty as to a birth or death date is indicated by a question mark.

- The *biographical and critical introduction* contains background information designed to introduce the reader to an author and to the critical debate surrounding his or her work. Parenthetical material following many of the introductions provides references to biographical and critical reference series published by Gale, including *Children's Literature Review, Contemporary Authors, Dictionary of Literary Biography, Something about the Author,* and past volumes of *TCLC.*

- Most *TCLC* entries include *portraits* of the author. Many entries also contain illustrations of materials pertinent to an author's career, including holographs of manuscript pages, title pages, dust jackets, letters, or representations of important people, places, and events in an author's life.

- The *list of principal works* is chronological by date of first book publication and identifies the genre of each work. In the case of foreign authors where there are both foreign language publications and English translations, the title and date of the first English-language edition are given in brackets. Unless otherwise indicated, dramas are dated by first performance, not first publication.

- *Criticism* is arranged chronologically in each author entry to provide a useful perspective on changes in critical evaluation over the years. All titles by the author featured in the critical entry are printed in boldface type to enable the user to ascertain without difficulty the works being discussed. Also for purposes of easier identification, the critic's name and the publication date of the essay are given at the beginning of each piece of criticism. Unsigned criticism is preceded by the title of the journal in which it appeared. When an anonymous essay is later attributed to a critic, the critic's name appears in brackets at the beginning of the excerpt and in the bibliographical citation. Many critical entries in *TCLC* also contain translated material to aid users. Unless otherwise noted, translations within brackets are by the editors; translations within parentheses are by the author of the excerpt.

- Critical essays are prefaced by *explanatory notes* as an additional aid to students using *TCLC.* The explanatory notes provide several types of useful information, including: the reputation of a critic; the importance of a work of criticism; the specific type of criticism (biographical, psychoanalytic, structuralist, etc.); a synopsis of the criticism; and the growth of critical controversy or changes in critical trends regarding an author's work. In many cases, these notes cross-reference the work of critics who agree or disagree with each other. Dates in parentheses within the explanatory notes refer to a book publication date when they follow a book title and to an essay date when they follow a critic's name.

- A complete *bibliographical citation* designed to facilitate location of the original essay or book by the interested reader follows each piece of criticism. An asterisk (*) at the end of a citation indicates that the essay is on more than one author.

- The *additional bibliography* appearing at the end of each author entry suggests further reading on the author. In some cases it includes essays for which the editors could not obtain reprint rights. An asterisk (*) at the end of a citation indicates that the essay is on more than one author.

An appendix lists the sources from which material in each volume has been reprinted. It does not, however, list every book or periodical consulted in the preparation of the volume.

Cumulative Indexes

Each volume of *TCLC* includes a cumulative index to authors listing all the authors who have appeared in *Contemporary Literary Criticism, Twentieth-Century Literary Criticism, Nineteenth-Century Literature Criticism,* and *Literature Criticism from 1400 to 1800,* along with cross-references to the Gale series *Children's Literature Review, Authors in the News, Contemporary Authors, Contemporary Authors Autobiography Series, Dictionary of Literary Biography, Something about the Author, Something about the Author Autobiography Series,* and *Yesterday's Authors of Books for Children.* Users will welcome this cumulated author index as a useful tool for locating an author within the various series. The index, which lists birth and death dates when available, will be particularly valuable for those authors who are identified with a certain period but whose death date causes them to be placed in another, or for those authors whose careers span two periods. For example, F. Scott Fitzgerald is found in *TCLC,* yet a writer often associated with him, Ernest Hemingway, is found in *CLC.*

Each volume of *TCLC* also includes a cumulative nationality index. Author names are arranged alphabetically under their respective nationalities and followed by the volume numbers in which they appear.

A cumulative index to critics is another useful feature in *TCLC*. Under each critic's name are listed the authors on whom the critic has written and the volume and page where the criticism may be found.

Acknowledgments

No work of this scope can be accomplished without the cooperation of many people. The editors especially wish to thank the copyright holders of the excerpted criticism included in this volume, the permissions managers of many book and magazine publishing companies for assisting us in securing reprint rights, and Anthony Bogucki for assistance with copyright research. We are also grateful to the staffs of the Detroit Public Library, the Library of Congress, University of Detroit Library, University of Michigan Library, and Wayne State University Library for making their resources available to us.

Suggestions Are Welcome

In response to various suggestions, several features have been added to *TCLC* since the series began, including: explanatory notes to excerpted criticism that provide important information regarding critics and their work; a cumulative author index listing authors in all Gale literary criticism series; entries devoted to criticism on a single work by a major author; and more extensive illustrations.

Readers who wish to suggest authors to appear in future volumes, or who have other suggestions, are cordially invited to write the editors.

Authors to Be Featured in *TCLC*, Volumes 22 and 23

Sherwood Anderson (American short story writer and novelist)—Among the most original and influential writers in early twentieth-century American literature, Anderson is the author of brooding, introspective works that explore the effects of the unconscious upon human life. Anderson's "hunger to see beneath the surface of lives" was best expressed in the short stories comprising *Winesburg, Ohio: A Group of Tales of Ohio Small Town Life. TCLC* will devote an entire entry to critical discussion of this work.

Henri Bergson (French philosopher)—One of the most influential philosophers of the twentieth century, Bergson is renowned for his opposition to the dominant materialist thought of his time and for his creation of theories that emphasize the supremacy and independence of supra-rational consciousness.

Edgar Rice Burroughs (American novelist)—Burroughs was a science fiction writer who is best known as the creator of Tarzan. His *Tarzan of the Apes* and its numerous sequels have sold over thirty-five million copies in fifty-six languages, making Burroughs one of the most popular authors in the world.

Joseph Conrad (Polish-born English novelist)—Considered an innovator of novel structure as well as one of the finest stylists of modern English literature, Conrad is the author of complex novels that examine the ambiguity of good and evil. *TCLC* will devote an entry to critical discussion of his *Nostromo*, a novel exploring Conrad's conviction that failure is a fact of human existence and that every ideal contains the possibilities for its own corruption.

Robert Desnos (French poet)—Desnos was one of the original members of the Surrealist movement and one of the most adept at its experimental techniques. Although he later broke with the group to explore more conventional literary forms, he is remembered as the poet whose work best realized the Surrealists' theoretical precepts.

Grazia Deledda (Italian novelist and short story writer)—Deledda was the second woman to win a Nobel Prize in literature, which she was awarded in 1926 for her naturalistic novels of passion and tragedy set in her native Sardinia.

Frank Harris (Welsh editor, critic, and biographer)—Prominent in English literary circles at the turn of the century, Harris was a flamboyant man of letters described by one critic as "seemingly offensive on principle." His greatest accomplishments—which were achieved as editor of the *Fortnightly Review,* the *Evening News,* and the *Saturday Review*—have been overshadowed by his scandalous life, his sensational biographical portraits of such contemporaries as Oscar Wilde and Bernard Shaw, and his massive autobiography, which portrays Edwardian life primarily as a background for Harris's near-Olympian sexual adventures.

Henry James (American novelist)—James is considered one of the most important novelists of the English language and his work is universally acclaimed for its stylistic distinction, complex psychological portraits, and originality of theme and technique. *TCLC* will devote an entire entry to critical discussion of his novella *The Turn of the Screw,* which is considered one of the most interesting and complex short novels in world literature.

Jerome K. Jerome (English novelist and dramatist)—Jerome was the author of humorous fiction and some of the most popular plays of the Edwardian era.

Sarah Orne Jewett (American novelist and short story writer)—One of the foremost American writers of regionalist fiction, Jewett is known for her sympathetic depiction of the characters and customs of nineteenth-century rural Maine.

Vladimir Korolenko (Russian short story writer and journalist)—Best known as a journalist and activist for social justice, Korolenko was also the author of fiction reflecting his sympathy for the outcasts of Russian society and his faith in human nature.

Alfred Kubin (Austrian novelist)—Known primarily as a graphic artist, Kubin is also the author of *The Other Side,* a fantastic novel that has been cited as an influence on Franz Kafka's *The Castle* and on the literary movements of Surrealism, Expressionism, and the Theater of the Absurd.

Sinclair Lewis (American novelist)—A prominent American novelist of the 1920s, Lewis is considered the author of some of the most effective satires in American literature. In his most important novels, which include *Main Street, Babbitt,* and *Arrowsmith,* he attacked the dullness, smug provincialism, and socially enforced conformity of the American middle class. *TCLC* will devote an entire entry to critical discussion of *Main Street.*

Dmitri Merezhkovsky (Russian novelist, philosopher, poet, and critic)—Although his poetry and criticism are credited with initiating the Symbolist movement in Russian literature, Merezhkovsky is best known as a religious philosopher who sought in numerous essays and historical novels to reconcile the values of pagan religions with the teachings of Christ.

Thomas Mofolo (Lesothan novelist)—Considered the first great writer in modern African literature, Mofolo is the author of novels depicting the radical effect of Christian teachings on traditional African society. His most highly regarded novel, *Chaka,* was suppressed at the time of its completion by missionary publishers who objected to the book's favorable portrayal of traditional African customs and beliefs; however, since its publication, the work has gained a reputation as an epic tragedy of both literary and historical significance.

Charles Nordhoff and James Norman Hall (American novelists, historians, and essayists)—Nordhoff and Hall collaborated on the novels *Mutiny on the Bounty, Men against the Sea,* and *Pitcairn's Island,* a trilogy comprising one of the most compelling and widely read maritime narratives in popular fiction.

Giovanni Papini (Italian essayist, journalist, and editor)—Papini was a man of letters whose work as an editor, journalist, and essayist was instrumental in shaping Italian social and cultural thought during the early years of the twentieth century.

Boris Pilnyak (Russian novelist and short story writer)—Pilnyak's *Naked Year* was the first important novel to depict the effect of the Bolshevik Revolution on Russian society. His energetic, episodic, and stylistically heterogeneous narratives were widely imitated by postrevolutionary writers, making Pilnyak one of the most influential Soviet literary figures of the 1920s.

Kenneth Roberts (American novelist)—Roberts's works, many of which are set in New England during the American Revolution, are considered among the best historical novels in American literature.

Romain Rolland (French novelist, biographer, and dramatist)—Rolland was a prominent man of letters and noted pacifist who is best known for his novel *Jean-Christophe,* a ten-volume life of a musical genius in which the author propounded his antinationalist and antimaterialist views. A distinguished musicologist and critic, Rolland also wrote many dramas that demonstrate his theory of a "theater of the people" devoted to the inspirationally heroic and to social change.

Oswald Spengler (German philosopher)—Spengler rose to international celebrity in the 1920s on the basis of *The Decline of the West,* a controversial examination of the cyclical nature of history. Although frequently deprecated by professional historians, *The Decline of the West* became one of the most influential philosophical works of the twentieth century.

Olaf Stapledon (English novelist)—An important influence on the works of C. S. Lewis, Arthur C. Clarke, and Stanislaw Lem, Stapledon was the author of what he described as "fantastic fiction of a semi-philosophical kind." Today, critics regard his novels as among the most significant and accomplished examples of science fiction and speculative writing.

Leslie Stephen (English biographer and critic)—A distinguished man of letters, Stephen is ranked among the most important literary critics of the late nineteenth century.

Leon Trotsky (Russian essayist and political philosopher)—A leader of the Bolshevik Revolution in Russia, Trotsky was also a historian, biographer, and one of the most influential political theorists of the twentieth century.

Beatrice and Sydney James Webb (English social writers)—Prominent members of the progressive Fabian society, the Webbs wrote sociological works significant to the advent of socialist reform in England and influenced the work of several major authors, including H. G. Wells and Bernard Shaw.

Simone Weil (French philosopher and essayist)—Weil was a social activist and mystic whose writings explore the nature of God, the individual, and human society.

Oscar Wilde (Anglo-Irish dramatist, novelist, and poet)—A crusader for aestheticism, Wilde was one of the most prominent members of the nineteenth-century "art for art's sake" movement. *TCLC* will devote an entire entry to his play *The Importance of Being Earnest,* which is considered his best and most characteristic work as well as the apogee of drawing-room farce.

Additional Authors to Appear
in Future Volumes

Abbey, Henry 1842-1911
Abercrombie, Lascelles 1881-1938
Adamic, Louis 1898-1951
Ade, George 1866-1944
Agustini, Delmira 1886-1914
Akers, Elizabeth Chase 1832-1911
Akiko, Yosano 1878-1942
Aldanov, Mark 1886-1957
Aldrich, Thomas Bailey 1836-1907
Aliyu, Dan Sidi 1902-1920
Allen, Hervey 1889-1949
Archer, William 1856-1924
Arlen, Michael 1895-1956
Attila, Jozsef 1905-1937
Austin, Alfred 1835-1913
Austin, Mary Hunter 1868-1934
Bahr, Hermann 1863-1934
Bailey, Philip James 1816-1902
Barbour, Ralph Henry 1870-1944
Barreto, Lima 1881-1922
Benét, William Rose 1886-1950
Benjamin, Walter 1892-1940
Bennett, James Gordon, Jr. 1841-1918
Benson, E(dward) F(rederic) 1867-1940
Berdyaev, Nikolai Aleksandrovich
    1874-1948
Beresford, J(ohn) D(avys) 1873-1947
Bergson, Henri 1859-1941
Bialit, Chaim 1873-1934
Binyon, Laurence 1869-1943
Bishop, John Peale 1892-1944
Blackmore, R(ichard) D(oddridge)
    1825-1900
Blake, Lillie Devereux 1835-1913
Blum, Leon 1872-1950
Bodenheim, Maxwell 1892-1954
Bowen, Marjorie 1886-1952
Byrne, Donn 1889-1928
Caine, Hall 1853-1931
Cannan, Gilbert 1884-1955
Carswell, Catherine 1879-1946
Chairil, Anwar 1922-1949
Chand, Prem 1880-1936
Churchill, Winston 1871-1947
Coppée, Francois 1842-1908
Corelli, Marie 1855-1924
Croce, Benedetto 1866-1952
Crofts, Freeman Wills 1879-1957
Cruze, James (Jens Cruz Bosen) 1884-
    1942
Curros, Enriquez Manuel 1851-1908
Dall, Caroline Wells (Healy) 1822-1912
Daudet, Leon 1867-1942
Davidson, John 1857-1909
Davis, Richard Harding 1864-1916
Day, Clarence 1874-1935

Delafield, E.M. (Edme Elizabeth Monica
    de la Pasture) 1890-1943
Deneson, Jacob 1836-1919
Devkota, Laxmiprasad 1909-1959
DeVoto, Bernard 1897-1955
Douglas, (George) Norman 1868-1952
Douglas, Lloyd C(assel) 1877-1951
Dovzhenko, Alexander 1894-1956
Drinkwater, John 1882-1937
Drummond, W.H. 1854-1907
Durkheim, Emile 1858-1917
Duun, Olav 1876-1939
Eaton, Walter Prichard 1878-1957
Eggleston, Edward 1837-1902
Erskine, John 1879-1951
Fadeyev, Alexander 1901-1956
Ferland, Albert 1872-1943
Feydeau, Georges 1862-1921
Field, Rachel 1894-1924
Flecker, James Elroy 1884-1915
Fletcher, John Gould 1886-1950
Fogazzaro, Antonio 1842-1911
Francos, Karl Emil 1848-1904
Frank, Bruno 1886-1945
Frazer, (Sir) George 1854-1941
Freud, Sigmund 1853-1939
Froding, Gustaf 1860-1911
Fuller, Henry Blake 1857-1929
Futabatei, Shimei 1864-1909
Gladkov, Fydor Vasilyevich 1883-1958
Glaspell, Susan 1876-1948
Glyn, Elinor 1864-1943
Golding, Louis 1895-1958
Gosse, Edmund 1849-1928
Gould, Gerald 1885-1936
Guest, Edgar 1881-1959
Gumilyov, Nikolay 1886-1921
Gyulai, Pal 1826-1909
Hale, Edward Everett 1822-1909
Hawthorne, Julian 1846-1934
Heijermans, Herman 1864-1924
Hernandez, Miguel 1910-1942
Hewlett, Maurice 1861-1923
Heyward, DuBose 1885-1940
Hope, Anthony 1863-1933
Hudson, W(illiam) H(enry) 1841-1922
Huidobro, Vincente 1893-1948
Hviezdoslav (Pavol Orszagh) 1849-1921
Ilyas, Abu Shabaka 1903-1947
Imbs, Bravig 1904-1946
Ivanov, Vyacheslav Ivanovich 1866-
    1949
Jacobs, W(illiam) W(ymark) 1863-1943
James, Will 1892-1942
Jammes, Francis 1868-1938
Johnson, Fenton 1888-1958

Johnston, Mary 1870-1936
Jorgensen, Johannes 1866-1956
King, Grace 1851-1932
Kirby, William 1817-1906
Kline, Otis Albert 1891-1946
Kohut, Adolph 1848-1916
Kuzmin, Mikhail Alexseyevich 1875-
    1936
Lamm, Martin 1880-1950
Lawson, Henry 1867-1922
Ledwidge, Francis 1887-1917
Leipoldt, C. Louis 1880-1947
Lemonnier, Camille 1844-1913
Lima, Jorge De 1895-1953
Locke, Alain 1886-1954
Long, Frank Belknap 1903-1959
Louys, Pierre 1870-1925
Lucas, E(dward) V(errall) 1868-1938
Lyall, Edna 1857-1903
Maghar, Josef Suatopluk 1864-1945
Manning, Frederic 1887-1935
Maragall, Joan 1860-1911
Marais, Eugene 1871-1936
Martin du Gard, Roger 1881-1958
Masaryk, Tomas 1850-1939
Mayor, Flora Macdonald 1872-1932
McClellan, George Marion 1860-1934
McCoy, Horace 1897-1955
Merezhkovsky, Dmitri 1865-1941
Mirbeau, Octave 1850-1917
Mistral, Frederic 1830-1914
Monro, Harold 1879-1932
Moore, Thomas Sturge 1870-1944
Morley, Christopher 1890-1957
Morley, S. Griswold 1883-1948
Mqhayi, S.E.K. 1875-1945
Murray, (George) Gilbert 1866-1957
Nansen, Peter 1861-1918
Nobre, Antonio 1867-1900
Norris, Frank 1870-1902
Obstfelder, Sigborn 1866-1900
O'Dowd, Bernard 1866-1959
Ophuls, Max 1902-1957
Orczy, Baroness 1865-1947
Owen, Seaman 1861-1936
Page, Thomas Nelson 1853-1922
Parrington, Vernon L. 1871-1929
Peck, George W. 1840-1916
Phillips, Ulrich B. 1877-1934
Pinero, Arthur Wing 1855-1934
Pontoppidan, Henrik 1857-1943
Powys, T. F. 1875-1953
Prévost, Marcel 1862-1941
Quiller-Couch, Arthur 1863-1944
Randall, James G. 1881-1953
Rappoport, Solomon 1863-1944

Read, Opie 1852-1939
Reisen (Reizen), Abraham 1875-1953
Remington, Frederic 1861-1909
Riley, James Whitcomb 1849-1916
Rinehart, Mary Roberts 1876-1958
Ring, Max 1817-1901
Roberts, Kenneth 1885-1957
Rohan, Kada 1867-1947
Rohmer, Sax 1883-1959
Rozanov, Vasily Vasilyevich 1856-1919
Saar, Ferdinand von 1833-1906
Sabatini, Rafael 1875-1950
Saintsbury, George 1845-1933
Sakutaro, Hagiwara 1886-1942
Sanborn, Franklin Benjamin 1831-1917
Santayana, George 1863-1952
Sardou, Victorien 1831-1908
Schickele, René 1885-1940
Seabrook, William 1886-1945
Seton, Ernest Thompson 1860-1946
Shestov, Lev 1866-1938

Shiels, George 1886-1949
Skram, Bertha Amalie 1847-1905
Smith, Pauline 1883-1959
Sodergran, Edith Irene 1892-1923
Solovyov, Vladimir 1853-1900
Sorel, Georges 1847-1922
Spector, Mordechai 1859-1922
Spengler, Oswald 1880-1936
Squire, J(ohn) C(ollings) 1884-1958
Stavenhagen, Fritz 1876-1906
Stockton, Frank R. 1834-1902
Subrahmanya Bharati, C. 1882-1921
Sully-Prudhomme, René 1839-1907
Sylva, Carmen 1843-1916
Thoma, Ludwig 1867-1927
Tomlinson, Henry Major 1873-1958
Trotsky, Leon 1870-1940
Tuchmann, Jules 1830-1901
Turner, W(alter) J(ames) R(edfern)
    1889-1946
Upward, Allen 1863-1926

Vachell, Horace Annesley 1861-1955
Van Dine, S. S. (William H. Wright)
    1888-1939
Van Dyke, Henry 1852-1933
Vazov, Ivan Minchov 1850-1921
Veblen, Thorstein 1857-1929
Villaespesa, Francisco 1877-1936
Wallace, Edgar 1874-1932
Wallace, Lewis 1827-1905
Walsh, Ernest 1895-1926
Webb, Mary 1881-1927
Webster, Jean 1876-1916
Whitlock, Brand 1869-1927
Wilson, Harry Leon 1867-1939
Wolf, Emma 1865-1932
Wood, Clement 1888-1950
Wren, P(ercival) C(hristopher) 1885-
    1941
Yonge, Charlotte Mary 1823-1901
Zecca, Ferdinand 1864-1947
Zeromski, Stefan 1864-1925

Readers are cordially invited to suggest additional authors to the editors.

Pierre Drieu La Rochelle

1893-1945

French novelist, poet, short story writer, and essayist.

A noted man of letters, Drieu was one of a number of French intellectuals who espoused fascist ideals during the period between the world wars, ideals which led eventually to his collaboration with German occupation forces in World War II. Drieu's reactionary views arose primarily from his conviction that the formation of a martial state based on moral vigor and physical fitness would remedy the profound spiritual malaise which plagued France as a result of the decay of traditional values. His portrayals of disillusioned, decadent, and alienated individuals, generally regarded as personae of the author himself, clearly illustrate this concept of malaise and have led critics to identify Drieu as the precursor of existentialist writers Jean-Paul Sartre and Albert Camus. Drieu's literary reputation was severely damaged by his political activities; for many years after the war, critics were reluctant to express admiration for the work of a fascist writer. However, recent translations of his works into English have revived critical interest in his fiction.

Born in Paris, Drieu was the son of an unsuccessful lawyer and his wife. According to Drieu's own account, his parents' marriage was a tempestuous one, undermined by frequent quarrels, financial instability, and adultery. As a result, their child was often left in the care of his maternal grandmother, a vigorous country woman who entertained him with tales of the heroic exploits of his countrymen. These tales had an enormous impact upon Drieu, who came to revere Napoleon and the martial spirit of Napoleonic France. Planning a career in the diplomatic service, Drieu attended the prestigious school of Political Science at the University of Paris, but his hopes were destroyed when he failed the examinations required for acquisition of a degree. He was, however, temporarily spared the task of choosing an alternate career by being drafted into the infantry a few days after his departure from the university.

Drieu had been in the army only a short time when the First World War began. Unlike the majority of his literary contemporaries, Drieu found war an exhilirating experience, and he revelled in the heroic élan and hearty camaraderie of men in wartime. When Drieu was wounded and confined to a hospital bed for several weeks, he began to write poetry in order to express the strong feelings aroused in him by the spectacle of an entire continent in conflict, but was dissatisfied with the result and discarded these early efforts. Then, during a second period of hospitalization for another injury, he read Paul Claudel's *Odes* and was impressed by their free verse forms. Inspired, he attempted once again to express his thoughts in poetry, this time with much success. These war poems, published in 1917 as *Interrogation*, gained critical acclaim, establishing Drieu as a major spokesman for his generation.

Drieu thus emerged from the war in considerably improved circumstances. He had proved himself as valiant a soldier as any of his ancestors and, despite his earlier academic failures, he had become a respected author. In 1919, he was asked to be a regular contributor to one of France's most renowned intellectual journals, *La nouvelle revue française,* then under

the direction of André Gide. Freed from the necessity of earning a living by his marriage to a wealthy woman, Drieu was able to devote most of his time to writing. After publishing a second volume of poetry in 1920, he concentrated his efforts on the composition of novels and essays, all of which explore the political questions that had come to dominate his attention. Drieu's study of French history and the events of the war had convinced him that France, and in fact all of Europe, had entered a period of decline characterized by political weakness, social chaos, and moral decadence. Believing that this condition posed a dire threat to the territorial integrity of the entire continent, which was likely to succumb to the domination of a younger, more dynamic state such as the Soviet Union, Drieu recommended the formation of a pan-European government. Throughout his writings of the twenties, Drieu wrestled with the question of exactly which ideological foundation would best serve his proposed new state and provide a cure for Europe's spiritual malaise. He was tempted to join his friends and colleagues the Surrealists in their endorsement of communism, but while he agreed with their contention that the old order must be destroyed, he saw in their credo primarily a materialistic impulse toward mediocrity. Drieu's inability to accept communism led him to break with the Surrealists in 1925, though he deeply regretted the loss of their friendship. Finally, in 1934, Drieu published *Socialisme fasciste,* an-

15

nouncing his decision that fascism would be the saving grace of Europe. Seeing in the infant Third Reich the kind of heroic spirit and unity of purpose he had been seeking, Drieu believed that a Europe united under German hegemony could thwart what he perceived as the imperialistic aims of both the United States and the Soviet Union. As a result of this position, which he maintained throughout the thirties despite the obvious abuses of power it justified, Drieu was offered a post in the Vichy government during the German occupation of France. He declined, stating that intellectuals were bound by duty to remain outside established regimes in order to preserve an unbiased perspective and the power to criticize. It was at this time that he assumed the directorship of the *Nouvelle revue française*. When the war ended, Drieu, conscious of having chosen the wrong side, felt compelled to regain his lost honor. Believing that the best way of doing so was to refuse to submit to trial and execution for collaboration with war criminals, he committed suicide in March of 1945.

Critics agree that the concept of decadence forms the thematic core of all Drieu's work and that this concept is a highly individualized synthesis of Drieu's own psychology and experiences. Drieu inherited from his grandmother the conviction that France had been gloriously powerful in earlier times, but had become weak and unable to defend itself as a result of the laziness and spiritual torpor of its people, who wanted only to immerse themselves in hedonistic pastimes. Critics note that this conviction was reinforced by Drieu's perception of his own immorality and inadequacy. Later, strongly influenced by the writings of Friedrich Nietzsche, Drieu came to view all existence in terms of "the will of power" and to equate spiritual vitality with moral superiority. Thus, the fact that France, England, and the Low Countries were very nearly absorbed into the young and vigorous republic of Germany during World War I, and were saved only by the intervention of the United States was for Drieu proof that the governments of Europe had degenerated to a state of moral decay and spiritual bankruptcy, leaving them weak and vulnerable.

In Drieu's fiction, the concept of decadence is explicitly manifested. The moral lassitude of society is mirrored in the characters, most of whom drift through purposeless lives, vainly attempting to find meaning and fulfillment in depravity. This technique dominates the early novels and stories, particularly *L'homme couvert de femmes,* in which Drieu frankly portrayed his own promiscuity, and *Le feu follet,* which features a drug-addicted gigolo as the protagonist. The characters of these novels all serve a single purpose: to illustrate the adverse effects of decadence upon the individual and thereby to criticize French society within the context of fiction. One novel of this period, *Bléche,* is the psychological study of a moral man's response to forced confrontation with the existence of evil and is generally considered Drieu's best work, revealing his growing sophistication as a writer in its depth of analysis and structural elegance. The later novels, *Gilles, L'homme à cheval,* and *Chiens de paille,* are more polemical in nature, causing some critics to regard these works as attempts on Drieu's part to justify his fascism. Much critical attention has also focused on Drieu's portrayals of male-female relationships, a central feature in all his fiction. Equating femininity with weakness and thus with inferiority, Drieu considered the only harmonious relationship to be one of male dominance and female submission.

Although Drieu's novels are strongly and consistently autobiographical, the development of his political thought is most easily traced through his essays. In *Mesure de la France,* the essay which established Drieu's reputation as an astute political commentator, he proposes the immediate and total annihilation of the old order, but presents no clear program for restructuring government, except the assertion that it will be young men like himself whose mettle has been tested in battle who will take the lead. This lack of constructive proposals is characteristic of all the early essays, reflecting Drieu's reticence to endorse any existing ideology and his inability or unwillingness to construct an alternate one. Even the declarations of *Socialisme fasciste* are tentative; while Drieu admired the collective spirit of fascism, he mistrusted the fierce nationalism and materialism of the two proto-fascist states, Italy and Germany. By the beginning of World War II, however, Drieu had come to believe that the hopeless decadence and apathy of the French people could only be remedied by a draconian transformation of society, much like the one being effected in Germany under Hitler. Conscious that the kind of state thus produced would fall far short of his proposed oligarchy of the young and vigorous, Drieu nevertheless applauded the German occupation of France and the resulting dissolution of the regime he found so distasteful. Drieu's wartime writings are largely endorsements of the Germans, chiding the French people for their xenophobic attitudes, denouncing Jews and communists, and pointing out the preferability of fascism to the kind of communism being practiced by Joseph Stalin. Many critics have attempted to explain Drieu's conversion to fascism, and the consensus is that the concept of a centralized government with nearly unlimited powers was simply amenable to Drieu's basically authoritarian personality and atavistic political ideals.

Always highly respected in France, Drieu's fiction did not come to the attention of English-speaking critics until the mid-1960s, when translations of his works began to appear. Although critics unanimously denounce his nonfiction for its political orientation, many praise his fiction. His characters, like those of Ernest Hemingway, are considered accurate, perceptive portraits of the post-World War I generation, and his explorations of their psychological states have been praised for depth of insight. While some maintain that the quality of Drieu's fiction is seriously marred by didacticism, he is regarded by many prominent critics as one of the most important figures in French literature of the interwar period.

(See also *Contemporary Authors,* Vol. 117.)

PRINCIPAL WORKS

Interrogation (poetry) 1917
Fond de cantine (poetry) 1920
Etat civil (novel) 1921
Mesure de la France (essays) 1922
Plainte contre inconnu (short stories)   1924
L'homme couvert de femmes (novel) 1925
Le jeune Européen (essays) 1927
Blèche (novel) 1928
Genève ou Moscou (essays) 1928
Une femme à sa fenêtre (novel) 1930
  [*Hotel Acropolis,* 1931]
L'Europe contre les patries (essays) 1931
Le feu follet (novel) 1931
  [*The Fire Within,* 1965; also translated as *Will o' the Wisp,* 1966]
Drôle de voyage (novel) 1933
La comédie de Charleroi (short stories) 1934
  [*The Comedy of Charleroi, and Other Stories,* 1973]

Journal d'un homme trompé (short stories) 1934
Socialisme Fasciste (essays) 1934
Beloukia (novel) 1936
Rêveuse bourgeoisie (novel) 1937
Gilles [censored edition] (novel) 1939; also published as
   Gilles [uncensored edition], 1942
Notes pour comprendre le siècle (essays) 1941
L'homme à cheval (novel) 1943
   [*The Man on Horseback,* 1978]
Charlotte Corday (drama) 1944
Le Chef (drama) 1944
Récit secret (journal) 1951
   [*Secret Journal, and Other Writings,* 1974]
**Les chiens de paille* (novel) 1964

*This novel was written in 1944 but was confiscated from the publisher
and not released until 1964.

MILTON H. STANSBURY (essay date 1935)

[*In the following excerpt, Stansbury surveys Drieu's fiction, detailing those aspects of modern life Drieu found repugnant.*]

If, according to the contention of some psychologists, it is only the unhappy, thwarted nature who seeks refuge in creative art, Drieu La Rochelle is another soul in pain who found relief in literary expression. Unfortunately the degree of pain is not the gauge of inspiration, and Drieu's is not a brilliant talent. He himself admits that he has no natural gifts, and in his autobiographical novel, **Le Jeune Européen,** he confesses it was because he gradually found himself without money, friends, children, and a vocation that he first turned to writing. Begging his public's indulgence for having embraced a literary career, he asks: "What was left but to become a writer if only to bid farewell to the human forms which one by one were disappearing over my horizon?" However, it was more than through cowardice and to earn his daily bread that Drieu became a man of letters. Idealistic and patriotic, he is fundamentally a moralist and a disciplinarian, whose instinct is to preach and reprimand. Drieu's characteristic note is acerbity and ill humor, which, without the saving grace of genius, makes him a dreary and forbidding writer.... A worthy bore, he must be reckoned with, for however chilling his attributes, Drieu demands recognition as a representative figure in contemporary French thought.

His first books, so many wails of complaint and dissatisfaction, reveal him as a Jeremiah, militant through his tears. He was a fault-finder from his earliest years, at least in retrospect, for it cannot be supposed that children are so hypercritical. His first *boutade* is **Etat-Civil** . . . , an autobiographical essay recounting his childhood and adolescence. In this series of monotonous and humorless pictures, in which he prescribes for his elders' shortcomings with the same zeal he devotes to his own grievances, the only period spared the long-suffering reader is the author's infancy between the years of one and three— too early, Drieu laments, to be recalled. Born of affluent, over-solicitous parents, he was brought up "in cotton-wool and the fear of draughts." He reproaches first his mother, for allowing him to remain an only child, for abandoning him too much as a little boy, and later guarding him too much a prisoner at her side. Having pilloried his father and his grandparents on various scores, he even reviles the family furniture which, being of

the department-store variety, lacked soul and was symbolic of the human slaves who manufactured it. He next rebukes his early teachers, old men "in whose veins flowed the meager sap of city trees" and who seemed bent on exterminating the last vestiges of childhood lingering in their unlucky pupils. Nor does Paris escape the universal ban, "that epitome of rottenness, senility, stagnation, and solitude," whose Sorbonne is "paltry and anonymous, new as a suburban *Hôtel de Ville,* open to every noxious fume and thronged with neglected adolescents soiled by their coarse puberty."

In the spotlight before this anathematized background stands the child Pierre, by no means too prepossessing a figure himself. To follow his own description: "An instinctive distrust, a determination contracted before my birth, made me rebel against everything my mother offered me. I remember that as early as my seventh year, every time I walked with her, I took virulent delight in thwarting all her kindness and in poisoning that day's happiness for her." Scarcely more appealing is Drieu the schoolboy, whose popularity must have been sadly impaired by his mania for meddling in his playmates' lives. "I had a passion for the public good. I wanted to see everyone around me bathed in a harmony pleasing to my soul. Forcing my comrades into what I considered paths to paradise, I experienced a profound emotion in imposing my religious ideas on them." To render the youthful zealot justice, it must be added that Drieu was also prepared to toil and suffer for his friends, provided that in return he was duly admired.

Drieu was twenty-one years old at the outbreak of the War. He had just completed his military service, to which he was to add four years of active service at the front. It was in the full flush of his youthful exaltation as a soldier, in 1915, that he wrote **Interrogations,** a little volume of free verse which glorifies war and its ally, death. Distrustful, like Montherlant and other belligerent spirits, of the enervating effects of peace, he writes: "I sing of the War because it is inseparably linked with grandeur. The War for men like me, born as we were in a long period of peace, was a fulfillment of our youth which the younger generation hailed with joy. Introducing into our lives a solemnity which human events no longer seemed to promise, it should never be looked upon as a catastrophe. And peace? Pacifists, what is your peace? Is man to end his days as a retired shopkeeper?" Obsessed by dreams of power, believing that might makes right, a partisan of "sword-intelligence," Drieu found the Germans a congenial race: "O Germans, I have never hated you! You have strength, the mother of all good!"

Against his own country, on the other hand, he directed the bitterest of philippics. There can be no doubt that at this period France was the greatest passion of his life. "I love her," he writes, "like a woman one follows in the streets. She is disturbing and fascinating like all chance encounters. I can also say that I love my countrymen, even when they are brutes, cowards, gluttons. Not because of a certain genius which may be theirs, but because they are the men with whom I've lived. If only for the privilege of making obscene jokes and of discussing women, I would willingly follow them into another planet." But Drieu's nature was that of the reformer who chastises what he most deeply loves. He thought France had sinned and deserved to be admonished. The more he berated her, the more he betrayed his ardent nationalism. His idol had toppled into the dust and must be kicked back upon the pedestal.

Having grown up in a period when France was still smarting under the Franco-Prussian War, Drieu added to the mortification felt by every Frenchman at this recent humiliation an exaggerated consciousness of his country's defeats throughout the centuries. He asserts that as a child he suffered acutely at the thought of disasters as remote as those of Crécy, Poitiers, and Agincourt. Hence his love of France was ever associated with pain. "Parents, why did you not keep silent on my country's ignominy? I was ill from France's illness, and everything around me reminded me of her insignificance in comparison with Great Britain, Russia, and the United States."

This is the theme of his political essay, *Mesure de la France* . . . , where in an alternating barrage of statistics and grandiloquence he draws up specific charges against his countrymen and prescribes panaceas for their ailments, whether these be flabby muscles or race suicide. "France held her head too high in this war. But her bloodless body would have been unable to sustain the weight had not the strength of twenty nations been added to her limbs. We French cannot claim to have been the sole possessors of this mistress Victory." And hurling his oft-repeated invective against his country for her sterility, he adds: "Unlike the Germans, our fathers were unwilling to have children, which is our crime. We tempted a proud and self-sufficient people, and by cynically displaying our weakness, invoked their scorn and hatred. France, ardent and dried-up mother, it is time for you to investigate the condition of your belly and your brains!" His lamentations pursue their lengthy course through the ills of capitalism and the various manifestations of modern materialism. Believing that money has become the universal god, he asserts that all classes of society have been reduced to the same level in a civilization of business men bent solely on gain. "Men of today are devoid of all passion, and share in common their system's resultant vices of alcoholism, inversion, and onanism. Does Lenin in his Kremlin differ from a Stinnes or a Schwab? What the world needs is a moral, intellectual, and political reintegration—not a revolution but a new birth."

This was also the conclusion of the hero in *Le Jeune Européen* . . . , easily recognized as Drieu, in spite of willful autobiographical disparities. The story concerns the career of a young dilettante of twenty-one, who after having dissipated his vitality in polo, skiing, hunting, and bejeweled adventuresses, having roamed to the four corners of Europe, "that great toy I should have liked to smash," finally yearns for a world upheaval to relieve the monotony of life. Suddenly at Deauville, in August 1914, his Hispano overturns, and this is coincident with the declaration of the World War: the playboy is metamorphosed into a trench-digger. "I had already exhausted motor racing, cocaine, and Alpinism; in this stripped and desolate Champagne I found the sinister sport I had so long been sensing in the air. Just as childbearing is the woman's mission, men are made for war."

Being a man of action, his hero enjoys the carnage. Moreover, being formed in Drieu's youthful image, he experiences his highest flights of mysticism in the midst of this human butchery. A victim of contradictory impulses, torn between the need to dream and the need to act, Drieu had once declared: "Along the misty shores of revery, I have lost all desire for life; languid but happy in my lethargic state, I should like to perpetuate a nocturnal navigation on the river of eternal bed-sheets." This theme, a recurring *motif* in the chaotic architecture of Drieu's life, throws light on much of the anomaly of his nature. It is responsible for the cigarette case he is said to possess, on which is pictured the meeting between Goethe and Napoleon. It accounts for the Young European in the trenches when, deprived

of worldly pleasure, he feeds his famished soul on Pascal. However, after a few months' contact with the monotonous reality of No Man's Land, Drieu's hero tires of both blood and prayer, and longs for something new. Deserting from the army, he arrives in America, only to become a prey to fresh disillusions. Drawn into what he calls America's national occupation of dollars and cents, he finds life in the New World as arduous as it had been at the front. He toils in an office, only to emerge at dusk into a labyrinth of narrow streets which, gorged with human flesh, remind him of the trenches: "The skyscrapers seemed no higher than the trajectories of our guns, and all this mass of humanity resembled soldiers hurling themselves forward to the assault of impregnable strongholds, as if in obedience to an absurd command dictated by an anonymous telephone. Americans cannonade nature; Europeans, deceived by ancient customs, fire upon each other. But let peace come, the world reverts only too eagerly to canned goods and cheap automobiles." Indeed, in the American, according to Drieu, may be recognized the worst type of European, who has only changed continents in order to play more easily the game of dollars. "The Americans are the oldest race I know; they are senile. In flocking to Europe, they are merely satisfying their nostalgia for the old. More advanced than we in their industrial evolution, further removed from the mysteries of nature, they are fifty years of age while we are only forty."

For those readers who are weary of battling with the political situation; who have long ago despaired of rehabilitating Europe, and realize their helplessness in face of either capitalism or communism; who hate dilemmas and the necessity of choosing between Moscow and Geneva; who refuse to become athletes or parents of numerous offspring, there remains a Drieu who, when he turns from public affairs to the study of social types, writes in a lighter, though always castigating, vein. By no means finished with problems, he has selected an insoluble one. The people he holds up to satire in his novels are thoroughly sophisticated men and women who have deliberately chosen the type of life they wish to lead. They are at once the fashioners and the victims of the corrupt society in which they move. Drieu places them in drawing-rooms, lends them a pseudocultured vocabulary, passes them as members of the smart set, and then says, Look at these awful things. Through this vitiated background of libertines, nymphomaniacs, drug addicts, and inverts, slips one central figure, for whom Drieu in a moment of inspiration found the name of "the empty suitcase." He sticks this label on only one of his heroes (*La Valise vide* in the four short stories comprising his *Plainte contre l'inconnu*), but the epithet applies equally to all the others, as they bear a striking family resemblance (*L'homme couvert de femmes; Feu Follet; Drôle de Voyage,* and others).

In *Le Jeune Européen,* where Drieu traces his literary career, is explained the origin of this *valise vide*. "When I finally decided to write of someone other than myself, I started to look around among my friends. Selecting the most conspicuous person I knew, a man called Jacques, I asked him to look at me fixedly for a moment. Then gazing obliquely at him through my spectacles, I was amazed to find him covered with a thousand little blemishes, as though he had suddenly contracted a skin disease, so that I accused him of having deceived me until that day. From this misunderstanding was born the heavy and lifeless caricature which I entitled the *valise vide* and which had no little success, since people always like a portrait in which they recognize the model."

From the character of Gonzague, we learn that the "empty suitcase" is a good-looking young man of twenty-two with the intelligence of a child of ten. Smartly dressed to the point of foppery, well mannered, alternately communicative or strangely reticent in regard to love-affairs which never seem to materialize, he is in comparatively straitened circumstances and, unable to persist in any occupation, in constant need of loans. An habitué of bars and resorts of frivolous entertainment, a collector of matchboxes, uniform buttons, and a thousand other baubles, he has never been known to read a book, attend a concert, or visit a picture gallery. He craves affection, but lacks the vitality, constancy, or emotional depth to attract either friendship or love. However, rather than be left to his own devices, he will attach himself to anyone. In short, he is an empty piece of luggage who creates an infectious emptiness around him. Drieu renders his hero's situation all the more pathetic by not entirely depriving him of nobler instincts, but he depicts him as so debauched that these instincts, far from constituting a regenerating force, merely serve to destroy his gratification in the sensual life he has no thought of renouncing.

Drieu's second "suitcase" is even more dilapidated. The hero of *L'homme couvert de femmes* has become so effete through erotic dissipation that he is no longer capable of experiencing love, his one obsession. Seeking the soul of a virgin in the body of a prostitute, he finds it impossible to enjoy the possession of either without evoking the image of the other absent one. Since in Drieu's books the woman of the salon has all the earmarks of the woman of the streets, it is difficult to understand the hero's hesitation between the two. Indeed, he does not hesitate but rushes with alarming rapidity from one to the other, the prostitute being the more difficult to acquire as she demands money. And so, the "man covered with women" is doomed to remain forever unappeased in his search for "esthetic concupiscence." Like the earlier *valise vide*, he aspires to higher things and secretly yearns to experience paternity. In the creation of a child, which he calls "the symbol of the physical union and tangible token of love's reality," he sees man's one opportunity "to participate in the divine mystery of life." Love without issue, on the other hand, he regards as little short of onanism. Deciding that solitude is his only refuge, he finally turns his back on brothel and boudoir. The book ends before he has had time to return to either.

The hero of *Le Feu Follet* is equally libertine and equally deprived of love. Being a man of greater action than either of the previous empty bags, he resorts to drugs and eventually to suicide. "If I kill myself," he says, "it is because I am not a successful beast. It is also because literature and the world of thinkers have wounded me with their abominable lies. Though they know full well that sincerity is impossible, they persist in talking of it."

A later novel, *Drôle de voyage*, is a semi-sardonic, semi-lugubrious version of the old story of Panurge. As in Rabelais' satire, the hero is alternately motivated by his desire to marry and his fear of the consequent loss of his liberty. Gille Gambier, this latest of Drieu's men of many women, is visiting for economy's sake at the country estate of some rich Jews. To quote a monologue: "It is true that I am thirty-five and for a fortnight have been living here in complete seclusion. I am not spending a cent, and at my forty-fifth year, when I shall no longer be attractive to women, the two hundred thousand francs which I have kept intact will provide for me. I shall remain a bachelor, forever separated from women, all of whom at heart are bourgeois. Whole days have passed since I have touched a human body. But I am so saturated with flesh that all I need is to close my eyes and—oh! what a relief, this close of day!

It is the hour when a great pipe organs melt, annul, and confound the vitality of life." Drieu's specialty is to write novels on love in which nobody loves, and, whether intentionally or not, the conversation never rises above a certain smartness. Perpetually philosophizing and generalizing, Gille, caustic but less penetrating perhaps than Drieu imagines him, concludes: "Women love nothing. Least of all do they love love. That is reserved for men. Women do nothing, are nothing. Even in the choice of their jewels and clothing they depend on men." Or again: "At bottom, girls and women are alike. Unmarried girls are unwilling to have too good a time because they wish to secure a husband; married women are just as unwilling to enjoy themselves because they wish to keep their husbands." When not only the hero, but each member of this rich and futile milieu joins in such reflections as: "Madame, you must resign yourself to seeing your daughter marry an attractive man who will be unfaithful to her, or an unattractive one to whom she will be unfaithful," the reader is apt to lose sight of the satiric import of the novel, to flounder aimlessly in its mire of tarnished epigram and cheap cynicism.

When the story is permitted to pursue its dismal course, we learn that Gille, haunted by the bitter sense of loneliness, has decided to punctuate his dreary life by marrying some innocent young girl. Beatrix, an English heiress, is at hand, to whom, after several days of half-hearted philandering, he finally considers himself engaged. When Beatrix departs for her home in Granada, Gille, morbidly depressed during his fiancée's temporary absence, engages in a liaison with a married woman in Paris. Thwarted in his efforts to inspire or experience love in this illicit union, he retreats to Spain to rejoin the ever hopeful Beatrix. No sooner arrived, however, than he plans to abandon her once more, alarmed as he is by her unsophistication and lack of voluptuous beauty. So he resumes his weary quest of that nonexistent woman who will satisfy at once his senses and his heart. *Drôle de voyage*, perhaps Drieu's masterpiece, is not without successful moments. Take this realistic picture of the desolate young couple: "Beatrix dragged her fiancé around the Spanish countryside: an old young man, long with an even longer face, a sort of imitation Englishman, imitation diplomat, imitation brother, who had no craving for her breasts or lips, who found her shoulders too thin, her face too dead, and whose least desire was to take in his her emaciated fingers." Gille's tragedy, like that of the average Drieu hero, is a fundamental inability to reach the heart of any woman, for his heart shrouded by morose egotism, his mind corroded by cynicism, and his intellect benumbed by laziness, condemn him to perpetual frustration. In short, the *valise vide*, Drieu's one original contribution as a portraitist, points a warning finger to the mental, moral, and emotional impotence of modern man.

Unlike his early peremptory strictures, when Drieu delineates this highly specialized social type, he speaks in tones of despairing pity rather than of blame. This was a milieu which he himself frequented, and he asks that no hatred or venom be detected in his portraits. (pp. 176-86)

An exasperated patriot and a nauseated spectator of society, Drieu is less a man of letters than a dynamic force. In 1924, when Drieu was first appearing on the horizon, one farsighted critic, Crémieux, prophesied for him a long career, but queried whether it should be one of literature or politics. Indeed, during the period when he was devoting himself almost exclusively to the *valise vide*, Drieu seemed to have lost all interest in public affairs to whirl in a frenzied social vortex. People wondered whether his "curiosity towards life, his fatalism, coquetry, obliging compliance, lassitude, and sense of justice,'' instead of leaving his repulsion intact, might finally cause him to dissipate his vitality, or perhaps flourish in this corrupt atmosphere. His recent conversion to fascism seems the reply to all these queries. If for years his pent-up energy found outlet only in fitful spurts of rage and spleen, a mine of strength was fermenting underneath, and that this wounded idealist should gravitate towards the rigid discipline of fascism was inevitable and fore-ordained. A logical entrenchment for the humorless man of action, it was the one and perfect answer to his lifelong quest. (pp. 186-87)

*Milton H. Stansbury, "Pierre Drieu La Rochelle,"
in his* French Novelists of Today, *University of Pennsylvania Press, 1935, pp. 175-87.*

FRÉDÉRIC J. GROVER   (essay date 1958)

[*In the following excerpt, Grover notes the themes and subjects of Drieu's fiction and assesses the importance of the works.*]

From **Etat-Civil** to **Les Chiens de paille,** Drieu's fiction offers a surprising variety of treatment in the exploitation of his basic subject—himself. When his novels and short stories are read chronologically they show the growth of an artist becoming more and more sure of himself and of his medium. They also produce a striking impression of unity for they really constitute a whole. As early as 1937, after **Rêveuse bourgeoisie,** Marcel Arland had noted this peculiar trait of Drieu's work: "Drieu La Rochelle undoubtedly is one of those writers in whose work one should not consider such or such successful book but the total sum in its inner relationship and rhythm." The three novels which followed only serve to make the unity more striking.

Many critics have complained of the limited inventiveness of Drieu as a novelist; others simply condemn most of his novels because they fall under the "autobiographical" category. Without starting a quarrel of language, the label "autobiographical" seems to me a contradiction in terms when applied to fiction. It is particularly inappropriate if used to describe Drieu's fiction as a whole. He himself has pointed out the classical and traditional aspect of this preoccupation with the self as a method of investigation.

> Actually one may perhaps distinguish two sorts of egotists: those who take a complacent enjoyment in the petty charm and fascination of being prisoners and of loving in the universe only what they find in their prisons; and those who, inclined to observe everything, keep analyzing their ego only because they count on finding in it the most tanglible and the least deceptive human substance. Confident in their good faith, they believe that in this *tête-a-tête* with themselves, holding both ends, nothing will escape them. This is also an illusion, of course, and yet it is an entirely different viewpoint from that of Narcissus, a viewpoint which has certainly been that of the most objective novelists and the most classic thinkers.

Who has complained—since Pascal—about the fact that Montaigne took himself as the subject of his book? In the same way that there are several Montaignes in the *Essais,* there are so many counterparts of Drieu in his fiction that the reproach of monotony is absurd.

It is true that he has not built a harmonious and impressive cathedral in the manner of Proust. But he belongs to the generation which at twenty saw the cathedrals fall under gunfire. He brought back from the war moral wounds much more difficult to heal than fleshly ones. He felt early that he was sick, that his country was sick and that nothing was more urgent than to expose the seriousness of the damage. Drieu, who is, with Apollinaire, the only poet of World War I, has also been the most reliable witness of the new *mal du siècle.* His testimony is indispensable to any historian of contemporary French sensibility.

The Drieu that emerges from a close analysis of the fiction is infinitely more complex than the human being who was sometimes so wrong and disappointing in actual life. Drieu's intimate thought is not to be found in his journalistic articles nor always in his political essays. He confided in his fiction all the things that he could not express as a public figure. An artist can be much more truthful under the veil of fiction. He must paint man in all his humanity; he must see the two sides of any questions; and if he is a great artist he sees more than two sides. A man like Drieu felt all the freer to show the various aspects of a problem in a novel if he had first taken a firm position in an article.

What broadens—and limits—the scope of his testimony is that his greatest passion was for his country. This passion had all the traits of an illness: it often betrayed anxiety, spite, and even hatred. But the disposition toward passionate attachments, for unbreakable ties, underlies all of Drieu's works as well as his life. The fictional testimony of Drieu's novels often provides an explanation or a prefiguration of what happened in his life. This is true of the real-life climax of Drieu's relationship with his country. Drieu's last novel indicated that in 1943 he had already chosen to be the Judas of France since he could not be its Savior. Constant's tale, which is, in a way, Drieu's testimony on the German occupation of France, shows that the tragedy of the enigmatic villain is not necessarily sordid. For the role of Judas cannot be filled by anyone; one of the requirements is that he must have been first a disciple. Drieu's nationalism had been as passionate as de Gaulle's. His nationalism, however, was not that of a stubborn man of action but that of an indecisive, hypercritical intellectual. If his great sensitivity led him sometimes to penetrating insights into France's illness, it led him also to despair. He remained a Frenchman to the last in spite of his efforts to reach the detachment of Hindu philosophy. He makes Constant, his last hero, say: "If I had to start my life all over again and if I were not more interested in Tibetan philosophy than in anything else, I would become American or Russian, but I would not linger among the petty spasms of a second-rate nation." When, however, the moment comes to make a choice and influence the events by decisive intervention, Constant is more than ever aware of his Westernism: "One then remains always the same, he thought. The animal is just as nervous in my fifty-year old carcass as in my body when I was a callow young man. Actually, I was more sure of myself when I was a soldier. Now would be the time for me to do a yoga exercise, but—to Hell with it! What is Salis going to do to Cormont? Which one do I prefer?" Constant must admit that he prefers Cormont, the idealistic, uncompromising French patriot with his "France, France alone" which sounds so much like de Gaulle.

In this last novel the admirer of Nietzsche also strips the intellectual hero of his legend and instead of mythifying him, in twentieth-century fashion, applies to him a clear-thinking analysis not very different, after all, from a Cartesian analysis and this despite the extensive irony Drieu had previously lavished on those who exploited the slogan: "France, the country of Descartes!"

In spite of the extreme positions he took in real life, in spite of his praise of French authors who showed some *démesure*, Drieu's fiction is a model of moderation, of "measure" both in form and content: "I said strictly what I saw . . . but with a movement toward diatribe . . . contained within strict limits, because, even though a great lover and defender of what is excessive, *démesuré*, in the history of French literature, I am a Norman, and like all Normans, scrupulously obedient to the disciplines of the Seine and the Loire."

Like Montaigne, Drieu could have said of his work: "This is a book of good faith." His outstanding contribution to French contemporary literature has been the tone of authenticity which is unmistakably his and which pervades all his writings. He has been as sincere, as honest, as he could be within the limits of his own personality. In a generation haunted by the obsession of sincerity, he has outdone Gide. This preoccupation with sincerity and his attachment to the French reality has prevented Drieu from belonging to the "heroic" or "Corneillean" tradition as Malraux describes it, and in which he places himself with Giono, Bernanos, and Montherlant. (pp. 247-51)

In his short stories and in great parts of his novels, Drieu has written many cruel tales denouncing the horror of life in contemporary civilization. He has detected decadence in all human activity: religion, art, sex, war, government. He has had the vision of humanity rushing to destruction. In its most somber aspects, Drieu's fiction, like Céline's *Voyage au bout de la nuit*, is an exploration of the miseries of the "abandoned" modern man in an urban civilization. He has denounced this misery with the violence of one who takes life seriously and who makes his protest in the manner of a prophet. Like Céline, he depicts painstakingly the deficiency of his contemporaries in order to emphasize the lack of humanity in modern man. He has been restrained, however, by a classical sense of measure, a Gidean tendency to understatement and a naturally impeccable taste which differentiate him markedly from the author of *Mort à crédit*. His bent toward diatribe has very little in common with the truculence of a Céline who in Drieu's words, "spits, only spits, but puts at least the whole Niagara in this salivation."

Drieu has depicted contemporary decadence from the inside. All the satirical part of his fiction could bear the title he intended for a book he never wrote: *Pamphlet contre moi et mes amis*. . . . [His] fiction constitutes a damning document against fascism in exposing the secret recesses of what has been labeled in our times a "fascist personality." Conversely, his fiction also provides a lesson in tolerance: it shows that a fascist is not entirely inhuman.

Drieu's style places him very high among his contemporaries. It partakes of the concision and restlessness of Malraux's without ever falling into obscurity. It is as elegant and lucid as Montherlant's but more consistently natural and rarely marred by rhetoric. It is popular, sometimes colloquial, faithful to the spoken language but it avoids the affectations and the vulgarity of Céline's. Drieu has written, along with Aragon, the best French of his generation.

Paradoxically, the development of Drieu's art as a novelist has brought the young rebel so opposed to all traditional literary forms to a typically French form of novel. Toward the end of his career, Drieu was reconciled to the fact; he pointed out himself how his fiction fits into the French tradition.

> The Russians and the English novels have been contrasted with the French novel, to the disadvantage of the latter. . . . But . . . the country which produced LaFayette, Marivaux, Voltaire, Stendhal, Constant, Balzac, Sand, Sue, Hugo, Flaubert, Zola, Maupassant, Barbey, les Goncourt, Villiers, Huysmans, Barrès, Proust has nothing to envy any other country. . . . In any case French techniques are as good as the English or Russian ones. They are, besides, very varied. What diversity between *Adolphe* and *Les Misérables,* Stendhal and Zola! The recent American novel seems to be a homage to French techniques more than to any other.
>
> I say all this in self-defense. Because my novels are made according to the most typically French tradition: that of the unilinear narration, egocentric, rather narrowly humanist, to the point of seeming abstract.

Although Drieu's novels have common traits which are rather accurately described in the passage just quoted, they offer a great variety of form. What difference, for instance, between the classic economy of *Le Feu follet* and the baroque profusion of *Gilles!* This variety stems mainly from the fact that Drieu was not imitating any preëxisting form but had to invent new forms to fit a new content. As Percy Lubbock pointed out: "The best form is that which makes the most of its subject—there is no other defintion of the meaning of form in fiction."

Drieu's central "subject" is primarily metaphysical: it is the plight of the modern man for whom "God is dead," and his efforts to find purely humanistic values in a universe which is not human, in a society cowardly and insincerely clinging to an obsolete order. But, for Drieu, to repeat with Nietzsche that God is dead is not the calm statement of fact of a materialist. He has a Romantic nostalgia for the time when a mystique was possible and his analysis of decadence consists to a large degree in showing the vacuum left by the disappearance of a mystique. It is significant that Drieu saw in Baudelaire one of the first and certainly one of the most conscious exponents of the idea of decadence in French letters. His summing up of Baudelaire's message applies to his own work: "No mystique is possible in our time, but no man is possible without a mystique. Therefore there cannot be a man in our time, therefore our time goes to nothingness."

In the same manner Drieu has summed up Nietzsche's philosophy in terms that apply to his own views while foreshadowing Camus' philosophy of the absurd and Sartre's existentialism: "Man is an accident in a world of accidents. The world has no general meaning. The only meaning it has is the one we give it one moment, for the development of our passion, of our action."

In such a perspective, politics assume a very important role in man's preoccupations since political anxiety replaces in concrete manner the problem of salvation and destiny. It is little wonder that political novels are so important in contemporary literature.

The novelty of his subjects made of Drieu more an innovator than a follower. We [see] in *Blèche* a case of conflict between form and content. And yet this novel which is not completely successful marks a transition toward the renewal of the genre in contemporary French literature because the conventional novel of psychological analysis is assuming metaphysical dimensions. In this respect both *Blèche* (1928) and *Le Feu follet* (1931), which illustrate Drieu's skill at portraying emptiness and the negativism resulting from this emptiness, are significant forerunners of *La Nausée* (1938). Doubtless, a recent novel like *Les Mandarins* (1954) owes much to the form and the technique originated by Drieu in *Gilles*. At an opposite extreme, an allegorical symbolistic fable like *La Peste* (1947) offers great similarities of form to *L'Homme à cheval* (1943).

Drieu can be considered a forerunner in the introduction of politics in the contemporary French novel. His philosophy of history lends itself well to fiction because he sees history in terms of the most immediate and concrete reality which he transfigures and transposes. By considering human events from the point of view of history, he justifies the importance of his testimony. In that respect what Drieu says of a "noble" writer like Alfred de Vigny applies to himself who, without belonging to the nobility, had a highly developed sense of aristocratic values: "Necessarily the noble writer has the feeling that he derives personally from history, from its rhythm of growth and recession, of grandeur and decadence both his strength and his weakness; in other words, his main reason to testify."

To see in Drieu the novelist only an author of transition, however, would be unfair. The elegant and cruelly ironic *Drôle de voyage* is a masterpiece of its kind and remains one of the best novels of the *entre-deux-guerres*. *Rêveuse bourgeoisie* alone would serve to establish a novelist's reputation. *La Comédie de Charleroi* can stand comparison with the best that has been written anywhere about war. *Les Chiens de paille* may well be a classic of the death agony of Europe.

Even though he always affected to despise the little world of men of letters, Drieu holds an important place in that world. Because of the intrinsic originality of the form of novel he developed, the novel of testimony, because of the opinions in the apparently autobiographical *Gilles,* critics have consistently been influenced by their opinion of the man in their literary judgment of the artist. They have forgotten the primary principle of all literary criticism: the work of art is turned toward us, not toward the author. (pp. 251-55)

> *Frédéric J. Grover, in his* Drieu La Rochelle and the Fiction of Testimony, *University of California Press, 1958, 275 p.*

WILLIAM R. TUCKER (essay date 1965)

[*Tucker is an American critic and educator whose particular field of interest is French right-wing politics. In the following excerpt, he discusses social criticism in Drieu's work.*]

Pol Vandromme has remarked that Drieu's thought commenced with facts but strayed off into a dream. That there was a dualism in his thought between reality and mysticism is clear. Given his artistic temperament, it was inevitable, perhaps, that the military defeat of Nazism, instead of confronting him with the physical and moral consequences of the regime and forcing him to make the realistic judgments that he had earlier been capable of, would only accentuate his search for the metaphysical ideal. Convinced that no hope was left for the West after the collapse of Nazism, he turned to Oriental philosophy, speculating on the soul in terms of Hindu mysticism.

Still, before reaching the stage of complete spirituality, he had not only marshaled statistics to buttress his arguments; he had speculated about problems that were of considerable social and political consequence. In particular, he gave voice to the fears of the independent "little man" who could see the shape of a future that he did not like looming on the horizon. Drieu was aware of the unsettling effect that the growth of bigness had on such individuals, just as he was aware of the important role that the *petite bourgeoisie* played in the rise of fascism in Germany and Italy. And it is possible that he expected some such overt class support for a fascist revolution in France. And yet in his writings Drieu gave not the slightest indication of having any capacity for sustained sociological analysis. While he used such terms as "elite" and "aristocracy," he seems not to have given the least attention to the writings of Pareto, Mosca, or Michels. Indeed, his speculations concerning the rebirth of European man were almost a model of the "soul-stuff" that Bentley disparaged.

In view of Drieu's bias against the world as it was, he would have allowed little in his utopia for sociologists—or economists—to analyze. The familiar scene of pressure groups, classes, parties, and even states, would have been, in his imagination, metamorphosized through fascism into a generalized anarchy in which the individual would have consulted only his own body and his own conscience. Despite his acute perception of the *malaise* that was stirring in the *petite bourgeoisie,* his conscious efforts, at least, seem to have been directed not so much toward the writing of a class doctrine as toward the simpler task of finding a method whereby the individual could leave the world while remaining in it. Thus, his interest in the *petite bourgeoisie* stemmed, apparently, only from his belief that this class had more individuals, like himself, who were uncontaminated by the capitalist-Marxist spirit of the age than did any other class. This assumption was never subjected to any systematic investigation. Nor did his dream of athletes and poets bear any discernible relationship to French grocers, wine merchants, or artisans.

There was implicit in his vision of the new type of man something like Stirner's egoist who would assert his "right"; but in Drieu's aesthetic imagination, the physical hero would also serve as an inspiration to the artists inhabiting his utopia. "Each hero nourishes ten great artists," he wrote. He never made clear the meaning of the relationship between heroes and artists apart from the union of action and thought, but merely suggested toward the end that the hero would inspire the artist with his beauty.

Such heroic and soulful figures might pursue their private ends under the inspiration of a visionary leader suggestive of Doriot or Hitler, and the state might continue a merely formal existence for a time; but as long as it did exist it would be a shell without any intervening social or economic layers separating the inner core, the savior and leader, from the people. Materialism would be eradicated, conflicts would be eliminated, leaving only the mystical interplay between the genius of the leader and the individuals under him. Both the leader and the led would allow no limits to their urge to self-fulfillment since, in Drieu's phrase, "Gods, like poets, need to live the blood of sacrifices."

Nevertheless, Drieu did not believe in the permanence of this relationship between the man of genius and the creative follower. Taking himself as a model of the latter, he could write in 1934:

I shall work perhaps, no doubt I have always been working, for the establishment of a fascist regime in France, but I shall remain as unencumbered by it tomorrow as I was yesterday. Fate, having involved me as an intellectual with its conception, will separate me from it from the moment of its birth, from the first steps of the new regime in the world.

And this independence was reaffirmed in 1942 in a statement that might have come from Alain: "I am not in power, I am never in power, my origins are not among those who are ever in power. I always arrange things so as to be on bad terms with those who are in power, even if they are on my side."

Drieu's temperament was that of the individualist who would have treasured his independence under any regime. It is doubtful that he could be identified as a totalitarian, as the term is ordinarily used in political discourse. He was far from accepting the *fuehrerprinzip* in all of its implications; his sense of nationalism was lukewarm at best; war was considered to be no longer defensible as an outlet for heroism; and even anti-semitism was, for him, not so much a racial bias as a dislike for Jews as the "representatives of the modern world." That politics, to him, was more a temptation than an object of serious study was underlined by his admission that political involvement was usually his antidote for seizures of depression. It has been suggested, in this context, that in Drieu's subjective drama he approached politics as a means of overcoming a part of himself that he disliked. But whatever the cause, his political involvement and his thought suggest more than anything else a nihilist's desire to destroy a world that he disliked. Thus his mania for predicting disasters to come.

His real talent was the use of devastating satire in his novels to depict the social and political life of what appeared to be a narrow, cramped society living on borrowed time. Even his vision of purity, insofar as it took on any tangible outline, was directed toward the opposite pole from the bourgeois France that he could not accept. Every authentically conservative sentiment of the day was made a target by the themes of his work, from his advocacy of socialism to his appeals to revolutionary violence and the abandonment of bourgeois goals. But, especially, a society dedicated in those years to inaction was urged to break with its main characteristic. That there was an air of unreality in his thought is undeniable; but paradoxes and contradictions can abound when the object is to shock the bourgeoisie. Drieu's work shows the spirit of adolescent rebellion against the comfortable mediocrity of the materialistic view of life, the politicians who articulate its values, and the myths associated with it. His views went beyond the spirit of *incivisme*, which permeates all classes in France. Indeed, it appears that his flight was not so much toward totalitarian political systems as it was away from any conceivable regime in France. To remain at least a nominal collaborationist to the end was to give proof of one's nonconformity and spirit of total opposition to the majority, even if that majority consisted of one's own countrymen undergoing the rigors of the Occupation. (pp. 172-75)

William R. Tucker, "Fascism and Individualism: The Political Thought of Pierre Drieu la Rochelle," in The Journal of Politics, *Vol. 27, No. 1, February, 1965, pp. 153-77.*

JOHN UPDIKE (essay date 1965)

[*Considered a perceptive observer of the human condition and an extraordinary stylist, Updike is one of America's most distin-* *guished men of letters. Best known for such novels as* Rabbit Run *(1960),* Rabbit Redux *(1971), and* Rabbit Is Rich *(1981), he is a chronicler of life in Protestant, middle-class America. Against this setting and in concurrence with his interpretation of the thought of Søren Kierkegaard and of Karl Barth, Updike presents people searching for meaning in their lives while facing the painful awareness of their mortality and basic powerlessness. In the following excerpt from an essay first published in the* New Yorker *in October, 1965, Updike reviews* The Fire Within.]

Drieu's *The Fire Within* is a brief, flickering novel issued in France in 1931 as *Le Feu Follet*—"playful fire," an idiom for "*ignis fatuus*," or "will-o'-the-wisp." The will-o'-the-wisp presumably is the hero himself, Alain, whose weak hold upon life finally yields to the pull of suicide. As Alain moves through his last few days vainly seeking an excuse to live, the author subjects him to a bewildering alternation of acute sympathy and stern lecturing. The sympathy probes emotional nihilism to its last dead end and self-defeating checkmate; the lecturing seems delivered from a standpoint nearly Christian:

> Alain had never looked at the sky or the house-fronts or the pavements—palpitating things; he had never looked at a river or a forest; he lived in the empty rooms of this morality: "The world is imperfect, the world is bad. I disapprove, I condemn, I annihilate the world."

Yet although he scolds him as a "fetishist" and a "naïve dandy," Drieu cannot in honesty construct a fictional world that at any point substantially resists Alain's premonitions of futility. So Alain's suicide, instead of afflicting us with the dizzying impression of waste we feel in, say, *Anna Karenina* or *Appointment in Samarra*, arrives serenely, as something appropriate and slightly overdue. It is a kind of happy ending: "A revolver is solid, it's made of steel. It's an object. To touch an object at last."

Alain is much concerned with objects, and part of Drieu's appeal to the modern young must be his flat objectivity, a dispassion that reduces people to a species of object opaque even in their psychology and mute even in speech. In Drieu, the tendency has not achieved the doctrinal purity of Robbe-Grillet; his flat narrative texture is bubbled by incongruous outbursts of sermonizing. But his sense of actuality rejects mankind's ancient claims of special importance, the conviction of spiritual destiny that inflames and inflates the living newspapers of Balzac and Dickens. *The Fire Within* ends a moment before death and begins a moment after coitus. The lover and beloved are discovered looking at each other with eyes dreadfully clear of illusions: "All she saw was a hairy chest, no head. It didn't matter: she had felt nothing very violent either, yet the switch had been tripped, and that was the only sensation she had ever known, not permeating but precise." *The switch had been tripped.* Drieu's mordant and entertaining characterizations—and there are many characters; the novel in form is picaresque—work to mechanize humanity, to chisel a series of hard-featured marionettes:

> Mademoiselle Farnoux smiled at Alain with meagre lust. . . . She was a little girl between forty and sixty, bald, with a black wig on her bloodless skull.

> The doctor was a nervous jailer. His huge round eyes swivelled above cheeks scored by the terror of losing his boarders, and the little beard that substituted for a chin trembled incessantly.

Brancion smiled. He wore his dentures with ostentation; women were not put off by them.

Even the beautiful women are rigid dolls, beyond desire:

[Eva] got up and slid her dress over her head. Then she pulled off her slip, her garter belt, her stockings. She was completely naked, a magnificent, bloodless plaster body.

Maria was Russian. A Russian peasant with a face and a body carved out of wood.

It is natural that Alain, who has some of the instincts of an artist, mocks this de-animated society with ironic collages and random assemblages of objects:

On the mantel, two objects: one a delicate piece of machinery, a perfectly flat platinum chronometer, the other a hideously vulgar painted plaster statuette of a naked woman that he had bought at a fair and took with him everywhere.

In his mirror he has arranged two photographs, a foreshortened man and woman, and between them "a news item pasted on the glass with four stamps reduced the human mind to two dimensions and left it no way out." The third dimension must be the supernatural.

Though *The Fire Within* takes place in Paris, its spiritual locale is the empire of disenchantment whose twin capitals are Paris and New York. The two chief women in Alain's life, his absent wife and his present mistress, are Americans, and his vices and weaknesses seem peculiarly American—drug addiction, sexual inadequacy, fear of losing his youth, a greedy awe of money, an enfeebling dependence upon women. He is described as a Puritan: "a man who saw the vices sprouting from his prejudices, but who was incapable, because of his prejudices, of enjoying his vices." He even has a psychiatrist, who sagely tells him, "A strong, healthy woman like these Americans will make you forget all this." But Americans, as represented in this book, are clearly also "a race exhausted by civilization." The only convinced spokesman for life is a scholar immersed in the study of the gods of ancient Egypt; "he would have liked to recite some of those Egyptian prayers distended with the fullness of being, in which the spiritual life, exploding, pours out all the sap of the earth." Perhaps the reason that the waning of the Christian faith is so peculiarly desolating in France and America is that in these nations the pagan gods, whether Hellenic or Teutonic, were never taken very seriously. The Christian bet was hardly hedged. Pascal and Cotton Mather alike theologize on the basis of a vast gamble, and their heirs feel cheated. "There was, after all, something of the Christian in Alain"—this something, which needs to act and refuses to embrace the mediocre muddle of living, produces, with a purity coolly mathematical, his self-destruction.

The New World to the Old is a hemisphere as disappointingly empty as the heavens. Alain, seeking to save himself, flees to New York and only deepens his plight. Of course, there are differences: Paris is a "lingering, low fever," whereas "New York, at least, was an open atrocity." But the two cities, as spiritual ciphers, are interchangeable. The faddish artistic scene of post-Surrealist Paris strikingly resembles the Camp of contemporary Manhattan:

Among other delusory projects, Alain had thought of opening a shop in Paris or New York to sell all those dated, ugly, or absurd objects

which industry, hovering between the popular and the vulgar, has produced in the last fifty years.

And the lean and sketchy style of the novel itself belongs to the Franco-American world of Hammett/Simenon detective novels and Bogart/Gabin movies and their Existentially fortified *nouvelle-vague* descendants; these things are thin with the thinness that implies a background of immense loss. Drieu La Rochelle is not as cool as his material—hence his erratic imprecations, his disturbing efforts to steer his tale toward an unsighted morality. But this roughness of tone touches the narrative from a source outside itself and recalls a context beyond the mechanical and mocked world Alain haunts, a context in which his extinction can be felt, momentarily, as a waste. . . . (pp. 260-63)

John Updike, "Death's Heads," in his Picked-Up Pieces, *Alfred A. Knopf, 1975, pp. 260-69.**

DOUGLAS GALLAGHER (essay date 1973)

[*In the following excerpt, Gallagher explains how Drieu's war stories reveal the author's conflicting attitudes toward warfare.*]

Drieu's immediate reactions to the war are to be found in the poems he published at that time: strange, brutal, lyrical. By comparison with his short stories the poems now appear somewhat juvenile; Drieu himself was well aware of their shortcomings, notably the final impression that he had welcomed the war unreservedly. He realised that the stark, even crude sentiments of the poems needed to be corrected by another work which would add the necessary nuances, lending greater depth and perspective to the harsh chiaroscuro of the poems; but it was not until 1934 that [*The Comedy of Charleroi, and Other Stories*] were published.

In the intervening period Drieu rapidly established himself as a writer. During the 'twenties he divided his talent between novels that attacked the decadence of Western European, especially French, society and political essays in which he expressed his hopes for the construction of a united Europe. These two themes—spiritual decadence and political reconstruction—were to dominate his writing all his life. (pp. x-xi)

[If] Drieu's war poems were the result of a reflex action, his short stories were the result of long and sober reflection on the fate of those values he had defended so grimly sixteen years before. As he wrote in the last of these stories:

Certainly, I am capable today of making distinctions that I did not make then, that I was incapable of making; a distinction between the war of the past and the war of the present, a distinction between present-day society, which produces present-day war, and another possible society.

Drieu's purpose in these stories is not essentially documentary. Although he describes the reality of combat, the boredom, the fatigue, the appalling conditions—"These communication trenches are filthy, full of the abominable debris that war accumulates as soon as it comes along: tins of food, arms, rifles, packs, boxes, legs, turds, shell cases, grenades, bits of clothing and even paper"—the terror, Drieu has rationalized the chaos of immediacy and ushers us into the calmer, clearer world of ideas.

Inevitably the prevailing idea is destruction.

Anyone who has not seen the emptiness of a
modern battlefield cannot begin to appreciate
the perfidious misery that has fallen on man
and that will destroy Europe. There are thousands of men out there, hundreds of thousands,
and you can't see them. Where are they? Hidden, buried in the earth, already buried. . . .
It's like a lunar landscape—no more houses,
no more trees, no more grass. No animals in
sight for miles around.

Destruction of nature, destruction of men, destruction of a
civilisation. Drieu had heard the ominous ring of Valéry's
famous phrase—"Nous autres, civilisations, nous savons
maintenant que nous sommes mortelles" ["We civilizations
now know that we too are mortal"].

Drieu was profoundly aware of "those million corpses under
our feet," and he realised that in modern warfare they were
not so much the corpses of men nor even soldiers but merely
statistics for another army, an army of civil servants. "It's
more a war for bureaucrats, engineers, an agony invented by
sadistic engineers for a bunch of melancholy bureaucrats."

In his poems Drieu had called upon the combatants to stand
up and show themselves, to meet and fight each other man to
man, instead of killing each other coldly from a distance. One
finds the same appeal in the stories but now the reply is clear:
"Men failed to stand up in the middle of the war—at least all
together. . . . Men failed to be human, they did not try to be
human." The reason for this is made equally clear: modern
war, the bureaucrats' war, is above all a war of machines, "a
war of iron and gas, and not of muscle," "of factories and
not of men," in which the combatants remain face down in
the mud, so much cannon fodder. Throughout the stories Drieu
returns to his attacks on the machinery of war, the artillery
especially, which transforms the would-be warrior into one of
a faceless herd being led to the slaughter, which makes the
cavalryman a horseless anachronism. It is important however
to note that the real object of Drieu's attacks is not the machine
itself but its effect on man, who has become the slave and
victim of his own inventions. The cry of exaltation of the
bayonet charge at Charleroi, one of the isolated examples of
human intervention, is drowned in the howl of terror under the
merciless and inhuman bombardments at Verdun. Verdun has
a terrifying and decisive revelation, for after Verdun war was
no longer a combat but a massacre. For Drieu there are only
two solutions in such circumstances: to stand up and run towards the enemy in a desperate assertion of one's humanity,
as in the charge at Charleroi; or if that is impossible to stand
up and run away from the inhumanity of war. The "hero" and
the "deserter" are from the same mold; both are ready to
sacrifice everything, including their lives, rather than resign
themselves to being shelled and gassed anonymously, rather
than submit to the mechanical annihilation of their human individuality. "How do you protect yourself from an earthquake?
By running away."

But in Drieu's case a puzzle remains. The young man who
was so keen to reach the front in 1914 and then so eager to
get away from it after the charge at Charleroi also chose, at a
time when the vast majority of his compatriots were trying
very hard to escape active service by transfer to the reserve
list, to return to the front line. In the explanation of this seeming
contradiction one finds the essential theme of these stories and
the nucleus of Drieu's attitude towards the Great War.

Above all else Drieu revolts against the destruction not of men
but of man. For if modern war had succeeded in destroying so
much—materially, physically, spiritually—it was because it
had first succeeded in destroying what for Drieu was the prime
value, man himself. Drieu welcomed the war because it presented man with an opportunity to assert himself as a warrior.
Here was an opportunity for Drieu to emulate his childhood
hero, Napoleon, and escape from the decadence and torpor of
pre-war French society. Like the young men of Agathon Drieu
longed for an "action which will absorb us, body and soul.
Only one thing is capable of doing that: war." The idea, though
it was not yet explicitly formulated, of a radical division between man's body and soul ("homo duplex") had begun to
figure as early as 1914 in Drieu's thinking; similar concepts
were to find expression in the work of D. H. Lawrence and
Aldous Huxley, both authors for whom Drieu had a particular
admiration; and by 1934, when these stories were completed,
Drieu had recognised the central importance of these two aspects of man.

Combat afforded a chance to resolve the internal psychological
conflict: hence Drieu's desire to return to the front. His awareness that such unity might be bought only at the price of death
served, if anything, to increase its value. Hence too Drieu's
dislike of the generals, who as leaders and men of action should
have been at the head of their troops but never were. Hence,
finally, the glorification of the hero and the deserter, who refuse
an anonymous death by an invisible piece of machinery, refuse
to allow themselves to become one of the anonymous herd,
and strive to assert themselves as men. Throughout these stories
Drieu returns to the same theme, generally expressed in the
conflict of his own two selves, on the one hand that part of
him dominated by the need for self-realisation in the spiritual
sense, on the other hand that part dominated by the instinct
for self-preservation in the physical sense. Drieu believed that
in order for this conflict to be resolved, for self-realisation to
predominate over self-preservation, it was necessary to seek
the ultimate sanction of death. But only if such an ultimate
sanction were human. Once the sanction becomes mechanical
and inhuman then its value is lost, the conflict itself becomes
meaningless, and man merely the tool of his own self-destruction. Drieu had exalted the notion of the warrior because his
conception of war was based on an idealisation of medieval
warfare and knightly chivalry, but the Great War had nothing
to do with such Quixotry, as the narrator of Charleroi discovered: "Your dream of the elegant, cleancut Middle Ages . . .
has been swallowed up in the fiendish dream of a crazy scientist, who mixes his poisons and stirs up all the fires of hell."
The Great War indeed had little to do with man.

Though Drieu utterly condemned modern war he remained
convinced, true to his dualist philosophy, that war is inevitable
and part of the unity of life itself: "There'll always be love,
always pain. Life and death, pain and joy, will always cancel
each other out so that the sum comes to the same each time."
By 1934 however Drieu could see to what extent the Great
War, by destroying the primacy of man, had undermined all
the other values of Western civilisation.

A soldier is a man. A man is a body. So what
became of my body? I had no call to use it. . . .
That absence of the enemy . . . nullified the
possibility of giving any meaning to my courage, it rendered anything I might do or say
pointless, and paralysed within me all freedom
to act. . . . My ancestors did not build up a

Drieu in 1933. From Pierre Drieu La Rochelle, *directed by* Marc Hanrez. © Editions de l'Herne.

civilisation for us to become incapable of doing anything further, for the movement to burn itself out in a blind absurd paroxysm of machinery.... When man invented the first machine, he sold his soul to the devil, and now the devil was taking his due.... Men who no longer know how to create statues or operas are only fit for cutting iron and steel into little pieces. They are busy hurling thunderstorms and earthquakes at each other, but they do not become gods for all that. They simply stop being men.

If Drieu was never to forget the moment of exhilaration at Charleroi, he also never forgot Verdun, the portent of whose ruins was, so he believed, the ruin of the modern world and modern man.

Sixteen years later, what Drieu recaptured was not so much the bare horror as the complexity of the emotions evoked by that horror. The memory of action works as a trigger for reflection, the one heightening the other, so that the differences and nuances are all the more distinct. Drieu's mastery of style can be seen in the effects he achieves by clever change of pace and rhythm. The charge at Charleroi surges forward in short panting phrases with deliberate repetitions in the vocabulary, the rolling wave abruptly halted by the startling change in tense which marks the end of the charge: "I was waving feebly, I was moaning. I stumbled. I fell." At the end of the last story, too, the staccato rhythms, the elliptical sentences serve to intensify the narrator's feelings of horror. On the other hand the breathlessness of the descriptions of the sacking of the Greek village in **"Expedition to the Dardanelles"** emulates the whirling carousel of alcoholic festivity: "The village was fast becoming a crazy merry-go-round. The people in the streets were becoming all mixed up, were going round in circles, greeting each other, swearing at each other, turning their backs on one another." This humour finds parallels in other stories: Madame Pragen's lorgnette, the antics of Pietro and Mauvier, Blow's ecstatic descriptions of food. It is often conveyed in subtle flashes of seemingly absurd detail, as when the intensity of an artillery bombardment is thus assessed: "There was even a cow that managed to survive until four o'clock in the afternoon." Or as in **"Expedition to the Dardanelles,"** where the narrator makes his advances "between two mouthfuls of chocolate éclair." But it is easy to see that this use of comic relief often conceals a macabre biting irony, as in the gloved hands and expensive cigarettes of Grummer, or the gruesome charade of Madame Pragen's visit by night to the cemetery.

Drieu also uses contrast and juxtaposition to surprise and shock the reader. The pastoral opening of the **"Expedition to the Dardanelles"** is irremediably shattered with two curt sentences—"We are at peace. No. We are at war."—and by the subsequent reversal of vision. The incongruous irruption of a prostitute in **"The Infantry Officer,"** who replies to the austere comment "This war's not made for me" with "Blimey, that's a good one chum! Who is it made for?" contains a wealth of overtones which Drieu leaves the reader to explore. Even when Drieu appears to repeat a theme he contrives to surprise the reader. The effect may be comic, as in **"Expedition to the Dardanelles,"** in which the narrator, having had one rendezvous in a hotel full of clergymen, sets off for a second, in advance of which he anticipates the reader's expectations, "Off I went, half expecting to find myself sitting at a high table of bishops" but disappoints them immediately afterwards. It can be much less comic, as in the two different charges at Charleroi, the one intersected with reflections and hesitations and fresh surges of rhythm, the second immediately cut short by the "Suddenly, bang! On the back of the neck. Ah, I'm dying." It can be grimly tragic, as in the final story, where the narrator meeting a first casualty comments, "Hullo, a casualty. In the arm, nothing serious. That's one bloke who's happy," adopting the same offhand tone when he meets the second, "Hullo, more casualties." The horror of what follows is intensified by the fact that expectations which have been aroused by the deliberate repetition of that opening phrase are shatteringly reversed.

The essential element of Drieu's style is its classicism; everything has been reduced to the significant detail; everything surplus has been pruned and only the salient features are left, these standing out the more starkly for their isolation. In this respect Drieu follows in the tradition of his Norman literary predecessors, Flaubert and Maupassant. One finds examples of his compressed power throughout these stories: for instance when he speaks of his "nice little wound" or of the "sentimental strolls" under enemy fire in the first story. His classicism also reveals itself in the eloquent image or metaphor: "The regiment itself stank to high heaven of filthy greased feet, the street returned the compliment with a stench of armpits"; or in **"The Infantry Officer"** where the meaning of Verdun is expressed in the image of a wristwatch: "I was looking at my watch, which represented my destiny, becoming simpler every minute, reduced to the calculation of probability"; and in the last story, the grim originality of the description of the wounded soldier: "And he was turning his head in all directions, with his habit of seeing. Somewhere there in the midst of that hideous pulp, in that chaos of flesh, there was a double habit of seeing that was looking for us.'' Above all, Drieu's classicism is to be seen in the remarkable economy of the story-teller. In a series of brief rapid master-strokes characters and situations are deftly drawn with a minimum of words, the story told with a maximum of effect. Just as Madame Pragen swings her lorgnette over the ''battlefields,'' so Drieu focuses his circular vision on the war and its effects, returning time and again to the same theme, the same point, but each time with added depth, with a fresh tint, until each element of the kaleidoscope is in place and the picture is complete. (pp. xi-xviii)

> *Douglas Gallagher, in an introduction to* The Comedy of Charleroi, and Other Stories *by Pierre Drieu La Rochelle, translated by Douglas Gallagher, Rivers Press, 1973, pp. vii-xix.*

JONATHAN DALE   (essay date 1976)

[*In the following excerpt, Dale maintains that in* The Comedy of Charleroi, and Other Stories, *Drieu's intention was not to realistically depict war, but rather to denounce the condition of contemporary civilization.*]

La Comédie de Charleroi comprises six stories which critics have tended to treat as independent entities. The few general interpretations have identified its unity with the continuity of the narrative viewpoint and have equated the first person narrator with Drieu himself. In this way the *Comédie* can be interpreted, aided by the legend of Drieu's egocentricity, as an inward-looking work of self-analysis.

Such an equation of first-person narrative with autobiography is particularly widespread in the case of war fiction, though often misleading. If, in the *Comédie,* Drieu does base his stories on his wartime experience, his account of it is not wholly accurate, still less complete. He omits, for example, all reference to a second infantry charge, in Champagne, and to a later heroic exploit for which he was awarded the *Croix de Guerre.* The discrepancy between Drieu's attitudes during the war and the narrator's in these stories is also, as has been suggested above, very wide. An analysis of the total change in Drieu's treatment of France confirms this. He had never been a narrow-minded nationalist; one would not expect him to present the war as a national crusade or war of justice, or to depict the Germans as objects of hatred. None the less a vibrant patriotism sounds in many of the poems of *Fond de Cantine,* which were written between 1915 and 1919, and is still present in 1922 in *Mesure de la France.* Not only did Drieu banish this note completely from the *Comédie* but in it he singled France out as an object of derision. He was clearly projecting on to the war his current preoccupations which included a conviction that France, in its mediocrity and indecisiveness, was the sick man of Europe *par excellence.*

If the essence of the *Comédie* is not autobiography, still less is it a portrayal of the war in its everyday reality. Drieu makes no attempt to rival the many powerful evocations of the war, in its horror or monotony, of his predecessors. This is no work of faithful record. It is rather a description of the world through the self and the self through the world. The static opposition of objectivity and introspection is transcended in the consciousness of a universal decadence, a disease manifested equally in self, war and modern society. The theme of the *Comédie* is that same comedy of decadence of Drieu's novels of sexual analysis.

Drieu, then, through the war is attacking contemporary civilisation as a whole, which has debased the ideal of war as all other ideals. The most categorical expression of this enlargement of the theme is the Infantry Officer's: ''All that's the modern world.'' . . . The disease afflicting war has likewise mutilated love and architecture. . . . When he describes the war as a huge metropolis . . . the nature of the parallel becomes clear: both are manifestations of mass society, where the anonymous individual is caught up in an impersonal structure. Such explicit statements and comparisons are strongly reinforced by symbolic elements in Drieu's descriptions, which have been largely disregarded. A battlefield becomes the battlefield of modern life in its anonymity . . . , its drab featureless uniformity . . . ; in the description of Verdun . . . it represents the void at the heart of modern life. There, the human form is buried out of sight and nature's forms destroyed by the bombardment. Later the narrator encounters a soldier with his face shot away . . . , the sight of which drives him from the battlefield never to return. The destruction of human and natural forms represents the death of Man and of human creativity in the decadence of the modern world.

A lapse of time may be expected to favour wider perspectives. That the wider perspective in Drieu's case should be that of universal decadence is hardly surprising. The current of cultural pessimism had run strong in Europe in the first quarter of this century and Drieu had bathed in it from the outset. Decadence had become a powerful myth in all his writing. During the mid and late twenties, however, it had been tempered by his belief in the feasibility of a federal Europe under the leadership of a reformed capitalism—a late spasm of creative energy in a dying civilisation. By 1933 this dream had become irrelevant; it was confronted on the one hand by a deteriorating international situation following Hitler's accession to power and on the other by the world slump, which had exposed the inability of capitalism to overcome its contradictions and had led to a severe political and social crisis destructive of reformist positions. Drieu's horror of modern war remained, but was now divorced from a convincing strategy for the preservation of peace. Politically he was in a no-man's land between his past reformism and his future fascism, turning perhaps towards the latter but paralysed by his strong reservations about its German and Italian forms, particularly about their militarism. In France itself, in any case, he saw no prospect of radical change. With the internal and international outlook so bleak, Drieu naturally painted his *Comédie* in his palette's darkest shades, expressing more powerfully than ever his mortification at the rottenness of the modern world.

A structural analysis confirms the existence of a concern for the unity of the work as a whole. Firstly, Drieu has multiplied cross references between the stories to bind them together. More important, his ordering of the episodes is not chronological. **"La Comédie de Charleroi"** treats August 1914 from a perspective in 1919; **"Le Chien de l'Ecriture"** moves from February 1916 to some time in the twenties; **"Le Voyage des Dardanelles"** is set in May 1915 and has no later fictionalised perspective; **"Le Lieutenant des Tirailleurs"** looks back at February 1916 from a vantage point in 1917; **"Le Déserteur,"** set in 1932, only cursorily glances back to August 1914; and **"La Fin d'une Guerre"** again has no later fictionalised perspective in its account of an event of October 1918.

He deliberately groups those which share common features: for example the first two stories have in common a narrative viewpoint which is doubly retrospective, and the two more theoretical episodes in dialogue form are placed together near the end. More fundamentally, these alterations to historical sequence are made in the interests of a progressive deepening of the mood of demoralisation. In this light "**La Fin d'une Guerre**" clearly forms a conclusion to the work as a whole rather than an independent episode, for its effect depends on a weakened resurgence of the zeal shown by the narrator in the opening story followed by its—this time—final extinction.

This structurally unifying movement between an initial exaltation and a growing disillusionment is only an aspect of the wider unity of the work which stems from its antithetical nature. This governs almost every aspect of the work, thematic and stylistic, and issues in a series of oppositions—between the *élan* of the charge and its negative counterpart of flight, between heroism and malingering, pride and cynicism, lyricism and its deflation. These oppositions, however, though vital, are contained within the yet more fundamental antithesis between both *élan* and flight on the one hand and the unheroic acceptance of a passive role in a dehumanising war on the other. In a world where choice is reduced to the passive acceptance of an inhuman event or its refusal, heroism, paradoxically, resides in flight. Yet, in relation to the initial dream of exaltation, the loss is immense.

The narrator's immediate response to the war is through a myth derived from childhood dreams and his reading of Nietzsche. He views it as an opportunity to break out of the mediocrity of his daily existence and to realise himself more completely, body and soul . . . , in the intensity of action at the risk of death. . . . In the energy generated and released he discovers a truer freedom and a creativity which arise in the refusal of the given, of the inert masses, of all that is a death-in-life. . . . The hero raises himself up above the prostrate around him in a movement in which his own self too is transcended. . . . (pp. 64-6)

The individualism of the myth is patent. Political perspectives are excluded; patriotism and justice are irrelevancies. In this Nietzschean world history marches on without rhyme or reason and war is but a noble occasion for the clash of conflicting energies. . . . The individual's action is not justified by any contribution it makes to meaningful historical development but by the mere fact of the mark it makes on the world. The essential image for such action is, as for Malraux's Adventurers, aesthetic or formal: the narrator describes himself as "sculpting the shapeless mass of the charge." . . . (pp. 66-7)

Sexuality provides an alternative image. The *élan* of the infantry charge at Charleroi, the principal embodiment of this myth of war, is masculine creativity or spirit wresting itself from its state of givenness and imposing its mark on formless matter just as, in Drieu's mythology, the male dominates and forms the female. If the *élan* is so short-lived it is not merely the effect of the German guns but because it is an ejaculation. . . . (p. 67)

Drieu demonstrates progressively the anachronistic nature of this myth in a world war with its scientifically organised mass slaughter at the hands of an unseen enemy. Such warfare is destructive of man's freedom and creative initiative; rigid hierarchies and organised masses of men leave little room for spontaneity: the test is of industrial power rather than human courage. . . . Men bury themselves deeper in the earth and wait inertly instead of raising themselves above it. . . . The war is an anti-war in every respect, a corruption of the dream. Its

anti-human nature is epitomised by the ruined face of the wounded man.

The same duality emerges in the transformation of the narrator's relationship with his comrades. He presents himelf as a self-conscious bourgeois intellectual. He is an outsider . . . , distrusted by the soldiers and N.C.O.s around him. He longs, however, for contact with the people . . . , is attracted to manual work—if only briefly . . .—and envies the physical strength of the labourer. . . . This desire for contact is rarely consummated. The *Comédie* contains almost nothing of that off-duty *camaraderie* which is so characteristic of the First World War novel. The narrator's one positive experience of a type of fraternity is of a quite different kind, occurring as it does in the intensity of action, during the charge. . . . A collection of individuals in dynamic action together fuses into an organic unity; shaping the world, the group itself is vouchsafed its form. Such a fraternity is distinctively hierarchical: the group recognises and adheres to a leader who has emerged spontaneously from it by virtue of his inner worth.

This mystical union of self and group in attack, this sense of wholeness never returns after the abortive charge at Charleroi. Its failure leads to the disintegration of the group and a consequential development of imagery of fragmentation. Each member turns back into a self-centered, isolated unit; the narrator himself tears away from the battle on his own. Binding love is replaced by divisive hatred, directed both at others and at the self: "Now I was beginning to feel disgusted with all those blokes around me. Or disgusted with myself." . . . (pp. 67-8)

There is one—inadequate—form of escape from the isolation of defeat. The individual, aware of his meaningless situation, may attempt to lose his consciousness of it by plunging into the frenzied tumult of the crowd, which is without form because it is devoid of purpose. This is debased fraternity, that of the urban crowd in all its anonymity and atomisation. The "**Voyage des Dardanelles**" provides many illustrations of this. The narrator exclaims during one such scene: "And I was there, lost in the middle of it all, exulting in my anonymity." . . . As the possibility of creative action vanishes the directional image of the charge is replaced by the whirling movements of a drunken crowd . . . , and of its symbolic counterpart, the spinning top. . . . (p. 68)

The antithetical structure of the world of the *Comédie* seems to suggest that modern life, in war as elsewhere, is destructive of the possibility of creative action without which there can be no organic community. Man is progressively reduced to the wretched alternative of frenzied immersion in the anonymous mass or the demoralising cynicism of the outsider isolated in an absurd world. In the *Comédie,* it is true, demoralisation is the only source of hope.

What can be the significance of the "comédie" of Drieu's title in this dark context? Most critics have interpreted it as "role-playing" and confined their analysis of it to the "**Comédie de Charleroi**" episode where the comedy of inauthentic roles is most in evidence. There the narrator's experience of the war is framed in the social comedy of Mme Pragen's exploitation of her son's death at Charleroi to nourish her own prestige. Her view of the war is wholly mythical, seen as it is through the role of heroic mother which she has since assumed and which blinds her to the reality of the decadence within herself and the war alike. The narrator is able to expose her self-deception but even his position is ambiguous since he is in her service as her secretary. Moreover, since his narration of the battle of Charleroi is from the perspective of 1919 when he returns to the battlefield with her, it is made obvious that neither the heroism of the charge, nor a healthy consciousness of the debased reality of war, have made any impact on the decadent social order of the peace.''

The narrator's own initial role of heroic warrior has been outlined above. Drieu is as concerned as in the case of Mme Pragen to reveal the hollowness of this myth through which the narrator views the war. The narrator himself comes to understand that the objective result of the charge is the senseless death of hundreds of his comrades. . . . The unreality of his nostalgic dream is further exposed by the irony of the rhetorical questions: "Where was the flag? Where are the flags of yesteryear? And the trumpets? And the colonel? And his horse?" . . . Drieu employs a range of comic devices, of which bathos is the most significant, to deflate these myths. A single example must suffice; the charge is lyrically evoked in a powerful rhythmic crescendo: "I was shouting, running forward. . . . With my arms I gathered the men up. I wrested them from the ground and threw them forward," but it is pulled up short by the bathetic: "There was nothing in front of us." . . . In Drieu's view the nostalgic perpetuation of anachronistic dreams is debilitating; restorative action must avoid such role-playing.

The "comédie" of the title, however, is not to be confined to the question of role-playing and the ironic contrast of dream and reality. In Drieu's view man acts out his destiny in different contexts which determine whether his performance will take place in a tragic, epic or comic mode. In an absurd world man's performance can only be comic, in a sense close to "derisory" ("comédie" tends to have pejorative overtones). War, which should be the *décor* for a dramatic figuration of man's heroic and generous nature, is a disillusionment: "One fights to express something . . . to give a performance." But "this particular performance was a flop." . . . The reality of the war, which had served to undermine the myths, is revealed as a degraded, essentially comic reality, which itself must be negated if Man is to be reborn.

In the **"Voyage des Dardanelles"** the "comédie" lies neither in role-playing nor in the ironic discrepancy between dream and reality; for the dream has disappeared and has not been replaced by any faith in the future. Perspectives are confined to the present. In the aimlessness, the absurdity of his situation, man's enactment of his destiny has lost its dynamic and dramatic forms—which the charge had represented—and has subsided into a formless stasis. The mood is one of demoralisation which generates the darker comedy of derision. Drieu significantly adopts a quite different style for much of this episode, one reminiscent of Céline in its cynicism and self-disgust. Its slangy, broken syntax is intended to convey the fragmentation and absurdity of contemporary life. But this slang differs radically from the usual slang of soldiers' speech in war fiction and has a quite different function. It is also significant that the narrator's squad now includes both a former acrobat and a clown and that he himself is seen busking to pay for his drink. . . . Scenes of mob intoxication and aimless riot pervade the episode, imbuing it with a coarse humour. The narrator, it is true, does eventually attempt to break free from this static, demoralised world. But his lone attempt to silence an enemy machine gun comes too late and the episode ends with the narrator awakening next morning "in a shell hole." . . . Far from escaping from the "comédie" of the world through such an instinctive resurgence of heroism, his act is itself, in its inef-

fective and short-lived nature, to be viewed in part with irony; at the most such a nostalgic spasm of heroism may preserve the narrator from the leprosy . . . of demoralisation. It is no real way forward for the shell hole is a reminder of its counterpart at Charleroi into which the charge tumbles when its impetus is broken and from which "we have never managed to get out to continue our advance." . . . (pp. 68-70)

Heroic zeal is treated with still deeper irony in the concluding episode, **"La Fin d'une Guerre."** This relates the narrator's temptation to risk his life again in a wholly gratuitous last visit to the front lines. The *élan* is here a mere theatrical gesture. . . . It is in all respects an ironic contrast to the charge at Charleroi: the narrator has no intention of fighting, walks rather than runs and is alone. This time his zeal is finally broken by his encounter with the man wounded in the face; he leaves the front never to return.

The novel ends on this negative note; there is no way back to an ideal in the past and no explicit orientation towards a future in which nobility, and hence tragedy, will again be possible. The *Comédie* is rather a work of demystification, preparatory to some future cultural renaissance. Drieu limits himself to furthering awareness of the anti-human nature of modern war and the modern world; the comedy, even farce . . . , of the work is an expression of this dehumanisation. Tragedy is impossible when men no longer express their passions in direct confrontations. Drieu may yearn for the epic and the tragic, but these are not real options since they depend upon faith and faith is absent from the *Comédie* and, in Drieu's eyes in 1933, incompatible with the modern world. This comedy of disenchantment, one might suggest, becomes inescapable from the moment when the charge is halted and the narrator separates from his men. That destruction of meaningful action creates a fundamentally ironic distance between the self and the world of war. Whether or not Drieu's innate talents were lyrical and epic as he sometimes claimed, his vision of the world was in fact compatible only with satire. Drieu came closer to reality when he envisaged his work as that of a satirist, a Daumier rather than a Delacroix.

It must already be apparent that the *Comédie* is no representative novel of the First World War. It does contain many of the habitual scenes, from the excitement of mobilisation to a gruelling night march and the officer shot in the back by his own men; but these do not begin to compare in descriptive power to similar scenes in many of Drieu's predecessors. His concern is not with realism in the sense of accurate observation and detailed description. His realism lies in a distillation of the experience of war in which non-essential elements are evaporated away, leaving behind a concentrated spirit—the significance of the war for modern Western culture. This explains the absence of other no less universal experiences, ones which Drieu himself had known, such as relaxed off-duty group conversations, contacts with friends and relations, etc. These simply do not accord with his interpretative framework with its emphasis on the atomisation inherent in mass society.

This wider interpretation of the war's significance, which distinguishes the *Comédie* from most earlier fiction of the war, relates it at the same time to important contemporary trends in the French novel, in particular to the many works which diagnose a disease of modernity spreading malignantly through the body of Western civilisation. This diagnosis is also an accusation. The works of Bernanos, Giono, Céline and Guilloux at this time constitute a "trial of bourgeois civilisation in its entirety." In so far as the war is widely seen as the most horrific manifestation of that disease it is natural that these writers should use it as evidence in the trial. Works such as Giono's *Le Grand Troupeau* (1931), Céline's *Voyage au bout de la nuit* (1932), Drieu's *Comédie* and Guilloux's *Le Sang Noir* (1935) represent a tendency for the War no longer to be "viewed in isolation as a thing in itself."

The anti-war novel, early predominant in France, seems to divide at this time, through the combined effects of distance from the war and a deepening social crisis, into two more distinct forms, both of which offer a larger interpretation of the war's significance. The rather helpless, if defiant, note of protest of much early war fiction is either subsumed in a wider and more coherent critique of our civilisation; or the defiance is sharpened into a more precise analysis of the political system held to have produced the war and a more positive conception of what could replace it. This is the contribution of Aragon's *Les Cloches de Bâle* (1934).

To simply submerge the *Comédie* in the current of literary history, however, is to neglect its originality. Amongst its most distinctive features are the retrospective elements in its narrative point of view and its essentially antithetical nature; for, however much it is a warning about modern warfare, it also contains a dream of ideal combat which, although inapplicable in present conditions, remains in its essence inviolate. Through the *Comédie* we are able to witness a transformation of the heroic mode of war fiction, under the pressure of reality, into pacifist protest.

The fact that Drieu was himself divided helps to prevent the *Comédie,* despite its warning function, from suffering from the ill-effects which the "will to prove" may produce. He has no simple answers; emotionally torn himself, he cannot be over-dogmatic. His structural and narrative techniques, moreover, in their constant shifts of viewpoint and scene, serve to fragment the narrator's conceptual analysis of the war and to integrate the fragments with the narration of a concrete episode in his war experience. Where theoretical discussion does predominate, in **"Le Lieutenant des Tirailleurs"** and **"Le Déserteur,"** the dialogue form reflects Drieu's divided attitudes. Finally, since the *Comédie* is limited to critical perspectives and eschews speculation about solutions it remains steeped in the experience of decadence which is a visceral reality for Drieu.

La Comédie de Charleroi which, in its very lack of vivid description, in its images compressed to the point of abstraction, in the importance of its ideological framework, would seem endangered as fiction by such didactic essay-like elements in Drieu's approach, is not in the end much weakened by these. Indeed the uniqueness of the work is largely derived from them. In almost all respects it is a thoroughly unified work. Structure, narrative and stylistic techniques all contribute to the exposure of the debased nature of modern war and society, the recognition of which, in Drieu's eyes, is an essential precondition for any renewal of the human spirit. If the *Comédie* has been so rarely examined both in itself and in terms of its place in the evolution of first world war fiction in France, it is because the unity and the wider implications of this apparently loose collection of war stories have been almost wholly disregarded. (pp. 70-2)

> Jonathan Dale, *"Drieu la Rochelle: The War as 'Comedy',"* in The First World War in Fiction: A Collection of Critical Essays, *edited by Holger Klein, The Macmillan Press Ltd., 1976, pp. 63-72.*

BARNETT SINGER   (essay date 1977)

[*In the following excerpt, Singer discusses the development of Drieu's fascist thought.*]

Drieu informs us that he had always wanted to be a man, but for readers schooled in the fiction of our century, with its sometimes suffocating individual focus, efforts in print to be a man cannot be considered original. Indeed, it is in his novels that Drieu's autobiographical prolixity becomes most irritating. Since the time of Zola, and particularly with the rise of Gide, a new dispensation allowed French novelists to discuss themselves at least as much as others in their work; and so Drieu, going beyond the more artistic Gide, made *all* his novels confessionals. For that reason it is unnecessary to read each one.

Perhaps most typical is *Gilles* . . . , the one he himself liked best and which used his own life most openly in the putative cause of human improvement. *Gilles* tells the story of how one man became a Fascist. It is a *Bildungs-roman,* as well as a didactic novel; in the preface Drieu says it is meant to demonstrate the course of decadence—the consequences of bad French blood in the twentieth century. The action begins near the end of World War I with an amorous conquest by the hero, the first of a succession; and we are introduced to the coming world of jazz and cocktails. The scene is somewhat reminiscent of Gide's earlier and pioneer novel, *L'Immoraliste* (1905). Having married a woman he does not love, Gilles not only takes mistresses on the side but he flaunts them before his wife. This causes her father to commit suicide and the marriage to break up. Many more women follow—of different kinds and nationalities—while in the meantime he is also compelled to embark on his intellectual odyssey toward Fascism. By the thirties he works on a literary review, and finally, renounces the life of pleasure and espouses the strict life of Fascist renewal. As the Nazis reacted against the flaccid spirit of Weimar, so Gilles renounces the frivolity and self-indulgence of the French 1920's. Thematically, the novel holds together; but in the execution—in character portrayal, plot, and sheer interest value—it does not escape mediocrity. Trying to shock the reader with a mixture of Huysmans and Nietzsche, he fails. The problem of a work of fiction resting too heavily on an individual and his ideas is also seen in a far better novel of the period, Malraux's *Man's Fate,* which, because of its outmoded Nietzscheism has not lasted as well as, say, *Darkness at Noon,* where ideas woven into character problems and plot still speak eloquently to us. Perhaps we have read too much and seen too much that is intended to shock; but even some of Drieu's contemporary readers may have been sated with the seamy personal traits he had already exposed in earlier novels. To dress up confession in ideas was not an adequate substitute for real fiction, and Drieu probably knew that.

Then there was his prolific and peppery journalism. In expository writing on issues of his day Drieu wished to join what Laura (Riding) Jackson calls "an intellectual-leader race of master minds"; or rather, he wished to *s'imposer.* Ironically, his fundamental desire was to be serious enough and patient enough to create art; in a last and unfinished novel, *Mémoires de Dirk Raspe,* Drieu's admiration for ascetic artists was clear. But as Alistair Hamilton notes, "he knew perfectly well that there was no surer recipe for mediocrity than political journalism." And he wrote too much of it.

Drieu's drift toward fascism in his journalism was, I suggest, a reaction against his own sense of impotence. For extreme right as well as for extreme left in the inter-war years, the bourgeois, middle-of-the-road, liberal democracy was the enemy. Thus in *Genève ou Moscou* . . . Drieu vowed a relentless struggle against all institutions, the first step in any authoritarian scheme. He noted that strength and beauty in present-day France could be felt only in evil and destruction; that entities like God, aristocracy, bourgeoisie, and even country no longer existed and that death encompassed everything. How seriously should we take this conventionally anti-bourgeois outburst? Rather seriously, if we are to discuss Drieu's philosophy; not too seriously if we contrast it with his actions and lifestyle. For to be a writer means almost by definition to be a bourgeois; in order to write one must have privacy; whereas Fascism, or any variant of it, means, in the view of scholars like Hannah Arendt, the total destruction of privacy.

This is only one of several contradictions in Drieu. His philosophy itself is unstable—sometimes moving toward socialism, sometimes toward internationalism, sometimes toward a medieval organicism. Like all authoritarians Drieu can perhaps best be understood, coherently summarized, in what he opposed, rather than in what he upheld. As a Barrèsian organicist he especially detested cold rationalism, which he thought had made France unadventurous and sclerotic. (Paradoxically, Drieu's own consistent attempts at irrational *tours de force* are tiresome and draining, in contrast to the energy of a rationalistic Voltaire or Descartes.) He also detested the middle class, as noted above, and disliked capitalism and Jews specifically as sustaining elements of middle-class values. In 1938 he wrote an often quoted line: "Ce que je reproche avant tout aux juifs, c'est d'être des bourgeois qui embourgeoisent tout ce qu'ils touchent" ["I reproach the Jews above all for being bourgeois who make bourgeois everything they touch"]. . . . He wanted to limit the number of emancipated Jews in professions and to put traditional Jews back in ghettoes. For the demise of French greatness he blamed not only Jews, but also teachers, professors, politicians of all stripes, Marxists, and even, in one breathtaking string of scapegoats, April 15 of that year, "les écrivains (comme moi) . . ." ["writers (like me)"]. . . . He also opposed the extension of mass culture, and increasingly viewed America and England, allied with the "judeo-masonic" international, as cultural manipulators "dans le monde du cinéma et de la presse, de la littérature et du sport" ["in the world of cinema and press, of literature and sport"]. . . . In some articles he derided and dismissed the workers, in others he discussed their possibilities for mobilization. Full of concepts and generalizations to support all this antipathy, Drieu never succeeded in disguising his tenuous positions.

But in addition to sheer opposition, there is in Drieu the classic Fascist exhortation of a return to origin and rebirth. In order to effect such change, there must be struggle—to call Drieu a neo-Darwinian is not an exaggeration. Where Drieu wishes to return is to mystical sources of French strength found in the countryside and its churches; to nature generally, and above all, to uprightness and health. As Bernard Frank correctly notes, the Fascist is "un homme sain" ["a healthy man"], a clear contrast to "le pâle Drieu" himself. It is no accident that Drieu begins a list of Fascist virtues with "santé" ["health"], followed by "dignité, plénitude, héroïsme". . . . Perhaps all psychically unhealthy people aspire finally to wholeness, though only a few wish to foist it upon others as well. When he joined Jacques Doriot's *Parti populaire français* in the mid-thirties, Drieu wrote of the need for a general health revolution, especially to counteract an overly mental existence such as his own. Both he and the P.P.F. called it specifically "Une Rév-

olution du corps" ["A revolution of the body"]. They demanded expanded sport facilities financed by the government and hiking associations modelled upon Hitler's "Strength through Joy" group. Clairvoyant in one sense, Drieu envisioned a future where people would live in the healthy, uncluttered countryside and commute by rapid transportation to work.

The importance of hero worship in Drieu's ethos has been mentioned, as well as a feeling or need in him that went back at least to his schoolboy reading of Napoleon's exploits. On the Hitlerian, Drieu wrote in 1941 that he is a man who rejects culture, steeling himself against sexual and alcoholic depravity, and dreaming of bringing physical discipline to the world. The hero rejects and defeats culture because, in Drieu's negative view, culture has been slipping anyway since the nineteenth century. At best, writers could only transcribe symptoms of decline, and not surmount them. In Zola Drieu saw fine portrayals of "la syphillis urbaine" ["urban syphillis"]; in Mallarmé's poetry "le chef-d'oeuvre de l'onanisme" ["the masterpiece of onanism"]; in Proust "la bourgeoisie finissante" ["the dying bourgeoisie"]; in Paul Valéry, whom he read and re-read, the genius of "la France finissante" ["dying France"]. . . . So if it comes down to a choice between culture and heroism, the latter, especially for Drieu of the thirties, wins out.

Drieu's main quarrel with culture was its effeminate nature, and like more conventional conservatives, he attacked the mass media and café's because they engendered passivity. The good hero personifies the virile struggle of authentic, linear culture against the random and passively accepted cosmopolitan culture. In a succinct way Drieu expressed this position during the late thirties: "Avec [Jacques Doriot] la France du camping vaincra la France de l'apéro et des congrès" ["with (Jacques Doriot) the France of camping out will vanquish the France of cocktails and of conferences"]. . . . This was written at the height of his admiration for Doriot and for the *Parti populaire français*, but even after that admiration waned and was replaced by collaboration during the war, he was still using the same kind of "struggle" metaphors. In *Notes pour comprendre le siècle* . . . , the most typical exposition of his Fascism, Drieu accounted for the defeat of 1940 in a series of Manichaean opposites, evil of course defeating good. The France of scouts, hikers, and skiers had been too weak to overcome the France of idlers, Pernod drinkers, river bank fishermen, and salon, committee, and syndicate charlatans; the France of Morocco and Indochina, of aviators and missionaries had succumbed to a France of the homey "pantouflard" type, of card players and bowlers. Each estate—a corrupt press, a middle-class nobility, a weak bourgeoisie, an avaricious peasantry—had contributed to the defeat.

When I first read these *Notes* years ago I was outraged. The same feeling of moral sickness came over me, such as one would have reading Koestler or Orwell, Mandelstam or Marc Bloch in the 1930's. There was not yet the feeling of sickness without catharsis that came from a closer inspection of La Rochelle. What scholars rarely point out, eschewing ambiguities, is that part of the original Fascist appeal was to the good and perfectly legitimate human impulses. No one can defend weakness, and modern man *is* prone to weakness, as Orwell, among many other non-Fascists, strongly emphasizes. Neither can one quarrel with the idea of improvement or with the idea of simply getting more exercise in the fresh air. Nor can one refuse at least to debate the idea of a return to origins in a century of dislocation and anomie. It is obvious that the

Nazis, in particular twisted their ''good'' ideals within the crucible of their many evil ones, and became quickly and wholly monstrous in the process. ''On ne badine pas avec l'histoire'' [''one doesn't take history lightly''] someone has said, and certainly the warning is most apt in our own century. It might be heeded by all contemporary writers who demonstrate what Edward Shils calls ''the aggrieved look.''

Now Drieu's writing, in particular, became increasingly the writing of a universal critic and accuser. A man who demanded constant change in the outside world, he also knew he could never change the face in the mirror, nor the weakness within himself. So he blamed, exhorted, yet did not set an example, either with accomplished prose or with meaningful action. In a confused decade that required clarity Drieu supplied the reverse: angry, hostile, polemical he confused more than he helped to clarify; and wailing continually about decline he helped only to bring on doom. His editorials left no room for good action nor for good judgment to assert itself. Particularly from the time of Munich his articles were so much in conflict and so muddled that they almost bring pain to a contemporary reader— pain for a civilization dying amid such confusion; and pain that far overshadows the slightest pity one might have for Drieu himself.

To be fair, he was far from the sole critic around, but just one more representative of a growing genre of French writers. It is hard to date the beginnings of this polemical trend with any precision, though the war of 1870 was undoubtedly a great stimulus. The causes of the French debacle at Sedan had been fiercely debated, and they brought forth explanations from obscure men (like de Gaulle's father) and famous men alike. Among the latter, Ernest Renan blamed the defeat on rising French mediocrity and materialism, as well as inadequate scientific knowledge and education; while Hippolyte Taine saw the roots of the disaster in the utopian cast of the French Revolution—a latent tendency toward abstraction that flowered in the nineteenth century. Many writers also considered German Protestantism as more apt to preserve manly and scientific virtues in modernity than French Catholicism; others harped on deficiencies of the French people. (pp. 406-10)

Perhaps Drieu was not as bad as the spiteful and deaf Maurras, or the limping and failed Goebbels, boiling with blame and full of revenge. Certainly he did not have the pomposity of a Maurras or Goebbels—he knew his deficiencies as well as anyone. But his obsessions festered and worsened with the war and the collapse of France. As editor of the war-time *Nouvelle Revue Française*, co-founder of *Le Fait*, and contributor to newspapers like *Je Suis Partout*, his articles grew more and more prolix on the subjects of race and nationality, taking to task now the Americans, now the British, now the beleaguered Jews. He continued to write of rotting capitalism, of the ruined bourgeois, ruined workers, and ruined Frenchmen generally. Already he had contemplated and even attempted suicide several times, always maintaining that after age fifty it was not worth living anyway, that baldness and rotting teeth were too much to bear. By 1943 he attained the half-century mark. Lonelier than ever toward the end, collaborating with the Germans yet sometimes secretly on the Allied side, knowing that the Allies now had a good chance of winning, knowing that if this were the case he would be punished severely and perhaps be executed, he saw no way out. As early as *Gilles* there had been in some of his prose an autumnal quality—bits that are lyrical and worth quoting: ''Gilles avait lié sa solitude à l'âme de France. A pied ou en voiture, il avait pèleriné dans tous les

lieux, dans tous les sites. Il avait interrogé les montagnes et les rivières, les arbres et les monuments'' [''Gilles had linked his solitude with the soul of France. On foot or in a car, he had made a pilgrimage to every port, every site. He had questioned the mountains and the rivers, the trees and the monuments'']. . . . Ah, he continued in the same passage, France can no longer build great cathedrals, and that is the crux of the problem. The past may be glorious but it is never the present—it is gone. And so, a few years later, was Drieu. (pp. 412-13)

Barnett Singer, ''The Prison of a Fascist Personality: Pierre Drieu La Rochelle,'' in Stanford French Review, *Vol. I, No. 3, Winter, 1977, pp. 403-14.*

THOMAS M. HINES   (essay date 1978)

[*In the following excerpt, Hines surveys Drieu's works, tracing his literary and political development.*]

Although Drieu first achieved recognition as a poet (*Interrogation,* 1917, his collection of war poems, is still highly regarded by critics), he quickly adopted the novel and essay as his preferred means of expression. His initial efforts at writing fiction were predictably awkward and somewhat erratic. Typical of most young writers, Drieu chose to portray aspects of his own life in his first ''novel,'' *Etat civil* (*Vital Statistics*), 1921. Mixing autobiographical references and childhood fantasies, Drieu compiled the first of his many fictional counterparts, young Cogle, rebellious child of the times. In this work, Drieu enunciated a primary theme of his writings—the yearning to be free from the bonds of a prescribed social and psychological identity. Like young Cogle, later protagonists in Drieu's novels would seek to go beyond the cumbersome weight of family heritage in order to achieve a new self-perception.

In 1922 Drieu's first book-length essay appeared, *Mesure de la France* (*A Close Look at France*), and his reputation as a provocative and controversial political analyst was immediately established. Contrary to popular opinion, Drieu warned his countrymen that victory over the Germans had not been exclusively a French triumph but the result of the timely intervention of foreign powers on their side. The inability of the French to control their destiny as a nation was caused, Drieu believed, by a profound decadence which had afflicted every aspect of society. In his eyes, the most deplorable signs of this lack of individual and national vitality were a declining birth rate and the attendant repercussions upon France's role as a world leader.

In his second novel, *L'Homme couvert de femmes* (*The Ladies' Man*), 1925, Drieu mercilessly dissects the moral emptiness and sexual excesses of the post-war generation in France. In this denunciation of the gilded youth of the ''Roaring Twenties,'' Drieu forged a style of writing that would become closely identified with his fiction: unfailingly tasteful, his novels were nonetheless negative in tone and harshly critical of society and the author himself. As an active participant in the drama of his era, Drieu infused his works with a spirit of personal commitment and undeniable sincerity. His truculence and urbane cynicism only served to mask a feeling of pervasive despair. The motivating force behind his literary activity was undoubtedly his quest for self-identity and a unified personality. As Drieu later explained in the autobiographical essay, ''L'itinéraire,'' he had always considered his inner self to be fertile ground for literary experimentation. By isolating certain of his own attributes (primarily negative ones) within various fictional characters, he could then manipulate and observe the interplay of these qualities and possibly arrive at a deeper understanding of his psyche through this method of self-analysis. Each novel, therefore, would portray a new but evanescent image of the author in search of himself.

One drawback to this autobiographical approach to literature was the inevitable tendency on the part of the reader to see in these fictional counterparts little more than a cleverly altered mirror-image of Drieu himself. In spite of the demonstrable artistry of his narrative technique and characterizations, Drieu would long be denied the title of authentic novelist. For later generations—and in some respects even today—Drieu would be the dissolute womanizer of *The Ladies' Man,* more libertine than dedicated artist, supremely callous and exploitative in his dealings with the opposite sex. Yet the fictional Drieu—i. e., the side of his personality he delineated in such unflattering terms—cannot be totally affiliated with the private Drieu. Rather than simple reflections of their creator, Drieu's characters were essentially prismatic in composition and effect. Although reasonably faithful to real-life prototypes, they would take on different shapes and colorations once engaged in the flow of action and subjected to the exigencies of plot and dramatic tempo. Fictional autobiography, therefore, was not so much a self-indulgent or narcissistic mode of expression as it was a genuine effort on Drieu's part to capture the essence of an entire generation through self-examination. In this capacity as a witness of his times, Drieu has been compared to the American expatriate writers of the post-war era, in particular Fitzgerald and Hemingway. Just as *The Sun Also Rises* heralded a new sensibility in American letters, *The Ladies' Man* was a work of ground-breaking dimensions as well in its portrayal of a new European *mal du siècle*—a sense of moral and spiritual void in a world fragmented by war and social alienation.

Although Drieu continued to write fiction during the late twenties and early thirties, his attention was turned more and more toward politics. In two major essays during this period—*Genève ou Moscou* (*Geneva or Moscow*), 1928, and *L'Europe contre les patries* (*Europe Against National Boundaries*), 1931—Drieu warned prophetically that the revival of nationalistic passions throughout Europe would only impede the creation of a unified continent. As a confederation of states (similar to the Helvetian model), Europe could then promote its best interests by counterbalancing the growing influence of the youthful American and Russian empires. Divided into opposing national groups, however, the nations of Europe would be unable to resist the "imperialistic" designs of American capitalism and Soviet communism. In this respect, it is worth noting that more than thirty years later the well-known French magazine editor and politician, Jean-Jacques Servan-Schreiber, in his best-selling book, *Le Défi américain* (*The American Challenge*), would dramatically catalog the extent to which American technocratic know-how had dangerously eroded both French and European autonomy in critical areas by a form of economic colonization—a trend that Drieu had intuitively grasped and decried years before. (pp. 4-6)

During the thirties, Drieu's talents as a novelist flourished in a most impressive fashion. After attempting a novel of manners with strong political overtones, *Une Femme à sa fenêtre* (*A Woman in the Window*), 1929, he turned for inspiration to the tragic existence of his friend and former surrealist companion, Jacques Rigaut. In the novel, *Le Feu follet* (*Will o' the Wisp*), 1931, Drieu reconstructs the last two days in the life of Alain, a drug addict, within a framework of Racinian concision and

purity. Just as Rigaut himself had done shortly before his suicide, Alain languishes in a rest home for wealthy neurotics in an unsuccessful effort to cure himself of his habit. Yet drug addiction is only a manifestation of a more profound social ill—that of decadence. As a child of the times, Alain has no reserve of self-discipline to draw upon. Appealing to his will power to overcome his difficulties, as the resident psychiatrist does, is a futile request. His friends cannot tolerate Alain's nihilistic despair which undermines their own sense of purpose and worth. Having spent his youth as an emotional and economic parasite, living off the generosity of his wealthy mistresses and estranged wife, Alain is now unable to endure the everyday pressures of life without the euphoric prophylaxis of drugs and easy money. His last gesture is one of total lucidity and resignation. He performs the only meaningful act he is still capable of accomplishing to lessen his anguish. He presses a revolver to his heart and pulls the trigger. Very few novels of this period have portrayed in such realistic terms the complete isolation of the individual in a world where even the most elementary communication is impossible. Ten years before the appearance of Camus' *The Stranger,* Drieu was examining, in *Will o' the Wisp,* the problem of man's inability to touch others around him or find meaning in a world where he no longer seems to belong. Retrospectively, Alain can be seen as one of the precursors of the existentialist anti-hero: the social misfit whose existence is stripped of essential values and defined in the end only by an extreme form of action.

In 1933, one of Drieu's most personally revealing novels was published, *Drôle de voyage* (*Strange Journey*). In much the same vein as *The Ladies' Man,* Drieu makes a romantic interlude in his own life the central focus of the work. While vacationing at the provincial home of a friend, Gille Gambier (Drieu's fictional counterpart), a young diplomat, becomes infatuated with a beautiful and wealthy Englishwoman, fleetingly contemplates marriage, but backs off at the last minute for fear of surrendering his freedom to the placid mediocrity of his fiancée's homelife. Disheartened by this experience, Gille resumes the "strange journey" of his affective odyssey, drifting from one casual affair to the next without being able to commit himself fully to another individual. In view of Drieu's use of literature as a means of self-awareness, the unsparing portrait he draws of Gille (i.e., his own reluctance toward any form of emotional involvement) tends to foreshadow the choice he will make the following year to escape the bondage of Parisian adultery and intrigue by devoting his life to a more exacting cause. This decision to forego dilettantism for political commitment was in part motivated by Drieu's horror of following in the footsteps of his father whose own life had been ruined by his sensual nature and lack of self-discipline.

Indeed, this obsessive concern with his youth and family background reaches its apogee in Drieu's next major novel, *Rêveuse bourgeoise* (*Middle-Class Illusions*), 1937. As though compelled to do so after his father's death in 1934 (his mother had died in 1925), Drieu undertook the painful task of recasting his youth and early manhood into fictional form. By reliving in this manner his bitterly unhappy childhood, Drieu hoped to view his formative years in a clearer perspective as well as demonstrate, in the last analysis, that hereditary character flaws could be overcome by decisive action. Thus, in the military hospital where he lies dying of gangrene, Yves Le Pesnel knows that courage is the product of a willful act and that, by his heroism in combat, he had dispelled his fears of being contaminated by his father's weakness and failure in life.

Although heavily autobiographical in its conception, *Middle-Class Illusions* is nonetheless a thoroughly imaginative work of art in which, contrary to his narrative style, Drieu switches unexpectedly from a third-person to a first-person perspective in the final section of the novel. In so doing, Drieu chooses to continue the story of the Le Pesnel family from the point of view of Yves' sister, Geneviève—the only time in his writings that Drieu ever adopted a first-person female vantage point. In *Middle-Class Illusions*, Drieu temporarily suspends his misogynistic tendencies and portrays Geneviève in a favorable light. As an actress, she must artfully lie to her audience in order to give the illusion of reality just as the novelist must necessarily distort the past he seeks to recreate in his writings. By means of this male-female duality of narration, Drieu was trying to probe and elucidate a certain sexual ambivalence within himself that lay at the very heart of his negative attitude toward women. Overall, *Middle-Class Illusions* is an impressive cornerstone in the autobiographical edifice that Drieu constructed, book by book, in an effort to objectify his innermost conflicts.

Gilles (1939), by far Drieu's most ambitious work of fiction, is a prime example of how the autobiographical novel can become, through its treatment of the important literary and political issues of the times, much more than a reflection of the authorial self. Taking over in a sense where *Middle-Class Illusions* left off, *Gilles* recounts the sentimental and ideological odyssey of Gilles Gambier (a similar version of the protagonist in *Strange Journey*) from the trenches of the First World War to the bloody skirmishes of the Spanish Civil War. As a satirical work, *Gilles* cruelly lampoons the idiosyncracies and bold pretentions of the surrealist movement. For several years after the First World War, Drieu had been close friends with Louis Aragon and had actively participated in the group's demonstrations, especially the mock trial of Maurice Barrès. On a political level, the novel shows how certain conservative elements of the post-war generation in France (namely Drieu and other anti-democratic intellectuals) were attracted to fascism in protest over the ineptitude and venality of the scandal-ridden Third Republic. At the end of the novel, Gilles Gambier leaves the French diplomatic corps and casts his lot with the Franco loyalists in central Spain, thereby rallying to the fascist cause and renouncing the republican ideal in the process. In a similar manner, Drieu himself would publicly announce his intentions to collaborate with the German occupational forces in Paris shortly after the Fall of France. Thus, *Gilles* can be viewed not only as a critical summing-up of Drieu's life but also as a prophetic novel that foreshadows his entry into the collaborationist ranks. (pp. 7-10)

In 1941 one of Drieu's most impressive essays appeared, *Notes pour comprendre le siècle* (*Notes For Understanding Our Times*). This apology of totalitarian man and his ethos analyzes the progressive loss of equilibrium between mind and body from the Middle Ages to modern times. It was Drieu's contention that the totalitarian (primarily fascist) revolution of the previous two decades had been in truth a therapeutic correction of a profound social and spiritual malady, created by the excessive emphasis that Western societies placed on analytical skills to the detriment of intuitive or affective knowledge. By not developing his body on a parity with his intellect, twentieth-century man—prior to the advent of fascism—had burdened himself with a divided self which was the heritage of eighteenth-century rationalistic thought. At present, however, the totalitarian countries had restored the body and its imperatives to their rightful place by stressing the importance of sports and

physical conditioning. In this manner, a new man—aggressive and vigorous—would arise and supplant his decadent predecessor of the rationalistic era. Together with a renewed physical dynamism, a sense of deep spiritual awareness would also reappear, fostered by the mystique of the new order. According to Drieu, therefore, fascism was primarily a restorative movement dedicated to purging Europe of its decadent spirit and introducing its people to an era of prolonged health—both politically and morally speaking.

As Drieu discovered shortly thereafter, Hitler's continental politics were unworthy of such encomiums. Progressively disillusioned over the imperalistic designs of the German armies and their disregard for the institution of a European confederation of national states, Drieu began to judge his political affinities and the Collaboration in a much harsher light. In 1943 Drieu published a novel of pivotal importance, *L'Homme à Cheval* (*The Man on Horseback*), which constitutes a symbolic farewell on his behalf to the concept of the heroic leader—or the fascist strongman—and a withdrawal from the political arena into an ascetic and contemplative existence. . . . (pp. 11-12)

After this renunciation of political activism, Drieu next turned his attention to the Collaboration, its failure, and the question of individual guilt and responsibility in a France soon to be overrun by foreign armies. Although hardly one of Drieu's more polished novels, *Les Chiens de paille* (*Straw Dogs*), 1944, does manage to capture the spirit and critical issues of the times with bitter clarity. In this work, Drieu views the last throes of the Occupation through the eyes of a politically neutral observer, Constant Trubert, erstwhile soldier of fortune who finds himself in the service of a Parisian black market racketeer. A large cache of arms, hidden by patriots near the Brittany coast after the armistice between France and Germany, exerts a magnetic attraction on the rival factions of an occupied France. Gaullists, collaborators, fascists, right-wing nationalists, petty thieves and others all converge on the concealed treasure, hoping to claim it for their own causes. Although he becomes deeply involved in the conflicting intrigues, Trubert considers such maneuvering futile and prefers to meditate in the dunes or discuss painting and religion. Very similar to Drieu's own attitude at the time, Trubert's apathy derives from his belief that Frenchmen have lost all control over their personal and national destinies. They have all become sacrificial lambs for the foreign empires they represent in various surrogate capacities—in brief, they are "straw dogs" of no concern to those outside powers seeking total domination of Europe. Nonetheless, to give their lives a semblance of meaning, they go about stalking the hidden weapons with deadly seriousness. In the end, Trubert decides to sacrifice both himself and the others by blowing up the munitions storeroom, but a stray bomb, dropped by a British bomber and intended for a nearby factory, does the work instead—ironical proof that, in spite of everything, no Frenchman was free to dispose of himself as he saw fit.

For Drieu, the last days of the Occupation were, oddly enough, peaceful ones during which he slowly withdrew from life, preparing himself for the final ordeal. On August 12, 1944, as the Allied troops were approaching Paris, Drieu tried to kill himself but was saved at the last minute by his maid who returned unexpectedly to his apartment. After being transferred to the American hospital at Neuilly outside Paris, Drieu again tried to commit suicide by slashing his wrists but was rescued *in extremis* by one of the hospital staff. As soon as he had

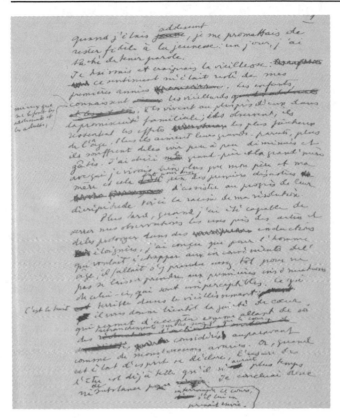

Holograph copy of the manuscript of the Secret Journal.
From Pierre Drieu La Rochelle, *directed by Marc Hanrez.*
© *Editions de l'Herne.*

recovered, Drieu took refuge for the next seven months at several hideaways in and around Paris.

It was during this period of forced leisure that Drieu began to write again. In the brief essay, *Récit secret* (*Secret Journal*), he examines his own reasons for attempting suicide and explains how, even in childhood, this profound self-negation had played a constant role in his life. While in seclusion, he was also composing the first four sections of a novel partially inspired by the life of Vincent Van Gogh, *Mémories de Dirk Raspe*. For his final self-portrait, Drieu chose an unlikely model (or so it seems at first glance) in this tormented genius whose very sanity and life were ultimately sacrificed to his art. By selecting this fraternal spirit as the wellspring of his work, Drieu renewed the quest for a total self, but this time in the domain of visual beauty. The former channels leading to inner knowledge and unity—i.e., war, eroticism, and political commitment—were thus abandoned in favor of an ascetic devotion to art and religious meditation. (pp. 12-13)

Like other introspective novelists before him, Drieu firmly believed that the ultimate secret of existence could be discovered within the recesses of the creative mind. His obsessive probings and questioning, however, unearthed little more than partial imitations of himself but no total image as he had hoped. In the end, Drieu failed in the quest to unite the opposing facets of his personality. Yet, in more ways than we would perhaps care to admit, his troubled spirit strikes a responsive chord within us. In the dark mirror he held up to himself and his era, we can easily recognize our own anxieties and nostalgic yearning for a more cohesive and fulfilling life. Although modest in scope, Drieu's contributions to modern French literature are undeniably authentic and should be valued above all for the light they help to shed on the political and social crises that France experienced from 1917 to 1945. (pp. 14-15)

Thomas M. Hines, in an introduction to The Man on Horseback *by Pierre Drieu la Rochelle, translated by Thomas M. Hines, French Literature Publications Company, 1978, pp. 1-24.*

ROBERT SOUCY　(essay date 1980)

[*Soucy, an American critic and educator, has written a comprehensive biography of Drieu. In the following excerpt, he explores the correlation between Drieu's Modernist literary ideas and his reactionary politics.*]

It should come as no surprise to readers of T. S. Eliot, Ezra Pound, Wyndham Lewis or Louis-Ferdinand Céline that modernist aesthetics and reactionary politics were often comfortable bedfellows in the 1920s and 30s. Pierre Drieu La Rochelle, a supporter of Jacques Doriot's fascist Parti Populaire Français in 1936 and a Nazi collaborator after 1940, is another case in point. An "avant-garde" critic of the cultural and political status quo of the Third Republic, affiliated in the early 1920s with Breton, Aragon and the French surrealists, and a defender in 1934 of fascist "socialism," he might seem at first glance to be impeccably anti-bourgeois in his radical credentials, a rebel against the old order, a man of the Left. But such a glance would be superficial indeed, ignoring as it does the traditionalist, conservative, anti-modernist ballast that underlay his rhetoric. His "advanced" views on art, culture, sex, and politics were the cosmetics used by a very insecure soul to hide the decadence which he felt within him and to achieve relationship with strong, reassuring, virile realities that would help him overcome that decadence. (p. 922)

Drieu admired writers like Claudel, Baudelaire, Rimbaud, Lautréamont and Apollinaire for their rejection of flowery rhetoric and stylized conceits and their commitment to a more "modern" approach to literature, and he was proud of the "sort of brutish quality" of his own poetry. Style in his case was part of the fundamental contrast he saw between the uncivilized toughness and existential profundity of wartime soldiers and the over-refinement and spiritual superficiality of decadent civilians. In 1914 he had led an infantry charge against a German machine gun position at Charleroi and the intoxication he came away with at having "proven" his manhood made him hunger for a more "masculine" literature as well. . . . (pp. 923-24)

In the postwar years Drieu's novels and essays were full of praise for all that was "new" and "young" and "modern"— as long as it was a virile, strong, and, paradoxically, *primitive* modernity. In truth, what Drieu wanted was a return to an earlier, pre-modern era where, he imagined, simple military virility and masculine toughness were all that was needed to win respect and keep society from sinking into decadence— hence his glorification of the Middle Ages in *Notes for Understanding the Century* . . . and his defense of a kind of macho petit bourgeois conservatism in *Fascist Socialism* . . . , the latter being a classic example of the disparity between the label of a product and its contents.

These contradictions created problems for Drieu when it came to addressing specific political issues, especially in the realm of foreign policy. For while he styled himself a modernist in literature, he was vehemently anti-modernist where "the Machine" was concerned. Many of the ills of the modern world, he reiterated throughout the 1930s, were due to industrialization and it was only by abandoning the machine and returning to a more craft-oriented society that French decadence could be completely eliminated. At the same time, he harped on the need to build up Europe's military might against the Bolshevik hordes of the East, even though reversing the industrial revolution and with it presumably the technological basis of Europe's military security seemed hardly the most astute way of accomplishing that end.

Drieu's modernistic anti-modernism was present in his views on war itself. In his novel *The Comedy of Charleroi* . . . he damned the impersonal, mechanized aspects of modern warfare which pitted men against machines instead of men against men, substituting artillery barrages for hand-to-hand combat. He wrote bitterly of "this modern war, this war of iron and not of muscles. This war of science and not of art. This war of industry and commerce. This war of bureaucrats. This war of journalists. . . . This war fought by everyone except by those who were actually there. This war of advanced civilization." Rather than being an anti-war diatribe, however, it was a pro-war diatribe—only in behalf of a *truly* "modern" warfare that was more natural, i.e. more animalistic and personal. Good "modernity" was primitive; bad "modernity" was mechanistic.

Clearly it would be foolish to take Drieu's sympathetic references to modernity at face value; it all depended on what he was referring to and on what values he attached to the term itself. He paid homage to both Lenin and Hitler for their "modern" approach to political means, by which he meant the utter ruthlessness they were willing to employ to attain their political ends (indeed, in 1944 he criticized Hitler for not having been ruthless enough!). In the 1920s and 30s Drieu saw parliamentarianism as passé and called for a more avant-garde approach to politics that would replace decrepit democracy with a newer, more youthful, more dynamic form of government: fascist authoritarianism. In 1938 he warned his countrymen that Nazi Germany had created a "new type of man" (in 1941 he called him "Hitlerian Man") who would overwhelm through the sheer force of his virility the decadent type of man produced by the democracies. "New" and "young" and "virile" were all part of Drieu's positive use of the word "modern." When used this way, it also included a strong note of violence, or potential violence, as part of the definition—violence to be directed against all that was physically or morally decadent in French life. In 1920 as a companion of the surrealists, Drieu extolled a violent futurism that bordered on the apocalyptic:

> We know an efficacious prayer.
> We call upon the future.
> We supplicate the future.
> We bribe the future.
> We submit to the future.
> Finally the future will descend upon us.

> There you will see the future is not the past.
> The past was the earth. The future will be heaven.
> Then we will come to know perfection and peace. Our passions will finally be consummated.

> But, my God, how they will flame during this consummation.

> The pulsing blood of a thousand bodies, beating like a thousand hammers, will forge the angry weapons of destruction.

It would be a great mistake, however, to see Drieu either before or after his conversion to fascism in 1934 as primarily a defender of futurism or modernism. While eager throughout his career to see the elimination of decadence from French life, his view of decadence itself was couched in profoundly anti-modernist terms. There was much that Drieu hated about the modern world, and many of his "avant-garde" political solutions amounted to little more than a nostalgic return to a simpler past. For Drieu the most decadent features of modernity were its materialism, hedonism, industrialism, scientism, communism, socialism, liberalism, egalitarianism, and feminism.

In his novel *Gilles* . . . he condemns Jews for being representatives of the modern world at its worst with their materialism, hedonism, and rationalism (elsewhere he condemns Americans on the same grounds: both reveal "the modern world terribly reduced to itself"). Gilles' downfall begins when he marries a Jewish medical student, Myriam, who corrupts him with her materialism and hedonism. In one scene, he visits his mentor, an old man named Carentan who had raised him as a boy and who lived in a primitive hut in Normandy, a noble savage returned to Nature. Speaking of Myriam, Carentan remarks: "I am not an anti-Semite, because I have a horror of politics. . . . But I cannot tolerate the Jews, since they are par excellence the modern world that I abhor. For me, a provincial, a rural bourgeois, who by instinct and study is attached to a complex and ancient universe, the Jew is as horrible as the *polytechnicien* or the *normalien*." Gilles replies: "You are terribly correct in what you say about the modern side of the Jews. Myriam is a 'scientific type.'"

Drieu applied the same standards to the Soviets. As early as 1922 he contended that communist Russia was as bad as capitalist America in its attachment to modern materialism. Like captains of industry in the United States, commissars of industry in the Soviet Union thought in pseudo-scientific terms, surrounded themselves with technocrats, and were blindly devoted to constantly raising the standard of living. Lenin was no different from the worst capitalists of the West in this regard: "He is bent upon sacrificing as much time as possible to the learned and debilitating religion of Europeans and Americans: Production." Twelve years later in *Fascist Socialism* Drieu returned to the same critique and praised Nazi Germany not for raising the standard of living but for lowering it. Modernity was characterized by too much materialism, and materialism was a major source of decadence; hence, Nazi anti-materialism was to be applauded.

Drieu's anti-modernism was evident in other aspects of his socio-economic thought as well. Critical of both big capitalism and big socialism for their materialistic goals, he preferred an earlier kind of capitalism: the small, free enterprise capitalism of the eighteenth and nineteenth centuries. In 1928 he wrote an article on the **"Metamorphosis of Capitalism"** in which he denounced modern monopoly capitalism and the submergence of the bourgeois elite of the past beneath a horde of technocratic bureaucrats. Once again the villain was the industrial revolution, or simply "the machine." According to Drieu, pre-industrial capitalism was anarchistic, competitive, and virile. The American pioneers of the frontier had been such capitalists, rugged individualists and noble savages, until the machine had ruined everything. The exigencies of a more primitive era had "pushed them toward risks and toward a moral enlargement of life." Early capitalism sprang from individualistic competition, later capitalism from bureaucratic organization. The "heroic" period of capitalism had been succeeded by an "era of trusts,'' by the ''pacifistic, administrative period.'' Production had become more rationally organized, but at the expense of ''combative energies'': ''The spirit of war has been annihilated in social relations, partly by the exhaustion of violence, partly by the rapidity of a general evolution toward pacifism.'' ''Capitalism is no longer a Klondike where the passion for gold led men to assault one another.'' The old, virile morality was dying out; a new, more decadent morality was taking its place.

Private property and individual initiative had given way to impersonal corporations and democratic conformity. No longer was capitalism characterized by men of independence and imagination, but by hierarchical administrations whose rules were slavishly followed by all. The feudal period of capitalism was ending, the bureaucratic period had begun. ''Capitalism,'' Drieu complained, ''is in the process of passing from the sphere of animal passions to the sphere of intellectual passions.'' The rugged individualist had been replaced by the white collar worker. ''Practically speaking, everybody has become a wage-earner.'' Anonymous corporations had replaced private, hereditary family property, and those who had worked for such corporations were mere employees, unable to bequeath what they had accomplished during their lifetimes to their offspring. ''Little by little under [modern] capitalism, the whole becomes more important than the parts,'' and its servants reduced to cogs in an administrative machine. Thus the bourgeoisie had become as much slaves of big capitalism as the proletariat. They, too, were dead souls, depersonalized by the same monotonous, machine-like routine.

The modern consumer was also regimented and manipulated to serve the system. Modern capitalism had become, in effect, a form of communism: ''Capitalism wishes to communize consumption, this is to say, it wants to render it egalitarian, standardization can mean nothing else. In order for the capitalist to accomplish his designs, everybody must buy and possess the same goods: the same auto, the same clothing, the same apartment, the same books. Whereas in former times men had devoted their lives to war or religion or art, today they ''want only to produce.'' Modern trade unionism had only hastened the process. ''Trade unionism arose and pushed democracy forward,'' and democracy meant consumerism. After a period of initial conflict, management and labor had become partners on the basis of a mutual materialism. Their goals were basically compatible: management was devoted to more and more production, labor to more and more consumption.

For Drieu such capitalism was reprehensible. The capitalism he honored was pre-modern, that of a scarcity economy which allowed man's highest ''moral'' qualities to flourish, a survival of the fittest where ''spiritual'' fulfillment through heroic struggle and anarchistic competition was still possible. *Fascist Socialism* . . . echoed the same themes.

Thus despite Drieu's ostensible commitment during the 1920s and 30s to the ''new'' and ''young'' and ''modern,'' he remained essentially traditionalist and backward-looking in his economic thought. Rather than identifying himself with the economic wave of the future—big business, corporate capitalism, and rationalized production—he extolled the same businessman, the petite bourgeoisie, and the family firm. Rather than siding with what modern economic historians have called the ''dynamic sector'' of the French economy (big, efficient firms), he backed the ''stagnant sector'' (small, inefficient firms). Despite his literary and political attacks on the ''old

order,'' his socio-economic thought was firmly rooted in the past.

His fascist ''socialism'' of 1934 was a variant of lower middle class traditionalism, and his praise of communist means was a defense of conservative ends. Like so many other fascist theoreticians of the period, he appealed to *petits bourgeois* who feared that modernization would reduce them to the level of the proletariat and deprive them of their former status and security. While he sometimes sided with youth against their elders, feeding the generational gap with colorful rhetoric, he made it clear in his economic proposals that a basic aim of this ''youth revolt'' was to serve the old, not to overthrow it. **''The Metamorphosis of Capitalism''** ends with praise for fascist Italy for launching a ''revolution'' against industrialism and sees it as a plus not a minus that Italy was largely an agricultural country poor in natural resources with an old culture superimposed on a medieval foundation. That Mussolini relied heavily on the petite bourgeoisie for support was also in his favor.

For Drieu the basic aim of the fascist ''revolution'' was always more spiritual than material. Modern hedonism was to be replaced with a more austere, virile way of life, in emulation of the tough warrior-knights of the Middle Ages. Drieu despised those who envisaged the ideal society in terms of a plethora of material goods and bodily comforts. It was people like these ''who like to eat and drink well, . . . to stretch out on the beach, . . . to contemplate . . . a fire and a shaggy crimson rug'' who were leading France to decadence. The goal of fascism was ''a restoration of the spiritual'' in modern life.

It was an ethic that affected Drieu's aesthetics as well. In one of his last novels, *Memoirs of Dirk Raspe,* the hero is modeled after Van Gogh. Raspe, a painter who is essentially interested in ''the religious time as pastor in a Belgium mining town, having deliberately chosen to abandon art for good works. But the poor disappoint him with their lack of an ''inner life''; shallow, materialistic, incapable of responding to deeper spiritual realities, they display none of the hunger for the divine which alone can make them human. ''The poor are poor in spirit: they do not know, they cannot know what is in the spirit, the spirit's power for transfiguration.'' Raspe had sought sainthood through acts of charity only to realize his mistake. Turning his back on the materialism of both the rich and the poor, he looks to art as the road to salvation. It is only in the lives of great artists that true spirituality can be found: ''a saint can be only an artist.'' And only an aestheticism that is fused with spiritual passion and impervious to political and social activism can serve the highest purpose of art, which is ''to help life pass over to death.'' To achieve this transcendence, Raspe renounces the material comforts of the world in behalf of self-imposed poverty, but unlike the philistine poor he brings to that poverty a metaphysical depth which they will never know. In one scene in the novel, he goes to a prostitute and asks to do a sketch of her. When he finally shows it to her, she dislikes it, being too aesthetically shallow to appreciate its non-representational aspects.

Drieu's aesthetics, like his politics, had an ascetic undertow. In *Straw Dogs* and *Memoirs of Dirk Raspe* the hero believes that art, not religion, is the best path to spirituality (modern Christianity having grown decadent), but only that art which transcends a concern for the physical alone. Thus in *Straw Dogs* the hero, Constant, finds the painting of Manet ''too directly erotic'' to be great art, even though he, Constant, had loved beautiful women in his life—''tall, large, and full-bodied, ample and glistening wardrobes with mirrors''—and therefore ''felt his nerves pinched by Daumier, Guys, and Manet.'' Still, he is much more impressed by a sculptor (Rodin?) who had done a statue of a beautiful female but had left the body largely unfinished (''Constant adored the breasts of women and yet before this figure he did not mind that there were not any''), because the sculptor had fulfilled one of the highest principles of art: he had achieved ''a perfect fusion of the ascetic and the sensual atmosphere: it caressed [Constant's] sense of religion.'' It was a modernist aesthetic that went perfectly with his reactionary politics.

Drieu's views on sexuality might also be dubbed ''modern'' in a sense—until one takes a closer look at their underlying traditionalism. On the face of it, Drieu might seem to have been an exceptionally ''liberated'' soul. Damning sexual repression, he wrote openly and repeatedly about sex, including his own numerous sexual relationships, scorned conventional hypocricies on the subject, and advocated sexual fulfillment as a major road to spiritual health. Two marriages, several love affairs, and considerable brothel-going characterized his own active sexuality. In 1921 he praised Frenchmen for surpassing their English counterparts in matters of love.

> The French are known all over the world for the taste which they have for physical love. They alone, in modern times, have courageously pursued the sentimental adventure and the quest for pleasure simultaneously and have admitted in their social behavior the progress that has resulted from it.

In *Man Covered with Women* . . . Drieu poked fun at Victorian prudishness and suggested that even the most enlightened Englishmen and Englishwomen had a certain linguistic path to travel before they could be fully emancipated. Dining with English visitors at a friend's estate, the hero (Drieu's alter ego in the novel) discourses on various kinds of love affairs—but is careful not to be too shocking: ''At the moment when an obscene word came to mind, he nevertheless held back a little and only spoke it after surrounding it with certain verbal precautions—appeals to freedom of speech and to a horror of all censorship—for our neighbors, dainty about immoralism, are still at the stage of timid conquests and surprising discoveries.'' In 1933 Drieu called D. H. Lawrence one of the great ''prophets'' of the twentieth century and berated philistines who ridiculed *Lady Chatterley's Lover*. (pp. 924-31)

In *Memoirs of Dirk Raspe* the hero is an unconventional pastor who sees nothing wrong with a village woman taking a lover: ''I had no sense of sin . . . and sin is no big thing, no matter what is said in the Gospels.'' Raspe sees ''nothing wrong with people making love'' and regards sexual abstinence not as a virtue but as a weakness. He himself has sex with prostitutes and with some of the women he visits on his religious errands: ''And none of them was scandalized, for my vigorous lack of hypocrisy, like that of an animal, impressed them immediately.'' He criticized prostitutes for not being shameless *enough,* particularly where nudity was concerned. . . .

In *Straw Dogs* the hero is proud of the way he had lived up to his highly erotic view of existence. ''He had made love in the four corners of the world. He had made love in the sand and in bed, with all classes and with all sexes, with women, men, children, animals, and gods. He had nothing more to learn.'' It was not a puritanical credo—on the face of it.

And yet Drieu's ''body consciousness'' and sexual libertarianism *were* deeply puritanical, as well as highly authoritarian, in important respects. Psychoanalytical literature has taught us to look not only for the most obvious kinds of sexual puritanism but also the more masked kinds, especially where ''authoritarian personalities'' are concerned. Sexual liberation on a superficial level is no guarantee of liberal politics or psychological health. In Drieu's case, sexual politics were fascist politics. Like a number of other authoritarian personalities, Drieu shrank from deep *emotional* contact with women even as he engaged in plentiful *physical* contact with them, practicing a kind of *affective* puritanism, an affectionless promiscuity common to his breed. Like other latent puritans before him, he was prone to the Madonna/prostitute syndrome, dividing women into two separate categories, ''decent'' and ''loose.'' As a young man he was often impotent with educated women of his own class (or higher) and could only perform successfully with prostitutes. At the end of his life he wrote in his diary: ''I liked prostitutes because they were mute. With what a good instinct have I always feared women. Which is why [I went to] the brothel.''

His fear of women had a number of consequences, not the least of which was to give his political and social thought a strongly misogynous cast. He depised all that was ''feminine'' in liberal and socialist ideology, associating women themselves with the major features of decadence: weakness, cowardice, comfort, materialism, hedonism, rationalism, pacifism, and luxury. Women themselves were repeatedly portrayed in his novels as lacking the spiritual and intellectual depth of men. In *Memoirs of Dirk Raspe* the hero concludes:

> A woman is not intellectual; she can at the most arrange her passions and feelings to accord with the masculine taste for the intellect. This is why great women may be merchants, politicians, or writers, but they are never creative in music or architecture or sculpture or painting. And in the field of writing, they can be neither philosophers nor true poets, nor even playwrights. They can be ''novelists'' or ''poetesses,'' but the essential genres are forbidden them. This is proven even by Nordic women who have gone the farthest, even by Emily Brontë.
>
> (pp. 932-33)

While Drieu pursued and approved of the *sexually* emancipated woman (her promiscuity was most desirable), he denounced the *intellectually* and *psychologically* emancipated woman. When denigrating women for lacking the intellectual qualities of men, he was irritated when they sought to assert these qualities. In *Gilles* we are told that the hero's first wife, Myriam, had been led astray by a schoolteacher who ''preached feminism to her, the most unfortunate of modern pretensions.''

> This Miss Dafre had the most pernicious influence on Myriam. Frightfully ugly, she offered her maxims of austerity and solitude as if Myriam had to be ugly also. . . . Myriam, in imitation, walked badly and dressed badly; she was ignorant of the graces, the pleasures, the outbursts of coquettishness [that befit a woman].

It was a traditionalist view: emancipated women were by definition ugly and sexless, having abandoned their proper role, which was to leave intellectual matters to the men.

At the heart of Drieu's sexism was his belief in male domination and female submission—emotional, intellectual, and "spiritual" as well as physical submission—and his fear that his own manhood was inadequate in this respect. In his highly autobiographical *Dreamy Bourgeoisie,* he tells how his father had reconquered his mother (after she had discovered his sexual infidelity) through the sheer force of his sexuality. In *Gilles* the hero's mistress, Dora, cannot break with her husband because of his dominating, even frightening, sexual mastery. When, before they were married, she had tried to break off her engagement to him, he had threatened her:

> But a threat can be felt by a woman as a kind of promise: he threatened never to let her go. Always to be held in a firm grip can fascinate a woman and can awaken in a young girl a confused hope of voluptuousness. He made her feel afraid, and that fear called to her like a secret road. . . . He took her with a violence that terrified her, wounded her, but subjected her in a very profound inaccessible region of her consciousness.

Gilles is deeply chagrined that he is unable to master Dora the way her husband does. He should have "led her away by force," but he had proven too weak, and in the end she had left him. "The only thing that counts is force," he concludes, "in love as in everything else." For the hero of *Man Covered with Women* . . . , the aim of sex is not pleasure but domination ("pleasure does not occupy a great place in my [sexual] memories or expectations.") But the domination he finds is usually with prostitutes—a bought domination. With women of his own class, it was another story.

Drieu's cult of male domination helps explain the ascetic element in his notion of ideal sexuality, often associated in his mind with military asceticism. A "true" man needed a strong, tough, virile, military body with which to master his woman and defeat his rivals. In *Wait No Longer* . . . , Drieu honored Frenchmen of the Middle Ages for retaining such bodies while he damned modern Frenchmen for preferring the bistro to the battlefield. In *Notes for Understanding the Century* . . . , he paid homage to the German soldier, "Hitlerian Man," for his fusion of various asceticisms: "the monk and the athlete, the saint and the hero come together in the soldier."

In the same work, Drieu agreed that sex could only remain healthy as long as the man retained the warrior spirit and virile possession of his woman.

> When society moves away from war, all passion and particularly all love soon die. What is a lover who can no longer kill his rival and whom his rival cannot kill? What is a man who is not stronger than a woman, who is not ready for greater challenges? How can a woman continue to put up with childbirth if her husband cannot put up with combat?
>
> (pp. 934-35)

A good deal of Drieu's political and social thought was rooted in a hatred of weakness and worship of virility that were the result of his own sense of weakness, his own lack of virility. His jeremiads against the decadence of others were also, on another level, exercises in self-flagellation. Drieu's novels abound with allusions to his own failure to command, to his own lack of "strength" in his relations with women. In Drieu's last novel, *Memoirs of Dirk Raspe,* the hero is repeatedly described as a "timid" person:

> This is my great weakness, my lack of profound faith [in myself]. . . .
>
> I have noticed this in men other than myself: they do not bring the same assurance to their sexual lives that they do to their professional lives. How is this possible? How can a man who knows what force he carries within him be troubled and not use this force against a woman? It is so easy to conquer, to dominate a woman! For other men.

Riddled with insecurities about his own masculinity, Drieu compensated by identifying with the "strong," "virile" ideals of fascism. His "liberated" sexuality—anti-Victorian, promiscuous, unhypocritical—was quite traditionalist at base. Fearful of intellectual or emotional equality on a woman's part, deeply misogynist, full of self-hatred at failing to be a "true" man, his emancipation was superficial. Beneath his "avant-garde" criticism of the "old" order was a nostalgia for a more primitive past—culturally, economically, and sexually. His fascist "socialism" denounced materialism, industrialism, and scientism and honored petit bourgeois, free enterprise capitalism and the rugged individualism of the American frontier. He honored sex but not pleasure and despised the hedonistic goals of liberalism and socialism. A metaphysical admirer of Van Gogh and the artist-as-saint, he scorned materialistic philistines who were unable to appreciate the profundities of abstract painting and "modern" literature, and he condemned a world that had abandoned the virile asceticism of the Middle Ages. His was a modernism shot through with anti-modernist longings. (pp. 936-37)

> *Robert Soucy, "Drieu La Rochelle and Modernist Anti-Modernism in French Fascism," in* MLN, *Vol. 95, No. 4, May, 1980, pp. 922-37.*

ROBERT BARRY LEAL (essay date 1982)

[*In the following excerpt, Leal discusses Drieu's attempt to resolve his ideals with what he considered the decadent modern world.*]

Drieu's imaginative writings of the interwar period show different attempts to investigate and to relate two constant thematic elements: the self, with its Romantic aspirations to the absolute; and the imperfect decadent society in which this self is set. . . . The resulting body of literature, to which Frédéric Grover attaches the name "literature of testimony" [see excerpt dated 1958], gives a many-faceted but highly individualistic vision of the age. It is, however, a vision with which some of the most perceptive and sensitive minds of the period have been able to identify. François Mauriac, for example, spoke in these terms of Drieu in 1958: "Drieu was at the center, not at the political center, but at the nervous center, at the magnetic center of the attractions and temptations of a generation. He felt very keenly all the currents, all the forces that passed through an entire age."

The main attraction of Drieu's works for the present-day reader, however, does not lie so much in their presentation of a particular interpretation of a fascinating historical period. It is to be found rather in the writer's imaginative efforts to face the enduring problem of how an individual relates to a society considered distasteful and decadent. Within the context of Drieu's vision of the interwar period the attempt to relate brings only dissatisfaction, frustration, and moral degradation.

The male self which traces its unhappy path through Drieu's fiction is deeply influenced by the decadence of the age and proves inadequate in matters of love as it demands from its partners greater vitality and commitment than it can itself provide. The catalog of sexual misery contained in *Journal d'un homme trompé* amply illustrates the situation as the author sees it. Contemporary political life, perhaps most vividly portrayed through Chanteau and his Radicals in *Gilles,* successfully resists attempts at change and alienates the efforts of those individuals with enterprise and courage enough to demand something better. The moral effects on those unable to adapt to the lack of challenge in political and social life are depicted most clearly in *Le Feu follet,* but also appear through Camille in *Rêveuse bourgeoisie.* The option sought by Blaquans in *Blèche:* intellectual and moral isolation, is, on the other hand, completely rejected as "bad faith," as a refusal to face the problems of life in society.

Only in the illumination of the charge at Charleroi does the eagerly sought unity between the self and the world prove possible. Here the self is experienced as fulfilled since momentarily it incorporates the richness of the world. The experience takes place outside normal society, however, and is, within the context of modern warfare, as rare and fleeting as a woman's separation from the values of her society.

The complexity of Drieu's presentation of the relationship between the self and society is seen most clearly through the character of Gille(s), who appears in three novels and numerous short stories. Afflicted by the inner demands of an idealistic self which seeks in life an experience of the absolute—a rather more dynamic version of Proust's "privileged moment"—Gille(s) finds himself conditioned in childhood and influenced in his adult life by social values which he instinctively rejects. This accounts for the sense of "lostness" which so mystifies yet attracts those with whom Gille(s) associates and which continues to exercise its fascination more than fifty years after the character's conception. A form of Barresian "déraciné," Gille(s) reflects some of the enigmatic qualities of Watteau's painting, which, as Dominique Desanti points out, bears a striking resemblance to Drieu himself!

The importance assumed by art and sacrifice in the three novels of the war years represents the ultimate and most significant stage in Drieu's efforts to reconcile the claims of the self and the facts of man's social and metaphysical situation. In common with his close friend André Malraux, Drieu, in the early 1940s, came to focus particular attention on the significance of artistic activity, especially in the visual arts. As early as 1934, in the first part of "**Journal d'un délicat,**" we read: "For me, a picture is the articulation of a prayer, a magical means of attaining the beyond, in the midst of the here and now." It is not until ten years later, however, in the pages of *Les Chiens de paille* and *Mémoires de Dirk Raspe* that the implications of this statement begin to be drawn out. Through the painting of Liassov and the different experiences that Dirk has in his formation as a painter, awareness comes that art, while firmly set in the world of man's activity, may serve as a means of access to the ideal world to which the self aspires. The same revelation, transposed to a different realm of art, may be inferred from *L'Homme à cheval.* Here its expression comes through the guitar and the experience of Felipe.

The theme of sacrifice, which dominates the closing pages not only of *Gilles* but also of *L'Homme à cheval* and *Les Chiens de paille,* and which would almost certainly have figured largely in the final sections of *Mémoires de Dirk Raspe* and the play *Judas,* emerges as a further means of achieving, at least symbolically, the elusive unity between the self and its social and metaphysical destiny. Gilles "finds himself" in an act of virtual suicide, which, by enabling thought and action to be finally linked, takes on the overtones of sacrifice. Similarly, Jaime's sacrifice of his horse Brave is conceived as a means of both affirming the ideal of action he has pursued in his social and political life and incorporating this social and political ideal into an eternal immutable world. Such a concept of sacrifice is pursued somewhat further in *Les Chiens de paille,* where the figure of Judas allows even closer incorporation of the individual: the role of traitor is willingly assumed as the path of human salvation; conscious human sacrifice of victim and priest replaces animal sacrifice; and the personal, the political, and the sacred are linked in an ultimate expression of unity of creation.

Constant's mystical vision highlights the concept of unity underlying all Drieu's thinking. The itinerary of Drieu's fictional heroes reveals a mind which needed to "vibrate in unison with the world" and which projected itself into literary creation to investigate the means by which this might be achieved. In consequence we have an everwidening conception of the self as it passes from relationships with family and school to those involving war, women, and politics before seeking to manifest in itself the fundamental processes of life. Within this general pattern the tensions between the self and society that are encountered result from frustration at the disparity between an ideal unity and the claims of the relative: the desire for the unity of "dream" and "action" in the first line of *Interrogation* is reflected in the very conception of Jaime in *L'Homme à cheval.* It is, however, precisely this tension, with the ideal of unity that it presupposes, that constitutes the essence of Drieu's works and serves to illuminate the fascinating personality of one whom not long ago many thought history had discarded. (pp. 142-45)

> *Robert Barry Leal, in his* Drieu la Rochelle, *Twayne Publishers, 1982, 156 p.*

ADDITIONAL BIBLIOGRAPHY

Balakian, Anna. "Hate the World, Destroy the Self." *Saturday Review* XLIII, No. 14 (3 April 1965): 42.
    Review of *The Fire Within* which discusses Drieu as one of the most formidable antecedents of the "angry young men" of post-World War II literature. Balakian notes: "His anger attributed all the world's ills to the white caste that ruled the Western world."

Bergonzi, Bernard. "Not So Novel." *The New York Review of Books* IV, No. 4 (25 March 1965): 14-15.*
    Review of *The Fire Within* which finds it "a cold, painful book, full of Baudelairian *misere,* which, if nothing else, shows that Drieu La Rochelle was a writer of very genuine talents." While he praises the novel's "intermittent poetic intensity," Bergonzi finds the work undeveloped as a whole.

Cadwallader, Barrie. *Crisis of the European Mind: A Study of André Malraux and Drieu La Rochelle.* Cardiff: University of Wales Press, 1981, 267 p.*
    Explores the political significance of Drieu's and Malraux's fiction.

Corrigan, Beatrice. "Drieu La Rochelle: Study of a Collaborator." *University of Toronto Quarterly* XIV, No. 2 (January 1945): 199-205.

Discusses Drieu's career, concentrating on his wartime activities.

Field, Frank. "Drieu La Rochelle and Fascism." In his *Three French Writers and the Great War*, pp. 81-135. Cambridge: Cambridge University Press, 1975.
  Examines the historical contexts of Drieu's political beliefs.

Green, Mary Jean. "Toward an Analysis of Fascist Fiction: The Contemptuous Narrator in the Works of Brasillach, Celine, and Drieu La Rochelle." *Studies in Twentieth Century Literature* 10, No. 1 (Fall 1985): 81-97.*
  Discusses Drieu's use of a "distanced and contemptuous narrator-protagonist" to create a social and political criticism.

Hines, Thomas M. "Myth, Mysogyny, and Fascism in the Works of Drieu La Rochelle." *Modern Fiction Studies* 24, No. 2 (Summer 1978): 197-207.
  Contends that the majority of Drieu's works reflect "a deep-rooted hostility toward women."

————. "The Concept of Friendship in Drieu La Rochelle." *South Atlantic Bulletin* XLI, No. 1 (January 1979): 19-26.
  Discusses the concept of collectivism in Drieu's fiction.

Leal, R. B. "Drieu La Rochelle and Huxley: Cross Channel Perspectives on Decadence." *Journal of European Studies* XV, No. 60 (December 1985): 247-59.*
  Finds elements of historical determinism in Drieu's concept of the decadence of contemporary society.

Merchant, Norris. "In Search of a Demanding Creed." *The Nation* 218, No. 14 (6 April 1974): 438-40.

Review of *Secret Journal, and Other Writings* in which Merchant considers Drieu's diaries "emblematic of an epoch that is very distant from us in spirit, one in which a sensitive French intelligence could choose the Fascist cause. . . ."

Sheed, Wilfrid. "We Know Everything, We Know Nothing." *The New York Times Book Review* (21 March 1965): 4.*
  Negative review of *The Fire Within* which notes the deserved obscurity of Drieu's works.

Soucy, Robert. "Psycho-Sexual Aspects of the Fascism of Drieu La Rochelle." *The Journal of Psychohistory* 4, No. 1 (Summer 1976): 71-89.
  Suggests possible motivations for Drieu's fascism.

————. *Fascist Intellectual: Drieu La Rochelle*. Berkeley: University of California Press, 1979, 451 p.
  Comprehensive biography.

Thiher, Allen. " *'Le feu follet'*: The Drug Addict as a Tragic Hero." *PMLA* 88, No. 1 (January 1973): 34-40.
  Explores elements of classical tragedy in *The Fire Within*.

"Dandy's Farewell." *The Times Literary Supplement*, No. 3733 (21 September 1973): 1074.
  Review of *Secret Journal, and Other Writings* which maintains: "Although they have no literary merit, they were worth translating as a document about the state of mind of a French intellectual who backed the wrong horse during the late 1930s and the German Occupation. . . ."

R(ichard) Austin Freeman

1862-1943

(Also wrote under pseudonym of Clifford Ashdown) English novelist, short story writer, essayist, and nonfiction writer.

Freeman is best known as the creator of Dr. Thorndyke, the first genuinely scientific investigator in detective fiction. The primary emphasis of most of Freeman's stories is the means of detection rather than the discovery of the criminal, a narrative scheme that is particularly evident in his "inverted" stories, which reveal the crime and criminal before presenting the detective's investigation and solution. Described by Howard Haycraft as the "true and undoubted 'parent' of the scientific detective story in the highest meaning of the phrase," Freeman is considered one of the classic figures in the history of the detective genre.

Freeman was born in London to a tailor and his wife. His interest in natural history and medicine, as well as his dislike of the tailoring trade, influenced him to begin medical training at Middlesex Hospital at the age of eighteen. In 1887, after qualifying as a physician and surgeon, he entered the Colonial Service as an Assistant Colonial Surgeon for the Gold Coast in Africa. Freeman joined a medical expedition to Ashanti and Bontuku in 1889, recounting his experiences there in his first book, published nine years later, *Travels and Life in Ashanti and Jaman*. In addition to being a physician for this expedition, he also served as a navigator and natural scientist. In 1891 Freeman was named Boundary Commissioner for a disputed border between British and German territories in Africa, but while in the Gold Coast awaiting the appointment, he contracted blackwater fever—a debilitating malarial disease—and returned to England an invalid. During the next ten years Freeman tried, with little success, to earn a living as a doctor. In his increasingly protracted intervals of free time, he also began writing articles and short stories, many of which appeared in *Cassell's Magazine*. In 1900, while serving as acting assistant medical officer in Holloway Prison, Freeman became acquainted with Dr. John James Pitcairn, with whom he collaborated under the pseudonym of Clifford Ashdown on the short detective stories included in his first collection, *The Adventures of Romney Pringle*. Although he maintained a small medical practice in Gravesend, Kent, where he moved with his family in 1903, Freeman afterward made fiction writing his full-time occupation. During the next four decades he published novels, short stories, and essays, as well as a biological-sociological study entitled *Social Decay and Regeneration*. Freeman died at Gravesend at the age of eighty-one.

Freeman's varied experience and extensive knowledge of many subjects are evident in his work. His first novel, *The Golden Pool,* is an adventure story set in the Gold Coast of West Africa, and both his nautical experience as well as his knowledge of medicine contributed to his early short stories. His background and training are especially reflected in the methods of Dr. Thorndyke, who is introduced in *The Red Thumb Mark,* Freeman's first detective novel. In this story, which is based on his experiences while working in Holloway Prison, Freeman asserted the possibility of fingerprint forgery. Having actually tested his theory by fabricating his own fingerprints, Freeman depicted Dr. Thorndyke conducting an experiment in a courtroom to expose the fallibility of using fingerprints as evidence in a case. The believability of both the characters and incidents in his fiction was important to Freeman, and he made a practice of performing in his workshop the tests and experiments which are part of his stories. Although his theory has been largely rejected by fingerprint experts and his novel did not receive much critical attention until years after its original publication, *The Red Thumb Mark* is particularly notable for introducing the first genuinely scientific investigator to the detective genre. Following this novel, most of Freeman's fiction was comprised of detective stories in which Dr. Thorndyke utilized his vast knowledge, deductive reasoning, and specialized tools to accomplish his work.

Although the character of Dr. Thorndyke is widely considered the single most interesting aspect of Freeman's work, critical opinions regarding his characterization are varied. Freeman's stories are often compared with the Sherlock Holmes adventures of Arthur Conan Doyle for their late-Victorian romanticism, their similar narrators, and for the detectives' impressive deductions. In critical comparisons with Holmes, Dr. Thorndyke is deemed the more accurate thinker and ranked superior as a scientific authority, whereas Holmes is considered the superior literary creation. Critics cite Dr. Thorndyke's encyclopedic knowledge, lack of eccentricities, and seemingly infallible abilities as both the basis of his fascination and as the source of his limited appeal. Nevertheless, the strong enthusiasm of some critics for this character is represented by Norman Donaldson's statement that Dr. Thorndyke has an "almost mystical quality," an "aura of omnipotence," and is "a noble, highly convincing, and thoroughly consistent character who was precisely fitted to his role." In general, Dr. Thorndyke is described as a fascinating though staid creation with exceptional ratiocinative ability, and his summations at the end of cases, which Raymond Chandler has described as "masterpieces of lucid analysis," are considered an especially interesting part of Freeman's stories.

It was Freeman's conviction that all other qualities of a good detective story are "subordinate to the intellectual interest" and that "conclusiveness . . . is the quality which, above all others, yields that intellectual satisfaction that the reader seeks." In his inverted stories, Freeman included almost no elements of mystery or surprise. These stories represent his theory that the process of detection and gradual illumination of the significance of data are of greater interest to a reader than is the discovery of who committed the crime. However, the critical reaction to these stories has been mixed. Many critics have praised Freeman's skillful and intriguing construction of stories which adhere to such difficult, unconventional requirements, but others debated the appeal of his storytelling technique and his theories of the detective story. For example, Alfred C. Ward states that "it is very doubtful whether there is any future for this method, or whether it does give even highbrow readers what in their heart of hearts they really want." H. Douglas Thomson concludes that Freeman became dogmatic about his theory of the detective story because of his excellent ability to construct the intermediate steps in such a story. Nevertheless,

Freeman's inverted stories are generally regarded as an important contribution to the genre.

Freeman's importance as an author of detective fiction rests primarily in his development of plots that utilize a variety of scientific material and arrive, with great consistency, at ingenious, convincing solutions. However, while Freeman is often credited with presenting to his readers the data required to be able, theoretically, to solve the crime with careful attention and analysis, some critics, such as Raymond Chandler and Dorothy Sayers, question the fairness of his presentation, contending that it would be very difficult for the ordinary reader to properly evaluate clues which are based on Freeman's specialized knowledge. Despite this objection, critics generally acclaim the scientific realism of his work and agree that Freeman was a conscientious craftsman. As Donaldson has stated of Freeman: "Whether his clues were magic caskets, tropical diseases, duckweed, or obscure minerals, he knew whereof he wrote, and if he did not know, he took the trouble to find out. Like Johnson's traveller, he regulated imagination by reality, thinking not of how things might be, but seeing them as they were."

(See also *Contemporary Authors*, Vol. 113.)

PRINCIPAL WORKS

Travels and Life in Ashanti and Jaman   (nonfiction)   1898
The Adventures of Romney Pringle [with J. J. Pitcairn under the joint pseudonym Clifford Ashdown]   (short stories) 1902
The Golden Pool   (novel)   1905
The Red Thumb Mark   (novel)   1907
John Thorndyke's Cases   (short stories)   1909; also published as *Dr. Thorndyke's Cases*, 1931
The Eye of Osiris   (novel)   1911; also published as *The Vanishing Man*, 1912
The Mystery of 31 New Inn   (novel)   1912
The Singing Bone   (short stories)   1912
The Unwilling Adventurer   (novel)   1913
A Silent Witness   (novel)   1914
The Uttermost Farthing   (novel)   1914; also published as *A Savant's Vendetta*, 1920
The Exploits of Danby Croker   (novel)   1916
Social Decay and Regeneration   (nonfiction)   1921
Helen Vardon's Confession   (novel)   1922
The Cat's Eye   (novel)   1923
Dr. Thorndyke's Case Book   (short stories)   1923; also published as *The Blue Scarab*, 1924
The Mystery of Angelina Frood   (novel)   1924
The Puzzle Lock   (short stories)   1925
The D'Arblay Mystery   (novel)   1926
A Certain Dr. Thorndyke   (novel)   1927
The Surprising Experiences of Mr. Shuttlebury Cobb (novel)   1927
As a Thief in the Night   (novel)   1928
Flighty Phyllis   (novel)   1928
Mr. Pottermack's Oversight   (novel)   1930
Pontifex, Son and Thorndyke   (novel)   1930
When Rogues Fall Out   (novel)   1932; also published as *Dr. Thorndyke's Discovery*, 1932
Dr. Thorndyke Intervenes   (novel)   1933
For the Defence: Dr. Thorndyke   (novel)   1934
The Penrose Mystery   (novel)   1936
The Stoneware Monkey   (novel)   1938
Mr. Polton Explains   (novel)   1940

The Jacob Street Mystery   (novel)   1942; also published as *The Unconscious Witness*, 1942
The Further Adventures of Romney Pringle [with J. J. Pitcairn under the joint pseudonym Clifford Ashdown] (short stories)   1970
From a Surgeon's Diary [with J. J. Pitcairn under the joint pseudonym Clifford Ashdown]   (short stories)   1975
The Queen's Treasure [with J. J. Pitcairn under the joint pseudonym Clifford Ashdown]   (short stories)   1975

*These volumes collect for the first time stories which appeared earlier in periodicals.

JOHN ADAMS   (essay date 1913)

[*In the following excerpt, Adams discusses Freeman's expertise and appeal as a writer of detective fiction.*]

In his preface to one of his detective books, **The Red Thumb Mark**, Mr. R. Austin Freeman adopts quite the attitude of the maker of "plausible yarns." It was written, he tells us, with "no purpose other than that of affording entertainment to such readers as are interested in problems of crime and their solutions; and the story itself differs in no respect from others of its class, excepting in that an effort has been made to keep within the probabilities of ordinary life, both in the characters and in the incidents." Few readers realise how much is implied in the apparently simple ideal of a "plausible yarn." There must be, to begin with, a vast background of accurate knowledge, but the knowledge must not be obtruded upon the attention of the reader. It is not sufficient that a certain incident is possible, or even that it actually happened, it must be such as to appear probable to the reader. Aristotle's view of the relative merits of the possible and the probable is as true to-day as it was when the "Poetics" was the book of the Year. Mr. Freeman obviously realises all this. He gives evidence of an unusually well-stored mind, he is master of many subjects, has read deeply and travelled widely. His is evidently a mind with a bias towards accuracy. To suit his purpose he sometimes takes certain liberties with facts, but his conscience is tender on the subject. If it is necessary to assume "a screw-pile lighthouse on the Girdler Sand in place of the light vessel," he is careful to note this, elsewhere than in the story itself, "to forestall criticism and save readers the trouble of writing to point out the error."

It appears that Mr. Freeman's critics do not all appreciate this love of accuracy and this endeavour to secure probability. In the preface to his recently published **The Mystery of 31 New Inn**, he tells us that one of his critics maintained that these things were "of no consequence so long as the story was amusing." Mr. Freeman's illustrative defence is not very happy, consisting as it does in showing that a particularly complicated method of orientation described in the story was actually used by himself in Ashanti. The critic would probably reply that the reader is not at all concerned about the actual use of the method, so long as it is intelligible and does not carry an obvious contradiction. The whole principle of the "plausible yarn," is here in question, the issue being practically the same as that raised in the various current discussions on artistic realism. The laws of perspective may show that a particular circular window that is open in a picture could never fit into the circular casement to which it belongs. What does it matter? ask critics of a certain school. The blunder is an offence to those who know perspective, but to the great majority of spectators it makes no difference. It would appear then that the degree of accuracy exacted from an artist, whether graphic or literary, must be determined by the knowledge of the persons to whom the artist appeals. Thus in stories of this class nothing must be introduced that is inconsistent with the ordinary experience of the average reader, or that is inconsistent with anything that appears in the story itself. This may be regarded as the minimum of accuracy necessary for successful work. On the other hand there cannot be an excess of accuracy, though there may well be an excessive display of accuracy. The author must . . . win [the reader's] confidence and thus let the question of accuracy drop out of consciousness altogether. It is here that Mr. Freeman is conspicuously successful. The ordinary reader is made to feel that he is in the hands of a man who is an authority on the subjects he is dealing with, and has a great deal of knowledge in reserve. Even the critical reader sees few traces of that shameless use of commonplace books of reference that marks journeyman work in mystery stories. Mr. Freeman draws from his store of knowledge, he does not usually hunt up knowledge *ad hoc*. It is true that one can sometimes reconstruct the origin of the plot. For example it is easy to imagine Mr. Freeman turning up some of his old biological notebooks or text-books, and glancing at a diagram of the unique oval-shaped bloodcorpuscle of the camel—obviously an infallible guide in a maze of evidence from blood stains. But his use of this basic fact is so skilful that the mechanical nature of the construction is completely hidden. While we follow the story of **"The Old Lag,"** we feel that we are reading of real men and women, though a cold-blooded critic might point out that they are all set in motion by the memory of a note or a drawing in an old college book.

As to narration, Mr. Freeman has, in three out of the four Thorndyke volumes, adopted the first personal presentation in that "second-fiddle" form typified in Dr. Watson of the Sherlock Holmes memoirs; in *The Eye of Osiris,* indeed, the narrator has to play even third fiddle. The purpose of this intermediary between the public and the really great man is no doubt to interpolate that amount of obscuration that is necessary to prevent the reader getting too soon on the right scent. The method necessarily condemns the intermediary to a somewhat humiliating grade of stupidity. The Dr. Jervis of these volumes is certainly not so dull as Dr. Watson, for his creator has had the advantage of Sir Conan Doyle's experience, and makes his secondary character much more of an active partner in the detection of crime. But, after all, Jervis is as inferior to Thorndyke as Watson was to Holmes. It must be acknowledged, however, that Jervis stands out more as an individual than does Watson. Indeed, one of the strong points of Mr. Freeman is the power he has of drawing real charcters; by no means a common mark of writers of such ingenuity in plot construction.

Three of the four books in which Dr. John Thorndyke is the central character [*The Red Thumb Mark, The Eye of Osiris, The Mystery of 31 New Inn,* and *John Thorndyke's Cases*] are written in the orthodox way. They are intrinsically of very great interest, and, indeed, stand out as conspicuously above the ordinary story of this type. They are the work of a master in this somewhat difficult craft. The fourth volume, however, *The Singing Bone,* has all the attractions of an experiment in literary form. It is apparent that Mr. Freeman has been worried in his other books, as his readers must necessarily be, by the necessity of continually keeping back certain bits of information that might precipitate the *dénouement,* so he put to

himself the question whether it would not be possible to write a detective story in which author and reader could play with the cards on the table. Accordingly, he set about writing the same story twice over—first from the point of view of the criminal, and then from the point of view of the detective. A by-product of this method is the elimination of the first personal form. The volume contains five such duplicated stories, and the result cannot be regarded as altogether successful. Were it not for Mr. Freeman's extraordinary power of telling a story the volume might have been a dismal failure. As it is, the author by a *tour de force* carries the reader right through the book, partly from sheer interest in the incidents, and partly from the interest in Thorndyke's methods. The objection to this duplicate method, which Mr. Freeman claims to have been justified by its success, is that it emphasises the purely logical aspects of the different cases. It is not so much a series of stories as a set of exercises. A teacher might be tempted to use them as problems in applied logic. This logical interest is no doubt prominent in the other books, notably in the summing up at the symposium at the end of *The Eye of Osiris,* but in the short stories it is deliberately brought forward as the chief matter. Nothing but the author's remarkable skill in character delineation and graphic narrative could save the stories from being regarded as technical studies, such as find a suitable place in a course on forensic medicine.

Indeed, the whole position of Mr. Freeman depends upon the class of readers to whom he appeals. His work is certainly beyond the range of the ordinary devourer of "sleuth" novels. He makes very great demands on the attention of his readers. To read these books intelligently implies a definite exercise in the use of Mill's Canons of Inductive Logic, and the books might form a very practical means of testing the student's mastery of these canons. A very obvious and natural criticism of the stories is that they are too clever: they ask too much of the reader. But, unlike some clever writers, Mr. Freeman is clever enough to carry off his cleverness. His exposition is so clear, his arrangement of events so methodical, that the reader is led along with the minimum amount of effort consistent with a very definite exercise of the reason. Stupid and lazy readers may be warned off, but the ordinary intelligent reader may rely upon having from Mr. Freeman a course in mental gymnastics conducted under the pleasantest conditions. (pp. 6-7)

[One] marked characteristic of Mr. Freeman's plots is that they justify themselves. In most mystery stories there is little difficulty in stating the mystery. As a rule, books of this kind have quite a piquant beginning. The failure comes later, when the mystery has to be unravelled. A great deal is usually left to the imagination of the reader, and not a little is entirely unexplained. Mr. Freeman leaves no such tangled threads. Everything is worked out with the greatest clearness and thoroughness. Where occasional obscurity occurs, as in the exposition of the principles of detection by fingermarks, the blame is thrown upon one of the characters: the author in his own person is eminently lucid. (p. 7)

John Adams, "Mr. R. Austin Freeman," in The Bookman, *London, Vol. XLIV, No. 259, April, 1913, pp. 6-7.*

THE NEW YORK TIMES BOOK REVIEW (essay date 1913)

[*The following essay is an early review of* The Mystery of 31 New Inn.]

For the man to whom the unraveling of intricate plots is a passion [*The Mystery of 31 New Inn*] suggests a problem after his own heart. It is a detective story, in which science ably assists John Thorndyke, lawyer and doctor of medicine, to evolve the truth from a seemingly impossible premise. Mr. Freeman has been careful to extract the full effect of reality from the jargon of scientific procedure through which his hero moves steadily to a solution of the mystery which it is his task to clear up. If the manner is thus made convincing, the mystery itself is also an attractive one.

To say that the method of the story was reminiscent of Sherlock Holmes would be putting it mildly—the unexpected, lightning deductions of Thorndyke, which promptly square with the facts, the character of the "I," who might easily be another Watson, and the whole manner of telling smacks strongly of Conan Doyle. But one need not quarrel with Mr. Freeman for that. He has at least followed the best of models, and he has, moreover, drawn a clever plot with several new twists, and written a story which is hard to lay down until its last page is turned.

> *"A Detective Story," in* The New York Times Book Review, *October 26, 1913, p. 584.*

PRESERVED SMITH   (essay date 1921)

[*In the following excerpt, Smith offers a largely negative review of* Social Decay and Regeneration, *citing aspects of the work that call into question the validity of Freeman's conclusions.*]

The most original part of [*Social Decay and Regeneration*] is the endeavor to prove that societies, like germs, have a life cycle. Just as a culture of yeast, or of typhoid bacilli, when introduced into a favorable environment, at first flourishes and multiplies, but finally produces toxins or antibodies fatal to itself, so Mr. Freeman thinks that all forms of life tend to give rise to a set of unfavorable conditions ultimately causing decay and death. Civilized societies are such organisms, in his opinion, and the antibodies set up by them are the machines and inventions of the last century and a half. The thesis that the race is degenerating due to the strains and stresses of a mechanical age is developed to much the same purpose as it was by Max Nordau some years ago, though with none of the wit or critical acumen of that author. If we may believe Mr. Freeman society is now going to the dogs, only (as Oliver Wendell Holmes said about physic) if it is in such a parlous state as the author thinks, no dog would touch it. Two considerations somewhat impair our confidence in Mr. Freeman's verdict. One is that he is evidently a rather crotchety gentleman, more interested in decrying what he does not like among his contemporaries than in establishing reliable scientific conclusions. He has gathered around him a large menagerie of pet aversions, and his favorite indoor sport is to give each of them in turn a flick of his whip while apparently talking of something else. Germany, politicians, cheap amusements, the taxes, socialism, the "battalions of parasites" now infesting society, and above all the laboring class come in for many a hard, but illogical, blow. In the second place Mr. Freeman is not always right in his economics and history. The ideas he has of over-production and the unemployment caused by technical improvements in machinery have been exploded long ago. His laments about the poor quality of the population as shown by the recruiting for the English army during the war might be paralleled in many a past age. Altogether they remind one of Falstaff's description of his company, containing Mouldy, Shadow, Wart, Feeble, and Bullcalf, as "pitiful rascals," "scarecrows," and

"food for powder," more than of anything else. So his laments about the intellectual poverty of this age recall similar comments by Ben Jonson on his own time. And yet the age of Elizabeth is held up by Mr. Freeman as an age of giants compared with the present. (pp. 323-24)

> *Preserved Smith, "The Future of the Race," in* The Nation, *Vol. CXIII, No. 2933, September 21, 1921, pp. 323-24.**

HAVELOCK ELLIS   (essay date 1921)

[*Ellis was a pioneering sexual psychologist and a respected English man of letters. His most famous work is his seven-volume* The Psychology of Sex *(1897-1928), a study containing frankly stated case histories of sex-related psychological abnormalities that was greatly responsible for changing British and American attitudes toward the hitherto forbidden subject of sexuality. In addition to his psychological writings, Ellis retained an active interest in literature throughout his life. As a critic, according to Desmond MacCarthy, Ellis looked for the expression of the individuality of the author under discussion. "The first question he asked himself as a critic," wrote MacCarthy, "was 'What does this writer affirm?' The next, 'How did he come to affirm precisely that?' His statement of a writer's 'message' was always trenchant and clear, his psychological analysis of the man extremely acute, and the estimate of the value of his contribution impartial. What moved him most in literature was the sincere expression of preferences and beliefs, and the energy which springs from sincerity." In the following excerpt, Ellis points out the social and political concerns addressed by Freeman in his book* Social Decay and Regeneration, *discussing some possible objections to Freeman's diagnosis of, and remedy for, the problems of modern civilization.*]

Some twenty years ago I chanced to come across a volume of *Travels and Life in Ashanti and Jaman,* presenting a fresh and vivid picture of a strong and primitive people just then being "civilized" off the earth. The author was evidently a man of penetrating observation, of independent judgment, capable of outspoken criticism when it was required, so that his name and his book remained in my memory. Therewith he passed out of my ken. But in the meanwhile, as I learn, and as indeed one might expect in a writer of so vigorous a mind, he has been active in another field, and now, with [*Social Decay and Regeneration*], he has again by chance come into my line of vision. It is incomparably a more mature book than the *Travels*. I realize how profitably the author must have spent the intervening years. On every page one feels that he has acquired a singularly wide, varied, and precise acquaintance with the phenomena of our social life; at the same time he shows a keen power in analyzing these phenomena as well as in demonstrating their wider bearings on the fate of mankind. Moreover, unlike the professional political economists, he gives the impression of having learnt to approach his task, not in the study, but by a large contact with human life and affairs and by a sensitive intellectual receptivity to that contact.

There are few whom [this book] can be said not to concern. To-day, indeed, when, as never perhaps before, there is so much searching of heart concerning the foundation on which we have based our civilization and so bitter a sense of disillusionment concerning the results so far attained, there may be many to heed the truths so clearly and so uncompromisingly set forth in this book. We are here shown what a Machine Age actually means, and what it must inevitably mean; how the machine which was meant to be the slave of man, its master, becomes itself the master and man its slave; how the effects of machinery on human welfare always tend to be illusory, for the "labour-saving" device increases labour, and the "time-saving" device destroys leisure; how the whole process is necessarily accompanied by a general and increasing degradation, not only in the products of machinery, but in the men and in the society which is responsible for them.

The prospect is not, therefore, hopeless. Dr. Flinders Petrie, in his notable and suggestive little book, "Revolutions in Civilization," points out the remarkable uniformity shown by the civilizations of the past in their progress from growth to decay, the final stage being marked by loss of artistic power and the general uprising of a restless democracy. We seem to see both these tendencies in our own civilization (although the author of [*Social Decay and Regeneration*], in agreement with Robert Michels in his remarkable and too seldom read study of *Political Parties,* finds the modern democratic tendency towards oligarchy), and we see them operating through the development of machinery and the general mechanization of life. Yet, however surely we may know that no civilization endures for ever, the fount of hope springs, and rightly springs, eternal in the human breast. The author of this book, at all events, believes that there is a way to prolong, or even to renew, the life of our civilization. Not everyone will accept his remedy as practicable, just as not everyone will agree at every point with his diagnosis. To some it may seem that, while we may approve his exposition of the aptitude of every social class, not excluding that of state-controllers, to act in antagonism to society, he yet scarcely makes clear enough the fact that the labouring class, while sometimes the victimizers, have beyond any class been in the past the victims of the Machine Age, and that Labour is now becoming recognized as a supremely important factor of Society. Some of us, also, may consider that Collectivism has claims under modern conditions to play in the social order a valuable part not incongruous with Individualism, and indeed as its indispensable ally, and that these claims are not discredited by setting forth the extravagancies of a wild Collectivism unbridled by Individualism. The fact, however, that the author's standpoint is evidently not that of the extremists on the Labour side obviously adds more point and force to his analysis of our social system, in which he has much in common with the latest social theorists in their revolt against the domination of the State and the spread of bureaucracy. To some readers, no doubt, it will seem that the author's plan of social regeneration is too Utopian in character. One would like to know his attitude towards the schemes of the Guild Socialists, with which his own scheme seems often to have points of contact, being like theirs an attempt to correct the faults of the present industrial system by introducing a maximum amount of individual freedom, responsibility, self-government, and the disappearance of State control, while at the same time he understands—as the Guild Socialists have often failed to understand—that the eugenic problem has now become the most fundamental of social problems.

Criticisms, however, so far as they merely qualify the arguments here set forth are but the legitimate outcome of our own special idiosyncracies, or the author's, and so far as they are merely negative they are futile. It is more to the point to consider what we ourselves propose to do about the matter. Whatever we propose to do about it, here, certainly, is a book which will help us to realize along what road our civilization is at present moving. (pp. vii-x)

> *Havelock Ellis, in an introduction to* Social Decay and Regeneration *by R. Austin Freeman, Houghton Mifflin Co., 1921, pp. v-x.*

R. AUSTIN FREEMAN   (essay date 1924)

[*In the following excerpt, Freeman argues that the most important quality a detective story can offer a reader is its intellectual interest, and he explains how the facts of a case should be presented to a reader in order to maximize this intellectual satisfaction.*]

The rarity of good detective fiction is to be explained by a fact which appears to be little recognised either by critics or by authors; the fact, namely, that a completely executed detective story is a very difficult and highly technical work, a work demanding in its creator the union of qualities which, if not mutually antagonistic, are at least seldom met with united in a single individual. On the one hand, it is a work of imagination, demanding the creative, artistic faculty; on the other, it is a work of ratiocination, demanding the power of logical analysis and subtle and acute reasoning; and, added to these inherent qualities, there must be a somewhat extensive outfit of special knowledge. (p. 714)

The distinctive quality of a detective story, in which it differs from all other types of fiction, is that the satisfaction that it offers to the reader is primarily an intellectual satisfaction. This is not to say that it need be deficient in the other qualities appertaining to good fiction: in grace of diction, in humour, in interesting characterisation, in picturesqueness of setting or in emotional presentation. On the contrary, it should possess all these qualities. It should be an interesting story, well and vivaciously told. But whereas in other fiction these are the primary, paramount qualities, in detective fiction they are secondary and subordinate to the intellectual interest, to which they must be, if necessary, sacrificed. The entertainment that the connoisseur looks for is an exhibition of mental gymnastics in which he is invited to take part; and the excellence of the entertainment must be judged by the completeness with which it satisfies the expectations of the type of reader to whom it is addressed. (pp. 715-16)

[Detective] fiction has a wide popularity. The general reader, however, is apt to be uncritical. He reads impartially the bad and the good, with no very clear perception of the difference, at least in the technical construction. The real connoisseurs, who avowedly prefer this type of fiction to all others, and who read it with close and critical attention, are to be found among men of the definitely intellectual class: theologians, scholars, lawyers, and to a less extent, perhaps, doctors and men of science. Judging by the letters which I have received from time to time, the enthusiast *par excellence* is the clergyman of a studious and scholarly habit.

Now the theologian, the scholar and the lawyer have a common characteristic: they are all men of a subtle type of mind. They find a pleasure in intricate arguments, in dialectical contests, in which the matter to be proved is usually of less consideration than the method of proving it. The pleasure is yielded by the argument itself and tends to be proportionate to the intricacy of the proof. The disputant enjoys the mental exercise, just as a muscular man enjoys particular kinds of physical exertion. But the satisfaction yielded by an argument is dependent upon a strict conformity with logical methods, upon freedom from fallacies of reasoning and especially upon freedom from any ambiguities as to the data. (p. 716)

[The] intellectual satisfaction of an argument is conditional on the complete establishment of the data. Disputes on questions of fact are of little, if any, intellectual interest; but in any case an argument—an orderly train of reasoning—cannot begin until the data have been clearly set forth and agreed upon by both parties. This very obvious truth is continually lost sight of by authors. Plots, *i.e.*, arguments, are frequently based upon alleged 'facts'—physical, chemical, and other—which the educated reader knows to be untrue, and of which the untruth totally invalidates conclusions drawn from them and thus destroys the intellectual interest of the argument.

The other indispensable factor is freedom from fallacies of reasoning. The conclusion must emerge truly and inevitably from the premises; it must be the only possible conclusion, and must leave the competent reader in no doubt as to its unimpeachable truth.

It is here that detective stories most commonly fail. They tend to be pervaded by logical fallacies, and especially by the fallacy of the undistributed middle term. The conclusion reached by the gifted investigator, and offered by him as inevitable, is seen by the reader to be merely one of a number of possible alternatives. The effect when the author's 'must have been' has to be corrected by the reader into 'might have been' is one of anti-climax. The promised and anticipated demonstration peters out into a mere suggestion; the argument is left in the air, and the reader is baulked of the intellectual satisfaction which he was seeking. (p. 717)

[The] plot of a detective novel is, in effect, an argument conducted under the guise of fiction. But it is a peculiar form of argument. The problem having been stated, the data for its solution are presented inconspicuously and in a sequence purposely dislocated so as to conceal their connection; and the reader's task is to collect the data, to rearrange them in their correct logical sequence and ascertain their relations, when the solution of the problem should at once become obvious. (p. 718)

The body of the work should be occupied with the telling of the story, in the course of which the data, or 'clues,' should be produced as inconspicuously as possible, but clearly and without ambiguity in regard to their essentials. The author should be scrupulously fair in his conduct of the game. Each card as it is played should be set down squarely, face upwards, in full view of the reader. Under no circumstances should there be any deception as to the facts. The reader should be quite clear as to what he may accept as true. In stories of the older type, the middle action is filled out with a succession of false clues and with the fixing of suspicion first on one character, then on another, and again on a third, and so on. The clues are patiently followed, one after another, and found to lead nowhere. There is feverish activity, but no result. All this is wearisome to the reader and is, in my opinion, bad technique. My practice is to avoid false clues entirely and to depend on keeping the reader occupied with the narrative. If the ice should become uncomfortably thin, a dramatic episode will distract the reader's attention and carry him safely over the perilous spot. Devices to confuse and mislead the reader are bad practice. They deaden the interest, and they are quite unnecessary; the reader can always be trusted to mislead himself, no matter how plainly the data are given. Some years ago I devised, as an experiment, an inverted detective story in two parts ["**The Case of Oscar Brodski**"]. The first part was a minute and detailed description of a crime, setting forth the antecedents, motives, and all attendant circumstances. The reader had seen the crime committed, knew all about the criminal, and was in possession of all the facts. It would have seemed that there was nothing left to tell. But I calculated that the reader would be so occupied with the crime that he would overlook the evidence. And so it turned out. The second part, which de-

scribed the investigation of the crime, had to most readers the effect of new matter. All the facts were known; but their evidential quality had not been recognised.

This failure of the reader to perceive the evidential value of facts is the foundation on which detective fiction is built. It may generally be taken that the author may exhibit his facts fearlessly provided only that he exhibits them separately and unconnected. And the more boldly he displays the data, the greater will be the intellectual interest of the story. For the tacit understanding of the author with the reader is that the problem is susceptible of solution by the latter by reasoning from the facts given; and such solution should be actually possible. Then the data should be produced as early in the story as is practicable. The reader should have a body of evidence to consider while the tale is telling. The production of a leading fact near the end of the book is unfair to the reader, while the introduction of capital evidence—such as that of an eye-witness—at the extreme end is radically bad technique, amounting to a breach of the implied covenant with the reader. (pp. 718-19)

[The] dramatic quality of the climax is strictly dependent on the intellectual conviction which accompanies it. This is frequently overlooked, especially by general novelists who experiment in detective fiction. In their eagerness to surprise the reader, they forget that he has also to be convinced. A literary friend of mine, commenting on a particularly conclusive detective story, declared that 'the rigid demonstration destroyed the artistic effect.' But the rigid demonstration *was* the artistic effect. The entire dramatic effect of the climax of a detective story is due to the sudden recognition by the reader of the significance of a number of hitherto uncomprehended facts; or if such recognition should not immediately occur, the effect of the climax becomes suspended until it is completed in the final stage. . . .

In all ordinary novels, the climax, or *dénouement*, finishes the story, and any continuation is anti-climax. But a detective story has a dual character. There is the story, with its dramatic interest, and enclosed in it, so to speak, is the logical problem; and the climax of the former may leave the latter apparently unsolved. It is then the duty of the author, through the medium of the investigator, to prove the solution by an analysis and exposition of the evidence. He has to demonstrate to the reader that the conclusion emerged naturally and reasonably from the facts known to him, and that no other conclusion was possible.

If it is satisfactorily done, this is to the critical reader usually the most interesting part of the book; and it is the part by which he—very properly—judges the quality of the whole work. Too often it yields nothing but disappointment and a sense of anti-climax. The author is unable to solve his own problem. Acting on the pernicious advice of the pilot in the old song to 'Fear not, but trust in Providence,' he has piled up his mysteries in the hope of being able to find a plausible explanation; and now, when he comes to settle his account with the reader, his logical assets are *nil*. What claims to be a demonstration turns out to be a mere specious attempt to persuade the reader that the inexplicable has been explained; that the fortunate guesses of an inspired investigator are examples of genuine reasoning. (p. 720)

It cannot be too much emphasised that to the critical reader the quality in a detective story which takes precedence of all others is conclusiveness. It is the quality which, above all others, yields that intellectual satisfaction that the reader seeks; and it is the quality which is the most difficult to attain, and which costs more than any other in care and labour to the author. (p. 721)

R. Austin Freeman, "The Art of the Detective Story," in The Nineteenth Century and After, Vol. XCV, No. 567, May, 1924, pp. 713-21.

ALFRED C. WARD   (essay date 1924)

[In the following excerpt, Ward discusses the genre of detective fiction and Freeman's short stories featuring Dr. Thorndyke. He also compares Freeman's character Dr. Thorndyke with Conan Doyle's Sherlock Holmes.]

Errand-boys and philosophers have one taste (if no more) in common—a strong liking for detective stories. In the hierarchy of literary society, moreover, it now requires more moral courage to confess ignorance of the latest detective story than of the newest philosophical theory!

Upon some understanding of the causes for the widespread popularity of detective stories depends the proper adjustment of a commentator's angle of vision. At what should the detective-story writer aim, in his desire to be widely read?—

(1) At a baffling involuted mystery, or thrilling hairbreadth adventures?

(2) At morbid details of criminal procedure?

(3) At the revelation of terrifying mental states in the remorseful criminal?

(4) At the detailed exposition of individual omniscience in the detective? *or*

(5) At an ordered setting-forth of the logical and reasoned processes by which the knot is untied and the mystery solved?

There can be little doubt that it is for (1) and (2) that the errand-boy clamours; and equally little doubt that the philosopher would justify his interest in this form of writing by classifying it wholly and altogether exclusively under (5). Readers with sadistic tendencies would probably find considerable satisfaction in (2) and (3); while no one, apparently, has any interest in (4).

The writer for errand-boys (a genus which embraces representatives of all ages and all social degrees) has the easier task, therefore. He may proceed to pile the Pelion of derring-do upon the Ossa of improbability, with only an occasional glance at the rules of the literary game. The writer who aims at the provision of a full body of facts, marshalled in accordance with the rules of evidence, has, however, a vastly different task and one which provides comparatively few opportunities for sensationalism. Indeed, there is perhaps no other branch of fiction which offers so numerous temptations to dullness as that type of detective story which depends upon deductive reasoning. (pp. 211-12)

What is it that the bulk of readers demands in detective fiction? Does the majority approximate to the errand-boy or to the philosopher? Are bafflement and mystery the primary sources of general pleasure? or are elucidation and logical unravelling? In theory, and very largely in practice, Austin Freeman definitely holds by the latter view. In a short preface to *John Thorndyke's Cases,* he avers that his stories constitute a new experiment in detective fiction; and while admitting that the entertainment of the reader is still the first consideration, he expresses the view that "careful adherence to the probable,

and a strict avoidance of physical impossibilities" serve to heighten the reader's interest, and therefore his entertainment also. These stories, he goes on to say, illustrate "the application to the detection of crime of the ordinary methods of scientific research." The main interest, therefore, is focussed by Austin Freeman upon the methods by which Thorndyke interprets the clues and constructs from them a formulated body of clear-cut evidence. So strongly does he feel that this is the most interesting aspect, that in *The Singing Bone* Freeman writes several stories which, deliberately, hold no mystery or surprise. We are allowed to be present at the actual commission of the crime; we are acquainted with the criminal's motives; we see his actions, and we know of any attempt made to cover the tracks. Then come the discovery of the crime, the investigation of the clues by Thorndyke, and the piecing together of the scraps of evidence until the whole thing is clearly worked out to form a sure case against the accused. Before the detective comes upon the scene at all, the reader knows all about the affair, and the interest is entirely in watching Thorndyke assemble the jig-saw puzzle, fragment by fragment. To plan the story thus is, of course, to cater fully to the type of reader who professes to have a purely philosophical interest in detective fiction; but it is very doubtful whether there is any future for this method, or whether it does give even highbrow readers what in their heart of hearts they really want.

Normally, a detective story opens with the discovery of a mysterious crime (1—*Discovery*); next, certain vague and dissociated pieces of evidence are found (2—*Clues*); then, frequently, an arrest is made as a result of the misreading of circumstantial evidence (3—*False Accusation*); thereupon the expert mind is brought to bear upon the problem, and other clues are found (4—*Investigation*); the expert argues back from his accumulated clues to a probable course of events (5—*Construction of a Hypothesis*); having put together a possible case, the expert tests its probability from all available standpoints (6—*The Hypothesis Examined*); by processes of deduction and induction, a substantial case is built up against the real criminal (7—*Solution*).

Still following the course of the average good detective story, it is necessary to hark back to consider the complications commonly introduced to provoke the maximum degree of excitement and thrill in the reader. These usually centre (*a*) around the falsely-accused person, about whom the threads of circumstantial evidence are drawn so tightly that the reader is kept in a state of sympathetic suspense; (*b*) around the detective, whose life is probably imperilled by the counter-activity of the actual criminal; (*c*) around the methods adopted by the criminal to evade arrest. Of course, there may not be any falsely-accused person; and then, usually, the reader's interest is stimulated by a series of blind-alley clues which point to various characters involved in the story. In this latter type, the author's success is in proportion to the skill with which he guards his secret until the concluding pages.

Austin Freeman's characteristic method simply lops off a number of these features, since his main aim is not to mystify or excite, but simply to present a view of practical logic working upon a definite problem—applied logic. He does not entirely abandon the more usual attractions, however, except in a particular group of stories in *The Singing Bone*. It is interesting and perhaps significant to note that only in the shorter stories does he keep at all closely to his own terms of reference: in the full-length novels, particularly in *A Silent Witness* and *The Eye of Osiris,* he gives full play to his dramatic and inventive faculties, while at the same time continuing to apply to the "detection of crime the ordinary methods of scientific research." (pp. 218-21)

[The] methods of Sherlock Holmes and Dr. Thorndyke can be compared in detail from their deductive procedure in relation to similar objects. In both Conan Doyle's "The Adventure of the Blue Carbuncle" and Austin Freeman's **"The Anthropologist at Large,"** the cases under investigation concern robberies. The main clue in each instance is a man's rather shabby felt hat, and Holmes and Thorndyke both profess to confine their attention to facts which can be gathered indisputably from the object under examination.

Let Sherlock Holmes begin. The hat before him is thus described: "It was a very ordinary black hat of the usual round shape, hard and much the worse for wear. The lining had been of red silk, but was a good deal discoloured. . . . It was pierced in the brim for a hat-securer, but the elastic was missing. For the rest, it was cracked, exceedingly dusty, and spotted in several places, although there seemed to have been some attempt to hide the discoloured patches by smearing them with ink." From these details as to the condition of the hat, Sherlock Holmes makes the following deductions:

(1) *That the man is intellectual.* The hat is a large one and "a man with so large a brain must have something in it."

(2) *That he was once well-to-do, but is so no longer.* The hat is of a style which was in vogue three years earlier. It is of the best quality, but is now shabby. Therefore, Holmes argues, the owner must have been able to buy an expensive hat three years ago, but has since been unable to replace it.

(3) *That he was a man of foresight, but has suffered moral retrogression, probably due to drink.* Because he had had a safety guard fixed to his hat, but had failed to renew the missing elastic.

(4) *That he is middle-aged, has grizzled hair which had recently been cut, and that he used lime cream.* Deduced from examination of the lining.

(5) *That his wife has ceased to love him.* "This hat has not been brushed for weeks. When I see you, my dear Watson, with a week's accumulation of dust upon your hat, and when your wife allows you to go out in such a state, I shall fear that you also have been unfortunate enough to lose your wife's affection." (There is other satisfactory evidence that the owner of the hat is not a bachelor.)

(6) *That he probably has not gas laid on in his house.* Because there are several tallow stains upon the hat—evidently fallen from a guttering candle.

Before Thorndyke begins to examine the hat which had come into his hands, he remarks, pertinently, that some misleading deductions as to the condition of the immediate owner may be made from a hat, unless very great care is exercised. In the first place, there is a considerable traffic in second-hand hats, and, consequently, the latest owner may not be identical with the original purchaser. (This explodes Sherlock Holmes's second deduction!) Among the observations and reasoned conclusions which Thorndyke then proceeds to make are:

(1) *That the man is a Japanese.* Because (*a*) his head (judged from the shape of the inside of the hat) is nearly as broad as it is long; and (*b*) the small pieces of hair behind the head-lining are circular in section and of exceptionally large diameter (typical Japanese characteristics).

(2) *That he is employed in a mother-of-pearl factory.* Because the dust from the hat when microscopically examined shows a large proportion of particles of pearl shell. (This strengthens the view that he was a Japanese, since the pearl-shell industry is largely conducted by Eastern races.)

(3) *That he is a decent orderly man.* Because there is no accumulation of old dust on the outside of the hat.

Thorndyke's main deductions are fewer than those of Sherlock Holmes, but they are sounder, less capricious, and more practical. From the evidence provided by the hat, Thorndyke does discover his man; but all that Holmes sets forth goes for nothing, since he has to advertise in all the evening papers before he can get in touch with his wanted person.

Particularly typical of the weak irrelevances which emanate from Holmes, is the allegation that the unknown man's wife no longer loves him, because his headgear is particularly dusty! (pp. 222-25)

The fact is, that Holmes was a *poseur* first and an amateur detective afterwards. His amazing success is rather a put-up job between him and his creator; and his occasional failures are a confidence trick, to suggest that there is really no deception in his triumphs. Thorndyke, on the other hand, is a straightforward scientific investigator, with very little nonsense about him. Perhaps he is a somewhat too-well-oiled piece of mechanism to be a satisfactory fictional character; and he has none of those memorable personal mannerisms which have made Sherlock Holmes more real to the multitude than is the whole police force. Story for the sake of story is more generously given by Conan Doyle than by Austin Freeman—so far as the latter's short tales are concerned. In the novels the position is probably reversed. (pp. 225-26)

Alfred C. Ward, "The Detective Story: Conan Doyle; Austin Freeman; H. C. Bailey," in his Aspects of the Modern Short Story: English and American, *University of London Press, Ltd., 1924, pp. 211-26.**

LIFE AND LETTERS, LONDON   **(essay date 1929)**

[*In the following excerpt, the critic compares Dr. Thorndyke with Sherlock Holmes and offers a mixed appraisal of* As a Thief in the Night.]

Now that Sherlock Holmes has at last been persuaded to issue his collected works in one volume (*The Complete Sherlock Holmes Stories* . . .), it is fitting that their appearance should coincide with Dr. Thorndyke's latest triumph (*As A Thief in the Night* . . .). For Dr. Thorndyke is unquestionably Holmes's chief successor in the rôle of expert (as distinguished from that of tracker or sleuth), and on internal evidence it looks very much as though the doctor's brilliant rivalry was partly responsible for the terrible decline in the Baker Street consultant. No one who had a respectable childhood can really criticize Sherlock Holmes in a dispassionate manner; yet no sentimentalist can be blind to the fact that the two last of the five groups of stories in this collection are simply very bad indeed. Nor is it entirely irrelevant to notice that Dr. Thorndyke's rise to fame took place between the publication of the third and fourth groups. For the plain fact is that, as an expert, Dr. Thorndyke has Holmes beaten at the post. If Holmes had had the death of Harold Monkhouse to investigate, he would not have come within a mile of finding the murderer. His equipment was not good enough; and even in re-reading some of his own earlier triumphs, we are uneasily conscious that Dr. Thorndyke would not have been satisfied with them. For instance, in that very early case, *The Musgrave Ritual,* we find that Holmes unearthed a treasure by means of a seventeenth-century *questionnaire,* part of which was concerned with the length of the shadow cast by an elm-tree. Holmes, learning the height of the elm from its nineteenth-century owner, measures with a tape and takes him straight to the spot; but Dr. Thorndyke, one is certain, would not so lightly have assumed that the top of an elm-tree would have remained in exactly the same place for over two hundred years. And this is only one of a series of cases in which Holmes, considered as an expert, was distinctly inferior. Yet from these two books it is equally plain why Dr. Thorndyke will never oust Holmes from his position as *the* detective of the world. Not only was Holmes the first-comer: he is a character, and Dr. Thorndyke is not. Dr. Thorndyke is an oyster, a block of teak, an Indian idol—or so his creator suffers him to be described—and though he is also, we are told, very handsome, very kind of heart, and always on the right side, one cannot have a really comradely affection for a block of teak, however handsome and kindhearted. A block of teak does not shoot bullets across the room, nor keep its tobacco in the Persian slipper, nor practise pig-sticking in order to trace a criminal, nor simulate epilepsy when on the chase, nor throw out immortal aphorisms such as that of the dog in the night-time; and it is the glory of Sir Arthur Conan Doyle to have created the man who did all these things. (pp. 63-4)

The solution in [*As a Thief in the Night*] is really a triumph of ingenuity, and the book is well worth seven and sixpence for the last chapter alone, in which it is expounded. Considered as a whole, however, it is certainly too long. The story would have been far better told in twenty-five thousand instead of eighty thousand words, and the middle part, which is pure padding, is distinctly dull. Nothing whatever happens in it beyond a certain manoeuvring of the characters, and as Mr. Freeman's characters, unless they are lawyers or old women, are invariably entirely without character, it is impossible to get up an interest in their manoeuvres. The whole business of the narrator in this novel could have been told in one chapter greatly to the novel's advantage. Mr. Freeman is one of the very few detective writers who are better at short stories than at long ones. But for the sheer brilliance of the crime and its discovery, it is well worth while to plough through the tedious parts. (pp. 64-5)

A review of "As a Thief in the Night," in Life and Letters, *London, Vol. II, No. 8, January, 1929, pp. 63-5.**

H. DOUGLAS THOMSON (essay date 1931)

[*An English critic, Thomson is the author of* Masters of Mystery: A Study of the Detective Story, *one of the earliest book-length studies of the mystery story. This work outlines the history of the genre, and is particularly useful as a guide to English detective story writers. In the following excerpt from that study, Thomson examines and challenges Freeman's contention that the most interesting aspect of a detective story is the detective's method of solving the problem.*]

Dr. Austin Freeman concerned himself more conscientiously than any of his predecessors with the scientific process of detection; and certain minutiae in the data which had been ignored up till then assumed a new significance. Concrete evidence was having its day. (pp. 70-1)

Dr. Austin Freeman started with a long handicap of specialised experience. *Who's Who* gives us some interesting facts:—

> Born in 1862; qualified as M.R.C.S. House physician at Middlesex Hospital; Acting Deputy Medical officer at Holloway Prison; Assistant Colonial Surgeon Gold Coast; Surveyor and Naturalist to the Expedition to Ashanti; Member of Anglo-German Boundary Commission, etc.
>
> Recreations: modelling in clay and wax.
>
> (pp. 168-69)

Dr. Freeman certainly makes the most of his varied experiences. Thus, in any of his novels there is the ring of authenticity in his description of an autopsy or when he is dealing with such a subject as toxicology. In *The Mystery of 31 New Inn* he gives us a way to find our bearings in the dark, a trick which he had learnt in his capacity as a surveyor. In *The Red Thumb Mark* he regales us with an inside picture of Holloway prison. His recreations allowed him to speak with authority in *The D'Arblay Mystery* on wax modelling. But that, as we shall see, is by no means all.

We read in the Preface to *The Singing Bone:*—

> In the conventional detective story the interest is made to focus on the question, Who did it? The identity of the criminal is a secret that is jealously guarded up to the very end of the book, and its disclosure forms the final climax.
>
> This I have always regarded as somewhat of a mistake. In real life the identity of the criminal is a question of supreme importance for practical reasons; but in fiction where no such reasons exist, I conceive the interest of the reader to be engaged chiefly by the demonstration of unexpected consequences of simple actions, of unsuspected casual connections, and by the evolution of an ordered train of evidence from a mass of facts apparently incoherent and unrelated. The reader's curiosity is concerned not so much with the question, Who did it? as with the question, How was the discovery achieved? That is to say the ingenious reader is interested more in the intermediate action than in the ultimate result.

Dr. Freeman is here laying down the general law to suit his own particular ideas. He knew very well that his power lay in the tracing of the intermediate steps; that this uncanny gift of his would constitute his main title to a seat among the worthies of the genre. So without turning a hair he became dogmatic. . . . "That is to say the ingenious reader is interested more. . . ." Now, I wonder why "ingenious." And what is an ingenious reader, anyway? I cannot bring myself to believe that Dr. Freeman implies that the reader's ingenuity is a reflection of the author's—the ingenuity being the capability to follow with interest the various steps. It sounds precious like self-advertisement; which, of course, it is not.

Yet is Dr. Freeman's theory a tenable one? We have regarded the problem of the detective story as the answer to the question, Who did it? . . . Now, we are informed that that is not so interesting a problem as "How did the detective solve the problem?" In the first we have, as it were, one known quantity—the data; and in the second two, the data and the conclusion.

With the latter it is as if we were set a problem and were told that we might look at the end of the book for the answer if we were so inclined. That very fact simplifies the problem, even although we have to cook the answer. Consider what we have to sacrifice if we are to be "ingenious." Suspense, excitement, the dramatic dénouement—all these go overboard. Instead we are asked to thrive on the vegetarian dish of science without tears!

In a first-rate detective story we expect both the interest of the intermediate action and the interest of the ultimate result. And as Dr. Freeman is one of the great artists of the genre, our expectations are not damped. The construction of the stories in *The Singing Bone* was a remarkably successful stunt (the last word is not used in a derogatory sense). The fact that Dr. Freeman has seldom essayed this type of story since seems to suggest that for him at least the novelty soon wore off. It remains, however, to repeat—and this was my reason for quoting at length—that whether the identity of the criminal is known or unknown, one's chief interest in an Austin Freeman novel is concerned with Thorndyke's methods.

Dr. Freeman's subordinates all else to the scientific treatment; and scientific, moreover, in the narrower sense, as all Thorndyke's triumphs are won in his laboratory or by means of his portable set, "the invaluable green case." This was a salutary reform. It was in fact the very best thing that could have happened to the detective story. The touches of academic pedantry, the chemical formulae, the microscope, Farrant, the forceps, the dusting powder—all these constituted an admirable reaction to the wild guesswork of some of Thorndyke's contemporaries.

But a general public uninitiated into the mysteries of chemistry and physics likes its doses in small quantities. In the preface to *John Thorndyke's Cases* the author politely informed his readers that the experiments detailed in the book had been personally carried out by himself—that Thorndyke's lustre was his own. A critic had evidently jumped at this opportunity; for in the preface of *The Mystery of 31 New Inn* Dr. Freeman sententiously takes up his cudgels in self-defence:—

> Commenting upon one of my earlier novels, in respect of which I had claimed to have been careful to adhere to common probabilities and to have made use only of really practicable methods of investigation, a critic remarked that this was of no consequence whatever, as long as the story was amusing.

> Few people, I imagine, will agree with him. To most readers, and certainly to the kind of reader for whom an author is willing to take trouble, complete realism in respect of incidents and methods is an essential factor in maintaining the interest of a detective story. Here it may be worth while to mention that Thorndyke's method of producing the track chart, described in Chapters II. and III., has actually been used in practice. . . .

The trouble with Dr. Freeman is just this: he takes too much pains. Taking trouble to please one's readers means taking trouble to please one's self. So far as one may gauge the average detective story fan's reaction to a Thorndyke novel, it is one of mild annoyance coupled with a genuine admiration for one who works at science and plays with it afterwards. But as regards the practicability of the experiments, the general public

would just as soon have him confess in a monthly magazine the impossibility of them. One and all would acclaim him as the perpetrator of a capital hoax. And this means that there was after all something in the critic's submission and that Dr. Freeman is apt to write above his public.

Dr. Freeman must have felt that so far he had been quite original enough and that for the rest he had better abide by the conventions. The Thorndyke household is based on Sherlock Holmes's. Thorndyke lives more doucely in chambers, but prospective clients show the same eagerness to ring his bell. As a character Thorndyke cannot hold a candle to Sherlock. He occupies the chair of Medical Jurisprudence at St. Margaret's; and he is a capital don, for he appears to have no eccentric weaknesses. (pp. 169-73)

Jervis, the medico, lacks Dr. Watson's humanity. But Dr. Freeman has shown great discretion in refusing to exaggerate the Dr. Watson characteristics in order to get a laugh from the gallery. Even Jervis knows too much.

"Excluding, quite properly, I think—Raynaud's disease, we arrive at frost-bite and ergotism."

I ask you, is it fair? Nor must we forget Polton, Thorndyke's laboratory assistant, photographer, butler, Jack-of-all-trades. Here Dr. Freeman has really missed the chance of his lifetime; for Polton might have introduced a welcome burst of comic relief between the experiments. What a character Mr. Edgar Wallace might have made of him!

It can easily be seen why Dr. Freeman is more successful in his short stories. He is an exponent of the unexpected means, not this time so much the unexpected means of inflicting death, but the unexpected means of detecting it. The narrative consists of experiment upon experiment based on facts which Thorndyke has singled out from his data with an unerring sense of their significance.

It is impossible to deny that Thorndyke is one of Fortune's favourites. He always finds some clue, or his microscope does—whether it is an infinitesimal piece of glass or a speck of dust. One's ignorance prevents one from questioning the probability of these finds. For example, in "**A Wastrel's Romance**" the criminal is traced to a certain locality from three different types of dust that are found in a discarded overcoat. In *The Red Thumb Mark* and "**The Old Lag**," Dr. Freeman describes a very clever method of forging finger-prints by a line-block process. Yet I have heard an authority on process-engraving express grave doubts as to the chances of such forgery proving really misleading. Now and again Dr. Freeman has the last laugh, as in "**The Moabite Cipher**," where the reader expects that one of the more complicated forms of "mathematical cipher" is to be solved, whereas the real message is written in invisible ink.

There are times, too, when Dr. Freeman can be attractively simple, as in *The Singing Bone,* where the main items in Thorndyke's deduction are as follows: A pipe is found near the body. But as the mouthpiece of this pipe indicates that its owner has a good strong set of teeth whereas the corpse certainly had not; and as the tobacco found inside the pouch was different from that found inside the pipe, the obvious conclusion—the one instance in a thousand where it is the right one—is that the pipe does not belong to the corpse. Then who else can be the owner but "the other?" Simple, my dear Jervis. I bless Dr. Freeman for *The Singing Bone,* for it is the one and only Thorndyke story which I have prematurely solved *in detail.*

The full length novels—in particular *The Red Thumb Mark, The Eye of Osiris, The Mystery of 31 New Inn, The D'Arblay Mystery*—suffer by reason of three serious faults.

(1) Two series of concurrent events are described as if they had no connection. Now although the characters cannot for a long time trace any inter-relation, the reader can.

(2) The excitement is provided by the numerous, sometimes quite unnecessary, attempts on the life of the secondary hero—in most cases a young doctor—who has come by some important evidence and thereby frightened the villain out of his mind. Austin Freeman villains always wax nervy after doing the deed. Their excessive zeal to cover up their tracks has been the efficient cause of their downfall.

(3) The minor characters have the "annoying" habit of falling in love. "Annoying" is E. M. Wrong's mild epithet; "exasperating" is perhaps a more fitting description. Perhaps on second thoughts Dr. Freeman concluded that he had misjudged the intensity of the scientific appeal. One cannot blame him for this decision. But love does not thrive in the laboratory, and the scientist is rarely an artist in analysing the emotions. Dr. Freeman's lovers are excessively wooden, excessively sensitive, and excessively honourable. *Helen Vardon's Confession* is the Victorian novelette in miniature. And all through *The Red Thumb Mark* the refrain of the music-hall ditty rang in one's ears—"O kiss the girl if you want to, but let her go home to bed." (pp. 173-76)

> H. Douglas Thomson, "The History of the Detective Story" and "The Realistic Detective Story," in his Masters of Mystery: A Study of the Detective Story, 1931. Reprint by Dover Publications, Inc., 1978, pp. 58-74, 168-92.*

HOWARD HAYCRAFT   (essay date 1941)

[*A perceptive and entertaining American critic of mystery fiction, Haycraft is the author of* Murder for Pleasure: The Life and Times of the Detective Story, *an authoritative study of detective fiction. In the following excerpt from that work, Haycraft praises Freeman's work and discusses his contribution to the genre of detective fiction.*]

From the earliest days of the police novel there has been a vast deal of high-flown talk about the "scientific" detective. The plain truth is that few of the sleuths of fiction wearing this designation would know which way to turn if they found themselves in a real-life laboratory. The shining exception for all time is R. Austin Freeman's Dr. John Thorndyke. No other literary criminologist, so far as this writer knows, has been paid the tribute of having his fictional methods put into use by the real police. (p. 67)

The Red Thumb Mark . . . was the book which marked [Freeman's] début in the form, at the age of forty-five. In respect to puzzle-and-solution, this remarkable volume remains one of the undisputed milestones of the genre. What is of but slightly less importance, it served to bring into existence the immortal Thorndyke and his delectable associates, Jervis and Polton. (p. 68)

The numerous Freeman books, still happily appearing at yearly intervals at this writing, are of a uniform detectival excellence, if slightly monotonous in their resemblance to each other. Special significance, however, attaches to *The Singing Bone* . . . , in which the author made the experiment of revealing to the reader the full stories of the crimes *first*, then describing the

steps leading up to the solutions by the detective. This rather dangerous departure—perilous in that it dispenses almost entirely with the puzzle and suspense elements—Freeman never repeated in toto; but in all the Thorndyke stories the revelation of the criminal will usually be found subordinated to the *means* of detection. In another writer this might be grounds for criticism, but in Freeman's skilled hands so fascinating is the business of investigation (based on actual experiments worked out in the author's extensive laboratory) that we scarcely notice the absence of mystification.

As a craftsman in the more literary sense, Dr. Freeman presents an interesting anomaly. His narrative style is so often that of late-Victorian romanticism that it is not unusual to find him unconsciously classified in the Doyle period. Indeed, the domestic trappings of a typical Freeman tale bring to the fire-lit chambers in King's Bench Walk much the same mood of snugness and nostalgic bachelor bonhommie which is destined to bespeak Baker Street to the end of time. But in his pioneer insistence on the fair-play method, the creator of John Thorndyke, M.D. was a Modern before the Moderns. He was the true and undoubted "parent" of the scientific detective story in the highest meaning of the phrase, and remains to-day the living dean of that form—if not, indeed, of all detective story writers of whatever style or persuasion. (pp. 69-70)

> Howard Haycraft, "England: 1890-1914 (The Romantic Era)," in his Murder for Pleasure: The Life and Times of the Detective Story, D. Appleton-Century Company, Incorporated, 1941, pp. 62-82.*

VINCENT STARRETT   (essay date 1943)

[*Starrett was a Canadian-born American journalist, critic, and novelist. Considered an authority on Sherlock Holmes, he is the author of* The Private Life of Sherlock Holmes (1933), *a compilation of Holmes lore and scholarship. Starrett also wrote numerous short stories, detective novels, and humorous sketches. During the 1920's, Starrett and Freeman corresponded intermittently for several years. In the following excerpt, originally published in the* Chicago Sunday Tribune *on 10 October 1943, Starrett discusses the high status of Dr. Thorndyke among fictional detectives.*]

Dr. Freeman's most important contribution to detective fiction as an art was made in a group of short-stories, published as *The Singing Bone* . . . , in which he invented the "inverted" detective story. In these engaging tales the reader is first shown the crime and the criminal—is put in possession of all the facts—before the detective takes over. Thereafter the interest lies in watching the investigator work backward, as it were, toward what the reader already knows. If you think this makes for any diminution of interest, just try reading the book. Try *rereading* it!

There are readers who find Thorndyke too painstaking, and Dr. Freeman—who has a flair for Dickensian caricature and a habit of permitting his minor figures to fall in love—too Victorian. I am not that ungrateful. Some fine detective stories are being written today; but, in general, the alcoholic blitheness and wisecracking sophistication of the current crop of fathomers is not the stuff of literature, and few of them will survive. When all the bright young things have performed their appointed task of flattering the complexes of neurotic semi-literates, and have gone their way to oblivion, the best of the Thorndyke stories will live on—minor classics on the shelf that holds the good books of the world. (pp. 110-11)

Vincent Starrett, "Good Bye, Dr. Thorndyke!" in his Books and Bipeds, *Argus Books, Inc., 1947, pp. 108-11.*

RAYMOND CHANDLER (letter date 1949)

[*Chandler was an American novelist and screenwriter who, along with Dashiell Hammett, elevated the genre known as the hard-boiled detective story into an American art form. His first and perhaps most famous novel,* The Big Sleep *(1939), introduced the detective hero Philip Marlowe, one of the most memorable characters in the field. In the following excerpt, Chandler expresses his high regard for Freeman's writing.*]

This man Austin Freeman is a wonderful performer. He has no equal in his genre and he is also a much better writer than you might think, if you were superficially inclined, because in spite of the immense leisure of his writing he accomplishes an even suspense which is quite unexpected. The apparatus of his writing makes for dullness, but he is not dull. There is even a gaslight charm about his Victorian love affairs, and those wonderful walks across London which the long-legged Dr Thorndyke takes like a stroll around a garden, accompanied by his cheerful and brainless Watson, Dr Jervis, whom no man in his senses would hire for any legal or medico-legal operation more exacting than counting the toes of a corpse.

Freeman has so many distinctions as a technician that one is apt to forget that within his literary tradition he is a damn good writer. He invented the inverted detective story. He proved the possibility of forging fingerprints and of detecting the forgeries long before the police thought of such a thing. His knowledge is vast and very real. The great scene would have been a courtroom battle between Thorndyke and Spilsbury, and for my money Thorndyke would have won hands down. (pp. 59-60)

Raymond Chandler, in an extract from a letter to Hamish Hamilton on December 13, 1949, in his Raymond Chandler Speaking, *edited by Dorothy Gardiner and Kathrine Sorley Walker, Houghton Mifflin Company, 1962, pp. 59-60.*

RAYMOND CHANDLER (letter date 1950)

[*In the following excerpt, Chandler offers a mixed appraisal of Freeman's work.*]

Yes, I know the books of Austin Freeman and Freeman Wills Crofts very well. I think my favorite Freemans are **Mr. Pottermack's Oversight** and **The Stoneware Monkey.** Freemans are very hard to get hold of. I haven't been able to get **The Stoneware Monkey** at all since I first read it. **Pontifex, Son and Thorndyke** is also very good. The hansom cab era appeals to me very much. And I always enjoy the long walks across London which Thorndyke and Jervis seem to take as a matter of course. Their legs never become tired apparently. As a matter of fact, Freeman is rather a poor writer compared with Conan Doyle. If you read him out loud he makes you laugh, he's so stilted. And Thorndyke at times is a bit of a bore, especially when explaining to Jervis that he now has all the facts and that if he sits down and studies them, he should come up with a few ideas. Can it be possible that the acute Dr. Thorndyke would ever think Jervis would ever come up with an idea? Dr. Watson, though no mental giant, was on occasion capable of a moderately sensible remark. But not Dr. Jervis. His mind is a complete blank. Some of the most delicious moments in Freeman to me are when Thorndyke politely in-

quires of Jervis whether he will be free from engagements on the following date to accompany him on some expedition. Jervis is always free of course. He will always be free. One can hardly imagine anybody employing him to do anything more exacting than copying out a laundry list. Whether or not Freeman writes really good detective stories is quite another matter. In cases where, as in the example of **The Mystery of 31 New Inn,** there is no analysis of scientific evidence, in spots they are extremely transparent. And where the solution of a mystery turns on the correct analysis of scientific evidence, there arises a question of honesty. I realize that this is a big problem in detective stories—just what honesty is. But if you accept the basic premise, as I do, that in a novel of detection the reader should have been able to solve the problem, if he had paid proper attention to all the clues as they were presented and drawn the right deductions from them, then I say that he had no such opportunity if, to evaluate said clues, he is required to have an expert knowledge of archaeology, physics, chemistry, microscopy, pathology, metallurgy, and various other sciences. If, in order to know where a man was drowned, I have to identify the fish scales found in his lungs, then I, as a reader, cannot be expected to tell you where he was drowned. I should not be expected to. And if to solve the mystery I must be able to solve this point, then so far as I am concerned the clue is suppressed just as effectively as though it had never been given. In spite of all this, I have a very high regard for Freeman. His writing is stilted, but it is never dull in the sense that Crofts's writing is dull. That is to say, it is never flat. It is merely old-fashioned. His problems are always interesting in themselves, and the expositions at the end are masterpieces of lucid analysis. Thorndyke is a far more accurate thinker than Sherlock Holmes. He is the only expert in fiction who would have been a match, and I think rather more than a match, for the real experts such as Sir Bernard Spilsbury. (pp. 225-26)

Raymond Chandler, in a letter to James Keddie on September 29, 1950, in his Selected Letters of Raymond Chandler, *edited by Frank MacShane, Columbia University Press, 1981, pp. 224-26.*

DOUGLAS G. BROWNE AND ALAN BROCK (essay date 1953)

[*In the following excerpt from their study* Fingerprints: Fifty Years of Scientific Crime Detection, *Browne and Brock examine Freeman's knowledge of fingerprinting as practiced in the late nineteenth and early twentieth centuries.*]

[It] is of interest to observe opinion on the subject [of fingerprinting and its use as evidence in court] as reflected in the mirror of contemporary fiction. . . . English writers of detective fiction on the whole faithfully followed popular trends of thought. Their classic characters of the period in this genre are Sherlock Holmes and Dr. Throndyke, whose creators were men with scientific knowledge; and if Holmes in his heyday is always a little behind the march of progress in this particular field, and Thorndyke usually abreast of it, Austin Freeman's technical interests covered a wider range than Conan Doyle's.

Holmes placed little confidence in fingerprinting, either as an aid to detection or as a means of registering convicted criminals. The years during which his famous *Adventures* and *Memoirs* appeared include the period that saw the first tentative consideration of the system, its adoption, and its vindication; yet there are only four references to fingerprints in the series—unless two casual remarks at an early date can be taken as proof that at that time the detective had some acquaintance with the subject. (p. 59)

In 1907 R. Austin Freeman's *The Red Thumb Mark* introduced Dr John Thorndyke to the reading public. It was the first full-length detective novel since [Mark Twain's] *Pudd'nhead Wilson* to deal with a question of fingerprint evidence. Thorndyke himself is the first truly scientific detective in fiction. A medico-legal expert who in technical attainments, extreme thoroughness, lucidity of mind and speech, and even physical appearance, foreshadowed the late Sir Bernard Spilsbury, he was less addicted to pure pathology than to other sciences helpful to criminal investigation—microscopy, microphotography, analysis of dust, and the like. In *The Red Thumb Mark* he employs his specialized knowledge to expose a conspiracy based on the fallacy that fingerprints can successfully be forged. (pp. 61-2)

This story appeared at a time when interest in fingerprints, and to some extent recognition of their individuality, had become sufficiently general to popularize such toys as "Thumbographs." Few people by then had not heard of the Fingerprint Branch at Scotland Yard, or read of cases in which fingerprint evidence figured. Austin Freeman, who later wrote a short story, **"The Old Lag,"** with a similar theme, was not only a man with some scientific knowledge, but also a practical craftsman who performed the tests and experiments he describes in his novels. *The Red Thumb Mark,* however, seems to-day as much of a museum piece as the Sherlock Holmes series. It is not merely that the characters drive about in hansoms and four-wheelers, but the police are always stupid. Superintendent Miller is little better than Lestrade. Sir Edward Henry might not have lived; in the C.I.D., so far as fingerprints are concerned, six years have gone for nothing. A forgery which, if only because it was made with a rigid stamp, should have been instantly detected, completely deceives the experts, who are blind, even with microscopes, to the importance of the S-shaped break in the ridge pattern. Nor do they appear to be aware that the natural greasy surface of the skin is caused by sweat exuded from pores situated between the ridges. It is in this grease that the latent finger-mark is imprinted, and in a photographic enlargement of a genuine fingerprint the pores are distinctly visible as rows of dots irregularly spaced. The experts should have known that successful reproduction of these pores is the chief difficulty facing the would-be forger, and that it is not ovecome by a gelatine stamp.

Austin Freeman himself must have been better informed about the efficiency of the Fingerprint Branch. But he was following the convention, established by Poe, adopted by Conan Doyle, and not yet outworn, of the brilliant amateur who must always score off the police. And he may unconsciously have reflected the attitude of his readers, who played with "Thumbographs," and talked of Loops and Whorls, without as yet fully accepting fingerprint evidence as an infallible means of identification. (pp. 63-4)

> *Douglas G. Browne and Alan Brock, "Fiction, Fact, and Fingers," in their* Fingerprints: Fifty Years of Scientific Crime Detection, *George G. Harrap & Co. Ltd., 1953, pp. 59-68.* *

NORMAN DONALDSON (essay date 1971)

[*An English-born American scientist, Donaldson was in his teens when he first discovered the Dr. Thorndyke stories. In the preface to his book-length study of Freeman and Dr. Thorndyke,* In Search of Dr. Thorndyke, *he states: "This volume . . . was originally planned as the first study to appear on Thorndyke, to parallel the many 'biographies' and studies of Sherlock Holmes. In the process I discovered just how difficult it is to separate Thorndyke from his creator, and inevitably my book has been the dual history of Freeman and his superlative detective." In the following excerpt from that work, Donaldson surveys Freeman's career.*]

One book which Freeman devotees sometimes overlook is his first hard-cover volume of fiction, *The Adventures of Romney Pringle,* written [in collaboration with John James Pitcairn] under the pseudonym, "Clifford Ashdown." It has been described [by Ellery Queen] as "the rarest volume of detective-crime short stories published in the twentieth century" [see Additional Bibliography]. (p. 52)

The hero of these collaborated stories, Romney Pringle, is an engaging villain, ostensibly a "literary agent" with shabby headquarters in Furnival's Inn (an obvious Freeman touch). He invariably used a bicycle in his travels from one spot of evil-doing to another (Pitcairn was an enthusiastic cyclist; Freeman, not at all). The division of plot construction and actual writing is difficult to apportion now. Freeman's hand is easily distinguished, but there are many unusual touches, for which Pitcairn was probably responsible. The stories are not brilliant, but the cool arrogant air with which Pringle mulcts his victims—usually dishonest people themselves, or else, like the Indian maharajah in the final story of the series, unpopular at the time and therefore fair game—has a dry, refreshing flavour lacking in most of Freeman's non-Thorndyke writings. (pp. 55-6)

It is not easy to determine just how important Pitcairn's help was to the struggling Freeman, but it was appreciable. Freeman working alone had never achieved anything more praiseworthy than anemic imitations of W. W. Jacobs. But in his association with Pitcairn, Freeman achieved his first sustained effort in fiction; twelve stories centering around one dominant character, Romney Pringle. Six of these appeared between hard covers, thereby elevating Freeman to the elite whose short stories of crime and detection have been published in book form. (p. 60)

More important than the Romney Pringle stories for Freeman's future development as a major detective novelist were the annals of medical sleuthing entitled *From a Surgeon's Diary,* published two or three years later. . . . These stories are reminiscent of the two series of *Stories from the Diary of a Doctor* by the profilic authoress L. T. Meade and her pseudonymous medical collaborator "Clifford Halifax" which had appeared a decade earlier. The Ashdown stories are superior in that they are based on rational motives and eschew such pseudoscientific "explanations" as telepathy and hypnotism. The latter stories, especially the *Diary* series, require only a recognizable detective hero to raise them to the level of classics. Previously, Freeman's work gave no promise of anything more remarkable than *Flighty Phyllis* or, on a more serious plane, *The Golden Pool.*

Pitcairn's friendship, coming when Freeman's medical aspirations were at an end, and when his own efforts to replace this career by a literary one were making slow headway, must have had inestimably heartening effects. If "J. J." [Pitcairn] and Freeman drifted apart just before the curtain rose on Thorndyke's debut, it is nevertheless true that together they set the stage for the greatest scientific detective of them all. (pp. 60-1)

In 1905, Freeman's first venture into book-length fiction of a serious nature was published by Cassell and Company. *The Golden Pool,* a thick, closely-printed tome, is set in the part of the world he knew best: the Gold Coast of West Africa. (p. 62)

The book is too slow-moving, too rich in native lore, to make an ideal adventure story, but it is the most significant of Freeman's non-Thorndyke works. Moreover, the publication of this lengthy story was important in promoting its author's self-confidence, despite the fact that the financial harvest was disappointing. . . . A dramatic new approach would be needed if Freeman were ever to raise himself to the ranks of the really popular authors. Detection and medicine were intermingled in *From a Surgeon's Diary;* crime—with a dash of detection added— was the theme of the Pringle stories. For some years past and for many years to come, the archetypical sleuth was and would be Sherlock Holmes. (p. 64)

Sherlock's little oddities—drug addiction, revolver practice in the living room, even his violin-playing—were distasteful to Freeman. His own investigator would rely on sound scientific reasoning and not at all on histrionics. (p. 65)

It was Freeman's experiences as Deputy Medical Officer at Holloway Prison which provided the theme around which his first Thorndyke novel was constructed. As he described the circumstances ten years later on the fly leaf of his own copy of *The Red Thumb Mark:*

> At that time the ''Thumbograph'' was on sale at all the railway book-stalls and I obtained a copy by purchase or gift, I forget which. As my observations in the Finger-print Department had convinced me that finger-prints could be quite easily reproduced, I regarded the ''Thumbograph'' as a rather dangerous publication and I projected this story as an instance of its possible misuse. But I tested my thesis that finger-prints could be fabricated by making a set of gelatine stamps from my own finger-tips and with these I was able to produce quite good prints.
>
> (pp. 75-6)

[The book] even now engenders sharp differences of opinion among those who read it. Fingerprint experts almost universally maintain that fingerprints cannot be successfully forged. They charge, in fact, that this, first of the many Thorndyke stories, is based upon a sham, and a mischievous one at that; for *The Red Thumb Mark,* famous in retrospect for its introduction of the greatest scientific investigator ever brought before the readers of detective stories, is concerned with one great central issue, the possibility that fingerprints can be successfully forged and the counterfeit impressions subsequently used to incriminate an innocent man. (p. 76)

Compared to the ingenuity and sheer complexity of such a subsequent novel as *The Cat's Eye* (1923), there is a simplicity and directness about the book which belongs to the turn of the century rather than to the more sophisticated 20's. There is a great deal of ''action'' in the story, in particular Thorndyke is assaulted twice—being injured rather badly in the first attack— and an attempt is made to poison him. There is a love interest (as usual), when Jervis meets his future wife, Juliet Gibson, who lives with John Hornby and his wife as a kind of adopted daughter. And there is much else to interest the student of ''Thorndykiana,'' for this is the debut of the immortal trio— Thorndyke, Jervis and Polton.

But in spite of these diversions, the mystery element is too concentrated. We may not know how the incriminating thumb-print got into the safe, and forgery may not occur to us; nevertheless, Thorndyke need but clear up this one matter in order to free Reuben and to substitute an alternative suspect (well in view from the beginning) in his miserable place. (p. 77)

Although *The Red Thumb Mark* did not set the Thames on fire, the book sold enough copies to warrant a paper-back edition the following year, 1908. (p. 90)

Freeman seems to have had little difficulty in selling *Pearson's* his first set of eight Thorndyke short stories, beginning with ''The Blue Sequin'' which appeared in the Christmas issue of 1908. (p. 91)

[The] stories were excellent examples of orthodox detection, often with surprise endings of a wholly satisfying character. That is to say, the reader is surprised in spite of Freeman's scrupulous fairness in providing clues. He is adept at directing the readers' attention away from the vital point while yet displaying it, like a stage conjurer. (p. 92)

Critics, including Miss Dorothy Sayers [see Additional Bibliography] and Raymond Chandler [see excerpt dated 1950], have suggested that Freeman is quite safe in presenting all the visible clues to his readers early in each story because they are not conspicuous to anyone not versed in scientific matters. This point is of doubtful validity. Even in Freeman's ''inverted'' presentation of stories something has to be left for telling later. In some of his early tales, moreover [such as ''The Blue Sequin'' and ''The Aluminum Dagger''], no special knowledge is needed and a sharp reader should have no difficulty in solving the mystery. (pp. 92-3)

Between the first group of stories and the second, seventeen months elapsed. (p. 98)

During this period [Freeman] had an inspiration, a happy thought which was to bring him fame in histories of detection. He had already made his mark—although the fact was evident to only a limited number of readers—by introducing the first real scientific investigator into the pages of detective fiction. Now he was to devise an entirely new form of story, in which he would give away the secret of the crime from the start and rely entirely on the ingenuity of his detective, and the sheer excitement of the deductive process in action, to draw the reader along to the end of the story.

It was a bold stroke for a writer with so little success behind him and such a tiny amount of money in the bank. ''Would there be any story left to tell when the reader had all the facts?'' wondered Freeman. ''I believed that there would; and, as an experiment to test the justice of my belief, I wrote 'The Case of Oscar Brodski.' Here, the usual conditions are reversed; the reader knows everything, the detective knows nothing, and the interest focuses on the unexpected significance of trivial circumstances.''

In the first part of this story (and of all his other stories in the same vein) the third-person narrative style is employed. We are able to view the murder scene as detached observers and also have the advantage of entering into the thoughts of one of the principals, usually the murderer. The second part of each story is related by Jervis, and describes how Thorndyke is brought into each case and, with remarkable dispatch, soon knows more about the crime than we do.

The first and best of the stories recounts the murder of Oscar Brodski, dealer in precious stones, in the home of a small-time burglar, Silas Hickler, near a country railway station. Hickler's motive is possession of the packet of diamonds he knows his victim to be carrying, and his method of disposing of the body is to lay it across the railway track shortly before a freight train is expected, thus simulating suicide or accidental death. His mistake is forgetting Brodski's felt hat, which he leaves behind at his home when he carries the body away; however, he remembers it when he returns to the house and is able to burn it in the fireplace.

There are many explanations for the fascination the story holds for connoisseurs of the detective story. If detection is what the customers like, here is detection in its purest form, with more inferences per page than in any other story up to that time or since. The dramatic impact is enhanced by Freeman's skillful construction. The first and second halves of the tale overlap and we see Thorndyke first through the murderer's eyes, as a stranger in the excited throng on the railway platform, and later as Jervis describes him, his antecedents nicely in place. Some of the dialogue of this scene is heard twice. It is all remarkably effective. Then there is striking unity of time and place. Thorndyke is on the spot when the body is brought into the station and he has the murder solved, thanks to his invaluable green research case, without ever leaving the scene.

Finally, there is that useful Thorndyke foil, the hostile local official, in this case a police inspector, eager to interfere with Thorndyke's activities at every turn, by means of sarcasm when all else fails. And against Thorndyke's imperturbable bonhomie, sarcasm invariably fails too. (pp. 98-9)

[All of Freeman's inverted stories published in *The Singing Bone*] are fine examples of detection, and most have convincing dramatic and human qualities. (p. 101)

Critical interest in *The Singing Bone* at the time of publication was moderate. It has taken many years for critics to appreciate Freeman's masterstroke and he has continued to appeal to a rather small but discriminating minority. (p. 103)

[In] recent years, with a new emphasis on the scientific method as opposed to the romantic or intuitive—in detection as in most other matters—Freeman can be said to be well suited to those modern readers who stumble upon his books. (p. 104)

Between publication of the inverted stories in *Pearson's* and *The Singing Bone, The Eye of Osiris* appeared. It is an excellent early Thorndyke novel and the first to employ a narrator other than Jervis, although he is awkwardly present, for he has no active role to play. The new story-teller, Paul Berkeley, is yet another young physician, and he is introduced to supply the story with a suitor for the heroine when the detection has been brought to a satisfactory conclusion by Thorndyke, Freeman having thoughtlessly removed Jervis from the matrimonial stakes by betrothing him to Juliet Gibson in *The Red Thumb Mark*. (p. 105)

[*The Mystery of 31 New Inn*] was born of Freeman's ophthalmic experiences at the Westminster Hospital. It was probably first written like *The Shadow of the Wolf* in novella form and lengthened for publication. (p. 107)

More than one critic of detective fiction has been annoyed by Freeman's preface to *The Mystery of 31 New Inn*, in which he observed:

Commenting upon [*The Red Thumb Mark*] in respect of which I had claimed to have been careful to adhere to common probabilities and to have made use only of really practicable methods of investigation, a critic remarked that this was of no consequence whatever so long as the story was amusing.

Few people, I imagine, will agree with him. To most readers, and certainly to the kind of reader for whom an author is willing to take trouble, complete realism in respect of incidents and methods is an essential factor in maintaining the interest of a detective story. Hence it may be worth while to mention that Thorndyke's method of producing a track chart, described in Chapters II and III, has been actually used in practice.

Freeman then explained that it was a modification of one devised by him in Ashanti, and that "the resulting route-map was surprisingly accurate." (pp. 107-08)

Readers can discover for themselves the reasons for Jervis's need of a track chart through the streets of London. The story is not one of Freeman's best, lacking the romance of *The Eye of Osiris* and depending too much on the reader's failure to discern a fairly obvious connection between two sets of ostensibly separate events. (p. 108)

[Freeman built] up a small reputation among thoughtful people by his carefully constructed detective stories, but the financial returns were modest. His novel *The Queen's Treasure*, written with Pitcairn, was an adventure story set in England, and for some reason it had not been sold. Still, he was satisfied that his only published adventure story up to this time, *The Golden Pool*, was sound. It had given him great satisfaction to write it and to do the small amount of historical research it demanded, and now it occurred to him to attempt something of a similar nature again. . . . Freeman loved the sea, and enjoyed visiting boat-building sheds around Gravesend to watch the men at work and engage them in conversation. (pp. 108-09)

When *The Unwilling Adventurer* was published . . . , many readers must have been disappointed to find it was not another detective mystery. Instead it is the story of young Robert Hawke of Shorne, a real village near Gravesend, in 1791. (p. 109)

As the reader closes the book, he is likely to reflect that this, the author's only historical romance, is well wrought. His technical mastery of sailing ships and natural history are sound and no less than we expect of him. His hero is never in mortal danger and suspense is as absent here as in most Thorndyke novels. On the other hand, *The Unwilling Adventurer* lacks also the frivolity which gravely mars *Danby Croker, Flighty Phyllis* and *Shuttlebury Cobb,* and comes close to duplicating the steady, informed pace of *The Golden Pool.*

I have found no corroboration of a statement, in a local obituary notice, that Freeman regarded *The Unwilling Adventurer* as his best book. It could be true. Conan Doyle rather despised Sherlock Holmes; Tschaikowsky hated his "Casse Noissette;" Sullivan resented the popularity of the Savoy operas, which he felt put his oratorios in the shade. "It is true," as Andrew Lang pointed out years ago, "that of all people authors appear to be their own worst critics."

On the other hand, what was undoubtedly Freeman's worst book had been appearing in serial form in *Pearson's* during the summer of 1913 as Freeman completed writing his sea story. Originally called *A Hunter of Criminals,* it was to have two other titles in its book editions—[*The Uttermost Farthing* and *A Savant's Vendetta.*] (p. 112)

The story is made up of a series of episodes. Professor Humphrey Challoner's wife has been killed by an unknown burglar. He thereafter devotes his life to enticing members of that nefarious profession to his home and therewith disposing of them. His wife's slayer, he knows, possesses ringed hair (an unusual condition, except in Freeman stories) and he examines the hair of each victim under the microscope before adding the skeleton and the shrunken head respectively to his two collections. Each chapter recounts a new killing, with remorseless monotony. The Professor, who dies a natural death as the story opens, leaves his private museum and diary to his physician, Wharton, who only then discovers the macabre story of his patient's last years. Wharton and, to some extent, Freeman seem to sympathize with Challoner's ends, if not with his means, and it is this which makes the book so chilling. A little-known pendant to this series of adventures appeared a few years later. In "**The Mystery of Hoo Marsh,**" Challoner was brought back to life in an episode involving fifteen anarchists. The Professor, disguised as a barber in the East End, blows them all up in a ramshackle shed to which he has lured them. The tale is, incredibly, even more tasteless than those in the main series in which, after all, the bereaved Professor had something approaching a reasonable motive for his overkill philosophy. The Challoner series, in short, is vastly inferior to Freeman's other work.

Before Freeman's routine was disrupted by the First World War he wrote one more Thorndyke novel, *A Silent Witness,* and it is one of his best. The opening became a favorite one with Freeman, who was to use variants of it in *The D'Arblay Mystery* (1926) and *The Stoneware Monkey* (1938). In *A Silent Witness,* published in the autumn of 1914, young Dr. Jardine stumbles on the dead body of a priest in a Hampstead lane one rainy midnight. While the police are being summoned the body vanishes and from there on the plot, as they say, thickens. . . . The nature of [Jardine's] concurrent emotional involvements with the two women deserves a separate study, and alone would raise *A Silent Witness* to a level decisively above most detective stories. Add to this the most convincing laboratory-workshop scene ever described and a superb summing-up by Thorndyke, and a remarkable book results. (pp. 113-14)

From Thorndyke's first appearance in *The Red Thumb Mark* (1907) until *A Silent Witness,* published in 1914, the stories in which the great detective appear show steady improvement. (This is more evident if they are placed in order of *composition.*)

Freeman's non-Thorndyke tales exhibit no parallel progression during the same period. *The Golden Pool* (1905) is a good, hearty adventure story, as is *The Unwilling Adventurer* (1913). Neither story is superior to the other, although this writer prefers the earlier book, which is based on a sounder sentiment. *The Uttermost Farthing* is a lamentable falling off, being not only technically poor but lacking Freeman's customary detachment and irony. (p. 115)

[While serving in the Royal Army Medical Corps during World War I, Freeman] busied himself, at Halton, with *The Exploits of Danby Croker,* a series of inconsequential adventures fittingly subtitled "Extracts from a somewhat disreputable autobiography." . . . (p. 120)

Freeman considered [fingerprint] forgery to be a real danger and therefore deplored the use of unsubstantiated fingerprint evidence to send men to prison or the gallows, even though the Court of Criminal Appeal in a 1909 decision had left the door open to such a possibility. However, *The Exploits of Danby Croker,* unlike *The Red Thumb Mark,* is not a serious treatment of the subject. It is, in fact, disturbingly flippant. The issue cannot be avoided: Freeman throughout most of his career assessed his literary worth at a low level. Most of us now accept Howard Haycraft's valuation of Freeman . . . as the "living dean" of scientific—and perhaps of all—detective story writers [see excerpt dated 1941]. We are pained therefore when we come across his slighter efforts. He is the creator of the immortal Thorndyke and, even in those of Freeman's books where the Great Fathomer is absent, his readers expect to find vestiges of the familiar magic. Alas, Thorndyke's presence, it seems, was as necessary to Freeman's proficiency as it is to his readers' delectation. He had attempted two serious adventure stories in *The Golden Pool* and *The Unwilling Adventurer* with considerable success, but in later years it almost seems that without "the Doctor" in the plot, Freeman didn't really try. (pp. 120-21)

[*The Exploits of Danby Croker*] has an outlook almost as immoral as *The Uttermost Farthing.* It has the advantage over the latter work of not involving murder, and its facetious tone allows one to take some of the more outrageous passages with a pinch of salt. The most striking character in the book, in spite of her small role, is undoubtedly Judith Lyon, the Jewish girl who helps Croker to run the antique shop, and who would, one feels, have made a better mate for him than the insipid creature whom he does marry. Despite its weaknesses, most Thorndyke enthusiasts will want to read *The Exploits of Danby Croker*—once! (pp. 122-23)

Freeman had always possessed a sharp social eye, as readers of his Ashanti book are aware. . . . His war service brought him into contact with physical and mental types of all kinds, as had his prison service earlier, and during his leisure hours he must have wondered whether he could not write a serious work on some subject related to these experiences.

Social Decay and Regeneration, which engaged Freeman's full energies for nearly two years, came out in March, 1921. (p. 125)

Freeman's thesis was twofold: first, that machines were ruinous to human physique, culture and environment and their use should be avoided, whenever possible. Second, that eugenic reform was essential if human life were to be preserved and enabled to evolve upwards. With regard to this latter objective, Freeman recognized that segregation of unfit members of the community was impracticable in a democratic society, and rejected compulsory sterilization and restrictions on marriage as being undesirable in the one case and ineffectual in the other.

His solution was the voluntary segregation of the fit. His aim was not the setting up of a small group of supermen, for such beings are rare. His "League," to use his own term, would simply exclude the obviously unfit, both physical and mental. Defectives born within the League would, after adolescence was reached and the subnormal condition verified, have the choice of undergoing sterilization or leaving the community. The adult members of the League would live utopian lives of farmers and skilled craftsmen. (p. 126)

Had he succeeded in his endeavor to strike out a new path, and had the resulting book been taken seriously by the scientific world, Thorndyke, most likely, would have been no more.

Luckily for us, if unluckily for Freeman, his book engendered respect rather than enthusiasm, and so Thorndyke survived to delight his readers for many more years. (p. 128)

During 1922 and at intervals during later years, Freeman wrote groups of stories for *Pearson's Magazine* which together made up the three collections entitled [*Dr. Thorndyke's Case Book, The Puzzle Lock,* and *The Magic Casket*]. . . . As Alfred C. Ward once observed [see excerpt dated 1924], while the short Sherlock Holmes stories are superior to the longer ones, the opposite is probably true of the Thorndyke tales. Nevertheless, all of Freeman's short detective stories hold one kind of fascination or another, and the omnibus volumes . . . offer unrivalled entertainment. (p. 141)

Towards the end of the series of forty Thorndyke short stories, Freeman was showing signs of weariness and repetition. None of the three collections published in the twenties can compete in quality with *The Singing Bone* stories written between 1909 and 1911. But on the whole the tales maintained a surprisingly high standard and often achieved an outstanding level of detection and dramatic invention, especially considering the speed with which each was written.

All the same, Freeman's working habits were better suited to the turning out of one novel a year, a rate which he almost maintained during the last two decades of his life, producing in that period eighteen novels—not all of them Thorndyke books—beginning with *The Cat's Eye* in 1923 and ending with his last work, *The Jacob Street Mystery,* in 1942. Add to this the various collections and the total reaches twenty-four, a surprising figure for a man who was past sixty when the period began. (pp. 145-46)

The Cat's Eye . . . is crammed with more ideas and incidents than any other Thorndyke novel, perhaps because it first appeared in serial form. . . . The labyrinthine plot also brings in dubious fingerprints (again), scriptural messages in a locket, blue hair in the same location, a porcupine anteater's third cervical vertebra, and a nearly fatal search for secret chambers by Thorndyke and Anstey. The way in which Freeman is able to juggle these disparate elements and keep them all ''in the air,'' as it were, until the end of the story, wins our admiration. (p. 148)

[Another] Thorndyke novel, *The Mystery of Angelina Frood,* [is] a commentary of sorts on incidents in Charles Dickens's unfinished novel, *The Mystery of Edwin Drood.* (p. 150)

The great Victorian novelist was a more emotional writer than Freeman; a man of infinitely deeper feelings, possessing, like Freeman, considerable legal knowledge but, unlike him, lacking any profound respect for legal niceties. (p. 151)

As to the quicklime, which Dickens apparently believed would destroy a human body completely, it was Freeman's main thesis that this was a fallacy well-known as such to modern medical jurists. . . .

Freeman's story is not an explanation of Dickens's story but is a fresh narrative using some of the earlier writer's materials as a starting point. The quicklime fallacy of the earlier work is transformed into the chief clue of the later one. Edwin Drood, the doomed young man, becomes Angelina Frood who, it may be said, is much the more attractive personality of the two. (p. 152)

[Freeman] had felt his age during the hot weather of 1926 and was without ideas for a new Thorndyke novel. *Pearson's* had asked him for a set of short stories, and he responded as best as he could. But although some of the stories, like ''The Naturalist at Law'' and ''The Magic Casket'' were among his most superior efforts, others, like ''Mr. Ponting's Alibi'' with its obvious phonograph clue, were hardly worthy of their author. . . . By midwinter, Freeman was at low ebb. For light relief he turned to *The Surprising Experiences of Mr. Shuttlebury Cobb,* one of his shortest works, though bearing the longest title of them all. It is a light romance in the form of a series of connected episodes, containing a dollop of mystery and a modicum of treasure-hunting in the Canterbury district. In a letter to Starrett . . . , Freeman described the book as a ''resuscitated pot-boiler'' which suggests that the story dates from some years earlier and may originally have appeared in some magazine.

He shortly afterwards did get down to work on another Thorndyke story, which may have begun life in Freeman's mind in the form of a straight adventure story. It ended as a hybrid; over half of *A Certain Dr. Thorndyke* is set in the Gold Coast area and deals with the adventures of John Osmond, a fugitive from English justice. The book is unique in opening in a foreign land and reverting to Thorndyke and the Temple only for the investigation of the mystery. (pp. 164-65)

On the whole, this is not one of the better Thorndyke mysteries. Unless the reader is a devotee of light-hearted adventure he will probably feel cheated at being given so little of Thorndyke. Moreover there is no capital crime to be cleared up, only a jewel robbery, and the hero's initial reason for flight can only be regarded as pretty unconvincing. The Thorndyke devotee, on the other hand, will be glad to read another episode in his champion's career, even though confined to half a book. (p. 165)

Freeman made up for his preoccupation with trivial fiction in his next work, *As a Thief in the Night,* one of the finest in the Thorndyke saga. The great man is seen from a distance by the narrator, a young lawyer called Rupert Mayfield. (pp. 167-68)

As a narrator, Mayfield views Thorndyke in the same detached, almost unfriendly fashion as that adopted by his fellow attorney, Anstey, in *The Cat's Eye.* Thus, after a search through the vacated Monkhouse residence, Mayfield reflects: ''In spite of my great confidence in Thorndyke, I was sensible of a chill of disappointment in respect alike of his words and his deeds. In this rather farcical grubbing about in the dismantled house there was a faint suggestion of charlatanism; of the vulgar, melodramatic sleuth, nosing out a trail. . . .'' So that, having commissioned Thorndyke to investigate, Mayfield becomes something like an adversary. But worse is to come, and the climax is reached in a nightmarish chase across London in the middle of the night after which an appalled Mayfield spies on Thorndyke's shocking activities in Highgate cemetery. A current of horror passes between narrator and reader. It is one of the few occasions when Freeman successfully appealed to his reader's emotions rather than their reason. If only he had chosen to do it more often! (pp. 168-69)

Many of the writers of the twenties surpassed Freeman in important aspects of technique and presentation. Thus, 1920 saw the first appearance of Mr. Fortune, H. C. Bailey's rather affected but highly effective physician-investigator, and the same year brought forth Agatha Christie's Hercule Poirot in *The Mysterious Affair at Styles* as well as Freeman Wills Crofts' first effort, *The Cask.* Lord Peter Wimsey made his entrance in 1923 in Dorothy Sayers' *Whose Body?* and Anthony Berkeley's *The Layton Court Mystery* (1925) marked the beginning for another notable writer in the genre. All these authors made important contributions to the modern detective story; some, notably Miss Sayers, were better writers than Freeman, and many of them told a more thrilling story than he did. Yet, on rereading even the best books of these masters, one cannot fairly say that their styles are more interesting than Freeman's. Crofts is frequently dull; Christie manipulates cardboard characters to enable the least expected—and often the least credible—solution to emerge. Bailey and Sayers created detectives whose manufactured affectations are difficult to tolerate nowadays, except in small doses. Thus, Lord Peter refers to indigestion as "the indijaggers" and much of his conversation is in the same embarrassing strain, while Reggie Fortune groans peevishly through his cases. By contrast, Thorndyke and his friends converse in a straightforward manner; in fact most of the time their conversational level is an echo of Freeman's own. Some critics have suggested that they sound too much like a textbook. (p. 172)

But after all, Thorndyke and his friends talk precisely as *scholarly* men talked during the early years of the century, and not so differently from the way they talk still. For this reason the style of the Thorndyke books and stories fails to jar where Sayers, Bailey and others—and, for that matter, Freeman himself in his lighter fiction—jar badly, for they use slang and transient forms of sub-standard English which have long since passed out of fashion.

So Freeman, ignoring other detective-story writers of the period, went on plowing his lonely furrow, assured of a steady but not massive audience in Britain and a small select one in the United States.

The Thorndyke book which engaged his labors throughout 1929 [*Mr. Pottermack's Oversight*] was one of his best. It is also something of a rarity in being a full length inverted story. (pp. 172-73)

Although the *quantity* of Thorndyke offered in *Pottermack* is somewhat less than the average, the *quality* leaves nothing to be desired. When he does appear he is at his most perceptive and most benign. He is never officially engaged in the case at all, his role being that of a detached observer. For all that, he leaves a thoroughly satisfying impression in the reader's mind. (pp. 173-74)

[The next Thorndyke novel, *Pontifex, Son and Thorndyke*] is a strange mixture. Although the book is a favorite of many Thorndyke devotees it is difficult to understand why. (p. 176)

Usually the lack of denouement, in the sense of exposure of the criminal, does not trouble the Freeman reader. He receives his satisfaction from learning *how* the crime was committed; *what* the essential clue was; *why* things happened as they did. In [*Pontifex*], though, there is a grave deficiency in almost every field. The intended climax—revelation of Jasper Gray's true identity—has been guessed early by even the dullest reader, and nothing is left with which to ring down the curtain with an appropriate flourish. Altogether it is disappointing. (p. 177)

Though some eminent critics have claimed that Freeman's books resemble one another too closely, it is not truer of Freeman's than of the works of other authors. The flavor of *Pottermack* is quite different from that of *Frood*, while *The Shadow of the Wolf* and *Helen Vardon's Confession* are completely distinct again. On the other hand, the stories and novels fall into groups, within which the resemblances are close, as Freeman would return to a type of plot he had used before. Moreover the rigid

format to which Freeman, by 1932, had perforce resigned himself made the conception of markedly novel plots difficult. At seventy his writing powers were not yet on the wane, but the launching of each new venture was a greater labor than it once had been. (pp. 179-80)

[Devised] under unusual circumstances, [*The Penrose Mystery*] was to become important beyond the ranks of mystery lovers. It concerns the disappearance of Daniel Penrose, an eccentric collector of archaeological and other specimens, as well as of apparent trash. . . . [The] hub of the whole affair is an ancient barrow or burial mound, called Julliberrie's Grave, near Chilham in Kent. Thorndyke harbors suspicions about what it might contain but, being an ancient monument, it was protected by law and therefore immune from unofficial investigation. In this impasse, Thorndyke calls in his archaeological friend Mr. Elmhurst and backs him in an officially sanctioned and exhaustive excavation of the barrow, and in due course a grisly discovery is made.

An interesting question immediately springs to the reader's mind. As Julliberrie's Grave is real enough and was possibly excavated at some time or another, just where does Freeman's fiction end and real life begin? A search of the archaeological literature soon brings to light two important papers on the matter. Both were written by Ronald F. Jessup, and describe two series of diggings in the summers of 1936 and 1937. Jessup's first paper begins: "The re-excavation of this well known barrow was undertaken at the suggestion and cost of Sir Edmund Davis (upon whose estate it is situated) after the recent publication of Dr. R. Austin Freeman's novel, *The Penrose Mystery*, in which it largely figures." (pp. 185-86)

The Jacob Street Mystery . . . , Freeman's final work, takes its name from the fictitious street off the Hampstead Road in which many of Freeman's characters (including the future Mrs. Anstey in *The Cat's Eye* and Peter Gannet in *The Stoneware Monkey*) had studio-residences. . . .

In many ways the story, more noticeably than any previous work, is a patchwork of earlier books: water-color painting, disguise, and the preservation of a tell-tale tress in a locket. We meet Inspector Blandy and Mr. Penfield once again, and Thorndyke is as satisfying as ever. If Freeman's originality was beginning to fade, the charm of the writing was undiminished. Polton's dexterity, whether in restoring a pewter tankard or repairing a pedometer, makes as lively reading as ever. (p. 198)

Though Dr. Joseph Bell of Edinburgh was the model on whom Sir Arthur Conan Doyle based Sherlock Holmes, the real Holmes was Conan Doyle himself. Similarly, though Freeman's intention was to create, in John Evelyn Thorndyke, an investigator without personal eccentricities of any kind, he succeeded in putting on paper an idealized Freeman, a Freeman with an augmented bonhomie and a diminished diffidence, but recognizable Freeman all the same. And if Thorndyke's manner and methods attract us, it is because Freeman's manner and methods are inherently attractive. (p. 202)

Of the host of details which make the Thorndyke canon distinctive, perhaps the first to come to mind is the Doctor's famous traveling research case covered with green Willesden canvas. In the very earliest stories the little case, "only a foot square by four inches deep," had not yet been devised. In **"The Old Lag,"** Thorndyke sets forth with "his queer outfit—something like that of a field geologist"; it it is more fully described in **"A Message from the Deep Sea"** as consisting of a small metal box containing "such requisites as cover-slips, capillary tubes, moulding wax, and other 'diagnostic materials'," as well as seed envelopes; in other words, nothing much more than a collecting box. The green research case, a much more sophisticated affair, was first glimpsed by the reader as it rested on the hat-rack of a train in **"The Case of Oscar Brodski."** By this time the detective never traveled from home without it; it was indispensable. Everything in it was minuscule—"little reagent bottles, tiny test-tubes, diminutive spirit-lamp, dwarf microscope and assorted instruments on the same Lilliputian scale." Asked whether the microscope is efficient, Thorndyke replies, convincingly enough: "Perfectly efficient at low and moderate magnifications. It looks like a toy, but it isn't one; the lenses are the best that can be had. Of course, a full-sized instrument would be infinitely more convenient—but I shouldn't have it with me, and should have to make shift with a pocket-lens. And so with the rest of the undersized appliances; they are the alternative to no appliances." Not only did the contents of the green case, which could be varied by Thorndyke according to the probable requirements of the situation, permit him to examine clues under the microscope, but also to employ other of his favorite techniques, among them the preservation of foot- and hand-prints in soft earth. "I now make a rule of securing a plaster cast of any object that I cannot retain in my possession," he once declared; and he used this method for bone fragments and the anteater's vertebra as well as foot-prints. An excellent example of Thorndyke's versatility is afforded by two incidents described by Freeman within a few months of one another in 1922. In *The Cat's Eye,* Thorndyke employs his normal method of copying footprints with plaster; all the details are there—dusting of dry plaster over the prints to avoid disturbing the earth; use of a ball-spray diffuser for gentle addition of water; prior addition of alum to the plaster of Paris for quicker setting; and so on. Freeman suspended the writing of the novel to produce a series of stories for magazine publication, and in one of them, **"The Touchstone,"** Thorndyke makes a cast of a toeprint half-way down a cliff. This time, though, he uses shredded wax and a blow-lamp. The only reason for the change in method would appear to be Freeman's dislike of repeating himself, and certainly, each method has its advantages.

Over and over again, Thorndyke's thoroughness, his sheer professionalism, overawe us. "All right," we may sometimes be tempted to say to ourselves, "Thorndyke's case is watertight: so why does he have to continue his explanation long after we are satisfied?" This . . . is H. Douglas Thomson's view [see excerpt dated 1931]: "The trouble with Dr. Freeman is just this: he takes too much pains. . . .' "

My own view is that Thorndyke's insistence on the need for an overwhelming case for presentation to a *jury* is in line with real-life practice and can hardly be criticized. Moreover, Thorndyke's summation of the case is usually the most satisfying part of the story. Thorndyke's opinions as they are exhibited to us are largely Freeman's opinions, slightly modified here and there. Thorndyke, like Freeman, was a nineteenth-century man adapting with difficulty to the twentieth. (pp. 212-14)

An implication met with in the few criticisms of Thorndyke to be found in historical reviews of detective fiction and the like is that his knowledge was just too encyclopedic to be genuine. It is certainly true that his apparent openness with the non-specialist reader often leaves the mystery as obscure as before, and this, of course, is intentional on Freeman's part,

for a premature uncovering of the mystery would destroy the story, and the reader would be the first to complain. . . .

[It] is one thing to possess Freeman's wide knowledge and another to harness it to the requirements of detective fiction. It is here that Freeman demonstrated remarkable ingenuity, constructing short stories, six at a time, dependent for their denouements on, respectively, such arcane matters as the specific gravity of lead and gold; the existence of four British species of duck-weed; parallax; the narrowly circumscribed habitat of a land mollusc; and the respective dyeing characteristics of methylene blue on cellulose and oxycellulose. Re-reading the stories, one is impressed by the incidental detail, characterization and additional detective interest. (p. 215)

Knowledge is one thing; wisdom is quite another. If Thorndyke had nothing to offer but quick-fire scientific diagnosis he would lack the preeminence as an investigator he has justly attained. The almost mystical quality of Thorndyke, the aura of omnipotence he exudes, is an exceedingly difficult thing to communicate to the reader unfamiliar with Freeman's books. It is a quality more evident in the novels than in the short stories, and largely accounts for Alfred C. Ward's remark, in his admirable comparison of Thorndyke with Sherlock Holmes, previously set out at length, that whereas "story for the sake of story is more generously given by Conan Doyle than by Austin Freeman [in the] short tales, . . . in the novels the position is probably reversed."

Largely, the reason is that Conan Doyle's inventive powers failed him when lengthy descriptions of the domestic life of Holmes and Watson was called for. Thus, if we eliminate *The Sign of Four* which is generally regarded as being inferior, two of the remaining long Holmes stories, *A Study in Scarlet* and *The Valley of Fear,* have recourse to lengthy American episodes. Nothing more alien to the tastes of true Sherlockians can possibly be imagined. They love nothing better than the cosy scenes between Holmes and Watson upstairs in their living room at No. 221B Baker Street, with a real London "particular" swirling outside and the muffled sounds of hansom cabs dimly heard through tightly shut windows.

Freeman's creative powers were under no such strain; he could have filled many volumes with the talk of Thorndyke, Jervis, Polton, Inspector Miller and the rest. And the reason, of course, is simple enough: having, in one master-stroke, created the great investigator, Freeman's major work was done. All Thorndyke's future actions flowed freely from the original conception; his creator needed only guide him through a series of diverse scientific investigations, the raw material for which, being almost entirely within Freeman's professional experience, was readily and convincingly at hand.

This, of course, fails to explain why Thorndyke, conceived as a matter-of-fact medical jurist without oddities of character, should exert such an impact on the reader. The answer can only be that Freeman was eminently successful in creating, in Thorndyke, a noble, highly convincing and thoroughly consistent character who was precisely fitted to his role.

What a superb executor Thorndyke would have made! He was not only capable, as a lawyer, in dealing with all one's business and legal affairs; but would have been the ideal person to detect any irregularities associated with one's demise. What a pity he is unavailable! (pp. 216-17)

Norman Donaldson, in his In Search of Dr. Thorndyke: The Story of R. Austin Freeman's Great Scientific Investigator and His Creator, *Bowling Green University Popular Press, 1971, 288 p.*

NORMAN DONALDSON (essay date 1972)

[*In the following excerpt, Donaldson discusses the scientific basis of Dr. Thorndyke's cases, commending the scientific intuition of Freeman.*]

A facet of R. Austin Freeman's work which admits of the most minute attention is the scientific foundation of Thorndyke's cases. It is enough for lesser detective-story authors to borrow chunks of undigested and poorly understood technical matter from books and to transplant them into their stories, often with bizarre results. ("Here," one fictional scientist is reported to have said to his laboratory assistant, "heat this liquid to forty degrees Beaumé!")

L. T. Meade and Dorothy Sayers went so far as to obtain professional scientific help and even, perhaps, collaboration at times, with passable results. But none of them could integrate legitimate science into its appropriate surroundings—until the final taste and smell were authentic to even the most sophisticated reader—as Freeman could. Still, he stood constantly in danger of one happenstance; the march of science could leave him behind. In the sense that his laboratory practice became dated, his apparatus less than the *dernier cri* ["latest thing"], this was unimportant. The period charm more than compensates. But in another way, science could leave him stranded. It could make new discoveries which disproved the old "facts" on which Freeman had based a story. That this seems scarcely ever—and perhaps never—to have happened, is a tribute to the soundness of Freeman's scientific intuition, which he demonstrated all his life. It is especially evident in his first and most revealing book, *Travels and Life in Ashanti and Jaman* . . . which was based on notes written when he was only twenty-six. When he turned in desperation to detective-story writing, he adopted no Craig Kennedy gadgetry. Instead, simple time-honored scientific principles were his stock-in-trade. His standards were high, to the extent that he was often hard put to find new motifs that satisfied him. The best ones had to be adapted to new circumstances and employed again. Nearly always, though, he clothed them with satisfying characterizations and set them in authentic surroundings. In one case, an archeological expedition was cleverly set afoot by his young friend Ronald Jessup solely because Freeman had described the "dig" in advance. Surely a *tour-de-force*?

In the first of the two scientific papers in the *Antiquaries Journal* which described the excavation (*after* it had really taken place), Jessup mentions Freeman's relevant novel (*The Penrose Mystery* . . .). Another scientist, the biologist Professor A. E. Boycott, cites a Freeman story in a 1929 paper in the *Journal of Conchology*. This paper came close to threatening the integrity of a Thorndyke short story and, though it did not succeed, it is the only case I know of in which later data put Freeman's scientific basis in question. Boycott's paper is titled "The Habitat of *Clausilia biplicata* Mont.," and Freeman's story, which first appeared (in *Pearson's Magazine*) as "**The Blue Diamond Mystery**" was later collected in *The Blue Scarab* (British title: *Dr. Thorndyke's Case Book*) as "**A Fisher of Men.**" The diamond thief had buried his loot near the towpath along the south bank of the Thames east of Hammersmith bridge, and had there pulled up some grass to serve as packing material for his leather bag (presumably to prevent his housebreaking tools from clinking). In this grass, Thorndyke later

discovered "a tiny, cigar-shaped object," a land-mollusc, which led him to the buried jewels. He explained it to Jervis this way:

There are four British species of these queer little univalves [*Clausilia biplicata*] (which are so named from the little spring door with which the entrance of the shell is furnished). . . . The first three species have what we may call a normal distribution, whereas the distribution of *biplicata* is abnormal. This seems to be a dying species. It is in process of becoming extinct in this island. But when a species of animal or plant becomes extinct, it does not fade away evenly over the whole of its *habitat*, but it disappears in patches, which gradually extend, leaving, as it were, islands of survival. This is what happened to *Clausilia biplicata*. It has disappeared from this country with the exception of two localities; one of these is in Wiltshire, and the other is the right bank of the Thames at Hammersmith. And this latter locality is extraordinarily restricted. Walk down a few hundred yards toward Putney, and you have walked out of its domain; walk up a few hundred yards towards the bridge, and again you have walked out of its territory. Yet within that little area it is fairly plentiful. If you know where to look—it lives on the bark and at the roots of willow trees—you can usually find one or two specimens. Thus, you see, the presence of that shell associated the handful of grass with a certain willow tree, and that willow was either in Wiltshire or by the Hammersmith towing-path. But there was nothing otherwise to connect it with Wiltshire, whereas there was something to connect it with Hammersmith.

Boycott's paper does not take issue with Freeman directly. Instead, he brings the *biplicata* story up to date (Freeman's information probably came from Swanton's Pocket Guide to the British Non-Marine Mollusca [1906]) and opens with the statement:

There seems to be a general impression that the characteristic habitat of *Clausilia biplicata* is a damp or marshy place near a river and that it has a special association with willow trees. The facts hardly bear this out.

He goes on to quote the authorities, beginning with the discoverer, Montagu (1803), and mentions findings in Wiltshire, "near London," and "on the banks of the Thames near London." He describes more recent findings at Purfleet (Essex) and Cambridge. As for the London habitat he stresses that, with the spread of urbanization up-river, *C. biplicata* in 1929 is found at Barnes, Chiswick and Mortlake rather than at Hammersmith. This is a distance of about two miles along the towpath, or half-an-hour's easy stroll for Thorndyke and Jervis, and, of course, the shift in domain refers to a period several years after the fictitious diamond robbery took place. Even if Boycott's account was precisely true at the date of the robbery, it seems likely that Thorndyke, aided by other clues (boot-prints and walking-stick impressions) would have got his man. The information regarding proximity to willow trees (as far as Thames-bank *C. biplicata* are concerned) is conflicting in the literature, but Thorndyke did not depend on it; his specimen came from the grassy bank. We can be fairly certain that Freeman, as he nearly always did, visited the site to verify his information. Professor Boycott's own accuracy is seriously in question; he certainly gives a poor summary of the Thorndyke story in his footnote:

> Made use of in a detective story by Dr. R. A. Freeman (*Pearson's Magazine* 1922, vol. liii, p. 379) when the villain is convicted of having been along the river bank at Hammersmith by the discovery of a *biplicata* in some grass he had picked up.

Of course, the thief is convicted, not of having visited a river bank, but of robbery with violence, and Thorndyke was certainly not foolish enough to engage the jury in consideration of so abstruse a clue as a tiny land-mollusc, however essential he himself had found it. Instead, he convincingly demonstrated the criminal's association with the buried spoils by means of impressions in the moist earth, aided by plaster casts he made on the scene.

To analyze all of the Thorndyke tales in this detail would, I daresay, be possible, but hardly worthwhile. It is important, on the other hand, to rebut the occasional suggestions . . . that Freeman was anything other than a most conscientious craftsman. Whether his clues were magic caskets, tropical diseases, duckweed, or obscure minerals, he knew whereof he wrote, and if he did not know, he took the trouble to find out. Like Johnson's traveller, he regulated imagination by reality, thinking not of how things might be, but seeing them as they were. (pp. 88-91)

> *Norman Donaldson, "A Freeman Postscript," in*
> The Mystery & Detection Annual, *1972, pp. 86-92.*

OLIVER MAYO   (essay date 1980)

[In the following excerpt, Mayo offers a general appraisal of Freeman's works.]

Despite holding [a] detached, sensible view of his detective stories . . . Freeman to some extent resented the fact that they were widely regarded as a second-rate form of literature.

In 1908, with **"The Case of Oscar Brodski"**, he had introduced, with considerable success, his "inverted" story whereby the reader was first given an account of the commission of the crime, with all relevant clues incorporated into the narrative, after which the solution of the crime was described. This innovation was interesting in Freeman's hands because of Dr. Thorndyke's virtuosity and the technicalities of the solution; as many critics have noted, Freeman was not good at creating suspense, nor at fashioning convincing interactions between "good" and "bad" characters, nor indeed was he good at creating villains. Thus, his denouements tended to be brief and sterotyped, mere preliminaries to Thorndyke's exposition of his solution. Partial exceptions to this, such as *Mr. Pottermack's Oversight* or *Mr. Polton Explains,* had sympathetic, not really evil men as Thorndyke's quarry, so that Freeman could describe them from within more satisfactorily. It was not in his power to imagine satisfactorily the dissembling, deceitful and hypocritical criminals who formed the villains of most detective stories at the time; where he used such figures, as in *The Unwilling Adventurer* (a mystery story rather than a detective story as such) or *The Red Thumb Mark,* he kept them offstage for most of the book.

It is not clear to what extent Freeman recognised that his limitations were in fact genuine deficiencies. In his article, **"The Art of the Detective Story"** [see excerpt dated 1924], he wrote that the:

> "distinctive quality of a detective story, in which it differs from all other types of fiction, is that the satisfaction that it offers to the reader is primarily an intellectual satisfaction."

While he agreed "that good detective fiction must be good fiction in general terms," he clearly regarded the exposition and solution of a puzzle as the key elements of the detective story: the:

> "construction thus tends to fall into four stages:
>
> 1. statement of the problem;
> 2. production of the data for its solution ('clues');
> 3. the discovery, i.e., completion of the inquiry by the investigator and declaration by him of the solution;
> 4. proof of the solution by an exposition of the evidence."

As he had done in developing his eugenic argument, Freeman was here reasoning from his own experience and practice far more than from the other detective fiction he had read. In the article, the only writers to whom he referred were himself, Poe (scathingly), and Dickens, who was one writer from whose work he never tired of quoting; and it was in the same year, 1924, that Freeman's solution of *The Mystery of Edwin Drood* was published, ***The Mystery of Angelina Frood.***

Connoisseurs of the detective story have frequently commented that the virtue—"conclusiveness"—which Freeman considered to be central to detective stories was one which he himself possessed in surplus and most thriller-writers in deficit. While it might have been the most difficult for him to achieve, as he claimed, this is not the appearance of the finished product. Rather, it appears as the part of the story on which Freeman lavished most care, giving the "love-interest" and so on perfunctory attention.

Angelina Frood is a good example of this. As Dorothy L. Sayers noted, Freeman's story turns on the ability of a woman to disguise herself as a man, one of the many "theories" advanced as to Dickens's intentions for the full story of *Edwin Drood* having had such a masquerade at its centre. This is carried through with great care; there is, for example, constant emphasis on the shortness and high voice of the man, Peter Bundy, and on the tallness and deep voice of Angelina Frood herself. However, Bundy's friendship with the narrator is most unconvincing. The latter is a young medical man who first treats Angelina after her husband "Mr. Johnson" (a parallel, no doubt, to John Jasper, Edwin Drood's uncle, whom Freeman considered the murderer) has attempted to strangle her in a frenzy induced by opiates. His attachment to the young actress in distress, and his subsequent liking for Bundy after Angelina's disappearance, are among the more awkward of the relationships created by Freeman. Perhaps Thorndyke's comments on the lack of manliness in Bundy's behaviour, which is whimsical and sportive to an embarrassing extent, showed that Freeman recognised a lack in the relationship of Bundy and John Strangeways, the narrator; but this is not certain. Possibly the false light shed by popular psychology on the close friendship of any two men makes it difficult for the modern reader to take the Bundy-Strangeways companionship seriously, especially when he reads of the rather feminine characteristics with which Freeman conscientiously endowed Bundy.

But while he failed to make this central relationship convincing, Freeman nevertheless told a good story, and introduced the essential features of *Edwin Drood* on which he wished to comment: first, Dickens might have intended the hero/heroine to escape from an impending murder by pretending to be dead and disguising himself/herself as a member of the opposite sex; secondly, how uncertain a method of disposal would be the dropping of a body into a tidal river; and thirdly, how burial of a body in quicklime would in fact preserve it by mummification. Angelina, not knowing as much as Thorndyke about the ways of rivers or quicklime, leaves relics of herself in impossible places, and buries a skeleton in lime in the town wall of Rochester. Thorndyke forces her to disclose her identity at the inquest on the skeleton, and all ends happily, or at least clearly, with a long dissertation by Thorndyke on the mechanics of detecting transvestites.

Thus, one is not left with the feeling of dissatisfaction which Freeman felt at closing the unfinished *Edwin Drood*. Equally, however, one has not been gripped from start to finish. As a whole, the book lacks vitality. (pp. 122-24)

> *Oliver Mayo, "The Art of the Detective Story," in his R. Austin Freeman: The Anthropologist at Large, Investigator Press, 1980, pp. 122-36.*

ADDITIONAL BIBLIOGRAPHY

Cuppy, Will. "*Dr. Thorndyke's Cases.*" *New York Herald Tribune Books* VII, No. 30 (5 April 1931): 15.

Positive review of a collection of Freeman's short stories entitled *Dr. Thorndyke's Cases.* Cuppy states: " After all these many moons [Dr. Thorndyke's] astounding powers of inference remain unimpaired; indeed, they improve with time. He is certainly the dean of omniscientist sleuths. In these eight adventures he is at his best."

"Notes of the Quarter." *The Eugenics Review* XXXV, Nos. 3 and 4 (October 1943 - January 1944): 51-6.

Eulogy of Freeman following his death. The critic notes Freeman's contribution to the Eugenics Society, both as a member and as a writer for the *Eugenics Review*, stating that "his reviews, models of their kind, were invariably informative, critical, and fair. They never left the reader in any doubt about the subject matter of the book or whether it had been worthily dealt with; and they could always be trusted to do justice to the author's opinions—and even more than justice if they were opinions which to Austin Freeman were antipathetic."

Heenan, Michael G. "A Note on the Chronology of the 'Dr. Thorndyke' Novels." *The Armchair Detective* IX, No. 1 (November 1975): 52-4.

Chronologizes the novels of Freeman according to the sequence of their narrative events, which differs from their order of publication. Heenan cites internal evidence from the novels which helps to determine when the action takes place.

Nelson, James. Introduction to *The Red Thumb Mark*, by R. Austin Freeman, p. vii-x. New York: W. W. Norton & Co., 1967.

Comments on the plot of *The Red Thumb Mark*, the medical and literary careers of Freeman, and the character of Dr. Thorndyke. The critic states: "R. Austin Freeman's appeal for readers, beyond his sound work in the laboratory, lies in his human, universal approach, his shrewd philosophy, and his dry humor."

"Man Devoured by His Machines." *New York Times Book Review* (2 October 1921): 14.

Discusses some of the social issues addressed by Freeman in his book *Social Decay and Regeneration*. The critic describes Freeman's manner of expression as "forceful, impressive and always interesting," but notes that his "ardor sometimes leads him to make statements rather too sweeping." The book is considered "of particular consequence because of the author's clearsightedness in linking up the eugenic problem . . . with collectivism and with the domination of man by mechanism."

"*The Singing Bone.*" *New York Times Book Review* (9 September 1923): 21-2.

Positive review of this collection. The critic considers this work to be better written than most volumes of short stories, asserting that "Mr. Freeman has proved his point: that it may be far more interesting to follow the methods of a detective when one's knowledge is greater than his than to proceed in ignorance."

"*The Blue Scarab.*" *New York Times Book Review* (20 January 1924). 17.

Positive review of the short story collection *The Blue Scarab*, describing the stories as "clever, interesting and well told."

"Dr. Thorndyke's Solution." *New York Times Book Review* (1 March 1925): 9.

Review of *The Mystery of Angelina Frood*. The critic states: "Mr. Freeman has contrived a particularly dark and puzzling plot and has solved its complications and its mystery in a very unexpected and unconventional way. The solution may not be wholly convincing as to its probabilities, but it is interesting and not without an element of humor."

Queen, Ellery. "The First Golden Era." In his *Queen's Quorum*, pp. 46-59. New York: Biblo and Tannen, 1969.*

Describes *The Adventures of Romney Pringle* as "the rarest volume of detective-crime short stories published in the twentieth century," listing the whereabouts of the then six known copies of the first edition of this book. Queen states that the copy autographed by Freeman is "one of the most prized volumes in the Ellery Queen collection."

"*The Mystery of 31 New Inn.*" *The Saturday Review* (London) CXV, No. 2995 (22 March 1913): 367.

Review of *The Mystery of 31 New Inn*, stating that "it is nothing more or less than a yarn, and a detective yarn. It is not highly ingenious nor startlingly original. . . . [The] plain facts of the case are made clear by the highly intuitive and ratiocinative mind of Thorndyke. All is set forth most engagingly, though at unnecessary length."

Sayers, Dorothy. Introduction to *Great Short Stories of Detection, Mystery and Horror*, edited by Dorothy Sayers, pp. 9-47. London: Victor Gollancz, 1928.*

Discusses the effect that the scientific nature of Freeman's fiction has on the reader's ability to solve the mystery. Sayers observes that "Thorndyke can cheerfully show you all his finds. You will be none the wiser, unless you happen to have an intimate acquaintance with the fauna of local ponds; the effect of belladonna on rabbits; the physical and chemical properties of blood; optics; tropical diseases; metallurgy; hieroglyphics, and a few other trifles." She also comments on the love interest in Freeman's stories, noting that "his secondary characters fall in love with distressing regularity . . . but they do not interfere with the course of the story."

Starrett, Vincent. Introduction to *The Singing Bone*, by R. Austin Freeman, pp. 4-8. New York: W. W. Norton & Co., 1965.

Commends Freeman for the entertainment value of his stories, the creation of Dr. Thorndyke, and the invention of the inverted detective story. Regarding *The Singing Bone* Starrett comments: "To waive the advantages of suspense and surprise is a severe test for any detective author, yet these are among Freeman's finest stories."

Sadeq Hedayat

1903-1951

(Also transliterated as Sādeq, Sadiq, Sadegh; also Hedāyat, Hidayat) Iranian novelist, short story writer, dramatist, essayist, critic, folklorist, and translator.

Regarded as the "father of modern Persian fiction," Hedayat employed Western literary forms of the novel and short story to provide the first great models of narrative prose in a literature previously dominated by verse. His work thus belongs to an international trend of the late nineteenth and early twentieth centuries which saw non-Western literatures strongly influenced by European authors and literary movements. However, like many of his counterparts in other countries, such as Sōseki Natsume in Japan and Munshi Premchand in India, Hedayat commands interest beyond his function as Iran's liaison with Europe. He was a highly individual writer whose works display both a scholar's erudition and a poet's imagination, as well as a philosophical insight which reveals an irremediable desolation at the heart of human existence. Indeed, although Hedayat sustained a sincere reverence for Iranian culture and often devoted himself to subjects of social relevance, his artistic vision is generally viewed by critics as antithetical to the values of his or any other society. Frequently associated with a literary tradition that includes Fedor Dostoevski, Edgar Allan Poe, and Franz Kafka, Hedayat's writings have been celebrated as expressions of literary genius and analyzed as documents of a troubled life that ended in suicide.

Relatively little is known about Hedayat's life, due to his simple and solitary manner of living. He was born in Tehran into a wealthy aristocratic family that had been active in Persian government and cultural life since the eighteenth century. After attending a French school in Tehran, Hedayat was sent to France in 1926 to study dentistry, which he subsequently replaced with a curriculum in engineering. Eventually he abandoned all plans for a conventional career to devote himself to the study of pre-Islamic Persian culture and to literature; his earliest works, tracts on vegetarianism and the mistreatment of animals, have been accorded little value among the author's writings. Returning to Tehran in 1930, Hedayat became associated with a group of artists and intellectuals, many of whom felt alienated under the monarchical dictatorship of Rezi Shah. At this time Hedayat also extended his scholarly studies to include Eastern religious philosophies, which are considered an important foundation of his creative works, and the twelfth-century Persian poet Omar Khayyam, whose poems of worldly hedonism and philosophical nihilism he examined in several critical works. "The philosophy of Khayyam," Hedayat wrote, "will never lose its freshness. . . . His cries are the reflections of tortures, worries, fears, hopes, and despairs that have successively racked the thoughts of millions of beings." Critics find a similarly universal importance in Hedayat's own works.

During the 1930s Hedayat published what are considered his best short stories, including the collections *Zendeh be-gur* and *Seh qatreh khun*, which contain the respective title stories "Buried Alive" and "Three Drops of Blood." He also issued his privately printed edition of the novel *Buf-e kur (The Blind Owl.)* Because of the repressive political climate in Iran, Hedayat traveled to India to have a few mimeographed copies of his

novel produced, clearly labelling them: NOT FOR SALE IN IRAN. With the abdication of Rezi Shah in 1941, Hedayat was able to publish *The Blind Owl* in his own country, four years after its private edition. Upon its appearance in serialized form in the daily *Iran, The Blind Owl* became the focus of social controversy among Iranian readers and critics even as it demanded attention as a revolutionary work in the history of Persian literature. The principal basis for its controversial reputation was the novel's pathologic narrator and his frantic discontent with life in general and Iranian life in particular. For a brief period after Rezi Shah's abdication Iranian writers were allowed greater freedom of expression, and it was at this time that Hedayat published *Haji Aqa (Haji Agha),* a satire of political, moral, and religious corruption in twentieth-century Iran. Considered Hedayat's most important novel after *The Blind Owl, Haji Agha* sold out several editions before it was outlawed by the government in 1945. This ban remained in force until 1979, when Rezi Shah's son was deposed and the Islamic Republic formed under the Ayatollah Khomeini. Between 1945 and his suicide in Paris six years later, Hedayat published only a few works, perhaps the most important of which was his commentary on the works of Franz Kafka, "Piyam-e Kafka." In a gesture regarded as typical of his personality, Hedayat left behind a macabre farewell note with his family before departing for Paris in 1951, apparently with the specific intention of ending his life there. The note read: "I left and broke your heart. See you on Doomsday. That's all."

Commentators on Hedayat's life and work often emphasize his extreme sensitivity to human suffering, a faculty which in his writings sometimes leads to a display of compassion for the downtrodden and other times is manifested in a world-rejecting pessimism that casts him among the ranting outsiders of modern literature. It is the latter quality that receives the most intense and artistic exposure in Hedayat's masterpiece *The Blind Owl,* the title of which has also been translated as "The Recluse." Told from the viewpoint of a hysterical drug addict whose private nightmares and outward life are indistinguishable, *The Blind Owl* is a confessional story that impresses readers with the force of its narrator's obsessions, which are frequently treated by critics as the author's expression of his own deepest feelings. This identification of the author and his work is considered especially valid in those passages of the novel which concern the narrator's hatred of those he calls "rabble-men," who to him epitomize the dominance of physical appetites among the greater part of humanity. They are thus described as animalistic figures consisting "only of a mouth and a wad of guts hanging from it, the whole terminating in a set of genitals." Elsewhere the narrator writes: "I felt that this world had not been made for me but for a tribe of brazen, money-grubbing, blustering louts, sellers of conscience." While he insists upon his exclusion from the common life of the world around him, he also empathizes with its misery and considers misery its essence. "For thousands of years," he writes "people have been saying the same words, performing the same sexual act, vexing themselves with the same childish worries. Is not life from beginning to end a ludicrous story, an improbable stupid yarn?" Outbursts such as this, along with the narrator's morbid reflections on death, are attributed by some critics to Hedayat's own emotional turmoil and by others to his reactions to the unstable and fear-ridden society in which he lived. Aside from these biographical or social interpretations, *The Blind Owl* is studied as a work in which a fugue-like recurrence of bizarre images and characters, a learned grounding in Eastern philosophy and religion, a complex symbolic relationship between the narrator and his nightmarish world, and a simple prose style binding the labyrinthine elements of the novel all combine to create a literary tour-de-force deserving of its reputation as Iran's most important contribution to modern world literature.

While *The Blind Owl* is a confessional monologue of a suffering self, most of Hedayat's fiction is less subjective and is often concerned with the misery and evil the author observed in the world around him. As H. Kamshad has stated: "No other writer in modern Persia has illustrated and analyzed with such mastery the life of the hungry peasant, the unfortunate beggar, hypocritical preacher, and greedy bazaar trader." It is to Hedayat's short stories that Kamshad's remark primarily applies. Representative among these works is "David the Hunchback," whose wretched title character, having been ridiculed and rejected by human society, looks to a stray dog for companionship at the very moment that the animal dies. Similar chronicles of tragic or atrocious lives are found in the stories "Buried Alive" and "The Doll behind the Curtain." In other stories, such as "The Man Who Killed His Passionate Self" and "Asking Absolution," Hedayat implicitly condemns the hypocritical behavior of characters who hide their crimes between layers of outward righteousness and inward self-deception. Hedayat's most extensive and successful work of this kind is *Haji Agha.* Subtitled "Portrait of an Iranian Confidence Man" in its English translation, this work is an anatomy of the various forms of corruption that Hedayat saw flourishing in his country, all of which are embodied in the eponymous character. Like the rabble-men of *The Blind Owl,* Haji Agha is a swindler, sensualist, and uncultured low-life who thrives in a society dominated by unprincipled materialism. Toward the end of the novel the poet Monadi ol-Hagh, in a confrontation with Haji Agha, castigates the wealthy powerbroker: "You and your like are just stupid creatures who eat and belch and sleep and beget children." The poet also foresees an approaching era in which the superior moral and cultural values of Iran's past will be reinstated, a reference to the brief period of political optimism following the abdication of Rezi Shah. *Haji Agha* considerably enhanced Hedayat's reputation during the 1940s; after the publication of this novel, it became standard practice among Iranian critics to measure new writers by the literary achievements of Hedayat, particularly *The Blind Owl.*

Writing in 1978, Michael Hillmann stated that in Iran *The Blind Owl* is considered "the most important Iranian literary document of the century." Translations of Hedayat's novel have also given it an international reputation unusual for a work of Persian literature. It was especially praised by André Breton and other Surrealist authors and has been compared for its visionary quality to the best examples of Surrealism. Having its sources in the author's own dreams and aberrations, as well as in a wide array of Eastern and Western philosophies, religions, and literatures, *The Blind Owl* is an exceptional instance of a work attaining significance far beyond the psychological or social context in which it was produced.

PRINCIPAL WORKS

Zendeh be-gur (short stories) 1930
Seh qatreh khun (short stories) 1932
'Alaviyeh Khanom (novel) 1933
Sayeh rowshan (short stories) 1933
Vagh Vagh Sahab [with M. Farzad] (short stories) 1933
Tarana-ha-yi Khayyam (criticism) 1934
Buf-e kur (novel) 1937
  [*The Blind Owl,* 1957]
Sag-e velgard (short stories) 1942
Haji Aqa (novel) 1945
  [*Haji Agha: Portrait of an Iranian Confidence Man,* 1979]
*"Piyam-e Kafka" (criticism) 1948
Parvin dukhtar-e Sasan (drama and short stories) 1954
Sadeq's Omnibus (short stories) 1972
An Introduction to Sadeq Hedayat (short stories) 1976
Sadeq Hedayat: An Anthology (short stories) 1979

*This work was published as the introduction to a Persian translation of Franz Kafka's *In der Strafkolonie (In the Penal Colony).*

HENRY D. G. LAW (essay date 1950)

[*In the following excerpt, Law evaluates Hedayat's literary importance in the context of modern Persian literature.*]

The sudden and tragic death of Sadiq Hedayat a few months ago has removed from the scene of contemporary Persian literature one of its most striking personalities and, so far as fiction is concerned, the most prolific, the most eminent and at the same time perhaps the most controversial writer in Persia. There will be many judgments passed on his work by his fellow countrymen; and these judgments will be based on an estimate of his place in Persian literature viewed from two standpoints: that of the conservatives who value tradition highly, who venerate the past and find it hard to adapt themselves to the notion of a "popular" literature: a literature written about and for the ordinary people; and a style of writing, in the manner and idiom of the common folk, which will be condemned by these critics as the debasement of a precious coinage. There will be others, however, who see in the work of Hedayat something new, exciting and alive; who regard his style as the enrichment of the Persian language and a source of fresh life and vigour.

It might seem prudent to leave it to the Persians themselves to fight out the issue and pass the final judgment. Nevertheless it is tempting to a foreigner who has read and enjoyed much of Hedayat's work to attempt an estimate of his contribution to the literature of his country. (pp. 109-10)

When Hedayat began writing his short stories the "aristocratic" tradition still had a firm hold on Persian literature. It dates from the old days when those who practised the art of writing did so mainly for the pleasure and edification of wealthy patrons. And it is in keeping with this tradition that the essays in fiction of Hejazi which are immensely popular in Persia today and, in the eyes of the most austere critics, entirely free from any taint of "vulgarity," are written for the most part about and for the gentility, the cultured classes. The only jar which this tradition had suffered till Hedayat appeared on the scenes had come from the distinguished and still very much alive Jamalzadeh, who startled (and at the same time delighted) many of his countrymen by a bold initiative. In the preface to his book *Yaki Bud Yaki Nabud* (*Once upon a Time*), a collection of short stories, Jamalzadeh advanced some entirely new theories about Persian culture and writing. Deploring the narrowness of culture in Persia, which was restricted to the elect few, the failure of education to reach the masses, and in consequence the complete inability of the people to understand and share the pleasures of reading (for what was written was obscure and unintelligible to them) he suggested that in order that culture might spread widely in all directions, thought should be clothed in the language which the mass of people would understand, in their own native idiom in fact, and presented in the guise of fiction which would interest and amuse and enlighten. Such writing would have the further merit of providing a record of the language of the people of Persia today, and of its gradually changing structure. This was a revolutionary idea; and Jamalzadeh the pioneer remained an isolated phenomenon till Hedayat started where Jamalzadeh had left off. Hedayat was well equipped for the role of disciple. He had an original and inventive mind; he had read and studied the work of French writers of fiction, he had a great gift of expression: but more important than all these he had genuine interest in and sympathy for the common people in Persia whose lot he deplored, and for the "under-dog" in general. Like George Eliot, herself a pioneer in the craft of fiction, Hedayat held the view that fiction should be based on real experience and enable readers to arrive at a deeper realization of the feelings and plight of common humanity. So he wrote about the lives of the ordinary people of his country, which he understood profoundly, and in their own language. His characters are the whole of humanity: the humble official, the beggar, the down and out, the villager, the rogues and scally-wags of Shiraz. He describes the rustics' marriage ceremonies, he quotes the people's songs, describes the wayside hostelries where the old men drink their tea, gossip, and smoke their pipes.

Many of Hedayat's tales have an obviously Western influence; some of them have their scene abroad. But it is the purely Persian tales which have the greatest interest for the foreign reader; for it is in these that Hedayat gives the fullest expression to his humanity, his sympathy for the masses with all the unhappiness and poverty they have to bear, his understanding of their minds and characters. In his story about Daud the hunchback Hedayat reveals that strain of pity for the outcast which is found so often in his stories—in the tale of the **"Stray Dog"** for example. The whole point lies in the last sentence. When Daud had sunk so low that he sought companionship with the utterly outcast, the dog (and he could sink no lower than that), the dog's death denied him even that consolation. The story of the woman who lost her husband is perhaps the most remarkable of all Hedayat's tales. It is the story of a young and pretty village girl who has a most unhappy life at home, with a mother who dislikes and bullies her and a married sister who despises her. She falls suddenly in love with a big, burly brute of a man whom she meets when the villagers are all working together in the vineyard gathering in the grapes. They marry; and after a few months of happiness with her husband Gul Baba, Zarin Kulah finds herself tied to a sadist who bullies her and beats her unmercifully with the whip he also uses for his donkey. He deserts her, and yet Zarin Kulah cannot get him, even the whip, out of her mind. Taking her child with her, so poor she can hardly keep herself and the child alive except by begging, she goes in search of Gul Baba; finds him at last; is roughly and harshly rejected by him. In despair, Zarin Kulah abandons her child; and then, aimless but free, tries to patch up her life by joining the first man she comes across who reminds her of Gul Baba—a man riding along the road, with a donkey and a whip: just like Gul Baba's donkey and Gul Baba's whip. And he will certainly treat her in exactly the same way; and every time he beats her it will be almost as if her beloved Gul Baba were beating her. It all sounds sordid enough told like this; yet it is, in fact, a profoundly enthralling psychological study; and the way in which Hedayat gets "under the skin" of the characters in this small and strange drama of village life is a secret which only the great writers share. It is due, one supposes, to his intense sincerity and understanding. And this habit of making his characters alive informs all his stories to a quite remarkable extent. It reflects Hedayat's power and his versatility; while the unchanging atmosphere of unhappiness, misery and frustration reflect a certain one-sidedness. To all protests at the monotonous gloom of his writing, Hedayat's answer was that such was life as he saw it and as he felt it. There is no trace of fun, scarcely a touch of humour in his writing. And that gives to his work a limitation which cannot be denied.

Hedayat began by being a follower in Jamalzadeh's path. He ended by being a master and a leader in his own right. He has founded a school in the difficult art of short story writing in Persia which is now strong and alive, and showing commendable variety in scope and treatment. The work of Sadiq Chubak, Ibrahim Gulistan and Jalal Al Ahmed must command the respect of any critic of Persian contemporary writing. Yet there is no longer a Hedayat: no longer that wide canvas, that penetrating understanding, that felicity of expression, and those passages of vivid description, of beauty and economy of style. One remembers especially the scene in **"Cul de Sac"** when Sharif watched his friend Muhsin, who was bathing in the Caspian Sea, drown in front of his eyes while he himself could do nothing to stop it, but remained on the shore helpless, or too timid to help. The whole incident, which haunted Sharif for the rest of his days and, in fact, shaped the whole of his life, has about it the quality of a nightmare, with a nightmare's sense of inevitability. "So it had to be" says Sharif, hoping thus to excuse himself; and "So it always is" say Hedayat. People are marked down by Destiny, and play the parts Destiny has assigned to them, without blame for they are without the power to shape or alter events: as Sharif was powerless to save his friend from death, or himself from endless shame and regret.

The heavy shadows which lie over almost everything Hedayat wrote are all too painfully reflected in the manner of his passing. He had always been curiously, even morbidly, interested in the subject of death. The hero of the story **"Zindeh bi Gur"** was born with an inclination to suicide, though he failed to achieve it. Hedayat himself was continually repeating that death is the only desirable thing in life. One of the characters in a story of Hedayat's describes life as a prison, or alternately, as a fraud. We deceive ourselves all the while; and the time comes when we tire of self-deceit and then must seek the only way out. Death is the fascinating mirage on the road which is called life. "Does the delight of this vision of death consist merely in the fact that it brings oblivion?" asks Hedayat.

Well: now, perhaps, he has the answer to the question he so often posed, the solution, by the way he had to choose, to the riddle which had always puzzled him. Thus ends, tragically but perhaps as inevitably as it happened to so many of the characters of Hedayat's own invention, a remarkable chapter in the history of Persian literature. To that literature in a small sphere may be, but in a very important one, he gave a real renascence of spirit and craftsmanship, and a striking originality. It now falls to others to carry on the work he began, and to follow his inspiring lead. The torch has been handed on; but something vital has gone; the light will no longer burn with Hedayat's vivid, if sombre, flame. (pp. 110-13)

Henry D. G. Law, "Sadiq Hedayat," in Journal of the Iran Society, *Vol. 1, No. 3, 1950, pp. 109-13.*

RAHMAT MOSTAFAVI (essay date 1951)

[*Mostafavi was an Iranian journalist and short story writer. In the following excerpt, he offers a description and appraisal of Hedayat's most important works.*]

"The most prominent Iranian writer" is the title given by a large part of the Iranian intelligentsia to Sadeq Hedayat; indeed, he could even be called the conscience of modern Iran. (p. 277)

His earliest books, **Shade and Light** and **Three Drops of Blood,** are collections of short stories covering a wide range of subjects. From the point of view of time they cover the story of mankind, starting with man when he was partly ape and ending with the imaginary collective suicide of the whole human race. Many of the stories deal with modern Iranian subjects; they show an amazing insight and keen sense of perception and they reveal the deep interest Hedayat took in the life of his countrymen. In his later works he concentrates on the latter subject, and in his novelettes **Hajj Agha** and **Alavia Khanom** he ridiculed, in sarcastic, biting and penetrating language, the ravages that superstition, hypocrisy and moral lawlessness have produced in Iranian society. **Hajj Agha** is the story of a religious man who has even made the pilgrimage to Mecca, thus acquiring the title Hajj. But all his religious devotions do not prevent him from committing all sorts of crimes, petty and large-scale, in order to acquire more wealth. In **Alavia Khanom** Hedayat depicts the pilgrimage of a supposedly devout woman

to a holy shrine; he probes her superstitious fears and hopes. Both books are masterpieces of characterization, psychological analysis and social criticism. Hedayat's profound knowledge of deep-rooted native superstitions and the mores and customs they originated was amazing. As a matter of fact, he compiled an informative and amusing book about them, **The Book of Tricks.**

His works also include some ghostly, haunted, bewildering stories and novels, similar to the works of Kafka, whom Hedayat admired. Most important is the novel **Blind Owl,** a story of frightful suffering, wild nightmares, reincarnations and murders. Some critics believe these works were the indirect fruit of the desperate, tragic mood in which Hedayat lived. (p. 278)

Rahmat Mostafavi, "Fiction in Contemporary Persian Literature," in Middle Eastern Affairs, *Vol. II, Nos. 8 & 9, August & September, 1951, pp. 273-79.**

JALAL AL-E AHMAD (essay date 1951)

[*Al-e Ahmad was an Iranian fiction writer and critic whose works focused on social problems in his country. In the following excerpt from an essay that is recognized as the first major statement in Persian on* The Blind Owl (*originally published in the journal* 'Elm va Zandegi *in 1951), Al-e Ahmad explores aspects of style and theme in Hedayat's novel.*]

There are only a few stories by Hedayat in which the first person is the speaker and agent. Hedayat seems to have experimented with this mode only five times. But in **The Blind Owl** he had no choice but this. The "blind owl" is Hedayat himself, or his own "self." Thus, in order to know Hedayat we should know **The Blind Owl** or "The Hedayat of **The Blind Owl**," Here the aim is an attempt to create this acquaintance, not literary criticism in the real sense.

The Blind Owl is not a short story (*nouvelle*). It is not a novel (*roman*) either. It is a dialogue. It is a conversation with the inner self. It is introspection. It is a deep search in recollections. It is an anecdote which contains the most intimate sensualities of an artist. It is a surrealistic and strange anecdote (*recit*) full of sorrow and nostalgia. But are these two or three sentences enough to know **The Blind Owl**? During the past few years it has become common for people to treat any work of art like a trunk full of luggage, to mark it with a couple of words ending in "ism" or "ic" and thus be done with it. Although **The Blind Owl** has been treated with this same destructive ignorance, it is not a trunk. The most succinct attempt at comprehending **The Blind Owl** or making it comprehensible ought to be at least as long as **The Blind Owl** itself because what is not in **The Blind Owl** is verbosity and artificiality.

What do we read in **The Blind Owl**? What does it mean? **The Blind Owl** is a miscellany and composite of ancient Aryan scepticism, of Buddha's nirvana, of Iranian gnosticism, of the Yogi-like seclusion of the oriental person, the scope of which an Iranian, an oriental with all his/her mental background, tries to achieve within his or her self. **The Blind Owl** is a refuge from the writer's disappointments, rejections, sighs, sorrows, and hopes. It is an attempt to comprehend the eternity of beauty. It is the vengeance of the mortal, short-lived man against this life, against this environment. It is the revenge of the mortal being against mortality and triviality. **The Blind Owl** is the cry of vengeance, the cry of revenge which arises only from within and causes a tumult only beneath the arch of the mind and descends like a whip on the back of the memories. **The Blind**

Owl is the image of all the hatred that the ''weak'' feel for the ''strong.'' It has all the spite that can arise from deprivation.

But how should we approach *The Blind Owl*? What is its form? What is its rhetoric?

The rhetoric of *The Blind Owl* is simple. The simplest phraseology has been used to explain the perplexities of the mind. *The Blind Owl* is an example for the proof of the fact that Persian, simple Persian, is capable of describing the most novel sensual states of a writer and can be employed for introspection. Even in surrealistic passages this simple language is preserved:

> All at once I found myself wandering free and unconstrained through an unknown town, along streets lined with weird houses of geometrical shapes—prisms, cones, cubes—with low, dark windows and doors and walls overgrown with vines of morning glory. All the inhabitants of the town had died by some strange death. Each and every one of them was standing motionless with two drops of blood from his mouth congealed upon his coat. When I touched one of them, his head toppled and fell to the ground. . . .

This strange nightmare, which reminds the reader of the strange paintings of Salvador Dali, is a result of a profound search into sensuality heretofore unprecedented in our literary tradition.

Sa'eb (seventeenth century A.D.), who has scattered verses in his poetry about this closeness to inner self, writes in such a complicated way that each line is rife with metaphors and allusions. But Hedayat does not even need to employ the simple device of simile to describe these difficult concepts. *The Blind Owl* is not a place for games with figures of speech. Hedayat, who sees resemblance as a sign of triviality overpowering life, shows not only a similarity between himself, the old odds-and-ends man, the butcher, the hearsedriver, and his uncle, but also a kind of unity and uniformity. He presents each one of these resemblances, each one of these trivialities with an original and new description. If similarities and trivialities exist in the world, they do not exist in art. This is the distinctiveness of Hedayat's work. All of the people who come and go in his various works, though a few of them may seem to be specific types or from a specific group, everyone of them has his or her own genuineness—this is one face of the revenge he takes from triviality. The realism of the opening scene of *The Blind Owl* seems more like the description of a dream, a dream which even if it has not happened should have happened, a dream which is more genuine for the writer than existing reality, that is, the writer needs it more. But in the representation of this dream the realism is so great that even for the reader it goes beyond a dream: ''My God, I hope that Hedayat didn't chop the girl's body into pieces with the knife of the old odds-and-ends man?'' Kafka uses this kind of realism in representing his imaginary worlds in *The Metamorphosis* and even more in *The Castle*. The reader of *The Blind Owl* sees himself or herself behind the hole above the shelf; and then he or she feels the ebbing warmth of the body of the girl who is dying; and when the golden bees start flying around the dead body of the ethereal girl, the reader comprehends the sense of disgust in the presence of a corpse.

In the second scene of *The Blind Owl* realism appears in the form of fantasy. The reader is returned to the world of childhood. The second scene of the book is a return, a return to disappointments, the disappointments that created the dream of the first scene. The detailed focus of this scene is so inquisitive that it even escapes from realism. A piece of plaster has fallen from the wall of the room, and the writer smells thousands of scents from this one piece of wall, smells that even a ''stray dog'' is not able to sense. Before Hedayat, only Rilke was able to display this exactness. Here, in any case, the reader is dealing with ''surrealism.''

The most appealing features of *The Blind Owl* are the repetitions of scenes, themes, and events. Here the past and the present are mingled. The characters also are mixed. Everybody becomes someone else. Each piece of life is diffused throughout it. The ethereal girl by the Suren River, who is submissive, shows the source of her growth in the person of the ''bitch,'' who has all sorts of lovers and who refuses to submit only to ''him.'' The flashback of the scene by the Suren River can be found everywhere: on the cover of the pen case, on the Rayy jar, on the printed curtain, in sleep and in consciousness, everywhere, exactly like a picture transfer. The drunken policemen constantly pass by beyond the house walls and keep the demon of fear awake inside the secluded painter. The people are not single, complete units. They don't have one face. Every character in *The Blind Owl* has two or three sides. The old hearsedriver is the second character of the painter of pen-case covers. The painter is the creator of beauties, and the old hearsedriver is their gravedigger. The ''bitch'' is the other side of the ethereal girl. It is her vulgar side, which is at everyone's disposal. In this way each of the characters in *The Blind Owl* is taken for each other. They are deliberately replaced by each other. It seems as if the writer is absentminded and in the course of describing his dreams repeats everything several times, forgetting that he has already mentioned them. This deliberate forgetfulness, which is the vehicle for representing the flashbacks, makes *The Blind Owl* melancholic.

The Blind Owl is not a work of realism. The world of existence has been set aside in *The Blind Owl*. The realities consist of a shabby house far from the city; and in the second scene they consist of yet another house, another ''four-walled place,'' whose windows open onto the butcher shop. Besides these, there are such realities as fear, anxieties, crumbled hopes, dreams, tales of existence, and introspections. But the characters and the events are so intermingled and repeated that they seem like wandering shadows that meet, separate, and meet again. There is no doubt about the existence of a special world ''full of poverty and misery. . . .'' . . . But in *The Blind Owl* there is doubt about existence itself:

> I do not know where I am at this moment, whether this patch of sky above my head and these few spans of ground on which I am sitting belong to Nishapur or to Balkh or to Benares. I feel sure of nothing in the world.
>
> (pp. 29-32)

Or elsewhere:

> Do not the rest of mankind who look like me, who appear to have the same needs and the same passions as I, exist only in order to cheat me? Are they not a mere handful of shadows which have come into existence only that they may mock and cheat me? Is not everything that I feel, see and think something entirely imaginary, something utterly different from reality? . . .

Not only with this frankness, which hitherto existed only in Khayyam's voice . . . and in the traces of *Illuminati* parables evident in the quote above, does Hedayat set aside the world of existence with gnostic doubt, but also whatever is figurative or metaphorical for him, for "The Hedayat of *The Blind Owl*," is more "real" than realities: ". . . on the wall inside my room hangs a mirror in which I look at my face, and in my circumscribed existence that mirror is a more important thing than the world of the rabble-men." . . . In Hedayat's words, the riffraff world means the world of realities. Elsewhere he writes: "The shadow that I cast upon the wall was much denser and more distinct than my real body. My shadow had become more real than my self." . . . Or:

> As my eyes closed a dim, indistinct world began to take shape around me . . . a world [that] . . . at any events . . . was far more real and natural to me than my waking world. . . .

He not only doubts the world of existence and the authenticity of realities and does not have any feeling for "place" (*makān*) (Balkh, Nishapur or Benares), but also time (*zamān*) for him—in his art—has lost its authenticity: "An incident of yesterday may for me be less significant, less recent, than something that happened a thousand years ago." . . . This is simple. Elsewhere he is much more frank: "Past, future, hour, day, month, year— these things are all the same for me. The various phases of childhood and maturity are to me nothing but futile words." . . .

In this fashion it is clear that the Hedayat of *The Blind Owl* is not a realist writer. His art does not find its basis in the existing realities. The basis of the art of *The Blind Owl* lies in the nonexistence of nonexistent things. It is in the nothingness, not in beings. True. But what connection does a person who finds such realities doubtful and deceitful see between those and himself or herself? Is it not a fact that he or she is part of the same doubted reality? The Hedayat of *The Blind Owl* has cut off his connection with the riffraff and has chosen seclusion, with a behavior which if not reminiscent of Buddha at least reminds us of the Indian yogis. He considers art not as a link between the artist and the outside world but as a means of connection between himself and his shadow: "The only thing that makes me write is the need, the overmastering need, at this moment more urgent than ever it was in the past, to create a channel between my thoughts and my unsubstantial self, my shadow." . . . This same shadow which has more reality than he himself: "This shadow surely understands better than I do. It is only to him that I can talk properly. It is he who compels me to talk." . . . The others, the rabble, not only do not know him and understand his words, they do not even have any relation with him. They consider him among the dead, and later we will see that he hates the rabble. Besides this, art is a consolation for him:

> Yes in the past only one consolation, and that a poor one, remained to me. Within the four walls of my room I painted my pictures on the pen cases and thereby, thanks to this ludicrous occupation of mine, managed to get through the day. . . .

(pp. 32-4)

In *The Blind Owl* the world of existence is doubted. It is a useless repetition of things and people and events. Actions are repeated. The characters are exactly repeated. Allegory and reality mingle. But that which has authenticity are the dreams, the recurring nightmares, the sickly deliriums, the dreams which can be dreamed between sleep and wakefulness, the dreams which are at the boundary between life and death.

In what should the idealism of *The Blind Owl* be sought? Why are the realities doubtful? Is this the reflection of ancient Aryan doubt which has been stated by Khayyam and immortalized in the form of quatrains? Why did Hedayat admire only Khayyam among the literary figures of the past? *Songs of Khayyam* (1934) should be read. But, the origin of Hedayat's doubt is not the "annihilation in God" and "achievement of the world of permanence" which the gnostics have talked about. He has freed himself from this idea by referring to "the pattern of earthly things being transferred to the sky." . . . To understand this, one should look at a more distant past, where Buddha, through Hedayat's voice, beckons to nirvana. . . . But can't we find the reason for this escape from realities in a simpler way? Yes. The idealism of *The Blind Owl* is a sign that criticizing the society alone does not satisfy the writer. Here the question is not about criticism but about negativism. The society that rejects Hedayat and *The Blind Owl* is necessarily rejected in Hedayat's works. Hedayat not only has no place in realities, but also the world of reality which is full of triviality and poverty and misery cannot be his place. The Hedayat of *The Blind Owl* is "alien." Let him speak: "I felt that this world had not been made for me but for a tribe of brazen, money-grubbing, blustering louts, sellers of conscience. . . ." . . . And when the world and life have rejected him in this way, he perforce seeks refuge in death, death which compelled him to attempt suicide several times, death whose epic *The Blind Owl* will be seen to be. (p. 34)

The death that invites the Hedayat of *The Blind Owl* is not merely a "refuge" or "shelter" that firmly embraces a person who is alienated from life and existence. Death is also the only obvious truth about which there can be no doubt. Look at these epic sentences: "Only death does not lie. The presence of death annihilates all superstitions. We are the children of death and it is death that rescues us from the deceptions of life." . . . This is Buddha's nirvana echoed in Hedayat's voice. Death is not an inaccessible thing for the blind owl. It is not a problem that can take him by surprise: "I was pleased with the change in my appearance. I had seen the dust of death sprinkled over my eyes. I had seen that I must go." . . . The thought of death is neither frightening nor horrible:

> I had many times reflected on the fact of death and the decomposition of the component parts of my body, so that this idea did not frighten me anymore. On the contrary, I genuinely longed to pass into oblivion and nonbeing. . . .

It is even consoling: "I murmured again and again: Death, death where are you? The thought of death soothed me and I fell asleep." . . . But this longing for death is also a wish for endlessness. Death is entreated because it is the gateway to "eternity."

> . . . if it were possible for my being to dissolve in one drop of ink, in one bar of music, in one ray of colored light, and then these waves and forms were to grow and grow to such infinite size that in the end they faded and disappeared—then I should have attained my desire. . . .

And this longing for eternity is at the same time an expression of the originality of beauty in art and in nature. In another place he has expressed similar sentiments in a different way.

In the first scene: the ethereal girl is dead; and he works with a kind of persistence and scrupulousness, which is suited to a painter of pen cases, until he paints her picture, and then he writes with serenity:

> . . . the essential was her face, or rather, her eyes—and now they were in my possesion. I had fixed on paper the spirit which had inhabited those eyes and I had no further need of the body that body which was worms and rats of the grave. Henceforth, she was in my power and I had ceased to be her creature. . . .

It is clear that death is the collateral for the authenticity of this eternal art. To die and to make your being immortal in a spot of ink or in a rhythmic tune or in a colorful ray, this is the message that has reached Hedayat from Khayyam. (pp. 40-1)

> *Jalal Al-e Ahmad, ''The Hedayat of 'The Blind Owl','' translated by Ali A. Eftekhary, in* Hedayat's ''The Blind Owl'' Forty Years After, *edited by Michael C. Hillmann, Center for Middle Eastern Studies, University of Texas at Austin, 1978, pp. 27-42.*

P. W. AVERY (essay date 1955)

[*Avery is an English critic and translator who has written extensively on Iranian literature and culture. In the following excerpt, he notes philosophic and stylistic characteristics of Hedayat's works.*]

Hedayat possessed the great writer's gift, which is the power to understand a wide range of emotions. He also had the absolute sincerity that must go with this gift if it is to lead to great literature. He fled from all forms of pretence. He believed that our lives are controlled by a blind destiny unconcerned with merit and justice, and he was incapable of pretending that there was room for hope in a world that filled him with gloom. Perhaps the reason for his suicide lies in his inability to deceive himself about final issues. Religion held no solace for him and, significantly, he was attracted by the quatrains of Omar Khayyàm. What interested him were the underdogs, the unfortunate and beaten. He wrote about these with superb mastery of Persian. Every word from the most wretched of men was of supreme importance to him when uttered in the hard unforgettable idiom of his own people. Every scene of misery and despair was ineffaceably printed on his vision, which was that of an absolute artist. Passages of great beauty resulted and, as is to be expected in the work of such a sincere writer, his style is quite free from any trace of artificiality and remains a splendid example of the abiding genius of Iran. (p. 320)

> *P. W. Avery, ''Developments in Modern Persian Prose,'' in* The Muslim World, *Vol. XLV, No. 4, October, 1955, pp. 313-23.**

WILLLIAM KAY ARCHER (essay date 1958)

[*In the following excerpt from the first American review of D. P. Costello's translation of* The Blind Owl, *Archer praises Hedayat's novel.*]

Possibly some understanding of the forces of change at work in Asia might be gained from reading **The Blind Owl**. Nor is it insolent to urge that statesmen fumbling at policy could profitably turn to the maturity and despair of Sadeq Hedayat. . . .

The Blind Owl is a nearly but not quite surrealistic story of the descent into madness of a poor painter of pen cases, and his repeated encounters in time and dream with a taunting old man, and with a dying girl with magnificent eyes, eyes such as are given to the maidens painted on pen cases. She is his love and his obsession. Surely the parable (or symbolism or myth, or whatever you choose to call it) is there: the artist of a declining and trivial craft meeting and meeting again with age, young love, madness, and death. But in the meticulous description and aureate language there is something else: the especially Persian sense of that beautiful quality which, without mysticism, poetry has but prose has not.

Sadeq Hedayat was a greatly gifted man. He wrote sensitive short stories, plays, studies of folklore and popular poetry and, most importantly, poetry. In the Persian tradition, he was acutely sensitive to the shades and graces of the marvelously expressive Persian language. He was aware of a great infinitude behind him. It was part of his gift that he had, with all the defects of its virtues, that terrible Persian awareness of time, of the past, of the direct burden of a great and antique culture. Despite its French influences, **The Blind Owl** is, above all, deeply Iranian.

As such, it makes shoddy most of our casual generalizations about ''the Middle East,'' not excluding our respect for a never-encountered oozy mystique. This is a product of that world of Firdausi and Hafiz and Omar Khyyám and other names we neither read nor recognize, which reached out and continues to reach out its seminal force as far as Turkey, as far as India, and has, in its time, reached farther still.

Yet there are dangers in store for **The Blind Owl**. It is susceptible to adoption by the coterie readers: tired of Vivaldi, fearing Beckett optimistic, wearying of Zen, they may easily find their newest *frisson* in this macabre Iranian sensibility, heightened by the author's romantic suicide in—how appropriate!—Paris. In the morbid, exhausted, depressing, anguished, frightful story itself, they may be overpowered by the oil lamp smell of Poe and Baudelaire, and in the filigree, arabesque, and inlay of the prose, a Scheherazade orientalism. (p. 24)

No reader, I think, will be bored by **The Blind Owl** nor left unhorrified at its end, though his literary judgment may be more reserved than mine. But the imperative to read it is other than literary. It is to confirm for us, once again, the affirmation contained in a gentle couplet of Hedayat's seventeenth-century compatriot, Sa'ib of Isphahan: ''All this chatter about religion and infidels at the last leads to one place, / Only the interpretations differ, the dream is the same dream.'' (pp. 24-5)

> *William Kay Archer, ''The Terrible Awareness of Time,'' in* Saturday Review, *Vol. XLI, No. 52, December 27, 1958, pp. 24-5.*

H. KAMSHAD (essay date 1966)

[*In the following excerpt, Kamshad offers a survey of Hedayat's short stories and novels.*]

Conscious of the fact that the writer, as Fielding maintained, is ''the historian of private life,'' Hedayat took a keen interest in the life of his countrymen, particularly the small man and the underdog. He penetrated into their monotonous lives, searched the dark corners of their souls, and with an amazing insight revealed their petty aspirations, anxieties, and sorrows. It is in the story of these people—farmers, workers, tradesmen, and the like—that we find not only Hedayat's masterpieces, but also some of the most beautiful passages of contemporary Persian literature. No other writer in modern Persia has illustrated and analysed with such mastery the life of the hungry peasant, the unfortunate beggar, hypocritical preacher, and greedy bazaar trader. Characters like Davud, Abji Khanum, Dash Akul, Mirza Husayn-'Ali, Mirza Yadulla, Gul Babu, Zarin Kula, 'Alaviya Khanum, Aqa Muchul, 'Ismat-Sadat, Hajji Aqa, and a host of others are so true to life that they are met again and again in any Persian town. Explaining the secret of Hedayat's power to depict his characters so skilfully, Henry D. G. Law writes:

> Firstly his sincerity. After that the magic of his prose . . . Hedayat does not write objectively; with his "reckless soaring genius" he infuses into each of his tales his own personality, his own mood of pity, indignation, or tenderness: so that you may enter fully into the mind and thoughts of his characters, whoever they may be—seeing them as he sees them. They live and they haunt you long after you have closed the book.

This is exactly the case when we read, for instance, **"Davud-i Kuzh-Pusht" ("David, the Hunchback")**, the story of a poor miserable creature who through no fault of his own is born a cripple. Everybody avoids him, people ridicule him and make fun of his love and sentiments:

> . . . from his earliest childhood up to now he had always been an object either of ridicule or of pity to others. He recalled how his teacher in a history class had said that the Spartans used to kill children who were born deformed or crippled. All the children had turned and looked at him, a strange feeling had taken hold of him then. But now he was wishing that the rule had been enforced everywhere in the world, or at least that as in most other places sick and unsound persons had been prevented from marrying, for he was well aware that all this was the fault of his father. He pictured his father . . . the old man, branded with syphilis, who had married a young wife and begot blind and palsied children, for that is what they had all been. One of his brothers had survived, but even he had been an idiot and dumb, till he died two years ago. He wondered if they had not been the lucky ones. . . . Some years ago he had twice made an offer of marriage, but both times the women had laughed at him.

So continues the story of Davud until the moving climax where he seeks the companionship of an outcast vagrant dog, but is denied even that consolation:

> He dragged himself along till he sat down beside the dog. . . . He pressed its head against his bulging chest. But the dog was dead.

At the end of the story the reader is no more an outsider, an impartial observer: he feels Davud's physical and mental sufferings as if they were his own.

This engagement in the characters' despair occurs with a great number of Hedayat's short stories, especially **"Abji Khanum" ("The Elder Sister")**, **"Dash Akul"** and **"Zani-ka Mardash ra Gum Kard" ("The Woman Who Lost Her Man")**, three masterpieces of modern Persian short-story writing. (pp. 151-52).

So far, writing about the people of his country Hedayat may have impressed us as a sympathetic writer with an amiable, even a mild, disposition. But all trace of mildness disappears when he handles themes like corruption, superstition, and especially religious hypocrisy. **"Talab-i Amurzish"** is an interesting description of the old-fashioned, long, and exhausting pilgrimages on camels and mules to holy shrines; it also shows the character of the pilgrims and their appalling conditions; but most of all, it is the sinister confession of a woman who, out of jealousy, murdered the rival wife (*havu*) and her children and has now come to Karbala to ask forgiveness and absolution from the *Imam*. 'Aziz Agha had been happily married but turned out to be barren. So with her consent the husband brought a second wife, a *Sigha* (a wife by temporary marriage), into the house. But as soon as the new wife became pregnant everything changed: "My husband paid all his attention to her. . . . I had become a ruined, unfortunate wife! . . . Then I realized what a mistake I had made." The child was finally born, and "one day when she [the second wife] went out to the public bath and the house was quiet, I went to the baby's cradle, drew out the pin I had below my neck, turned my head aside and pressed it to the end into the child's fontanel. . . . For two days and nights the child did not stop crying . . . and died on the second night." She murdered the second child and finally the mother.

When she confided her secrets to other pilgrims, they simply laughed and assured her that they had committed similar crimes. After all, "What do you think we have come here for?," asked Mashdi Ramazan-'Ali, shaking the ashes out of his clay pipe. . . . (pp. 154-55)

After hearing the cynical confessions of other fellow pilgrims, 'Aziz Agha starts rejoicing and says: "Then . . . then, you too? . . ." The other lady traveller pronounces: "Did you not hear from the pulpit that as soon as the pilgrims specify their intention and set out, they become chaste and purified even if the number of their sins is as many as the leaves of a tree?" (p. 155)

Sympathetic or wicked, mostly from the lower strata of society, these are the kinds of characters we have so far met in Hedayat's stories. They are not the only types that appear in his works. In fact . . . in his later works, Hedayat wrote about people from almost every walk of life. However, in this period of his life [1930-37] there does emerge another important type of character: the eccentric. Usually belonging to the middle class, the *petite bourgeoisie,* he is very often trying to imitate the European way of life; but, as usually happens in a changing society, he can neither hold on to his own cultural heritage nor grasp European ideas properly. It is the confusion, desperation, and pessimism of these people that form the subject matter of short stories such as **"Zinda Bi-gur" ("Buried Alive")**, **"Sa Qatra Khun" ("Three Drops of Blood")**, **"Girdab" ("The Whirlpool")**, **"Suratak-ha" ("The Masks")**, **"'Arusak-i Pust-i Parda" ("The Puppet Behind the Curtain")** and **"Shab-ha-yi Varamin" ("The Nights of Varamin")**. In all these stories the abnormalities of the characters are striking. They are the deformities produced by a deformed society, and it is therefore not surprising that Hedayat should make them all either die violently, by committing suicide perhaps, or end up in a lunatic asylum. The hero of **"Zinda Bi-gur,"** for example, is a suicidal maniac who tries a variety of methods of self-destruction, but none is effective: "Yes, I have become invulnerable. . . . Nothing effects me. Took cyanide didn't affect me. Tried opium but I'm still alive. If a dragon bites me, it's the dragon that will die." And the eccentric man in **"Sa Qaṭra Khun"** who is detained in a madhouse wants to have the authority of the asylum doctor, for: "If I were in his position [the doctor's] I would poison the food one night and feed them all with it. Then in the morning I would stand in the garden, hands on my waist, and watch the dead bodies being carried away."

Or there is the sentimental lover in **"Ṣuratak-ha,"** who, suspecting the faithlessness of his girl friend, leaves her and decides to take his revenge; and in an impressive way:

> He would make a reconciliation with Khujasta
> [the girl friend] and exchange this life, which
> his parents had one night given him in bed, for
> another. Khujasta would be there, they would
> take poison and die in each others' arms. This
> idea sounded beautiful and poetical to him.

The lugubrious nature of this writing is best seen against the background of social conditions in modern Iran, where traditional patterns of life have been violently disrupted and the superficial aspects of alien patterns acquired. Thus besides creating great literature, Hedayat has provided a commentary on the mental condition of sensitive people in a period of rapid transition. It is in this role of commentator on the tragedy of twentieth-century Iranian society, notably its urban society, that Hedayat is at his best. Where he attempted a different type of writing—in stories like **"Asir-i Faransavi"** (**"The French Prisoner of War"**), **"Madlin"** (**"Madeleine"**) and **"Ayina-yi Shikasta"** (**"The Broken Mirror"**), concerned mostly with characters and events outside Iran—he proved himself much less effective. (pp. 157-58)

We can sum up this phase of Hedayat's writing by saying that he unfolded a panorama of the habits, traditions, and dialects of various groups of Persian people. And yet, having known Hedayat as a lonely figure, as a man who constantly held himself aloof from people and public life, and bearing in mind that he grew up in the restricted circle of an aristocratic and extremely conventional family, it is puzzling how he captured such a gallery of "typical" characters from various walks of life; how he reproduced their language and described their habits and preoccupations with such precision. That he had the artist's gift of exact observation helps to solve the puzzle. Sensitive to other people's feelings, he identified with their suffering and could therefore comprehend, share, and re-create their plight and tragedy. He also possessed, as his careful annotations of his own and other people's books prove, the scholar's fastidious love of exactitude. He thus observed things as they are, not as he thought they should be. He watched his fellow-creatures, or, as he would put it, his fellow-sufferers, with the painstaking attention of a scientist looking down his microscope. Inform this power of observation with an extraordinary feeling of sympathetic anguish for the plight of men on earth, and perhaps we have the answer to how Hedayat managed to record experience so accurately and with such universal validity. (pp. 159-60)

Satire is one of the prevailing traits in Hedayat's art. Not only in his completely facetious works but in most of his other writings one can trace a melancholy derision.

Satirical criticism has been frequently used in Persian literature, usually when political circumstances have prevented the writer from approaching his readers directly. Dihkhuda, we recall, was the first modern Persian writer to make use of this weapon for social criticism; this was in the post-Constitutional period, when Muḥammad 'Ali Shah's autocracy was opposing the rights

granted by the Constitution. A similar tyranny, though far better established and in many respects much more effective, existed during the second decade of Riza Shah's reign. Here, Hedayat's gift for satire, mockery, and lampooning grew and flourished. And he employed this technique in an entirely new way.

Apart from one earlier attempt (*Afsana-yi Afarinish*) his main achievements in this field are: the novelette *'Alaviya Khanum* (**"Madame 'Alaviya"** . . .), followed by a miscellany of rather bizarre pieces called *Vagh Vagh Sahab* (**"Mister Bow Wow"** . . .) and, later in his life, *Vilinq ari* (**"Tittle-tattle"** . . .) and finally *Tup-i Murvari* (**"The Pearl Cannon"** . . .). At present, however, we are concerned with only two of these: *'Alaviya Khanum* and *Vagh Vagh Sahab*. Both books are criticisms of the old customs, deep-rooted superstitions, and social and cultural conditions of modern Iran. In them the solemn and sometimes apparently nonchalant Hedayat becomes a sarcastic critic who gives not an inch to hacks and humbugs, and who ridicules the naïve beliefs and reactionary mental habits of the masses.

'Alaviya Khanum is about a woman's pilgrimage to the shrine of *Imam* Riza at Meshed, one of the most important Iranian centres of pilgrimage. Stage by stage, from Tehran to Meshed, we follow the route of four carts (*gari*) loaded with simple men, women, and children. The hopes and fears, the intrigues, quarrels, and shocking accusations of these people form the backbone of the story; and not only the story's amusing incidents but every word, phrase, and passage carries the odour of Persia and the high sense of tragedy that is a feature of the life of the masses. It is, however, 'Alaviya Khanum—an outwardly pious but inwardly vicious woman—who dominates the story and whose speech, consisting mostly of abuse, affords one of the most unusual pieces of modern Persian writing. Hedayat makes the submerged masses come to life by reproducing their speech in all its vividness. Yet while he does this with consummate skill, his disgust for the ignorance and degradation of these characters is not concealed. (pp. 161-62)

Vagh Vagh Sahab is of an entirely different pattern. It is a rather tart criticism of conditions during Riza Shah's reign, especially in art and culture. It also served, at the same time it was written, as a riposte to the pampered scholars of that "golden era." During this period of Hedayat's life, triviality was not only the stimulus for fashionable art and letters but also a dominating factor in the whole pattern of Persian life. Poetry was the strictly guarded domain of a handful of "high-minded dignitaries" whose essential merit was to copy the great classics. Cinemas presented the public with every piece of rubbish Hollywood produced, and the theatre was the scene of cock-and-bull stories mainly about clumsy lovemaking. In the literary field, apart from a few "established" scholars, two groups of upstart novelists and translators had emerged: the first group produced with breathless haste genial stories for the popular papers. The second group, the translators, faithfully followed the direction Hedayat had ironically pointed out to them:

> After you have been to a school for a few months
> and have learnt a few of the foreigners' words
> so that you can read just the name of the author
> or the title of an article, you are in a position
> to push yourself among the distinguished translators. Then try to know who has written the
> book and what it is about. Having done that,
> write whatever nonsense comes to your pen and

publish it under the name of the well-known original writer.

(pp. 162-63)

When *Vagh Vagh Sahab* first appeared in 1933 it was denounced as a wicked piece of nonsense by the established men of letters, but of course welcomed by the younger intelligentsia as a superb exposure of the lack of taste and the false criteria of the men who were supposed to be their teachers. Yet at the time the full significance of the work was missed, because many took it to be concerned with follies that would soon be corrected; they thought Hedayat and Farzad quixotic in their profound pessimism. Time has shown that now, more than three decades after this book was written, its criticisms remain valid. (p. 164)

Hedayat turned from the evils of society to self-analysis in one book. *Buf-i Kur* ("**The Recluse**") means literally "blind owl"; and its signficance lies in Persian folk-lore:

> The owl is commonly regarded as a sinister and lonesome bird and an omen of ill-luck. Normally lives in ruined and desolate places away from cities and people. The bird is supposed to be afraid of light, hiding in dark crevices or thick trees in day time. When the sun sets, it emerges from its seclusion in search of prey. The owl has a dismal and hideous appearance, with peculiar screams turning to hisses and snarls at night. The belief in the inauspiciousness of this bird in Iranian tradition and folklore goes back to the advent of Islam and the Arab influence. Damiri, in *Ḥayatu'l Hayvan* ("The Life of Animals"), relates that according to Arab fables when a man dies, or is killed, he sees himself metamorphosed into an owl sitting on his own grave and moaning his bodily death. And in the *History of Ibn-i Najjar* we read that Chosroes ordered his functionary to hunt for the worst bird, whereupon he caught an owl. Stories and references of this kind pertaining to the obnoxiousness of the owl are also found in abundance in the classical prose and poetry of Persia.

To quote from the opening sentences of the book, Hedayat's *Blind Owl* is the story of "the wounds that eat into the soul like cancer and grind it down little by little in seclusion." (p. 165)

To understand and analyse the repellent, unpeopled life of Buf-i Kur, it is necessary to remember the writer's life and environment. And besides reading carefully one should also keep one's head clear and steer a straight course through this strange book. For the reader, despite all his awareness, is constantly driven into an hypnotic dream-state. He starts reading with a determined critical approach, but gradually an atmosphere of obscurity creeps in; the thread of events becomes blurred, and in the end an attitude of uncritical acceptance prevails. The critic of *Buf-i Kur* is like a surgeon who becomes affected by the anaesthetic every time he starts to operate. Like Kafka, Hedayat deliberately applies a "dream technique" to evoke this sense of unreality. (p. 167)

The influence of Buddha can be easily detected in the book. Buddha seems to have been Hedayat's last refuge during this period, and, as we shall see in the next chapter, Buddhism and Hinduism remained his main preoccupation all through the later

period of his life. In *Buf-i Kur* Buddhist ideas are mostly infused with Hedayat's own pessimistic views. The whole story revolves round Buddha's *inward contemplation and meditation*, i.e. the command to "look within." The ideas of past lives, oneness of existence, contempt for earthly life, rebirth, and "ceasing to be of the not-self" are plainly discernible. (p. 172)

The Buddhist philosophy of death and suffering dominates the whole book. Buddha believed that:

> Birth is suffering, decay is suffering, disease is suffering, association with unpleasant is suffering, separation from pleasing is suffering, not to get what one wants is suffering. . . . Buddhism is, therefore, to some extent a philosophy of suffering. If life is filled with suffering, and if suffering is the means by which we learn to put an end to suffering, is it not foolish to attempt to run away from school?
> [Christmas Humphreys, *Buddhism*].

In this light Buf-i Kur proves to be an ardent student.

On the crucial question of death—Hedayat's obsession throughout his life—Buf-i Kur sounds somewhat uncertain. Expressing his disbelief in religion and in the existence of an almighty god, he observes: "All my teachings on the reward and punishment of the soul and the Day of Resurrection had become an insipid deceit and the prayers they had taught me were of no value against *the fear of death*."

A few pages later he contradicts himself:

> I had so often thought of death and the decay of the particles of my body, that *this thought frightened me no more*. Quite the opposite, *I sincerely aspired to non-existence*.

Buddhism regards death as "a gateway to a different form of life," whereas the idea of rebirth and a second life is sometimes unbearable for Buf-i Kur: "My only consolation was the hope of nothingness after death. The thought of a second life exhausted and terrified me." And yet there are passages in the book where he praises and identifies himself completely with the Buddhist conception of death and Nirvana. Take for instance these impassioned sentences:

> It is death alone which does not lie! The presence of death destroys all illusions. We are all the children of death and death is our salvation from the deceptions of life, and it is death which stands at the bottom of life, calling and beckoning us.

Buddha's compassion for animals and the Buddhist prohibition against killing animals for food are also vividly reflected in *Buf-i Kur*. The butcher whose shop is across the street from Būf-i Kūr's house is portrayed as the symbol of cruelty and evil. (Hedayat himself was a vegetarian.)

The whole plot, and especially the climax of the story, seems to derive from Buddhist ideas. While Lakkata (the name he has given his wife) represents a vile creature at everyone's disposal, the ethereal girl is the image of grace and innocent virtue beyond the reach of the *rajjala-ha*: the unearthly counterpart of Lakkata. Buf-i Kur kills Lakkata at the end of the book; and despite all his love and admiration for her counterpart, she must also be killed. "Death," say the Buddhists, "is the death of the body and its invisible counterpart."

Besides Buddhism and other oriental ideas, the book carries the mark of certain Western writers, particularly Poe, Dostoevsky and Kafka. Its hero also has much in common with some Western characters who have a contemptuous attitude towards life. There is Barbusse's hero in *L'Enfer*, for example, "who shuts himself away from the world in his hotel bedroom and lives vicariously by spying through a hole in the wall." Or Shelley's Alastor, "who pines away and dies because he can find no earthly counterpart of the beautiful girl who had embraced him once in a dream." There is also Dostoevsky's Raskolnikov, who confines himself alone in a room, morose, self-conscious, panic-stricken at the thought of arrest, hating the human condition and human weakness. Even more striking is Buf-i Kur's resemblance to another of Dostoevsky's characters, the peculiar creature portrayed in *Notes from Underground*. Both men are under the strain of unsatisfied desires, both indulge in suffering, loathe human beings, shun society, and take shelter in seclusion. One is pictured as a beetleman, the other as a blind owl. (pp. 172-74)

The last decade of Hedayat's life coincided with an exceptionally eventful period in the history of Persia, and most of his works during this period are a reflection of that period.

Following the abdication of Riza Shah and the beginning of the new era, Hedayat, after years of silence and resignation, brought out a new collection of short stories, *Sag-i Vilgard* ("The Stray Dog" . . .). Most of these eight stories were apparently written during the earlier years, for they carry the familiar gloom and melancholoy so characteristic of Hedayat's earlier works. Two of the pieces, **"Sag-i Vilgard"** and **"Bun Bast"** ("The Dead End") rank among Hedayat's best short stories.

"Sag-i Vilgard" is the story of a dog who loses his master and, in contrast to the comfort and compassion he formerly enjoyed, becomes the victim of brutality. To a Westerner, and especially to an English reader brought up to love and care for animals, the story might sound somewhat unrealistic and overdramatized; but if we remember that dogs are considered unclean in the Islamic world, then the sad story of Pat, the unfortunate Scottish terrier, is given its true perspective. (p. 184)

The story is written with a close-knit texture; it leaves the reader with a feeling of distress and irritation as he broods over the nostalgic sentiments of the dog and comes to the creature's pathetic end.

Distress, irritation, nostalgia, and a pathetic end also form the substance of the second story, **"Bun Bast,"** one of the grimmest of Hedayat's grim stories. Here, as in so many other stories, he reaffirms his belief in destiny as an inexorable, foreordained fate. (p. 185)

The reader of the story may not care much for fate and predestination; he may even favour Gertrude Bell's view that "oriental fatalism, which sounds fine in theory, breaks down woefully in practice. It is mainly based upon the hopelessness of a people to whom it has never occurred to take hold of life with vigorous hands"; yet having reached the end of **"Bun Bast,"** he cannot but sympathize with [the protagonist] Sharif. This, indeed, is one of Hedayat's outstanding gifts: the ability to make the fate of his characters seem inevitable. His stories may repel us, but our repulsion is not directed against the characters, for no matter what their dispositions may be, they always have the disarming force of conviction.

None the less, Hedayat has been severely criticized, both at home and abroad, for the negativity and sullen temperament of his characters, the unhappy finale of his stories, the black pessimism, boredom, and affliction that permeate most of his works. These *are* the prevailing traits in his writings, but to charge them against him is to isolate his work from the social conditions that nurtured it. Similarly, one could forget the philosophical pessimism that existed in Europe between the two world wars: ". . . everywhere there arose thinkers who deepened this pessimism and who built up their *weltanschauung* on some philosophical generalization of despair." Hedayat, too, susceptible to the conditions in his country, built up his *weltanschauung* thus; and . . . when these conditions changed, Hedayat's world outlook also changed—though, alas, temporarily. (pp. 187-88)

[The] last story of [*Sag-i Vilgard*], **"Mihan-Parast" ("The Patriot"),** was a landmark in Hedayat's career, for it heralded a phase that was to embrace all but the last of his future creations. Once again, however, the change can be understood only against the background of social and political changes that took place in Persia during the post-war years. For when the régime changed, a new, democratic era was heralded. In the following years there was a good deal of demonstration, oratory, and political manoeuvring everywhere in the country; and on the surface it looked as though the history of Iran had been given an abrupt twist.

The younger generation was naturally very impressed by these developments. This group included many who were fully aware of the needs and defects of their country. They knew, for instance, that during the past century and a half the country had been "a pawn of international diplomacy," that "the life of peasants has changed little in the past thousand years"; and that "it was not difficult for a foreign legation to 'buy' a newspaper, an editorial writer or an underpaid employee in one of the administrations." They not only knew of these flagrant evils, but for many years they had cherished the desire to rid the country of them. Now their chance had come. After long years of silence, resignation, and frustration, they were suddenly free: free to express their opinions and release their pent-up desires. Here the role of intellectuals was of special significance: in fact, they stimulated the whole movement of political reform. For two decades they had been denied freedom of expression, but now that they had it they could not use it judiciously, and their first outpourings were, naturally, directed against the atrocities of the former régime.

Hedayat could not stay out of this conflict. Under the old régime he had endured enough suffering to make him raise his voice against it now; and before he realized it, he was swimming with the currents of the time. **"Mihan-Parast"** was his first contribution to this new theme. It is an ironical account of the sea voyage of Sayyid Naṣrulla, one of the die-hard connoisseurs of the ministry of education who is sent on a commission to India to unfold the "dazzling cultural progress" in Iran during the "golden era." The plot is commonplace, but the wit, the sharp irony, and violent humour make the story memorable. The reader, especially if he is Persian, can hardly help savouring the portrayal of the conceited, ludicrous Sayyid Naṣrulla, for he is so utterly typical of his species. He claims to be erudite in French, Arabic, Persian literature, in oriental as well as occidental philosophy, in gnosticism, and in the ancient and modern sciences; he regards himself as "the pride of mankind," and he delivers such pronouncements as: "English is in fact French, only they have spoiled the spelling and pronunciation." The story also contains bitter attacks on the Far-hangistan (The Iranian Academy) and its "ludicrous, non-sensical coinages," as well as some derisive criticism of the general plight of culture and education during the reign of Riża Shah and of the way in which ministers and high officials achieved promotion.

Though full of hope, humour, and spirit, Hedayat's writings during this period often lack the depth, the grace, and pathos of his earlier works. His fastidious economy of words is aban-doned, and in its place are an unsparing sense of humour, a great deal of journalese, and (as with the work of all the in-tellectuals during these critical years) an unrestrained liking for babbling and bitter sarcasm. These habits dominate **"Qaẓiya-hi Namak-i Turki"** (**"The Case of the Rock-salt"**) published in the collection *Vilingari* (**"Tittle-tattle"** . . .): forty pages of sardonic gibing and medley. It is useless to look for any specific purport, relevance, or consistency: he just goes on and on, playing the fool, writing whatever comes to his mind; and yet every line, every word is a sharp prick at the ironies of human life—like Lucky's tirade in Beckett's *Waiting for Godot*. Of the same pattern, though with more substance, are two other pieces in this collection: **"Murgh-i Ruh"** (**"The Soul-Bird"**) and **"Zir-i Buta"** (**"In the Wild"**), the first a witty piece teasing a friend and the second a somewhat obscure allegory against the racial theories of Fascists. In the same volume there is also **"Dast-i Bar Qaẓa"** (**"It Happened That"**), written in the style of the celebrated *Vagh Vagh Sahab*, a masterly jux-taposition of words, with lots of drollery and little sense.

An exception among the pieces in this miscellany is **"Qaẓiya-hi Khar Dajjal"** (**"The Case of the Antichrist's Donkey"**), a very refined, clever, and suggestive allegory about the politics and general state of affairs in Persia from the early days of Riża Shah's rise to power until the period when the work was written. In its characterizations the piece resembles George Orwell's satire, *Animal Farm*.

The language used in this collection, as in the rest of his works during this period, is that of the ordinary man. Hedayat, we remarked, took pride in bringing the songs, idioms, and slang of the common people into literature. (pp. 188-90)

The legendary tale *Ab-i Zindigi* (**"The Elixir of Life"**), which appeared at this time, is a good example of these qualities. The unadorned beauty and ease of style, the flow of words and the simplicity of the story are probably unprecedented in Per-sian prose. The story is based on an old nursery tale, and Hedayat, faithful to the original, envelopes it in a fairy tale atmosphere. Hence on the surface *Ab-i Zindigi* appears to be a children's story, while underneath, some of the most fun-damental sociological problems are being dealt with. One im-mediately notices that a new Hedayat has been born, with hardly a trace of despair or gloom left in him. We now see a social crusader who shows amazing insight, clairvoyance and understanding of a society in transformation. He portrays the emancipating class struggle and ends his attractive story with the victory of knowledge and humanity over the black forces of ignorance, tyranny and enslavement to gold. (pp. 191-92)

Hajji Aqa . . . , a one-character novelette, was the culmination of his optimism and the perfection of his new themes and style. Abandoning depth, pathos, and different kinds of mysticism, he shows a tendency for babbling and journalistic invective: these are the dominant tones in this masterpiece of sarcasm and denunciation. Ḥajji Aqa himself is a monstrous phenom-enon whose prototype might be found nowhere except in Per-sian society of the time. The son of a tobacconist, with little education and no solid background, Ḥajji Aqa has managed, through fraud, pretension and political charlatanism, to acquire a vast fortune as well as considerable social status. A prominent figure in the country, he now owns estates, factories, and houses, has a business in the bazaar, trades in opium, hoards medicine and foodstuffs, and contrives various kinds of smug-gling through his connections with ambassadors abroad. At the same time he is stingy and frugal to excess: "I counted the plums," he says when interrogating his old servant, "then the stones: four were missing." (pp. 192-93)

Hajji Aqa is not a close-knit story but a rather extended com-mentary; a bitter exposure of moral decline and social crimes. . . . [There] are, in fact, no incidents, not even a central plot, in the book. But despite all its rancour, none of Hedayat's books is so full of humour as this one. There are passages that will make even the most unsympathetic reader laugh. One of the novelties in the book is that, although primarily a one-character work, it *introduces* the reader to thirty different characters without actually letting him meet them. This Hedayat achieves by his genius for coining names. People like Falakhunu'd-Dawla, Sarhang Buland Parvaz, Banda-yi Dargah, Muntakhab Darbar, Ḥizqil Mash'al, and many others never appear in the story, but their names immediately illustrate and colour their characters for us. [The critic adds in a footnote: Although translation deprives such names of their full allusive flavour, a rough English version might aid the non-Persian reader. Hence the above five mean: "The state's catapult," "Colonel climb-high," "The slave of your threshold," "The Court's nomi-nee" and the last a Jewish name, to imply greed and usury.].

Hajji Aqa was by far Hedayat's most popular work, especially among the general public. At the same time it met with dis-approval by the establishment and by carping, highbrow schol ars. The latter suggested that it was not a work of art; that the character of Ḥajji Aqa is a mere caricature, more exaggerated than typical. None of these charges is based on a real critical judgement. For, in the first place, Hedayat never intended *Hajji Aqa* to be a work of art; his aim, like that of most young writers of the period, was to appeal to the taste of the time, and to open his fellow-countrymen's eyes to the blemishes and scan-dals in their society. Secondly, given that Ḥajji Aqa *is* a car-icature, he can also be a literary creation provided he remains forceful and vigorous. To go even further, "Where there is no character there can be no caricature. Caricature is an artistic excess of character." And lastly, the question of type versus individual is, in fact, the old argument in literature: whether the character should be the photographic reflection of an or-dinary man in everyday life, with all his average qualities; or an artistically magnified creation, with all his human impulses there, but presented in the extreme. In *Hajji Aqa,* Hedayat has employed the latter conception. (pp. 196-97)

Other works during this period show that Hedayat has become more and more a militant humanist, conscious of the class struggle in society; while trying to disgrace the people's ene-mies, he fights vigorously for the rights of the downtrodden. For instance, the short story **"Farda"** (**"To-morrow"** . . .), which appeared after *Hajji Aqa*, is purely proletarian in nature. It sketches the turbulent dreams of two workmen, who, in their insomnia, picture for us the inner lives of a group of workers in a printing-shop: their political wranglings and petty tiffs, their hopes, anxieties, and comradeship. The story is in two complementary parts. In the first, one of the workers, who has to leave his job and go hunting for another in a distant town, tells us of his fears and perplexities; in the second part he has been killed in a strike, and a fellow-worker meditates on the life and character of his deceased friend. Both parts merge into the workers' worried glance at the future, with the word "tomorrow" rippling on their lips. (p. 198)

Between 1947 and 1951, the year of his suicide, [Hedayat] wrote two books: *Tup-i Murvari* ("The Pearl Cannon" . . .) and *Piyam-i Kafka* ("The Message of Kafka" . . .). The first is an indiscreet narrative, probably his shrug of the shoulder at what was happening in his country. The book is not yet published, and its profane and maledictory language will most likely prevent its publication in the near future. (p. 200)

Piyam-i Kafka is both a brilliant introduction to the Persian translation of Kafka's *The Penal Colony* and a description of Hedayat's own pessimism. A mature work both in thought and style, it is the complete expression of a philosophy of despair.

> Before the last World War [he states] there still existed a vague hope of freedom and respect for the rights of mankind. The supporters of dictatorship had not yet openly replaced freedom by slavery, the rights of humanity by the atomic bomb and justice by injustice. The masses of the people had not yet been transformed by politicians and robbers into cattle, and living men into half-dead creatures.

Hedayat's grim philosophy is recited in *Piyam-i Kafka* with a mastery and confidence that denote the great artist at the height of his powers. But having reached this height, Hedayat had also made up his mind on a problem that had engaged him all his mature life: the problem of whether or not the highly sensitive and idealistic individual could sustain the experience of mortal life; that is of a solitary life where all pain is perceived and loneliness suffered, which becomes all the more complete for its being so largely incommunicable. This was the predicament of an artist whose temperament was made for pessimism and for whom neither religion nor philosophy held any consolation. For Hedayat, life could not be borne; he had to shed it. (pp. 200-01)

The "blind owl" could not stand the ugliness that his psychology and brand of introspection revealed to him in the harsh light of day. This was a failure, of course. But the final giving up must not blind us to his importance in continuing the greatest that is in Iran's literary heritage. Hedayat above all others has proved the endurance of Iran's literary genius. No reference to this genius will ever again be possible without his name. (p. 201)

> *H. Kamshad, in his* Modern Persian Prose Literature, *Cambridge at the University Press, 1966, 226 p.**

MICHAEL BEARD (essay date 1976)

[*In the following excerpt, Beard provides a psychological reading of* The Blind Owl.]

In Sadeq Hedayat's short story, "Gojaste Dezh" (in *Se Qatre Khun* . . .), the protagonist Khashtun characterizes the human condition in terms of a prison:

> We're all alone. We shouldn't fool ourselves: life is a prison, a series of prisons [*zendegi yek zendan ast, Zendan-ha-ye gunagun*]. Some people paint figures on the prison walls and keep themselves busy with that; some try to

escape and scrape their fingers to no avail. Some just cry, but in the final analysis we're forced to fool ourselves, just fool ourselves. . . .

Here the prison is human individuality—as the pun in the words of *zendegi* and *zendan* suggests, it is life itself—and there is no way out of it but death. In the period of Hedayat's writing which precedes the Second World War, such images of isolation—of barriers, walls, dead ends, prisons, madhouses—occur everywhere, and *Buf-e Kur (The Blind Owl)* is the work in which this imagery coalesces in its most intense and compressed form. For this reason *Buf-e Kur* is often read as evidence of the propensity towards Schopenhauerian pessimism which we know Hedayat to have been afflicted with in life. Hedayat's suicide (1951) is often cited as an essential fact for our understanding of his work, or as a sufficient explanation for it.

It might be more accurate to regard Hedayat's suicide as a barrier between us and his fictional works. For those who wish to attack him, the manner of his death becomes evidence that his personality was unbalanced, an excuse for discounting the pessimism expressed in his stories. For those of the opposite persuasion, his suicide is used to give validity to the pain we read in him. In either case, however, biographical information offers itself as a substitute for understanding what is on the page. *Buf-e Kur* is Hedayat's most withdrawn and hermetic work, but it is also his most complex and consistent one. It deserves to be read as more than the testament of an eccentric. Whatever the mysteries of the author's life, *Buf-e Kur* is a work of literature growing out of specific identifiable literary traditions. Literature is not so much created out of life as it is made out of other literature. The forms and techniques Hedayat devised for his story have precedents and sources: in the 19th century Gothic novel, in the French *conte fantastique* and in any number of works which were current in Europe during the years 1928 to 1930 when he was living in Belgium and France. Al-e Ahmad noted twenty years ago in his essay on Hedayat [see excerpt dated 1951] that there are references to Rilke's *The Notebooks of Malte Laurids Brigge* in *Buf-e Kur,* and the passages which Hedayat paraphrases from Rilke have since been quoted in detail in a 1971 article by Manoutchehr Mohandessi. Elaborate references to Edgar Allan Poe can be traced in it as well. The particular line of influences I have chosen to trace below follows the sources I feel to be most central to the structural difficulties of the story.

It is to be expected that a young writer who had lived in France in the late 1920s would be familiar with the writings of the Surrealists, and at least one passage in *Buf-e Kur* suggests that this was true of Hedayat. When the speaker of *Buf-e Kur* says, "I had acquired a new life. For it seemed a miracle to me that I had not dissolved in the bath like a lump of salt," . . . he seems to be referring obliquely to this passage in Jean Cocteau's *Opium* (1930): "Picasso said that everything was a miracle, and it was a miracle that one did not dissolve in one's bath like a lump of sugar." *Buf-e Kur* has reminded many readers of surrealism, but it seems likely that its antirealistic elements derive not from surrealism itself but from the intellectual background of surrealism, namely, the early writings of Freud and the psychoanalytic school. Mohammad Yusef Qotbi's 1973 study, *Inast Buf-e Kur,* suggests this directly. "It has been established," he says in his introduction,

> that Hedayat's inspiration in writing *Buf-e Kur* was first his deep studies in the ancient literature of Iran and India and then the two famous

books of Freud called *The Interpretation of Dreams* [*Ta bir-e Khab*] and *The Future of an Illusion* [*Ayande-ye Yek Pandar*]. . . .

Qotbi unfortunately gives no reference to show how he knows this. We know from the section called "The Case of Freudism" (*Qazie-ye Froidism*) in **"Vaq Vaq Sahab"** . . . , for instance, that Hedayat was at least interested in the new science of psychoanalysis, but more illuminating evidence is textual.

André Breton, when he reviewed Roger Lescot's 1953 translation of *Buf-e Kur,* compared it in passing to a German novella by Wilhelm Jensen called *Gradiva* (1903). The possible relation between the two books is particularly interesting because *Gradiva* is the only fictional work to which Freud ever devoted a full-length study (in *Delusion and Dream,* 1906), and the only place a French-speaking reader would be likely to run into *Gradiva* is the 1931 translation of it which was part of the French edition of *Delusion and Dream.* The plot, described briefly, is that Norbert Hanold, a German archeologist who is a bachelor with no interest in the opposite sex, develops an obsession with a bas-relief in a Roman museum. He dubs the sculpture "Gradiva," and his obsession leads him to Pompeii, where he is suddenly confronted with its living counterpart, a mysterious woman he believes to have been resurrected from the last days of Pompeii. In fact, the woman is someone he has known all his life — his own childhood sweetheart — but his obsession prevents him from recognizing her. She gradually brings Hanold around to realize her actual identity, and to acknowledge that his obsession was a substitute for romantic desire, a disguised searching for her, with the predictable result that the childhood lovers become adult ones. In *Buf-e Kur* we also have an obsession with a work of art (the drawing on the pen cases, and later the portrait on the Rhages vase), and the materialization of the image into a human being (the mysterious female apparition who comes to visit the narrator at twilight). There are similarities of superficial detail as well. Norbert Hanold's walks around Pompeii, like the narrator's walk near the end of *Buf-e Kur,* take place in a landscape of midday sun. The sun, which in *Buf-e Kur* "like a golden knife, was steadily paring away the edge of the shade beside the walls," . . . is visualized with a similar comparison in *Gradiva:* "As with a golden eraser, [the sun] . . . effaced from the edges of the houses on the *semitae* and *crepidine viarum,* as the sidewalks were once called, every slight shadow. . . ." The flower which the recurring figure of the woman carries in *Buf-e Kur* has a counterpart in the leitmotif of the asphodel in *Gradiva,* which the girl is repeatedly seen carrying. Hanold imagines his "Gradiva" to be a Greek among Romans, and we may see this idea as analogous to the idea of the woman in *Buf-e Kur* as a Turkoman among Iranians. Both stories take place on the site of buried cities, Pompeii and the ancient city of Rey, and this, as Freud points out, is appropriate to stories about repressed desire.

Gradiva is a charming but shallow story of the type still found in popular magazines. If Hedayat consciously utilized techniques found in it, he used them for different purposes than Jensen's. The most significant difference is that the speaker of *Buf-e Kur,* unlike Norbert Hanold, is never cured of his obsession. As a result, we are never explicitly told the identity of the mysterious woman who appears in the opening section of *Buf-e Kur,* although we are able to tell from the repeated descriptions that she must be a fantasied distortion of his own wife (also, as in *Gradiva,* a kind of childhood sweeetheart). By making the entire story the monologue of the obsessed

individual, Hedayat refuses us the opportunity of seeing him from the outside. Instead, he has the speaker circle around a single repressed, guilty memory, gradually dredging up the fact that he is unwilling to admit except momentarily. The fact, which he refers to twice as "that which should not have happened" (*anche ke na-bayad beshavad . . .*), is the killing of his wife. He describes it twice, once in the fantasy of the woman who drinks the poisoned wine and later at the conclusion of the book, where he describes the murder but portrays it as an accident. In other words, up to the episode ending with the return from Shah Abdo'l-Azim graveyard and the opium dream, the speaker is describing a fantasy self and imaginary events. After the opium dream, which leads to the central break in the narrative . . . , he is the actual self who has imagined the events.

The contradictions between the narrator's description of himself in the first and second parts can be shown most easily in his references to his house. In Part One he emphasizes its affinity with his own being and its separation from men:

> I am fortunate in that the house where I live is situated beyond the edge of the city in a quiet district far from the noise and bustle of life. It is completely isolated and around it lie ruins. Only on the far side of the gully one can see a number of squat mud-brick houses which mark the extreme limit of the city. . . .

The introduction to his new life after the opium dream, in the beginning of Part Two, also begins with the description of a house, but notice its location:

> The room itself has two windows facing out onto the world of the rabble. One of them looks onto our own courtyard, the other onto the street, forming thereby a link between me and the city of Rey. . . .

At the end of the same paragraph we learn that he lives across from a butcher shop on a busy city street. The confining rooms in the first and second parts, then, are not the same. (Al-e Ahmad notes this briefly in his article on Hedayat.) Moreover, the speaker in the first part imagines himself to be a painter of pen-cases. After the break in the narrative following the opium dream there is no mention of his being an artist, and in fact when he sees the pen-case described in Part One, in a passage near the end of the story, here is how it looks to him:

> My life appeared to me just as strange, as unnatural, as inexplicable, as the picture on the pen-case that I am using this moment as I write. I feel that the design on the lid of this pen-case must have been drawn by an artist in the grip of some mad obsession. . . .

For those who are skeptical about the split in the narrator's identity, there are a number of mutually exclusive memories between Part One and Part Two which serve as further evidence. The uncle who appears on the 13th of *Now Ruz* at the opening of the story is at that point a mystery: "I seem to remember that he was a sea-captain." . . . He is given a detailed life history in the Bugam Dasi story, with which Part Two begins. Names of people and specific terms that seem to have been repressed in the first section materialize in the second, such as the word *rajjale* ("rabble"), which during the introduction to Part Two he abruptly announces is the word he was been looking for. . . . The nickname *lakate* ("bitch"), which he uses for his wife, does not appear until just before the story of his Indian mother Bugam Dasi in Part Two.

The terms *lakate* and *rajjale,* representing the wife and her lovers respectively, stand out from the text, and the reader tends to consider them together in an imagistic unit that underlines the triangular situation of the narrator's household. (His gratuitous use of the unusual word *taslis* ["trinity"] in a different context, at the conclusion of the passage explaining why he calls her *lakate* . . . is perhaps meant to tip us off to the schematic nature of the dramatis personae.) Indeed, there scarcely seem to be more than three characters in the story. Adaline Glasheen, describing the complex shifting of characters in Joyce's *Finnegans Wake,* refers to a quotation from Bernard Shaw about a Dublin stock company:

> . . . a readymade cast that had to fit all plays, from *Hamlet* down to the latest burlesque; and as it never fitted any of them completely, and seldom fitted at all, the casts were more or less grotesque misfits . . . each claimed . . . the part which came nearest to his or her speciality; and each played all his parts in exactly the same way.

Hedayat's family drama is, to be sure, simpler and more somber than Joyce's, and the parts assigned to the three players are much more limited, but the principle is the same. The ingenue of the troupe is clearly both the ethereal visitor and the girl in the picture. We know that from repeated descriptions. When the narrator describes his mother Bugam Dasi in Part Two, we may think we have a new actor:

> . . . a girl called Bugam Dasi, a dancer in a lingam temple. Besides performing ritual dances before the great lingam idol she served as a temple attendant. She was a hot-blooded, olive-skinned girl, with lemon-shaped breasts . . .

but as we reach the end of the description we begin to see a familiar face behind the make-up, the face of the mysterious woman in the opening fantasy: ". . . great, slanting eyes and slender eyebrows which met in the middle. . . ." . . . Perhaps the wife's brother is a part for the same actress, since she and he (like the father and the uncle . . .) are as alike "as two halves of one apple" . . . and since his lips have the same bitter taste as the ethereal visitor's. In any case, if Part Two is the reality from which Part One diverges, the prototype for the ingenue figures can only be, as we have suggested, the speaker's wife.

By distorting the events of his life, the speaker exerts the power of a tyrannic director over the stage of his imagination. The actress whom he forces into the female roles is the speaker's wife, but there is evidence that the wife we meet in Part Two, whose courtship is described after the Bugam Dasi story, the wife who deserves the title *lakate,* is simply another role and not the actress herself. Most of her appearances are filtered through the speaker's selective memory, but on three occasions she does enter the room in which he writes, and in none of them does she confirm his characterization of her. The first, which is also the first actual event (after the long introduction) of Part Two, is the nocturnal visit described by his nurse: "'My daughter'—she meant the bitch, my wife—'came to your bedside and took your head in her lap and rocked you like a baby.'" . . . It is, significantly, at this point that we learn she is pregnant. In her second visit he merely glimpses her at the door of his room after he has upset his soup bowl and

shrieked. . . . In her third visit there is a sign of hostility toward the narrator, but it is only the tone of her voice:

> She asked me in a sarcastic tone [*be tane*], "how are you feeling?" I replied, "Aren't you perfectly free? Don't you do everything you feel like doing? What does my health matter to you?"
>
> She left the room, slamming the door behind her. She did not turn to look at me. It seems as though I have forgotten how to talk to the people of this world, to living people. . . .

A lot rests on the words *be tane*. His sudden change of tone after her departure and her return on the next page (as well as the detail that she is dressed up in her best clothes [*ba haft qalam-e arayesh*]) indicate that he may have willfully misheard her. If we count the two visits he makes to her bedroom, there are five confrontations in all, one for each of the five days described in Part Two. Although her reaction on the two occasions when he comes to her room indicates that she is waiting for someone to come sleep with her, there is evidence (to be dealt with presently) that she is waiting for him. In any event the fact of her infidelity has its problematical overtones. At one point he refers to "all the things people said about her" . . . ; at another he speaks of her affairs as hidden: "No one knew the secret which existed between us. Even my nurse . . . used to reproach me—on account of the bitch." . . . (207-13)

The nature of her sin depends, of course, on the identity of the old man who turns up as her ultimate lover. In the Gothic setting of Part One he plays the visiting uncle and a humorous gravedigger: when in Part Two the mode switches to realism he plays an odds-and-ends man. In India we see him momentarily young, but after his experience in the cobra pit he is the same old man again, complete with his fearful laugh, in the guise we first met him on the pen-case: "a bent old man like an Indian fakir." . . . That he also plays the role of the wife's father we know from his fearful laugh in the "courting" scene by the bier of the *lakate*'s mother. If, to take the stage metaphor a step farther, the old men break down into a single actor, that actor can only be the speaker himself. He says as much at the opening of Part Two, though he draws our attention away from it immediately afterwards:

> Whoever saw me yesterday saw a wasted, sickly young man. Today he would see a bent old man with white hair, burnt-out eyes and a hare-lip. I am afraid to look out of the window of my room or to look at myself in the mirror for everywhere I see my own shadow multiplied indefinitely. . . .

He draws our attention away from this in order to intensify the reader's shock at the climax of the story when, after twice producing the old man's laugh, the narrator looks into the mirror and sees his other self there. ("I had become the old odds-and-ends man." . . .) Students of 19th century fiction are familiar with this theme as the motif of the double, or doppelganger, in which a mysterious figure who haunts the hero of the story is discovered at some point to be an image of the hero's self: examples are to be found throughout E.T.A. Hoffmann's stories, in Dostoevsky's "The Double," Edgar Allan Poe's "William Wilson" and in any number of more contemporary works. The classic study of the doppelganger theme, by Freud's disciple Otto Rank (*The Double,* 1914), for example, opens with a chapter on the use of the double in a popular film of the time, Paul Wegener's *The Student of Prague.*

Otto Rank's theory interprets the double as a personification of forbidden, repressed desires:

> The most prominent symptom of the forms which the double takes is a powerful consciousness of guilt which forces the hero no longer to accept the responsibility for certain actions of his ego, but to place it upon another ego, a double who is . . . [a] detached personification of instincts and desires which were once felt to be unacceptable, but which can be satisfied without responsibility in this indirect way. . . .

There is much in *Buf-e Kur* to suggest that Rank's theory applies here, and that the particular desires which the old man embodies are sexual in nature. Frequently his role is to intrude between the narrator and the girl, literally in the tableau glimpsed through the air-hole . . . and figuratively in such scenes as when he interrupts the embrace near the mother's coffin . . . ; he appears as if spontaneously called forth whenever a potentially erotic scene begins. Notice, in his role as the odds-and-ends man, when he came into the narrator's life:

> And, now I came to think of it, why was it that this man had been hanging about outside our house ever since I had got married? . . .

The link between the figure of the old man and the narrator's sexual anxieties is made most nearly explicit in the Bugam Dasi story. There too we find doubling of characters, in the two merchant brothers who are as alike "as two halves of one apple." . . . Again one of the two is transformed into the guise of a fearsome old man, and the agent of that transformation is his exposure to the snake in the trial by cobra scene. If we speak of the cobra as a sexual image, it is not simply because snakes have a phallic shape. The trial by cobra is after all punishment for a sexual transgression, and it takes place at a lingam temple. The cobra kills one of the twins; it leaves the other insane and prematurely aged. Applying this as a parallel to the narrator's two selves elsewhere in the book, we can say that under the pressure of his own venomous sexual anxieties he has split into a self that feels he is a living corpse (*morde-ye motaharrek . . .*) and another self who is the old man that haunts him. It is as if we were reading the story of the narrator's life superimposed on the figures of his parents. Otto Rank has dealt in another book, *The Myth of the Birth of the Hero,* with recurrent themes in accounts of heroes' parentage in folklore and mythology, many of which seem relevant here. Rank's interpretation points out that folk-heroes often have two sets of parents: real parents who are respected and admired, and false parents who are humble, or even threatening and sinister. Such doubling, Rank argues, is a means of objectifying the contradictory emotions we feel towards our parents, and of course the orgin of those feelings according to the psychoanalytic system is our discovery of the sexual life of our parents. The device of giving the father a twin brother in the Bugam Dasi story in effect creates two father figures, and the element which creates the difference between them is the cobra. Hedayat has cunningly remodeled the folktale device Rank describes by applying it to both the self and the father, so that the evil father and the double become the same figure. The speaker's guilt, in other words, stems from his imagined identity with his father, and this in turn is his sexuality. What he

has undergone is not a trial by cobra, but simply the anxiety of his own marriage.

Hedayat may have used both of Rank's studies in the preparation of *Buf-e Kur;* he almost certainly used *The Double.* Mostafa Farzane, in his recollections of Hedayat's last days in Paris in 1951, describes going to a number of films at a cinema club. Hedayat, he says, introduced him to the classic films of German Expressionism, including Paul Wegener's *Student of Prague,* "a description and analysis of which he had read in a book by some German psychoanalyst." This would be Rank's *The Double,* which begins with a discussion of that film. As it turns out, there is also a specific substantive relation between *The Double* and the text of *Buf-e Kur,* as both allude to the superstition of the headless shadow (that "if anyone cast a headless shadow . . . that person would die before the year was out" . . .), Rank in a chapter on the double motif in anthropology and Hedayat in the scene where the narrator returns from his walk outside of town.

In other words, *Buf-e Kur* can be read as a gradual materialization of the repressed memory of the murder. The opening situation represents a kind of stasis, in which the painting of the obsessive scene is (as in a dream image) both outlet and disguise for the repressed material. The events which begin with the uncle's visit set off a process of escalation after which the picture is no longer a sufficient outlet. The vision through the ventilation hole is a more persistent version of the obsessive scene in the painting, though the world of that vision does not close in on him until the evening of the ethereal woman's visit. As more and more of the speaker's actual world is admitted to his consciousness, the hallucination of the old man looms more tangibly on the scene. He is paradoxically the speaker's last refuge from what he has done, and as an odds-and-ends man he plays a role analogous to that of dream images in psychoanalysis: he offers an array of objects no one wants to buy, but which have a curious significance waiting to be fathomed. ("Those dead objects left a far deeper imprint upon my mind than living people could ever had done." . . .) Since among his wares is an old jar, apparently the one that was discovered when the grave was dug for the ethereal girl at the climax of Part One, we may conclude that he is, like our dream life, offering for sale the key to unifying the narrator's two worlds. If so, it is significant that the speaker's attempt to buy it took place on his own wedding day. . . . (pp. 213-16)

Instead of unifying his two worlds, however, the narrator finds himself unable to rise beyond a certain level of self-awareness. The situation of the domestic triangle and his consequent rage at his wife are two delusions he cannot break through. Once he has translated his disgust towards his own sexuality into personal rage at his wife, the dilemma remains which side of the imagined triangle to remove. He could kill his wife's lover, but the wife's lover is secretly himself. The other answer, killing the wife, achieves only the retranslation of the problem into its original terms, because once she is gone his jealous rage is left without an object and turns back into guilt. What it achieves for the reader is an understanding of the forces that led to the crime; for the speaker it achieves only the completion of the book. The epilogue leaves no doubt that he has relapsed into fantasy, for after having become the odds-and-ends man he wakes up "as if from a long, deep sleep," . . . and the narration connects, without a break, to where the fantasy of Part One left off. The fog on the window panes suggests that the outside world is again blocked out, and again he is separated from the double, while the double disappears with the Rhages vase.

The narrator's relapse throws the responsibility for understanding his blindness on the reader. We have found the speaker to be at the center of a complex network of illusions, and this returns us to the image of a prison with which we began. It is a prison of mirrors, mirrors because all his illusions reflect his own image, a prison because by the end of the book we are sure that the speaker cannot see beyond those reflections. Yet if we sense an inexplicable current of affirmation running through **Buf-e Kur** which cannot be accounted for by the events of the story it is because the walls of that prison are transparent from the outside. Perhaps a final example is in the title. The word *buf* does not appear in the text of the story, but its synonym *joghd* does in connection with the shadow:

> My shadow on the wall had become exactly like an owl [*joghd*] and, leaning forward, read intently every word I wrote. Without doubt he understood perfectly. Only he was capable of understanding. . . .

The suggestion is that the owl of the title is not the speaker but his shadow, the dark shape which the sputtering lamp of his reason throws against the surface of reality. But the shadow is not alone; we are reading the story too, and when we remember this the passage quoted becomes one of those disturbing moments in literature when the fictional creation seems almost to look out and see the reader's eye peering in at him. It reminds us that from our side the shadow is transparent, the prison walls collapse and (from our side) the owl need not be blind. (pp. 216-17)

> *Michael Beard, "Character and Psychology in Hedayat's 'Buf-e Kur'," in* Edebiyât, *Vol. I, No. 2, 1976, pp. 207-18.*

HOMAYOUN KATOUZIAN (essay date 1977)

[*In the following excerpt, Katouzian discusses* "The Man Who Killed His Passionate Self" *as an example of what he calls Hedayat's "psycho-fictional" stories.*]

Sadeq Hedayat's life and works have been subjected to numerous comments and criticisms of both a general and particular nature. But, with the possible exception of **The Blind Owl,** there have been very few detailed studies of his individual short stories. This has created two major defects in the understanding of the man and his works: on the one hand, it has resulted in a serious neglect of many of Hedayat's stories which are well worth studying in their own right; and, on the other hand, it has contributed to an imbalance in the overall assessment of his socio-literary achievements. Indeed, it can be argued that a full appreciation of **The Blind Owl** itself is not quite possible without a careful study of Hedayat's earlier and—to some extent—later works. . . . [Among Hedayat's works is a] group of psycho-fictional stories. It consists of such pieces of prose fiction as **The Blind Owl,** "Seh qatreh khun" ("Three Drops of Blood"), etc., in which the basic question or theme is ontological rather than sociological. In these stories the main characters ask questions which know no cultural boundaries, and seek solutions to problems which are not specific to any given socio-historical framework; they look for a *raison d'etre,* or at least an excuse for living which cannot simply be achieved by the removal of specific socio-economic constraints or a change in social atmosphere. **"The Man Who Killed His Passionate Self"** is one of the most interesting of those stories which fall into this category.

A schoolmaster becomes interested in sufism and tries to "kill" all his worldly desires, in the hope of attaining the ultimate truth; but, in the end, he gets disillusioned and kills himself. What remains of the story is typically some minimum character development of the *salik* ("seeker") and his hypocritical *murshid* ("guide"), a modest background and a number of quotations from some masters of classical Persian mysticism. Nonetheless, this must be regarded as one of the most profound pieces of Hedayat's prose fiction. It is simple, lucid and—putting aside its rather repetitive and disproportionate use of classical verse—quite terse. And it uses an authentically Persian setting for the exposition and analysis of a remarkably universal predicament. Like **The Blind Owl,** the psycho-philosophical undercurrent is developed in such a way that it becomes almost indistinguishable from the narrative. Unlike **The Blind Owl,** the narrative does not betray any "hallucinatory," "psychedelic" or surrealistic quality. It gives a familiar theme an unfamiliar ending with a simple, unsubtle, but devastating realism.

Mirza Hussein Ali was an intellectual who believed that the secrets of life had been discovered by the great sufis. As a child he had displayed a noticeable tendency and talent for learning sufi literature and philosophy. This had been greatly encouraged by his private tutor who himself had a deep knowledge and interest in the subject. For example, he had been told by his tutor how, upon leading a pure and ascetic life, Hussein, son of Mansur-i Hallaj, had reached the exalted position of claiming to be The Truth even from the top of the gallows: "Mansur-i Hallaj, that whale of the high seas," who (in the quartrain of Abu Said) "when crying from high on the gallows 'I am The Truth,' was Mansur no more but god incarnate.'" And this cry—described by Hafiz as "revelation of the secrets"—was precisely "The offence" for which he was punished.

[The critic adds in footnote: "The author has apparently misunderstood the Hafiz verse from which the latter quotation comes. He does not seem to be aware of its implicit reference to Hallaj, and he interprets it so as to mean that the seeker must always ask for advice before he reveals the 'secrets'!"]

But Hussein Ali was still a novice, and he had only begun the process which Hallaj had completed by his martyrdom: he was still on the road to discover the Secrets. So, unlike his younger brother (and in spite of his tauntings), he decided to shun material ends and became a schoolmaster. But a mere preference for a materially modest, though intellectually rewarding, life of scholarship in itself would be no more than a declaration of intent for the great "enterprise." In his candid gropings for ultimate Reality, the seeker is in need of the guidance of a *pir* or *murshid* who would goad him on to the correct path at successive stages of the process. And our seeker discovers this guide in the person of Sheikh Abulfazl (Abulfazl) the opinionated Arabic master at the same school. However, we are told that his acceptance of the Sheikh's spiritual leadership is not quite without reservation. In particular he finds the sheikh, "hardly capable of anything else than setting the rules and, when faced with a difficult problem, declaring, as if addressing a child, that it was as yet too early to discuss it." The reader is left wondering why in that case Hussein Ali continues to accept his leadership.

It is not, of course, difficult to imagine why it does not apparently occur to our seeker to join one of the numerous sufi orders which are still quite active within their traditional frameworks. He is not merely looking for some kind of comfort or reassurance, however spiritual that may be. Otherwise, he would not have looked the truth in the eye at the bitter end with the same seriousness of purpose with which he had begun. At any rate, if he had adopted the institutionalized method, there would have been little chance of such a bitter harvest. It is well-known that institutions have a life, character, history and purpose of their own, not necessarily in accord with the original intentions of their founders. Hussein Ali is one of those few mystics who, in the words of Tolstoy, seek to discover "the kingdom of God within themselves"; and he might therefore be excused for prefering to do so outside the channels of any institution. But it is still odd that he embarks upon his search under the guidance of someone who does not perfectly fit the role. Perhaps he ascribed the sheikh's shortcomings to a high-mindedness which reflected his own inexperience, hoping that in later stages the master would be more forthcoming. Alternatively, he might have regarded the sheikh as no more than an enlightened, sympathetic and morally acceptable audience, in association with whom he would indirectly manage to clear up some of the problems which he encountered. Finally, it is perfectly possible that he did not have much choice in the matter, and the sheikh was "all the guide that he could have." Still, the point remains rather obscure and it may well be nothing but a structural weakness which leaves vague the pattern of motivation and makes it difficult for us to believe the author as he continues to unfold the story. Such "technical weaknesses" are not unfamiliar in Hedayat's psycho-fictional works where his primary aim is not to produce a piece of prose fiction but to use this as a cover for his own ontological reflections.

Indeed, the sheikh's "positive contributions" are not all that impressive either, for his main (or sole) guidance to Hussein Ali is rather commonplace: the latter is simply advised to embark on a process of subjugating, or "killing," his *nafs*—his "passionate self." In classical Arabic the word *nafs* simply means person or "soul." For example, it occurs in the Koranic verse "he who kills a *nafs* on purpose shall be punished by Hell," which prohibits murder and, by implication, suicide too. But, in its sufi usage, this word acquires a very special, if not wholly different, significance. For, in this context, *nafs* is the symbol of all that is materialistic and this worldly in the desires, hopes and aspirations of a person.

This is not merely the arithmetic sum of an individual's worldly needs and passions, but a person's own self with an identity of its own. It is not his *real self,* however. It is the product of estrangement, of banishment, of the fall; and its continued existence justifies the persistence of the exile and alienation. It is a "cage" which imprisons man's *real self*—that "bird of the heavenly garden" of which Hafiz speaks—for as long as he is content to be busy painting its walls. The bird would be free to fly away only if—as Rumi tells us—"The door of the eternal prison cell" is "smashed into pieces." Man's passionate self, his false sense of identity, his confusion of appearance with reality, of the "false love" with the "true love"; and his struggle for the fulfillment of his deceptive desires, of the needs of the flesh, of all that is worthless, perishable and passing—these are the very qualities which blind him to the vast horizons of verity, love and eternity and—in short—of the realization of his "true" or "real" self. Hence the "killing" of the one is a necessary condition for the realization of the other. "You co-habit with an enemy which is your own *nafs,*" Saadi tells us, "why then do you bother to fight the external enemy?" It must be emphasized that it is not only the "killing" of the individual passions which is intended, but the destruction of a whole personal identity which is regarded as the false self. Thus, the seeker does not merely set out to kill his "passion"—as its title has been rendered in some English translations of this story—since, in any case, it is the passion which shall be destroyed in the process; rather, he aims at destroying the totality of his passionate, his carnal and carnivorous, self.

Therefore, Hussein Ali set about to kill his passionate self, especially as he found ample evidence for the sheikh's guidance in the works of leading sufi classics. [The critic adds in a footnote: "It is rather strange that he had had to wait for the sheikh's guidance to take such an obvious course of action, or to find it suggested in the writings of classical theorists and practitioners. This may be yet another 'technical flaw' or further evidence for the author's lack of interest in telling a technically consistent *story* (as opposed to reflecting on the subject matter). In this connection, it is even more strange when we read that *a week* after Hussein Ali had received his guidance, he was pondering upon 'the twelve years' in which 'he had subjected himself to suffering and hardship.'"] He did not exactly become a hermit, for he lived in "a small clean house just like an egg," which he probably owned, and he had two domestic servants. This is a point which is worth a moment's pause. Hussein Ali clearly comes from a comfortable, if not aristocratic, background, or he would not have had a private tutor in his childhood. It is therefore likely that his present mode of existence—though far from being ascetic—is comparatively modest. One way of interpreting his psychology is to claim that he was rejecting what he could afford because he had realized that there was no salvation in material power and possession; another way is to argue that he could afford the luxury of such a rejection itself. Perhaps his comfortable background gave him a natural advantage in realizing, sooner than the less fortunate, that the pursuit of material goals, and the indulgence of mortal passions would afford no lasting solution to the basic problem of existence (or a reason for it). On the other hand, he might have been simply spoiled by his upbringing, and even bored with possession of what he had not really earned. But the latter possibility becomes less and less likely as the story develops, although it retains some validity as a *partial* explanation of Hussein Ali's mental processes.

Hussein Ali becomes, if not a perfect recluse—which would have been impossible in the circumstances—then at least an internal *emigré.* He lives virtually alone and talks only to the Arabic master. He subjects himself to hardship, so we are told, but these are not spelled out in much detail: he did not go out, did not drink, and certainly did not indulge in normal sexual gratification. But we learn that sometimes in his sleep "all sorts of demons would begin to tempt him." Had he *ever* experienced a normal sexual relationship? This is a crucial question to which no answer may be found in the text. The problem is very familiar from many of Hedayat's short stories, and especially those which make up his psycho-fictional works. In *The Blind Owl* the recluse is likely to be impotent although he nowhere admits it; in **"S.G.L.L."** the man is accused of loving merely for its psychological satisfaction and, in any case, declines his beloved's invitation to go to bed with her; in **"Puppet Behind the Curtain"** a soulless manikin becomes the object of the hero's obsessive passion; in **"Dead End"** the man fails to consummate his marriage on the wedding night for some obscure reason; in **"Buried Alive,"** the Persian student fails to turn up on the first day on which his French girlfriend plans to visit his room, without adequate explanation. And there are plenty of other examples.

However, Hussein Ali is the only such character in Hedayat's works who is claimed to practice self-denial with the implication that he is otherwise a sexually normal person. If this had not been the case, we would not have found him regretting his years of self-denial at the moment of his disillusionment. Yet, how can a young man abstain from normal sexual relations for twelve years and still remain sexually normal? Was this perhaps the cause rather than an effect of his attempt at "self-purification": an unconscious urge to adopt a mode of existence which would camouflage and, indeed, raise to a high moral level what was after all nothing but an incurable psychological defect? To put the question briefly, was it not all a mere lie in the soul? And if this is true, are we not justified in thinking that he must have failed himself on that fateful night when in bitter disappointment he broke all his vows and finally took a prostitute home to bed? And if so, did he not subsequently kill himself not as an act of defiance against a shallow and hypocritical world (which is apparently the author's interpretation) but in disgust with his own pathetic disability. Or, to put it more subtly, was this not a revolt *against himself* on the discovery of his own unconscious hypocrisy which he might have regarded as being even uglier than the sheikh's, who, though deceiving others, had been perfectly honest with himself? All these speculations are perfectly plausible, but whatever may have been the truth, Hussein Ali's suicide was *intended* as a judgment on man and his predicament.

Some of the above hypotheses may be strengthened by the discovery that, in spite of his best intentions, Hussein Ali had never become wholly convinced of the rightness of his course. And, they may be even further reinforced when we find that his self-doubt was generally bound up with his carnal desire. This, at any rate, is the only reference to be found in the text itself: "having been deprived from the pleasures of youth, he was now completely empty-handed, looking for an illusory idea." The demons kept visiting him in his sleep, and the quatrains of Omar Khayyam tended to encourage general philosophical skepticism.

In fear of losing everything through a "slip" (or was he asking for one?) he rushes to the sheikh's house, without previous warning, to seek further guidance and reassurance. But he hears the sheikh publicly accused in front of his own house of having made his maid-servant pregnant. And, when in disbelief he goes in to investigate, he watches the cook running to take a roasted partridge off the mouth of a hungry cat, whereupon the sheikh drops all pretense to be having bread and onions for supper and joins the chase, explaining that, according to Islamic law, "if a cat causes more than seven-hundred *dinars* worth of damage, its execution is obligatory." The rest we have seen already: disillusionment, depression, rebellion and suicide.

The story is rather eventless in that it contains much more reflection than action. There are structural weaknesses and formal errors of syntax. Its real value is not so much in its fictional, let alone formal, appeal as it is in the psycho-philosophical undercurrent.

Unlike most of the characters in similar short stories by Hedayat, Hussein Ali's search for the "lost paradise" is conscious and deliberate. He sets out to kill his *nafs* not only to escape from "the rotten human society"—as does the recluse in **"The House of Darkness"**—but to reach out beyond the needs of the flesh, to discover the Hidden Truth, and so to realize his real self. Perhaps even more significantly, his method is entirely conventional. There is nothing original in this approach which

finally fails him. On the contrary, this is a familiar and, in some ways, established and institutionalized method of approaching the problem. In nearly all the similar short stories the "heros" have already given up the search when the story begins. They are already convinced of the rottenness both of human society and, more especially, of life itself. Their problem is not so much where to reach as it is how to escape. But Hussein Ali's case is different. He begins by believing that there is a road to salvation, even though he is not completely free from doubt; and he ends by concluding that even this is nothing but an illusion among others. The Rumi verse which the author has rather ironically quoted as the epitaph is singularly appropriate for the occasion:

> The *nafs* is a dragon how can it be dead? It is
> (merely) lying dormant for lack of opportunity!

Hussein Ali tries to kill his "passionate self" in order to attain a higher existence. He negates in order to prove, rejects in order to achieve. But the simple dialectic turns out to have been false. He therefore ends up where other characters in the similar short stories begin; that is, in complete negation and denial. He intends to kill his *nafs* and *he does so* by killing himself. There are no noble Truths hidden behind the ugly "appearance," and there is no salvation but death. This is a highly original, even though devastating and merciless, judgment upon the whole idea of mystic self-purification: you can only kill your *nafs* by killing your*self*. The rest is either hypocrisy or self-deception. (pp. 196-204)

> *Homayoun Katouzian, "Sadeq Hedayat's 'The Man Who Killed His Passionate Self': A Critical Exposition," in* Iranian Studies, *Vol. X, No. 3, Summer, 1977, pp. 196-206.*

LEONARD BOGLE   (essay date 1978)

[*In the following excerpt, Bogle explicates Hedayat's interpretation of the poetry and philosophy of Omar Khayyam and demonstrates the influence of Khayyam's thought on* The Blind Owl.]

Sadeq Hedayat's first publication, an edition of quatrains attributed to 'Omar Khayyam entitled **Quatrains of the Philosopher 'Omar Khayyam** (1923), marked the beginning of a lifelong interest in Khayyam. In 1934, Hedayat published **Songs of Khayyam,** an important new critical edition of Khayyamic quatrains with a long introduction in which he elaborated his views on Khayyam's philosophy. (p. 87)

In the introduction to **Songs of Khayyam,** Hedayat points out that almost all of the collections of quatrains attributed to Khayyam contain a bewildering variety of philosophical and religious ideas many of which are incompatible with each other. Hedayat concluded that a man like Khayyam, who was a systematic thinker and mathematician, could not possibly have held such heterogeneous ideas; thus he searched the oldest extant sources in an effort to find a group of quatrains which expresses a coherent philosophy.

He found two sources that seemed to him to contain authentic quatrains. The oldest, a book entitled *Mersad al-'Ebad* by the famous Sufi Najm al-Din Razi, cites two quatrains which attributes to Khayyam. Razi states that philosophy, materialism, and naturalism will never be as elevated as intuition and gnosticism, and that they are, in fact, misleading. He calls 'Omar Khayyam one of the philosophers famous among the "blind" and then accuses him of having written the quatrains "from the depths of bewilderment and error." Razi's criticism of these two quatrains convinced Hedayat that Khayyam was not a Sufi, as many people have speculated, but, on the contrary, was antagonistic to Sufism. Razi's book was written approximately one hundred years after Khayyam's death. In Hedayat's opinion, this makes the author more familiar with Khayyam's life, thought, and works than later writers.

The other source, a book entitled *Munes al-Ahrar,* was written more than two hundred years after Khayyam's death. It contains thirteen quatrains attributed to Khayyam, one of which is quoted by Razi. Hedayat has the following to say about the quatrains:

> In addition to being very old, [they] are compatible with Khayyam's soul, philosophy, and style, and the criticism of the author of *Mersad al-'Ebad* is also valid for them. So there is no doubt about the authenticity of these thirteen quatrains and the two quatrains in *Mersad al-'Ebad,* one of which is in both. It is apparent that their composer has an independent philosophy and a definite mode of thinking and style and it shows that we are dealing with a materialistic and naturalistic philosopher. Thus we can say with complete certainty that these fourteen quatrains belong to Khayyam himself and consider them as the key and criteria for recognizing Khayyam's other quatrains. Therefore, these fourteen quatrains will be the basis of this book, and any quatrain which has one dubious word or metaphor or a Sufistic flavor cannot be attributed to Khayyam.

Hedayat devoted the rest of the introduction to *Songs of Khayyam* to an exposition of his views on the philosophy of Khayyam. His belief that Khayyam was a materialistic and naturalistic philosopher was partially based on the commentary in *Mersad al-'Ebad* mentioned above. Further, he believed that Khayyam was a pessimist who hated the Arabs and their religion and longed for the glories of pre-Islamic Iran.

Khayyam's supposed theory of creation is another subject treated by Hedayat in *Songs of Khayyam.* According to Hedayat, Khayyam believed the universe came into existence accidently; the right conditions existed and things happened spontaneously. He cites the tractate *Nowruz' nameh,* which he mistakenly attributes to Khayyam, as a source of this doctrine. Khayyam is alleged to have written that "at the command of the most high God conditions on the earth changed and new things came into existence. That which remained was suitable for the changing world." Hedayat concludes from this that Khayyam "denies that God has created all creatures separately and believes that they have come into existence in accordance with the changing states of the world." He also attributes to Khayyam the belief that "the world came into existence as a result of the joining of molecules and worked by accident. This stream [of events] is continual and eternal. The molecules continually enter into and come out of different forms and types."

The existence of man is also accidental, which is to say that "as a result of the combination of molecules, the four elements and the seven planets [mankind] came into existence and his soul is like a material body which does not survive after death." At a time when man was believed to be the mirror of God and the ultimate reason for creation, Khayyam declared him to be an accident and of no more importance than a fly.

> A drop of water merged with the sea,
> A speck of dust became one with the earth,
> What is your coming into the world?
> A fly appears and disappears.

According to Hedayat, Khayyam rejected the Islamic faith and held the Arabs in contempt. "For the reader there is no doubt that the speaker of the quatrains views all religious questions with disdain and contemptuously attacks the religious leaders of Islam." And again: "From his angry laughter [and] allusions to Iran's past, it is apparent that he hates the brigand Arabs and their vulgar ideas from the bottom of his heart." Khayyam did not limit his contempt to the Arabs alone. According to Hedayat, he was "disgusted with the people of his time, with a sharp tongue he condemns their morals, thoughts and customs. In no way does he approve of the opinions of society."

As a result of his astronomical studies, Khayyam believed that "our lives are under the influence of the harsh laws of the revolving firmament. His complaint is more against the revolving firmament and fate than God. Khayyam finally came to believe that all the stars are sinister and that a lucky one doesn't exist."

Khayyam, in Hedayat's opinion, was a thoroughgoing determinist. He rejected the Semitic concept of God because, for him, there was "no god but fate." Obviously, in a world where fate is the only god and all the stars are sinister, evil will dominate. "In addition to the tangible and material realities, Khayyam believed in a larger truth, the existence of evil which prevails over happiness and good."

The only thing that is certain is death, an omnipresent shadow that continually threatens humankind. "One of the characteristics of Khayyam's thought is that it is always mixed with sorrow, non-existence and death." For Khayyam, death is no more than a transformation of molecules. "On the subject of the permanence of the soul, he believes in the transformation of the particles of the body after death . . . the particles of the body find new life in other bodies. But there is no independent soul which has a separate existence after death."

What recourse does mankind have in the face of fate and death? The Khayyam which Hedayat paints for us answers that is would be better never to have been born. Mankind is in a helpless position, ignorant of his origin and final destiny, and under the control of a fate which has no compassion. There is no need to work for success since, in the end, kings and commoners alike return to dust and the molecules of their bodies are transformed and carry on a painful existence in plants and other objects. Man's only recourse is to live for the moment, to "know this instant and be happy. The aim of life is pleasure and enjoyment. As long as we can we must hold sorrow and suffering far from us."

There are two vehicles of pleasure in this life: women and wine. "Moonfaced beauties alone are the perfect means of pleasure." Wine, however, is the better source of pleasure because it not only brings pleasure but also "causes drunkeness and forgetfulness." Its purpose is to alleviate "the sorrow and grief of life." And, the only path to happiness is to forget everything except the present moment because "a fearful shadow hovers around our parties of pleasure—this shadow is death." (pp. 87-90)

A summary of Hedayat's views of Khayyam's philosophy has these salient features: (a) death, an omnipresent shadow, continually threatens our existence, (b) the molecules of man's body are transformed at death and continue to exist in plants and other objects, (c) the Arabs and their religion are objects of contempt, (d) our lives are controlled by fate, (e) women and wine are the only sources of pleasure, (f) mankind's only recourse is to live for the present moment, and (g) the existence of the world is accidental.

Turning to *The Blind Owl,* one finds that it is pervaded by shadows and shadowy figures. The narrator says his only reason for writing his experiences is to "introduce myself to my shadow—a shadow which is bent on the wall and seemingly devours everything I write." . . . The narrator questions the reality of the visible world and wonders if other men are illusory, if they are not just "a handful of shadows who only came into existence to deceive and trick me? Isn't that which I feel, see and measure completely imaginary and different from reality?" . . . [The] narrator is tormented throughout the book by shadowy figures who seem to be intent on destroying all his pleasurable experiences. (pp. 91-2)

> The heavens add nothing but grief
> And only give to take away again.
> If the unborn knew what we
> suffer in life, they wouldn't come.

Thus to Hedayat, and to the Khayyam that he presents to us, life is nothing but a cruel joke. Fate teases us with a glimmer of happiness, only to dash our hopes mercilessly on the ground. Whether or not Khayyam actually held these views is not at issue here. What is significant is that some of the quatrains attributed to him can be interpreted as expressing these views and that Hedayat gained inspiration from them, an inspiration which found its most significant expression in *The Blind Owl.* (p. 97)

> Leonard Bogle, "The Khayyamic Influence in 'The Blind Owl'," in Hedayat's "The Blind Owl" Forty Years After, *edited by Michael C. Hillmann, Center for Middle Eastern Studies, University of Texas at Austin, 1978, pp. 87-98.*

DARYUSH MEHRJOOI (essay date 1978)

[*In the following excerpt, Mehrjooi explicates various aspects of* The Blind Owl, *including its symbolism, the psychology of its narrator, the importance of death in the novel, and the work's value as a social document of Hedayat's time.*]

Every fiction is a reality, even more so than our own empirical world, for it is a mirror image in which we see life in its diverse complexities—at once beautiful and ugly, sad and joyous. The poet, the creator, is not a moralist but one in search of morality; and we only participate in his search and as such come to know him and ourselves and acknowledge the truth which was hidden from us. The participation, however, generally proves to be not as fruitful as one expects, for the work is complex and life full of riddles, especially when we have a novel as colorful and rich with multidimensions as *The Blind Owl* and an author as subtle as Sadeq Hedayat. Yet one's participation must begin somewhere, and with a good deal of vigilance in order not to misinterpret or overlook those concealed dimensions which elucidate so much of the author's temperament and the peculiarities of his world. (p. 185)

From the outset, the narrator of *The Blind Owl* makes it clear that he is writing for his shadow, stretched across the wall, and that he is attempting to make himself known to it. Such a preference is not a whimsical trick, nor does it suggest extra artistic merit—at best it defines an aesthetic choice instantly appropriate to the overall construction of the novel. As such, art, in Hedayat's case, assumes its singleness of purpose: it becomes more a means for self-identity rather than a mere tool for communication. For indeed, the world Hedayat creates is a "shadowy" world rich with subjective dimensions, primarily seen through a particular perspective, defined and interpreted within a particular set of metaphors. In this world the real and the illusive are not separate, but constitute aspects of a whole. The empirical world and the world of dreams and bygone memories are combined. Events, free of history to confine them to specifics, flow and overshadow one another. Characters likewise merge and emerge and eventually dissolve into the self of the narrator. In short, in this particular world, logic (rational—not necessarily emotive) is absent, and everything seems to be possible. Yet the irrational side of this world is only one phase of Hedayat's art. One may rationally approach irrationality, breed order out of disorder, or meaningfully explain absurdity. In that respect, chaos and obscurity cease to be primary constituents, but tend to form secondary aspects of a mind, a self that consciously or unconsciously produced them. Hence, in *The Blind Owl,* underlying all perplexities, disorders, illogicalities of the surface, one may easily discern the solidarity of a mind unifying muliplicity of forms, connecting various images and rendering them aspects of a whole. That whole, of course, springs from the mind of the author or, more explicitly in this case, the narrator. He, the blind owl, is in the center of his world; everything else, whether people, objects or space and time generates out of him, and eventually returns to him.

Identity is the key to the novel. It is a cumbersome, even impossible task to divide things into distinct, unmelting entities; for everything resembles the narrator and mirrors him. On a concrete level, the narrator is a bent old man engaged in a fruitless activity—he is a painter of sterility, a painter of spiritless subjects. What he paints consists of a bent old man squatting beneath a cypress tree, a cloak wrapped about him and wearing a turban on his head, like an Indian fakir, biting the index finger of his left hand in a gesture of surprise; before him stands a girl in a long black dress, leaning toward him, offering a morning glory; and there runs a stream between them which, with its constant flow, separates the two. This is what he paints, and ironically enough the subject matter never changes. This pose is essential to the novel; it mirrors not only his own particular life condition, but extends to an overwhelming generality, encompassing at once peculiarities of a society—or a circumscribed world that encircles him; it is a sterile, immobile pose, dead in appearance but pregnant with concealed emotions of longings, fears, and anxieties. In order to understand the novel, one has to understand this pose.

The Blind Owl, both as a novel and as a character, deals with a quest after a transcendent, the nature of which, as it were, remains uncertain. All the tensions, dreads, and vacillations are there to implement such a quest. The pose not only symbolizes this quest, it very vividly provides the answer: the man, reduced to an arid, useless body, will continue staring at his "ethereal" maiden without the ability or will to capture her with full certitude. Hence, from the outset, we can guess the ending, for "that" has never belonged to this world and if one goes on absurdly, yet stubbornly to insist upon some ultimate form of attainment, this attainment must be achieved only in death—through death or with death. And *The Blind Owl* is just that—a slow, painful process of dying.

A symbol is a fascinating thing; it can be specific as well as general, depending on the viewpoint of the observer. In *The Blind Owl,* the ethereal girl may symbolize the absolute, eternal beauty, but at the same time it can be something else, or perhaps just what she is: a girl, only extremely beautiful to the narrator's eyes. But by virtue of her being a symbol, she can always illuminate the shadows and give the work and Hedayat's thinking proper form. However, unlike other ideals (both occidental and oriental) which are generally endowed with all precious excellences that the human mind in its innocence is capable of imagining, the narrator's ideal is exceptional, for it possesses in one breath the very core of a dual existence. She is a spirit, but carries marks of flesh; she is heavenly, yet is infinitely tied up to earth; she is light, but wears a black gown. At last we confront a celestial beauty that is not free of ugliness. In describing the ethereal girl, the narrator begins with the spiritual, superhuman side and ends up with her voluptuous body, the lines of her legs, her arms, her breasts. . . . When the ethereal girl finally comes to him of her own volition, he has her corpse and now he must immortalize something of her eternity; he draws her eyes. Her eyes, likewise, possess a dual quality. On the one hand, they are capable of transporting him beyond the world of the given: "One glance from her and mysteries and secrets would no longer have existed for me.". . . But on the other hand, they are demoniacal and would reflect his own wretchedness: "As I looked upon those closed eyes it was as though the demon which had been torturing me, the incubus which had been oppressing my heart with its iron paw, had fallen asleep for awhile." . . . "In the depth of her immense eyes I beheld in one moment all the wretchedness of my life." . . . In this way, the image of the ethereal girl as an ideal loses all its traditional, mystico-theological attributes: she falls into distortion; she becomes an anthropomorphic mirage of an abstractly distorted imagination. Absolute, hence becomes what it has been and what it should be: a mirror image of the human self. She exists not as a detached external divinity but primarily in the mind and anticipation of the agent. As such, she may demonstrate, though indirectly, peculiarities of self that creates and desires her.

The narrator is an underground man *par excellence*. He carries within him appropriately and sufficiently all the attributes associated with an undergroundling. Early in his intellectual development, the narrator comes to realize that he has no place within the rational, practical schemes of a reasonable world and that the peculiarities of his self, his abilities are such that they cannot be of use to realms of human activity. He willingly cuts himself off from the rest of the world—the "crystal palaces"; or better, his dark, horrid and dingy room becomes the world itself. The four walls of his room set the margin of his world, beyond which there is nothing, or else only objects of indifferent values, one or two of which would sufficiently epitomize the rest—like the odds-and-ends man, like the dog, like his father. Against these walls he is utterly helpless. This is part of his contradictory self. Although the walls are willed and constructed for the purpose of final disconnection from outside reality, yet he obstinately continues knocking his head against them, he suffers them, he wishes to surpass them. And when he does actually surpass his walls, he finds himself in the same prison, fetid, depressing—the same prison, only larger in space and varied in content—with the "rabble-men" lining up as unshakable walls, echoing a "gruesome laughter." He

immediately turns back to his room. The room, besides being a dungeon, can be a grave or a womb as well. In any case, it has no access to life; it inhibits growth and its inhabitant, therefore, becomes either a corpse or an infant. Both these variants are significant symbols of a dissociated self. At best they demonstrate incapacity of a self to achieve a healthy form of self-completion, a general development both paternal and biological. As such, the man is highly vulnerable and susceptible to "others" whose varied selves he adopts and nurtures (he becomes the odds-and-ends man, the bitch, Bugam Dasi, the butcher, the uncle and even the ethereal girl). But at the same time, he rejects and despises them violently for being perverse enemies of his true, ideal self. But underlying all these alterations, the man preserves a single image which, in implication, is most true and most revealing of his life reality: a despairing and, as it were, an isolated owl. This owl image is not willed: it is simply known and accepted by the man. That is why he never directly refers to it or mentions it. The man is extremely aware that he is in a state of "reduced" existence—a Kafkaesque or a Dostoevskian figure, both in the degree of a metamorphosis and the consciousness that accompanies it. This time, however, Hedayat's is not an "awkward insect" or a "disgusting fly," but a lonely owl, yet equally miserable, perhaps more so, for he is denied the single virtue of being an owl: the power of vision. But unlike Gregor Samsa, and much in tune with the Dostoevskian anti-hero of the underground, the awareness of leading a reduced mode of existence is always countered by an assertion of superiority over and above the others. In Hedayat, this sense of superiority, contrary to Dostoevksy's, has a peculiar merit, for it is not celebrated or heightened by the rhetoric of rebellion. The man accepts his lot and suffers it because of the circumstances of his personal temperament, but simultaneously falls into most vociferous rejection of the self for being no different, both in biological perversion and spiritual defectiveness, from that of others.

This ambivalence, the acceptance-rejection process of the self, characterizes the most crucial aspect of the novel, and more implicitly, Hedayat's thinking. The man is thrown into, or exposed to, a dualistic setting of a highly fatal tempo. He hangs between polarities over which he seems to have no control, although they are positively willed and nurtured on a grand scale. As a contradictory man, he is destined from the outset to search and discover a means by which he may either solve the tension, resulting from the clash of the two poles, or destroy one at the cost of retaining the other. And he ends up doing both, perhaps out of pure confusion and helplessness: he reaches out for drugs in the hope of losing himself in a peaceful surrogate world and he does not. For in each move, he finds himself and his suffering mounting. On the other hand, he kills—and it turns out to be that which he cherishes most: the ethereal girl, or by implication, himself.

The symbol of the "rabble-men," personified in all bent old men capable of laughing a "hollow grating laugh, of a quality to make the hairs of one's body stand on end: a harsh, sinister, mocking laugh," stands out as a demon containing all the perverted values of his world. This demon is in constant conflict with the ethereal girl: he is presumably a monster who would emerge always triumphant in his destruction of whatever there is of beauty and innocence. Both the demon and the girl are intrinsic to the self and the conflict, therefore, has for its battleground the heart of the man. He, in short, is prey to a persistent and hopeless defiance of the two. But this defiance, being primarily initiated and accentuated from within, leads into diverse forms of confusion and vacillation. Thus characters who were to symbolize the demoniacal side of the man fade into the image of the ethereal girl and vice versa; the ethereal girl and her variants (Bugam Dasi, Nanny, himself in his childhood) show signs of perversion and become "rabble-stricken." The overall picture is, therefore, a vast panorama of confused blending of faces and images beneath which the man remains crumbled, indecisive, and deeply anguished.

Throughout the novel, the narrator proclaims that he has been carrying and is still carrying heavy burdens. Among manifold types of burdens, that which is most immediately felt and dreaded is an awesome awareness of mortality. And there are circumstantial factors to intensify this awareness—the fact that the narrator is actually living in a large tomb, that he cannot transcend the limits of his prison in its space and his body in its scope. The body is not heavenly: it is constrained by an inevitable mortality and moves inexorably toward annihilation, to become a "disintegrated corpse." However, by means of a dream, drugs or a fantasy, the walls become transparent and the man can surpass the conditions of his tomb without really leaving it. These excursions consist of free but distorted maneuverings within a surrogate world, wherein the narrator is able to reenact his search and become a mystic. They are a brief flight from reality to appearance. But the latter cannot help but mirror the former. Hence, he is caught up again with the variants of the self, as cumbersome and potentially tormenting as in real life. The move towards the beyond, the illusive, therefore terminates with a helpless return to the room and an unavoidable confrontation with death. Forever he is impelled to carry the weight of a dead body, a "decomposed corpse" on his chest. The corpse, in a narrow sense, is the ethereal girl, the ideal whom he kills. But the ethereal girl, as we saw, being a mirror image of the narrator's self and the circumstances of his life, can only function in a dichotomized pattern. She is the object of his search and his love, but she is also something else: a potential source of evil—precisely when she dies, when the spirit leaves and the body becomes nothing but a stinking corpse like the rest of the rabble-men. Thus, the corpse symbolizes not only death in its naked ontological form, but all the diabolical values that he despises in life condensed in the image of the "rabble-men." In this sense, the novel moves away, again and again, from a mere personal indulgence, or an observation on the imperfectability of human self, to an authentic, though in this case, rather oblique (and for a good reason) study of the social diseases of a particular society.

The rabble-men are a fearsome herd, who like his walls, press against him and darken his life. He cannot avoid them, for they are everywhere, in his fantasies, in his real world, in the people around him, in the ethereal girl, and in a peculiar way, even in himself. One is a model for the others: "Each and every one of them consisted only of a mouth and a wad of guts hanging from it, the whole terminating in a set of genitals." . . . These rabble-men pollute the world, cause him suffering and are directly responsible for the destruction and corruption of his ethereal girl. Therefore, they are worthy of a supreme resentment—they must be murdered to purge the world. The narrator's resentment, however, must be seen, at least in this context, independent of the naggings of a deprived soul. He detests them not because they are capable of doing things that he is not, but because these rabble-men consist only of what they are: defunct bodies, for whose protection, in their decomposed states, they must lie, cheat, and rob one another. In this sense, they are not human but mere hungry dogs "wagging their tails in the hope of receiving a fragment of offal." To this herd all that is human and noble is foreign; everything about them comprises cheapness and mediocrity: cheap, they remain in their actions; cheap, in their judgments, in their aspirations. He says, "I felt that this world was not made for me but for a tribe of brazen, money-grubbing, blustering louts, sellers of conscience, hungry of eye and heart." . . . In *Hajji Aqa* . . . he has a better metaphor, "we are living in the gutter of the world," a gutter created by people like Hajji Aqa, whose life is summed up in one effort: to cheat, to steal lest he might cease to exist. But these rabble-men are all on the verge of decomposition, both physically and spiritually, and the stifling odor of the gutter and the rabble-thieves who occupy it, is choking to death the few others who manage to stay aside— to melt away in their impoverishment. Yet these few, despite their nobility, acknowledge with despair that they are part of the whole, and that, in fact, they are the ones who must pay for the inhuman acts of others by shouldering the whole weight of *the corpse*. Only in this light can one appreciate the depth of the blind owl's agony. The resemblance that he constantly returns to is a fatal one:

> A thought which I found intolerably painful was this: whereas I felt that I was far removed from all the people whom I saw and among whom I lived; yet at the same time I was related to them by an external similarity which was both remote and close. . . .

This is the point: "both remote and close." He is close to them because of the consequences of his flesh, his body; in this respect he is a rabble-man, too. He may metamorphosize into many faces of the rabble-herd, but at bottom his real self demands a distinction; he knows that he does not belong to them:

> All of these grimacing faces existed inside me and formed part of me: horrible, criminal, ludicrous masks which changed at a single movement of my fingertip. The old Koran-reader, the butcher, my wife . . . I saw all of them within me. They were reflected in me as in a mirror; the forms of all of them existed inside me but none of them belonged to me. . . .

Hence, he is always held back by the consciousness of detachment, and he is deeply agitated to prove his superiority— so he can say that he is above the rabble-men and even superior to gods. He becomes a man-god but only on an imaginary level, because the consciousness that commands distinction at the same time reveals the similarities. He can never overcome the feeling or the obsession that he, in one way or the other, is actually a rabble-man. So he is drawn to act like them: he imitates them brutally, obscenely: he cuts the flesh (of the ethereal girl) in the manner of the butcher, laughs as the old Koran-reader would laugh, wags his tail for his wife just like the dog. He becomes an apparition of them. But again, we must emphasize, what reduces him to the level of others is not humility, but the highest form of consciousness. He is a blind owl, but capable of seeing beyond the walls and ruins surrounding his room. A special touch of Hedayat's irony: blind, dumb in appearance (like the rabble-men), but, in reality, endowed with supreme intelligence and vision; he can penetrate into the very "sores" that uproot society, that generate the rabble-herd. And the consequence of this vision is not rebellion, as one expects, but only resentment. Any gesture of rebellion in him is doomed to failure; he can imagine it or enact it in his reveries but only momentarily, for he is instantly thrashed by that strange yet highly concentrated sameness. As such he parts company with the demoniac men of Western literature, the "supermen," "man-gods," the "superfluous" heroes. The final recognition, which summarizes the pinnacle of Hedayat's sensibility and his anguish, is therefore this: that to be different by virtue of one's awareness is not enough, that the show includes him too; that he is sharing the same fate, the same slow, painful disintegration along with the others. His lot is to carry the rabble-men's burdens and to suffer them: he is bound to assume the responsibility of their inhumanity—because he is part of the whole—without recognizing the possibility either of elevating himself above them, being content with an insane pleasure of superiority, or destroying them. Thus, like the others, he will remain bent, old, and death-ridden; but unlike them, he will continue staring, though sightlessly, at the ideal—no matter how difficult it is to rise, leap over the stream and *move* that eternal immobility. . . .

The ceaseless and unyielding quest for the ideal and its concomitant urge for drugs and an illusive world can be seen, aside from its private implications, in other contexts: not so much mystico-metaphysical (as we shall see), but social and historical. It can be said that the purpose of the narrator's attempt at idealizations is to find a means of escape from the temporal into the eternal. The temporal embodies, by implication, the historical present, and the eternal, the historical past.

Hedayat was a child of chaos; he was born into a social climate which, like the corpse of his ethereal girl, was fast engaged in a process of decay. A long time had passed since history had seen great men at the head of a great nation. The country had been handed to a host of feeble Qajar monarchs (1796-1925) who had only their courts to worry about and their women to extol. Everything had to be decided for them by the outside powers who were naturally more inclined to delude than assist. In his childhood, he sees, on the one hand, the end of rivalry between the powers (thanks to the inefficiency and ignorance of the government, the country is now cut up into regions of influence): and on the other hand, he is witness to a short period of upheaval ending with the tantalizing name of Constitutionalism, which turned into illusion and full of contradictions, like his own private world. There follows a period of restlessness and intolerance when he must go away, to Europe. But in exile, he is as tormented as at home—he returns; goes to India, where he publishes *The Blind Owl;* comes back; goes to Europe again; returns, wonders, fluctuates until he puts an end to his life. And at all times he cherishes, like a homeless orphan, the splendor of the past. What is the meaning of so much allusion to the ancient city of Rayy, which once had its glory but now is a pile of ruins surrounding his four walls of a tomb—wherein he must bury the deformed body of his ethereal maiden? We are familiar with the extent of Hedayat's passion for the Pahlavi language and the riches of historical Iran. In this respect, his groping towards the ideal is to find consolation in the past which is, of course, an illusion but has sufficient truth to expose the squalor of the present. In referring to the eyes of the ethereal girl, is he not speaking about the eyes of history which so brilliantly reflect the "wretchedness" of the present? As I said, a symbol always transcends itself. *The Blind Owl* is not only a story about a tormented soul, it is a valuable social document of the time.

In this sense we see how different Hedayat's outlook on life is from that of Khayyam, to whom some have compared him. No doubt he was influenced or, better, charmed by the sort of metaphysical grotesquery that dominates Khayyam's thinking. The latter's keenness of vision and wit and, above all, his rebellious pose in the midst of drooping sychophants absolutely delighted Hedayat. In so far as Heaven was concerned, Hedayat followed Khayyam in his rather imperturbable debunking of the old Harmony, in his shaking the theretofore unshakable spectacle of God and His creation. Khayyam was a scientist and a metaphysician. In his astronomical adventures, he had come to acknowledge the immutable laws of the cosmos and their anthropomorphic orders. But he was also shocked by their eternal silence; beneath the harmony he had sensed the germ of an absurdity fundamentally incomprehensible to mankind. Against this monstrosity of the infinite, he saw the pettiness of man momentarily flickering on the surface of the "grain-earth," subject to a fatal determinism which was absurd yet inevitable. Thus, he saw man as being basically innocent and morally helpless, condemned to pursue a preordained pattern of existence. For Khayyam, in short, humanism was a point of departure and freedom of choice, a meaningless echo.

Unlike Khayyam, Hedayat's anguish, as Taqi Modarresi correctly puts it, essentially begins with the people and ends with their suffering and wretchedness. His vision does not go beyond the immediate society and its people. He finds them responsible and condemns them for the tremendous misery that they, through their ignorance and pettiness, have brought about. With God and Heaven, in all their transcendental manifestations, he has little to do. As for a religious move, he has vowed to be honest with himself. Thus, he bows down humbly to the supreme paradoxes that reign over the heavenly show; he comes to get rid of God with one polite stroke: he prefers to speak to a friend or an acquaintance rather than God. "The high and mighty one" is too important a personage for him. And as regards a mystical move, he starts it off with good faith: he becomes a vegetarian, delves into Hindu wisdom, pretends to be squatting under the tree, in the manner of Buddha, contemplating the eternal. But soon he recognizes the futility of the attempt—no, he can never surpass the limits of his human measure; this gesture is too comical; the "gruesome laughter" never ceases—he descends with additional suffering. But on earth, he is face to face with the ephemeral. Everywhere he turns he finds gigantic contradiction, no wonder why he should doubt so fully:

> I have seen so many contradictory things and
> have heard so many words of different sorts,
> my eyes have seen so much of the worn-out
> surface of various objects—the thin, tough rind
> behind which the spirit is hidden—that now I
> believe nothing. At this very moment I doubt
> the existence of tangible, solid things, I doubt
> clear, manifest truths. If I were to strike my
> hand against the stone mortar that stands in the
> corner of our courtyard and were to ask it "are
> you real and solid?" and the mortar were to
> reply "yes" I do not know whether I should
> take its word or not. . . .

If Khayyam was haunted with the absurd universe, he could at least draw some joys on earth. Hedayat was incapable of even that. In final analysis, he was the victim of a double denial. He was denied the comforts of a reposed mind as a devout or a mystic; and he was also denied the small pleasures of life—he could not drink "the wine"; he could not forget the past nor ignore the present. Wine and opium, in his own terms, only intensified his pains. Khayyam, sensing the touch of the absurd, left heaven and its paradoxes alone and dived full-heartedly into earth in search of some meaning. He found it, like many others, in the scent of a rose petal, in a soft breeze, in the smile of a lovely woman. For him, misery on earth was the product of a cruel heaven—he had best not get entangled in it—though he could amuse himself and others with its farce. Hedayat, likewise, made the leap, but nothing was gained. All pleasures had lost their meanings to him. Indifference is what could have saved him, but this was foreign, if not a curse to his temperament. His lot, in short, was unconditional suffering without redemption.

The same holds for the narrator of *The Blind Owl.* Now the man, in total deprivation, concentrates his passion in one longing: "Death, death . . . where are you?" With the hope that death alone will not lie to him—the only reality. But he wants of death its nothingness, its everlasting lifelessness. He fears life after death; he wants nothing of immortality.

Consider the remarkable irony: the man who commenced with a full "being," swallowing life with an extraordinary passion and whose self disseminated to the extent of engulfing and even bearing the defective deeds of his humanity, ends up with a sole desire for "naught"—he wants to become just a cipher—and succeeds, if not concretely in the novel, in his real life.

Hedayat's story, like that of the blind owl, is another "Season in Hell." He seats Beauty on his knees and finds her bitter, thus, he continues cursing her. But this curse has for its root a good deal of knowledge—only those who know what blessing is can curse. Any optimism in the midst of hell comprises blindness and ignorance. Hedayat was too saturated with that hell, and he was not ignorant, he went on screaming, but no one would hear him, for he was surrounded by phantoms.

In this drained atmosphere, naively happy with a far removed past, wherein at present a bit of "spirit" is such a rarity, he glowed but soon faded out. There was no room for him. He was of no use to a society wherein, as he put it, "people compete for debauchery and lewdness." His suicide, therefore, was only too legitimate an act—no, he was dead long before. . . . (pp. 186-96)

> *Daryush Mehrjooi, "On Sadeq Hedayat's 'The Blind Owl'," in* Hedayat's "The Blind Owl" Forty Years After, *edited by Michael C. Hillmann, Center for Middle Eastern Studies, University of Texas at Austin, 1978, pp. 185-97.*

EHSAN YARSHATER (essay date 1979)

[*In the following excerpt, Yarshater discusses Hedayat in relation to the traditions of Persian literature and the characteristic attitudes of modern Iranians.*]

Hedayat's importance in Persian literature derives primarily from his pioneering position and the vast influence he has exercised on Persian writers after World War II. But his popularity owes much to the fact that, despite his oddities and notwithstanding the harsh criticism leveled against his work as being perverted and alien to Persian tradition, Hedayat is essentially a writer of moods and sentiments that are deeply rooted in Persian life and tradition.

First, the melancholy tenor of his writings is common not only to Persian lyric poetry and Persian music—the two most intimate voices of the Persian soul—but also to the Persian religious outlook in Islamic times, with its emphasis on the martyrdom and passions of the saints. . . . [If] for no other reason,

the vicissitudes of Persian historical experience appear to fully justify it. Although Hedayat's grim despondency born of his depressive nature exaggerates the mood, nevertheless it is an expression of a genuine and widely shared Persian feeling.

Second, Hedayat's fatalism, perhaps best expressed in his short story, "Blind Alley," coincides with a cherished mode of thinking in Persia. Islam preached an absolute belief in the will of God and in predestination as a manifestation of God's will, and Persian literature is replete with the notion of the futility of human struggle against destiny. Hedayat's personal predicament and inner helplessness favored this belief. It is succinctly reflected in a recurrent phrase in "Blind Alley": "it had to happen." In those fleeting moments of hope, when Hedayat denounced a belief in fate, as in *Haji Aqa,* he was indeed writing against the grain.

Third, Hedayat's ardent, if often distorted, romantic pride in the Persian past ties him intimately to his native culture. Since the turn of the century the Persian national consciousness had increasingly stressed, on the one hand, the weaknesses of the present, and on the other, the splendor of a romanticized past. An awareness of the decline of traditional Persian society often prompts a nostalgic flight into the accomplishments, real or fancied, of ancient and medieval Persian nation. Both Hedayat's romantic view of the past and his cynical notion of the present find a ready response among his countrymen, who display the same ambivalent feelings towards their society. Love turned into resentment and disgust colors the attitude of many Persian intellectuals and is echoed only too often in the works of modern Persian writers.

Finally, Hedayat's sarcastic humor and mocking parodies express the impotent outrage and thwarted expectations that underlie the satirical literature of Persia throughout many centuries. Thus, in the last analysis Hedayat is a thoroughly genuine Persian writer who voices native attitudes in a new guise. While breaking with the tradition in genre, technique, and style, he reflects the basic sentiments of that tradition. (pp. xii-xiii)

> *Ehsan Yarshater, in an introduction to* Sadeq Hedayat: An Anthology, *edited by Ehsan Yarshater, Bibliotheca Persica, 1979, pp. vii-xiv.*

MICHAEL BEARD (essay date 1981)

[*In the following excerpt, Beard reviews the English translation of* Haji Agha.]

Sadeq Hedayat's political side has not attracted as much commentary as his personal eccentricities, his interest in folklore or the hermetic modernism of his *The Blind Owl.* . . . [*Haji Agha: Portrait of an Iranian Confidence Man*] his portrait of a hypocritical miser, a sinister capitalist speculator who embodies the evil of a corrupt and exploited society, is the most substantial of his political creations. For years during the Shah's regime it was unavailable, and there were even rumors that copies were being stolen from American universities and destroyed by the Shah's eyes and ears (SAVAK). . . .

Haji is not the good-natured scoundrel the English subtitle (which has no counterpart in Farsi) may suggest, but a figure so repulsive both morally and physically that he becomes a caricature. Instead of the richly detailed background we may expect from socialist realism, most of the action takes place in Haji's courtyard, and aside from the endless conversations in which he engages with local citizens who have dropped by to do business—conversations whose endless distortions and self-serving prevarications represent indirectly the world outside Haji's doors—very little happens. Haji is denounced in a climactic speech by a noble, uncorrupted poet who has been called in to write a eulogy. Haji has an operation for swelling of the testicles and under the anesthetic sees a vision of the other world in which he is comically humiliated.

Hedayat's sympathies with the Left are unmistakable; but the narrative takes the form of a series of satirical tableaux rather than a story, and it is difficult to say whether his title character is an appropriate vehicle for any political program. Haji is a soundrel of such intense and concentrated evil that we hardly have any indignation to spare for the system he represents. (At times social systems seem not be be at issue. In one scene Haji sends a clergyman on a mission to the provinces, speaking momentarily without prevarication and flattery, in stage-capitalist maxims like "It's our duty to keep the people stupid," thus reducing our social vision to a simple conspiracy theory.) The Hedayat of *Haji Agha* is a satirist in the Swiftian vein, whose savage indignation scatters so liberally that it would not be surprising to see it banned again.

> *Michael Beard, in a review of "Haji Agha: Portrait of an Iranian Confidence Man," in* World Literature Today, *Vol. 55, No. 1, Winter, 1981, p. 169.*

ADDITIONAL BIBLIOGRAPHY

Baraheni, Reza. "Masculine History." In his *The Crowned Cannibals: Writings on Repression in Iran*, pp. 19-84. New York: Vintage Books, 1977.*

Discussion of *The Blind Owl* as an allegory of Iran's history of patriarchal authority.

Bashiri, Iraj. *Hedayat's Ivory Tower: Structural Analysis of "The Blind Owl."* Minneapolis: Manor House, 1974, 221 p.

Analysis of the influences upon, and structure of, *The Blind Owl*. This study includes Bashiri's full translation of the novel.

Beck, Lois. Introduction to *Haji Agha*, by Sadeq Hedayat, pp. xv-xxxvii. Middle East Monographs, No. 6. Austin, Tex.: Center for Middle Eastern Studies, 1979.

Provides background to the social and political climate satirized in *Haji Agha*.

Hillmann, Michael C., ed. *Hedayat's "The Blind Owl" Forty Years After*. Middle East Monographs, No. 4. Austin, Tex.: Center for Middle Eastern Studies, 1978, 210 p.

Collection of essays growing out of a 1975 conference on Hedayat's novel, two of which are excerpted in this volume. Other essays include "History as a Theme of *The Blind Owl*," by Elton Daniel; "Hindu Imagery in *The Blind Owl*," by David C. Champagne; and "Hedayat's Psychoanalysis of a Nation," by Carter Bryant.

Komissarov, D. S. "Sadeq Hedayat: On His Seventieth Birthday." In *Critical Perspectives on Modern Persian Literature*, edited by Thomas M. Ricks, pp. 266-73. Washington, D.C.: Three Continents Press, 1984.

Survey of Iranian views of Hedayat and his works.

Mohandessi, Manoutchehr. "Hedayat and Rilke." *Comparative Literature* XXIII, No. 3 (Summer 1971): 209-16.*

Compares passages from Rainer Maria Rilke's *The Notebooks of Malte Laurids Brigge* and *The Blind Owl*, proposing the influence of Rilke's work on Hedayat.

James Hilton

1900-1954

(Also wrote under pseudonym of Glen Trevor) English novelist, screenwriter, journalist, essayist, dramatist, biographer, and short story writer.

A highly successful English novelist, Hilton is best known as the author of *Lost Horizon* and *Good-bye, Mr. Chips*. Like much of his work, these two novels focus on the experiences of people faced with the events and consequent problems of the twentieth century. Presented in his generally sentimental, fluent, and somewhat philosophical narratives are heroes whose integrity reflects Hilton's faith in human nature and whose values echo his nostalgia for the traditions and way of life which were prevalent in England before World War I.

Hilton was born in Leigh, Lancashire, and moved at an early age to London, where his father became headmaster of an elementary school. As part of his early education, Hilton attended Leys School, Cambridge, during World War I. Despite the sobering impact of the war on school life, and although he disliked the competitive sports in which he was required to participate, Hilton enjoyed his school days. While at Leys, he wrote articles, stories, and poems for, and served as editor of, the school magazine. His lifelong antiwar sentiments, later expressed in his novels, appeared at this time in his poetry. In 1921 Hilton received a B.A. in English and History at Christ's College, Cambridge, where he also began his professional writing career, publishing an article in the *Manchester Guardian* at the age of seventeen and his first novel, *Catherine Herself*, two years later. For a number of years following his graduation, Hilton was an instructor at Cambridge, as well as a journalist for Dublin's *Irish Independent* and the London *Daily Telegraph*. Although he also published six novels during the 1920s, they received little attention. It was not until 1931 that Hilton's first financially successful novel, *And Now Good-bye*, enabled him to make writing his full-time career. Following the moderate success of his other novels published at this time—among them *Murder at School*, a thriller published under the pseudonym of Glen Trevor—Hilton received the Hawthornden Prize, awarded annually to the most imaginative work by an English author under the age of forty-one, for *Lost Horizon*. However, a much more significant effect on his career resulted from the enormous popularity of his next novel, *Good-bye, Mr. Chips*, which revived interest in Hilton's earlier works and marked the beginning of his lasting success as a novelist. In addition to his novel writing, Hilton became a successful screenwriter, and eight of his novels were adapted into motion pictures, generally with his supervision. Having settled in California during the mid-1930s, he became an American citizen in 1948 and spent his last years writing and lecturing. He died of cancer in 1954.

Hilton wrote *Good-bye, Mr. Chips* for the 1933 Christmas supplement of the *British Weekly*. It was written in just four days—"more quickly, more easily, and with fewer subsequent alterations than anything I had ever written before," according to Hilton. Facing a deadline, he conceived the idea for the story while riding his bicycle through the English countryside and reminiscing about his school days. A few months after its appearance in the *British Weekly*, the story was published in

Photograph by Robert Disraeli

the *Atlantic Monthly* and shortly thereafter in book form. Although the story was favorably received by English critics, the American public—prompted by the influential recommendation of Alexander Woollcott in both the *New Yorker* and on a radio broadcast—responded very enthusiastically to *Good-bye, Mr. Chips*, and it became an overnight best-seller. As described by Edward Weeks, "Everywhere you went you heard people talking about Mr. Chips as if he were someone they had known." *Good-bye, Mr. Chips*—the title character of which is based in part on Hilton's father—presents the career and personal life of a kindly schoolmaster at Brookfield, a respectable but second-rank English boarding school, from his arrival on the campus in the late nineteenth century to his death in the early 1930s. Mr. Chips is loyal to the classics, Brookfield, and England, resistant to change, eccentric, good-humored, and interested in his students. His youthful ambition—to someday secure a high position at a first-rank school—gradually diminishes as he becomes a vital, beloved, and irksome part of Brookfield, where eventually he is respected as the embodiment of a fading but cherished tradition. *Good-bye, Mr. Chips* has generally been regarded as emotionally moving, engaging, and pleasantly sentimental, although a few critics have considered the sentimentality excessive, with Clifton Fadiman describing it as "mile-thick," and T. S. Matthews, who deemed the work "harmless" but unrealistic, noting, "The world outside is not so neatly framed.'' Similarly, while the character of Mr. Chips has generally received a favorable response from critics as a memorable portrait of a dedicated and compassionate schoolmaster, William Rose Benét has challenged the view that he is wholly admirable and considers him an example of teachers who muddle the problems faced by educational systems. However, the public enthusiasm for *Good-bye, Mr. Chips* was evident not only in the best-seller status of this work, but in the many letters Hilton received from readers all over the world claiming to have been taught by the original Mr. Chips.

Throughout Hilton's novels, war and its consequences are common themes. *Good-bye, Mr. Chips,* for example, portrays the effects of World War I on an English boarding school, and *Nothing So Strange* depicts the dilemmas of an atomic scientist during World War II. *Lost Horizon,* which developed out of Hilton's anxiety over the European situation prior to World War II, conveys the message that war is a threat to all civilization. In this novel, four people from Western culture are mysteriously transported to Shangri-la, a secret paradise in the Tibetan mountains. Here the lamas, who have discovered a way to prolong human life, create an ideal world, hoping to escape the world war they foresee and to preserve the treasures of civilization—including art, music, and literature—for a future renaissance. The novel recounts the experiences of the four visitors, particularly those of the hero, Hugh Conway, and the drama arises from the contrast between Eastern and Western philosophies, as well as from the visitors' differing reactions to Shangri-la.

Early critics of *Lost Horizon* praised the originality and engaging style of this novel, finding the content imaginative and thought-provoking. However, they have also noted that the four visitors to Shangri-la lack development as individuals. According to James Poling, the characters are ''typical representatives of four modes of Western thinking'' who often function more as ''mental concepts'' than as individuals. George Dangerfield, on the other hand, while citing problems in the narrative which detract from the reader's acceptance of the fantasy, maintains that the novel is a diversion which should not be taken too seriously. More recent critics have discussed *Lost Horizon* in relation to utopian literature, analyzing the appeal of Hilton's novel from this perspective. Harold Martin contends that although Hilton's primary interest was in telling a story, nevertheless ''the two impulses that produce utopias— discontent with the present and hope for the future—lie at the heart of this novel.'' Unlike Dangerfield, Martin considers *Lost Horizon* a serious work, arguing that Hilton tried to persuade his readers to accept the possibility of Shangri-la. He attributes the success of this novel with the readers of Hilton's day (who lived in an economically depressed, politically turbulent era) to the timely theme and the dream of escape, as well as to Hilton's skillful construction of the story and his characterization of the hero. Crawford discusses the ''Eden motif'' in *Lost Horizon,* comparing and contrasting aspects of the biblical Eden with the world of Shangri-la in Hilton's story. He states that even though Hilton's utopia is unattainable, *Lost Horizon* inspires a feeling of hope and a vision that man has the freedom to strive—a vision which ''helps give meaning to life.'' *Lost Horizon* became Hilton's most successful work, and, as pointed out by Martin, ''Shangri-la'' has become ''a synonym for peace and reflection and a synonym for the hope for a world free from war.''

In a review of *Time and Time Again,* Hilton's last novel, John Barkham observed, ''Mr. Hilton has long since attained that plateau of success where readers take it for granted that all his books will be good.'' This statement concurs with the critical consensus throughout Hilton's career that, despite the flaws in his works, Hilton was an exceptional storyteller. As expressed by Martin, ''While Hilton may not be a great writer, he has a knack for making a story move.''

(See also *Contemporary Authors,* Vol. 108; *Something about the Author,* Vol. 34; and *Dictionary of Literary Biography,* Vol. 34: *British Novelists, 1890-1929: Traditionalists.*)

PRINCIPAL WORKS

Catherine Herself (novel) 1920
The Passionate Year (novel) 1923
And Now Good-bye (novel) 1931
Murder at School [as Glen Trevor] (novel) 1931; also
   published as *Was It Murder?* 1933
Contango (novel) 1932; also published as *Ill Wind,* 1932
Lost Horizon (novel) 1933
Good-bye, Mr. Chips (novel) 1934
Camille [with Z. Atkins and F. Marion] (screenplay)
   1936
We Are Not Alone (novel) 1937
To You, Mr. Chips (short stories) 1938
To You, Mr. Chips [with Barbara Burnham] (drama)
   1938
''What Mr. Chips Taught Me'' (essay) 1938; published
   in journal *The Atlantic Monthly*
We Are Not Alone [with Milton Krims] (screenplay) 1939
Random Harvest (novel) 1941
Mrs. Miniver [with A. Wimperis, G. Froeschel, and C.
   West] (screenplay) 1942
''Literature and Hollywood'' (essay) 1946; published in
   journal *The Atlantic Monthly*
Nothing So Strange (novel) 1947
Morning Journey (novel) 1951
Time and Time Again (novel) 1953
H. R. H.: The Story of Philip, Duke of Edinburgh
   (biography) 1956

KONRAD BERCOVICI (essay date 1924)

[*Bercovici was a Romanian-born American fiction writer, dramatist, and critic. In the following excerpt, he offers a largely negative appraisal of* The Passionate Year.]

A new novel out of England is ***The Passionate Year*** . . . , but if the reader concludes from the title that the narrative is one more addition to the already long catalogue of stories with a sex-interest let him disabuse his mind of the notion at once. Mr. Hilton's story is one involving the eternal triangle; but sex-interest not only is not dominate, it is almost specifically debarred. The chemical nature of the affinity between the young husband of the triangle and the young woman who completes the Euclidean figure is, we are definitely warned, primarily intellectual, with only a dash of sex in solution.

There is nothing highly original in Mr. Hilton's story. The author seems to have taken somewhat literally the dictum that there are not more than two or three dozen plots in the world, and has failed to perceive that, even were this true, the possible permutations of three dozen leave at least room for a semblance of originality. The narration is, however, off the beaten track in that most of the action takes place in one of the great "public" schools of England, a field which has been more or less neglected of late years. . . .

Mr. Hilton's plot, by its very bareness, calls for psychological treatment or the story must fall. There is no objection to the hero of a novel being a cad but it is incumbent on the author to justify the caddishness with a psychology which is thoroughgoing and convincing. The author of *The Passionate Year* manfully attempts the rôle of psychologist now and again, but it is evidently distasteful to him, and he quickly reverts to the pure externalities of a starkly naturalistic treatment and style.

In the final quarter of the book, when the tragedy of the mismated couple hurries to its conclusion, Mr. Hilton achieves some considerable degree of poignancy; but the earlier portions drag woefully.

> *Konrad Bercovici, "The Triangle Plot," in* The New York Times Book Review, *April 20, 1924, p. 27.*

THE NEW YORK TIMES BOOK REVIEW (essay date 1932)

[*In the following excerpt, the critic offers a positive review of* And Now Good-bye.]

Beautifully written, deftly constructed, tense, dramatic and with a leading character who lingers in one's memory, *And Now Good-Bye* is a genuine work of art. Its author, James Hilton, is a new English writer, hitherto unknown in this country. If this novel is to be taken as indicating his quality, he should soon become very well known indeed. Sensitive, fine, delicate yet strong, his book appeals to the reader's emotions, and to his brain also. Moreover, Mr. Hilton has the gift of being able to draw character in a few brief strokes.

It is all very vivid, deeply appealing. . . . The novel has sentiment without sentimentality, a fine and spiritual atmosphere devoid of cant or twaddle; even in its most emotional moments it never slops over. . . . As unpretentious as it is exquisite, *And Now Good-Bye* is a novel of high quality.

> *"A Real Christian," in* The New York Times Book Review, *February 21, 1932, p. 7.*

THE TIMES LITERARY SUPPLEMENT (essay date 1933)

[*In the following excerpt, the critic offers an ambivalent review of* Lost Horizon.]

Mr. James Hilton seems determined to leave no part of our little earth unexploited as setting for his fictional inventions. In *Contango* he girdled the globe, north and south, with easy versatility, and *Knight Without Armour* led one into strange unexpected places in Eastern Europe and Northern Asia. The principal background in *Lost Horizon* . . . is a particularly remote portion of Tibet, but minor episodes are staged in Berlin, China, India and elsewhere. In earlier books Mr. Hilton has proved amply his possession of the storyteller's gift of continuous new invention always adequately and often brilliantly clothed in the flesh-and-blood of convincing circumstance. For once, in the present case, he has perhaps exercised that gift too easily. He tells his story of the mysterious kidnapping of four passengers of—and in—an aeroplane on the Indian frontier with a sketchiness which the conditions indicated in the Prologue do not entirely excuse. Here he is nearer fantasy than perhaps anywhere in his earlier works; but he appears at times

to forget that the fantastic above all demands the aid of concrete realization if it is to pass muster, and that to fit a lamasery in mid-Tibet with green porcelain baths from Akron, Ohio, and the works of George Moore, "and even Old Moore," is to make it rather more than less incredible. . . .

Certainly the book makes, if in its conception rather than its execution, the most of its opportunities. Mr. Hilton always writes well and with imagination; his characters are clearly drawn and revealed in constant dramatic movement; his dialogue is excellent. He does, however, having created a situation, rather get out of it than resolve it; and one is not entirely convinced by Conway's final return to action, nor is the rather abrupt ending really satisfactory.

> *"Lost Horizon," in* The Times Literary Supplement, *No. 1652, September 28, 1933, p. 648.*

GEORGE DANGERFIELD (essay date 1933)

[*In the following excerpt, Dangerfield reviews* Lost Horizon.]

[In *Lost Horizon* Mr. Hilton] joins those many writers who have made the alluring and usually fatal journey into Xanadu. He has already shown a certain fondness for the fortuitous and the improbable, and it is not surprising that his latest book should be about a mysterious lamasery in one of those familiar, uncharted, and inaccessible valleys of Thibet. There are grim opportunities for nonsense in such a theme, and it is pleasant to record that Mr. Hilton has avoided all of them. . . .

Mr. Hilton, as an Anglo-Saxon writer, is inclined to treat [Shangri-la] and its inhabitants with an exaggerated courtesy; his fantasy is sometimes too studiously delicate, too ponderously fragile.

But only sometimes. The enjoyment of fantasy is not a matter of belief but of acquiescence, and it is all to Mr. Hilton's credit that for the most part we are quite willing to acquiesce. True, there are dangerous moments. The almost inaccessible "pale pavilions" of Shangri-la have central heating, modern American bathrooms, the best books up to 1930, and a grand piano. All travelers in Xanadu, however delicately they walk, are in great peril of bathos: and in the matter of pianos and plumbing Mr. Hilton stumbles into something of a pit—as indeed, lacking that exquisite sense of humor which is essential to perfect fantasy, it was almost inevitable that he should. But he manages to climb out with a good deal of skill.

In any case, it would be a pity to spoil one's very real pleasure in this book by taking it too seriously. It is diversion, all the more charming because it is written by a man who knows how to think, none the less pleasant because it is very slight. It quite definitely establishes Mr. Hilton as a writer to read now and to watch for in the future.

> *George Dangerfield, "James Hilton's Fantasy," in* The Saturday Review of Literature, *Vol. X, No. 13, October 14, 1933, p. 181.*

JAMES W. POLING (essay date 1933)

[*In the following excerpt, Poling praises the conception, theme, and prose style of* Lost Horizon, *but criticizes its characters as stereotypes.*]

In *Lost Horizon* James Hilton, playing Alice, takes us through the Looking Glass into a land of make-believe. This novel, so fantastic and incredible in conception, is a strange and interesting example of that romantic "escape" literature which, today, many of our better writers are turning to. . . .

[During a revolution in Baskul four people are kidnaped and conveyed] to the mysterious lamasery of Shangri-La, located at the base of the Mountain of the Blue Moon and overlooking the Valley of the Blue Moon, in the inaccessible Kuen-Lun mountains of southern Tibet. They are made welcome at Shangri-La, and in that setting—with the addition to the cast of Chang, a postulant lama; Lo-Tsen, a beautiful Chinese girl who has not yet attained full initiation, and the High Lama—the intellectual and spiritual melodrama of the story occurs. . . .

Lost Horizon is in conception an extremely original novel. But its characters are intellectually, not emotionally, realized; more gray matter than red corpuscles has entered into their composition. And they have a tendency to run to type. As typical representatives of four modes of Western thinking, they heighten the contrast with the Eastern wisdom of the lamas of Shangri-La, but in so doing they frequently cease to be individuals and become, instead, mental concepts. And so the book is not completely convincing. I think the author has labored too strenuously at the task of trying to make the implausible sound credible. He isn't willing to transport the reader completely through the Looking Glass. Instead, we are caught half way, unable wholly to escape our every-day world and unable to enter entirely into the fantastic world the author has created.

Not that the novel hasn't much to offer; the gold outweighs the alloy. There are several truly dramatic moments, some moments of quiet beauty and others of pleasant satire and humor. The idea behind the book and its implied philosophy are mentally provocative, and it is all told in the same terse and imaginative prose which distinguish the author's earlier work.

> *James W. Poling, in a review of "Lost Horizon," in* New York Herald Tribune Books, *October 15, 1933, p. 14.*

THE NEW YORK TIMES BOOK REVIEW   (essay date 1933)

[*In the following excerpt, the critic offers a largely negative review of* Lost Horizon.]

James Hilton, whose *And Now Good-Bye* brought him flattering attention from the critical world, contrives in [*Lost Horizon*] a mixture of Wellsian fantasy, Eastern mysticism and an adventure yarn. It is engagingly written for the most part, it is often effective, but it seems to be little more than an intellectual tour de force.

One suspects Mr. Hilton of not having arrived at the age where the pangs of growing old are genuinely felt, of not having himself yet experienced the painful, unreasoning clutch at the kind of security which means only not to die. Instead, he seems to have speculated about the human craving for imperishability. And there is a synthetic quality about this story of an intellectually ripe Englishman in his late thirties who is precipitated into a Tibetan monastery whose lamas have learned to prolong their lives for several centuries.

By means of a somewhat inept prologue, we learn that in Baskul a native made off with a luxurious plane intended to carry its four passengers from that spot of uprisings to a safe Indian city. The plane disappeared. Then the novelist present tells the neurologist that their old school friend Glory Conway was the

English consul among the missing passengers. More, he discovered Conway some time later, a victim of amnesia, in China, where the latter on regaining his memory tells part of his adventures and then disappears.

Conway, the American, the woman missionary and the young vice consul found themselves stranded in the wilds of Tibet with their inexplicable pilot dead. They are led to Shangri-La, the exquisite, unaccountable lamasery with American bathtubs. Conway, the only one who shows himself truly appreciative of this fabulously beautiful hidden world, learns from the Head Lama that the four of them are to be kept there forever. (pp. 8-9)

Of the four new visitors, only the young vice consul is impatient to leave. It is his frenzy and his love affair with a Manchu princess there (a lovely young girl around 90) that bring about the dénouement. But this is a climax merely so far as excitement and action are concerned; it resolves nothing. Nor does the epilogue, which, as inadroit as the prologue, tells merely of the novelist's unsuccessful search for Conway. So doing, Mr. Hilton may be obliquely warning us that Conway dreamed this. Perhaps he is saying that Conway experienced what de Soto and Great-grandfather, drowsing in the sun, and the human race dreams of. If this was his intention, he has not matched it with his execution.

What remains in the memory of the reader is a delicately imaginative picture of the lamasery and its ideals. The characters in the book were too vaguely realized and their problems were too evasive to matter then or now. (p. 9)

> *"Utopia in Tibet," in* The New York Times Book Review, *October 15, 1933, pp. 8-9.*

WILLIAM ROSE BENÉT   (essay date 1934)

[*In the following excerpt, Benét challenges the view that Mr. Chips is a wholly admirable, lovable character.*]

To judge by the jacket of [*Good-bye, Mr. Chips*] . . . , its principal sponsor is Alexander Woollcott, though the story caused widespread comment when it originally appeared in *The Atlantic Monthly*. It proved precisely the sort of story that those rheumy old eyes of Mr. Woollcott's delighted to see in print. And it *is* a graceful character study. It is sentimental in a most pleasant fashion. But several hours after one has closed the book, the little doubts begin their creaking in the mind. Was the dear old fellow, after all, so wholly admirable? Isn't the charming tale a celebration of a mere muddler-through?

Not that "Chips" did not have admirable qualities. And yet, though it be heresy, one somehow sympathizes a bit with the snappy science man who at one time took charge of the school. H. G. Wells could have presented his point of view so as to make Mr. Chips look rather as though he were hardly playing the game. And Sinclair Lewis would—in one mood—have blown him off the face of the earth in a single detonating sentence. Not that one forgets *Our Mr. Wrenn* by Sinclair Lewis. He also had his day with quaint and lovable little men.

Everyone can recall some schoolmaster in his own personal experience for whom he still feels a glow of affection. The headmaster of my old school was such a one. But after all, though he believed "everlastingly" in Latin and Greek, he was a character of almost Rooseveltian drive and gusto, quite other than Mr. Chips.

Mr. Chips is a genuine creation and I am glad the story was written about him. But I am rather of the H. G. Wells party when it comes to problems of education. The Mr. Chipses of this world, for all their quaintness and humor, serve only to muddle the matter. All of which discussion may be loading a slight story with far more than the traffic should be called upon to bear; and yet such a story, picturing as it does an educational system that apparently appeals to the headmasters of the most exclusive schools in America—to judge by their quoted comments—must necessarily provoke controversy. If you are content simply to take Mr. Chips in the old Dickensian spirit, as did Mr. Woollcott, he is wholly lovable; and perhaps you are better off. I admit I should have liked the kind of easy-going life he led, and to be beloved as was he for my dear old eccentricities. But my dear old eccentricities, from the beginning, have merely aroused family criticism. And oh, to be a quaint character!

> William Rose Benét, "A Quaint Character," in The Saturday Review of Literature, *Vol. X, No. 47, June 9, 1934, p. 739.*

FLORENCE HAXTON BRITTEN   (essay date 1934)

[*In the following essay, Britten discusses the plot and main character of* Good-bye, Mr. Chips, *expressing high regard for the novel.*]

Good-bye Mr. Chips is a little masterpiece. Reading time: a couple of hours, perhaps, for even the very slow reader who savors in leisurely fashion as he goes.

And what satisfaction such a reader will take in the grace and style and sympathetic delicacy of this gently told story of the uneventful, yet richly influential long life of Mr. Chipping, classical master of "Brookfield," an English public school for boys.

A good school of the second rank, was Brookfield. A few notable families supported it; it supplied fair samples of the history-making men of the age—judges, members of parliament and the like. But mostly it turned out merchants and manufacturers, professional men and country squires. Mr. Chipping taught these boys benignly, humorously, Latin and Greek and a point of view unto the third and post-war generation.

Yes, surely, "Mr. Chips" was a humanist, and the flavor of his personality and point of view seeped through Brookfield and tempered with the gentilities of an old-fashioned attitude the brash new harshness of the onrushing social changes. Mr. "Chips" didn't hold back the flood; he didn't, in fact, consciously try to. But to Brookfield boys he gave a little and very salutary taste of the best of the old and the pre-war which must so inevitably yield its place to the new.

All of the important events in Mr. "Chips's" life are caught up and delivered to us in retrospect in the course of this story. His first coming to Brookfield, his early ordeals with discipline, his belated happy marriage and the death of his wife and child, his retirement, the war and his recall to the classroom to support the morale at Brookfield during those poise-destroying times, his declining days—all these are deftly manipulated into an easy, full-flowing stream of interest. Not only does **Good-bye Mr. Chips** stand very high, intrinsically, as a fine piece of fiction, but I should think that Mr. Hilton's little book might well find a place in writing courses, alongside Edith Wharton's novelettes, as an outstanding example of perfect finesse in the handling of the long short story and as a first-class specimen of the methods of that subtler, yet still somewhat technical matter, literary "charm."

> Florence Haxton Britten, "A Quiet Little Masterpiece," in New York Herald Tribune Books, *June 10, 1934, p. 5.*

THE NEW YORK TIMES BOOK REVIEW   (essay date 1934)

[*In the following excerpt, the critic praises various aspects of* Good-bye, Mr. Chips, *a work which he describes, in an unexcerpted portion of this essay, as an "unclassifiable little story."*]

One might, perhaps, call [**Good-Bye, Mr. Chips**] a novelette, except that it has nothing at all of that machine-made briskness one ordinarily associates with novelettes, which too often in the proof turn out to be neither flesh nor fowl nor good red herring. Still less does it deserve to be ranked with the plotless inanities that fall under the general, if rather vague, heading of "character sketch."

In its way, **Good-Bye, Mr. Chips,** is a minor miracle—one of those rare and living pieces of writing which transcend classification, which require no precedent and are certain to have no successful imitators. To convey the precise flavor of this piece by attempting to describe it would be impossible. It is written with such economy and exactness that the substance of a 600-page chronicle and a shrewd commentary on life have been compressed into a few thousand words—yet one is not conscious, while reading it, of any undue condensation. It has tenderness and humor, and smoothly avoids the pitfalls of sentimentality and bathos. Above all, it creates in Mr. Chips himself a memorable and living character. . . .

The reticent story of Chips's life—of his tragically brief marriage, his clash with innovation in the person of a new headmaster and his victory (for, whatever the headmaster thought, Brookfield by now couldn't get on without Chips), his retirement at the age of 65, and his emergence from that retirement during the war to assume the active headship—forms an unexpectedly touching chronicle. How Chips, a shy fellow with no particularly marked traits of personality, came through the mellowness of time to represent an embodiment of beloved tradition, forms an unexpectedly acute and interesting commentary on the ways of the world. Mr. Chips himself, with his jokes, familiar to three generations of school boys, with the eccentricities and liberties he permitted himself as his years advanced, with his crusty but deeply rooted loyalties—to the classics, to Brookfield, and to England—is a figure to cherish in one's memory.

> "A Memorable Character," in The New York Times Book Review, *June 17, 1934, p. 9.*

JAMES HILTON AND GRANT UDEN   (interview date 1934)

[*Uden is an English author of numerous works on historical subjects. In the following excerpt, Hilton discusses* Lost Horizon *and his view of the future with Uden.*]

[I] asked [James Hilton] how **Lost Horizon** came to be written.

"At the back of my mind I have a feeling that it is the duty of every writer to deal with current problems and the anomalies he finds around him. That had something to do with it. Then the subject and setting had a great imaginative appeal. Obscure places and peoples have a great attraction for me, and Tibet is one of the few places on earth that is still comparatively inaccessible.''

"Have you ever travelled there?'' I asked.

"No. I don't think I shall ever try to do so. I entertain a lot of dreams and illusions about it that would probably be rudely shattered. I prefer to keep them intact.''

"But your descriptions of the country and its people are not purely imaginative?''

"No; there is a large amount of reading behind them. The mountain of Karakal is imaginary—I don't suppose there is so lovely a mountain anywhere—and it would be difficult to find in Tibet a lamasery as clean as Shangri-La, but much of what I have written about it is true. There is plenty of evidence, for instance, to support the ideas I have introduced of longevity and telepathy. It is something yet unexplained that in a country half the size of Europe, and with the population of Sheffield, no stranger can cross the border without being deliberately met by somebody and sent back. The incident I mentioned of a priest who, by means of special breathing exercises, could sit on a river-bank stark naked in the middle of winter and dry by the warmth of his body sheets dipped in the frozen river, is perfectly genuine.''

The talk switched off to the modern novel, criticism and poetry. I asked him if he has written any poetry.

"Yes, a little. Carefully polished, eighteenth century sort of stuff. But I am not really tempted in that direction at all. I can say all I want in prose. I should hate to be thought a stylist. I'm not very interested in what words sound like so long as they express my meaning adequately.''

Some of those words came back to me vividly from the pages of *Lost Horizon*:

> He saw the nations strengthening, not in wisdom, but in vulgar passions and the will to destroy; he saw their machine power multiplying until a single weaponed man might have matched a whole army of the Grand Monarque.... He foresaw a time when men, exultant in the technique of homicide, would rage so hotly over the world that every precious thing would be in danger, every book and picture and harmony, every treasure garnered through two millenniums, the small, the delicate, the defenceless—all would be lost like the lost books of Livy, or wrecked as the English wrecked the Summer Palace in Pekin.

"Is that a reflection of a personal belief?'' I asked him.

"Yes. I don't think it will happen in my time, possibly not for a considerable period after. But if humanity rushes on at its present headlong speed it must inevitably crash sooner or later. When that time comes I'm afraid all the precious things in this world will be lost—books, pictures, music. . . .''

I remembered repeated references to music, particularly Mozart, in his novels, and interjected:

"You are very fond of music?''

"Yes. I used to play a good deal. In fact I once contemplated taking it up professionally, but wiser counsels prevailed.''

"To come back to the debacle, you think the upheaval will take the form of a world-war?''

"On a far more colossal scale than we can dream about. There was a time when war seemed to have some sort of resultant cultural value, in that it impressed fresh ideas and a wider outlook on the conquered people. The Norman Conquest, after all, gave us Norman architecture and enriched our language considerably. That sort of thing is past, and that in itself, if you like, is a sign of decadence. The last war was little but a white civil war. From one point of view the wrong side won. Don't think I'm being pro-German. I mean that geographically and ethnically unification and federalisation of Europe would have been far more practicable if we had lost. As it is, the whole four years was simply an incredible waste. The next war will be more than a waste—it will mean practically total annihilation of everything decent and beautiful.''

And then, following his own train of thought:

"The Industrial Revolution was the most terrible thing in English history.''

"And after? Surely there must be a renaissance of sorts. Surely you believe, as Perrault in *Lost Horizon* believed, that a new world will arise from the ruins?''

"Yes, I suppose there will be a renaissance of sorts. What form it will take I can't determine. Perhaps we shall go back to a mammalian stage and work through the whole cycle again.''

"And if a new civilisation does arise, who will be responsible for it?''

"I am not a religious man, but I think the world's salvation may lie in the hands of the Church. The Church, particularly the Roman Catholic Church, has always been a sort of repository of culture. Perhaps from such a source will be recreated some of the old beauty.''

It may seem strange to say that Mr. Hilton outlined this gloomy future with an entire lack of pessimism. He has a gift for saying pessimistic things optimistically. I cannot imagine him ever being depressed by his own theories. Rather is he very much in love with life, pleasant-voiced, quickly laughing, and frankly enjoying success.

Let me say one other thing. Mr. Hilton has established a landmark in literary history. Lo-Tsen, the heroine of *Lost Horizon,* does not speak a word from first page to last.

It is a precedent which was well worth establishing.

> *James Hilton and Grant Uden, in an interview in* The Bookman, *London, Vol. LXXXVI, No. 514, July, 1934, p. 192.*

T. S. MATTHEWS (essay date 1934)

[*An American journalist, poet, and novelist, Matthews served as the editor of* Time *magazine from 1949 to 1953. In the following excerpt, he offers an ambivalent review of* Good-bye, Mr. Chips.]

[*Goodbye, Mr. Chips* is] a little watercolor of the sentimental English schools and an excellent example of its type. No tears will flow over this story of a schoolmaster who gradually turned into a mythical salty character instead of a drone, but everybody will feel like crying, and that does us all good. The little tale gives us the soft English character in a hard nutshell. Mr. Chips is a mediocre classics master in a good but not-quite-first-rate public school. His tragic marriage (of course his perfect wife dies in her first childbed) adds the touch of Anglo-Saxon irony to his backbone that lifts him out of mediocrity into that omni-popular but lonely priesthood that made the British Empire what it was yesterday—the kind of dry, stuttering, helplessly warm-hearted man with whom no one is intimate but whom everyone chaffs to his face and applauds behind his back. This is a hard-boiled view of a harmless little story which Alexander Woollcott is quite within his rights in calling "tender and gentle," but let us not forget, ladies and gentlemen, that we are in a picture gallery. The outside world is not so nicely framed. (p. 271)

> T. S. Matthews, "A Gallery of Novels," in The New Republic, Vol. LXXIX, No. 1024, July 18, 1934, pp. 271-72.*

E. B. C. JONES (essay date 1934)

[*Jones was an English novelist and critic. In the following excerpt, she strongly criticizes* Good-bye, Mr. Chips.]

[**Good-bye, Mr. Chips**] is a short, sickly story about the life and death of a dear, funny old schoolmaster, whose Latin tags, jokes and puns so delighted the dear old school:

> And once, Chips had got into trouble because of some joke he had made about the name and ancestry of a boy named Isaacstein. The boy wrote home about it, and Isaacstein *père* sent an angry letter to Ralston—touchy, no sense of humour, no sense of proportion; that was the matter with them, these new fellows.

If that is Mr. Hilton's notion of a sense of humour and a sense of proportion, silence appears to be the only adequate reply. **Good-bye, Mr. Chips** bears no relation to literature whatever. (pp. 550, 552)

> E. B. C. Jones, in a review of "Good-bye, Mr. Chips!" in The New Statesman & Nation, n.s. Vol. VIII, No. 191, October 20, 1934, pp. 550, 552.

THE TIMES LITERARY SUPPLEMENT (essay date 1934)

[*In the following excerpt,* Good-bye, Mr. Chips *receives a favorable review.*]

Sunset of a schoolmaster! The little tale of Mr. Chips dreaming away his last days within sight and sound of the school that has absorbed his life is very much a true story and very moving, although it trembles on the edge of an uncomfortable sentimentality once or twice—**Goodbye Mr. Chips!** by James Hilton. . . . Mr. Chips, very old but still happy to have the grandsons of his boys to tea and ready to tell them in what way they resemble the earlier generation of boys who have passed through his hands, is something of a celebrity by dint of having lived so long and kept such close touch with Brookfield. Indeed he *is* Brookfield, having lived its life, retired, and emerged again to take on the duties of acting Head while the War is on. He is a legend, a glorious tradition. And the last cheeky new boy to call out "Goodbye Mr. Chips" to him before he slips quietly away cherishes a feeling of pride and glory never to be resigned. But the tale has to be told first, the history of Chips's life as he recalls it in snatches of memory, walking through the village or dozing in his chair before Mrs. Wickett's fire. Mr. Chips is an admirable portrait.

> "Boy's School Stories," in The Times Literary Supplement, November 22, 1934, p. 826.*

V. S. PRITCHETT (essay date 1937)

[*Pritchett is a highly esteemed English novelist, short story writer, and critic. Considered one of the modern masters of the short story, he is also one of the world's most respected and well-read literary critics. His criticism is often described as fair, reliable, and insightful. In the following excerpt, Pritchett discusses the intriguing plot and effective characterization of the hero in* We Are Not Alone, *while pointing out a major flaw in the construction of the novel.*]

A reviewer in these columns some time ago suggested that writers of detective novels are obsessed with the detection of crime. Was crime the only thing to be detected? Why not a detective novel which sets out to discover the innocent and not the guilty, a good man and not a criminal? It would, the reviewer saw clearly, be a far more difficult task. Something of the kind has been attempted (and very ingeniously) by Mr. James Hilton in [**We Are Not Alone**]. Primarily, it is a study of gentleness and goodness pitted against malevolence, stupidity and chance.

In writing about books of detection and suspense, we must not give away the author's secret. The quiet cathedral town can be indicated, the plodding little doctor and the foreign dancer who is stranded there and whom he befriends. There is also the doctor's grim, managing wife and their difficult son. They are a dull little group of provincial people, the wife set in her routine of committees, the doctor gentle and, in all that is important, alone; the dancer alone, too, shut away behind the barrier of another language and inarticulate.

But what the truth about the relationship of the doctor and the dancer is, what interpretation must be put upon his visits to her at a seaside resort near by, upon his introducing her into his home and then upon their "flight" together on a certain evening, is for the reader to discover. Public opinion and, finally, a court declare that he is guilty of a crime. Is he? The evidence is heavily against him. How, given that evidence, could you establish that he is a good man and not a criminal? It is for the reader to work his way back over the clues under Mr. Hilton's expert guidance.

The reason why virtue is so often inspired in novels is that novelists have such a vast respect for it. They pour all the perfection they can imagine into a single mold; they attempt to stand the attribute in petticoats or in trousers. Alternatively, the virtuous character is merely a peg on which to hang long moral essays. The novelist forgets—in his commendable fervor—that goodness and badness are but aspects when seen in terms of people.

Mr. Hilton has managed to avoid these traps. The doctor is a dull, workaday fellow, indeed dangerously near to being "a little man," shown not with the flush of virtue aware of itself upon him, but in the loneliness of goodness. And it is a goodness not of striking acts or sentimental indulgences, but of quiet integrity. So positive is the portrait of the doctor that it is the stupid and malevolent people around him, those ready with the automatic judgment, who are, if anything, unreal. They are the lay figures.

The real difficulty, the reader foresees, will be the trial of the doctor. Eager for this showdown, the reader pushes swiftly on to see how Mr. Hilton rises to this crucial occasion. Alas, he does not rise, and this is the one flaw in the book's construction. In detective novels, one acquires a morbid eye for such flaws, where the author has failed to face the big moment by which all his ingenious management of evidence will stand or fall.

Publisher's advertisement for We Are Not Alone. *By permission of Little, Brown and Company in association with The Atlantic Monthly Press.*

Mr. Hilton dodges the drama of the trial, the great clash between the good and the stupid, and is content with scraps of its findings. We will give him credit for not being afraid of the difficulties. They would indeed be an attraction to a novelist of his competence. No, he has not been aware of the necessity of dramatizing this trial scene.

And the reason for this is that, like all detective novels, *We Are Not Alone* is based far more upon an idea than upon life, and the idea in its eager logic hurries life out of the picture. The fundamental criticism of detective fiction of all kinds—if one is not ascending to the plane of *The Brothers Karamazov*—is that it is a parlor game, a game of chess. It is based on living determined by an idea, and not an idea assimilated into living. This limitation is characteristic of all Mr. Hilton's work; it does not detract from his readability and the pleasure we always get from sheer skill.

> V. S. Pritchett, "*A Detective Story that Sets Out to Discover the Innocent,*" in The Christian Science Monitor, *June 23, 1937, p. 10.*

CLIFTON FADIMAN (essay date 1941)

[*Fadiman became one of the most prominent American literary critics during the 1930s with his insightful and often caustic book*

reviews for the Nation *and the* New Yorker *magazines. In the following excerpt, Fadiman commends* Random Harvest *as an example of Hilton's storytelling ability.*]

James Hilton's new offering, *Random Harvest,* is likely to baffle any conscientious reviewer. The only important thing about it is its plot, and the plot is of such a nature that were I to tell it to you, I'd deserve drawing and quartering. . . .

So I had better content myself with saying that Mr. Hilton has cranked out another deft piece of storytelling, combining the suspense of *Lost Horizon* with the mile-thick sentimentality of *Goodbye, Mr. Chips,* and that anyone who starts it will read it to the very end, impossible as that end is.

The yarn is full of clever things: an upper-class industrialist English family, very neatly hit off; a troupe of traveling actors done in the jolly Priestley vein; two love affairs, quite affecting; and some satire on the world situation and English decadence, rather mildly expressed, for Mr. Hilton is hardly a heavyweight thinker. There's also an eccentric clergyman, Blampied, who might have stepped out of Chesterton, and who sticks in the mind, though I won't say for how long.

Hilton the moralist (he *is* a moralist) interests me rather less than Hilton the plot-maker. There are certainly very few writers as sheerly ingenious as he is, or as able to cut out and put together the complex jigsaw-puzzle kind of story of which *Random Harvest* is so good an example. His storytelling capacity shows no sign of diminution and, for me, that's enough. (p. 60)

> Clifton Fadiman, "*Messrs. Hilton, Powys, Collier,*" in The New Yorker, *Vol. XVI, No. 50, January 25, 1941, pp. 60, 62.**

ROSE FELD (essay date 1941)

[*Feld was a Romanian-born American journalist and writer. In the following excerpt, she offers a largely positive review of* Random Harvest, *praising above all the characterization of the hero, Charles Rainier.*]

James Hilton has an enormous preoccupation with the past and the hidden, both in terms of civilization and of human beings. Wedded to that preoccupation is a masterly ability to create a mood in his writing which carries the reader along with him. Shangri-La became almost trite in its implications, so deeply did it attack the popular mind. Similarly the lovable Mr. Chips became a sentimental fixture in the hearts of all men and women who looked back into their childhood and youth with nostalgia.

Charles Rainier, the hero of *Random Harvest,* Hilton's new novel, will probably take his place with Mr. Chips and Hugh Conway. . . . For though he stands foursquare as an individual and a character, he is built of the same emotional texture that gave them distinction, that made them real, however they were touched by romantic unreality. Charles Rainier, brilliant English industrialist, lived with the torturing need of recapturing a period in his life that had vanished from his memory.

Between the time he had left Cambridge and entered the World War and the time he rediscovered himself as Charles Rainier on a bench in a Liverpool park in 1919 there was a dark corridor. The last thing he could remember on that fateful day in Liverpool was hearing and seeing a bomb shatter near him as he lay wounded in a field in France three years before. But who he was, what he had done, where he had been in the intervening time he did not know. Out of Rainier's effort to throw the light of knowledge upon this period Hilton weaves his strange tale. There are times in his telling when Hilton almost slips into the technique of the mystery thriller. . . .

It is in his portrayal of Rainier that Hilton is at his best. Rainier is no creature lost in dreams, no wraith seeking its bourne. He is an Englishman of solid worth, aware of his responsibilities as head of the family and head of the Rainier interests. His inclinations are scholarly; he would have preferred to continue his studies at Cambridge when he returned to the family at Stourton, but his brother's mismanagement of the Rainier works forced him to give that up. . . .

Because it would be unfair to Mr. Hilton to divulge the end, it is difficult to state what makes it unconvincing. But one can with clear conscience ask why Mrs. Rainier, knowing what she did, made no recorded effort to pierce the darkness of her husband's mind.

The book takes its title from garbled German reports of present-day events—"bombs fell at random." In telling the story of Rainier, Hilton tells the story of the consequences of wars in terms of human disaster. Just as Mr. Chips, just as Conway, Rainier is strongly and self-consciously English. Seemingly unemotional, he feels deeply the barbs of criticism thrown at England's imperialism. "A time may come," he says in bitter forecast, "when a cowed and brutalized world may look back on the period of English domination as one of the golden ages of history."

Random Harvest is, as a whole, so good a book that one forgets its minor flaws. It is Rainier who makes the tale and he is completely real and convincing.

> Rose Feld, "The New Novel by James Hilton," in The New York Times Book Review, *January 26, 1941, p. 4.*

ISABELLE MALLET   (essay date 1945)

[*In the following excerpt, Mallet reviews* So Well Remembered.]

James Hilton's gift as a raconteur has reached a pitch where he could if necessary tell an absorbing and expert story about almost nothing. He has now perfected a technique for keeping an everyday secret until it flowers into a full-blown enigma. He has evolved a smooth blend of worldly wisdom, charming simplicity and delightful ease with words which could conceivably carry the multiplication table to dramatic heights. But the moralist in Mr. Hilton demands that, however cunning the design of his embroidery, the material used must project its author's straightforward belief in human nature, his positive reverence for decency.

Thus he asks us to enter an enchanted circle where kindly decent motives are triumphant in the face of all that clever twists of plot can do to them. His favorite characters lose no whit of integrity through whatever misadventures arranged for them. They emerge as they began, sturdy, responsible and representative of the world Mr. Hilton believes in. It is a good world and we like it.

So Well Remembered, the latest charming, leisurely contribution to Hilton fans, has a pattern slightly reminiscent of *Random Harvest.* A puzzle is assembled before our eyes, lacking one missing piece which is sought with increasing tension throughout the book. In this case the missing link is the personality of a *femme fatale* named Livia. Livia is rendered fascinating by being kept at arm's length from the reader's understanding.

From the impression we have of her through a great part of the story, she seems to be one of the most likely feminine characters created by Mr. Hilton.

There are glimpses of her childhood, haunted and appealing; moments when she is a recognizable adolescent, diving into self-contemplation with haphazard fervor to emerge with a bit of bewildered perception. Later there are flashes of humor and a hint of originality. But as the author's artistry deepens the mystery about Livia, we begin to expect too much of her. By the time we have caught up with her total character, we are disappointed to discover that she is merely unbalanced, with predatory vampire habits which crop up too frequently in fiction nowadays. Still the pursuit of her personality has provided a great deal of entertainment.

And in the meantime, George, Livia's first husband, bears the brunt of his author's affection and ours. Here is the Hilton morality at its best. George is the kind of politician who might reasonably be expected to produce a formula for permanent peace. His integrity rings through some unbelievably good actions; his quiet common sense takes hold of his dialogue and our imaginations. He has an immaculate sanity which easily defeats the machinations of a contrived creature like Livia. Since the author allows his characters to act at a temperature of sentiment rather than emotion, we can never enter deeply into George's conflicts. But we like him. He is, like all Mr. Hilton's pleasant people, a very possible fellow.

Above characterization, and the clever manipulation of dialogue and plot, Mr. Hilton brings us the quiet spirit of a small English town. The descriptive atmosphere of his books is born of pure realization. A row of shabby houses on the wrong side of town, a quiet garden outside a cottage window, a sullen, wet, November day; he gives us the inner feel of these things. And his conception of England under threat of war and later under war itself is a nice core of integrity, believable and satisfying. This seems more durable than all the Maughamish goings-on of the principals in the drama.

> Isabelle Mallet, "Mr. Hilton's Cunning Embroidery," in The New York Times Book Review, *August 5, 1945, p. 5.*

FLORENCE HAXTON BULLOCK   (essay date 1947)

[*In the following excerpt, Bullock discusses* Nothing So Strange, *noting the more realistic nature of this novel as compared with Hilton's previous works and commending its moral and intellectual content as well as the interest of the mystery presented.*]

Consistently James Hilton has been on the side of the angels. In *Lost Horizon, Good-bye Mr. Chips, So Well Remembered,* he was engaged not merely in telling engrossingly good human stories but in bearing steadfast witness to his own faith in the lifting power, measured in spiritual foot-pounds of force, released by the life of a good man. These novels had in common also a strong, though progressively diminishing, mystic approach which—so great was Mr. Hilton's eagerness to beget in his readers some of his own compulsive sense of the potency of good in man's affairs—slipped over rather readily into that shortest, easiest way into the popular heart, frank sentimentality. But as Mr. Hilton has matured as a novelist he has accepted the fact that the battle against Lucifer cannot by any trickery be won in a single blow—or a single novel. So that now, in *Nothing So Strange,* he is prepared to confront reality without benefit of any tempering rosy glow, and to let truth—his novelist's sense of truth—speak for itself.

The story told in *Nothing So Strange* has its beginning in 1936 in a well-set-up pre-war London house, and its ending on an emergency landing field in the California desert on the day the atom bomb was dropped on Hiroshima. And in the mean time, consonant with the mobility of its time and spirit, it moves from London to a laboratory in Vienna, to Prague, to an F.B.I. office in New York City, to Washington, to Oak Ridge, Tenn., and to Hollywood. So warmly and artfully has Mr. Hilton built his story, so skilfully has he made use of interesting character and tense suspense . . . that *Nothing So Strange,* in spite of its serious moral and intellectual intent, has all the dynamic interest of one of the better imagined, better written mystery stories.

Nothing So Strange—the title is drawn from Daniel Webster's "There is nothing so powerful as truth—and often nothing so strange"—tells the story of two exceptionally able, modern young people, both Americans: of Dr. Mark Bradley, originally a North Dakota boy, who both as a scientist and as a man faced some of the biggest problems of our time, and of Jane Waring, an immensely intelligent and attractive young woman whose path crossed and recrossed Bradley's in an ever deepening spiral, to the true and permanent advantage of them both. . . .

Mr. Hilton's conviction of the importance of science and of the responsibility of the scientist to the world dominates his book. A scientist is his mouthpiece:

> They never invite us to use the scientific method plus unlimited funds on the general problems of world affairs or the organization of society. . . . Yet you can't exaggerate the mess we're in—a technological crisis bringing to a head the moral crisis we've shirked for centuries. . . . Atomic energy is such a big thing it's the curse of Cain that we should be thinking first of bombs. It could make heaven and earth if we'd only let it—if only we'd use it for peace with a tenth of the energy we've worked on it for war. And there's where research comes in—open research inside a framework of free science. So far as I'm concerned, free science is the fifth freedom, and if we don't get it back and hang onto it, then count me out of science altogether—I'd rather go fishing for the little time that's left.

And a little later:

> The future's not a club you can resign from! It's part of the whole world's problem, and, as you say, we've shirked it for centuries. But now we've got to stop shirking it, and in that fight count me in.

Mr. Hilton has made the long trip back from Shangri-la to take his manful place in this crisis among the responsible citizens of the world. And *Nothing So Strange* is a man-sized job.

> Florence Haxton Bullock, "Truth Escapes the Laboratory," in New York Herald Tribune Weekly Book Review, *October 19, 1947, p. 4.*

JOHN BARKHAM   (essay date 1953)

[*In the following excerpt, Barkham offers a positive review of* Time and Time Again, *commending the authentic characterization of the English diplomat who is the hero of this novel.*]

Mr. Hilton has long since attained that plateau of success where readers take it for granted that all his books will be good. The fact is that *Time and Time Again* is better than that: it is the most thoughtful novel he has written in years. It is an expertly crafted, well-proportioned study of an English diplomat which gets deep enough beneath that icy aplomb to expose the human being behind it. Anderson becomes so authentic a character in the reader's mind that one tends to forget that he is only a figment of the author's imagination. Usually an English diplomat is a two-dimensional figure—all appearance and behavior. Mr. Hilton's feat lies in having explained the motivation as well.

Anderson will no doubt be compared with H. M. Pulham, Esq., and in truth the portraits have much in common in their dissection of an aloof patrician. The reader has the same feeling that he is watching the author peel layer after layer off his character's epidermis till the true man stands revealed. . . .

Charles Anderson has seen his beloved Britain buffeted by the winds of war and unexpected penury. With no stardust in his eyes, he says: "Perhaps we shall solve the trick of all tricks for this millennium—how to stop down without falling backward, and then how to build a new must be on the foundations of the old has-been." No Briton could hope to sum up the facts of his country's future more succinctly.

The book offers many such felicities. The reader will find himself gripped from the opening by Mr. Hilton's fluent narrative and mature understanding. Yet in the last resort this book belongs to Charles Anderson, a man to remember, if only for his wartime crack about Winston Churchill: "I wouldn't let him get into uniform, to requiescat in khaki."

> John Barkham, "Mr. Anderson, British Diplomat," in The New York Times Book Review, *August 23, 1953, p. 4.*

HAROLD C. MARTIN   (essay date 1962)

[*Martin is an American educator and critic. In the following excerpt, he discusses themes and characters in* Lost Horizon.]

During World War II, when President Franklin Roosevelt needed a quiet place away from Washington in which to think and relax, he selected a cottage in the hills of Maryland and named it *Shangri-La*. The name he chose came from [*Lost Horizon*], and by the time he chose it the name needed no explanation to Americans. Millions of them had read *Lost Horizon,* as millions have done since, and the name had become a synonym for peace and reflection and a synonym as well for the hope of a world free from war.

Lost Horizon is a romance—not a love-story (though it contains one briefly) but the story of an ideal world. To such stories we commonly give the name "Utopia," after a book written in 1516 by Sir Thomas More. The name comes from the Greek *ou,* meaning "no" and *topos* meaning "place." It is therefore, by definition, no place that has ever existed. At the same time, it represents the world as men have dreamed it should be or might become if wise men realized their wishes. As a Utopia, then, *Lost Horizon* is part of a great tradition in world literature. . . . (p. vii)

[When James Hilton began to write *Lost Horizon*, he] was primarily interested in telling a story. Yet it is clear from the story itself that the two impulses that produce utopias—discontent with the present and hope for a better future—lie at the heart of his novel. Born in 1900, Hilton was old enough by the time of the First World War to understand that the invention of the airplane had made world-wide destruction possible. It is true that he did not foresee, as H. G. Wells did, the fullest possibilities of aerial warfare, but he saw enough to be sure that the future held great danger to all mankind. Before he was thirty, Hilton was also fully aware of the fact that the relatively stable economic and social structure of the England he knew as a boy and as a young man at Oxford was falling apart. The Wall Street Crash of 1929, which toppled governments and shook the financial foundations of all Europe, and the Great Depression that followed were events of immediate concern to him, events he must have studied with growing apprehension in his years as a journalist. So, too, was the revolutionary activity in India, long England's most important colony and a great reservoir of its overseas wealth. To a man of Hilton's tastes and turn of mind, these events must have seemed not only dreadful in themselves but a threat to the way of life he most cherished. (pp. ix-x)

Looking back on the sensational success of *Lost Horizon*, a reader can see readily enough why it became at once so popular. In the first place, it deals with a matter uppermost in men's minds, the dire possibility of another war foreshadowed by the turbulent political activity apparent throughout the world. In the second, it offers the easiest way of putting the thought of war out of mind, a dream of escape. To be sure, the dream is fantastic, but dreams often are, and readers weary of the hard

Typescript, with Hilton's revisions, of Lost Horizon.

struggle to make a living in the depression-harried world must have found in it a sense of the peace and stability so lacking in their own lives. Moreover, while Hilton may not be a great writer, he has a knack for making a story move. He draws his characters swiftly and with considerable humor. He knows how to exploit the mysterious and how to keep a story taut with tension by placing clues adroitly with his left hand while the right goes on with the central narrative. Finally, in his hero he has managed to incorporate virtues dear to the English, and to a lesser extent to the American, mind. Conway is brave before danger, cool in emergency, but so unassuming and laconic in ordinary affairs that a rash observer, like his impetuous young friend Mallinson, even thinks him cowardly. In those characteristics, he is very like the soft-spoken, gun-toting deputy sheriff of our Westerns. But he is also cultivated and gentlemanly like the ideal of the liberally educated man; and like all romantic heroes he is handsome and daring.

What distinguishes Conway from the ordinary Englishman and American are two characteristics, and they distinguish him as well from his traveling companions. He believes that duty and self-denial are overrated virtues, and he neither admires work for its own sake nor cares about the possessions that are the fruit of work. He travels light, accepts what he cannot alter, is content with less than perfection. These characteristics are essential to the story, for they set Conway off from the main emphasis and direction of Western culture for the past thousand years, and it is for that reason, as well as for reasons of geography, that the utopian land of *Lost Horizon* is located in the fastnesses of Tibet.

You will want to keep two questions in mind as you read *Lost Horizon*. How much is fantastic and how much is real? To put it another way, how much are we expected to take seriously in this tale of a never-never-land? The second question is related to the first: how much is the author himself convinced of the worth of the ideal world he creates?

The answer to the first question requires that the reader make large allowance for the nature of fiction at the outset. To use the words of Coleridge, all fiction demands that we temporarily suspend our disbelief, that we agree to accept for the duration of the story whatever extraordinary situation or events the author chooses for his starting point. Hilton has taken care in this novel to persuade us to accept his premises. The story itself is "boxed" between a Prologue and an Epilogue which not only attach the central plot to everyday reality but insist, by the inconclusive fate of the hero, both on the possibility and the mysterious attractiveness of life at Shangri-La. The first chapters of the story proper are, moreover, calculated to reassure us that it is real and possible. In a sense, we fly with the quartet of Westerners from the hard realities of Europe into the misty wonders of the East and, with them, gradually consent to the unlikely and the fantastic. The heterogeneous foursome also keep us in touch with the world we are sure of. Three of them are like people we know, and their characteristics are those we can readily find in ourselves if we look. The fourth, our hero, is no more alien, for he mirrors what we can at least dream ourselves to be. The utopia itself will raise questions each reader must answer according to his tastes and beliefs. Is this a place of wisdom and strength or, instead, as Mallinson insists, an "unhealthy and unclean" society of "awful creatures"? Is the principle of life at Shangri-La, or is it not, one that has meaning even for men's dreams?

The second question, that about the author's commitment to his own utopia, is a matter of the art of the story. When John

Dryden took Shakespeare's play about the great love of Anthony and Cleopatra as the theme for a play of his own, he entitled it, *All for Love, or The World Well Lost.* Is Conway's decision about the future of the world *versus* youth and love in the last chapter really the author's way of rejecting the utopia he has created? Or is it, perhaps, only his way of saying that men are not yet ready for such wisdom, that every man is, like Conway "a wanderer between two worlds, and must ever wander; doomed . . . to flee from wisdom and be a hero"? (pp. xi-xiii)

> *Harold C. Martin, "The Road to Shangri-La," in* Lost Horizon *by James Hilton, Houghton Mifflin, 1962, pp. vii-xiii.*

SAMUEL IRVING BELLMAN (essay date 1973)

[*Bellman is an American critic and educator. In the following excerpt from his essay "The Apocalypse in Literature," Bellman uses an episode from* Good-bye, Mr. Chips *to illustrate a "subtle type of apocalypse."*]

The word *apocalypse* means revelation, disclosure, discovery . . . in short, a remarkable and in a sense unlooked-for divulgence of information that was formerly kept hidden, or at least was not made available to the curious. *There is a prophetic and shockingly unfamiliar quality to a real apocalypse.* In order to feel a genuine apocalyptic effect, the beholder cannot have been prepared in any way, through cumulative foreshadowings or conscious anticipation. Functionally, the experience should be unsettling and it should have a profound influence of some sort on the beholder's subsequent view of his surroundings and his life-course. (p. 13)

A . . . subtle type of apocalypse—. . . submerged in a deceptively simple setting—is to be found in James Hilton's story of a kindly teacher named Chipping at a fashionable English public school in the later nineteenth century and early twentieth century. Familiar to millions of readers and movie viewers who have seen two excellent film versions of the story, *Mr. Chips* for all his fitting in so harmoniously at Brookfield is essentially a solitary figure who lives on the periphery of society. Even his lighthearted remark about his actually having had children (despite his childlessness)—thousands of children, all boys—cannot disguise the privation and muted sadness that characterize his life. Once, at the end of the 1890's, after he had married a charming woman young enough to be his daughter, there was a chance for the kind of deep bliss that is accorded few men. But this opportunity is dashed in a matter of minutes, when his wife dies in childbirth, together with her baby. The scene is perhaps the most memorable scene in the entire story. However, a certain feature of the scene may easily escape the reader's or viewer's notice.

The day is April 1, 1898: April Fool's Day, and Chips has just learned that his wife and baby have died. Hardly able to cope with the disaster, he stumbles somehow through Brookfield village on his way to his fourth-form grammar class. For a moment he is detained by a student who asks for the afternoon off. Thus Chips is a little late, and as he walks into the classroom, overcome with grief, his mind is in a fog. Before his arrival, the waiting boys have decided to play an April Fool's joke on their teacher. They place a pile of envelopes on his desk, each envelope carefully addressed to him, but containing only a blank sheet of paper. As Chips tries, distractedly, to begin the grammar lesson, one of the boys calls his attention to the mail on his desk. He opens the envelopes, and the boys'

laughter fills the room. Chips does not seem to understand that the blank sheets represent a schoolboy prank, and is even more dazed than he was when he entered. More loud laughter. A perfect April Fool's stunt. (The movie versions, admittedly, treated this scene more dramatically, and consequently with far greater effectiveness, than did Mr. Hilton himself. For some reason, his handling of the situation was really too low-keyed to give it the intensity it deserved.)

Hilton's description of Chips's reaction is stark, simple, and ultimately quite deceptive: Chips "thought in a distant way that it was rather peculiar, but he made no comment; the incident gave hardly an impact upon his vastly greater preoccupations. Not till days afterward did he realize that it had been a piece of April foolery." On the surface, this seemingly innocuous if bitterly ironic episode shows us that *Chips was not being communicated with . . . by his pupils.* Their one statement to him was, in effect, a very cheeky "April Fool!" And Chips did not even realize that this was being said to him, through the blank envelopes. More importantly, however, those same messageless letters represent another broken communication. In a sense they serve as a kind of objective correlative for his wife's and baby's being out of touch with Chips from this moment onward . . . but (through a process of literary displacement) being linked for the last time with him by the most tenuous tie: blank sheets of writing paper.

It is not enough though, to say that those blank sheets contain the formula of that particular action. There is a radical difference between what Hilton (perhaps unconsciously) is suggesting and the *attempted,* forceful but quite ineffective communication with the Unseen that we find in the popular song of the early twentieth century, "Hello Central, Give Me Heaven" ("'Cause my daddy's there") . . . or that we find in Walt Whitman's "Song of Myself": Walt guesses that the grass "is the handkerchief of the Lord, / A scented gift and remembrancer designedly dropt, / Bearing the owner's name someway in the corners, that we may see and remark, and say *Whose?*"

Dramatically, literarily, the blank sheets were *no* coincidence. Two planes of existence, the *seen* and the *lost-and-hence-never-again visible,* touch, if only for a fleeting instant. And because they touch, so maddeningly, for that all too brief interval, the sensitive reader may be given a mere glimpse of the ultimate horror of human estrangement. Unless there is this apocalyptic glimpse on the part of the reader, 'the incident will give hardly an impact on his vastly greater preoccupations,' and he will wonder, if he wonders at all, only why the schoolboys had not written "April Fool!" on the papers. . . . (pp. 23-5)

> *Samuel Irving Bellman, "The Apocalypse in Literature," in* Costerus, *Vol. 7, 1973, pp. 13-25.**

JOHN W. CRAWFORD (essay date 1981)

[*Crawford is an American poet, critic, and educator. In the following excerpt from his essay on "The Utopian Dream," Crawford discusses* Lost Horizon *as an example of humanity's dream of a perfect world.*]

World War I, followed by world-wide depression, caused a melancholy mood in the West. The tremendous spirit of optimism inherited from the Victorian era suffered its greatest jolt from these two closely related events. As one writer comments in retrospect, "Just as the whole world is accepting it, Western civilization begins to totter. The World War was more than a gesture toward suicide; and the present economic debacle is no accidental or transient crisis; it is the culminative collapse of competitive capitalism. . . . The old sureties in religion and morals and goals of life are crumbling.''

This is, of course, not a new sound in the Western world social order. John Donne's ''All Coherence Gone'' sums up quite well the attitude of the seventeenth-century thinker in the wake of apparent social disorder, and Matthew Arnold's poetic comment that late Victorians are ''living between two worlds / one dead, the other powerless to be born'' suggests the dilemma of the changing order of the nineteenth. And as in all such crises, there is a frantic search for security. Often that security is found in another order, usually a primitive one immune to the decay of the present scene, in fact, another Eden. For the early twentieth century, this Eden is the East.

Just as eighteenth-century England became enamored of Orientalism, so does the twentieth-century Englishman begin seeing man's hope resting in the isolated, primitive setting of marble palaces, running streams, flowing fountains, and afternoon teas in shady bowers—a virtual Edenic Shangri-La. (pp. 186-87)

[In *Lost Horizon*] Hilton uses a journey as the vehicle for his story. The journey is that of ''Glory'' Conway, suave diplomat, adventurer, and patriot, who, with others, is kidnapped to Shangri-La, a lamasery in unexplored Tibet, which bears many striking resemblances to the utopia of Eden. The story is not relayed by Conway, however, but by Rutherford, a friend who has experienced his own journey searching for Conway but has been unsuccessful in bringing him back to England.

The vanguard of Shangri-La is a cone-shaped, snowcapped mountain, standing higher than all the rest. Its perfection is in direct contrast to the wild, rugged, uncontrolled terrain which surrounds the valley for thousands of miles in every direction. Conway thinks of the mountain as a lighthouse. . . . The valley is very isolated and is reached either by aid of the valley people, or by accident, by those just on the point of death. If Eden was guarded by its immortal angel, Shangri-La is guarded almost as effectively by the ageless rocky crags, snow, and strong wind of the Tibetan plateau.

The valley is ''an enclosed paradise of amazing fertility.'' . . . An abundance of vegetation and water are to be found, along with almost unlimited time for rest and freedom to pursue whatever task is meaningful to the individual. The very highest attainments in all fields are possible. Besides meeting the basic needs, the most exquisite things are to be found here—from collections of art, to music, to knowledge, to religion. The whole illustrates a balance and rarity so fragile that it could be easily destroyed at any time by those who do not understand or appreciate its worth. ''Beauty,'' says Conway, ''lies at the mercy of those who do not know how to value it. It is a fragile thing that can only live where fragile things are loved.'' . . . And over all is Karakal, the mountain of the Blue Moon, whose massive force could some day fill the valley and destroy everything, adding to the outside threat of perverted humanity.

The dominant belief among the people is that of moderation or balance in all things, avoiding every kind of excess or stress. ''Including, if you will pardon the paradox, excess of virtue itself,'' comments Chang, Conway's guide in Shangri-La. The lamas are, characteristically, moderate even in pursuit of their individual tasks, as there are no time pressures. If each of the lamas has a purpose in life, so does the lamasery as a whole: in effect, to be a sanctuary for all the treasures of civilization, so that when war has destroyed all, man can ''seek its lost and

legendary treasures. And they will all be here, hidden in the valley of the Blue Moon, preserved as by a miracle for a new Renaissance. . . .'' (pp. 188-89)

The High Lama is the highest wisdom, next to God, in the valley. Although he is considered a legend by the valley people, and capable of miracles, the Lama himself knows very well his weaknesses and his mortality. It is interesting that the same kind of misunderstanding is also applied to Conway, who is considered both a hero and a coward at various times and knows himself to be neither. Conway is so in sympathy with the concepts of the valley, that for him ''the name Blue Moon took on a symbolic meaning, as if the future, so delicately plausible were of a kind that might happen once in a blue moon only.'' . . . (p. 189)

But if Eden had its serpent, its outside evil influence, Shangri-La also has its element of discontent. It comes in the form of Mallinson, the deputy counsel. While the others see beauty in the valley and want to stay, Mallinson sees only filth and evil. He sees the lamas as ''wizened old men crouching like spiders for anyone who comes near.'' . . . His distrust causes Conway to ''fall,'' that is, to leave Shangri-La. This is not because of ambition on Conway's part, but because he feels that he must protect Mallinson from the rigors of the mountain and guide him back to the outside world where he can be happy. Of the ones who leave Shangri-La, only Conway survives, and only he with great physical difficulty. As soon as he is able, he does everything he can to regain his lost paradise, his Eden. It is theoretically possible for man to reenter Shangri-La, although the journey is extremely difficult and few survive. Conway is willing to give up everything, even his life, in order to attempt the recovery.

Hilton's purpose in *Lost Horizon* is very similar to that of H. G. Wells in much of his future-oriented writing. Wells had lived through World War I as had Hilton, and both had seen the devastation not only to England, but to mankind all over the European world. The useless bloodshed and horror and the unchangeableness of man's thirst for war led Wells and Hilton both to make predictions regarding the possibility of another great war. Although Wells's *Men Like Gods* and Hilton's *Lost Horizon* take different approaches to the same problem, they both seek a similar Eden of bliss. In Wells's story we find the Samurai have become self-reliant, noble supermen-leaders through education, the ''food'' of the gods. In Hilton's story, the lamas have achieved mastery through dedication to moderation, a recurring eighteenth-century Rasselassian idea, a scientific approach in its attention to following the laws of nature. Both writers believed that man could look at the future scientifically. Wells expresses this effectively in *The Discovery of the Future:*

> All applied mathematics resolves into computation to foretell things which otherwise can only be determined by trial. Even in so unscientific a science as economics there have been forecasts. And if I am right in saying that science aims at prophecy, and if the specialist in each science is in fact doing his best now to prophecy within the limits of his field, what is there to stand in the way of our building up this body of forecast into an ordered picture of the future that will be just as certain, just as strictly science, and perhaps just as detailed as the picture that has been built up within the last hundred years of the geological past?

There are obvious differences between Eden and Shangri-La. The settings, although very similar, are of a separate place and time. Eden is certainly more primitive in its appeal, while Shangri-La takes into account the sophistication and complexities of the modern world and its people. In effect, it has built, in Wells's words, the forecast of the future into an ordered picture which man wants to hold tenaciously to.

Even though all this is true, both Edenic utopias go back to the basic needs of men. In their separate ways they provide both the basic stuff of life, and the satisfaction of the highest longings. Both utopias are literally unattainable; they are dreams that "dissolve like all too lovely things, at the first touch of reality." . . . But in their wake, they leave a feeling of hope, so that man is never entirely destitute. He is free to strive, and this alone helps to give meaning to life. (pp. 189-90)

> *John W. Crawford, "Utopian Eden of 'Lost Horizon'," in* Extrapolation, *Vol. 22, No. 2, Summer, 1981, pp. 186-90.*

ADDITIONAL BIBLIOGRAPHY

Lowry, Malcolm. "The Real Mr. Chips." *Malcolm Lowry Newsletter* XI (Fall 1982): 7-10.

> Compares and contrasts Mr. Chips, the character, with "the Hooley," one of Hilton's masters at The Leys, Cambridge. According to Lowry, "the facts relating the Hooley to Mr. Chips either directly or by implication are too many to be accidental."

Matthews, T. S. "Three Professionals." *The New Republic* LXXXX, No. 1163 (17 March 1937): 173-74.*

> Summarizes the plot of *We Are Not Alone*, describing the novel as "a pathetic mess rather than a tragedy." Matthews states, "If you are part of the bull's eye he was aiming for, you will be reduced to tears. But there won't be many of you—not nearly so many of you as smiled bravely with swimming eyes over *Mr. Chips*."

Mott, Frank Luther. "Books of the New Era." In his *Golden Multitudes: The Story of Best Sellers in the United States*, pp. 279-85. New York: The Macmillan Co., 1947.*

> Discusses the success of four best-selling Hilton novels—*Good-bye, Mr. Chips, Lost Horizon, We Are Not Alone,* and *Random Harvest*.

"Russia's Civil War." *New York Times Book Review* (11 March 1934): 24.

> Surveys several of Hilton's novels, focussing primarily on *Knight without Armour*. Comparing this novel unfavorably with *Between Red and White* by Erich Dwinger, the critic describes *Knight without Armour* as "an unimportant but entertaining novel of adventure set amidst Russia's civil war."

Pritchett, V. S. Review of *Contango*. *The New Statesman and Nation* n. s. IV, No. 80 (3 September 1932): 262-3.

> Appraises *Contango* as "on the whole, an interesting, exciting and varied book, with some ideas and many entertaining notions." However, Pritchett also points out that the many loosely-related episodes cause the novel to be incohesive.

Sibley, Carrol. "James Hilton." In his *Barrie and His Contemporaries: Cameo Portraits of Ten Living Authors*, pp. 38-43. Missouri: International Mark Twain Society, 1936.

> Interviews Hilton regarding such topics as *Good-bye, Mr. Chips*, Hilton's work in progress, and the possibility of his visiting the United States. About Hilton, Sibley comments, "I somehow knew that the man who gave to the world the lovable Mr. Chips, could hardly be less engaging himself. For that delicate sensitivity of *Lost Horizon*, and indeed of every book he's ever written, was too sincere, too intimately personal, to have come from anyone who wasn't himself eminently, and above all, a human being."

Stevens, George. Chapter Six. In his *Lincoln's Doctor's Dog and Other Famous Best Sellers*, pp. 38-42. Philadelphia: J. B. Lippincott Co., 1938.*

> Discusses the effect of publicity on the sale of books, relating the sales history of *Lost Horizon*, a novel which was enthusiastically recommended by Alexander Woollcott on a radio show about a year after its original publication. Stevens points out that this publicity resulted in the greatly increased sales of *Lost Horizon*.

Review of *The Passionate Year*, by James Hilton. *The Times Literary Supplement*, No. 1142 (6 December 1923): 853.

> Summarizes the plot of *The Passionate Year* and offers a mixed review of the novel. The critic states, "Though the story may fairly be called extravagant, the emotions over-wrought, and the style verbose, that is not all that should be said of it by any means. There is a true feeling for character in the descriptions of its persons, a sense of atmosphere about all the scenes in which they take part."

Weeks, Edward. Foreword to *Good-bye, Mr. Chips*, by James Hilton. pp. v-viii. Boston: Little, Brown and Co., 1962.

> Editor of the *Atlantic Monthly* reminisces about his acquaintance with Hilton, recounts the public response to *Good-bye, Mr. Chips*, and comments on the characterization of Mr. Chips. According to Weeks, "Everywhere you went you heard people talk as if [Mr. Chips] were someone they had known."

Julia Ward Howe

1819-1910

American poet, dramatist, biographer, autobiographer, and essayist.

Howe is best remembered as the author of "The Battle Hymn of the Republic," one of the most memorable and enduring martial lyrics ever composed. She was also a social activist who contributed her time, the efforts of her pen, and her skills as an orator to the causes of abolition, black suffrage and enfranchisement, and women's rights. Although Howe published several volumes of poetry, mostly on topical themes, and contributed many essays to the periodical press supporting her various causes, she was most widely known throughout her lifetime for the single work which for millions has come to convey the righteousness of the Northern cause during the American Civil War.

Howe was born in New York City to the wealthy and socially prominent banker Samuel Ward and his wife. She attended a private "school for young ladies" for seven years, learning primarily social skills, and at sixteen abandoned formal schooling for private tutoring in a wide variety of fields, especially music and languages. A popular belle, Howe was noted for a degree of seriousness and intellectualism uncommon in a young woman of her age and social class. At twenty-three she met and married the eminent doctor, social reformer, and educator Samuel Gridley Howe, a man eighteen years her senior. Dr. Howe was a dashing and romantic figure: a hero of the Greek Revolution, he had assumed directorship of Boston's Perkins Institute for the Blind and had formulated landmark reform measures in the care, treatment, and education of the blind, deaf, and mentally ill.

From early childhood Julia Ward Howe had possessed a predilection for composing verses. During the early years of her marriage she was left alone much of the time by the active and outgoing Dr. Howe, who did not approve of married women functioning in public or professional areas. Further housebound by frequent pregnancies, she began writing poetry again with the idea of submitting it for publication. A selection of these poems was edited by James T. Fields for anonymous publication under the title *Passion Flowers*. Julia kept the knowledge of the forthcoming book from her husband, but the author's identity was generally known before the book appeared for sale. Dr. Howe was furious, the more so when it was laughingly hinted that the poem "Mind Versus Mill-Stream"—about a miller unable to dam a freely-flowing stream, actually a parable about a man unable to control a willful wife—was a comment on his own marriage. At this time, according to papers found by Julia after his death, Howe took a mistress. He also began to press for a separation or divorce from Julia, but one of his conditions was that he be given their oldest daughter and son to raise alone, and Julia would not consent to this. Despite the many discordances between the Howes, they remained married—though often traveling, and sometimes living, apart. According to most major biographers, when Dr. Howe entered into a decline in health that led to his death in 1876, the couple drew together in a new-found closeness, discussing and resolving many of their past differences and spending at least a few years in concord.

In 1854 and 1855 Dr. Howe was becoming increasingly involved in the abolitionist cause, and Julia, publishing poetry anonymously in the *Atlantic Monthly* under the editorship of James Russell Lowell, drew many of her themes from the antislavery movement. The Civil War furnished her with martial themes for her verses, including the most famous product of her pen, "The Battle Hymn of the Republic," which was composed as an indirect result of her husband's involvement with the war effort. Anxious to contribute to the Union cause, Dr. Howe had been instrumental in identifying the need for and helping to form the "sanitary commission" to establish and maintain hygienic conditions in field hospitals and military camps. This organization—the forerunner of the American Red Cross—was at first viewed askance by military and political factions alike; even President Lincoln believed such long-range planning unnecessary for what was expected to be a short-term dispute. However, the reality of war conditions soon demonstrated the need for the sanitary commission, and the group began to receive financial support from the government. In his capacity as an organizer of the commission, Dr. Howe was invited to visit military installations in and around Washington, D.C., in 1861. At this time the war was still perceived somewhat romantically and unrealistically, with officers' families visiting encampments very near the front in what was almost a picnic atmosphere. In fact, Julia Ward Howe accompanied her husband to the Capitol and was permitted to ride out and witness reviews of battle-ready Union troops. On November 18, Julia was one of a horde of sightseers whose pastoral ideas of warfare were jolted when, during a review at Munson's Hill, Virginia, the troops suddenly had to be mobilized to meet a nearby attack. During the long trek by carriage back to Washington, Julia and her companions sang patriotic and martial songs to pass the time, and an acquaintance suggested that she write some new words to the stirring tune of "John Brown's Body." According to the often-repeated story, she awoke before dawn the next day and wrote the "Battle Hymn" without hesitation, returning to bed with a feeling of great accomplishment. The untitled lyric was submitted to Lowell at the *Atlantic Monthly*, who named the work and reportedly paid her some four or five dollars for it.

Throughout the years of the Civil War and after, Howe continued to pursue her literary ambitions, publishing essays as well as poetry in various periodicals. While her contributions nearly always appeared anonymously, her identity as the author of a growing number of essays and verses on religious, moral, ethical, and political themes was well known within the Howes' closely knit, upper-class circle of Boston intellectuals. As her children approached adulthood and Howe was left with more free time, she became interested in another outlet for her social and intellectual needs: women's clubs. Although the activities of the women's groups that she joined or helped to organize were often limited to such traditional concerns as bandage-rolling, sewing hospital garments, or holding charity bazaars, Howe witnessed a level of competence and professionalism in herself and in the women of her acquaintance that led her to object to discrepancies in the treatment of women and men under existing laws. Many women's groups had worked toward the cause of black enfranchisement; that battle won, they began to agitate for voting rights for women. Howe's involvement with women's groups led her to a new phase in her career and to the area in which she made her most enduring mark. Persuaded to address a suffrage meeting, she discovered a talent for forceful, convincing public speaking. Howe quickly became a much sought-after lecturer, noted for skillfully combining conventionally accepted truisms, Biblical teaching, her knowledge of trends in philosophical thought, and a quick wit to argue persuasively for women's rights. Public speaking occupied Howe for most of the latter part of her life. She was a regular fixture on the platforms of public meetings well into her eighties, traveling widely in the United States and in England, lecturing on women's rights and often establishing women's clubs in the cities she visited. During her husband's lifetime Howe had acquiesced to his wish that she not accept payment for her public appearances; however, after his death she began to ask a lecture fee and it was largely through her earnings as a speaker that she supported her household thereafter.

In the few critical considerations of Howe as a writer, commentators have found that in all of her works—poetry, essays, and lectures—her appeal was largely to the emotions rather than the intellect. Her early poetry has been especially noted for such elements as religious sentiment, moral tone, and lyricism. "The art is subordinate to the feeling," wrote an early anonymous reviewer who found the "artistic inaccuracies" of the poems secondary to "the ability, the earnestness, and the intensity of the writer." Howe biographer Deborah Pickman Clifford has noted that while it was the responses and encouragement from established poets that most heartened Howe following the publication of *Passion Flowers*, even such friends

as Ralph Waldo Emerson "refrained from commenting at all on her poetic powers, preferring rather to emphasize the insight the verses gave into her inmost thoughts and feelings. The fact is that except for a few intense poems which touch on then-forbidden subjects, there is little true poetry in *Passion Flowers*."

"The Battle Hymn of the Republic" remains Howe's only work to have received much comment, although it is primarily the "miraculous" nature of the lyrics' inception and its emotional appeal that are most often discussed. According to Edward D. Snyder, the predawn composition of "this masterpiece among all Civil War poems" was an "apparently unprepared stroke of genius." Snyder cites Howe's knowledge of the Bible and her conviction of the justice of the Northern cause as the elements that enabled her to spontaneously create the memorable lyric. Snyder notes that Howe drew specifically from references in the prophetic books of the Old Testament and in the Book of Revelation to the "Day of Jehovah," a Hebrew day of vengeance and purification similar to that which Howe believed would be visited upon the United States with the inevitable triumph of the Union army. The "Battle Hymn" closely resembled the language and imagery of many Biblical passages. Edmund Wilson has also noted the parallels to Biblical imagery in the lyric, but stresses Howe's equation of the righteousness of the Northern cause with the Calvinist doctrines of determinism and predestination. Although some modern commentators have come to deplore and regret the aggressive tone of the "Battle Hymn" and its glorification of warfare, it remains the pinnacle of Howe's career and a stirring reminder of nationalistic fervor and popular sentiment during the American Civil War.

(See also *Contemporary Authors*, Vol. 117 and *Dictionary of Literary Biography*, Vol. 1: *The American Renaissance in New England*.)

PRINCIPAL WORKS

Passion Flowers (poetry) 1854
Words for the Hour (poetry) 1857
The World's Own (drama) 1857
"The Battle Hymn of the Republic" (poetry) 1862;
    published in journal *The Atlantic Monthly*
Later Lyrics (poetry) 1866
Memoir of Dr. Samuel Gridley Howe (biography) 1876
Margaret Fuller (biography) 1883
Is Polite Society Polite? (essays) 1895
From Sunset Ridge (poetry) 1898
Reminiscences (autobiography) 1899
*Hippolytus (drama) 1911
Julia Ward Howe and the Woman Suffrage Movement
    (speeches and essays) 1913

*This work was written in the 1850s.

JOHN GREENLEAF WHITTIER (essay date 1853)

[*Whittier was a noted American poet, essayist, and editor. Most widely known in his own time for his antislavery poetry and abolitionist essays and tracts, he is best remembered for such nostalgic pastoral poetry as "Snow-bound: A Winter Idyl" (1866). In the following excerpt Whittier, a longtime acquaintance of*

Howe, writes to acknowledge receipt of her first volume of poetry, Passion Flowers.]

My Dear Fd.—

A thousand thanks for thy volume! I rec'd it some days ago, but was too ill to read it. I glanced at **"Rome," "Newport and Rome,"** and they excited me like a war-trumpet. To-day, with the wild storm drifting without, my sister and I have been busy with thy book, basking in the warm atmosphere of its flowers of passion. It is a great book—it has placed thee at the head of us all. I like its noble aims, its scorn and hate of priestcraft and Slavery. It speaks out bravely, beautifully all I have *felt*, but could not express, when contemplating the condition of Europe. God bless thee for it! . . .

I wish I *could* tell thee how glad thy volume has made me. I have marked it all over with notes of admiration. I dare say it has faults enough, but thee need not fear on that account. It had beauty enough to save thy "slender neck" from the axe of the critical headsman. The veriest "de'il"—as Burns says— "wad look into thy face and swear he could na wrang thee."

> *John Greenleaf Whittier, in a letter to Julia Ward Howe on December 29, 1853, in his* The Letters of John Greenleaf Whittier: 1846-1860, Vol. II, *edited by John B. Pickard, Cambridge, Mass.: The Belknap Press of Harvard University Press, 1975, p. 246.*

THE KNICKERBOCKER (essay date 1854)

[*The following excerpt is taken from an early anonymous review of Howe's first poetry collection,* Passion Flowers. *The critic praises the originality and high order of lyricism in Howe's work, comparing Howe favorably with Elizabeth Barrett Browning.*]

Macaulay tells a story of an Italian convict, who was allowed to take his choice of punishments—to read [Italian historian Francesco] Guiccardini or go to the galleys. At first, he chose the former, but the *History of Pisa* was too much for him, and he cried out to be taken to the docks. Something of the feeling which this much-enduring man must have had toward Guiccardini comes over us when we see a book—splendid in blue muslin or crimson morocco, perhaps—lettered on the back, "Female Poets of America." So many maidenly and matronly platitudes; so much second-hand finery; so much general prettiness and insipidity of thought, go to make up a book with that name, that we instinctively avoid it. For in spite of the many single poems of great beauty which American women have written, hardly any of our countrywomen, as yet, have shown a good title to the sacred name of poet. (p. 353)

It would seem as if poetry were specially adapted to the nature of woman. Her fine soul, trembling alive to all harmony, and catching at those vanishing, unattainable beauties of sound which are apt to escape the ruder ear of man, fits her well for the form, at least, of poetry; while the sea of affection in her heart, when stirred by the strong blasts of passion that sweep over it, ought to find voice, one would think, in true poetical utterances. What poems in themselves are the lives of many women, perhaps of most! And yet, since the days of Sappho, of whom every body talks and few know any thing, how few have been the really great female poets! The very greatest, to our mind, who has ever lived, ennobles our age by her life: the loving wife of one who is himself in high honor among bards. Elizabeth Barrett Browning, in spite of great harshness of metre, oftentimes an unconscious pedantry, and a half morbid recurrence to certain pet themes and forms of expression,

seems to us to stand as high as any living poet of either sex. Next to her in her own sex, although widely different, and in some respects very much inferior, we are inclined to place the author of *Passion Flowers*.

To many this will seem preposterous; a few will think it scanty praise. (pp. 353-54)

Oftentimes one notices in female poets a lack of earnestness and depth of thought, exhibiting a wide contrast to the majority of eminent poets of the other sex. In this respect Mrs. Browning is greatly superior to her rivals; nor is the author of *Passion Flowers* wanting in merit of this kind. . . . She has written nothing which has much claim to notice as a work of art; nothing to compare with Mrs. Browning's "Romanists" and dramas; and it is in these, perhaps, that the latter excels. . . . [The] author of *Passion Flowers,* to judge by what this volume contains, is simply lyrical, and as such, her merit is of a high order. (p. 354)

The poems in the volume under notice are not of [the] highest character. We call them lyrical, because they are such as the poet, singing from his own breast the songs of love, or sorrow, or indignation, or devotion, as they rise there, would naturally write; because, too, they have a full, musical flow of verse, fitting well to the thought.

The name of the book is well chosen, for through it all there runs a strong under-current of passion, breaking forth now and then in sharp and wild expression. Or if the author intended the symbolical passion flower as the emblem of her flowers of song, there is a singular beauty in the choice. As that sacred flower, by the very gorgeousness of its hues, makes more intense the sorrowful signal stamped upon it, so does the warm, brilliant life which colors these poems make the sad, sombre thought of many of them more keenly felt. It makes us think of that princess who under her flashing robes wore the heavy cross studded with sharp points, pressed close to her bleeding breast. We feel as we read that these are the revelations of one of those electric natures whose love and disdain, whose joy and grief, are alike keen and thorough. We are constantly reminded of the traditional Sappho, and never more so than in the remarkable poem **"Mid-night."** . . . (pp. 354-55)

This is the "vision and the faculty divine," unquestionably. How well do the verses suggest the thrilling intoxication of mid-night—the rush of life through the veins of all who drink from that mysterious cup! We wonder that a woman could so well have felt and expressed it. Yet, above all the passionate music of the poem rises the clear, spiritual tone of the woman's untroubled voice, as in some wild orchestral din, one sweet, reed-like note, growing fuller and fuller, at last overcomes the tumult, and the shrill and loud become hushed before it. (pp. 355-56)

It is in such a poem as [**"Mid-night"**] that we see the immense superiority of a modern poetess over the famous singers of old. Sappho of Lesbos was a woman on fire with passion and conquered by it, wasting both her life and her song on unworthy objects. Our Sappho is a clear-eyed, noble woman, lifting us nearer heaven by the purity of her soul. With such a nature she can treat of themes often left unsung, and, by the tone which she uses, bring them strongly and naturally before us, without incurring the reproach of speaking an unwomanly word. (p. 356)

[The] author of *Passion Flowers* draws every thing that she touches into some sort of relation to herself and her life. Not a poem in the book but has this true woman's mark stamped upon it. Even the one most free from it—**"Handsome Harry,"** one of the most charming, freshest of sketches—could never have been written by any but a woman. (p. 357)

[In] many of these poems it is not so much the words which attract notice—they often seem almost commonplace—but somehow the vivid thought *behind* the words forces itself upon your attention. This is a rare merit; for now-a-days poets, for the most part, elaborate the metrical form which they use, and make it in itself musical and pleasing; but the form is not, as it should be, the natural growth of the thought; it has much that is superfluous and without meaning. Emerson says of Shakspeare and the poets of his age, that the secret of their unequalled rhythm is this: it was the simplest expression which their idea could take; never redundant or overlaid with foreign ornament. As compared with later poets, this is undoubtedly true of them; for the defect that comes from using more words than are supported by ideas, is painfully felt in nearly every recent poet. We see the same defect in *Passion Flowers,* but in no great degree. Oftener there are not words enough to express the thought fully; it therefore forces itself through, half unpleasantly. Both faults—although the latter is rather a virtue in these days—sometimes coëxist in the same poem, as in the one called **"Wherefore?"** and **"The Death of the Slave Lewis."** But usually there is a singular fitness in the verse to express the thought which it is meant to embody, a fitness which is not perceived at first, any more than we at first take notice of the nice blending of colors by which the painter sets face or landscape living before us. So, as the picture which at first and always pleases us by its effect, does so still more when we examine it more closely, do these poems grow upon our admiration the more we read them. What seemed at first commonplace, or passed without notice, is seen to have a merit above the more ambitious style of the great mass of versifiers. (pp. 357-58)

It seems as if we could all write poetry as good, so simple is the construction and so easy the language. We have no doubt that many young ladies who take up the book think it inferior to their own warblings, and wonder what it is that people find to admire in it.

But we have not yet alluded to the chief merits of the book before us, which are: its independence, its originality, and its hearty sympathy with the cause of humanity. It shows fewer traces of imitation than any book of the kind which we remember for this long time. Take up the poem of almost any American writer of either sex, and how strongly they hint of Byron, or Shelley, or Tennyson, or Mrs. Browning, or some other pet poet across the water. (p. 358)

Passion Flowers, as we have said, is clear of all accusations of [imitation]. You could not say from reading it whether or not the fashionable poets are on the author's shelves; or whether, like some of her sex, she prefers the sonorous Greek of Homer, and Aeschylus, and Pindar to all the later bards have sung. Our own guess is, that as one of Ben Jonson's characters says, "Although she speaks no Greek, she loves the sound on 't;" and is not skilled in the classics, notwithstanding a single Greek word which she uses for the title of one of her best pieces, and which is one of the few affectations in the volume. But however this may be, she certainly has not copied her rhythm or her thought from any ancient or modern singer. It is true there are, in many parts of the book, marks of the influence on her religious sentiments and her ways of thinking, which one great New-England mind has exerted; but this influence has been a guide and an impulse, rather than a tyrant to her own spirit. It were hardly possible for a person, living within the sphere of one of the foremost reformers and strongest men of the age, to escape the noble contagion of his character; nor are we sorry to see in this volume such well-deserved tributes to his elevating friendship. (pp. 358-59)

But we are wandering from the subject—the fearless freedom of speech which the book everywhere manifests. This is none the less to be admired because it is so rare in America. Strangely enough, in the freest country of the world there is more timidity and servility in literature than under many a despotic government. The dread of censure, the fear of offending that dear public whom we ought to love well enough to tell it the truth, makes cowards of our writers, from the newspaper editor to the dignified historian, appealing to posterity. (p. 359)

Our author spurns this general subordination, and insists, not only on singing her song in her own way, but also on saying what she pleases in her song. We have looked with some curiosity to see her sin visited upon her with the heaviest punishment which the American press can inflict; but she has hitherto escaped detection, it would seem. It is true, a very commendable change in this particular is taking place among us; nor do we (being still young) despair of seeing the day when thought shall be as free in democratic America as in England. Never till then shall we have anything which can rightly be called a national literature.

The crowning excellence of the book is its unwavering devotion to the cause of progress, manifested without parade, yet manly, womanly, and commanding respect even from those who differ from her. Since Margaret Fuller, no countrywoman of ours has so well supported the cause of the brave republicans of Europe. Yet American women have not been cold in their sympathy for Hungarian and Italian liberty. What friend of humanity can ever forget the true-hearted woman who so triumphantly vindicated the cause of Hungary and her hero against the attacks of suspicious and bigoted American critics? It is with Italy and the Italians that these poems have to do. Warm love for that fair land, endeared to her by so many memories, impels her to cry out against its oppressors with almost an exile's vehemence.

So, too, when she has occasion to speak of the stirring questions which agitate the social and political and theological life of our countrymen—of the New-Englanders especially—she shows a tender, womanly enthusiasm for the cause of justice and mankind. With no little vigor of intellect and comprehensiveness of thought, she aims shrewd blows at what she takes for the fortress of wrong. This will make her book especially dear to those whose side she espouses, while it may, perhaps, offend their antagonists. But one thing is certain: it gives an air of reality and conviction to all she says, which cannot fail to impress the reader.

Of the lesser beauties of the book one could say much. There is a vein of playful satire in some parts, and of trenchant sarcasm in others, both of them admirable. For the first, we may mention, **"Mind *versus* Mill-stream;"** for the other, **"Whitsunday in the Church;"** and **"A Picnic Among the Ruins of Ostia."** Her descriptions are often marvellously beautiful. . . . (p. 360)

Of pure description, however, there is very little. Every thing, as has been said, is touched and colored by its relation to herself. . . .

Countless felicities of expression are there in the volume, as full of meaning and of music as those single-line beauties of Tennyson which every one notices. (p. 361)

Neither are these the results of labor and a striving for effect, but they have an appearance of ease, as if said without premeditation.

The strength of religious feeling shown in many of the poems is not their least attraction. Among the many we notice especially **"Santa Susanna,"** **"The Dead Christ,"** and the concluding piece. In fact, the whole book is marked by a fervid religious character, as the work of one to whom the ideas of God and Duty are familiar and clear.

It remains to speak of the faults of the book—by no means a faultless one. There is too little variety in this large collection; too frequent reference to certain favorite topics. This is true of the matter, and the same may be said of the manner. The verse sometimes becomes monotonous and wearies the reader. Then there is some meddling with metres which are evidently unmanageable; such as the pitiable hexametre of **"Wherefore."** And although the language is, for the most part, pure and vigorous English, there are a few instances of a remarkable use of words. . . . There is a touch of affectation, too, in some of the titles.

But in comparison with the many beauties of the book, its faults seem trivial. We hail with joy its appearance, not only as introducing us to a poet of power and originality, but because it is a work of which we may be proud as Americans. It owes its birth to influences which are wholly American; it faithfully adheres to the American idea; nor can it be mistaken for the work of any but a true American woman. Our country might well afford to be represented abroad by such as she has shown herself to be.

And who is she? The book is published anonymously, but the author is understood to be the wife of an honored citizen of Massachusetts, famous for his early heroism in the cause of Greece, and for his more recent and more arduous labors in behalf of the blind and the unfortunate of every class. He has won for himself a name nobler than that of the warrior or the politician: she, too, may now claim her share of fame, and well maintain the honor of the name which she bears by marriage. (pp. 361-62)

> *A review of "Passion Flowers," in* The Knicker-bocker, *Vol. XLIII, No. 4, April, 1854, pp. 353-62.*

JULIA WARD HOWE   (essay date 1899)

[*In the following excerpt from her* Reminiscences—*probably the most often-reprinted of Howe's works after the "Battle Hymn" itself—Howe recounts the events leading to the writing of her famous poem.*]

It would be impossible for me to say how many times I have been called upon to rehearse the circumstances under which I wrote the **"Battle Hymn of the Republic."** I have also had occasion more than once to state the simple story in writing. As this oft-told tale has no unimportant part in the story of my life, I will briefly add it to these records. I distinctly remember that a feeling of discouragement came over me as I drew near the city of Washington [in the autumn of 1861]. I thought of the women of my acquaintance whose sons or husbands were fighting our great battle; the women themselves serving in the

hospitals, or busying themselves with the work of the Sanitary Commission. My husband . . . was beyond the age of military service, my eldest son but a stripling; my youngest was a child of not more than two years. I could not leave my nursery to follow the march of our armies, neither had I the practical deftness which the preparing and packing of sanitary stores demanded. Something seemed to say to me, "You would be glad to serve, but you cannot help any one; you have nothing to give, and there is nothing for you to do." Yet, because of my sincere desire, a word was given me to say, which did strengthen the hearts of those who fought in the field and of those who languished in the prison.

We were invited, one day, to attend a review of troops at some distance from the town. While we were engaged in watching the manoeuvres, a sudden movement of the enemy necessitated immediate action. The review was discontinued, and we saw a detachment of soldiers gallop to the assistance of a small body of our men who were in imminent danger of being surrounded and cut off from retreat. The regiments remaining on the field were ordered to march to their cantonments. We returned to the city very slowly, of necessity, for the troops nearly filled the road. My dear minister was in the carriage with me, as were several other friends. To beguile the rather tedious drive, we sang from time to time snatches of the army songs so popular at that time, concluding, I think, with

THE

ATLANTIC MONTHLY.

A MAGAZINE OF LITERATURE, ART, AND POLITICS.

VOL. IX.—FEBRUARY, 1862.—NO. LII.

BATTLE HYMN OF THE REPUBLIC.

MINE eyes have seen the glory of the coming of the Lord :
He is trampling out the vintage where the grapes of wrath are stored ;
He hath loosed the fateful lightning of His terrible swift sword :
    His truth is marching on.

I have seen Him in the watch-fires of a hundred circling camps ;
They have builded Him an altar in the evening dews and damps ;
I can read His righteous sentence by the dim and flaring lamps :
    His day is marching on.

I have read a fiery gospel writ in burnished rows of steel :
" As ye deal with my contemners, so with you my grace shall deal ;
Let the Hero, born of woman, crush the serpent with his heel,
    Since God is marching on."

He has sounded forth the trumpet that shall never call retreat ;
He is sifting out the hearts of men before His judgment-seat ;
Oh, be swift, my soul, to answer Him ! be jubilant, my feet !
    Our God is marching on.

In the beauty of the lilies Christ was born across the sea,
With a glory in his bosom that transfigures you and me :
As he died to make men holy, let us die to make men free,
    While God is marching on.

Entered according to Act of Congress, in the year 1862, by TICKNOR AND FIELDS, in the Clerk's Office of the District Court of the District of Massachusetts.
VOL. IX.   10

The "Battle Hymn" as it first appeared in the Atlantic Monthly *in February, 1862.*

John Brown's body lies a-mouldering in the ground;
His soul is marching on.

The soldiers seemed to like this, and answered back, "Good for you!" Mr. Clarke said, "Mrs. Howe, why do you not write some good words for that stirring tune?" I replied that I had often wished to do this, but had not as yet found in my mind any leading toward it.

I went to bed that night as usual, and slept, according to my wont, quite soundly. I awoke in the gray of the morning twilight; and as I lay waiting for the dawn, the long lines of the desired poem began to twine themselves in my mind. Having thought out all the stanzas, I said to myself, "I must get up and write these verses down, lest I fall asleep again and forget them." So, with a sudden effort, I sprang out of bed, and found in the dimness an old stump of a pen which I remembered to have used the day before. I scrawled the verses almost without looking at the paper. I had learned to do this when, on previous occasions, attacks of versification had visited me in the night, and I feared to have recourse to a light lest I should wake the baby, who slept near me. I was always obliged to decipher my scrawl before another night should intervene, as it was only legible while the matter was fresh in my mind. At this time, having completed my writing, I returned to bed and fell asleep, saying to myself, "I like this better than most things that I have written." (pp. 273-75)

> *Julia Ward Howe, in her* Reminiscences: 1819-1899,
> *Houghton, Mifflin and Company, 1899, 465 p.*

JULIA WARD HOWE   (poem date 1909)

[On the occasion of her eighty-ninth birthday, a number of Howe's friends composed commemorative poems in her honor. The following is Howe's response and a summary of her eighty-nine years.]

Why, bless you, I ain't nothing, nor nobody, nor
   much,
If you look in your Directory you'll find a thousand such.
I walk upon the level ground, I breathe upon the
   air,
I study at a table and reflect upon a chair.

I know a casual mixture of the Latin and the
   Greek,
I know the Frenchman's *parlez-vous,* and how the
   Germans speak;
Well can I add, and well subtract, and say twice
   two is four,
But of those direful sums and proofs remember
   nothing more.

I wrote a poetry book one time, and then I wrote
   a play,
And a friend who went to see it said she fainted
   right way.
Then I got up high to speculate upon the Universe,
And folks who heard me found themselves no
   better and no worse.

Yes, I've had a lot of birthdays and I'm growing
   very old,
That's why they make so much of me, if once the
   truth were told.

And I love the shade in summer, and in winter
   love the sun,
And I'm just learning how to live, my wisdom's
   just begun.

Don't trouble more to celebrate this natal day of
   mine,
But keep the grasp of fellowship which warms us
   more than wine.
Let us thank the lavish hand that gives world
   beauty to our eyes,
And bless the days that saw us young, and years
   that make us wise.

(pp. 311-12)

> *Julia Ward Howe, in a poem in* Carlyle's Laugh, and
> Other Surprises *by Thomas Wentworth Higginson,
> Houghton Mifflin Company, 1909, pp. 311-12.*

JEANNE ROBERT   (essay date 1911)

[In the following excerpt, Robert summarizes Howe's career.]

Mrs. Julia Ward Howe's posthumous volume of verse, *At Sunset,* will endure the test of true poetry—that it must stir the imagination and speak to the heart. It seems quite fitting that we should incidentally call to mind, along with some comment on this volume, the major incidents of the life and career of this distinguished woman of letters, philanthropist and reformer. Mrs. Howe's life was an outpouring of the passion that ever remains an attribute of the good and the great—the passion for "carrying, from one end of society to the other, the best knowledge, the best ideas of their time." . . .

Mrs. Howe became a contributor to many periodicals, writing many lyrics and two plays. Previous to this last collection of verse she had issued two volumes of poems, *Passion Flowers* and *Words for the Hour.* Of the two plays, the most pretentious, *Hippolytus,* written for Edwin Booth, was never brought out—much to Mrs. Howe's disappointment. *The World's Own* was produced at Wallack's in 1855, but was not a decided success.

Mrs. Howe's permanent contribution to literature will in all probability be only a few lyrics, of which the popular **"Battle Hymn of the Republic"** is the most noteworthy. These fervid lines, sung to the tune of "John Brown's Body," were written in the spring of 1861, while Mrs. Howe was visiting the scenes of war in the outskirts of Washington. . . . The *Atlantic Monthly* published the poem and it circulated rapidly throughout the country, in camp, in hospital, in prison—wherever men listened to the call of freedom. The popularity of the **"Battle Hymn"** has only been paralleled by that of Mrs. Harriet Beecher Stowe's "Uncle Tom's Cabin." It is our "Marseillaise." It sank like a diver into the hearts of men to bring forth the pearl of absolute heroism—the heroism which is the essence of the old Celtic spirit that goes to death with smiling eyes and a song upon the lips. . . .

The opening line, "Mine eyes have seen a vision" [sic], is an utterance that gives one an understanding of the tremendous influence she exerted upon her times. She was inspired; her poems were prophecies up-leaping like flames from the altar of her soul to light the way to things eternal.

Mrs. Howe was intimate of the most intellectual men and women of her time and a great attraction as a public speaker. As years passed the people of New England came to regard her as an institution—the "Grand Old Woman of America." She outlived most of her contemporaries. (p. 252)

Most women realize their responsibility to the family, to the community, even to the state and to the country; Mrs. Howe, with a recognition of a far off ideal of womanhood, realized her responsibility to the world,—to the Cosmos. This sense of spiritual kinship with humanity gave her courage for the independence of thought and action so manifest in her life. She believed, with Nietzsche, that "only the minority is capable of independence." . . . At the time of her death she was engaged in arranging the poems included in the volume *At Sunset.* This collection embraces many poems written for public occasions, such as the Hudson-Fulton celebration, the Lincoln centennial, and the Peace Congress. There are also many personal tributes to friends like Whittier, Dr. Holmes, Phillips Brooks, James Freeman Clarke, and others. To analyze Mrs. Howe as a poet is difficult. She is at her best when she attempts least, namely, in her simple, spontaneous lyrics. There is a feeling of a loss of power in her longer poems, where spontaneity is sacrificed to content. For pure, lyrical beauty there is nothing that surpasses the lovely lines **"Looking Down on the White Heads of My Contemporaries."** (pp. 252-53)

Another lyric breathing the mother spirit that so eloquently characterized Mrs. Howe, beginning "I have tended six pretty cradles," is of exceptional sweetness. . . . It is proposed to hang a life-sized portrait of Mrs. Howe in Faneuil Hall and also to erect a bust in the Boston Public Library. It is right that she should be venerated; for she was in the truest sense a liberator and a reformer; she pleaded for the rights of womanhood with audacity and eloquence. In a century of marvelous achievement she was eminently useful; she stands for the noblest womanhood and the highest standard of citizenship. (p. 253)

Jeanne Robert, "Julia Ward Howe As a Writer," in The American Review of Reviews, *Vol. XLIII, No. 2, February, 1911, pp. 252-53.*

FLORENCE HOWE HALL   (essay date 1913)

[In the following excerpt, one of Howe's daughters outlines Julia Ward Howe's contributions to the women's suffrage movement and the early twentieth-century women's peace movement.]

My mother tells us, in her *Reminiscences,* that she first became interested in the woman suffrage movement when she was nearing the half-century mark. Up to that time, as she says, "I looked to the masculine ideal of character as the only true one. I sought its inspiration, and referred my merits and demerits to its judicial verdict." (p. 11)

Throughout her long life of more than ninety years, Mrs. Howe devoted much time to serious study. In reading the writings of the great philosophers, she pondered deeply on life and its meaning.

Gradually her views changed. "I at length reached the conclusion that woman must be the moral and spiritual equivalent of man. How, otherwise, could she be entrusted with the awful and inevitable responsibilities of maternity?"

While my mother thus reasoned out for herself the equality of the sexes, the events of the day brought home to her, as to others, the injustice of longer denying the franchise to women. The negro was now "admitted to freedom and its safeguard, the ballot." Should the women, who had helped him gain his liberty, be refused the rights and privileges granted to the black man?

Whatever our views about the bestowal of citizenship on the negroes may be, we must bear in mind the fact that it had a very important influence on the woman suffrage movement immediately after the Civil War. Mrs. Howe and her fellow-workers all acted in the hope and belief that their turn would come next.

A woman who delighted in communing with the great minds of the past as well as of the present, who had studied the works of Kant, Hegel, Spinoza, Plato, Goethe and many others, could not look at this great question in any narrow spirit.

She did not consider the matter of granting the suffrage to her sex as a single isolated subject to be treated and discussed by itself. She felt rather that it was only one albeit the most important feature of a great movement for the advancement of women and for the uplift of all mankind. In the change in the position of women, she saw the unfolding of a divine purpose and plan. Hence her writings on the subject breathe a deeply religious spirit.

The hope of success which animated her first efforts to obtain the suffrage never deserted her, although at times she realized that victory might not come in her lifetime. (pp. 13-15)

But my mother was happy in living long enough to see her hopes realized in four states of the Union and to predict new gains to the suffrage cause. (p. 17)

Her faith in the ultimate victory of the cause of woman was strengthened by the wonderful changes she had already beheld. It owed its inspiration, however, to the poetic, one might indeed say religious, fervor which at times lifted her out of herself and her surroundings, enabling her to see visions of future truth and good. I do not use the word "vision" in a supernatural sense, but in that of spiritual exaltation. It was in such a mood that she wrote:

> Mine eyes have seen the glory of the coming of the Lord.

(p. 18)

The warmth and enthusiasm with which she advocated the advancement of women were characteristic of her ardent and poetic temperament. There are passages, written for the most part in the earlier days of her connection with the movement, filled with indignation at the opponents of the new and nobler order of things. With advancing age came an ever-increasing serenity of soul. Yet she retained to the end of her life the spirit of the Crusader, and was ever ready to defend the cause in which she had such deep faith. (p. 19)

My mother began her work for suffrage and for women's clubs in 1868, and for the Association for the Advancement of Women, a few years later. These were indeed three branches of the feminist movement. For a time, as she tells us, the cause of woman suffrage was predominant among her new interests and activities. In those early days, the number of its adherents was comparatively small, and my mother was called upon for active service. It was now necessary for her to address large audiences and preside over conventions. But like many of her countrywomen, she learned readily to do these things and to do them well.

The advocates of the cause of equal suffrage all acted at the time "under the powerful stimulus of hope." While the movement was decidedly unfashionable, nevertheless it aroused popular interest. (pp. 25-6)

Among my mother's activities in behalf of equal suffrage were her many pilgrimages to the State House in Boston. In Massachusetts, the custom of bringing this subject before the legislature every year has long prevailed. To these legislative hearings she was accustomed to go, despite the most formidable obstacles. (pp. 26-7)

She considered it a privilege to take part in these hearings. The memory of them she counted "among her most valued recollections." They extended over a period of forty years or more. Indeed, the last one which she attended took place only a few months before her death.

The excursions to the Capitol often involved vexation of spirit, as well as fatigue. Among the remonstrants, as the early anti-suffragists were called, there was no woman equal to Mrs. Howe in mental grasp or vigor, and some of the opponents were ignorant persons. The constant repetition of the same time-worn arguments, many of which had been disproved, was certainly trying to a woman of my mother's temperament. Fortunately, these difficulties served only to quicken the operations of her active mind.

"If I were mad enough, I could speak in Hebrew," she once said, jestingly.

She had the lawyer's faculty of seeing and seizing upon the weak point in the statements of her opponents, and was always noted for her power of keen and witty repartee. (pp. 27-8)

During the last few years of her life, when she was in the neighborhood of ninety years of age, her friends succeeded in persuading her to leave the State House after the suffragists had presented their arguments and before the "anti's" had spoken, since it was found that the reaction following the excitement of listening to the speeches of the opposition, especially when she was not permitted to reply, produced a degree of fatigue dangerous to so old a person.

The statements of the anti-suffragists were often in direct contradiction of my mother's own personal experience. She did not fail to point this out when opportunity was allowed her, and to chronicle the victories for justice won by those many weary pilgrimages to the State House.

The reader will find certain of these mentioned in **"The Change in the Position of Women."** Sometimes there is a note of triumph. "Our bill passed the legislature and became a part of the laws of Massachusetts." Elsewhere we are made to feel the length and weariness of the struggles necessary to achieve some small measure of success.

"In Massachusetts the suffragists worked for fifty-five years before they succeeded in getting a law making mothers equal guardians of their minor children with the fathers. . . .

"In Colorado, when the women were enfranchised, the very next legislature passed such a bill." (pp. 31-2)

My mother took an active part in the woman's club movement and was greatly interested in it. She founded so many of these societies as to earn the title of the "Mother of Clubs." "I have one every year," she jokingly said. (pp. 38-9)

Not long after the Franco-Prussian War, my mother undertook a Peace Crusade. "The question forced itself upon me, 'Why do not the mothers of mankind interfere in these matters, to prevent the waste of that human life of which they alone know the cost?'"

She devoted two years almost entirely to correspondence with leading women in various countries, having first issued an appeal, translated into several languages. In the spring of 1872 she visited England and held a Woman's Peace Congress in London. While the undertaking did not prosper so well as she had hoped, it had some success and helped pave the way for the modern peace movement. (p. 41)

I have now given in brief outline, the principal features of my mother's work for women. . . . It should be said that [her many activities in behalf of her sex] included the granting of many interviews and the writing of endless letters to all sorts and conditions of women, many of whom were entire strangers to her. Her daughters sometimes fretted because so much of her valuable time and strength were spent in this way. My mother herself was wiser in her day and generation than we, and realized the value of the personal relation. She received her reward. The sympathy which she extended to others was returned to her an hundredfold in the beautiful affection of her countrymen and women. This affection and the consciousness that she could still be of use, prolonged her life and contributed greatly to the happiness of her serene old age.

In the last years of my mother's life, the question of extending the franchise to women became a very live one. She was often called upon to uphold, with her ready pen and tongue, the cause in which she so fervently believed. (pp. 42-4)

> *Florence Howe Hall, "Mrs. Julia Ward Howe's Work for Women," in* Julia Ward Howe and the Woman Suffrage Movement *by Julia Ward Howe, edited by Florence Howe Hall, Dana Estes & Company Publishers, 1913, pp. 11-47.*

LAURA E. RICHARDS AND MAUD HOWE ELLIOTT WITH FLORENCE HOWE HALL (essay date 1915)

[*In the following excerpt from their Pulitzer prize-winning biography of their mother, two of Howe's daughters briefly discuss Howe's two earliest published literary works, the poetry collection* Passion Flowers *and the drama* The World's Own.]

[From] her earliest childhood Julia Ward's need of expressing herself in verse was imperative. Every emotion, deep or trivial, must take metrical shape; she laughed, wept, prayed—even stormed—in verse.

Walking with her one day, her sister Annie, always half angel, half sprite, pointed to an object in the road. "Dudie dear," she said; "squashed frog! little verse, dear?"

We may laugh with the two sisters, but under the laughter lies a deep sense of the poet's nature.

As in her dreamy girlhood she prayed—

> Oh! give me back my golden lyre!—

so in later life she was to pray—

> On the Matron's time-worn mantle
> Let the Poet's wreath be laid.

The tide of song had been checked for a time; after the second visit to Rome, it flowed more freely than ever. By the winter of 1853-54, a volume was ready (the poems chosen and arranged with the help of James T. Fields), and was published by Ticknor and Fields under the title of *Passion Flowers*.

No name appeared on the title-page; she had thought to keep her *incognito*, but she was recognized at once as the author, and the book became the literary sensation of the hour. It passed rapidly through three editions; was, she says, "much praised, much blamed, and much called in question." (p. 66)

The warmest praise came from the poets,—the "high, impassioned few" of her "**Salutatory.**" (p. 67)

Emerson wrote:—

CONCORD, MASS., 30 Dec., 1853.

DEAR MRS. HOWE,—

I am just leaving home with much ado of happy preparation for an absence of five weeks, but must take a few moments to thank you for the happiness your gift brings me. It was very kind [of] you to send it to me, who have forfeited all apparent claims to such favor, by breaking all the laws of good neighborhood in these years. But you were entirely right in sending it, because, I fancy, that among all your friends, few had so earnest a desire to know your thoughts, and, I may say, so much regret at never seeing you, as I. And the book, as I read in it, meets this curiosity of mine, by its poems of character and confidence, private lyrics, whose air and words [are] all your own. I have not gone so far in them as to have any criticism to offer you, and like better the pure pleasure I find in a new book of poetry so warm with life. Perhaps, when I have finished the book, I shall ask the privilege of saying something further. At present I content myself with thanking you.

With great regard,

R. W. EMERSON.

(p. 68)

Speaking of the volume long after, she says, "It was a timid performance upon a slender reed."

Three years later a second volume of verse was published by Ticknor and Fields under the title of *Words for the Hour.* Of this George William Curtis wrote, "It is a better book than its predecessor, but will probably not meet with the same success."

She had written plays ever since she was nine years old. In 1857, the same year which saw the publication of *Words for the Hour,* she produced her first serious dramatic work, a five-act drama entitled *The World's Own.* . . .

She notes that one critic pronounced the play "full of literary merits and of dramatic defects"; and she adds, "It did not, as they say, 'keep the stage.'" (pp. 70-1)

Some of the critics blamed the author severely for her choice of a subject—the betrayal and abandonment of an innocent girl by a villain; they thought it unfeminine, not to say indelicate, for a woman to write of such matters.

At that time nothing could be farther from her thoughts than to be classed with the advocates of Women's Rights as they then appeared; yet in *The World's Own* are passages which

show that already her heart cherished the high ideal of her sex, for which her later voice was to be uplifted. (p. 71)

> *Laura E. Richards and Maud Howe Elliott with Florence Howe Hall, in their* Julia Ward Howe: 1819-1910, 1915. *Reprint by Houghton Mifflin Company, 1925, pp. 66-84.*

FLORENCE HOWE HALL (essay date 1916)

[*In the following excerpt, one of Howe's daughters briefly notes the circumstances surrounding the writing of much of Howe's war poetry.*]

My mother's natural mode of expressing herself was by poetry rather than by prose. She wrote verses from her earliest years up to the time of her death. It is true that some of her best work took the form of prose in her essays, lectures, and speeches, yet whenever her feelings were deeply moved she turned to verse as the fittest vehicle for her use. (p. 107)

[She] began to write poems protesting against human slavery at an early period of her career. Thus her first published "**On the Death of the Slave Lewis.**" In *Words for the Hour* we find several poems dealing with slavery, the struggle in Kansas, the attack on Sumner, and kindred subjects. (pp. 107-08)

Howe at the time of writing the "Battle Hymn."

When the Civil War broke out, she poured forth the feelings that so deeply moved her in a number of poems. **"The Battle Hymn of the Republic"** is the best known of these, as it deserves to be. The others, however, while varying as to merit, show the same patriotism, indignation against wrong, and elevation of spirit. The woman's tenderness of heart breathes through them, too, as in the story of the dying soldier [**"Left Behind."**] (p. 108)

It will be remembered that the first blood shed in the Civil War was in Baltimore. There the Massachusetts troops, while on their way to defend the national capital, were attacked by "Plug-Uglies" and several soldiers were killed. My mother . . . [described] the funeral in Boston [in the poem **"Our Orders."**] (p. 109)

Other verses published in *Later Lyrics* under the title **"April 19"** commemorate the same event. They were evidently written in the first heat of indignation at the breaking out of the rebellion, yet her righteous wrath always gave way to a second thought, tenderer and more merciful than the first. We see this in the last verse of the **"Battle Hymn"** and in various other poems of hers. . . . Of her **"Poems of the War"** **"The Flag"** ranks second in popular esteem and has a place in many anthologies. (pp. 110-11)

"Our Country" contains no word about the civil strife, although it is classed with **"Poems of the War"** in her volume entitled *Later Lyrics*. A prize was offered for a national song while the war was in progress, and Mrs. Howe sent in this poem, Otto Dresel composing the music. (p. 114)

The news of Lincoln's assassination dealt a stunning blow to our people. The rejoicings over the end of the Civil War were suddenly changed to deep sorrow, indignation, and fear. How widely the conspiracy spread we did not know. It will be remembered that other officers of the Federal Government were attacked. My mother wrote that nothing since the death of her little boy had given her so much personal pain. As usual, she sought relief for her feelings in verse. **"The Parricide,"** written on the day of Lincoln's funeral, expresses her love and reverence for the great man, her horror of the "Fair assassin, murder—white," whom she bids:

> With thy serpent speed avoid
>   Each unsullied household light,
> Every conscience unalloyed.

As usual, compassion followed anger. **"Pardon,"** written a few days later, after the death of Wilkes Booth, is the better poem of the two. (p. 116)

The other **"Poems of the War"** published in *Later Lyrics* are entitled **"Requital," "The Question," "One and Many," "Hymn for a Spring Festival," 'The Jeweller's Shop in Wartime,"** and **"The Battle Eucharist."**

In these we see how deeply the writer's soul was oppressed by the sorrow of the war and the horrors of the battle-field. We see, too, how it turned ever for comfort and encouragement to the Cross and to the Lord of Hosts. (pp. 119-20)

> *Florence Howe Hall, in her* The Story of the Battle Hymn of the Republic, *Harper & Brothers, 1916, 130 p.*

EDMUND WILSON (essay date 1962)

[*Wilson, considered America's foremost man of letters in the twentieth century, wrote widely on cultural, historical, and literary matters, authoring several seminal critical studies. He is often credited with bringing an international perspective to American letters through his widely read discussions of European literature. Wilson was allied to no critical school; however, several dominant concerns serve as guiding motifs throughout his work. He invariably examined the social and historical implications of a work of literature, particularly literature's significance as "an attempt to give meaning to our experience" and its value for the improvement of humanity. Although he was not a moralist, his criticism displays a deep concern with moral values. Another constant was his discussion of a work of literature as a revelation of its author's personality. In* Axel's Castle (1931), *a seminal study of literary symbolism, Wilson wrote: "The real elements, of course, of any work of fiction are the elements of the author's personality: his imagination embodies in the images of characters, situations and scenes the fundamental conflicts of his nature." However, though Wilson examined the historical and psychological implications of a work of literature, he rarely did so at the expense of a discussion of its literary qualities. In* Patriotic Gore: Studies in the Literature of the American Civil War, *Wilson surveys some of the written works produced in the United States between 1861 and 1865, focusing upon the speeches, pamphlets, memoirs, and newspaper reports that dealt specifically with issues and personalities connected with war activities. In the following excerpt, Wilson examines the probable Biblical source for the "Battle Hymn" and provides his own explication of Howe's lyrics.*]

The real causes of war still remain out of range of our rational thought; but the minds of nations at war are invariably dominated by myths, which turn the conflict into melodrama and make it possible for each side to feel that it is combatting some form of evil. This vision of Judgment was the myth of the North. If we study the Civil War as a political or an economic phenomenon, we may fail to be aware of the apocalyptic aspect it wore for many defenders of the Union; but this myth possessed the minds of the publicists, the soldiers and the politicians to an extent of which the talk about "Armageddon" at the time of the first World War can give only a feeble idea, and the literature of the time is full of it. Though Calvinism was being displaced by more liberal forms of religion—Unitarianism in New England dates from 1820—the old fierceness, the old Scriptural assertiveness of the founders of the New England theocracy had not yet been wholly tamed by their children, and were ready to spring out at a challenge. William Lloyd Garrison, the leader of the Boston Abolitionists, had since 1834 been preaching in his paper, the *Liberator*, his intransigent crusade against slavery. Though he had broken with the traditional New England church, he exhibited all the old fanaticism, and when faced with the argument that the Constitution did guarantee property in slaves and provided no way of freeing them, he denounced it, in the language of Isaiah, as "a covenant with death and an agreement with hell." And this semi-religious fervor is felt in the passionate enthusiasm—a spirit that has not been displayed in any of our subsequent wars—with which the more idealistic of the Northern youth threw themselves into the regional conflict.

The songs these soldiers sang were like psalms. It is significant that in "John Brown's Body," the Federals' favorite song, John Brown should be "a soldier in the army of the Lord"; and that Julia Ward Howe, when asked to provide for the popular tune a more dignified set of words, should have produced, in **"The Battle Hymn of the Republic,"** a more exalted version of the same idea. It will be worthwhile to scrutinize this poem, which, carried along by the old rousing rhythm, has persisted so long and become so familiar that we have ceased to pay attention to its sense. The **"Battle Hymn"** seems to have burst into life as uncontrollably as *Uncle Tom's Cabin*. The day after the suggestion was made, says Mrs. Howe in her *Reminiscences* [see excerpt dated 1899], she woke in the early dawn, and "the long lines of the desired poem began to twine themselves in my mind." Fearing she might forget them, she made herself get out of bed and write them down "in the dimness" with "an old stump of a pen which I remembered to have used the day before. I scrawled the verses almost without looking at the paper."

Now, there were probably two influences at work in the just-awakened mind of Mrs. Howe when she composed "**The Battle Hymn of the Republic.**" She must certainly have taken her cue from Isaiah 63.1-6:

> 1. Who is this that cometh from Edom, with dyed garments from Bozrah? this that is glorious in his apparel, travelling in the greatness of his strength? I that speak in righteousness, mighty to save. 2. Wherefore art thou red in thine apparel, and thy garments like him that treadeth in the winefat? 3. I have trodden the wine-press alone; and of the peoples there was none with me: for I will tread them in mine anger, and trample them in my fury; and their blood shall be sprinkled upon my garments, and I will stain all my raiment. 4. For the day of vengeance is in mine heart, and the year of my redeemed is come. 5. And I looked, and there was none to help; and I wondered that there was none to uphold: therefore mine own arm brought salvation unto me; and my fury, it upheld me. 6. And I will tread down the people in mine anger, and make them drunk in my fury, and I will bring down their strength to the earth.

Macaulay had already made use of this passage in one of his *Songs of the Civil War:*

> THE BATTLE OF NASEBY, BY OBADIAH BIND-THEIR-KINGS-IN-CHAINS-AND-THEIR-NOBLES-WITH-LINKS-OF-IRON, SERJEANT IN IRETON'S REGIMENT 1824
>
> Oh! wherefore come ye forth in triumph from the North,
> With your hands, and your feet, and your raiment all red?
> And wherefore doth your rout send forth a joyous shout?
> And whence be the grapes of the wine-press which ye tread?

(pp. 91-3)

That Mrs. Howe, in what was doubtless unconscious memory, went back directly to Isaiah is proved by her writing "the grapes of wrath" instead of merely Macaulay's "grapes," and the meter of the "**Battle Hymn**" is different from Macaulay's; but the "**Hymn**" does have something in common with the poem on the Battle of Naseby and may well have been suggested by it. In this case, the cause of the North was associated by Julia Ward Howe not merely with God's punishment of the enemies of Israel but also with the victory over the Royalists and Papists of Ireton's Cromwellian army.

Let us examine now the "**Battle Hymn**" itself:

> Mine eyes have seen the glory of the coming of the Lord:
> He is trampling out the vintage where the grapes of wrath are stored;
> He hath loosed the fateful lightning of his terrible swift sword:
> His truth is marching on.

The advent of the Union armies represents, then, the coming of the Lord, and their cause is the cause of God's truth.

> I have seen Him in the watch-fires of a hundred circling camps;
> They have builded Him an altar in the evening dews and damps;
> I can read His righteous sentence by the dim and flaring lamps.
> His day is marching on.
>
> I have read a fiery gospel, writ in burnished rows of steel:
> "As ye deal with my contemners, so with you my grace shall deal;
> Let the Hero, born of woman, crush the serpent with his heel,
> Since God is marching on."

The Confederacy is a serpent, which God's Hero must slay, and in proportion to the punishment inflicted by this Hero on God's enemies, who are also his own, the Deity will reward the Hero.

> He has sounded forth the trumpet that shall never call retreat;
> He is sifting out the hearts of men before his judgment-seat:
> Oh! be swift, my soul, to answer Him! be jubilant, my feet!
> Our God is marching on.

The Lord is apparently checking on those who do and those who do not enlist, so hurry up and join the Lord's army!

> In the beauty of the lilies Christ was born across the sea,
> With a glory in his bosom that transfigures you and me:
> As he died to make men holy, let us die to make men free,
> While God is marching on.

This stanza is particularly interesting on account of its treatment of Jesus, so characteristic of Calvinism. As is often the case with Calvinists, Mrs. Howe, though she feels she must bring Him in, gives Him a place which is merely peripheral. He is really irrelevant to her picture, for Christ died to make men holy; but this is not what God is having *us* do: He is a militant, a military God, and far from wanting us to love our enemies, He gives "the Hero" orders to "crush the serpent with his heel." The righteous object of this is to "make men [the Negroes] free," and we must die to accomplish this. Note that Christ is situated "across the sea"; he is not present on the battlefield with His Father, yet, intent on our grisly work, we somehow still share in His "glory." I have not been able to guess where Julia Ward Howe got these lilies in the beauty of which Jesus is supposed to have been born. The only lilies mentioned in the Gospels are those that toil not neither do they spin. Was she thinking of Easter lilies? But these are associated not with Christ's birth but with His resurrection. In any case, they serve to place Him in a setting that is effeminate as well as remote. The gentle and no doubt very estimable Jesus is trampling no grapes of wrath. And now come on, New England boys, get in step with the marching God! If you succeed in crushing the serpent, God will reward you with ''grace.'' (This cheats on Predestination, but Mrs. Howe, ''brought up,'' as she says, ''after the strictest rule of New England Puritanism,'' had afterwards become more liberal.) (pp. 94-6)

> *Edmund Wilson, ''Calvin Stowe; Francis Grierson; 'The Battle Hymn of the Republic': The Union as Religious Mysticism,'' in his* Patriotic Gore: Studies in the Literature of the American Civil War, *Oxford University Press, 1962, pp. 59-98.**

ADDITIONAL BIBLIOGRAPHY

Brooks, Van Wyck. ''The Radical Club.'' In his *New England: Indian Summer, 1865-1915*, pp. 115-39. New York: E. P. Dutton & Co., 1940.*
    Rambling reminiscence of Boston intellectual society during the mid-to-late 1800s, with mention of Howe.

Chapman, John Jay. ''Julia Ward Howe.'' In his *Memories and Milestones*, pp. 235-45. New York: Moffat, Yard and Co., 1915.
    Character sketch of Howe and background to her social milieu.

Clifford, Deborah Pickman. *Mine Eyes Have Seen the Glory: A Biography of Julia Ward Howe*. Boston: Little, Brown and Co., 1978, 313 p.
    Insightful major biography, focusing on the impact of Howe's marriage and family on her public life.

Grant, Mary H. ''Domestic Experience and Feminist Theory: The Case of Julia Ward Howe.'' In *Woman's Being, Woman's Place: Female Identity and Vocation in American History,* edited by Mary Kelley, pp. 220-32. Boston: G. K. Hall & Co., 1979.
    Examination of the religious, philosophical, and social influences that contributed to the formation of Howe's thought and character, as well as the impact of her often unhappy marriage upon her career as a public figure.

Howe, Maud. ''Authors at Home: Mrs. Howe at Oak Glen, Newport.'' *The Critic* 10, No. 180 (11 June 1887): 191.
    Description of Howe's life at her summer residence in Newport, Rhode Island, by her youngest daughter.

O'Neill, William L. ''The Origins of American Feminism.'' In his *Everyone Was Brave: The Rise and Fall of Feminism in America,* pp. 3-48. Chicago: Quadrangle Books, 1969.*
    Briefly notes Howe's position of prominence among the conservative Bostonian founders of the American Woman Suffrage Association.

Snyder, Edward D. ''The Biblical Background of the 'Battle Hymn of the Republic'.'' *The New England Quarterly* XXIV, No. 2 (June 1951): 231-38.
    Line-by-line explication of the ''Battle Hymn,'' offering Biblical parallels to the language and often to specific phrases used by Howe in the lyric.

Tharpe, Louise Hall. ''The Song that Wrote Itself.'' *American Heritage* VIII, No. 1 (December 1956): 10-13, 100-01.
    Tribute to Howe and her most famous work.

————. *Three Saints and a Sinner: Julia Ward Howe, Louisa, Annie and Sam Ward*. Boston: Little, Brown and Co., 1956, 406 p.*
    Extensive biographical and historical study of the lives of the rich, powerful, and influential Ward and Howe families.

T(homas) E(rnest) Hulme

1883-1917

(Also wrote under pseudonyms of Thomas Gratton and North Staffs) English poet, essayist, and philosopher.

Hulme was one of the most important theorists of Modernist poetry and an influential figure among English intellectuals during the first two decades of the twentieth century. Breaking sharply with the dominant thought of his contemporaries, Hulme denounced Romantic aesthetics and humanist philosophy. He correspondingly advocated classical standards of art, including precision of statement and simplicity of form, and affirmed the superiority of Christian theology and ethics. In poetry, Hulme proposed the use of clear, visual imagery to replace the lofty metaphors of the Romantics. Although Hulme's poetic output was slight, he exerted enormous influence on modern art and literature through his associations with such major twentieth-century artists as Ezra Pound, Wyndham Lewis, and Jacob Epstein, and through his erudite essays, many of which appeared in widely read journals of the day.

Born in the village of Endon, in central England, Hulme was the son of a moderately wealthy landowner and his wife. Contemporaries describe him as a precocious child who displayed an early interest in philosophy and mathematics, while demonstrating a natural ability to lead and influence others. At nineteen, he was admitted to St. John's College at Cambridge, where he distinguished himself as an excellent student, passionately concerned with questions of metaphysics and ethics and willing to debate such topics at great length. Two years later, however, he was expelled from Cambridge when he allegedly struck a policeman. Upon his expulsion, Hulme was disowned by his father, who felt that he had irrevocably disgraced the family name. A small allowance provided by a sympathetic cousin enabled him to settle in London and continue his studies of philosophy and science at University College. There followed a brief period of travel, during which he visited Canada, Belgium, and Italy. Returning to London in 1908, Hulme immediately introduced himself into the city's thriving intellectual community. By the end of the year, he was a regular contributor to the *New Age,* a magazine noted for its high standards and tolerance of extremist viewpoints, and had helped form the Poet's Club, which was intended as a forum for the reading and discussion of its members' poetry. Through his participation in that group, Hulme attempted to disseminate his iconoclastic literary opinions, but he soon tired of the rigid format of the meetings and broke away to create a salon in which he could dominate the proceedings. With other prominent artists and writers, including F. S. Flint and Francis Tancred, Hulme espoused a new philosophy of art which rejected the aesthetic tenets of the Renaissance and all later artistic developments, including realism, impressionism, and expressionism, as invalid, promoting a form of abstract art as the only true vehicle for creation. One particularly notable member of Hulme's circle was the American poet Ezra Pound, who had just arrived in England and who agreed with Hulme's contention that visual image was the preferable method of poetic communication. Hulme's opinions, however, reached far beyond the limits of art. In his many *New Age* articles, he discussed religion, politics, and metaphysics with equal elo-

quence. Even after his induction into the infantry in 1914, Hulme continued to submit essays for publication, but he now turned his attention to philosophical justifications of the war, which were written even as he endured the misery of the trenches. He was killed in action in 1917.

Although Hulme's poetic output was small, his work in that area has been highly praised. T. S. Eliot wrote that "the poems of T. E. Hulme needed only to be read aloud to have immediate effect." Nevertheless, it is generally thought that he wrote poetry primarily to illustrate his theories, and it is as a theorist and essayist that he is best known. Critics agree that his desire was not to present a consistent philosophical system, but rather to effect a transformation of art. Hulme's vision of modern art was based on a complex web of convictions about the nature of humankind, existence, and the world. His philosophical approach has been called fragmentary, for he chose to address only specific aspects of large, intricate questions, treating philosophy as a creative rather than a scientific endeavor. Underlying all of Hulme's rational constructs is his view of the history of ideas. He divided history into two distinct periods, calling them the "classical" and the "romantic" eras and using the Renaissance as the point of demarcation. The Renaissance, he argued, marked the demise of true religion, which he regarded as a basic human need, and the rise of humanism, which he called "a specious substitute for religion." Hulme's dislike for humanism centered primarily on its concept of the inherent perfectibility and goodness of human beings, which was in sharp contrast to his own highly orthodox belief in the doctrine of Original Sin. Hulme believed that human nature is fundamentally evil and that only the restraints of civil and religious law prevent humanity from destroying itself. Lamenting the pervasive influence of humanist thinking, Hulme called for a return to the values of antiquity.

Hulme's early work clearly reflects his absorption in the metaphysics of Henri Bergson, a French philosopher who opposed the prevailing materialist views of the period. Hulme offers an explanation for this obsession in "Notes on Bergson I," in which he relates how the desolation he felt as a result of the conflict between his religious faith and his belief in the mechanistic universe of the scientific determinists was eased by his discovery of Bergson's thought, which asserted that rational cognition is not the only valid means of knowledge, and that through a suprarational process of intuition conclusions which transcend or contradict logic may be reached. This approach to knowledge allowed Hulme to embrace religion through the precepts of a philosophy which claimed to surpass, rather than betray or neglect, reason. While Hulme never abandoned Bergson's views, he gradually shifted the focus of his essays from metaphysics to aesthetics, and it is in these writings that he set down his most influential ideas. Hulme's aesthetic theories arise logically from his ideology; in his essay "Romanticism and Classicism," he separated all art into two categories, the "vital" and the "geometric," with vital art corresponding to romanticism and geometric to classicism. He considered vital art to be that which attempts either realistic or impressionistic re-creation, both methods reflecting humanist presuppositions of the beauty in natural objects and the validity of human perception. Conversely, Hulme considers geometric or non-representational art to be the response of a limited being to the overwhelming complexity of a universe which can never be fully comprehended and in which humanity plays an obviously peripheral role. All art, Hulme asserts, manifests this dichotomy. In poetry, the romantic celebrates the triumph of the individual ego while "the classical poet is always aware of his own insignificance as compared to the infinity of God's power." Hulme thought that poetry should reflect the limited nature of humanity through simplicity of form and humility of tone. Moreover, he considered humanity's limited powers of observation and comprehension best utilized in the creation of clear, simple visual images, as exemplified in the following lines from one of his poems: "Above the quiet dock at midnight, / Tangled in the mast's corded height, / Hangs the moon. . . ." Subject matter, then, would necessarily be limited to those objects which lent themselves naturally to such simple descriptions, thus discouraging the kind of heroic verse of which Hulme disapproved so heartily, believing that there was much beauty in "small, dry things."

After the outbreak of war in 1914, Hulme turned his attention to problems of politics, writing a series of articles for the *New Age* entitled "War Notes by North Staffs." In addition, he engaged in a lengthy debate about warfare with pacifist philosopher Bertrand Russell in the pages of the *Cambridge Magazine*. Although Hulme's belief in the inherently evil nature of human beings placed him in direct opposition to the democratic principles for which the war was ostensibly being fought, he supported war in itself as a proper instrument of the state. Considering individuals to be incapable of correct behavior without the external restraint of a political system, he understood the necessity of the exercise of coercive power, and, by extension, of warfare.

Negative criticism of Hulme's work has traditionally focused on his rhetorical methods rather than on his conclusions, except in the case of his political beliefs, which are regarded as dangerously naive. He has been accused of disregarding those facts which do not support his conclusions, and most critics agree that his tendency to view reality as a series of dichotomies is a case of oversimplification to the point of distortion. Furthermore, some critics find the value of his work severely reduced by its derivative nature, since he usually preferred to comment upon the theories of other philosophers rather than construct his own. Hulme's artistic and poetic theories are, however, generally acknowledged as concise, well-argued reflections of the classicist spirit that eventually came to dominate Modernist poetry. While the exact magnitude of Hulme's influence on twentieth-century art is still being disputed, the fact that he did exert such influence is unquestioned, and his essays are regarded as definitive statements of Modernist poetic theory.

(See also *Contemporary Authors*, Vol. 117, and *Dictionary of Literary Biography*, Vol. 19: *British Poets, 1880-1914*.)

PRINCIPAL WORKS

"The Complete Poetical Works of T. E. Hulme" (poetry) 1912; published in journal *The New Age;* also published as an appendix to *Ripostes* by Ezra Pound
Speculations (essays and poetry) 1924
Further Speculations (essays) 1955

Many of Hulme's unpublished poems and fragments of poems can be found in *The Life and Opinions of T. E. Hulme*, by Alun R. Jones.

CRITES [PSEUDONYM OF T. S. ELIOT] (essay date 1924)

[*Perhaps the most influential poet and critic of the first half of the twentieth century, Eliot is closely identified with many of the qualities denoted by the term Modernism: experimentation, formal complexity, artistic and intellectual eclecticism, and a classicist view of the artist working at an emotional distance from his or her creation. He introduced a number of terms and concepts that strongly affected critical thought in his lifetime, among them the idea that poets must be conscious of the living tradition of literature in order for their work to have artistic and spiritual validity. In general, Eliot upheld values of traditionalism and discipline, and in 1928 he annexed Christian theology to his overall conservative world view. Of his criticism, he stated: "It is a by-product of my private poetry-workshop: or a prolongation of the thinking that went into the formation of my verse." In the following excerpt, Eliot reviews* Speculations.]

The posthumous volume of *Speculations* of T. E. Hulme . . . appears to have fallen like a stone to the bottom of the sea of print. With its peculiar merits, this book is most unlikely to meet with the slightest comprehension from the usual reviewer: with all its defects—it is an outline of work to be done, and not an accomplished philosophy—it is a book of very great significance. When Hulme was killed in Flanders in 1917, he was known to a few people as a brilliant talker, a brilliant amateur of metaphysics, and the author of two or three of the most beautiful short poems in the language. In this volume he appears as the forerunner of a new attitude of mind, which should be the twentieth-century mind, if the twentieth century is to have a mind of its own. Hulme is classical, reactionary, and revolutionary; he is the antipodes of the eclectic, tolerant, and democratic mind of the end of the last century. And his writing, his fragmentary notes and his outlines, is the writing of an individual who wished to satisfy himself before he cared to enchant a cultivated public.

Hulme is a solitary figure in this country: his closest affinities are in France, with Charles Maurras, Albert Sorel, and Pierre Lasserre. Compared with these men, Hulme is immature and unsubstantial; but he had the great advantage of a creative gift. The weakness from which the classical movement in France has suffered is that it has been a critique rather than a creation; the movement may claim Paul Valéry, but that elusive genius will hardly allow itself to be placed. It would be as tenable, and as dubious, to claim James Joyce in England. Of both of these writers it may be cogently be said that they belong to a new age chiefly by representing, and perhaps precipitating, consummately in their different ways the close of the previous epoch. Classicism is in a sense reactionary, but it must be in a profounder sense revolutionary. A new classical age will be reached when the dogma, or *ideology*, of the critics is so modified by contact with creative writing, and when the creative writers are so permeated by the new dogma, that a state of equilibrium is reached. (pp. 231-32)

> *Crites [pseudonym of T. S. Eliot], "A Commentary," in* The Criterion, *Vol. II, No. VII, April, 1924, pp. 231-35.**

I. A. RICHARDS   (essay date 1924)

[*Richards was an English poet and critic who has been called the founder of modern literary criticism. Primarily a theorist, he encouraged the growth of textual analysis and, during the 1920s, formulated many of the principles that would later become the basis of New Criticism, one of the most important schools of modern critical thought. In an attempt to make literary criticism a more scientific endeavor, Richards proposed the systematic application of objective principles to the interpretation of literature, stressing careful textual analysis as the primary means of explication. In the following excerpt, Richards reviews* Speculations.]

T. E. Hulme . . . was no ordinary amateur. He had an acute and rather audacious mind, and, what is rarer, that ability to persist in thought which usually leads to interesting work. We have had many collections of the poetry of those who were killed before they came to their full powers. This assemblage of Essays, Lectures, Papers read to various societies, Notes, and Jottings [*Speculations*] is the only example which has been published of the analogous thing in philosophy. (p. 469)

People both able and interested in philosophy seem to be rarer than poets; certainly the material for the study of the earlier stages of philosophical development in good minds is scanty. The tasks of pupils are too much influenced by the teachers to whom they are presented to be very valuable evidence, and there are strong reasons why the early jottings of philosophers who later publish their maturely considered works find their way to the wastepaper basket. Records, such as those here collected, of the processes by which views actually come in the first instance to be adopted and to be formed, have a special interest, apart from that of the views, which in some instances here is considerable.

There is nothing tentative or hesitating, however, though there is much which is incomplete and confused, in the opinions set forth. Hulme had to an exceptional degree the gift of dramatic presentation. He makes his arguments exciting without using illegitimate appeals. About half the book consists of an interpretation of Bergson; the rest is divided between essays or sketches for essays upon recent art, and an attack upon what Hulme called the Humanist ideology, the view, roughly, that the human mind is the measure of all things. Hulme's attempts to reconcile and combine the Realism, or Absolutism, which he found in *Principia Ethica* with the elements which attracted him in Bergson are representative of many people's struggles with these two chief influences of the years immediately preceding the War. This in itself would make them well worth preserving. There are also scattered throughout the book many highly original if cryptic utterances upon important matters, remarks of a kind which fully justify the title, for the author was one of those who can suggest new problems of interest as well as discuss the old. (pp. 469-70)

> *I. A. Richards, in a review of "Speculations: Essays on Humanism and the Philosophy of Art," in* Mind, *Vol. XXXIII, No. 132, October, 1924, pp. 469-70.*

HENRY KING [PSEUDONYM OF J. MIDDLETON MURRY]   (essay date 1925)

[*Murry is recognized as one of the most significant English critics and editors of the twentieth century. Anticipating later scholarly opinion, he championed the writings of Marcel Proust, James Joyce, Paul Valéry, D. H. Lawrence, and the poetry of Thomas Hardy through his positions as the editor of the* Athenaeum *and as a longtime contributor to the* Times Literary Supplement *and other periodicals. As with his magazine essays, Murry's book-length critical works are noted for their unusually impassioned tone and startling discoveries; such biographically centered critical studies as* Keats and Shakespeare: A Study of Keats' Poetic Life from 1816-1820 *(1925) and* Son of Woman: The Story of D. H. Lawrence *(1931) contain esoteric, controversial conclusions that have angered scholars who favor more traditional approaches. Nevertheless, Murry is cited for his perspicuity, clarity, and supportive argumentation. His early exposition on literary appreciation,* The Problem of Style *(1922), is widely revered as an informed guidebook for both critics and readers to employ when considering not only the style of a literary work, but its theme and viewpoint as well. In it Murry espouses a theoretical premise which underlies all of his criticism: that in order to fully evaluate a writer's achievement the critic must search for crucial passages which effectively "crystallize" the writer's innermost impressions and convictions regarding life. In the following excerpt, Murry criticizes Hulme's rhetorical methods.*]

Hulme possessed an original and vigorous philosophical mind. He was not what professional philosophers would call a philosopher: the phrase he used for himself was "philosophic amateur." But indeed we have no word for the genus Hulme in English, probably because we have not felt the need of one. The phenomenon is pretty rare among us. Hulme was a critic of ideas, a critic of philosophies, a critic of critiques—into whatever phrase we use for him, the words "critic" or "critical" must enter somewhere. But what the precise province of his criticism was must be left vague. That was Hulme's misfortune. In his writings one quickly becomes conscious of a lack of *engrenage* somewhere. This keen and vigorous mind is, after all, not cutting very much ice. He insists on clarity, and is himself rather vague. He stimulates, but fails to satisfy.

Take, for instance, his leading idea of a fundamental antithesis between the Humanist and the Religious attitudes of mind. He directs all his criticism against Humanism, arguing, I believe truly, that the humanist presupposition has been implicit in all European thought since the Renaissance. At that moment, he says, man began to regard himself as perfectible, or even as naturally perfect. Whereas under the dispensation of mediaeval Christianity he had profoundly acknowledged himself the victim of original sin, under the new dispensation he repudiated any such essential disability, and held that man was, by his own effort, capable of perfection. On this instinctive category of thought the modern consciousness and modern life is based.

As a general statement of the antithesis this is acceptable. But, implicitly during a great deal of his argument—which is rather tedious, chiefly because it is not so original as he believed it—and explicitly at the conclusion, Hulme declares himself an anti-humanist. He is on the side of the religious attitude, and he foresees (on slender evidence) the advent of a new religious epoch, when men will abandon this unconscious assumption of their own perfectibility and once more regard perfection as an abstract and unattainable ideal.

But the question Hulme seems to have failed to ask himself was: Why did *he* take up this position? Quite possibly man is not perfectible by his own efforts. But to make of this possibility a certainty is an extraordinary step for a sceptical critic to take without recognizing its implications. The mediaeval Christian could be certain of man's imperfectibility because he knew God who was perfect, and because he knew by the scriptures, which were the veritable word of God, how sin entered into the world; and finally, because he knew how man's original sin was and might always be redeemed. But of these certainties Hulme had none. His assertion of man's imperfectibility was nothing more than an expression of opinion; he had no basis for any critique of imperfectibility. And, in fact, at this crucial point he begins to strike us as a mere dilettante, although he emphatically repudiates any tendency in himself towards a sentimental return to mediaeval Christianity.

> I have none of the feelings of *nostalgia,* the reverence for tradition, the desire to recapture the sentiment of Fra Angelico, which seems to animate most modern defenders of religion. All that seems to me to be bosh. What is important, is—what nobody seems to realize—the dogmas like that of Original Sin, which are the closest expression of the categories of the religious attitude.

"What nobody seems to realize"! There speaks intellectual arrogance and not a little ignorance as well. Sainte-Beuve, then, wrote "Port-Royal" for nothing, and the Catholic Church in France was rent in twain at the end of the seventeenth century for nothing also. And Hulme himself appears to be standing "aloof from the entire point," by not being able to see that to speak of accepting the dogma of Original Sin is hardly more than a romantic phrase unless the acceptance is based on a knowledge of the nature of God.

So when it comes to the real issue Hulme fails rather badly. He becomes much too much like a pale English version of the acrobats of *L'Action Française,* who want the Church without the religion, and the tradition without the sacrifice. Whatever substance there may have been in Hulme's criticism of modern humanism begins most ingloriously to evaporate so soon as we realise that *he* has not the right to make it. He is, in spite

of all his repudiations, almost exactly in the position of the man who has a sentimental preference for conditions different from those in which his lot is cast. And perhaps in Hulme's case it was an aesthetic preference of the same order as that which a generation ago moved the decadents in France and England to dabble with Catholicism. He preferred the modern "abstract" art of the cubists to the traditional art which has its origins in the Renaissance; he also preferred Byzantine mosaic to Italian fresco. Perhaps he elaborated his critique of humanism merely to substantiate his aesthetic preferences.

Anyhow, it is certain that an atmosphere of futility begins to descend upon his writing when he approaches problems of applied criticism. His essay on Romanticism and Classicism in English poetry only satisfies so long as you refuse to think about it. He declares himself the enemy of Romantic vagueness and infinitude, and the champion of the vivid and precise visual image. In other words, instead of being a critic, he is merely the apologist of the school of poets who called themselves "The Imagists." Had he been critical, he would have realised that this question of "vagueness" cannot be so lightly disposed of, and that a talent for exact visual description is only a small part of the make-up of a poet. How much exact description is there, for instance, in those "Elizabethans" whom Hulme (with the large and sweeping gesture familiar in such arguments) pitted against the Romantic poets of the early nineteenth century? In actual fact, very little—much less, indeed, than there is in the generality of nineteenth-century English poets. How many times do Shakespeare's superlative effects depend upon precise visual imagery? The number could probably be counted on the fingers of one hand.

And in this failure to realise, first, that this insistence upon exact visual imagery is a comparatively modern invention, and secondly that the real power of a work of literature, whether in poetry or prose, depends upon a hundred other elements, which need a much more thorough-going analysis than Hulme's for their elucidation,—he reveals once more the limitations of his dilettantism.

Nevertheless, though in his longer essays he is rather a specious than a satisfying writer, he is in his smaller pieces often provocative of thought. Some of his aphorisms are admirable, and his definition of ordinary Romanticism as "spilt religion" is simply masterly. Unfortunately the critical aphorism is a genre which receives very little encouragement in England. Had it been otherwise Hulme might have left behind him a remarkable book. (pp. 848-51)

> *Henry King [pseudonym of J. Middleton Murry], "The Contributors' Club," in* The Adelphi, *Vol. II, No. 10, March, 1925, pp. 848-51.*

W. E. COLLIN (essay date 1930)

[*Collin was an English-born Canadian critic and poet who wrote the first book-length critical work on Canadian literature,* The White Savannahs *(1936). In the following excerpt, he summarizes the basic tenets of Hulme's philosophy.*]

Hulme was . . . a prophet. He prophesied a change in our outlook on life and a renunciation of the romantic spirit in literature.

"Actual philosophy," he states, and this is where his method begins, "is not a pure but a *mixed* subject. It results from a confusion between two subjects which stand in no essential or necessary relation to each other, though they may be combined together for a practical end. One of these subjects is a science, and the other is not.'' These two subjects he denotes as: Pure Philosophy (L), the scientific, and a more *personal* subject (h) made up of ideals, standards or *canons of satisfaction* which ''should be subject to a *critique*.'' It is to (h) that he has given ''the somewhat grotesque title of the Critique of Satisfaction.'' Much of Hulme's thinking turns upon (h) and because literature eventually comes within its boundaries it is pertinent to take note of its scope.

''In his last chapter, in his 'conclusion,' the philosopher presents us with his reconstructed world as it is in *reality*. . . . He undertakes to show that the world is other than it appears to me; and as he takes the trouble to prove this, we should expect to find that consciously or unconsciously the *final* picture he presents will to some degree or other *satisfy* him.'' That is the word Hulme makes use of. He and others who have exposed the nineteenth century, for example Lasserre, are inclined to think that the standards which satisfy a particular age are unconscious standards, which no intelligent individual is expected to question, but which, taken for granted, lead to a characteristic view of life and a characteristic literature. Hulme puts it like this: ''In order to understand a period it is necessary not so much to be acquainted with its more defined opinions as with the doctrines which are thought of not as doctrines, but FACTS. There are certain doctrines which for a particular period seem not doctrines, but inevitable categories of the human mind. Men do not look on them merely as correct opinion, for they have become so much a part of the mind, and lie so far back, that they are never really conscious of them at all. They do not see them, but other things *through* them. It is these abstract ideas at the centre, the things which they take for granted, that characterise a period.'' Therefore a complete understanding of any period involves an examination of these pseudo-categories which ''lie so far back,'' their origin and development. As regards the modern age it involves an inquiry into the origins of our belief in personality and progress.

''The fundamental error is in placing *Perfection* in humanity.'' And in tracing it to its source Hulme does not stop at Romanticism and Rousseau, he goes back to the stoics, Epicureans, and Pantheists of the Renaissance. At the Renaissance ''men's categories changed; the things they took for granted changed. Everything followed from that.'' From this point of view we comprehend two periods of history: The Middle Ages, and the period from the Renaissance to us. The canons of satisfaction in these two periods, Hulme states, are: in the one case, a belief in the imperfection of man, the subordination of man to certain absolute values, the doctrine of Original Sin, immortality; in the second case, a belief in the perfection of man, in personality and ''all the bunkum that follows from it.'' His notes are sufficient to indicate that a very interesting history of modern literature could be written with these canons as guides. The two periods may be denominated Religious and Human. Of the two Hulme inclines to the Religious. ''I hold, quite coldly and intellectually as it were, that the way of thinking about the world and man, the conception of sin and the categories which ultimately make up the religious attitude, are the true categories and the right way of thinking . . . the important thing is that this attitude is not merely a *contrasted* attitude, which I am interested in, as it were, for the purpose of *symmetry* in historical exposition, but a real attitude, perfectly possible for us today. To see this is a kind of conversion.'' Hulme, therefore, turned to St. Thomas Aquinas. And by his ''conversion'' is it too much to say that he has shown the way for our restless and disillusioned generation of poets

who had pinned their faith to the doctrine of evolution and to a machine only too capable of enslaving their souls? He has made possible a return to religious poetry in England. Mr. T. S. Eliot is his disciple. There is a parallel case abroad. In France, and for the same reasons, we have philosophers like Jacques Maritain and poets like Jean Cocteau. Maritain, brought up a Protestant and Bergsonian but a convert to the Catholic Church, since 1914 has not ceased to advocate the realism of St. Thomas as a solution for all our problems.

Hulme was convinced that we were at the end of a period which had lasted for four hundred years, during which time the Greek attitude had prevailed. He saw signs of a renunciation of that attitude in Philosophy and Art: in the neo-realism of G. E. Moore and Husserl, in the art of Jacob Epstein and Wyndham Lewis. He prophesied a corresponding return to the classical spirit in literature.

Speaking on Modern Art and its Philosophy (1914) he applied the same kind of historical hypotheses to art:

(1) There are two kinds of art, geometrical and vital, absolutely distinct in kind from one another.

(2) Each of these arts springs from and corresponds to a certain general attitude towards the world.

(3) The re-emergence of geometrical art may be the precursor of the re-emergence of the corresponding attitude towards the world, and so, of the break-up of the Renaissance humanistic attitude.

Convinced as he was of a return to the religious attitude, he was just as certain that we were emerging into a period when we should find pleasure in rigid lines, geometrical, crystalline forms away from the confusion and accidental details of things as they exist. But he is also sure that the new period will bear the evidences of having come out by way of the Greek. ''Compare a Byzantine relief of the best period with the design on a Greek vase, and an Egyptian relief. The abstract geometrical character of the Byzantine relief makes it much nearer to the Egyptian than to the Greek work; yet a certain elegance in the line ornament shows that it has developed out of the Greek. If the Greek had never existed it could not have the character it has. In the same way, a new anti-humanist ideology could not be a mere revival of medievalism. The humanist period has developed an honesty in science, and a certain conception of freedom of thought and action which will remain.''

Then we may come to the two kinds of literature and say that because Romanticism is exhausted we shall have a revival of Classicism. ''Here is the root of all romanticism: that man, the individual, is an infinite reservoir of possibilities. . . . One can define the classical quite clearly as the exact opposite to this. Man is an extraordinarily fixed and limited animal whose nature is absolutely constant. It is only by tradition and organization that anything decent can be got out of him.'' As representatives of the classical spirit he takes ''such diverse people as Horace, most of the Elizabethans and the writers of the Augustan age.'' We are to expect, then, a return to these. But, as with philosophy and art, the new classicism will show signs of having come through romanticism. In poetry its instrument will be fancy; it will use romantic material but instead of damp, moaning, whining poetry, and emotions grouped round the word infinite, and the vague mysterious light that never was on land or sea, we shall have dry, hard, definite, physical, and cheerful poetry and ordinary daylight, we shall have poems which resemble mosaics and we shall certainly have others more typically reflecting the mechanical age in which we live.

We have only to look a little ahead to know that Hulme's words have come true; to the Sitwells and T. S. Eliot with their Elizabethan and Augustan pretensions, their disregard for conventional poetic diction, their pranks with metaphors, images and fanciful mosaics, the bright, geometrical lines and shrill steely noises of their poetry. (pp. 333-37)

We are beginning to realize fully what a supreme loss Hulme was to our generation. Not the poet so much as the philosopher and critic. More intelligently than we did, he felt our feelings and understood our responses to life and art; when we were still confused and baffled, he spoke out with conviction and with the voice of prophesy. (pp. 338-39)

> W. E. Collin, "Beyond Humanism: Some Notes on T. E. Hulme," in The Sewanee Review, Vol. XXXVIII, No. 3, Summer, 1930, pp. 332-39.

MICHAEL ROBERTS   (essay date 1938)

[*Roberts, an English poet and critic, wrote extensively on English poets of the early Modernist period, including Ezra Pound and T. S. Eliot. His critical work is generally informed by his interest in philosophy. In the following excerpt, Roberts discusses some of the salient features of Hulme's philosophical thought.*]

There is scarcely a single statement in Hulme that is not borrowed: his distinction between scientific philosophy and *Weltanschauung* comes from Husserl and Dilthey, his "classical" conception of man and his notion of the three worlds come from Pascal, his view of the world as flux from Bergson, his doctrine of intrinsic moral values from G. E. Moore, his talk about geometrical and vital art comes from Worringer, his interpretation of romanticism from Lasserre, his defence of violence from Sorel, and his conception of poetry as a logic of images might have been taken from any one of half a dozen French or German writers. Hulme's merits are seldom those of originality, but originality is more often a vice than a virtue, and Hulme, though he added little to the European tradition, did something to preserve it. He writes with a brilliant metaphysical style, very different from Husserl's abominable sludge, he seizes important points and puts them pungently, he knows more of philosophy than most art critics do, and his judgments in art are worth more than those of most philosophers. He writes more vividly and more coherently than Sorel, but like his master he does not pause to answer an objection. He has the enthusiasm and the naïveté of the amateur, and rushes on with the same dogmatic and incisive style and the same air of excitement and exploration, whether he is discussing the familiar quaysides of New York or the wilds of an unexplored Kamchatka.

In Hulme's philosophy, there is little that can properly be called scientific, and much that is personal. He admires systematic philosophers like Moore and Husserl, who try to doubt every statement they are tempted to make, and do not pass over a possibility until it has been shown to lead to a contradiction or other absurdity; but his own method is to assert impetuously his views, and only when those views contradict common beliefs does he set to work to make an ingenious, and often useful, distinction. He echoes Dilthey's plea for a critique of historical reason, but he seldom uses the historical approach to test his own ideas. He uses suitably chosen historical examples to show other people that the set of terms they use in speaking of the

world is not the only possible one, but he does not use the method in order to transcend particular interpretations.

The unity of Hulme's work is temperamental rather than logical, and one important point about him is that men of Hulme's temperament seldom write philosophy at all. He was active and restless, rather than sedentary and contemplative; he was a man of exceptionally wide interests and not only knew something of the arts and sciences, but enjoyed them and showed ability and taste in their pursuit; there was a touch of personal arrogance in his attitude to humanity in general, and some reverence for tradition when the tradition was old enough and could be used against his own contemporaries. Like Sorel, he seemed to hate followers quite as bitterly as he hated his opponents. An audience, yes, but not followers, because followers would corrupt and vulgarize all that he had said. He even speaks, in his notebooks, of the danger "that when all these notes are arranged, the order will kill them in commonplace."

It would be absurd to claim that Hulme was a very original thinker or that his motives were always philosophically "pure," but it would be equally absurd to dismiss his writing as a mere scrap-book of favorite quotations. Hulme has three great merits. First of all, the ideas that he borrowed are important and not as widely known in England as they ought to be. Secondly, he expressed those ideas with great vigor and clarity. Thirdly, though Hulme was temperamental and unsystematic, his ideas are far less contradictory and incoherent than they appear to be. (pp. 117-19)

Hulme's **"Sketch for a New Weltanschauung"** is a mixture of moral principles, definitions, assertions about history, and assumptions that belong to systematic philosophy. It is not an orthodox philosophy, but it resembles the Thomist philosophy in not recognizing any distinction between moral and aesthetic values. Hulme says that a work of art is an intuition of reality, and the standards by which he condemns romantic art and commends classical art are always moral and intellectual. This, perhaps, is what one might expect from a follower of Worringer, who is more interested in works of art regarded as parables or allegories expressing intellectual and moral beliefs than in art simply as a thing in itself, valuable quite apart from its ascertainable meaning.

The metaphysical assertions are derived from Bergson, but are modified by Hulme's tendency to describe everything in spatial metaphors, even when he is talking about time. Further, these metaphysical assumptions imply others that are never explicitly stated. No doubt the position is tenable, but it is a description of the raw material of a metaphysics, rather than a metaphysics itself: it offers a framework for Hulme's assertion of his personal creed, but the creed could be expressed just as well within quite a different framework.

Hulme sometimes allows his metaphor about cinders ["The absolute is to be described, not as perfect, but if existent, as essentially imperfect, chaotic, and cinder-like."] to run away with his judgment: he then says that the whole of the world is wholly chaotic. In more sober moments, he seems to believe that the whole of our experience is a featured continuum like a landscape: some patches of that continuum resemble others, as one hill resembles another, and so we can divide the continuum up into features, such as hills, rivers, towns, counties, that are arbitrary but yet objective. Different maps of the continuum can be drawn (like rainfall maps, population maps, and so on); and these are related to each other, but often in a very complex way. And though experience is partly ordered, we cannot accurately represent it by sharply defined symbols, because the things we try to represent merge into each other as hills merge into valleys, and rivers into glaciers and seas.

This description of experience leaves unanswered all the old problems about the nature of knowledge and the relation of language to reality; but there seems to be no devastating objection to it; and it has one great merit: it keeps the attention firmly directed to the existence of *people*. Hulme did not base an argument on it—it was the vehicle of his thought and not the thought itself—and his other assumptions and arguments might have been stated in other terms without losing their force. In any case, if we are going to say that there is no means of knowing whether a particular perception of order is really a perception of external reality, or an impression common to all reasonable people, it does not matter whether we describe the order as external or not; it is objective; that is to say, it can be shown to anyone and does not vary from one person to another. If we go on to say that in addition to these objective perceptions of order, there are others, which are not common to everybody, but only to people in one place, or living at one time, or educated in one special way, or speaking one special language, and if we add that these perceptions common to one group of people cannot readily be distinguished from perceptions of truly objective truth, then we admit all that is needed for the development of the rest of Hulme's outlook.

As we have seen, Hulme does not set up aesthetic judgment as something distinct from moral and intellectual judgment; furthermore, he does not separate moral and intellectual judgment. He does not assert that there are two kinds of truth or that there is a realm of values distinct from the realm of things. In place of the humanist's absolute distinction between things and their value, Hulme sets his distinction between three orders of reality. This he derives from Pascal. . . . (pp. 122-25)

Hulme's distinction, however, is not quite the same as Pascal's: in Hulme's description the three regions are not those of body, mind, and charity, but those of inorganic matter, the organic world, and the world of religious values. Pascal's distinction between mind and body raises one of the perennial problems of philosophy, but Hulme confuses the problem instead of clarifying it when he replaces it by the distinction between the vital and the mechanical worlds, which he tries to make clear by an example. "A mechanical complexity is the sum of its parts. Put them side by side and you get the whole. Now vital or organic is merely a convenient metaphor for a complexity of a different kind, that in which the parts cannot be said to be elements as each one is modified by the other's presence, and each one to a certain extent is the whole. The leg of a chair by itself is still a leg. My leg by itself wouldn't be."

This useful common-sense distinction works fairly well as long as we are talking about bricks and tables on the one hand, and eels and rabbits on the other; but when the scientist begins to study things that are neither seen nor felt directly, he becomes less confident. The "atom" of theoretical chemistry is assumed to be "mechanical" in Hulme's sense, but in atomic physics it shows nasty signs of being something more than the sum of its parts. "Vital events are not completely *determined* and mechanical", says Hulme. But neither are physical events: they cannot be foreseen in detail. There is always a margin of uncertainty, and the smaller the system the bigger the uncertainty. The only world that completely satisfies Hulme's conditions is the ideal world of theoretical reasoning: theoretical mechanics may indeed be mechanical, but the real world that is partially and more or less accurately represented by the theory

is not "mechanical" in the same sense. We cannot detach portions of reality either physically or mentally without altering or misrepresenting reality itself. A hill is a hill *in situ* not *in vacuo*.

Again, not only is the mechanical world ("the leg of a chair") quite as organic as Hulme's own leg, but also the world of theoretical biology is quite as mechanical as the world of theoretical physics. The scientist always tries to find a formula, that is to say, to find concepts that when manipulated according to fixed rules will represent the behaviour of the empirical world. The arguments for and against vitalism in biology therefore have nothing to do with this discussion. If a special concept such as "organism" is ultimately found to be necessary in the biological sciences, it will be like any other scientific concept: it will be a new concept modifying all the others, as the notion of an electron modifies the notion of an atom. It will not belong to a world apart, but will take a place in a definite technique for describing and forecasting the behaviour of some aspects of the world.

When we talk in this way, we are in danger of confusing the literal and the figurative senses of the word "mechanical": there is a plain sense in which it is ridiculous to say that a human leg is mechanical. Hulme himself does confuse these two senses, and he adds to the difficulty by combining a figurative meaning of "mechanical" with one, or perhaps two, of the meanings of "determined." This combination must be rejected, and unless Hulme's distinction between the "vital" and the "mechanical" worlds is nothing more than the usual rough and ready division between the vegetable and mineral kingdoms, it must be taken as a distinction between the real world of the senses and an ideal world that more or less represents one part of it. The one is an objective reality (the real cinders), the other is a world of discourse (the built-up picture of the cinders). This possible interpretation leads us to ask whether the world of ethical and religious values is also a world of discourse, a symbolic picture of a natural cindery world.

The question is this: can we distinguish between a "natural" world (the vital and mechanical worlds) and some other world? In what sense can we say that there is no "natural" objective justice, if we nevertheless believe that there is a world of religious values that is objective and accessible to everybody? Furthermore, if something good can be got out of man by tradition and discipline, and the tradition and discipline are supplied by other men, how can you say that "man is not naturally good?" The only way out seems to be to say that there are two kinds of knowledge, the one "natural" and the other "revealed", and that the tradition and discipline come from this "revealed" knowledge. But how can revealed knowledge be established, and how can true "revealed" knowledge be distinguished from false?

It is here that Hulme invokes his **"Critique of Satisfaction."** It seems (though Hulme never makes this clear) that in one sense the critique is as "natural" as the special sciences: the ordinary process of reasoning, if it is applied to our natural knowledge, and if it is pursued long enough, shows the vanity of desire; but by an intuition, as certain as any knowledge that we have, we know that this conclusion cannot be final. This intuition marks the boundary between "natural" knowledge and the knowledge of what Hulme would call the world of religion: it leads us to recognize the existence of an absolute moral imperative, and once this is admitted a new development of our knowledge becomes possible. By appealing to history and authority we can guard against personal errors in the application of this intuition, and thus our knowledge in the new region is as reliable as our scientific knowledge. Interpreted in this way, it seems that the distinction between the three worlds does not imply that there are two kinds of knowledge: the knowledge of the world of religion is as "natural" as any other, though it rests on a process of criticism that seems unusual to the humanist, and on an intuition that he does not question but is reluctant to use.

Hulme's assertion that we can have absolute and certain knowledge of the mechanical and religious worlds, and that this knowledge can be exactly reflected in logical terms, seems to rest on a misunderstanding of the nature of mechanics, and on a confusion of knowledge about the structure of ethics with knowledge of ethical values. The scientist himself does not claim that he arrives at absolute knowledge even in mechanics: "A scientific belief is a policy, not a creed." Of course, the fact that the ideal world of mechanics does more or less represent one part of our experience may be taken to show that there is some kind of order in that part; although we can only know that order more or less roughly, partly because our language does not really fit it, and partly because our own observation always alters it to an unknowable extent. (pp. 125-30)

Hulme is confused at this point: he has tried to combine Bergson's distinction between what can be said in logical language and what cannot, with Pascal's distinction between the material, intellectual and spiritual worlds. Pascal's distinction is valid and useful; but there is no reason whatever for saying that the first and third are mechanical, and the second organic, or that absolute knowledge is possible in the first and third and only relative knowledge in the second. Each of these three "worlds" can be discussed, more or less adequately, in logical language and in poetic language: the difficulties and the advantages vary only in degree.

Part of Hulme's difficulty comes from the fact that he never properly distinguishes between "intrinsic values", "objective values", and "absolute values". If for some people something is good in itself, he at once assumes that it can be treated as a detached inorganic entity, that its existence and value can be demonstrated to other people, and that it can be given a definite place in a hierarchy of values. This is the outcome of his passion for geometrical images, and combined with his limited knowledge of physical and biological science it leads him to say that the "mechanical" and "religious" worlds share some quality which they do not share with the "vital" world.

All that is really essential to Hulme's position seems to be this: all our reasoning about empirical knowledge does nothing more than show the structure of experience; it does not strengthen our motives or set them in order, but rather weakens them and destroys their order. All is vanity and uncertainty, if reasoning and empirical knowledge are the only sources of truth. "All bodies together, and all minds together, and all their products, are not equal to the least feeling of charity." The confidence that gives reality to courage and love, and all the things we value, cannot be known solely through the description of mind and body, though our language nearly always forces us to speak in terms of mind and body. To represent the relations of this source of value to the world of mind and body, which is the field of "natural" knowledge, we must use metaphors; we can talk, for example, of a "world" of values or a "sphere" or "plane" of values distinct from the material and intellectual regions, but this is always, and only, a metaphor.

When Hulme says that the world of religion is like the world of theoretical mechanics, he is needlessly adding to his own difficulties. It might equally well be argued that religious values cannot be described in logical terms, and must always be expressed in parable or poetic metaphor; and this view would in no sense weaken Hulme's essential doctrine that these values are objective and absolute. Pascal's statement is more judicious than Hulme's; he keeps closer to the fundamental contention that all is vanity unless the values of religion are objective. The assertion that there is a world of religious values, distinct from the world of mind and body, presents difficulties like any other fundamental distinction; but these difficulties need not be confused with those that follow from the assertion that the distinction between logical and poetic language is the same as the distinction between inorganic and organic matter.

The doctrine of the three worlds certainly enables Hulme to state very clearly his view that man is neither fundamentally good nor naturally progressive; it has a metaphorical value, and it points the way by which we can pass beyond the conclusion that all is vanity. If we believe not only that there is only one kind of knowledge, and one kind of reality, but also that everything of value must be justified by its consequences, we are led to this conclusion of vanity, for a morality of this kind becomes nothing but a matter of prudence unless we back it up with a belief in the desirability of human survival, and human survival hardly seems worth while unless we can point to some intrinsic goods that are incidental to it.

In order to make it clear that the value of any action or experience depends, not on its consequences in the world that is of a piece with the world of matter and thought, but on itself alone, Hulme says that the value is a manifestation of another, quite different, world; and by saying that this other world is disparate, he denies the relevance of the consequences altogether. He speaks as if "intrinsic" values were necessarily "isolated"—as if the Weisshorn, being beautiful, existed by itself, apart from the Dent Blanche and the Rothorn and the earth and sky. But there is no need to choose between the one assertion, that the object or its value exists utterly alone, and the other, that the object or its value exists only as a wholly undetachable feature of the whole universe. It is better to say that as we can *focus* on the Weisshorn, so we can focus on an "intrinsic" value; we need not ignore completely the relations between it and the rest of the world. In this matter there is a sort of law of inverse squares ("charity begins at home" expresses the notion) and in practice we all recognize this law and act upon it.

When Hulme attacks an error he is always inclined to assume that its opposite must be true; he seldom asks whether it is based on a false antithesis. Thus in dealing with the view that man is naturally good he does not examine the word "naturally", but goes to the other extreme and says that man is naturally bad. This doctrine he identifies with the dogma of original sin; but in Christianity the dogma of original sin is inseparable from the doctrine of redemption, and this last involves the possibility that man may recognize and accept redemption. Pascal insists on this: "It is equally dangerous for man to know God without knowing his own wretchedness, and to know his own wretchedness without knowing the Redeemer who can free him from it."

Hulme, in spite of his Bergsonian ideas, has a passion for making those distinctions that are the basis of all logical thought; and having made his distinctions, he has a quite un-Bergsonian belief that they are universal and unalterable. This belief he reinforces by running two or three distinctions into one: he speaks as if the distinction between the spiritual and the natural world were the same as the distinction between logic and poetry or between physics and biology. Hulme's combination of different antitheses often does more to confuse issues than to clarify them. (pp. 132-34)

> *Michael Roberts, in his* T. E. Hulme, *Faber and Faber Ltd., 1938, 310 p.*

DIXON WECTER (essay date 1939)

[*An American historian, biographer, and literary critic, Wecter wrote extensively on American cultural history. In the following excerpt, he discusses Hulme's tragic view of existence.*]

Hulme's posthumous volume [*Speculations*] is . . . the notebook of a keen mind dredging the depths of modern German and French speculation about which most Englishmen of his day knew nothing, and gathering into his net a variety of fish which he did not have time really to sort or appraise. To expect any very logical system of thought to emerge from this learned young eclecticism is vain; Hulme's originality might have begun after he had thought through all the ideas which he restated with such pungency, wit, and recklessness of their contradictions, but at the age of thirty-four he was dead. Hulme the literary artist and critic reached his majority, but Hulme the philosopher was still green timber.

Yet he did much to sow these borrowed ideas upon English soil, and specially to render them attractive to the world of art and aesthetics. But in the ears of most contemporaries his words sounded both impudent and pessimistic, the gospel of a graceless young Jeremiah. Most of the intellectual Edwardians believed that science and the spirit of brotherhood had conquered all the major problems, and that human life henceforth would be a kind of Fabian garden-party lit by the paper lanterns of idealism and set to the waltz music of inevitable progress.

From Max Weber, Hulme took his thesis that ever since the Renaissance the doctrines of humanism, Protestantism, and capitalism have grown thickly together to overshadow and destroy the truly religious attitude which once fed the wisdom and humility of man. In its place they have put the idol of progress, supposedly the spiral traced upward by successive ages of civilization, but in truth only a vicious circle. They have brought back the old pagan hedonism in the guise of "the happiness of posterity." Yet the ancient classical virtue of *pietas,* of simple reverence for values greater than individual man in his fleeting context, has been canceled out, along with the medieval concept of man as a sinful and wretchedly imperfect creature who by Divine help alone might apprehend perfection. To the Middle Ages man was neither a beast nor a god, but an immortal soul struggling precariously yet hopefully toward a state of grace. Pride was therefore the deadliest of the Seven Deadly Sins. Although Ruskin was anathema to Hulme, his remarks on the humility of Gothic architecture would have been fitting here.

But the self-sufficient spirit of the Renaissance, the age of romanticism, and the temper of modern science have filled man with a false security; he has been told that he is the measure of all things, and that outside his own health and wealth and contentment all else is relative or unimportant. To take an illustration not found in Hulme, one might say that the attitude of medieval man even at its most naïve was nothing more than an astronomical egoism—since he believed that his earth was the bull's-eye of the material universe, and that the stars in their courses fought for his salvation. But the man of the Renaissance, although disabused of this more or less harmless delusion by Copernicus and Galileo, gained in its place a much more baleful kind of vainglory—a temporal rather than a spatial egoism, which allowed him to see himself as heir of all the ages, in the foremost files of time, and thus smugly slighted both past and future. The result of this focus upon the here and now was an ethic of expediency, a philosophy of pragmatism, which forgot many of the hard-won lessons of error and self-limitation which medieval man crystallized into such a dogma as that of Original Sin.

Such things were said of course before Hulme, by Newman and others; they have been repeated since his time in the controversies over humanism. Nobody, however, has been more aware than Hulme of the deep and almost hopeless penetration with which the spirit of the Renaissance has sunk into the modern mind. During these last few centuries, he says, we have lived and breathed humanism; it is the ambient of our lives, and we are almost unable to return our thoughts to an age whose art and religion sprang from a sense of man's sinfulness rather than his perfectibility. Hulme tells us that we suffer from the complacence of the contemporary, that it is well for us to remember, for example, that "other ages have not been industrial, not because they lacked the capacity, the scientific intelligence, but because on the whole they did not desire to be industrial because they lacked this particular 'spirit,'"—i.e., capitalism.

In his attempt to explain this radical change Hulme falls back upon Pascal, the philosopher whose blend of hard-headed mathematical logic and religious faith makes him peculiarly congenial to the author of *Speculations,* who freely acknowledges in his chapter on "Humanism" that "these notes [are] to be regarded merely as a (*sic*) prolegomena to the reading of Pascal." Pascal's three orders of reality, explained in Fragment 792 of the *Pensées,* are those of body, mind, and "charity" or the grace and love of God. Hulme calls his three regions the realm of inorganic matter, the organic world, and the sphere of religious values. His distinction between organic and inorganic, even less defensible than Pascal's between mind and body, is drawn with more ingenuity than logic; thus he seeks to differentiate what he calls "mechanical" from "vital" complexity by remarking, "The leg of a chair by itself is still a leg. My leg by itself wouldn't be." As Mr. Roberts observes [see excerpt dated 1938], this common-sense distinction—useful enough when one is talking about furniture and animals—seems to break down when the scientist begins to study things which are not perceived directly, such as the atom of physics, which when considered *in situ* and not merely *in vacuo* is seen in Hulme's sense to be both mechanical and vital.

Hulme however seems to have been satisfied with this naïve classification of the three worlds, in his haste to link it with Bergson's contention that man's mind tends to see all phenomena in a mechanistic pattern—not because such is their real nature, but because human reason is made for analysis rather than synthesis (creation). Hence, says Hulme, a subjective trick of our minds reduces to a false simplicity and order the "extensive manifolds" which lie about us. We learn to trace a mechanical or spatial configuration upon the surface of a world of disorganized reality or "cinders." Such unity as the scientists and nominalist philosophers have devised is at best "an extremely artificial and fragile bridge, a garden net," which allows much of the real world of cinders to sift through. "All clear cut ideas turn out to be wrong," he wrote with typical overstatement in his notebook.

Following Bergson, Hulme maintains that there is another path to knowledge, intuition, by which alone we can apprehend an "intensive manifold," such as the idea of Free Will, which refuses to fit into any mechanical or spatial scheme, or the concept of the *élan vital*. It is not surprising that scientists and humanists, having an instrument of no such finesse and penetration as intuition at their command, are apt to ignore or deny the existence of a third world which it alone can lay bare. Hulme's ideas about intuition stem from Bergson, or ultimately Heraclitus, in the belief that all things flow, that "all reality is tendency," and hence that the truth about this ever-changing flux cannot be represented in rigid abstract terms. "All expression is vulgar," Hulme wrote with his usual drastic terseness. Yet he admits that the poet and the philosopher may capture by intuition something of the paradox of reality—of an ever-fluid world rushing between the banks of eternal and absolute value yet somehow never touching those banks.

Hulme believed that just as science by failing to keep the organic and inorganic clear and apart has led us into the fantasy of a mechanistic universe, so humanism is plunging us into the flux of vital phenomena so that we lose sight of the eternal banks. It has well-nigh drowned us in the welter of romantic perfectionism:

> You don't believe in a God, so you begin to believe that man is a god. You don't believe in Heaven, so you begin to believe in a heaven on earth. In other words, you get romanticism. The concepts that are right and proper in their own sphere are spread over, and so mess up, falsify and blur the clear outlines of human experience. It is like pouring a pot of treacle over the dinner table. Romanticism then . . . is spilt religion.

Hulme's attack upon romanticism is brilliant and withering, but in the midst of our applause it dawns upon us that the term means for him what French romanticism and Rousseau meant to the late Irving Babbitt—an epithet to which he has pegged all the disagreeable or irritating associations of a lifetime. It is sticky sentimentalism—hence the analogy of the treacle pot—but it is also the sense of wonder which springs from mere ignorance. It is the spirit of all lukewarm liberalism and utopianism, belonging to the people whom Shaw has described as "having minds so open that there is nothing left but a draft." It includes alike the "vulgarism of 'my unconquerable soul'" and also the spineless pacifism which does not thrill to "the long note of the bugle."

Hulme is ready cheerfully to sacrifice Hugo, Lamartine, Swinburne, and other poets he detests to the romantic holocaust, but snatches Shakespeare and the Elizabethans back to the safety of the "classical" ranks. . . . His borrowing of Nietzsche's phrase "dynamic classicism" gives him a shield with which to protect all his miscellaneous favorites—including Egyptian, Indian, and Byzantine rather than Greek art—against his own critical arrows. Whatever Hulme likes is "classical." Yet this is not to refuse our sympathy for Hulme's detestation of such statements as "art is the revelation of the infinite in the finite," reflecting the vague, misty *sehnsucht* of a certain brand of romanticism, or his demand that "it is essential to prove that beauty may be in small, dry things"—although Hulme himself hardly went farther in this direction than the Imagist Credo of 1915.

Hulme's desire in aesthetic criticism to "speak of verse in a plain way as I would of pigs" accords with his attitude toward the mysteries of religion. His viewpoint here is a "sensible" one, perhaps a shade too self-conscious but very refreshing. His distrust of sentiment and prettiness saves him from a kind of High Church posturing into which, with his hunger after authority, he might otherwise have fallen. His attitude is much like Chesterton's recognition of "the fact of sin, a fact as plain as potatoes." In defending the religious conception of ultimate values he writes:

> I have none of the feelings of *nostalgia*, the reverence for tradition, the desire to recapture the sentiment of Fra Angelico, which seems to animate most modern defenders of religion. All that seems to me to be bosh. What is important, is what nobody seems to realise—the dogmas like that of Original Sin, which are the closest expression of the categories of the religious attitude. That man is in no sense perfect, but a wretched creature, who can yet apprehend perfection. It is not, then, that I put up with the dogma for the sake of sentiment, but that I may possibly swallow the sentiment for the sake of the dogma.

Hulme finds that most moderns, including churchmen, "chatter about matters which are in comparison with this, quite secondary notions—God, Freedom, and Immortality." (pp. 143-48)

In thus paying attention exclusively to the sinfulness of man Hulme illustrates what Chesterton and others have pointed out as the essence of heresy—the plucking of a single dogma out of its rightful place in the larger harmony of doctrine. Similarly the Arians overemphasized the humanity of Christ, and Calvin the prescience of God, to the damage of other equally vital truths. Though one of Hulme's best friends, Ramiro de Maeztu, insists that he was a Catholic *in petto* at the time of his death, and although Roberts upon his own responsibility amplifies Hulme's viewpoint until it comes into the ken of the critic's own Christian outlook, the author of *Speculations* is often closer to the grave pagan disenchantment of Marcus Aurelius than to the faith and passion of his avowed master Pascal. By Hulme, . . . "religion" is used to describe "not a state of faith, but a state that may lead to faith."

Hulme is even more destructive toward his own case for objective authoritarianism when he contends that "all a writer's generalisations and truths can be traced to the personal circumstances and prejudices of his class, experience, capacity and body," that any attempt precisely to define the values he has seemed so bravely to defend will reveal that they, like all others, are but "amplifications of man's appetites." . . . Hulme insists that to reveal the feet of clay we apply rigorously to any philosopher's conclusions what he calls the critique of satisfaction. He says for example that after all the precision and refinement of Croce's philosophy we reach his grand summation on the note of the "mystery of infinite progress and the infinite perfectibility of man," and then detect the "commonplaceness" and "vulgarity" at the bottom of his dialectic. We perceive the shallow foundation of current humanism, thinks Hulme, when we begin to examine its canons of satisfaction, and find that all its pretentious rhetoric is grounded not upon eternal truth but upon some disguised personal fulfillment or the blind urge of racial survival. Believing that modern man is self-centered and crass because he has forgotten so much, Hulme warns us to carry "a library of a thousand years as a balancing pole" at the same time that we are searching our hearts.

Yet it is hard to resist the conviction that Hulme's logic, for all its residue of wisdom, is somewhat muddled. When we find the self-styled Valet to the Absolute making fun of metaphysical armor we grow a little puzzled. Hulme indeed fails to apply the critique of satisfaction to his own philosophy, gone awry between the will to believe and the fear of believing too much, and at all times suspicious—as a middle-class son of the Victorians might be—of betraying himself into undue enthusiasm or any symptom of "vulgarity." Hulme is in the unhappy plight of believing that absolute ethical values are the only ultimate good-and-truth, yet of having a skeptic nominalist imp forever at his elbow whispering that it is impossible actually to define these values in any terms save those of wishfulness. In *Speculations* he remarks that "all English amateurs in philosophy are, as it were, *racially* empiric and nominalist," and hence bog down when they come to intellectualist and realist philosophy—a remark well illustrated by the lineage of Bacon, Locke, Shaftesbury, and Hume as contrasted with the Continental tradition of Descartes, Spinoza, Kant, and Hegel. It was Hulme's misfortune, perhaps, that his racial heritage and his personal sympathies were at variance. This discord Mr. Roberts, out of his admiration for Hulme, seems to pass over rather lightly, although his awareness of it is shown perhaps in his admission that "the unity of Hulme's work is temperamental rather than logical."

After rejecting with a show of violence the humanism which tries to interpret the universe in terms of reason, Hulme smuggles through the back door another kind of humanism garbed in irrational dogma, even though this dogma is never very clearly explained. Hulme is prone to forget that—lacking mystical or at least supernatural assumptions—he is still dealing with the fallibility of the human mind, and has not yet come to grips with the absolute. But being essentially an artist rather than a philosopher, Hulme feels that he has bartered well in exchanging rationality for intuition. Intuition is the path of the mystic and the artist, but is hardly the highroad to objective and authoritarian truth; the reader of Hulme is tempted to regard it as a compromise somewhere between reason and faith but lacking the impregnability of either. (pp. 148-50)

Hulme's recognition of man's sinfulness and proneness to error—a sort of fatal heliotropism which makes him blunder whenever he aspires to the heaven of ultimate truth, the eternal failure of Icarus, Prometheus, Faust—leads him not to the religious but to the tragic view.

He sees that human life is not the well-ordered game of man against an invisible opponent about which Thomas Henry Huxley wrote a little unctuously, where "the chess-board is the world, the pieces are the phenomena of the universe, the rules of the game are what we call the laws of nature." Hulme, like Kafka, suspects that the rules cannot be known with much certitude, that the game is shot through with unexpected passages of comedy and irony but overshadowed throughout by tragedy, and that the Heavenly Powers in "the Castle" who allow man to play with them demand a humility of spirit that is more vital than the rational knowledge which Huxley and his bumptious generation thought was attainable. Boastfulness, sentimentalism, cynicism, and despair are equally foolish; the tragic view makes for a deep sense of personal responsibility, but never for self-pity or bravado. "Blessed are the poor in spirit, for theirs is the kingdom of Heaven."

Such is the tragic view of Hulme, founded upon the honest recognition that evil exists not only in the world but in ourselves, and even more honestly admitting that we are often unable to tell the evil from the good. It is a view of tragedy which springs from humility as well as *hubris,* since none can escape some sense of bafflement and overthrow, but it inspires feelings akin to the pity and terror of the ancient Greek drama, now mixed with the self-consciousness and more desperate skepticisms of modern man. The tragic view becomes Christian only when the redemptive and penitential motif is added, as for example in T. S. Eliot; but whatever its many guises may be, it seems to offer us the key to the most sensitive and profound art of our time. "It is the closing of all roads," wrote Hulme, "this realization of the *tragic* significance of life, which makes it legitimate to call all other attitudes shallow." (pp. 150-51)

Dixon Wecter, "Hulme and the Tragic View," in The Southern Review, *Vol. V, No. 1, Summer, 1939, pp. 141-52.*

J. F. HENDRY   (essay date 1942)

[*Hendry is a Scottish poet, novelist, and critic. His poetic work is comprised primarily of longer poems and he has noted that he "dislikes 'I' poetry, prose poetry, 'descriptive' poetry, and all poetry that does not create a world of its own." In the following excerpt, he examines the flaws inherent in Hulme's philosophical constructs.*]

Hulme was possessed by the image of "Cinders." "The absolute," he says, "is to be described, not as perfect, but if existent, as essentially imperfect, chaotic, and cinder-like."

His constant use of this metaphor reveals that to him it was of great significance. We shall not attempt here to find out exactly what that significance was, nor to relate it to his general philosophy, a task already ably carried out by Michael Roberts [see excerpt dated 1938]. Rather shall we try to place that image in time, and relate it to others of like date, in the hope that thereby we may gain some conception of where *we* are going.

The first thing to note is that Hulme's vision of reality is closely akin to T. S. Eliot's image of "The Waste Land." The common quality seems to be their belief that reality is brittle, possibly even breaking up, and more than that, their interpretation of this "reality" in terms which are always wholly material and inorganic, "broken glass in a dry cellar." Thus their historical significance seems to lie in the fact that in them, as individuals, a "scientific-materialist" outlook on the world is coming to an end, if indeed it is not already dead. Their imagery implies a whole superstructure of philosophy and experience known to be outmoded. Both therefore sought something to replace the excessively objective outlook which was in process of collapse. Mr. Eliot embraced the Anglican faith. Hulme thought he had found his panacea in a philosophy, the core of which, perhaps, was Bergson's conception of intuition.

Bergson, however, in describing the use of images, also revealed his mental attitude, since he regarded the advantage of imagery as being "that it keeps us in the concrete." Here again is seen the cindery vision peculiar to Hulme and Eliot. "By choosing images as dissimilar as possible," wrote Bergson, "we shall prevent any one of them from usurping the place of the intuition it is intended to call up, since it would be driven away by its rivals."

This, of course, is precisely Rimbaud's technique of dissociation and not association at all. It is reminiscent of the surrealists whose juxtaposition of images drawn from the concrete is designed, often deliberately, to provide the shock of "surprise," that is, of intuition. Even in thought Hulme was breaking-down, therefore, not building.

The weakness of these attitudes is their failure to establish any kind of absolute, though such was Bergson's aim and Hulme's desire. "What is relative is the symbolic knowledge by pre-existing concepts, which proceeds from the fixed to the moving, and not the intuitive knowledge which installs itself in that which is moving, and adopts the very life of things. This intuition attains the absolute."

That it failed to do so in the case of surrealism and of Hulme may be due precisely to this fact, that it *is* an attitude, a pre-existing concept (Hulme's "cinders"; Bergson's "concrete") which may actually become the symbolic knowledge Bergson says is relative. Many of the surrealist designs notoriously fail because they are deliberate, fixed, and not a spontaneous re-lease of the unconscious at all. Truth, Hulme seems to say, with Krieck the Nazi philosopher, depends on the pre-existent image in the spectator's mind. Actually, the pre-existent image should be regarded as a subject for study, and intuition may come with investigation.

If, however, such images are not "intuitive" in so far as they are partly conditioned, the question arises how they have been thus conditioned, these visions of deadness against which both Hulme and surrealists revolt. They seem to be the result of the psychological twist inherited from the Age of Enlightenment, and especially from the Industrial Revolution, which prevents us seeing reality essentially in terms of people, but which clings to the objective world of matter for its own sake, in the belief that somehow, in ruins as it is, it must yet be the sole significant standard of value, a power illimitable. By "twist" I mean no more than "way of looking at things," what Americans call "angle." No revolt against reason as such is involved, only against the "angle" which has turned that reason outwards.

Thus, while Hulme rejects the nineteenth-century concept of the inevitability of progress, he still retained the nineteenth-century concept of the intrinsic value of the material world, and his cindery-imagery reveals this clearly. Equally, his con-stant attempt to think in a straight line, the line of progress, betrays his mental approach. He fought of course against this, as can be seen in his notes. These are full of what I might call thinking in clots, in lumps. The thoughts are thrown up like gold nuggets and turned over for testing. This is organic think-ing, *real* intuition because quite free of pre-existing concepts or attitudes. If, too often, the nuggets turned out to be mere cinders instead of gold, it can only have been because of the historical colouring of his mind, because the soil contained more ash than precious metal. Hulme is therefore, unknown perhaps to himself, the philsopher of the materialist world in decline as Eliot was its poet.

His search for a new classicism and ethereal absolute is the counterpart of Mr. T. S. Eliot's conversion, and its error con-sists in its assumption that man must be deserted for the ab-stract, because of the failure of an abstraction.

"There is," says Hulme, "no bridge from the finite to the Infinite; the world is finite and we cannot escape from its surface." Here, unmistakably, the soil of historical materialism clings to the nugget. Thus he enunciates his famous three cat-egories of reality, the organic, the inorganic, and the religious, and declares them separate, not as a mere technique of thought, but absolutely and eternally.

In practice, whatever Hulme may assert, it seems that at various times myths serve as a bridge, and the Christian myth in fact did so in Hulme's case, whether he recognized it or not. "The Revolutionary objective will serve the purpose of a myth and so lead to the establishment of absolute ethical values, whereas Utopian myths lead to day-dreaming."

Hulme's concept is as Utopian, more Utopian, than those of outworn liberalism because he *denies* the bridge. Pope is to be independent of Emperor, and Emperor of Pope, but both Mi-lords Spiritual and Temporal shall reign by Divine Right, and the earth shall be divided between them. Such was Dante's original Utopia. No bridge, no communication between spirit and matter was permitted or recognized. Thus Hulme strangled his own intuition at birth. The images that did come forth from it were, like those of Rimbaud, images of dissociation, of disintegration, cinders. What might have been the foundation of a new and absolute Humanism, becomes the definition of an ancient and inverted materialism.

This inversion is seen for example in Hulme's conception of the Deity. Belief in Him is inevitable, like belief in the ob-jective world and matter. The analogy is significant, and hints at identity. "When the fixed instincts are repressed, they burst out in some abnormal direction. If you are not allowed to believe in Heaven, you begin to believe in Heaven on earth. If you don't believe in God, you begin to believe that man is a god."

This is all right as far as it goes, but it does not go very far. Belief in a heaven on earth is a myth as belief in Heaven is a myth, and Hulme is not interested in myths, or their relative validities and social roles. He is dealing in absolutes, or trying to. Having therefore established to his own satisfaction that humanism involves belief in man as a god, he discards it and flies at once to the other extreme. Man is limited. The Deity forever separate from him.

Yet somehow man is to be ruled by the Deity. There's the rub, for if the Deity is out of touch with man, yet must rule man, He can surely do it only through a representative, and we are back at the Divine Right of Kings, where the Divine Right is in question since there is no bridge! Without the concept of myth we are lost, and the myth of humanism is as valid as the myth of Divine Right. Even Hulme asserts that all men are equal.

The trouble with this new classicism that rejected, and rightly so, Romantic Art, Pragmatic Philosophy, Modernist Religion, and Utopian Liberalism, was that it provided us in their stead with a cindery art answered in Germany with "Blubo"; a fascist-academic philosophy with none of the dynamism of nazism; cloistral religion; and the medieval utopianism of the Holy Roman Empire. It did not, as Hulme would agree, carry forward enough from Humanism. Denying the bridge, it fails to make its artifices work.

Yet because man's attempted conquest of nature, and his at-tempt to express himself in terms of caesarism, have failed, there is no valid ground for believing man to be a fundamentally limited creature *in himself*. To do so, as Hulme did, is to leave out of account the very aspirations which, he warned us, would "burst out" if repressed. Nevertheless, although only man's orientation has been shown to be wrong, his previous pattern of behaviour, perhaps because it was a pattern, Hulme would have us subjected to a new pattern, one just as "objective-mechanical," thus inviting not a new world of glorious order, but a new nihilism.

Never is there a word of human attempt at self-expression through a new set of human relations. We are simply invited to exchange human exploitation in the interests of a materialist absolute, for human exploitation in the interests of mechanist idealism. And this in spite of Hulme's professed belief that "there is no average or real truth to be discovered among the different fronts of prejudice." No attempt is made to incorporate even this last important concept in any new political order. That might mean delegation of responsibility, or a new social myth of democracy, but Hulme denies bridges. He is a poor Horatio, especially for these days when the Channel is a very real bridge with an Infinite Darkness.

> Experience shows that the framing of a future in some indeterminate time may, when it is done in a certain way, be very effective, and have very few inconveniences; this happens when the anticipations of the future take the form of those myths which enclose within them all the strongest inclinations of a people, of a party, or of a class, inclinations which recur to the mind with the insistence of instincts in all the circumstances of life.

This is a demonstration of how a myth, representing "in the consciousness the image of which it feels the attraction," may act as a bridge, as did the myth of the French Revolution, of the Russian Revolution; in England the myth of Christianity, of human freedom. Myth, we say, because it is not yet realized but held to be capable of realization, "justifying, sustaining, and inspiring the existence of a community," a bridge with what at any moment is the infinite because it is not yet attained. This is the dynamic of progression—not the old easy "progress"—active intuition, not Hulme's static surrender of that intuition to external forces.

Yet though he denied the bridge, he did in practice demonstrate his belief in the defence of the bridge. He lived in an era when Imperialism was on the defensive in his own state. To go forward he held to be utopian. He preferred to go back, though how far back that would have taken him he did not completely realize. He was defending the bridge as an Ideal alone.

"To Hulme," says Michael Roberts, "the prospect of a German Europe was intolerable because it meant the extinction of ideals of liberty and democracy; and though he was opposed to the ideas with which the democratic movement was associated, he was willing to fight for democracy as an 'ideal.' In its ideas, the German outlook resembled his own, but his 'ideals' were those of English democrats." This is very interesting. To-day we should say that whilst his "ideals" were English— a phrase that means little if anything—his "idealogy" was German, which means a great deal indeed. I doubt if we should find this comforting, however much it may seem to approximate to unofficial war-aims.

Graham Wallas has incidentally thrown some light on the fundamental weakness of his position. "Philosophers should give us a conception of the relation between freedom and determinism which shall apply to the whole living universe, and not draw an arbitrary line as some do, dividing certain facts of psychology, which are legitimate subjects of scientific inquiry, from others which are not. . . ."

This strikes directly at Hulme's arbitrary division of reality into three categories, a division which in any case, like the reason he revolted against, is based on fear, for whilst it might be acceptable as a methodology, with the proviso that it should not be watertight, and that myth or imagination should operate between the three, there are no grounds whatever for declaring it absolute.

Fear is admitted by Hulme when he writes, of art in the future, "They live in a world whose lack of order and seeming arbitrariness must inspire them with a certain fear. . . . In art this state of mind results in a desire to create a certain abstract geometrical shape, which, being durable and permanent, shall be a refuge from the flux and impermanence of outside nature."

Here again he does not face up to the question of *why* such an art may be expected, if indeed it now may. He denies that fear is a necessary pre-supposition for this development, but his alternative motivation, the "idea of disharmony or separation between man and nature" is but another way of expressing that same fear. It is also in flat contradiction with his introductory idea of the inevitability of separation between man and nature. Having himself declared them absolutely separate, he proceeds to look for an art which shall overcome that separation—and finds incidentally an *inorganic* one, a pyramid cinder. Had he denied the separation in the first place he might have had a clearer conception both of his own motives, and of the function of the art he described.

Again in his actual consideration of the geometrical nature of Egyptian arts, he was too content perhaps to take these for granted as isolated phenomena, ignoring the other side of the picture; Thoth of the ibis-head; the deification of animals and birds; and their identification in many cases with man. His philosophy, "scientific" though it is, leaves out of account too much of anthropology, psychology, and in this case Egyptology. There are grounds at least for supposing that these Egyptian myths and legends are the expression of the fear felt by the society for just these outside elements, the crocodile, and the scarab; and the fact that man is himself often identified with these forces, capable of destroying him, further shows that the *geometrical* art was less a reaction to external flux than the expression of *inner* instability, just as our own institutions and cultivation of the reason are forms of inhibition, repression, or objectifications of inner conflicts. That our art is more vital than Egyptian or Byzantine therefore, may be due to the fact that we are more aware of the real nature of the conflict than were these primitive peoples, and hence better able to express it in vital terms. Our myths have more individual and social content. Only when they prove deficient in this, will a "geometric" art become likely. It is noteworthy that in Hulme the myth has become very non-human indeed.

It seems therefore that Egyptian art, and the others which Hulme considers to be purely geometrical, did in fact express in the totality of their civilizations, a deep-seated conflict, which for want of more precise terms we must call a conflict between inner and outer worlds, but one which was based essentially on *fear* of the outside world owing to its instability and flux. There is therefore less difference between the arts leading up to the Classical period, and our Renaissance and modern art, than Hulme supposed, since its vital nature is merely a consequence of recognition that the conflict is in reality an inner one, and incapable of *solution* in external, geometrical, non-human terms.

Again though the work of Epstein is continually cited in support of his thesis, it is overlooked that in addition to the geometrical, "cubism" in Picasso, Cezanne, or Epstein, there is present a great deal of irrationality and myth. The expression of the faces, of the eyes, the choice of themes, of people and acts such as procreation, show that Epstein is as close to myth and symbolism as were the primitive Egyptians, and this is as significant as the geometrical element *per se*.

Furthermore the distinction between the Byzantine-Egyptian-Indian and the Western civilizations becomes less still when we consider their achievement. The pyramids represented to the Egyptians, as Hulme shows, precisely that conquest of space and time which we attempt to achieve to-day in industrial development, the railway, the aeroplane, the giant liner, and which the Middle Ages attempted to achieve in the cathedral and the chronicle. The psychological trend in both cases is the same, inhibition, objectification of the inner feeling of insecurity. Hence wars become bigger and better, not only outside the society in question but inside, since no amount of objectification in modern times can abolish or disguise man's awareness of inner conflict. Thus, as well as military wars on the grand scale we may, if we yield to Hulme, expect petty gangsterdom, violence in private life, lawless anarchy, the jitterbug with a gun.

This Hulme also admits when he envisages the break-up of the Renaissance humanistic attitude. And make no mistake, this is a process much more fundamentally disastrous than the superficial scratching implied in the phrase "break-down of liberalism." It has political implications, of course, totalitarianism, for example; but the effects inside man are liable to be even more devastating, for it must be remembered that the societies to which Hulme looks back were helot-states of the worst type, so that ultimately the break-up of humanism must result inevitably in a slow and ineluctable return to slavery, literal and inescapable, the most frightful victory in fact, of the *forces* (not necessarily the nation) which we are now fighting against.

It is to be hoped that he miscalculated.

The intuition which Hulme neglected, can be seen therefore to be of extreme psychological importance, and the core of the internal conflict at work in modern society. No attempt at external solutions based on purely materialist or abstract conceptions, can go very far towards solving it, though they may for a time repress it. This "intuition" seems therefore to be the dynamic, that driving-force which, he held, derived from the religious sense of absolute obligation, but which seems to have an immediate origin in the Unconscious. The latest theories of Jung make it seem likely that it is of an affective nature, precisely that "palpable and obvious love of man for man" dismissed by Michael Roberts. The human problem must therefore be conceived in terms of human relations first.

Hulme's insistence on the Absolute, however, that psychological twist, leads him into the strange impasse in which, criticizing man for failing to express himself entirely through matter, he interprets man through that matter. "Nothing is what it is, alone." Thus he climbs from the cinders to deny that the world can be considered as separate fragments at all! Here he is linking man to the inorganic world, as he was forced earlier to link him to the Divine, in a new philosophical tyranny.

More consideration of the purely human, might have shown him that fragmentary outlooks are irrelevant where the question of changing "reality" is concerned, at least "reality," devoid as it is of people. Language and a space between words does not break up "reality," though it may break up our reactions to it, or reform them. The error lies again in excessively objective thinking which allows no place to man, the psychological twist which sees "reality" in a heap of stones, but none

in a crowd. The need is therefore now for a philosophy which shall include psychology, instead of roping it off, and by integrating man, do something to integrate his society, from the individual upwards into institutions. For that, we shall need a Horatio with belief in the bridge, for to disbelieve in it now is the essence of psychological Fifth-Columnism. (pp. 136-47)

> *J. F. Hendry, "Hulme As Horatio," in* Life and Letters To-Day, *London, Vol. 35, December, 1942, pp. 136-47.*

HERBERT READ　(essay date 1945)

[*Read was a prolific English poet, critic, and novelist. Several convictions are central to his discussions of literature, the foremost being his belief that art is a seminal force in society and human development, and that a perfect society would be one in which work and art are one. He also believed that art and material progress are the result of conflicting forms of thought. In literature, the most dynamic conflict is between classicism and romanticism: "categories usually known as classicism and romanticism are related to their psychological origins in the individual, and shown to be, not alternatives equivalent to right and wrong, but tendencies which must be accepted as equally inevitable and reconciled in some more universal concept, which with due caution might be described as Humanism." Read's work as a poet and novelist gave him special insight into the creative process, and his tolerance of various literary theories enabled him to appreciate the works of many diverse artists. In the following excerpt, he discusses and criticizes Hulme's conception of the opposition between romanticism and classicism.*]

Hulme recognized two orders of reality, the one divine, a hierarchy of absolute ethical values represented by religion; the other human, the world of our physical existence, inevitably limited, imperfect, and only saved from brutishness by some perception of the nature of the divine order. Hulme, like many philosophers before him, naturally drew the conclusion that if humanity is to enjoy any degree of civilization, it must be disciplined by an order or tradition established in accordance with the absolute ethical values. He was never, however, very precise as to the way in which this was to be done. He combined a belief in absolute values with a nominalism which would normally lead a philosopher to deny their existence. That is to say, though he might admit the existence of the values, he was equally convinced that it was impossible to define them, or rather, that any attempts to define them would necessarily be only "amplifications of man's appetites." There is an abyss between the human and divine, and we can only bridge it with approximations—that is to say, with the intuitions of the poet and the mystic.

If we look at Hulme's dilemma a little closer, we find that one of its terms is equivocal. There can be no question about the first proposition—that man is inherently limited, a mixture of good and evil impulses, incapable of progress unless controlled. That proposition must either be accepted or rejected—it cannot be qualified. Hulme accepted it and based on it his destructive attacks on humanism. The second proposition, that man, on account of his inherent weakness, must submit to the authority of a religious tradition, he held with the same conviction but with less consistency. Tradition in art, the subject in which Hulme was chiefly interested, meant classicism. Hulme hastened to adopt classical art. Without putting too much strain on his natural preferences, he could exalt fancy at the expense of imagination, and a German art historian, Wilhelm Worringer, provided him with a distinction between geometric and organic form which enabled him to divide contemporary painting and sculpture along similar lines. War was declared against romanticism, and by defining romanticism as spilt religion and confusing it with sentimentality, he was able to manoeuvre all his enemies into the same false position. But when he came to review his own forces he found not only Horace, Racine and the English Augustans on his side, but also Shakespeare and the Elizabethans. Nietzsche provided him with a phrase— dynamic classicism—to hide the discrepancy, but it was a palpable begging of the question. Actually, when he is discussing this weary question of romanticism and classicism, Hulme is apt to forget his fundamental distinction, which is philosophical, and lose himself among the secondary characteristics of aesthetic expression. That is to say, having decided on philosophical grounds that Horace, Racine and Shakespeare are acceptable poets, he proceeds to lump their very diverse literary qualities together as classicism; and having decided on the same grounds that Lamartine, Hugo and Swinburne are bad poets, he proceeds to call their qualities romantic. But it is doubtful if stylistic criteria have much to do with the question. The underlying distinction, which is never so consciously philosophical as Hulme would have it, is between two social attitudes—between those poets on the one hand who wish to devote their artistic talents to the conservation of existing social values, and those on the other hand who wish to devote them to the disruption of these values and to the establishment of new ones. A revolutionary poet will often introduce a revolutionary technique, but not necessarily so. The youthful and revolutionary Wordsworth revolted against an artificial poetic diction, but the equally youthful and revolutionary Swinburne restored it.

From the point of view of art, there is not something which we can call tradition: there are two traditions, the romantic tradition and the classical tradition, and the prevalence or urgency of one or the other at any particular time will depend on the distribution of social forces. The only conditions which would ensure a stable form of art, that is to say, a disappearance of the conflict between classical and romantic tendencies, would be a state embodying the principles of absolute justice. But to suppose that such a state can ever exist is to accept that very doctrine of human perfectibility against which Hulme brings his most destructive arguments.

This contradiction is inherent in every form of the traditionalist doctrine—even the religious. Unless a religion is based on mystical revelation, on an irrational authoritarianism which can in no sense be called "an act of the intellect," the traditional dogmas of that religion can only be established and elaborated and sustained by fallible human agents; and that this human fallibility extends to such doctrinaire products of the mind is evident enough from the whole course of history. The choice, therefore, is not between humanism and an absolute ethical order free from human taint; it is between a humanism that strives after a rational interpretation of the universe and a humanism that accepts an irrational dogma. And an irrational dogma can only survive as a tradition by virtue of an external authority. The life of reason, which also has every right to be called a tradition, is a life of change, of growth and decay; but the stabilization of a human interpretation of ethical values, which is the only meaning we can give to a religious tradition of a rational kind, is an arbitrary act of the human will. Even if we believe with Kant that a moral sense is implicit in the nature of reason, we are still bound to the limitations of a human faculty. Michael Roberts, in his study of Hulme, says finely that reason is not complete unless it includes humility, and that humility involves a recognition of tradition and authority. But reason also includes doubt—humility involves doubt;

Bronze of Hulme by his friend Jacob Epstein.

and finally we may accept all Hulme's criticisms of humanism, romanticism and liberalism and still be no nearer the shelter of a Church. Between the feebleness of mankind and the perfection of the divine Hulme saw nothing but a tragic discord— a discord to be resolved by the fallible processes of human reason, or to be affirmed by an act of intuition—by the highest of all human modes of expression, the art of tragedy.

Hulme's predominant interest, as I have already said, was aesthetic. . . . There is little doubt that in the course of his development Hulme would have encountered Kierkegaard, and would have had to deal with that philosopher's contention that the aesthetic attitude can only lead to despair. If he had accepted that conclusion, the real problem would then have been to reconcile the aesthetic with the ethical attitude. Kierkegaard believed that they could only be reconciled in religion, but he could not reconcile his conception of religion with the tradition of the Established Church.

If we would secure the free assent of men we must appeal to them by myth rather than by precept—by art rather than by dogma. Perfect things teach hope, said Nietzsche. In the perfection of tragedy we transcend our fate. This realization of the tragic significance of life is the prerequisite of any measure of human greatness, but it is not specifically religious. Or if it is, the religion is in the ritual, in the drama, in the creation of the poet. To interchange tragedy and religion is to confuse what is perhaps the greatest of all issues. Between tragedy and religion the burden shifts. Redemption, which is inseparable from religion as understood in the Western world, introduces the idea of divine pity. Tragedy is not so humane; its catharsis is a healing process, but the most that it promises is serenity. (pp. 295-99)

Herbert Read, "T. E. Hulme," in his A Coat of Many Colours: Occasional Essays, *George Routledge & Sons, Ltd., 1945, pp. 294-99.*

WALTER JACKSON BATE (essay date 1952)

[*Bate is an American critic and biographer who has written a definitive study of the life and works of John Keats as well as several important surveys of literary criticism. He is particularly interested in late eighteenth-century literature, which he considers a watershed in the history of ideas, marking the transition from classical to romantic influences. In the following excerpt, originally published in 1952 in* Criticism: The Major Texts, *Bate briefly explains Hulme's aesthetic theories.*]

Hulme has extensively influenced modern criticism because he stated, in brief and vigorous fashion, a variety of views that were to prove congenial to the modern temper but had not yet been theoretically expressed (at least in this particular combination) and critically applied to art. His critical writing, in fact, is more in the nature of a brief manifesto or declaration of principles than it is an analysis or development of a position. Hence he is not, perhaps, read so frequently now as in the late 1920's and early 1930's, even by critics and readers who repeat the same views in terms originally popularized by Hulme.

To begin with, Hulme offered to English and American critics a general credo for modern abstract *formalism*. The reaction already beginning against nineteenth-century art—against romantic vagueness and the romantic exploiting of emotion for its own sake—was carried further by Hulme, and expressed in more drastic and thoroughgoing terms. In his provocative essay, **"Modern Art,"** he divided art, rather abruptly, into two varieties, "geometrical" and "vital," each of which expresses a basic way of regarding life. Because it leads so directly to the premises of an important modern movement, Hulme's notes on this subject deserve a fuller discussion than does his superior essay, **"Romanticism and Classicism."** "Vital" art tries to disclose the living and organic process of nature, though Hulme would say that it does not "disclose" but rather that it invents the quality it prizes and then projects it upon nature. This sort of art, which tends toward a "naturalistic" or "realistic" rendering of its subject, arises when man feels that he has a satisfactory and indeed organic connection with the external world. It is found in classical antiquity, and it returns in the Renaissance as the dominant form of art. Romanticism is its last stage, and, at the close of the nineteenth century, it culminated in a loose and meaningless sentimentality—"in the state of slush in which we have the misfortune to live." On the other hand, "geometrical" or abstract art—such as we find in primitive, Byzantine, and some kinds of Oriental art—arises when man feels his separateness from the external world and from other men. Here, with a feeling of "space-shyness," he *imposes* form—rigid, lifeless, abstract form—thus trying to order his experience in such a way as to control it. It is into such a state of mind that the twentieth century, Hulme believed, has been moving. And he buttressed his argument by connecting it with a religious outlook which stresses man's separateness, and in which the central dogma is that of "original sin."

Hulme's division of art into these two types may be accepted as a suggestive hypothesis. But it is hardly an argument, in the form that he left it, and it leaves unanswered some of the central problems of critical theory. The foremost is that involved in the classical belief that form of any sort is nothing except as it is objectively *real*—except as it is found working through nature itself—and that art is of value to the degree that it reveals this form, conveying or recasting it through its own medium. Hulme's implication that the form in "vital" art is a happy delusion and a subjective creation of one's own mind is, of course, a possible interpretation. But the "geometrical" art he opposed to it is openly admitted to be subjective. It is imposed directly on nature: indeed, its principal merit, as Hulme urged it, is that it is anti-natural. Nor is the attitude of "space-shyness" that underlies it developed by Hulme: he simply assumed it is inevitable, and half advocated it on romantic grounds as being "of greater intensity." If both forms of art are subjective, the difference for Hulme seemed to be that abstract art openly admits it. Like that of Irving Babbitt, if only in this one respect, Hulme's central position was thus arrived at negatively, through reacting strongly against the nineteenth century. The difference is that, for Hulme, the classic and the romantic were both of a piece in contrast to the abstract art which he urged. For Babbitt, on the other hand, the abstract formalism of Hulme would simply be one side of the same coin of which romanticism comprises the other side. Both, that is, would show a concern with the medium of art at the expense of its subject; both would illustrate the disintegration of the classical tradition by retreating from actual life, the romantic showing a subjective withdrawal from reality into an art of sentimental stock responses, while abstractionism continues this withdrawal but protests against the sentimentality of the romantic and seeks to substitute instead a more ingenious and demanding method of arousing response.

A less extreme treatment of Hulme's theory of art is that offered in his influential **"Romanticism and Classicism."** Here he repeated his protest against the romantic without handicapping his argument by connecting what he disliked in it with the entire Western tradition. In fact, what he here theoretically opposed to romantic art is a conception of classicism broad enough to include not only classical antiquity, but also Shakespeare, most of the Elizabethans, and the neoclassic tradition of the seventeenth and earlier eighteenth centuries. Still, the tone of his discussion suggests an ideal that may more aptly be described as neoclassic—an ideal achieved by "fancy" rather than "imagination," and characterized by a "dryness" and "hardness" of style. Both directly, and also indirectly through T. S. Eliot, this conception of poetic style was taken over and adapted in the revival of "metaphysical" poetry in the 1920's and 1930's. But its more general influence was to encourage the search, by both critics and poets, for a sophisticated urbanity of style that had not been common in English poetry since the death of Pope. (pp. 560-62)

Walter Jackson Bate, "Thomas Ernest Hulme," in Criticism: The Major Texts, *edited by Walter Jackson Bate, revised edition, Harcourt Brace Jovanovich, Inc., 1970, pp. 560-62.*

MURRAY KRIEGER (essay date 1956)

[*Krieger is an American critic who has written numerous books and articles on modern critical theory. In the following excerpt, he examines the differences between Hulme's conceptions of artistic imagination, which set the tone for much Modernist poetry, and those of Samuel Taylor Coleridge, which provided the theoretical foundation of nineteenth-century Romantic thought.*]

Hulme feels that the essence of romanticism is located in its idolatry of the individual who, for the romantics, should have unlimited aspirations since he has unlimited powers. The transcendental faculties given the individual by German Idealism and by Coleridge embody these unlimited powers and therefore must be denied by the classicist for whose advent Hulme prays. For the classicist, according to Hulme, sees man as an extremely limited being who needs all kinds of severely imposed disciplines if he is to function as he should in his proper sphere. Thus Hulme, defending the view of the classicist, rejects a concept of imagination which would substitute a monism for Christian dualism and would make of man a god. For the attribution to man of the power to create absolutely, *ex nihilo*, could mean little less. Thus Hulme explicitly calls for a poetry of fancy rather than the poetry of unbounded imagination which he feels contaminated English verse in the nineteenth and early twentieth centuries. [Of these two terms Krieger notes: Seen through the interests of twentieth-century critics, the meaning Coleridge attached to these two terms may be briefly summarized. "Imagination" is that spontaneous power of mind which allows it to express itself in a literally creative way; through imagination the mind infuses organic life into the lifeless mental impressions it has gathered from a lifeless world. "Fancy" is the faculty which, while it also chooses among the many impressions stored by the mind, remains essentially passive; bound by the law of association, it can only bind together additively the selections it has made from the mind's associative memories. For these critics, the imagination, thus derived from Coleridge, is the empowering faculty for our best poetry. Hulme] calls for a poetry that is formally precise and whose pretentions are limited to simple and vivid description. One might say he calls for a return to a theory of imitation and opposes the reigning theory of expression, the introduction of which was so largely Coleridge's responsibility.

But there is also a quite different side of Hulme. In his essay on Bergson, in which he expounds sympathetically the aesthetic of his master in philosophy, there is a description of the poet's activity that seems nearly as transcendental as Coleridge's. Here Hulme distinguishes between intuition and stock perception and characterizes artistic creativity as the former. It is only the artist, he claims, who can break through the mere static recognition of the world about us which practical life demands; he alone can see through to the dynamic flux which characterizes essential reality. And as artist he makes this vision available to others who, without the artist, could never see beyond the stereotyped world of practicality.

This conception gives the poet a far higher and more romantic function than Hulme has assigned him in his severe **"Romanticism and Classicism,"** which repeats, in more narrowly literary terms, the general argument of his more ambitious **"Humanism and the Religious Attitude."** For while Hulme, as influenced by Bergson, still wants the poet to be descriptive, he adds a metaphysical dimension to this objective. He would have the poet describe the world about him not merely as it seems to be but rather as it really is behind the veil that hides it from most of us. The poet must not give us as the world "the film of familiarity and selfish solicitude" (note how apt this Coleridgean phrase is here) which our senses normally allow to us; rather he must give us the rare world beyond, which he somehow intuits. Now this is a handsome objective; and the intuitive faculty which is to fulfill it for Hulme seems not far removed from the imagination invoked by Coleridge. Surely we may doubt the power of fancy to operate at these profound levels. Hence, we cannot accept Hulme's plea for a

poetry of fancy and his condemnation of a poetry of imagination as his final or his only word. Similarly we may be disposed to categorize Hulme as a severe classicist who wants to return poetic theory to the well-ordered stalls of classical imitation from its chaotic refuge of romantic expressionism; but again Hulme's essay on Bergson should give us pause. For while the poet, as envisaged by Hulme in this essay, may in some metaphysical sense be said to imitate reality, only if we stretch the traditional meaning of the concept of imitation in an extraordinary way—one which would make it broad enough to accommodate anti-classicists as extreme as Schelling—can we make it apply here.

Of course, we can dismiss the entire problem by calling Hulme's two positions the damning inconsistency of a muddled mind. But even if this were true, as it very well may be, the problem simply takes another form, since we are still left with the need to account for this inconsistency if we are to see its significance for modern poetic theory. And Hulme's enormous influence on the direction this criticism has taken, an influence that stems from both aspects of his speculations, cannot be gainsaid. For, if we follow down the line that starts with Hulme, we find the same seemingly contradictory duality in most of its major exponents: an uncompromising prejudice against romanticism coupled with an invocation of romantic and Coleridgean concepts, even when Coleridge has been slandered by name. For example, the attraction of these critics to romantic theory is betrayed by their constant use of the now common "organic" concept in discussions of either creative activity or poetry itself, as they either use Coleridge's psychologizing or seek to transform it into objective criticism.

Thus, having forced a disjunction between romanticism and classicism, recent theorists, in the footsteps of Hulme, desire to justify classicism with the theoretical tools of romanticism, yet without permitting a reconciliation between the two. Perhaps their reasoning may become clearer if we examine, from another perspective, their general attitude toward this concept of imagination which some, like Hulme, explicitly reject even as they smuggle it into their theory. (pp. 33-5)

To begin with, although it is true that Hulme does not accept Ruskin's concept of imagination as necessarily identical with that of Coleridge (and it is the latter against which he intends to argue), he still carries along many of Ruskin's connotations in his own uses of the word. For example, late in the essay, when Hulme is discussing fancy, he says, "where . . . your only objection to this kind of fancy is that it is not serious in the effect it produces, then I think the objection to be entirely invalid." But an objection of this kind could come only from a defender of a concept of imagination that is close to Ruskin's. Elsewhere in this essay Hulme disparagingly characterizes all theories that derive from German romantic aesthetics as conceiving that the artist partakes in a vague infinite. Similarly, he says, although in another connection, ". . . there you seem to me to have the highest kind of verse, even though the subject be trivial and the emotions of the infinite far away." He distinguishes in yet another way between imagination and fancy: ". . . where you get this quality [of concrete and fresh imagery] exhibited in the realm of the emotions you get imagination, and . . . where you get this quality exhibited in the contemplation of finite things you get fancy." It is evident in these passages that Hulme considers the imagination to be distinguished from fancy because it is serious rather than witty, because it reveals the infinite rather than the limited, and because it deals with vague emotions rather than with concrete things. Now the former characteristics of these pairs follow from Ruskin's concept of imagination—and, to some extent, perhaps, from the imagination we could derive from Coleridge's practical criticism. But none of them appears as the defining quality of the imagination delineated in Coleridge's theory.

Yet at the end of the essay, when Hulme speaks of Coleridge's distinction between vital or organic complexity and mechanical complexity—which has seemed to be the essential feature of Coleridge's distinction between imagination and fancy—he treats this distinction sympathetically, strangely enough, and proceeds, on the basis of a careful analysis of this distinction, to outlaw romanticism and the poetry of the imagination. In other words, he seems to be defending organicism even as he attacks the romantic theory of imagination. Obviously Hulme does not intend to judge against this concept of imagination by using a law furnished him by this very concept. It should be clear, then, that Hulme is not defining imagination, as Coleridge originally did, in terms of the organic concept; that instead he is still characterizing the imagination largely by the traits attributed to it by Ruskin. In this way Hulme can both favor organicism and oppose the imagination, despite the fact that Coleridge's importance to us lies in the fact that he firmly identified the two. Further, in this last discussion, Hulme, as a faithful Bergsonian, uses "vital" complexity to characterize *all* art, in contrast to the mechanical complexity by which he characterizes the operations of the intellect. For he is as anxious to avoid "the old classical view," which defines beauty "as lying in conformity to certain standard fixed forms" (any such fixity would be abhorrent to Bergson), as he is to avoid "the romantic view which drags in the infinite." In a similar vein, Hulme earlier says of fancy that it "is not mere decoration added on to plain speech. Plain speech is essentially inaccurate. It is only by new metaphors, that is, by fancy, that it can be made precise." Then he goes on to describe a form of fancy that is inferior to imagination. So here he is defining fancy (as "not mere decoration") in the very way that Richards and Brooks, for example, taking their lead from Coleridge, define imagination. For it is the concept of the functional, rather than the merely decorative, metaphor which characterizes that modern criticism which is admittedly Coleridgean.

It follows from these various passages, first, that the imagination excluded by Hulme is not excluded by reason of the definition Coleridge gave to it. On the contrary, the differentia established by Coleridge for the imagination is the very one Hulme uses to define all art—and here Hulme properly sees Coleridge and Bergson as agreeing. Secondly, Hulme's idea of fancy appears to be essentially no different from Coleridge's imagination, unless we import Ruskin's claims about the kinds of attitudes and subjects appropriate to each. In manner of operation, or in the kind of mental faculty involved, there is no important difference. To put it another way, if we look at the problem from the point of view of the Coleridgean imagination, Hulme is not actually calling for a different faculty; he is calling for a different use of the same faculty. He wants it to be addressed to different subject matter, to be at the service of different attitudes.

Hulme is reacting against a "Weltanschauung" and a metaphysic more than against a literary theory. And this realization leads to another source of his confusion. In many of his essays Hulme uses the term "romanticism" to cover a multitude of sins. He collapses within this single term two quite antithetical movements, which would involve two quite different meta-

physics and aesthetics. He often sees romanticism as best typified by the ideas behind the French Revolution—by what might be termed rationalistic progressivism. "Here is the root of all romanticism: that man, the individual, is an infinite reservoir of possibilities; and if you can so rearrange society by the destruction of oppressive order then these possibilities will have a chance and you will get Progress." He opposes to this political romanticism the belief in order and tradition, just as he opposes to the self-indulgent seriousness of literary romanticism the toughness of his proposed classical poetry.

But having established his definition of romanticism on the ideas, let us say, of a Thomas Paine, he proceeds to use the derogatory term to put what I shall term Germanic romanticism in its place. But this is not entirely just. It perhaps springs from a confusion which commonly lumps all English and German romanticism together without first making the necessary distinctions. For example, Edmund Burke, who is indeed one of the earlier Germanic romantics, opposed to the rationalistic defenses of the French Revolution the very virtues—order and tradition—which Hulme claims to be the antidotes to romanticism. And the German romantics are equally conservative and equally traditional. Indeed, the number of converts they gave to Catholicism should certainly have pleased Hulme. With Burke they stood for the organic concept, which resists the mechanism of the rationalistic progressive. If segments of British romanticism were Godwinian, this is hardly reason to damn as a Godwinian anyone who has ever been called a romantic. Hulme has earned the right to condemn romanticism only by his arguments against the antitraditional progressives; he proceeds to prosecute the Germanic romantics (including, of course, Coleridge) on the wrong grounds, therefore. He would need a new series of objections to press the case. Similarly, when he disparages literary romanticism by citing its unleavened seriousness, we must conclude that he is unmindful of the sometimes tough-minded self-criticism of romantic irony (not entirely unlike the "irony" of modern criticism), which is displayed in some German romantic literature and proclaimed in much of its literary theory. Again he seems not to have realized sufficiently that much of English and Germanic romanticism has little in common beside the not very judiciously applied name. In failing to classify the enemy more carefully, he fails also to note the points on which there may be some agreement between them and him. In his anxiety to make the romantic-classical cleavage too clean, he ignores certain all-important overlappings—all-important because so many of his followers are heavily dependent upon the romantic (Germanic romantic) concepts they have adapted to their own uses.

This is not to say that Hulme, had he seen the necessary distinctions among romantics, would have felt very much kinship with the Germanic variety. There still would remain the problem of metaphysics; and certainly few thinkers in the history of philosophy are more open to Hulme's charge that they "drag in the infinite" than these romantics are. Their frequent recourse to metaphysical monism, which would detract from God's transcendence in order to exalt His immanence, must have seemed sufficient reason for Hulme to give them the label of romanticism. And certainly they deserved it, at least on these grounds. But aesthetically, and often politically too, he would, and unconsciously did, find many of their ideas congenial to his own. And in his literary theory, like Bergson before him, he put their dynamic organicism to good use. (pp. 38-43)

Clearly it would seem that Hulme is trying to maintain a position which at once includes classical imitation and romantic expressionism, obedience to mechanical rules and individual creativity. His distaste for nineteenth-century poetry, as well as for nineteenth-century criticism and philosophy, forces him to think of himself as a defender of another neoclassicism. But at the same time his devotion to Bergson forces him to adopt the principle of an organicism or vitalism that must resist all fixity. To say merely that Hulme tries to stand between these extremes and to utilize the best that each has to offer would be radically incomplete; it would make of him no more than a reckless eclectic who would have little to contribute. Instead he made his way to a completely independent position which, to use his words again, avoids the "standard fixed forms" of "the old classical view" as well as "the romantic view which drags in the infinite." To clarify this position and the direction it has given, it is necessary to add yet another element to those shown to be at work so far.

As imagist, Hulme is especially concerned with language. We have seen that for Hulme, the disciple of Bergson, the poet must break through the stock recognitions which plague practical life and thus must make it possible for us to see things in their uniqueness. But Hulme does not allow these intuitions to take place in a vacuum; he is anti-romanticist enough not to believe in the self-sufficiency of the mind. Not only do intuitions take linguistic form, he claims, but they are dependent upon language. For just as most of us look at the world through stereotypes, so do we speak of the world through the equally fixed forms of language. Since thinking can take place only in a medium, it may very well be that we cannot have a fresh perception of the world unless we have first dislocated language in order to force fresh ways of expression from it. Thus, to the problem with which Hulme was seen to be concerned earlier—the artist's need to see the world in a new way—another must now be added which is perhaps prior to, or at least inseparable from, the first: the artist's need to use his language in a new way. (pp. 43-4)

> *Murray Krieger, "T. E. Hulme: 'Classicism and the Imagination',"* in his The New Apologists for Poetry, *The University of Minnesota Press, 1956, pp. 31-45.*

FRANK KERMODE   (essay date 1957)

[*Kermode is an English critic whose career combines modern critical methods with expert traditional scholarship, particularly in his work on Shakespeare. In his critical discussions of modern literature, Kermode has embraced many of the conceptions of structuralism and phenomenology. Kermode characterizes all human knowledge as poetic, or fictive: constructed by humans and affected by the perceptual and emotional limitations of human consciousness. Because perceptions of life and the world change, so does human knowledge and the meaning attached to things and events. Thus, there is no single fixed reality over time. Similarly, for Kermode, a work of art has no single fixed meaning, but a multiplicity of possible interpretations; in fact, the best of modern writing is constructed so that it invites a variety of interpretations, all of which depend upon the sensibility of the reader. Kermode believes his critical writings exist to stimulate thought, to offer possible interpretations, but not to fix a single meaning to a work of art. True or "classic" literature, to Kermode, is thus a constantly reinterpreted living text, "complex and indeterminate enough to allow us our necessary pluralities." In the following excerpt, Kermode explores Hulme's theories of the image in poetry.*]

For Hulme, the epoch of humanism, anti-religious in every department of life, but visibly so in art, was ending. He lavishes his contempt upon it; with a sort of doctrinaire fury he elim-

inates as bad and anti-religious (because on the side of life) even Michelangelo. Nor does he care for the kind of thing other Roman Catholics like—Fra Angelico, for instance. His Catholicism is intellectual in the extreme, almost to the point of being a dogmatic abstract from the religion; without its support he cannot have the world-picture he wants, but he will have none of its tenderness and sentiment. The art he cares for is that of the period which the Renaissance ended, an epoch which believed in Original Sin and produced, at its best, a geometric art quite distinct from the vitalism of Renaissance art, which ministered to the spectator's pleasure in being alive, his desire to be *acting*. The art of Byzantium abhors all this, being concerned with absolute non-human values; being life-alien, remote from organic life and even detesting it. This art resembled not that humanist art which began in Athens, but Egyptian religious sculpture and the art of primitive peoples. Geometrical abstraction is a characteristic of cultures which understand the human lot as tragic, and distinguish sharply between the human and the divine, never confusing them, as the "vitalist" art he hated did. Hulme applies to philosophies and art alike what he calls his *critique of satisfaction*. Never mind what the philosophers say, he advises; ask instead, what emotional requirement in themselves are they trying to satisfy. And all post-Renaissance philosophy is the same, so considered; it satisfies only the need for an assurance of human centrality. But new needs are now, he adds, appearing, and we are beginning, with Epstein and Wyndham Lewis, to get that anti-vitalist, geometric art of which the beginnings were to be perceived in Cézanne.

Whenever Hulme generalises about historical periods he goes wrong. The critique of satisfaction apparently fails to distinguish between Descartes and Schopenhauer, and it tells us that Hartley and the later Coleridge were seeking the same answers. It is impossible to understand how anybody who had read the *Essay on Man* could possibly regard Pope as exempt from the heresy (which Hulme called "Romantic") of denying the *absolute* inaccessibility of ethics to the reason; Pope's trace of scepticism has very little to do with the chilly fideism of Hulme, and he has far more of Montaigne than Pascal in him. Much more important than the numerous minor objections of this sort that one could bring against Hulme is the well-established fact (ably presented in Michael Roberts's book) that he disastrously misrepresents Romantic philosophy. For Hulme, as we have seen, Romanticism was a calamity however you looked at it: politically, philosophically, aesthetically. It was the anthropocentric assumption of the Renaissance at the stage of mania, all Rousseauistic rubbish about personality, progress and freedom, all a denial of human limit and imperfection. (In fact it would be truer to say that the movement was obsessed by Original Sin than to say, as Hulme does, that it completely ignored it, and made life the measure of all values.) For Hulme, as for all seers, the moment at which he was thinking was the perfect one for seeing the whole matter in perspective, and so breaking history into two parts (Augustine to the Renaissance, the Renaissance to Hulme). He did not even see how inconsistent he was about Coleridge, whose "vital" he sometimes uses in its original Coleridgean sense, and sometimes in Worringer's sense, with great confusion—a confusion, incidentally, which reflects the Paterian life-and-death ambiguity which we have already looked at, and which turns up again in the aesthetic of Vortex. Nor did he see how dependent he was upon the tradition he was attacking, despite his avowed and enormous debt to Bergson. In so far as he was merely doing propaganda for a new abstract art which had already got under way he was primarily a reporter of Worringer, and that is consistent and defensible as far as it goes, which is not so far as the main historical generalisation; but in so far as he was introducing a new "classical" poetry—anti-humanist poetry he means, which is a pretty paradox in itself—his position is complex and unsatisfactory, because he has not found out what it really is. We shall see more clearly where he stood if we consider the theory of the image which is central to his whole aesthetic. It is closely related to the concept of discontinuity, with its attendant rejection of empathic, *vital* art; but, as we shall see, it fits much more neatly into the old Romantic-Symbolist theory with its dualist implication (*two* discontinuous orders related to reason and imagination) than into the triplex structure of his own Bergsonian-Pascalian hypothesis.

Let us, then, look at Hulme's requirements for good poetry. Negatively, it must not be concerned with the myth of human perfection or perfectibility in any form; it must accept the strict limitations of human powers, be life-alien. (Note that Hulme is evasive and inconsistent about Coleridge's Imagination, fearing that there is some connection between it and the hated divinisation of human intellect that denies limit; he seems to have been unaware of the controlling force over Coleridge's thought of his refusal to give up the doctrine of Original Sin, whatever metaphysical labour this refusal might involve him in. In fact Hulme's "intellect" is much the same as the Coleridgean and Wordsworthian "reason," the reflective faculty that partakes of death.) The acceptance of limit will at once cut out the ecstatic meaning and hysterical aspiration Hulme regards as characteristic of Romantic poetry. The first positive requirement is for *precise description* (Hulme might have reflected that it is also the first requirement of Wordsworth's *Preface* of 1815). For Hulme, however, this precision concerns the recording of images; and here we are at the core of Hulmian aesthetics. (pp. 124-27)

Poetry, by virtue of the image, *is;* prose merely describes. One is end, the other means. What poetry seems to be *about* is therefore irrelevant to its value. "Subject doesn't matter." Poetry is bad when it directs the attention away from the physical uniqueness and oneness of the image (the poem itself of course is an image, if it is good) and enables the reader "to glide through an abstract process." It is concrete, because the Image can be represented only as concrete, and entirely devoid of discursive meanings and appeals to the intellect; it is the direct representation of what is intuited. Whether the poem is good or not depends upon the accuracy of the representation, and upon that alone. (pp. 127-28)

But this does not mean that good poems are about "the infinite" or "the ineffable"—that would be to fall into the Romantic heresy in a slightly different form. We return to Bergson's two orders. What *is* intuited in terms of the Image? In what circumstances does this act of intuition occur? Hulme's answer is Bergson's. The sphere in which intuition operates is that reality which is conceived "as a flux of interpenetrated elements unseizable by the intellect." What normally debars our entry into this sphere is the usual orientation of the human mind towards action. If that were not so we should have easy commerce with it, and there would be no need for art at all; as it is, the artist is "a man who is emancipated from the ways of perception engendered by action." (p. 128)

[It] is hardly necessary to point out how richly "Romantic" this formulation of the artist's function is, but it is worth emphasising that the twin concepts of isolation and image occur in Hulme as surely as in the poetry he despised. But we must return to the question of the intuited image.

Hulme's metaphysical justification of his image-theory is borrowed from Bergson. The human intellect tends to explain (*explico,* unfold) everything in a manner fitting its limitations; it analyses, because "that is the only way in which the intellect can deal with things"; "we reduce everything to extensive manifolds." We unfold everything out in space, and we tend to think that everything that cannot be so unfolded must be unknowable. But of course this is not so, and anybody can think of things which are somehow known but resist this form of knowing them. How do such things differ from the others which allow themselves to be treated as extensive manifolds? Bergson argues that such things, "while incomprehensible by our ordinary standards" are nevertheless finite. The nature of their complexity is qualitative, not quantitative; they simply do not yield to explanation, to discursive methods of analysis; they resist the intellect. Their parts are "interpenetrated in such a manner that they could not be separated or analysed out." And yet one should not even speak of parts, because the complex thing is a continuous whole, and it is impossible to conceive of its parts as having a separate existence. This is the intensive manifold, by the very terms of the argument impossible to define; it is accessible only to intuition, belonging to a different order of reality. It is "indescribable but not unknowable." The artist knows it; it is his Image. It is finite; hence the need for precision. Its meaning is the same thing as its form, and the artist is absolved from participation with the discursive powers of the intellect.

This theory, as Hulme explains it, makes a show of being in opposition to Romantic imprecision—hence the emphasis on finiteness, and the lack of reference to the third, Pascalian order—but in fact it is fundamentally a new statement of the old defence of poetry against positivism and the universe of death. It is a revised form of the old proclamation that poetry has special access to truth, and is not merely light entertainment for minds tired out by physics. Poets, excluded from action, are enabled to achieve the special form of cognition and pierce the veil and intuit truth; this is communicated in the Image. (pp. 128-30)

Hulme remained committed to this view so long as he persisted in his opinion of language as—in poetry—a mode of communicating *visual* images, "a compromise for a language of intuition—to make you continuously see a physical thing"; the poet strictly as *voyant*. There seems no doubt that the next step forward in Romantic aesthetic depended upon a new theory of language. Hulme was very deficient here, though there are possibilities in his work of a development which have rendered superfluous the awkward implications of the view he professed. The problem was to preserve the Symbol (the "aesthetic monad," the Image alogical yet meaningful, or as Sir Herbert Read has recently called it, "the poetic Gestalt") and yet to be rid of magic. This could not be done so long as the Image was thought of as a thing seen only, or so long as language was considered as a means of handing over visual concreteness only. In his anxiety to distinguish between symbolic and non-symbolic language Hulme commits himself absolutely to this visual hypothesis. His Symbol is a visual thing, and its opposite is just the dead sign of an abstract prose process. (p. 132)

Hulme stands conveniently between the generation of Symons and our own time; and, what is more, his influence has proved hardy. It remains perceptible in the American "New" Criticism; it plays its part in the work of the younger Poundian critics of the present moment; even as far afield as Japan, I notice, there is a Hulmian movement. For what he owed to the past, and for what his successors have taken from him (without, as I think, fully understanding the history of what they had got) he demands attention. (p. 137)

Frank Kermode, "T. E. Hulme," in his Romantic Image, *The Macmillan Company, 1957, pp. 119-37.*

GRAHAM HOUGH   (lecture date 1959)

[*Hough is an English poet and critic who has written a major study of the Imagist movement entitled* Image and Experience: Studies in a Literary Revolution. *In the following excerpt from that work, which was originally delivered as a series of lectures in 1959, Hough disputes Hulme's association of classical literature with Christian dogma.*]

I do not want to enter into the question of how great Hulme's personal influence on his contemporaries actually was. Pound tends to play it down, and Eliot had no personal contact with him. But Hulme's ideas, either in his own formulation or in some diffusion, or by pointing back to Hulme's own sources, or to analogues elsewhere, are fundamental to the criticism of this time; and the brash confidence with which he exposes them makes his work a particularly convenient field for inspection.

The celebrated essay **"Romanticism and Classicism"** is both typical and central. Words fail me to record the number of fallacies and contradictions in these twenty pages; or rather, any reasonable number of words fail; it could be done at inordinate length. But the central notion is plain. It is the same idea that was made familiar a little later (Hulme's essay was written about 1914) by Irving Babbit's *Rousseau and Romanticism* (1917)—that Romanticism has a single root, the Rousseauist doctrine "that man was by nature good, that it was only bad laws and customs that had suppressed him". Hulme identifies himself with the opposite; with what he calls the classical point of view, which accepts the finite and limited nature of man; and this, he says, is also the religious view.

> Here is the root of all romanticism: that man, the individual, is an infinite reservoir of possibilities. . . . One can define the classical quite clearly as the exact opposite to this. Man is an extraordinarily fixed and limited animal whose nature is absolutely constant. It is only by tradition and organisation that anything decent can be got out of him. . . . It would be a mistake to identify the classical view with that of materialism. On the contrary it is identical with the normal religious attitude.

The essential of the religious attitude for Hulme is what he calls the sane classical dogma of original sin; and this is the essential of the classical attitude too. I will not pause to wonder at the strange realignment of forces that this alliance of classicism with Christian dogma brought about, though anyone who was following these matters in the twenties will remember it as bewildering. I have only two points to make; one is the extraordinary impoverishment of the religious attitude that would follow from Hulme's formulation; the other is concerned with the literary consequences that he draws from it.

It is not worth wasting much time on Hulme's religious attitude. "Man is an extraordinarily fixed and limited animal whose nature is absolutely constant." "Extraordinarily" can only mean "more than is ordinary with animals". Man is more fixed and limited than the lion or the horse or the duck-billed platypus? This is surely nonsense both culturally and biologically. "It is

only by tradition and organisation that anything decent can be got out of him"; and this represents the religious attitude? But all the higher religions have come with the promise of bringing man deliverance from the law. It was not Rousseau, it was the Psalmist who said *Emitte spiritum tuum et creabunter: et renovabis faciem terrae.* It was not Rousseau, it was St. Paul who spoke of Abraham "who against hope believed in hope, that he might become the father of many nations according to that which was spoken. . . . He staggered not at the promise of God through unbelief, but was strong in faith, giving glory to God; and being fully persuaded that what he had promised he was able to perform." And it was not Rousseau who was the witness of the Apocalypse. If religion were a contemplation of the natural world as a closed order—if, that is to say, faith and hope were omitted—Hulme's account of it would be true. But why go on? Anti-Rousseauism may have been a needed tonic, but when it is used to reduce religion to a depressed cosmic Toryism the limited efficacy of this nostrum becomes apparent.

And of course Hulme gives the game away himself. He is not at heart concerned with religion. His version of original sin is a political doctrine, and his performance is a projection of political doctrine into the religious sphere. One cannot accuse him of lacking candour. The names he invokes in the early paragraphs of his essay are those of "Maurras, Laserre and all the group connected with *L'Action Française*". It is they, he says, who have made romanticism and classicism into political catchwords. It is they whose main use for classicism was as a stick to beat the Revolution. As he accurately remarked, the distinction had become a party symbol. "If you asked a man of a certain set whether he preferred the classics or the romantics, you could deduce from that what his politics were." And, though Hulme does not mention this, it was of course Maurras and the *Action Française* group who did notoriously and openly what many have been willing to do covertly—used Catholic Christendom in a purely political sense, were willing to employ Christianity simply as a right-wing political weapon. If Hulme's notion of the religious attitude came to him from this source it is not surprising that it would be an eccentric one.

The literary deductions from this are still more eccentric. Hulme foresees the arrival of a "classical" period in poetry; and this is apparently a straightforward piece of historical prognostication, such as men of letters with their ears to the ground are often liable to make. What are the qualities that the classic-religious attitude will produce in poetry? Since man is a limited creature his verse must also be limited in its aims. The literary vice of romanticism was a continual attempt at commerce with the infinite. This deplorable traffic will now cease. Ruskin wrote, "Those who have so pierced and seen the melancholy deeps of things are filled with intense passion and gentleness and sympathy." But when he did so he was thinking in the corrupt Romantic mode. For the new classical poetry "it is essential to prove that beauty may be in small, dry things": and "the particular poetry we are going to get will be cheerful, dry and sophisticated". Now in the course of developing this argument Hulme, who writes with great liveliness, if not without vulgarity, scores many effective literary hits. And his Imagist propaganda is of great interest from another point of view. But the main drift of his argument is a foolish paradox. The essential of the religious attitude is the dogma of original sin, and this is the essential of the classical attitude too. It is about to become influential again and will produce a kind of verse that is small, dry, cheerful and sophisticated. This is the natural consequence of the religious attitude, which has nothing to do with the infinite—and, I suppose we might add, has produced in the past such small, dry, cheerful and sophisticated words as the *Aeneid, Dies Irae,* the *Paradiso, Piers Plowman* and *Phèdre.* The examples are mine, but they will be enough, I imagine, to indicate the abyss of nonsense into which Hulme would lead us, by a skilful manipulations of half-truths; and into which he did lead a good many literary theorists of the generation succeeding his own.

Now all these operations of Hulme's are conducted in the name of tradition; and tradition, the word and the idea, was to become a spell to conjure with in the coming literary upheaval. What we can learn from Hulme's essay is how anomalous, how eccentric, the relation to tradition is. A fragmentary version of the Christian religious tradition is seized on. It is equated with a partial notion of classicism derived from a group of politically-minded Frenchmen. (There is no indication that Hulme has thought about ancient classical literature at all, and if he had cared to look at English classicism he would surely have had to relate it to Deism rather than to traditional Christianity.) And from this mish-mash is drawn a set of literary deductions which are both logically uncompelling and historically false. When we consider the influence that ideas of this sort had, we may suspect that an eccentric and anomalous idea of tradition is generally at work. (pp. 32-6)

Graham Hough, *"Reflections on a Literary Revolution,"* in his Image and Experience: Studies in a Literary Revolution, *Gerald Duckworth & Co. Ltd., 1960, pp. 3-83.*

ALUN R. JONES   (essay date 1960)

[In the following excerpt, Jones discusses some general features of Hulme's poetry.]

Although Hulme was mainly responsible for working out the principles on which the Imagist movement was founded, his poetic theory is not to be valued on the success or failure of that movement, but on the possibilities of its general application. Ezra Pound is largely responsible for adapting and publicising Hulme's ideas but before the movement had got under way, Hulme himself had withdrawn from it. His poems do not belong to the Imagist movement as such but are to be regarded primarily as experiments in which he attempted to illustrate his own theories. In fact, his theory of poetry finds its most coherent expression neither in the poems of the Imagists, nor in his own poems, but in the early poetry of T. S. Eliot. In spite of his overt rejection of romanticism, Hulme never really succeeds in breaking free from its poetic conventions. He never really escapes from the conventional poeticisms and the rhetorical apostrophes which he hated in the work of his contemporaries. He is still under the influence of the Victorian romantics. Even the sense of wonder with its associations of infinity, which he finds so distressing in the poetry of the romantics, is still present in his poetry, though certainly in disguise. Although, by personification, he interprets the infinite in terms of the finite, the strange in terms of the familiar, his poetry is nevertheless, like that of Wordsworth, calculated to excite "a feeling analogous to the supernatural." He does, however, skilfully accommodate the more traditional cosmic symbols within the homely, urban orbit of everyday life; the stars have "white faces like town children," and the sunset is nothing more than "a vain maid, lingering, loth to go." The symbols are fixed and hardened out into precise images and,

by limiting their vague aura of suggestion, he has managed to reclaim their force—but that force remains one of wonder. In his poem **"The Man in the Crow's Nest,"** the wind at sea on a lonely night is overlaid with the idea of a boy whistling to hide his fear. The two ideas are accurately and precisely delineated but the effect is to heighten the reader's awareness of man's fear before the infinity of the unknown. The fear is given concrete expression, as is the loneliness of man, and this alone indicates a change of poetic style. Hulme has deliberately set out to achieve an effect of dramatic impersonality in which the emotions are not stated but are given objectivity in terms of familiar things. Hulme's poetry, like his theory, announces a change, but not of the subject of poetry or, basically, of attitude towards the subject, but a change of poetic technique. The most remarkable aspect of the new technique is the disappearance of the poetic "I". The poet no longer speaks out in his own voice and person but seeks for an analogy or a number of analogies which, separately or working together, will represent his own inner world of private emotions.

For the most part, Hulme's poems are urbane, witty exercises within this new technique and they achieve a dry, cheerful sophistication. They are often characterised by an element of surprise, held back but carefully worked for, which give the poems a disturbing beauty of their own. By juxtaposing contrasted but related images, he compels the reader to close the gap between one image and the next and thus achieves a kind of imaginative logic; and he also manages to suggest his own oblique comment on the human predicament. If we may be allowed to adapt the verdict of F. R. Leavis passed on the minor poems of Wordsworth, we can say that although the substance of Hulme's poetry in paraphrase would not amount to very much, his success depends upon his conveying the peculiarly private value, the intense personal significance, of the concrete incident—of the experience in immediacy. The freshness, the immediacy, the feeling which poetry can give of handing over sensations bodily—these are the qualities which Hulme values in his theory and which he achieves in his poetry. T. S. Eliot, during his brief career as a schoolmaster, discovered that "the poems of T. E. Hulme only needed to be read aloud to have immediate effect," and this testimonial alone might well justify their preservation. Hulme himself, however, did not set much value on his own poems, except as exercises which he hoped would illustrate his attitude towards poetry as a whole and indicate something of the method by which twentieth-century poets might be led out of the *cul-de-sac* of nineteenth-century romanticism. As exercises of this kind they are never wholly satisfactory. He never completely threw off the influence of the nineteenth-century romantics against whose poetry his theories were so strenuously directed. They were, none the less, highly valued by his friends and followers in so far as they offered, together with his poetic theory, a fresh direction and a new start for poetry. They were welcomed also in themselves for their charm, freshness and physical immediacy and, above all, for their wit which seemed to offer a real opening for the readmittance of the free intelligence and of humour into poetry. In the work of the predecessors solemnity was all too often confused with seriousness, whimsy with humour; Ruskin pronounced for the Victorians generally when he spoke of poetry and "the awful undercurrent of meaning, and the evidence and shadow upon it of the deep places out of which it had come." Hulme did much to destroy this Gothic, pseudo-religious high-seriousness in which the Victorians had stifled poetry. For Hulme, the analogy or image, which he saw to be central to poetry, was always the presentation of a resemblance which, like the resemblance between the mother and her baby, was to be taken half-seriously, with a smile.

Hulme's interest in language did not slacken with the cessation of his writing of poetry but was, in fact, widened to include an examination of language itself as a means of expression and communication. He came to distrust language as being an unreliable and inflexible medium which imposed false categories upon thought and feeling and distorted the nature of reality itself. His later work, which survives only in random notes, marks a clear break with the uncompromising theories of his earlier writings. Indeed, he came to hold that, "The cosmos is only organised in parts; the rest is cinders," and that all theories, which are merely toys, attempt to throw an artificial network over the cinders of reality. These notes suggest an originality quite different from that usually associated with him. The notes on **"Expression, etc.,"** clearly indicate the direction in which in the last years of his life his mind was moving. Had he written the books he planned he would, undoubtedly, have produced a significant metaphysic of an existentialist kind. His notes on his reading of Meinong and Scheler indicate a more profound and tolerant approach to the work of writers of quite a different order than those who previously occupied him.

Although Hulme did much to prepare the ground on which twentieth-century poetry has been built, he is, in many ways, the last of the Victorians. His work must be placed against the background of late Victorianism before its significance can be fully appreciated. He was never really part of the new anti-Humanist, anti-Romantic age which he prophesied would come; his anti-Humanism is directed against T. E. Huxley, and his anti-Romanticism against Ruskin. At the centre of his attack in philosophy, politics and poetry there is always a hard, solid core of Victorian parochialism. In the fragmentary notes which he left at his death there is every indication that he might have thrown off the dead hand of the Victorians. (pp. 53-6)

Alun R. Jones, in his The Life and Opinions of T. E. Hulme, *Beacon Press, 1960, 233 p.*

C. H. SISSON   (essay date 1971)

[*Sisson is an English poet, novelist, and critic. His work often satirizes British society and government with savage wit, reflecting the author's ultimately pessimistic view of existence, which is exemplified in his assertion that he judges his writings to be "no more than an ironic contribution to a hopeless situation." Nevertheless, Sisson has a devout Christian perspective which stresses a purpose that transcends the desolate condition of humanity. In the following excerpt, Sisson discusses Hulme's poetry and its relationship to the Imagist movement.*]

A . . . powerful figure of the renascence loosely connected with imagism, an instigator indeed of that as of much else, was T. E. Hulme. It is hardly too much to say that Hulme has been, in this country, one of the dominant minds of the century. Certainly there can be no understanding of the literature of the age without some grasp of what he stood for. Hulme had his sources, like another man, and I am not suggesting that everything which shows signs of the change of temper Hulme represents has his personal mark upon it. It is evident that Wyndham Lewis, in particular—a much greater figure and one whose influence is still far from having been fully absorbed—arrived by his own intuitions at related positions. Hulme, however, because of his short life and limited scope, stands as a monument at a certain point reached in the century. One may

say that Hardy, Shaw and Kipling were incurably pre-Hulme, whereas Eliot and Pound were post-. (p. 64)

The water-shed Hulme represents is indicated in the essay on **"Humanism and the Religious Attitude"** which stands first in the volume of *Speculations*. . . . The underlying notion is the rejection of the principle of *continuity*, the "elaboration and universal application" of which was "one of the main achievements of the nineteenth century" while "the destruction of this conception" was "an urgent necessity of the present." The nineteenth-century doctrine—still widely held now, of course—was that there are no breaks in reality, that it is all of the same kind. The "popular conception of evolution" is an obvious illustration of the idea. The point is, however, that "continuity" is a preconception, not a conclusion drawn from reality, but it is so prevalent a notion that it is thought of not as a notion but as if it were reality itself. "We now absorb it unconsciously," says Hulme,

> from an environment already completely soaked in it; so we regard it not as a principle in the light of which certain regions of fact can be conveniently ordered, but as an inevitable constituent of reality itself. When any fact seems to contradict this principle, we are inclined to deny that the fact really exists. We constantly tend to think that the discontinuities in nature are only *apparent*, and that a fuller investigation would reveal the underlying continuity. This shrinking from a gap or jump in nature has developed to a degree which paralyses any objective perception.

Against this Hulme set the conception of an absolute discontinuity, a chasm, between the various zones of reality. Thus one might assume a division into "(1) the inorganic world, of mathematical and physical science, (2) the organic world, dealt with by biology, psychology and history, and (3) the world of ethical and religious values." The division between (1) and (2) is still fairly generally recognized—though it could be said that the recognition of the difference has faded a little since Hulme's day—because it "falls easily into line with humanism," which is the superstition of the Renaissance, while the division between (2) and (3) "breaks with the whole Renaissance tradition." It was this break which Hulme was seeking to get people to understand. For Hulme "the *divine* is not *life* at its intensest. It contains in a way an almost *anti-vital* element; quite different of course from the non-vital character of the outside physical region." The art he was concerned to recommend was inhuman and geometrical. The cosy world of sentiment and progress was left behind. There is no need to insist on the kinship of this view with the formalizing inventions of the visual art of the period, and in particular with the work of Wyndham Lewis.

In its application to literature, Hulme's view meant that "after a hundred years of romanticism, we are in for a classical revival," and that, for the purposes of this revolution, "fancy will be superior to imagination." He recommended "the dry hardness which you get in the classics," and which was "absolutely repugnant" to most people, to whom "poetry that isn't damp isn't poetry at all." It was a limited and definite poetry he wanted to see, something that would do without the "strange light" of romanticism, which had the effect of a drug. It is a programme which defines, despite some deviations, the main movement of English poetry in the twentieth century. Hulme was himself an uncompromising practitioner of the art he recommended, no doubt because his theories were of a piece with his impulses. He had a brain which he could use in verse.

The *Complete Poetical Works* of T. E. Hulme, consisting of five poems, were first printed as an appendix to Ezra Pound's *Ripostes* . . . , and reprinted in Hulme's posthumous *Speculations*. . . . The five poems were not quite all, however. A couple of dozen poems, and some fragments, with a textual introduction for good measure, are to be found in *The Life and Opinions of Thomas Ernest Hulme* (1960) by Alun R. Jones. It would be a service if some publisher would give this tiny collection a little volume on its own. It would be of impressive weight for its size. The success of the word imagism has been such that it is generally taken that the interest of the poems is simply as illustrating this dead movement. On the contrary, the verse has intellectual and rhythmic qualities not found elsewhere in English verse. The images are there, of course:

> The lark crawls on the cloud
> Like a flea on a white body.

Or, from the *Complete Poetical Works,* published by Pound:

> Above the quiet dock in midnight,
> Tangled in the tall mast's corded height,
> Hangs the moon. What seemed so far away
> Is but a child's balloon, forgotten after play.

The verse has the throw-away rhythm of talk and—unless it is in the "forgotten after play" which however is also part of the visual impression—there is no concession to sentiment. There is such concentration that one feels one has the complete content of the mind at the moment of the poem. As in this, called **"Susan Ann and Immortality"**:

> Her head hung down
> Gazed at earth, fixedly keen,
> As the rabbit at the stoat
> Till the earth was sky,
> Sky that was green,
> And brown clouds past,
> Like chestnut leaves arching the ground.

In **"A Tall Woman"** we have such a combination of sensual absorption with the disjunction of the intellectual man as is hardly to be paralleled since Donne:

> The same promise to many eyes.
> Yet when she forward leans, in a room,
> And by seeming accident her breasts brush against me,
> Then is the axle of the world twisted.

Each poem of Hulme is a sort of instantaneous carving cut out of reality with a knife. If there is a contemporary parallel, it is with certain work of Gaudier-Brzeska rather than with that of the official imagists. But a line of verse can carry with it a world of thoughts as a drawing cannot:

> A rough wind rises, dark cliffs stare down.
> Sour-faced Calvin—art thou whining still?

A man walking on the sea-shore has to have something in his head. The romantic is, so to speak, a holiday-maker, with vague thoughts of luxurious beauty. The classic is a man no less serious than the fisherman mending his nets. His preoccupations do not leave him. He does not turn aside for beauty. No good writer does. In a sense Hulme's distinction between "classic" and "romantic" is merely the distinction between good writing and bad. (pp. 65-8)

C. H. Sisson, "Imagism: F. S. Flint, Richard Aldington, T. E. Hulme, the Verse of James Joyce," in his English Poetry, 1900-1950: An Assessment, St. Martin's Press, 1971, pp. 54-70.*

SAMUEL HYNES   (essay date 1972)

[*An American critic, Hynes has written and edited numerous studies of English literature, including a compilation of previously uncollected essays by Hulme,* Further Speculations. *In the following excerpt, he summarizes Hulme's political and poetical beliefs, demonstrating that they were neither original nor revolutionary.*]

To many of his contemporaries Hulme seemed to have genius, but if he had it was a genius for simplifying complex social and intellectual processes so as to fit them into apparently ordered systems, rather than for original thought. He was one of the great simplifiers, the kind of writer who makes intellectual history look easy. He saw history as a road composed of alternate straight stretches and right-angle turns, and himself as a sort of intellectual policeman, posted at one of history's corners to direct traffic into the twentieth century.

Hulme's particular corner was the turn from Victorianism to what, for the time being, we may call "modernism." He chose, however, to see this turning in rather more grandiloquent terms, as a change from a continuous humanistic tradition stretching back to the Renaissance, to a revival of "the religious attitude." This humanist-religious antithesis was Hulme's first principle, and underlies virtually everything he wrote; he saw the changes of his own time—in philosophy, in art, in poetry, in politics—as constituting a single change, "the break-up of the Renaissance." (pp. 123-24)

The one political principle which we can deduce from Hulme's writings is that he was a convinced authoritarian. "Nothing is bad in itself," he wrote, "except disorder; all that is put in order in a hierarchy is good"; and one of the ideas that he found most attractive in Bergson was that "man's primary need is not *knowledge* but *action*." These two principles—order for its own sake and action for its own sake—are at the bottom of any authoritarian philosophy, but Hulme did not seem conscious of their uglier possibilities. Because he habitually reduced human choice to simple alternatives, he assumed that the only alternative to liberal humanism was a return to a religious view of existence. . . .

But even the religious view, as Hulme defined it, has little that is attractive (or for that matter religious) about it. Hulme employed certain religious terms because they were useful to him, but he showed no sign of the faith that should attend the terms. Thus he used the dogma of Original Sin as a support for his authoritarianism and as a weapon against humanism and romanticism; man's radical imperfection was the important thing, but humanists "chatter about matters which are in comparison with this, quite secondary notions—God, Freedom, and Immortality." Most religionists would surely reject this, as they would reject Hulme's cognate notion that religious values are anti-vital and opposed to life. Hulme's religion was a sanction for imposing discipline, but the discipline he urged was a secular, not a spiritual one.

"It is my aim," Hulme wrote in **"A Tory Philosophy,"** "to explain in this article why I believe in original sin, why I can't stand romanticism, and why I am a certain kind of Tory." The answer to all these questions was essentially the same: Hulme did not regard theology, literary criticism and politics as distinct disciplines, but as aspects of the single question of one's beliefs about the nature of man and his relation to the world. Starting from a belief in human perfectibility, one *must* arrive at humanism, romanticism, and liberalism. Starting from original sin, one must arrive at religion, classicism, and Toryism. Thus romanticism could alternately be regarded as bad politics or as, "split religion," and original sin as a "sane classical dogma."

The starting point in all Hulme's distinctions is metaphysics; in his best-known essay, **"Romanticism and Classicism,"** for example, the distinction is between a bad metaphysic of art (romanticism) and a good one (classicism). "Here is the root of all romanticism," he wrote,

> that man, the individual, is an infinite reservoir of possibilities; and if you can so rearrange society by the destruction of oppressive order then these possibilities will have a chance and you will get Progress.

> One can define the classical quite clearly as the exact opposite to this. Man is an extraordinarily fixed and limited animal whose nature is absolutely constant. It is only by tradition and organization that anything decent can be got out of him.

It is difficult to apply this distinction to either literary or intellectual history, and Hulme had a good deal of trouble in doing so himself. His romanticism, for example, stretches back to the Renaissance (though he saved Shakespeare for classicism by calling him "dynamically" classic); and even classical Greek art seems to share in certain romantic qualities. On the other hand, Hulme's "good" metaphysic of art has some profoundly romantic characteristics.

The point of **"Romanticism and Classicism,"** however, is that it is not so much philosophical as propagandist—it is the "conceptual clothing" in which Hulme sought to dress the change of taste which he discerned in his own time. The standard critical terms were useful, just as the language of theology was useful, to give names to the change; but Hulme was primarily interested in the change itself rather than in its philosophical ancestry. He sensed a new spirit in the arts—a turn away from the romantic and the rhetorical, and toward the abstract, the geometrical, and the precise—and he described it in the terms that were at hand.

It was in poetry, however, that Hulme most directly influenced the course of the new spirit, through the Imagist movement. In retrospect Imagism seems at most a brief chapter in the history of modern poetry; but because it had a name and a manifesto it gained considerable attention in its time, and it has since been taken more seriously than it deserves by the professors and academic historians of literature. The exact origins of the movement are now too obscure to be sorted out, and in fact it is unhistorical to suppose that it had a single originator—individuals never invent changes of taste. Poets were reacting against nineteenth-century rhetoric before the Imagists appeared; Verlaine had said, "Prends l'éloquence et tords-lui son cou" ["Take eloquence and wring its neck"] a long time before Hulme cried "*Smoothness*. Hate it," and Yeats and Henley, each in his own way, had already wrung rhetoric's neck in English.

Hulme's contribution to Imagism was the authority and dignity of a philosophy, or rather the notes for a philosophy which are scattered through his **"Notes on Language and Style"** and other essays—notes like the following:

> Thought is prior to language and consists in the simultaneous presentation to the mind of two different images.

> Language is only a more or less feeble way of doing this.

> Thought is the joining together of new analogies, and so inspiration is a matter of an accidentally seen analogy or unlooked-for resemblance.

Here we may apparently read *intuition* for *analogy* ("this is all worked out in Bergson," Hulme said); the essential poetic datum is unsought-for intuition, out of which the poet, by "a deliberate choosing and working-up of analogies" makes literature. To express his intuition of reality, the poet must use visual images; plain speech is not precise enough for poets.

This is an acceptable enough account of the poetic process as far as it goes, but one can scarcely call it revolutionary, or even original. Hulme did not invent the poetic image, nor was he the first to observe its importance in poetic discourse. What he did do was to elevate the image to the level of a poetic principle, and thus to emphasize the power of imagery divorced from abstract emotive language.

Hulme's own poems are useful examples of his theories in action; they do juxtapose visual images, and they are unrhetorical, hard and dry. They also demonstrate what one might guess from Hulme's remarks on metre—that he had no ear at all for the sound of poetry, and regarded metre as simply a tiresome restraint on free expression. They are at best trivial pieces, and it comes as a bit of a shock to be reminded that Mr Eliot once described Hulme as "the author of two or three of the most beautiful short poems in the language" [see excerpt dated 1924]. It is perhaps an indication of Mr Eliot's critical authority that Hulme has managed, on the basis of the five poems that Pound included in *The Complete Poetical Works of T. E. Hulme,* to find his way into a great many anthologies of modern poetry; surely no other poet has done so well with so little. (pp. 125-28)

> Samuel Hynes, "T. E. Hulme: The Intellectual Po-
> liceman," in his Edwardian Occasions: Essays on
> English Writing in the Early Twentieth Century, Ox-
> ford University Press, 1972, pp. 123-28.

MIRIAM HANSEN   (essay date 1980)

[*In the following excerpt, Hansen places Hulme's aesthetic theories within the context of early twentieth-century avante-garde thought.*]

Hulme's propensity for direct action and his frank espousal of sensual immediacy express a more general intention pervading his poetics, aesthetics and ideology alike—a radical urge to promote the eclipse of the "symbolic." (p. 365)

Hulme's impulse to destroy the symbolic link makes itself felt on a very basic level in his concept of poetry, the level of language and perception. Like Pound and Flint, he relied heavily on turn-of-the century French psychology and philosophy, including Rémy de Gourmont and Théodule Ribot. His most obvious debt, as he rarely fails to acknowledge, is to Bergson. In the tradition of a Romantic critique of the encroachment of science on all spheres of life, Bergson had pitted his concept of "intuition" against the quantification of time and reification of experience, discarding intellect, the faculty on which these developments rely, as an inferior mode of cognition. The medium of intuition—for Bergson as for Hulme—is the "Image": the simultaneous presentation to the mind of two distinct, often disparate, sense impressions. Perception by "analogy," as Hulme also refers to it, is prior to language and therefore superior, since language itself has become the vehicle of intellectual modes of thought.

Hulme's critique of language takes up on a basically Romantic distinction between "poetry" and "prose." "Prose," by which he means everyday discourse as well as that of traditional philosophy and scholarship, is a language of "signs" and "counters" which are used and exchanged almost automatically. . . . Thus ordinary discourse allows us "to pass to conclusions without thinking" . . . ; in another instance, Hulme even compares it to the "reflex speech" observed in "certain cases of dementia." . . . Mistrust of everyday (including academic) language, as it were, also informed the beginnings of analytic language philosophy whose English representatives, Russell and G. E. Moore, Hulme knew from his studies in Cambridge. But whereas Russell and Moore, each in a different way, did not give up belief in the powers of language—reconstructed—to represent reality, Hulme's critique lapsed into a "contempt for language" as such. . . . In his blunt rejection of "prose," Hulme denies language its arbitrary, conventional and systematic properties—the very properties that constitute language as a symbolic medium. Just as his opposition to the ideology of Progress does not allow him to acknowledge the cognitive and self-reflective potential of ordinary language, so does his anti-democratic stance rule out the social universality of speech. The fact that language is a "communal apparatus" which "only conveys over that part of the emotion which is common to all of us" prevents it, in Hulme's view, from expressing the individuality of actual experience. . . .

The medium of poetry, accordingly, is not, as it was for Pound, the beginning of a new language that would regenerate itself as well as public speech—but only a compromise, "a compromise for a language of intuition which would hand over sensations bodily." . . . Given the importance of physical experience in Hulme's biography and presentation of self, this statement has to be taken rather literally. Poetry is an "affair of the body" . . . , i.e. it should affect the human organism in much the same way as fighting, dancing, marching and sex. The organ to be affected is the eye, not the ear; poetry should be read not "chanted." . . . Its language is a "visual concrete one"—"words seen as physical things like a piece of string." . . . Therefore, accepting the terms of the "compromise," the poet should aim for "accurate, precise and definite description." . . . Considering the snapshot-like, or sometimes telescopic, quality of Hulme's poetic "visions," one might wonder, however, if this poet would not have been better equipped with a camera. Yet even a photographic language, in the end, can only offer a "compromise."

The ecstatic, unmediated impact of the poetic experience is a matter of "freshness" . . .—surprise but also transience. Intuition may grasp the most trivial of objects, fragments of scattered totality, and combine them in an artificial unity of effect: "a method of sudden arrangement of commonplaces. The *suddenness* makes us forget the commonplace." . . . What counts is the intensity of the emotion that is communicated. "Subject doesn't matter. . . . It isn't the scale or kind of emotion produced that decides, but this one fact: Is there any real zest in it?" . . . The source of this zest is not some kind of divine inspiration but a consciously cultivated poetic perceptiveness:

A transitory artificial impression is deliberately cultivated into an emotion and written about. Reason here creates and modifies an emotion, e.g. standing at street corners. Hence the sudden joy these produce in the reader when he remembers a half forgotten impression: "How true!" . . .

Poetic images are no longer sought for to illustrate pre-existing feelings; they arrive in the poet's mind and project a new emotional meaning. "In a sense poetry writes itself." . . . Hulme's "creation by happy chance" may prefigure the surrealists' experiments in automatic writing, but his psychological premises would not have allowed him to participate. Rather than plunging into the depths of the poet's psyche—a relic of Romanticism, a possible link to the infinite—Hulme conceives of the poetic disposition as a momentary, temporal pose. "The inner psychology of a poet at such a creative moment is like that of a drunkard who pushes his hand forward along a table, with an important gesture, and remains there pondering over it." . . .

Hulme not only debunks the concept of the poet as divinely inspired genius but also discards the concept of the poet as craftsman or technician—Pound's "engraver" or "stone-cutter."

> We no longer believe in perfection, either in verse or in thought, we frankly acknowledge the relative. We shall no longer strive to attain the absolutely perfect form in poetry. Instead of these minute perfections of phrase and words, the tendency will be rather towards the production of a general effect. . . . We are no longer concerned that stanzas shall be shaped and polished like gems, but rather that some vague mood shall be communicated. . . .

Such poems are no longer made to join the great tradition of masterpieces. An "Image" relying on surprise, suddenness, effect implicitly defeats the notion of timelessness associated with traditional works of art. If the "succession of visual images should exhaust" the reader . . . , as Hulme claims, these images will also exhaust themselves in the process; yet at the same time, by the very principle of their creation, they can also be infinitely reproduced. Given the "natural" decline of metaphors, of new, "original" analogies, from poetry into prose, Hulme prefers the Futurists' solution: "Personally I am of course in favour of the complete destruction of all verse more than twenty years old." . . .

The deliberate reduction of poetic vision to a *déjà-vu* effect ("How true!") also suspends, if only in tendency, traditional demarcations between author and reader. Hulme speaks of the "new art of the Reader" and goes so far as to consider the reader as "brother," as *unexpressed* author": "all the effects that can be produced by the literary man . . . are to be found dormant, unused in the reader, and are thus awakened." . . . It should be noted, however, that Hulme limits that notion to a small privileged audience—people who are exempt from the necessities of everyday life:

> Poetry after all for the amusement of bankers and other sedentary arm-chair people in after-dinner moods. No other. (Not for inspiration of progress.) So no infinite nobleness and function about that. (For one person in a thousand hence uselessness of school teaching.) . . .

The juxtaposition of poetry and dessert unintentionally reflects on the actual low level of Imperialist culture, at the same time, it presents an attack on the ideology still effective in concealing that state-of-affairs—the ideology which linked art to higher revelation and ulterior purposes, whether in the service of national sentiment, Victorian morality, or Fabian reformism.

Tracing Hulme's attack on the symbolic through his concept of poetry, I have stressed those elements which align him most closely with contemporary—and slightly later—avantgarde movements on the continent: the attack on the transcendental and unique character of artistic creation, on the special status of the work-of-art associated with both timelessness and tradition, on traditional modes of reception linking contemplation with exaltation and passivity. The question of the extent to which Hulme's concept of the "Image"—or, for that matter, Imagism in general—partakes in the non-organic, anti-organic determination of the most advanced continental avantgarde works would require a closer look at Imagist poetry, including Hulme's own. The ephemeral, artificial character of poetic vision, the dwelling on commonplace and detail, the fragmentary, emblematic shape of the Image, the emphasis on effect, surprise and diversion would certainly place Imagism in the context of avantgarde poetics. Yet does the juxtaposition of an image of the moon with that of a child's balloon or a farmer's ruddy face present a conceit in itself so incompatible as to potentially explode the organic unity of a poem from within? A comparison of the semantic structure of the "Image" with that of, say, the Futurist "analogia" or the Surrealist metaphor might help to elucidate the organicist limitations of their English counterpart. But we need not even resort to poetic practice to discover the inconsistencies of Hulme's avantgarde endeavor: at the end of the same pamphlet against Romantic imagination he advocates Coleridge's notion of "vital" or "organic" (vs. "mechanical") "complexities," equating them to Bergson's "intensive" (vs. "extensive") "manifolds" . . .—a non-discursive whole uniquely capable of grasping reality.

A number of critics from Krieger to Kermode have called attention to Hulme's Romantic relapses—yet I would like to stress one point: false totality is not just reintroduced on the level of poetic form, but seems predetermined by Hulme's ideological predilections. His insistence on the discontinuity of reality notwithstanding, he makes poetry again a merger of human experience with the sphere of absolute values—by subjecting it to the service of "the classical ideal of the fixed and constant nature of man." . . . Whether the moon is pulled down to earth or whether the lark on the cloud is turned into a flea on a white body, the internal dynamic of such Imagist conceits is to remind us that "man is always man and never a god." . . . But since the world view of the seventeenth century allegorist or—to mention one of Hulme's philosophical landmarks—the pessimism of a Pascal no longer presents a set of values shared by society as a whole or by influential social groups, Hulme attempts to restore this world view by force of dogma. From that angle, any kind of poetry, even the most spontaneous, personal vision physically transcribed becomes an affirmation of the religious attitude. . . . Admitting to the arbitrary, voluntaristic character of his enterprise, Hulme turns his criticism of prevailing ideology into an ideology of its own, or—in the sense of Sorel's concept of ideology—into a political stratagem. . . . Yet the political values Hulme wants to see implemented are not those of revolutionary Syndicalism, but are explicitly derived from his **"A Tory Philosophy"**: order, discipline, hierarchy, and tradition. (pp. 367-72)

The reductionist bent of Hulme's aesthetics reflects a general tendency of his conception of reality. In revolt against a present that claims to fulfill the course of history, he denies historical development as such; and protesting against a society that blindly reproduces injustice and stupidity, he categorically eliminates the conventional middle ground of social interaction (except for a few extraordinary individuals who are able to communicate). History is reduced to a conflict of "fundamental attitudes": the "humanistic" attitude (which Hulme rejects as a "false" or "pseudo-category") on the one hand, and the "religious" attitude on the other. . . . The basic immutability of those attitudes derives from the very constancy of human nature:

> It is as impossible to discover anything new about the ways of man in regard to the cosmos as it is to observe anything new about the ways of a kitten. The general conceptions we can form are as limited in number as the possible gestures of a dance, and as fixed in type as is the physiology of man himself. . . .

Here, as in other instances, Hulme's critique of evolutionist ideology lapses into a primitivist ontology.

By a similar logic of reduction, Hulme's radical critique of language finally dissociates into cognitive pessimism, solipsism and voluntarism. "All general statements about truth, etc., are in the end only amplifications of man's appetites." . . . All particular statements are handicapped by the "disease of the symbolic language": "world indescribable, that is not reducible to counters." . . . Distinguishing himself from animals only by the illusory medium of "symbolic language," . . . man finds himself thrown into the chaos of empirical reality, the world of **"Cinders,"** Hulme's "Sketch of a New Weltanschauung."

> There is an *objective* world (?), a chaos, a cinder-heap. Gradually oases have been built up. Egos have grown as organised trees. . . . A landscape, with occasional oases. So now and then we are moved—at the theatre, action, a love. But mainly deserts of dirt, ash-pits of the cosmos, grass on ash-pits. No universal ego, but a few definite persons gradually built up. . . .

This select company of Stirnerian egos emerges as the only meaning and purpose of history: "Through all the ages, the conversation of ten men sitting together is what holds the world together." . . . Their unifying capabilities result from the presence of their consciousness, for *"only in the fact of consciousness is there a unity in the world."* . . . The principles governing that unity, however, seem as posited and arbitrary as those of modern urban or industrial planning: "Unity is made in the world by drawing squares over it. . . . No unity of laws, but merely of the sorting machine." . . . (pp. 375-76)

Against the vast desolate background of Hulme's **"Cinders,"** the antinomies of his poetics can be seen in a better light. On the one hand, poetic intuition does offer a method for the structuring of experience: ". . . an infinity of analogues which help us along, and give us a feeling of power over the chaos when we perceive them." Whereas the empirical world is absolutely finite, the production of Images is virtually infinite: ". . . herein lies the chance for originality. Here there are some new things under the sun." . . . On the other hand, whenever Hulme insists on the temporality of poetic expression, he emphasizes its accidental and contingent character—"a happy escape from platitude. Nothing new under the sun." . . . From that angle, poetic activity appears as meaningless as any other human activity in Hulme's bleak view of life. The aphorism "Most of our life is spent in buttoning and unbuttoning" . . . and the phrase "Life composed of exquisite moments and the rest shadows of them" . . . are two sides of the same coin. Life presents a haphazard collection of sensations, gestures, acts and rituals; the individual experience no longer relates to any other experience, let alone to anyone else's. The images that contain those isolated "exquisite moments" are fragments, their meaning is contrived. If nothing else, they signify the disappearance of meaning from history, the evanescence and contingency even of aesthetic experience. "The eyes, the beauty of the world, have been organized out of faeces. Man returns to dust. So does the face of the world to primeval cinders." . . . (pp. 376-77)

Hulme's fragments and sketches clearly reflect a melancholic disposition—as he himself puts it in the last paragraph of **"Cinders"**: "A melancholy spirit, the mind like a great desert lifeless, and the sound of march music in the street, passes like a wave over that desert, unifies it, but then goes." The fundamental "ennui"—a term the Surrealists were to apply to a similar disposition—in Hulme's case coincides with a cynical indifference to existing social hierarchies. . . . (p. 377)

With his melancholic vision, Hulme seems even further removed from contemporary social and political developments than were the Guild Socialists with their idealistic medievalism. In their attack on the Labour Party and Trade Unionism they had replaced "class" by "culture" and "values." Hulme no longer even pretends to refer to social and economic conditions but makes it clear that his only interest in the Middle Ages is in certain "abstract things" at the "centre" of their civilization, "doctrines felt as facts." "The only thing the new period will have in common with medievalism will be the subordination of man to certain absolute values." . . . Clearly preferring the notion of direct action to the cultural idealism of the *New Age* medievalists, Hulme related to Syndicalism in an equally abstract manner. In his introduction to *Reflections on Violence* he professes an interest in Sorel's "ideology," particularly his emphasis on "absolute" (or "heroic") "values" and the tactical value of "myths," yet relegates Sorel's concept of class struggle to the realm of "facts" with which he, Hulme, firmly avows not to be concerned. . . . Hulme's dogmatism appears as the reverse side of his melancholic disposition; his bent for direct action reflects the militant isolation of an intellectual at war with the more established parts of the intelligentsia. The abstractness of his rebellion and his dogmatic short-cuts led him to render service to the dominant forces. Like the vorticists, he can be called a "mercenary" in more than a metaphorical sense: literally, he pledged his life to a state, a nation, an Imperialist power whose culture he had not only criticized but violently attacked.

On the other hand, Hulme had a much keener awareness of the present than, for example, the *New Age* medievalists or, for that matter, Pound. His poetics of sensual immediacy and fragmentary vision, the physical concreteness of his war diary, the abstract bleakness of his **"Cinders,"** all prefigure a modernist sensibility which was to come to full reign only after World War I. If cultural innovations can be attributed to the individual intellectual at all, Hulme has to be credited for his strange allegorical intuitions rather than his restoration of false totalities. [Wyndham] Lewis's play "Enemy of the Stars" (1914) comes to mind for a contemporary vision of comparable allegorical intensity; the *Waste Land* had yet to be written. For the visual arts, Hulme underlined the anti-organic tendencies of contemporary non-mimetic works by a concept of "abstraction" updated with technology. Whatever the political implications of that concept may have been, the works in question clearly reflect a definite change in human perception—a change relating to industrial methods of production, urban traffic, mechanical techniques of reproduction. The impact of these fundamental changes on British avantgarde art may have been curbed—for political reasons as well as aesthetic ones—yet they yielded a "new sense of form," a sense of "construction" (Pound) which also made its way into the fields of poetry and criticism.

Hulme single-handedly produced and lived out a number of inconsistencies in store for the avantgarde state of mind. The fumbling articulation of a modern sensibility through reactionary dogmatism and melancholic immediacy provides a meaningful contradiction—a contradiction which so often got lost in the course of Hulme's critical (or rather less critical) reception or was transmuted into the smooth cultural conservatism of Eliot or Hulme's New Critical successors. (pp. 378-79)

> *Miriam Hansen, "T. E. Hulme, Mercenary of Modernism; or, Fragments of Avantgarde Sensibility in Pre-World War I Britain," in* ELH, *Vol. 47, No. 2, Summer, 1980, pp. 355-85.*

MICHAEL H. LEVENSON   (essay date 1984)

[*In the following excerpt, Levenson discusses the development of Hulme's poetic theories.*]

The posthumous publication of *Speculations* . . . had its intended results: the rescuing of Hulme's work from obscurity, and the return of his thought, if not to the modernist foreground, at least to its looming background. Almost as soon as the volume appeared, it won its author the comfortable status of an acknowledged precedent. Eliot, reviewing the work in the *Criterion*, praised Hulme as a "solitary figure . . . the forerunner of a new attitude of mind, which should be the twentieth-century mind, if the twentieth century is to have a mind of its own" [see excerpt dated 1924]. This is the place which has since been Hulme's, the valued predecessor, the cherished forerunner of modernism. It is no meagre role; other forerunners have fared worse; and *Speculations* is in large measure responsible for the reputation. It remains the work through which he is known.

But while *Speculations* has gained Hulme a certain prominence, it has done so at increasing expense. Herbert Read, who assembled the volume, drew on published, unpublished and unfinished writings, early, late and undated—presumably, in order to show the range of Hulme's attitudes and interests. But the result has been that Hulme has the appearance of a wildly inconsistent enthusiast, a follower of Bergson, Nietzsche and Sorel, and as if that were an insufficiently heterogeneous lot, an equally fervent admirer of Husserl, G. E. Moore and Charles Maurras. In recent years this has begun to undermine Hulme's standing—to the extent that Herbert Schneidau can write that "it is now generally recognized that Hulme was not an original or serious thinker, nor even a literary critic."

That he was not "even" a literary critic seems to me the least telling of the charges. It is a point happily conceded. Nor is it necessary to insist on Hulme's originality. It may be true, as a biographer [Michael Roberts] has held, that "there is scarcely an argument or instance in Hulme's writing'' that does not derive from someone else [see excerpt dated 1938]. But that does not diminish Hulme's interest. Indeed, he turns out to be interesting just insofar as he is derivative, just insofar as he submitted himself to a range of influences not previously conjoined. ''T. E. Hulme'' might be seen merely as the name of an intellectual site, a place where intellectual currents converged. If that does not make him a ''serious thinker,'' it at least makes him worth treating seriously.

That Hulme is eclectic is evident. But he was by no means as capricious, as indiscriminate, as intellectually fitful, as it may appear. The intention here is to restore some of the lost coherence, and thereby the seriousness, of his thought. This would be a limited exercise were it not that Hulme's intellectual development was so closely bound to the vicissitudes of early modernism.

Much of the interpretive confusion has derived from a single, apparently trivial, editorial lapse: Read's failure to fix correct chronology for the texts. The essays in *Speculations,* thus appearing together, gave an air of simultaneity to Hulme's opinions. Certainly, if he had held all those opinions all at once, then the persistent complaints of paradox and contradiction would be fair and telling. In fact, he did not, though this has escaped critical attention. What have appeared as contradictions were almost without exception changes of mind. His thought passed through a number of distinct and irreconcilable phases, and in separating what has been too casually agglomerated, it will become possible to see Hulme's career, and early modernism more generally, as something more than a welter of passionate opinion. (pp. 38-9)

Not atypically, Hulme had passed his early intellectual life preoccupied with the growth of science and its moral and religious consequences. The issue was for him, in William James' phrase, ''living,'' ''forced,'' and ''momentous.'' Hulme seems to have been unable to turn elsewhere until he had discovered a satisfactory position on the subject. Nor was he evasive or sentimental about the matter. He took the materialist position seriously and addressed it in its extreme form, often identifying it by means of this remark from Munsterberg:

> Science is to me not a mass of disconnected information, but the certainty that there is no change in the universe, no motion of an atom, and no sensation of a consciousness which does not come and go absolutely in accordance with natural laws; the certainty that nothing can exist outside the gigantic mechanism of causes and effects; necessity moves the emotions in my mind.

Hulme found this kind of claim completely unsettling. If it were accepted, it would threaten not only religious belief but the possibility of any moral realm at all: ''it is impossible, if mechanism be a true account of the world, for us to believe in any preservation of values.'' Within the materialist perspective, ''the word 'value' has clearly no meaning. There cannot be any good or bad in such a turmoil of atoms.''

Against this background Hulme discovered the work of Bergson, which seems to have produced a miraculous cure. Reading Bergson ''put an end to an intolerable state''; ''I had been released from a nightmare which had long troubled my mind''; it was ''an almost physical sense of exhilaration, a sudden expansion, a kind of mental explosion.'' The important step was simple. It involved Bergson's attack on materialist expla-

nation on the grounds that it neglects or distorts crucial aspects of conscious experience. Materialism introduces into consciousness factors only appropriate to the external world— quantity, causality—and attempts to make the inner and ''intensive'' realm continuous with the outer and ''extensive'' sphere. But, according to Bergson, no such continuity obtains. He does not dispute the soundness of science within its own boundaries; the error of materialist explanation is that it mistakes this part of reality for the whole. Hulme describes the ''general idea'' behind Bergson's work as the ''endeavor to prove that we seem inevitably to arrive at the mechanistic theory simply because the intellect, in dealing with a certain aspect of reality, distorts it in that direction. It can deal with matter but it is absolutely incapable of understanding life.'' (pp. 40-1)

Bergson's refutation of materialism was the first issue to seize Hulme's attention, but the implications of the argument went further, and Hulme willingly accepted them. If reason was ''inevitably'' distorting, then the project of a comprehensive rational understanding of the world was pointless and naive. Such an attitude led quickly to an anti-intellectualism, which Bergson accepted with equanimity and Hulme with enthusiasm. On its basis Hulme constructed a general Anglo-Bergsonian perspective: a scepticism towards the claims of traditional metaphysics, and a rejection of the rationalist belief in historical and social progress. Attending meetings of the Aristotelian Society in London, he appears to have sat in uncharacteristic silence and more characteristic contempt. In 1911, he travelled to Bologna for an international philosophic conference, and sent his impressions to the *New Age.* They typify his attitudes of the time.

Hulme asserts his ''rather sceptical opinion of philosophy,'' which he considers ''not a science but an art,'' and he indicates his contempt for the rationalist pursuit of the ''one Truth, one Good.'' ''I am a pluralist,'' insists Hulme. ''There is no Unity, no Truth, but forces which have different aims. . . .'' To the rationalist, ''this is an absolutely horrible position.'' The essay becomes a carping satire of the naive ambitions of philosophers. Hulme himself, he tells us, would rather watch a parade in the street than attend the opening conference of ''Reality,'' since ''they would be certain to talk inside of progress, while the only progress I can stand is the progress of princes and troops, for they, though they move, make no pretence of moving 'upward.'''

Hulme's career as a poet ended in 1912. His oeuvre comprised six published poems, none of them more than nine lines. In his lifetime he published no essay specifically devoted to literature or literary theory. His importance for the modern movement came from a few telling contributions that appeared at opportune moments. As early as 1908, he belonged to The Poets' Club, and served as its honorary secretary. He left the club the following year but continued in a literary discussion group, of which, according to F. S. Flint, he was the ''ringleader.'' During this period, he published two poems, delivered **''A Lecture on Modern Poetry,''** and contributed an essay on Haldane to the *New Age.* These are among his earliest surviving texts, and they contain the outline of a distinct literary posture.

The lecture, presumably delivered to The Poets' Club, provides the most extensive formulation, and deserves the most attention. It is an effort to establish a large-scale historical context within which modern poetry can be understood. As will become his habit, Hulme passes casually over vast intellectual epochs in the pursuit of even vaster generalizations. According to his scheme, the "ancients" had attempted to evade the fluidity and instability of the world by constructing "things of permanence which would stand fast in this universal flux which frightened them." In their poetry, for instance, they wished "to embody in a few lines a perfection of thought . . . hence the fixity of the form of a poem and the elaborate rules of regular metre." The same desire manifested itself in the building of the pyramids, and the "hypostatized ideas of Plato." The claim, in brief, is this: "Living in a dynamic world they wished to create a static fixity where their souls might rest." Purity of form became a refuge. But with the advent of "modernity" (the date of which is left unspecified) a thorough change in perspective occurred. "The whole trend of the modern spirit" is away from "absolute duty" and "absolute truth": "we no longer believe in perfection, either in verse or in thought, we frankly acknowledge the relative." In Hulme's scheme, the history of thought, most broadly conceived, is from Platonic fixity to Bergsonian fluidity. With this shift in *Weltanschauung,* Hulme associates a corresponding change in literary forms. Since poets will "no longer strive to attain the absolutely perfect form in poetry," the predominance of "metre and a regular number of syllables" disappears. From the perspective of the new "impressionist poetry," regular metre is "cramping, jangling, meaningless, and out of place," a remnant that has become constraining. Hulme betrays no nostalgia for the fading past: "Each age must have its own special form of expression, and any period that deliberately goes out of it is an age of insincerity."

Poetic subject-matter undergoes a similar shift. Traditional poetry treated "big things," "epic subjects," and thus fit easily into metrical regularity. But such grand poetic statements have become obsolete. Even the lyrical perfection of Shelley, Keats and Tennyson is outmoded. The modern poet remains "tentative and half-shy." Whistler's paintings are a paradigm; what has "found expression in painting as Impressionism will soon find expression in poetry as free verse." Modern poetry, in short, "has become definitely and finally introspective and deals with expression and communication of momentary phases in the poet's mind." We are no longer concerned that stanzas shall be shaped and polished like gems, but rather that some vague mood shall be communicated. In all the arts, we seek for the maximum of individual and personal expression, rather than for the attainment of any absolute beauty."

That is one movement in the lecture, and in Hulme's thought generally: the confining of poetry to the restricted sphere of personal expression. It corresponds to the negative aspect of Bergson's philosophy: the rejection of any large-scale metaphysical system, or of any comprehensive intellectual schema. But there is a second movement, no less Bergsonian, no less crucial. It is best described as the attempt to escape the bounds of the ordinary, the conventional, the commonplace. The attitude appears most clearly in Hulme's antagonism to prose.

Prose, insists Hulme, represents language in a stage of decline; it uses "images that have died and become figures of speech." He compares it to a "reflex action" such as the lacing of one's boots, an action accomplished with an "economy of effort" and "almost without thinking." That is how prose treats language: "we get words divorced from any real vision," words used as mere "counters" in order "to pass to conclusions without thinking." The aim of poetry is precisely to resist such a tendency: "It always endeavors to arrest you, and to make you continuously see a physical thing, to prevent you gliding through an abstract process." Where prose is indirect and conventional, poetry is vivid, physical, direct. Condensed to an aphorism: "Prose is in fact the museum where the dead images of verse are preserved."

This second emphasis, then, leads Hulme to large claims on behalf of poetry—poetry as "the advance guard of language"—even while his other emphasis insists on restricting the poet's range. As we shall see, this is a characteristic modern strategy: to narrow the domain of the literary, even as the claims for literature increase. In Hulme's case, the dual movement reflects still more general aims, which derive from his Bergsonian perspective: first, to abandon any obsolete metaphysical or epic pretensions; and second, to escape the constraints of ordinary and prosaic reality in order to see a deeper truth.

For Bergson, and consequently for Hulme, the two great dangers coincide, as do their solutions. Both systematic philosophy and ordinary thought are subject to the same distortion, since both depend on the constructs of reason and the conventions of language. The pressing need is to recognize the reality which exceeds these rational conventions, because "by intellect one can construct approximate models, by intuition one can identify oneself with the flux." The transcendence which "intuition" provides in Bergson's philosophy is furnished by the "image" in Hulme's literary theory.

The concept is best approached through example. Hulme's poem "Autumn" appeared in the first volume of Poets' Club verse (1909):

> A touch of cold in the Autumn night
> I walked abroad,
> And saw the ruddy moon lean over a hedge
> Like a red-faced farmer.
> I did not stop to speak, but nodded,
> And round about were the wistful stars
> With white faces like town children.

Two characteristics of the poem will lead us to the point. First is its self-conscious restraint, the deliberate avoidance of the grand scale. The scene is slight, the tone conversational, the diction homely; there is only a "touch" of cold; the narrator's activities are reduced to the most commonplace: "walked," "saw," "nodded." "I did not stop to speak, but nodded,"—that puts the issue nicely. There is no pause for speech, no lyric flight, no pantheistic interchange with nature, only a terse acknowledgement: a nod. The second point concerns the use of metaphoric image. Take, for instance, the poem's fourth line. The moon/farmer simile is introduced with a sudden deflation of rhythm; the image occupies the whole line and ends the poem's first sentence. The effect is to foreground the comparison and to make it bear considerable poetic weight. The same technique occurs in the metaphor and simile which end the poem: "With white faces like town children." Again the comparison obtrudes, this time as the conclusion of the poem, and again the result is to bestow privileged attention on the trope.

Of importance here is the relation between these two, fairly obvious, characteristics. For just to the extent that the poetic subject remains muted and slight does the role of the image become predominant. In the absence of any narrative, any development of ideas, any articulation of character, the images themselves come to attract the poetic regard. Further, in being so stressed, they stand against the triviality of the poetic scene.

What is enacted in the poetry is enacted in the theory. On the one hand, Hulme sees the image as part of the modern retreat from "epic subjects," "heroic action," "big things." It is an expression of the new "tentative and half-shy" temperament, whose poetry has abandoned "absolute beauty" in favour of "personal expression." The image is to be visual and concrete, replacing large-scale philosophic vision, emotional effusion, the declamatory impulse. Instead of momentous sentiments unfolding in regular verse, the modern method is simply to be the "piling-up and juxtaposition of distinct images in different lines." The image reflects the modesty of modernism.

On the other hand, the image, though perhaps modest, is by no means shy. Images are "the very essence of an intuitive language," because they disrupt the habitual patterns of thought, producing what Hulme calls the "other-world through-the-glass effect," the sense of strangeness which makes possible a deeper and more intuitive vision. 'Ordinary language communicates nothing of the individuality and freshness of things"—only poetry can produce the "exhilaration" of "direct and unusual communication." Thus the importance of the image: it allows poetry to avoid literary excess without succumbing to the commonplace.

The insistence on the primacy of the image is the specific literary point that has been Hulme's most influential. But what should by now be clear is that for Hulme the image was not a matter of merely formal poetic concern. It was part of the attempt, indeed a considerable part, to find a satisfactory definition for modern poetry. In this regard Hulme makes three points which are central to his literary position: that poetry is to avoid pursuit of the epic, the absolute and the permanent; that it is likewise to avoid the prosaic and conventional; that a poetry of images is therefore the appropriate literary method. There is a fourth point, which has so far been submerged but which will come into increasing prominence: namely that the poetic strategy is to be founded on a radical literary individualism. Throughout, Hulme depends on notions such as "sincerity," "feeling," "personality," "introspection," "expression." These are the qualities which characterize the new poetry, which, indeed, distinguish modern from ancient and poetry from prose. And Hulme's particular formal enthusiasms—for free verse and the image—are consistently defended in terms of the drive toward the "maximum of individual and personal expression." Free verse makes it possible to communicate "some vague mood"; the arrangement of images allows the poet "to suggest and to evoke the state he feels."

In trying to establish a literary position that is at once antimetaphysical and nontrivial, anti-heroic and yet not commonplace, Hulme takes emotional subtlety as the basis for modern poetry. In this he remains a faithful Bergsonian. As metaphysics becomes untenable, it is the intuiting subject which becomes pre-eminent. Similarly, as the epic aspiration disappears from literature, personal expression takes its place. The struggle of modern poetry becomes the struggle of *le moi profond*: against language, against convention, against habit, against the seductions of metaphysics, in order to achieve satisfactory expression. (pp. 41-7)

> Michael H. Levenson, "Dating Hulme / Parsing Modernism," in his A Genealogy of Modernism: A Study of English Literary Doctrine 1908-1922, Cambridge University Press, 1984, pp. 37-47.

RENÉ WELLEK (essay date 1986)

[*Wellek's* A History of Modern Criticism (1955-86) *is a major, comprehensive study of the literary critics of the last three centuries. Wellek's critical method, as demonstrated in* A History *and outlined in his* Theory of Literature (1949), *is one of describing, analyzing, and evaluating a work solely in terms of the problems it poses for itself and how the writer solves them. For Wellek, biographical, historical, and psychological information is incidental. Although many of Wellek's critical methods are reflected in the work of the New Critics, he was not a member of that group, and rejected their more formalistic tendencies. In the following excerpt, Wellek points out some inconsistencies in Hulme's aesthetic ideas.*]

When [Herbert] Read published *Speculations,* [T. S.] Eliot hailed the book in the *Criterion* [see excerpt dated 1924] as "a work of very great significance. In this volume he appears the fore-runner of a new attitude of mind which should be the twentieth-century mind, if the twentieth century is to have a mind of its own." Since then Hulme has attracted biographers and a large body of comment wherever English criticism is discussed, which seems to me totally out of proportion to the quality and originality of his writings on literary matters.

Michael Roberts, whose sympathetic, expository book [see excerpt dated 1938] was the first full-length study of Hulme, makes many admissions that are far more damaging than he seems to realize. "A hostile critic might say that Hulme's sole merit was that he could read French and German. He was not an original thinker he solved no problems." ... "There is scarcely a single statement in Hulme that is not borrowed." ... In philosophy, Hulme has merits as a propagandist, translator, and expounder of Bergson and Georges Sorel. He was one of the Englishmen impressed by Lasserre, the *Action française,* and the whole French antiromanticism. Though less systematically, he later showed an awareness of new German philosophical and aesthetic trends: he speaks of the neo-Kantianism of Hermann Cohen, of the so-called Marburg school, he has read and paraphrases something of Wilhelm Dilthey and Max Scheler, he knows the beginnings of phenomenology in Husserl, and he uses Wilhelm Worringer's *Abstraction und Einfühlung* (1908) to justify his artistic tastes. Hulme wanted to write a book on modern theories of art, which in addition to Bergson and Croce would have emphasized the German theoreticians—"this astonishing and intensely interesting literature entirely unknown in England" ...—centering on Theodor Lipps, "the greatest writer in aesthetics." ... But it is hard to see how these different motifs of thought could have been assimilated into anything else except some kind of superior *reportage.* His adherence to the philosophy of Bergson cannot be reconciled with the abstract classicism Hulme's taste demanded. He himself seems to have been worried about this. In 1911 he wrote:

> I noticed early this year that M. Pierre Lasserre, ... one of the most interesting of the group, had made an attack on Bergson. I was very much in sympathy with the anti-romanticism of his two books, *La morale de Nietzsche* and *Le Romantisme français,* and I wondered from what point of view exactly he was attacking Bergson. I was in agreement with both sides, and so I wondered whether there was any real inconsistency in my own position. When I was in Paris, then, last April I went to see Lasserre and talk to him about it. . . .

Roberts does not record the outcome, if any, of this discussion. It seems to me that there could not have been any: one cannot believe in a highly irrational philosophy of flux and at the same time believe in ethical absolutes, classicism, order, and abstract geometrical art.

But it is best to look at the more strictly literary and aesthetic pronouncements by Hulme. There are only a few documents that have any bearing on our main interests: **"Modern Art and Its Philosophy,"** . . . **"Romanticism and Classicism," "A Lecture on Modern Poetry,"** and **"Notes on Language and Style."** Each must, I think, be discussed separately. **"Modern Art and Its Philosophy"** is, as Hulme himself points out, "practically an abstract of Worringer's views." . . . It seems to me totally incompatible with Hulme's Bergsonism, but it satisfied a personal need of his taste. Hulme found in Worringer a defense for his interest in abstract art: in Egyptian art, in Byzantine mosaics (he must have visited Ravenna), and in Epstein, whom he knew personally and greatly admired. The thesis of the paper is that of Worringer's book; there are two kinds of art: one vitalistic, based on sympathy or empathy with nature and living forms—organic—and the other abstract, abstracting, geometrical, "searching after an austerity, a monumental stability and permanence, a perfection and rigidity which vital things can never have." . . . Hulme sympathizes with abstract art and hails its reemergence: its "desire for austerity and bareness, a striving towards structure and away from the messiness and confusion of nature and natural things." . . . It is an exposition and a plea for a kind of art disparaged and neglected by vitalistic, organistic art, produced by the Greeks, the Renaissance, and the German classics.

Things became much more complex when Hulme writes on **"Romanticism and Classicism."** He starts, as he himself indicated, with the antiromanticism of Maurras and Lasserre . . . ; he interprets romanticism in the general political sense of the French antiromantics, endorsing, for example, the view that "romanticism has made the revolution. They hate the revolution, so they hate romanticism." . . . Romanticism is conceived to be simply optimistic liberalism, belief in progress, and so on, just the theories that most of the great romantics hated most. Romanticism, in this view, is a lower form of the Enlightenment—something that can be possibly found in Rousseau, Hugo, or Shelley, but surely not in the Schlegels, or any German romantic, or Leopardi, Chateaubriand, Vigny, Blake, Wordsworth, or Coleridge. Romanticism, according to Hulme, is "spilt religion," . . . a sentimental trust in human nature, a yearning for the vaguely infinite. Against this Hulme poses classicism, which implies a belief in original sin, in the stability of human nature, the impossibility of progress, and lack of interest in the vague infinite. The contrast is pinned then to the Coleridgean distinction between imagination and fancy. Hulme does not, however, come to grips with Coleridge's own distinction but fastens on Ruskin's later development of the terms to disparage imagination as a solemn yearning for the vague and to recommend fancy. Fancy is preoccupied with the finite; fanciful poetry is dry and hard. Beauty, Hulme pleads, "can be in small, dry things." . . . "The great aim is accurate, precise and definite description." . . . The aim of art is to catch the "exact curve" of the thing, complete "sincerity"—"the fundamental quality of good art without dragging in the infinite or serious." "I prophesy that a period of dry, hard, classical verse is coming." . . . A visual concrete language is the aim, which makes the reader see a physical thing. But this "making the reader see" cannot be achieved by simple description. "It is only by new metaphors, that is, by fancy, that it can be made precise." . . . So far, so good—one can speak of a theory of imagism, but then suddenly an astonishing attempt is made to recruit Coleridge and Bergson into the camp of this "clas-

sicism": Hulme argues that this classical art is still somehow vital, "intuitive," organic, though "vital"—or "organic"—is "merely a convenient metaphor for a complexity of a different kind, that in which the parts cannot be said to be elements as each one is modified by the other's presence, and each one to a certain extent is the whole." . . . But this is, of course, a false interpretation of Coleridge. "Organic" in Coleridge surely implies a metaphysics, a concept of creative imagination, and I cannot see how Bergsonian "intuition" can be brought in to defend such a "classicism." The bridge seems to be provided by the implied concept of the "characteristic," in which the artist seizes intuitively, a notion acceptable to Hulme, Bergson, and most romantics. The essay is of great interest as a statement of aversion to a complex of ideas that Hulme quite unhistorically calls "romantic" and as a prophecy of an imagistic, unemotional, fanciful poetry of hard, dry things. But it is hardly a piece that can be recommended as a full and fair discussion of the issue.

We come nearer to Hulme's concrete taste in the **"Lecture on Modern Poetry."** It starts out with a repudiation of the metaphysical claims of poetry. "A reviewer writing in the *Saturday Review* last week spoke of poetry as the means by which the soul soared into higher regions, and as a means of expression by which it became merged into a higher kind of reality. Well, that is the kind of statement that I utterly detest." . . . Hulme states boldly, "I have not a catholic taste, but a violently personal prejudiced one. I have no reverence for tradition," . . . and then explains his views: "Poetry no longer deals with heroic action, it has become definitely and finally introspective and deals with expression and communication of momentary phases in the poet's mind. It was well put by Mr. G. K. Chesterton in this way—that where the old dealt with the Siege of Troy, the new attempts to express the emotions of a boy fishing." . . . Hulme himself recognizes that what he demands here is something like impressionism in painting. He remembers that "the first time [he] ever felt the necessity and inevitableness of verse, was in the desire to reproduce the peculiar quality of feeling which is induced by the flat spaces and wide horizons of the virgin prairie of western Canada." . . . What poetry is after is the precise image: "This method of recording impressions by visual images in distinct lines does not require the old metric system." . . . Hulme disapproves of chanting, hypnotic verse. "Regular meter to this impressionistic poetry is cramping, jangling, meaningless, and out of place. Into the delicate pattern of images and colour, it introduces the heavy, crude pattern of rhetorical verse." . . . The differentia between poetry and prose is not meter but imagery. With a reversal of the usual terminology, Hulme argues that "the direct language is poetry, because it deals in images. The indirect language is prose, because it uses images that have died and become figures of speech." . . . "Images are born in poetry. They are used in prose, and finally die a long, lingering death in journalists' English. Now this process is very rapid, so that the poet must continually be creating new images, and his sincerity may be measured by the number of his images." . . . "This new verse resembles sculpture rather than music; it appeals to the eye rather than to the ear." . . . But who can ever measure sincerity by the number of images, and why should impressionist poetry resemble sculpture rather than painting?

These ideas can be supplemented by aphorisms in the **"Notes on Language and Style."** Much says the same as the **"Lecture."** Poetry should be visual, "each word must be an image *seen*, not a counter." . . . "Poetry is neither more nor less than a mosaic of words, so great is exactness required for each one." . . . But poetry must be metaphorical. "Never, never, never a simple statement. It has no effect." . . . Astonishingly enough, metaphor leads Hulme to recommend analogy, and analogy to a hint of a romantic metaphysics of symbolism and correspondences. "It is not sufficient to find analogies. It is necessary to find those that add something to each, and give a sense of wonder, a sense of being united in another mystic world." . . . The **"Notes"** contain assertions much in the style of late nineteenth-century aestheticism. Poetry "must be absolutely removed from reality." . . . "Poetry is not for others, but for the poet"; "expression builds up personality"; poetry comes "in moments of ecstasy," "with the jumps, cf. love, fighting, dancing." . . . "The literary man deliberately perpetrates a hypocrisy, in that he fits together his own isolated moments of ecstasy," some of them "perhaps brought on by drink." The last entry is "All theories are toys," . . . and it would be easy to conclude on this note. All theories were toys to Hulme, but it is both more charitable and more accurate to say that Hulme was a young man groping for a view of the world, with a definite taste in art for which he was trying to find defenses. There seems to me an undeniable contradiction between his Bergsonism and his "classicism," but as in Eliot, the classicism is only an ideological superstructure: the taste is for the imagistic, the "characteristic," the "sincere," the fanciful, and that is really not incompatible with Bergsonism, whose metaphysics Hulme had embraced with such conviction. (pp. 148-52)

> *René Wellek, "The Innovators," in his* A History of Modern Criticism, 1750-1950: English Criticism, 1900-1950, Vol. 5, *Yale University Press, 1986, pp. 144-75.**

ADDITIONAL BIBLIOGRAPHY

Brandabur, Edward. "The Eye in the Ceiling and the Eye in the Mud: T. E. Hulme's Comedy of Perception." *Papers on Language and Literature* 9, No. 4 (Fall 1973): 420-27.
    Explicates Hulme's theory of imagery.

Csengeri, K. E. "T. E. Hulme's Borrowings from the French." *Comparative Literature* XXIV, No. 1 (Winter 1982): 16-27.
    Explains the influence of French thinkers on Hulme.

Daiches, David. "T. E. Hulme and T. S. Eliot." In his *Poetry and the Modern World*, pp. 90-105. Chicago: University of Chicago Press, 1940.*
    Discussion of the similarity between the artistic theories of Hulme and Eliot.

Flint, F. S. "The *Ripostes* of Ezra Pound with 'The Complete Poetical Works of T. E. Hulme'." *Poetry and Drama* I, No. 1 (March 1913): 60-2.*
    Review of *Ripostes* and *Complete Poetical Works*.

Kamerbeek, J., Jr. "T. E. Hulme and German Philosophy: Dilthey and Scheler." *Comparative Literature* XXI, No. 3 (Summer 1969): 193-212.
    Discussion of the impact of German philosophers upon Hulme's thinking.

Kishler, Thomas C. "Original Sin and T. E. Hulme's Aesthetics." *Journal of Aesthetic Education* 10, No. 2 (1976): 99-106.
    Analysis of Hulme's ideas about religion and art.

Lewis, Wyndham. "Hulme of Original Sin." In his *Blasting and Bombardiering*, pp. 99-104. Los Angeles: University of California Press, 1967.
    Personal reminiscences of a close friend.

Nott, Kathleen. "Mr. Hulme's Sloppy Dregs." In her *The Emperor's Clothes*, pp. 56-104. Bloomington: Indiana University Press, 1958.
    Refutation of Hulme's philosophical position.

Paliwal, B. B. "T. E. Hulme's Poetics." *The Literary Criterion* VIII, No. 1 (Winter 1967): 33-8.
    Explicates Hulme's theories of poetry.

Pound, Ezra. "Preface to 'The Complete Poetical Works of T. E. Hulme'." In his *Ripostes of Ezra Pound*, pp. 58-9. London: Stephen Swift and Co., 1912.
    Considers Hulme's poetry "an enviable example."

――――. "This Hulme Business." In *The Poetry of Ezra Pound*, edited by Hugh Kenner, pp. 307-09. London: Faber and Faber, 1951.
    Maintains "the critical light during the years immediately prewar in London shone not from Hulme but from [Ford Madox] Ford."

Primeau, Ronald. "On the Discrimination of Hulmes: Toward a Theory of the 'Anti-romantic' Romanticism of Modern Poetry." *Journal of Modern Literature* 3, No. 5 (July 1974): 1104-22.
    Clarification of terms "romantic" and "anti-romantic" and their relevance to modern poetry.

Read, Herbert. "The Isolation of the Image: T. E. Hulme." In his *The True Voice of Feeling*, pp. 101-15. New York: Pantheon, 1953.
    Examination of Hulme's theories.

Riding, Laura. "T. E. Hulme, the New Barbarism, and Gertrude Stein." In her *Contemporaries and Snobs*, pp. 123-99. Garden City, N.J.: Doubleday Doran, 1928.*
    A poet on "neo-classical" criticism.

Robinson, A. D. "New Sources for Imagism." *Notes and Queries* n.s. 27, No. 3 (June 1980): 238-40.*
    Suggests the writings of Jean-Marie Guyau as possible source of Imagist theory.

Schuchard, Ronald. "Eliot and Hulme in 1916: Toward a Revaluation of Eliot's Critical and Spiritual Development." *PMLA* 88, No. 5 (October 1973): 1083-94.*
    Discussion of Hulme's impact upon Eliot.

Wees, William C. "Ford and Hulme." In his *Vorticism and the English Avant-Garde*, pp. 73-85. Toronto: University of Toronto Press, 1972.*
    Consideration of Hulme's place in early twentieth-century literary thought.

Ilya (Arnoldovich) Ilf
1897-1937

Evgeny (Petrovich) Petrov
1903-1942

Ilya Ilf

Evgeny Petrov

(Also transliterated as Ilia; also Eugene, Evgeni, Evgenii, Yevgeni, Yevgenii, Yevgeniy, Yevgeny, and Yevgueniy; pseudonyms of Ilya Arnoldovich Fainzilberg and Evgeny Petrovich Kataev) Russian novelists, short story writers, travel writers, and dramatists.

Ilf and Petrov were popular post-Revolutionary humorists whose entertaining but pointed fiction satirizing human weakness and governmental inefficiency earned them a reputation as the "Soviet Mark Twains." Their most famous works, the novels *Dvenadtsat stulyev (The Twelve Chairs)* and *Zolotoi telenok (The Little Golden Calf)*, depict the adventures of Ostap Bender, an ingenious rogue who is among the best-loved characters in Soviet literature. These novels demonstrate the influence of Nikolai Gogol in their mixture of realism, satire, and fantasy, and Ostap Bender is often compared to the protagonists of Gogol's *Inspector General* and *Dead Souls*.

Ilf, the son of a Jewish bank clerk and his wife, was born in

Odessa. After completing his formal education at a technical school in 1913, he held jobs in a draftsman's office, an aviation plant, and a hand-grenade factory before beginning his literary career as a writer and editor for the local humorous journal *Sindektikon*. He moved to Moscow in 1923, where he contributed humorous pieces to newspapers and satirical magazines. Like Ilf, Petrov was born in Odessa and held a variety of jobs before moving to Moscow to write for the satirical journal *Krasny perets* and other magazines. He met his future collaborator in 1925 in the offices of *Gudok,* the daily organ of the railroad workers' union, which became famous during the 1920s for the contributions of such talented writers as Mikhail Bulgakov, Yuri Olesha, and Petrov's brother Valentin Kataev. According to Petrov, his collaboration with Ilf began at the casual suggestion of Kataev that the pair write an adventure novel concerning the search for a set of chairs in which diamonds are hidden. Within six months Ilf and Petrov had completed *The Twelve Chairs,* which became an immediate

149

success and sealed their collaboration for the next ten years. The partnership proved one of the most fruitful in Soviet letters, and critics praise the harmony and consistency of style that the pair achieved in their writings. In addition to *The Twelve Chairs* and *The Little Golden Calf,* their works include numerous short stories, two dramas written in collaboration with Kataev, and a volume recording impressions of a trip to the United States in 1935. After Ilf's death from tuberculosis in 1937, Petrov published the notebooks in which his friend had recorded reflections, short sketches, and ideas for future stories. Critics praise these writings for their intelligence, wit, and vivid style; according to Georgy Munblit, "subtlety, keenness of observation, charming lyricism, and sparkling humor make them real literary gems." In the five years following Ilf's death Petrov composed several film scenarios, none of which are as highly regarded as the works he wrote in collaboration with Ilf. During World War II Petrov worked as a correspondent for the newspaper *Pravda;* while serving in that capacity, he died in an airplane crash in 1942.

The Twelve Chairs and *The Little Golden Calf* are closely modeled on Gogol's most famous works, utilizing simple plots in which realism and fantasy are intermingled to ridicule negative aspects of Russian society. Written in a witty, colorful style, they also demonstrate the influence of Mark Twain, O. Henry, and, in their numerous slapstick sequences, American silent films. Beneath the comic surface of the novels, however, critics often discern an underlying sadness and bitterness. One critic has written that the humor in *The Twelve Chairs,* although "innocent on the surface, is often of an extraordinarily biting kind, and the grotesque situations frequently verge on tragicomedy." Both novels recount the adventures of the irresponsible, unscrupulous, yet lovable Ostap Bender as he travels throughout Russia in search of fortune: in the first novel he vies with competing fortune hunters to locate the missing chairs; in the second he collects evidence with which to extort a million rubles from a wealthy black-marketeer. By means of these picaresque plots the authors were able to present a vivid portrait of Russia in the late 1920s, relating the hero's encounters with characters from all walks of Soviet life. Critics are unanimous in their praise for Ilf and Petrov's portrayal of these minor figures, which have been described by M. K. Argus as "a host of queer, silly, repulsive, lovely, pathetic Russian characters."

Ilf and Petrov depicted a period during which state control of commerce, industry, and agriculture was diminished to allow limited private enterprise. *The Twelve Chairs* and *The Little Golden Calf* mock the widespread speculation and black-marketeering characteristic of those years, as well as official ceremonies, Soviet propaganda, and bureaucratic inefficiency, stupidity, and fraudulence. Western critics have often speculated as to the reason such irreverent novels were allowed publication. Some attribute the publication of *The Twelve Chairs* to the political climate in Russia in the late 1920s, when relatively liberal economic policies were paralleled by less restrictive attitudes toward the arts. In addition, it has often been maintained that both novels express a fundamental sympathy with socialism, reserving ridicule for those whose graft and stupidity threaten to undermine the system. At least one critic, however, has taken issue with this view: according to Joshua Kunitz in his essay on *The Little Golden Calf,* the satire "is more than Bolshevik self-criticism. In places [the authors] challenge the basic principles of collectivism and the communist state." Vyacheslav Zavalishin has put forth a similar view of Ilf and Petrov's short stories, noting that "their hero is the common man crushed by impossible living conditions and over-

work and bemazed by the official directives regulating even his private life and his thoughts." Typical of these stories is "A Soviet Robinson Crusoe," in which an author's tale of individual struggle for survival on a desert island is revised by a censor to include workers, activists, trade unions, and an island party committee.

The last major work on which Ilf and Petrov collaborated is *Odnoetazhnaya Amerika (Little Golden America),* a travel memoir recounting the authors' four-month journey to the United States. *Little Golden America* is written in a lighthearted style similar to that of the novels; however, commentators note that the biting satire characteristic of Ilf and Petrov's fiction is absent from the travel essay. Although Zavalishin contends that *Little Golden America* is "a piece of biased journalism rather than literature," most Western critics praise the objectivity with which the authors depicted both positive and negative aspects of the United States. Alayne P. Reilly has written that Ilf and Petrov did not "let their political leanings interfere with their craftsmanship as writers or with the honesty of their reporting," and Robert van Gelder asserts that the authors were "never guilty of sacrificing the facts as they saw them for the sake of a quip."

Although popular with readers from the time of their publication, Ilf and Petrov's works have often been disparaged by Soviet critics, particularly during the 1940s and early 1950s when increasingly repressive restrictions were applied to literature in order to prevent the dissemination of political unorthodoxies. Typical of the attacks leveled against them are the views of an anonymous critic who condemned *The Twelve Chairs* and *The Little Golden Calf* as "ideologically pernicious," and that of Boris Gorbatov, who judged the authors themselves to be, "like much of their humor, empty and without principle." Their works were rehabilitated by Soviet officials in the late 1950s, a period of relative artistic freedom, and Ilf and Petrov have remained among the most popular Russian authors of the twentieth century. Their admirers contend that the pair's comic tales reflect reality in much the same way as the works of Gogol, depicting a world one critic described as "grotesque, confused, improbable, and yet real."

*PRINCIPAL WORKS

Dvenadtsat stulyev (novel) 1928
  [*Diamonds to Sit On,* 1930; also published as *The Twelve Chairs,* 1961]
Zolotoi telenok (novel) 1931
  [*The Little Golden Calf,* 1932]
Kak sozdavalsia Robinzon (short stories) 1933
Chudesnie gosti (short stories) 1934
Bogataya nevesta [with Valentin Kataev] (drama) 1936
Odnoetazhnaya Amerika (travel essay) 1936
  [*Little Golden America,* 1937]
Tonya (short stories) 1937
Zapisnie knizhki [by Ilya Ilf] (notebooks) 1939
Sobranie Sochenenie. 5 vols. (novels, dramas, travel essay, and short stories) 1961
**The Complete Adventures of Ostap Bender* (novels) 1962

*Unless otherwise noted, all works are by Ilya Ilf and Evgeny Petrov.

**This work comprises the novels *The Twelve Chairs* and *The Little Golden Calf.*

Translated selections of Ilf and Petrov's short stories have appeared in the following publications: *Soviet Short Stories;* Lavrin, Janko, ed., *Russian Humorous Stories;* and Van Doren, Carl Clinton, ed., *An Anthology of World Prose.*

THE TIMES LITERARY SUPPLEMENT (essay date 1930)

[*In the following excerpt the critic reviews* The Twelve Chairs, *which was first translated into English under the title* Diamonds to Sit On.]

Diamonds to Sit On . . . is a humorous novel in the Russian tradition—the tradition of Gogol. It is a genuinely amusing story, spiced with a pretty turn of satire and more than a trace of malice; the humour, in fact, innocent on the surface, is often of an extraordinarily biting kind, and the grotesque situations frequently verge on tragi-comedy. Hippolyte Matveyevitch Vorobianinov, a widower of fifty-two, formerly a member of the petty nobility, now a registrar of births, deaths and marriages in a small provincial town in Soviet Russia, makes a surprising discovery. His mother-in-law, an unpleasant, grasping old woman, is taken seriously ill and confesses to him that the family jewels, which he had always supposed were stolen during the revolution of 1917, were hidden, when they were forced to abandon their old home in Stargorod, in the seat of one of the drawing-room chairs. There were a dozen such chairs, elegant walnut pieces covered in English chintz. The unfortunate Hippolyte completely loses his head; he throws up his job and at once sets out for Stargorod to trace the chairs and the treasure concealed in the seat of one of them.

He is not the only person to engage in the search for the hidden diamonds. The avaricious Father Theodore, the priest who had attended the dying woman, is also in hot pursuit; and before long there is a third fortune-hunter, the bouncing, impudent Ostap Bender (a portrait recognizably on the model of Hlestakov, the hero of *The Government Inspector*), almost the first person Hippolyte meets in Stargorod, and with whom he is compelled to enter into an uneasy sort of profit-sharing alliance. There are some delicious moments of comedy in the first stages of the quest, which slowly assumes an increasingly ludicrous and pathetic complexion. The dark and rather cruel aspect of the comedy is oppressive towards the end, though it is relieved by shafts of satire directed at the Government and the Press, and everything else within reach.

A *review of "Diamonds to Sit On," in* The Times Literary Supplement, *No. 1481, June 19, 1930, p. 512.*

JOSHUA KUNITZ (essay date 1933)

[*A Polish-born American critic, Kunitz was the author of several respected works on Russian history and literature. He also served as literary editor of* New Masses, *one of America's leading socialist journals between 1926 and 1948. In the following excerpt, Kunitz favorably reviews* The Little Golden Calf.]

The picaresque novel is, like the comedy, a weapon particularly serviceable to the social satirist in times of rigid official vigilance, when cap and bells are not infrequently the only way of achieving a measure of free expression. Under all govern-

ments the jester is more or less privileged. This, on the whole, has applied to the Soviet government as well.

Among the Soviet jesters, Ilf and Petrov, the authors of *The Little Golden Calf,* first attracted universal attention with their uproarious Soviet extravaganza *The Twelve Chairs.* The central hero in both of these works is Ostap Bender, a delightfully unscrupulous rogue who, in the company of a few mercurial aides, roams through the highways and byways of the vast Union in pursuit of a hidden treasure. In the first book the hero is frustrated, for he finally discovers that a Soviet organization had accidentally unearthed the treasure and used it for building a workers' sumptuous club. In the second book, the "great schemer" is more successful: he finally tracks down his quarry—a sub-rosa Soviet millionaire—and extorts a million dollars from him. But his success is illusory. To be a millionaire in Soviet Russia means neither power nor glory nor leisure. To remain unexposed and unmolested, the Soviet millionaire is condemned to toil hard at a miserable wage, wear tattered apparel, eat nondescript food and keep eternal watch over his money-laden satchel. Profoundly disappointed, the new plutocrat with the dream of a resplendent and remote Rio de Janeiro glowing in his breast, attempts to steal across the Rumanian border, but he is nabbed by the myrmidons of capitalist law and order and stripped of all his valuables. At the end we behold our jovial, dextrous, daring, ingenious and, in his own way, great-hearted rogue, now ragged and beaten, his romantic notions of Rio de Janeiro shattered, crawling back to his native Soviet shores. "No ovations necessary, citizens," he shouts into the stillness of the night. "I have not become the Count of Monte Cristo. Methinks I shall have to master the trade of janitor!"

One does not know whether to exult or grieve over the hero's sudden resolution to learn the janitor's trade, for, to confess, behind the resolution of this blithe, casual, effervescent, romantic, irresponsible, irrepressible, individualistic and rather lovable schemer, one feels not a deeply inevitable conviction of the sublimity of labor and good citizenship, but a melancholy resignation to the drabness of Soviet life and an ironical bow to the demands of Soviet morality. In the final analysis, the authors manage to give the reader a feeling, not of a stirring moral conversion, but of a shameful spiritual collapse, a collapse too pathetic to be comic and too mean to be tragic.

More than the plot, it is the satirical depiction of various negative aspects of Soviet reality that make *The Little Golden Calf* significant—inefficiency, bureaucracy, peculation, petty graft, nepotism, hypocrisy, toadying, cant. Particularly caustic is the portrait of the Soviet careerist Yegor Skumbrievich, whom "it was beyond anyone's power to expose . . . for he delivered the correct speeches about Soviet life, about cultural work, about vocational guidance, about various active circles . . . all of which was a mirage" existing in his own "swollen imagination." Then there is the hilarious delineation of the munificently paid, unutilized, and therefore frantically indignant, German specialist. "You know," remarks one of the Russian managers, "I think he is simply quarrelsome. So help me God! All the man has to do is to sit at his desk, do absolutely nothing, receive a heap of money. And still he complains!"

The novel is full of such titbits. "In Soviet Russia," asserts one of the officials who simulates madness so as to escape prosecution, "the insane asylum is the only place where a normal man can live. Everything else is superbedlam. I prefer to live here with genuine madmen. At least they are not trying to build socialism. Besides, here they give you to eat, while there, in the bedlam, you merely work. . . . Here at least there is personal liberty, freedom of conscience, freedom of speech. . . .''

Clearly, Anatole Lunacharsky is altogether wrong when in his Introduction he assures us that ''Ilf and Petrov are very gay people . . . not baffled by the sordidness of life.'' Wrong, too, are the American publishers when they refer to *The Little Golden Calf* as ''the book that's too funny to be published in Russia.'' Under their mask of gayety, superficiality and innocuous buffoonery, Ilf and Petrov have written a very serious book. The authors aim to hit, and hit hard, at the most vulnerable spots. Theirs is more than Bolshevik self-criticism. In places they challenge the basic principles of collectivism and the communist state, a thing the Bolsheviks, who have no pretensions to liberalism, have always frankly refused to tolerate. Certainly, in declining to publish this book, the Soviet authorities were more consistent than was Lunacharsky in recommending it. Yet it may be plausibly suggested that in matters as delicate as creative art consistency is not necessarily the greatest of virtues, especially when it threatens to, and often actually does, degenerate into the application of mechanical formulas. In matters of art, the victorious workers, sustained by their faith in the inspiring and cleansing power of the proletarian revolution, can certainly afford to be more or less indulgent.

> Joshua Kunitz, ''Commissar of Monte Cristo,'' in The New Republic, *Vol. LXXIII, No. 945, January 11, 1933, p. 250.*

ROBERT van GELDER (essay date 1937)

[*Van Gelder was an American journalist, novelist, and critic who served as editor of the* New York Times Book Review *from 1943 to 1946. In the following excerpt, he favorably reviews* Little Golden America.]

Ilya Ilf and Eugene Petrov toured 10,000 miles of America two years ago. They went to football games, visited Sing Sing, talked to Henry Ford, kibitzed while J. P. Morgan answered questions for a Senate committee, studied burlesque shows, saw well over 100 movies, oh-ed about bridges and tunnels, wondered at the Grand Canyon, listened to Aimée McPherson, had a drink with Ernest Hemingway, attended one of President Roosevelt's press conferences, ate dinners in drug stores and conducted dozens of interviews with hitchhikers. Their conclusion [in *Little Golden America*] is that the United States is a great place to visit, but that they'd hate to live here.

Back in Moscow they closed their eyes and focused their minds for a single picture of the United States. The mental vision resulting was of a crossroads and a gasoline station against a background of telephone wires and advertising billboards. They found much to admire over here. They liked the ''service'' idea; they tremendously admired the technological efficiency of American business. They were amazed and delighted to find that Americans have a tendency to keep their promises—even the most casually given ones. And they heartily recommend the outward forms of democracy as an oil for human relations.

But they are sorry for Americans because of the food, the dullness, the lack of patriotism. The food in the drug stores and cafeterias, they complain, is cheap enough certainly, the helpings are generous, the preparation clean, but the taste of this food isn't exciting. People should have black bread, herring, vodka—not the tasteless stuff that capitalism forces on them. And they should read Tolstoy, look at the work of Van

Gogh, study Einstein—not read magazines, look at movies, do crossword puzzles. This, they say, is another crime of capitalism. It keeps the best for the few, and so the rest are dull.

This viewpoint, so young as to bring up memories of grammar school logic, is developed with: ''The average American cannot endure abstract conversations, nor does he touch upon themes too far removed from him. He is interested only in what is directly connected with his house, his automobile or his nearest neighbors.'' And this is so because he does not understand real patriotism as a Soviet man does, to whom ''a native land is tangible, where to him belong the soil, the factories, the stores, the banks, the dreadnoughts, the airplanes, the theatres and the books, where he himself is the politician and the master of all.''

Yet, though they feel sorry for Americans, they looked at the people and the country with more tolerance and with better humor than might be expected of a pair coming from a State so new as theirs and one in which their gifts as humorists had been so highly applauded. They are never guilty of sacrificing the facts as they saw them for the sake of a quip.

They did collect considerable misinformation—some one seems to have told them that snow stays on skyscrapers because they are so high; that there are more books about Hollywood than about Shakespeare; that the average American weighs 180 pounds; that gangster automobiles are equipped with sirens—but there is not enough of this kind of thing to spoil their book, which is, on the whole, a good job of reporting. Their humor is extremely mild and never bites.

> Robert van Gelder, ''Two Soviet Humorists in America,'' in The New York Times Book Review, *October 31, 1937, p. 10.*

GEORGY MUNBLIT (essay date 1947)

[*In the following excerpt, Munblit discusses the contents of Ilf's notebooks, which were collected and published as* Zapisnie knizhki.]

In 1939 Ilf's journals and diaries were collected and published. They cover the period between 1925 and 1937. The first entries occur irregularly, jotted down when the occasion arose in leather-bound notebooks which he invariably carried around with him for that purpose. In the years right before his death, his journals assumed a different character. Illness kept him away from Petrov for long periods of time. The urge to write did not leave him, however, for a single day. Yet he did not wish to undertake a serious work alone and he assuaged his hunger for writing with brief jottings of the things he saw, ideas in the rough, meditations, reminiscences, entries in his diary, sketches for future stories, and numerous tiny, quite finished miniatures—gems of brevity, craftsmanship and wit.

From Ilf's notes the reader learns what an observant traveller he was, what remarkable feeling he possessed for words and their different shades, how exacting he was in his work, how rich was his imagination and how appropriate his humour.

Here are some of the jottings picked at random: . . .

> Cold, noble and chaste, like a beam of artificial ice, towered the Empire State Building. . . .
>
> It's easy enough to write: ''No ray of light penetrated into his cell.'' You didn't copy it from anybody yet the words are not yours.

Went for a walk with Sasha on a clear but chilly day in spring. Overturned dustbins, shabby coats, frozen spittle, damp plaster on the walls of the houses—I was always fond of ice-clad, red-nosed spring.

Upon discovering that he had no tail the Pithecanthropus grew frightfully upset. That, he reasoned, would make him inferior to the apes. It did not even occur to him that he was the master of the world. His spouse, the young lady Pithecanthropus, kept nagging him about it, quite openly declaring that she regretted she had not married the orangoutang who courted her the previous summer.

A certain fear possesses mankind—it immures gramophone records and films, anxious to leave the memory that it lived, that there was such a thing as civilization.

The above give only a fragmentary idea of the contents of Ilf's journals and diaries. What is remarkable about his notes which cover a period of twelve years is that now that they have been put together they give the impression of a single, carefully conceived composition. In turn they plunge the reader into melancholy, laughter, and serious thought. With their vivid word pictures like some smooth and rythmic verse they become deeply ingrained in the memory. Subtlety, keenness of observation, charming lyricism and sparkling humour make them real literary gems. And what is most important, from them emerges a picture of the man himself, complex, clever and talented—the personality of the writer, which was hitherto fused in the mind of the reader with that of his constant collaborator and friend. (p. 71)

Georgy Munblit, "Ilya Ilf and Evgeni Petrov," in Soviet Literature, *No. 7, July, 1947, pp. 69-72.*

VYACHESLAV ZAVALISHIN   (essay date 1958)

[*In the following excerpt, Zavalishin discusses Ilf and Petrov's most important works.*]

Ilf and Petrov are known primarily for *The Twelve Chairs* and its companion piece, *The Golden Calf.* . . . Both books stem from Gogol's *Dead Souls*, but reflect also the authors' admiration of Mark Twain, O. Henry, and American movies—Harold Lloyd's and Monty Banks' rapid tempo and the touching quality of Chaplin's films.

"Into our two novels we have crammed enough observations, thoughts and imagination . . . to suffice for ten books," commented the authors. "That's how uneconomical we are."

The hero of both novels is the business genius Ostap Bender. Lacking a legal outlet for his talents he becomes a crook—pitting his wits against the crooked Soviet system and displaying astonishing ingenuity. What develops is, as it were, a competition between a lone pirate and the organized pirating of the state. Unlike Gogol's Chichikov, Bender does not inspire real hostility in the reader. The other characters he encounters are mostly Soviet "has-beens"—a poverty-stricken priest, a former marshal of nobility, bankrupt NEP-men, criminals, a hapless owner of an automobile that gives endless trouble. Incredible adventures take place all over Russia, and the impression is conveyed that everywhere in the vast land the common people lived in unspoken fear and mystery.

The Twelve Chairs came out while literature was not yet strictly controlled, but with *The Golden Calf* the authors ran into considerable difficulties, and the novel was published only because of Gorki's personal intervention.

Many of Ilf and Petrov's sketches which were first published in newspapers and magazines are collected in the books [*The Writing of "Robinson," The Serene Blockhead*, and *Tonya*]. . . . Their hero is the common man crushed by impossible living conditions and overwork and bemazed by the official directives regulating even his private life and his thoughts. Trifling real-life events are embroidered upon to the point of absurdity, and their implications well driven home. One of the authors' targets is the stupidity of state control over literature. In the story **"The Writing of 'Robinson,'"** a novelist is commissioned to write a Russian version of *Robinson Crusoe*. When the book is finished, the censor finds that it lacks ideological and social significance, and directs the author to put in a few Party members, also washed ashore. Otherwise, who will watch Robinson's ideology and collect dues from him? (pp. 342-43)

Vyacheslav Zavalishin, "Satirists and Humorists," in his Early Soviet Writers, *Frederick A. Praeger Publishers, 1958, pp. 329-48.**

MAURICE FRIEDBERG   (essay date 1960)

[*Friedberg is a Polish-born American critic, editor, and writer on international affairs, as well as a former director of the Russian and East European Institute. In his critical studies, Friedberg focuses on the relationship between political and social conditions in the Soviet Union and literature produced by Soviet writers. In the following excerpt from an introduction to* The Twelve Chairs *written in 1960, he discusses the novel's principal themes and techniques.*]

The hero of *The Twelve Chairs* (and also, it might be added, of *The Little Golden Calf*) is Ostap Bender, "the smooth operator," a resourceful rogue and confidence man. Unlike the nobleman Vorobyaninov and the priest Vostrikov, Bender is not a representative of the *ancien regime*. Only twenty-odd years old, he does not even remember prerevolutionary Russia: at the first meeting of the "alliance of the Sword and the Plowshare" Bender has some difficulty playing the role of a tsarist officer. Ostap Bender is a Soviet crook, born of Soviet conditions and quite willing to coexist with the Soviet system to which he has no ideological or even economic objections. Ostap Bender's inimitable slangy Russian is heavily spiced with clichés of the Communist jargon. Bender knows the vulnerabilities of Soviet state functionaries and exploits them for his own purposes. He also knows that the Soviet Man is not very different from the Capitalist Man—that he is just as greedy, lazy, snobbish, cowardly, and gullible—and uses these weaknesses to his, Ostap Bender's, advantage. And yet, in spite of Ostap Bender's dishonesty and lack of scruples, we somehow get to like him. Bender is gay, carefree, and clever, and when we see him matching his wits with those of Soviet bureaucrats, we hope that he wins.

In the end Ostap Bender and his accomplices lose; yet, strangely enough, the end of the novel seems forced, much like the cliché happy ending of a mediocre Hollywood film. One must understand, however, that even in the comparatively "liberal" 1920's it was difficult for a Soviet author not to supply a happy *Soviet* ending to a book otherwise as aloof from Soviet ideology as *The Twelve Chairs*. And so, at the end of the novel, one of the greedy fortune-hunters is killed by his partner, while the

Manuscript page of The Little Golden Calf.

other two end up in a psychiatric ward. But at least Ilf and Petrov have spared us from seeing Ostap Bender contrasted with a virtuous upright Soviet hero, and for this we should be grateful. Much as in Gogol's *Inspector General* and *Dead Souls* and in the satires of Saltykov-Shchedrin, we observe with fascination a Russia of embezzlers, knaves, and stupid government officials. We understand their weaknesses and vices, for they are common to all men. Indeed, we can even get to like these people, as we could not like the stuffy embodiments of Communist virtues who inhabit the great majority of Soviet novels.

Inevitably, some of the humor must get lost in the process of translation. The protagonists in **The Twelve Chairs** are for the most part semi-educated men, but they all aspire to *kulturnost,* and love to refer to classics of Russian literature—which they usually misquote. They also frequently mispronounce foreign words with comical effect. These no translator could possibly salvage. But the English-speaking reader won't miss the ridiculous quality of the "updated" version of *The Marriage* on a Soviet stage, even if he has never seen a traditional performance of Gogol's comedy; he will detect with equal ease the hilarious scheme of Ostap Bender to "modernize" a famous canvas by Repin even if he has never seen the original painting. Fortunately, most of the comic qualities of the novel are inherent in the actions of the protagonists, and these are not affected by being translated. They will only serve to prove once again that, basically, Soviet Russians are "fed with the same food, hurt with the same weapons, subject to the same diseases, healed by the same means, warmed and cooled by the same winter and summer" as all men are. (pp. xi-xii)

Maurice Friedberg, in an introduction to The Twelve Chairs *by Ilya Ilf and Eugene Petrov, translated by John H. C. Richardson, Vintage Books, 1961, pp. v-xii.*

ALAYNE P. REILLY   (essay date 1971)

[In the following excerpt, Reilly examines Ilf and Petrov's depiction of the United States in Little Golden America *and the short stories* "Tonya" *and* "Columbus Moors to the Shore."]*

The well-known Soviet humorists, Ilya Ilf and Evgeny Petrov, offered the Russian reader a trifold image of America in three very different works that resulted from their trip to America in the midthirties: a fairly objective and comprehensive description of the land, its people, and its everyday life in their travel memoir, *One-Storied America* [published in translation as *Little Golden America*]; a tendentious short story about a young Soviet girl's experiences in capitalist America, **"Tonya"**; and a humorous satirical sketch describing Columbus' impressions of twentieth-century America, **"Columbus Moors to the Shore."** By far the most significant work, for the image of America it presents to the Soviet reading public, is the lengthy account of their travels in America, *One-Storied America.*

Ilf and Petrov visited America for four months in late 1935. Purchasing an automobile, they drove across America covering some ten thousand miles and visiting twenty-five states. They explored everything from stock car races, rodeos, and boxing matches to prisons, factories, and film studios. *One-Storied*

America is an informal and intimate account of their trip which involves the reader in the details of their planning, their setbacks, and their adventures. The style is straight-forward and sober—there is almost no trace of the renowned satirical style of their earlier works. *One-Storied America* is a serious assignment for the pair. The authors come as devoted Communists to report firsthand on the life of a country whose capitalist way of life they consider alien to their own. But unlike their predecessors, they do not let their political leanings interfere with their craftsmanship as writers or with the honesty of their reporting. What they do not like in America is reported calmly and for the most part rationally. They do not harp repeatedly on the tiresome themes of propaganda.

Thus, *One-Storied America* marks the beginning of a three-dimensional image of America in Soviet writings. Ilf and Petrov unhesitatingly report the good along with the bad. The work also marks the discovery of rural America for the Russian reading public, heretofore acquainted mainly with the skyscrapers and slums of New York City. Now a whole new panorama lay before them: "America is basically a country of one and two-storied buildings. The great majority of the American population lives in small towns of three, five, ten or fifteen thousand people." It is this America, the land of small towns, the "land of automobiles and electricity," that the authors describe for their reader:

> When we shut our eyes and try to resurrect in memory the country in which we spent four months, we do not see before us Washington with its gardens, columns, and assorted monuments, nor New York with its skyscrapers, its poverty and its wealth, nor San Francisco with its steep streets and suspension bridges, nor hills nor factories nor canyons, but a crossroads with a gasoline station set against a background of telegraph wires and advertising signs.

Ilf and Petrov's guide to America is the middle-aged, good-natured, and absent-minded Mr. Adams. He and his wife Becky, who serves as chauffeur for the group, are used by the authors as a device to weld the narrative as well as to provide comic relief with their petty squabbles over Mr. Adams' forgetfulness—he continually misplaces his hat and glasses, walks through a plate glass window, loses the car keys, neglects to return motel keys, and so forth. He also acts as a spokesman for American accomplishments, as a critic of American injustices, and as an admirer of the Soviet Union.

One-Storied America is divided into five parts covering different regions of the authors' travels: New York City; the Eastern states; across the nation to the Pacific Ocean; the West; and the relatively quick trip back to New York. The book is written from their carefully kept diary notes and follows the time and geographical sequence of their travels. The most important impressions of their trip are related.

The authors found car travel through America to be convenient and inexpensive. Their accommodations were always comfortable and clean: "We became so accustomed to good roads, and good facilities, cleanliness, and comfort, that we stopped paying attention to them." American food, however, is a major complaint: "Generally speaking, if one may speak of bad taste in food, then American cuisine undoubtedly appears as an expression of bad, absurd, and eccentric taste."

American movies are another subject of major criticism. The authors went to the movies almost every night during the trip and saw over a hundred films. They devote quite a few pages to a discussion of Hollywood. Although they admired the technological brilliance of the film industry, they deplored the content of its product: "All of these films are below the level of human dignity. It seems to us that to watch such movies is a humiliating occupation for a human being."

The contrast between poverty and plenty under the capitalist system, a frequent criticism of America, is also noted by Ilf and Petrov. They comment about it quite strongly, but do not dwell repeatedly upon it.

> Even from the point of view of capitalism that has elevated the simultaneous coexistence of wealth and poverty to the status of law, Chicago must appear a dreary, clumsy, uncomfortable city. There is probably nowhere else on earth where heaven and hell are so intimately intertwined as in Chicago. Side by side with the marble and granite facing of skyscrapers on Michigan Avenue are disgusting sidestreets, filthy and stinking.

Interestingly enough, they do not note any such contrasts in the smaller towns and cities they visit. The contrast between rich and poor, between skyscrapers and slums, seems to be their main objection to the big cities such as New York and Chicago. The Negro problem is mentioned only in passing. Ilf and Petrov also visited Indian reservations in New Mexico, and describe the Indians as poor but proud of their own heritage and refusing to participate in the white man's world. In general, there is little of the exploitation-caricature that is so prevalent in earlier and later Soviet works on America.

Ilf and Petrov are especially delighted by the natural beauty of America, and by her National Parks in particular. Some of their descriptive passages of the American landscape are quite lyrical, and their vivid imagery recalls the style of the ornamental school to which they, like Pilnyak, belong. Here they describe the painted desert:

> Smooth sandhills stretched to the horizon like a stormy ocean whose waves had suddenly turned to stone. They crept upon one another, forming crests and thick round folds. They were magnificent, brilliantly painted by nature in blue, pink, reddish-brown, and pale yellow. The tones were dazzlingly pure.

> The word "desert" is frequently used as a symbol of monotony. But the American desert is unusually varied. The appearance of the desert changes every two or three hours. We passed hills and cliffs that resembled pyramids, towers, recumbent elephants, and antediluvian pangolins.

> (pp. 30-4)

Ilf and Petrov find the Americans themselves to be hospitable, reliable, sociable, helpful, good workers, and uncomplaining in adversity:

> When we left for America there was one thing we did not take into account—American hospitality. It is boundless, and far outshines any other, including even Russian, Siberian, or Georgian hospitality.

There are many wonderful and attractive features in the character of the American people. They are superb workers with hands of gold. Our engineers say that working with Americans is sheer pleasure. Americans are accurate, but far from pedantic. They are precise. They know how to keep their word and trust the word of others. They are always ready to come to your assistance. They are good comrades, easygoing people.

Much of the negative side of America for Ilf and Petrov, as with most Soviets, is the seeming preponderance of "bandits," "racketeers," and "bankers"—all of whom they consider one and the same. Adhering to the Marxist premise that capitalism is the root of all evil, they see the profit motive behind almost everything:

> The persistent advertising has conditioned the American to drink juice at breakfast and at lunch. The juice contains vitamins that are very beneficial for the consumer; but the sale of the juice is beneficial for the fruit growers.

They also believe that the automat was invented not to serve the public better, but to deprive waitresses of their jobs and increase profits.

The authors frankly report their habit of comparing what they saw in America with life in the Soviet Union:

> We constantly talked about the Soviet Union, drew parallels, made comparisons. We noticed that the Soviets whom we often met in America were possessed by the same feelings. There was not a single conversation that did not lead in the end to a reference to the Soviet Union. "We have this." "And we have that." "We could use this." "We do that better." "This we can't do yet." "This we have already mastered."

The objectivity and honesty of this passage is rare in Soviet writings which are usually not disposed to admit that they do not have or would like to acquire something that America already has. They are more inclined to claim that they do everything better. Ilf and Petrov explain their faith in the Communist cause:

> At the foundation of Soviet life lies the Communist idea. We have a definite goal toward which our country is moving. That is why we, people of only moderate achievement in comparison to the Americans, are much calmer and happier than the people of the land of Morgan and Ford, the land of twenty-five million automobiles, of a million and a half miles of roads, of hot and cold running water, rooms with baths, and service. The slogan that technology solves everything was coined by Stalin after the Communist idea had triumphed. That is why technology does not seem to us an evil genie that cannot be returned to its bottle. On the contrary we want to catch up with American technology and surpass it. America does not know what will happen to it tomorrow. We know and can predict with definite accuracy what will happen with us in fifty years.

It is interesting to compare this passage with Mayakovsky's arrogant assertion that "Soviets look down upon the bourgeois." Ilf and Petrov explain their feelings without resorting to name calling or inflammatory statements. The simple and grammatical exposition of their thoughts contrasts with the emotional and repetitive banter of propaganda. There is also no feeling of ill will toward America in *One-Storied America*. (pp. 35-7)

The tone of *One-Storied America* is essentially that of objective reporters in contrast to the polemical tone of Gorky, Mayakovsky, and Pilnyak. This is evidenced in the general lack of emotionality, the absence of satiric hyperbole and stereotypes, and the fact that the authors report the good they saw as well as the bad. While preferring their own country, Ilf and Petrov approach America with open curiosity, explore her from coast to coast, and describe what they find. When criticizing something they usually explain their objections, and seldom indulge in rhetoric or hysteria. Like many visitors to New York they find the city dark and depressing:

> New York is astonishingly beautiful! But why does one feel sad in this great city? The buildings are so high that the sunlight lies only on the upper stories, and throughout the day one has the impression that the sun is setting. A morning sunset. No doubt that is why one feels so sad in New York.

The fault is not proclaimed in emotional exaggeration but rationally explained as an inevitable consequence of closely constructed tall buildings.

However, while marking a new dimension and direction for the Soviet image of America in their *One-Storied America*, Ilf and Petrov also helped to propagate the conventional caricature of capitalism in a little known story, "Tonya.". . . Tonya is a young Soviet girl, newly married, who comes to America with her husband, a junior officer in the Embassy in Washington, D.C. Tonya's excitement and happiness are short-lived, however, as she and her husband fall prey to the capitalist way of life. Medical expenses deplete their budget when Tonya's husband finds a society doctor who cures his colds by a $200 tonsillectomy. This blow forces them to do without new winter coats (the authors do not explain why their old Muscovite coats will not do). They must also forego a baby carriage and crib, settling for a common cradle "like those used by the poor Negroes." When the baby arrives, further hospital expenses all but devastate the hapless couple. The "moral" that such terrible things would never have happened in Moscow where such things are free is repeatedly emphasized. Tonya learns a vivid and bitter lesson:

> Tonya, who had understood from her Pioneer days what capitalism meant, and had even given small reports about it at school and in the factory, suddenly confronted it in real life. And you can imagine how furious she was. The capitalist system interfered with her life. Although it was harmful for her to get upset, she excitedly cursed this system every night.

The pedantic moralizing of this paragraph is clearly addressed to the reader: "And you can imagine how furious she was."

"Tonya" is so different from *One-Storied America* in style and in content that it is hard to believe both works were written by the same authors about the same country. **"Tonya"** is completely different from any other work of Ilf and Petrov as well. It is a poorly written publicist sketch, full of bathetic distortion that betrays the craftsmanship of these two literary masters. The work may have been written, or at least finished, by Petrov as it appeared some eight months after the death of Ilf in April of 1937. It may possibly be an attempt to atone for the objectivity of **One-Storied America.** The notes to the latest edition of their works comment on this "new genre" of the writers: "The political school of *Pravda* taught the writers to widen the use of the publicist weapon as a means of satirical denunciation."

The two works contain many discrepancies in their portrayals of the American way of life. For example, the Adamses, not wealthy people, apparently have no difficulty in finding a nursemaid for their two-year-old daughter and taking off for two months to tour America with the authors. Ilf and Petrov repeatedly state how easy, inexpensive, and comfortable it is to travel across America, and how many Americans themselves are on the roads at all hours. They are also continually impressed with American hospitality and helpfulness. In light of these observations it seems a bit strange that Tonya has almost no contact with America outside the Embassy walls and cannot afford a baby sitter for an occasional evening out with her husband.

The moralistic tone and sharply negative portrayal of American life in "Tonya" thus continue the caricature tradition of Gorky, Mayakovsky, and Pilnyak. This interesting dichotomy in Ilf and Petrov's writings on America marks the beginning of a double image of America in Soviet writings. On one hand we have negative caricature that condemns all of America as an ideological enemy. On the other hand we have an objective commentary that reports the good as well as the bad in America. The latter presentation, however, was to lie dormant until the 1960's.

Ilf and Petrov also wrote a humorous sketch on life in America in 1936, "Columbus Moors to the Shore." This is a description of contemporary New York through the eyes of the fifteenth century Columbus, who writes the Spanish King about his new discovery:

> I have sailed many seas but never before have I encountered such original natives. They absolutely cannot tolerate quiet. In order to enjoy noise as much as possible, they have constructed special roads on iron stems where iron carriages roll day and night, producing the clamor so beloved by the natives.
>
> I still have not been able to determine whether or not they are cannibals. However, they do eat hot dogs. With my own eyes I saw many eating places that invite passers-by to eat these hot dogs. They even praise their taste.
>
> I have come to the conclusion that the natives are pagans. They have many gods whose names are written in fire on their huts. Their most important gods seem to be the goddess Coca-Cola, the god Drug Store, the goddess Cafeteria and the great god of gasoline fumes, Ford. He seems to be their Zeus.

This work is typical of the imaginative wit of the pair and of the style that made them famous. The satire of Ilf and Petrov is never sarcastic or denigrating but is exercised with the true

artist's delicate sense of balance and harmony between form and content. Their satire is derived from a deep love of man, a Horatian satire that stems from the humanist's conception of evil as a moral failing as well as from his desire to help man recognize his weaknesses. (pp. 38-41)

> *Alayne P. Reilly, "Four Early Impressions: Gorky, Mayakovsky, Pilnyak, Ilf and Petrov," in his* America in Contemporary Soviet Literature, *New York University Press, 1971, pp. 3-45.**

GLEB STRUVE (essay date 1971)

[*A Russian-born educator, Struve is internationally known for his critical studies of Slavic literature. In the following excerpt, he discusses Ilf and Petrov's most important works.*]

Twelve Chairs is a gay, picaresque novel. It is also a satire. In the center of it stands the irrepressible Ostap Bender, who was originally meant as a purely episodic character, but grew into a real hero. He is one of the most memorable creations in Soviet literature, a modern Chichikov, a cunning and ingenious rogue, who leads the fantastic, breath-taking race for the diamonds which their pre-Revolutionary owner hid in one of a set of twelve chairs. The set having been dispersed, the search for the right chair takes Bender, his assistants and his rivals, among whom is a former priest, through all sorts of fantastic and farcical adventures, against the background of grotesquely satirized Soviet life in the NEP period. The hunt for the chair has an appropriate ideological ending: the chair with the diamonds in it turns out to have become the property of a Soviet club and the money used for cultural purposes. As for Bender, he is killed by one of his fellow diamond hunters just before the denouement of the novel. The authors afterward regretted having disposed of their hero and decided to bring him back to life in their second novel, **Zolotoy telyonok** (**The Little Golden Calf**. . .). This sequel to **Twelve Chairs** is just as entertaining and just as recklessly fantastic, while the satire in it is even more serious and biting. It also has a neater and better balanced plot, revolving around several competing pretenders to the role of the son of Lieutenant Schmidt, the famous hero of the *Potyomkin* mutiny in 1905, with Ostap Bender acting as the sponsor and impressario of one of these pretenders. Here again everyday Soviet life can be seen through a grotesquely distorting mirror.

In **Twelve Chairs** and its sequel we see a procession of Soviet gangsters, confidence men, corrupt and unscrupulous officials, and gullible, ordinary citizens. The authors let their fancy run loose, while at the same time drawing upon real life for their characters and situations. As the Communist review *Oktyabr* put it, life in **Twelve Chairs** is "grotesque, confused, improbable, and yet real."

Ilf and Petrov also wrote together a number of humorous and satirical stories, again for the most part satirizing various aspects of Soviet life. However, two of the stories in the volume **Tonya** . . . are satires on American life. "**Tonya**" describes the first steps of a young Soviet couple in America and contrasts American and Soviet life (it is written more seriously than is usual with Ilf and Petrov and is spoiled by its obvious didacticism), while "**Kolumb prichalivayet k beregu**" ("**Columbus Puts To**") is an amusing short skit on modern-day United States, describing what happens to Christopher Columbus when he rediscovers twentieth-century America, with her reporters, her publicity, her burlesques.

Ilf and Petrov's last major joint work, *Odnoètazhnaya Amerika* (*One-Storied America* . . .), is also about the United States. It is a witty, satirical account of their visit to the United States and their transcontinental automobile trip. In writing it, they adopted a new method: twenty chapters were written by Ilf, twenty by Petrov, and seven by both of them in the old way. The original intention of the authors was to take Ostap Bender, the "Great Combiner" of their two novels, to the United States and describe his adventures there—they even sold the idea in advance to their American publisher—but instead they decribed, in a mildly satirical vein, their own impressions of American life, many aspects of which obviously appealed to them. (pp. 166-67)

> Gleb Struve, *"Writers about Everyday Life and Satirists," in his* Russian Literature under Lenin and Stalin, 1917-1953, *University of Oklahoma Press, 1971, pp. 152-67.**

JOHN L. WRIGHT   (essay date 1974)

[*Wright is an American educator. In the following essay, he examines the ways in which Ostap Bender resembles the traditional picaresque hero.*]

Ilf and Petrov's novels, *The Twelve Chairs* . . . and *The Golden Calf,* . . . have often been referred to as picaresque novels. Soviet scholars have published many articles and several books on Ilf and Petrov, but only one significant study of these novels has been made outside the Soviet Union. None of the major studies approaches these novels from the standpoint of the picaresque tradition. Although there is no evidence that Ilf and Petrov intended to write picaresque novels, both *The Twelve Chairs* and *The Golden Calf* contain many elements which justify the appellation "picaresque." This paper will treat only the hero of the novels, Ostap Bender, as a picaroon.

The dominating element in any picaresque novel is the hero, the picaroon. The picaroon is a rogue, or more properly a delinquent, but he never becomes a hardened criminal. If he steals, it is usually because he has to in order to survive in the chaotic world into which he is born. He lives according to his own set of morals if he has any at all; but he is always true to himself. Since he has no place in society, the picaroon does not have to follow society's moral code. The picaroon is usually drawn from a low social level, and his origins are obscure and unfavorable. It is this unstable family situation which sends him out into the world to fend for himself. When he begins his picaresque journey, he is still innocent. The world teaches him to be a delinquent. The only position in society which a person of the picaroon's background could obtain honestly would be that of a servant. However, the picaroon is ordinarily not satisfied with his social position, and he can better himself only by assuming disguises and becoming a trickster. Thus, his very ability to successfully wear masks is of the first importance.

Although the hero is the single most important character in a picaresque novel—since the reader's attention is focused on him throughout—he shows little, if any, character development in the course of the novel. This lack of internal development has several manifestations which can be recognized immediately in the picaroon. One of these is his inability to love. As a result, he becomes a very lonely figure. Yet no matter how self-reliant he desires to be, he cannot get along without the help of others, some of whom are as destitute as he. If a picaroon should marry, it will most often be for reasons of

security; however, such a marriage rarely lasts. The picaroon's role-playing is a further manifestation of his lack of character development. This again demonstrates his internal instability. He is unable to learn from life's experiences and, therefore, cannot formulate any set course to follow. Directly related to this is the picaroon's curiosity and love of adventure, which frequently lead him into trouble.

Finally, the picaresque novel is usually narrated by the picaroon himself. This first-person narration performs several functions. First, the recollected or later point of view of the narrator helps to give the story an air of authenticity. Second, the narrator may emphasize only those things about the picaroon which will make a favorable impression on the reader, while attempting to conceal those things which he does not want the reader to learn. As a result, the reader will tend to sympathize and even identify with the picaroon. Third, the first-person narration by the picaroon allows the author to make comments about society which, because they come from the picaroon, will throw dust in the eyes of the censor. However, according to critical opinion, the first-person point of view is not absolutely essential in a picaresque novel.

It is apparent from the beginning that *The Twelve Chairs* differs from the typical picaresque novel, since it is not autobiographical or even biographical in form. The picaroon himself does not appear until the fifth chapter. Instead, the reader is introduced to several other characters, including the former marshal of the nobility, Ippolit Matveevič Vorobjaninov, and the Orthodox priest Father Fedor. The reason for this, according to Petrov, is that Ostap Bender was originally conceived as a secondary character, almost an episodic figure. But he grew beyond the limits set for him and soon took over.

Ostap Bender enters the plot of *The Twelve Chairs* in medias res. The chapter or chapters devoted to a background sketch of the picaroon are absent. Rather, Bender gives only one detail about his origins, namely that he is the son of a Turkish citizen: "Moj papa . . . byl turecko-poddannyj." Perhaps Ilf and Petrov are parodying the traditional picaresque novel by including this single fact. On the other hand, Bender's having no family history is even more inauspicious than the origins of the traditional picaroon. The narrator describes Bender's past experiences in one additional sentence. The hero has spent his life thus far as an adventurer, unable to pursue any one thing for very long. The narrator ironically attributes this instability to the liveliness of Bender's character. Thus, the reader meets the hero for the first time after the picaroon has reached adulthood. The picaroon's initiation into the world and his picaresque education are not even within the scope of these novels.

The fifth chapter of *The Twelve Chairs* is appropriately titled "The Great Schemer" ("Velikij kombinator"), since this epithet for Ostap Bender becomes synonymous with his name as the plot progresses. In effect, Bender takes command soon after he is introduced to the reader. He immediately becomes involved in Vorobjaninov's quest for Madame Petuxova's diamonds, hidden in one of a set of twelve walnut chairs. From here on, Bender proves himself to be a rogue and, even more, a swindler. Unlike earlier picaroons, however, he is not willing to play the role of servant and instead, expects Vorobjaninov to serve him. Viktor Šklovskij asserts, unjustifiably it seems, that Bender begins as a traditional servant and grows with the events until he becomes the element of *the* novel, the motivation of the adventures. It is true that Bender's importance grows as the plot progresses, but he never plays the role of servant to Vorobjaninov. It is only the former marshal's intention that Bender serve him. As soon as the "great schemer" is told of the existence of the jewels, he begins to bargain with Vorobjaninov about his percentage of the expected profits because he considers himself a direct partner.

Like the earlier picaroons, Ostap Bender plays a large number of roles in both novels. In *The Twelve Chairs* he plays the majority of these roles for the non-picaresque purpose of obtaining the chairs. Few, if any, disguises are assumed by him for reasons of survival. Even his marriage to the widow Gricacueva is accomplished solely for the purpose of gaining access to a chair. It would seem that Ilf and Petrov are poking fun here at the traditional picaresque marriage for financial security, especially since Bender's marriage lasts one day— just long enough for him to procure the chair! Some of his disguises also give the authors the opportunity to satirize the exploiters of the NEP and the remnants of pre-revolutionary Russia.

Ostap Bender proves to be a master swindler. In the role of Vorobjaninov's son, for example, he outsmarts the chief of the Stargorod records department—also a well-known swindler— by obtaining information leading to the location of the remaining chairs and not paying the records-keeper anything for this information. Significantly, Bender never becomes a hardened criminal, although he is the petty thief which he accuses Vorobjaninov of being. By the end of the novel Bender has moved through a series of episodes, but his character has remained fixed.

Like many picaresque novelists, Ilf and Petrov had difficulty in deciding their hero's fate at the end of the novel. In deciding whether to have Bender killed or to keep him alive, they placed two pieces of paper in a sugar bowl. On one of them they drew a skull and crossbones. It happened that this was the one which was drawn out; thus, their hero's fate was to be death. Nevertheless, Ilf and Petrov apparently were not able to part with Ostap Bender so easily. They resurrected him for their second novel, *The Golden Calf*.

When Bender enters the plot of *The Golden Calf* early in the first chapter he seems at once to be the familiar "great schemer" of *The Twelve Chairs,* with the exception of a scar appearing across his throat. Indeed, his entrance here is reminiscent of his entrance in the earlier work. On both occasions he is walking on a city street. In each instance he makes a remark which will have a special significance throughout the novel. In *The Twelve Chairs* it is "the key to the apartment where the money is" (". . . ključ ot kvartiry, gde den'gi ležat''); in *The Golden Calf*: "No, this is not Rio de Janeiro." ("Net, èto ne Rio-de-Žanejro.''), which Bender repeats three times in the first chapter alone. This phrase has a deeper meaning for the hero than its counterpart had in *The Twelve Chairs*. Rio de Janeiro is for Ostap Bender a paradise he is seriously seeking. In a picaresque novel the hero often has his own "vision of paradise." Bender sees Rio de Janeiro clearly: a magical city on the bay, populated with good-natured mulattoes, most of whom wear white trousers. The "great schemer's" aspirations, however, are not simply to live in Rio, but to become a gentleman in a society of gentlemen. These aspirations are also not unlike those of earlier picaroons.

The roles which Ostap Bender plays in *The Golden Calf* are nearly as numerous and diversified as those in *The Twelve Chairs*. His first role, son of the revolutionary hero Lieutenant Schmidt, is an especially significant one for him. While playing this role Bender learns of the means by which he can achieve his goal, his dream. This is not due to the nature of the role itself, but to the fact that Bender is not the sole impersonator in it. There are as many as thirty imposters, as the hero finds out from Balaganov, the second "son of Lieutenant Schmidt." The complexity of the project which Balaganov and his associates have contrived is shown in humorous contrast to Bender's simple pose, which he thought up at a moment of expediency. Therefore, it is ironic that Bender, and not Balaganov, gains from the role. His gain is not merely the eight rubles and three meal coupons which he receives from the chairman of the Arbatov executive committee, but indirectly it is the fortune of the underground millionaire Korejko. Many of the hero's disguises are assumed for the purpose of attaining his immediate goal. All the same, even after he has received the million rubles and has parted with Korejko, Bender still has to wear masks in order to be accepted in Soviet society.

More illuminating than any of Ostap Bender's roles is his relationship with the other characters in the novel and the development (or lack of it) of his own personality. Emphasis on these things rather than on disguises may at first seem contrary to notions about the picaresque genre. However, if one views *The Golden Calf* as a continuation of *The Twelve Chairs*, he will discover that it has much in common with the continuations or "second parts" of the early picaresque novels where the authors attempted a moral or religious conversion of their heroes. Instability of character and an attempted conversion become the main features of the hero in *The Golden Calf*, too.

In *The Twelve Chairs* Bender has one companion, Vorobjaninov. In *The Golden Calf* he has three: Balaganov, Panikovskij, and Kozlevič. They travel with him throughout much of the first two parts of the novel. Bender assumes an air of superiority over his fellow-travellers as he did over Vorobjaninov before. This is, of course, a mark of his insecurity. However, having three to deal with instead of one, he treats each of the Antelopians individually. Only Panikovskij is as low in his esteem as Vorobjaninov was. He is more tolerant of Balaganov because it was Balaganov who told him about Korejko's fortune in the first place. Bender is considerate of Kozlevič and even shows him some respect because Kozlevič has the "Antelope-Gnu," the automobile that will take Bender to Korejko. At the same time, the Antelopians work together as a team with Bender as their leader. Like a true picaroon Bender has chosen companions as destitute as he and ones which will be of some benefit to him. They are all rogues at heart. As one critic pointed out, Bender belongs to the same type as his colleagues—the differences are merely quantitative, individual differences, not social ones. Bender is simply a more resourceful rogue who finds himself in more advantageous situations. In the case of Korejko, however, Bender is dealing with a schemer as formidable as he himself. It is mainly through his persistence that he finally convinces Korejko to hand over the million rubles.

The one additional character who plays an important, albeit limited, role in Ostap Bender's experiences is Zosja Sinickaja. At first, Bender uses her by "falling in love" with her so that she will tell him exactly where her former lover, Korejko, has gone. Then after Bender becomes disillusioned about the happiness which a million rubles is supposed to have brought him, he sends Zosja telegrams declaring his love to her. This again exemplifies the picaroon's basic insecurity. It is likewise only natural for Bender to return to the post office for his money after he finds that Zosja is married to a member of a collective. It would have violated artistic truth, as Boris Galanov points out, if Ilf and Petrov had brought harmony to Bender's life by having him give up his fortune and marry Zosja as they did in several variants of the novel's ending. After all, Ostap Bender lacks the ability to love.

Before parting with their hero, Ilf and Petrov put him through the struggle of attempting a "religious" conversion. The religion here, of course, is that of socialism. The authors' attempt at converting Bender is not handled hastily, but is approached gradually. The "golden calf" has not brought Bender the security of recognition and fame which he had so desired. In fact, he is not even able to get a hotel room or be served in a restaurant because of the priority given to such groups as a congress of soil scientists and the Komsomol. Still worse, the hero is not permitted to be as generous as he would like to be. His desire to buy Kozlevič a new automobile never materializes because the Soviet government will not sell automobiles to private citizens. Bender becomes so downcast that he momentarily gives up his dream of Rio de Janeiro, as if it were a figment of his imagination. After he fails to impress a group of polytechnic students with his money, he concludes that the "golden calf" was not meant for him after all. So he takes it to the post office to be sent "To the People's Commissar of Finance, Moscow." Here he seems about to be converted; but after his fateful encounter with Zosja and her husband, he rushes back to retrieve his money in one of the novel's great comic scenes. Once again his dreams are of Rio de Janeiro.

The last chapter accomplishes little more than to place another obstacle in Bender's way. He is robbed by the Rumanian border guards and forced to return to his native land. But he fights to the very end to save his "golden calf." His final remark about having to train himself to be a janitor is at best ironic and ambiguous. One can only surmise what will happen to Bender next. The authors themselves did not know what to do with him; and although they planned to write a third novel about Ostap Bender, they did not fulfill their intentions. As it stands, Bender's adventures only stop. They do not really end. Thus, like many picaresque novels, *The Golden Calf* remains open-ended.

In conclusion, there is much in the character of Ostap Bender which is reminiscent of the early picaroons. This is especially true concerning Bender's basic insecurity, exemplified by his role-playing, love of adventure, and ability as a swindler. However, unlike the majority of picaroons, he does not narrate his own story and does not comment on the shortcomings and evils of society himself to the extent that the earlier picaroons did. For all that, the adventures are his, and through his experiences the reader gets a good glimpse of Soviet society in the late 1920's. (pp. 265-68)

John L. Wright, "Ostap Bender As a Picaroon," in
Proceedings: Pacific Northwest Conference on For-

eign Languages, *Vol. XXV, Part 1, April 19-20, 1974, pp. 265-68.*

ADDITIONAL BIBLIOGRAPHY

Argus, M. K. "Ostap Bender's Quest for a Million Rubles." *The New York Times Book Review* (18 November 1962): 4, 18.
Favorable review of *The Little Golden Calf* which maintains that "every character, even the least significant one, has been drawn with meticulous (and devastating) care and remains forever ingrained in the reader's mind."

Cukierman, Walenty. "The Odessan Myth and Idiom in Some Early Works of Odessa Writers." *Canadian-American Slavic Studies* 14, No. 1 (Spring 1980): 36-51.*
Examines typically Odessan situations, themes, characters, and language in the works of Ilf and other authors from the Russian city of Odessa. Cukierman analyzes Ilf's early short stories "Galife Feni-Loksh" and "Milaia Odessa," which he considers unique among Ilf's writings for their characteristically Odessan atmosphere.

Hingley, Ronald. "Control Mechanisms." In his *Russian Writers and Soviet Society: 1917-1978*, pp. 205-25. New York: Random House, 1979.*
Describes the short story "A Soviet Robinson Crusoe" as "a minor masterpiece" on the theme of Soviet censorship.

Ilf, Ilya, and Petrov, Evgeni. "Pages from the Past." *Soviet Literature*, No. 3 (1967): 159-65.
Petrov's recollections of Ilf, followed by excerpts from Ilf's notebooks.

Rahv, Philip. "Golden Calves." *The Nation* 145, No. 13 (25 September 1937): 326.
Review of *Little Golden America* stressing Ilf and Petrov's enthusiasm for America's technological achievements.

Reeve, F. D. "The Autobiography of a World." *The Hudson Review* XVI, No. 4 (Winter 1963-64): 610-17.*
Notes a change in the character Ostap Bender from a sympathetic rogue in *The Twelve Chairs* to a misfit in *The Little Golden Calf* and praises the latter as "a sharper and broader book than *The Twelve Chairs.*"

Sillen, Samuel. "The Life and Death of Eugene Petrov." *New Masses* XLIV, No. 3 (21 July 1942): 22-3.
Tribute to Petrov.

Wolfe, Tom. "Dignity, Yes, But Above All, Not to Go Hungry." *New York Herald Tribune* CXXII, No. 42,326 (21 October 1962): 7.*
Favorable review of *The Little Golden Calf* disputing the opinion of many critics that Ilf and Petrov were sympathetic to socialism.

Thomas Mann

1875-1955

German novelist, short story writer, essayist, and critic.

The following entry presents criticism of Mann's novel *Der Zauberberg* (*The Magic Mountain*). For a complete discussion of Mann's career, see *TCLC*, Volumes 2, 8, and 14.

The Magic Mountain is considered one of the greatest novels of ideas as well as the foremost German *Bildungsroman,* or "novel of education," of the twentieth century. Set in a tuberculosis sanatorium, which many critics have seen as a symbol of diseased and decaying Western society, the novel depicts the intellectual and spiritual maturation of its young protagonist, Hans Castorp, during his seven-year sojourn there. His development is effected primarily by his exposure to various characters whose political and philosophical convictions create an interplay of ideologies representing the intellectual temper of Europe in the years preceding World War I. Mann rendered this portrait of his age with characteristic irony tempered by sympathy for humanity, while simultaneously exploring such themes as the nature of time and the seductiveness of death. The complexity of *The Magic Mountain* has led to interpretations from a variety of perspectives—including readings of the work as historiography, philosophical novel, spiritual autobiography, and political allegory—and the novel has received universal praise for its depth and vision. According to Kuno Francke, *The Magic Mountain* represents "the most subtle spiritual reflex of an age of convulsions, disruptions, and cataclysms," and upon its publication in 1924 Ludwig Lewisohn proclaimed the book "the *Divine Comedy* . . . of our disastrous age."

Mann began writing *The Magic Mountain* in 1912, inspired by a visit to a sanatorium in Davos, Switzerland, where his wife was being treated for a lung ailment. He envisioned the work as a satire on sanatorium life that would form a humorous counterpart to his tragic novella *Der Tod in Venedig* (*Death in Venice*), similarly depicting a protagonist whose orderly life is transformed by disease and repressed passions. However, Mann was distracted from his writing by an intellectual crisis that was precipitated by the events of World War I and exacerbated by a long-standing difference of opinion between Mann and his brother, novelist Heinrich Mann, over the role of art and the artist in society. Thomas Mann's literary response to the war was a series of nationalistic essays supporting Germany's role in the hostilities. Heinrich Mann attacked his brother's position, and that of numerous other German intellectuals, in the 1915 essay *Zola,* an account of novelist Emile Zola's stand against militant nationalism in nineteenth-century France. The essay constituted a thinly-veiled condemnation of those members of the German intellectual community who denied their country's responsibility for the war and who asserted Germany's moral superiority over its antagonists, with Mann labeling such intellectuals political opportunists. *Zola* also contained numerous pointed personal allusions to Thomas Mann's characteristic ideas, and commentators maintain that the essay had a dramatic effect on Mann, plunging him into an extended period of intense self-examination. He set aside *The Magic Mountain* to formulate a response in the essay collection *Betrachtungen eines Unpolitischen* (*Reflections of a Nonpolitical*

Man), maintaining that "I must write the *Betrachtungen* simply because, as a result of the war, the novel would otherwise have been intellectually intolerably overloaded." In the *Betrachtungen* Mann sought to defend Germany against its critics in elaborate arguments demonstrating Germany's moral and cultural superiority, emphasizing a particular contrast between the subtlety and profundity of the German Romantic tradition and what he considered the shallowness of Western progressive humanism. According to T. J. Reed, he presented "Romanticism as the higher art born of disease, and reaction as a less facile outlook on life," in opposition to "humanitarian commitment and shallow progressivism." These oppositions were later to form the principal ideological conflict in *The Magic Mountain*. Despite the militancy of his arguments in the *Betrachtungen*, as the war progressed Mann gradually abandoned his reactionary stance for a democratic humanism markedly similar to that advocated by his brother and the Western critics against whom he had earlier railed. He resumed work on *The Magic Mountain* after the war, and by the time of its publication in 1924 the novel had grown from a short satire on sanatorium life to a massive and complex narrative, the dominant themes of which derived from Mann's disagreement with his brother and his own ideological reversal in the preceding decade.

In the novel, the conflict between progress and reaction is embodied in two characters, Ludovico Settembrini and Leo

Naphta, who are among the primary forces in Hans Castorp's education. Settembrini, a liberal humanist whose views resemble those of Heinrich Mann, is an exponent of rationalism, democracy, and enlightenment; his spiritual antagonist Naphta conversely advocates mysticism, despotism, and discipline. Throughout much of the novel the two contend for Castorp's allegiance in repeated and lengthy theoretical debates. Much of the criticism of the novel centers on these debates, which, along with detailed accounts of the books Castorp reads, contribute to the reputation of *The Magic Mountain* as a particularly intimidating "novel of ideas." Marshall Montgomery, among others, has criticized Mann's "only-too-German habit of turning the novel into a vehicle for conveying a heavy cargo of psychological, philosophical, and pedagogical reflections." Other critics, however, dismiss these objections, praising Mann's brilliant craftsmanship and maintaining that the abstract theorizing is skillfully integrated into the narrative. Joseph Wood Krutch observes that "'ideas' are there in plenty, but they are always seen through a temperament and used as the materials of art." Like Settembrini and Naphta, the novel's other main characters, Clawdia Chauchat and Mynheer Peeperkorn, are clearly delineated representatives of philosophical positions or attitudes, and they play an equally important role in Castorp's education. Chauchat, a Russian woman with whom Castorp falls in love, introduces him to the mystical temper of non-Western culture. Like Naphta, she both represents and actively advocates the unconscious and nonrational aspects of existence, forming an opposition to Settembrini's unflagging rationalism. This opposition has led many critics to view Castorp as a symbol of Germany's geographic and ideological position between the cultures of Western and Eastern Europe, with their divergent tendencies of intellectualism on the one hand and intuitiveness on the other. According to Hermann J. Weigand, Mann envisaged "spiritual Germany, in contrast to the stark reality of the War, as steering its course between East and West, between vociferous individualistic liberalism and equally vociferous communistic radicalism, inclining its ear to both in turn, but selling its soul to neither." Peeperkorn, an inarticulate Dutch plantation owner, is the fourth decisive influence on Castorp's development. Peeperkorn, who is unable to form a coherent sentence yet dominates the narrative from the moment of his appearance through the sheer force of his personality, is generally considered the embodiment of pure feeling. With Chauchat, Peeperkorn represents life's vital aspects, in direct contrast to Settembrini and Naphta's obsessive intellectualizing. Hans Castorp is not completely won over to the position of any of these characters, and critics observe that none of them serve a didactic function in the novel as the representative of a position that Mann himself seeks to propound. According to Theodore Ziolkowski, the characters instead symbolize various potentialities that "exist timelessly as eternal positions," and serve in the narrative to "awaken within Hans Castorp an awareness of certain human possibilities."

The eternal nature of Hans Castorp's experiences on the Magic Mountain is emphasized by the novel's atmosphere of being set in a realm beyond time. The concepts of time and timelessness are central preoccupations of the novel, as evidenced by numerous theoretical discussions of these concepts and by the author's manipulation of the narrative to reflect the subjectivity with which an individual experiences time's passage. Maintaining that his novel "depicts the hermetic enchantment of its young hero within the timeless, and thus seeks complete presentness at any given moment to the entire world of ideas that it comprises," Mann also sought to establish the timeless quality of Castorp's experiences through various technical de-

vices emphasizing the "presentness" of the entire story at each point in its narration, thereby allowing the form of the narrative to reflect his conception of an eternal present. He achieved this goal in part through utilization of the leitmotif, a technique whereby the repeated use of a particular phrase or image recalls to the reader related events or situations. Calling the leitmotif "the magic formula that works both ways, and links the past with the future, the future with the past," the author explained that in *The Magic Mountain* "the leitmotif is the technique employed to preserve the inward unity and abiding presentness of the whole at each moment." Mann acknowledged his indebtedness to classical music for such techniques as the leitmotif and for the system of thematic development used in *The Magic Mountain,* a system whereby simple themes are combined and played against one another with ever-increasing complexity in a manner resembling musical counterpoint. Like the author, the novel's protagonist also exhibits extraordinary receptivity to music. Throughout the book, music is viewed as a dangerously seductive power, and is continually associated with one of the novel's dominant themes, the similarly seductive powers of disease and death.

According to Stefan Schultz, "the 'mark of disease' has always been, in Thomas Mann's thinking, a badge of intelligence; the stupid may be healthy, but it takes a special mind to be struck by disease." Like Mann, Hans Castorp exhibits from the time of his arrival on the Magic Mountain a reverence for disease similar to that of the nineteenth-century German Romantics. Although his stay at the tuberculosis sanatorium is originally planned as a brief visit to his cousin, Castorp soon develops symptoms of the disease himself, the effects of which stimulate him to higher levels of perception and awareness. His fascination with disease gradually becomes an obsession, prompting research into the biological and chemical bases of life and death and eventually leading him to maintain that "there are two ways to life: one is the regular, direct and good way; the other is bad, it leads through death, and that is the way of genius." Citing this "notion of disease and death as a necessary route to knowledge, health, and life," Mann and many critics have placed *The Magic Mountain* in the tradition of Grail or "quester" legends in which the protagonist strikes a pact with the unknown in order to attain knowledge or salvation. Weigand writes that "Castorp's surrendering to disease has the same symbolical significance as Faust's concluding his pact with the devil," in that he places "not only his body but the integrity of his whole mental-moral personality" at risk in exchange for a heightened awareness of life.

Castorp's attraction to death reaches its climax in the chapter "Snow," which critics generally consider the novel's intellectual center. Lost in a snowstorm and freezing to death, he dreams of a classical Mediterranean landscape populated by serenely beautiful "People of the Sun," who treat each other with an extraordinary reverence and civility that stands in sharp contrast to the scene in a nearby temple where two old, hideous women are dismembering and consuming a small child. Castorp views this dream as a synthesis of the forces of life and death, in which the People of the Sun are "so sweetly courteous to each other in silent recognition of the horror." Realizing that neither Settembrini's affirmation of life to the complete exclusion of death nor Naphta's devotion to the dark mysteries of existence is sufficient, Castorp renounces his sympathy with death and reconciles the extreme world views of his pedagogues into a position that affirms life and love yet respects death as a necessary adjunct to life. Mann called this realization Castorp's Grail, which is described in Mann's essay "The Making of *The Magic Mountain*'' as ''the conception of a future humanity that has passed through and survived the profoundest knowledge of disease and death.'' Although most commentators agree that the episode marks a turning point in Castorp's education, noting that in this scene he forms an independent world view, critical opinion is divided over the episode's artistic success. Hatfield considers it ''perhaps the most magnificent passage in all Mann's work, and certainly the high point of the novel.'' T. E. Apter, however, has dismissed the scene as ''hopelessly trite,'' and Martin Swales contends that ''the dream sequence is overwritten to the point of being a melodramatic scenario.''

Commentators also disagree over the significance of the episode to the meaning of the novel as a whole. Some critics condemn the indifference to cruelty exhibited by the People of the Sun and fault the ''Snow'' chapter for its implication that horror and cruelty must be tolerated as an integral part of life; Ronald Gray notes that ''it is strange to find Mann describing all this as a dream of love.'' Other critics who accept the episode as an affirmation of love and life are nevertheless unable to reconcile this philosophical position with the novel's final scene, in which Castorp appears likely to die in battle in World War I. Roman S. Struc speculates that Mann may have sought through this ending to express the fundamental incompatibility between a mystic experience and reality, or between an ideal and its realization. Some critics argue that the ending expresses Mann's view that humanity's redemption will be rendered possible only through a cataclysm of death and destruction such as World War I, and that Castorp's likely death in battle prefigures society's resurrection as well as his own. Yet another position is taken by Ziolkowski, who disputes the prevailing opinion that the purpose of Castorp's education is to convince him of the importance of love and the sanctity of life. Ziolkowski argues that the protagonist's development is designed instead to lead him to ''a position of neutral objectivity and awareness beyond any ideological position,'' and that the novel itself is Mann's symbol of the supremacy of aesthetic form to ideology in a world where ideology is ultimately meaningless.

These differences of interpretation notwithstanding, critics have uniformly found *The Magic Mountain* to be one of the most challenging and profound works in literature, a novel whose vision encompasses both the perennial ordeals of the human spirit and the specific traumas of modern history. In addition, the novel is praised as an exemplary artistic creation. Summarizing this relationship between the aesthetic and ideological intricacies of *The Magic Mountain*, Ziolkowski has stated: ''The book remains as a symbol of the aesthetic attitude that is capable of reconciling the conflicting positions not accessible of resolution by the forces portrayed individually within the novel. For this reason its meaning will never be exhausted by a statement of theme and of plot, or by an analysis of structure or content. The book as a whole is a symbol of the life represented within the book. Like that life, it is hermetic and timeless; like that life, it has an existence independent of reality; like that life, it represents an enhancement and intensification of life itself.''

(See also *Contemporary Authors*, Vol. 104.)

LUDWIG LEWISOHN   (essay date 1925)

[*A German-born American novelist and critic, Lewisohn was considered an authority on German literature, and his translations of Gerhart Hauptmann, Rainer Maria Rilke, and Jakob Wassermann are widely respected. In 1919 he became the drama critic for the* Nation, *serving as its associate editor until 1924, when he joined a group of expatriates in Paris. After his return to the United States in 1934, Lewisohn became a prominent sympathizer with the Zionist movement, and served as editor of the Jewish magazine* New Palestine *for five years. Many of his later works reflect his humanistic concern for the plight of the Jewish people. In the following excerpt from a review of* The Magic Mountain, *Lewisohn praises the novel's profound vision as well as its style and structure.*]

In *Buddenbrooks* and in *Tonio Kroeger* and elsewhere Thomas Mann sought to give a responsible accounting of himself and so of the creative artist in human society. In *Der Zauberberg* he turns to human society itself—to the European world on the edge of the great war but unconscious of it—and lets that society, under his philosophic and emotional guidance, render an accounting of itself. He accomplishes his purpose not by telling many stories of many men nor by dealing in incident or even primarily in character. In a sanatorium near Davos, in a high, isolated world, where nature abandons the very march of the accustomed seasons and time, grown relative in actual fact, stands icily still, Thomas Mann has staged the great debate of all the psychical forces that govern man, the great research concerning our knowledge and our ignorance of our fate, the great speculation concerning the health and the disease of mind and body, the nature of both and their relation, the high and ultimate secrets of love and death. His protagonists are men and voices, too: Settembrini, the humanist, bourgeois liberal, *rhetor*, who with all his fine truths and fine sentiments concerning the dignity and liberty of man cannot save for man either that dignity or that liberty; Naphta, the apostate Jew turned Jesuit, who strangely yet logically enough symbolizes the reactions toward power and obedience, so-called discipline and so-called order, that unite the hierarch and the proletarian, the Fascist and the Communist; Behrens, the physician, the scientist pure and simple, quite honest in intent yet forced, by the inevitable gaps in our knowledge, into a measure of charlatanism. And all these voices, as well as the morbid siren song of Clawdia Chauchat and the indomitable vitality of the self-sufficing force of Mynheer Peeperkorn, hurtle about the head of that once simple young man and titular hero, Hans Castorp, engineer of Hamburg. Once simple and straightforward and almost unreflective but now cast, with his abnormal temperature and acuter sensitiveness, into the midst of this severe and rarefied world wherein all emotions are more direct and terrible and all ideas more trenchant and ultimate and in which the confusion of time, no longer cut and divided by business or pleasure, invites to an hourly facing of last and absolute issues. And Hans Castorp, held by this spiritualization of his inner self, held by the timelessness of time, held, too, by the fatal siren voice of the Russian temptress, clings to these strange heights of snow and pine and eternity. But the great, foul, blasting thunder that cleft through the midst of the world blasts him loose from his speculative eminence and hurls him into the mud and shame and falseness of the war.

Thus ends this book—a book so packed with the deepest experience of mankind, so broad in its philosophic range and profound in its vision, so intricate despite the superb clarity and order—*lucidus ordo*—of style and structure, that it will not reveal all its fulness or greatness to one year or even to one generation of readers. It is, as Goethe said of Faust, incommensurable. It is hard to define or describe. Much nonsense will be talked about it and I shall be living from now on in some fear of the English translation, which only a great artist and a trained thinker could undertake with any hope of measurable success. But it is with the fullest sense of sober, critical responsibility that I may, on the one hand, call *Der Zauberberg* the Divine Comedy, no less perfect for its prose form, of our disastrous age, and, on the other hand, liken the great debates in it to those Platonic dialogues that have carried both thoughts and voices across the millennia, and yet assert that the book remains a novel, an epic narrative, enlarging and also heightening, of course, the very concept of the novel by what it is. And if our age is indeed a disastrous one, the disaster is mitigated by the vigilant nobility of such a spirit as that of Thomas Mann. (pp. 667-68)

Ludwig Lewisohn, "Thomas Mann at Fifty," in The Nation, Vol. CXXI, No. 3153, December 9, 1925, pp. 667-68.

KUNO FRANCKE   (essay date 1926)

[*Francke was a German-American poet and literary historian. In the following excerpt from an essay written in 1926, he discusses the plot, principal themes, and main characters of* The Magic Mountain.]

[Among] all contemporary German writers of fiction, Thomas Mann stands out as a solitary and unique figure. From the year 1901, the date of his first great novel, *Die Buddenbrooks*, until the beginning of the war, keeping conspicuously aloof from the sentimental emotionalism of the Herzogs and Frenssens, steadfastly maintaining his careful, serious, austere manner of observation, his profound insight into character, his sure grasp of the things of the outer world, he allowed to be published only such productions of his as came fully up to the standard of his own judicious and severe self-scrutiny. During the war, he refused to be drawn into any kind of hysteria, seeking solace in retirement and in deep studies upon the basic qualities of German national achievements and failures. But not until a year ago, seven years after the armistice, as a man of fifty, has he given us, as the finished product of a whole decade of work, thought, investigation, suffering, and striving, what perhaps will go down in history as the most subtle spiritual reflex of an age of convulsions, disruptions, and cataclysms—the two-volume novel *Der Zauberberg*.

I shall not attempt the impossible by trying to give an account of the extraordinary variety of characters and happenings which Thomas Mann crowds together on the stage of this "Mount of Enchantment," a luxurious international tuberculosis sanatorium in the midst of the snow and icefields of Davos. The author himself, in an answer to critics, has admitted that it was meant by him as representative of the diseased capitalistic society of pre-war Europe, the very society upon which rests the ultimate guilt of having made the war inevitable. But this social symbolism of the underlying conception reveals itself only now and then to the more deeply searching eye, and then only dimly; it does not in the least take away from the vividness and reality of the individual experiences brought before us. What most palpably is the common theme of all these individual experiences is Death—death and its relation to life.

At first sight it is the grimly farcical aspect of death that forces itself upon us as the prevailing impression of this picture. The society congregated on lonely Alpine heights in its flight from the fatal result of disease, contracted in the conflux and tumult of modern civilization, seems habitually to be engaged in a veritable *Danse Macabre*. Although bearing the mark of Death upon their faces, the majority of them keep on following the course of their mean and worthless habits. Indeed, the disease only accentuates their weaknesses and their appetites; it makes them caricatures of life; and all their eating, drinking, flirting, gossiping, bragging, slandering, and intriguing is nothing but one continuous, though constantly changing, collective grimace. A few figures, however, stand out by contrast from this mass of frivolity and vulgarity.

There is the young German officer, Joachim Ziemssen, instinctively guarding himself against the weakening influences of his illness and the equivocal charms of his effete surroundings, holding himself inwardly and outwardly erect, bent only upon regaining his health and rejoining the colors: his final succumbing to the fatal disease has a fine human touch and affects us like a soldier's death on the battlefield. There is the ascetic Italian humanist and philosopher, Signor Settembrini, a champion of the spirit, an enthusiastic advocate of freedom, enlightenment, and progress, a living protest against self-indulgence and weakness of the flesh: his brilliant speeches on human dignity and the necessity of resisting bodily conditions dispel for the moment the enervating air of the sick-room. There is Settembrini's spiritual antagonist, the Galician ex-Jew and revolutionary Jesuit Naphta, a fanatic of skepticism, nihilism, terrorism, despotism: his provoking and defiant attacks against phrases and fashions and the whole existing order of things stimulate intellectual independence and courage, although they lead to his own rash and unhappy end. There is the aged Dutch tobacco-king, Mynheer Peeperkorn, a giant of living, of enjoyment, of feeling, truly Gargantuesque in his proportions: his primitive massiveness and impressiveness seem to contradict all impotence and inactivity, and his suicide impresses us like the blasting of rocks. And there is the principal figure of the novel, the young Hamburg patrician Hans Castorp, in whom all the fantastic sights and experiences of this world of fever, decay, and death produce a complete reversal of his former commonplace states of mind and views of life.

He is an ingenuous youth of aristocratic and refined instincts, not in any way remarkable intellectually, dreamy and indolent, highly impressionable. He joins the sanatorium company in the first place on a brief vacation trip as the guest of his cousin, Joachim Ziemssen, is therefore in the first place only a sympathetic observer of the effects of disease upon different natures and tempers. But soon he finds himself a patient too, and gradually drifts into a state where disease as such comes to be his all-absorbing study and occupation. Of striking outward experiences there is very little. The weeks, seasons, years come and go. Time seems to lose all distinguishing features. An immeasurable sameness of arrival and departure, of X-ray examinations and lung operations, of dying and recovering, of frivolous amusement and of lonely despair, of superlatively blue sky and savagely violent snowstorms envelops all things. The silence of eternity seems to descend. But in this silent sameness of things Hans Castorp hears voices and sees sights which stir his innermost being.

Soon after his arrival he has noticed in the dining room, at the "Russian table," far from his own, a young woman whose face, manner, motions strangely attract him. He learns that she is the wife of a Russian official beyond the Caucasus whom, however, no one has ever seen here, that she is tubercular, that she is a frequenter of all the fashionable European health resorts—Madame Chauchat. For months and months he makes no attempt to be introduced to her, nor does she speak to him when they accidentally meet in the halls or the parkways. But her seductive image pursues him always and everywhere; at meal times his glance is constantly trying to meet hers, sometimes successfully; in his room he examines his temperature and is delighted to find that his fever rises at the thought of her; he dreams of her kiss at night. He knows that all this is immoral, that it is disease. But is not disease a heightened condition of life? Does it not open your eyes to the mystery of things? Does it not give you a freedom of which the workaday world has no conception? And are not love and disease the same thing? Do they not both disintegrate the body? Do they not both lead to death—death, the glorifier of all things, the solemn and majestic power which transforms life and surrounds it with eternity? By such and similar sophistries does this modern Tristan try to justify to himself his inner looseness and to assimilate the poison from which he cannot escape.

That this hysterical state of mind does indeed expand and heighten his soul life is apparent. It makes him peculiarly susceptible to the suffering round about him and induces him to shower all kinds of attention and kindnesses upon particularly distressing cases among his fellow patients, the incurable, the moribund, the utterly lonely. It makes him listen with feverish eagerness to the debates of his philosophic friends about human freedom and destiny. It makes him delve in an amateurish way into the abstruse recesses of modern biology and chemistry. But everywhere he finds a confirmation of the conviction which more and more firmly and inevitably is settling upon him— the conviction that his whole previous life of health and activity had been a delusion, that only on this Mount of Enchantment has he come to understand the source of all our highest feelings and deepest insights: death.

So he drifts on, dreaming and longing. Only twice in the book is there a meeting of the lovers, if lovers they can be called. The first time at a fancy-dress party on Carnival Tuesday, the evening before Madame Chauchat's departure. Here Hans Castorp, emboldened by the Bohemian license of the fête, approaches her without ceremony, addresses her with "Du," blurts out before her his fantastic philosophy, and trembling, on his knees, stammers insane words about the wondrous mystery of her body and the raptures of eternal communion; while she, stroking his hair, half tempting, half pitying, calls him "petit bourgeois" and "mon prince Carnaval."

The second meeting, years later, is after her return with another "travelling companion," the Gargantuesque Mynheer Peeperkorn. This time it is she who makes the first approach. On the basis of their common feelings for the marvellous old man who has impressed his personality upon both of them, she asks and receives Hans Castorp's consent to a treaty of friendship; and she seals this treaty with a kiss. But although these are the only two scenes in which the Russian adventuress and the young German ingénu engage in intimate conversation, we feel her spell throughout the book and are made to understand why with her final departure all incentive seems to have gone from him.

He now sinks back into what the author calls "the great dullness"—the ordinary dallying away of time by the sanatorium company, stamp-collecting, amateur photography, esperanto, playing patience, and what not; he becomes a victrola fanatic, a victim of hypnotism and spiritistic séances; he even takes an interest in all the silly and stupid altercations and enmities which infest the hospital atmosphere. He seems to have lost his individuality.

What at last arouses and restores him to himself is the great historic thunderclap which rocks the foundations of the Mount of Enchantment and scatters its inhabitants to the four winds: the declaration of war.

> The dreamer stood up and looked about himself. He felt disenchanted, redeemed, delivered—not through his own will power, as he had to confess to himself with a sense of shame, but hurled into space by elemental forces to which his deliverance was an entirely accidental and secondary matter. But although his little fate vanished into nothing before the universal disaster, was here not after all a revelation of something like personal, that is, divine justice and grace? If life was to accept once more her sinful child of sorrows—not on easy terms, but in the hard and harsh manner of a visitation which perhaps did not mean bodily life, but three volleys of honor over his, the sinner's, grave, then he was ready for it. And thus he sank down on his knees, face and hands lifted up to a sky which was sulphurous and dark, but not any longer the grotto ceiling of the Mount of Sin.

The final scene shows him on the battlefield, as a private, mudbespattered, gun in hand, in the midst of falling comrades, blindly plunging on into shot and shell.

I know that I have given only a very imperfect impression of a book crowded—possibly overcrowded—with thought, with knowledge, with characters, with incidents. But perhaps I have made it clear that it is essentially an epic of the inner life, and that, morbid and irrational as is its subject, it appeals altogether to the striving for health and reason. In reading it, I could not help recalling the sensations aroused in me by the masterpieces of San Marco and San Lorenzo; for here also I felt the power of an artist who, concentrating his whole being upon his work, disciplining his will and his imagination, presenting life with perfect detachment and sovereignty of mind, has by this mastery of himself created something which communicates to those who enter into his work the same firm and self-controlled state of feeling. And, as a German, I could not help being proud that a work of such calm greatness and fundamental nobility should have sprung from the soil of harassed and distracted Germany. (pp. 117-27)

*Kuno Francke, "German After-War Imagination,"
in his* German After-War Problems, *Cambridge,
Mass.: Harvard University Press, 1927, pp. 95-128.**

JOSEPH WOOD KRUTCH   (essay date 1927)

[Krutch is widely regarded as one of America's most respected literary and drama critics. A conservative and idealistic thinker, he was a consistent proponent of human dignity and the preeminence of literary art. His literary criticism is characterized by such concerns: in The Modern Temper *(1929) he argued that because scientific thought has denied human worth, tragedy had become obsolete, and in* The Measure of Man *(1954) he attacked modern culture for depriving humanity of the sense of individual responsibility necessary for making important decisions in an increasingly complex age. In the following excerpt from a review of the English translation of* The Magic Mountain, *Krutch praises*

Mann's skillful incorporation into the narrative of ideas extraneous to the plot and applauds the novel's technical and stylistic achievements.]

[**The Magic Mountain**] is a massive work which represents several years of labor on the part of a novelist whose fame was already great, and it is worthy of him—but this is not all that can be said of it. Other established writers have recently issued books which sustain their reputations, but none have this year published anything so new and so vital. The extraordinary, almost morbid sensitivity which Mann has before exhibited is here again revealed, and so, too, is the mastery of detail which marked **Buddenbrooks,** his other massive novel; but here also it is made evident that his style, beautiful and individual though it was, had not before and probably has not even now completed its evolution. For not since Marcel Proust published the first volume of *A la Récherche du Temps Perdu* has anything appeared in which a new form was so completely mastered.

Mann has come nearer than any other contemporary writer to solving a problem of which innumerable students of contemporary fiction have been acutely aware. Obviously "ideas" cannot be neglected in the writing of modern fiction; they are, as H. G. Wells has argued, quite as much a part of the life of a modern hero as deeds; and yet most people now feel that Mr. Wells and his followers succeeded in introducing "ideas" only by destroying fiction, which became in their hands little more than a sugar-coated treatise supplied with an exordium. Mann, on the other hand, though his novel is concerned with intellectual movements more, perhaps, than it is concerned with anything else, has succeeded in remembering always that his business is with the imagination. In his novel "ideas" appear not so much for themselves as for the moods which they generate, and what one gets is not argument but a diffused sense of the effect which the intellectual atmosphere of their times has upon the characters. "Ideas" are there in plenty, but they are always seen through a temperament and used as the materials of art.

Vast as is its scale one does not get from it the impression of anything unwieldy or sprawling. So perfectly is it proportioned and so completely are all its details held in hand by the author that when one has finished it one seems to have read not one of the longest modern novels but a perfectly rounded conte, since the thing which is left in the mind is an absolutely unified impression. And yet this perfection of execution is achieved in the case of a work planned in a radically new way and intended to accomplish something never accomplished before. Readers of the story called **"Tristram"** in the collection entitled **Death in Venice** will find the mood of the book there foreshadowed, but they will get from it alone no conception of the magnitude of the new book nor of the astonishing art which has enabled its author to tell the whole story of the modern mind without violating the unity of the single impression which he creates.

The Magic Mountain does not lend itself easily to imitation. It is a creation, not a formula, and very likely it will not, for that very reason, serve as the beginning of a new school. One cannot easily imagine another work of fiction "like it"; but so great is its achievement in an essentially new direction that it will, I fancy, be the most influential as well as the greatest of the season's novels.

> *Joseph Wood Krutch, "Spring Novels and 'The Magic Mountain'," in* The Nation, *Vol. CXXIV, No. 3231, June 8, 1927, p. 437.**

MARSHALL MONTGOMERY   (essay date 1927)

[*In the following essay, Montgomery summarizes a negative review of* The Magic Mountain *that appeared in the German magazine* Der neue Merkur *in 1925.*]

A writer in the leading Zurich daily newspaper has remarked rather contemptuously that Thomas Mann's great novel **Der Zauberberg,** even in its new English dress, is too "hard" for English readers, and has achieved among us only a *succès d'estime.* It may be so; at least no statistics are available to prove the contrary. But it may not be amiss to recall the impression made by this book in Germany when it appeared some three years ago. The other day I mentioned the work to a young German Ph.D., who took his degree in German literature, and asked if he had read it. He replied, "Oh, yes, as a German, one must have read that!" I ventured to remark that the book seemed to me "interesting and boring." He answered, without hesitation, "Yes, both at the same time." I have turned back to see what Conrad Wandrey wrote about the novel in the February number of *Der neue Merkur* for 1925. This review is now extinct, but at that time was considered by intelligent people the leading German periodical, so far as literature is concerned.

Wandrey does not pretend to deny the importance of Mann's work; he finds in him essentially a strong will, coupled with an agile intellect and keen analytical powers. There is no greater example in German prose of these special gifts. But his epics have never showed the marks of natural growth, were never nourished by the secret magic of the irrational that flows from the blood of the writer by the grace of God and not merely from the brain of the finished author. So it was even in **Buddenbrooks,** Mann's earlier (and greater?) novel of epic breadth. So it is still more with **Der Zauberberg,** the painful product of ten years' labour. Even the language of these works, rhythmical as it undeniably is, is not the musical flow that some have pretended. The forms of Mann's imagination again are "two-dimensional." "His talent is that of the draughtsman, but it is not plastic" like the sculptor's. Hence the calligraphic thinness of his masks and faces. They "never are anything, but are always representing something." In **Der Zauberberg,** Hans Castorp himself is, as it were, a shadow of (a younger) Thomas Mann, for whose soul the struggle is carried on between those two thinner pedagogue shadows, Settembrini and Naphta. It is all "faithful, diligent artist's work." It gives us a "real symbol of civilized progress" in this wonderful sanatorium. It is a remarkable performance, it does honour to its author and to his country, but it remains "a toilsome book much loaded-down." On the other hand, "none is the equal of the master who drew the portraits of Mynheer Peeperkorn, Hofrat Behrens, and Hermine Stöhr." May he soon finish that of Felix Krull, so admirably begun! May he now shake off the excessive influence of the long-winded Dostoievsky and the only-too-German habit of turning the novel into a vehicle for conveying a heavy cargo of psychological, philosophical, and pedagogical reflexions. Does not Mann himself appear to make light of them all in the end, when Hans Castorp, after seven years of painful listening and arguing, reaches, at last, a conclusion which was obvious to his simple, honest cousin Joachim from the beginning: "Der Mensch soll um der Güte und Liebe willen dem Tode keine Herrschaft einräumen über seine Gedanken" ("Man, for the sake of goodness and love, should not permit death to become master of his thoughts"). A clear formula, indeed, but one that only sick minds need, a tiny packet of ethical gold to bring home after seven years on the magic mountain. All this wit and wisdom—Naphta's, Settembrini's, Peeperkorn's and the rest—expended to prove a law that all healthy men and women take for granted! What immense art has gone into cooking and spreading out so thin a layer of moral doctrine over a thousand pages of rolling sentences! What juggling with the simple everyday concept of time! What architectural ingenuity in the use of curious materials from botanical science to psycho-analysis! What exactitude and fulness in the description of chairs, tables, and washstands! What unwearied care in the recounting of odd slips of the tongue and tremblings of the neck! Would now that Thomas Mann leave the discussion of political and philosophical problems to the professors and the journalists, and finish those brilliant "Memoirs of a Swindler," in which, with such a masterly hand, he has set about parodying "the great German form of autobiography."

But, one asks oneself doubtfully, can a thoughtful German cease from being a pedagogue, even when he turns parodist? It remains to be proved. (pp. 16-18)

> Marshall Montgomery, "'The Magic Mountain' through German Eyes," in Modern Languages, *Vol. IX, No. 1, October, 1927, pp. 16-18.*

HERBERT MULLER (essay date 1937)

[*An American critic and educator, Muller is the author of works on such diverse topics and figures as the modern novel, Adlai Stevenson, the philosophy of modern science, Thomas Wolfe, and Byzantine history. In the following essay, he presents* The Magic Mountain *as Mann's attempt to synthesize life's contradictory aspects, examining how the humanistic world view expressed in the novel integrates the rational and nonrational natures of the individual.*]

"All mere pronouncements," Thomas Mann has written, "are relative and vulnerable, regardless of the pretensions to absoluteness and finality with which they may be felt and uttered . . . only the shapes of esthetic creation are impervious to the ravages of time." In discussing the thought of the author of *The Magic Mountain,* one should accordingly remember that this novel is not a philosophical treatise. Its immense intellectual content is dramatized, concretely objectified in character and incident, made timeless by its place in a majestic compositional scheme. Mann not only makes the novel hold more than all except a few writers have attempted to pack into it, but holds all this fact and thought in the solution of a brilliant artistry. Hence his work constantly suggests even more than it represents; it is not only wide, solid, and deep, but resonant, rich in the overtones of poetry. It is, I believe, one of the indubitably great novels of the ages.

Yet it is also clearly a product of the twentieth century and of special significance to contemporaries. Mann faces squarely the central problem of modern life and literature underlying all immediate issues. In a chaotic, devaluated age, he seeks to establish a firm basis of solidarity, to order a system of values, to build up unobstructed lines of communication both with the past and between the isolated outposts of the present. He seeks, in short, to provide a whole scheme of reorientation for the world at once unimaginably old and disconcertingly new in which men now find themselves, and then to vitalize it in the enduring shapes of art. This is a task of unprecedented difficulty. It demands great intellectual as well as great imaginative powers—powers such as we do not expect of the geniuses of the past, and find in very few of them. So ambitious an artist

must today embrace an immense profusion of perspectives, an immense range, diversity, and complexity of specialized thought and experience; and unlike the artist of the past he can take nothing for granted. Accordingly, the importance of Thomas Mann lies in the fact that he is not only better equipped for this task than any other contemporary writer, but less oppressed by its necessity, less appalled by its conditions. It is interesting to speculate upon what he might have accomplished in a simpler, stabler, more homogeneous age; meanwhile he appears to fulfill himself as completely in this one as did Dante in his.

Mann found himself, indeed, only after most arduous self-education. He could not be content with the hand-to-mouth solutions by which less critical artists manage to live, but had to justify his seemingly remote, unworldly activity. The sociological chronicle of *Buddenbrooks,* the exquisite psychological study of *Death in Venice,* some distinguished short stories—he did not rest on these performances but continued to wrestle with the problem of his responsibility to himself, his kind, and, above all, to his society. With the catastrophe of the World War, this soul-searching became a desperate business, the very condition of his survival. For some years he was as artist completely paralyzed. In a series of treatises he painfully examined his conscience, groped towards enlightenment. And of this spiritual travail *The Magic Mountain* is the magnificent summation and the epilogue. Here Mann finally exorcised his demons, sublimated his distress, converted the confusion and the din into imperishable beauty.

Commentators have already appeared with keys to open the many entrances to *The Magic Mountain;* for if it is immediately impressive, it is also bewildering. At first glance it might be taken simply as a realistic account of a young man's experience in a sanatorium—another of the pathological studies in which this age specializes. It is always leisurely and solid; Mann carefully individualizes every character, minutely annotates every experience. His novel is indeed a triumph in the realistic method. And his detail is especially interesting because of his deliberate emphasis upon certain machine products, like the thermometer, the pencil, the phonograph, the watch, and the X-ray machine. Through these Mann conveys the deepest experience of his hero, thus accomplishing what Hart Crane attempted in "The Bridge": through a new set of symbols, unprepossessing in themselves but an inseparable part of modern experience, he realizes the timeless purposes once served by the nightingale and the daffodil. He makes good the prophecy of Wordsworth and achieves a vital synthesis of poetry and science.

Yet Mann's intention plainly goes deeper than this. The simplest reader recognizes *The Magic Mountain* as a philosophical novel, highly charged with meanings not visible on the surface. When it is most concrete it still carries a haunting suggestion of symbolism; the very sharpness of the contours of the characters makes their shadows stand out more boldly. The title itself suggests allegory: this is the Magic Mountain of the *Siebenschläfer* ["Seven Sleepers"]. The greatness of Mann's novel lies in just this wealth of implication, the many layers of meaning under its vivid surface.

One of the more obvious of these deeper purposes is spiritual autobiography: in his most significant traits and concerns, his hero represents Mann himself. Hans Castorp seeks the meaning of life, and he goes about this exalted metaphysical business in a manner at once phlegmatic and impassioned that is typical of his author. Many readers are misled by Mann's Olympian irony, an irony that turns in on itself, smiles at its own image, gives the impression of lightness and mockery when he is in holiest earnest. Thus he constantly calls Hans "mediocre" and makes him appear ludicrously naïve. Yet his "mediocrity," Mann adds, is a by-product of a scrambled, viewless, profoundly uncertain age: an age in which "a man who is capable of achievement over and above the average and expected modicum must be equipped either with a moral remoteness and single-mindedness which is rare indeed and of heroic mould, or else with an exceptionally robust vitality." In the end, moreover, Hans turns out to be *not* mediocre. His simplicity is noble as well as amusing. He is a better man than either of the brilliant dialecticians, Settembrini and Naphta, and finally comes closer to the truth than all the apparently superior men who fight over his honest soul. "You must have more in you than we thought," writes his creator in an affectionate farewell. "Life's delicate child" has proved to be a "genius in the realm of experience," a hero worthy of even so heroic an adventure as that of *The Magic Mountain.*

This adventure is not, however, a purely personal one. Mann is not seeking a way of salvation for himself alone, or for a few superior spirits like him. He is seeking to express the consciousness of the race, to integrate the whole experience of modern man. Hence the setting of his novel. The International Sanatorium Berghof incidentally provides an opportunity for a study of disease and its effects—a subject that has always fascinated Mann; its tubercular patients may incidentally symbolize, as some critics think, the sickness of bourgeois society; but it is essential to Mann's epical intention. In the first place, the rarefied atmosphere of the mountain accelerates the metabolism of Hans Castorp—with his habitual irony, Mann takes pleasure in pointing out this simple physiological basis of lofty endeavor. More important, this is the *International* Sanatorium, located in Switzerland, most cosmopolitan of European countries. Thus Mann is able to assemble naturally representatives of many nationalities and submit for synthesis many different points of view. He is also able to put Hans Castorp beyond Time itself. Time ceases to exist for the patients of the Berghof; it is one of the dominant themes of *The Magic Mountain* as of *Remembrance of Things Past,* and Mann seeks as earnestly as Proust to escape its tyranny. But, above all, in the isolation of this setting the simple nature of Hans can be distilled and redistilled until nothing remains but its pure essence. He is cut free from all the snarls and tangles, the shifting appearances and ceaseless distractions of the world of practical affairs. If, accordingly, Mann pays little attention to immediate political or economic problems, it is only to go behind them to the last and absolute issues of human life.

Hence the failure of Hans Castorp to leave the sanatorium is not to be considered mere weakness, nor the novel interpreted as an "epic of disease," a fatal spell or morbid dream from which the hero is awakened only by the World War. Although death and disease have a dangerous lure for Hans, he presently shakes off their unhealthy influence. He returns to the "flatland" unmistakably a better man for his prolonged stay on the Magic Mountain. His refusal to leave proves to have been no flabby self-indulgence but an obscure devotion to the law of his nature. It enabled him to "take stock" once and for all.

When one inquires, however, specifically what Hans found out after seven years of taking stock, one discovers a whole new range of meanings, a whole new set of symbols. As Professor Wiegand makes clear, Hans Castorp also represents the German nation, and his story is an elaborate allegorical statement of its ideal destiny [see *TCLC*, Vol. 2]. If the present regime in Germany makes this intention appear grotesque, it is nevertheless unmistakable and governs the conception of character and invention of incident down almost to the last detail of the novel. Unlike the Odyssey motif in Joyce's *Ulysses,* it is not superstructure but foundation, not an incidental overlay but a vital animating principle. Its main outlines stand out boldly, and its significance to a German is attested by the otherwise surprising popularity of *The Magic Mountain* in Central Europe.

Upon the outbreak of the World War, Mann felt a profound obligation to become the spokesman for spiritual Germany. In this rôle he adopted the traditional national view (of Adam Müller, Nietzsche, and others) in which Germany is the mediator between Western and Eastern civilization, more particularly between French rationalism and Russian mysticism—"*das Volk der Mitte*" ["the nation of the middle"]. Hence the two most persistent influences upon his typically Teutonic hero in *The Magic Mountain* are the eloquent Settembrini, symbol of the Western enlightenment, and the slovenly, alluring Clavdia Chauchat, symbol of the mysticism of the East. Hans Castorp learns much from both—but he succumbs to neither; in the end he goes his own way, following the laws of his own nature. Symbolically he achieves an ideal synthesis of the opposing cultures while retaining his peculiar native genius. He realizes the exalted destiny of the German people: "the race," as Mann declares in his essay **"Goethe and Tolstoy,"** "that practices a sly and ironic reserve toward both sides, that moves between extremes, easily, with non-commital benevolence; with the morality, no, the simplicity of that elusive 'betweenness' of theirs." Yet this pretty wish-fulfillment is also a challenge. Like Nietzsche, Mann combats the excesses of the German romantics and calls for more rationality, more devotion to logic and the habit of analysis. Germany must complement its splendid romanticism, qualify its peculiar genius. And Mann is himself, more clearly than the Nietzsche he admires, the embodiment of his cosmopolitan ideal: he has blended the native genius of music with a logical, analytical prose.

These meanings, unmistakable and important though they are, the unaided English reader is likely to miss entirely. He can even afford to miss them. For they are but a part of still larger, more universal intentions. Mann's very conception of the ideal destiny of Germany demands that he transcend the specifically German. The "mediocre" Hans Castorp, "life's delicate child," proves great enough and robust enough to represent not only Thomas Mann and his race but all inquiring, aspiring mankind. His spiritual adventures carry him beyond the borders not merely of self but of nation; he "takes stock" as *Homo Dei.*

What in the final analysis governs the pattern of *The Magic Mountain* is, accordingly, the effort at an all-inclusive synthesis. Themes and characters are arranged in pairs. Settembrini is balanced by Naphta, Clavdia by Joachim. Behrens represents the physiological, Krokowski the psychological approach to the problem of disease and finally to the principle of life. The metaphysical speculations of Hans are supplemented by his intensive scientific studies. In this welter of opposites only a few elementary forces stand out singly: the force of pure, inarticulate feeling in the magnificent personality of Mynheer Peeperkorn; the force of Nature, a sublime and abiding presence; and always at the center the force of Hans Castorp himself, an absurd, appealing little figure busying itself on a vast stage, a piping voice in a confused uproar, a pin-point of flickering but unquenchable light in the illimitable darkness—the human spirit on its forlorn, gallant, preposterous adventure among the immensities.

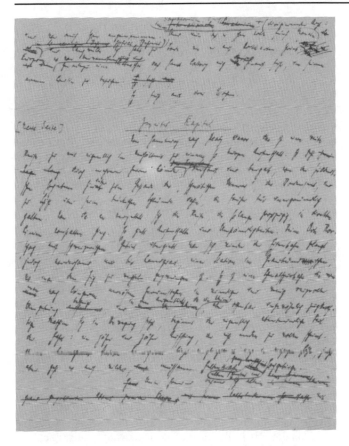

Manuscript page of The Magic Mountain. *Yale Collection of German Literature, Beinecke Rare Book and Manuscript Library.*

Now, the spirit that conceived and broods over every page of *The Magic Mountain* is in the deepest sense of the word humanistic. In an age of cultural specialization and violent partisanship, Mann is conspicuous for his tolerance, urbanity, and catholicity, the range and depth of his understanding and sympathy. He has suggested that the two most significant experiences of the nineteenth century were those of Nietzsche and of the Russian soul: Nietzsche is a symbol of pride and freedom, Dostoyevsky of humility and reverence. Mann has succeeded in reconciling and fusing these experiences; and because both are natural to him, his synthesis does not seem synthetic. He has the piety of the great Russian writers, their deep conviction of the dignity and worth of the human spirit even in degradation; despite his unfailing irony, he always pities, respects, and loves his people. At the same time his spirit is not that of resignation or meek submission; he has Nietzsche's love of reckless spiritual challenge and adventure, his willingness to risk his soul in hazardous inquiry. He is at once tender and austere, mild and lofty, ironical and earnest. And this attitude leads him to break down all rigid dualisms, the analytical abstractions that separate men from the living truth of experience. Flesh and spirit, mind and matter, reason and emotion—such antitheses are as artificial as one between belly and lungs; and to make them sharp and absolute, Mann considers not "genial," even "inept." He is fundamentally idealistic, he is primarily concerned with spiritual values, but these he would draw from the totality of man's relations to the universe. They are both flower and root, not merely choice distillations.

To state these meanings and values more specifically, however, is not easy. Many readers leave *The Magic Mountain* perplexed.

Mann raises innumerable questions and indicates their urgency—but he does not answer them. The novel ends, in fact, on a question. Hans Castorp goes to war, presumably to his death: "Out of this universal feast of death, out of this extremity of fever, kindling the rain-washed evening sky to a fiery glow, may it be that Love one day shall mount?" Mann does not say. He refuses to be stampeded into judgment or prophecy. "I am neither learned nor a teacher, rather a dreamer and a doubter who is hard put to it to save and justify his own life."

Mann's skepticism and irony nevertheless are not simply a refuge. In his essay "Thomas Mann and André Gide" Kenneth Burke asks, "Are not these men trying to make us at home in indecision, are they not trying to humanize the state of doubt?" In a sense they are—and it is a humane vocation. It is also a realistic one; as Mr. Burke adds, becoming certain too quickly is perhaps an evasion, a shirking of responsibility. Yet this proposition is likely to give a false impression of the work of Mann. With him, skepticism is included within a larger frame and serves as a means to an end. Although he does not hope to attain absolute truth, he earnestly seeks some measure of certainty; although suspended judgment is for the present needful, it must be accompanied by a sense of responsibility and a deep concern for values if it is not to become sheer evasion. A confirmed and complacent skeptic would not have suffered his travail during the war years, nor could he have written *The Magic Mountain.*

Hence, if one can find a wealth of meanings in Mann's novel, one cannot find whatever one wants. The limitations of his fiery pedagogues, for example, are obvious enough. Settembrini blows too hard on "the penny pipe of reason"; he gets intoxicated on his own eloquence, blown from his moorings by his own windy rhetoric. His idealism is noble, but it is also vague, shallow, ultimately illiberal—Woodrow Wilson was a tragic example of both its insolence and its insufficiency. On the other hand, Naphta, who brilliantly exposes Settembrini's inconsistencies, himself illustrates the absurdity of the logical extreme. He is too often merely negative—his suicide is symbolical, his only positive affirmation is an inhumanly rigorous dualism that justifies Settembrini's criticism: "His form is logic, but his essence is confusion." Even before the entrance of Mynheer Peeperkorn, Hans Castorp has rejected them both, found his own way "between two intolerable positions, between bombastic humanism and analphabetic barbarism." With the coming of the magnificent Dutchman, however, Settembrini and Naphta seem like wrangling schoolboys. Inarticulate, incoherent, beyond the reach of the most eloquent rhetoric or the most incisive argument, Peeperkorn is the embodiment of pure feeling—feeling that makes possible the "roused and intoxicated life" in which man appears godlike. By the sheer force of personality, simple, elemental, unanalyzable, he overshadows their most brilliant talk, dwarfs them into insignificance.

Why, then, does Peeperkorn kill himself? Because, says one commentator, the principle of Life could not exist in this sickly atmosphere. But a deeper reason is the inadequacy of his sublimely simple way of life. As an old man, he could no longer follow it. "He was built on such a grand scale," Hans Castorp explains reverently, "that he considered it a blasphemy, a cosmic catastrophe, to be found wanting in feeling." Yet a complete, harmonious way of life should not demand even such majestic martyrdom. Simple feeling, however godlike, is not enough. Mynheer Peeperkorn failed to see that the rational faculty must also play a part in the ideal life, and is also a sign of divinity.

It is thus left to the unassuming, undistinguished, unheroic Hans Castorp, the plastic pupil of a dozen tutors, to correct all their distortions and point the way to truth. Lost on the mountain during a snowstorm, he achieves what none of his tutors was able to achieve: a vital, all-inclusive synthesis, a view of life in which all the faculties of man are divinely fused. Here he harmonizes all that he has learned, here he escapes the orbit of disease and triumphs over death. In this transport he affirms life once and for all:

> There is both rhyme and reason in what I say, I have made a dream poem of humanity. I will cling to it. I will be good. I will let death have no mastery over my thoughts. For therein lies goodness and love of humankind, and in nothing else. . . . It is love, not reason, that is stronger than death. Only love, not reason, gives sweet thoughts. And from love and sweetness alone can form come: form and civilization, friendly, enlightened, beautiful human intercourse. . . . *For the sake of goodness and love, man shall let death have no sovereignty over his thoughts.*

The vision fades—but it leaves a residue. "I will remember," Hans promises himself in his ecstasy; and he does remember. Henceforth he is consistently a better man.

Despite his discreet habit of skepticism and irony, then, Mann is not merely a skeptic, and certainly not a defeatist. This scene is plainly the spiritual climax of the novel, and as plainly it is a lyrical affirmation of life. Even the question at the end now takes on a positive implication; it remains, significantly and fittingly, a question, but in the light of the experience of Hans in the snowstorm it is a sign of hope, not of despair. And it is also plain that with all his intellectual interests and remarkable powers of thought, Mann has strong mystical leanings. The vision of Hans is a kind of communion with a "wholly-knowing All-soul," a communion that takes place through the channels of intuitive sympathy, not of reason. Throughout the novel, moreover, Mann displays a readiness to leave the "saner, chaster realms of thought" and embark upon "highly questionable" speculations, such as those on spiritualism in the strange scene of the séance.

Yet Mann does not join in the popular crusade against, or flight from, intellect. His hero exercises the rational faculty most freely, with great pleasure, pride, and profit. Mann's attitude is most clearly stated in his essay on **"Freud's Position in the History of Modern Thought."** Freud, he points out, was among the first to announce "the powerlessness of mind and reason by contrast with the forces marshalled in the depth of the soul, with the dynamic of passion, the irrational, the unconscious." Many converts then proceeded to grovel before the throne of the dark powers. Instead of pitying this poor intellect and trying to protect it in its weakness, they despised it as a base illusion, gloated over its defeats, performed a witch dance about its remains. Paradoxically, they came even to fear it—while proclaiming its powerlessness, they still pointed to it as a menace. But Freud does not join in these obscene rites that his researches helped to instigate; he does not himself glorify the affective at the expense of the intellectual. His own summation is this:

> We may emphasize as often as we like the fact that intellect is powerless compared with im-

pulse in human life—we shall be right. But after all there is something peculiar about this weakness; the voice of the intellect is low, but it rests not till it gets a hearing. In the end, after countless repulses, it gets one after all.

And this is essentially the view of Mann himself. He recommends an attitude of research "in which feeling, intuition, spiritual implications reassert their right, and art secures its position as a genuine instrument of knowledge." But he also clings to the "large and trusting and enduring conviction" that the power of reason, which has played so great and honorable a rôle in historical enlightenment, will continue to do so. He exalts the need of "conscious possession . . . the culture of men developed to complete self-consciousness."

The humanism of Mann is, accordingly, an effort to embrace all our faculties, integrate all that is valuable in our new knowledge and experience, in the hope of securing a full, free, harmonious development of human possibilities. He seeks to reconcile the many conflicting claims of specialists and partisans. In the disorder of the present, when the immense accumulations of scientific investigation have been incorporated neither in the practical administration of society nor in the spiritual attitudes of the individual, he recognizes the necessity of re-examining and redefining the whole humanistic tradition. But he wishes, above all, to preserve the essential values of this tradition. In **"Goethe and Tolstoy"** he declares that "it is time for us to lay all possible stress upon our great humane inheritance and to cultivate it with all the means at our command." He praises Goethe particularly for his reverence for the past and his strong communal spirit in the face of an increasingly anarchical individualism: his call for tradition, piety, discipline, conformity of the ego within a noble and estimable community. To those who would dismiss our "great humane inheritance" as mere irrelevance, or as a luxury that the contemporary cannot afford while practical problems are so urgent, he answers that modern socialism, for example, "has all too long allowed its spiritual life to languish in the shallows of a crude economic materialism," and has no greater need than to find access to this inheritance. His criticism is pertinent simply because he does not lose sight of immediate realities but maintains an admirable balance between the old and the new, the heritage of the past and the needs of the present.

Thus his humanism makes plain how shallow and artificial are such brands as that of the New Humanists, who simply block off all that will not fit cozily into their arbitrary categories. They appear to regard culture as a hothouse plant that does not have its roots in the vulgar realities of biology, psychology, economics. They nurture their spiritual values as if they were tender flowers that must wither under the foul breath of democracy, industrialism, or scientific investigation. They talk abstractedly of the "great tradition," as it has come down from Greece, as if it were not an organic social growth and could be kept alive in a vacuum. But Mann, with as pious a devotion to this tradition, refuses to isolate it or make it the exclusive property of a few gentlemanly scholars. He is unafraid to reinterpret it, as it has constantly been reinterpreted in the past, in the terms of new knowledge and a new cultural context. He seeks to relate it vitally to the special interests and inescapable conditions of modern life, in the faith that it is still noble and valid even when working men have the ballot and ride in Ford cars, and when even gentlemen are conditioned by reflexes and complexes.

At the same time, Mann respects the methods and accepts the findings of scientific investigation without swallowing them whole. He embraces many perspectives, such as the Freudian and the Marxist, but he recognizes them for what they are: illuminating perspectives, not exclusive avenues to truth. He takes a genuinely organic view, perceiving that the rationale of science is a splendid means but not a sufficient end, that it must be subordinated to the emotional needs of a naturally ethical animal to whom purpose and piety are more important than fact, and that the view of man as a perfectly rational creature who can live on knowledge alone is the most oppressive of all superstitions.

This whole attitude may seem pretty vague and provisional—and necessarily it is. The humanistic tradition has never supplied specific weights and measures or elaborate blueprints for a spiritual home; to sign on the dotted line of Thomas Mann is not to achieve success within a thirty-day or even a thirty-year trial period. He himself pays the penalty of his breadth, his freedom from partisanship, his habit of doubt and humble inquiry. At times he takes almost too cool and abstracted a view of imperious problems, which cannot be dispelled by the loftiest thinking; in the interests of his Olympian pursuits he seemed for a time too willing to compromise with such temporal monstrosities as Hitlerism. At best, tolerance is a beautiful but not a dynamic virtue. It is not the way to get things done. Active measures, for better or worse, are taken care of by the zealots, the one-idea men; if too many doctors love to operate, operations are nevertheless often unavoidable. Yet Mann has not lost touch with his age, nor is his thought ever irrelevant. If there is always a need for the practical reformer, there is also a need for the man who detaches himself from the immediate present to gain perspective, to return to first principles, to grapple with final issues—to clarify meanings and establish values to which the reformer can appeal in the course of his more "practical" activity. Marxists have the habit of appropriating the "long view" for themselves; Mann's is clearly a still longer view.

The Magic Mountain is indeed not even the final solution of the problems of Thomas Mann himself. He is one of the few important writers today who continue to grow, to shoot arrows at a farther shore. He is still an inquirer, a self-questioner, and still follows the path of the middle, the path of irony. He is still wary, perhaps too wary, of anything like finality; as he wrote some years ago, "In matters of humanity every decision may prove premature." He is convinced only of the dignity of man, the worth of human aspirations and possibilities. But if he is not a witch doctor or wonder-worker, we can dispense with this one absence from the host we already have. Through both his profoundest convictions and his profoundest doubts he carries himself with absolute integrity; and if he offers no dogmatic assurances, at least he points steadily, austerely, to a way. (pp. 302-13)

> *Herbert Muller, "The Humanism of Thomas Mann,"*
> in South Atlantic Quarterly, *Vol. XXXVI, No. 3, July,*
> *1937, pp. 302-13.*

ELIZABETH E. BOHNING   (essay date 1945)

[*In the following excerpt, Bohning examines the depiction and narrative function of minor characters in* The Magic Mountain.]

The presentation of the environment, an important means of revealing character and motivating action, is conceded to be a significant aspect of a writer's novelistic technique. It is our purpose . . . to study Thomas Mann's procedure in presenting the "milieu" in his *Magic Mountain* and also to consider the minor characters which compose it.

The *Magic Mountain* is, like Goethe's *Wilhelm Meister,* a "Bildungsroman." In both novels the hero develops through the help of the persons with whom he comes in contact from an egocentric existence to useful membership in a community. Hans Castorp, who appears at the beginning of the novel as a sensitive, unsettled youth, represents at the end of his development an integrated personality who thoroughly understands the "Kunst des Schauens" ["art of seeing"]. . . . (p. 189)

The characters to offer Castorp the "grosses Erlebnis" ["great experience"] through which he develops into a mature spectator in life are Settembrini, Naphta, Clawdia Chauchat and Peeperkorn. Castorp is, to be sure, . . . simply a tractable dilettante, without special talents, a youth like Wilhelm Meister, but he is at the same time, as Kastorff emphasizes, exceptional. He is exceptionally capable of development. Only the influence of the four main characters is needed to bring about this development.

The two adversaries, Settembrini and Naphta, are responsible for the development of his reason. These two complement each other. Naphta, with his interest directed primarily towards the world to come, is the avowed enemy of Western civilization, which the Humanist Settembrini champions with complete conviction. The impressionable Castorp is buffeted to and fro between these two who have selected him as the object of their pedagogical drives.

This theoretical education through Settembrini's "plastische Redensarten" ["plastic way of speaking"] and Naphta's penetrating dialectic would surely never suffice to mold Castorp into an integrated personality, if he did not experience in addition the "bildende Kraft des Eros" ["formative power of Eros"]. For this experience he is indebted to the Kirghiz-eyed Russian woman, who is living separated from her husband and without a wedding ring. The Northern exoticism of this unconventional, licentious woman, who smiles down, superior but understanding and patient, upon his passion, enchants Castorp. . . . Hans Castorp matures emotionally through this experience in love.

The fourth character to whom a part in Castorp's education is ascribed is the regal Peeperkorn. In Walzel's opinion the latter is the most interesting figure in the *Magic Mountain.* In Peeperkorn the hero comes in contact for the first time with a vital "Persönlichkeit" ["personality"]. This great personality, acquainted with life in all its richness and abundance, needs not even to speak in order to impress others with his wealth of experience. . . . That this man offers Castorp the brotherhood, which is signified by the intimate form of address, the "du," represents symbolically how far the latter has already advanced along the path of his development. If Peeperkorn had made his acquaintance when Castorp entered the sanatorium for the first time, these fraternal bonds would have been impossible.

These four characters are the true educational factors in Castorp's life. There are, however, many other persons whose only claim to significance is the part they play as the background of his development. Instead of changing the background in agreement with the growth of the main character, as Goethe does in *Wilhelm Meister,* Mann has the tone of the background set by characters who play no rôle of any importance in the hero's development and who by and large remain unchanged themselves. (pp. 189-91)

In **Buddenbrooks** all—at least after the first generation, which is still able to preserve the "gute alte Form" ["good old form"]—are included in the same biological degeneration. In the **Magic Mountain,** on the other hand, the secondary characters do not participate in the formation of the hero's personality. Rather they are static figures, representing a static "milieu," whose constant reappearance serves the unity of the work.

Thomas Mann describes these characters in minute detail. (p. 191)

Naumann calls attention to the painful exactness of Mann's description of all that is characteristic of a person: figure, appearance, clothing, mannerisms. Every one of the countless commonplace gestures, apparently so banal, he adds, has a certain symbolic value.

Solothurn gives as an illustration of characteristic facial expressions among the "Hintergrundsgestalten" ["background figures"] the fact that Blumenkohl always looks as if he had a bad taste in his mouth, and as [an example] of the detailed description of clothes he mentions . . . the expression of Behrens' suspicious character through his clothes at Fasching: the clinic uniform in combination with a red Turkish fez.

Often conversation is used as a means of portraying the character who is either speaking or under discussion, as Petsch mentions in *Wesen und Formen*. Weigand stresses the fact that in the **Magic Mountain** the author neither presents the characters to us directly nor gives an even more or less complete account of the characteristics of each individual, as he does twenty-five years earlier in **Buddenbrooks.** We make the acquaintance of the figures in the **Magic Mountain** in an unsystematic and fragmentary way through Castorp's own reactions.

> At the first breakfast, Hans takes note of his companions in a cursory and provisional way. Five strangers are seated at the table, in addition to himself and Joachim, four women and one man. Only one name, that of Frau Stöhr, is noted. This female bears from the outset the definite stamp of crass vulgarity and ridiculous affectation. The others remain vaguely defined types, differentiated by a few general characteristics. At the second breakfast Hans Castorp's impressions of some of his table companions become somewhat more defined by the repeated perception of characteristics already noted, and his attention is focused in a certain degree on two new faces, an elderly Russian lady and, beside her, a pretty girl of striking features and manner whom he hears addressed as Marusja.

The conversation following this second breakfast might also have been cited as an example: the two cousins discuss their table companions while walking to the village, and that evening, when the group gathers again, Castorp is in a position to take careful note of everyone.

The constant recurrence of the "Leitmotiv" is typical of Mann's character delineation. In his introduction to *Tönio Kröger* Kelly says of the use of the "Leitmotiv":

> This consists in coining a phrase, usually picturesque, representative of a character or an idea and in repeating the phrase judiciously from time to time when the character appears or the idea is suggested. . . . In repeating the phrase, however, he (Mann) usually varies it slightly,

after the manner of Chopin, who quite as much for the negative purpose of avoiding hackneyed effects as to gain positively new ones, seldom repeats a passage in his piano compositions without at least introducing into it a new embellishment.

(pp. 192-93)

The following may be mentioned as examples of "Leitmotiv" in the **Magic Mountain.** The grand niece is always ladling out Yoghurt when she appears, while Anton Karlowitch Ferge, the simple man who lacks all feeling for higher things, recalls to the attention of his audience again and again the suffering caused him by the "Pleurochok." An allusion to her similarity to a wax figure constantly accompanies the ivory-complexioned Levi. Marusja, ever fond of mirth, always wears the orange kerchief and the little ruby ring on her pretty finger.

Now let us consider the "Hintergrundspersonen" ["background characters"] themselves. Weigand characterizes the clientèle of the sanatorium as "a giddy, frivolous, squirrel-brained lot, thrill-hunters and sensualists without the inhibitions that tend ordinarily to hold the appetites of the healthy in check" [see *TCLC*, Vol. 2]. In another passage he calls these people "flighty, thrill-hungry and insincere." Weigand's words remind us at once of a figure like Frau von Mallinckrodt, so fond of dress and so coquettish, "die in der Frühe mit Korallen beginnt und abends mit Perlen endet" ["who begins in the mornings with coral and ends in the evenings with pearls"], or perhaps of the incurable Mr. Albin and his morbid joy in playing with murderous weapons. The latter horrifies all the women by his implication that he will soon liberate himself by an act of suicide from his unbearable condition, but he continues to eat his chocolate, smoke and laugh calmly at everything, like the pupil who already knows that he will not be promoted and therefore no longer feels inclined to exert himself. Weigand's "diseased thrill-hunger" is perhaps best exemplified in little Ellen Brand's passionate interest in the supernatural.

It may seem at first astonishing that the same adjectives may be applied to so large a group. We might expect individual characteristics in each of the various persons. But we must bear in mind that the disease from which all are suffering has to a certain extent a leveling effect, and that furthermore the prerequisite for membership in this group is a considerable fortune. Castorp's first bill convinces the reader that the Berghof sanatorium is exclusively for the moneyed "bourgeoisie." The patients in Davos all belong, after all, to the same stratum of society, a fact which also tends to make them similar.

There are to be sure a few exceptions to whom we should be doing an injustice if we applied Weigand's adjectives to them: if we called the women "frivolous," "vain," "distracted" and "coquettish," and if we, in regard to the men, emphasized simply "the absurd clinging to the banal business interests of the world about to be left behind." Karen Karstedt, the little girl who is so grateful for the brief change offered her by Hans Castorp and Joachim Ziemssen, must be mentioned as one of these exceptions. We should not forget, however, that there exists a financial difference between her and the others. The prosaic, sober and tactless Alfreda Schildknecht and the dull Miss Robinson are hardly to be described as "giddy," and the modest, uncommunicative Dr. Blumenkohl, with the worried expression, has no longer any interest whatsoever in the business affairs of the "Flachland" ["flatland"]. But despite these exceptions Weigand's description of the patients in Berghof is strikingly accurate.

Sickness seems to be "eine Form der Liederlichkeit" ["a form of dissoluteness"] among these people. Weigand suggests that Pópow's madness is to be interpreted as a flight from responsibility. . . . (pp. 194-95)

Of the "Verinnerlichung" ["spiritualization"] often associated with sickness, as in the case of Goethe's Fräulein von Klettenberg, we find hardly a trace among the characters who form the background in the *Magic Mountain.* In the small world of the sanatorium, where necessarily many of the opportunities for activity and sublimation offered in normal life are eliminated, all emotions mount to a maximum. Therefore there is a constantly feverish atmosphere at Davos. . . .

This tremendous excess of all animal passions gives the impression of a caricaturing of the "Hintergrundsgestalten." The tantrum of Weidemann and Sonnenschein is perhaps the most pertinent example. Weidemann's lurking, furtive gaze is his most striking external characteristic, and the stress upon his malicious leer gives us an insight into the soul of this anti-Semitic fanatic. . . .

In the merchant Sonnenschein the disease has produced a pathological sensitivity, and one fine day these two men, Weidemann and Sonnenschein, are found in a scuffle, just as if they were two small boys. . . . (p. 196)

A tendency to fits of temper is likewise apparent in the Czech, known simply as Wenzel because of his unpronounceable name, and in the brewer from Halle, Mr. Magnus,—these two, who for reasons political and otherwise, "feindlich zusammenstossen" ["clash antagonistically"].

An atmosphere of melancholy surrounds the Magnus couple, the talkative husband and the stupid wife. This pathological melancholy appears in Marjorin Gerngross in the form of an exaggerated feeling of guilt. The Mexican lady falls prey to this same sadness: dressed in black and with a pallid, sorrowful face, she wanders restlessly about, until her sole expression ["*Tous les deux*" ("both of them")], gradually becomes her nickname.

Erotic feelings mount to excess in the *Magic Mountain.* The first "Hintergrundspersonen" to appear seem to set the tone in this regard. Their sensuality reaches the bestial. Such an exaggeration of the voluptuous is especially evident in Wehsal: this otherwise humble, self-effacing creature loses every trace of composure as he describes the suffering caused him by his unbridled yearning for Clawdia Chauchat.

We are told again and again of the ample meals in the sanatorium and of the colossal voracity of the patients, a gluttony which seems to be a phenomenon concomitant with their disease. Mr. Wenzel is an example of this. Greediness has long been a favorite subject of caricature.

Love of gossip is another trait which plays an important rôle in caricature. The offensive babble of the coarse, ill-bred Mrs. Stöhr is an illustration which recurs throughout the novel.

Many of the characters of the background, as for instance the former public prosecutor Paravant, have an "idée fixe" about which their whole life revolves. Paravant's enthusiasm is devoted to a complicated mathematical problem: he works incessantly to discover the secret of the circle. The young lady from Siebenbürgen seeks to direct the interest of the whole sanatorium to her brother-in-law, a stranger to everyone in

Davos, and an Austrian sculptor has devised an—in his opinion—epoch-making plan of a financial-political nature. Others study Esperanto, while several Englishmen enthusiastically play a completely nonsensical game, which consists simply in the repetition of this question and answer: "Did you ever see the devil with a night-cap on?" "No, I never saw the devil with a night-cap on."

In the last analysis Weigand seems to be justified in calling these people a "squirrel-brained lot of sensualists and thrill-hunters."

There is present another group in Haus Berghof, not subjected to the levelling effects of disease and financial security, namely the doctors and the nurse. Mann has, however, not permitted the feverishness of the atmosphere to be interrupted by these characters: they all somehow fit into the atmosphere he has created. The same exaggeration which we find stressed in the patients is likewise strikingly evident in the staff. The prim, careless nurse with her somewhat pert manner of speaking has something mechanical about her. She is part of this world of caricatures. From the very beginning Mann's treatment of the self-centered Krokowski imparts a vague foreboding to the reader that the constant preoccupation of the psychoanalyst with his interpretation of disease as a result of unsatisfied love is closely connected with a hope for personal advantage. Krokowski gives the impression of being, even if not physically ill, at least psychically unhealthy. Lack of balance is perhaps most striking in the most congenial of the staff members, in Behrens. There is something unhealthy even in the latter's appearance. His blood-shot eyes are a veritable "Leitmotiv." His cheeks are constantly blue, and, to judge by his appearance, his temperature is always slightly above normal. Even in his hearty, good-natured speech there is a strange exaltation which also serves to convince us of his constant feverishness. After the death of his wife he is said to have developed many surprising habits and mannerisms. Her grave binds him to Davos. "War er gesund und unzweideutig gesonnen, die Leute gesund zu machen, damit sie recht bald ins Flachland zurückkehren und Dienst tun könnten?" ["Was he healthily and unequivocally disposed to curing people so that they could return right away to the flatland and serve?"] Castorp asks himself, as he realizes how impossible it is for him to regard the doctor with child-like confidence, regardless of how great his need for fatherly authority may be. In Behrens, as in so many of the patients, a definite propensity to attacks of melancholy is noticeable, and his control of sudden anger is hardly superior to that of the invalids themselves. The doctors and the nurse are all fundamentally diseased. None of them is the embodiment of "Vollmenschentum" ["full humanity"] as is Mynheer Peeperkorn.

Although all the background characters are well-to-do sick people, Thomas Mann has nevertheless made an effort to preserve certain differences within the group. Various classifications would be possible, for instance according to sex, age, profession and nationality, according to the length of their part in the novel, the degree of their affliction, or—what is of particular interest—their relationship to Hans Castorp.

Nearly all possible types of the diseased rich "Bourgeoisie" are represented in Berghof. While they are, generally speaking, fairly young, still we can find a few representatives, both among the men and among the women, of various age groups. Among the children we might mention the wealthy, elegant little Teddy and the charming, golden-haired girl, Leila Gerngross. These children are not permitted to grow up: the background remains static. Only at her deathbed do we make the acquaintance of little Leila. Teddy, to be sure, appears a second time, and we discover suddenly that he is no longer a child. The ladies no longer hold him on their laps; rather the relationship is now reversed. . . . But Teddy is not intended to develop into manhood, and he dies in his twenty-first year. The twenty-year-old Mr. Rotwein, an active, business-like young man, introduced to us just before his death, and the nineteen-year-old Elly Brand, the gentle, flaxen-haired girl with the uncanny ability to lift the veil from the world of the supernatural, are representatives of youth. In middle age we find, for example, Mr. and Mrs. Magnus. Their malady, however, does not allow these people to become old. There are, therefore no really aged members of the group.

Although not many professions are open to women of this stratum of society, there is considerable variation in the pursuits of the men of Davos. The women, who are not, like Miss Engelhart, teachers, are for the most part married. Many—and here we cannot help but think of Frau von Mallinckrodt—have, however, not permitted themselves to be bound very tightly by the bonds of matrimony. Elly Brand has been employed in a provincial affiliate of a large bank. Among the men we find, to mention only a few examples, a lawyer, a teacher, several merchants, a manufacturer, the owner of a sugar beet plantation, a brewer, and a travelling salesman in the service of a fire insurance company. Most of the patients have belonged to the business world. Intellectual achievements are rare, and a laborer would be out of the question in this society.

There is a greater possibility of diversity in the nationalities of the inmates. Quite justifiably the adjective "international" appears on the door-plate of the sanatorium. The Orient is represented by Dr. Ting-Fu. There is also an Egyptian princess in Berghof. Peeperkorn himself, who to be sure does not belong to the "Hintergrund," is a colonial Dutchman, the owner of a coffee plantation in Java, and not to be overlooked is the Italian, Settembrini, although he is likewise a "Hauptperson zweiten Ranges" ["main character of the second rank"]. There are understandably many Germans and Austrians and also numerous Russians and Englishmen. Denmark, Mexico, Bohemia, and other lands as well have their representatives in Davos. We must bear in mind of course that all these invalids are sufficiently affluent for considerable travelling about, so that we are hardly justified in regarding any one of them as belonging to one single country. All in all, we meet a thoroughly cosmopolitan group in the *Magic Mountain.* The greatest diversity among these people is geographical, for their home is not, as is to a certain extent their age, limited by their affliction, nor does it, like their profession, depend upon their income.

As already indicated, another grouping of these characters is possible, namely according to the length of their rôle in the novel. A few appear only once like fleeting shadows. Many of the "moribundi" belong to this category. Leila Gerngross and Mrs. Zimmermann may serve as examples. In the works of other authors the background frequently is made up of these meteor-like characters, as for instance the peasant in Eichendorff's *Taugenichts,* but in the *Magic Mountain* there are on the other hand many more who recur again and again throughout the entire book. Mrs. Stöhr and Mr. Albin are important members of this latter group. There is, however, of course no question of a development in their character or personality. Alfreda Schildknecht and the Russian couple are examples of those who play their rôle in the first part of the book and then

disappear. Ellen Brand and Paravant belong on the other hand exclusively to the end of the book. A few figures, like Teddy or the Mexican lady, are used by the author almost as connecting links. We encounter them in the early chapters of the book, and then they are lost for awhile, only to reappear suddenly towards the close.

Extreme care is everywhere evident in Mann's portrayal of the "nuances" of the disease. There are the "moribundi," like Frau von Mallinckrodt, the members of the "Half Lung Club," like Hermine Kleefeld, and those unfortunates, who are losing vital products of metabolism, like the brewer and his wife. For others, like Marusja, there is no immediate danger; they can, however, never return to the Plains in a healthy condition. The patients look down in a superior way upon those among their companions who are suffering from only light cases and who, like Miss Robinson, are discharged as cured before the end of the book.

It is interesting to note at what point in Castorp's development the various figures appear. Upon his arrival at Berghof he comes in contact with characters like Miss Engelhart, with her correct grammar and her voluptuous talk, like Miss Robinson, to whom life's ecstatic moments are so completely foreign, or like the Russian couple.

Castorp's "Sympathie mit dem Tode" ["sympathy with death"] is the fundamental reason for his subsequent enthusiasm in visiting the dying. He has begun to be aware of his love, and he has undergone the influence of the pedagogical Settembrini. In this state he makes the acquaintance of the "moribundi."

Ferge and Wehsal do not appear until his development is nearly complete. His intellectual and his emotional education lies behind him, and he is facing the great formative experience offered him by Peeperkorn; he is ready to absorb certain elements of this great personality.

An important function of the "Hintergrundsgestalten" consists in the mirroring of the main characters. The similarity between Marusja and Clawdia, for instance, is most striking where the two Russian ladies, both of whom are described as having a somewhat girlish appearance, sit together and laugh in the car. Marusja reflects Clawdia on a lower plane; she lacks Clawdia's knowledge of life in all its fullness.

A parallel relationship exists between Joachim and Hans. The author's purpose in introducing Joachim and the grandfather is to round out the character of Hans Castorp. The extraction of Hans and Joachim is the same, and in both young men the same restraint is apparent, a restraint inherent in their family, which is particularly striking in the bashful, well-bred James Tienappel. These people come from a "geschlossene Kultur" ["closed culture"]. The difference between Joachim and Hans consists in the fact that the former is incapable of overcoming this hereditary shyness, as Hans does. Joachim follows the path of least resistance, while Hans experiences almost a second birth in the sanatorium. It is significant that Joachim, silent to the last, is inclined toward a sweet and simple girl, while Hans loves a woman familiar with life in all its abundance. Typical of Thomas Mann's literary technique is this shading: a characteristic reappears over and over again, but always in a different degree.

To sum up, the background of Castorp's progress towards mature contemplation of life is a static one, determined by static characters. Mann presents these characters by means of the most minutely detailed descriptions and the lavish use of

"Leitmotiv." He caricatures them through the tremendous exaggeration of their passions, in this way emphasizing the hysteria of the atmosphere in which the development of the hero takes place. Although both the physical and the financial condition of these people exerts a levelling influence upon them, we find nevertheless extraordinary "nuances." This fine shading is evidence of the truth of Mann's own words: "Im Handumdrehen also wird der Erzähler mit Hansens Geschichte nicht fertig werden. Die sieben Tage einer Woche werden dazu nicht reichen und auch seiben Monate nicht" ["Not all in a minute, then, will the narrator be finished with the story of our Hans. The seven days of a week will not suffice, no, nor seven months either" (Translation by H. T. Lowe-Porter)]. (pp. 197-202)

Elizabeth E. Bohning, "The 'Hintergrundsgestalten' in the 'Magic Mountain'," in The German Quarterly, Vol. XVIII, No. 4, November, 1945, pp. 189-202.

H. STEFAN SCHULTZ (essay date 1954)

[*In the following excerpt, Schultz examines how Mann's symbolic depiction in* The Magic Mountain *of the intellectual temper of Europe before World War I was influenced by Friedrich Nietzsche's writings on nihilism.*]

As a consequence of the struggle between East and West, it has almost become fashionable to interpret Thomas Mann's **The Magic Mountain** as a historical document portraying the clash of political and social ideologies. Depending on the critic's point of view, the novel is taken either as a positive declaration of the author's conversion to democracy or as Mann's warning of the decadence into which the bourgeois world of the West was sinking.

According to the first viewpoint, the novel is "undoubtedly . . . the signal document of Mann's struggle for the re-orientation of his nation in the democratic spirit. . . . This book, if any, is the preeminent literary testament of the Weimar Republic." Mann himself gave credence to such an interpretation when he said in his 1950 speech at the University of Chicago, that The **Magic Mountain** "embraced . . . the entire Western politico-moral dialectic," that "politics had become dominant," and that "two antagonists were locked in struggle, in pedagogic dispute over . . . the soul of the West." (p. 110)

Hermann J. Weigand . . . understood the novel as a twentieth-century *comédie humaine* of the decade before the first World War. For he wrote: "Thus the *clientèle* of Haus Berghof—this motley international group drawn from the middle and upper strata of society, all of them stamped with the mark of disease—is readily felt as a symbol representing pre-war Europe. The analysis of the prevailing mental attitude, flighty, frivolous, thrill-hungry, and insincere, becomes a searching indictment of Western civilization, and the **Zauberberg** thereby reveals itself as a *Zeitroman* ["time novel"], in that it strives to express the psychic temper of a whole age" [see *TCLC*, Vol. 2].

I have never been convinced of the soundness of Professor Weigand's assertion. For, to begin with, the "mark of disease" has always been, in Thomas Mann's thinking, a badge of intelligence; the stupid may be healthy, but it takes a special mind to be struck by disease. Furthermore, the indictment of Western civilization as "flighty, frivolous, thrill-hungry, and insincere" is not to be found in the novel. To be sure, the prevailing mental attitude, or, rather, "attitudes," in the novel are described with irony and humor, but we should not overlook the deadly and sometimes pathetic seriousness of the charac-

ters. Not one of Professor Weigand's epithets would fit Hans Castorp or Joachim, Behrens or Krokowski, Settembrini or Naphta, Peeperkorn or Madame Chauchat. Perhaps the philistine, with his average morality, would call the hero's intellectual adventures and moral experiments in immorality "frivolous"; but the sympathetic reader, while being amused, would have to grant that *placet experiri* ["it's worth a try"] is serious business.

Consequently, it seems necessary to abandon the simple theory of the **Zauberberg** as an indictment of Western civilization and to interpret the *Zeit* of the *Zeitroman* less literally than has been the custom. Possibly, this time is as far removed from the actual date of events (1907-14) as the locality of the Mountain of Venus is removed from the ordinary flatlands in which Western society was and is still living. Slyly and with tongue in check, Mann himself has hinted at such a possibility in the "Vorsatz" ["preface"] to his novel: "This story happened long long ago; it is, so to speak, already covered with the noble patina of history and must perforce be narrated in the tense of the deepest past." Admittedly, this quality of being long past is, in the author's words, the result of the fact that all the events took place before the deep chasm that the first World War opened in Western life and consciousness. Yet the character of the novel has something of the fairy tale; Mann himself remarked: "Furthermore, it might be possible that our story, by its inner nature, has something or other to do with the fairy tale."

We are here not concerned with the element of the fairy tale in the novel but shall look at those instances in which the "times" are analyzed. At a crucial point in the story, the mood of the "present time" is used in order to prove that Hans Castorp was "mediocre, although in a very honorable sense." A man, we are told, lives not only his personal life but also, whether consciously or unconsciously, the life of his epoch and his contemporaries. Hence the deficiencies of the times may well have a disturbing effect on the moral well-being of a person. So it was with Hans Castorp, whose passive character the author traces back not to personal traits but to the impersonal (*unpersönlich*) temper of the times. Although these times were outwardly busy, they were actually bare of hopes and prospects; they were hopeless and helpless; they opposed nothing but a hollow silence to the eternal question of a final, suprapersonal, and absolute meaning for all activity and exertion. These times had no satisfactory answer to the question of "What for?"

Later in the novel, before the distemper of the times culminates in the outbreak of the war, we are once more informed of the difficulty of differentiating Hans Castorp's case from the general case: Everything, the whole world, had arrived at a dead end; there was something uncanny about life and the world; in a special and increasing way, things were awry and alarming; a demon had taken over, which for a long time had already exercised considerable influence; its name was *Stumpfsinn* ["dullness"]:

> The reader will accuse the writer of laying it on pretty thick and in a romantic fashion when he connects the name of "staleness" or "dullness" with the demonic and ascribes to it the effect of mystical terror. . . . Hans Castorp looked about him. . . . He saw on every side the uncanny and the malign and he knew what it was he saw: life without time; life without care or hope; life as a busy and slovenly stagnation;

dead life. Busy-ness was there, activities of all kinds took place simultaneously.

But, in spite of this "busy-ness," Hans Castorp's innermost being was horribly touched by the uncanny state of a world awry, by the grin of the demon and monkey-god whose apocalyptic name was "Der grosse Stumpfsinn" ["the great stupor"]. He felt that a catastrophe would be the end, a rebellion of patient nature, a thunderstorm and a cleansing hurricane.

What epoch's psychic temper can be accurately described by such language? Certainly not the years after the turn of the century, which, according to the prevalent opinion, were supposed to usher in a new era. The words in *The Magic Mountain* remind us, rather, of negative attitudes toward the *fin de siècle* expressed, for instance, in Albert Jay Nock's surly *Memoirs of a Superfluous Man* or in the works of Nock's admired predecessor, Max Nordau. The latter wrote in his *Entartung:*

> The mood of the times is strangely confused, a mixture of febrile restlessness and dull discouragement, of fear of the future and a resigned cynicism. The prevailing feeling is one of going-down and being extinguished. *Fin-de-siècle* is at once a confession and a dirge.... In our days there arises in the more highly developed minds a dark foreboding of a dusk of nations when all the suns and stars are gradually extinguished, and mankind with all its institutions and creations vanishes in the midst of a dying nature.

Albert Jay Nock quoted this passage freely from the English edition of Nordau's work and supplemented it with Aratov's dream from Turgenev's novel *Clara Militch* (1883). Similarly, Nock's countryman, Ralph Adams Cram, spoke of the present condition of this happy world as of one very like the Puritan idea of hell; but he found "the preserving factor if not the original cause of this pleasant state of affairs" in the modern theory of economics and its resulting industrial and commercial systems.

Some aspects of the *Zeitstimmung* ["mood of the times"] as described by Nordau, Nock, or Cram certainly agree with the picture we find in *The Magic Mountain:* in Mann's account of *Der grosse Stumpfsinn*, too, is the curious confusion of feverish restlessness and blunted discouragement in all the busy fads and fanatic hobbies to which the inhabitants of Haus Berghof dedicate themselves, from amateur photography to stamp-collecting, from the munching of chocolate to the drawing of pigs with eyes closed, from the squaring of the circle to plans for an economic golden age through the collection of old newspapers, from stupid social games to the playing of solitaire. In all these activities we find "the uncanny air of futility and even a sort of sinister imbecility." But, in spite of this agreement, there is no indication that the author of *The Magic Mountain* believed, like the writers quoted, that the dusk of nations was the result either of a capitalistic economic system or of the spirit of materialism or of "degeneration." On the contrary, the economic system of a capitalist leisure class is the very foundation on which life in the sanitarium rests. Although a moralist like Settembrini might call such life loose and idle, Hans Castorp felt that nothing could be clearer than his own presentation of the matter: "A young man of his social class and in his circumstances did something for himself, when it seemed advisable; he made use of the comforts which had expressly been prepared for him and his like. So it was only

fitting. . . . At the end [of his letter] he asked that the necessary monetary means be supplied regularly; eight hundred marks per month would cover everything."

Thomas Mann's analysis of the spirit of the times in *The Magic Mountain* has, therefore, nothing to do with theories of degeneration advanced by Nordau and similar prophets of doom. Mann, unlike Nordau, is not a disciple of Herbert Spencer's positivism. He has never seen in "Verfall" ["decay"] an unmitigated evil, nor has he found the reason for the insufficiency of the times either in *fin de race* or in the "decay of the rich inhabitants of the great cities and the leading classes." He belongs to European decadence in a different and more intellectual sense. He has remarked of himself:

> Intellectually I belong to that generation of writers that is spread all over Europe. They stem from *décadence,* they have been called to be the chroniclers and analysts of *décadence,* and carry at the same time in their hearts the will to emancipate themselves from it and to renounce it. Or let us put it pessimistically: they carry in their hearts the stray impulse to renounce it and would like at least to experiment with the conquest of decadence and nihilism.

The foremost German—and, we may add, European—"chronicler" and analyst of decadence and nihilism was Friedrich Nietzsche. And Nietzsche had said before Thomas Mann that a philosopher wishes, above all other things, to overcome him-

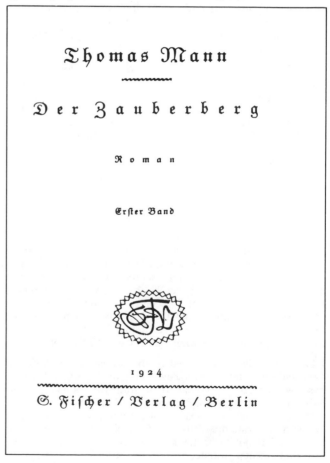

Title page of the first edition of The Magic Mountain. *Courtesy of S. Fischer Verlag.*

self but that his hardest struggle is that with the very things in which he is a child of his time, "to wit, a *décadent*." It is well known that Nietzsche, along with Schopenhauer and Wagner, was one of the three guiding stars on Mann's intellectual path. But some critics think that Mann, by the time of writing *The Magic Mountain,* had conclusively vanquished the worlds of Nietzsche and Schopenhauer. In contrast to such views, it can, I believe, be shown that, in one aspect at least, *The Magic Mountain* faithfully preserves the Nietzschean mood. If we trust Mann's own statement that the novel is "a *Riesensuppe* basically removed from reality," we ought not to look for its "times" in any reality of politics or economics but in the intellectual vision which Nietzsche had proclaimed in aphoristic prose. For the description of the mental atmosphere of the times in *The Magic Mountain* seems to be nothing but the artist's version of that phenomenon which Nietzsche had named "European nihilism" in the title of the first book of *The Will to Power.*

The close connection between *The Magic Mountain* and Nietzsche is, however, not so apparent as Mann's relation to his "sources" in some other works. Notably in *The Beloved Returns* and also to some degree in *Dr. Faustus,* direct quotations, even when not marked as such, point immediately to the method by which the novels were "com-posed." But it is different with *The Magic Mountain.* For Mann has lived so long and intimately in Nietzsche's climate that we ought not to speak of Nietzsche's "influence" but rather of an elective affinity or "secret magnetism" by which the pupil, with surprise perhaps and delight, discovered in his predecessor ideas which were also his own.

That Nietzschean ideas figure in *The Magic Mountain* was first suggested by Bernhard Blume. . . . Professor Blume mentioned Mann's quoting Dostoevski as a prophet of an impending European catastrophe and remarked that Mann, with greater right, might have called upon his teacher Nietzsche, "the first one to describe the threatening danger of a general European intellectual collapse." Professor Blume's insight was correct, but an explicit reference to Nietzsche on the part of Thomas Mann was unnecessary, since Nietzsche's words were actually paraphrased in the passage. For, according to Nietzsche, nihilism is a psychological state in which man becomes conscious of the lack of a goal; he receives no answer to the questions "Why?" or "What for?"; he feels all happenings to be without meaning; he is tortured by the "In vain"; he is disappointed and feels the modern world to be useless. Furthermore, we suffer because of the very time into which we have been thrown; our nihilism is a pathological state, pathological because of our tremendous generalization that comes to the conclusion of the utter meaninglessness of all things. This is exactly the mood or, stated objectively, the "time" which causes Hans Castorp's suffering. Nietzsche mentions especially the younger generation that suffers from the times as from a severe illness. According to him, the falling-apart, that is to say, the uncertainty, is the characteristic quality of this time: nothing stands any longer on firm feet. Here one is forced to think of the conclusion of Mann's chapter "The Dance of Death"; the dead in the mountain cemetery are usually twenty years of age, or little more; almost exclusively youth populated the spot; unsure folk had at last turned to the horizontal position of existence.

While it is obvious that Mann has always been convinced of the productive powers of illness and that he did not need a Nietzsche in order to write a novel centered in a sanitarium, it may not be quite accidental that our "joli bourgeois à la petite tache humide" ["pretty bourgeois with the little moist

spot"] lives as a sick man among other sick. For Nietzsche considered physiological decadence one of the causes of nihilism and remarked that the decadent "selects, while believing that he is choosing a curative, the very thing which hastens the exhaustion." This is what Hans Castorp does.

Thomas Mann does not always evaluate a phenomenon in the same way in which Nietzsche judges its worth. Nietzsche, for instance, thinks that a characteristic element in *décadence* is the fact that an individual's powers of resistance against stimuli are weakened; one result of this is an altruistic morality, which speaks constantly of sympathy; the personality is weakened to such an extent that it trembles continuously like an overexcited chord and, with extreme irritability, vibrates in consonance with other vibrations. Mann exemplified this sympathetic altruism by Hans Castorp's visits to the moribund patients but called Castorp's action a "protest against the ruling egotism," while Nietzsche considered this altruism a deceptive kind of egotism, viz., sentimental egotism.

The hero's charitable endeavors belong, of course, to the sphere of *placet experiri,* that often repeated and, at times, flippant phrase with which Hans Castorp defends actions which could in no way be condoned by a more responsible and rational pedagogue like Settembrini, who might well have quoted Nietzsche's dictum: "If this is not an epoch of decay and of decreasing vitality, it is at least an epoch of thoughtless and undisciplined experimenting." Nietzsche linked the will to experiment, to "attempt," and therewith to "tempt" to other characteristics of European nihilism, such as an infinite increase in sensitivity reacting to a multitude of disparate impressions; a cosmopolitanism of foods, literature, newspapers, forms, tastes, and even landscapes. Man adapts himself to this overabundance of impressions, he unlearns to act and instead merely reacts to stimuli from the outside. He spends his energy partly in the appropriation of impressions, partly in the defense against impressions, and partly in responding to impressions. He artificially makes his own nature a "mirror"; he is "interested," but, so to speak, interested only with his "epidermis." On the surface there are warmth and movement; below this thin surface are a basic coolness and a permanent low temperature. There is a contrast between external mobility and a certain inner heaviness and tiredness.

It seems as though Nietzsche had furnished in these remarks an outline for *The Magic Mountain*—Haus Berghof gives the cosmopolitan setting. The "problem child of life" is like a mirror collecting impressions from all sides: Behrens and Krokowski present scientific experiences, Settembrini and Naphta provide ethicophilosophical experiences, Madame Chauchat and Peeperkorn introduce the hero to "vitalistic" experiences. Hans Castorp reacts to all of them intelligently partly by learning and thus appropriating, partly by defending himself; if things go too far, he is even able to say "Enough of this," as in the chapter "Fragwürdigstes." Sometimes he merely "responds," as in the discussions with Settembrini and Naphta. But Castorp's interest is literally skin deep; witness the amusing discussion of the epidermis in the chapter "Humaniora," first the epidermis of cigars and then the epidermis of Madame Chauchat. The hero's temperature, too, indicates no more than a superficial disturbance of his health. Representative of a deep heaviness and tiredness is Hofrath Behrens, who is frequently seized by melancholy and has to lie down on his sofa.

In addition, Mann seems to have incorporated in the novel Nietzsche's "oversupply of intellectual traffikers and middlemen," those "in-between-persons" belonging partly to the natural sciences and partly to philosophy or being semitheologians. What Nietzsche, however, had meant as a stricture and a characteristic fault of the age becomes in the novel a strength and a means to heighten the intellectual interest. Castorp's deliberations about the origin of matter and of life, for instance, are none the worse for their skilful blend of science and theology.

In Nietzsche's view, nihilism is of two kinds: an active nihilism and a passive nihilism. The former is the result of heightened intellectual powers, it has gone beyond the ordinary morality, it is a pessimism of strength through the energy of its logic. The latter is of Hamlet's kind and shows itself in an extreme self-consciousness and in an inability to act; it understands everything and parades as "la largeur de sympathie" ["expansive sympathy"] willing to forgive everything, while it actually consists of equal parts of indifference, curiosity, and pathological sensitivity. Both kinds, however, stem from the same root, namely, modern man's will to truth: we do not rest until we have analyzed everything and seen through it. Nietzsche's disjointed passages, in which he speaks alternately of pessimism, anarchism, nihilism, or "analytics" and their advantages and disadvantages, have been reduced to one clear statement in *The Magic Mountain* when Settembrini warns Castorp:

> Analysis as an instrument of enlightenment and civilization is good, in so far as it shatters absurd convictions, dissolves natural prejudices, and undermines authority; good in other words, in that it sets free, refines, humanizes, and makes slaves ripe for freedom. But analysis is bad, very bad, in so far as it impedes action and is incapable of shaping life, but maims it at its roots.

There remains one more problem of major importance for both *The Magic Mountain* and for Nietzsche, namely, the problem of "the Romantic." Nietzsche's pessimism of weakness and of weariness also goes under the name of "Romantic pessimism," in contrast to the "Classic pessimism" of strength. Generally, for Nietzsche, the Romantic movement means a manifestation of nihilism in the realm of art and not romanticism only, but also the anti-Romantic attitude which dislikes Romantic ideals and lies. For Nietzsche believes that antiromanticism, while being more moral on account of its greater sense for truthfulness, is still pessimistic and hence nihilistic. He remarks that this aesthetic pessimism, be it Romantic or anti-Romantic, expresses itself in the form of "l'art pour l'art" ["art for art's sake"]; it is an art which is satisfied with "description" and indifferent to content, an art of Romanticists who have lost their faith and now would like at least to see how everything goes and works. It is scarcely necessary to cite *Tonio Kröger* as one of Mann's works in which this "philosophy of disappointment" has been molded into a literary work of art.

In *The Magic Mountain* the Romantic mood and attitude are introduced toward the end of the novel, its culmination, so to speak, and the author's final word. Among Castorp's five favorite records is Schubert's "Lindenbaum," "a song for the people and a masterpiece as well," something German in a special and exemplary fashion, a song marked by a peculiar spiritual stamp which reflected a whole world. Mann goes to great lengths to tell his readers what a "ticklish undertaking" it is to explain the meaning of this last musical piece for Hans Castorp, and says at last:

> Let us put it this way: A conception which is of the spirit and hence meaningful is "meaningful" by the very fact that it points beyond itself, that it is the expression and the exponent of a more general spirit, a whole world of feeling and sentiment, which has found its more or less perfect symbolic expression in the particular creation. . . . Furthermore, the love for such a creation is in itself also "meaningful." It tells us something of the person who cherishes it; it characterizes his relationship to that larger world for which the particular creation stands, which world he loves, consciously or unconsciously, in that creation itself.

In Mann's account, Castorp is quite conscious of the love for that—as yet unnamed—world for which the "Lindenbaum" stands and for the whole realm of sentiment and the intellectual attitude which are concentrated in the song in such a heartfelt and mystical fashion. At the same time, he is aware that his conscience ought to question the propriety of this love; he ought to have misgivings and doubts about the enchanting song and the world whence it stemmed. For the world of this forbidden love was death, and a love and passion for this world was nothing less than sympathy with death. Castorp remembers Settembrini's warnings about "spiritual backsliding," a symptom of disease, just as the intellectual epoch to which one "backslid" would appear "diseased" to any responsible pedagogue.

What was that intellectual epoch? Thomas Mann does not have to tell, because every German schoolboy knew that Goethe had called the Romantic attitude "diseased" and the Classic attitude "healthy." Instead of naming the Romantic epoch, Mann presents the following analysis of the nostalgic lay and of the mental sphere to which it belonged:

> This was a fruit, fresh and splendidly healthy at one instant or barely so, yet in an extraordinary manner prone to decay and rottenness. The purest refreshment of the mind when enjoyed at the right moment, yet at the next and wrong moment spreading corruption and disaster among a mankind that ate of it. It was a fruit of life, conceived of death and pregnant with death. It was a miracle of the soul—perhaps the greatest in the eyes of beauty that lacks a conscience. It was blessed by beauty, but was, on good grounds, to be viewed with mistrust by the eyes of responsible friendship for life and of love for the organic. It was at the final verdict of conscience a subject for self-conquest.

> Yes, self-conquest, that might well be the essence of the conquest of this love—this magic enchanter of the soul with sinister consequences! . . . Ah, how powerful was this enchanter of the soul! We were all its sons and in its service could achieve mighty things on earth. One need have no more genius, only much more talent than the author of the *Lindenbaum* to be an artist of soul-enchantment and to give the song a gigantic magnitude by which it should subjugate the world. Quite possibly even kingdoms might be founded upon it, earthly, all-too-earthly kingdoms, very robust

and "progressive" and not at all nostalgic—in which the song degenerated to a piece played on an electric gramophone. But its best son might still be he who consumed his life in self-conquest and died, on his lips the new word of love which he did not yet know how to pronounce. It was worth dying for it, the magic song! But whoever died for it, died fundamentally no longer for it and was a hero only because basically he died for something new, in his heart the new word of love and of the future.

This is the song that Castorp sings with gasping breath when we meet him again on the field of battle. The chances are that he will die. Will he die for the nostalgic lay and hence basically no longer for it? What are the new world and the new word of love and of the future? We cannot tell. But it is quite clear which intellectual epoch is symbolized by the song of *Heimweh* ["homesickness"] and of death. It is the "Romantic" nineteenth century, which, Mann said in 1933, was characterized by pessimism and musical sympathy with death. If there is any doubt about this identification, one has only to read Mann's Nietzsche speech of 1924. Probably on October 15 of that year, the eightieth return of Nietzsche's birth was commemorated in Munich through a musical celebration; Mann had been asked to say a few words. He repeated—or, better, anticipated—almost verbatim the words about the "Lindenbaum" which were to be published in *The Magic Mountain*. But the subject of his talk was no longer Hans Castorp's "holdes Heimwehlied" ["sweet song of homesickness"], it was "das Romantische" ["the Romantic"]. Verb tenses have been changed from the present to the past; the reference to the author of the "Lindenbaum" is, of course, omitted; the phrase about the degeneration to gramophone music is marked as a quotation by the insertion of "if I may say so." The conclusion has been so altered that it fits Nietzsche and expresses Mann's love for him: "But its [i.e., romanticism's] best son may still be he who, for all of us, consumed his life in the conquest of it and died, on his lips the new word of love that he scarcely yet knew how to speak, that even we scarcely know how to stammer, the prophetic word of friendship for life and of the future."

When these words were spoken, the text of *The Magic Mountain* must have been already at the printers'. Hans Castorp, mediocre in a thoroughly honorable sense, but not unintelligent, would probably have been slyly amused, had he discovered that his conscientious qualms about the fruits of romanticism were weighty enough to be associated with a mind like Nietzsche's. For Mann said in the Nietzsche speech, with unmistakable reference to Castorp's "governmental" problems:

> Whence the prophetic pedagogic doubts of conscience and of responsible government that gave to his [i.e., Nietzsche's] love of music the stings of doubt and of the problematic?—They stemmed from the fact that he—in a truly German fashion—almost equated music with Romanticism. It was his fate and his heroic calling to stand the test of this mighty complex of the highest magic of the soul, the Musical-Romantic or the Romantic-Musical—and, thereby, almost the test of that which is *German*. His heroism, however, was self-conquest.

Nietzsche, like Wagner, is, for Mann, a late son of romanticism, but, unlike Wagner, he was a revolutionary self-con-

queror. Mann considered him in 1924 "a friend of life, a seer of a higher humanity, a leader into the future, a teacher of the conquest of all that in us which stands in the way of life and of the future, to wit the Romantic." By 1947, Nietzsche reappeared as Adrian Leverkühn in *Dr. Faustus*. He had become a musician and was no longer a comparatively harmless Romantic or a conqueror of the Romantic mood. In a sense, he had returned to what he was in his life: a truly tragic figure and, through his very striving, bound to the devil. (pp. 112-21)

Nietzsche in the mask of Hans Castorp and Nietzsche in the mask of Adrian Leverkühn correspond to the picture that Mann had of the German during 1914-18 and during 1939-45: while "das Bürgerliche" ["the bourgeois"] was characteristic of Germany during the earlier period, "das Teuflische" ["the diabolical"] had become predominant during the times of Adolf Hitler. In each case, Mann was inclined to equate the great complex that goes by the name of Nietzsche "almost" with the complex of "that which is German." We do not have to go so far. As literary historians, however, we may record how deeply the questions raised by the "late Romantic" stirred the creative imagination of the foremost modern writer in the German tongue. (p. 122)

> *H. Stefan Schultz, "On the Interpretation of Thomas Mann's 'Der Zauberberg'," in* Modern Philology, *Vol. LII, No. 2, November, 1954, pp. 110-22.*

RONALD GRAY (essay date 1965)

[*Gray is an English educator and critic specializing in German literature. In the following excerpt, he criticizes* The Magic Mountain *for what he considers Mann's ambiguous and equivocal treatment of the novel's dominant themes.*]

Der Zauberberg represents Mann's contribution to the solution of Germany's troubling problems in the period immediately after the First World War. He had led himself into some difficulties in the Weimar Republic by his wartime advocacy of the Imperialist cause both at home and abroad. For some, he was a symbol of an attitude which the new Republic would replace. The more liberal and humane beliefs, which *Der Zauberberg* was (and still is) thought to express, were thus seemingly in accordance with the change in the general mood.

Der Zauberberg is remarkable for the introduction of more explicit speculation than had hitherto appeared in Mann's fiction. There had been almost none in *Buddenbrooks,* in which the ideas expressed were on the whole incorporated into the incidents: into Thomas's vision, Hanno's music, the whole decline of the family. In *Tonio Kröger* the central passage is a fairly lengthy discussion about art and society; in *Der Tod in Venedig,* the first section contains a good deal of argument on the same topic, but again the story continues from there mainly in terms of incident and plot. In *Der Zauberberg,* by contrast with *Buddenbrooks,* one is struck by the very large amount of space taken up by reports of lectures and of the contents of books read, and by long arguments between the protagonists, all of which is relevant to the general themes of the novel and yet makes it less of a novelistic unity, more of a collection of essays and reflections loosely linked to the course of events. This tendency increases until in *Doktor Faustus* incident and plot play a very small part indeed, and some two hundred pages of reported lectures and discussions pass before the narration begins at all. (After *Doktor Faustus,* it is true, in *Der Erwählte, Felix Krull* and *Die Betrogene,* the story again becomes the real vehicle of expression.)

This tendency accords with [the tendency] . . . to adapt the incidents to the ideas, and yet to do so in such a way that there is often only an apparent correlation. It is clear, from the way in which Mann omits to give information from time to time, and the way in which he makes statements about his characters contrary to the impression we receive of them, that he was more concerned to set forth a pattern of ideas than to allow characters to develop more freely with their situations. His increasing use of abstract discussion is a further sign of his preference for communicating a group of extremely complex beliefs which he already holds, rather than for exploring an imagined situation to discover what its fullest implications may be. The comparatively few incidents in *Der Zauberberg* also show a disregard for the importance of events, which Mann seems increasingly to have treated as he treated human actions generally in his fiction, as irrelevant trifles from the standpoint of the Spirit. Thus it is noticeable, in a novel of which Mann said that its hero learned how "knowledge of sin is a condition of salvation," and in which one principal form of sinning is taken to be sexual love, that very little of the action really concerns sexual love. Hans Castorp falls in love with Clawdia Chauchat, it is true; in his inward eye he sees her naked body projected on to the night sky, and engages in mystical speculations on its geometrical proportions. She becomes for him a symbol of the Body, which is associated with Life, and Death, and corruption and temptation and deliverance; she plays Venus to his Tannhäuser. But in the only scene of love between them, Mann literally puts a dunce's hat on Castorp's head, pushes him on to his knees, and has him pronounce an absurd declaration in French, partly a translation of a poem by Whitman, in which he worships her physical form in anatomical detail. "Parler français," Hans is made to say, "c'est parler sans parler" ["To speak French is to speak without speaking"]: his passion seems to him too absurd for direct expression. More important, we never really get to know whether Hans sleeps with Clawdia or not. She leaves him after his declaration with a reminder to return her pencil, which sounds like an invitation to her bedroom—the pencil has played an obtrusively symbolical role for some time before this incident—but the chapter ends here, and the remainder of the novel gives only the barest ambiguous hints. Hans never thinks of that night again, nor does Clawdia refer to it, and we are left to suppose whatever we please. Yet, without expecting Mann to write as Lawrence did, we have good reason to experience a strange lacuna here. Hans and Clawdia do not strike us as people in love but rather as a man pretending devotion and a woman playing the part of a *femme fatale*. If any kind of salvation were to come from this play-acting it would need a careful definition which it does not receive from Mann.

The climax of *Der Zauberberg* is just as much a matter of pretence and equivocation. As with the climax of Thomas Buddenbrook's vision, the point has been disputed whether it is really a climax or not, and that there should be any dispute about the matter is in itself a sign of some uncertainty in the structure. Thomas Mann, in a lecture on his novel delivered at Princeton University, later printed as a foreword, was quite explicit: in the chapter entitled "Snow," he told his audience, they would see Hans Castorp "divine" (erahnen) the Grail: "You will find out too what the Grail is—knowledge, initiation, that supreme summit in quest of which not only the 'simple' hero but also the book itself is involved. You will find it particularly in the chapter entitled 'Snow' where Hans Castorp, lost amid deathly mountain-peaks, dreams his dream of Man" [see *TCLC*, Vol. 8]. In other words, while Hans Castorp does not himself truly find the Grail, only seeing it and failing to

profit by the vision (or so we assume, for he forgets about his dream very shortly after it has happened), the Grail is made visible both to the reader and to him: it is "the Idea of Man, the conception of a humanity of the future that shall have passed through the profoundest knowledge of disease and death." It is true, of course, that what the author said is not evidence, and Mann himself confessed that the idea that Hans's dream symbolized the Grail had come to him from reading a research thesis about his novel—"if I thought of it myself, it was both more and less than thinking." Nevertheless, his words do indicate the importance of this chapter in Mann's estimation; they underline a second time the italicized, didactic passage, which, like the passage on Thomas Buddenbrook's dream, it contains.

In any case, the position of the "Snow" chapter indicates its function as a fusion of the ideas which have gone before. So far, there has been a continual opposition between the ideas of Settembrini on the one hand and Naphta on the other, the Italian humanist advocating social reform, shunning all forms of irrationalism, which for him is symbolical of "Death," and the Jewish, communistic Jesuit advocating a mystical and deathlike seclusion, together with a terroristic violence, in the interests of what he sees as true Life. Hans wearies at length of these diametrically opposed, yet often paradoxically similar standpoints. He perceives, as the reader has probably done long since, that there is "no lack of inner contradictions" in the arguments of both sides, and that it is extraordinarily difficult "not only to choose between the opposites, but even to keep them clear and distinct in one's mind." He objects to "the general crossing over of lines, the great confusion," and indeed the two opponents have taken so little trouble to sort out their positions that they do frequently appear to be holding identical views. The "Snow" chapter, immediately following on these reflections of Hans's, thus represents the moment in which he seems to free himself from the confusion, at least temporarily. It is the end of that process which Mann described in his lecture as "Steigerung," an "intensification" and "heightening" of the polar opposites towards a higher synthesis.

It is no longer by means of intellectual discussion that Hans foresees a solution. On the contrary, he abandons the society of his two mentors and the "civilized" atmosphere of the hotel to confront the elemental powers of Nature. He sets out on an afternoon's skiing expedition in the mountains, in the course of which, temporarily halted by a snowstorm, he enjoys his dream. During the snowstorm, but before the dream, there occurs an episode which is evidently meant to have a suggestive significance. The sequence of events from the moment that he loses his way until he sinks exhausted by the Alpine hut is, like Hanno's improvisation, a résumé of the novel up to this point in symbolical terms, although without the same sexual undertones. Hans starts in a resolute mood, akin to that in which he first came to the Davos sanatorium, and quickly comes to enjoy the freedom of movement, unhindered by the need to keep to conventional paths, offered to him by the open snowfields—again, rather as he began to enjoy the contrast between the easy-going mode of life at Davos and the stricter code of his home in Hamburg. From here onwards, many of the words take on a double sense: "he pressed on deeper into the wild silence, the monstrous and the menacing," as he earlier pushed his way into troubled regions of thought; and as the snow begins to fall, obscuring his view, he reflects (or the author reflects for him), "It was nothingness, white, whirling nothingness, into which he looked": one thinks here, perhaps (especially at the "planted" words, "kein Weg" ["no path"]), of Faust's descent to the spaceless, timeless world of the "Mothers." A little later, Hans begins to doubt whether he is making any progress: "But whether in the right direction, whether there was any point in this progress, remained to be seen"—"he laboured deeper and deeper into this grim and callously indifferent sphere." He begins to become indifferent whether he is making his way homewards or not, and trembles with excitement "as often after a colloquy with Settembrini and Naphta, only to a far greater degree." And at length, having continued to struggle onwards without hope of getting anywhere, he finds himself back at the Alpine hut which he passed an hour ago, having travelled round in a circle. "That was the very devil" expresses Hans's first reaction to this, and although he certainly means to curse his bad luck, it seems quite probable that Mann would have us read this in a double sense also, for all his principal characters come back in one sense or another to the starting-place, and Mann would seem to count this as bad in one way, since they merely affirm an existence whose inadequacy they have already perceived, and good in another, since to make such an affirmation is wise. Thus Hans's further reflection, that for the last hour he has accomplished "a sheer waste of time and effort," while it may sound severe if taken to refer to the recent happenings as a résumé of the novel, may yet be meant to read in this sense—it is, after all, no more severe than the sexual connotations of Hans's music in its implications for the whole, and we have seen how low an estimate Castorp has formed of the arguments which take up so much of the preceding seven hundred pages.

As though to remove any doubt we may have about the symbolical nature of this passage, Hans himself now becomes aware of it. The succession of double meanings continues into explicit punning:

> Wenn auch außen verklammt, habe ich doch innerlich Wärme gesammelt bei der Bewegung, die ich gemacht, und so war die Exkursion doch nicht ganz nutzlos, wenn ich auch umgekommen bin und von der Hütte zur Hütte geschweift . . . "Umkommen," was ist denn das für ein Ausdruck? Man braucht ihn gar nicht, er ist nicht üblich für das, was mir zugestoßen, ganz willkürlich setze ich ihn dafür ein, weil ich nicht so ganz klar im Kopfe bin; und doch ist es in seiner Art ein richtiges Wort, wie mir scheint.

> (I'm rather stiff, naturally, but the effort I made has accumulated some inner warmth, so after all it was not quite in vain, that I have come round all this way, started at the hut and finished at the hut. "Come round"—what am I saying? That's not the proper usage, not at all what people say for what has happened to me, I'm saying it quite off my own bat, because I'm not quite clear in the head, and yet in its way it's the proper word, I feel. [I translate literally, where the standard translation becomes free, in order to convey the sense of the pun.])

The pun is naturally untranslatable, depending as it does on the fact that "umkommen," normally meaning "to die," can be divided into a verb and a prefix meaning "to come" and "round," although the whole word, as Hans remarks, is never used in any such sense. The dream-vision is about to come,

and Hans must in some sense "die" before it is vouchsafed to him; before he is reborn in the pure world of the Spirit, if only for a moment, he must deny the Will to live. But in fact he has only "come round" in a circle, the significance is entirely in the pun. Hans has died neither in a physical nor in a metaphorical sense, neither in his life hitherto nor in the recent events which symbolize it. He had become confused by incoherent arguments to the point where he no longer knew what to think, but his mood after that has been a determined one: he meant to challenge the elements in his brief expedition, and having challenged them he has gone on struggling to keep alive at all costs. His pun is thus an empty formula, the proper move to make in a pattern which is known beforehand; there is no pain of relinquishment in it, no exercise of will. All that happens is, as he says, exactly what the books say should happen: "But there it was, just as the books said"—he means the explorer's narrative in which he has read how lost travellers return to their starting-point, but he may equally well be understood to mean some religious or philosophical work. The strangest aspect of all this, however, is that Mann himself provides the words which reveal what looks like a rejection of his own accomplishment. Was he not aware of them, was some unconscious artistic impulse, at a level of integrity deeper than the conscious mind, responsible for such phrases as "a waste of time and effort" ("nichtsnützigsten Unsinn," which also suggests wickedness)? He probably was aware; the motif in Hanno's music, it will be remembered, was both "stupid" and "mysterious," the "Bürger" was in Tonio's eyes both "stupid" and the supreme expression of unreflective life. These repetitions in various works seem to show that Mann consciously approved of what he thought unworthy of approval.

The dream-vision too shows bookish qualities, seeming to have been evolved from the last paragraph of Nietzsche's *Birth of Tragedy* rather than from experience in either the life of reality or an imagined world. Hans sees now a conventionally drawn Mediterranean landscape filled with happy people, the "People of the Sun," Apolline in their serene composure and fraternal reverence for one another. At their backs is a Greek temple within which, he discovers when he enters, two grisly hags are silently crunching the bones and flesh of a small child, Dionysian in their savage and cruel indifference. The "opposites" emerge in sharp contrast: Settembrini's clarity, and Naphta's devotion to dark mysteries, the dream of human happiness, and the evil which constantly frustrates it. Hans admires the one and shudders with horror at the other. What he remembers best, however, when the dream is over, is the expression on the face of one of the young men by the sea-shore, who turns round as though in recollection of the mysteries and gazes at the temple steps beyond which they are hidden. Or rather we should say not the expression, but the lack of any, for the young man's face, although "grave" and showing a "deathly reserve," is in the same sentence said to be "expressionless" and "unfathomable." It is clear at least from this paradox that the young man is in some way aware of the grisliness in the temple. It is also a disappointment that no more is said, for much depends on the attitude conveyed by this unfathomable gaze. As so often happens, Mann withdraws behind a convenient vagueness. How necessary it was to penetrate a little further, if anything of value was to be had from the dream, is shown by the fact that the People of the Sun are shortly taken by Hans as inspiring models. These people, he concludes, were courteous and charming to one another not because they did not know of the "blood-feast" in the temple, but because, knowing of it, they were able to regard it with equanimity and continue with their happy lives. . . .

I have dreamed of man's state, of his courteous and enlightened social state; behind which, in the temple, the horrible blood-sacrifice was consummated. Were they, those children of the sun, so sweetly courteous to each other, in silent recognition of that horror? It would be a fine and right conclusion they drew. I will hold to them, in my soul, I will hold with them and not with Naphta, neither with Settembrini. They are both talkers.

It would have been interesting to know what this 'silent contemplation of the hideous' implied. So far as can be seen from the events of the dream, which is not to say very much, the happy people know to the full what is going on in the temple and quietly disregard it. (A more favourable, though ultimately no less objectionable phrase would be "they accept it.") Their attitude is not quite that of the happy people in Thomas Buddenbrook's dream, who drove the unhappy to despair: the deliberate cruelty has disappeared, and yet they are capable of indifference to cruelty. It is strange to find Mann describing all this as a dream of love. As in *Tonio Kröger,* his interpretation of the word seems to be based on the idea of preserving one's self-regard rather than on compassion or mutual forgiveness. At times, indeed, he seems to revert to the earlier notion, whereby all good and evil are parts of one whole which exists to be affirmed. "The great soul of which we are a part," in Hans Castorp's words after the dream, "may dream through us, in our manner of dreaming, its own secret dreams, of its youth, its hope, its joy and peace—and its blood-feast." From this it might seem that the indifference of the People of the Sun is the indifference of the "great Soul" itself. Theirs is a kind of godlike indifference.

It is not even clear, however, what Castorp himself makes of the dream. The scene described seems to make a sharp cleavage between the temple and the people on the beach, yet for Castorp it represents some form of synthesis. "Man," he reflects, "is lord of the counter-positions, they can be only through him, and thus he is more aristocratic than they." Yet neither he nor the people of his dream are masters of the opposites, for they have no control over the happenings in the temple, nor can they except by some sophistry pretend that these do not happen. Certainly, Hans, whom we know to have been inside the temple and to have shuddered with horror at the gruesome rites, does not deny their existence; what he does deny and thrust out of his mind (or at any rate forget) is the recollection of the horror he felt. And when he comes to the thought italicized for our special attention, he generalizes so much that the origin of the thought is scarcely discernible. *"Der Mensch soll um der Güte und Liebe willen dem Tode keine Herrschaft einräumen über seine Gedanken." "For the sake of goodness and love, man shall let death have no mastery over his thoughts."* But it was not death which the scene in the temple brought to mind so much as savage cruelty, the "blood-feast." Settembrini, for that matter, would not allow death to have mastery over his thoughts, in fact his purpose was to promote all forms of healthiness. It is not clear why Castorp so emphatically rejected him, or why the paraphernalia of the dream was needed for so obscure or platitudinous a conclusion. The dream is now disregarded, or else, perhaps one should say, Mann's habit of making loose associations between ideas lets him down once again: "death" means not only cessation of life but also everything that makes it more difficult to live in untroubled serenity. But whether we take the one view or the other, we are still in the dark as to the meaning of the dream as Hans interprets it: does

he really side with the People of the Sun, as it were with Settembrini against Naphta, or does he associate himself with the "great Soul," as it were combining Settembrini and Naphta in one? Is he another Tonio Kröger, rejecting the daemonic and all forms of intellectual inquiry or artistic scruple ("death" is occasionally associated with these in the novel), or is he still secretly hankering after the "total acceptance" of Naphta?

Mann's own attitude to these events lends colour at times to the latter interpretation. The scene in the temple is a case in point, for it is not sheerly horrible, though it has the ingredients which make for horror. It is self-consciously portrayed, by one who looks with some detachment at the whole situation....

> The bronze door of the sanctuary stood open, and the poor soul's knees all but gave way beneath him at the sight within. Two grey old women, witchlike, with hanging breasts and dugs of finger-length, were busy there, between flaming braziers, most horribly. They were dismembering a child. In dreadful silence they tore it apart with their bare hands—Hans Castorp saw the bright hair blood-smeared—and cracked the tender bones between their jaws, their dreadful lips dripped blood. An icy coldness held him. He would have covered his eyes and fled, but could not. They at their gory business had already seen him, they shook their reeking fists and uttered curses—soundlessly, most vilely, with the utmost vulgarity, and in the dialect of Hans Castorp's native Hamburg. It made him sick, sick as never before. He tried desperately to escape; knocked into a column with his shoulder—and found himself, with the sound of that dreadful whispered screech still in his ears, still wrapped in the cold horror of it, lying by his hut, in the snow, leaning against one arm, with his head upon it, his feet in their skis stretched out before him.

(pp. 157-68)

Phrases such as "the poor soul," "were busy . . . most horribly," "their gory business" convey a certain detachment, "placing" the scene for the reader as a classifiable phenomenon. The portrayal itself has a melodramatic note: the witches are in their appearance conventional figures calculated to impress rather than freshly perceived realities, and even the description of their actions, horrible as they are, strikes a note of unreality: "und verschlangen die Stücke, daß die spröden Knöchlein ihnen im Munde knackten und das Blut von ihren wüsten Lippen troff" ["and cracked the tender bones between their jaws, their dreadful lips dripped blood"]. There is an excessiveness about this onomatopoeic rendering which makes it capable, when read aloud, of sending even a large audience into a fit of laughter: it is too plainly a matter of deliberate "artistry," with a "deliberate imprint" akin to that of Aschenbach's style. The anticlimax of the witches' swearing at Castorp with "the utmost vulgarity"—the contrast between this offensiveness to his social upbringing, reproved in such a phrase of lofty disdain, and the real offence to his deepest feelings—is a further indication of Mann's intentions. And this is capped by the words "und zwar im Volksdialekt von Hans Castorps Heimat" [translated above as "and in the dialect of Hans Castorp's native Hamburg"], in which "und zwar" [a phrase roughly equivalent to the English "moreover"] has an untranslatable note of pedantic exactitude. The progression downwards, from the savage cannibalism to the crowning insult of being obscenely sworn at in local dialect, from an offence against humane feeling to one against social convention, shows that despite the importance of this scene for the whole dream and thereby for the whole novel, Mann could either not resist the temptation to make it sound comic or else was not enough of an artist to avoid a clash of tones. His own attitude is not the indifference of the People of the Sun, but an amused contemplation or an immature determination to compensate for melodramatic grotesquery by a snigger.

One notices, indeed, that the dream, and even Castorp's thoughts on awakening from it, the thoughts in which the famous italicized passage occurs, are not more esteemed by Mann than was the dream of Socrates in *Der Tod in Venedig*. Lying against the side of the hut, Hans is scarcely aware whether it is a hut or a temple, "and after a fashion he continued to dream, no longer in pictures, but in thoughts hardly less fantastic and confused [kraus]." The last word here should not be overlooked. Hans has sought to escape from the "große Konfusion" ["great confusion"] brought about by Settembrini and Naphta in his mind, but both his dream and his reflections on it remain, as we have observed ourselves, in at least as much confusion. Mann is not seriously concerned to make anything else of them; from the heights of the Spirit it is all a sin or a bit of a joke, though any reader who cares to read deep meaning into this discovery of the Grail is welcome to do so. Small wonder that the dream has so little effect on Hans's later life, or that he forgets it so quickly.

The same indifference continues to the end of the novel. We need not refer, except in passing, to the intervening episodes, in which the same confusion of ideas spins on for another three hundred pages: to Hans's reflections on the "nunc stans," which is the "infinite present" of Thomas Buddenbrook's dream; to Mynheer Peeperkorn, the symbol of Life who commits suicide by means of a poison derived from a life-giving substance; to the discussion of Hans's musical preferences, in which the same ambiguity of life and death is brought out. (One notices, however, that the epithet of "the great Personality," attached to Peeperkorn, is belied by the actual presence of this incoherent and amusing windbag—he is no more what he is said to be than is usually the case with Mann's characters.) Let us move on, instead, to the final chapter, in which Hans takes what is often regarded as an important decision, to leave the Davos sanatorium and enlist in the German Army at the beginning of the First World War. Here, it is argued, is a resolution to act, a movement away from the irresolute speculations of the magic mountain: Hans ceases to sit on the fence or above it, and takes sides. And it is quite true, he does, though whether this has any decisive significance is still doubtful. He is last seen stumbling across a battlefield under shrapnel fire, singing the words of the "Lindenbaum" song, which have been analysed at length some pages earlier and shown to be the expression of a secret yearning for death. He does not know he is singing, this is made explicit more than once. And in this way, his decision to act and to take sides with Life is shown to be as ambiguous as any of his experiences on the mountain.

What, then, is to be made of the sentence with which the novel ends? "Out of this universal feast of death," the author asks, "out of this extremity of fever, kindling the rain-washed evening sky to a fiery glow, may it be that Love one day shall mount?" Here at least—apart from the inflated expression, which may after all be Mann's own—there seems to be an unambiguous question, implying an unambiguous attachment. Yet it comes strangely from the pen of one who has just declared that he does not much mind whether Hans survives the battle or not ("We even confess that it is without great concern we leave the question open"), and who has just expressed an inclination, no more, to dab the corner of his eye at the thought of never seeing his hero again. The reasons for this indifference are also relevant but strange. Hans has, it now appears, experienced something of such great value that his mortal life is of no importance. "Adventures of the flesh and in the Spirit, while enhancing thy simplicity, granted thee to know in the Spirit what in the flesh thou scarcely couldst have done. Moments there were, when out of death, and the rebellion of the flesh, there came to thee, as thou tookest stock of thyself, a dream of love." In other words, the dream was supremely valuable despite the impression it made on us, Hans Castorp, and Mann himself; its confusions were not, or not only, grounds for rejecting it. In that case, however, what can be meant by the word "love" in the final sentence? In terms of the dream it means for Hans the "silent recognition of the horror." It means continuing a life of happiness, as most people try to do anyway, while knowing that the blood-feast continues, perhaps knowing too that the blood-feast is merely one part of the dream of the "great Soul." There is nothing in it which would suggest any desire that the blood-feast should end, rather at best a grave resignation at its continuance. In terms of the ending of the novel, the battlefield is the blood-feast, and the attitude of the People of the Sun towards it would presumably remain what it was towards the knowledge of the temple's mysteries. Yet the final sentence clearly hopes for an end to the war; "love" means here not acceptance of things as they are, and not an embracing of opposites in a single unity, but the triumph over, or the emergence out of death. The ending looks very much like a conventional bow to the proprieties, vaguely Christian like that in *Tonio Kröger* or the more ironically treated ending in *Buddenbrooks*. To take it at all seriously, we would have to disregard all the meaning accumulated by the word throughout the novel as far as the last sentence but one, and if we did that we should really have cause to ask why we had been led such a dance.

The answer to our difficulties must be that for Mann such contradictions are the very stuff of life as well as of art. Both life and art are in his eyes worthless and yet valuable, so that he constantly both denies and affirms the value of what he writes. But it is his own picture of things which he thus denies, not a picture to which we can attach a general validity. It is he who makes of the "Snow" episode a confusion as great as that of the events and arguments preceding it. His account, nobody else's, makes the "discovery of the Grail" a matter of contradictions, platitudes, and cruel mockeries, so that his ironical attitude towards it becomes tautologous. If we are not impressed in the first place, we are not likely to become more so when the author observes that he has written nothing that should impress us, and we can only be baffled when he then adds that it is highly impressive all the same.

To understand Mann better, however, we need to realize that, as he saw things, there was indeed a general validity attaching to the picture he drew, a validity which would be recognized by the greater number of his contemporaries in the German-speaking world, whether men of letters or politicians. In other words, Mann was and had a right to think of himself as being representative of his times, at least within the limitations described earlier. In the tradition within which he wrote, such a form of argument as he used was commonly accepted, while the need to express it through concrete realities was scarcely felt. His language thus remains unfulfilled, a promissory note without valid backing. (pp. 168-72)

Ronald Gray, "'The Magic Mountain'," in his The German Tradition in Literature: 1871-1945, Cambridge at the University Press, 1965, pp. 157-72.

THEODORE ZIOLKOWSKI   (essay date 1969)

[*Ziolkowski is an American critic who is best known as the author of* The Novels of Hermann Hesse *(1965) and as the editor of numerous English translations of Hesse's works. Also a professor of German language and literature, Ziolkowski contends that literature cannot be studied from a single national perspective; accordingly, throughout his career he has promoted the value of comparative literary studies. In the following excerpt, he discusses the relationship between the form, content, and substance of* The Magic Mountain *and examines the importance of that relationship to the work's ultimate meaning.*]

[Rainer Maria Rilke's] *The Notebooks of Malte Laurids Brigge* is about a young man who comes to Paris and, jolted there by the shock of reality into a reassessment of all his values, begins to write a journal in order to bring at least some semblance of aesthetic order to a threatening, disorderly world. [Franz Kafka's] *The Trial* is about a young man who is awakened by his arrest to a consideration of the problem of personal guilt and who, after he commits moral suicide by denying his guilt, is punished by execution. *The Magic Mountain* is about a young man who goes to a tuberculosis sanatorium in Switzerland to visit his cousin for three weeks and—and what? Remains for seven years? Falls in love with a Russian woman who reminds him of a childhood friend? Listens to interminable philosophical debates between an Italian humanist and a Jewish-Jesuit-communist-terrorist? Studies physiology, botany, astronomy? Makes friends with an inarticulate Dutch plantation owner with an imposing personality? Goes skiing in snowstorms? Attends séances and listens to music?

This simple exercise that can be demanded of any reasonably competent student—the statement of theme—highlights one of the difficulties involved in any discussion of Thomas Mann's masterpiece. In the novels by Rilke and Kafka the theme is roughly reflected in the action: there is a correlation between substance and content. *The Magic Mountain,* by contrast, is *about* one set of things, but it *says* something quite different. The entire ideological framework of this perhaps greatest novel of ideas is, ultimately, irrelevant to the meaning of the novel. This detachability of content is not a shortcoming but rather, as we shall see, is implicit in the meaning of the work. It merely emphasizes the fact that we are dealing here with a symbolic novel par excellence, with an absolute novel, with a hermetic novel. This distinguishes it from such works as *The Trial,* which might be described as an extended metaphor. The symbolic novel, by way of distinction, does not have the referential quality of the metaphorical or parabolic novel. In the symbolic novel it is not the content that matters. To state the case most bluntly, its ingredients are virtually interchangeable; they are not important in themselves. It is the tensions and relations obtaining *between* them that reflect the author's meaning. This can be demonstrated most clearly, perhaps, if we resort to what may strike some readers initially as a rather unsophisticated approach: namely, an old-fashioned distinction between the form, the content, and the substance of *The Magic Mountain.* By these I mean simply the organization and structure of the chapters, the ideological texture of the work, and

the development of the hero. These three aspects, it turns out, are in themselves only casually related; their true relationship emerges in a *tertium comparationis* ["a characteristic which two basically different things have in common"]. It is in every case the theme of timelessness that provides the link between otherwise disparate elements.

Critics have sometimes objected to what they call the excessive intellectual baggage of Thomas Mann's novels, and especially of *The Magic Mountain,* maintaining that the ideologies are derivative and that their obtrusion delays the denouement of the action. This is not the proper place to discuss to what extent the intellectual contents of the works of most major writers—from Dante to Sartre—are ultimately derivative. In the case of Thomas Mann, the fact that we learn something or nothing new is largely irrelevant, of course. What matters is the fact that the ideologies constitute the intellectual framework through which and within which the development of the hero takes place. It is not the ideas in themselves that contribute to Hans Castorp's spiritual education, but rather the tensions between them.

For the reader with a taste for erudition and "civilized" conversation—and, it must be conceded, with the time and patience to read at the leisurely pace demanded by Mann's novels—there is nothing more delightful than the scintillating, highly articulate ideological fireworks that explode in the conversations of Settembrini and Naphta. Yet few readers, probably, are capable of recapitulating afterwards the main points of the arguments. Certain general attitudes emerge clearly, of course. Settembrini, the humanist, defends the classics and the Renaissance against the fanatic medievalism of the Jewish-Jesuit Naphta. He upholds reason against Naphta's advocacy of faith and discipline, monism against the latter's dualism, nationalism against a communistic church, and humanism in the face of Naphta's endorsement of blind terrorism. In these intellectual duels the flashing stiletto of Naphta usually wins out over the graceful rapier of Settembrini. Yet the reader is no more convinced by one side or the other than is Hans Castorp, who looks rapidly from one disputant to the other as he follows the debate, "roguishly" interjecting from time to time a seemingly innocent remark that spurs them on to ever greater intellectual bravura. For the whole point of these debates is not to persuade Hans Castorp or the reader; they exist for their own sake, for the sake of the dialectical interplay. Hence the subtleties of argumentation rapidly recede in the reader's mind into a loose rhythm of tensions.

The careful structuring of ideologies becomes most apparent if we disregard fine points and concentrate on the main representatives of these ideologies in the two parts of the novel. The first half of the book is dominated largely by the tension obtaining between the oriental temptations of sleepy-eyed Clawdia Chauchat and the Western rationalism of Settembrini, who turns on the brightest lights when he enters a room and constantly "disturbs" Hans Castorp in his acquiescence to the seductiveness of the East. Here the dialectical positions seem to break down into an opposition of East and West, emotion and reason, passivity and action.

In the second half of the book these elements are reshuffled and complicated, for the characters of Naphta and Mynheer Peeperkorn have been added to the game. Various geometrical alignments become evident; or, to use another analogy, the forces are polarized into different configurations in the electrical field. For before the magnitude of Peeperkorn's imposing gestures (*Kulturgebärde*) and mighty cult of feeling, all the posturings and subtly articulated distinctions of Naphta and Settembrini are lumped together into a position that Peeperkorn jocularly and contemptuously calls "cerebrum, cerebral." The utter irrelevancy of their lucubrations is nowhere more apparent than in the magnificent scene where Mynheer, standing before the thundering waterfall, holds forth in a grandiloquent speech that no one can understand—but which nevertheless, through the force of his personality, is more impressive than all the finesse of the two disputants. The tension that originated as a juxtaposition of East and West, then shifted to a battle between reason and faith, is transmuted finally into an opposition of intellect and feeling. In the face of this rhythm of tensions the details of the ideologies become unimportant.

All these positions hold each other in check or cancel one another out. No ideology is left intact at the end of the novel. Peeperkorn, the advocate of blind feeling who regards himself as "God's marriage organ," commits suicide because his sexual powers have receded. Naphta, the vigilante of terror, faith, and discipline, shoots himself in the head in a fit of frustration and rage. Settembrini, the spokesman for work and progress, is reduced by his illness to a bedridden existence. And Madame Chauchat, whose orientalism results in such passivity that she never acts but only responds to others, simply goes away after Peeperkorn's death. (pp. 68-72)

What matters ultimately is not, say, that Naphta wins a certain argument with Settembrini or that Hans Castorp's allegiance, in the "Walpurgis Night" chapter, swerves from Settembrini toward Clawdia Chauchat. As one looks back over the thousand pages of the novel, one becomes aware that there has been no dialectical progress; no true belief has emerged. Instead, we see these various ideological possibilities spread out like constant forces in a magnetic field. Hans Castorp does not, in other words, begin as a *tabula rasa* and progress from Settembrini to Clawdia, past Naphta, to Peeperkorn. Rather, through these symbolic figures he encounters various potentialities of being that exist eternally. They awaken within him an awareness of certain human possibilities; it is an expansion, a heightening, a *Steigerung*, in Mann's own expression, but not a progress in the sense of movement through time. (p. 73)

[An] intellectual lability marks a fundamental difference between the writer and other men, Thomas Mann stresses in [his essay **"Politik"**]. "It must be clearly understood that someone who is accustomed not to speaking directly and on his own responsibility but, instead, to causing people and objects to speak—that someone who is accustomed to making *art*, never can take the spirit and intellect in full seriousness since it has always been his affair, rather, to treat them as material and playthings, to represent points of view, to practice dialectics, always to allow the person who is speaking to be right. . . . The intellectual thought in the work of art is not understood if one takes it to be its own purpose . . . it is purposeful with respect to the composition, it affirms itself only with reference to the composition. It can be banal, from an absolute and literary point of view, but brilliant within the composition."

This aesthetic attitude, which Mann, borrowing a term from Strindberg, calls "stereoscopic" vision, constitutes the inherent superiority of art over the merely intellectual. Art vouchsafes a certain spiritual freedom and flexibility not to be enjoyed by the intellectual who is bound to his own unyielding position. It is in this light, then, that we must regard the ideological framework of *The Magic Mountain*. None of the positions represents the author's own point of view, but all of them together symbolize potentialities of his own mind, which exist time-lessly as eternal positions. More important, however: the stereoscopic or aesthetic vision also characterizes the hero of the novel, Hans Castorp, who takes cognizance of all the positions thrust upon him by the various figures of the novel but commits himself to none. For the most essential element of his personality is a great sense of freedom. His "development" can be regarded not as the acquisition of new ideas, but rather as a series of liberations. And from the structural point of view, the entire novel is constructed in such a way as to heighten the reader's experience of the freedom which characterizes the state of timeless suspension in which Hans Castorp spends seven years on the Magic Mountain.

Erich Heller once remarked that Hans Castorp, should he survive the war, would have no choice but to become a writer [see Additional Bibliography]. He certainly could not go back to the career as a nautical designer that he left behind when he departed from Hamburg for his little visit to the Magic Mountain. This comment reveals the connection between the ideology, or the content, of the novel and the development of its hero, or its substance. For the point of view with which Hans Castorp emerges from his seven "hermetic" years is essentially the "stereoscopic" view that Thomas Mann claims for the writer. While it is perfectly true, as Weigand demonstrates, that Hans Castorp's development consists in an "exposure" to the world in the concentrated, "escalated" compression of the feverish atmosphere of the sanatorium, it is equally true that the ultimate effect of his ideal education at the hands of various mentors is to liberate him successively from all bonds and ties until he emerges, toward the end of the novel, in perfect freedom. And since this absolute freedom is symbolized by a suspension of time, Hans Castorp's development can be regarded in another sense as a movement from time to timelessness.

In this connection the setting of the novel is of central importance. Isolated from the world "down below," existing almost in a different time system, the sanatorium is a realm which recognizes the month as its smallest unit of time, where popular usage reduces even such a measure as the year (*Jahr*) to a diminutive form (*Jährchen*). It is an "Asiatic style of time consumption," as Settembrini complains in a formulation that renders even time in ideological terms. The seasons, virtually indistinguishable, "do not adhere to the calendar." It is a world with laws of its own, where the main concerns, as Mann remarks, are one's temperature and flirtation. The mountain is "magic" not least because it is independent of the rules of everyday life, of the reality which binds the world on the plains below. . . . Only in an atmosphere of this sort can Hans Castorp be liberated in the sense mentioned above. For in the world below, the concerns and responsibilities of everyday life absorb one's time and attention; the individual is caught up in the flow of temporality and rendered incapable of the pure reflection ensured by the hermetically enclosed world of the sanatorium.

From the very start the motif of detachment is sounded, anticipating to a remarkable extent the third volume of Broch's *The Sleepwalkers*, where the action also takes place during a "vacation period" of six months in which the hero, Huguenau, wanders through life "as though under a glass bell." For Hans Castorp, as well, the time on the Magic Mountain is a vacation time, both literally and figuratively. On concluding his studies he has taken off three weeks, before beginning his practical apprenticeship on the wharves, in order to regain his strength and visit his ailing cousin. It is quite literally a vacation that brings him to the mountain. This circumstance causes the narrator to reflect, on the second page of the novel, that "Two days of journeys remove a man—and especially a young man who is still not firmly rooted in life—from the everyday world, from all that he called duty, interests, worries, prospects. . . . [Space] contains powers that one generally believes are reserved for time."

Even after Hans Castorp has become a resident, long after his imagined "visit" has ended, the motif continues to reappear throughout the novel. . . . On [one] occasion he senses what it is that permits him to listen to Settembrini's discourses: "that holiday irresponsibility of the traveler and visitor who doesn't close himself off from any impression and who lets everything approach him, in the awareness that tomorrow or the day after tomorrow he will again air his wings and return to his accustomed order." It is this mood of ferial lability, then, that permits Hans Castorp to profit from his experiences on the Magic Mountain. At the same time—and this should be borne in mind—this mood anticipates his precipitate return to the plains and its war at the end of the book. For all holidays must come to an end, even such a spiritual vacation as Hans Castorp's.

Hans Castorp does not succumb immediately to the "advantages of shame" that he discovers in Davos. Everything in his solid bourgeois upbringing impels him to resist, at first, the laxity of the life that he witnesses during his first days and weeks. On the one hand, he is all that Mme. Chauchat calls him: "un petit bonhomme convenable, de bonne famille, d'une tenue appétissante, disciple docile de ses précepteurs" ["an

Heinrich (left) and Thomas Mann, about 1900.

agreeable and good-natured little offspring of a good family, likeable in his manner; the docile disciple of his teachers"]. It is this tension between freedom and the restraint of Hans Castorp's training that produces many of the novel's humorous situations, upon which the narrator comments with delicious irony. On the other hand there exist, deeper in his character, qualities that respond inchoately to the appeal of the Magic Mountain. Weigand speaks in this connection of four *Urerlebnisse*, primal experiences rooted at the core of Hans Castorp's being: continuity, death, freedom, and Eros. Like the ideological content discussed above, these experiences also coexist in a state of tension, of dialectical interplay. The sense of continuity, for instance, is associated in Hans Castorp's mind with the memory of his grandfather holding the family baptismal bowl, murmuring the syllables "great-, great-, great-, great-, great-" to indicate how many generations of the family had been baptized in this same bowl. This sense makes Castorp receptive, on the mountain, to the entire cultural tradition spread out before him through the persons of Settembrini, Naphta, and Peeperkorn; somehow, he feels, it belongs to his own heritage. At the same time, this sense represents a certain loyalty to his specific origins on the "plains" below and his responsibility to life. Certainly, this feeling of continuity and tradition functions as a timeless constant, an eternal presence of values that contrasts with the bourgeois obsession with temporality.

The same ambivalence attaches to his sense of death. . . . Exposed to death from his earliest years, Hans Castorp is both attracted to death with a romantic morbidity and at the same time imbued with a certain reverence for death. In any case, his attitude does not allow him simply to ignore the fact of death, as do most of the inhabitants of the sanatorium. He even seeks out the "moribundi" in the hope of bringing some comfort to their last days and hours. Death, moreover, is associated in his mind with a state of timelessness. When Naphta, in a discourse on alchemic transmutations, speaks of the grave as the symbol of hermetic purification, Hans Castorp recalls the vacuum jars on the shelves at home in Hamburg, in which fruits and meats are preserved. "They sit there for years and years, and if you open one the contents are quite fresh and unspoiled; neither years nor days have been able to affect them. You can partake of them just as they are. This is not alchemy and purification, to be sure, it is simply preservation, hence the name 'preserves.' But the enchanting thing is, that the preserves were lifted out of time, hermetically sealed off; time passed them by, they had no time but stood outside of it on their shelf. Well, that's enough about the vacuum jars."

Even Eros assumes a certain quality of timeless irreality in Hans Castorp's mind. This becomes clear through the terms in which he explains and justifies to Peeperkorn his single night of intimacy with Madame Chauchat. He argues that that particular evening was "an evening that falls out of all order and almost out of the calendar, an *hors d'oeuvre,* so to speak, an extra evening, a leap-year evening, the twenty-ninth of February."

The primal experiences of tradition and death, along with freedom and Eros, act as counter-impulses to the more superficial elements of his training and upbringing, and establish in him a subliminal sympathy for the new experiences that he encounters on the Magic Mountain. At first Hans Castorp attempts to resist this appeal. His gradual acclimatization is marked by a series of trivial "liberations" that cut him off from his own past. (pp. 75-82)

The first definitive liberation occurs in the seventh week of his stay. It is only at this point that he commits himself to an indefinite sojourn in the sanatorium as a patient, and in his third letter to his uncle he makes arrangements to have a certain sum forwarded to him regularly at monthly intervals. The chapter is entitled "Freedom," and this is the word that reverberates in his mind as he writes the fateful lines. Up to this point his future had lain in the balance: he could easily have decided to follow Settembrini's admonishments and return home to his existence in the plains. But the first taste of the freedom of the Magic Mountain has exerted its attraction, and he is determined to remain.

It has often been remarked that in this "hermetic" novel, which delights in references to mystical initiation rites, the number seven and its multiples play a central symbolic role. Hans Castorp comes for three weeks (twenty-one days) and remains for seven years. Four times a day he takes his temperature for seven minutes. He occupies Room 34 (three plus four), and during the course of his stay sits at each of the seven tables in the dining room. The entire novel has seven chapters, and the first part (Chapters 1 through 5) covers a period of seven months. His cousin Joachim dies in the twenty-eighth month of his visit. It is not surprising to find, therefore, that this inner or mystical, symbolic rhythm of the novel is punctuated essentially by intervals of seven. Thus the association of Madame Chauchat with his childhood friend Hippe comes to Hans Castorp in a vision on his seventh day in Davos. At the end of three weeks (twenty-one days) Hans Castorp discovers that he has a fever, and is easily persuaded to stay on and submit to three more weeks of bed rest for the purposes of diagnosis.

At the end of seven weeks, then, Hans Castorp has completed his first liberation. He has cut himself off from his home below and committed himself to the hermetic life of the sanatorium, to a life given over to the motto that Settembrini quotes from Petrarch: *Placet Experiri*. The ideological confrontation presented in the first half of the novel, as we have seen, is that of Settembrini and Madame Chauchat. It is perfectly in keeping with the inner rhythm of the novel that the culmination of this phase occurs at the end of Hans Castorp's seventh month on the Magic Mountain, on the "Walpurgis Night" of the Mardi Gras festivities—that timeless twenty-ninth of February that Hans Castorp later discusses with Peeperkorn. For it is on this occasion that he frees himself from the glib rationalism of his mentor and "tastes the pomegranate" of Eros. Love, he argues in his inspired French, must be "une aventure dans le mal" ["an adventure in evil"]. But it is important to remember that this episode is more one of liberation than of commitment. Clawdia and her morality of sin—"Il nous semble qu'il est plus moral de se perdre et même de se laisser dépérir que de se conserver" ["It seems to us that it is more moral to lose oneself and even to allow oneself to waste away than to preserve oneself"]—help to free him from the bland humanism of Settembrini. But even though he repeats the same sentence later in the book, it must not be assumed that he accepts it. He quotes it in a subsequent conversation with Clawdia for rhetorical effect, to impress her. As an absolute point of view, it runs directly counter to his own primal experience of continuity and tradition.

During the early part of the second half of the novel, the opposing ideological positions are represented by Naphta and Settembrini. But between their radical antitheses of spirit and nature, life and death, sickness and health, freedom and piety, Hans Castorp works out his own position during his vision in the snow. Though the time element has become less specific by this point in the novel, it is not unlikely that this episode falls in Hans Castorp's twenty-first month on the mountain, in the April of his second year; nothing, in any case, speaks against this assumption, since it is late in the winter snow-season when he finally makes his way up to the mountains on skis. Since this vision is the high point of the entire work, the circumstances should be recalled. It is important, first, that his journey through the snow carries him higher than any other walk during his sojourn, that is, farther away from all past attachments. Moreover, it carries him outside the periphery of the sanatorium as such, to a symbolic spot high above, where he is free of and superior to the ideas represented there. Finally, the vision is akin, symbolically, to fleeting visions at the moment of death, since Hans Castorp is very much in danger of succumbing to exhaustion and dying of exposure at the moment of epiphany.

The vision that Hans Castorp experiences—that of an Apollonian People of the Sun carrying on their serene activities side by side with the enactment of the most bloody Dionysian horror—leads him intuitively to the synthesis that all the lucubrations of Settembrini and Naphta are unable to attain. "I am going to keep faith with them in my soul and not with Naphta—and not with Settembrini either. They are both chatterers." He arrives at a conception of man as "Lord of the Antinomies," capable through his freedom and piety of respecting both death and life, of paying allegiance to both. "Love opposes death; only love and not reason is stronger than death," he concludes. The resolution that emerges from the play of ideologies, then, is love of man. *"Man shall, for the sake of goodness and love, concede to death no power over his thoughts"* is the maxim that Thomas Mann sets in italics as the single position that he endorses in the novel. It is for the sake of this vision that Hans Castorp required the absolute freedom of the Magic Mountain, for this that he needed all the experiences of ideologies, love, and death that have preceded. They have supplied the materials for his own great synthesis. But it is a synthesis that can be reached—and maintained—only in absolute freedom. For as he moves back through the clearing evening toward the sanatorium, the ecstatic vision fades in his memory and he recollects only vaguely the position at which he had arrived. The entire vision took place outside of time. When Hans Castorp looks at his watch, he discovers that the whole experience had lasted barely ten minutes.

In the descending rhythm of the last chapter, however, even the positive factors of love and freedom are canceled out in the dialectics of the book. The dominant figure here is Mynheer Peeperkorn, half-buffoon and half-priest in his curious mixture of Dionysus and Christ, who represents a travesty of the vision in the snow. It is as though the absolute truth that Hans Castorp had experienced were possible only in the complete isolation of the mountaintop, as though such a truth were not tenable in reality, where every absolute is degraded and relativized. (pp. 83-6)

The final years on the Magic Mountain lose all temporal structure; the events are not clearly articulated. The "eternal sameness" has asserted its full prerogative. But after the apex of the snow vision, even the timeless freedom has lost its charm for the hero. Hans Castorp looks around, "and he knew what he was seeing: life without time, life without cares and hope, life as a stagnating and busybody slovenliness, a dead life."

Hans Castorp has long since given up calendars, and he no longer even carries his watch, which broke one day when it fell from his night table. The vision in the snow was not only a high point, but also a turning point. All that happens afterwards reveals to Hans Castorp the negative side of his most affirmative insights. Now he perceives that even the absolute freedom that he has attained can also be viewed as death and stagnation rather than freedom. The interplay of ideas has become so complex that it is no longer reduced to simple ideological positions. Instead Mann allows us, toward the end, to sense the hero's feelings by experiencing with him the intricate associations which various pieces of music hold for him. In *Aïda* he hears his own confused emotions echoed: Rhadames has broken his oath to fatherland and king for the sake of love and must now be buried alive with his beloved in a tomb. Through this *mêlée* of associations, we grasp intuitively the conflict between love and duty, between life and death in Hans Castorp's own soul. The haunting harmonies of *L'Après-midi d'un faun* seem to him to justify "the innocence of timelessness," whereas *Carmen* again proclaims the almost criminal irresponsibility of a freedom attained at the cost of honor and duty. In a simple folksong by Schubert, "Unterm Lindenbaum," he hears the appeal of home, fatherland, and death.

It is such blurred associations as these that finally impel Hans Castorp to leave the mountain after seven years and to return to serve his country in the war that has broken out below. All the conflicting ideologies have canceled one another out. Even the ideal of life in the face of chaos and horror has been somehow trivialized by its materialization in the person of Peeperkorn. And the ideal of a timeless freedom has revealed its verso: tedium and criminal irresponsibility. The Hans Castorp who goes back down the mountain is not a whit richer in beliefs than the one who came up: as a matter of fact, he is in a sense poorer, since the convictions of his upbringing, his faith in the simple facts of bourgeois life, have been wiped out. And this is indicated by the author's attitude at the end. He does not venture a prediction regarding the future, but merely asks tentatively: Will love emerge once more from the holocaust now engulfing the world? The novel has shattered every illusion, every conviction, every ideal. It has left only frustrating questions.

But Hans Castorp is immeasurably richer in insights and awareness. He is immensely conscious of the world as it exists around him in all its contradictions. And though he is committed to no one position, he is able to view all these antinomies critically. He emerges from his intellectual adventure much like Franz Biberkopf [in Alfred Döblin's *Alexanderplatz, Berlin*], who returns to reality "with his eyes open." Or like Huguenau in Broch's *The Sleepwalkers,* he represents a new "objectivity" which rejects all traditional values and views the world with a sober sense of reality. So the substance of the novel, the hero's education, has actually travestied the traditional *Bildungsroman*. For Hans Castorp is not educated to the acceptance of any ideal; rather, he is led to a position of neutral objectivity and awareness beyond any ideological position.

All that we have said about the substance and content of *The Magic Mountain* would be mere verbiage, and the objections of the critics to its excessive intellectuality justified, were not the meaning so perfectly realized in the structure of the work. *The Magic Mountain* is *the* time novel of the twentieth century. As Thomas Mann has pointed out, it is a time novel in several senses. It is one in that it reflects its time, the period from 1907 to the outbreak of World War I. It is one in that it contains a mass of reflections about time. But this is less important, since these reflections, which are not really very original, be-

long to the content of the novel, along with the elaborate ideologies. It is a time novel above all, however, because of the brilliant way in which the author structures his narrative. It is time and time alone that provides the framework within which everything else becomes meaningful. "Time is the element of narrative, just as it is the element of life," the author reflects at the beginning of the extensive digression on time in the chapter "Walk on the Beach." And the narrative requires time for its manifestation, "even if it should attempt to be constantly present at every moment."

This is the principle from which the tension of the structure derives. The action, the substance, progresses through time, through the seven years of Hans Castorp's stay on the mountain. At the same time the author must render the loss of time, the movement toward timelessness; and he does this by attempting to keep the entire novel constantly in the reader's mind as a continual present. Thus in the novel's structure, as well as in its content and substance, there is a tension between temporality and timelessness, between direction and presence. It is this tension that provides the essential link between content, substance, and form. Only the tension between time and timelessness keeps the structure from being more than a matter of mere technical brilliance, more than a literary tour de force.

Through the organization of the novel, the reader is led to experience time in a variety of ways. The principle upon which the organization of chapters is based is anything but profound: it is the simple perception that our attention, when first we enter a new situation, is focused upon myriad details that are gradually, as we adjust to the new surroundings, simplified into an accustomed routine of even texture. (pp. 87-90)

The temporal sequence begins with Chapter 3, which contains a detailed account of the first day at the sanatorium. This chapter begins with Hans Castorp's awakening and concludes when he retires that same evening, and is punctuated by the five mealtimes in the main dining room of the Sanatorium Berghof: breakfast at eight o'clock; midmorning lunch at eleven; dinner at one; tea at four; and supper at seven. The intervals are filled, for the most part, with walks and rest periods on the balcony. We see—indeed, since everything is narrated from Hans Castorp's point of view, we *experience*—how the new environment and particularly the many people there first obtrude upon his consciousness as a blurred mass and how, by the meal at the end of the day, a few individuals gradually emerge in sharper outline. At the same time we receive a highly detailed report of the daily routine, which, as we are constantly assured, is invariable. This element is highly important. First, it helps to reduce time to a cycle of perpetual recurrences, beginning the movement toward timelessness. And second, it provides the background for the hundreds of pages that follow. For the reader always knows, after this chapter, precisely what is going on at any given time of day that the author may single out as a context for subsequent scenes.

Whereas the third chapter relates the events of one day in a rhythm of hours, the fourth chapter covers three weeks in a rhythm of days. Yet the number of pages required to describe these three weeks is only twice the number required for the single first day. The events of the individual days are effaced here, as we are exposed to the routine of the week with its Sunday concerts and, in the case of Joachim and Hans Castorp, the Saturday examination. In Chapter 5 the process of temporal leveling is carried even further: here we have the events of the first seven months (exclusive of the first three weeks) related in a rhythm of weeks. Individual days are scarcely mentioned.

Instead, Hans Castorp lies in bed for the assigned three weeks; a week later he has a second examination. The scenic description that has been the main technique up to now gives way at this point to frequent chapters of iterative-durative time. A particular scene, for instance that of Hans Castorp reading at night on his balcony, is described as representative, as recurring every night; and then the substance of his reading over the course of a full month is related by the narrator. As the length of time expands, scenic description is replaced more and more by iterative-durative narrative.

Chapter 5 and Part One conclude with leap year, which falls at the end of Hans' first seven months on the Magic Mountain. We have experienced the first day in a rhythm of hours, the first three weeks in a rhythm of days, and the first seven months in a rhythm of weeks. The same pattern continues in the two long chapters of Part Two. Chapter 6 covers the year and nine months from that leap year until the November of Hans Castorp's third year at the sanatorium. Here we experience time in a rhythm of months: Naphta is introduced in June, Uncle James Tienappel arrives in October, and so forth. The sequence of months is kept quite clear until the second winter, when even the articulation of months is blurred in the eternal winter depicted in the chapter entitled "Snow." This blurring of months, finally, leads to the introduction of the rhythm of years in Chapter 7, which covers the last four and a half years before the outbreak of World War I and Hans Castorp's departure.

Thomas Mann has constructed this temporal sequence with supreme artistic consciousness. It is quite apparent how, at the end of each chapter, the rhythm of time (hours, days, weeks, months, years) begins to blur into the rhythm of the succeeding chapter, gradually producing the effect of "eternal sameness" that is mentioned in the various digressions on time. The tendency of the novel "to be constantly present" is enhanced, of course, by Thomas Mann's much-discussed use of leitmotif. Settembrini's checkered trousers, Frau Stöhr's malapropisms and her lip drawn back from her teeth, Hans Castorp's habit of staring openmouthed, his head tilted to one side, and dozens of other set descriptions of this sort recur from start to finish; with each mention they call to mind similar situations earlier in the book and stress the repetitive structure of life at the sanatorium. (pp. 91-3)

On a structural level there are major devices that correspond to the repetitive effect of the leitmotif. The "Attack and Repulse," in which Uncle James Tienappel attempts to persuade Hans Castorp to return to Hamburg, is carefully constructed in such a way as to parallel the events of Chapters 1 and 3, Hans Castorp's arrival and first day at Berghof. Indeed, the whole chapter can be regarded as a brief recapitulation of the two earlier chapters. The same applies to Joachim's return to the sanatorium a year after his flight. The events are repetitive; but here the mood of the scene is shifted from major to minor, as it were, by the sad circumstances surrounding Joachim's return. And we have already noted that the entire second part is a complex parallel, on a grand scale, to the first part.

Finally, the effect of timeless suspension and eternal recurrence is vastly heightened by structural references to broad realms that lie outside the novel altogether. Thus, the Walpurgis Night scene, carefully constructed around quotations from Goethe's *Faust,* suddenly thrusts the novel into another complex of associations altogether.... All these devices, to which attention has often been called, contribute ultimately to the effect of timeless suspension: the actions taking place here, one feels, are not unique actions happening just this once in this specific situation, but rather part of certain patterns which in turn belong to an eternal process of repetition.

In all of this, of course, the role of the narrator is of central importance. An omniscient narrator would regard these seven years on the Magic Mountain as a definite point in time, preceded and followed by other events of history that would locate Hans Castorp's sojourn in a temporal sequence. That is not the case here. Instead, Thomas Mann has created for his novel a narrator who very distinctly fills the specific needs of this particular work with its movement toward timelessness. The narrator, to be sure, does not tell us all that he knows; but he does not know everything.... [The] narrator's omniscience is limited to the hermetic seven years on the Magic Mountain. He is tied to the locale; he is the *genius loci.*

It is precisely this hermetic quality of the narrator that lends credence to the timelessness of the events told there: they are not connected in any way, through the narrator, with events taking place on any other plane of time or life. Yet although the narrator "knows" his story before he begins to tell it, he again carefully restricts his point of view to that of the hero. All that we experience happens within Hans Castorp's sight or hearing.... This point of view is, of course, essential to the time effects of the story. For if, at any point, the narrator should reach ahead and anticipate events by means of his omniscience, then the carefully structured rhythm of exposure, progressing through hours, days, weeks, months, and years, would be destroyed—not so much for Hans Castorp himself as for the reader. Thus the narrator's position is conceived more with an eye to the reader and the effect of the narrative on him than to Hans Castorp. Through the narrator, so to speak, we are permitted to experience the unfolding of time exactly as Hans Castorp does.

The narrator, at the same time, possesses a conspicuous degree of ironic detachment and objectivity. He criticizes, comments, and (in the chapter "Walk on the Beach") even interposes an entire chapter of his own reflections. But his role changes noticeably in the course of the novel. During the early chapters he rather conspicuously keeps himself in the background. His occasional ironic notes are usually enclosed in parentheses. It is not until Chapter 7 that he emerges in the full glory of his narrative sovereignty. He interjects himself far more boldly into the narrative, dropping the coy parenthetical pose that he had maintained up to this point. In the last chapter, indeed, it is only the figure of the narrator who holds the story together. There are good reasons for this. The temporal framework of the novel begins to collapse in the last chapter, where the rhythm of years, according to the scheme of the work, moves gradually toward a rhythm of indefinite suspension of time.... In order to save the situation, the narrator must assume an ever greater role. He becomes a much more clearly defined figure here than was the case earlier, holding together by the strength of his own personality the structure of the otherwise disintegrating action. It is clear that the role of the narrator is conceived in such a way as to complement, indeed to make possible, the illusion of timeless suspension toward which Thomas Mann moves in the course of a thousand pages; and finally it is the narrator who gives the novel, once it has become timeless, the structure of his own personality.

Can we pat ourselves on the back at this point and feel that we have done justice to the novel by our analysis of its content, substance, and structure, and of their interaction in the movement toward the common goal of timeless suspension? Not at all. For this novel is a more delicately woven fabric than most.

If we pull one thread in order to follow it to its end, we merely unravel the entire tissue and are left with a meaningless pile of material instead of the meaningful design of the whole. *The Magic Mountain* is not merely a certain rhythm of development toward a suspension of time, through a magnetic field of polarized ideologies, presented by an ironic storyteller. Frau Stöhr remains. Hofrat Behrens remains. The narrative beauty of the vision in the snow and of Hans Castorp's sight of the sun and moon in the evening sky remains. To put matters most bluntly: after all the ideologies have canceled each other out, after the ideal of love and a reconciliation of life and death has turned out to be trivial in its realization or, at best, of questionable value for the future of Hans Castorp, even after the freedom of timelessness has been unmasked as the mere license of indolence—after all this, the novel remains as the one absolute. This is surely what Thomas Mann had in mind when he wrote that "only form is unassailable."

This is perhaps the final irony of this ironic work: absolutely no position is left intact. Only the work remains. But the work, as a work of art, approaches perfection to a degree rarely achieved on such a monumental scale. In its own way, then, *The Magic Mountain* stands in the same relation to reality as do the various prose poems of Malte Laurids Brigge. Though the world represented within the novel turns out to be ultimately meaningless, *The Magic Mountain* gives meaning to this world by ordering it according to the novel's own principles of organization. In an ideologically meaningless world, only aesthetic order is capable of producing meaning. And so Erich Heller was completely right when he suggested that Hans Castorp could only have become a novelist, for only a writer could come to grips with the reality that he encountered on the Magic Mountain.

We see, then, that this is not merely a symbolic novel; it is also the novel *as a symbol*. For if there is any meaning left intact after we have read the last page and closed the volume, it is the book itself. It exists; its aesthetic meaning is there, hermetically sealed within its covers like the timeless atmosphere of the sanatorium on its isolated mountain top. The book remains as a symbol of the aesthetic attitude that is capable of reconciling the conflicting positions not accessible of resolution by the forces portrayed individually within the novel. For this reason its meaning will never be exhausted by a statement of theme and of plot, or by an analysis of structure or content. The book as a whole is a symbol of the life represented within the book. Like that life, it is hermetic and timeless; like that life, it has an existence independent of reality; like that life, it represents an enhancement and intensification of life itself. (pp. 93-8)

> Theodore Ziolkowski, "Thomas Mann: 'The Magic
> Mountain'," in his Dimensions of the Modern Novel:
> German Texts and European Contexts, *Princeton
> University Press, 1969, pp. 68-98.*

ANDRÉ von GRONICKA   (essay date 1970)

[*An American educator and critic, Gronicka has written widely on German literature and Russo-German literary relations. In the following excerpt, he discusses the ways in which* The Magic Mountain *reflects the evolution of Mann's thought from conservatism to democratic humanism.*]

It is easy to forget that *The Magic Mountain,* the inception of which, to be sure, dates back to the years preceding World War I, is nevertheless, in large part, the product of develop-

ments on the European scene and in Mann's life during the war and during the first crucial years of the struggling Weimar Republic. The novel was finished late in 1923. From the point of plot-chronology, the "peal of thunder" of the outbreak of war that casts Hans Castorp down upon the flaming battlefields of the *Flachland* (the lowlands) in August of the fateful year, 1914, is a most deceptive finale to a narrative which, in significant measure, records and analyzes the author's impressions and thoughts that postdate the war, and are the *result* of the apocalyptic cataclysm. The protagonists in the pages of this novel are portrayed by a poet matured beyond the emotional and intellectual stance that had been his at the beginning of the war or even at its end. Thus, Settembrini is clearly the product of Mann's greatly mellowed view of the once hated *Zivilisationsliterat* and generally of Mann's progress toward a democratic, cosmopolitan stance. This figure is drawn with an eye not focused on the past but on the future. And so is his antagonist, the Jesuit Jew Naphta. In him Mann created a figure not, primarily, typical of bourgeois prewar society but rather of the postwar scene. In Naphta's world view the author sounds his warning of an ideological development which, though rooted in war and revolution, had grown beyond these, to threaten in the form of modern totalitarianism the very foundations of Western civilization with a ruthless and insidious force more devastating than even the brutality of war. Naphta is Mann's portrayal of the modern ideologue ready to sacrifice man on the altar of utopia, enjoying his dialectical triumphs but ending in self-destruction.

It has been suggested that the Marxist literary and social historian, Georg Lukács, has furnished some traits for the figure of Naphta. That may well be. However, Lukács' Marxian thoughts had little if any influence on Naphta's basic philosophy. That philosophy is far more the anticipation of the type of Fascist reactionary neo-barbarism which Mann was to present, some two decades later, in its full-blown form in the racist rantings of Dr. Chaim Braisacher in his *Faustus* novel. Braisacher was drawn in retrospect, after the dread event. With Naphta, however, Mann furnished in the early twenties striking proof of his uncommon skill at sociopolitical and cultural diagnosis and even prognosis.

The Magic Mountain presents an extensive record of Mann's growing awareness of the poet's responsibilities in the social and political life of his time. It reveals this development at least as impressively as Mann's voluminous correspondence of those years or his seminal essay **"Goethe and Tolstoy,"** which he subtitled "Fragments Toward the Problem of Humanism." Written in 1921, this essay is an apt companion piece to the novel, which in its own way is also a great fragment toward the solution of the problem of humanism. Interpreters who seek to establish the *locus classicus* in the work of Mann's rejection of his former conservative stance in favor of a democratic dedication in the service of life generally focus on the chapter "Snow." Without denying its central importance, we would draw the readers' attention to another statement of Mann's painful liberation from a seductively alluring Romanticism and dedication in the service to humanity. We find it in the chapter *"Fülle des Wohllauts"* ("Plenitude of Euphony"). Here Hans Castorp muses on the meaning of Franz Schubert's famous song of the "Linden Tree" ("Am Brunnen vor dem Tore"). Through the "alchemical enhancement (alchemische Steigerung)" experienced by Hans Castorp in the Hermetic, pedagogical sphere of the mountain, he is enabled to penetrate to the morbid essence of that magical song which had held him spellbound. In his state of "illumination" he realizes that this beloved melody, despite its enchantment, or rather precisely by the very power of its spell, was a

> . . . life-fruit begotten of death and pregnant with death. It was a miracle of the soul—the loftiest perhaps in the sight of a beauty devoid of conscience. . . . And yet a miracle viewed with distrust by a responsible sense of friend-ship to life . . . and this for good reasons.

In the final judgment of conscience, Castorp now finds this miracle of a song "standing condemned as an allurement that had to be overcome in an act of self-conquest." This is a most painful truth that has dawned on our humble hero, for it amounts to the sacrifice of a part of his very self. "Yes," Castorp muses, "self-conquest might well be the essence of this re-nunciation of my 'love,' of that soul-magic fraught with such ominous consequences."

In distant retrospect, in a letter to his friend and confidante Agnes Meyer, written in 1943, two decades after the novel's completion, Mann makes it abundantly clear that Castorp's musings on the enchanting song and his painful self-conquest in its renunciation were Mann's very own. "This song," he explains to his friend, "had become a symbol for me of all that is lovable, but also of all that is seductive, of all that harbors the secret seed of corruption." Mann still admits, at this late date, that "Romanticism is far more attractive, even richer, spiritually, than humanism." But he knows now beyond a doubt that "intellect has no right to devote itself to the 'attractive' at a time when it is so emphatically a matter of serving *mankind* as it is today. And," he concludes, "for me that 'today' was even then," even in those early years when he was composing the linden tree scene, lending artistic form to his painful self-conquest in service to mankind.

Another central scene in the novel, expressive of Mann's basic reorientation, is Hans Castorp's conversation with Madame Chauchat, which takes place shortly after the reappearance of Castorp's paramour in the company of Mynheer Peeperkorn. In this scene we have a splendid example of the author's ex-traordinary ability to enhance the meticulously detailed por-trayal of his characters into a significance that transcends the individual and imbues the specific with a paradigmatical im-portance. In the richly delineated personality of Clavdia Chau-chat, Mann succeeds admirably to present, literally to embody, his conception of Russian national characteristics. The ex-change between Clavdia and Castorp reveals impressively his dream of a creative interaction of the aristocratic Western spirit with Russia's democracy-of-the-heart to create Mann's fer-vently hoped for ideal of an aristo-democratic society of the future.

No doubt the poet used both Clavdia Chauchat and Hans Cas-torp as his spokesmen to deliver an urgent message, a warning to his fellow-Germans, his fellow-Westerners. And yet, in using his figures for this openly ideological purpose, the poet did not abuse their integrity as fictional personae. The message springs organically from the medium; Mann's thoughts are quite naturally those of the protagonists of his novel, who remain true to their basic character throughout the work.

Clavdia's Slavic personality and Castorp's German, Western make-up are effectively counterposed to one another as anti-thetical world views. Chauchat accuses her conversation part-ner of selfishness and of egocentricity, arguing that his is a way of life totally devoid of *passion*. She remarks with biting irony:

> I am extraordinarily relieved to hear that you are not a passionate man. But how could you be passionate? You would have to become es-tranged from your kin and kind. To be pas-sionate means living for the sake of life. But it is well known that you, all of you, live for the sake of experience. Passion is self-forget-fulness. But what you all want is self-enrich-ment. *C'est ça.* You don't realize what revolt-ing egoism it is, and that one day this egoism will turn you into an enemy of the human race!

In this significant passage, with its various strata of implication, Thomas Mann placed his finger squarely on the central weak-ness, not of the German character alone, but of the make-up of humanism in all Western countries. It is the inherent indi-vidualistic egocentricity and aristocratic exclusiveness of hu-manism which Mann exposed here, significantly, through the medium of the Slav's differently conditioned and oriented psy-che. To be sure, Mann was not the first to discover this fateful shortcoming in humanism. Goethe in the wisdom of his old age became very conscious of it and sought to correct it in *Wilhelm Meisters Wanderjahre* as well as in the second part of *Faust*, where, all too abruptly, perhaps, Faust, that highest incarnation of man bent on self-perfection and self-enrichment, seeks his salvation in altruistic social activity. Yet it was Mann's contribution to have shown in the Slavic temperament a pos-sible cure to the West's malady of solipsism and to have called for the fusion of the East's passionate antiegocentricity with the West's conscious glorification and cultivation of the great personality, its dignity and inviolability. Mann was to empha-size this thought by frequent repetition. Years later, in 1941, he still considered the reconciliation and fusion of these two world views a central concern of the day:

> The reconciliation of two principles, *intra mu-ros et extra*, is an urgent matter: The "sover-eign" individual must make social concessions to the collective, Socialism and Democracy, "Russia" and "America" must be fused in union.
>
> (pp. 159-64)

André von Gronicka, in his Thomas Mann: Profile and Perspectives, *Random House, 1970, 237 p.*

ROMAN S. STRUC   (essay date 1971)

[*In the following excerpt, Struc examines the concepts of time and timelessness in* The Magic Mountain.]

One of the thorniest problems involved in the study of Thomas Mann's *Magic Mountain* is the puzzling ending of the novel. The serious reader is perplexed by the casual manner in which the author dismisses his *Sorgenkind* ["problem child"], who is thrust into the storm of steel and machines of the First World War. If the reader cannot comprehend the dispassionate manner in which the author releases his protagonist into the world, he is also tempted to regard the protagonist as a character who, after seven years' exposure to various pedagogues and influ-ences, appears to have learned nothing and abandons himself wholeheartedly to the *danse macabre* of the war. Not unlike Josef K. of Kafka's *Trial*, who has not learned anything after a year's lawsuit, Hans Castorp of Mann's novel "concludes" his career as *der Tor* he was when he embarked on his trip to the sanatorium in Davos. Even his momentous experiences in the "Snow" chapter have not left a lasting impression. The italicized sentence (*Der Mensch soll um der Güte und Liebe willen dem Tode keine Herrschaft einräumen über seine Gedanken*) ["For the sake of goodness and love, man shall let death have no sovereignty over his thoughts" (Translation by H. T. Lowe-Porter)]—the only one in the entire novel—seems to have been erased by the routine of the virtually meaningless remaining years in the sanatorium.

Is Hans Castorp a failure? A man who has a unique opportunity in the microcosm of the sanatorium to experience the widest range of existential phenomena apparently fails to draw the obvious conclusions. Our disappointment with Castorp's performance is particularly acute, for we have been told of the great tradition of the *Bildung* and/or *Entwicklung* novel, a genre involving the harmonious resolution of conflicts, and the self-realization of the protagonist as an individual and social being, who, most important, with his initiation into life completed, is capable of living with a greater awareness of his own worth and that of his fellowmen. From his knowledge of that genre the reader will recall that the gentle guidance of the *Turmgesellschaft* ["tower society"] in Goethe's *Wilhelm Meisters Lehrjahre* has an effect on the protagonist, that Heinrich Lee of Keller's *Der grüne Heinrich* turns away from romantic, self-indulgent, and self-defeating artistic pursuits to communal service and local politics, and thereby realizes his true potential, and that Heinrich Drendorf of Stifter's *Der Nachsommer,* who is guided by the gentle pedagogy of his tutor, sails through his apprenticeship without trials or tribulations. The reader begins to suspect that he is not dealing with a classical German novel; indeed, he might even believe from the clues given in the novel itself that the author is playing a cruel if humorous game with him. The all-pervasive presence of irony and of motifs of classical vintage expressed with tongue in cheek makes the reader suspect the presence of a parody on this venerable classical German genre. In any case, he has probably been cautioned to read Thomas Mann with such a possibility in mind.

Thomas Mann writing on Thomas Mann in the Princeton introduction to his novel [see *TCLC*, Vol. 8] is quite explicit in placing it in the context of the literary tradition of the *Bildungsroman*. By implication, Mann would have the reader place his *Sorgenkind* in the company of Parzifal and Wilhelm Meister. But is the author necessarily the best authority on his works? And does the "intention" of the author find its "objective correlative" in the novel? I would like to examine the pertinent aspects of the novel in an attempt to answer these and other questions implied in my introductory remarks.

The retrospective chapters of the novel ("Von der Taufschale und vom Grossvater in zwiefacher Gestalt" and "Bei Tienappels. Und von Hans Castorps sittlichem Befinden" ["Of the Christening Basin, and of Grandfather in His Twofold Guise" and "At the Tienappels', and of Hans Castorp's Moral State"]), dealing with Hans Castorp's formative and traumatic childhood experiences, establish two important points. First, they graphically convey the world Castorp came from, that is, a tradition-bound and settled world, conscious of time and history. They make abundantly clear how radical is the change to which Castorp is subjected when he ventures into the High Alps and loses himself in the atmosphere of the sanatorium. Second, these chapters also bring into sharp focus another point which can be appreciated only retrospectively. Castorp does not enter the world of the "Magic Mountain" altogether unprepared for his adventure and quest since, significant as the difference between his bourgeois past and adventuresome present is, his venture into the realm of irresponsibility, love, and death is predetermined by his childhood experiences. These are described in the two chapters, and later in the dream episode concerning Pribislav Hippe and Castorp's fascination by him. Just as the retrospective chapters prefigure Castorp's development in the sanatorium, his Hippe dream definitely anticipates his passion for Chauchat, the most significant happening in the novel. Hermann J. Weigand in his study of the novel [see *TCLC*, Vol. 2] singles out four "Urerlebnisse" (Continuity, Death, Freedom, and Eros) which predispose Castorp to enter on the perilous path of experimentation, but also—here the matter concerns his awareness of traditional values—allow him in the end to return to his bourgeois matrix or at least to tear himself away from the sanatorium and its temptations. Weigand, too, places the novel in the tradition of the *Bildungsroman* and asserts that the process of development and cultivation of consciousness is both a process and the goal of that process. Experimentation and the heightening of consciousness represent the ever-unfolding goal of Hans Castorp's progress.

It is impossible to disagree with Weigand; still, I would like to add some qualifications and argumentations of my own. The question of the specific results of Castorp's apprenticeship was answered by Theodore Ziolkowski perhaps more clearly than by anyone else [see excerpt dated 1969]. According to Ziolkowski, the essence of Hans Castorp's existence before his trip to Davos was a state of being in time—the bourgeois, historical time; with his trip to the Swiss sanatorium begins his exposure to the illusory nature of time. In the teaching process the lessons are varied in form and intensity. At the very beginning he learns of the relativity of time in such simple terms as the relative speed of the passage of time. "Kurzweile" and "Langeweile" turn out to be misnomers, for it is precisely the time filled with events, the traditional "Kurzweile," that turns out to be "lange Weile," while time unpunctuated by events "passes" rapidly, for there are no signposts by which to measure it. Gradually, Castorp begins to realize that the trip from the lowlands into the heights of the "Magic Mountain" is ultimately not so much a change in life-style, but is rather a byproduct of a much more momentous change, namely in one's perception of time and awareness of various time dimensions. Several formulations of this problem come to mind, such as Einstein's theory of relativity and Bergson's notions of the nature of time; perhaps even more germane to this problem, however, is Heidegger's philosophy in which "Sein" ["existence"] and "Zeit" ["time"] are bound inextricably together so that time dimensions are functions of human existence and human existence is a manifestation of time and in time.

It is not surprising, therefore, that Hans Castorp's views on a number of philosophical, political, and ethical matters undergo a change as his perception of time changes. Thus, he can abandon himself irresponsibly to his passion for Claudia Chauchat; he observes no longer the standards and strictures of the life he has left behind; with a superior and rather arrogant smile, he can dismiss his uncle on the "rescue mission"; he can reflect vis à vis Settembrini that kind of irresponsible, nonclassical, nonrhetorical irony, while he manifests increasingly that newly acquired "freedom" allowing him willfully to shuttle back and forth between paradoxes and polarities, apparent and real. In other words, Hans Castorp the bourgeois becomes the philosopher, but with a difference: his speculations are not tempered by the traditional discipline of enlightened humanism postulated by Settembrini, but are marked by the spirit of an irreverent questioning of all traditional concepts. This attitude does make him a philosopher, but not necessarily a humanist in the traditional sense of the word. For the learning process, commencing with his break with the time concepts he had known as an engineer and member of a loose community in Hamburg, insidiously acquaints him with a view of life, inadequately termed *sub specie aeternitatis*. In other words, the conventional, but still very human point of view is gradually abandoned, and all the usual distinctions are obliterated or obscured with the help of those essentially hostile to the humanistic bourgeois tradition of occidental thinking embodied in the novel primarily by Settembrini and, with certain qualifications, Hofrat Behrens.

In one way or another the questioning of those traditional concepts proceeds to a most radical examination, *i.e.*, to the critique of the conventional concept of time. Madame Chauchat and her secret ally, Naphta, view this conventional concept with a haughty irony or ire, respectively, since they both realize the illusory characteristic of time. Claudia Chauchat experientially, intuitively, and, by virtue of her background, both as a Russian and patient; in Naphta's case, the natively sceptical attitude toward time is reinforced by his training as a theologian for whom time exists only on the lowest intellectual level. The background of the two emphasizes that cultural geography introduced by Thomas Mann as early as *Buddenbrooks* (1900) in which East and West as geographical concepts extensively determine the individual's *Weltanschauung* ["world view"]. If Hans Castorp as a German is geographically located between East and West, his spiritual destiny as well is to stand in the middle, or, more accurately, to shuttle back and forth between various polarities traditionally and, in the case of Thomas Mann, most consciously associated with such distinctions. This is another reason why those characters, whose allegiances consciously or unconsciously are given to that complex of thought and emotionality designated in the novel as oriental, assume in the awareness of the protagonist a role different from that of other characters.

Most characters in this novel, apart from the specifics of their background and personality, are endowed with a mythical analogy. The author draws on Classical, Germanic, and psychoanalytic lore to establish these mythical identifications. In making such additional distinctions we might come to understand more fully the configuration of the novel. Let us take, for example, four characters: Joachim Ziemssen, Claudia Chauchat, Settembrini, and Naphta. Both the cousin of Hans Castorp and the Italian mentor are portrayed primarily within the framework of Western referential tradition: Joachim whose figure recalls such *literary* analogies as Goethe's Valentin in *Faust*, embodies the Prussian concept of honor and the military. Settembrini is entirely a *literati*. He introduces himself as a man of letters, who associates himself with the tradition of European enlightenment, and even the sparse mythological identifications point to the literary-humanistic tradition (Satana-Lucifer). Analogies for Chauchat and Naphta, on the other hand, are much more amorphous: they lack the precision evident in the former two characters. For that very reason, however, they are no less poignant or effective. The "temptress" Claudia brings to mind all the temptresses of the myth, fairy tale, and literature generally; she is indeed the Siren, the *Urnymphe*, an archetypal phenomenon, just as Naphta's principal quality is perversion or, in the original Greek, he is the "diabolos" of all the myths, legends, and literary works. These last two characters owe more to primitive or chthonic mythology than to the essentially literary and humanistic tradition drawn on for the first two. We can discern the lines in the configuration of the characters in the novel. Those that we have taken as an example generally belong to two camps differentiated as to geographic background (East and West), attitude toward time, mythical identification (classical-humanistic versus primitive-chthonic), and ethical considerations (duty, progress versus irresponsibility, freedom, and questioning the very possibility of progress). Another category of identification and differentiation should be added. The first group of characters in our example is associated with reason and consciousness, while the second can easily be regarded as representative of that other, diametrically opposed dimension, *i.e.*, the unconscious.

Let us now return to the main argument. From the beginning Hans Castorp is exposed to a concept of time which radically differs from the one to which he was accustomed and which largely determined the quality of his life. What he learns on the "Magic Mountain" is to measure time differently, in units increasingly diverging from the familiar standards. One could again refer to Ziolkowski's book, which views Hans Castorp as learning a new concept of time—timelessness. Such a concept stands beyond human imagination. Its ontology is primarily of a semantic nature, and its literary manifestation is as impossible and elusive as the concept itself. For that matter the very embodiment of time in literature is an extremely daring undertaking. Enough has been written about this concept, especially in regard to Thomas Mann's uniquely successful techniques in *The Magic Mountain*. . . . What should be restated here is that the author's accomplishment arises from a total subordination of all available means to the attainment of this end.

As the author explores various aspects of time in both the speculative essays of the novel and in the descriptions of the protagonist's existential experience, he also touches on a dimension which in modern scientific theory is inextricably tied to the concept of time—the concept of space. Thus, in an early encounter with Settembrini, Castorp is informed that his arrival at the sanatorium could be interpreted as a trip downward. At this juncture Settembrini's remark contains exclusively moral implications. He views the sanatorium as a pit of depravity and moral licentiousness, and, therefore, the physical ascent may figuratively be construed as a moral descent. This figurative relativization of apparently exclusive concepts is expanded in various ways. Thus, the relativity of time and space is explicitly asserted, as is the relativity of the moral concepts. Furthermore, physical dimensions are accorded a symbolic value; for example, the characters associated with the subconscious or unconscious—Chauchat, Naphta, and Dr. Krokowski—are alternately identified with the physical "below" and "underneath." The first decisive meeting between Castorp and Chauchat takes place in the basement of the sanatorium building, where the offices of the psychoanalyst Krokowski are located, just as Naphta's very name hints at his subterranean origin and character. Retrospectively, then, Settembrini's remark on Castorp's journey gains another perspective which can be understood symbolically as a descent into the unconscious, into the self, or, to use the romantic formulation, it is "der Weg nach Innen" ["the way inward"].

Manifestations of the unconscious naturally move upward to the surface, but these are mostly in the form of gestures, insignificant slips, and are generally those actions which defy explanation in terms of conventional psychological plausibility. The unconscious reveals itself in an equally elusive and symbolic manner, as dreams, visions, and experiences in which the intellect is dormant, being relegated, as it were, to a minor role in the concert of existence. Dreams and visions punctuate the structure of the novel. They perform in a limited way the literary function of prefiguring certain motifs, characters, and events, but primarily they advance the intellectual movement of the novel. If the numerous forces contesting for the soul of Hans Castorp could be schematically categorized as those of humanistic self-assertion, and those of Eastern passivism and acceptance of death as deliverance to the ''perfection'' of Nirvana, and if this distinction could hypothetically represent consciousness and the unconscious, one could say that it is the latter that expresses itself in those significant dreams. As an example, the hidden identity of love and death comprises the subject of the Pribislav Hippe dream. It indicates the protagonist's love involvement with Chauchat and his accompanying wish for moral abdication and abandonment to disease and death. Just as ordinary existence is bound up with the concept of time, with chronology, the realm of the unconscious, the dream and the vision, wreaks havoc on time or, to put it more directly, knows no time. Chronology is confused, the terms early and late, now and then, these distinctions men usually apply are nonexistent; and the same is true of spatial dimensions.

The modern European novel (for example, the works of Dostoevsky, Kafka, Joyce, and Proust) made increasing use of the insights of modern science, depth psychology, and the novelistic techniques partly resulting from such insights and partly anticipating them. Kafka, Proust, and Joyce are all most adept at incorporating these insights arrived at personally or with the aid of various disciplines, while in Kafka, for instance, phenomenal reality functions exclusively as a projection of the characters' consciousness in its most comprehensive sense. Thus Thomas Mann's artistic practice has to be carefully qualified. Mann, an essentially nineteenth-century humanist, allows the unconscious just so much room in his ideational framework and in his art. There is a constant interplay between the two, between dream and reality, the conscious and the unconscious, the intellect and the Will. The balance is often upset, yet neither aspect ever entirely disappears from the scope of his writings. Besides, the primary conflict in the novels of Thomas Mann is the contest between the spirit and the Will—to use Schopenhauerian terms—in its most varied configurations and variations.

Let me summarize some of the points made so far: the hero's progress can be seen as a movement away from the tradition-bound, morally strict societal context of the lowlands, toward a state of moral indifference, toward a position of questioning bourgeois morality and ethics, toward a lassitude in erotic involvements, and the relentless, if somewhat ''irresponsible'' philosophical speculation influenced by various tutors of opposing points of view. Further, this development is paralleled by the experience of the relativity of time and, with some reservations, of space, which in the course of the novel becomes more and more explicit and culminates finally in an obliteration of these concepts (this is especially so in the ''Snow'' chapter, which in many respects represents the heart of the novel). I would also like to emphasize that an analogy to the important ethical and philosophical experiences is to be found in certain manifestations of the protagonist's unconscious, specifically in his dreams. These concepts clearly undergo a radical change in the dreams, a change which, as I hope to show, determines also the ending of the novel. On the following pages I propose to concentrate on the chapter ''Snow,'' which by the author's own admission contains the quintessence of the novel.

The chapter ''Snow'' is placed in the last third of the novel. Significant events still to come include the appearance of Mynheer Peeperkorn, his suicide, the duel between Settembrini and Naphta, Naphta's exit, the occult scenes, and Castorp's strange return to the homeland. In comparison with the first half of the novel, which is primarily concerned with the taciturn and rather one-sided romance between Castorp and Madame Chauchat, the second half, with the possible exception of the Peeperkorn incident, is deficient in drama and excitement. Some critics have objected to the monotonous second part of the novel. But if the novel is considered as a whole, the monotony of the second part is justified. As monotony and boredom invade the life of the protagonist, the sluggish progression of Castorp's routine existence is paralleled by the form of the novel. The monotony of the protagonist's life has its correlative in the endless and inconclusive debates between Settembrini and Naphta, in the frequently long descriptions of the sanatorium affairs, in the quarrels among the patients, and in other ''digressions.'' Just as time in the first half of the novel seems to pass rapidly, or slowly, since it is filled with events, later, depending on Hans Castorp's attitudes, it flows slowly or ''rapidly,'' as the case may be. The chronology becomes blurred, the punctuation is obscured, since routine and sameness reign. Thus, movement resulting from that rapid succession of events abates, and the weeks, months, and years leading to the end pass unnoticed. Time seems to come to a standstill. At this point Castorp decides to take stock of himself, ''mit seinen Gedanken und Regierungsgeschäften allein zu sein'' [''to be alone with his thoughts and his stock-taking projects'' (Translation by H. T. Lowe-Porter)]. . . . This escape from the lethargy and passivity of the earlier days is mistakenly welcomed by Settembrini as an act of self-assertion, as a rebellion against the evil influences of the sanatorium surroundings. ''Zwei Jahre hier und noch dieses Einfalls fähig—ah, nein, Ihr Kern ist gut, man hat keinen Grund, an Ihnen zu verzweifeln. Bravo, bravo!'' [''Two years up here, and still capable of such projects—ah, yes, your heart is sound, no need to despair of you. Bravo, bravo!'' (Translation by H. T. Lowe-Porter)]. . . . Settembrini's applause is based on a misunderstanding of Castorp's intention. The trip to the mountains is explained as a skiing excursion. Something rather trivial like *mens sana in corpore sano* [''a sound mind in a sound body''] might have occurred to Settembrini. In retrospect, both Settembrini's assessment and Castorp's statement seem to be true. Castorp's undertaking is both a break from the routine of the sanatorium and a somewhat irresponsible venture into the realm of danger and into a dimension—timelessness—far removed from the familiar realities of the protagonist.

Up to this point the author was endeavoring to convey the relativity of time and concepts through the experiences, reflections, and discussions of his protagonist; in the ''Snow'' chapter this trend reaches its culmination. Hans Castorp experiences the cosmos stripped of its civilizing attributes, the world without the directional signals of anthropomorphic projection. Mann uses modifiers which make the snowfall appear ''unnatural'': ''monströs und masslos'' [''monstrous and measureless''] . . . ''nicht geheuer'' [''uncanny'']. . . . The snow obliterates the familiar distinctions of time and space, and the protagonist is confronted with the ''Chaos von weisser Finsternis'' [''chaos of white darkness'']. . . . The author speaks explicitly of the ''Aufhebung der Zeit'' [''arrest of time''] . . . and of the relativity of motion and progress. . . . Anyone knowing Thomas Mann's philosophical bend of mind, painstaking workmanship, and density of thought cannot assume that such clusters of utterances and imagery are accidental. Time and again many critics, including Mann himself, have regarded the ''Snow'' chapter as the intellectual center of the novel. It is

The Hotel Schatzalp in Davos, Switzerland, which, with the Waldsanatorium in Davos, served as a model for the Sanatorium Berghof in The Magic Mountain. *Dr. Hans-Otto Mayer.*

the culmination of the *Bildung* of the protagonist, and, at the same time, the turning point in the career of Hans Castorp. In this chapter he is introduced to that realm to which he aspired and for which he was prepared by his assorted mentors, specifically those representing the East with all its connotations. It is no accident that the chapter in which Castorp arrives at the synthesis contains an unusually extensive employment of oxymora functioning not merely to emphasize the irreconcilability of the positions borrowed from his tutors, but also to anticipate the synoptic vision confronting the protagonist and obliterating the contradictions in his teachers' positions. Two visions, two archetypal realms, stand before him: the bright and harmonious picture of the classical landscape, with the ideals of the Greek *Paideia,* and the chthonian vision of the Dionysian underworld.

Yet Castorp realizes that man is not helplessly turned over to the struggling opposites: man can rule, mediate, challenge, make war, and even triumph. He cannot legislate "night" and death out of his life, but can hold these forces in check. "*Der Mensch ist Herr der Gegensätze, sie sind durch ihn, und also er ist vornehmer als sie. Vornehmer als der Tod, zu vornehm für diesen—das ist die Freiheit seines Kopfes*" ["Man is the lord of counter-positions, they can be only through him, and thus he is more aristocratic than they. More so than death, too aristocratic for death—that is the freedom of his mind"], and

further: "*Der Mensch soll um der Güte und Liebe willen dem Tode keine Herrschaft einräumen über seine Gedanken*" ["For the sake of goodness and love, man shall let death have no sovereignty over his thoughts" (Translations by H. T. Lowe-Porter)].... This sentence must necessarily be understood as Thomas Mann's own concurrence in the position at which his protagonist evolves. For this reason it is even more surprising and disappointing, if not shocking, that so little is made of this realization. For before long, as the narrator claims, what remains of this vision of humanity is a mere shadow, only an indistinct memory in the mind of the protagonist. The distance (or time) between the snow episode and the novel's conclusion is considerable. The Peeperkorn incident, the conjuring up of Castorp's cousin Joachim, the endless quarrels among the patients, and other variously important occurrences intervene. For Castorp these incidents eliminate or neutralize that physical and spiritual experience manifesting the potential for a break with the hothouse atmosphere of the sanatorium in the direction of the humanism envisaged in the snow dream. And yet this vision is not realized, for it is half forgotten, half abandoned. Does this fact mean that Mann was having second thoughts about the vision, that he realized the basic incompatibility between an ideal and its realization? To some extent, yes. But the reasons for the author's decision to direct his protagonist's life may have been infinitely more complex.... It is true that

Castorp's vision has something in common with a genuine mystic experience. Thomas Mann does realize that such an experience cannot be projected into phenomenal reality since this would violate its very mysticism. . . . Is then the primary function of the "Snow" chapter one of revealing the existence of experiences which cannot be integrated into the fabric of life as it is lived? If so, one must then explain why the author does make this chapter the indisputable centerpiece of his novel only to discard it in the end. As I mentioned before, *The Magic Mountain* owes a good deal to the whole tradition of the *Bildungsroman*, and here especially the author would likely subscribe to the efficacy of the individual experience of the "Bildungsprozess."

Alternate reasons should be considered as well. Often enough the point has been made that *The Magic Mountain* is a *Zeitroman* ["time novel"] in the dual sense of the word. It is a novel which deals with time as subject matter, but it is also a time novel in the more ordinary sense; roughly speaking, it is a historical novel dealing with a specific period of time. In the first sense the novel affords the reader the opportunity to experience various time levels at "first-hand," since this is part of the process of Hans Castorp's acclimatization to the sanatorium. Linear time, with which Castorp had been most familiar in the past, now recedes before the realization of utter subjectivity in experiencing time. Subsequently, Castorp learns of the cyclical nature of time, which is especially evident in the chapter "Ewigkeitssuppe," an ironic reinterpretation of Nietzsche's "eternal return." Moreover, another time dimension seems to emerge from the novel. I am not persuaded that terminology is of the utmost importance here, and am cautiously tempted to call this dimension timelessness. Naturally, in the strict sense, such a word is nonsensical. One of the key attributes of existence is its being conceivable only in time, to which all aspects of human existence are subject. The unconscious is, however, an area in which the experience of time is suspended. Freud commented on this phenomenon:

> In the Id there is nothing corresponding to the idea of time, and (a thing which is very remarkable and awaits adequate attention in philosophic thought) no alteration of mental processes by the passage of time. Conative impulses which have never got beyond the Id, and even impressions which have been pushed down into the Id by repression, are virtually immortal and are preserved for whole decades as though they had only occurred. . . . It is constantly being borne in upon me that we have made far too little use in our theory of undubitable fact that the repressed remains unaltered by the passage of time. This seems to offer us the possibility of an approach to some really profound truths.

Commenting on this passage, Hans Meyerhoff quotes an article by Marie Bonaparte, who "distinguishes three senses of 'timelessness': (1) the unconscious has no knowledge of time; (2) the unconscious is completely unaffected by the process of time; (3) the unconscious does not perceive time." She further qualifies Freud's thesis by saying that "repressed psychic content undergoes *some* modification, however unalterable it may appear to our conscious minds."

The most obvious manifestation of the unconscious is the dream. *The Magic Mountain* abounds in dreams, of which the most important are the Hippe dream and the visionary dream in the snow. These dreams cannot be entirely assessed in terms of the above quotations; they afford us, however, a useful point of departure. The Hippe dream is functional in the structure of the novel as an anticipation of Castorp's involvement with Claudia Chauchat. Its secondary function is to reveal from what depths such engagements arise, from the puberterian homoerotic inclinations of the protagonist. The important thing is that the repressed sequence recurs in all its immediacy and vividness in response to a clue supplied by the meeting with Chauchat. Time has not destroyed any of its acuteness. Were we to use the psychoanalytic terms, we should call this dream a manifestation of the repressed personal unconscious. For when we look at the vision in the snow, it becomes obvious that the personal is reduced to negligible dimensions and to the fore comes that quality which in Jungian terminology we would call the "collective unconscious." These are terms we choose for the sake of convenience and not because they are particularly suitable for assessing the realities of the novel. Besides, there is no test by which one with sufficient discrimination could discern which manifestations belong to what layer of the psyche, even if we were to accept its basic structure arrived at by psychoanalysis.

One can indeed question the psychoanalytical "authenticity" of the snow dream. For the vision in the snow has the characteristics of an ideational statement whose sources in part could be traced in German intellectual history. More important to us than the actual content of the dream are the circumstances surrounding it. Namely, time and space in this case are suspended most thoroughly. If the entire novel is a representation of time and, to some extent, space relativized, the dream sequences and, specifically, the snow dream are removed from the context of time and space only to enhance the impression of "timelessness." The baffling remark at the end of the chapter, "Was er geträumt, war im Verbleichen begriffen. Was er gedacht, verstand er schon diesen Abend nicht mehr so recht" ["What he had dreamed was already fading from his mind. What he had thought—even that selfsame evening it was no longer so clear as it had been at first" (Translation by H. T. Lowe-Porter)] . . . , now becomes clearer. It is not that the "Mysterium" of the envisioned truth will be destroyed by its transfer to everyday reality, but that the dream introduces a level of "reality" at absolute odds with that reality to which Castorp descends after the dream. Timelessness and time are mutually exclusive. The unconscious has no time dimension, and therefore dream insights cannot be accepted into a reality circumscribed by time.

Concerning the other meaning of "Zeitroman," *The Magic Mountain* is, with the necessary qualifications, defined as a historical novel. Hans Castorp enters the novel from a realm which partakes of the historical process. To be sure, Castorp's awareness of this process is dim. As a graduate shipbuilding engineer one would expect more of him; though by virtue of his character, his social status, and the fact that he is an "unpolitical" German, his indifference to, and ignorance of, historical forces is understandable and plausible. Ironically, when he is thrust into the ahistorical realm of the "Magic Mountain," he is subjected to the subtle persuasiveness of quietism and Eastern inactivity and, on the other hand, to the somewhat simpleminded, socio-political activism of Settembrini. The climate of the sanatorium, Castorp's own inclinations, and his consuming passion for Madame Chauchat, all contribute to the choice of *vita contemplativa* over the alternatives advanced by Settembrini. These alternatives are presented with irony, for their spokesman, the Italian humanist and perennial patient himself, has no choice in the matter. Castorp's own brand of humanism, which slowly evolves in the course of his stay in the sanatorium and reaches its peak in his visionary dream in the snow, is an indirect result of his "horizontal" existence, of his contemplative efforts, rather than of his view of the human condition as part of the historical process. In this respect the vision in the snow indeed represents the timeless, mythical view of the condition of mankind, rather than its dynamic here and now. And yet history and its processes have their own laws and dynamism as we see at the end of the novel. The First World War breaks out, and Hans Castorp is drawn into it more as a victim than an agent. As the reader leaves the protagonist, he sees him stumble and fall, raise himself and charge over one of the battlefields of war-torn Europe. For the decision to return and take part in the conflict is not his own. History, so long ignored by Hans Castorp, catches up with him. . . . Thus, what is presented as a vision of all-conquering love in the snow does not seem to find its way into the consciousness of everyday reality; to put it differently, the mythical dimension is at odds with history, whose laws operate independently of the timeless vision of man.

If the reader is disappointed with the inconclusive issue of the novel, he must bear in mind that it has its own terms and operative laws. The "vacation" land of the sanatorium is rudely confronted with reality, history, and with a time in which the dream of mankind has no place. To pass judgment on Castorp or his authorial progenitor is as foolish as to pass judgment on reality. The perspective of the novel does not allow such judgment, for it is polyphonic in its structure: many voices resound but are not resolved in a symphony. They are allowed to sound continuously in witness to man's infinite capacity for versatility in thoughts and emotions, goodness and evil. This approach suggests a pessimistic view of man and his works; it may also result in attributing the nihilistic view of art to Thomas Mann. Although such a charge is tempting, it is also much too facile.

If the author somewhat cruelly abandons his *Sorgenkind* in the midst of the European bloodbath, the vision of humanism based on love is not relinquished. The very last sentence of the novel reaffirms the vision, albeit as a question, as hope so precarious and fragile that it is hope against hope. But if Hans Castorp is to be seen as representing European consciousness and if he was possessed of this vision for but a moment, soon to be forgotten, then the novel, despite its ironies and ambiguities, bears witnesses to the reality of the vision in the snow. "Wird auch aus diesem Weltfest des Todes, auch aus der schlimmen Fieberbrunst, die rings den regnerischen Abendhimmel entzündet, einmal die Liebe steigen?" ["Out of this universal feast of death, out of this extremity of fever, kindling the rainwashed evening sky to a fiery glow, may it be that Love one day shall mount?" (Translation by H. T. Lowe-Porter)]. . . . To this the novel says: yes. (pp. 83-95)

> *Roman S. Struc, "'The Magic Mountain': Time and Timelessness," in* Research Studies, *Vol. 39, No. 2, June, 1971, pp. 83-95.*

MARTIN SWALES (essay date 1978)

[*A Canadian educator and critic, Swales is the author of* The German Novelle *(1977) and* The German Bildungsroman *(1978). In the following excerpt from the latter work, which first appeared in a different form in* Deutsche Vierteljahrsschrift für Literaturwissenschaft und Geistesgeschichte *(1972), Swales discusses Hans Castorp's intellectual and spiritual development and the relationship of* The Magic Mountain *to the Bildungsroman tradition.*]

Critical discussion of *The Magic Mountain* continues with unabated energy. Despite the multiplicity of diverging viewpoints and approaches, however, there is still an approximate consensus of opinion about the function of the hero, Hans Castorp, and about the thematic import of the experiences he undergoes in the rarefied air of the sanatorium world. This consensus could be summarized as follows: Hans Castorp, a simple, somewhat mediocre young man leaves the world of good Hamburg society to which he belongs and travels to Davos in order to visit his cousin Joachim, who is a patient in the Berghof sanatorium. His short visit turns into a seven-year sojourn when it is discovered that he himself is suffering from tuberculosis. In the hermetic, feverish atmosphere of the enchanted mountain the ordinary stuff of which Hans Castorp is made undergoes a heightening and enhancing process that makes him capable of adventures in sensual, moral, and intellectual spheres he would never have dreamed of in the flatland. Narratively, this process is intimated through Castorp's contact with various characters who are in effect exponents, representatives, emissaries from domains of the spirit. The macabre adventures through which Hans Castorp passes are a pedagogic instrument, used to accomplish the heightening and enhancement of the hero to a point far beyond his original competence. And pedagogically, the Magic Mountain experience works. Castorp learns to overcome his inborn attraction to death and arrives at an understanding of humanity that does not simply ignore death nor scorn the dark, mysterious side of life. He takes account of death, but without letting it gain control of his mind. It is this notion of disease, and of death as a necessary route to knowledge, health, and life, that makes *The Magic Mountain* a novel of initiation. Like the traditional seeker after the Grail, Hans Castorp has to undergo various terrible ordeals before he may approach his goal. And that goal, the Grail of his quest, is to be found in the chapter "Snow," where, lost in perilous heights, he dreams his dream of humanity. If he does not find the Grail, yet he divines it in his deathly dream before he is snatched downward from his heights into the European catastrophe.

That most Mann critics would agree on this kind of outline of the basic theme of *The Magic Mountain* is perhaps hardly surprising, because the foregoing summary of the novel's thematic purpose is taken, for the greater part word for word, from Thomas Mann himself, from his paper, **"The Making of The Magic Mountain"** [see *TCLC*, Vol. 8]. . . . In my view, however, Mann's own remarks on his novel capture only one part of the total meaning of the work. *The Magic Mountain* is much more complex and differentiated than this simple summary of Hans Castorp's development suggests. I might here summarize my reasons for believing that this outline of Hans Castorp's function is misleading. There are four aspects which trouble me, and none more so than the pedagogic notion that the hero develops in the course of the novel to a "point far beyond his original competence." In the first place, what kind of competence is involved here? Intellectual, imaginative, moral competence? Furthermore, do the last three chapters or so of the novel show us a hero who is manifestly in possession of certain values which he did not have at the beginning? My second objection concerns the whole question of *The Magic Mountain* as a novel of initiation, as a novel with a Grail. I can see that there are insight moments in the novel, moments when Hans Castorp perceives some aspect or aspects of the human condition. Yet, each time, the insight moment is forgotten, is relativized by what follows it. And this fact leads me to question whether there is an explicit value center to Mann's novel. If such a center does exist, then it may indeed be the "Snow" chapter. But does Hans Castorp's dream vision of the Sun People function as the climactic wisdom of this massive novel? Does the hero's vision stand up intellectually and stylistically within the context of the novel? My final objection concerns the structure of the novel. If the snow vision does stand up, why does it not come nearer to the end of the novel? It is significant in this context to note that Mann's remarks about the "Snow" chapter being the Grail of the novel operate with a misleading time scale. He writes that Hans Castorp "divines [the Grail] in his deathly dream, before he is snatched downward from his heights into the European catastrophe." In fact, however, some two hundred pages follow the "Snow" chapter, and in these pages one of the most crucial characters of the whole novel makes his appearance: Mynheer Peeperkorn. (pp. 105-07)

In order to clarify the remarkable elusiveness of the hero's development in *The Magic Mountain* it is necessary to examine in some detail those insight points that do occur in the course of Hans Castorp's seven years spent in the sanatorium. One aspect should be stressed at the outset: Hans Castorp is vouchsafed these moments of insight as a result of his confrontation with a quite specific world, with the world of extremes that is the Berghof. The comment the narrator makes about Frau Ziemssen's attempt to moderate the hilarity of the cousins when they are reunited is pertinent here: "It was essentially for reasons of propriety that she had wanted to introduce a little moderate seriousness, not knowing that precisely the moderate, the middle way was completely unknown here and only a choice between extremes was offered." . . . (p. 108)

The sense in which the sanatorium represents a world of extremes is suggested at several points in the novel: it is a world that makes the intellectual more purely intellectual (that is, cerebral) in that there are no everyday practicalities to relativize the articulation of certain intellectual positions; it is also a world that makes the physical more purely physical in that sickness invites acquiescence in the body's complete domination of the human personality. (pp. 108-09)

The interaction of Hans Castorp, in all his problematic mediocrity, with the Berghof world of extremes is the subject matter of *The Magic Mountain*. A complex of thematic strands interweave to form the texture of the novel as a whole. And the strands constantly interact in the sense that they comment on and relativize each other. At crucial points along the plot thread the strands emerge and constitute a focus, a moment of insight, a new understanding for Castorp. Common to these focus points is the notion of man as a being greater than any of the dualisms his reflective faculty perceives. And yet Hans Castorp forgets the insight he has gained, the focus point fades, the themes become submerged in the general texture—only to reappear elsewhere.

I wish to comment in detail on four of these focus points. The first concerns Hans Castorp and medicine. Its explicit formulation is to be found in the chapter "Researches," where Castorp, largely under the impetus of a recent conversation with Hofrat Behrens, devotes his attention to the study of medical textbooks. In their conversation Castorp had learned that the life process is chemically identical with the dying process (oxidation). The only difference is that in life the organic form is preserved and constantly renews itself. This chemical fact, Castorp reflects, is a precondition of man's being, and of his entire reflective, analytical, speculative capacity. . . . Insight, intellectual understanding, is a function of the material constitution of man and can therefore never fully understand the

process of which it is a part because it cannot stand outside the context of its own functioning. This crucial notion relativizes much of Naphta's and Settembrini's endless debates about spirit and matter. It reveals their intellectualism as a process of bloodless cerebration, as operating with the false postulation of the spirit of man, his self-awareness, as something over against and contemplatively separate from his material selfhood. Furthermore, this notion questions the whole nature of human insight in that it suggests the incompleteness of any intellectual construct that claims to know and understand life. Hence, it is the purpose of this particular moment of insight that Hans Castorp be made to question how much can be learned from moments of reflective analysis.

The second focus point involves Castorp and the notion of form. Its explicit center is the chapter "Dance of Death," where Castorp decides to take an interest in the dying patients in the sanatorium. The purpose behind his visits is to offer formal expressions of sympathy and condolence. In the chapter that depicts the death of Joachim the point is made that this capacity for compassion linked with formal observances of decency and decorum distinguishes man from animals, that is, man is able to answer death by form and therein expresses his humanity. The theme of form is something we have already encountered in the "medical" focus point: form is that which distinguishes living from dying. Man's capacity for giving form to experience is what makes him truly human. Form is also seen as central to the medical profession: doctors formalize by means of Latinate categorizations the multifarious possibilities of sickness. In this sense they answer the process of dissolution, decay, and loss of form by strict formality. Form, Castorp comes to realize, is at the heart of any humane morality, for human dignity resides in the ability to know of the abyss and to answer it with form, with ceremony and observances (a notion inherent in Castorp's reverence for the "baptismal bowl"). Form, then, represents control and order; it is purposive, it is morally good.

But, as with the previous focus point, this moment of insight too cannot simply be possessed as a stable intimation of abiding value. Once glimpsed, it is to be forgotten. The theme of form finds its own relativization in the notion of Spanish court etiquette (Castorp's references to *Don Carlos*), which emerges as both the ultimate expression of human dignity and willpower, and also as a constriction of life, a schematization of human behavior to the point of lifelessness. This relativization of the theme of form becomes explicit in the introduction to the next thematic crystallization point, the "Snow" chapter: as Hans Castorp blunders through the swirling snowflakes he reflects that the snowflake in its total formal perfection represents a *deathly* perfection, an order to which all dynamic and flux has been sacrificed.

The "Snow" chapter begins with a journey into obliterating death, a journey that involves a process of *umkommen* (the etymological pun—"to come in a circle" and "to die"—is made explicit). And yet this journey to the edge of the abyss yields a dream of perfect humanity, of the Sun People, who live a life of sensuous beauty and ordered, serene social intercourse, while yet knowing of the dark, mysterious horrors embedded in the very heart of life. Before commenting on the substance of this dream image of human wholeness and perfection, it is, I think, appropriate to review the conclusions that Hans Castorp draws from it. There can be no doubt that these conclusions are important, not only to Castorp himself— he desperately tries to hammer them into his brain—but also to the narrator, who resorts to italics in order to emphasize the importance of the insights gained.

Castorp concludes that man truly is the problem child of life because of the inescapable ambiguity of his situation, an ambiguity that informs even the values by which he seeks to live. There is no one answer to life's complexities because there are no one-dimensional, abiding certainties. This leads Castorp to reject both Naphta and Settembrini as empty talkers, as windbags, as false propounders of easy doctrines. Their falsity resides in the exclusive extremism of their respective positions, for as Castorp comes to realize, so many polar opposites are not necessarily antagonists. Rather, they are subsumable under a meaningful, coherent, and humane wholeness. This is the center of Castorp's insight: because man's being houses and encompasses multiple dualisms, his being is greater than all the dualisms and contradictions which his reflective faculty so relentlessly perceives. Here we are in effect concerned with a reworking of the "medical" insight: man is in danger of postulating a free-floating mind separate from the physical organism whose existence and functioning is a precondition of his thinking at all. To talk of a dualism between matter and spirit is therefore cerebral nonsense; the mind needs the body in order to be able to formulate its denial of and withdrawal from the body. The lesson to be learned, then, is love of man, love of that process—life—which enables him to know himself to the extent that he does, and above all, love of that process which makes him so much more of a totality than he is ever able to perceive intellectually. This is the italicized message of the "Snow" chapter: *"for the sake of goodness and love man should not allow death to take charge of his thoughts."* . . . It would seem, then, that the "Snow" chapter is a point of climactic insight within the novel. But intellectually, it says no more than the other focus points. It reaches the same conclusion, a conclusion which is then, as we are quite explicitly told, forgotten by Hans Castorp. In other words, it is as valid as the other focus points, no more and no less.

What distinguishes this section from all the other insight points, however, is that the moment of insight is not simply formulated discursively and stated in conceptual terms, but is also made concrete in an image of human existence and activity, the Sun People. It is this concretization that I find questionable. In my view, the dream sequence is overwritten to the point of being a melodramatic scenario. It is in part a euphoric wish-dream emanating from the mind of a young man lost in a blizzard. The vision is not without touches of irony, as when the witches hurl obscenities at Castorp in his native Hamburg dialect. The dream derives from the hero's present longing for warmth and sunlight, from his craving for an image of human wholeness and integration as opposed to the partial and extreme figures of the Berghof. But whether the Sun People are an intellectually satisfying embodiment of this wholeness seems to me questionable. Hans Castorp's fevered brain attempts to construct an image which can express such wholeness in visible and concrete terms. The Sun People on the beach know of the horror of the human sacrifice—the boy's gaze darkens as his eyes alight on the temple—but they make no attempt to halt the monstrousness of the human sacrifice. They simply acquiesce in the fact that it is, and thereby, surely, they lay themselves open to the charge of smugness and callousness.

It is, then, the dream image which I find stylistically and intellectually questionable. The conclusions that Hans Castorp draws—which the narrator describes as a continuation of the dream "no longer in images, but in thoughts, although for all

that no less venturesome and confused" . . .—are acceptable in that they represent, as elsewhere in the novel, a grappling on the conceptual level with the antinomies that make up existence, and with the human totality under which they are ultimately subsumable. Yet this insight fades like all the others.

The fourth insight point centers upon the theme of love. The theme of course appears in a variety of guises throughout the novel, but it finds its focus—surprisingly perhaps, but importantly in my view—not with reference to Hans Castorp's love for another human being, but rather in the context of his love for a human construct, for a song, the "Lindenbaum." The song itself, we are told, has simple strength and energy, a folksy sturdiness, but it knows of death. The return for which it longs is the return to a simple state, return to a peace that obliterates everything, all sorrow, all joy, all individuation, the peace of death. Castorp's love for this intrinsically ambiguous song is equal to and aware of the ambiguity of the thing loved. His love encompasses detachment and attraction, passionate assent and critical distance; it is self-aware, yet profound. The narrator explicitly describes the nature of Hans Castorp's love, that it is an eros deeply ironic and self-critical:

> Is one to believe that our simple hero after so and so many years a hermetic-pedagogic enhancement has penetrated sufficiently deeply into spiritual matters in order to be *aware* of the significance of his love and of its object. We assert and tell that he was. The song meant a great deal to him, a whole world, indeed a world which he perforce loved, otherwise he could not have been so infatuated with its representative symbol. We know what we are saying when we—perhaps somewhat obscurely— add that his fate would have shaped itself very differently if his heart had not been excessively responsive to the charms of that emotional world, of that general spiritual attitude which the song summarized in its heartfelt, mysterious way. But precisely this fate had brought with it enhancements, adventures, insights, had caused reflective difficulties within him, which had made him capable of perceptive criticism of this world, of this its admittedly admirable symbol, of this his love—such that all three became the object of moral scruple. . . .
>
> (pp. 109-15)

And yet, here again the moment of insight is taken back, is relativized, as Castorp goes on to falsify his insight, his love. In the passage I have just quoted the narrator asserts the clarity—and the rightness—of Hans Castorp's perception. But our hero cannot leave it at that:

> Hans Castorp's thoughts or intuitive half-thoughts flew high as he sat in night and loneliness in front of his silent musical sarcophagus. They flew higher than his reason could go, they were alchemistically enhanced thoughts. Oh it was powerful this magic of the soul. We all were its sons and we could achieve mighty things on earth by serving it. . . . But its best son might be whosoever in self-transcendence consumed his own life and died, on his lips the new word of love which he could not yet utter. It was so worth dying for, this magic song! But he who died for it, did not actually die for it anymore—

he was a hero insofar as he died for the new,
for the new word of love, of the future in his
heart. . . .

This is a passionate and rhetorical passage. In it, Hans Castorp dreams of a love beyond, outside this his present love for the "Lindenbaum." He postulates a distant, future realm in which a truly regenerate love will be possible, some mystical future which promises release from present ambiguity. But this is false reasoning. Because Hans Castorp can apprehend the contradictions at work within his own person he is a being greater than those contradictions. The synthesis is there already, now, in the fact of his being, in the differentiated love of which it is capable. And yet it is a synthesis, a totality, rarely known for what it is because it can only be glimpsed and then forgotten. It does not show itself in a sustained and cumulative revelatory process to the eager mind of the self-examining Castorp. Hence, that very process of examination leads Hans Castorp to project his longing for present wholeness onto some temporally distant mode of fulfillment. He postulates a time sequence, a direction, that will in the future yield synthesis. And the future of which he dreams is, typically, a speculative and imaginative construct, a future beyond the present ambiguity of his situation, a future that promises synthesis by evasion, by obliterating the mode of being that yields the antinomies that cry out for synthesis.

Such musings on Hans Castorp's part are described as "alchemistically enhanced." They represent the point at which his capacity for self-examination, which is heightened by the extreme world of the Berghof, succumbs to the rarefied atmosphere of the sanatorium, to the luxury of juggling endlessly with speculative cerebralities. This, then, is the value and the danger of the hermetic pedagogy to which Hans Castorp is exposed. The process of alchemistic enhancing has its value: it intensifies and crystallizes certain aspects of Hans Castorp's being; it makes him aware of what he is. But the awareness is always questioned by what goes before and what comes after, and such awareness as Castorp gains emerges briefly, only to be forgotten, or falsified, or relativized almost as soon as it has appeared. This rhythmic pattern is central to the novel, to the meaning it yields, and to the question of how far and in what way Hans Castorp develops, if he develops at all. There would seem to be considerable evidence for a conclusion that Castorp does not develop. One thinks particularly of the remarks with which the narrator opens and closes his story: the story is worth telling for its own sake and not on account of the hero, who is a simple but engaging young man, although, as it is *his* story and no one else's, he must be entitled to some credit for his participation. What does one make of such remarks, of the constant stress on our hero's *Mittelmässigkeit* (mediocrity)?

Quite obviously, Hans Castorp is the focus of the novel in the simple sense that his presence at the Berghof is the precise precondition of the plot. If we follow the plot thread through the novel, we find that there are certain points along that sequence of events, related in chronological order, where the whole process yields purpose and values are revealed. This is, of course, what we traditionally expect of plot: events in sequence that coalesce to yield meaning. As I have suggested in my discussion of four of the thematic focus points, we do encounter moments in the plot that are unmistakably value heavy. All these moments of insight are associated with Hans Castorp. The conceptualizations of meaning are his or are specifically imputed to him by the narrator. It is therefore very

tempting to assume that Castorp derives an abiding insight from these experiences. Oddly enough, however, he seems to forget them.

Perhaps one can best illuminate this elusive quality about the hero's progression through the novel by constructing a different ending. *The Magic Mountain* would be a very different novel if after the "Snow" chapter Hans Castorp left the sanatorium of his own accord and returned to the plains in order to become a doctor (in terms of cultural tradition, a very respectable conclusion; one thinks of Goethe's *Wilhelm Meister's Travels*), or if the closing chapter showed him as a member of a field hospital, surrounded by bursting shells, with little chance of survival, but with the narratively intimated certainty that the values which he has learned and which he is enacting in his work will outlive him. I cannot help but feel that this is the kind of conclusion many people would have wished Thomas Mann to reach. But emphatically he did not. In other words, it seems to me questionable whether Hans Castorp develops in the traditional sense in which we understand a novel hero's development, that is, learning consistently and cumulatively from his experience to the point where he can then enact the values he has acquired. Hans Castorp is and remains "mittelmässig," mediocre, or perhaps more accurately, undistinguished by any dominant characteristic, propensity, or quality.

Therein, of course, resides his crucial importance. When Hans Castorp arrives at the Berghof, all the experiences and values he meets are present implicitly, latently within him (just as, for example, the Clawdia experience is already inherent in his being, as we know from his boyhood infatuation with Pribislav Hippe). What the Berghof does is to confront him with these values and experiences in extreme, heightened form. It intensifies an aspect of his being by confronting him with the explicit articulation of that aspect. But Hans Castorp himself is and remains "mittelmässig"; he is and remains the "Mittel-mass," the middle way, in which all the extremes potentially are present. In this sense one can in part see Castorp as a catalyst: his presence forces the interaction, confrontation, and, ultimately, relativization of those values and attitudes which find their exclusive and extreme exponents in the rarefied air of the Berghof sanatorium. But like any catalyst, Castorp himself remains unchanged. Of course, Hans Castorp is a special kind of catalyst: he is a human being, and the values which interact so busily around him are all present and coexistent within him in a way that is not true of any of the other characters in the novel. Hence the paradox with which Mann begins and ends his novel: the story matters more than Castorp himself; the interaction of values matters. But without Castorp's presence the interaction would not take place in the explicit and overt way that it does. And without his presence the interdependence of these values, their coexistence as a corpus of human possibilities of which no one constellation automatically excludes the others, would not reveal itself. Hence, central to the meaning of the four focus points I have discussed is that Hans Castorp should forget the insight he has gained. Any insight into the wholeness of man is immediately relativized by the fact that this moment of insight represents the luxury of a contemplative relationship to experience. The moment of insight cannot be prolonged because it is the nature of the insight that the intellect, the faculty for conceptualizing experience, is only part of man and part of his experience. It may briefly apprehend the whole truth, but it cannot *be* the whole truth because the whole truth is a totally interacting dynamic. Any attempt to prolong the moment of insight into a serenely contemplative relationship to experience falsifies the insight and leads to a simple indulgence in cerebralizings about life.

It is this notion of human wholeness that *The Magic Mountain,* in my view, is concerned to intimate. It accounts for the curiously dominant stature which Hans Castorp in all his indeterminateness acquires. But Castorp's dominance can only be implied. It defies concrete enactment and depiction for reasons which are important for an understanding of Mann's whole relationship to the novel form. To these reasons I want to return later. Suffice it to say at this stage that there is no one event, no one situation, no one human confrontation that functions as the novel's explicit value center. In this belief I find myself at variance with most Thomas Mann critics, even with those who have questioned the validity of the Sun People vision in "Snow." Indeed, it seems to me central to the novel's meaning that there can be no concretization of the wholeness of humanity that transcends all dualisms. The one attempt at explicit depiction and embodiment of this wholeness leads to the dream sequence in "Snow." In other words, we are concerned with a totality that can only be focused conceptually—this is what happens at the moments of insight. But the insights are discursive *statements* concerning the nature of this wholeness, they do not embody it in a concrete image. Similarly, none of the characters whom Castorp meets during his stay at the Berghof is allowed to represent the total interacting complexity of man's being. The "medical" theme does not find its explicit enactment in Krokowski or Behrens; the "form" theme is not concretized by the figure of Joachim; the "love" theme is not embodied in the person of Frau Chauchat. Nor indeed does Peeperkorn stand for the sum total of life's experience. The nearest we get to an image of this sum total (and with it to the value center of the novel) is the implicit dominance of Hans Castorp himself. The reason why this dominance is implicit rather than explicit, suggested rather than stated, lies above all in the function of the narrative voice.

Throughout *The Magic Mountain* one is aware of the narrator's lofty, pedagogically patronizing relationship to the main character. The tone is all important because it suggests that the narrator is part of the Berghof world. He is, as Theodore Ziolkowski aptly puts it, "tied to the locale; he is the *genius loci*" [see excerpt dated 1969]. It is interesting to note that at the end of the novel, when the narrator bids farewell to his main character, his voice sounds like Settembrini's, and he even repeats the latter's gesture of touching the corner of his eye with his finger tip. The narrator's voice is located in and works through a world of extremes. It verbalizes these extremes with the irony appropriate to such extremes, thereby intimating both the excitement and the human questionableness of the hermetic pedagogy of the Berghof world. It implicitly suggests the curious richness of the indeterminate figure of Hans Castorp, a richness that derives from the unutterable complexity of life in all its contradictions, so much richer than the other characters—ultimately, so much more a totality than the narrative voice can say.

In the last sentence of the novel the narrator asks whether love will one day rise from the insane holocaust of the war. His plea reminds us of Hans Castorp's "alchemistically enhanced" thoughts at the end of the "Lindenbaum" section. There Castorp postulated some removed future, some new world of love, as an image of a distant totality for which man strives. But these thoughts were a falsity, just as the narrator's question is a falsity. The love of which the pedagogically heightened Hans Castorp and the pedagogic narrator speak is, like man himself,

the father and child of contradictions. It is the sum total of life experience, a totality that can never be possessed in terms of a specific turning point within a linear time sequence. Hence, the narrator's question at the end of the novel, a question that operates within a linear time scale—"will love ever arise?" . . .—is relativized by the whole novel. Love will not come at some time. It is *now* in life, unsayable, intimated through a narrative irony, through an unspoken relationship to the main character that ultimately ironizes its own presence as traditional narrator, as spinner of the plot thread, as "intoning wizard of the imperfect." . . . (pp. 116-22)

The narrative voice tells a story in time sequence. In order to do this it refracts life through the prism of the hero's confrontation with the Berghof world into some of its component values, concepts, ideologies, and attitudes. The novel can narrate the temporal sequence within which these strands of being appear, but the totality of Hans Castorp's "mediocrity" cannot be narrated as such because it is not straightforwardly realizable in plot, in linear concretization. The unexceptional indeterminateness of Hans Castorp cannot say its own sum total, it can only *be* it. Thus the narrative voice is imprisoned within its own function as a reporter of events in chronological sequence. The only way out of this constriction is irony and the intimation through irony that what can be said is only a small part of what needs to be said. This ironic intimation, this narrative that questions its own function as novel narrative, is the only way of making the spark of meaning jump the gap between language and silence.

Of course, the process of ironic intimation also involves plot. Obviously, *The Magic Mountain* does have a plot thread, a chain of events arranged in the *Nacheinander* ["succession"] of linear time sequence. Yet the relationship between the narrative voice and the person of the hero is not the only feature of the novel's construction and theme that relativizes the validity of the traditional presuppositions of plot. For example, the recurring routine of the Berghof, its hermetic quality, sealed off from time like preserves in a jar (Hans Castorp's image), the whole theme of time, of time as subjective perception, of time as its own dimension, as a continuum rather than a transparent vessel for containing and pigeonholing human activities—these and many other aspects contribute to the process. They find ample discursive treatment in the novel itself, and critics have analyzed them fully.

In the sense that *The Magic Mountain* has a *Nacheinander* but is centrally concerned with a *Nebeneinander* ["simultaneity"], with a complex coexistence of possibilities, with the value-heavy *nunc stans* of Hans Castorp's being, it is a novel which questions what can be said by the traditional novel form of narrative sequence. *The Magic Mountain* is, then, very much part of that cardinal experience of the modern novel which Theodor W. Adorno has aphoristically summarized: "It is no longer possible to tell a story, while the novel form demands story telling." One must ask, however, why so many major writers of the twentieth century, Mann included, have not taken the final step of dissolving the narrative sequence altogether, why many novels cling tenaciously to some sort of plot, if only in order to parody it. Perhaps the reason for this remarkably persistent residue of events in time sequence is that, whatever happens, man is obliged to live out his life, and to conceive of it, within the linear temporality of practical existence. He may not be able to affirm this sequence, to see it as in any way expressing that which is valid, important, or necessary, but like it or not, he is still caught up in this mode of existence.

It is central to the honesty of **The Magic Mountain** that Hans Castorp is, in the last resort, powerless. The crucial decisions as to what happens with his life are not his: world history decides for him. Mann carefully documents the growing seediness of the Berghof; the hysteria enveloping the plains is felt even in the Magic Mountain. In the last analysis, Hans Castorp's complexity means nothing when he is sucked into the worldwide death feast. That the problem child of life ends up as cannon fodder gives **The Magic Mountain** a tragic resonance.

It is by now a truism in discussion of **The Magic Mountain** to describe it as a parodistic Bildungsroman. There are two immediate senses in which the parody is manifest: first, the real social world which Hans Castorp enters at the end of the novel is a chaotic and violent confusion which simply does not allow him to see his way clear to a fulfilling relationship with human society; second, the educative environment bears no relationship to the common realm of ordinary human encounters and interaction but is rather the "hermetic" and sick world of the sanatorium. The relationship to the Bildungsroman is admittedly parodistic, but there is more to it than this. **The Magic Mountain** involves not simply an exploration of the tradition and a critique of it, but also a precarious reinstatement of it. It is this latter aspect which deserves special attention, the sense in which Mann's novel in part fulfills the genre because it illuminates aspects of it which were always more tentative and problematic than traditional literary history has allowed. The question of plot is an obvious example of what I mean. The traditional Bildungsroman at one level always tends to question the linear time sequence of narrative, that is, the characters the hero meets exist for the most part in order to bring out strands within his being. This accounts for the curious lack of experiential finality in the Bildungsroman: one rarely has the sense of an irrevocable interaction between the hero and the world in which he moves. This tentative relationship to experience, this lack of immediacy in the hero's confrontation with events, goes back a long way. As Schiller wrote to Goethe in 1796:

> Wilhelm Meister is of course the most necessary, but not the most important person: precisely that is one of the peculiarities of your novel that it neither has nor needs such a most important person. *To* him and *around* him everything happens, but not essentially *for his sake*. Because the things around him represent and express energies and he embodies educability, he has to stand in quite a different relationship to the other characters from that which the hero in other novels has.

The paradox Schiller recognized is the same paradox with which Mann opens and closes his novel: the story is told for its own sake, not for the hero's, because the hero is not a clearly defined character, he is not a "personality" in the accepted sense of the term. Yet the hero is the precondition of the story; everything that happens in fact befalls *him*.

In effect, the hero both has and does not have a story. This is the characteristic tension of the Bildungsroman . . . , that between the *Nacheinander* of plot and the *Nebeneinander* of human potentiality and wholeness. Both *Wilhelm Meister's Apprenticeship* and **The Magic Mountain** enact this tension: the "Snow" vision as a discursive perception of human wholeness is as surely relativized by the ongoing flow of events as is the Society of the Tower in *Wilhelm Meister*. In my view, Mann's novel, like all sophisticated parody, represents a last-ditch fulfillment—and illumination—of the thing it parodies.

T. J. Reed has shown how Mann's whole conception of **The Magic Mountain** changed in the course of its composition [see Additional Bibliography]. Mann began work on the project in 1913, at which time it was intended as a humorous companion piece to **Death in Venice**. But the material grew in resonance as Mann, under the pressure of the early months of the war, found that "its figures and story irresistibly became . . . representative of the issues he believed the war was about." In other words, "if he had been able to complete the novel during the war, it would certainly have been a fictional expression of his Romantic anti-westernism." But Mann was not able to finish the novel during the war years. The completed version, which did not appear until 1924, bears the imprint of his decisive change of mind and heart. For he came to abjure the unpolitical attitudes of German conservatism and to plead for a commitment to practical affairs, to politics, to parliamentary democracy. For Reed, the genesis of **The Magic Mountain** shows a process of growth and education undergone by the author; hence Mann "himself had completed the education which **The Magic Mountain** relates. This is how the Bildungsroman became possible, and necessary." Clearly, on numerous points Reed is right. However, I think that Mann's employment of the Bildungsroman genre should be seen less as an announcement of an unambiguously didactic intention than as a precise engagement with a German tradition to which, under the impact of political events, his allegiance had become ever more critical. One can see this dual relationship with particular clarity in the last few pages of the novel. We are told that Hans Castorp had "allowed himself, to be sure, to dream this and that about the spiritual shadows of things in his usual reflective way, but had paid no attention to the things themselves—in fact out of the arrogant propensity to take shadows for things, but to see in things merely shadows . . ."... . This sounds like a very thoroughgoing repudiation of that complex inwardness which the Bildungsroman is so often concerned both to explore and to validate. It would seem, then, that the novel's end takes back all that precedes it, that the massively (and lovingly) chronicled debate about human values, with its omnipresent concern for the wholeness of man, amounts in the last resort to nothing in a world where the mud of the Somme has the last word for a whole European generation.

Yet—and not surprisingly when one is concerned with something from Thomas Mann's pen—the issues are not so simple. The narrator does indeed make his devastating criticism of Castorp's "arrogance" (and, by implication, of the arrogance of the fastidiously unpolitical German tradition), but then immediately goes on to qualify his strictures: "out of the arrogant propensity to take shadows for things, but to see in things only shadows—for which one should not scold him too harshly, since the relationship between the two has not been finally settled." . . . So perhaps, in spite of the irrevocable inroads made by world history into the fastness of Hans Castorp's retreat in the Berghof, there is after all a distinction and value to that process which this novel, like all Bildungsromane, chronicles. The *Nacheinander* of practical and physical existence is the ultimate arbiter of an individual life, but the *Nebeneinander* of human inwardness is the source of human complexity and interest. Outwardly, Hans Castorp is swallowed up without trace; inwardly, he has the distinction of trying to know himself more strenuously than the practical world of the flatlands would ever have permitted. This is Thomas Mann's grudging—and in its grudgingness, wonderfully right—engagement with the Bildungsroman tradition. (pp. 122-28)

> *Martin Swales, "Mann: 'The Magic Mountain' (1924)," in his* The German Bildungsroman from

The Waldsanatorium in Davos. Dr. Hans-Otto Mayer.

Wieland to Hesse, *Princeton University Press, 1978, pp. 105-28.*

T. E. APTER (essay date 1978)

[In the following excerpt, Apter examines Mann's treatment of disease and death in The Magic Mountain.]

"So sweet was ne'er so fatal," Othello muses in despair as Iago, the anti-spirit, penetrates his soul. This mingling of sweetness and fatality issues in a violent, destructive ecstasy, as it would in the case of a Romanticist; yet Othello's genuine horror at this identification separates Shakespeare's conception from that of the Romanticist. Othello's sensuous vision becomes devoid of tenderness once he is convinced that his senses are grossly misleading, even mocking his spirit. His abuse of Desdemona is a means of rooting out his love for her. He must destroy his emotional world because the anti-spirit Iago has destroyed the harmony between goodness and beauty, between, that is, what satisfies his senses and what satisfies his spirit.

In Romanticism, however, the connections between sweetness and fatality are explored with delight and intrigue. Sometimes this affinity is endorsed because sweetness is more poignant when set beside death, or because only in death will the sweetness—which in life would be short—be preserved. In *The Magic Mountain* Mann avoids this sentimental ploy. In his critical investigation of Romanticism he turns aside from its appreciation of a loveliness that cannot last and turns towards the quick decay and deadliness which are shown to be attractive in their own right. The view that death and disease are lovely

things is presented with relentless irony, and their disgusting aspects are continually underlined; but the disgust itself has an irrefutable appeal. Fatality is sweet, and nothing can be other than banal without its aid.

The point and good of life in the Berghof Sanatorium, and the power of its attraction are one with its feverish, decaying atmosphere:

> Rendered torpid, as often, by the beer and music, [Hans Castorp] sat with his head to one side and his mouth slightly open, watching the gay, spa-like scene, feeling, not as a disturbing influence, but rather as a heightening of the general singularity, and lending it one mental fillip the more, the fact that all these people were inwardly attacked by nearly resistless decay, and that most of them were feverish. . . .

When Hans Castorp learns that he belongs to this feverish crowd, that he, too, has the disease, the will to corruption—which is the impetus of the entire novel—erupts with a terrible joy:

> For as he lay he would be shaken from deep within by a frantic burst of triumphant laughter, while his heart stood still and suffered something he had never before known, an extravagant joy and hope; then again he grew pale from shock and fear, and it was conscience itself that knocked, in the very throbs of his heart as it pulsed against his ribs. . . .

But conscience (*Gewissens*)—as conscience rather than as fear or habit—can function only upon the belief of some good, and the will to corruption makes the corrupt seem good. Therefore conscience cannot protect him.

In the sanatorium all moral notions are stripped of their practical, resolute, "Buddenbrook" content. Respect for decay develops its own moral language. The director of the sanatorium speaks of the air on the mountain as being good for disease. In ordinary language this would mean that the air was a good cure for disease, but Hofrat Behrens means that the air speeds up the course of the disease, that the air brings out the symptoms, so that many people who pass for healthy people in the ordinary world below, reveal the disease when they come to the sanatorium. When the Hofrat speaks of some one as a "good patient" he does not mean that the patient does what is necessary to bring him back to health, but that the patient has a respect for his illness and a talent for exhibiting its symptoms. When the Hofrat congratulates Hans Castorp for doing well, he means to praise him for the way the disease is manifesting itself; he congratulates him not for getting well but for showing the "normal" symptoms of the disease.

Not only is the Hofrat's notion of good determined by his respect for disease, but, also, his notion of life is derived from the notion of decay. Hans Castorp asks him, "What is life?" and he replies that it is combustion, a breaking down of chemicals; that it is, in short, decay and dissolution. The Hofrat gloats over this paradox, and though Mann does not endorse this definition, he does see more in it than what it actually is— a shallow play upon words. Indeed, this view of life is tied to Mann's definition of Romanticism as "the fruit of life, conceived by death, pregnant of dissolution." Unlike the Hofrat, however, Mann imagines a finer world in which the captivating focus upon decay will be overcome. In this novel the overpowering of the Romantic enchantment involves more than the simple, robust practical nature of first generation Buddenbrooks. The goodness and fascination of decay and death have to be faced. The Romantic enchantment has to have its consummation. The world must be destroyed by it and then, from the ashes, a rebirth of love and hope is possible. Hans Castorp, the commonplace German burgher, susceptible to the will to corruption through his love for music and his respect for illness and death, spends the seven years preceding the First World War on this mountain. He is able to return to the ordinary world only when it, too, is shaken by the forces that have been at work among the inmates of the sanatorium. The cataclysm of the War provides the fulfilment of Mann's apocalyptic Romanticism. (pp. 58-60)

In *The Magic Mountain* Mann makes disease a central Romantic concept. In *Death in Venice* Aschenbach's vision of the reeking jungle that leads to his restless travels and, finally, to the abyss of his own imagination, mirrors the source of the disease which sweeps through Venice. Aschenbach's yearning for a widening of the inner barriers is a desire for the dissolution of his personality. Mann takes this desire for dissolution out of the usual Romantic schema in which dissolution is seen as spiritual release, and presents this desire as desire for spiritual and physical decay. Mann wants to expose the corruption inherent in a longing for release; in *The Magic Mountain* its spiritual aspect is undermined even more thoroughly than in the earlier novella. Here, the love of beauty, the mystical yearning, which can go wrong and result in decay, is superseded by the love of decay itself:

But in the first storey Hans Castorp stopped suddenly, rooted to the spot by a perfectly ghastly sound coming from a little distance off round a bend in the corridor. It was not a loud sound, but so distinctly horrible that Hans Castorp made a wry face and looked wide-eyed at his cousin. It was coughing, obviously—a man coughing; but coughing like no other Hans Castorp had ever heard and compared to which any other had been a magnificently and healthy manifestation of life: a coughing that had no conviction and gave no relief, that did not even come out in paroxysms, but was just a feeble, dreadful welling up of the juices of organic dissolution. . . . Hans Castorp could not get over the coughing he had heard. He kept repeating that he could see right into the gentleman rider's vitals; when they reached the restaurant his travel-weary eyes had an excited glitter. . . .

He might, indeed, be listening to *Tristan und Isolde* as Nietzsche described the opera's effect in *The Birth of Tragedy;* his ear is aware of the secret, deep inner functions of the world, and his consciousness is overwhelmed by the revelation.

To make a connection between a ghastly, transfixing sound of coughing and a transfixing beauty is in itself ironic, but Mann increases the tension of this identification by continually setting up an opposition between the sympathy disease demands and the frantic comedy of its practical difficulties. Joachim tells the new visitor that in winter, when the inmates of the various mountain sanatoriums die, the bodies have to be carried down on a bobsled. This news arouses in Hans Castorp an uncontrollable and embarrassing fit of laughter: Romanticism's fascination with death, when applied to actual death, is confused by death's ugliness and absurdity. Hans Castorp, as an incipient Romanticist, believes there is something ennobling and edifying about death and disease. He is offended to see that severe disease occurs in coarse, common people. He believes that a corrupt body should make one more spiritual, but Settembrini, the humanist who pretends to value all life (though in fact he underestimates the power of the darker, destructive aspects of human nature) says that a diseased person is primarily body, for disease brings a person's physical aspects to the forefront of his consciousness and that therefore, on the contrary, disease is degrading. The behaviour of the sanatorium patients supports Settembrini's claim. This undermining of Hans Castorp's initial regard for disease, however, gives way to a more profound regard for disease. Its indignities and horrors actually increase its fascination; and this attraction to that which is inherently repulsive, reveals a basic and undeniable impulse to corrupt and destroy one's self. (pp. 61-3)

Mann presents one argument for the love of the ugly and repulsive through Naphta. The Jesuit is contemptuous of health and beauty, and of Settembrini's notion of good as comfort, with all the crass materialism and industrialism such an identification implies. Naphta cites stories of saints' sufferings and the grotesque details of their tortures to prove that people crave the hideous and the repulsive. He believes that the driving force of the world is the hostility between spirit and matter. Beauty—the glorification of matter—is therefore antipathetic to the spirit, and people love ugliness—the denigration of matter—because it heightens their sense of the spiritual. He declares that people want to believe that salvation can be achieved only through pain, for only through physical degradation can they conceive spiritual beauty.

Naphta's views have some affinity to those of Nietzsche. The philosopher saw pain and adversity as necessary to achievement. He therefore rejected the notion of comfort as a good because comfort undermines creative achievement. The Jesuit, however, advocates pain not because it stimulates the imagination but because it satisfies the imagination. He is not interested in improving or invigorating the quality of mankind, for his view of the world as a constant battle allows for neither advance nor retreat. Naphta's similarity to the anti-religious Marxist emphasises the destructive conservatism in any world view based upon continuous hostility. Such a view, however apparently noble its purpose, is ultimately sadistic. Naphta's disdain for the material world is also a spiritual nihilism. His theory of truth (which he shares with the Marxist) is that truth is determined by man's interests and survival; and this theory, combined with his conservative and reductive suppositions about man's interests and salvation, paves the way—Settembrini rightly points out—to cruelty and suppression. Yet Settembrini himself is no less despotic. He cannot tolerate the Jesuit's emphasis upon the dark, corrupt aspect of man. He cannot permit, in his libertarian world, sympathy with the irrational forces of man's psyche. The two men are forced into a duel. Settembrini shoots into the air with a gallant flourish. His shallow optimism cannot be effective against the sadistic nihilist disguised as a man of spirit. Such a man, whose nature is deathly, is powerful against himself, too; and Naphta ends the duel by shooting himself. (pp. 63-4)

In this novel there is no fundamental resistance to the attractions of disease and death. If, somewhere along Hans Castorp's journey to the underworld, he came upon a dynamic "no"— if, that is, the fascination with death, decay and disease was shown in the end to violate man's deepest interests and needs (as it is shown to do in *Doctor Faustus*) the spiritual drama would be more intense and the final apocalyptic vision might be more convincing. As it is, Mann's portrayal of the daemonic sometimes has the cheapness of a haunted house atmosphere (as in the séance). In his treatment of disease, too, the thrill of horror, rather than horror itself, emerges. Disease, as Mann presents it, is something of a luxury; it comforts one and protects one from life's responsibilities and decisions. There is no indication that the life-alienating effects of disease are directly, deeply painful, or that such alienation involves an absolute loss. In *Buddenbrooks* Mann showed artistic sensibility to cut one off from life, and his sympathies were on the side of artistic sensibility. In *The Magic Mountain* his view is not fundamentally changed. It is interesting to compare this novel with Solzhenitsyn's *Cancer Ward* which also describes the way illness cuts a person off from life, but this loss of interest is an undeniable human loss, and the characters fight to maintain their involvement with other people and with their work. Part of Solzhenitsyn's greatness arises from his understanding of the need to work and to love and to participate in one's immediate world, however unsatisfactory that world happens to be, as human strengths. This view is alien to Mann's imagination. At the time of Hans Castorp's visit to the sanatorium he is preparing for a career as an engineer for a shipbuilding firm. This prospective employment is shown to be thoroughly mediocre, and in abandoning his career for the mountain's licence, he is not seen to be abandoning anything of real value. In fact, Hans Castorp avoids being a totally commonplace burgher through his awareness that the world, as he knows it, is not worth the practical man's exertion; and his love for Clawdia Chauchat, the love that binds him to the mountain, is like a "frightfully alluring dream of a man whose unconscious questioning of the universe has received no answer save a hollow

silence." The fascination with disease, and the debilitating passion bred by disease, provide compensation for an empty life rather than a threat to ultimate fulfilment.

The battle between life and death forces, therefore, is itself ambivalently conceived, and Mann's moral resolution to life is not quite integrated with what in the novel is felt to be man's greatest good. The ambivalence results in uneven writing, for Mann presents the resolution in morally satisfactory (that is, life-oriented) terms, but in terms in which he does not quite believe. A visionary resolution between these forces is presented in the section "Snow." Hans Castorp has summoned up sufficient initiative and energy to learn how to ski, for the alpine landscape intrigues him and he defies the sanatorium's prejudice against active, individual exploration. First Mann introduces the keen nostalgia of winter, but then lapses into a merely virtuoso description. His presentation of the snow-covered mountains as comic and fairy like is over extended; it is meant to balance the awe and sublimity of the high Alps in the distance, but this careful balancing of opposing views defeats them both. Gradually, however, the finer, majestic aspects of the scene blend with the confusing, compelling death wish:

> The snow fell silently. Everything blurred more and more. The glance, as it sank into the padded nothingness, inclined one to slumber. A shiver accompanied this view of distant places, yet there could be no sleep purer than this in the ice-cold, this dreamless reprieve from any unconscious feeling of organic life, as little aware of an effort to breathe this contentless, weightless, imperceptible air as is the breathless sleep of the dead. . . .

Here the danger and the enchantment are at one with the reverence. The identity is not a combination of opposites which cancel one another, but a successfully disturbing presentation of the seduction of stasis. Yet this tender release from consciousness and from the pressures of organic life, is only one face of the death-wish; its other aspect is violent and destructive: the snowstorm continues to come as a "mad dance, a white—dark, a monstrous dereliction" and Hans Castorp craves for contact with these violent, desolate mountains. But amid this wild, inhuman landscape, he feels his heart beating: "A naïve reverence filled him for that organ of his, for the pulsating human heart, up here alone in the icy void, alone with its question and its riddle."

The cross-references to Hans Castorp's beating heart extend from his feverish passion for Clawdia Chauchat to that paltry, grotesque organ Hofrat Behrens describes whose function can be summed up as dissolution; but here the immediacy of Hans Castorp's organic humanity overcomes the distrust and ambiguity felt in the associated themes. The organic burden is straightforwardly embraced in protection against the seductive and destructive alpine landscape.

Subsequently, however, Mann forces a resolution upon Hans Castorp's musings. The young man rejects the uncanny, anti-organic perfection of the snow-flakes, and then sets out to lose his way in the white expanse of the mountains, which is so much like the expanse of the sea. Like the sea in *Death in Venice,* this cold desert represents the imagination which, for Mann, magnetises the elemental wildness and excesses of human nature, and is more appealing than normal human fulfilment. While Hans Castorp presses close to a hay-hut to keep warm, while he tries to resist the temptation to sleep—a sleep which would be his death—he has a hopelessly trite vision of young lads and lasses fishing, riding, engaging in archery, eating grapes and generally doing their best to present a Neo-classical image of the harmony between beauty and spirit, and what Mann calls a high seriousness without austerity. This happy vision is replaced by a disgusting scene within a temple where two old hags dismember a child and fight over the remains. In horror Hans Castorp wakes, but he continues to muse in a dream-like trance. He concludes that neither Settembrini, who insists upon the unqualified dignity of man, nor Naphta, who advocates man's degradation, is correct. From love and sweetness alone, he now realises, not from death and destruction, can beauty and civilisation arise; but one must nonetheless give recognition to the blood sacrifice, to the destructive will, and one must keep faith with one's connection with death, with one's longing for dissolution and release, but one must also prevent these darker tendencies from dominating one's thoughts.

This vision is similar, in its Neoclassical representation and its themes of harmony versus destructiveness, to Aschenbach's dream in which he believes he is waging a successful battle against desire until a terrifying howling, interspersed with sweet flutelike tones, infects him with savage lust. The allegory of Aschenbach's dream has an effectiveness lacking in Hans Castorp's vision, because the dream in *Death in Venice* clearly defines the battle that is actually waged within the writer's soul, whereas Hans Castorp's vision lacks the real spiritual tension that would make it a plausible drama. Hans Castorp is merely musing upon various theories about human nature; he himself stakes nothing upon the battle. (pp. 64-7)

Hans Castorp's musings are often presented in highly schematic images, without convincing participation in or expression of the character's emotional drama. Connections between science and daemonic investigations, or between death and music, are thrust forward by a memory or simile or repetition of a character's gesture. The darkened room in which the séance is held reminds Hans Castorp of the darkened X-ray laboratory which, in turn, has been said to be similar to Faust's study. When Hans Castorp looks at his own skeleton and realises, for the first time, that he will actually die, his face assumes the sleepy and pious expression he habitually wears as he listens to music. This use of *leitmotif* forces rather than explores the associations. It does not justify or explain the connections between music, death, science and the daemonic.

The lack of dramatic necessity in Hans Castorp's confrontations with death and decay is consistent with Mann's presentation of such preoccupations as indulgences. It is boredom and discontent that corrupts the inmates of the sanatorium—not the painful, inescapable soul conflict that destroys Aschenbach. In this novel Mann is interested in the languid effect of Romantic fascination, and the fascination of indulgence itself. Loving, rapt attention to detail indicates in itself the sinister nature of an object. Hans Castorp's perusal of his thermometer—which is his membership card to the sanatorium and therefore to the world of licence and irresponsibility—provides a delight which signals danger:

> Smiling he took up the case and opened it. The glass instrument lay like a jewel within, fitted neatly into its red velvet groove. The degrees were marked by red strokes, the tenths by black ones; the figures were in red and the tapering end was full of glittering quicksilver. . . .

Also, the attention given to the gramophone indicates an importance far beyond that of a mere mechanical object; through the almost comically rich description of the object Mann makes the gramophone itself uncanny. . . . (pp. 68-9)

The most compelling object on the mountain, however, the most vivid embodiment of lawlessness and intrigue and disease-ridden loveliness, is Clawdia Chauchat; and the features of her face are meticulously recorded, for the detail itself reflects Hans Castorp's fascination with the face. . . . The objects that fascinate seem also to hypnotise, and desire is almost no more than a desire to be enchanted in his rapt, passive manner. This rapture breeds idleness and stagnation which, in turn, provide a breeding ground for passion and enchantment. Fascination is like a door closing upon the normal world and normal activity; and, in isolation and idleness, fascination becomes frenzied excitement. It is when Hans Castorp is resting in bed, having been proclaimed to be ill, that his attraction to Clawdia becomes an overwhelming infatuation:

> The day, artificially shortened, broken into small bits, had literally crumbled in his hands and was reduced to nothing. . . . In each hour of his diminished day he thought of her: her mouth, her cheek-bones, her eyes, whose colour, shape and position bit into his very soul. . . . Possessed of these thoughts, his hours passed on soundless feet. . . . Yes, he felt both terror and dread; he felt a vague and boundless, utterly mad and extravagant anticipation, a nameless anguish of joy. . . .

(pp. 70-1)

The misgiving and the anguish are essential to this passionate infatuation. Passion in spite of the world's opposition, passion which battles with self control, passion which defies consequences are common themes for the Romanticist; but Mann presents as the point and danger of Romantic passion not its disregard for the world or for ordinary life but its will to destroy ordinary life and discipline. Mann is not interested in specific social contexts which thwart specific passions. There is no social or indeed any external ban against Hans Castorp's love for Clawdia, for there are no moral restraints on the mountain. He keeps his distance from her until just before she leaves the sanatorium not because circumstances frustrate his passion but because his passion craves this secrecy and isolation. Only a passion which reaches out into the world, towards another person, can suffer from the more usual Romantic constraints of the world's censure. In Mann it is passion that censures the world—the total normal world. Passion cannot partake of spoken language, for language is tied to reason and rational communication; passion communicates only with smiles and glances, and would be destroyed by speech. Passion rejects the world because it sees itself as the greatest good: "But he was enraptured not so much because she looked so charming, as because her charm added strength to the sweet intoxication of his brain, the intoxication that willed to be, that cared only to be justified and nourished." Passion is a longing to intensify desire, not to satisfy it. The drama of passion is a drama of the inward, isolating, destructive will and of purely private joy.

As in *Death in Venice* the precarious balance between the physical and the spiritual is a prominent theme, though in this novel the relation between the two seems to be total opposition; whereas, in the novella, there was at least a possibility that beauty—a material, sensuous manifestation—would lead to or express the spirit. Here the sensuous, even in its most promising state, borders on the disgusting. Hans Castorp's first acquaintance with sensual love in the sanatorium is made as he hears, from the next room, sounds of vulgar, playful lovemaking. And the entire subject of physical love is treated with this false objectivity, this half-unwilling voyeurism. Sexual love is deliberately taken out of the more usual contexts of affection and family bonds and breeding. In investigating sexual love among the diseased inmates of the sanatorium, Mann presents such love as ultimately perverse. As Hans Castorp admires the fine upward curve of Clawdia's arm he muses upon the efforts women take to achieve the illusion of beauty—efforts, he feels, which would be justified only if such illusion led to the preservation of the species, but which are immoral if the woman is diseased and therefore unfit for motherhood. This attitude obviously extends to sex beyond the walls of the sanatorium, for it implies that attraction is illusion and that its only justification is propagation. The distaste with all physical love and the sense that it is never healthy, is underlined by the fact that while Hans Castorp is admiring Clawdia's arm and considering the immorality of beauty in a woman unfit for childbearing, he is listening to Dr Krokowski (the assistant director of the sanatorium, whose interests range freely over forbidden areas—hypnotism, psychoanalysis, somnambulism, and the supernatural) lecture on the absurdity of physical love and its proneness to perversion. There is, the doctor says, a continual battle between chastity and love; and if chastity wins, then love emerges as symptoms of a disease. In a subsequent lecture, Krokowski suggests that love itself is a disease. His theory is that there is a poisoning, a sort of auto-infection of the organism caused by the disintegration of some as yet unknown substance which is present everywhere in the body. The products of this disintegration operate like an intoxicant upon the nerve centres of the spinal cord, with an effect similar to that of certain poisons, such as morphia or cocaine. Such is the chemistry of love, which explains its feverish, stagnant qualities.

Feverish and stagnant: Mann focuses upon the properties of love that Romanticism endorses both advertently (feverish—through Romanticism's esteem for intensity) and inadvertently (stagnant—through the Romanticist's desire to maintain intensity and therefore his need to avoid distractions and fluctuations of feeling). He presents qualities which combine the worse possible connotations of these terms, and continues to insist upon the attraction and power of such qualities. It is not that Mann actually endorses Krokowski's views. Clearly he shows the sadism that motivates the doctor's theories and the corruption in the will to place everything in a corrupt light. Nonetheless, Krokowski's poison has a truth, in Mann's view, for it enforces the criticisms of love which emerge from the novel as a whole. (pp. 71-3)

Repeatedly Mann overestimates the relevance of chemical explanation to descriptions and evaluations of emotion. The Hofrat's scientific analyses of the skin tissue, as Hans Castorp admires the skin tones in the Hofrat's portrait of Clawdia, pretends to supplant the immediate sensuous appreciation of skin and to make that sensuousness appear something like a cheat because skin tones, the object of Hans Castorp's admiration, are susceptible to cold, detailed scientific explanation. Yet to give a chemical analysis of the paints on a canvas would not be to explain away or to undermine the aesthetic qualities of the painting, and a purely physical description of skin tissue does not deny the reality of its sensuous properties. . . . Mann often accompanies a description of Hans Castorp's emotional state with a reference to the Hofrat's various analyses of physical responses, and this reference is meant to deflate Hans

Castorp's emotional state, to show that it is merely a physical response and that the emotional or spiritual value is illusory. Yet the fact—if it is one—that the body's responses to various stimuli are identical, simply shows the poverty of purely physical descriptions and their inability to indicate spiritual or emotional differences; it does not prove the emotional or spiritual content of such states to be illusory.

Mann does not actually deny the possibility of spirituality in emotion. He claims to find the image of spiritual emotion irrefutably compelling, yet he is suspicious of the value or reality of this vision. As Hans Castorp listens to the final duet of *Aïda* in which Radames and Aïda sing of their unity in heaven, it seems to him so beautiful that Aïda has come to die with her lover. The real, objective fact, however, is that two bodies, their lungs filled with pit gas, will die and putrefy and become two skeletons totally indifferent to one another. In spite of this, Mann says, the music provides an irrefutable alleviation of the physical horror. The undeniable comfort of the music, then, is seen to be opposed to the real, objective situation. The spiritual vision is endorsed, but only as a perverse stand against reason. (pp. 74-5)

Mann takes every opportunity to underline the repulsive aspects of that which fascinates and attracts. He defines passion as the organic sympathy, the sense embrace of that which is doomed to decay; and thus he mocks the Romantic image of passion as an eternal soul-embrace. The emphasis on decay—on decay in its most physical, disgusting aspects—does not, however, enable him to conquer his Romantic imagination. Decay does not diminish passion, but heightens it. In the world of ***The Magic Mountain*** excitement feeds upon decay; there is no possibility of healthy passion—either morally or physically healthy—because passion is aroused only in disease and only by something that is diseased or decaying. In ***Death in Venice*** disease was a symbolic manifestation of Aschenbach's inner life; in this novel it has become a real object of desire and fascination.

The Romanticist's desire for dissolution has been wrest from its metaphorical setting; the desire for dissolution is no longer seen as a longing for mystical union but for literal dissolution, with all the ghastliness of decay. Yet at the end of this novel in which, ceaselessly, the total deadliness of the Romanticist's desires has been exposed, Mann proposes the possibility of redemption through a cataclysm of death and destruction. His relentless criticism of Romanticism has resulted only in a corrupt Romanticism, and Mann ends by endorsing the Romantic schema of love arising through utter annihilation.

The final section of the novel presents a naïve and sentimental picture of a battlefield on which courageous young men, who crave neither the food nor the sleep they have been denied, pass willingly through mud and flame and explosions. Hans Castorp is among them. The First World War has shaken him from the idleness and indulgence of the mountain sanatorium, as it has shaken that world which answered his need for meaning with only a hollow silence. The cataclysm of destruction and death is proposed as a resolution of the death-disease fascination.

As Hans Castorp passes across the battlefield he has on his lips a song from Schubert's *Die Winterreise*, "Lindenbaum," and this song represents the paradox of Romanticism. The sentiments expressed by the song seem to be the sanest in the world. The song expresses the desire for rest and comfort and release from pain. For one moment, Mann says, the song provides refreshment which seems human and healthy, but the refreshment lasts only for a moment: "it was the fruit of life, conceived of death, pregnant of dissolution." It begins with true sadness and longing and tenderness, but the expression of these sentiments is so striking, so beautiful, that the beauty leads to soul enchantment. Sorrow is no longer seen as a human ill, but as a fine excuse for beautiful expression. The beauty contains a longing which is a longing for release, for death. The song, in short, begins in life and conflict, and then leads to the Romantic impasse. The only path out of Romanticism lies in self-conquest, in a conscience that overcomes this seductive languor; but, Romanticist that he was, it was only in death that Mann could imagine resolution and rebirth: "It was so worthy, one could die for it, this enchanted song. But he who died for it, really died no longer for it, and was a hero only because in dying he lay the groundwork for the new, the new word of love and the future in his heart."

Mann tried to defend himself against the allegation that he was hostile to life by citing (in a letter to Joseph Poten, 5 February 1925) his relentless mockery of death's dignity in *The Magic Mountain*. For all its indignity, however, death is no less fascinating and attractive; and, in conclusion, Mann gestures towards hope through this "world-feast of death," and "wicked feverish lust." There is a clear parallel here with the end of *Götterdämmerung*, where Brünnhilde's love motive arises from the deluge of the Rhine; yet love and passion, in Wagner's *Ring*, have been shown to be positive, revitalising forces, whereas, in *The Magic Mountain*, Mann has presented them as debilitating and destructive influences. His concluding, hopeful vision is as unsatisfactory, as untrue to the substance of this work, as would be the suggestion of redemption through love at the end of Strauss's *Salomé*. (pp. 75-7)

T. E. Apter, in his Thomas Mann: The Devil's Advocate, *The Macmillan Press Ltd., 1978, 165 p.*

VALERIE D. GREENBERG   (essay date 1985)

[*In the following excerpt, Greenberg discusses scientific themes and motifs in* The Magic Mountain.]

Increasingly, it has become commonplace for students of the philosophy of science to examine science less in terms of its separateness than in terms of its common features with the supposedly antithetical discourse of literature and art. This has been particularly true since the publication in 1969 of Thomas S. Kuhn's *The Structure of Scientific Revolutions* that contradicts the conventional view of science as taking place in a realm of "objectivity," purified of potential contaminants from society, personality, emotions, or beliefs. According to Kuhn: "An apparently arbitrary element, compounded of personal and historical accident, is always a formative ingredient of the beliefs espoused by a given scientific community at a given time." . . . Other thinkers, such as Michel Foucault, have interpreted science as a feature of the episteme that dominates an historical era, rather than as an objective system that transcends the vicissitudes of history.

These and other studies encourage closer examination across conventionally accepted boundaries of the disciplines to see whether art can be as infected by science as science apparently is by modes of thought once considered exclusively "artistic," that is, subjective, intuitive, value-laden. The notion of boundaries is new, of crossing, old: "For the Romantics, science and literature were reciprocally interactive modes of thought and discourse, a dialectic of reason and imagination benefiting

both" [Stephen Leo Carr, "The Ideology of Antithesis: Science versus Literature and the Exemplary Case of J. S. Mill"].

In German literature Goethe is the predominant representative of this dialectic. His studies in biology, to name only one of his scientific pursuits, reflect "his ambition of making the most rigorous research into nature harmonious with the poet's search for beauty and the philosopher's search for wisdom" [John F. Cornell, "Goethe's Classical Biology"]. (p. 59)

During the extended composition of *The Magic Mountain*—from 1912 to 1924—Thomas Mann frequently made reference in his diary to his preoccupation with Goethe in relation to *The Magic Mountain*. In an entry of 15 June 1921 he notes: "In the evening as I read Bielschowsky's chapter on Goethe as a scientist (*Naturforscher*) the meaning and the idea of *The Magic Mountain* became clear to me." . . . *The Magic Mountain* is steeped in science to the end, I propose, of achieving a modern version of the Goethean ideal described above. . . .

The intent of this article . . . is to cast into relief those aspects of *The Magic Mountain* which are paradigmatic for the ways a work of art can integrate the supposedly alien discourse of science. This article seeks to demonstrate that in the course of achieving a synthesis of modes of discourse, Mann has raised questions which still occupy integrative thinkers today. (p. 60)

On one level *The Magic Mountain* is a compendium of the known science of its time, complete with the limitations of early twentieth-century science. Astronomy, biology, botany, chemistry, anatomy, physiology, physics, meteorology, and others are the subjects of private study by protagonist Hans Castorp, but more importantly, they are the warp and woof of the monumental novel, elements of its structure like veins in a leaf.

The opening description of Hans Castorp's travel in 1907 to the Swiss alpine resort of Davos sounds like the launching of an astronaut into space—into realms where expected relations of time and space are suspended. And this is exactly what happens to Hans once he arrives at the international sanitorium Berghof; he learns there to question conventional notions of time and space.

The Magic Mountain is, among other things, about time (and many critical studies have explored it). The narrator tells the reader that the subject is time, and in several theoretical digressions examines and questions notions of time. The author manipulates and confuses the reader's sense of time by frequently switching the means of measuring time passed in the story and by creating a disproportion between fictional time passed and pages devoted to that time, so that the reader's pace becomes another signal of relativity. In a dream Hans Castorp is granted insight into the true nature of time itself: it is nothing more than a so-called "silent nurse," a thermometer without degrees to be used by those who wanted to cheat.

In 1932 Thomas Mann wrote a letter to German scholar Käte Hamburger in which he maintained that the ruminations on time in *The Magic Mountain* were Romantic in origin, and that he hit upon the relationship of time and space without having closely read Einstein. . . . (pp. 60-1)

However, it is not necessary to prove the connection—ideas which are "in the air" may exert their influence without being consciously adopted—in order to see that the viewpoint of *The Magic Mountain* is consonant with Einstein's theory: that the measurement of time and space is dependent upon the position of the observer. Nigel Calder wrote in *Einstein's Universe:*

''The chief merit of the name 'relativity' is in reminding us that a scientist is unavoidably a participant in the system he is studying. Einstein gave 'the observer' his proper status in modern science.'' . . . If we replace the word scientist we see that this statement applies to *The Magic Mountain* as well, for perceptions are dependent upon the observer, whether the observer be the intrusive narrator, Hans Castorp, or the reader. The reader experiences (and is told he ought to experience) something akin to the relativity that is the subject of theoretical speculations.

Hans Castorp's search for the meaning of life (in the section called ''Research'') moves via his scientific studies from the beginning of the universe to the origin of matter, transformation from inorganic to organic matter, simple cells to complex species, and on to the vastness of the universe and speculations on the stars. The progression is analogous to Hans Castorp's own coming to life, his growth and increasing complexity. Throughout the novel he subjects himself and is subjected to a pedagogical version of a chemical laboratory experiment in which his person is tested by several reagents, namely his own studies, the philosophies of his advisers, Settembrini and Naphta, the perilous influence of the mysterious Russian woman Clavdia Chauchat, and the world view of Mynheer Peeperkorn.

Hans has a talisman of his love for Clavdia. It is a wallet-sized x-ray of her chest. This product of science stands for all the seething connections in his mind between his studies of anatomy, physiology, and the principle of life as expressed in the human body with its marvelous workings, and his passion for Clavdia. Clavdia is the stimulus for and the product of his scientific studies; love and science enhance each other as Hans searches for reasons why he feels the way he does about a collection of cells organized into soft arms, Slavic features, and cat-like grace of movement. In *The Magic Mountain,* as in a scientific view of life itself, love and sex are phenomena of anatomy, bone structure, nerve endings, blood vessels and pores, brain cells and lymph glands. Even death is subjected to the dispassionate scrutiny of science. In the most moving scene, the tears Hans sheds when his beloved cousin Joachim dies are subjected to chemical analysis, as is the process of decay of Joachim's body.

A central theme of *The Magic Mountain* is the relationship of science to art. It is most obvious in a scene that takes place in the quarters of the director of the sanatorium, Dr. Behrens. Hans and Joachim are ostensibly there for a casual visit; actually Hans has wormed the invitation so that he can view Dr. Behrens's oil portrait of Mme. Chauchat. Dr. Behrens turns out to be an inferior painter. However, what he *was* able to render extraordinarily well on canvas was Clavdia's skin. The reason, he explains, is that he is a physician and therefore has a comprehension that extends beneath the surface. Hans praises the realization of the skin with all the fervor of his love-sickness, which prompts Dr. Behrens to interpret his success in medical terms:

> That birthday suit there (''That bodily covering'' is a better translation) is painted with science, it is organically correct, you can examine it under the microscope. You can see not only the horny and mucous strata of the epidermis, but I've suggested the texture of the corium underneath, with the oil- and sweat-glands, the blood-vessels and tubercles—and then under that still the layer of fat, the upholstering, you

> know, full of oil ducts, the underpinning of the lovely female form. . . .

Commentators on this scene accept Dr. Behrens's explanation of his art. Yet it would be ridiculous to believe that his modest talents surpassed the great masters—Titian or Rubens, for example—in portraying human skin, merely because Behrens is a physician. One would have to be credulous indeed to suppose that his laboratory grasp of the composition of skin could be transferred via his brush strokes to the canvas.

Art is illusion, this scene implies, thrice removed from the mystery of life. Behrens himself advises that in order to capture Clavdia Chauchat's Mongolian-like eyes on canvas, one must do as nature does with the skin on the bridge of the nose to create the effect of those eyes: practice illusion within illusion; the hand of the artist can play tricks as nature does if the artist understands nature's tricks.

Scientific analysis has supported the multiple layers of meaning in this scene, beginning with explaining the natural phenomenon itself, going on to the knowledge and practice of the physician-painter combined with the properties of the canvas (that lent the skin the illusion of reality), and finally the interpretive language that presents sequentially and therefore imposes logical form on what in its visual form leapt directly to Hans Castorp's emotions (whose impression is that if one pressed one's lips to the canvas, the fragrance would be of human flesh rather than of paint and varnish). This scene serves as an ironic preview of the sublime ideas that are to follow in the ''Research'' section.

Hans Castorp's enthusiastic response to the physician's idea that the knowledge of medicine contributes to art, is to conclude that they are fundamentally one and the same: '' you can see how the things of the mind and the love of beauty come together, and that they always really have been one and the same—in other words, science and art.'' . . . Thus an overview of themes and aspects of structure points to the weight and function of science in *The Magic Mountain.*

The parallels that Hans has drawn between the intellect and beauty, science and art, are those he will explore on long winter nights, lying on his balcony wrapped in blankets like a cocoon, as the temperature drops and a heavy snowfall hermetically seals the world of the Berghof. Nature liberates Hans into isolation, his mind stimulated by the cold and the magical winter night. Like a scientist isolated in a laboratory, he can freely explore the question he poses for himself: What is life?

To convey what Hans is doing we can borrow from a book on contemporary physics a description of what physicists do: ''. . . wonder what the universe is really made of, how it works, what we are doing in it, and where it is going, if it is going anyplace at all. In short, they do the same things that we do on starry nights when we look up at the vastness of the universe and feel overwhelmed by it and a part of it at the same time'' [Gary Zukav, *The Dancing Wu Li Masters: An Overview of the New Physics*]. It is not important for our purposes to test the validity of the scientific principles that Hans finds in his winter nights' readings of textbooks on biology, anatomy, embryology, physiology, physics, and astronomy. From today's perspective there are errors in the science, and the narrator refers to fundamental mistakes known then. Science is not presented as omniscient but as one avenue—albeit strewn with unanswered questions—to the heart of profound connections.

The twenty-page "Research" section of the novel is so complex and tightly organized, so profound in its implications, and exemplary for the whole, that it would hardly be possible to do it justice, even in a long study. Therefore two fundamental structures serve to illustrate what Thomas Mann has done to fuse in the crucible of craft and imagination the conventionally separated disciplines of science and art and thereby to realize the vision of his model, Goethe. The structures are the cell and the atom. They are analogues to the work as a whole in their functions of organization and recapitulation, and in their function as symbols for Hans Castorp of self-reflection.

It is commonplace for critics to note that *The Magic Mountain* is a highly organized work. In his classic study Hermann J. Weigand wrote: ". . . of all the attempts ever undertaken to express life on a large scale through the medium of literary creation, the *Zauberberg* is the most highly integrated" [see *TCLC*, Vol. 2]. . . . One organizing principle is the recapitulation of the whole in its constituent units. Chapters or sections of chapters, or even paragraphs repeat central developments in analogue form. The section "Research" corresponds to Hans Castorp's development over the course of the entire novel. That can be said of individual paragraphs as well. One such paragraph is the description of the pathological process of disease that is analogous to Hans's process of subjugation to the decadent Clavdia. The terms used to describe the reaction of an organism to disease include terms from the spheres of sex and morality: "voluptuous forms of tissue," "dissolute," "corruption;" the diseased organism ". . . staggered—so to speak with heaving bosom—toward dissolution." . . . Mann's characteristic equation of sex, sickness, and death reaches in these paragraphs an apotheosis as the pathology of disease reiterates the moral and emotional infection of Hans Castorp by the decadent, terminally ill Clavdia: "Thus far pathology, the theory of disease, the accentuation of the physical through pain; yet, in so far as it was the accentuation of the physical, at the same time accentuation through desire." . . . Here, in summary, is the saga of everyman Hans Castorp's awakening to life, to sensation, to knowledge, insight, and death:

> The first step toward evil, toward desire and death, was taken precisely then, when there took place that first increase in the density of the spiritual, that pathologically luxuriant morbid growth, produced by the irritant of some unknown infiltration; this, in part pleasurable, in part a motion of self-defence, was the primeval stage of matter, the transition from the insubstantial to the substance. This was the Fall. The second creation, the birth of the organic out of the inorganic, was only another fatal stage in the progress of the corporeal toward consciousness, just as disease in the organism was an intoxication, a heightening and unlicensed accentuation of its physical state; and life, life was nothing but the next step on the reckless path of the spirit dishonoured; nothing but the automatic blush of matter roused to sensation and become receptive for that which awakened it. . . .

Another paragraph, which begins with the question what is life and answers it is warmth or a kind of fever of matter, recapitulates Hans's quest in the above-mentioned scene with Behrens for the answer to the mystery of the beauty of the flesh as personified in Clavdia.

The primary structural principles are reiterated in the nature and behavior of the individual cell. In contemplating his mind's image of a naked human body—Clavdia's—Hans concludes after reviewing its biological structure: "This body which hovered before him, this individual being and living [ego] was an enormous multiplicity of breathing and self-nourishing individuals which, through organic adjustment and adaptation to special purposes, had parted . . . with their essential individuality." . . . (pp. 61-5)

The cell, as Hans recognizes, is a world unto itself: "However these events [fertilization of the egg by the sperm] are organized, they force us to accept the idea that the cell is not fundamentally different from the more complex body that it makes up; that the cell is already an advanced form, composed in its turn by division of living bodies, individual units of life." . . . Life itself, Hans thinks, is based upon organization: ". . . for the concept of an individual unit of life is identical with being structured out of smaller, subordinate units that are organized for the sake of the higher form of life." . . . The living organism, made up of cooperating units of individual cells, is the equivalent of the entire work of art with its reiterative and cooperating units.

Hans is convinced of the "unity of all branches of learning." . . . Trained as an engineer, he contemplates the functioning of bones and their mechanical properties, and realizes that he relates to the femur, in fact to all of "organic nature" in three ways, or from three points of view: the lyrical, the medical, and the technical. He sees again the unity in diversity which he recognized in the notions behind Behrens's painting. For Hans and the narrator, organization and recapitulation are principles of life, of art, and therefore of beauty; for the reader they are principles of this work of art, *The Magic Mountain*.

For all the talk of organization, it is not precision or sterile symmetry that is being advocated. In the famous section "Snow," Hans contemplates snowflakes, and as beautiful as they are, rejects the idea of crystalline symmetry. It is organization perfect, pure, and cold, and therefore related to death (which it would literally mean for Hans if he were to give in to the temptation to sleep in the snow). A snowed-in world is also described in "Research": "The world seemed spellbound in icy purity, its earthly blemishes veiled; it lay fixed in a deathlike, enchanted trance." . . . Life, on the contrary, is organic, by definition profoundly impure; its beauty is the sensual beauty of desire.

When he first asks the rhetorical question: What is life? Hans answers that it is consciousness of itself. In his review of the biological nature of consciousness—"consciousness as sensitivity to stimulus" . . .—he provides an analogy to his own situation as contemplator of life and of himself. For another organizing principle of this section is its self-referential nature. At intervals during the theoretical speculations the reader is reminded of the controlling consciousness by reference to the heavy scientific tomes resting uncomfortably on Hans Castorp's stomach or chest (a reminder also of the dependence of the workings of the intellect on the state of the whole organism). At the center of the contemplation of the universe and life is a sentient being whose mind directs and orders these speculations.

The atom in its inconceivable smallness, Hans thinks, is also a microcosm of the universe—on its own scale a functioning solar system. Just as the organization of society recapitulates the organization of organisms, so in innermost nature, in the atom, is recapitulated the macrocosm of the universe itself, of the moon and stars over Hans's head in Davos as he contemplates them. Since there might be life on distant planets, he thinks, might there not also be life on one of those "internal" planets? Large and small, after all, are relative, as are external and internal. "The world of the atom was an 'outside,' as very probably, the earthly star which we inhabited was, viewed organically, deeply 'inside'." . . . Might there not be inside the atoms that composed him another Hans Castorp, in the same position, thinking the same thoughts?

> Then perhaps in the very innermost of his being and the inmost of that innermost there was young Hans Castorp, again and a hundred times Hans Castorp, lying warmly muffled on a balcony with a view of the moonlit high mountain frosty night, and studying with stiffened fingers and flushed face and humanistic as well as medical sympathy, the life of the body?

These dizzying thoughts of unending reflection are central to the novel. Hans Castorp is outside as an observer, but he is also inside the events. He is examining phenomena as through a microscope, but is also a participant. The narrator and the reader are in both positions as well. In an unending series of recapitulations, self-consciousness is reflecting upon itself.

The intellectual, emotional, and erotic fulfillment for Hans of his investigations is the vision of a beautiful woman—Clavdia—who bends over him to embrace him. As once before in "Research," he comprehends not the mere surface of her, but her palpitating life, her internal organs, her physiology: "He beheld the image of life in flower, its structure, its flesh-borne loveliness." . . . (pp. 65-7)

Beauty (and therefore art, as the scene with Dr. Behrens that was discussed above demonstrates) resides in the mystery of life. It is to be approached via the path of understanding. Understanding is achieved by knowing, through science, what is beyond and beneath the surface, what is there but not seen: the structure and organization of life. The climax of Hans's research appears to be captured in two of the most famous lines of Romantic poetry:

> "Beauty is truth, truth beauty,"—that is all
> Ye know on earth, and all ye need to know.

Yet Keats's contemplation of the Grecian urn is a contemplation of its surface—not its atomic structure, for example, or the chemistry of the paints that created the images. It is an expansion, to be sure, of the poetic imagination to include the past and future—a time machine-like leap that suspends time and conjoins life long gone with the mortality of the observer and future observers.

The true analogy to *The Magic Mountain* is to be found in "truth" and "beauty" of a more recent time. (pp. 67-8)

[A] biography of 1983 Nobel Laureate, geneticist Barbara McClintock, contains passages of description that reformulated into Mann's language, could almost have been lifted from or served as guidelines for the "Research" section. Perhaps most remarkable about McClintock is her willingness to think beyond the boundaries of what Kuhn calls "normal science" to accept the limitations of scientific "knowing":

> A deep reverence for nature, a capacity for union with that which is to be known—these reflect a different image of science from that

of a purely rational enterprise. Yet the two images have coexisted throughout history. We are familiar with the idea that a form of mysticism—a commitment to the unity of experience, the oneness of nature, the fundamental mystery underlying the laws of nature—plays an essential role in the process of scientific discovery. Einstein called it "cosmic religiosity." In turn, the experience of creative insight reinforces these commitments, fostering a sense of the limitations of the scientific method, and an appreciation of other ways of knowing. . . . [according to McClintock] . . . what we call the scientific method ". . . gives us relationships which are useful, valid, and technically marvelous; however, they are not the truth." And it is by no means the only way of acquiring knowledge. . . .

This paragraph could be an introduction to the last stage of Mann's use of science: the step beyond to events and realms unexplainable by science. On the intellectual level, Mann has the devil's advocate, the Communist, Jesuit and blood-thirsty fanatic Naphta attack modern science as subjective. There is no such thing as objective science and value-free inquiry, he argues. Everything is predicated on a worldview, a set of beliefs. To contemporary readers these points have validity. Toward the end of *The Magic Mountain* Naphta accuses science of being a faith like any other. He rejects notions of space, time, and causality as illusions dependent upon the illusion that the world of the senses really exists. He rejects the notions of evolution, the atom, and measurement by light years as incompatible with the idea of eternity and therefore illogical. He is acting in defense of what according to Reiss may be called pre-modern, pre-scientific discourse, when he asserts that he prefers the naivete of a child who believes that the stars are holes in the canopy of heaven. . . . (pp. 68-9)

These views are clearly beyond what even the modern explorer of science would subscribe to and indeed, Naphta, the moral inferior of his opponent, Settembrini, loses his battle. He carries his convictions to their logical conclusion by shooting himself when the duel to which he had challenged Settembrini is foiled by Settembrini's refusal to shoot at Naphta.

However, in terms of Mann's technique, Naphta's excoriations must be viewed in the context of the whole work as references and correspondences to the transcendence of the known laws of nature that occurs when Joachim—whose death from tuberculosis was analyzed in scientific terms—is summoned back as a spirit during the seance conducted by the Berghof's psychiatrist, Dr. Krokowski. The poignant whisper "Forgive me" that Hans addresses to the apparition is never subjected to Mann's customary relativization by irony. The summoning back into the world of this most tender relationship subjects Hans to unbearable pain and he must leave the room. The event is of unmitigated seriousness, transcends accepted laws of science, and remains an open wound, an unanswered question.

The unanswered questions of science, the fundamental mysteries of the universe and life, the limitations of the human capacity to know constitute the governing perspective of *The Magic Mountain*. It is realized in the relation of the observer to the observed, in particular the roles of the involved narrator and the protagonist-contemplator, and captured in the image of Hans Castorp's unending reflections of himself in an infinite series of universes within universes. The role of the observer is only one of the issues raised in *The Magic Mountain* that are still being grappled with by thinkers on the frontiers of the sciences. (p. 69)

Physicists who are seeking to explain the origin of the universe are finding that they meet on common ground with particle physicists—the cosmic or very largest scale meets the scale of the sub-atomic particle—because they must understand the properties and behavior of matter during the first fractions of a second after the big bang in which the universe is believed to have originated. The connection is obvious to Hans Castorp's theorizing on the origin of matter, parallel worlds on an atomic and a cosmic scale, and the relativity of notions of size.

It is fitting to conclude with a comment by mathematician and scholar of the humanities, Jacob Bronowski, who recognized a pattern shared by science and art. It is the pattern of Hans Castorp's scientific investigations that proceed from gross internal structure as revealed by x-rays to fine structure on the smallest scale. It is the weave of *The Magic Mountain:*

> For fifty years we have been living in an intellectual revolution, in which interest has shifted from the surface appearance to the underlying structure, and then from the gross structure to the fine organization of minute parts in which only the total pattern expresses an order. And while critics have argued who has the monopoly of the new vision, and which culture ought to scorn the other, artists and scientists have gone quietly about their business of feeling and expressing the same common revolution.
>
> (p. 70)

Valerie D. Greenberg, "Literature and the Discourse of Science: The Paradigm of Thomas Mann's 'The Magic Mountain'," in South Atlantic Review, *Vol. 50, No. 1, January, 1985, pp. 59-73.*

ADDITIONAL BIBLIOGRAPHY

Abbott, Scott H. "*Der Zauberberg* and the German Romantic Novel." *The Germanic Review* LV, No. 4 (Fall 1980): 139-45.*
>   Maintains that in writing the final chapters of *The Magic Mountain* Mann drew heavily on Marianne Thalmann's description of the Romantic novel in her *Trivialroman des 18. Jahrhunderts und der romantische Roman.*

Beach, Joseph Warren. "Philosophy: Zola, Thomas Mann." In his *The Twentieth Century Novel*, pp. 103-17. New York: Century, 1932.*
>   Discusses *The Magic Mountain* as a novel of ideas, maintaining that "an enormous amount of discursive philosophy can be conveyed in the form of fiction if the writer has the genius of Thomas Mann for 'dramatizing' it, for rendering it in the proper terms of the story."

Behrendson, Walter E. "Writings to 1943." In his *Thomas Mann: Artist and Partisan in Troubled Times*, translated by George C. Buck, pp. 65-132. University: University of Alabama Press, 1973.
>   General discussion of *The Magic Mountain.*

Berland, Alwyn. "In Search of Thomas Mann." *Symposium* XVIII, No. 3 (Fall 1964): 215-28.
>   Contrasts the European romantic tradition with its American counterpart by examining the reception of *The Magic Mountain* by American students.

Blackmur, R. P. "The Lord of Small Counterpositions: Mann's *The Magic Mountain.*" In his *Eleven Essays in the European Novel*, pp. 75-96. New York: Harcourt, Brace & World, 1964.
>   Investigates the ways in which Mann "dramatises the actual thought—thought in all its senses—of his own time."

Bravermann, Albert S., and Nachman, Larry. "Nature and the Moral Order in *The Magic Mountain.*" *The Germanic Review* LIII, No. 1 (January 1978): 1-12.
>   Discusses Hans Castorp's struggle to reconcile his conceptions of the physical and spiritual natures of the individual.

Brennan, Joseph Gerard. "Heard and Unheard Speech in *The Magic Mountain.*" *Novel* 3, No. 2 (Winter 1970): 129-38.
>   Examines the manner of speech of each of the novel's main characters.

——. "Fifty Years of *The Magic Mountain.*" *Columbia Forum* III, No. 3 (Summer 1974): 31-9.
>   General discussion of the novel and personal reminiscence of the author's meetings with Mann and his wife.

Bruford, W. H. "Thomas Mann: *Der Zauberberg.*" In his *The German Tradition of Self-Cultivation: 'Bildung' from Humbolt to Thomas Mann*, pp. 206-25. Cambridge: University of Cambridge Press, 1975.
>   Discusses the novel as a representative and parody of the German *Bildungsroman*. Bruford observes that while the traditional *Bildungsroman* deals with the hero's developing awareness of life, *The Magic Mountain* parodies "this kind of novel in that the hero comes to terms, in the course of it, not so much with life as with death."

Bulhof, Francis. "Zauberberg, Magic Mountain, Toverberg." *Babel* XXI, No. 4 (1975): 173-79.
>   Evaluates Dutch and English translations of the novel. While Bulhof contends that Helen Lowe-Porter's English translation violates the "cross-referential integration of the text," he ultimately judges both translations to be "formidable performances."

Egri, Peter. "*Der Zauberberg.*" In his *Avantgardism and Modernity*, edited by H. Frew Waidner III, translated by Paul Aston, pp. 73-100. Budapest: Akadémiai Kiadó, 1972.*
>   Compares the form and thematic content of *The Magic Mountain* with that of James Joyce's *Ulysses.*

Enright, D. J. "Thomas Mann and 'The Novel of Ideas'." In his *The Apothecary's Shop: Essays on Literature*, pp. 113-20. London: Secker & Warburg, 1957.
>   Observes that despite its abstract theorizing *The Magic Mountain* is an integrated work of fiction rather than a patchwork of ideological arguments and attributes this to Mann's skill as a novelist.

Ezergailis, Inta. "Thomas Mann's Resort." *Modern Language Notes* 90, No. 3 (April 1975): 345-62.
>   Examines Mann's frequent use of resorts, spas, and sanatoriums as settings for his fiction, observing that in *The Magic Mountain* "the combination of resort and healing institution" appears "in its climactic embodiment, with infinite concrete detail yet charged with the widest possible symbolic associations."

Firchow, Peter. "Mental Music: Huxley's *Point Counter Point* and Mann's *Magic Mountain* as Novels of Ideas." *Studies in the Novel* IX, No. 4 (Winter 1977): 518-36.*
>   Presents numerous technical and thematic similarities between the novels, observing that their "resemblances are the result, not of influence, but of the *Zeitgeist* and the profound affinity of Mann's and Huxley's minds."

Ford, William J. "A Note on Hans Castorp." *Newsletter of the Conference on Literature & Psychology of the Modern Language Association of America* II, No. 4 (September 1952): 2-5.
>   Argues that the novel's main character is motivated primarily by a regressive desire to avoid responsibility.

Harvey, W. J. "Time and Identity." In his *Character and the Novel*, pp. 100-29. Ithaca, N.Y.: Cornell University Press, 1965.*
>   Discusses the passage of time in *The Magic Mountain.*

Hatfield, Henry. "Germany and Europe." In his *Thomas Mann*, pp. 64-94. Norfolk, Conn.: New Directions Books, 1951.
Analyzes the novel's principal themes and techniques.

Heller, Erich. "Conversation on *The Magic Mountain*." In his *The Ironic German: A Study of Thomas Mann*, pp. 169-214. Boston: Little, Brown, 1958.
Informal discussion of the novel in the form of an interview, with Heller taking both parts.

Hirschbach, Frank D. "The Education of Hans Castorp." *Monatshefte* XLVI, No. 1 (January 1954): 25-34.
Examines Hans Castorp's growing awareness that "love and death are closely related, that to love means to surrender a vital part of oneself, that death is innate in life."

Holesovsky, Hanne Weill. "Hint and Incantation: The Preface to Thomas Mann's *Zauberberg*." *Symposium* XXXIV, No. 3 (Fall 1980): 217-32.
Detailed analysis of the preface, which Holesovsky considers "a small work of art in itself."

Hunt, Joel A. "The *Walpurgisnacht* Chapter: Thomas Mann's First Conclusion." *Modern Language Notes* LXXVI, No. 8 (December 1961): 826-29.
Analyzes a passage appearing in the novel's first draft that was deleted before publication and contrasts Mann's original intention to write a humorous satirical work with the profundity of his actual achievement.

Koepke, Wulf. "Frisch's *I'm Not Stiller* as a Parody of *The Magic Mountain*." In *Perspectives on Max Frisch*, edited by Gerhard R. Probst and Jay F. Bodine, pp. 79-92. Lexington: University Press of Kentucky, 1982.*
Discusses Frisch's novel as "a parody of a parody."

Kowalik, Jill Anne. "'Sympathy with Death': Hans Castorp's Nietzschean Resentment." *The German Quarterly* 58, No. 1 (Winter 1985): 27-48.*
Analyzes Friedrich Nietzsche's writings on suffering and demonstrates their importance to the interpretation of the theme of suffering in *The Magic Mountain*.

Krieger, Murray. "Disease and Health: The Tragic and the Human Realms of Thomas Mann." In his *The Tragic Vision: Variations on a Theme in Literary Interpretation*, pp. 86-113. New York: Holt, Rinehart and Winston, 1960.
Considers *The Magic Mountain* a partial failure, arguing that the protagonist is not deep enough "to earn the stature needed for vision and for pronouncement."

Latta, Alan D. "The Mystery of Life: A Theme in *Der Zauberberg*." *Monatshefte* LXVI, No. 1 (Spring 1974): 19-32.
Discusses how the appearance of Joachim's spirit at the séance refutes Settembrini's contention that the universe can be explained in strictly social and political terms.

————. "Symbolic Structure: Toward an Understanding of the Structure of Thomas Mann's *Zauberberg*." *The Germanic Review* L, No. 1 (January 1975): 34-54.
Analyzes "the intricate network of symbolic systems in *Der Zauberberg*, systems which link specific elements of the novel such as figures, objects, landscapes, or actions with abstractions of a higher order."

Loose, Gerhard. "Ludovico Settembrini und *Soziologie der Leiden*: Notes on Thomas Mann's *Zauberberg*." *Modern Language Notes* 83, No. 3 (April 1968): 420-29.*
Examines the sources of the character Ludovico Settembrini. Loose presents Luigi Settembrini, a nineteenth-century Italian author, educator, and political figure, as the character's probable prototype, and locates the basis of much of the character's ideology in *Soziologie der Leiden* (1914), a treatise on suffering by sociologist Franz Carl Müller-Lyer.

Miller, R. D. *The Two Faces of Hermes: A Study of Thomas Mann's Novel, "The Magic Mountain."* Harrogate, England: Duchy Press, 1962, 124 p.

Discusses various oppositions in the novel, including Humanism and Romanticism, progress and reaction, politicism and apoliticism, and health and disease, and analyzes these oppositions as embodiments of the principles of form and formlessness.

Mueller, William R. "Thomas Mann's *The Magic Mountain*." *Thought* XLIX, No. 195 (December 1974): 419-35.
Calls *The Magic Mountain* a novel of education "in the most exalted sense," maintaining that "Thomas Mann's novel teaches us what it means to be educated, bringing us to a closer understanding of our own humanity and our own world."

Mumford, Lewis. "Barbarism and Dissolution." In his *The Condition of Man*, pp. 343-90. New York: Harcourt, Brace, 1944.*
Cites evidence of the cultural decay of industrial society after World War I and maintains that the novel's depiction of an ailing world is "perhaps the most satisfactory esthetic symbol of [its] period."

Nehamas, Alexander. "'Getting Used to Not Getting Used to It': Nietzsche in *The Magic Mountain*." *Philosophy and Literature* 5, No. 1 (Spring 1981): 73-90.*
Contends that "Nietzsche's Socrates, who espouses rationality out of a fear of his own instincts, is the paradigmatic reactive character of whom Mann's heroes are variations." Nehamas maintains that each of the main characters in *The Magic Mountain* represents a particular attitude toward life, such as rationality or reactionism, and that the characters "represent these as specific attempts to escape from what they perceive human nature to be, and of which they are afraid."

Newsom, Jon. "Hans Pfitzner, Thomas Mann and *The Magic Mountain*." *Music & Letters* 55, No. 2 (April 1974): 136-50.*
Attempts to depict German cultural and political attitudes in the years preceding the rise of nazism by examining political differences between Mann and German composer Hans Pfitzner and by analyzing musical motifs in *The Magic Mountain*.

Panaghis, Afroditi P. "Thomas Mann's *The Magic Mountain*: A Point of View." *Germanic Notes* 14, No. 1 (1983): 3-4.
Asserts that "to see the novel as a requiem for a moribund world beyond hope is to miss its entire point," arguing that Hans Castorp is successful in his quest for salvation and that his likely death in battle "predicts not only his resurrection, but society's as well."

Pascal, Roy. "Thomas Mann: *The Magic Mountain*." In his *The German Novel: Studies*, pp. 76-98. Toronto: University of Toronto Press, 1956.
Analyzes the novel's principal themes and techniques.

Passage, Charles E. "Hans Castorp's Musical Incantation." *The Germanic Review* XXXVIII, No. 3 (May 1963): 238-56.
Discusses the episode in which Hans selects five pieces of music from gramophone records placed at his disposal, analyzing the literary themes of the selections and demonstrating their relationship to the novel's thematic development.

Priestley, J. B. "Between the Wars." In his *Literature and Western Man*, pp. 376-440. New York: Harper & Brothers, 1960.*
Contends that Settembrini and Naphta's lengthy debates mar the novel's artistry, but nevertheless considers *The Magic Mountain* "a novel of marvelous solidity, richness, complexity."

Prusok, Rudi. "Science in Mann's *Zauberberg*: The Concept of Space." *PMLA* 88, No. 1 (January 1973): 52-61.
Investigates Mann's use of modern science and technology in *The Magic Mountain*, maintaining that the novel "refutes the very existence" of a distinction between the sciences and the humanities "by making literature out of the sciences and by fitting modern science into the continuum of technological evolution that reaches back into mythology."

Reed, T. J. "Education: *Der Zauberberg*." In his *Thomas Mann: The Uses of Tradition*, pp. 226-74. Oxford: Oxford University Press, 1974.
Examines the novel's development over a twelve-year period, the nature of Hans Castorp's education, and the relationship of the

protagonist's intellectual and spiritual development to that of the author.

————. "Thomas Mann: The Writer As Historian of His Time." *Modern Language Review* 71, No. 1 (January 1976): 82-96.
    Contends that in *The Magic Mountain* Mann sought to chronicle the evolution of his own convictions as well as to "speak critically about the sins of a generation and a culture."

Seidlin, Oskar. "The Lofty Game of Numbers: The Mynheer Peeperkorn Episode in Thomas Mann's *Der Zauberberg*." *PMLA* 86, No. 5 (October 1971): 924-39.
    Examines Mann's repeated use of the number seven in the novel.

Struc, Roman S. "*Sanatorium Arktur:* Fedin's Polemic against Thomas Mann's *Magic Mountain*." *Research Studies* 35, No. 4 (December 1967): 301-07.*
    Maintains that Konstantin Fedin's novel *Sanatorium Arktur*, which was expressly written as a refutation of the philosophical views presented in *The Magic Mountain*, fails its objective because of "the author's conscious or unwitting disregard of Mann's philosophical premises."

Thayer, Terence K. "Hans Castorp's Hermetic Adventures." *The Germanic Review* XLVI, No. 4 (November 1971): 299-312.
    Investigates "those main traits of Hermes' mythical existence" which in *The Magic Mountain* "become formulae of character and conduct, namely as a sort of mythical underlay for Hans Castorp himself."

Webb, Eugene. "The Perilous Journey to Wholeness in Thomas Mann." In his *The Dark Dove: The Sacred and Secular in Modern Literature*, pp. 157-93. Seattle: University of Washington Press, 1975.
    Examines allusions to mythology and the Christian tradition in *The Magic Mountain*, maintaining that in his novels Mann sought "an understanding of life that would unite the sacred and the secular."

White, I. A., and White, J. J. "The Importance of F. C. Müller-Lyer's Ideas for *Der Zauberberg*." *The Modern Language Review* 75, No. 2 (April 1980): 333-48.*
    Expands the argument of Gerhard Loose [see Additional Bibliography] to demonstrate that the work of Franz Carl Müller-Lyer is "of interest not merely as a source specifically for Settembrini's own sociological project (in the way in which Loose suggests)," but is also "aesthetically functional as part of a much wider pattern of montage in Mann's novel."

Wilson, John R. "Tuberculosis and the Creative Writer." *Journal of the American Medical Association* 196, No. 1 (14 April 1966): 161-64.*
    Discusses the association between tuberculosis and creative activity and examines *The Magic Mountain* as an example of "sanatorium literature."

Zinberg, Dorothy S., and Zinberg, Norman E. "Hans Castorp: Identity Crisis without Resolution." *The American Image* 20, No. 4 (Winter 1963): 393-402.
    Psychoanalytic study demonstrating that Hans Castorp "used his whole life to search for an identity" but "never achieved more than a pseudo-identity."

Gustav Meyrink

1868-1932

(Born Gustav Meyer) Austrian novelist, short story writer, dramatist, and translator.

Meyrink is recognized as one of the foremost twentieth-century novelists of the supernatural. His novels, which often depict an individual's quest for spiritual enlightenment, utilize elements of Christian and Jewish mysticism, Eastern philosophy, and such branches of occultism as the tarot, alchemy, and spiritualism. His most popular novel, *Der Golem (The Golem),* is considered by many critics to be a masterpiece of supernatural literature. Like many of his protagonists, Meyrink spent his life in pursuit of spiritual knowledge, and his works often demonstrate the animosity he felt toward materialistic modern society. His hostility to modern social and political institutions was also voiced in numerous satirical writings that earned him a reputation as one of the leading satirists of his day.

The illegitimate son of an actress at the Austrian court theater and a German minister of state, Meyrink was born in Vienna and raised primarily in Munich and Hamburg. He attended a business college in Prague, and in 1889 opened a bank there in partnership with a nephew of German poet Christian Morgenstern. Meyrink, who called himself "the most frivolous and systematic dandy in Prague," was a prominent playboy who delighted in offending the city's conservative middle class. He was also a talented athlete who once held the sculling championship of the Austro-Hungarian Empire. According to scholars, at the age of twenty-three Meyrink became disgusted with the shallowness of his life and resolved to commit suicide. Meyrink maintained later that he had been in the process of placing a pistol to his head when a pamphlet advertising a series of books on the occult was pushed under his door. Interpreting this as an indication of the course he should take, Meyrink refrained from suicide and renounced his devotion to materialism in favor of what would become a lifelong pursuit of higher knowledge. His subsequent studies encompassed spiritualism, theosophy, Christian and Jewish mysticism, and various areas of Indian and Far Eastern thought, and although Meyrink eventually came to regard occultism as "the religion of the stupid," he incorporated aspects of each of these systems into the independent philosophy that dominated his later writings.

In 1901 Meyrink was stricken by an illness that was diagnosed as spinal tuberculosis, and while recuperating in a sanatorium he was encouraged by author Oskar Schmitz to begin writing. His first story, "Der heisse Soldat," was published in October of that year in *Simplizissimus,* a prominent literary journal. Also in 1901, Meyrink became involved in a highly public dispute with a military officer named Bauer. Stemming from a slanderous remark directed by Bauer at Meyrink's mistress, this incident ultimately involved: other members of the officer corps, with whom Meyrink exchanged challenges to duel; a court of honor, which ruled on the grounds of Meyrink's illegitimate birth that he was ineligible for redress; the Prague press, which sided with Bauer; and the police, who began harassing Meyrink. In January of the following year Meyrink was jailed on charges of embezzlement, and although the exact grounds for the charges are not known, many commentators

believe his arrest to be the result of personal grudges borne Meyrink by police and military officials as a result of the Bauer affair. After a three-month investigation of his financial dealings Meyrink was cleared of all charges; however, public confidence in his bank had been destroyed and he was financially ruined. For the next ten years Meyrink earned a meager living from his writing. He served for a short time as editor of *Der liebe Augustin,* a literary journal whose contributors included Max Brod, Alfred Kubin, Stefan Zweig, and Frank Wedekind, but which nevertheless failed for lack of sufficient financial backing. During this period Meyrink wrote most of his short stories, which were published in *Simplizissimus* and other prominent literary journals. He also began translating the works of Charles Dickens into German, eventually completing twenty volumes, and critics observe the influence of grotesque elements in Dickens's works on Meyrink's later fiction. Between 1912 and 1914 he wrote four plays in collaboration with Rumanian dramatist Roda Roda, none of which were critically or financially successful.

In 1913 and 1914, Meyrink suddenly achieved popular and critical acclaim with the serial publication of his first novel, *The Golem.* Issued as a book in 1915, *The Golem* sold over 200,000 copies, establishing Meyrink as one of the bestselling authors of his day. With the outbreak of the war, his increase in popularity was paralleled by escalating notoriety, as Meyrink came under attack for his early satirical short stories—three volumes of which were reissued under the collective title *Des deutschen Spiessers Wunderhorn*—and for his outspoken opposition to the war. Many of his short stories were considered dangerously antinational for their international perspective, extreme individualism, and explicit mockery of the Kaiser, the police, the military, and such bourgeois institutions as university professors and pastors' wives. A writers' association denounced him as "a public enemy," and Albert Zimmerman proclaimed him "one of the most dangerous opponents of German folk-thought," maintaining that "he will corrupt thousands and tens of thousands, just as Heine did." Both Meyrink and his house were stoned, and, according to E. F. Bleiler, "when his friends in Munich planned to give him a gigantic fiftieth birthday party in 1918, it was necessary to ask for police protection against riots." Although *Des deutschen Spiessers Wunderhorn* was banned by the Austrian government in 1916, *The Golem* and Meyrink's subsequent novels continued to be popular with readers through the early 1920s. After the war Meyrink went into semiseclusion in Bavaria, where he wrote fiction, translated works by St. Thomas Aquinas, Lafcadio Hearn, and others, and edited books on occult subjects. His financial situation again became difficult during the 1920s as his works declined in popularity with the reading public. While some critics attribute this loss of readers to the greater obscurity of Meyrink's later works, others maintain that Meyrink was simply abandoned by readers as the German fascination with fantasy and the occult that characterized the first two decades of the century gave way to other interests. In the late 1920s Meyrink suffered a debilitating recurrence of the spinal ailment that had plagued him throughout his life. He died in 1932.

Meyrink's short stories are predominantly fantastic and horrific, replete with vampires, anatomical experiments, supernatural occurrences, gruesome and imaginative murders, and characters in the grip of unusual psychological states. Typical of his horrific tales are "Das Präparat," in which two men discover that an anatomist has dismembered their friend and incorporated the body parts into his decor, and "Der Man auf der Flasche," in which a husband suffocates his rival in a huge glass bottle in full view of unsuspecting guests at a masquerade ball. In other stories Meyrink achieved absurd effects by relying more heavily on fantasy than horror, as in "Der violette Tod," in which hearing a particular word transforms listeners into small, conical piles of purple jelly. Approximately half of Meyrink's short stories utilize similarly grotesque and fantastic elements for the purpose of social satire. Frequently exposing what Meyrink saw as the inadequacies of a materialistic way of life, his satires are often directed at the institutions and representatives of the modern society with which he felt himself at odds. These targets included the medical profession, modern science, academia, the clergy, and financiers, as well as the German literary establishment. He reserved his sharpest satire for the police and the military, who are portrayed in "Das verdunstete Gehirn" and numerous other stories as blustering buffoons. Scholars disagree over the impulse prompting these satirical attacks. While some critics maintain that the author was a spiritual leader who sought to destroy his readers' complacency and adherence to false values in order to awaken in them an awareness of higher realities, others point out that Meyrink's satirical targets were most often the elements of society by whom the author felt he had been wronged, and contend that his satire sprang from vindictiveness rather than from a desire for either political or moral reform. Eduard Frank has asserted that Meyrink's only goal in writing satire was to gain a forum in *Simplizissimus* and a readership for his meta-physical writings. Whether or not these allegations are true, critics agree that Meyrink was among the most effective satirists of the early twentieth century, one who, according to Bleiler, "had the ability to prick his victims into a frenzy."

Meyrink's works of social criticism were written early in his career. Critics observe in his later works what Christine Rosner has described as a shift "from polemical, satirical, personal attacks to the impersonal and the timeless." This trend is particularly evident in his novels, most of which were written during the latter half of his career and all of which are dominated by spiritual matters. Foremost among these is *The Golem,* in which mysticism and occultism are combined with earthly romance and intrigue. The most widely praised aspects of the novel are its skillful evocation of the nineteenth-century Prague ghetto and its creation of a nightmare atmosphere, which is produced by a masterful intermingling of dream and reality that has prompted comparisons to works by Franz Kafka. Expressionistic in style, *The Golem* has also been praised for its narrative grace and what one critic called an "uncommon power to evoke eerie reactions by nebulous suggestion." The book's plot concerns the gradual revelation of spiritual knowledge to its protagonist, Athanasius Pernath, through a series of dreamlike visions and encounters with emissaries of a superior order of being. Among these is the title character, a mystical apparition loosely based on Jewish legend, who appears in the novel both as the materialized collective psyche of the ghetto's inhabitants and as Pernath's doppelgänger, a spiritual double who confronts the protagonist with hitherto unknown aspects of himself. Commentators observe that Meyrink's golem has little in common with the figure of Jewish legend, and many have criticized the novel for its similarly distorted rendering of Kabbalah, the traditional system of Jewish mysticism which forms the novel's ostensible philosophical basis. Other critics have called *The Golem* a confused muddle of Jewish legend, Eastern philosophy, and Western occultism. Lee B. Jennings, however, maintains that while Meyrink's "eclectic use of such lore makes it difficult to trace the provenance of any particular motif or idea," the suspicion that he is guilty of "an exploitative popularization of the occult" is "uncalled for, since Meyrink, like C. G. Jung, treats occult and arcane doctrines as a general repository of archetypal symbols of psychic change." Meyrink's other novels are dominated by spiritual matters to an even greater extent than *The Golem.* According to Verna Schuetz, in *The Golem* "the ghetto and its miseries provide an important background for Pernath's development and his final release into the spiritual realm." In *Der weisse Dominikaner* and *Der Engel vom westlichen Fenster,* however, the narrative "no longer encompasses an extended milieu but is limited solely to isolated incidents leading the hero to his final goal of release from the material into the spiritual sphere." Critics generally consider these works to be of lesser literary merit than *The Golem,* contending that they sacrifice artistry to philosophical didacticism.

Composed as they are of elements taken from widely diverse areas of philosophical speculation, it is not surprising that Meyrink's works have inspired contradictory interpretations and critical evaluations. While some commentators assert that his writings exhibit a fundamental concern for humanity and belief in a supreme being, others see in his works a profoundly pessimistic view of humankind and a rejection of all theistic philosophies. Representative of the latter position is the assertion of Theodor Schwarz that in Meyrink's world "one no longer needs the rest of mankind. . . . His mysticism finally culminates in the deification of the self." A similar dichotomy exists between those who accuse Meyrink of exploitation of the occult and consider his works pulp, and those who attribute to Meyrink the highest spiritual ideals and literary achievement: critics in the first group argue that Meyrink's works are marred by stereotypical characters, contrived plots, sensationalism, and sentimentality, while those in the second group maintain that the author's subtle juxtaposition of reality and unreality, masterful use of the grotesque, and biting satire warrant comparison to works by Kafka, Edgar Allan Poe, and E. T. A. Hoffman. During Meyrink's lifetime his writings also inspired contradictory views of his ideological position, prompting attacks both by conservative critics who considered his works antinationalist and by socialist critics who deprecated his abandonment of social criticism for what they considered self-indulgent spiritualism. Since that time much of the controversy surrounding Meyrink's writings has subsided, and most of his works have fallen into neglect with readers and critics. Meyrink's literary reputation today rests almost exclusively on *The Golem*, which remains one of the most famous supernatural novels in modern European literature.

(See also *Contemporary Authors*, Vol. 117.)

PRINCIPAL WORKS

*Der heisse Soldat   (short stories)   1903
*Orchideen   (short stories)   1904
*Das Wachsfigurenkabinett   (short stories)   1907
Die Sklavin aus Rhodos [with Roda Roda]   (drama)   1912
Gesammelte Werke. 6 vols.   (novels and short stories)
    1913-17
Der Golem   (novel)   1915
    [The Golem, 1928]
Fledermäuse   (short stories)   1916
Das grüne Gesicht   (novel)   1916
Der Löwe Alois, und andere Geschichten   (short stories)
    1917
Walpurgisnacht   (novel)   1917
Der weisse Dominikaner   (novel)   1921
Der violette Tod, und andere Novellen   (novellas)   1922
Goldmachergeschichten   (short stories)   1925
Die heimtükischen Champignons, und andere Geschichten
    (short stories)   1925
Der Engel vom westlichen Fenster   (novel)   1927

*These volumes were published collectively as *Des deutschen Spiessers Wunderhorn* in 1913.

THE NEW YORK TIMES BOOK REVIEW   (essay date 1928)

[*In the following excerpt, the critic favorably reviews* The Golem.]

Out of the ghoulish legend of the Golem, out of bestial hatreds, unendurable miseries, and villainy in the ghetto of Prague, out of the fundamental properties of sinister mystery—secret passages, apparitions, black sorcery—Gustav Meyrink has created a phantasmagoria of horror. The plot becomes irritatingly muddled at intervals, but at the end one sees that there is a definite pattern. And whatever the category, the book is a superb addition to the literature of the supernatural in its more spectacular aspects.

The Golem (that Frankenstein variant ascribed to a seventeenth century rabbi, who put him together by magic formula in the shape of a man), who escaped and spread havoc until his power was destroyed, is only one of the many sources of terror in the book. The plot rests on the possession of a hat acquired by mistake. The man who got it in place of his own went through all the horrible experiences that the owner had endured.

He found himself in the ghetto, working as a fine engraver, being gradually drawn into the destiny that went with the hat, fulfilling the prophecy that once every thirty-three years the Golem apparition comes through the streets of the Jewish quarter.

Across the street from his house lived Aaron Wassertrum, the pawnbroker, malevolent and powerful, about whom clustered stories of ghastly occurrences in the past, and who presently became the principal villain of the subsequent action. Wassertrum had had a son who rose to eminence by performing fiendishly ingenious eye operations. He had been exposed by a Dr. Savioli, and had taken poison. So Wassertrum was waiting for the chance to revenge his son's death. That chance seemed close at hand, because Dr. Savioli had taken a room in the house across the street where he had rendezvous with a married lady of noble birth. But there were further complications to the situation—infinities of complications strew every chapter—since it was a fanatic beggar student called Charousek who had led to the exposure of Wassertrum's son, really. And his reason for that was that Wassertrum was actually his father, and he hated him with a special venom based on family and racial reasons.

There, then, is an indication of the course of the external circumstances that faced the man who wore the hat. Subjectively, he had to face horrible nightmares, the knowledge that he was supposed to be mad, encounters with supernatural creatures, appalling revelations from a book of illimitable magic powers, and episodes in which these two fields of horror overlapped. Written with grace and an uncommon power to evoke eerie reactions by nebulous suggestion, these passages are apt to give one moments of what is vulgarly known as the creeps.

The man in the hat—he took the name of Penrath that he found inside it—was now not only carrying the varied burden of horrors, but he was serving as knight protector to one lovely lady in the case and serving another as well. He went to taverns with neighborhood characters and there heard more tales of the grim and the supernatural. He was making sorties governed by both physics and metaphysics at a bewildering and engrossing rate when the murder of a man was laid at his door, and he was thrown into jail. All skeins were completely tangled. Gradually they began to unravel—at the same pace—and with much the same effect.

> "'The Golem' and Other Recent Works," in The New York Times Book Review, *December 30, 1928, pp. 12-13, 15.*

JETHRO BITHELL   (essay date 1959)

[*In the following excerpt, Bithell discusses* The Golem *and* Der Engel vom westlichen Fenster.]

Gustav Meyrink's [*Der Golem*] is by reason of its allusive handling of the robot-theme one of the most readable tales of the period. The Golem is an artificial man made according to a lost specification of the cabbala by a rabbi of Prague in the seventeenth century, to help him ring the bells of the synagogue. The creature lives only with a 'half-conscious vegetable life' by the virtue of a magic card (*Zettel*) inserted behind his teeth; this draws down the sidereal powers (the symbol is apparently that of the automatism of modern society; Heaven still moves us, though in our limp life of routine we are unconscious of it). When, one evening, the rabbi forgets to remove this card from the creature's mouth he runs amok through the streets, smashing whatever comes in his way, until the rabbi captures him and removes the card (symbolically: reduces the robot to brute matter—there is not much difference; and also—if we lose priestly direction we are raging brutes). When the card is removed the Golem falls all of a heap, and nothing remains of him but the figure of a clay dwarf which is still shown in the Altneusynagoge at Prague. But the people in the ghetto of Prague believe the Golem still appears in the streets at intervals—*'ein vollkommen fremder Mensch, bartlos, von gelber Gesichtsfarbe und mongolischem Typus—in altmodische, verschossene Kleider gehüllt—mit schiefgestellten Augen und gespaltener Lippe'* ['an utterly strange man, beardless, of yellow complexion and Mongolian type—enveloped in old-fashioned, faded clothes—with slanting eyes and cleft lip']. One person who has seen the Golem maintains that it can only have been her own soul which had stepped out of her body to face her; this, of course, is E. T. A. Hoffmann's *Doppelgänger-Motiv*, of which there is much in the book. A curiosity of Meyrink's tale *Das grüne Gesicht* . . . is that the post-War topsyturviness is foreseen. In all his other tales [*Orchideen, Das Wachsfigurenkabinett, Walpurgisnacht, Der weisse Dominikaner*] . . . there is the same sensation-mongering in the guise of occultism or spiritism.

To English readers there is probably more appeal in his *Der Engel vom westlichen Fenster* . . . , for the scene of a great part of the tale is in England, and in the chain of magicians are St. Dunstan and Queen Elizabeth, while the hero is Sir John Dee, the descendant of a Welsh chieftain whose desire is to win Greenland for Gloriana. ('Greenland', as the tale unfolds, is the deep dead past, from which come ghosts and all mediumistic visions and succubi and the mirages of sexual desire.) The scene changes to Prague, where another *Teufelsbündner*, Kaiser Rudolf, wise and wily but in the toils of priests, directs the ever elusive quest for the philosopher's stone. The actual theme of the novel is the secret of existence, and this is revealed (darkly) by the complicated action as man's ceaseless battle with sex: a good man by his very nature strives frantically to achieve wisdom and selflessness, but this masculine ideal is thwarted by the demonic fascination of the female, in this tale sensationally embodied, obscene and divinely lovely, as the Pontine Isis (*die schwarze Isaïs*), with lithe limbs and panther's smell (*das Pantherweib*). Isis is eternal, for she is in the blood and is the blood of the male, whose only hope is to be mothered by some domestic woman, from whose shielding arms he is lured, however, by this vampire who is lust, not love. The demon may, when man's senses are cold, fill him with loathing of her functions, but her magic lies in the heating of his senses; and even if he would destroy her she seizes him in the very frenzy of his hate, for sexual desire is the adoration she craves. There is much play with elusive symbols: particularly with the dagger, or spear-head, of the hero's Welsh ancestor, which is at the same time an attribute of the cat-headed goddess (= phallus): the hero, in his successive incarnations, can only save his soul—and even then only when life is ending—by preserving this instrument from the greed of the evil powers. The mystic illumination of the problem of life comes from a weird rabbi who is versed in cabbalistic lore: and the lesson is (apparently) that man must choose between suppression after death or

supression in life of the brute element of sex—in other words between flesh and spirit, and that the true alchemistic *transmutatio* is achieved by the hermaphroditic marriage of the male with the female (element) within himself: thus Sir John Dee might win 'the Queen'; not, as he deludes himself, Queen Elizabeth—who gives herself to him only as Isis in the shape of a succubus and lures his descendant in our own days as the medieval Dame World, fair in front and with hollow back wreathed with slimy snakes—, but the irradiation through strain and suffering of personality. (pp. 72-4)

Jethro Bithell, ''Humorists, Satirists, Satanists and Visionaries,'' in his Modern German Literature: 1880-1950, *revised edition, Methuen & Co. Ltd., 1959, pp. 54-74.**

GERSHOM G. SCHOLEM   (essay date 1960)

[*A German-born Israeli scholar specializing in Jewish mysticism, Scholem was the author of over five hundred books and articles. His work is generally credited with raising the study of Kabbalah from its previous disreputability to what the* London Times *called ''a position of central importance'' in Jewish scholarly thought. In the following excerpt from his study* On the Kabbalah and Its Symbolism, *originally published in Switzerland in 1960, Scholem discusses Meyrink's adaptation of Jewish legend in* The Golem.]

Some forty years ago Gustav Meyrink published his fantastic novel, *The Golem*. By taking up a figure of Kabbalistic legend and transforming it in a very peculiar way, Meyrink tried to draw a kind of symbolic picture of the way to redemption. Such literary adaptations and transformations of the golem legend have been frequent, particularly in the Jewish and German literature of the nineteenth century, since Jakob Grimm, Achim von Arnim, and E. Th. Hoffmann. They bear witness to the special fascination exerted by this figure, in which so many authors found a symbol of the struggles and conflicts that were nearest their hearts. Meyrink's work, however, far outdoes the rest. In it everything is fantastic to the point of the grotesque. Behind the façade of an exotic and futuristic Prague ghetto, Indian rather than Jewish ideas of redemption are expounded. The alleged Kabbalah that pervades the book suffers from an overdose of Madame Blavatsky's turbid theosophy. Still, despite all this muddle and confusion, Meyrink's *Golem* has an inimitable atmosphere, compounded of unverifiable depth, a rare gift for mystical charlatanism, and an overpowering urge to *épater le bourgeois*. In Meyrink's interpretation, the golem is a kind of Wandering Jew, who every thirty-three years—it would seem to be no accident that this was the age of Jesus when he was crucified—appears at the window of an inaccessible room in the Prague ghetto. This golem is in part the materialized, but still very spooky, collective soul of the ghetto, and in part the double of the hero, an artist, who in the course of his struggles to redeem himself purifies the golem, who is of course his own unredeemed self. This literary figure, which has achieved considerable fame, owes very little to the Jewish tradition even in its corrupt, legendary form. (pp. 158-59)

Gershom G. Scholem, ''The Idea of the Golem,'' in his On the Kabbalah and Its Symbolism, *translated by Ralph Manheim, Schocken Books, 1965, pp. 158-204.*

JACK HIRSCHMAN   (essay date 1971)

[*In the following excerpt from an essay originally written in 1971, Hirschman emphasizes Meyrink's vision of psychic and spiritual evil in* The Golem.]

Advertising leaflet for the first edition of The Golem.

Meyrink's book, all of Meyrink's books, are deeply influenced by Poe, that count in urban sheeps clothing whose *de*-transcendentalizing works represent the wrist of realism and a cross-legged irony cutting through the continents of religion and apocalypse like a stiletto.

For it is the process of a *darkness* that concerns Meyrink in his work. The Buddha image which opens the book is bathed in no gloriously meditated white light of silence. The architecture of the mind, like the chops of the rooftops of the Prague ghetto that locates the story, is in a state of collapse. In a word, Meyrink begins at the point where, so to speak, all the drugs have been 'taken'—there is *only* the darkness of the confusion of one's divided soul. Something, someone, has split. The remaining fissure, the crack, the abyss between the two lobes of the skull, is where his book is woven, as if to be a bridge between the two, but a bridge that at the same time records, as a grimoire, the dark angels that took up their places in a magic theater of the mind at the outset of the parting of the curtains.

Meyrink's world does have something of the same tonalities as that of Hesse, but it is less swissed i.e., euphorically neutral, and as such less sophisticated from a pacifist point of view. Gershom Scholem, the leading Kabbalist mentality, has written (in his essay on golemics, in *On the Kabbalah and Its Symbolism*) of the redemption at the novel's end as being related

to Indian theosophies [see essay dated 1960], and the reincarnative conclusions at the end of *Magister Ludi* come to mind, as does the sublime laughter at the end of *Steppenwolf*. But both Hesse's novels were written more than a decade after *The Golem*, a decade moreover in which post-war depressions and the deeper understanding that there was, in reality, no *post-war*, that consciousness of an endless war would be man's revolutionary fate, drove many writers to the east in search of 'teachings.' Meyrink's novel, composed synchronically with the onset of the Russian Revolution and the First World War, reflects both the collapse *backward* and the futuristic despair of magical disorientation which marks this entire ironically exalted epoch. An inheritor of the aristocratic-to-dandyistic stance of irony, and even satire, in the face of his perceptions of the world, Meyrink was spared the fate of the contemporary poet or novelist: he was not turned *completely* against himself, was not the abundant fanatic that most important writers of our time either write to, or become; but then, Meyrink is pre-radio, and, visually, in the domain of *The Cabinet of Dr. Caligari*, i.e., silent movies.

In short, he writes to and of those who believe that evil is a necessary part of existence rather than that which has to be 'cleaned up.' His novel is not the mirror of the newspaper expose. The repertory company of his Prague ghetto is a microcosm of the world of the tortured soul, but the macrocosm it reflects is not yet the mass or collectively medacritized gnosis of our time. As such *The Golem*, as here presented, is meant to serve as a talisman or shield as one carries on his encounters in the psychic darkness which conditions them. In this Meyrink touches upon an essential of kabbalist thought: that evil was created *in order* to *punish the wicked*, that without it, there would be no cosmic drama, no paradox of energy,—all would be equal to godhead; but since godhead, in kabbalism as in eastern theophanies, stems from the sustaining endlessness of a silence surpassing all definition and all sensible life, and 'equilibrium of balance,' which pays ultimate homage to what is beyond the human comprehension that it originates and keeps abundantly alive, all would be (without evil) presumption, arrogance, and, ultimately, unredeemed. Thus, kabbalists from Luria to Luzzato to Kook and Krakovsky stress the element of evil not as simplistic iniquity, but, paradoxically, as that locus or center of descent from (and by) which one can experience with pleasure (that is, humility) the *conscious life* of *everything ascending.*

In most literature of our time, evil has been popularized into detective work, and the cathartic terror that is part of its purifying process has been reduced to tracking down some objective fact, usually identified with an actor, the perpetrator of the crime. In *The Golem*, though murders are committed in the ghetto, the all-pervading sense is not that of life and death as crucial elements, but rather the aural planes on which their interlinked dramatic processes are played, in the name of a purification by the magic realism of the imagination. Even in that most extraordinary encounter, between the hero-narrator and the admitted rapist-murderer Amadeus Laponder, it is not the act for which he soon will be executed that Laponder is created to be remembered, but the extra-sensory perception which his dream-life exhibits in jail. Everywhere objective acts are made to appear inferior to inner events, dreams, evocations of ESP; and in this, Meyrink—whose biography touches upon elements of freemasonry, kabbalisms Judaic and Christian, etc.— must be regarded as a forerunner of that occult fanaticism that is part of the socializing function of the times, a condition of contemporary poemic man in his struggle with and against the computations of a statistical death. In all three of his major novels (*The Green Face,* a magical realist work set in Amsterdam, and *The Angel at the Western Window,* a work based upon the relationship of the alchemists Kelley and Dee, are the other two key works), Meyrink engages elements of the bizarre and quackdoctorly in order to affirm dimensions of consciousness that *literally* are sub-cult-ural. These works represent at one and the same time a recoil from the pressure of his own historical moment and a foreshadow of that ironic consolation of magic (as I write this, in 1971, the visual mediums of motionpictures and television provide for most that governmental boobyprize of opiation by which totalitarian powers 'entertainingly' guide their peoples to scientific and electronic submission) by which the robbery of unconscious life is done up to look like the greatest salvation man can hope for, as supernal joints, needles, images, pills, are shoved into the orifices of his body.

Meyrink's golem, not yet a robot and certainly not designed to destroy anything but the walls of armour within the damned imagination, turns out to be a book within the book, a book called *Ibbur* (the term comes from Chaim Vital's *Book of Transmigrations* and means an impregnation, or pregnancy, in the sense of being fecundated) through which the narrator of the story enters, as Orpheus entering the mirror, engaging elements of a dark journey leading to purification.

Such an inward journey, since *The Divine Comedy,* has been repeated with every shade of variation for centuries. In the case of *The Golem,* the soul of the *Ibbur* book is mated to the soul of the Wandering Jew mythos, which is said to inhabit the soul of the ghetto every 33 years. The Wandering Jew is thus wedded—in Meyrink's arcana—to the notion of a ghetto resurrection along the track of a kabbalism that becomes Christian, if not Buddhist, in scope. And, one might add, racial in evocation, from the point of dark political blaze which everywhere triggers the current generation.

Jack Hirschman, in an afterword to The Golem *by Gustav Meyrink, translated by Madge Pemberton, Mudra, 1972.*

VERNA SCHUETZ (essay date 1974)

[*Schuetz is an American educator. The following excerpt, in which she discusses grotesque and fantastic elements in Meyrink's short stories, is taken from a doctoral dissertation examining themes and motifs in the fantastic fiction of Meyrink, Hanns Heinz Ewers, Alfred Kubin, and Karl Hans Strobl.*]

The largest single group of motifs these authors employed was that dealing with the human body: its parts, illness, death, burial, and decay. That which is commonplace in occurrences of sickness, death, and burial—events grim enough in themselves—seldom interested these writers. Instead, they dealt with unusual or improbable aspects of these motifs. Many of their stories are clearly predicated on the assumption that horror possesses a certain fascination for man. (pp. 119-20)

Meyrink's first published story, "**Der heisse Soldat,**" [deals with illness]. . . . The temperature of a foreign legionnaire rises to a phenomenal ninety degrees Centigrade after he drinks an opalescent fluid he found in a fakir's hut. The head military physician, Professor Mostschädel, is incompetent and totally unconcerned with the well-being of the patient. When the soldier's medical history is reported to him and the opalescent liquid is mentioned, Mostschädel interrupts the report to dis-

miss this information as an irrelevant digression. On a purely theoretical basis, without examining the patient or taking into account the fluid he drank, the professor diagnoses the case as a disturbance of the brain's thermal center. After the announcement of the diagnosis, all the army doctors are happy and act as though with the diagnosis their responsibility in the case were over. They gather that night for an evening's entertainment and never undertake anything to cure the patient. In the meantime, the soldier's clothes catch fire because of his extreme body heat, and he is given an asbestos suit by attendants. After a period of time, reports state that he is cooling off and that he plans to return home to Bohemia when he reaches fifty degrees Centigrade. (pp. 121-22)

Meyrink does not seek to shock or repulse by portraying a real illness and its effect or a possible variation thereof. Nor does he want to arouse sympathy for the soldier as a suffering human being. For this reason, he creates an absurd, impossible ailment. Professor Mostschädel, on the other hand, is revealed in all his real arrogance, incompetence, and inhumaneness. Meyrink intended to ridicule military doctors and simply employed fantastic elements, primarily an imaginary illness, to fashion his satire. Contempt of military physicians is a recurrent theme in his satiric stories and stemmed from an unpleasant personal experience in Prague. (pp. 122-23)

As they did with sickness, death, and burial, so too Ewers, Strobl, and Meyrink sought out unusual, grotesque, and absurd aspects of physical decomposition for their strange tales. (p. 127)

[The] motif of sudden decomposition is more comical than bloodcurdling in Meyrink's story "**Der violette Tod.**" . . . As with sickness in "**Der heisse Soldat,**" Meyrink does not emphasize the repulsive aspects of his motif. Instead, he treats it as an absurdity. It is but a vehicle through which he exposes and ridicules the stupidity of the masses in general and scholars in particular.

Meyrink's story begins in a remote valley in India. A deaf servant sees his master turn into a tiny conical heap of purple jelly before his eyes when the members of a mysterious tribe, covering their own ears, yell something. The servant reads the lips of the natives and repeats the word "Ämälän." At this, the natives also turn into heaps of jelly, but not before they wound the servant with a poison spear. He manages to escape the valley and write an account of his adventure before he dies. His story finds its way into the newspapers, and around the world people disappear and leave behind only a pile of purple slime. The masses are so stupid that nearly half the world population is decimated before a German scholar realizes the connection between the mysterious deaths and the word "Ämälän." The scholar holds a lecture to explain that in the light of modern vibration and radiation theory such a phenomenon is possible. He warns his audience not to say "Ämälän" and immediately dissolves, with all his listeners, into a shimmering cone of jelly.

The purpose of Meyrink's story is to satirize the scientist-scholar with his lack of worldly practicality just as he had ridiculed the physician-professor in "**Der heisse Soldat.**" . . . Meyrink has the process of decomposition occur repeatedly and at totally indifferent moments in the story so that each single instance in itself is of relatively little importance. Meyrink further minimizes any possible horror effect from the motif of physical decay by avoiding all realism of depiction. The decomposition results from a magic word as in a fairy tale, and it bypasses death. Without the realistic intermediary steps of illness and death, the victims change immediately from healthy living beings into neat, colorful, odorless little piles of purple jelly. (pp. 133-34)

Besides dealing with the entire body, its death and decay, Ewers, Strobl, and Meyrink all portray individual body fragments that lead an independent existence apart from the body as a whole, a frequent motif in Kubin's early pictures also. Among the three writers, this motif occurs by far the most frequently in Meryink's works. He uses it both for horror effect as in ["**Das Präparat,**" "**Der Opal,**" and "**Das Wachsfigurenkabinett**"] . . . and for satire as in ["**Das verdunstete Gehirn**" and "**Coagulum**"]. . . . (p. 141)

In the story "**Das Präparat,**" the two friends Ottokar and Sinclair break into the house of the Persian anatomist Dr. Darasche-Koh after Sinclair hears the voice of their dead friend Axel emanating from the doctor's house. They had been surprised some time before when Darasche-Koh, Axel's mortal enemy, had claimed their friend's body and proved his right to it by producing a certificate of payment signed by the dead man. Ottokar and Sinclair, suspecting foul play, have sent Darasche-Koh a bogus telegram that lures him out of town to Berlin. In a room containing stuffed monkeys and snakes, they find Axel's head suspended from the ceiling and attached to a functioning heart and lungs. The heart is surrounded by wires leading to an electrical apparatus, and veins supply it with blood from two bottles on the floor. When the eyes perceive a blue spark from a mirror opposite the head, the mouth opens and begins to count aloud. Ottokar and Sinclair want to flee, but the door has fallen shut, and in place of a doorknob, they find the hand of their dead friend. Meyrink's use of a hand as a doorknob has been severely criticized: "Diese kunstgewerbliche Verwendung des anatomischen Fragments als Türgriff ist banal und in der Kumulation der Reize ('menschliche Hand'—'mit Ringen geschmückt'—'Hand des Toten'—'Weissen Finger'—'krallten ins Leere') kitschig. Die Übertragung funktions- und materialfremder Formen auf Gebrauchsgegenstände ist ein Stilzug büngerlichen Kitsches" ["This artistic use of the anatomical fragment as a doorknob is banal and in the aggregation of stimuli ('human hand'—'adorned with rings'—'hand of the dead man'—'white fingers'—'clawed into space') kitschy. The transference of functionally and substantively alien forms into common objects is a characteristic of bourgeois kitsch" [Siegfried Schöde, *Studien zu den phantastischen Erzählungen Gustav Meyrinks*].

While Meyrink bestows a superfluity of bizarre detail on his description of the doorknob-hand, at a later point in the story, he tries to arouse horror by total lack of detail. "**Das Präparat**" is intended to appeal to the reader who delights in grim tales. Meyrink is only interested in deriving the maximum shock effect from his material. In case he has failed to call forth the desired response through the depiction of the independently functioning heart, lungs, and head of a dissected body or through the detailed description of a human-hand doorknob, he makes one last attempt to satisfy his reader's desire for gruesomeness by appealing to the reader's own imagination. Once Ottokar and Sinclair are outside, they notice the bell cord, utter a scream, drop their candle, and race away with their hair standing on end. Instead of stating specifically what Ottokar and Sinclair see when they look at the bell cord, Meyrink simply reports their terrified reaction and leaves it to the reader to imagine whatever he himself finds most ghastly. Meyrink thus, in effect, declares artistic bankruptcy by tacitly admitting he has to rely on his reader to compensate for his own creative inadequacy.

In the story "**Das Gehirn,**" . . . Meyrink tries to combine the ghastliness of an anatomical fragment with the parody of a medical professor. Brains appear as: a bloody calf brain, a human brain that falls to the ground and splatters, and a bloody human brain into which a witch doctor sticks needles. Instead of contributing to the satirical goal of the story, the body-fragment motif becomes a gory end in itself and counteracts the humor of the rest of the story.

"**Das Gehirn**" is an early tale and rather the exception than the rule among Meyrink's works. Although he employs the same motifs in both his satirical stories and his horror tales, his treatment of a given motif generally varies according to the purpose of the story. Without a doubt, Meyrink often captures his reader's initial attention in both types of stories by appealing to the reader's fascination with horror. But in the satires, Meyrink, for the most part, either underplays the hair-raising aspects of motifs like sickness and anatomical fragments, or he topsy-turvily converts these motifs into sources of humor themselves. This is the case with the story "**Das verdunstete Gehirn.**" . . . (pp. 141-43)

Meyrink's ridicule in this tale is directed at military officers, and the story itself is fittingly dedicated to the shoemaker Voigt. At the beginning, the reader learns that Hiram Witt has discovered a way to produce brains from animal cells by subjecting them to the dual influence of a magnetic field and mechanical rotation. In contrast to "**Das Gehirn,**" the brains are never described. Witt's discovery has aroused little scientific interest, for, as the narrator muses, "Was sollte man in Deutsch sprechenden Ländern mit selbständig denkenden Gehirnen?!'' ["What would be done with independently thinking brains in German-speaking lands?!''] Witt has sent some brains to a scientific institute, but they died when given a lecture by a Gymnasium professor. However, the most amazing occurrence in connection with the artificial brains unfolds before the reader's eyes. A military officer comes into Witt's room and places his helmet over one of the brains while talking with Witt. When the officer picks up the helmet, the brain has disappeared and in its place lies a mouth topped by a moustache. Witt draws the conclusion: "So schnell also verwandelt der Einfluss eines Helmes ein Gehirn in ein Maul!!'' ["So quickly does the influence of a helmet transform a brain into a mouth!!''] Meyrink's implication is clear: intelligent brains cannot survive in the society of either mindless military officers or lethally boring pedagogues. Not only Witt's creations, but also his own mind falls prey to the brain-destroying forces around him. He goes insane and ends in an asylum singing "Deutschland, Deutschland, über alles.'' (pp. 143-44)

Motifs of sex are of major significance for Ewers' and Strobl's short stories; they are almost totally lacking in Meyrink's. Only in Meyrink's novels does the male-female relationship play a role, and then not as a physical relationship but rather as a highly idealized, etheralized partnership that culminates in the merging of a man and a woman into a single hermaphroditic being in spheres beyond the confines of the real world. (p. 147)

In turning to psychological material, Ewers, Meyrink, and Strobl were reflecting the interests of their age as well as following the lead of earlier authors of the grotesque, among them Edgar Allan Poe. Meyrink's tale "**Eine Suggestion**" . . . deals with exactly the same psychological phenomenon as Poe's "The Imp of the Perverse.'' In both stories, the first-person narrator has committed a murder without being detected, but under the influence of an idea he implants in his own mind, he is led to betray himself. Poe specifically raises the question of the sanity of a person so dominated by a single idea that he is compelled to act on that idea even though such action endangers his very existence. Meyrink does not explicitly question his narrator's saneness. However, whether a man who commits murder, one who is then preoccupied to the exclusion of all else with the effects of that murder on his mind, and who is willing to murder again in order to learn why his mind has reacted as it has, the question of whether such a man is demented or not is implicit in the material itself. (p. 158)

Ewers', Strobl's, and Meyrink's works range over a wide spectrum of psychological and parapsychological phenomena: the power of suggestion, obsession, religious insanity, possession, split personalities, hallucinations resulting from physical illness, and the aberrations of a deranged mind. (p. 159)

Meyrink's story ["**Die Pflanzen des Dr. Cinderella**"] is told by a first-person narrator who relates in retrospect events that have led up to his present confusion regarding the dividing line between reality and illusion. . . . [Meyrink] attributes his narrator's loss of his grasp on reality to supernatural forces, in this case of occult origin.

A series of strange experiences has followed the narrator's imitating the posture of a bronze statuette he once found in the sands of Thebes. One night, he felt himself driven to a house in the old part of Prague. He went into the cellar and found eye-bearing arteries growing like vines on trellises. In addition, he also saw a pinecone of human fingernails and mushrooms growing from flesh. Outside the house, the narrator was arrested without explanation and taken to the local police station. There he heard for the first time the name of Dr. Cinderella, a great scholar and Egyptologist who is supposedly raising a new meat-eating plant. While the narrator was musing over what he had heard, an Egyptian Anubis walked in and whispered the name Dr. Cinderella to him. Then the Anubis suddenly turned into a police clerk who returned some calling cards imprinted with the name Dr. Cinderella to the startled narrator. He was told that he himself was Cinderella, and the police clerk advised him to stay home at night.

The narrator states that these events occurred three weeks ago and since then he has been lame. He has two different face halves and drags his left leg. Furthermore, he has been unable to locate the house with the strange vines in the basement, and no one at the police station knows anything about his having been at the station that night. In language at once reminiscent of the religious ecstatic, the occultist, and the drug user, the narrator speaks of breaking through the boundaries of earthly knowledge, of being outside his body, and of hearing sounds and seeing colors and figures that no one else perceives. He says his soul is on a long, dark trip away from mankind. The narrator's extraordinary experiences occur only in his own mind. His mental distortions do, however, manifest themselves externally through the psychosomatically induced changes in his physical body. As in the case of Ewers' story ["Aus dem Tagebuche eines Orangenbaumes"], it is essentially irrelevant whether the cause of the narrator's delusions is a magical or an occult force, insanity or drugs. What both authors are endeavoring is to depict a person in the process of losing touch with reality. The incipient moment and the consequent development are of greater importance than the germ itself. (pp. 161-62)

Meyrink offers a glance into the conceptual world of a deranged mind when he has the narrator write about eyes growing on vines, pinecones of fingernails, and mythological gods turning

Title page by Andre Lambert for Das Wachsfigurenkabinett. *From* Gustave Meyrink, *directed by Yvonne Caroutch.* © *Editions de l'Herne.*

into human beings. Meyrink nowhere states that the narrator is insane. And instead of warning the reader directly from the beginning about the veracity of the narrator, Meyrink lets the reader discover for himself that the narrator does not differentiate between reality and illusion. (p. 163)

Like motifs of death and decay, those of physical and mental abuse offer, by their very nature, especial opportunity for horror. (p. 165)

Only a small percent of Meyrink's stories deals with either physical violence or mental cruelty, but of those few works, several rival Ewers' most gruesome tales in ghastliness. Meyrink's murderers display great ingenuity in devising torturous deaths for their victims. In the story "**Der Opal,**" . . . an Indian fakir, a worshiper of the goddess Dhurga, uses magic in sacrificing two servant boys to the destroyer of all organic life. The boys are found with their heads severed from their bodies and their faces contorted in an insane laugh, their eyes have turned into opals. A man in "**Die Urne von St. Gingolph**" . . . leaves his own child to suffocate in a sealed stone urn in order to punish his wife for her infidelity. And "**Der Mann auf der Flasche,**" . . . like Edgar Allan Poe's "The Cask of Amontillado," is the story of a revenge murder executed in the midst of a masquerade. Meyrink's ball has been planned in every detail from the costumes to the entertainment as a backdrop for murder. As part of the floor show, a man plays the role of Pierrot in a huge glass bottle. He gradually suffocates in full view of the unsuspecting ball participants when the host secretly closes the air vent and thus avenges himself for his wife's unfaithfulness. The murderer disappears without a trace.

In all of Meyrink's tales dealing with man's inhumanity to man, the gruesomeness of the deed is intended to horrify the reader. However, Meyrink neither dwells on detailed descriptions of gore as does Ewers, nor does he have the perpetrators of frightful deeds encounter the retribution of poetic justice as does Strobl. From Meyrink's stories emerges an extremely pessimistic picture of the world. Fiendish brutality strikes with the speed and unexpectedness of lightning and then vanishes from view equally as quickly. Evil is innate in the beings who inhabit this world, and, under certain conditions, this evil becomes the dominant factor of personality.

In two different stories, Meyrink depicts a being of absolute depravity created through controlled mutation of the physical body. One of these stories, **"Das Wachsfigurenkabinett,"** . . . tells of three friends who recognize the missing child of an acquaintance in two children they see in an exhibit of curiosities at a fair. They vainly attempt to locate the mysterious Persian Mohammed Daraschekoh who is responsible for splitting the child into two separate beings. However, the plot of the story is only incidental. It simply provides Meyrink with an opportunity to horrify by portraying a person, in this case even a child, who embodies evil absolutely. Not a single element of goodness mitigates this total depravity. Daraschekoh has made one child into two separate beings by separating the electrical currents determining character that normally are united in and surround one body. The result is one stupid eight-year-old child with a puffy, full-grown body and a second child who is not much more than a head. The second child has no skin and has to be preserved in a fluid. This child is unthinkably depraved, and the expression on its face is described as "tückisch, hass-verzerrt, . . . boshaft und voll . . . unbeschreiblicher Laster-haftigkeit" ["malicious, distorted by hate, . . . wicked and filled with . . . indescribable viciousness"]. The motif is that of the personality split into its good and evil components as in Robert Louis Stevenson's *The Strange Case of Dr. Jekyll and Mr. Hyde*

The malevolent child in **"Das Wachsfigurenkabinett"** is itself the victim of mutilation and, in spite of its degenerate nature, causes no harm to anyone else. In **"Der Albino,"** . . . a similar victim of malicious mutation itself then inflicts injury on another person. The creation of the albino has already taken place before the beginning of the story and is explained in the course of the action. Dr. Kassekanari, a physiologist whose forefathers were from Haiti, experimented on a child his wife conceived with his best friend Ariost. Kassekanari operated to remove those portions of the brain responsible for the gentler feelings of man and transfused the blood of white degenerate animals into the child until he created a being of physical and spiritual degeneration: a white Negro who is also "ein seelisch Ges-torbener" ["a spiritually dead man"].

At the beginning of the story, the albino is a grown man living as a sculptor under the assumed name of Pasqual Iranak-Essak (Kassekanari spelled backwards). Corvinus, Ariost's legitimate son, goes to Iranak-Essak to have a plaster cast made of his face. The albino murders him by leaving out the straws for ventilation. Furthermore, Iranak-Essak has developed a plaster as hard as granite, and it is impossible for Corvinus' friends to remove the mask from his head and save him. Iranak-Essak escapes. The framework within which this action occurs is the fulfillment of a prophecy concerning a secret lodge to which Ariost and Corvinus belong. According to the prophecy, the visage of the person who tries to open a certain sealed letter before the appointed time will be blotted out of the world forever without a trace. As a joke, Corvinus plans to have his friends relate that he has opened the letter but that the impres-

sion of his face has nevertheless been preserved in the plaster mask. The lodge with its forbidding prophecies and elaborate robes adorned with mystical signs provides an exotic background for the story of a jealous husband's revenge just as had the masked ball in **"Der Mann auf der Flasche."** Again, the dreadfulness of that revenge, here the perversion of one of Ariost's sons into a fiend who gruesomely murders the other son, is the point of the story.

In both **"Der Albino"** and **"Das Wachsfigurenkabinett,"** each fiendish being is artificially created by eliminating all counterbalancing elements of gentleness and goodness. Meyrink starts from the assumption that man is a mixture of good and evil, and when the force of good is removed as a restraint on evil, man degenerates into a spiritually and physically deformed monster.

In all of Meyrink's stories of physical abuse, with the exception of **"Die Urne von St. Gingolph,"** the persons resorting to violence are all non-Europeans: an Indian, a Persian, a Haitian. In part, Meyrink was simply taking advantage of the cliché association of horrible, torturous practices with certain other cultures. In addition, he could hope for a more willing suspension of disbelief on the part of his reader by having characters with an exotic, mysterious background perform the deeds of dastardliness he portrayed. Meyrink certainly did not intend to imply that his European brethren treated each other any less inhumanely, as indicated by the tale **"Ohrensausen."** . . . (pp. 171-75)

The plotless narrative **"Ohrensausen"** relates how, at night, the vulture souls of men leave their sleeping bodies. "Die Menschen sind ermattet vom Tagewerk, das sie Pflicht nennen, und suchen frische Kraft im Schlaf, um ihren Brüdern das Glück zu stören,—um neuen Mord zu sinnen im nächsten Son-nenschein" ["The people are exhausted from the day's work, which they call duty, and seek fresh strength in sleep,—in order to disrupt the happiness of their brethren,—in order to plot new murder by the light of the next day"]. The souls fly to a cellar in which Satan's emery wheel turns day and night. The stone has been hardened in the fire of hate for thousands of years, and here the souls sharpen the claws their owners have scratched dull during the day. According to Meyrink, the wheel will turn until time stands still. The tale's closing sentence makes clear that Meyrink does not exempt a single living person from his damning judgment of man: "Wer die Ohren verstopft, der kann ihn [den Stein] sausen hören im Innern" ["He who plugs his ears can hear it (the stone) rumbling within him"]. (pp. 175-76)

Meyrink, Ewers, and Strobl employed motifs of death, sex, mental distortion, and man's maltreatment of his fellow man because of their potential for thrilling titillation and their appeal to man's immemorial fascination with horror and the grotesque. . . . Roughly half of Meyrink's stories are satires in which he uses the fantastic as an initial allurement and as a vehicle for ridicule, usually of specific groups in society. However, others of his fantastic tales are calculated to cause his reader's blood to curdle. The pessimistic view of man Meyrink expresses in the process is often more spine chilling than the gruesome deeds he depicts. (pp. 176-77)

Verna Schuetz, "Bizarre Motifs in the Tales," in her The Bizarre Literature of Hanns Heinz Ewers, Alfred Kubin, Gustav Meyrink, and Karl Hans Strobl, *The University of Wisconsin, 1974, pp. 119-77.**

CHRISTINE ROSNER   (essay date 1974)

[In the following excerpt from a doctoral dissertation, Rosner summarizes several important commentaries on Meyrink's works and analyzes the use of the grotesque in his short stories.]

The first objective and comprehensive essay about Meyrink appeared anonymously in 1917 at the end of the last volume of his collected works. It bears the title, ''Zu Gustav Meyrinks Werken.'' [Siegfried] Schödel claims that the author of this lengthy essay was Kurt Pinthus, then lector of the Kurt Wolff-Verlag in Leipzig. Pinthus discusses Meyrink's short stories in the first part of the essay and the novels written up to that time in the second. He points out the bond between Meyrink and the Romanticists, especially with E.T.A. Hoffman whose abounding imagination and hatred of the *petit bourgeois* (*Spießbürger*) Meyrink shares. In his satires and grotesques Meyrink also derides militarism, corrupt officers, and the shallowness of rationalistic theology and of *Heimatkunst*—forces and figures which he considers inimical to his life. Pinthus sees Meyrink as a master at the organ of horror, a horror which may serve as guide to another, higher world if it is combined with the occult. (p. 6)

[Pinthus'] essay concentrates on inner development, interpreting Meyrink's works as a breviary of the secret teachings of all times and all peoples. Pinthus sees Meyrink's concern for the occult as a search for a deep and serene philosophy shared by the peoples of East and West alike. Although Meyrink had never been to India, he avidly studied Oriental philosophy as well as the Jewish Cabbala and came into contact with a group of Christian mystics. Pinthus contends that Meyrink's occultism is atheistic: the guide to life is our inner self. His contention is later rejected by Frank, who discovers in Meyrink's works three stages on the way to God.

In his stylistic investigation, ''Motiv and Wort bei Gustav Meyrink,'' [Hans] Sperber traces various recurrent motifs: death by suffocation, death by hanging, and the motif of the vampire. Equating recurrence with intense preoccupation, Sperber interprets each case as a kind of emotional release. Sperber sees in Meyrink's work a good example of his theory that literary creation provides psychic release. Defining a true poet—in contrast to a writer of Schundliteratur [''trash'']—as a person who creates from an inner urge, he regards Meyrink with favor and describes Meyrink's imaginative gift as ''mythenbildende Phantasie'' [''myth-creating fancy''].

The only book-length treatment of Meyrink, Dr. Eduard Frank's eighty-page appreciative, positive, psychologically-oriented study, accords Meyrink a special place between literature and psychology. Dr. Frank writes as a former friend; he presents a considerably detailed biography and a concise review of the psychological interpretations of Meyrink's works (e.g., those of C. G. Jung, J. J. Hablitz, and Herbert Fritsche). Contemplating Meyrink's spiritual development, Frank notes two aspects, the parapsychological and the esoteric: during the time Meyrink experimented with spiritualism, he was primarily a parapsychologist; when yoga dominated his interest, he became an esoteric.

Frank also traces Meyrink's literary development. Emphasizing the novels and noting an unusual maturity even in the early works, Frank claims Meyrink began to write only after his inner development had been completed. Frank sees Meyrink's works as a literary ''historische Angelegenheit'' [''historical matter''] but predicts that psychologists and parapsychologists will renew their interest in them. Whatever one may think of

Meyrink, Frank states, he was a restless, incredibly serious seeker.

In her dissertation, Marga-Eveline Thierfelder examines Meyrink's philosophy, mainly as it is set forth in his novels. According to Thierfelder, Meyrink the satirist and seeker wants to arouse the complacent and self-content from their deceptive dreams and lead them to a higher form of existence. To achieve this he dons the mask of the satirist. The types he chooses for his satires represent visible symptoms of the spiritual malaise of his time. Thierfelder contrasts Meyrink's skeptical view of man with Adalbert Stifter's concept of man as an image of God. Noting the difference between Meyrink and the Romantic poets, she quotes Nietzsche's ''Ihr leidet mir noch nicht am *Menschen*. Ihr würdet lügen, wenn Ihr's anders sagtet! Ihr leidet alle nicht, woran ich litt,'' and regards both Meyrink and Nietzsche as suffering from a religious crisis. Like Nietzsche, Meyrink conquered his despair by creating a new ethos of man, that of the superman.

[Marga-Eveline] Thierfelder traces the several stages which lead to this new being: the first decisive step is doubt in the being and value of man. Doubt is followed by recognition of the insecurity of human existence and of the physical world. Having lost his transcendental anchorage and reverence for nature, modern man, *homo faber*, feels cast out from all ordered existence and thus becomes prey to the demonic forces in nature. In Meyrink's poetic world man is constantly threatened by such demonic forces and by insanity. Satiric and ironic laughter provides some protection from the world of demons and chaos and serves as a means towards self-preservation, but in order for man to attain the absolute he must first despair. Thierfelder relates Kierkegaard's philosophy to Meyrink. Since the renewal of man must come from within he must first come to a knowledge and acceptance of his limitations. This ''know thyself'' forms the basis of all religions. Knowledge leads to awareness. Thierfelder equates the man who has become aware of himself with the superman who has exchanged the active world for a pure, spiritual realm where external events mean nothing and inner experience everything. Dreams form a significant part in a new life in which spiritual strength overcomes fear. It does not become altogether clear whether Thierfelder sees a traditional image of God evolving in Meyrink's works or whether she equates the force within man with God.

Thierfelder associates Meyrink with the art and literature of the early Expressionist movement. To confirm her thesis she quotes liberally and convincingly from pertinent writers. She points out that Meyrink's use of the grotesque constitutes a further tie with Expressionist writers. Satire and irony have a twofold function: to jolt the bourgeois out of his complacency and to preserve the poet's sanity in an unreliable world. Thierfelder's thorough and positive appraisal of Meyrink and his work opens the door to an understanding of Meyrink's novels, although she believes that the insertion of mystical and occult teachings weakens the compactness of the novels. Her classification of Meyrink as a writer between Neo-romanticism and early Expressionism is shared by [William R. van] Buskirk.

Buskirk attempts to establish the bases of satire in Meyrink's work. An extensive biography and a discussion of the history and definition of satire precede the examination of specific satires. Buskirk tries to show that ''a combination of circumstance and spiritual necessity'' made a Meyrink a satirist and that the bases of his satire can be found in his life, especially in his Prague experiences and in his reactions to a materialistic society. (pp. 6-12)

For purposes of analysis, Buskirk groups the satires into various types. A brief history of each type precedes analysis. Of the nine stories assigned to the group of "grotesque satire," he discusses two: **"Der heiße Soldat"** because it was the first one published and because of the physical exaggeration, and **"Schöpsoglobin"** "for its wide variety of satirical targets in addition to its grotesque content." In his treatment of Meyrink as social satirist Buskirk agrees with Thierfelder's conclusion that a concern for mankind and for moral values underlies Meyrink's work, but he also notes that Meyrink's "otherwise high motives are marred by the injection of personal, often petty hatreds." (pp. 12-13)

In his dissertation, *Studien zu den phantastischen Erzählungen Gustav Meyrinks,* Schödel denies that Meyrink's works are serious literature ("Dichtung"). He claims that to write of Meyrink as a *Dichter* means uncritically accepting Meyrink's own claims. Schödel examines Meyrink's style but admits that he is concerned only with the "façade" and not with the essence of Meyrink's works. (It does not become clear what he means by "essence.") Schödel concedes to Meyrink a position between *Dichtung* und *Schundliteratur.* In his survey of the literature of the fantastic during the first decades of the twentieth century he notes the tendency of the entire genre towards *Trivialliteratur.* Schödel succeeds in relating Meyrink to other contemporary writers and artists on the subject of the fantastic but his criticism of Meyrink as a writer is open to question. Though copious quotes from authors concerned with stylistic literary criticism—for example, E. R. Curtius, R. Wellek and A. Warren, W. Kayser, F. Martini, M. Bense—are given to support his negative evaluation, he does not always convince. No distinction is made between the fantastic, the grotesque, and the bizarre, and Schödel's working definition of the fantastic, a brief quote from Gradmann's book *Phantastik und Komik* (1957), begs the question: the fantastic "entzieht sich einer strengen Definition" ["eludes a strict definition"]. In conclusion Schödel discusses Meyrink's works as an unsuccessful combination of "*Dünnromantik* und *Gottessehnsucht*" ["thin Romanticism and yearning for God"]. (pp. 13-14)

In this dissertation three types of grotesques will be distinguished in the works of Gustav Meyrink: the horrifying, the fantastic, and the satiric.

The three categories will be defined as follows: the grotesque in literature entails the presentation of highly unusual events or phenomena in a greatly exaggerated way to produce 1) fear or loathing (horrifying grotesque), 2) a feeling of the uncanny and of strange delight (fantastic grotesque), 3) laughter or mirth (satiric grotesque).

Elements such as the monstrous, the hideous, the demonic, the fearful, the abnormal, the incongruous, and the extravagant, which are generally acknowledged to be aspects of the grotesque, may be found within each type. (p. 47)

The plot of [the horrifying grotesque tale **"Das Präparat"**] concerns the search for Axel, a supposedly dead man, and his being discovered by two friends, one of whom believes he has heard Axel's voice through an open window at the residence of the famous Persian anatomist, Dr. Mohammed Darasche-Koh. His claim marks the beginning of the suspense because the two suspect the Persian of having done away with their friend. The suspense is increased by the suspicion that the Persian, an expert in anatomical preparations, did not really kill Axel but merely induced a state of *rigor mortis* by means of a poison. The horror begins here with the introduction of the possibility of the "living dead," i.e., with a human being placed in a supposedly inanimate state. It is not unheard of for people to sell their bodies to medical schools for dissection; nevertheless, when the reader learns that Axel has done so, the sensation of fear and horror increases. A feeling of apprehension arises when one learns that the Persian has acquired legal possession of the corpse and was, moreover, Axel's fiercest enemy.

By a ruse the two friends make certain the anatomist is out of Prague before they proceed to his residence in order to find their friend. The accumulation of horrifying and grotesque details gradually increases in intensity. There is, first of all, the location of the Persian's house in the vicinity of the Hradschin, the Chapel of St. Wenzeslaus and the Cathedral of St. Vitus, the Starvation Tower and the Alchemyst's Lane, "diese alten, fremdartigen Bauten mit ihren Skulpturen wie aus geronnenem Blut, die immer von neuem einen so tiefen, unerhörten Eindruck auf unsere Seele machen" ["these old, unknown structures with their sculptures as if of coagulated blood, that make ever anew such a deep, shocking impression on our soul"]. The mention of these locations conjures up pictures of dark bygone times—of emperors and alchemists pacing underground passages of the castle in search of gold; of St. Wenzeslaus, Duke of Bohemia, who was murdered in the tenth century, and of St. Vitus, the fourth-century martyr. By an inevitable association with the name of the saint, the reader's imagination turns to the St. Vitus's dance and its convulsive jerking movements. Similarly, mention of the Starvation Tower brings to mind the slow death of guilty murderers and innocent victims alike. These associations, belonging to a remote past which is unfamiliar to the reader, evoke a sensation of eerie and uncanny fascination at the same time, as does the anthropomorphic simile of clotted blood, a simile which, furthermore, points more directly to the central grotesque revelation of the story.

For the house of the anatomist, Meyrink chooses another grotesque anthropomorphic simile to heighten the feeling of horror: "Das Gebäude—einsam auf der Anhöhe des Fürstenbergschen Parkes—lehnt wie ein toter Wächter an der Seitenmauer der grasbewachsenen Schloßstiege" ["The building—solitary on the rise of the Fürstenbergschen Park—leans like a dead watchman on the sidewall of the manor house staircase"]. . . . The house is not only solitary, but it is situated in the seclusion of a private park. Adding to the already uncanny locale is the paradoxical comparision of the house with a dead guard. The loneliness of the place is enhanced by the description of the castle staircase as being overgrown with grass. The surrounding garden is seen as indescribably horrifying: "Dieser Garten, diese alten Ulmen da unten haben etwas namenlos Grauenhaftes" ["This garden, these old elms down below have something unspeakably horrible about them"]. . . . Here, as frequently in his stories, Meyrink suggests how the reader is to react. In the above quote he implies that the reader is supposed to feel the horror he mentions. The Hradschin itself is depicted as standing out threateningly against the sky; even the air seems strange, as if all life had retreated deep into the earth from fear of a lurking death. . . . The entire Hradschin area is perceived in a vision, projected into the future, in which the sleeping, crouching life would reawaken like a ghostly animal to something new and horrifying. . . . (pp. 53-6)

The exposure to weird visual impressions is continued inside the house and acoustic sensations are added which intensify the grotesque aspects and the mood of horror. . . . (p. 56)

During Ottokar's terrified attempt to light a match, the friends hear the sluggish counting continued from a niche ("—vier—fünf—sssechss—siiiieben"). At last they discover the source of the voice:

> Von der Decke der Wandvertiefung an einem Kupferstab hing ein menschlicher Kopf mit blondem Haar. Der Stab drang mitten in die Scheitelwölbung. Der Hals unter dem Kinn mit einer seidenen Schärpe umwickelt—und darunter mit Luftröhren und Bronchien die zwei rötlichen Lungenflügel. Dazwischen bewegte sich rhythmicsh das Herz—mit goldenen Drähten unwunden, die auf den Boden zu einem kleinen elektrischen Apparat führten. Die Adern, straff gefüllt, leiteten Blut aus zwei dünnhalsigen Flaschen empor. . . .
>
> Das war Axels Kopf, die Lippen rot, mit blühender Gesichtsfarbe, wie lebend—die Augen, weit aufgerissen, starrten mit einem gräßlichen Ausdruck auf einen Brennspiegel an der gegenüberliegenden Wand, die mit turkmenischen und kirgisischen Waffen und Tüchern bedeckt schien. Überall die bizarren Muster orientalischer Gewebe. . . .
>
> [From the ceiling of the niche, on a copper rod, hung a human head with blond hair. The rod passed through the top of the head. The neck under the chin was draped with a silken shawl—and beneath that with windpipes and bronchia the two reddish lobes of the lungs. Between them the heart moved rhythmically—wrapped with gold wires that led to a small electrical apparatus on the floor. The veins, filled taut, conveyed blood upward from two narrow-necked bottles on the floor.
>
> It was Axel's head, the lips red, with rosy complexion, as if alive—the eyes, wide open, stared with a hideous expression at a concave mirror on the opposite wall, which appeared to be covered with Turkoman and Kirghiz weapons and cloths. Everywhere the bizarre patterns of oriental weavings.]

The grotesque character of the preceding paragraphs lies chiefly in the ghastly arrangement of the anatomical parts. A particularly striking feature is the clash of incompatibles, between animate and inanimate. Though Axel's cranial center is pierced by a rod, a voice issues from his head and some parts of his anatomy seem to function. A further grotesque image results from the unexpected and startling draping of a silken shawl around the victim's throat. Gold wires enclose the rhythmically-beating heart and hook it up to an electrical apparatus. The incongruity of the decor enhances the grotesque effect: one does not expect to find in an anatomical laboratory an Oriental atmosphere created by Turkoman weapons and bizarre tapestry.

While the imagination of the reader can perhaps accept stuffed snakes and monkeys in that environment without feeling disgust, the description of a human belly floating in a bluish liquid in a glass tub induces a feeling of nausea. Similarly, the impaled fragments of Axel which function as a talking clock are repulsive. The reader's reaction may be explained by the process of identification with the anatomist's victim.

The two frightened friends are making for the door when they again hear a grating sound that seems to emanate from their friend's lips. His brain, too, seems to function:

> Seine Lippen öffneten sich—schwerfällig streckte sich die Zunge vor—bog sich hinter die Vorderzähne—, und die Stimme röchelte:
>
> Ein Vier—rrr—tel.
>
> Dann schloß sich der Mund, und das Gesicht stierte wieder geradeaus. . . .
>
> [Its lips opened—the tongue stretched ponderously forward—bent behind the front teeth—and its voice rattled:
>
> A quar—rrr—ter past.
>
> Then the mouth closed, and the face once again stared straight ahead.]

The slowness and laboriousness with which the speech organ still functions, indeed, the fact that it functions at all; the minute description of this functioning; the contrast of motion versus abrupt rigidity ("das Gesicht stierte wieder geradeaus")—all these factors contribute to the enhancement of the sensation of horror and the grotesque.

The grotesque horror reaches its climax when the friends encounter two more of Axel's anatomical parts, the door handle and the bell rope on the stairway:

> Die innere Türklinke war eine menschliche Hand, mit Ringen geschmückt. Die Hand des Toten; die weißen Finger krallten ins Leere. . . .
>
> "Hier! das da—", er wies auf den Glockenzug. . . .
>
> [The inner doorknob was a human hand, adorned with rings. The hand of the dead man, its white fingers clawing into space. . . .
>
> "Here! this here—," and he pointed at the bell pull.]

The choice of two parts of human anatomy in isolation is sufficiently hideous. Yet the grotesque aspect is rendered even more effective by the manner of presentation. The lifeless hand, instead of hanging limply, claws into space. The fingers are bedecked with rings which create an impression of color and of contrast between the whiteness of the hand and the hue of the rings (though no specific color is mentioned, the impression of color is evoked).

The feelings suggested by the narrator in presenting the last grotesque item are as strong as they are unambiguous. Although the identification of the limb that functions as a bell pull is left to the reader, the usual shape of the utensil and the highly emotional reaction of the two men leave little doubt that the light of the flickering candle reveals Axel's penis. Ottokar groans and his knees give way, Sinclair drops the candle, and both take to flight." . . . (pp. 57-60)

Meyrink makes use of the customary elements of the grotesque in this tale: the accumulation of very unusual and abnormal occurrences in a strange, exotic environment. The extravagant anatomical experiments are performed, moreover, by a foreigner, a Persian, who, like most Asiatics in Meyrink's works, is seen as an evil, cunning, inscrutable creature. By choosing an exotic character, Meyrink perhaps wished to lend credibility to the depraved nature of the Oriental's experiments. Had Meyrink written a few decennia later, he could have found an equally horrible reality almost at his doorstep. The language, especially the choice of dramatic verbs and adjectives, such as *fremdartig, altertümlich, drohend, zusammengekauert, röchelnd, grauenhaft* ["strange, ancient, menacing, huddled together, rattling, hideous"], ... etc., serves to heighten the grotesque impression. (p. 60)

When unnatural, uncanny or imaginary phenomena appear in a story to such a degree as to produce a shudder or a feeling of strange delight, the fantastic grotesque is produced.

While the effect of the horrifying grotesque is strongly emotional and that of the satiric grotesque strongly intellectual, the effect created by the fantastic grotesque may be experienced on both levels. If the uncanny elements predominate in a story, the effect will be primarily emotional; if the fantastic or the unreal stands out, the effect may be more intellectual.

Like the fairy-tale, the fantastic grotesque takes place in the world of the imagination as constructed by the writer. The absence of any firm connection with reality permits the emotion of laughter or amusement at the poet's fantastic creations. What distinguishes the fantastic grotesque from other tales of fantasy is the high degree of exaggeration. (pp. 80-1)

A graveyard, a dream, an animal fable, and a feverish somnambulist are the components of [the fantastic grotesque tale **"Das Fieber"**]. The fairy-tale "once-upon-a-time" beginning removes it one step further into the realm of the unreal where a sleepwalker dreams of a raven who hatches hearts. At sundown he observes from his window a moving black wing-shaped cloud with feathery edges. The sleepwalker decides to follow the wing to find out to whom it belongs. He climbs out of bed and, clad only in his nightshirt, walks out into the street towards the setting sun. Having arrived at the cemetery, he sits down to wait for the full moon. The cemetery comes uncannily alive:

> Wie der Mondglanz grell auf den Flächen schwamm, schlüpften hinter den Grabsteinen, an den Seiten, die dem Lichte abgewandt waren, blau-schwarze Vögel aus der Erde und flogen lautlos in Scharen auf die kalkbetünchte Mauer. . . .

> [As the moonlight swam glaringly on the surfaces, behind the gravestones, on the sides where the light was averted, blue-black birds slipped out of the earth and flew soundlessly in flocks to the whitewashed wall.]

The bright light that emanates from the moon, the flocks of bluish-black birds who emerge from the earth on the dark side of the gravestones to sit on the white-washed cemetery wall, the sharply contrasting images of light and shadow, of black and white, startle the reader. The eerie mood is produced by the visual associations of two unusual verbs (the moonlight "swimming," the birds "slipping" out from behind the gravestones), and by startling adverbs like flying "soundlessly" and moonlight shining "glaringly." The adjective "blau-schwarz" ["blue-black"] modifying "Vögel" ["birds"] gives an impression of metallic luster and heightens the uncanny atmosphere.

Against a background of mist-shrouded forest the sleepwalker sees a gigantic raven sitting on a wall, with wings outspread. Grotesquely, the raven speaks with a human voice. Following the rules of fairy-tale etiquette, it introduces itself as the raven who hatches hearts from dead humans. . . . The weird idea of a raven hatching hearts is intensified by the olfactory sensation suggested by the scent of withered flowers, given off as the raven beats his wings. The reference to withered flowers also underscores the association with funerals and cemeteries.

The raven flies to the marble gravestone of a recently buried philanthropist, who is described with a touch of satiric malice as having been forever active in "enlightenment," in doing and speaking good, and in bowdlerizing the Bible. His guileless eyes had looked like "Spiegeleier," ["fried eggs"], giving the impression of blank staring stupidity.

Even though the somnambulist expects to see a white raven hatched, a pitch-black one emerges from the heart of the deceased "Menschenfreund" ["philanthropist"]. In fact, all the hatched ravens are black, with one exception, a snowy white one, of which it is said "es schien, als käme all der Schimmer der Nacht von ihm" ["it appeared as if all the brightness of the night came from it"]. . . . It sits on the grave of an idler. The man in his nightshirt recalls how the idler had been brought to the gallows three times and each time the mechanism had refused to function. The uncanny concept of an idler for whom the gallows goes on strike is rendered more grotesque, almost magical, by the triple repetition. When asked by the man what became of the idler, the white raven states: "Ich habe sein Fleisch gefressen und seine Gebeine, die Erde ist kleiner geworden um das Stück, das sein Leib groß war" ["I have eaten his flesh and his bones, and the earth has sunk at the spot he was buried"]. The feeling elicited upon reading this passage is one of eerieness, almost of horror. These elements do not predominate, however, and the fever-dream atmosphere places the story in the realm of the fantastic grotesque. (pp. 82-4)

Anthropomorphic grotesque descriptions also contribute to the uncanny atmosphere. A few such passages may serve as examples: "Eine breite, goldgelbe Wunde klaffte quer über den Himmel unter einem dunkeln Wolkenkopf hervor" ["a broad, gold-yellow wound gaped across the sky beneath a dark cloud"]. . . . To see the sunset as a golden-yellow wound gaping across the sky beneath a dark cloud is a far cry from Goethe's harmonious view of nature as expressed, for example, in the poem "An den Mond." By likening the sunset to a festering wound—one is reminded of Büchner and of the poets of Expressionism—all pleasant associations are destroyed. The stars and the moon fare but slightly better: "Und wie er empor zum Himmel blickte, standen die Sterne voll Tränen und blinzelten. Nur der Mond glotzte vor sich hin und begriff nicht" ["And as he glanced up at the sky, the stars stood full of tears and squinted. Only the moon goggled silently and understood nothing"]. . . . The conventional romantic sees the stars as bright, smiling and friendly, but Meyrink makes them squint and fills them with tears. The moon, whose light seemed soft and dreamlike to Eichendorff, is here personified as a dull-witted goggling being (the verb "glotzen" connotes stupidity), an unfriendly image much like the sun and moon images in the grandmother's fairy-tale in Büchner's *Woyzeck*, where the moon is nothing but a piece of rotting wood, the sun a withered sunflower.

The raven is the central image in this tale. As a creature believed to have the gift of prophecy, it arouses a feeling of the uncanny, of fear. This feeling is intensified when one recalls that the raven is also considered a bird of ill omen and a companion of the devil. The raven is mentioned in the unidentified quote prefacing the tale: An alchemist asks a black substance in its retort: "Wer bist du, trübes Ding im Glase hier, sag an" ["Who are you, turbid thing here in the glass, tell me"]. The substance answers: "Ater corvus sum." . . . This response casts a dark spell over the tale. It is perhaps not too far-fetched to draw a parallel between Meyrink's presentation of sun, moon, and stars on the one hand and of the raven on the other. Just as Meyrink destroys the romantic aspects of these natural phenomena, the raven destroys the dreamer's belief in the goodness of the philanthropist and the worthlessness of the idler.

The ending of this tale is rather Heinesque (cf. Dr. Saul Ascher). The Herr Medizinalrat appears in black frock coat, takes the patient's temperature,—the patient has awakened from his tortured sleep—and writes out a nonsensical prescription in Latin and Greek. As he departs, with his index-finger dignifiedly uplifted, he murmurs in a tone of great secrecy and importance: "Gögön das Fübör, gögön das Fübör. . . . The solemn dress of the doctor, his pompous demeanour and his exaggerated language destroy the uncanny mood. (pp. 86-8)

[The effect of Meyrink's stories of satiric grotesque] is mainly intellectual and derives from the recognition of the objects or conditions satirized, as well as from the appreciation of the writer's wit and imagination. The reader reacts with laughter which will differ in quality depending on his mood and temperament. (p. 111)

["**Das verdunstete Gehirn**"] is an example of Meyrink's attacks on those social classes where conceitedness tends to be most rife: the military, civil servants, scientists, professors, and physicians. The satire is aimed at deflating the egos of specimens of these classes and at unmasking their ignorance and bad manners. In addition to his loathing of pomposity, Meyrink had a personal reason for his dislike of the military and the police. His second wife's brother, who was an officer, and a police commissioner were both instrumental in jailing the innocent Meyrink. (pp. 111-12)

Hiram Witt, an experimental research scientist, has been growing brains for the past twenty years. Disappointed in the reception of his scientific endeavors, he sells his products for human consumption to Kempinski's restaurant. Success seems to come at last when after a night of research he observes the formation of tiny neural fibers on the brains. All his previous achievements appear trivial by comparison. At this very moment, however, the military forces its way into his room, confiscates and destroys his accomplishments. The realization of the irresistible influence of the military in all spheres of life causes the researcher to lose his sanity. This grotesque satire derides the uncouth manners which the military men exhibit when they break into Hiram Witt's home. It also satirizes the scholarly establishment in the person of the scientist who, despite his supposedly superior intellect, follows the intruder's orders unquestioningly and resignedly. At the same time it directs its taunts at secondary-school teachers and medical specialists. (p. 112)

The house is first invaded by a vagabond posing as the Captain of Köpenick, accompanied by a baboon whom he identifies as the Mayor, and later by genuine representatives of the military. Witt willingly hands over his "valuables" to the former invaders and reaches obediently for the seams of his trousers at the command of the latter. Meyrink mocks the scientist's limitless conceit in endeavoring to reduce the wonders of the universe to a mathematical formula while his superior training is useless when dealing with the cruder forces of life.

What renders the satire grotesque is Meyrink's combining of incongruous elements and his distortion of reality. One device Meyrink delights in is the combination of unlikely names. Frequently he uses a distinguished first name and an ordinary last name, e.g. Hiram Witt. While Hiram was King of Tyre, Witt is renowned in German areas adjacent to the Czech border as the name of a large textile firm in Weiden. Meyrink was most likely familiar with the name. . . . Another grotesque feature is Hiram Witt's address, "Schnedderedengstraße." Rather than inventing a realistic street name, Meyrink preferred an onomatopoeic word imitating the sound of trumpets. The name also has military associations appropriate for a story in which soldiers play so ludicrous a role.

The incongruity in Hiram Witt's name is reinforced by the juxtaposing of fame and obscurity. Hiram Witt is introduced as follows:

> Hiram Witt war ein Geistesriese und als Denker gewaltiger und tiefsinniger noch als Parmenides. Offenbar,—denn über seine Werke sprach überhaupt nicht ein einziger Europäer.
>
> [Hiram Witt was a mental giant and as a thinker even more powerful than Parmenides. Manifestly,—since not even a single European discussed his works.]

The satire lies in the erroneous deduction: If Parmenides is read by few people because his philosophy is so difficult, then Hiram Witt's even greater "exclusiveness" must be due to the even greater depth of his works. (The officer later refers to Hiram Witt in a far less complimentary way as "Jehirnfatzke," the brain nut).

Witt's lack of fame seems astonishing in view of the information that he had succeeded, twenty years earlier, in growing brains capable of thought from animal cells on glass plates. (pp. 113-16)

Hiram Witt's scientific achievement has aroused no interest; for "was sollte man in Deutsch sprechenden Ländern mit selbständig denkenden Gehirnen?!" ["what would be done with independently thinking brains in German-speaking lands?!"]. . . . What, indeed, would such brains have been useful for when even a perfect specimen almost instantly turns into a "Maul" ["mouth"] when brought into contact with a helmet? (p. 116)

The Street of Alchemists. From Gustave Meyrink, *directed by Yvonne Caroutch.* © *Editions de l'Herne.*

The medical profession is satirized in the person of the great surgeon, Professor Wasenmeister, who makes the profound observation that brains have no appendices to remove. His comments mocks the obsession of some surgeons with cutting. The caliber of Professor Wasenmeister's competence becomes apparent in his fondness for appendectomy—one of the easiest of operations. He views Hiram Witt's attempts to grow brains with disparagement, since brain operations would seem to be beyond his scope.

Next the police and the military become the butt of Meyrink's satire. He satirizes the misplaced reverence of the police, who generally consider themselves superior to civilians, for a still "higher" social group, the military. The latter represented by the "Captain of Köpenick," a vagabond with a soldier's cap, and a baboon in an officer's uniform. The following scene takes place outside Hiram Witt's window:

> Ein Strolch mit einer Soldatenmütze und ein Pavian in Offiziersuniform waren in einer Droschke vorgefahren und musterten . . . die Fassade des Hauses.
>
> —Und gleich darauf begannen die beiden, der Affe voran, den Blitzableiter hinaufzuklettern, bis sie im ersten Stock anlangten, die Scheiben zerschlugen und einstiegen. . . .
>
> [A tramp with a solider's cap and a baboon in officers' clothing drove up in a cab . . . and inspected the facade of the house. The pair immediately began, the monkey in front, to climb up the lightning rod, until they reached the second floor, smashed the window, and climbed in.] . . .

The playful grotesque effect is achieved by the incongruity in dress and behavior: The two intruders arrive on the scene in a taxicab. They quickly climb up a lightning rod, smash the second-floor window-panes and climb in. The satire becomes even more pronounced because the baboon is thought to be comic on account of his colorful behind.

Hiram Witt's scholarly acumen identifies the intruders even before the Captain introduces himself politely and proffers his credentials by pointing at the baboon's multicolored posterior. Because Witt knows what would be in store for him otherwise, he willingly hands over four marks and fifty pfennigs, a watch chain of silver, and three golden tooth fillings, with the explanation that this is all he has. . . . The incongruous objects sharpen the satire's wit, the implication is that there is nothing the military won't take. (pp. 118-19)

A hilarious grotesque incident concludes the story and the mockery of the military. The officer wants to draft Witt's creation, the result of twenty years of effort: a still brainless, naked artificial man, propped against a wall. When the officer learns that the creature has not yet been registered for military service, he becomes enraged . . . and has his men confiscate Witt's belongings, including the artificial man. Witt's resigned suggestion that he should put some brains into the mannequin now that it is to join the military the officer answers with a contemptuous "no." The officer clearly thinks enlisted men need no brains but only a "Maul" to say "zu Befehl" ["very good, sir!"]. When Witt picks up the officer's helmet, which he had carelessly put down on the plate that held the "prächtig lebende Gehirn" ["splendidly living brain"], he encounters a surprise:

> Was sich da nun zeigte, war derart überraschend und unheimlich, daß dem Gelehrten der Helm aus der hand fiel.
>
> Das Gehirn, das sich darunter befunden, war nämlich nicht mehr vorhanden, und an seiner Stelle lag—an seiner Stelle lag—ein Maul!
>
> Ja, ja, ein Maul.
>
> Ein schiefes Maul mit eckig aufwärts gebogenem Schnurrbart.
>
> [What now appeared was so startling and uncanny that the helmet fell out of the scholar's hand.
>
> The brain that had lain below existed no longer, and in its place lay—in its place lay—a mouth!
>
> Yes, yes, a mouth.
>
> A crooked mouth with an angular, upwardly bent mustache.]
>
> (pp. 120-21)

The discovery that a brain quickly metamorphoses into a mouth in proximity to a helmet drives Witt insane. He is taken to an asylum where on quiet Sundays he can still be heard singing Germany's national anthem, "Deutschland, Deutschland üü—ber a—ha—lles . . ." . . . . Even genius must succumb in an atmosphere of chauvinism and ubiquitous militarism. If it were not for the light tone of most of the story this ending might have a terrifying effect.

In addition to the grotesque satire there are two other instances of the grotesque in the story. One is the description of how Witt tries to produce more brains for Kempinski's restaurant to make up for the money he has lost to the Captain. . . . The thought of manufacturing live brains for a hotel keeper's guests is as hilarious as it is disgusting. No less grotesque is Witt's storing his magnificent live brains beneath his bed where one would suspect the presence of a chamber pot. (pp. 120-22)

The grotesque in the works of Meyrink may be seen as expressing three functions: didacticism, fear of the unknown, and the delight in fantasizing. In its didactic role, the grotesque is an instrument in the service of the writer's creative mission: the transformation of man from a materially oriented to a spiritually guided being. In its pessimistic aspect (especially favored in modern definitions of the grotesque), the grotesque can be seen as an expression of a crisis, of demonic and inimical forces of life, of existential fears that beset the writer. Interpreters of Meyrink's works tend to find evidence that both roles can go hand in hand. In its sheer pleasure of giving free rein to the imagination, the grotesque expresses life's exuberance and a strong sense of humor. It is this function of the grotesque (emphasized by earlier writers on the grotesque, and particularly stressed by Meyrink's contemporary Strobl), that is often overlooked.

Writers on Meyrink generally assign him a place in literary history between Neoromanticism and Expressionism and relate him to other authors of fantastic tales. Most scholars concur that a concern for man's moral and spiritual life underlies Meyrink's works. His use of the grotesque can be understood as an effective manifestation of this concern, coupled with a desire to bring about a change in man and society. This sense of moral mission provides the link between Meyrink's early grotesque stories and his later works. At the same time, it serves to connect him with the literary movements of his time. Like the Expressionists, Meyrink has a great deal in common with the Romanticists, including their love of the fantastic, the macabre, and the grotesque.

Whether delight in the play of unfettered fantasy, existential dread, or didactic intention underlies the creation of Meyrink's grotesque tales, they constitute a meaningful and substantial part of his work and link Meyrink to his contemporary Franz Kafka—despite Kafka's dislike for Meyrink—as well as to later writers like Friedrich Dürrenmatt. (pp. 145-47)

> Christine Rosner, in her Grotesque Elements in Se-
> lected Prose Works of Gustav Meyrink, *The Uni-
> versity of Connecticut, 1974, 159 p.*

E. F. BLEILER (essay date 1976)

[*Bleiler is an American editor, biographer, and critic prominent
for his work in the genres of science fiction, fantasy, supernatural
horror, and detective fiction. In the following excerpt, he examines
the principal themes and techniques of Meyrink's fiction.*]

Many of the details in **The Golem** might have been recognized by Meyrink's contemporaries in Bohemia. Vriesländer the painter, who appears as one of the background figures, was a friend of Meyrink's, a fellow contributor to many periodicals; Loisitschek's dive existed, as did the blind centenarian Schaf-franek and the woman who accompanied him; the student Char-ousek is obviously reminiscent of Charousek the chess master, while the Brigade of Thieves existed, as did the renegade privy councillor who renounced his honors to become the mastermind of a gang. The brutal police chief who interrogates Pernath was Meyrink's revenge on the police chief, Olič, who had hounded him, and in all probability a host of smaller details and personalities could have been found in the Prague of Mey-rink's own life.

This Prague, however, was Romantic Prague, which Meyrink seems to have been the first to perceive and record. It was a comfortable, decaying city, not yet a center of Czech nation-alism, a living museum where ancient fortresses and palaces projected memories of the Bohemian kings and Holy Roman Emperors, particularly the mad Habsburg Rudolf II. There were the quaint, ancient architecture and narrow twisting streets of the old quarter—the Stag's Ditch, where criminals were flung in the old days, and the Hunger Tower, where other criminals were suspended in baskets—the Street of the Alchemists, where Rudolf's assorted quacks and fanatics tried to manufacture gold—the insular, decadent German patricians and nobility, who knew no Czech and only incorrect German—the Moldau and the old statue-adorned bridge (which was partly washed away in 1890, the year that *Der Golem* takes place)—and of course the Ghetto, a strange city within a city. Surrounded by invisible psychic walls the Ghetto was still living in the experience of the great sixteenth-century cabbalist Rabbi Judah Löwe or Loew, who had created the golem of folklore. Meyrink may have hated Prague as much as he loved it, but he was obviously fascinated by it and Prague enters into his works over and over. The experiences of Pernath, just released from prison, as he wan-ders over the devastated Ghetto (in process of "urban re-newal") looking in vain for familiar streets are obviously based on Meyrink's own experience on leaving prison.

After Prague itself, which Meyrink often considered anthro-pomorphically, the most striking element in *Der Golem* is the "being" that gives the novel its name. Yet the presence of the

Golem is really more a matter of local color than of necessity. While Meyrink gives the "standard" version of the Golem legend in the puppeteer's narrative, he makes little use of the legend. The Golem might have been called many other things without too much loss. Indeed, Meyrink has been criticized by historians of religion like Gershom Scholem for inadequacy in both the Golem and the comments on the Cabbala [see excerpt dated 1960]. The criticism has some justification, since Mey-rink in his desire to retain an element of place gave a historical name to a private symbol.

As the figure of the Golem assumed final form in 1913-14 for Meyrink, it consisted of two supernatural elements. It was the collective psyche of the Ghetto, a strange mixture of saintliness and squalid evil, first evoked by Rabbi Löwe; it was a soul that sums up the experience of the humanoid old buildings and the organic city within and below a city. On the second and more important level the Golem was the principle of individ-uation, the split soul within us, which could awaken and emerge under certain circumstances, and must be faced and mastered. The Golem is freedom from matter, freedom from organic limitations (and thereby all restraint), and he is the etheric body of the occultists. In this sense *Der Golem* anticipates the spir-itual quests of the later novels.

In *Der Golem* the emergence of this second self may occur through various means: the nameless narrator of the frame story experiences it through a dream experience caused by indirect contact with the adept Athanasius Pernath; Pernath experiences it through mental illness and a hypnotic treatment that divided his mind into two compartments; Pernath's counterfigure La-ponder the sex criminal experiences it after years of ascetic training and occult study. Pernath succeeds, while Laponder fails, or perhaps the Laponder facet of the larger personality is cast out. Above and beyond the Golem, however, stands the persistent theme of most of Meyrink's major fiction: the sur-mounting of death by death in life or life in death, as Pernath and the dead Miriam find one another and live in a never-ever world.

Der Golem was Meyrink's first novel, and now, 70 years after its conception, it is mostly a love story in faded old rose, with occasional flashes of fire to be seen behind the fabric. Mey-rink's later novels are more individualized and more timeless. As novels of mystical exploration and occult adventure in the mind they form a unique grouping.

Das grüne Gesicht **(The Green Face),** which first appeared in 1916 when World War One was still in progress, in some superficial aspects embodies the frustrations and miseries of life in Austria and Germany. It is set in Amsterdam in the near future just after the World War has ended in a stalemate of exhaustion. The Netherlands are filled with refugees from Cen-tral Europe, and both social and physical dimensions are strained. The world is about to collapse; the Great War was only a symptom of this collapse; and the Kaliyug is about to end. A great spiritual revolution is about to burst upon mankind, ac-companied, but not caused, by a physical catastrophe.

The plot line, following a technique that Meyrink often used, starts in a very sedate manner, with only slight hintings and murmurings of fantasy, as a German engineer, Hauberrisser by name, comes upon a magic supply shop in Amsterdam. Within a short time the engineer is whirled along at unbeliev-able pace through bewildering experiences: the Wandering Jew, the embodied soteric personality of the universe, supernatural judgments, the gods of ancient Egypt, reincarnation, prophecy, madness, voodoo, glamour, doppelgängers, eternal life in death, confrontation with the female principle of the universe, Cabbalism, and many other motives. This listing may sound strange and jumbled, but such is Meyrink's power of internal logic that all these strange concepts are harmonized and flow logically from the basic premises. The novel ends with the destruction of Western Europe by a tremendous wind storm paralleling the spiritual storm, and with the transcendence of life and death by Hauberrisser and his bride. It is a novel of great scope, filled with marvelous touches of style, satirical humor on occasion, and strange personalities.

In *Walpurgisnacht* (**Walpurgis Night**), which was first published in Leipzig in 1917, Meyrink returned to the curious lore of the strange old city on the Moldau for a wild, chiliastic fantasy. Again it is a collapsing world that he depicts. A physical and spiritual cataclysm (this time motivated from the Orient) brings an age to an end. In German Prague, set among the precious and futile older nobility, whom Meyrink satirizes with his usual savage humor, an upwelling of psychic reversion takes place. The unfulfilled personal past, the criminal, suppressed past, the ancestral past all emerge. The young noblewoman Polyxena Zahradka is possessed by a personality fragment of a wicked ancestress. By magical means she assumes control of the emergent forces of terror and raises her lover to the position of a stump king, in a situation reminiscent of Jan of Leiden. The local Czechs, roused to wild enthusiasm, revert to Ziska's medieval Taborites, and a welter of terror begins, to end horribly. Telepathy, reincarnation, psychic control (aveysha, as Meyrink calls it), prophecy all interpermeate the pathetic story of an elderly privy councillor, the Penguin, who discovers all too late that he may have been purposed for flying. He perishes in the attempt. As a strange Manchu sage reveals, just as there are yearly Walpurgis nights, there are also cosmic Walpurgis nights. All in all *Walpurgisnacht*, with its combination of local color, wild imagination and mockery is a remarkable work.

With *Der weisse Dominikaner* (**The White Dominican**), published in Vienna and elsewhere in 1921, Meyrink began to abandon the external story of event and action, and began to concentrate more on the inner story of mind and idea, in a combination of occult and mystical themes. A somewhat Hoffmannesque story set vaguely in a small German or Austrian town, it is heavily symbolic in detail and plot, so much so that a summary cannot represent the story fairly. It is a study of psychic evolution through the development (by mental disciplines) of an etheric body; this concept is combined with transmigratory linkages with the past. It is a story of the psychic way of life and psychic way of death; of the battle with the Medusa force of matter, illusion, constraint, and Maya that permeates the universe, and of the narrator's reception into an eternal line of adepts. It is a strangely serene story, filled with odd detail, thought-provoking for the reader who wishes to try to unravel its symbolic threads in detail, but highly personal for Meyrink, and much less accessible than the earlier novels.

Meyrink's last novel, *Der Engel vom westlichen Fenster* (**The Angel from the Western Window**), published in Leipzig in 1927, is a curious compound of genius and flatfooted banality. The explanation for its defects is quite simple: Meyrink was too ill to work out all his scenario, and much of the novel was written by an occultist associate and friend.

Der Engel vom westlichen Fenster is magnificent in concept, a novel of fate and reincarnation, occult perils and developments, strange linkages of past and present, occult brotherhoods with secret wisdom, black magic, alchemy, Maya, and astounding drugs. It is a double novel set in two worlds which are linked magically: sixteenth-century England and Prague, and twentieth-century Vienna and Prague. Baron Müller, the last descendant of John Dee, the English renaissance scholar and magician, receives an inheritance from his remote ancestor and discovers that he has become involved in Dee's tragedy. Dee's scrying stone, the alchemical stone, mind-expanding drugs, angelic revelations, and a supernatural weapon all play a part in the story, as the novel alternates back and forth in time, yet reveals the meaningless of time. Müller experiences episodes from the life of Dee (freely fantasized from history). He is present as Dee encounters black magic and an Isiac cult flourishing in England and he relives Dee's association with the charlatan Edward Kelly: their mystical séances, the transformation of metals, the revelations they receive from the Angel Il, and their pilgrimage to Prague. There, in Prague, they meet the Emperor Rudolf and encounter the wisdom of Rabbi Löwe. But the Dee facet of the eternal personality is defeated by the evil powers of the universe and perishes miserably. In the twentieth-century facet Müller must redeem the eternal personality by overcoming the Black Isais, the evil principle of duality that destroyed Dee. Müller emerges into a strange transcendence and interpermeation of life and death that cannot be summarized.

Those portions of *Der Engel vom westlichen Fenster* that seem obviously by Meyrink (most of the twentieth-century episodes) are remarkable, and show Meyrink at his best. If one can survive the maunderings of John Dee (which I would speculate were not written by Meyrink), one will never forget the beautiful and charmingly evil Princess Chotokalungin, certainly the most fascinating female figure in occult literature, nor the enigmatic, timeless Mascee, nor the strange wonderland when Prague and Mortlake, past and present, myth and symbol of the cosmic drama all interpermeate one another almost indistinguishably in a misty syncrasy.

In addition to the five important novels, *Der Golem, Walpurgisnacht, Der weisse Dominikaner, Das grüne Gesicht*, and *Der Engel vom westlichen Fenster*, Meyrink wrote a fair amount of shorter material that can be considered fantastic in one manner or another. His book *Goldmachergeschichten* (**Tales of Alchemists**) . . . plays semifictionally over historical moments in eighteenth-century alchemy, including the careers of Böttger and Sendivogius. Meyrink wrote with the assumption that alchemy was valid, and cited contemporary documents in the guise of narrative, a practice for which he was criticized. It is not an important book. Meyrink also left an unfinished novel, *Das Haus des Alchimisten* (**The Alchemist's House**), which, to my knowledge, has not been published; I know it only from a description of the manuscript. One of its themes is the use, in a motion picture, of an emblem of Melek Taos to enslave men's minds.

Many of Meyrink's short stories use the motives of fantasy for purposes of social satire, literary parody, polemics, or as fables. These do not concern us, despite their occasional brilliance; most of them were based on issues or ideas that are now forgotten except to specialists, and much of their point is now inaccessible to a lay reader.

Certain of Meyrink's short stories, however, conform more to English-American standards of a weird tale. To mention a few: "**Der Opal**," a Tantric adept changes the human eye into an opal of peculiar brilliance; "**Bal Macabre**," visions caused by the hallucinogen *Amanita muscaria*, and vampirism; "**Bolog-**

neser Tränen,'' a witch uses Prince Rupert's drops to kill her lover; and a short series of fantastic *contes cruels* based on the remarkably wicked Dr. Mohammed Darasche-Koh, a Persian master who holds the lost wisdom of Atlantis: **''Der Mann auf der Flasche,'' ''Das Präparat,''** and **''Das Wachsfigurenkabinett.''** Dr. Darasche-Koh also appears in *Das Haus des Alchimisten*, where he is revealed to be a Yezidee. Also worthy of mention are three of the stories in *Fledermäuse*: **''Meister Leonhard,'' ''Der Kardinal Napellus,''** and **''Die vier Mondbrüder.''**

Meyrink's later short stories, such as those in *Fledermäuse* and the few that were written in the 1920's, tend to approach symbolism and planned allegory and bear out his statement that he wrote, as he put it, not by the rules of art, but by the rules of magic. Stories like **''Der Uhrmacher''** . . . are a closed system. At times they remind one of Goethe's ''Maerchen,'' and at other times they seem to be a Renaissance or Baroque magical diagrammatic illustration turned into prose. I know of nothing else quite like **''Der Uhrmacher.''**

For some years after his death in 1932 Meyrink suffered a critical eclipse. The generation that had laughed or snorted at his jibes in *Simplicissimus* in the first decade of the century grew old, and probably forgot Meyrink for more important day-to-day things. His occult romances, so highly personal in his later years, grew less and less intelligible. And then there was the problem of finding texts. The Nazis had been rather thorough in destroying his books. Even today it is very difficult to find them. I still do not have a full set of his fiction, after some twenty years of (admittedly intermittent) search.

There was the further problem of the Golem itself. I suspect that just as *Der Golem*'s partial concern with the Prague ghetto and Judaism capped Meyrink's puncturing of *Spiesser* for the Third Reich, it also served as a point of recoil in post-war years. How was Aaron Wassertrum to be taken? Or how Rosina? Are these to be read as anti-Semitism in Meyrink? Do Meyrink's comments about the horror-soul of the Ghetto indicate hatred in his mind? It is quite conceivable that these questions should be raised. Yet the answer is obvious and clear: no. Meyrink portrayed saints as well as villains, and he said no more about the Ghetto than has been said about ghettos of all sorts by generations of sociologists.

One peculiar aspect about Meyrink has, to my knowledge, never been pointed out. It is generally accepted, almost as a truism, that aspects of the German mystical and romantic traditions gave birth to Nazism, in a linkage from the early nineteenth-century storytellers, poets and philosophers through the Victorian romantics, up into the Neo-romanticism of the early twentieth century. ''From Caligari to Hitler'' is the phrase that sums up this interpretation of history.

An examination of the work and life of Gustav Meyrink, on the other hand, offers an opposite picture. Here we see the writer of fantasy and expressionist critic lambasting the reactionaries, the military, the totalitarians of the early twentieth century, the men who either lived to become Nazis or anticipated their counterparts who became Nazis. In Meyrink we see occultism and mysticism interpreted as the utmost in the evolution of the free spirit, the ultimate freedom of speech, action and thought. It was the uniformed *Spiesser* of the 1930's who became the final enemy of this mode of thought.

Meyrink reached his position of freedom via occultism and mysticism. Part of his system came from his personal psychic experience; part of it came from external sources. His system,

unfortunately, will never be known in detail, since so much of it was lived month by month by Meyrink in his own mind, and would only occasionally be recorded. In all probability Meyrink would have followed the common practice of occultists and initiates in maintaining a level of esotericism that could not be revealed until proofs of advancement had been shown. Yet it is possible, in the most general way, to characterize his thought in historical terms: a background of neo-Paracelsian interpretation of the components of the pysche; a mixture of Renaissance alchemy and psychoanalysis for certain aspects of spiritual praxis; and an equally strong component from Indian thought, particularly the later yogic and tantric systems for physical exercises. To this would have been added interpretations from the various lodges emergent from Madame Blavatsky.

I do not know if too many people today take Meyrink's occult ideas seriously (I should add that I do not), but this does not change the fact that they offer a wonderful source of images, rich in imaginative possibilities. One can read Meyrink's novels on the thrill level, or on the level of art and ideas. As Hermann Hesse said of him, ''He is a man with something to say.'' (pp. xi-xviii)

> *E. F. Bleiler, in an introduction to* The Golem [*and*] The Man Who Was Born Again: Two Supernatural Novels *by Gustave Meyrink* [*and*] *Paul Busson, edited by E. F. Bleiler, translated by Madge Pemberton* [*and*] *Prince Mirski and Thomas Moult, Dover Publications, Inc., 1976, pp. iii-xxiv.*

NEIL W. RUSSACK   (essay date 1978)

[*In the following essay, Russack offers a reading of* The Golem *based on the psychological theories of Carl Gustav Jung.*]

The Golem, a novel by Gustav Meyrink first published in Germany in 1915, is narrated in the first person. We do not know much about the narrator. He does not even have a name. He is a stonecutter working in the ghetto of Prague; he is also able to restore old manuscripts. He is suffering from amnesia, and that means loss of personal identity. We do not know till the end of the story that this loss of identity is due to his having taken Athanasius Pernath's hat by mistake. We only know he is under some strange influence. It is a sort of psychosis. His memory of his personal unconscious has been eclipsed, and therefore he has a direct connection with the unconscious images in their pure form. In this sense, his strange experiences are similar to those of a patient in a mental hospital.

The main characters include Hillel, a Kabbalist, who helps the narrator put the experiences he has into a natural order. There is also Hillel's daughter, Miriam, with whom he falls in love and who helps him to appreciate the mystery of the spiritual aspect of life. And there is Athanasius Pernath, whose name Jung says means the ''immortal one'', clearly one of the images of the self. There are too many other figures and all too many experiences to relate here. But I thought I would relate four important scenes that will give a sense of the story. The central figure is the golem. It is known that somewhere in the ghetto there exists an autonomous figure known as the Golem, and there is a window to an unknown room in one of the houses where he is supposed to live. The narrator, in a strange state of mind, encounters the Golem without knowing it and only later realizes that it is causing evil things to happen whenever it appears.

Gershom Scholem, in *On the Kabbalah and Its Symbolism*, presents the legend of the Golem as it was described by Jakob Grimm in 1808.

> After saying certain prayers and observing certain fast days, the Polish Jews make the figure of a man from clay or mud, and when they pronounce the miraculous Shemhamphoras (the name of God) over him, he must come to life. He cannot speak, but he understands fairly well what is said or commanded. They call him golem and use him as a servant to do all sorts of housework. But he must never leave the house. On his forehead is written *emeth* (truth); every day he gains weight and becomes somewhat larger and stronger than all the others in the house, regardless of how little he was to begin with. For fear of him, they therefore erase the first letter, so that nothing remains but *meth* (he is dead), whereupon he collapses and turns to clay again.

Meyrink portrays the Golem as one who has escaped, a form the Polish Jews recognized. Instead of being a servant, he has become an autonomous being similar to Frankenstein's monster. This is a figure not in itself evil but having an evil effect because it is an unrecognized bearer of self-realization.

Scholem compares the Golem to Adam, the first man:

> At a certain stage in his creation Adam is designated as "golem." "Golem" is a Hebrew word that occurs only once in the Bible, in Psalm 139:16, which Psalm the Jewish tradition put into the mouth of Adam himself. Here probably, and certainly in the later sources, "golem" means the unformed, amorphous. There is no evidence to the effect that it meant "embryo," as has sometimes been claimed. In the philosophical literature of the Middle Ages it is used as a Hebrew term for matter, formless *hyle*.... In this sense, Adam was said to be "golem" before the breath of God had touched him.

In Scholem's description of the first creation of Adam as Golem, which indicates the long history of the legend, we see that the Golem represents medieval man—in contrast to psychic or spiritual man, in the Kabbalistic tradition.

In Meyrink's novel, the first indication that the problem to be solved is redemption of the archetypal shadow comes in the chapter called "Awake." The narrator has been in a psychotic condition, with catatonic symptoms, in the previous chapter.

Hillel speaks to the narrator:

> "Hear and understand. The man who sought you out, and whom you call the Golem, signifies the awakening of the soul through the innermost life of the spirit. Each thing that earth contains is nothing more than an everlasting symbol clothed in dust.... Nothing that takes shape unto itself but was once a spirit.

> "Two paths there are, running parallel courses— the way of life and the way of death. You took unto yourself the book of *Ibbur* and read therein. Your soul is fecund now with the Spirit of Life.

> "Men tread not a path at all, neither that of life nor death. They drive like chaff before the wind. In the Talmud it is written: 'Before God made the world, he held a mirror to his creatures, that in it they might behold the sufferings of the spirit and the raptures that ensue therefrom. Some of them took up the burden of suffering. But others refused, and those God struck out of the Book of Life.' But you tread a path you have chosen of your own free will, even though as yet you know it not. You are self-elected. Do not torture yourself. As knowledge comes, so comes also recollection. *Knowledge and recollection are one and the same thing.*"

Hillel explains to the narrator that the Golem has sought him out in order to awaken him, and the healing experience is described as a death and rebirth, which means an awakening to consciousness. Hillel is his guru here, and, although Hillel is not old (only forty-five), he has the wisdom of the Wise Old Man archetype, when he says "knowledge and recollection are one and the same thing."

The narrator then has the following vision.

> I looked up, and suddenly became aware that the room was full of forms that stood round us in a circle. Some were in white robes like grave-clothes, as worn by rabbis of olden days; others wore three-cornered hats, and shoes with silver buckles.

This is the vision of former rabbis who seem to be emerging from the past in a revival of life from death. In other words, the spirit of resurrection is evoked, along with the memory of previous ancestors from the eighteenth century (thus the three-cornered hats). At the end of the chapter he has another vision.

> The book of *Ibbur* rose before me, with two letters flaming in it: one signifying the Archetype Woman with the pulse that beat like an earthquake, the other, at an infinite distance, the hermaphrodite on the pearly throne, with the crown of red wood upon its head.

The reconciling symbol appears first as the "Archetype Woman with the pulse that beats like an earthquake," presumably to counteract the negative power of the shadow, but then it gives way to the "hermaphrodite on the pearly throne" as reconciling the opposites. The word "Ibbur," according to Meyrink, means "The Soul's Conception."

But all this is anticipatory, like initial dreams in analysis. The hero still has to encounter the full force of the archetypal shadow.

Then he meets the Golem in his human form in prison. His name is Laponder.

> A little, slender, still youngish man, carefully clad, though without his hat, like all newly introduced prisoners, stood bowing politely before me.

> He was clean shaven, like an actor, and his large, almond-shaped eyes, with a bright green gleam in them had the strange peculiarity of not seeming to see me, for all they gazed at me so directly. Almost as though his spirit were absent from the body.

Laponder admits to the crimes of murder and rape. Meyrink makes us realize that the narrator is now somewhat identified with Athanasius Pernath, whose hat he took by mistake. Athanasius tells Laponder of his earlier vision in which he encounters a headless man. The headless man is the Golem in the general archetypal image of the shadow, while Laponder is its human form. In place of a head, there is a nebulous globe-shaped mist. Athanasius tries to put many sorts of heads on the torso, but the only one that fits is that of the Egyptian Ibis. Ibis is the emblem of the Egyptian god Thoth, who resembles, in classical mythology, Hermes or Mercurius, the bringer of change. The headless man offers Athanasius a handful of little red and black seed pods. Instead of accepting them, however, Athanasius knocks them out of his hand. Laponder, the murderer-rapist, tells Athanasius that he too had experienced the same vision but says that he took the pods.

> "So you struck them out of his hand?" he murmured thoughtfully to himself. "Never would I have believed that a third way could have been found."

Had Athanasius accepted the pods, he would have chosen the path of death as did the murderer. Meyrink labels the colors red and black, both colors of death, which he calls bad. If Athanasius had simply refused them, he would have chosen the path of life. But he neither accepts nor rejects them; instead he knocks them out of his hand, thereby choosing a third way. He does not accept the offer as it is presented. By refusing to accept an either/or situation, he denies the validity of the offer. He will not even allow himself to enter into a dialogue with the Golem. He refuses the situation that the Golem puts before him.

By denying the Golem, he seems to redeem the whole history of man. At this point in the story, the images of all the faces of his ancestors pass by him, century after century. It is not only himself that he is saving but all mankind. The conscious work the individual does has an impact upon the world. By denying the shadow, the hero finds a new religious attitude. Laponder says,

> "If you had refused them, then would you most certainly have chosen the path of life, but the pods, that signify the powers of magic, would not in that case have remained behind. You tell me they rolled on the ground. That is to say, they stayed behind here, and will be in the custody of your forefathers until the time of their ripening. Then will the faculties still latent within you spring into being."
>
> I could not understand. "My forefathers . . . you say, those pods will be in their custody?"
>
> "All those things you have experienced," explained Laponder, "you must partly interpret in the way of symbol. That circle of blue luminous entities that closed you around was the chain of the diverse inherited personalities each mother's son is born into the world with. The soul is not 'one and indivisible'; it will ultimately become so, and thereby attain what man calls immortality; your soul consists of infinite component parts—egos innumerable, like an ant-heap is composed of multitudinous ants. You bear within yourself the *spiritual vestiges* of thousands of your forebears, the original pro-

genitors of the face from which you sprang. It is the same with all creation. How otherwise could a chicken hatched from an incubator instantly seek forth its own peculiar nourishment, did it not contain, innate within itself, the accumulated experience of hundreds of centuries? The presence of 'instinct' reveals in both one's body and one's soul the undeniable fact of our own ancestors."

If Athanasius had accepted the pods, he would be identifying with the shadow. He would then have become the shadow. Psychologically, that would mean that, if one had bad thoughts, he would identify with them. He says, "Those thoughts are who I am." If he takes them literally, he would fall into a depression. If I think I am what I feel, then I am accepting the seed pods. Identification with the shadow causes depression. The shadow takes over the ego.

By not accepting them, he chooses the path of life. He says, I am not the shadow. I do not have to be that thing. But it is the opposite and is too one-sided. It does not include death. He is not even conscious of the shadow.

It is a paradox. He has to accept it and reject it at the same time. That is the third way. It is the path of immortality, or individuation. It is neither death nor life. The third way is not accepting one or the other. To accept a thing means to become identified with it. One must keep one's own ego. He must accept neither death nor life and thereby become identified with neither. By knocking the seeds out of his hand down onto the earth, new life can come. Something new comes out of the destructiveness of the past. It is the path of redemption. That is the point of the book, to redeem the Golem. To bring spiritual life into man, to put the spirit into matter; that is the task of us all.

God created Adam like clay. The old Adam is unchanging and sinful. It is Adam before he has a soul. The Golem is Adam in his first creation. The Golem is the archetypal shadow. He is mechanical man. The new Adam is regenerated man. He has been redeemed.

Jung says,

> The Golem is an entirely negative figure, the complete shadow of the immortal one. He began as a lump of clay and was brought to life by black magic, by writing the holy name on his brow. So he is a living being that has no soul,—a mechanism which can only be killed by wiping out the holy name. The figure occurs in many ancient Jewish legends, and Meyrink used it in free form, a personification of the horrible troubles that befall the hero through those visions.

There is a third shadow figure in addition to the image of the headless man and Laponder. This person is Aaron Wassertrum, the old Jewish pawnbroker. He embodies the Golem-like materialistic man in whom no soul is apparent. He might represent that aspect of the cultural Jewish shadow.

In Meyrink's novel, the beginning of the healing process occurs with the emergence of the rabbi, a Kabbalist named Hillel, who embodies the archetypal image of the Wise Old Man, and his daughter, Miriam, who embodies the spiritual aspect of the anima. This is in contrast to the worldly aspect represented by Angelina, the other woman Athanasius cared about. It is through

Alleyway in the Prague ghetto in 1898.

his relationships to these two women that he learns to love. It is the wisdom embodied in the archetypal image of the Wise Old Man and the life and love of the anima which is compensating to the ego and shadow. But real healing and redemption can only come through the ego's relation to the self. Athanasius is, of course, the self-image.

At the end of the story, the narrator comes to the simple house where Hillel and Miriam are supposed to be living. But in the morning he sees the house has been transformed.

> The night before it had been the same place. Now in the morning I see that it is by no means a simple place but a very beautiful gilt gate, quite an elaborate thing, and there are two yew trees that rise up from low bushes or flowering shrubs, flanking the entrance. I see now that the wall around the garden is covered with a beautiful mosaic, made out of lapis lazuli. The God himself, an hermaphrodite, forms the two wings of the gate, the left side male, the right side female. The God is seated on a precious throne of mother-of-pearl, and his golden head is the head of a hare. The ears are erect and close together, looking like the two pages of an open book. The air is full of the smell of dew and hyacinths and I stand there a long time, astonished. It is as if a foreign world were opening before my eyes. Suddenly an old gardener or servant in the costume of the 18th century opens the gate and asks me what I want. I give him the hat of Athanasius Pernath, which I had wrapped up in paper. The servant disappears with it, but in that moment before he shuts the gate behind him, I look inside and see not a house, but a sort of marble temple, and on the steps leading up to it, I see Athanasius with Miriam leaning on his arm. Both are looking down upon the town. Miriam catches sight of me, smiles and whispers something to Athanasius. I am fascinated by her beauty. She is so young, just as young as I saw her in the dream. Athanasius then turns his head towards me and my heart almost ceases to beat. It is as if I should see myself in a mirror, such is the similarity of his face to mine. Then the gate shuts and I only see the resplendent figure of the

hermaphroditic God. After a while the servant brings my hat which was in the possession of Athanasius and I hear his voice, deep, as if from the depths of the earth. He says, "Mr. Pernath is much obliged and asks you not to hold him inhospitable that he does not invite you in, since it is a strict law of the house since old that guests are not invited. He also says he has not used your hat as he noticed at once that it was not his, and he hopes that his has not caused you headache."

Meyrink ends the story with a humorous touch. This lets the reader know that these archetypal images originate in the collective unconscious and belong there. We could say the hat belonged to that principle of renewal connected with immortality. Under the influence of the hat, the hero is able to experience the death-and-rebirth archetype. Like many people, he has a close relationship with his unconscious in which he is able to identify with these archetypal images and learn from them. The danger lies in becoming inflated from a permanent identification with them. This does not happen to the hero in *The Golem*. The gate in the form of the hermaphrodite indicates a way of entering into a certain kind of knowledge, which means that, in a relative sense, the opposites are joined. (pp. 158-64)

> *Neil W. Russack, "A Psychological Interpretation of Meyrink's 'The Golem'," in* The Shaman from Elko: Papers in Honor of Joseph L. Henderson on His Seventy-Fifth Birthday, *edited by Gareth Hill & others, C. G. Jung Institute of San Francisco, 1978, pp. 158-64.*

LEE B. JENNINGS (essay date 1981)

[*Jennings is an American educator and critic who has written extensively on myth, archetype, and the grotesque in German literature. In the following excerpt from a paper delivered at a 1981 conference on fantastic literature, Jennings analyzes the theme of spiritual awakening in* The Golem.]

Writers sympathetic toward Gustav Meyrink's work have stressed that he was a serious and devoted student of mystical and esoteric doctrine. Less sympathetic critics, especially those favoring a sociological approach, have tended rather to treat his work under the rubric of "*Trivialliteratur*." We should bear in mind, however, that for this latter school any dominant concern with inward self-realization or affairs of the soul, let alone a receptivity toward occultist thought, is likely to appear as evidence of counterproductive, asocial subjectivism and is bound to be entered on the debit side of the ledger when the overall merit of a work is considered.

To be sure, Meyrink's *Der Golem* does show some naively awkward features. Because of the basic premise of the novel, no clear line can be drawn between visionary and paranoid perceptions, and the hero's tendency to sense menace in the most innocuous objects approaches the ludicrous at times. Ghostly messengers appear as if on cue. The inner narrator, Pernath, may seem an unlikely candidate for enlightenment, since he suffers throughout from a frenzied, expressionistic befuddlement. The erotic relationships smack of wish-fulfillment fantasy, and the overt story line, with its adventure and intrigue, appears contrived. The subsidiary characters are little more than stereotypes, and the depiction of some of the Prague ghetto dwellers as saintly figures does not quite outweigh the predictable depravity of the Jewish villains.

Nonetheless, even a casual reading should bear out the author's serious endeavor to provide a fictonalized account of the mythical struggle toward the higher self. In various works, Meyrink draws upon different areas of esoteric lore to symbolize this struggle; in this novel, the Kabbala, the tarot, gnosticism, and alchemy are favored. His eclectic use of such lore makes it difficult to trace the provenance of any one motif or idea, arousing, no doubt, the suspicion of an exploitative popularization of the occult as well. This suspicion is uncalled-for, since Meyrink, like C. G. Jung, treats occult and arcane doctrines as a general repository of archetypal symbols of psychic change. The symbolic nature of visions is expressly mentioned in the novel, and within it they attain a quasi-objectivity as glimpses, shared by different observers, of a hyper-real order of things.

A summary of the action may be helpful. A man troubled by puzzling dreams gradually resolves into the figure of Athanasius Pernath, a gem engraver living in the Prague ghetto. He is recovering from mental illness and cannot remember his past life because of amnesia hypnotically induced in the course of therapy. Just this amnesia, however, is said to be a prerequisite for his awakening to a higher state of being, the first step of which occurs when an uncanny stranger, later identified as the dread Golem, delivers a mysterious old book for him to repair. Pernath finds that he can now better grasp the hidden connections of events, especially as they are revealed to him in dreams and visions and in remarks of his mentor, the saintly quasi-rabbi Hillel. Hillel's daughter Mirjam, to whom Pernath is increasingly attracted, is nearly as spiritual as her father and is a naive believer in miraculous coincidences. The diabolical schemes of the obsequious, harelipped secondhand dealer, Aaron Wassertrum, are opposed by his natural son, the half-crazed, impoverished, tubercular student, Charousek, who has sworn blood revenge against Wassertrum and aids Pernath to the extent that it furthers his own cause. Less significant figures are the coquettish, aristocratic Angelina, who is carrying on an extramarital affair in a room adjoining Pernath's quarters, and Pernath's tavern cronies, wry commentators on the ghetto scene. The subplots (there is no main one except for Pernath's meandering quest) involve the protection of Angelina's secret (and Pernath's temporary infatuation with her) and Charousek's revenge-plotting.

Due to Wassertrum's conniving, Pernath is eventually imprisoned on a false charge of murder. On being released, he finds that the ghetto has been largely torn down, and he sets about seeking Hillel and Mirjam, who now seem in some way to hold the key to his fate. He apparently glimpses them as he is fleeing a burning building by climbing down a rope. They are in a mysterious, doorless (but windowed) room which the Golem was once reputed to inhabit and in which he himself once spent an eerie and sleepless night. He loses his hold, the rope breaks, and he falls.

At this point we discover that Pernath's history, though apparently true, was dreamed by yet another man, who now awakes. The dream was caused by his inadvertently wearing Pernath's hat. This unnamed frame-narrator sets out to trace Pernath and finds that approximately forty years have passed since the last events of his dream. Nevertheless, he finds Pernath and Mirjam, untouched by the ravages of time, living in a mysterious house familiar to him from his dream. The house is now a kind of shrine, decorated with symbolic depictions

of the hermaphrodite and the god Osiris. He is not allowed to enter this sanctuary, but he glimpses the pair from a distance and is able to exchange hats. In a note brought by a somewhat golemesque servant, Pernath expresses the hope that his hat has not caused its bearer any headaches.

The peculiarly depressing tenor of the work seems to arise not only from its questioning of reality, but also from its nearly complete separation of spiritual awakening from the conventional moral values. The path of awakening is said to depend on a free decision, a vocation from within, but in effect this vocation seems little more than a blind and arbitrary urge, the small manifestation of a vast ultramundane plan extending over generations. Life, for Pernath, is predominantly absurd, perhaps more so after his "awakening," which, although it increases his sensitivity and intuitive understanding, does nothing to improve his poor judgment or to dampen his occasional murderous urges. No indulgent deity presides over his obscure strivings, only the stern god Osiris. A powerful virtue emanates from his mentor, Hillel, who, however, is separated even from his own family by a glass wall of sanctity. A synthesis of the infinite and finite worlds is hinted at, but the dominant concept is that of a spirituality quite incompatible with the world of the senses.

Hillel's delineation of the Ways of Life and Death evidently is intended to provide the key to the world order presented here. There are those "bitten by the serpent," "pregnant with the spirit of life," who are destined to awaken from the sleep of ordinary consciousness. Others go the Way of Death, though most humans follow no particular path in their aimless drifting. . . . The Way of Death in its pure form, then, is rare. We gain insight into its nature from one of the novel's visionary events. Pernath, in a trancelike state, is accosted by a phantom with stumps for legs, its head a nebulous globe (a classical Jungian archetype of the whole self). The Phantom proffers seven seeds; not knowing whether his salvation lies in accepting or rejecting them, Pernath hits upon a third alternative and knocks them out of the Phantom's hand. . . . (pp. 55-7)

The exegesis of the vision is provided by Laponder, a confessed rapist-murderer and somnambulist who shares Pernath's prison cell, a saintly figure in the Dostoevskian sense. Laponder once had the same vision; in his version, he accepted the seeds and was forced to go the Way of Death. Accordingly, during his moon-induced trances, he becomes a robotlike instrument of alien spiritual forces. It is hinted that his crime represented a dim realization of the hermaphrodite image, the symbolic incarnation of the whole human being. By knocking the seeds out of the Phantom's hand, Laponder explains, Pernath has mobilized magical powers that will remain in the custody of his ancestral spirit counterparts until ready for use. . . . (p. 57)

Thus, in Meyrink's usage, the concept of "life" is largely limited to the domain of the spirit. All of the things we regard as vital connote mortality and thus belong to the realm of death. When Pernath experiences vernal stirrings of the blood, he is distracted from his quest. The path of Eros is a false one. In this light, the figure of the Golem becomes more understandable. Though thematically central, this figure is rather subsidiary to the action. It is only loosely related to the legendary animated clay figure of Rabbi Loew and his predecessors. Its manifestations are explained in two fairly unrelated ways. First, the Golem incorporates the collective unconscious of the ghetto in times of spiritual crisis. The speculation here is that the legendary rabbi created a mental image which has ever since craved some form of embodiment. Usually it appears as a vaguely Asiatic, zombilike figure wearing old-fashioned clothes. Second, the Golem acts as a psychic double or alter ego for some individual, in which case it appears as a frightening but not altogether malevolent figure. . . . To Hillel, who sees self-confrontation as the ultimate mystery, the Golem-double is "breath of the bones" . . . a puzzling term since the figure actually represents "bones" (corporcality) of the "breath" (spirit).

The doppelgänger aspect is forcibly driven home. Pernath imagines himself to be the Golem on two occasions, and when he stays in the doorless room (which he recognizes as a symbol for the recesses of his own psyche) he dons what appear to be the Golem's cast-off clothes to keep warm, causing general consternation upon his emergence. . . . In this respect, the Golem is like the Jungian "shadow," which is often confronted at the beginning of a crisis of psychic growth, but it lacks the individual features that might bear out such a function. Perhaps it stands as a general reminder of the deadness of merely physical things and of the basic abstractness of the animating life-force, thus signifying the ultimate separateness of body and spirit.

Though the dread accompanying the Golem's appearances is stressed nearly to excess, Hillel explains that such demonic apparitions are not to be taken altogether seriously. They are the psychic growing pains of those who witness them, and their mental abrasiveness can be compared to the polishing of a silver mirror. When the mirror is completely reflective, that is, when the soul is clear, the unpleasantness will cease. . . . Hillel thus anticipates the classic psychedelic enthusiast's explanation of a "bad trip": the demons represent the ego's struggle in the face of its own temporary or permanent extinction. Likewise, although evil is clearly manifested in the rascally Wassertrum, its role in the cosmic scheme is slight. Evil is a chance imperfection, as Laponder suggests in his elaborate likening of human minds to glass tubes with different colored balls rolling through them. . . . (pp. 57-8)

To further illustrate his arcane thesis, Meyrink calls upon the symbolism of the tarot cards. According to Hillel, these cards contain the entire wisdom of the Kabbala in the form best suited to its communication. . . . Pernath, while shivering in the doorless room, passes the time by contemplating the Pagad or Fool, the joker of the tarot deck, and this figure seems to materialize before his eyes. The Fool can be understood in two ways: as the materialist and sensualist, oblivious to the treasures of wisdom in his knapsack, about to walk over a precipice; or as the pure innocent whose wisdom is still undeveloped. In either case, he represents man as yet unawakened.

The second tarot card mentioned, the Hanging Man, is somewhat more complex in its significance. . . . It depicts a man hanging upside down by one foot, his left leg folded behind the right, with a halo around his head. Pernath is unable to guess at its meaning. The symbol seems to be objectified twice in the novel. According to local legend, a workman helping to search for the Golem was lowered on a rope to look into the window of the concealed room. Just as he reached his destination, the rope broke and he plunged to his death. . . . Pernath reenacts the scene in his fall at the end of the dream narrative. For a moment he hangs "head down, legs crossed, between heaven and earth." . . . Strangely, this is the one detail that the frame-narrator is unable to substantiate; the house had never burned. . . . The meaning of the image, in any case, is clear. The breaking of the rope means the severing of connections with the world of the senses. The Hanging Man is a

Prometheus or redeemer figure, the immortal self temporarily enmeshed in the tangled yarn of mortal karma. Pernath, when the frame-narrator last sees him, apparently has shuffled off, or at least loosened, the mortal coil. In his union with Mirjam in the hermaphrodite-temple he is the world but not of it, an Immortal, demonstrating in his own being the fusion of male and female elements to form a purified and complete entity.

Meyrink's symbolization of the psychic integration process is no less valid because it draws upon occultist lore. Pernath may seem an unworthy recipient of higher wisdom, but the archtypes of psychic transformation play no favorites and mock our moralistic expectations. Jung has noted Meyrink's use of the hat motif in connection with assumed identities. Trite as it may first appear, the device conveys a legitimate message. Illumination, by its very nature, cannot readily be conveyed. The reader-pupil can vicariously follow the process, as the dreamer can understand awakening, only up to a point. Beyond that, he must discard the spurious headpiece and wear his own hat or go forth bareheaded. (pp. 58-9)

> *Lee B. Jennings, "Meyrink's 'Der Golem': The Self As the Other," in* Aspects of Fantasy: Selected Essays from the Second International Conference on the Fantastic in Literature and Film, *edited by William Coyle, Greenwood Press, 1986, pp. 55-60.*

ROBERT IRWIN (essay date 1985)

[*Irwin is an English historian, novelist, and critic. In the following excerpt from an introduction to the most recent edition of the English translation of* The Golem, *he discusses the enduring points of interest of Meyrink's novel.*]

The Golem has been generally acknowledged to be Meyrink's masterpiece. In it we have the Castle which is not Kafka's Castle, The Trial which is not Kafka's Trial, and a Prague which is not Kafka's Prague. Kafka and Meyrink were contemporaries in Prague in the years before World War I. Max Brod knew and admired them both. By the time Brod met him, Meyrink was already a published writer with a life of mystery and scandal behind him, an eerie presence among the chess players and political dabblers of the city's cafe society. (Two of Meyrink's drinking companions, Teschner the puppeteer and Vrieslander the painter appear in *The Golem*—Teschner as Zwakh, Vrieslander under his own name.) Meyrink's novel powerfully evokes the physical presence of Prague three quarters of a century ago—Hradčany Castle, the Street of the Alchemists, the Charles Bridge, the Jewish Quarter. As Kafka acknowledged, Meyrink brilliantly reproduced the atmosphere of the place.

But if this were all, then the novel could only have a limited interest for us today. More importantly, *The Golem,* like Meyrink's earlier and shorter satirical pieces, was written to be an assault on the dubiously "safe" values of the bourgeoisie of the Austro-Hungarian Empire in its last days. In an expressionist and melodramatic mode it anticipates the anxieties of Karl Kraus's *Die Letzen Tage der Menscheit* (1919) and Robert Musil's *Der Mann ohne Eigenschaften* (1930-43). It must be admitted though that Meyrink's intellectual position was a great deal more eccentric than Kraus's or Musil's and his mode of expression willfully distorted and bizarre, for *The Golem* is, before all else a masterpiece of fantasy. It and Meyrink's later novels and short stories were to serve as sources of inspiration for the fantastic and expressionist movement in the German cinema—most notably, of course, for Paul Wegener's two film versions of *Der Golem*. Equally Meyrink's haunted visualisation of the Prague ghetto—a sunless quarter where architecture and action alike are distended, fragmented and exaggerated for expressive effect—was to inspire artists like Hugo Steiner-Prag and Alfred Kubin.

The sources of Meyrink's fantasy do not lie in whimsy or in self-reflective literary jokes. Rather he drew upon the experiences of his own life (and here the reader is referred to the chronology at the beginning of this volume). His life was a great deal stranger than fiction, though his fictions were in all conscience stranger than fiction, though his fictions were in all conscience strange enough. In particular he drew upon his own active involvement in the intellectual and occultist movements—cabalistic, masonic and theosophical—which secretly fermented in Central Europe at the beginning of the century. The Great War was to throw all into turmoil. Artists and occultists dispersed and recombined in new centres after the War and, within a few decades the world which had given birth to *The Golem* would be annihilated by the Third Reich. This book then leads back into a world we have lost. Indeed it has passed away so utterly that we have not even been conscious of its passing.

What is the Golem? What is a Golem? In Old Testament Hebrew the word seems to have meant the unformed embryo. In medieval Jewish philosophy the term designated *hyle* or matter which had not been shaped by form. More curiously Hassidic mystics in twelfth-thirteenth century Germany are known to have practised an obscure ritual which aimed to use the Cabalistic power of the Hebrew alphabet and manipulate the material form of the universe to create a "golem." It was from these philosophical and mystical usages that a group of legends about the golem evolved to become one of the stock themes of Jewish folklore and Yiddish literature. In these legends a man-like monster of clay is created by a rabbi or other student of the Cabala and is given life by inscribing *Emeth* (Truth) on its brow. The creature can be deactivated by removing the first letter, leaving it immobilised under the power of *Meth* (Death). In some stories the attraction of this primitive Jewish version of the robot is that it can labour in the synagogue on Saturdays, though in the golem story attached to the sixteenth century Rabbi Loew of Prague the Rabbi is careful to remove the crucial letter every Saturday evening. In most of the tales there comes a point where the rabbi or occultist forgets to remove the letter of power and the creature grows in power and goes on the rampage. In some stories it is only disabled at the cost of its creator's life as the monstrous thing of clay tumbles down upon its master. There are clear affinities in the legend of the golem with tales about the Paracelsean homunculus and the Sorcerer's Apprentice and with Mary Shelley's *Frankenstein*— and for that matter with stories of Tibetan *tulpas* who escape their mystic masters' control.

However in yet other legends the golem operates as the defender of the ghetto against anti-Semitic libels and pogroms. Tales about the golem and anti-Semitic libels both enjoyed a vogue at the turn of the century. The Russian monk Nilus published his version of *The Protocols of the Elders of Zion* in 1905. More locally anti-semitism and accusations of ritual murder were rife in Bohemia from the 1890's onwards. It is possible that Meyrink, whose mother was Jewish, suffered in some measure from the revival of this prejudice. Certainly his Golem has been seen by some as the embodiment of the spirit of the Jewish ghetto.

Perhaps. But Meyrink's Golem has distinctive features. It manifests itself in Prague, in a room with no doors, once every thirty three years. The novelist has gone back to older Jewish sources to transform them and create a spirit figure which seeks materialisation. It emerges that the Golem's features are those of the artist Athanasius Pernath, who is the novel's protagonist. The Golem is Pernath's doppelganger and it manifests itself in a room with no doors—that is, in an area of the mind which is inaccessible to normal consciousness. *The Golem* is before all else an exploration of the problem of identity, a "painful quest for that eternal stone that in some mysterious fashion lurks in the dim recesses of . . . memory in the guise of a lump of fat."

Exploration of consciousness . . . deep currents of European thought! It is not compulsory to be so serious about it all. *The Golem* is also the glittering farrago of a master of charlatanry in which all the props of melodrama are skillfully deployed. Besides the artificial monster or doppelganger, we have the mysterious murder, the one woman who is all women—the Eternal Woman—, the puppets, the hermaphrodite, the tarot cards, revenge for love, the secret society of criminals and much else besides. The plotting is all wild and preposterous. Some of the characters wear rags, others wear shiny opera hats and white gloves but they all—Pernath the amnesiac hero, Jaromir the deaf mute sillhouette artist, Wassertum the pawnbroker, Zwakh the marrionetteer, Rosins the prostitute, Hillel the Cabalist, Chanousek the poor student, Habal Garmin "Breath of Bones"—they all are driven through dark and narrow streets of Prague like playing cards before the wind. (pp. 11-14)

Some novels—and the novels of David Lindsay and Charles Williams are examples—achieve an effect which is not a purely literary one and an effect which lingers on in the mind of the reader long after the reading of the book has been concluded. *The Golem* is one of these novels. "The path I am pointing out to you is strewn with strange happenings: dead people you have known will rise up and talk with you! They are only images!" (p. 16)

Robert Irwin, "Gustav Meyrink and His Golem," in The Golem *by Gustav Meyrink, translated by M. Pemberton, Dedalus, 1985, pp. 11-16.*

ADDITIONAL BIBLIOGRAPHY

Lovecraft, H. P. Letter to James F. Morton. In his *Selected Letters,* edited by August Derleth and James Turner, pp. 137-38. Sauk City, Wis.: Arkham House Publishers, 1976.

    Calls *The Golem* "the most magnificent weird thing I've run across in aeons!" and comments that "as a study in lurking, insidious, regional horror it has scarcely a peer."

Monegal, Emir Rodriguez. "The Philosopher's Code." In his *Jorge Luis Borges: A Literary Biography,* pp. 134-43. New York: E. P. Dutton, 1978.*

    Quotes a 1936 essay in which Borges called *The Golem* "an extraordinarily visual book which graciously put together mythology, eroticism, tourism, Prague's local color, premonitory dreams, dreams of alien or previous lives, and even reality."

"Two Legends." *The New Statesman* XXXI, No. 792 (30 June 1928): 398.*

    Review of *The Golem* maintaining that the book's virtue is "its good though sometimes too strident writing, and the unity of its nightmare atmosphere,'' while its defect is ''that the author has failed to decide between writing a pure tale of mystery and imagination and composing an explicable psychological fantasia.''

Review of *The Golem*, by Gustav Meyrink. *The Times Literary Supplement*, No. 1380 (12 July 1928): 518.

Considers the novel ''a genuinely weird and impressive tale'' that is worthy of comparison to works by Edgar Allan Poe.

''Revelling in Romantic Horror.'' *The Times Literary Supplement*, No. 3568 (16 July 1970): 766.

Discusses Meyrink's blend in *The Golem* of themes and motifs characteristic of eighteenth-century Gothic novels, nineteenth-century horror stories, and twentieth-century fiction, drama, and film.

Marjorie (Lowry Christie) Pickthall

1883-1922

English-born Canadian poet, novelist, dramatist, and short story writer.

Called by Desmond Pacey "the best poetic craftsman of her Canadian generation," Pickthall is considered a poet of somewhat archaic style and sensibility whose works nevertheless form a distinguished chapter in the history of modern literature in English Canada. She is often compared with figures of the Celtic Renaissance, particularly W. B. Yeats and Fiona Macleod (William Sharp), and with such Catholic Revival poets as Francis Thompson and Katherine Tynan. Like the works of these authors, her poetry is frequently concerned with mystical subjects and contains a wealth of imagery and symbolism from religion and folklore. Pickthall's work has been especially praised for its technical accomplishment, masterful portrayal of nature, and refined sentiment. While Pickthall also attained some success as a novelist during her life, she is best remembered for the poetry collections *The Drift of Pinions* and *The Lamp of Poor Souls*.

An only child, Pickthall was born in Middlesex, England, though soon afterward the family moved to Southwater, Sussex. There, in "Shelley's Country," Pickthall developed the kinship with nature that would become a significant characteristic of her poetry. A precocious child whose delicate health kept her indoors much of the time, by the age of four or five she had decided to become a writer, illustrator, and publisher. Throughout her childhood she produced books of her own stories, poems, and illustrations, inspired in part by her love of the Sussex countryside. In 1889, the Pickthalls moved to Canada and settled in Toronto. Characteristic of her single-mindedness, Pickthall applied herself scholastically only in those subjects that related to her future as a writer and artist. At sixteen she wrote: "It is to be glorious for I am to write famous books and illustrate them myself." At the age of fifteen she sold her first story to the *Toronto Globe* for three dollars, and real success followed in December 1899, when she won first prize in both categories of an annual poetry and short story competition for young Canadians. At the time, she confidently remarked that it was "the first step, and a very splendid stride at that, to Success with a capital letter."

Over the next several years, Pickthall's stories, poems, articles, illustrations, and photographs appeared in numerous newspapers and periodicals. Her prolific output was interrupted, however, in the spring of 1910 by the sudden death of her mother. Pickthall was deeply affected by the loss and stopped writing altogether. Gradually, through the encouragement of friends, she began writing again. In particular, Sir Andrew MacPhail, editor of *University Magazine,* was instrumental in persuading Pickthall to prepare a collection of her verse for publication. As her manuscript neared completion, it became apparent to Pickthall's friends and advisors that she should leave her job at the Victoria College library to devote herself solely to writing. While she was persuaded to do so, she also knew that a full-time literary career would tax her frail health. Hoping that a change of environment would improve her physical condition, she returned to England shortly before *The Drift of Pinions* was published. In London, she received news that the first

edition of *The Drift of Pinions* had sold out in only ten days, an event which fortified her desire to write for a living. She devoted the rest of her life to poetry and fiction, interrupting her writing only to contribute to the war effort during the First World War. She held various positions during the war, including farm worker and office librarian, but, because of her delicate health, could not work for more than a few months at a time. After the war, she returned to writing and had completed manuscripts of *The Bridge* and *The Wood Carver's Wife* before she left England. Proclaiming herself "Canada sick," she returned to Toronto in May, 1920, and soon after settled in British Columbia, where she went to work in earnest, revising the poetic drama *The Wood Carver's Wife* and the novel *The Bridge*. In April, 1922, one month before the publication of *The Bridge*, Pickthall suffered an embolism and died in a Vancouver hospital.

Pickthall's poetry had an established audience even before her first collection appeared, but it was not until *The Drift of Pinions* was published in 1913 that she fulfilled the expectations of her early literary supporters. When she won national poetry competitions in both 1899 and 1900, she was hailed by many Canadian critics as a young author of undeniable ability and remarkable polish. Independent of systematic poetic theories, she relied upon her innate aesthetic sense to create works noted for their keen perceptions, delicate imagery, and graceful cadences. Influenced by Yeats and the Celtic Renaissance, she also utilized folkloric motifs, pastoral images, and mystic symbolism. According to some critics, Pickthall's importance rests on her skillful portrayal of nature; but other critics are less exuberant, noting that it is an ethereal nature, imagined, not observed, that is evoked by her impressionistic descriptions. Generally, critics agree that Pickthall's best work is contained in her first two collections, *The Drift of Pinions* and *The Lamp of Poor Souls.* Related to her poetry is the poetic drama *The Wood Carver's Wife,* which some critics regard as her greatest achievement. Similarly high in Pickthall's own estimation, the one-act play is representative of her verse writing in its mysticism and its rich symbolism.

Pickthall often selected religious or mystical themes, leading many critics to compare her work with that of the Catholic mystical poets Francis Thompson, Katherine Tynan, and Christina Rossetti. Pickthall was continually drawn to biblical motifs and found inspiration in what she called "the two greatest poems in existence," the *Song of Songs* and the *Book of Job.* Although deeply religious, she subscribed to no doctrine other than her own devotion to Christ, which has been described by her biographer, Lorne Pierce: "His gentleness in the face of wrong, courage in the midst of danger, serenity in sorrow and his indomitable independence, these were dear to her own heart." Pickthall developed a similar, though less numinous, attachment to the national pioneering spirit and natural grandeur of Canada. Having identified herself firmly as a Canadian writer, Pickthall took subjects from Canadian history and folk legend. In two such works, "Père Lalemant" and "On Lac Sainte Irénée," she used Canadian settings to treat themes prominent throughout her works—separation and loneliness. These, together with death, grief, and regret, are subjects to which she returned regularly. She presented them with characteristic grace and wistfulness, recognizing the inevitability of suffering, yet seeing in it also the way to spiritual fulfillment. In her own words: "Without winter there is no spring; there is no resurrection that is not purchased by death." Some critics have suggested that her own frail health and her failure to overcome the deep grief she experienced at her mother's death led to Pickthall's preoccupation with these dark themes. To Pickthall, however, beauty could be found in all things, and she sought to render it poetically with reverence and imagination.

The scope of attention given to Pickthall's poetry has not been afforded her fictional works. Although she published a novel and numerous short stories during her years in England, upon her return to Canada in 1920, Pickthall was disappointed to find that she was thought of as a "writer of verse only." Commenting on Pickthall as a fiction writer, Pierce has stated: "Only in her novels and short stories did she ever try to come to grips with mankind, and even then she tended to submerge her intimate thoughts and feelings in romantic situations from which the tangible and the real too often escaped." The subjects of her fiction are often highly dramatic and regularly involve high adventure, something unattainable in Pickthall's sheltered life. At the same time, Pickthall's novels and short stories are described by critics as strongly psychological: often constructed around a physical, though metaphorically spiritual journey, such as the pursuit of refuge from the merciless elements of nature, these works typically follow the development of a single character. Pickthall's two novels demonstrate a difficulty in handling many characters at once, an ability she admired in Charles Dickens. Although this has led some critics to suggest that she was never comfortable with the novel form, her fiction

has been praised for its lucid narrative style, successfully maintained suspense, and underlying humor.

A critical and popular success during her lifetime, Pickthall is today regarded as an important contributor to early twentieth-century Canadian poetry on the basis of her technical proficiency, her spiritual insight, and the unsurpassed delicacy of her pastoral imagery. In an appreciation of Pickthall's work, Robert Max Garrett has written: "Her vision of life is such as is granted only to three classes of people: women, poets, and mystics, and she is all three."

(See also *Contemporary Authors,* Vol. 107.)

PRINCIPAL WORKS

Dick's Desertion: A Boy's Adventures in Canadian Forests
   (juvenile fiction) 1905
The Drift of Pinions (poetry) 1913
The Worker in Sandalwood (short story) 1914
Little Hearts (novel) 1915
The Lamp of Poor Souls, and Other Poems (poetry) 1916
The Wood Carver's Wife (drama) 1921
The Bridge (novel) 1922
The Wood Carver's Wife, and Later Poems (drama and
   poetry) 1922
Angels' Shoes, and Other Stories (short stories) 1923
The Complete Poems of Marjorie Pickthall (poetry) 1927

ODELL SHEPARD (essay date 1917)

[*An American critic, biographer, and poet, Shepard is best remembered for his Pulitzer Prize-winning biography* Pedlar's Progress: The Life of Bronson Alcott *(1937). In the following excerpt, Shepard favorably reviews Pickthall's* The Lamp of Poor Souls.]

Most of [the poems in *The Lamp of Poor Souls*] appeared in Miss Pickthall's earlier collection, *A Drift of Pinions,* which was far less read in the United States than it deserved to be. Here is another name to be added to the long list of Canadian poets of the last twenty years. In music and magic of line, in range and delicacy of imagination, Miss Pickthall yields to none. The rarest and finest thing about her poems is their strong clear music. Sheer beauty—"about the best thing God invents" or lets his children discover—is here in abundance. It should be said that the singing line is notably absent in all the other books I have mentioned, and this, to one who believes that whatever else a poet may do, he *must* sing, is a sad commentary.

The themes and materials of these poems are as various as the forms. They are drawn from many sources—Greek, Hebrew, Japanese, Irish, French, Canadian, English. The chief sources of literary inspiration seem to have been the works of Swinburne and of Bliss Carman. (p. 140)

Odell Shepard, "Stops of Various Quills," in The Dial, *Vol. LXII, No. 736, February 22, 1917, pp. 137-40.**

ANNE ELIZABETH WILSON (essay date 1922)

[In the following excerpt, Wilson discusses Pickthall's prose.]

Marjorie Pickthall was the mistress of one of the rarest gifts of prose expression it has been this country's good fortune to witness, much less to claim.

It is simply that Canadians have not yet fully learned of that powerful turn of her talent. It has not been called sufficiently to their attention. The fact, however, that the last book . . . [*The Bridge*] is now leading the fiction lists in Great Britain, and is creating more comment throughout the English-speaking world than any Canadian novel has heretofore so much as approached, is proof that it has not lacked recognition. The fact also that the three or four Canadian editions are now almost completely exhausted, is further proof that there has been recognition in Canada too, of that last work and, as many say, masterpiece.

But it would be better to forget all that in the writing itself, wherein it is possible to see humanity with new strength and clarity, and also heaven. In her prose writing Marjorie Pickthall assumed a new touch. *It is not the touch with which she has approached any of her poems.* It is here, in my opinion, that Canadian critics have fallen short in the classification of her work. Comparison of any sort is a poor basis for judgment, and it has been singularly inadequate between the two forms of this writer's expression. It is absurd to say that Marjorie Pickthall's prose is not enriched [by] her innate poesy; it is, as Haendel's oratorios were vivified by his dalliance with the opera; but it is a greater absurdity and a slight upon another power equally great and stronger in its simplicity, to call it a *product* of her poesy. Her prose is narrative drama, decorated by a hand made light with exquisite practice. Her poetry is a lyric manifestation of grace and sentiment—and her mastery of the one (the poetry) has tremendously aided in the perfection and enlargement of the other (the prose).

When I come to express, as I so often have occasion, just what quality or quantity fills the two novels (and the stories as well) I am continually brought up upon a muteness of utter insufficiency. What to say? The best I can usually manage is, "Read them." It is splendid advice but literary cowardice. Perhaps this time I shall write it, although I have my doubts.

The first quality, and that too is quantity, is understanding—a most unfailing understanding; the second is a magnetic power, as of a foreknowledge of all circumstance big and little, a closeness with destiny; the third is beauty—beauty of conception, beauty of phrase, beauty of sadness and nature; and the fourth is a finely-chased but most satisfying humorousness—as though at times the page were written under a constant smile. . . .

For those who have not made the discovery of Miss Pickthall's novels, let me proclaim them. *Little Hearts* is a story of England in the old days—the time of Prince Charles, and there are silks and powdered hair *about* it—but *in* it—just a handful of "little hearts" in poverty, in the pathetic brave philosophy of poverty, in good and ill adventure and in loss of what little they have found to lose—but finally one heart in triumph. Out of the book I take one quotation which is part of an entry in young Mr. Sampson's *Philosophy Book*: "Without winter there is no spring; there is no resurrection that is not purchased by death." You will never forget *Little Hearts.*

Of *The Bridge,* there is much to say for Canadians. One of the things which must be said, is that it leads in the vanguard of truly great literary production which our country may give the world. It is the story of a man who was lost in cowardice of mind, but found himself in sacrifice and self-knowledge. Laid in the magnificence of the Great Lakes, it is filled with the spells of love, romance and good battle that must be present in any book that is to be truly sufficient. The scenes of storm, on the water, the sand, and in the hearts of its characters make it an epic. If there runs close towards its close a sorrowful theme of unfulfilled seeking, it is justified in the beauty of the ending of all suspense. If one might speak at length of mysticism, one could dwell longer on *The Bridge,* and its significance spiritually. It has already been mentioned from the pulpit, and I hope it may bring its message to the many who may not hear any message from the pulpit. I wonder as I read this last published work of that great and knowing woman who has died, whether she can have more to say of God since she has seen Him.

> Anne Elizabeth Wilson, "Magnificent Prose of Marjorie Pickthall," in The Canadian Bookman, *Vol. IV, No. 7, June, 1922, p. 185.*

E. RITCHIE (essay date 1922)

[In the following excerpt from an obituary tribute, Ritchie offers an appreciation of Pickthall's verse.]

To Miss Pickthall . . . , more than to some much greater poets, was it granted to bring her reader into a very intimate relation with her own mood and her own imaginative vision, so that—if susceptible to such influences at all—he could not fail to have his own sense of beauty renewed and quickened by the spiritual contact. Hence her verse possessed a quality which, without exaggeration, we may call lovable. (p. 157)

[It] might have been supposed that she would have given to Canadian sentiment and Canadian scenery prominent places in her poetry, but only to a very slight extent are such influences apparent. Contemporary events seldom inspired her pen; and there is little of what is commonly called "local colour" in her lyrics, except where, as in **"Père Lalement,"** the theme itself requires it. Even the birds and flowers which she weaves so deftly into the web of her fancy are not quite realistically treated; they are not the product of "Nature study," but of that artistic imagination which is creative as well as receptive. It is, indeed, only in that world which we half perceive and half create that such a lyrical poet feels at home. It was not realistic accuracy, but the deeper and higher truths of emotional life, at which she aimed; so that whether she writes about Palestine or Japan, of Canada or Greece, while the "mise en scène" is indicated with much skill, the delicate charm which gives atmosphere to the verse comes more from the soul of the writer than from the environment described.

For Marjorie Pickthall as for Keats, Beauty is Truth,—Truth, Beauty. In all her verse whatever the theme, beauty is the inspiring motive: religion, love, sorrow and death,—all come to her clothed in beauty as in a garment. . . . (pp. 157-58)

There are no doubt clearly marked limitations to her work. It is graceful rather than vigorous, and emotional rather than intellectual. But, within its limits, it is good work. It shows no carelessness in technique, no over-emphasis in expression, no indulgence in mere sentimentality. She gave us of her best in her song.

In her prose she was less successful. Her short stories and novels are written with characteristic refinement and delicacy of feeling, and contain not a few passages of real charm, but she was lacking in that firm grasp of character and mastery of incident that belong to the true teller of tales. It is by her lyrical genius that Marjorie Pickthall will be remembered. To indicate which are the best of her poems can only be to express a personal preference. Time, like a good gardener, "thins out" the too plentiful growths that spring from the soul of even the best of poets. Some things the world willingly, and rightly, lets die. But surely such lyrics as **"The Little Fauns to Proserpine,"** **"A Mother in Egypt,"** **"Swallows,"** and **"Mary Shepherdess,"** are destined to endure. Marjorie Pickthall's verse had the sweet freshness that comes with the dawn in springtime, and her voice will be sadly missed from our too scanty choir of singing birds. (p. 158)

> E. Ritchie, "Marjorie Pickthall: In Memoriam," in
> The Dalhousie Review, *Vol. 2, No. 2, July, 1922,*
> *pp. 157-58.*

J. D. LOGAN (essay date 1922)

[*In the following excerpt, Logan compares Pickthall's work to that of her contemporaries in Canadian poetry.*]

What first brought Marjorie Pickthall to appreciative public notice, and distinguished her from other contemporary poets in Canada, was a singular *precocious virtuosity* in verbal painting of Nature and in verbal music. When she began to write verse, Lampman had been dead a decade, Roberts had gone over to fiction, Campbell had turned to poetic drama, Duncan Campbell Scott had achieved a first-rate name for exquisite artistry in verse, Bliss Carman was internationally known as one of the world's sweetest warblers of wood-notes wild; and her contemporaries, of a near age to her own, and chiefly the members of "the Vaudeville School of Canadian Poetry," led by R. W. Service, had neither aesthetic taste nor the artistic conscience. Naturally, those on "the *qui vive*" for New Voices in the poetic choir of Canada, heard the free, happy, pure pipings of a newcomer to the choir—Marjorie Pickthall, singing shyly from the corner of a daily newspaper, but singing with a rare lilt—so rare in Canada indeed that the little world which heard her first warblings wondered if the singer were a Canadian person, but felt that her song was not autochthonous to Canada, that the singer would create poetry which would be *more* than Canadian, which would be a contribution to literature as such, to world-literature.

What, then, caused Marjorie Pickthall, from the beginning, to win public notice, and to stand out from the Vaudevillian crew of poetasters in Canada, was, as I said, her precocious virtuosity as a word-painter, verbal colorist, and melodist. From the start, even in the sixteenth year of her age, she was a remarkable artist in colorful and musical language—original and adroit in poetic craftsmanship, in "the mastery of rhythm and the management of rhyme." It is as an adroit and exquisite *craftswoman* (or "artist," if one prefer the term), not for originality of imaginative conception, that, from her first printed essays in verse to the last, Marjorie Pickthall must be noted as a specially gifted poet in Canada, and must be accorded a relatively honorable, possibly high, place in the history of English literature—not "world literature," as we shall see—produced in Canada. (pp. 14-15)

It will be found, I believe, that she made no advance in poetry, from her first essays, say, in her sixteenth year to her thirty-ninth (or last), save in perfection of craftsmanship, gaining, that is, in artistic finish of form and structure, mastery of rhythm and rhyme, delicate sensuousness, grace of diction, charm of color and pure verbal music. Let us say, then, that the poetry of Marjorie Pickthall is assured of immortality as an Ideal for future poets of Canada to emulate in technical perfection, and that when she sang of Nature, the afflatus in that case being natural to her genius, she created authentic poetry as such, poetry that was arresting, airy, bright, liquid, limpid, and, to use her own words with reference to Keats—

> . . . . . of fragrance made,
> Woven and rhymed of light.

But we must be critically careful not to give Marjorie Pickthall, as the *singer* and nature-*painter,* which she was *par excellence,* undue distinction, as if she had no peers in Canada. "For thirty years," said Dr. Archibald MacMechan in a lecture on our poet, as reported in the daily press (*The Evening Echo,* Halifax, December 10, 1918)—"for thirty years I have been a student of Canadian Literature, and a watcher of the skies for the appearing of new [poetic] stars. In that time four only have arisen, the greatest of whom is a woman—Marjorie Pickthall."

Of the other three, Lampman, I know, was one. The remaining two must be chosen from Roberts, Campbell, Duncan Campbell Scott, and Bliss Carman. If Dr. MacMechan had in mind four "stars" in the technic of poetry, in the demesne of Canada, the four Canadian poets who can be regarded as pervasively technical artists in beauty of diction, imagery, color, and verbal and rhythmic music, are—Carman and Duncan Campbell Scott among the still living, and Lampman and Marjorie Pickthall amongst the deceased. Of these four, the late poet, whose genuinely lamented death has caused to disappear from Canadian literature—or literature as such—the re-incarnation of the spirit of Titania or of Ariel, must be reckoned the least, or, at best, not the greatest, even in craftsmanship.

Let me be just to others while yielding to none in my admiration of her genius and her artistry. It may be true that, as Mr. Laurence E. Jones says (*The University Magazine,* December, 1913), we may search in vain "for a lame or halting line, for a strained or dissonant rhyme. It is all careful and clean-cut, but perfectly free and flowing none the less." But it is absurd to make her *sui generis* as a technical artist, excluding even Sappho, Alcaeus, Horace, Catullus, Gray, Shelley, Keats, Tennyson, Arnold, Meredith, and Swinburne, by saying, as Dr. MacMechan has said (*vid. loc. cit.*), that her poetry, as he finds, exhibits "a flawless technique. Her verse is as musical as Carman's, and as sincere as Lampman's; but, unlike both, it contains no failures. Her feeling for the right, the inevitable word ('le mot juste') is exquisite and sure . . . It is not too much to call her work impeccable."

Dr. MacMechan's view would be important if it were not an uncritical opinion when it should state a matter of fact. No poet born of woman has been flawless, impeccable, in technique. Certainly Lampman, Carman, Duncan Campbell Scott are not; and there is certainly not flawless technique in these two lines, to take but two, by Marjorie Pickthall—

> In those fair coves where tempests *ne'er* should be.

This line is from **"Dawn,"** the poem which, under the name **"A Prayer,"** according to Dr. MacMechan, led Professor Mavor to the exclusive discovery of the new star in the poetic heavens of Canada. Next, consider the impeccability (?) of this line from Marjorie Pickthall's **"Vale"**—

> And when immortal morning *opes* her door.

Technically, her poetry is distinguished musically by an extraordinarily successful use of alliteration; but the defect in it is that, on the whole, her verse lacks *style*. I do not mean that it is not written in the grand style. Technically her verse is free, flowing, musical, airy, tripping, graceful, "woven and rhymed of light"—in a word, *feminine*. But, by thus much, does it lack originality and substance of style—the subtle quality which gives us the sense of having met with beauty that is memorably, unforgettably fine and pervasive as a spiritual essence. The supreme Canadian artist in the fine style in poetry, in substantial manner, is, in my view, Duncan Campbell Scott. He is rivalled, at times, in substance as well as technical style, by Lampman. But neither of these poets has had the singing or lyrical gift that is Carman's or was Marjorie Pickthall's— but her lyrical gift was not in the same absolute degree or quality as is Carman's, which always has the sheer ecstatic lilt of the lark, while Marjorie Pickthall's was less above the earth, more confined, like the linnet's sweet, sensuous reaches in song. Lampman, Carman, and Scott may be technically at fault oftener than was Marjorie Pickthall; but when they are technically perfect, it is a finer perfection than hers, and their subtleties and sheer reaches in the technique of poetic style, and form, and in substance were not hers.

Yet I have no doubt that, had this darling of the gods, as her genius and, from the human point of view, untimely death, proved her to be—I have no doubt that had Marjorie Pickthall lived, she would have learned the finest technical reaches of Lampman, Carman and Scott; and that she would have come to take a place in English literature deservedly beside Elizabeth Barrett Browning, Christina Rossetti, and Alice Meynell. Amongst her contemporaries in the homeland, there shall abide a green and sweet memory of her as "th' eclipse and glory of her kind" in the technical artistry of exquisite lyrical singing and fanciful painting of Nature's face, and moods, and life. (pp. 17-19)

> *J. D. Logan, in his* Marjorie Pickthall, Her Poetic Genius and Art: An Appreciation and an Analysis of Aesthetic Paradox, *T. C. Allen & Co., 1922, 44 p.*

DUNCAN CAMPBELL SCOTT   (essay date 1923)

[*Scott was a Canadian poet, novelist, and critic. He is best remembered as one of the leading poets of the "Confederation group." Writing in an era following the formation of the Dominion of Canada, Scott, along with poets Bliss Carman, Archibald Lampman, and Charles G. D. Roberts, helped create and cultivate a sense of national identity. Early cast as a regional writer of the northern wilderness, especially its Indian life, Scott has been reappraised as a writer of great diversity with a complex vision and a distinctly Canadian spirit. As Desmond Pacey has said, "Is it too much to suggest that in these quietly powerful poems . . . we catch an authentic glimpse of the Canadian spirit at its finest?" In the following excerpt, Scott discusses Pickthall in the context of modern Canadian literature and offers a general appraisal of her poetry.*]

It is now twenty-three years since [Archibald] Lampman died, and the period is marked by the [recent] death of Marjorie Pickthall. . . . She was of English parentage, born in England, but educated in Canada, and she was in training and sentiment a good Canadian.

If one were looking for evidence of progress in Canadian literature during the period . . . just referred to, one positive item would be the difference in the reception of the first books published by these two authors. Until the generous review by

William Dean Howells, of Lampman's book had been published in *Harper's Magazine,* it was here considered, when any consideration whatever was given to the subject, a matter of local importance. But the warm-hearted welcome of Howells led to sudden recognition of the fact that the book was an acquisition to general literature, and was not merely parochial. After that incident, and others like it, we find that recognition of Miss Pickthall's first book [*The Drift of Pinions*] took place at once, and from our independent judgment, as an important addition to poetical literature. Advance is clearly shown by this fact; for until we have faith in the power of our writers we can have no literature worth speaking about; our position in arts and letters will be secured when we find foreign critics accepting a clear lead from us. We accepted Miss Pickthall, and our opinion was confirmed very generally afterwards.

It is to be deeply regretted that her career is closed and that we shall not again hear, or overhear, that strain of melody, so firm, so sure, floating towards us, to use a phrase of Lampman's, "as if from the closing door of another world and another lovelier mood." "Overhear" is, I think, the right word, for there was a tone of privacy, of seclusion, in her most individual poems, not the seclusion of a cloister, but the seclusion of a walled garden with an outlook towards the sea and the mountains. Life was beyond the garden somewhere, and murmurously, rumors of it came between the walls and caused longing and disquiet. The voice could be heard mingling the real appearance of the garden with the imagined forms of life beyond it and with remembrances from dim legends and from the untarnished old romances of the world. Her work was built on a ground base of folk melody, and wreathed about it were Greek phrases and glamors from the "Song of Songs". But composite of all these influences, it was yet original and reached the heart with a wistfulness of comfort. She had a feeling for our little brothers of the air and the woods that was sometimes classical, sometimes mediaeval. Fauns and hamadryads peopled her moods, and our familiar birds and flowers took on quaint forms like the conventional shapes and mellow colors of tapestries woven long ago. "Bind above your breaking heart the echo of a Song"—that was her cadence, the peculiar touch that gives a feeling of loneliness and then heals it, and if one might have said to her any words at parting, they would have been her own words—"Take, ere yet you say good-bye, the love of all the earth". (p. 189)

> *Duncan Campbell Scott, "Poetry and Progress," in* The Canadian Magazine of Politics, Science, Art and Literature, *Vol. LX, No. 3, January, 1923, pp. 187-95.**

ROBERT MAX GARRETT   (essay date 1924)

[*In the following excerpt, Garrett discusses prominent characteristics of Pickthall's fiction and poetry.*]

At first it seems that the quantity of [Marjorie Pickthall's] work is pitiably small: Two thin books of verse [*The Lamp of Poor Souls* and *The Woodcarver's Wife*, two novels *Little Hearts* and *The Bridge*] . . . , a little uncollected verse, some thirty short stories in various magazines—that is all. But when one weighs the quality of the work, one's standard quickly alters. From the very first one recognizes that one has to do with no ordinary or second-rate writer, while soon one discovers that her best work stands the most rigid tests that can be applied to it. In her presence one feels that he is in the presence of greatness. Her vision of life is such as is granted only to three classes of people: women, poets and mystics, and she is all three. That intensity of feeling which is one of her great powers, bears within it her most serious shortcoming—her inability to interpret group consciousness; she is too intensely personal to be able to handle many characters. It is because of this that her latest novel, ***The Bridge,*** fails of being a really great novel. The passion is narrowed down to the single problem of bridging the gulf which separates the selfish, handsome Maclear from humanity. The novel is hailed as being a *best seller,* but it will, I think, disappoint its heralds. It has none of the qualities demanded by the *best seller.* Its plot is not lurid enough, and its canvas is not full enough of figures. It has not the public graces demanded of the moving picture star or of the prima donna. Its action comes once in a while dangerously near the grotesque, as in the avowal of love between Maclear and Sombra after the storm. Nevertheless, the book will live, for it has less obvious charms which completely outweigh its defects. Miss Pickthall shows that love of exquisite pattern in it which she does in her short stories, a ruthlessness and a delicacy of drawing which will be more and more appreciated as time goes by. The three divisions of the novel, Sand, Mist and Snow, are powerful symbols which are made actors in the story. The shifting sands upon which Maclear has based his character and his work, and which have betrayed him, which hunt him into the arms of Sombra, which at length give her to him again as from the dead; the mist through which their love struggles, and which typifies his moral outlook, which finally separates them; the snow which brings at first danger, almost death, but finally cleanness of soul and a wholesome new outlook upon life—all this is delicate art which the true lover of letters will not consent to have forgotten. But to call it a popular novel is like calling a novel of Jane Austen a popular novel.

In the same way, to call her first novel, ***Little Hearts,*** a novel which can never be a popular novel, is to give it high praise. It is a well-sustained story with a good plot, but it is written with such beauty that it will be constantly discovered afresh by lovers of the choice in literature, and will be read with rich appreciation decades after the popular novels, its contemporaries, have ceased to exist.

If one were to enumerate the qualities which impress him in Miss Pickthall's work, he would probably mention first her fine ability to portray nature. Pure landscape delights her. The little apprentice in **"The Worker in Sandalwood"** thought of the country where the stranger had been a boy, of the flowers on the hills, of the laughing leaves of the aspen and poplar, of the golden flowering anise, and the golden sun upon the dusty road. (pp. 18-20)

One trait which she possesses in splendid measure, but which she is chary of showing, is humor. There is an underlying delicious humor in many of her situations, which does not break out into laughter, and she rarely makes use of such farcical elements as the cabbage fight in ***Little Hearts***; but now and again sly shafts are sent unexpectedly, such as M. le Curé in **"The Worker in Sandalwood,"** who was tainted with the infidelities of cities, good man, having been three times to Montreal, and once in an electric car to Sainte Anne. Again, the minister [in another story], when caught in the rapids above the Île de Paradis, tries to think of some Scripture to aid him, but could think of none but the Forty-second Psalm, "which, he explained, in that situation, was irony." "Like as the hart desireth the waterbrooks!" (p. 23)

One exceedingly interesting aspect of Miss Pickthall's art is her Catholicism. She is a Catholic, an Anglo-Catholic, a mystic, one who has drunk of those springs reopened for us by the leaders of the so-called Oxford Movement. To her as to countless others came a new hope and strength when they were assured that as members of the old Church of England they were heirs to all the Catholic ages with their wealth of devotion and of sacramental life, and that the Reformation was valid for them only in-so-far as it purified the life of the Church, not when it attempted to nullify vital currents and beliefs and associations which were of the very life of the Church. One can almost trace the devotional reading of her youth—the *Little Flowers of St. Francis,* Law's *Serious Call,* the *Spiritual Letters of St. Francis de Sales,* John Inglesant, Christina Rossetti, Michael Fairless. She must have been deeply impressed by the work of the Pre-Raphaelites, especially, it would seem to me, by Holman Hunt and Ford Madox Brown. (p. 24)

It is with the group of mystical writers, Anglo-Catholic and Roman,—Francis Thompson, Katherine Tynan, Christina Rossetti, Michael Fairless, Evelyn Underhill, Alice Meynell, that we must class a good deal of her work in order to see its true significance. Here belong such poems as **"The Lamp of Poor Souls,"** and that magnificent **"Salutaris Hostia"**; **"When the Moon Is Last Awake"**; **"Mary Shepherdess"**; **"The Young Baptist"**; **"The Bridegroom of Cana"**; **"A Mother in Egypt"**; **"St. Yves' Poor"**; **"Père Lalement"**; **"Bega"**; **"In a Monastery Garden"**—all from the volume *The Lamp of Poor Souls;* **"Mary Tired"**; **"Christ in the Museum"**; **"Sleep"**; **"The Gardener's Boy"**; **"Singing Children"**—all from the volume *The Woodcarver's Wife;* and her short stories **"The Eye of the Needle,"** and **"The Worker in Sandalwood"**—that delightful Little Flower. Then, too, her novel ***Little Hearts,*** is worthy of standing by the work of Charlotte Yonge, W. M. Letts, and J. M. Shorthouse, the tale of the simple-hearted Mr. Sampson, who writes in his journal of his bride the Lady Poverty purely as a philosophic pastime, but who at last after the world has shown itself ashes to him, embraces her with true Franciscan ardor.

It was this fellowship which taught her that philosophy which is the keynote of so much that is beautiful in her work, the principle of sacramentalism. As she learned in her catechism, a sacrament is the outward and visible sign of an inward and spiritual grace; since to her, God was so close to his creatures that He comes to them in homely guise of food and drink, so all creation is a cloak of his glory. (pp. 25-6)

She is keenly sensitive to symbolism. To her, as to Anthony, the commonest sticks and straws would be the symbols of something forgotten, to be relearned. It is the true mystic who can express things like this: "A great crop of little crosses, both of Thorn and Rosemary, may be nourished up in our spiritual Gardens; but only One besides ourselves hath the Key to these walled Plots."

It is this delicate poise between immanence and pantheism which St. Francis knew but which he never destroyed, this very note of the oneness of the soul with nature that reminds her of her Greek training, which she uses with such skill now and then. How finely she blends the two in the poem **"The Shepherd Boy."** . . . (pp. 26-7)

And then in **"Jasper's Song,"** she achieves a rare thing—a Gypsy Canticle of the Sun. But she can write a perfect epigram in the classical manner, as when Mr. Sampson [in ***Little Hearts***] cuts into the chalk above the ancient trough, "what any wandering shepherd might have read there years afterwards: 'I am forgotten of man, but the bees and the woodpigeons remember me. Wherefore pass by, O traveller, if thou wilt, sparing no offerings. For these have given me of their first-fruits, a grain of honey-meal and one grey feather.'" She gives us more of this same exquisite stuff in two pages "From a Lost Anthology," which for sheer beauty is hard to surpass. (p. 28)

That power of feeling oneself into the hearts of one's characters which belongs to very great creative art, is hers. Malachi, the faithful old servant, who found the strayed horse, "drank in the kindly smell of horse and it went to his starved heart like wine." . . . And in the short story "The Eye of the Needle," where the blessed old Curé who knows himself a hardened sinner because he has hoarded to buy a crucifix which he has coveted, how marvellously she paints his despair. "Père Michel ate his supper. Outside, in the narrowed garden, the red phlox and the hollyhocks were in bloom; tobacco flowers shone in the night like stars, and the great moths passed driftingly across the beam of light from his reverence's lamp. The crickets whirred in the long, sun-scented grass, and the bull-frogs croaked in the pool below the bridge. A cow moved far down the road, and it was so dewily still that Père Michel could hear her tearing at the clover between the muffled tinkles of her bell. It was an hour that had been used to bring him peace."

It is possibly in her short stories that Miss Pickthall's work is most perfect. It is true that she has not herein the space for those delicate touches which may be found in her novels, nor is there opportunity therein for the heights which she reaches in her poems. But the form as she uses it has a fresh power. . . . [The geography of her short stories] is world-wide, ranging from French Canada to Central America, Central Africa, the East Indies, the wilds of Northern Canada. And the plots are just as varied. "La Tristesse," falsely accused of being a *loup garou*, whose master loves her so that he calls forth a corresponding passion in Felice, who leaves all she has known and shares the fate of the banished man and his dog—a love idyl of great power—"But think of the wonder of it—a flower of Greece in her golden days, a vision of Italy, a dream of ancient France, there suddenly showing forth for all men to see;" the tender charm of the story of "O-Jii-San," where the master painter, now grown old, loses his skill, and his master-piece is completed by his little pupil who makes him believe that his hand has lost none of its cunning . . . ; and that exquisite story of the "Worker in Sandalwood" who was no other than Christ himself come to help the tired little apprentice who found himself on Christmas Eve with an impossible task to finish. These short stories, sketches, whatever one may choose to call them, are marvellous not only in conception, but in execution—the carving being done with the precision and the grace of a gem.

To a certain limited extent, Miss Pickthall reminds one of the Brontës—there is the same passion and high emotional expectancy, the same spiritual isolation reaching yearningly forth for a companionship which is too likely to be unworthy its high gift; but in the Brontës there is always a feverish and starved anxiety and an intellectual and spiritual thinness which makes one always just a little nervous in their proximity; whereas Miss Pickthall shows a culture deep and broad, and a spiritual vision of such a calibre that one receives her work as having an authority which is not to be questioned. In the presence of work like hers, we can only feel a thankfulness that we have it at all. (pp. 28-32)

Robert Max Garrett, "Marjorie L. C. Pickthall," in The Personalist, Vol. V, No. 1, January 24, 1924, pp. 18-32.

ARCHIBALD MacMECHAN (essay date 1924)

[*MacMechan was a Canadian critic, poet, and historian. His works include studies in Nova Scotia history, collections of sea stories, and the critical survey* Head-waters of Canadian Literature, *from which the following excerpt is taken. In an unexcerpted portion of that survey, MacMechan describes the work of the Canadian poet Robert W. Service as "sourdough" verse, which he defines as a "willfully violent kind of verse without the power to redeem the squalid themes it treats," and contrasts this type of verse with Pickthall's work.*]

If the critic were to judge the taste of the Canadian public solely by the prairie fire success of the sourdough verse, he might rashly conclude that the tender idealism, the Keats-like love of beauty which distinguish the dawn of Canadian national poetry had fled from the land for ever. But he would have to correct his judgment by taking into account success of another kind. In the autumn of 1913, there appeared, through the good offices of Andrew Macphail, a slim little dove-colored volume of less than a hundred pages, called *The Drift of Pinions*, by Marjorie L. C. Pickthall. An impression of a thousand copies was absorbed almost at once by the discerning; and this must also be reckoned as a popular success. (p. 221)

The common complaint of the critic was that Canadian poets proffered their music to the world before they had mastered their instrument. They were apt to produce involuntary discords; but here was a singer who from her first prelude was incapable of uttering a false note. Open her little book at random, and harmony comes forth. . . . If technical perfection were all, *The Drift of Pinions* would stand alone in Canadian literature beside [Bliss Carman's] *Low Tide on Grand Pré*, but the verbal music is only the accompaniment of inner harmonies which these true poems release. Miss Pickthall is a singer of spiritual songs, a dreamer of such dreams as haunted St. Agnes. The title is significantly drawn from Francis Thompson's lines,

> The drift of pinions, would we hearken,
> Beats at our own clay-shuttered doors.

Her consciousness of the unseen is the heart of all her poetry. Perhaps the most significant of all her poems is "St. Yves Poor." It is a mediaeval theophany, the scene being laid in Brittany; the very name is mystical. . . . Christina Rossetti and Blake would have felt their spiritual kinship with the author of this poem. Narrative is the exception. Her poems are essentially songs, the purest form of poetry, "purest" meaning "freest from admixture of anything else." These lyrics are not of the earth; their element is air; they never touch the ground, but wheel like swallows in an enchanted crystal-clear ether of their own. For this poetess, the jar and fret of this present evil world, the tempest of human sorrow, the clamor of social war, the tumult of discontent, the roaring wheels of industry and commerce are as if they had never been. Apart and aloof from it all, she sits and weaves her spells, admitting within the magic circle of her verse nothing harsh, nothing ugly, nothing common or unclean. Creeds, opinions, philosophies which unite or divide men cast no shadow here. Most poetry is human sadness, human emotion and brooding charged with the sense of tears, but these fairy roundels are full of quiet joy, such as an innocent child might feel in a world that had never known sin.

Though *The Drift of Pinions* is not "a contribution to Canadian literature," Canada has brought her own subtle contribution to its making. Maple leaves are entwined in a song of the Nativity; choke-cherries and milk-weed are decorations borrowed from Canadian fields; the heart of Lalemant, the Jesuit martyr, is laid bare in one poignant soliloquy; and the cruelty of Charnisay in another. Such a lyric as **"Frost Song"** in an intimate interpretation of the norland winter, and fit tribute to Our Lady of the Snows—a little love by the blazing fire with the frost barricading the doors against all intruders. . . . It may not perhaps be mere fancy to suggest that clear Canadian skies and hopeful air may have had some influence on the serene tone of all Miss Pickthall's poetry.

Prose has also engaged her pen. Since returning to England, she has produced a novel, *Little Hearts* . . . of much promise. The scene is laid in eighteenth-century England, the coarse, shallow, self-complacent world of Horace Walpole. But Miss Pickthall is incapable of representing that world as it really was. Over all she casts the opalescent mists of her own temperament, softening, irradiating, etherealising the harsh features of that prosaic time. Her novel has the same qualities as her poetry, a refined and flawless style, with its centre in the things of the spirit. *Little Hearts* is not a costume novel, nor a Stevensonian story of adventure. It deals with problems which cannot vary from age to age—love for a woman, friendship for a man, loyalty to a trust, speaking truth or living a lie—and it handles these problems with rare and delicate skill. In the technique of the story-teller's art, Miss Pickthall has little to learn; the characters are pastels, the narrative moves freely, suspense is well maintained, the climax is a complete surprise, deep and touching. A certain patrician distinction attends all Miss Pickthall's work. Her prose is gentle, unforced, clear, penetrating; sentence following sentence "with the moon's beauty and the moon's soft pace." The patriotic critic is wistfully conscious that Canada has neither part nor lot in this achievement, and he wishes his country could lay claim to it. (pp. 222-29)

In spite of excellent passages, *The Bridge* cannot be considered a successful novel. The Canadian setting seemed to make the tale unreal; and it is doubtful if she would have ever succeeded as a novelist. Her legacy to Canada is a tiny sheaf of true poems. (p. 229)

> *Archibald MacMechan, "East and West," in his* Head-Waters of Canadian Literature, *McClelland and Stewart Publishers, 1924, pp. 187-229.**

LORNE PIERCE (essay date 1925)

[*Pierce was a Canadian biographer and literary historian. Editor-in-chief of the Ryerson Press from 1920 to 1960, he was an influential champion of Canadian literature. Under his direction, the "Makers of Canadian Literature" biography series and the Ryerson chapbooks were published, gaining recognition for many Canadian writers. In addition, Pierce established several awards for literature, including the Lorne Pierce Medal of the Royal Society of Canada, and made Canadian authors and subjects the focus of his own works. In the following excerpt from his critical biography of Pickthall, Pierce discusses the major themes of, and influences on, Pickthall's poetry.*]

Although entitled to take her place among the great women writers of the world, Marjorie Pickthall owes little to them. The objects of her adoration were to the end—Swinburne, Fiona MacLeod, Conrad, Scott, Dickens and Christina Rossetti. As for her contemporaries who boasted every conceit, and raucously descanted, saying that they had "lived," she had no use at all. She did not return often to the classics, possibly for the same reason that she took no active part in the established systems of politics, sociology or religion, namely, that her chief desire was for liberation from all abstract ideas,

systems and forms, and for the welling fulness of life. Classic forms to her were empty and must be rehabilitated, not with Homeric hexameters nor with the toga of Cicero, but with new themes, new loves and fresh beauty. It is interesting to note that she preferred rather the sublime figures of history and legend, for she believed that every fresh advance humanity has made has been through a liberation by the imagination, thought transfigured into passion and made operative in the will. The real problems of life can never be solved by philosophy, pedagogy or theology, but by the imagination alone. (pp. 155-56)

It is not necessary to make the claim for [Marjorie Pickthall] that she was profound, for profound she was not, in the sense in which Browning, Wordsworth, Ibsen or Goethe were. She believed that poetry or prose, no matter how realistic they both might be, should never be "merely horrid and never grubby." She was rather an Ariel, and remarkable chiefly for the elfin magic of her music, the wizardry of her fragile beauty, the sensitiveness of her spiritual insight, and for the intangible beauty and subtle meanings she discovered hidden in all things. Her mind was not concerned exclusively with the physical, nor was her thought entirely absorbed with the metaphysical. "Her consciousness of the unseen is the heart of all her poetry" [see MacMechan excerpt dated 1924]. . . . She possesses little of what one might call a system of thought, and yet her passionate pursuit of all the forms of loveliness took her straight to the heart of the love, melody and beauty that throbs at the centre of the universe. To report what she saw and heard and felt there, she employs a wealth of descriptive imagery and symbolism, of tonal and colour effects, rarely equalled in our language. (pp. 156-57)

Like Yeats and "A. E.," [Marjorie Pickthall] had studied art first, and, like Synge, she was a musician before she was a poet. Therefore, we may expect word pictures and verbal harmonies. This quest for the lovely objects of her adoration she made alone. There was a holy of holies where none might intrude; and there alone she beheld that beauty not revealed to the uninitiated, and listened to the voices in the unspeakable harmonies. (p. 157)

She was of a reflective turn of mind, and it became a passion with her to give her thought its most inevitable and beautiful utterance. She seems to have been ever in search of symbols, upon which to hang her beautiful creations. The great variety of these symbols have led some to look at certain groups of them and declare her to be now this and now that, but the fact is that she was either consciously or unconsciously not a systematic philosopher, sociologist, or theologian. She chose pictures and patterns corresponding to her moods, and around these built up colourful and toneful creations. The bond that held flesh and spirit together was always fragile, and possibly this developed in her an early other-worldliness. At any rate, she seems ever sensitive to the beauty about her, for the ultimate beauty to which it led her. (pp. 157-58)

W. B. Yeats has suggested that the artist reveals not his "self," but his "anti-self"—a complementary or contrary self. Meredith is a striking proof of this, for in actual life he was an egoist, but in his books he was always an anti-egoist. Synge, too, sorrowful, lonely and ill, loved brutal strength; and frail R. L. Stevenson, as every one knows, delighted in ruffians. From the beginning there had been fairies, of course, for Marjorie Pickthall was "of imagination all compact"; but into this ideal world there came death, terrible grief, then war and more loss, and finally failing health. To offset this she seems to have found relief in spiritual confession, for which she chose religious, mythical and aesthetic themes. On the other hand she found escape in romance, in creations of the imagination, which are occasionally sheer bravado and melodrama. There are deserts, jungles and interminable forests; terrible loneliness and heartbreaking, endless trails; savage enemies, malignant cold, blasting heat, and wasting sickness; but always overhead moved the pale, lone star, a consolation and a challenge.

Marjorie Pickthall never stopped to reason with death, war, ugliness, falsehood or disappointment; she simply made her escape from them, either into some sanctuary of loveliness, or else through the imagination into some thrilling adventure which took her to the Arctic circle, the tropical jungle, or climbing all but inaccessible mountain peaks. (pp. 158-59)

Believing as she did in the unending beauty of life, and the ineffable loveliness with which God clothed his magic universe, these vandals seemed to violate what was too precious to name save in symbols, as the Hebrew spoke of Jehovah. Her sadness is not the disillusionment of Anatole France, or the hopelessness of Synge, or the cynicism of Villon or Papini. It is due rather to the rift between poetry (i.e., beauty) and life, between the actual real and the ultimate ideal. (p. 159)

The genius of Marjorie Pickthall will ever remain associated with a rich and sumptuous attitude towards all that is loveliest and most beautiful. She went in search of these through many lands and literatures, and recorded each new discovery with a certainty, freshness and originality, entirely in keeping with a nature so rarely sensitive and sympathetic. What she lacked in intellectual precocity she made up in spontaneous sympathy and insight. Her heart was precocious, and its costly expenditure of itself wore her out. (p. 161)

We have already seen one aspect of the Oriental quality of Marjorie Pickthall's thought, revealed in that pervading tone of sadness and other-worldliness which marks most of her work. But more than that, in mood and phraseology, the sumptuousness of her expression, the sheer joy in overpowering beauty as it caresses every sense—in these she approached the Oriental attitude towards life and art. But she was too individualistic, too nonconformist to sink into any mere emotionalism. She disliked and feared the inclemency of the northern climate, and she was instinctively drawn to the warm, spiced airs of the south and east, but only in imagination did she ever inhabit those friendly zones.

Marjorie Pickthall was not an Oriental. She possessed the colour and richness of the East, as in **"The Little Sister of the Prophet," "The Worker in Sandalwood,"** etc., and could interpret the emotional and æsthetic experiences of the Orient with remarkable fidelity, but she had none of the languorous luxuriousness of the East. She was too wholesomely independent, too alert, too restlessly inquisitive to be completely Oriental. She urged her publisher to think of her as a Canadian. She was not essentially an imperialist or a nationalist, but she was of the very soil and spirit of Canada. Her ideas, her people, her landscapes, disguise them as she might with foreign word patterns, still remained eloquent of Canada. From her dreaming on the Orient her work acquired a kind of disciplined sensuousness, a heightened colour, warmth and softness, a certain indefinable magic of music, but in spirit and in idealism her work remained, to the last, Canadian. Canada was the scene of her first triumphs, and thither she returned, homesick, to die. (p. 162)

Allied to this Oriental quality in her work, which was chiefly associated with the adornment of her finest conceptions, and

therefore may be considered a part of the external aspect of her work, was her mysticism. If mysticism means a quiescent, voluptuous enjoyment of the emotional experiences, then she certainly was not a mystic. If it means a vital and intuitive experience of the heart of all reality, if it means a God-intoxicated passion by which one looks at the world from within outward, from the centre to the circumference, then she was a mystic. And just as the buoyancy of her own nature, her individualism, her kindly humour and her romantic impulse saved her from the dangers of Orientalism, so the practical and pressing emergencies of the hour saved her from unfruitful emotional experiences. Her melancholy must not be confused with mysticism. By temperament she could identify herself with the very heart of all goodness and beauty, enter into direct and loving contact with them; but she never remained in selfish enjoyment of these experiences. The struggle for existence and the discipline of suffering and sorrow—these tempered her mysticism; and in these, too, she found other inspiring experiences and the wonder of larger life. From them all she learned the secret of glorifying the commonplace.

Her mysticism will have to be taken seriously, however, for it is essentially the quality which distinguishes poets and seers from the rest of humanity. She instinctively fashioned her art around every symbol of the spirit. (pp. 163-64)

Marjorie Pickthall's wealth of symbolism might be treated at length, for it is an unerring index to the quality of her spirit, but an illustration or two must suffice. For example, one of her characters, Sol, stumbles on a fence in a snow-storm. "Because men's hands had made it, suddenly it became a human thing. He clung to it a moment as though it would warm him." Death and sleep become something else to her, "Death the lover and Sleep the friend." Her mind goes back to a carpenter shop in Nazareth.

> A woman sits there in the shadow of leaves,
> Watching her men at work, two carpenters,
> While mirrored angels move in her still eyes.

Folk tales were a constant delight to her. They fascinated her because she felt that in them she was somehow near to the elemental, secret source of things. It was not to be wondered at, therefore, that she should imitate folk lore; but she was too much alive to the present, too humanitarian, to lose herself in useless eccentricities.

This is the distinguishing feature of her mysticism; inwardly it sought the justification of her sensitive spirit; outwardly it desired verification in humanity. Every symbol, picture and image, however "woven and shaped of light" they might be, was erected over some living reality, and discovered its final vindication in the lives of men.

Some critics have discovered pagan elements in the writings of Marjorie Pickthall. In a sense this is true. She was a lover of nature in the widest sense. Her adoration of nature included all external beauty; it regarded the human body as the chalice of the divine spirit; it possessed the exuberance of youth, but it never divorced soul from body. It was a sanctified sensuousness. Her paganism was typically Canadian. It partook of the pioneer spirit, exulting in the primitive and elemental forms of life. It spoke of youth, the youth of a new country, with all its effervescence, superabundance and uncontrollable love of the romance of life in all its forms. It glorified power, immensity, the colossal outlines and natural grandeur of an unlimited demesne. It prided itself upon the strong, clear and courageous manhood of the north. It exulted in independence, in selfhood, in the widest freedom untrammelled by old conventionalities. Idealism there must be, but likewise realism, stark if necessary; the cold that leaps at one menacingly from the winter forests; and a livelihood that has to be wrung from Mother Earth, prodigal provider only to those who suffer for her treasures; and then, too, nature almost moral in its austere grandeur, something to be loved in its kindlier moments, but always something to be worshipped—eternal, unconquerable, serene.

But Marjorie Pickthall was not pure pagan. The beauty of Canada's natural grandeur awakes a constrained pantheism in many of her poets, as, for example, Bliss Carman's poem, "The Wall." C. G. D. Roberts was awakened to a cosmic consciousness in "Beyond the Tops of Time," and "In the Wide Awe and Wisdom of the Night." The same effect may be seen in Albert Durrant Watson's "Under the Open Sky" and "One Consciousness." But with Marjorie Pickthall nature acted as a kindly mentor who conducts her into the innermost secrets, into the abiding place, of the Most High. Call it paganism or whatever you please, its dominant note was simplicity and naturalness, a quiet certainty that all life is holy and fundamentally beautiful, and that among the lovely things of life the gods still break through and surprise. While some might be content with rapturous ecstasy over the forms of nature, and some might identify themselves with nature, and others still conceive themselves to transcend nature, she was saved from excess by her own unfailing common sense, and by her urbanity and cosmopolitanism. As we have tried to show, she adopted an attitude of eager expectancy towards life in general, listened to its many voices, and permitted herself to be initiated into any experience from which she might hope to derive fresh intimations of a higher beauty. Her contact with nature purified her spirit, cleansed it of all morbidity, and thus, while her contemporaries were wearing themselves out in inartistic disputations over sex, psycho-analysis, and kindred concerns, she was pursuing essential truth and beauty to their happiest and holiest hiding-place. (pp. 164-66)

Again it may be claimed that Marjorie Pickthall exhibits unmistakable Greek qualities in her poetry. Certainly her love of the beautiful and the highest truth entitle her to Attic lineage. But she was not a classicist. One might as well claim that she was Roman in her passion for perfection and symmetry, or Gothic in the certain substantial lightness and upward soaring of her religious meditations, or Keltic in the dream patterns of her purest idylls, as to claim her for a classicist. She exhibits no high, austere and sustained pursuit of beauty in and for itself. She speaks often of beauty, and frequently uses Greek names borrowed from antiquity, but her subjects deal with experiences of her immediate acquaintance. (pp. 166-67)

She followed beauty with breathlessness, but she pursued it through the clear Canadian atmosphere, where beauty never evaporates into subtleties, where it always makes actual and helpful contacts with the experiences of real human beings. (p. 167)

[Marjorie Pickthall] showed how beauty may become transcendental without becoming lost in the stars; ethical without sogginess; lovely without voluptuousness. Beauty for her never decorated or disguised homely facts. It reached in and was satisfying, sincere. It reached out and set a new star in the heavens, gave a new orientation to thought and life. It set a song in the heart and a goal to be attained.

Was Marjorie Pickthall Catholic in her religious belief? This claim has frequently been made for her, but we believe that

Holograph copy of Pickthall's poem "Ebb Tide."

the reason for this is the same as that which has been given for the appellations, mystic, pagan, classicist, etc., namely, her work has not been considered as a whole, and quite innocent symbols and fugitive fancies have been taken as part of a systematic belief.

She was a Christian of the most simple and unassuming type. It was but natural that since she was a cosmopolitan in her art she should be a catholic in her creed, but Roman or Greek she was not, neither was she strictly orthodox in her Anglo-Catholicism. She borrowed her symbolism from the Mass, just as she did from folk-lore, mythology, or anywhere else, and for the simple reason that she found something beautiful about them, and because she intended to use them in her own way.

While a member of the Protestant faith, she was not such in the old sense. Protestantism in its emphasis upon theological and social values did not interest her. Indeed she was too positive and independent to be a good Catholic, and too broadly catholic to be a good Protestant. The fact is that she was enamoured of the Gospel story, chiefly with its utter simplicity, quiet beauty and tender humanity. But there was no quietism, no miraculous, no organized system of belief about her religious experience. While she discovered new implications in old religious ideas and ceremonies, as for example **"The Bridegroom of Cana"** and **"Mons Angelorum,"** it was not their doctrinal or ecclesiastical associations which attracted her, but rather some suggestion of a higher beauty that touched her and loosed her art. She was constantly unorthodox as concerning the symbol of faith, and ever orthodox as affecting the heart.

Of the kin of Francis Thompson, Katherine Tynan and Christina Rossetti, she possessed none of their knowledge of Roman Catholic dogma, and also none of their veneration. She could not be said to have had any love for Catholic theology any more than for Catholic tradition. Her use of certain sacramental ideas was of the widest and freest nature. No Catholic will claim **"Pieter Marinus"** as the true idea of the doctrine of purgatory, or **"The Lamp of Poor Souls"** and **"Père Lalemant"** as reflecting the orthodox idea of the Mass and prayer for the dead. Certainly **"Child's Song at Christmas"** is as far from the doctrine of the incarnation as can be.

Then take any one of the religious poems. **"When the Moon is Last Awake," "Mary Shepherdess," "Mary Tired," "The Young Baptist," "St. Yves' Poor," "Bega," "In a Monastery Garden," "Christ in the Museum," "Sleep," "The Gardener's Boy,"** they are not any more Catholic than they are neo-pagan, mystical or Protestant. It is just as correct for one to talk of the Franciscan ardour of Mr. Sampson in *Little Hearts,* working out his philosophy of poverty, as it is to insist upon the principle of sacramentalism in **"Birds at Evening"** or **"Père Lalemant."** Marjorie Pickthall was not one, but many things. (pp. 167-69)

A definite faith, in that sense which the Church, Catholic or Protestant, demands, she had not, but she saw the one essential value at the heart of life so clearly that she pursued it through every avenue, maintaining an even balance between immanence and pantheism, using the symbols of paganism, mysticism, mythology, classicism and Christianity as they served her purpose, and all the while never losing her identity in the agony of individualism. In this connection one ought to read **"The Shepherd Boy"** and **"Shut-in."**

If one could sum up the main ideas of Marjorie Pickthall's religious faith possibly it would read something like this:

> I believe in the supremacy of thought.
> I believe in the immortality of beauty.
> I believe in the final triumph of goodness.
> I believe in the refining culture of suffering.
> I believe in the saviourhood of Love.

(pp. 169-70)

At any rate she was before all else Christian. She was fascinated by the Christ. Those things which she saw in Him she felt in herself. He was very man of very man and never at any time a fetish. His triumphant faith in His own ideals; His ability to discover the beautiful in the heart of things unwholesome and ugly; His sweetness, dignity, truthfulness and unfailing kindness; His gentleness in the face of wrong, courage in the midst of danger, serenity in sorrow and his indomitable independence, these were dear to her own heart. It were safer to say that Marjorie Pickthall grew up in orthodox Protestant Christianity, but found the Christ for herself. Every fresh beauty led her back to Him by a new way, every return sent her on other quests, until if Christianity can speak a universal language much of it will be found in her poetry. Possibly we shall not err if we call her simply a Christian *wandervogel.* (p. 170)

Marjorie Pickthall is a constant challenge to Canadian literature. She is a challenge to bad artists dealing in cheap sentimentality, in muttering compromise and bad taste, and to all those who stress commonplace and subsidiary things, who mistake luxury for beauty, "gripping romance" for the strength and reality of an experimental search for the absolute, and who imagine that genius will excuse them from the agonizing pains of finished craftsmanship. (p. 197)

Dr. A. C. Bradley, in his Oxford inaugural lecture, "Poetry for Poetry's Sake," emphasized the fact that the ultimate worth of a poem does not consist in any or all of its sounds, forms, images, thoughts or emotions, but that it must be judged from within as "a satisfying imaginative experience." A great poem achieves this quite apart from any contribution it may make to religion, sociology, botany, astronomy or government. A poem must have both substance and form fused in one transcending æsthetic experience.

In Marjorie Pickthall we have an excellent illustration of this. The meaning and the sound are one. "There is a resonant meaning, or a meaning resonance." Her ideas are neither profound nor startlingly original; her verse forms are those endorsed by good usage, and are handled with restrained freedom, but the total effect of her poetic expression lifts us into a different kind of existence.

Many of her poems are not orderly developments of an idea, but rather wisps of melody, scattered phrases, intriguing images and subtle symbols, appearing, as in **"The Immortal,"** beautifully inchoate. The total effect, however, seems to beckon away beyond itself, or rather to expand into something boundless which is only focused in it, something also which we feel would satisfy not only the imagination but the whole of us. . . . (pp. 198-200)

The chief character of this imaginative experience through which Marjorie Pickthall leads us is distinctly and uniquely beautiful. Sheer beauty—this is the centre and circumference of her work. On every page the marvellous blending of beautiful images and haunting cadences, "tantalize us to their own inaccessible homes," possessing an unusually rich capacity for sensuous experience and an equally rich accumulation of sensuous perceptions. . . .

The quality of her beauty is timeless. The total effect is a purifying and ennobling of the whole nature, and yet this is not produced by any doctrinal system of ideas, nor by reasoning of any kind, but whatever it is, it is produced through the imagination alone, an imaginative experience through which we are identified with the beautiful, which is not only felicitous but also loving and true. Through this lies her real interpretation of life. She, too, like Keats, "had loved the principle of beauty in all things," which, in a world of decay and disillusionment, defies death and constitutes the one living reality. (p. 200)

> *Lorne Pierce, in his* Marjorie Pickthall: A Book of Remembrance, *The Ryerson Press, 1925, 217 p.*

E. J. PRATT   (essay date 1933)

[*Pratt is considered a major figure in modern Canadian poetry. While his earliest poems overtly display his training as a philosopher and, in Pratt's own words, are "full of theories and reflections of theories about life," he soon developed the simple, concrete, and vigorous manner characteristic of his best works. Pratt has been especially praised for his skill as a narrative poet in such works as* Brébeuf and His Brethren *(1940) and* Towards the Last Spike *(1952), which are epic works based on events in Canadian history. As in these narrative poems, Pratt's other works often return to subjects that allow him to explore the strengths and weaknesses of individuals who are struggling against the*

*forces of nature and society. In the following excerpt, Pratt offers
a general discussion of Pickthall's work.]*

It is not difficult to understand the impression which the work of Marjorie Pickthall made upon the Canadian public when her first volume, *The Drift of Pinions,* appeared in 1913. The poetic taste, of the kind which would appreciate her quality, had been greatly stimulated by two factors—the Celtic Renaissance, and the Pre-Raphaelite influence energized for a short period by the immense vogue of Francis Thompson. The library counters were busy dispensing *The Countess Cathleen, Deirdre of The Sorrows, The Blessed Damosel, The Shepherdess of Sleep,* and *The Hound of Heaven.* The New Poetry, whether of the Imagists like Amy Lowell, Ezra Pound, and H. D., or of the Realists as represented by the Georgian Anthologies, had effected little, if any, infiltration, while the industrial blasts from Chicago, even granted they were heard, were repudiated as outside the province of art.

That Miss Pickthall had mastered the prevailing styles was clear from an examination of both the form and content of her work. The title of the first volume was taken from *In No Strange Land* of Thompson, and the influence of this poet was seen not only in her fondness for religious themes, but in the "mystical approach," and in the sumptuous imagery with which she invested and sometimes over-apparelled the idea. The Celtic spell was upon her in the definite Yeatsian rhymes and in her mythopoeic tendencies, though she turned her face to Palestine rather than to Galway for her poetic lore.

There are two strands discernible in the texture of her verse on the metrical side—the Swinburnian prosody combined with the earlier and decorative Yeats, this second feature being a phase which the Irish poet later abandoned in theory and practice. The chorus in Atalanta—the "hounds of Spring," and "the lisp of leaves and rattle of rain"—echoes in the excessive alliteration and assonance, in the deluge of liquids and sibilants, though of course the vast tonal effects of Swinburne were impossible because of the nature of Miss Pickthall's briefer compositions. The Yeats influence was a somewhat dangerous one, though quite intelligible in a young writer working under the glow of the contagion. . . . As Miss Pickthall's first published material consisted of poems whose writing covered a term of many years without conscious reference to their integration in a printed volume, these discrepancies stand out the more prominently. Mannerisms strike the eye on every second page. Multitudes of moths flutter through the poems. The horns of elfland are blowing persistently, if faintly. Phrases of the lush variety are recurrent: "Little lilting linnets; elfin trills; honeying pipes of pearl; honeyed dark; moth-winged winds of sleep." The alliterative structures, though beautiful taken separately, cloy when they are pyramided. Examples of such "verbal felicity" are **"Bega"** and **"Armorel."** This latter poem Yeats, twenty years ago, described as his favourite in the collection. Nevertheless, the value of these and kindred compositions resides more in the mechanics of the movement than in the emotional rendering of the ideas.

It is not in this type of verse where Miss Pickthall does her best work. It is rather when she forgets Swinburne and leaves to other writers the task of attending to the flight of wild swans over the Irish loughs that she takes on significance. And poems like **"The Mother in Egypt,"** **"The Shepherd Boy,"** **"The Lamp of Poor Souls"** started her reputation for the expression and control of tender moods, which no poet in Canada has surpassed. Certainly, no one has succeeded so well in exploring the sources of pathos and at the same time avoiding the slough

of sentimentality. Whether it is the death of a bird or the death of a child, it is the utter simplicity of the speech which conveys the poignancy—a simplicity which unerringly finds its appropriate melodic setting. Strung to her own measures, her child themes have the authenticity of folk-songs, as rooted in natural feeling as the best poems of Moira O'Neil, Katherine Tynan, or Charlotte Mew.

In 1919 she achieved a notable success in *The Wood-Carver's Wife,* a one-act play based upon a French-Canadian scene. . . . This play, the finest single accomplishment of her life, and hailed by so many critics as the one outstanding drama of Canada, may be taken as the best approach to the evaluation of her gifts. It was her own favourite and she lavished her resources on it. It exhibits her excellences and her limitations. As poetic drama, with the tonal climaxes of its blank verse sections, with its lovely fashioned phrases and the general harmony of the mood, it secured unstinted praise. And it might be unjust to demand qualities precluded by the form. Still, the impression left is that it is ideas rather than persons that are on the stage. It is the Andrea del Sarto conception presented again as an artistic thesis, but the dialogue, beautiful as it is, sacrifices dramatic tang and intimate characterization—always the peril of the mode unless superbly executed. Local colour has vanished. The scene, despite the references to familiar fauna and flora, might have been placed in Fiesole as in Quebec. . . . (pp. 334-35)

The permanent value of [Miss Pickthall's] prose work consists in her sympathetic portrayal of child life and in the poetry of her nature descriptions. She can people the air with tanagers and blue-bills, etch shadows under poplars and birches, make kingfishers dive through a circle of lily-pads till the splash is audible, describe brown snakes crawling with the "rustle of dry leaves," and unfold over pages at a stretch a panorama surpassed in richness of colour only by a Hudson or a Conrad. What she lacked was the broad psychological interpretation. Desirous of describing human struggle on wide areas, she never quite realized the oscillating crises. Nature was too close at hand with her medicinal plants to allow wounds to bleed sufficiently. And her Celtic love of symbolism was continually blurring our vision of the protagonists by intercepting barriers not less tantalizing because composed of ivory or sandalwood. The unlovely phases of life were repellent to her. Her expressed dislike of Ibsen and his school, the absence of any analysis of life on the side of its civilized contradictions, her complete immunity to cynical and satirical moods reveal a temperament which, common enough only twenty-five years ago, seems as far removed from contemporary psychology as the mental horizon of Galen would be from the thought of experimentation on the ductless glands. (p. 335)

*E. J. Pratt, "Marjorie Pickthall," in The Canadian
Forum, Vol. XIII, No. 153, June, 1933, pp. 334-35.*

W. E. COLLIN   (essay date 1936)

*[Collin is a Canadian critic, biographer, and poet. His The White
Savannahs is the first book-length critical study of English-Canadian
literature and remains one of the most important works on this
subject. In writing his survey of Canadian poets, Collin took a
highly subjective, rather than analytic, approach to critical discussion of an author's works. As Germaine Warkentin explains:
"The White Savannahs emerges from a French tradition in which
the critic aims to identify and reveal, in an iridescent and subjective prose, the central motifs of a writer's art." Challenging
the conventional academic methods of criticism, Collin himself*

wrote: "What guarantee have we that analysis and comparison will yield the truth of poetry? Is poetry a matter of literary elements, formal beauty, influence, and reputations? Are these not things imposed from without by the contemplating critic?" In the following excerpt from The White Savannahs, *Collins discusses the chief traits of Pickthall's poetry and drama.*]

Nature and fortune predisposed [Marjorie Pickthall] to visionariness. She was a very shy girl. Had she been born a decade or so later when hardly any form of activity was regarded as the exclusive preserve of the male she might have lost some of her reserve. But as it was, the life of adventure for which she yearned all her days was denied her. (p. 45)

She felt like a spirit in a tower on the brink of a tall cliff listening perpetually "to the soft winds full of voices, night and day, but she cannot follow, for she has no wings."

It was wanderers like Kipling and Stevenson, and Celts like Yeats and Macleod, who sang to her "the song of the calling voices, the mystery of the road, the vision behind the unattained hill, the star of all quests that lights the following feet." The loneliness which gnawed silently into her heart is epitomized in Macleod's line, which she copied in her notebook: "My heart is a lonely hunter that hunts on a lonely hill"—while her body was shut in. She loved the *Song of Songs* not only, we may divine, for its poetic beauty but, as other poets and mystics have loved it, because it passionately chanted her most secret and insatiable hunger. Whatever permanent and perhaps unsatisfactory results that hunger may have had in other ways, it found some relief by passing out of her heart into her work in the form of emotional symbols.

Her shyness of the world, her fear of the full light of day find perfect expression in a poem which she wrote at seventeen: "**Dawn.**" Each of the stanzas of nine and eleven lines begins with a group of three lines of five feet and continues with lines of three and five feet as though she had deliberately fashioned her poem on the principles laid down in Verlaine's "Art poétique." It is a miracle of rhythmic feeling, whispering melody and intangible nuances: "opals, cobweb-strung," sea-pearls veiled in "pearlier mist," "shadows lingering dim," "half-seen beauties," "airy tremors." It is not a picture that Lampman or any human eye would see. It is not visible; it is emotion clinging to trembling things; it is the poem of trembling adolescent femininity. Quietly as a faun she comes to the forest pool "where fragrant lilies are," and where the world is "hushed, as if the miracle of morn were trembling in its dream." Every line is softened by the muted emotion in her voice exulting in the birth of beauty, tremulously clinging to the happiness she fears is doomed, pleading: O keep . . . keep all things hushed in promise "too sweet to be fulfilled." (pp. 45-7)

The language of *Solomon's Song* is her native air; her poems are, as it were, ozonized by all that Oriental and Jacobite lyricism: some owe their life to it.

At this time she is about to explore the fascinating domain of folklore which "has always been very much to her taste." "Shortly," she writes in 1904, "I expect to go in for a course of Norse, Irish and American folklore." Her reading of Indian legends served as a basis for the stories she wrote for *The Globe* in 1905 and 1907.

She saw the old Celtic world through Yeats and Macleod as, at a later date, about 1911, she saw the Norse sagas in the "strange, gay, stiff word-embroideries" of William Morris.

Yeats' shorter poems are "simply lovely." Some of her own lyrics at this time ("**Wanderlied,**" "**My Father He Was a Fisherman,**" "**Duna**") are flavoured with a wistful Irish idiom. "**Armorel**" is "Mr. Yeats' favourite." No wonder. It is so like his "Stolen Child." There is moonlight in it and bats, and elfin voices, and "Gates o' dream are held ajar." There is a garden in it, and Mary-lilies, and a white moth. The Celtic call is there at its loudest. "**The Immortal,**" composed of the melancholy last oozings of pretty things that pass away yet perpetuate "that immortal which we call Beauty," is the Celtic, twilight counterpart to "**Dawn.**" "**Kerry**" deals with purely Celtic emotions which she has not deeply felt; yet the music is as sweet as Yeats', and sweeter than Masefield's "Sorrow of Mydath."

Since Masefield's first sea-ballads are still steeped in the music of Yeats, Marjorie Pickthall easily slipped into Masefield who, she writes, "always seems nearer to me as a writer than anyone else." He who wrote "D'Avalos' Prayer," "The Dead Knight," "A Wanderer's Song" and "Vagabond" would recognize his own vintage in "**Pieter Marinus,**" "**The Tramper's Grave,**" "**The Rover**" and "**Ebb-Tide**"; even after the piquancy has been dulled by the addition of elfin voices and the special word "fain."

Compared to Masefield's genuine pictures of the sea, the sea as Dauber would paint it, Miss Pickthall's might be hung in a nursery. Here are some:

> The tides go up and the tides go down.
>
> In vain the long-ridged swell shall raise the
> keel.
>
> No more our prow shall leap above the foam.
>
> Gods! how the keel cut seaward through the
> blue
> When the long galley raced the roving stars!
>
> Out of the winds' and the waves' riot,
> Out of the loud foam.

There is no storm at sea in her pictures; no picture of men in ships battling with mountainous waves, no glory of battle, no cry of conquest, but soft, unexciting pictures, and the old trick of wringing the sentiment out of "last" and "no more." But the swing of the old sea-chanties is there, and the interior rhymes and endings of an old Irish song:

> And a dawn will *break* when my soul shall *wake*
> and call from the isles to me—
> "Come gather me *up* like a silver *cup* from the
> heart of the swaying sea,
> Like wave-washed *gold* from a wreck of *old,*
> and hide me safe in your breast."

The call from the isles or to the isles of the west is mournful and clear:

> No more the winds shall call us to the west.
>
> Drowned like a shell in the tides that swell
> by the dim sweet isles o' the west.
>
> O, there I'd lie and watch the sails go shining
> to the west.

Miss Pickthall chose mariners, as she chose certain landsmen, not to picture the sea, certainly not to picture it buffeting men and ships, but to show how strongly man is attached to nature.

All her heroes are bound to wild nature by a spell. They are like that wild swan which, as he passed the sea witch's tower,

> Was laggard through her loveliness.

Ole Varenne [in **"The Inevitable Hour"**] had no kin but the trees and the wild birds. He carried with him "the glamour of wandering, the gipsy charm that draws the heart of youth." To the author, he was one of those "wild swans calling up the spring."

The scene shifts, names change, but the symbol of the "wild swans" remains almost constant, linking up her emotional being with the wild life of Canada. It is a definitely Canadian symbol, as in Brittany the wild duck. The "call" is perhaps most diffused in Macleod.

> When the day darkens,
> When dusk grows light,
> When the dew is falling,
>   When silence dreams . . .
> I hear a wind
> Calling, calling,
> By day and by night.

is representative of his lullabies.

The Celt does not describe nature in "the faithful way," as Matthew Arnold puts it, not as Lampman describes it. He looks at it with ecstasy. "(Corona) stared into the silver moonlight, doubtful a little, a little afraid." So Miss Pickthall wrote in 1910. "A while ago she had known of nothing there but the frost-mist and the little wind of the high pasture, which even in summer kept the cows cool. Now it seemed she saw wings, shadowy faces, white feet that were never still." That is Celtic vision. That is the way Macleod looks at the world. Once she heard Macleod, she was in the Isles. What she saw there, saw with his eyes, hallucinated eyes, she confided to readers of [her monthly column] "The Shadow on the Dial":

> People said that Evan was fey, and that when he went to drink at a pool *a face* looked over his shoulder *that no other christened soul could see.* "And that is a very true thing," said little Evan, "for it is *white feet among the foam* and *a following shadow* in the thick of the heather, and *the eyes of beauty* in the stars at night, and *the lips of her* in the curve of a flower."

Celtic writers are hyper-romantic, they dissociate attributes and qualities from the objects to which they belong and look upon them as persons—in order to create mystery. White feet, a face, eyes, lips are not flotsam, they are mermaids. Macleod commits the arch-atrocity when he says "it is Loveliness I seek, not lovely things"; as though Loveliness were a girl that one could find and pick up in one's arms. But no; she is a *white vision,* a *haunting voice,* or that *Dim face of Beauty haunting all the world.* (pp. 47-53)

Macleod more especially sought to express the conflict between natural and spiritual religion, to give impassioned utterance to "our deep primeval longing for earth-kinship with every life in Nature" in revolt against the Christian ethic of renunciation. Marjorie Pickthall may have had Macleod in mind when she wrote of those discontented souls who "fled to the caverns of the hills and the dark hearthstones of an older race." She who suffered abrasions from an ill-fitting and imposed ethic was on the side of those discontented souls. Had she not created a little rebel of a Geronimo? Had she not felt that "Amun is

gentle and Hathor the mother is mild;" that the Lord of Israel's judgment against the gods of Egypt was harsh and cruel? Had she not seen Moses on Pisgah, after Joshua had relieved him of the burden of the Lord, looking back to his boyhood days in Egypt and thinking

> on old forgotten things—
> A song within the temple-court, to her,
> Isis, the Lady of Love?

When she turned to the Western World, there was much in the circumstances attending the Christianizing of Europe to remind her of Israel's contact with the gods of Egypt. If the religion of the Celts was "the ancient religion of the world, the ancient worship of nature and that troubled ecstacy before her," then Marjorie Pickthall wanted nothing with fashionable gods. "Thou hast conquered, O pale Galilean." But her Joachim and Jasper are there to testify how difficult a thing it is to stifle the call in a young pagan's heart. Those lads may have seen some coracles coming ashore on Iona and, wide-eyed and open-mouthed, watched Colomba and his monks, even helped them to build their church and small wattled huts about a green court. For it was in surroundings such as these that Joachim and Jasper listened to Christ's missionaries and changed their names and became brothers in the monastery.

> Over the long salt ridges
> And the gold sea-poppies between,
> They builded them wild-briar hedges,
> A church and a cloistered green.
> And when they were done with their praises,
> And the tides on the Fore beat slow,
> Under the white cliff daisies
> They laid them down in a row.
>
> Porphyry, Paul, and Peter,
> Jasper, and Joachim,—
> Was the psaltery music sweeter
> Than the throat of the thrush to him?

(pp. 56-8)

And in dreams the incessant calling monastic discipline could not stop!

> I can hear the wild swan calling
> From the marshes broad and dim,
> "Follow, follow, Joachim."

He is brother to that other cloistered gipsy, Jasper, who sings:

> follow, O follow the white spring home.

How many of Macleod's people have "the gloom" upon them? One often had "the light in his eyes . . . it was the sea he was dreaming of." He tells of a "man who went (from Iona) to the mainland, but could not see to plough, because the brown fallows became waves that splashed noisily about him. The same man went to Canada, and got work in a great warehouse; but among the bales of merchandise he heard the singular note of the sandpiper, and every hour the sea-fowl confused him with their crying." The same kinship with nature is the theme of Marjorie Pickthall's **"Forest Born"** and **"The Woodsman in the Foundry."**

Anatole France took great delight in tormenting religious ascetics by hallucinations of that sort. His monks have enough of the old Adam and the old pagan religion in their blood to get into ludicrous situations, exquisitely amusing to Gauls and Saxons alike. The Celt, on the other hand, is serious; he is a rebel and he is sad. Macleod's "Cathal of the Woods," when he falls in love with the pagan girl, Ardanna, spurns the very hymns that Colomba had taught him. "They are idle, foolish songs . . . It is a madness, all that. See, it is gone; it is beneath my feet. I am a man now."

Perhaps it was through Macleod, who wrote on Villemarqué's *Barsas Breiz* (Ballads of Brittany), that Marjorie Pickthall was led to read Tom Taylor's translation (1865). Some of her prettiest names are in that book, Breton and French names: Jannedik (little Jean), Jeffik (little Jeff), Mathieu, Franch, Bran, Marchaid. As she brooded on the Golden Legend of Saint Yves of Brittany, those pretty names became dramatis personæ, "suffretous and poor," in the old English of William Caxton, "that ran to him from all sides, followed him, for all that he had was ready to their behoof as their own," even to God's need, whom he recognized in the form or likeness of a poor man holding out his hands towards the steaming soup bowl. But **"St. Yves' Poor"** bears the unmistakable marks of her own art: the familiar dove, heron, curlew, wild swan, the picturesque detail, the rhythmic cadences of Old Testament poetry, the trance in which is revealed a resplendent vision of Christ's face.

> A thin, white blaze of wings, a face of flame

are images that Macleod uses to describe rapt vision. The difference is that this "face of flame" is Christ's face—which it never is in Macleod. True, in *The Wayfarer* and *The Fisher of Men* he tells how Christ comes among the islanders in the guise of a strange visitor, "ill-clad and weary, pale, too, with dreaming eyes," who "hath not where to lay his head." But Christ is still an outland god even in those stories, which are quite exceptional in Macleod's work. Much of the beauty of Celtic legend derives from the blending of Christianity with pagan nature-worship but Macleod, wholly dazzled by the glamour of the nature-worship, ignores the other. It is here, then, that Marjorie Pickthall leaves him. She is dazzled by that "face of flame," which is Christ's face.

The Celtic call, as Macleod apprehends it, is a call to Beauty. An old man of the Isles, standing looking seaward with his bonnet in his hand, said to him: "Every morning like this I take my hat off to the beauty of the world." And Marjorie Pickthall's **"Prophet"** has the "gloom" upon him, his head is "all misty with dreams, and his eyes on fire." Looking out over the valley he sees nature ecstatically, but—here he differs from the Celt—he sees it as "the strength and beauty of God out-rolled in a fiery screed." He hardly remembers that there are common duties to be done: cattle to be fed and watered. The secret of his rapture and his apparent indifference to his sister's affectionate services is that he is a man who is already dead to the world. (pp. 58-62)

Concurrently with the poems we have been considering, Marjorie Pickthall was producing stories at a rapid rate. In the wake of her master-adventurers she concocted stories of men's adventures in regions more or less remote from prosaic Toronto; derivatives of a yearning to slip the noose of the conventions and set her sails for "those fair countries far away" where she could "stir things up *fine*."

Not so far away were French Canada and the Canadian Northland, but she had a magic carpet on which she could go in search of rubber and strange Mexican gods, hover around a Japanese garden, or follow the mirage across the deserts of the East and South.

Some of her stories are marred by a too liberal dose of the sensational, some by meretricious sentiment, some again are perfect. The most significant of them are those in which love is calling. The dramatic force in stories of the type of **"The Voice and the Shadow," "The Interlude," "The Lost Orchard"** and **"The Seventh Dream"** is love's call to happiness. Wild nature, woods or desert symbolize happiness; the accompanying mirage or dream occasion disillusionment; a gun or sword (an arrow in *The Wood-Carver's Wife*) represent the ever-present menace of death to love. (pp. 68-9)

[*The Wood-Carver's Wife*] is a drama which aspires to poetry and it has the shortcomings of a hybrid form. We are not persuaded that Jean talked like that; that language is Marjorie Pickthall's. Although she chose for her scene a picturesque craft which flourished, and still flourishes, in Quebec, the dramatic interest is independent of the craft: it results from the clash of two passions. A wood-carver has willed to make his wood incarnate with a perfect resemblance of a human form. The ideal Mary in its perfect expression is there set up before his mind's eye. In front of him is his wife and model, Dorette, who is in love with a young nobleman and has no interest in the carving. But Jean's artistic conscience makes everything bend before its ideal.

> "You are hard,"

Dorette reproaches him.

> "You love your cold woods more than loveliness
> Of look and touch."

And that artistic conscience retorts with the implication: "Yes, but imagine yourself elevated to a shrine prepared for you in the Church!"

> "They'll see you there between the candle flames
> A hundred years. The lads will worship you
> And maids with innocent eyes will wonder at you.
> Your beauty will lift many souls to God."

> "They will hail you mystic rose,
> The tower of ivory, the golden house,
> Sea-star and vase of honour."

So he taunts and martyrs Dorette till he has her sitting with her dead lover's sword across her knees looking down upon it with eyes "the barren houses of despair," like those of Mary looking down upon the dead Christ. Under his hand the cedar wood, after the ultimate gashes of his tools, becomes the ideal reality. And if Jean, the perfect craftsman, is a symbol, so are they all, all symbols. Dorette has no desire to be a wooden Madonna in a shrine. She craves a human love and . . . she has heard love's call to the forest. . . . But we are not surprised that she is afraid of the shadows in the forest, afraid of Shagonas' knife, afraid of the thought of blood. They are Aphrodite's intuitions that her Adonis will be slain in the forest, and that those white flowers will change to red anemones.

This piece of work stood high in her estimation because it is the drama of her own soul. The time-distance from the subjects is sufficient to permit her to lend them her own idiom, which is exquisitely imaged; but since they all speak as poets, the author could not be satisfied with them as real persons. (pp. 73-5)

To hold it down to matter-of-fact human reality was an almost impossible achievement for an artist of her genius, which revolted against the sovereignty of present fact and reacted to stories of "old, unhappy, far-off things."

She looked at nature, then at her own heart. Her troubled ecstacy before nature passed into the ecstacy of passion and so into the drama of frustrated love. In the sense that it bodies forth those emotions, her poetry is pure experience. For those were the emotions that wore her heart. They were her reality. Since *The Song of Solomon* is an ecstatic yearning for love as for earth's fragrant spices and most luscious fruits, it is not strange that her poetry constantly trembles with the accents of that most familiar and unexcelled love-song. Yet all that possessed her senses and mind, things in nature and what she absorbed by reading, was so thoroughly assimilated into her emotional and imaginative experience that when it passed out into her poetry it was dissociated from all legend; it was warmed and tinted when it left her pen, for her feminine heart had yearned over it and thrown around it the festoons of a poet's symbolism. Whence the delight and the pathos which we feel in her work. The power thus to transmute emotion into poetic reality was her great gift. Her imagination was as keen as her physical vision, but it could only be nourished by a great variety of experience. She possessed exquisite artistic sensibility. Had she been gifted with as resourceful a social instinct her fame and fortune would have been immense. (pp. 78-9)

> *W. E. Collin, in a chapter in his* The White Savannahs, *1936. Reprint by University of Toronto Press, 1975, pp. 43-79.*

E. K. BROWN (essay date 1944)

[*Brown was a Canadian critic and educator. Chief among his works is the critical survey* On Canadian Poetry, *in which Brown traces the development of Canadian poetry from its pre-confederation era to the notable achievements of its three major figures, Archibald Lampman, Duncan Campbell Scott, and E. J. Pratt. In the following excerpt from that survey, Brown assesses Pickthall's poetry.*]

More than any other Canadian poet of this century [Marjorie Pickthall] was the object of a cult: the kind of comment she evoked is exemplified in Professor Broadus's claim: "The untimely death of Marjorie Pickthall (April 19, 1922) deprived Canadian literature of its purest poet. The two slender volumes, *The Drift of Pinions* and *The Lamp of Poor Souls,* contain nothing that will place her among 'the few, the immortal names,' but they do reveal a singing voice and a delicate perception of beauty unparalleled in contemporary Canadian poetry." Unacademic critics boldly placed her among the few, the immortal names. It is now clear that the praise she received was exuberant. Her perception of beauty has not the clarity which is so constant a trait of Lampman and its range is slighter than Roberts's or Duncan Campbell Scott's. It is almost purely Celtic, and indeed the essential influence pervading her work, as Mr. W. E. Collin has shown abundantly [see excerpt dated 1936], is that of the Irish poetry of the 'nineties. She likes to write of:

> The cloud-white thorn and the white cloud
> blowing together

or

> a wild swan calling
> From the marshes broad and dim

Of her, as of Cameron, it must be conceded that where there is deviation from the main stream of Canadian poetry, it is not because of originality, but because of closer contact with movements in other countries. Still, Canada was . . . the country of her imagination, the setting which now and then does enable her to make her pictures clear and her feelings sharp and strong.

It is not an accident that the work which is most remembered, the poetic play called *The Wood-Carver's Wife,* has a Canadian setting. More moving than this play, which is shot through with misty Celtic symbolism weakening to its dramatic force and pictorial sharpness, are a few pieces in which Miss Pickthall deals more simply and forcefully with Canadian history and legend. There is, for example, **"On Lac Sainte Irénée,"** where despite a softish beginning,

> On Lac Sainte Irénée the morn
> Lay rimmed with pine and roped with mist

the theme of an Indian fleeing from justice is handled with intensity, the picture of nature and the very rhythm co-operating to strengthen the effect, as in such a stanza as this:

> On Lac Sainte Irénée the moose
> Broke from his balsams, breathing hot.
> The bittern and the great wild goose
> Fled south before the sudden shot.
> One fled with them like a hunted soul,
> And followed ever
> By ford and river
> The little canoe of the lake patrol.

The virtue of that last line, which may seem a little pat, and even melodramatic, can be appreciated when the poem is read as a whole: with slight variation it ends each stanza. (pp. 64-5)

After the Celtic influence, the biblical is next in strength. She is bewitched by the biblical parallelisms, and by the biblical imagery melting into music. Biblical themes attract her again and again; and she treats them with a rich orientalism and a never-failing delight in what is very much of the past. All her poetry, except a few brief lyrics, is poetry of the past: the immediate present she was quite helpless to apprehend in its poetic significance. Even when the war forced itself upon her consciousness and she wrote a once famous sonnet, **"Canada to England,"** she began by hailing

> Great names of thy great captains gone before

and ended by evoking

>   the invulnerable ghosts
> Of all past greatnesses.

When she thought of what the war was fought to preserve she symbolized what she valued by a daffodil. When she thought of what soldiers in German prisons were deprived of, she gathered together images of birds and squirrels, stars and the new moon, trees, the aroma of burning leaves and of the rich earth, and the play of the sun on English beeches. When she was faced with the need to sum up civilization, she summed up nature; for her there was nothing else. And the nature she loved was nature in her exquisite little details.

Naturism could go no farther. Marjorie Pickthall had worked the last and smallest lode. It was time for a change. (pp. 66-7)

> *E. K. Brown, "The Development of Poetry in Canada," in his* On Canadian Poetry, *revised edition, 1944. Reprint by The Tecumseh Press, 1977, pp. 28-87.**

DESMOND PACEY (essay date 1952)

[*Pacey is a Canadian critic, short story writer, and educator. He is best known as the author of* Creative Writing in Canada: A Short History of English-Canadian Literature, *a pioneering critical survey of Canadian literature since 1750. In the following excerpt from that work, Pacey offers an appraisal of Pickthall's poetry and drama.*]

Miss Pickthall, in spite of her obvious limitations, was a craftsman sincerely devoted to her calling. Her work is slight in extent and shallow in thought and emotion, but it has a delicate lyricism and an easy grace. She was—like many Canadians—a highly derivative poet, whose work is full of echoes of the pre-Raphaelites and of the poets of the Irish Renaissance, but she at least chose serious models and studied them assiduously. And in her best work she achieves a vision which, if never very penetrating, is clear and individual.

It is not surprising that she should have leaned so heavily upon other writers, for Marjorie Pickthall had little direct experience of life upon which to draw. Always a delicate girl, she was brought up in a sheltered home in Toronto, educated at a fashionable school for young ladies (the Bishop Strachan School), worked in the Victoria College Library, spent the war years in England, and died at the age of thirty-nine in Vancouver. Knowing little of the world of men and affairs, she was compelled to draw her inspiration from books, and about all her work there is a bookish, indoor atmosphere.

Her first book, *The Drift of Pinions* . . . , contains almost all her best poetry. In its ninety-four pages are forty-three poems, including such well-known ones as "**The Bridegroom of Cana,**" "**The Little Sister of the Prophet,**" "**Père Lalemant,**" "**Duna**" and "**Saxon Epitaph.**" As this list of titles suggests, most of her poems are set in remote times and places, in the Palestine of biblical days or the Canada of the early Jesuit missionaries. Only in her nature lyrics does she show any awareness of the immediate world about her, and in them she treats this world in such a romantic fashion that it is almost unrecognizable. Here is one of her nature lyrics which, in its delicate impressionism, its unreal atmosphere, its lush diction, and its incantatory rhythms is typical of her work of this sort.

> Wind-silvered willows hedge the stream,
> And all within is hushed and cool.
> The water, in an endless dream,
> Goes sliding down from pool to pool
> And every pool a sapphire is
> From shadowy deep to sunlit edge,
> Ribboned around with irises
> And cleft with emerald spears of sedge.
>
> O, every morning the winds are stilled,
> The sunlight falls in amber bars.
> O, every night the pools are filled
> With brede of shaken stars.
> O, every morn the sparrow flings
> His elfin thrills athwart the hush,
> And here unseen at eve there sings
> One crystal-throated hermit thrush.

"**Dream River**"

There are so many poems of this type that they become monotonous. Always the same dreamy, unreal atmosphere is evoked, always the same tremulous note struck, always the same sad-sweet mood established. Her diction in particular is monotonous. She has certain words which she uses over and over again—silver, dream, gold, shadowy, hushed, fairy, sweet—

and they are all words of the same rich, lush, romantic quality. One word especially she loves, and in it we can see all her weaknesses brought to a focus—the word "little". Everything in Marjorie Pickthall's vision is "little"—which means that it is made the object of sentimental pathos, reduced to the dimensions of a fairy-tale.

The only variety in the volume is provided by the narrative poems, which are usually cast in the form of dramatic monologues à la Browning. They differ sharply from Browning's monologues, however, in that there is no effort to attain psychological complexity or subtlety. They seek, like her lyrics, rather to evoke a mood of longing, regret, or gentle sadness. They have not the strength or substance of great poetry, but they have occasional haunting lines and images:

> Thy lips are bright as the edge of a sword . . .
>
> The shaft of the dawn strikes clear and sharp. . . .
>
> Like lotus petals adrift on the swing of the tide. . . .

The best of the poems, undoubtedly, is "**The Bridegroom of Cana.**" The setting of the poem is vague and shadowy. Palestine becomes a dim Garden of Eden:

> Slenderly hang the olive leaves
> Sighing apart;
> The rose and silver doves in the eaves
> With a murmur of music bind our house.

But in spite of the unreality which results from this shadowy setting, the poem rises to a moving climax, in which the bridegroom is torn between the love of his bride and the call of Christ. . . . (pp. 91-3)

Of the other poems of this kind, the best are "**Little Sister of the Prophet**" and "**Père Lalemant.**" The latter is the only narrative with a Canadian setting. As we might expect, the characteristic ruggedness of the wilderness has been reduced to a gentle softness:

> I lift the Lord on high,
> Under the murmuring hemlock boughs, and see
> The small birds of the forest lingering by
> And making melody.

The poem, stressing the priest's loneliness, attains a mild pathos but not tragedy. It is all too soft and muted and unreal—very unlike the great treatment of a similar theme in Pratt's *Brébeuf and His Brethren.*

Marjorie Pickthall's subsequent volumes of verse—[*The Lamp of Poor Souls, The Wood Carver's Wife,* and *Complete Poems*] . . .—sustained rather than enhanced her reputation. Most of the later poems closely resemble the early ones in both theme and form. There are a few interesting experiments—"**On Amaryllis, A Tortoyse,**" for example, which has a seventeenth century quaintness, and "**Wiltshire,**" which is an amusing dialect poem—and a handful of poems which rival her early best. Of the latter group, "**Resurgam,**" with its soaring anapaestic rhythm and its quietly triumphant close, is probably the finest example. Her patriotic and war poems are, on the other hand, her least successful productions. *The Wood Carver's Wife,* a verse drama of a tragic love-feud in the days of the French régime, is a brave experiment which does not quite come off. Apart from its melodramatic plot, its worst fault is its style. She employs throughout the play her characteristically ornate diction and imagery, and although this style enables her to create some fine descriptive and atmospheric effects, it is fundamentally unsuitable for dialogue.

Marjorie Pickthall was not a great poet: her work lacked the imaginative power, the disciplined intensity, of the best romantic verse. But she was a genuine if minor artist, and easily the best poetic craftsman of her Canadian generation. (pp. 93-4)

> Desmond Pacey, "The Early Twentieth Century: 1897-1920," in his Creative Writing in Canada: A Short History of English-Canadian Literature, *The Ryerson Press, 1952, pp. 82-109.*

LORNE PIERCE   (essay date 1957)

[*In the following excerpt from his introduction to* The Selected Poems of Marjorie Pickthall, *Pierce surveys the principal themes of Pickthall's work. Pierce prefaced his remarks with a quote from Pickthall's poem "Resurgam": "I shall say, Lord, 'is it music, is it morning, / Song that is fresh as sunrise, light that sings?' / When on some hill there breaks the immortal warning / Of half-forgotten springs."*]

"**Resurgam**" sums up, in a way, the strength and weakness of Marjorie Pickthall. On the one hand, there are grace and charm, restrained Christian mysticism, and unfailing cadence; on the other, preoccupation with the unearthly, with death and regret, with loneliness and grief, where the tendency is toward emotional interpretations of life, and rapture and intuition are substituted for the discipline of reason. Something of a pagan in the classical sense, as well as part Protestant and part Anglo-Catholic, she took beauty where she found it and believed that it held all of goodness and truth. Her faith could be summed up in a quotation from the Bible which she treasured: "Mine eyes shall see the King in His glory!" Her favourite saint was Francis of Assisi. Her poems very often seem to be private acts of devotion—reticent, wistful, and personal, a kind of oblation jewelled with symbolism, bright with imagery, and always softly cadenced as if joining in the age-old litany of the Mass. Passion, grief, feelings of injustice or outrage, were nearly always muted in her verse. Only in her novels and short stories did she ever try to come to grips with mankind, and even then she tended to submerge her intimate thoughts and feelings in romantic situations from which the tangible and the real too often escaped. In both prose and verse her humour remained more or less constant, a fundamental fact in both her art and life that partook of her blitheness and gaiety, sometimes a commentary upon life and sometimes a kind of anodyne to still the hurts of reality. (p. 15)

From her prize poem of 1900 to "**Bega,**" "**The Little Sister of the Prophet,**" and "**The Bridegroom of Cana,**" all published in 1909, the distance was great and illustrates her progress from a beginner to the full maturity of her powers. When *Drift of Pinions,* her first book, appeared in 1913, she had already written much of her best poetry, and was to continue not only the repetition of her favourite attitudes and metaphors, but even the vocabulary that included such words as *gray, little, silver, rose, dreams, mist, dove,* and *moth.* (p. 16)

With Marjorie Pickthall the old poetic tradition in Canada may be said to have come to its foreordained end. It came to its end at Victoria College. With a young student, E. J. Pratt, who borrowed books from the Library where Marjorie Pickthall was assistant, the new tradition began. She who helped move the books from the old stacks to the new building, and was not a little lost amid it all, was shortly to enter the chaos of the First World War, and would scarcely survive it. The new

day demanded other gifts than hers. Like Bliss Carman, she found the firmament dissolving beneath her feet. What she had to say, and the lyric way she said it, were fast going out of style. (p. 19)

In her poetry she carried the old tradition as far as it could reasonably be expected to go, and certainly as far as the transplanted Celtic motif was desirable in the new world. There seems to be no place now for the historic sorrows of Deirdre, dim and inconsolable, or for the luxurious grief of a Celtic Sappho regretting absent love. There is not a little of this in the poetry of Marjorie Pickthall, as well as her own variations on the theme of *The Song of Songs,* a blending of passion and reverence, always rather wistful, and very beautiful at its best. Her poems based upon the Mass reveal her imperfect understanding of both doctrine and symbol, and reflect, instead of a deep religious experience, her prevailing attitudes, sincere enough but emotional, toward death, love, and separation, a passionate longing for fulfilment and peace. Whatever theology she possessed was, like her understanding of people—both as individuals and in their social relationships—almost always intuitive and not derived from reason or profound personal experience. (pp. 19-20)

In her early work she dealt with humanity, but it was man out of the past, remote, idealized, and legendary. She faced away from her own age. In her first novel, *Little Hearts,* she retreated to the Jacobean period, just as elsewhere she was intrigued by mediaeval Brittany or in love with the Cavaliers. Her difficulty, in both prose and poetry, was in not being able to see mankind as it really was.... When she wrote, the spell, the imagery, the very rhythms of far-off times and ways, dominated the cadences of her lines. (p. 20)

Within the same poem one might expect to meet Armorel or Mary the Mother, Adonis or the Light of the World. Her poetry is saturated with religious sentiment and often reveals swift spiritual insights. Some have suggested that the apparent confusion of symbol and creed in her work anticipated the religious and intellectual fuzziness of our own time. Certainly she was not orthodox, either Protestant or Catholic, and her faith had no consistent theological or philosophical foundations. But it is also true that religion was the deepest thing in her experience, and she spoke about it as naturally as she did the weather. It was valid and real for her, and transcended the bewildering divisions of creeds in the only way she knew, that is, the way of the true artist, and as such provided a meeting ground for all. (pp. 21-2)

> Lorne Pierce, in an introduction to The Selected Poems of Marjorie Pickthall *by Marjorie Pickthall, edited by Lorne Pierce, McClelland and Stewart Limited Publishers, 1957, pp. 15-22.*

NORTHROP FRYE   (essay date 1958)

[*A Canadian critic, Frye has exerted a tremendous influence in the field of twentieth-century literary scholarship, mainly through his study* Anatomy of Criticism (1957). *In this seminal work, he makes controversial claims for literature and literary critics, arguing that judgments are not inherent in the critical process and asserting that literary criticism can be "scientific" in its methods and its results without borrowing concepts from other fields of study. In the following review of Lorne Pierce's edition of Marjorie Pickthall's selected poems, Frye discusses Pickthall's role in the development of Canadian poetry.*]

The Selected Poems of Marjorie Pickthall . . . has an introduction by Dr. Lorne Pierce [see excerpt dated 1957]. The introduction is written with much sympathy, but tends to confirm the usual view of this poet as a diaphanous late romantic whose tradition died with her. "With Marjorie Pickthall the old poetic tradition in Canada may be said to have come to its foreordained end. It came to its end at Victoria College. With a young student, E. J. Pratt, who borrowed books from the Library where Marjorie Pickthall was assistant, the new tradition began." Dr. Pierce knows far more about Marjorie Pickthall than I do, but still I have some reservations about this. She died at thirty-nine: if Yeats had died at the same age, in 1904, we should have had an overwhelming impression of the end of a road to Miltown that we now realize would have been pretty inadequate. Marjorie Pickthall was, of course, no Yeats, but her Biblical-Oriental pastiches were not so unlike the kind of thing that Ezra Pound was producing at about the same time, and there are many signs of undeveloped possibilities in this book. For some reason I had not read her little play, *The Wood Carver's Wife*, before, and I expected to find it Celtic twilight with a lot of early Yeats in it. It turned out to be a violent, almost brutal melodrama with a lot of Browning in it. Also, it is an example of a very common type of critical fallacy which ascribes to vagueness in her theoretical grasp of religion what is really, at worst, second-hand Swinburne, and, at best, the requirements of her *genre*. When she writes of Père Lalemant, she is subtle and elusive, not because her religion was fuzzy, but because she was writing lyric; when Pratt writes of Brébeuf he is dry and hard, not because his religion is dogmatic, but because he is writing narrative. Anyway, I think she handed rather more over to Pratt, besides library books, than simply her own resignation. (p. 450)

> *Northrop Frye, "Letters in Canada, 1957: Poetry," in* University of Toronto Quarterly, *Vol. XXVII, No. 4, July, 1958, pp. 434-50.**

ADDITIONAL BIBLIOGRAPHY

Adcock, A. St. John. "Marjorie Pickthall." *The Bookman*, London LXII, No. 369 (June 1922): 127-29.
Recounts Pickthall's life and literary career. Adcock calls *The Wood Carver's Wife* and *The Bridge* Pickthall's "highest achievements in poetry and in fiction. . . . The same psychological insight, the same breadth of imaginative and emotional power are potent in both; each has a certain bigness and grandeur of idea, and a strong individuality of style."

Gordon, Alfred. "Marjorie Pickthall As Artist." *The Canadian Bookman* IV, No. 6 (May 1922): 157-59.
Excerpts from Pickthall's letters to Gordon demonstrating her preference for lyric poetry and her views on such poets as Sidney Lanier, John Masefield, and Duncan Campbell Scott.

Hassard, Albert R. "The Dawn of Marjorie Pickthall's Genius." *The Canadian Bookman* IV, No. 6 (May 1922): 159-61.
Reminiscence of Pickthall as a young woman, with excerpts from her letters to Hassard.

Lugrin, N. de Bertrand. "Marjorie Pickthall As a Companion." *The Canadian Magazine* LXIV, No. 3 (April 1925): 72-3.
An account of the author's friendship with Pickthall and of their vacation together on Vancouver Island.

"The Bridge." *The New York Times Book Review* (12 February 1922): 14.
Calls Pickthall's novel "a strong story with a distinct moral tendency, relieved by a strain of poetic description, intensified by an elemental love affair and enlivened by dramatic action."

Rhodenizer, V. B. "Canadian Poets since Service." In his *A Handbook of Canadian Literature*, pp. 232-42. Ottawa: Graphic Publishers, 1930.*
Characterizes Pickthall as an "essentially lyric" genius more distinguished for her poetry and short stories than her novels. Of Pickthall's poetry, Rhodenizer comments: "Whether her poetic themes are pagan or Christian, her musical language and her beautiful, and usually Canadian, imagery rank her high among the women poets of Canada. . . ."

Stringer, Arthur. "Wild Poets I've Known: Marjorie Pickthall." *Saturday Night* 56, No. 40, part 2 (14 June 1941): 41.
An account of Stringer's May, 1921, visit to Pickthall.

Thomas, Clara. "Marjorie Lowry Christie Pickthall." In her *Canadian Novelists: 1920-1945*, pp. 98-9. Toronto: Longmans, Green & Co., 1946.
Biographical and critical sketch.

Gene(va Grace) Stratton Porter

1863-1924

(Also Stratton-Porter) American novelist, short story writer, nonfiction writer, essayist, and poet.

Porter was one of the early twentieth-century's foremost practitioners of sentimental fiction, and ranks among the best-selling authors in the history of publishing in the United States. Intended to be both morally uplifting and entertaining, her works usually portrayed characters overcoming the trials of life and love through a combination of decency, hard work, and a renewed relationship with nature. These values struck a responsive chord among readers in a rapidly industrializing America just after the turn of the century. In that sense she was, according to Bertrand F. Richards, "the right writer for her time," one who "helped ease the strain of a life which was rapidly becoming too mechanical." In addition to her novels she wrote numerous nature studies, most notably about bird life in Indiana.

Porter was the youngest of twelve children born to an Indiana farmer and his semi-invalid wife. During her childhood, Porter spent much of her time outdoors in the company of her father and brothers, and she quickly developed an abiding passion for nature and wildlife, particularly birds. Her father's hopes for a successor to the farm were dashed by the drowning death of Leander, his oldest son living at home and Porter's model for the principal character in her novel *Laddie*. The family moved to the closest town, Wabash, in 1874, and Porter's mother died shortly thereafter. For these reasons, Porter was compelled to relinquish leisurely lessons at home, where she was tutored by her father, and began attending public school, which she heartily disliked even though her performance was creditable. She left high school in her final year to nurse an ailing sister and never completed her formal education. Nonetheless, Porter continued the course of omnivorous reading—including the works of nature writers and literary classics—which she had begun in childhood.

In 1884 Porter engaged in a correspondence with Charles Dorwin Porter, a druggist twelve years her senior. The following year they met at Rome City, Indiana, and were married soon afterward. In 1890 the couple moved to Geneva, which lay on the borders of the Limberlost swamp region of northeast central Indiana. From her girlhood Porter had been interested in writing, and she busied herself with poems, essays, and short fiction. Meanwhile she was attracted to the natural beauties of the Limberlost swamp, devoting much time to exploring the region and observing its wildlife. She quickly mastered the difficult art of nature photography and became very skilled at photographing birds in their natural habitats. The Limberlost in the 1890s, despite inroads recently carved by the lumber and oil industries, was still a formidable swampland and not entirely safe to travel. The crews of men working in the region were tolerant and even helpful to Porter, often telling her of unusual wildlife sightings. When the increased prosperity of the area was shared by the Porters through their own investment in the oil industry, they designed and had built a spacious house of cedar and redwood named Limberlost Cabin.

Porter's nature studies intensified her already existing concern for wildlife causes and inspired a desire to share her findings with others. Her first published article, deploring the slaughter of birds for their plumage, appeared in the February, 1900, issue of *Recreation* magazine, and afterward she often published articles on the Limberlost swamp, accompanied by her photographs. At the same time, Porter also began to publish fiction based on childhood memories. By the time of the appearance of her first novel, *The Song of the Cardinal*, the story of a farm couple paralleled by that of a bird and its mate, Porter was established as a professional writer, photographer, and illustrator. Her popularity with reading audiences resulted in invitations for public speaking engagements, particularly regarding wildlife causes.

The Porters remained in Geneva until 1913. By that time the Limberlost, drained of its resources, had ceased to be productive for Porter's fieldwork. The Porters relocated to an extensive lakeside estate in Rome City and built a second Limberlost Cabin, where Porter continued to work as naturalist and writer. Unfortunately, the same forces which had destroyed the first Limberlost site were rapidly encroaching upon the second. When her struggle to oppose a drainage project failed, Porter herself undertook the conservation of much local plant life, transplanting to her own property the widely scattered flowers, shrubs, and small trees threatened with destruction. Porter's impact as a conservationist can be felt today, as Wildflower Woods remains a protected area. Nevertheless, Porter's grasp of conservation was not one-sided: she realized, throughout her efforts, that urban expansion also had its rightful priorities.

In 1919 Porter contracted influenza. Her bout with the illness left her in a weakened condition which necessitated living in a milder climate with ready access to medical care. Porter began wintering in California and by 1923 had made it her year-round home. There she became increasingly gregarious and, by virtue of her wealth and literary reputation, associated freely with the affluent and cultured, including those in the motion picture industry. After much urging from various firms interested in the film rights to her books, Porter permitted the film production of her novel *Freckles*. Dissatisfied with the resulting adaptation, she determined to undertake any future projects herself and formed her own film company, which produced adaptations of many of her novels. The high standards of morality she had always desired to instill in her books became integral to Porter's campaign for decency in the movie industry as well. Porter continued to write prolifically until her death in an automobile accident in 1924.

The predominant critical response to Porter's work challenges what has been called her simplistic view of life, which insists that goodness will eventually prevail over evil and happiness emerge from adversity. Critics have also found her characters to be one-dimensional, particularly her persistently courageous heroes and heroines whose resolve to help others and to succeed through honest hard work is unwavering. Her technique, which has been called cloying, was colorfully described by Carl Van Doren, who noted that Porter "piled sentimentalism upon descriptions of nature in soft, sweet heaps." Critics maintain that Porter has insufficiently supported what they consider an untenable premise—that good is indomitable. Porter was, however, as warmly embraced by her readers as she was scorned by many of her reviewers. Regarding Porter and other sentimentalists, Margaret MacMullen observes that their works afforded "an insane optimism adapted to beguile those who spend much of their lives averting their gaze from the glare of reality. When the theme was regeneration, the uphill road was pleasantly graded and florally landscaped, with the love nest on the summit always in sight. No matter how the forces of evil might plague from without, internally the hero and heroine suffered no setback of humiliation."

In one of her most successful novels, *Freckles,* Porter employed the formulaic elements which delighted her readers and which she continued to utilize throughout her career: a homeless waif later discovered to be the foundling son of wealthy and titled parents, majestic natural settings symbolic of moral rectitude, and a deus ex machina conclusion bringing about a dramatic reversal of fortune to the protagonist's benefit. All work together to substantiate Porter's basic theme—that any obstacle can be overcome through goodness and determination—though some critics have complained that Porter unfairly stacks the deck in favor of her hero by bestowing wealthy and influential parents upon him in a late plot twist. The same formula of triumph over adversity, with some variation, is present in *Laddie,* in which the main character, an earnest young farmer intent on marrying a girl of aristocratic birth, is aided by the unexpected disclosure of his own family's nobility. Again, in *A Girl of the Limberlost,* a struggling young heroine strengthened by her love of nature finds romance and wins her estranged mother's love while gladdening the hearts of all who know her.

Nature studies, though not so numerous as her fictional works, figure significantly in Porter's career. Porter considered her work as a naturalist very important, and took her own photographs for the books. Although these volumes were more costly to produce than her novels and did not sell as well, Porter refused to comply with her publisher's suggestion that she curtail her nonfiction and omit the scrupulous nature details from her fictional works. *Homing with the Birds,* one of her more ambitious efforts and thought by some critics to be her best, follows autobiographical introductory chapters with others addressing Porter's unusual experiences in the field, her interpretations of various aspects of bird life, and pleas for the protection of certain species. One commentator commended it without reserve for its "fine spirit of accuracy and trustworthiness." Birds were not her only subjects for observation: *Moths of the Limberlost,* Porter's personal favorite, has been acknowledged by critics to be a reliable introductory guide to identifying and collecting these insects. While her nature studies have sometimes been faulted for their scientific unorthodoxy and unabashed sentimentality, Porter's dedication and keen powers of observation and description remain unchallenged.

During her career, Porter was chiefly concerned with writing for a middle class, traditionally-minded, and largely female readership which enthusiastically accepted her work. However, she was criticized by many reviewers for her sentimentality, effusiveness, and an unscientific approach to natural subjects. Lack of critical respect annoyed her; to the charge that her fiction was unrealistic she once responded sharply that her stories "do not contain what I know to be true of all life, but what I do know to be true of a much larger part of life than any critic I have ever known will admit." While her once overwhelming acclaim has been somewhat diminished by changing popular taste in fiction, some of her novels are still

read today. Richards has observed that although "Porter somehow failed to develop major powers of fiction, . . . it must be remembered that she never intended her work to be judged solely as fiction but as *story* carrying a nature message. It was her undeniably fine portrayal of a region and her excellent discernment of the wonders of nature which sustained her through many successful years. If she neither knew nor cared how to construct a novel, she certainly possessed the power to weave a narrative and to tell a story."

(See also *Contemporary Authors,* Vol. 112.)

PRINCIPAL WORKS

The Song of the Cardinal   (novel)   1903
Freckles   (novel)   1904
What I Have Done with Birds   (nonfiction)   1907; also
    published as *Friends in Feathers* [revised and enlarged
    edition], 1917
A Girl of the Limberlost   (novel)   1909
*Music of the Wild, with Reproductions of the Performers,
    Their Instruments and Festival Halls*   (nonfiction)
    1910
The Harvester   (novel)   1911
Moths of the Limberlost   (nonfiction)   1912
Laddie: A True Blue Story   (novel)   1913
Birds of the Limberlost   (prose and poetry)   1914
Michael O'Halloran   (novel)   1915
Morning Face   (prose and poetry)   1916
A Daughter of the Land   (novel)   1918
Homing with the Birds   (nonfiction)   1919
Her Father's Daughter   (novel)   1921
The White Flag   (novel)   1923
Let Us Highly Resolve   (essays)   1927
The Magic Garden   (novel)   1927

THE NEW YORK TIMES BOOK REVIEW   (essay date 1904)

[*In the following excerpt, an anonymous reviewer summarizes the plot of* Freckles, *noting that the unreality of the novel does not render it less pleasing.*]

In a way [*Freckles*] combines the old plot of the waif who found his lost name with the more modern nature cult, but it takes most of its spirit from old-fashioned romance—and is all the better for that. The hero is a little Irish boy lacking a hand, but all there in the matter of courage, cheerfulness, and freckles. He walks ragamuffinwise into a lumber camp and is set to patrol a piece of valuable timber land, to walk around the seven-mile circuit of it twice a day, and see that no marauders steal the curly maple trees. So the boy grows strong in body and soul and makes friends with the birds and the beasts, and has in particular a tremendous fight with one ugly thief. Then comes to the wood, when the snows are gone and the Spring is come, all that's idyllic in the shape of a pretty girl, just sixteen, a pretty girl whom the boy names the Swamp Angel. She comes under the protection of a naturalist lady (called the Bird Woman) who is indefatigable in taking photographs of wild creatures by which means she becomes the most delightful kind of chaperon, one who is much of the time clear out of the way, busy with her camera. And there in the woods the girl plays the banjo and the boy sings Irish songs in a fine Irish voice. Really it is a very pretty idyl. Then come the timber thieves in real earnest—villainous, bad men—and capture Freckles and truss him up to a sapling and set to work with crosscut saws on the very finest curly maple of all, worth a thousand dollars or so. But the Angel appears out of the blue and uses girlish wiles upon those wicked men and flatters the boss villain into a state of softness of heart most unusual in villains and most inconvenient to the prosecution of villainy. Then come yet other adventures and at last the discovery of who this brave little Freckles is. It is a very pleasing story, the unreality of which has nothing whatever to do with the case. In the forest of Arden one does not bother with brute probabilities, nor does one or need one in the Limberlost Swamp, where also the world is younger and kinder than most people find it outside of enchanted places.

> *"The Timber-Guard's Paradise," in* The New York Times Book Review, *December 3, 1904, p. 839.*

GEORGE GLADDEN (essay date 1907)

[*In the following excerpt, Gladden disparagingly reviews* What I Have Done with Birds.]

The idea that supply can create demand may make certain "dismal science" expounders roll over in their graves, but it seems a fair question whether, after all, the "nature fakirs" are not chiefly responsible for the ever-increasing supply of nature books. Clearly there are many more of these books nowadays than there were before Mr. Seton began to tell us about the lions and bears he had known who had committed suicide rather than bear the ills they had; or Mr. Long watched that woodcock stand still for half an hour on one leg, waiting for the clay cast it had applied to the other broken one to get hard.

And it isn't surprising that of the mass of such matter now getting between covers an appreciable amount should be of a kind which will not stand scrutiny either as natural history, or as plain common or garden "literature."

Of the strictly bird books now under consideration, the most remarkable, so far as text is concerned, is Mrs. Gene Stratton-Porter's **What I Have Done with Birds**. If the reader expects from the form the title to find a self-effacing account of what the author has done, he will be disappointed. "A deep love for, and a comprehension of, wild things runs through the thread [sic] of my disposition, peculiarly equipping me to do these things," modestly declares Mrs. Porter. And again: "No man has ever had the patience to remain with a bird until he has secured a real character study of it," which will be interesting news to Mr. Finley, Mr. Dugmore, Mr. Baynes, Mr. Loring, Mr. Job (of Connecticut, not of the Old Testament), and various other impatient and bungling bird-photographers. Similar self-appreciation or self-consciousness constantly reappears throughout the book. . . . If one can be patient with the text, the book, which is very handsomely printed, is worth having.

> *George Gladden, in a review of "What I Have Done with Birds," in* The Bookman, New York, *Vol. XXV, No. 6, August, 1907, p. 622.*

THE NATION (essay date 1912)

[*In the following excerpt, an anonymous critic provides a balanced appraisal of* Moths of the Limberlost.]

Mrs. Gene Stratton-Porter's **Moths of the Limberlost** . . . is a happy relief from the made-to-order nature books which flood the market at the present time. Instead of a mass of good, bad, and indifferent photographs, purchased by some publisher and turned over to a hack writer who is supposed to supply enough text to tie the series together, we have a collection of exceptional photographs made by the author herself, and by her colored in the most life-like manner. It is virtually true, as she states in her introduction, that the illustration of every moth book that has attempted colored reproduction proves by shrivelled bodies and unnatural position of the wings that it has been painted from subjects mounted from weeks to years in private collections and museums, and that a lifeless moth fades rapidly under the most favorable conditions. Her own illustrations are, in nearly every case, of moths photographed before they had taken flight, and their colors were copied as soon as the down was dry and fluffy. They have been reproduced with remarkable fidelity in the beautiful book before us. It goes without saying that the author of **The Harvester, A Girl of the Limberlost,** and other stories, has written entertainingly of her insect friends. The life-long interest in nature which shows in all of her writings, is here given free rein, and we have many experiences recounted which have been elsewhere interwoven with her fiction. The habits and the life-histories of the large moths which she has studied, are described with the same accuracy and charm which are shown in her illustrations. When it comes to generalizing, Mrs. Porter is not so fortunate. Like all careful students of insect life, she has been able to observe many facts not recorded in the textbooks, and even to correct some commonly accepted statements. This has hardly qualified her to pass upon moot questions of insect psychology, morphology, or metamorphosis, or to criticise so freely the writers who "fail to explain the absolutely essential points over which an amateur has trouble." However, the few faults of the book are such as may be attributed to over-enthusiasm. Author and publisher have coöperated in producing a book which is attractive from cover to cover, and which will do much to stimulate study of a group full of interest for the nature lover.

> *A review of "Moths of the Limberlost," in* The Nation, *Vol. XCV, No. 2462, September 5, 1912, p. 217.*

H. L. MENCKEN (essay date 1913)

[*From the era of World War I until the early years of the Great Depression, Mencken was one of the most influential figures in American letters. His strongly individualistic, irreverent outlook on life and his vigorous, invective-charged writing style helped establish the iconoclastic spirit of the Jazz Age and significantly shaped the direction of American literature. In his literary criticism, Mencken encouraged American writers to shun the anglophilic, moralistic bent of the nineteenth century and to practice realism, an artistic call-to-arms that is most fully developed in his essay "Puritanism as a Literary Force," one of the seminal essays in modern literary criticism. In the following excerpt from a review of* Laddie, *Mencken acknowledges Porter's artistic skill but criticizes what he considers the essential banality of the novel's plot.*]

[A] gifted manufacturer of popular confectionery is Mrs. Gene Stratton-Porter, of Indiana, whose latest volume, **Laddie** . . . , is crossing the 200,000 mark as I write. . . . The foundation of **Laddie** (what a ghastly name for a hero!) is the ancient tale of Romeo Montague and Julia Capulet, but Mrs. Porter has given it a happy ending and added a number of well esteemed characters, including the Infant Terrible, the Innocent Condemned and Old Mother Hubbard. This, however, is not her only, nor even her chief addition to the literary *pot-au-feu:* what she principally contributes is a deft and delectable compound of homely humor and sweet, sweet sentiment—in brief, the sort of stuff that makes an honest American smile through his tears. This is what Americans most esteem in a humorist: the gift of pathos, the talent for concealing a sob in a snicker. That explains, I dare say, the success of such things as *Mrs. Wiggs of the Cabbage Patch* and the national veneration for Dickens, despite his uncomfortable plain speaking in his serious moods; and it explains, too, the national distrust of satirists. The Puritanical feeling that mirth is somehow discreditable still lingers in the subcellars of the national consciousness. But if it can be given a moral, a sentimental, a lachrymal quality, then it escapes excommunication. Mrs Porter . . . is a highly dexterous performer. She writes so well, indeed, that large sections of her book have genuine merit as prose fiction. It is only when she sets the old machinery in motion and exposes the fundamental banality of her "story" that she becomes commonplace and tedious. (pp. 154-55)

> H. L. Mencken, "Marie Corelli's Sparring Partner," in The Smart Set, *Vol. XLI, No. 3, November, 1913, pp. 153-60.**

FREDERIC TABER COOPER (essay date 1915)

[*An American educator, biographer, and editor, Cooper served for many years as literary critic at* The Bookman, *a popular early twentieth-century literary magazine. In the following essay, he explores the appeal of Porter's writing to her reading audience and notes the reasons for the lack of critical regard for her work. For Porter's reaction to Cooper's criticism, see the excerpt dated 1916.*]

Serious critical opinion is fairly well agreed as to the general qualities that distinguish the confessedly popular stories of Gene Stratton-Porter, who in private life is Mrs. Charles Dorwin Porter. She has a certain specialised knowledge of the fauna and flora of her own home section of the State of Indiana; she has a gift for vivid and at times over-florid landscape painting in words; and she uses these talents as backgrounds for innocuous and rather thin narratives, usually much too long drawn out, which one unsympathetic reviewer has labelled the "sugar cookie" brand. All of which, while fairly accurate, quite fails to account for the rather large audience that Mrs. Porter undoubtedly reaches.

If we are to solve the problem at all, it is necessary to examine somewhat closer the nature of Mrs. Porter's literary interests. Her earliest writings were not fiction, but articles embodying her own patient and prolonged observations of wild life, in meadow, swamp and woodland; and her two most ambitious books are *Moths of the Limberlost* and *Music of the Wild,* the latter divided into three parts, "The Chorus of the Forest," "Songs of the Fields," and "The Music of the Marsh." No one can read these volumes without realising that minute nature study is, with this author, not so much a fad as a fanaticism, and the scientific value of her labours is largely discounted by the open and unabashed self-satisfaction of her style. Even more plainly can her foibles and shortcomings be seen in *The Song of the Cardinal,* her first attempt at anything approaching fiction,—although, in spite of the introduction of two or three human beings, it is really the story of a pair of Cardinal birds, and distinctly, albeit unconsciously, of the nature-faking sort. The author expressly states that all her facts are the result of three years' patient watching, from a hiding place in a tangle

of sweet-briar and blackberry vines, of a certain nest, in which the drama of the tale was enacted; yet she lets her imagination constantly translate the actions of these birds into human emotions, such as they could not possibly have had, and at times her imagery is unconsciously grotesque, as when she tells us that the female bird "blushed with embarrassment to a colour even brighter than her natural red." Incidentally, she anathematises the brutality of man considered as a species, and glorifies the other works of the Creator with all the ardour if not the quality of the great Psalmist.

It is necessary to dwell upon these characteristics in discussing Gene Stratton-Porter's claim to consideration as a novelist, because it has been generally conceded that their interest lies, not in the story, but in the background and atmosphere, in the sense of outdoor life and sunshine and the sheer jubilant joy of living. In point of fact, she does achieve these effects, even though at times she inclines toward verboseness and redundancy, and there is a cloying sweetness in her nature worship that puts a matter-of-fact reader somewhat out of patience. And in this respect her books are all precisely alike, for she has a single talent of rather limited range,—and so the reader who liked *Freckles* can safely count upon getting pretty much the same sort of placid entertainment from *The Harvester* or *Laddie* or *A Girl of the Limberlost.* As for the author's plot sense, the kindest thing to say about it is that it has remained in a rudimentary state. She does not seem to realise that her oversentimentalised characters act for the most part in a manner half way between melodrama and a grown-up fairy tale. Take, for instance, *A Girl of the Limberlost,* which is probably the least convincing of her books. Here, in Elnora Comstock we have the only child of a widowed mother who treats her with a systematic and vindictive cruelty more improbable even than that meted out to poor little Cinderella of the old nursery tale. Yet although no fairy godmother appears on the scene, fate nevertheless takes a kindly hand in straightening out her troubles, so that, penniless and without friends, she accomplishes the miracle of clothing and educating herself in spite of all the obstacles her mother can put in the way. And after we have racked our brains through several hundred pages for an adequate reason for such unnatural motherhood, we learn that the girl's father was drowned years ago in the swamp lying almost at the door of their cabin, and that because the hour of his death happened to coincide with that of his daughter's birth, the mother always held her to be responsible for her own inability to save him. People act that way in melodrama, and a certain type of audience loves them for it. But in real life a normal human being does not live for the sole purpose of taking a slow revenge upon an innocent child, while an abnormal one would not be cured by the belated discovery that the dead husband was unworthy of her love.

Yet, even though we recognise that Mrs. Porter sees life through convex mirrors and distorting lenses, making her good people incredibly good and her wicked people superlatively bad, the fact remains that she has a rather big audience and has no difficulty in holding it. And the reason seems to be a twofold one. In the first place, there is more sentimentality in the world than is generally admitted; and secondly, it is human nature to enjoy by proxy many things which would be a sad bore if we had to do them ourselves. Forty years ago thousands of readers spent happy hours in the company of "Adirondack" Murray, whipping the streams for elusive trout and gloating over the marvellous weight of his captures,—and as likely as not half of these readers never had a rod in their hands and never meant to. In the same way, it is rather pleasant to return to nature vicariously through the pages of Mrs. Porter's stories, explore the woodlands and swamps quite safely, with no danger of getting our clothing soiled or our shoes muddy, picnic on the grass, untroubled by crawling ants or persistent mosquitoes, and persuade ourselves that the Music of the Wild is very near to our hearts, when as a matter of fact if the canary sings too loudly, we usually put a handkerchief over its cage.

This, then, is the real secret of the appeal of *Freckles* and its numerous successors. Their author does have the faculty of making us hear the birds and smell the flowers and watch the shifting seasons and the alternating sunshine and rain. She is sincere in her passionate love of the outdoors, and because that sort of sincerity is contagious, she does for the time being trick us into imagining that we too would revel in just that sort of a life and that all the pageantry of city streets is not worth one apple-tree in bloom, or the feathery wings of one of those huge, slumberous moths that make the month of June in the Limberlost a memorable epoch. The effect that she gets may be transitory, but she certainly does get it, in spite of some crudeness and affectation and over luxuriance of style. (pp. 670-71)

> Frederic Taber Cooper, "The Popularity of Gene Stratton-Porter," in The Bookman, *New York, Vol. XLI, No. 6, August, 1915, pp. 670-71.*

GENE STRATTON-PORTER (essay date 1916)

[*In the following excerpt, Porter challenges criticism by Frederic Taber Cooper (see excerpt dated 1915). In an unexcerpted portion of the essay, she relates scattered childhood reminiscences which deal with her interest in nature, as well as personal convictions regarding several of her works.*]

Nothing could better prove my contention that some of my critics shoot their bolts wide of the mark, than a recent effort by a man who does not deserve the prominence the mention of his name would give him. He attempts in the beginning to bolster his article by the ambiguous statement that "serious critical opinion is fairly well agreed on the merits of the work," done by me. This would seem to indicate that he desires his criticism to be taken "seriously" and I will so take it. His first statement to which I "seriously" object is that "the scientific value of her labours is largely discounted by the open and unabashed self-satisfaction of her style"; which proves that my critic had not read my books, for I was not writing about myself, but the miracles of natural evolution with which I admit I am amply satisfied, for I believe with Whitman that "a mouse is miracle enough to stagger a sectillion infidels."

This critic classes *The Song of the Cardinal* as fiction, and then immediately turns and attacks it as "nature-faking." He says I "constantly allowed her imagination to translate the actions of the birds into human emotions," which I grant; not "unconsciously," as he takes the liberty to assert, but deliberately and to the last degree permissible. That my critic feels I carried this too far can be seen from his statement: "At times her imagery is unconsciously grotesque, as when she tells us that the female bird 'blushed with embarrassment to a colour even brighter than her natural red.'" "Grotesque," I will concede, if it were a true quotation; but the "faking" applies to my critic, not to my work. William Sharp wrote that the work of a critic was a thing rare and fine: "the marriage of science which knows, and of spirit that discerns."

Now if my critic had been possessed of "the science which knows," he would have known that a hen cardinal is grey; and had he been endowed with even a glimmering of "the spirit that discerns," he would have seen that the poorest naturalist alive would not have attributed a "blush," to a feathered creature. Not in *The Song of the Cardinal,* or in any line I ever wrote, can any one find the statement by me that any feathered or furred creature "blushed with embarrassment." If "serious critical opinion is agreed" concerning me, where does it stand concerning a critic who will pronounce the work of a nature writer "grotesque" and "faking," and then himself fakes an entire quotation in an attempt to prove his point?

He goes on to state that I have "a single talent of rather limited range." And here I had been thinking that when I went afield and brought in the first-hand material for five nature books, illustrated them with half-tones from life, and water-colour paintings; wrote stories containing thousands of natural history references none of which have as yet been authoritatively contradicted, designed my covers and front matter, and furnished the bird work for the New International Standard Biblical Encyclopaedia, that I was doing several things well enough for some of the world's best editors to accept them.

He writes that my "plot sense has remained in a rudimentary state." This cuts me out of all volition in the matter of writing my books. It makes my work what I *can* do, *not* what I *design and deliberately plan to do.* I am not wholly devoid of conception and imagination. I could weave an intricate plot of rankest realism, an I chose; I merely decline to set my name to work of that sort, and stick to the thing I set out to do in the beginning. Again, had he been possessed of "the spirit that discerns," he would have seen that he broke every canon of the true critic's art when he pronounced *A Girl of the Limberlost* the poorest work I had done, and then selected it for review, in an article devoted to setting me in my proper literary place.

Had he been writing of the work of either of two men of my State, will anyone believe that he would have passed over *A Hoosier Chronicle,* and *The Poet,* and made an estimate of the literary values of Nicholson based on a former indiscretion, *The Siege of Seven Suitors*? Or would he have ignored *Beaucaire* and *The Turmoil,* and judged Tarkington by *Cherry* or *The Two Van Revels*?

Now for the *justice* of his review of this book. He champions realism, yet he disavows that any mother would treat her daughter in the manner described, for the reasons adduced. I was familiar with the Comstock incident, under another name, and will vouch for it. When we read this review my daughter and I sat down and counted up six instances we could recall among our immediate acquaintances, where parents and children were farther estranged than this book recounts, for much less reason. At this instant among my girl acquaintances there is one whose father treated her with such vindictive cruelty for years, merely because she was not a son. She so craved his love and appreciation that she took a course of training in his profession, and when she proved that she understood and could be of great assistance to him in his business, she won him completely, and now she is the subject of prideful boasting on his part, not in melodrama, but in my nearest city.

Of *A Girl of the Limberlost,* this critic makes the statement that no fairy god-mother appeared on the scene yet "penniless and without friends she accomplishes a miracle of clothing and educating herself." To anyone who has read the book this is even a more flagrant breach of the ethics of true criticism, than that of making up a quotation to suit his convenience. To those who have not, I will explain that the first chapter introduces a man who had loved and fended for the "Girl" all her life, the second brings in the man's wife who buys and makes the clothing the girl needs; at almost the same time appears a professor who helps her to books; and shortly after she comes into contact with the "Bird Woman," which is where I come in; while throughout the book almost each day brings her some new helper, just as life brings such a girl as I described the thing she bravely and persistently sets out to win. Further, the "miracle of clothing" was some country made gingham dresses, and of "education," graduation in a small town high school.

The next accusation against me by this critic is that I "see life through convex mirrors and distorted lenses"; which leads me to the strictly feminine comment that this is exactly the way he sees my books. He calls me a "nature faker," then himself fakes a quotation to prove it; which leaves my natural history of a brand acceptable to the doctors of science compiling the Encyclopaedia I mentioned—and they had the ornithologists of the world from whom to make a choice to do the work. As for my stories, they do not contain what I know to be true of all life, but what I do know to be true of a much larger part of life than any critic I have ever known will admit. It is exactly what could be true of all life if all men would put up the fight for clean morals that *The Harvester* did. Fifty years of such life on the part of every man would empty our feeble-minded homes, alms houses, and prisons, and, barring accidents, would practically do away with hospitals and sanatoriums. This is no Utopian dream: ask any responsible physician. (pp. 152-53)

> Gene Stratton-Porter, *"My Work and My Critics,"* in The Bookman, *London, Vol. XLIX, No. 293, February, 1916, pp. 147-55.*

GRANT M. OVERTON (essay date 1918)

[*Overton was an American novelist and literary journalist known for his biographical and critical essays on American authors. In the following excerpt, he unconditionally praises the moral value of Porter's work.*]

Because Gene Stratton-Porter cares for the truth that is in her, she is the most widely read and most widely loved author in America today, with the probable exception of Harold Bell Wright. She is absolutely sincere in all her work, she is in dead earnest, she does not care primarily for money, but for certain ideas and ideals. Let no one underestimate the tremendous power that is hers because of these things, let no one underestimate her hold upon millions of readers; let none undervalue the influence she has exerted and continues to exert, an influence always for good, for clean living, for manly men, for womanly women, for love of nature, for sane and reasonable human hopes and aspirations, for honest affection, for wholesome laughter, for a healthy emotionalism as the basis and justification of humble and invaluable lives.

If Mrs. Porter has egoism it is the sort of egoism that the world needs. It is nothing more or less than a firm and sustaining belief in one's self, in the worth of one's work, and is bred of a passionate conviction that you must always give the best of yourself without stint. Is it egoistical to believe that? Is it self-centeredness to be proud of that? Is it wrong, having set the world the best example of which you are capable, to call it to the world's attention? You will not get the present reporter to say so! You will get from him nothing but an expression of his own conviction that while literature, aesthetically viewed,

may not have been enriched by Mrs. Porter's writings, thousands, yes, tens of thousands of men and women have been made happier and better by her stories. And that just about sweeps any other possible accomplishment into limbo!

The secret of Mrs. Porter's success is sincerity, complete sincerity; doing one's best work and doing it to the top of one's bent. It is not a question of art. There is no art about it. The finest literary artist in the world could not duplicate her performance unless he were a duplicate of *her*. It's not a literary matter at all; the thing has its roots in the personality, in the mind and heart and nervous organization of the writer. If you could be a Gene Stratton-Porter you could write the novels she writes and achieve just the success she achieves, a success which is improperly measured by earnings of $500,000 to $750,000 from her books, a success of which the true measure can never be taken because it is a success in human lives and not in dollars. (pp. 88-9)

Freckles took three years to find its audience. The marginal illustrations made people think it purely a nature book. The news that it was a novel of the kind you simply must read had to get about by word of mouth. The copy that lies beside us as we write this sketch was printed in 1914, ten years after the story's first appearance. The jacket says that by 1914 exactly 670,733 copies had been sold. And the most important three of the ten years were largely wasted!

Publishers told Mrs. Porter then and afterward, repeatedly and emphatically, that if she wanted to sell her best and make the most money she must cut out the nature stuff. But, as she says, her real reason in writing her novels was to bring natural history attractively before the people who wouldn't touch it in its pure state.

"'I had had one year's experience with *The Song of the Cardinal,* frankly a nature book, and from the start I realized that I never could reach the audience I wanted with a book on nature alone. To spend time writing a book based wholly upon human passion and its outworking I would not. So I compromised on a book into which I put all the nature work that came naturally within its scope, and seasoned it with little bits of imagination and straight copy from the lives of men and women I had known intimately, folk who lived in a simple, common way with which I was familiar. So I said to my publishers: "I will write the books exactly as they take shape in my mind. You publish them. I know they will sell enough that you will not lose. If I do not make over $600 on a book I shall never utter a complaint. Make up my work as I think it should be and leave it to the people as to what kind of book they will take into their hearts and homes." I altered *Freckles* slightly, but from that time on we worked on this agreement.

"'My years of nature work have not been without considerable insight into human nature, as well,' continues Mrs. Porter. 'I know its failings, its inborn tendencies, its weaknesses, its failures, its depth of crime; and the people who feel called upon to spend their time analyzing, digging into, and uncovering these sources of depravity have that privilege, more's the pity! If I had my way about it, this is a privilege no one could have in books intended for indiscriminate circulation. I stand squarely for book censorship, and I firmly believe that with a few more years of such books as half a dozen I could mention, public opinion will demand this very thing. My life has been fortunate in one glad way: I have lived mostly in the country and worked in the woods. For every bad man and woman I have ever known, I have met, lived with, and am intimately acquainted with an overwhelming number of thoroughly clean and decent people who still believe in God and cherish high ideals, and it is *upon the lives of these that I base what I write.* To contend that this does not produce a picture true to life is idiocy. It does. It produces a picture true to ideal life; to the best that good men and good women can do at level best.

"'I care very little for the magazine or newspaper critics who proclaim that there is no such thing as a moral man, and that my pictures of life are sentimental and idealized. They are! And I glory in them! They are straight, living pictures from the lives of men and women of morals, honor, and loving kindness. They form "idealized pictures of life" because they are copies from life where it touches religion, chastity, love, home, and hope of Heaven ultimately. None of these roads leads to publicity and the divorce court. They all end in the shelter and seclusion of a home.

"'Such a big majority of book critics and authors have begun to teach, whether they really believe it or not, that no book is *true to life* unless it is true to the *worst in life*, that the idea has infected even the women.'"

A Girl of the Limberlost "'comes fairly close to my idea of a good book. No possible harm can be done any one in reading it. The book can, and does, present a hundred pictures that will draw any reader in closer touch with nature and the Almighty, my primal object in each line I write. The human side of the book is as close a character study as I am capable of making. I regard the character of Mrs. Comstock as the best thought-out and the cleanest-cut study of human nature I have so far been able to do.'"

Prior to the appearance of *A Daughter of the Land*, [*A Girl of the Limberlost*] was Mrs. Porter's best book, unquestionably . . . There is much humor in it and the delineation of Kate Comstock, particularly in the first half of the book, has the sharpness of line and the sureness of handling visible in a fine etching. Consciously or subconsciously Mrs. Porter created at the very outset of her story, in the second chapter, a situation which appeals to the most thrilling and satisfying instinct in the human breast. Elnora, pitifully dressed, has spent a humiliating first day at high school in town. Since her mother will not provide them, Margaret and Wesley Sinton go forth at nightfall to buy the clothes the girl needs to wear and sit up half the night to get them ready quickly. It is both humorous and genuinely moving. The reader shares their burst of generosity. He shops with them and sits up with them and worries with them and rejoices and partakes of their happiness in "doing for" the girl; he is all the while quite conscious of the humor of the situation without any abatement of the tenderness and delight that is his as well as theirs. This is great work; it may not be great literature; whether it is or not depends on what you require "literature" to give you. The innumerable readers who require literature to give them what life gives them (or even more, what life unjustly withholds from them)—emotion, pure, deep, contenting and cleansing—these will ask no more than Mrs. Porter gives them here. (pp. 98-102)

[Mrs. Porter's stories] call for no special survey one by one. The one supremely significant thing to grasp is her sincerity and her giving of the best that is in her. Now, the mass of people possess, in respect of these qualities in a writer, a sort of sixth sense, a perfectly infallible instinct that tells them when a writer is sincere, when he is giving of his best. It is the faculty aptly described in the phrase: "I don't know much about literature, *but I know what I like.*" To be sure you do!

And that's as near as ready characterization can come to the secret! The person who has achieved a certain measure of sophistication or who has cultivated his taste (which may mean improving it but always means narrowing it) does *not* know what he likes! He knows only what he doesn't like—or at least he is always finding it. He pays the price of every refiner in the loss of broad and basic satisfaction. Cultivate a tongue for caviar and you lose the honest and healthful enjoyment of corned beef and cabbage. When you appreciate Bach you can no longer get thrilling pleasure hearing a military band. It's the same way everywhere and with everybody.

If some people find no pleasure or benefit in Gene Stratton-Porter's stories, that is exclusively their own fault. They are looking for certain aesthetic satisfactions in what they read and they require them so absolutely that the writer's best and the writer's sincerity cannot compensate for their absence. Is it good to have come to such a state? Every one must make up his own mind about that, even as he must make his own decision whether he will strive to attain it. Everything of this sort is to be had for a price,—if you want to pay so much.

"'To my way of thinking and working the greatest service a piece of fiction can do any reader is to leave him with a higher ideal of life than he had when he began. If in one small degree it shows him where he can be a gentler, saner, cleaner, kindlier man, it is a wonder-working book.'"

Thus Gene Stratton-Porter. There is incontestable evidence that her books have done these very things. Literature, we have been told, is "a criticism of life." How about molding lives? (pp. 105-07)

Grant M. Overton, "Gene Stratton-Porter," in his The Women Who Make Our Novels, *1918. Reprint by Dodd, Mead and Company, 1927, pp. 88-107.*

THE NEW YORK TIMES BOOK REVIEW (essay date 1919)

[*In the following excerpt, an anonymous critic commends* Homing with the Birds.]

The fairies who presided over the birth of Mrs. Stratton-Porter endowed her with a rare and wonderful gift. From her early childhood she seems to have been able to secure the trust and affection of even the wildest and fiercest of birds, and to have felt for all feathered creatures a surpassing degree of interest, compassion, and love. Those who have read any one of her dozen and more previous volumes, either of fiction or nature study, have learned something about how steeped her mind is in birdlore and her soul in love of birds. But even to those who know her books well this new volume [*Homing With the Birds*] will be in the nature of a revelation, so early in life does it show her interest in birds to have begun, so constantly to have continued ever since, so wide and thorough-going her observations to have been, so voluminous her knowledge of birds, and so deep her love for them. No one who has any interest in the feathered denizens of the air can afford to miss her book, for he will find in it all manner of accurate information about bird habits, gleaned wholly from the author's lifelong study of birds, an immense number of those anecdotes and bits of observation in which bird lovers always delight, and running all through it a fine spirit of accuracy and trustworthiness that adds greatly to the reader's enjoyment. Mrs. Stratton-Porter does not belong to the ranks of either the nature fakers or the nature romancers. She describes what she has herself seen and knows to be true, and she has seen so many and so fascinating things that she does not need to draw on her imagination to dress them up in more amazing colors, nor does she attempt to interpret and describe bird life in terms of human intelligence, and so make of them human beings dressed in feathers instead of clothes. The honesty and sincerity of the work inspire the reader who is familiar with the romancings and imaginings in which so many nature writers indulge with a peculiar gratitude. (pp. 678, 681)

> *A review of "Homing with the Birds," in* The New York Times Book Review, *November 23, 1919, pp. 678, 681.*

REBECCA WEST (essay date 1921)

[*West is considered one of the foremost English novelists and critics to write during the twentieth century. Born Cecily Isabel Fairfield, she began her career as an actress—taking the name Rebecca West from the emancipated heroine of Henrik Ibsen's drama* Rosmersholm—*and as a book reviewer for the* Free-woman. *Her early criticism was noted for its militantly feminist stance and its reflection of West's Fabian socialist concerns. Her first novel,* The Return of the Soldier (1918), *evidences a concern that entered into much of her later work: the psychology of the individual. West's literary criticism is noted for its wit, its aversion to cant, and its perceptiveness. Of her own work, West has commented: "I have always written in order to discover the truth for my own use, on the one hand, and on the other hand to earn money for myself and my family, and in this department of my work I hope I have honoured the truth I had already discovered. I have like most women written only a quarter of what I might have written, owing to my family responsibilities. I dislike heartily the literary philosophy and practice of my time, which I think has lagged behind in the past and has little relevance to the present, and it distresses me that so much contemporary work is dominated by the ideas (particularly the political and religious ideas) of the late eighteenth or nineteenth century, and those misunderstood." In the following excerpt, West disparagingly reviews* Her Father's Daughter.]

It is not always with exultation that one says, "This book could only have been written by a woman." There are times when the meaning behind that sentence is not, "Listen to the Woman Soul revealing its secrets," but, "I think the cork has come out." There are times when one's ear is vexed by the low buzzing hum of the female maunderer or the shrill insistent note of the female chucklehead. . . .

[The feminist will not] boast about Mrs. Gene Stratton Porter's *Her Father's Daughter,* though it is distinctively feminine and undeniably gives great pleasure of a certain sort. Linda, the heroine, is an American schoolgirl of seventeen with a white, pure, flagwagging soul. She is, perhaps, at the top of her form when she rebukes a young man who is building a house because there is not a nursery in it, since, "if every home in Lilac Valley has at least six sturdy boys and girls growing up in it with the proper love of country and the proper realisation of the white man's right to supremacy, and if all the world, now occupied by white men, could make an equal record, where would be the talk of the yellow peril?" The young man is so moved by this that he abandons his previous objection that he has not yet found "his dream lady" and orders nurseries for six children to be added to his house. Needless to say, Linda marries him in the end; in forcing the nurseries into his house she was only driving in the thick end of the wedge. There is a curious dietetic twist to the book. When Linda rushes up to her own bedroom, overcome with emotion, as she frequently does, she invariably draws towards her a sheet of paper and

begins writing. But it is not, as one might expect, a poem or a diary that she writes. Instead, it is a solid thousand words of this sort of thing: "Take the most succulent young bloom stems of the yucca when they have exactly the appearance of an asparagus head at its moment of delicious perfection. With a sharp knife cut them in circles an inch in depth. Arrange these in a shallow porcelain baking dish, sprinkle with salt, dot them with butter, add enough water to keep them from sticking and burning. . . ." The girl is solving certain financial difficulties by writing cookery articles for a magazine, and we are given at least six of these articles at length. Tantalising as this is to English readers, whom the sundering seas prevent from taking a yucca, it must be a great help in the business of authorship. If the technique of other domestic arts were called upon, this artifice might be useful to many writers. It might have enabled Miss E.C.B. Jones, for instance, to give substance to *The Singing Captives.* As it is, one feels, when one reads it, that a character whom Henry James conceived and rejected on account of its vagueness, has married nothingness, and these people are their children. It would be a great relief if Caroline Peel, instead of blowing in a shuddering draught of refinement across the scene of her father's ruin, occasionally went up to her bedroom and immersed herself and the story in the technique, say, of jumper knitting. "She picked up a ball of wool and cast on stitches, two purl, two plain. She intended to do this for seventeen rows, and then to divide, decrease two stitches in every alternate row for ten rows. . . ." No, we should not be too proud to learn from Gene Stratton Porter. From the back of the wrapper, which gives the titles of her other works (of which I find, ***Laddie, a True Blue Story*** and ***Homing with the Birds: A History of a Lifetime of Personal Experience,*** the most inviting), I learn that the sale of her books amounts to over nine millions. It looks as if humanity had more sense of fun than one had suspected. . . .

> *Rebecca West, in a review of "Her Father's Daughter," in* New Statesman, *Vol. XVII, No. 442, October 1, 1921, p. 706.*

WILLIAM LYON PHELPS (essay date 1921)

[*An American critic and educator, Phelps was for over forty years a lecturer on English literature at Yale. His early study* The Beginnings of the English Romantic Movement (1893) *is still considered an important work and his* Essays on Russian Novelists (1911) *was one of the first influential studies in English of the Russian realists. From 1922 until his death in 1943 he wrote a regular column for* Scribner's Magazine *and a nationally syndicated newspaper column. During this period, his criticism became less scholarly and more journalistic, and is notable for its generally enthusiastic tone. In the following excerpt, Phelps notes some strengths and weaknesses of Porter's work.*]

The two novelists whose books enjoy the biggest sales in America are Gene Stratton-Porter and Harold Bell Wright. In part they owe their circulation to the invincible sentimentality in the human breast. America has no monopoly of this emotion. These two authors are surely not inferior to the beknighted Hall Caine, Marie Corelli, and the late Mrs. Barclay in England, to the late Georges Ohnet in France, to a hundred sloppy novelists in Germany. Every human heart has a percentage of slush. (p. 299)

[Harold Bell Wright] knows well enough that the shortest cut to the ordinary intelligence is by the sentimental route, and like a spellbinder, his muzzle velocity is very high. The difficulty is that if the world could be saved by sentimental melodrama, we should have been saved long ago. Nearly all sentimental melodramas are on the side of virtue; as were the novels of Oliver Optic and Horatio Alger, Jr.

I have no particular desire to join the army of those who satirize virtue. As between virtue and vice, even in this ridiculous world, virtue actually seems to me less absurd than vice.

The case of Gene Stratton-Porter is not quite so easy as that of her running mate. The publishers tell us that nine million copies of her books have been sold. With five readers to each copy, this means a circulation of forty-five million. She is a public institution, like Yellowstone Park, and I should not think she would care any more than a mountain for adverse criticism. She does, though. Wise men know that more than half the things that appear in print are not true, and yet many have such a superstitious reverence for type that an attack or a misrepresentation fills them with real agony. Even those whose position seems immovable—Pope, Tennyson, Henry James—suffered torture when they read an adverse criticism printed in an ephemeral paper, and written by a nobody. One of Yale's greatest presidents, in the eighteenth century, saw an unfavorable criticism of his book in an English journal, and he immediately fainted away.

Gene Stratton-Porter lives in a swamp, arrays herself in man's clothes, and sallies forth in all weathers to study the secrets of nature. I believe she knows every bug, bird, and beast in the woods. I believe she recognizes every sound in a forest, and can tell you what caused it. She is primarily a naturalist, one of the foremost in America, and has published a number of books on flora and fauna, illustrated with photographs of her own taking. These books—which are closest to her heart—have only a moderate sale. Thus she hit upon the plan of writing sentimental novels, in which her observation of nature is brought to the attention of America. I have no doubt that she has led millions of boys and girls into the study of natural objects; that she has accomplished in this way much permanent good.

She is as full of energy as Roosevelt, and as hearty an American. She could have retired on a fortune long ago, but she will never retire until the day of her death, which I hope may be long distant. She is eaten up with ambition, and with the joy of life; few have more fun in their daily existence than she. I have no doubt that if the public could see some of the letters which she receives by the cartload, they would share her belief that she has not lived in vain.

I have read three of her novels—*A Girl of the Limberlost, A Daughter of the Land,* and the one just published, *Her Father's Daughter.* The first of these with all its nature lore, was rather too sentimental for me, and the third impossible; but I defy any unprejudiced person to read *A Daughter of the Land* to the end, without enthusiasm for the story. The style is so crude that one must determine not to be stopped by it; one must not quit. Apart from the lack of stylistic art, one will find an admirable story, with a real plot and real characters; nothing is shirked or softened in the course of the novel, and the heroine is a girl that holds one's attention, not merely by what happens to her, but by what she is. There is a certain grandeur in the conception of the tale, like a great architectural idea disguised by bad drawing. Furthermore, just now, when everybody thinks everybody else ought to be a farmer, this epic of the farm has a particular importance. Here was a girl who really loved the country; loved living on a farm; loved all kinds of agricultural work; loved to make and see things grow. And, as presented in the novel, this love is understandable and intelligible. There

are not many such girls. But it would be well if there were more.

Living all her life in daily contact with nature, there is an elemental force in Gene Stratton-Porter which partly accounts for the hitting power of her novels. But in her latest story, *Her Father's Daughter,* her passion for the California mountains and deserts has made her neglect not only the graces of style but the reality of her supposedly human beings. Linda, the high school wonder, is an impossible person; and the contrast between her, as a child of nature, and her suppositious sister, Eileen, stands out too grossly. By far the best things in this book are the cooking receipts and the intimate facts about the desert. Here the reader feels like a child in the author's hands.

In addition to the literary shortcomings of this novel, it is sadly marred by anti-Japanese propaganda. Somebody in California has been stuffing our novelist, who is more gullible in international politics than in the study of nature. The villain of the story is a Japanese, who, enraged at losing his place at the head of his class in the high school, attempts to murder the boy who outpaced him, and is himself done to death by Katherine O'Donovan, the Strong Cook, otherwise the best character in the novel.

Despite my disappointment in *Her Father's Daughter,* I shall read Gene Stratton-Porter's next novel. If she is not a literary artist, she is anyhow a wonderful woman. No one lives closer to nature than she; and her undoubted vigor comes partly from this contact. (pp. 300-02)

> *William Lyon Phelps, "The Why of the Best Seller," in* The Bookman, *New York, Vol. LIV, No. 4, December, 1921, pp. 298-302.**

HERBERT S. GORMAN (essay date 1922)

[*Gorman was an American critic, historical novelist, and biographer who reviewed books for several major New York publications, among them the* Times. *His works include biographies of Henry Wadsworth Longfellow, Nathaniel Hawthorne, and James Joyce. In the following excerpt from a review of* The Fire Bird, *Gorman questions Porter's poetic ability.*]

If the test of inspired literature be ecstasy, as Arthur Machen affirms, both Alfred Noyes and Gene Stratton-Porter may, with all logic, be established as authentic creators. Certainly there is enough ecstasy in *Watchers of the Sky* and *The Fire Bird.* Yet a reading of both long poems curiously enough leaves the reader with unquickened pulses. Passion and a vibrant idealism have passed in colorful array before him, yet the books are calmly put down and immediately forgotten. There is obviously something the matter with the ecstasy of Mr. Noyes and Mrs. Stratton-Porter. It does not communicate itself to the reader. It is an ingrowing ecstasy. Although it may keep both the versifiers awake it possesses quite the reverse urge for its readers. Perhaps a brief investigation of the reasons why this ecstasy does not function may not be amiss.

The case of Mrs. Stratton-Porter is simple. In spite of *The Fire Bird* and her publishers, she is not a poet. It remains but to be pointed out that her book contains an interesting Indian legend which rises to its climax in excellent style but which does not possess a single line that may properly be offered as containing that divine substance which we call poetry. The only lift in *The Fire Bird* is the tautened interest as the reader dashes on through the lines. Color and movement are to be discerned compact with an admirable use of Indian properties. The stage is well set but the actors do not sing. (pp. 96-7)

Herbert S. Gorman, "Ingrowing Ecstasy," in The Bookman, *New York, Vol. LVI, No. 1, September, 1922, pp. 96-8.**

THE NEW YORK TIMES BOOK REVIEW   (essay date 1923)

[*In the following excerpt from a review of* The White Flag, *an anonymous critic discusses Porter's work as an "agony novel" and questions the verisimilitude of her characters.*]

Readers who love a good cry will find ample material in *The White Flag* to set them sobbing. Little Mahala is so sweet, Jason is so poor and noble, and the Morelands, sire and son, are so hard hearted that the tears flow in almost every chapter. If the novel is ever screened, the movie actress who takes the leading part will not need to resort to drops of glycerine on her lily cheeks. She will only need to read the book.

The ease with which people are killed off in agony novels must excite the admiration of the most bloodthirsty European militarist. There are a good many deaths in *The White Flag*.

Mahala's father dies of grief when Banker Moreland forecloses the mortgage.

Mahala's mother dies of grief when Mahala is arrested on suspicion of stealing the purse—a single sentence accounts for her removal from the scene.

Edith falls over the porch rail and breaks her neck when she discovers Junior Moreland paying money to the hotel maid in exchange for a hug.

Rebecca dies when it is time to bring the Morelands to book for their atrocities.

Black Jemima's son dies, and Jemima has to go to look after his children, just at the moment when it seems expedient to rob Mahala of her last faithful friend.

The farmer's daughter whom Jason marries in an unguarded physical moment (though his heart, please understand, is true to Mahala) dies when she discovers that Mahala is Jason's real love. She runs out into a thunderstorm and is struck by lightning at Mahala's door. Nothing could be more convenient.

And Junior Moreland dies in time to escape a beating from Jason. The book fills a small cemetery as handily as anything. Department stores should note that handkerchiefs will be in large demand this Fall.

Gene Stratton-Porter is said to be the most popular of American woman writers. Perhaps an explanation of the bigness of her sales is that her villains are so terrifically villainous that the ordinary wicked person, reading about their evil deeds, can feel milk-white by contrast.

Martin Moreland is such a villain. Through the sweet pages of *The White Flag* he leaves a ghastly trail of greed, lust, hate and cruelty. The blackness of Judas Iscariot, Benedict Arnold, Nero, Iago and a certain United States Senator is pale gray alongside the blackness of Martin Moreland. He certainly gets away with murder.

He is the village banker, of course, as most villains are in the stories of this school of literature. He prospers by ruining his neighbors in purse, if they are men; in morals, if they are women; in reputation, if they are fair young girls like Mahala.

His meannesses are past counting; their recital is like a visit to the Chamber of Horrors plus a busy Monday morning in the Traffic Court.

Martin cannot open his mouth without screaming in angry passion, save when he addresses his spoiled son. And Junior is a vulture like his father—as if one such bird were not enough in any book, even an emotional novel. Junior has everything he wants except, be sure, the love of the gentle Mahala, who loves the washerwoman's son, as a true Gene Stratton-Porter heroine should.

Mrs. Porter has been happy in some of her character drawing, and her picture of the high school commencement, in which Mahala speaks her mind to the tight minds of the town, is a commendable piece of work. But the author seems to tire toward the last. Perhaps the emotional strain is too much even for her. The last chapters are bare framework and read like a movie scenario.

Her readers will not mind that. They will want to know whether Mahala will get over the typhoid fever, and whether Junior will confess about the purse, and how in the world Jason and Mahala can ever marry when Jason has gone and espoused the wrong girl. All in all, the book is one of Mrs. Porter's best. (pp. 17, 24)

A review of "The White Flag," in The New York Times Book Review, *August 26, 1923, pp. 17, 24.*

CARL VAN DOREN   (essay date 1940)

[*Van Doren is considered one of the most perceptive critics of the first half of the twentieth century. He worked for many years as a professor of English at Columbia University and served as literary editor and critic of the* Nation *and the* Century *during the 1920s. A founder of the Literary Guild and author or editor of several American literary histories, Van Doren was also a critically acclaimed historian and biographer. In the following excerpt, he places Porter in the forefront of sentimentalized popular literature.*]

After 1900 the stream of American fiction was so broad that any brief record of it can do no more than hint at its volume and variety. Since the popular writers did not belong to conscious schools they can be classified only approximately. But most of them worked in kinds of fiction that had been established before them. The domestic sentimentalism with which the American novel had begun was still a staple, though no longer Richardsonian in manner, of Gene Stratton Porter, who piled sentimentalism upon descriptions of nature in soft, sweet heaps, and Harold Bell Wright, who cannily mixed sentimentalism with valor and prudence. They throbbed with all the current impulses; they laughed and wept with the uncritical multitude; and they had the gift of attracting and exciting that multitude with their books in which was displayed, as in a consoling mirror, the rosy, empty features of banality. These two novelists were first among dozens who practised their tearful, perishable mode of art. (p. 269)

Carl Van Doren, "Tradition and Transition," in his The American Novel: 1789-1939, *revised edition, The Macmillan Company, 1940, pp. 246-73.**

MARGARET MacMULLEN   (essay date 1947)

[*In the following excerpt, MacMullen utilizes the works of Porter in a discussion of the artistic and philosophic weaknesses of popular literature of the early twentieth century.*]

In the early years of the present century, when *Sons and Lovers* was jeered at, *Of Human Bondage* neglected, and *Sister Carrie* banned, a number of beautiful masterpieces of a very different sort were flowing like a thick, pink wave of tomato soup into the stream of current fiction. On the crest of this wave, three surprised and discordant Venuses, rode Mrs. Gene Stratton Porter, Mrs. Florence Barclay, and Mr. Harold Bell Wright.

We can visualize them as in a Botticelli canvas, slightly revised. No frail cockleshell would bear them up, and no amorini blow secular trumpets. Instead, with their feet set on a stout raft and with music pumped from an ornamented melodeon, Mrs. Barclay would be stately in black velvet with "soft old lace at the bosom," Mrs. Porter winsome in white, and on her head "a pure white creation of fancy braid, with folds and folds of tulle, soft and silken as cobwebs, lining the brim; and a great mass of white roses [which] clustered against . . . her hair, crept about the crown, and fell in a riot to her shoulders at the back." Thus they embellished their heroines. Why not themselves? Mr. Wright would be manly in chaps, a clerical collar, and a ten-gallon hat. They would be well dressed and triumphant, and rightly so, for each had the supreme felicity of being born at the right time.

The elements of what we idly call Victorianism—class pride, bad taste, false sentiment, and an excess of optimism and paper-lace piety—though undoubtedly present in the day of King Assurbanipal, had not before been assembled into this particular blend. It wanted industrialism and general education to bring out its full flavor, and in addition to have been preserved to the point of incipient decay. These three novelists, with the best intentions in the world and by a stroke of luck they confused with Providence, seized on the prescription and out of it brewed results of unparalleled bathos and popularity. The movies had not yet diverted the public from reading, tabloids and picture magazines hardly existed, and the radio was still a laboratory dream. The field, therefore, was wide open to them. They had only to move into it with the assured gait of the born storyteller.

It may be argued quite reasonably that such gifts will always command an audience and that the special kind of florid bad taste which we associate with the early nineteen-hundreds is almost as prevalent today. Is a bronze nymph with a clock set in her stomach any worse than the white plaster poodle sitting on a cushion, with a lamp springing from his head, which these charmed eyes beheld only yesterday in a New York decorator's shop? Is the hat lovingly described by Mrs. Porter more unnerving than plaid slacks and high-heeled sandals? . . . The human instinct for the tawdry and absurd is whimsical in its choice of outlets, but it flows on forever.

The generation which steered its course by the Wright-Porter-Barclay constellation now finds guidance in the soap operas, the movies, and the romance magazines. Even so late as 1920, Sinclair Lewis put on a parlor table in *Main Street* the latest novel of Mrs. Gene Stratton Porter and gave to an elderly couple in Gopher Prairie a literary philosophy summarized thus: "Harold Bell Wright is a lovely writer, and he teaches such good morals in his novels, and folks say he's made pretty near a million dollars out of 'em." Today on that table—smaller, because of the space taken up by the cabinet radio-phonograph—would lie the movie magazines, and the elderly couple would exclaim over the earnings of the Fitzgeralds and Bing Crosby. But nowadays, alas, lovely writers who teach good morals find the best-selling novel a somewhat corrupted channel. Readers who have lived through two major wars and one major depression, having forgotten what security feels like, will no longer take their optimism undiluted. And with education more general, the public demands more competent workmanship and an increase in intellectual content. Nevertheless, education acting upon a basic soft-mindedness does little to change the true quality of that content. We have all known people who were both very learned and very silly. In the case of this particular trio of novelists, it is an open question whether the intellectual training which they did not undergo—in contrast to the more skillful and better equipped modern writers—would have had much effect on their natural tendency to let emotion seep through and moisten the whole fabric of their thinking, like damp on a cellar wall. (pp. 371-72)

[Here] were three very good people, who forfeit immunity from criticism only because their great popularity and influence form a footnote to literary history. If they wrote very bad books, they did so with innocence, and since they themselves remained incurably adolescent no one could accuse them of trading on a like quality in their readers. Indeed, any such attempt would have been detected. Granted that it is easy to write down to a public if what you give them is love or adventure or comedy—the movie producers have proved that—when it comes to moralizing about things you yourself do not believe in, that instinct by which immature minds are, rather feebly, guarded, and which our politicians call native intelligence will spot the fraud.

Sentimentalism is essentially a disease of decadence. Among the American pioneers, whose noses were perhaps so close to the earth that they could not lift them to sniff at wistful lavendar, the ailment either did not exist or did not find expression, but with the beneficent growth of education and some relaxation of the fiercer demands of survival, it expanded toward the turn of this century with the spongy fecundity of unhealthy cells. In the English novel of the mid-nineteenth century, it was tidily compartmented. In a kind of holy vacuum, Amelia Sedley, Bella Wilfer, and the lesser-known heroines of Miss Yonge, Mrs. Wood, and Mrs. Oliphant shook their curls, kept albums and anniversaries, wept for grief and pleasure, and surprised their husbands with a ninth baby. Though the world might wound, it could not sully them. By the end of the century, however, realism began to threaten the excesses of sentimentalism, not merely in "good" novels but in popular fiction. Some authors, like Anthony Hope and George Barr McCutcheon, dodged it by the road of pure romance in Ruritanian kingdoms; others, like Robert Hichens, neutralized the effects of passion on the human frame by placing their characters in foreign countries, where, as everyone knows, things are different. Still others, like Robert W. Chambers, to the extent permitted by the women's magazines, and Elinor Glyn, whose books lived in bureau drawers, faced the facts of life in a flurry of tiger-skin rugs and polo ponies.

Though one cannot picture either Mrs. Porter or Mrs. Barclay curled up in front of the fire with *Three Weeks,* and Mr. Wright would have blown a boiler at the very mention of it, they could not and apparently did not want to by-pass the new literary tendencies. By nature and by training they were so concerned with the ethical aspect of life that it was impossible for them to bar the flesh and the devil from their pages. In sentimental and moral tales of the earlier Victorians the problem of evil had been handled with extreme gentility. The deceptions, frailties, and broken hearts had been kept remote from any taint of explicit carnality. One gets the impression of lots of heaving, struggling, and humping going on behind a heavy plush curtain. Our particular authors, on uplift bent and living in an age of greater frankness, disdained such cowardice, and introduced with a certain succulence the sins they intended to fight. In a word, they progressed from the bosom to the breasts school of literature. This is less true of Mrs. Porter, whose young couples made love in a lusty girl-scout fashion suggestive of middy blouses and khaki pants, than of Mrs. Barclay and Mr. Wright. He, in fact, went so far as to land one of his heroines in a most unfortunate establishment—of which he gave an enthralling description—and made her accept the prospect of a life of shame as casually as she would a jujube.

For the most part the background was simple and familiar. The girls worried over their clothes, the boys played games, chickens were fed and stock watered, young and old struggled to make ends meet and talked about their neighbors. Mrs. Barclay's county families ate strawberries with their tea and the rector came to call. If only the plots and the character-drawing matched the surroundings we might have had something of merit, for the ability to tell a story was there. (pp. 374-75)

If living people step out of it, a novel can rise above awkward style and construction, as a good actor, handicapped but not obliterated, can surmount a poor play poorly staged; but our trio, with all their output and with all their conviction to the contrary, created only characters flatly "good" or "bad" or "quaint." Though both Mrs. Porter and Mr. Wright had an ear for the vernacular with which they were familiar, their local characters could under pressure of plot make quite dressy speeches, while those blessed with superior education expressed themselves with an almost Attic glory. Unlike most of us, who even on ordinary occasions bog down in "I mean" and "we-e-ll," and in emotional ones end in just plain babbling, they were never at a loss for the rounded sentence and the punctuated paragraph. Mrs. Porter's Laddie, a farm boy, described his best girl to his little sister with remarkable detail: "Her face is oval and her cheeks are bright. Her eyes are big moonlit pools of darkness, and silken curls fall over her shoulders. One hair is strong enough for a lifeline that will draw a drowning man ashore, or strangle an unhappy one."

Equally startling, though in a milder way, was her admiring version of the speech of a cultivated young Englishman. He used "fawct" for fact, "hoss" for horse, "uth" for earth, "cawn" for can. He also dropped his aitches. . . .

How could such books sell by the million? Why were extra freight cars needed to distribute *The Winning of Barbara Worth* on the day of its publication? Why were countless readers comforted and amused, excited and exalted?

The first and most important reason was the writers' unconquerable gusto. Not only did they believe every word they wrote, but they gave the impression of having torn off their books as a locomotive blows off steam. Puerilities, bad style, shaky grammar, contradictions, all dissolved in a fiery vigor that was irresistible to an uncritical reader and could not be entirely withstood by the critical. . . .

And there was sound reason in the works themselves for this success which begot success. The fairy tale happy ending, the cheerful moral lesson, the salt of sex were combined in a perfect formula. In these novels was an insane optimism adapted to beguile those who spend much of their lives averting their gaze from the glare of reality. When the theme was regeneration, the uphill road was pleasantly graded and florally landscaped, with the love nest on the summit always in sight. No matter how the forces of evil might plague from without, internally

the hero and heroine suffered no setback of humiliation. Love conquered at the last—and in a chinchilla dolman.

The ladies were seldom in need of any moral remodeling. They were as pure as they were beautiful—pathologically so, in fact. For purity is a virtue which may be said to exist only in the negative state; any definite affirmation suggests coldness, self-righteousness, overlong preservation. The vapor of pruriency, of something not quite fresh, creeps in. The traces of it in Mrs. Porter's work, a mere cream-cheese whiff, ripened to the full power of Gorgonzola in that of Mr. Wright and Mrs. Barclay. *The Eyes of the World* was condemned on its appearance by more than one reviewer as pornographic, which it was not, except in a most infantile and disarming way, and only as a result of the author's unflagging effort to drive home a moral lesson. (pp. 378-79)

The scale of values was actually a first-class muddle. On the one hand there was an exaltation of simple faith and plain living; on the other, a worldliness less knowing but as complete as Edith Wharton's. Mrs. Barclay, whose formative years were passed near the slums of London and who did valiant social service there and later in her husband's country parish, peopled her stage exclusively with the crustiest of the upper crust. Her duchesses were paralleled by Mr. Wright's "fashionable hardware merchant." If his or Mrs. Porter's characters entered the scene nameless or unidentified, their origins proved in the last chapter to be the height of elegance; an avowed contempt for social labels was outweighed by a strong bias in favor of aristocratic background. Moreover, the final affluence assuring the future of the young lovers was often inherited rather than earned. It seems to have had more *ton* that way.

Confusion is inevitable when art and ethics are awash with the sentimentalism which flourishes equally in those who don't like what they have but don't know what they want, and those whose minds are so padded with sanctities that there is no room left for ideas. Either type may be counted on to supply a boundless patronage of bad art. Certainly the devotees of *Freckles* and *The Rosary* liked these soda-fountain concoctions all the more because so many artificial moral or social implications had been stirred into them. . . .

The average reader of novels will no longer throb to such an appeal, though he may accept a chromium-plated version on the screen or over the radio. Unabashed sentimentality can expand only in an atmosphere of security, and that we have lost. With the exception of *A Shepherd of the Hills*, which because of its production as a movie has reappeared in a twenty-five cent reprint, you will find the stories of Mrs. Barclay, Mrs. Porter, and Mr. Wright only in small, old-fashioned libraries, from which the elderly subscriber will once in a long while draw *The Winning of Barbara Worth* or *The Rosary* on a sleepy summer afternoon.

It may be that from their pages floats an image of that lost world in which some of us grew up; of the hammocks hung under apple-trees and lemonade pink with squashed strawberries. But the lemonade is too freely sugared, and the motion of the hammock makes one a trifle queasy. (p. 380)

Margaret MacMullen, "Love's Old Sweetish Song," in Harper's Magazine, *Vol. 195, No. 1169, October, 1947, pp. 371-80.**

EDWARD IFKOVIC (essay date 1975)

[*In the following essay, Ifkovic discusses the idealistic portrayals of God, nature, family life, and American values in Porter's fiction.*]

For many readers, Gene Stratton-Porter . . . was *the* writer of domestic romance in pre-World War I America. With Harold Bell Wright she was a household word, a woman whose books delighted millions of readers. She helped lead a school of domestic romance which peaked just before America's entry into World War I. With assuring, homely portraits, such writers as Harold Bell Wright (*The Shepherd of the Hills,* 1907), Kathleen Norris (*Mother,* 1911), and Eleanor H. Porter (*Pollyanna,* 1913), told middle-class white America that its homes were safe—secure in a new America that was torn by industrial mechanization, ghetto-ridden cities, violent anarchism, and non-WASP immigration. Mrs. Porter presented an alternate portrait of America—escapist to be sure, but idyllic salve for a confused America at the end of the genteel age. One of the most successful domestic writers in American history, she was at her peak from 1909 until 1915. In these years she produced five books that are all-time best sellers—*Freckles, A Girl of the Limberlost, The Harvester, Laddie,* and *Michael O'Halloran*—which rank her, in terms of number of best-selling books, with James Fenimore Cooper and Harold Bell Wright as fourth place behind Dickens, Scott, and Erle Stanley Gardner.

So successful was Mrs. Porter that she profited over two million dollars, viewed her work as a profession, and even organized a movie company to film her romances. She was a woman of affairs in a time when women like her were unique. The irony emerges when we realize that she evolved to such a professional state by means of her domestic message: a woman belongs in the home. She condemned the suffragettes and believed that women could best vote through their husbands—hers always voted as she wished. She became for millions of readers the singer of the hearth—a sugary, sickly sweet sentimentalist whose home-portraits were as far from reality as she could manage. She evolved a formula of Nature, God, domestic problems, ideal love and confectioned rhetoric—stirred with the loving care of Mother—and the American middle class (not necessarily economically middle class, but a rural America which long accepted middle class values, inculcated throughout the nineteenth century: God and the home, provincial Americanism, and Christian morality), bought her books in unprecedented numbers. Harold Bell Wright wrote her a letter of appreciation, thanking her "for our race that, in this day, so much needs the sort of stories you are writing." As she stated: "My formula for a book was damned by three of our foremost publishers in the beginning, *and I never have changed it a particle.*" Only a change in popular taste after World War I would stop the well-oiled machinery of her romance.

Born in Indiana, the twelfth child of a Dutch-American mother and an English father, she very early came to love the great Limberlost forest where her parents built their home. Here she studied and loved nature, collecting specimens of moths and butterflies, photographing birds and flowers. Her strong Christian upbringing told her that God was the force behind nature, and she could not see the happy American family unless it was strengthened by the outdoors. She was as much an apostle of the outdoors as Roosevelt whom she revered as a man of action and man of family. Man needed to return to communion with simple nature:

> If possible, I would advocate holding services
> out-of-doors in summer, giving as my reason
> that God so manifests Himself in the trees,
> flowers, and grass that to be among His crea-
> tions puts one in a devotional frame of mind,
> gives better air to breathe, and puts worship on

> a natural basis, as it was in the beginning, when
> Christ taught the people beside the sea and in
> the open.

She described herself as a creature "saturate with earth, water, and air," and indeed this passionate commitment to nature must have given her romances the spark of freshness which excited the reader. When she began a story, she knew only that she needed "an outdoor setting of land," and she would serve as the funnel through which the divine message would sing: "I am nothing but a machine of transmission." She felt a kinship with those who loved nature and wrote of it—a kinship which made her see Whitman as "the most democratic man that ever lived" because he understood the God behind nature.

A sympathy with nature was the first step to a reverence for the home. Man and his woman forging their home and producing children were the beautiful extension—God's noblest extension—of the natural life processes of the forest. The ferns, the flowers, the deer, the squirrels—all flourish and reproduce in their season, and they have an unalterable harmony with man. Natural man, that is. As Mrs. Porter wrote in a letter to her future husband: "to have a home—God's greatest blessing on earth—a beautiful, cozy place to live in, to love in, to come from the world's toil and care to the tender love of one who will look beautiful to you at least." Such domestic felicity was possible only when man was in communion with nature. She felt that the world already knew too much corruption of natural man, and the city especially had polluted his basic goodness until he was filled with the black pus of evil ambition and desire. There are no families in the city. "No man can love the *home* he rents," she said. They knew no God in the narrow green-less streets of the city; God made His home where there was air to breathe, the scent of early mosses and late harvests, where the expanse of wide sky was blue and white. Here man's home was a living ideal:

> . . . in the plain, old-fashioned country homes
> where I have lived, I have known such wealth
> of loving consideration, such fidelity between
> husband and wife, such obedience in children,
> such constancy to purpose, such whole-souled
> love for friends and neighbors, such absence
> of jealousy, pettiness, and rivalry, as my city
> critics do not know is in existence.

The world of nature is an honest one, and a timeless one. Despising schedules and deadlines, she kept no clocks in her home: "I hate having the time of day stare me in the face from every room I enter." The forest is the time before time, a land without machinery: America before the fall.

She realized very early that she could reach people with her message of nature by adding a sentimental love story—layers of purposely sweet confection which would attract the reader. With *A Girl of the Limberlost* . . . , she began to ride the crest of a tremendous wave which was to make her one of the important spokesmen of the much-beleaguered home. "I wrote *A Girl of the Limberlost,*" she said, "to carry to workers inside city walls, to hospital cots, to those behind prison bars, and to scholars in their libraries, my story of earth and sky." She posited a different American identity for those who were far from the natural world. Given the choice of American identities, America chose her buoyant one, an America in which evil has been destroyed. Even in the midst of shattering reality, America could believe (for a few minutes at least) in her pictures. A soldier, deep in battle in France in World War I, paused to write Mrs. Porter about *A Girl of the Limberlost:* "I surely enjoyed it. It sounded so American, and the nature suggestions brought me back to myself again." His letter is testimony to the strong hold of the sentimental romancer's ideal America on the popular imagination—even in the midst of war and dying, an ideal America is the means of consolation.

In *A Girl of the Limberlost* the heroine, Elnora Comstock, "who collects moths to pay for her education, and lives the Golden Rule," is a beautiful young country girl who lives alone with an embittered, puritanical mother. Living in the vast Limberlost forest, Elnora has found a home in nature. But she sorrows: she lacks the love of a real mother. To bring humanity back to the saddened mother is the challenge for the Young Girl. So begins the romance, and we see how Elnora's natural goodness softens her severe mother and, indeed, transforms the whole world (city and country) into a happy state—simply by her happy presence among people. In the end she finds the loving mother she has so desperately wanted. Mrs. Porter is clearly tapping the traditional fairy tale formula, so popular a device for girls. But the standard pattern is now used to reinforce the question of American identity. The plot formula of a particular adolescent fantasy is manipulated now for an adult audience.

The romance is simply the young girl's journey to love and success, all her problems falling away from her sainted presence. In such a parable there is virtually no evil. Mrs. Porter does not build her plots by confrontation with evil; rather, the obstacles she sets up are only minor domestic matters—getting money for tuition, for example—and they are achievable goals. And because these goals are within reach, paradise can be obtained. The posing of domestic obstacles doubtless satisfied the middle-class reader whose life was filled with a rush of petty concerns and small economic problems. The plot structure paralleled his own life, and the solving of the small nagging problems in fiction was solace indeed for the reader who would then view his own problems which, once eradicated, insure the security of the home in paradise. People speak of evil but the world is really a place filled with good people. Average man in Average American Home is the good, contented man. "The world is full of happy people," Elnora states, "but no one ever hears of them. You have to fight and make a scandal to get into the paper. No one knows about all the happy people. I am happy myself, and just look how perfectly inconspicuous I am." . . . This statement, then, is Mrs. Porter's testimony to America that a different America did exist; here was plenty evidence to counter the black headlines of American strife. The average American is Elnora, living without evil, without difficult problems, in the country home. With husband and loving mother, she abides in the quiet of her happy days.

If *A Girl of the Limberlost* is Mrs. Porter's ideal of young womanhood, then *The Harvester* . . . is her ideal of young manhood. The Harvester, David Langston, lives in the Limberlost forest where he collects medical specimens to be sold to the drug firms in the city. He is content with his life, a complete immersion in the splendor of nature, but the time for him to marry arrives: the natural function of man. So the novel becomes one long song of marriage with every action revolving around the pursuit of a woman. The life of solitary man is not good, for the Harvester knows that procreation is a fact of nature. Like Elnora, David is a domestic country man who helps rejuvenate tainted city people, showing them the way to home and love. The love of nature and of nature's God has

given both a gentleness which cannot help but influence others. While Elnora is a conventional heroine of domestic romance, the Harvester is an intriguing male character, a man who is not orphaned boy, minister, wise old man; but he is legitimately a hero of domestic romance by virtue of his character. He is a tender man, described in terms conventionally "feminine": a soft heart, a gentle way with animals, a sense of the niceties of life. "Why you are more like a woman!" one character tells him when he will not hurt a moth. The Harvester answers: "To appreciate beauty or to try to be just commonly decent is not exclusively feminine." . . . Mrs. Porter is putting forth her ideal of man—one who has a tender regard for all life, who understands the beauty of nature and God, but one who is always ready to fight and do hard work when the need arises. This is Mrs. Porter's definition of American man: a combination of gentleness and boldness, quietness and aggressiveness, a man of peace and a man of war when honor is on the line. Such men do exist, she claimed. Every "tender, loving, thoughtful, chivalrous thing" in *The Harvester* was done by her father and two brothers "for my mother and sister in my own home." Such characters are thus "true to life." Mrs. Porter wanted her book to be a guide for the men of the nation. Men wrote to her that their lives had been changed by the novel; the book was used in reform schools and prisons; and the president of a railroad company gave three hundred copies to young men in his employ. The Harvester's long address on "clean living" was often quoted in the homiletic press.

Inevitably, Mrs. Porter merged her portraits of ideal man and woman into her ideal of the family, a culmination seen in *Laddie: A True Blue Story.* . . . Mr. and Mrs. Stanton are clearly based on Mrs. Porter's own family, the Strattons. Little Sister tells the story which centers around an older brother, Laddie, and his love for the "Princess," the daughter of a new English family in the neighborhood. The story has about it an ethereal quality, as Laddie and his Princess romp through the splendid woods with talk of Fairies and Magic Carpets. The Princess shows how "to make sunshine on dark days," and Laddie adores her. The Limberlost has become the Enchanted Land. The Stanton family is happy, carefree, the children virtually tumbling up. Little Sister, like Mrs. Porter herself, is the twelfth child to arrive. The book is filled with nostalgic, warm family memories—church recitations, family dinners, minor heartaches. One girl gets married ("If he kisses her when he leaves, of course they are engaged" . . .), and a wedding is celebrated. The bond of love is so strong among the members of the family that it casts a romantic glow over the entire autobiographical rendering. God is mentioned often as the spirit behind the family, and the Stanton children play at going to church. . . . The parents have created a blissful paradise, entire in itself, where their children can know the taste of Eden. A child's fantasy world, this inviolate state of grace is called an Eden by Mrs. Porter herself. . . . No hells exist here, no suggestion of hell—when Laddie refers to hell he calls it "the Bad Place." . . . Here is the Family in its quintessential form: untainted, strong, loving, numerous, secure and happy.

The ideal family occupies, to use one of the chapter headings, "The Garden of the Lord," where the family feels one with the rhythms of day and night. The awe they sense when the day is beautiful is "The Home Feeling," according to the author, a feeling filling them "with the spirit of worship." . . . This Home Feeling makes Laddie decide to stay on the land. "I stick to the soil." . . . An allegiance to the land can cause no harm to come to man—the failure of banks and the upheavals of industry do not touch the land—or so the author says. Laddie's father, a pioneer himself, is pleased with his son's decision.

> I hate to see a son of mine thriving on law, literally making their living at the fruit of other men's discord. I dislike seeing them sharpen their wits in trade, buying at the lowest limit, extorting the highest. I don't want their horizons limited by city blocks, their feet on pavements, everything under the sun in their heads that concerns a scheme to make money; not room for an hour's thought or study in the whole day, about the really valid things of life. After all, land and its products are the basis of everything; the city couldn't exist a day unless we feed and clothe it. In the things I consider important, you are a king among men, with your feet on soil of your own. . . .

Laddie inherits the domestic felicity of his father, the desire to both *use* the land as well as beautify it. "You have made it all a garden," Mrs. Stanton tells her husband. "You have made it a garden growing under the smile of the Master; a very garden of the Lord, father." . . . Here the family will live and die, part of the natural world where they live, buried in the lap of nature when they die.

When the bitter Mr. Pryor, an atheist and emigré Englishman, is concerned with the worthiness of Laddie for his daughter, the "Princess," Mrs. Stanton defends the democratic ideal: "Men are men, and Laddie is as much above the customary timber found in kings and princes, physically and mentally, as the sky is above the earth . . . the real question is, whether she's fit to be his wife." . . . Mr. Pryor comes to understand American values, just as he finds God again in America, influenced by the prayers of the Stanton family. Until he realizes that he can only suffer anguish so long as he refuses to accept God and the democratic notion that "All men are brothers," . . . he is doomed to unhappiness. His narrow, inward torture cannot understand at first why the Stantons are concerned for his welfare, why he is a burden on their souls. Why do they not simply ignore him—let him stay with his bitterness and blasphemy? But the Stantons are conscious of their duty to fellow man: in a democratic land all men are capable of being saved. The encounter with the ideal home must save anyone. Mrs. Porter, however, cannot escape the easy trick of the romancer to make Mr. Pryor's transformation the result of a deus ex machina: the return of a prodigal son whose disappearance had precipitated Mr. Pryor's turning from God. Had she allowed him to change simply because of the domestic philosophy, her domestic message could have had more strength behind it. Insecurity with her vision (and the machinery of romance) made her introduce coincidence into the plot.

This same insecurity made her stress the noble lineage of the Stanton name. The family possesses the crest of the Earl of Eastbrooke, master of Stanton house. Ancestors had distinguished themselves on the Crusades—four times in fact; and the blood of the Crusaders flows in the Stanton veins. Although they express the democratic ideal and say they put no faith in ancestry, the pride of blood pervades the romance. The Stantons are *not* the average people Mrs. Porter proclaims them to be; they are distinguished gentry, part of the Anglo-Saxon nobility which has always gone forth to conquer the world. In her own life Mrs. Porter spoke of the noble connections of her family, the long lineage of British blood of the house of Northbrooke. Her father, although a pioneer in the American wilderness, clung "with the rigid tenacity" to British tradition and custom: "He believed in God, in courtesy, in honour, in cleanliness, in beauty, in education." Democratic confrontation with the wilderness was not enough: the heightened distinction of the privileged British gentry was necessary to validate the professed American ideals.

The romance is one long hymn to the family, and the emotional symbol is the mother, whose dedication and warmth hover, like the wings of one of the Limberlost moths, over the land. The mother holds the family together; she prepares her daughters for motherhood and the comfort of the husband, teaching them every domestic duty—from housecleaning to the making of a garden—which will insure their skill as leaders of the family. Her girls, like herself, have no other wants in life other than that of the home: "To be a good wife and mother is the end toward which I aspire. To hold the respect and love of my husband is the greatest object of my life." . . . She hopes she has washed enough sheets to make a pile high enough to reach heaven; for domestic accomplishment is the surest road to paradise. Mrs. Porter was countering the contemporary movement of women out of the home and into the office, fearing the effects on the race. *Laddie* was her vehement response to the New Woman: "So long as women are the mothers of the race, what happens to them is absolutely vital to the race." Mrs. Porter aimed all her syrupy guns at the change in American society, and told her women readers that the old American woman was the Christian woman—and, it followed, the New Woman was a betrayal of God's desire. She found justification in her view of women in the Bible, still the standard of conduct in the middle-class American home:

> One could take the Bible and outline the duties of women as they are set forth. I take women because women are the mothers, and are primarily responsible for the atmosphere of our homes and the religious training of our families. . . . The things that make them shirk motherhood, that make them narrow and selfish, that set them to drinking and gambling, that drive them to find their entertainment in cabarets, cafes and hotels instead of at home, are greatly to be deplored. I put my ideal of a wife and mother into a book of mine entitled *Laddie*. To my mind, my mother was an example of the highest type of housekeeper, a proud woman, beautifully dressed, interested in politics, religion, and all social problems; and at the same time mothering her dozen, keeping an immaculate house, and lending her influence and experience to the education of each and every one of her children.

So *Laddie* is the natural extension of the Biblical word, the new tablet of commandments of the domestic hearth—to break the commandments was to invite the death of the race.

In the romance itself there is no evil, for in the American family, as Mrs. Porter depicts it, evil has been killed—significantly, evil has been destroyed by mother. Here in the Garden of Eden (and the author makes free use of edenic imagery), the serpent did not destroy but was itself destroyed. Mrs. Stanton recalls that she once insured the preservation of prelapsarian Eden; for in her earlier pioneer days, she spotted a snake crawling next to her first child, "It was my job to throw the first thing I could lay my hands on so straight and true that I would break the snake's neck, and send its deadly fangs away from my baby." . . . The serpent which would destroy Eden is itself destroyed. Man does not fall; the mother has saved the purity and future of the race, and only paradise can follow. Such a twisting of Biblical tradition—if we can entertain this symbolic rendering—helps reinforce Mrs. Porter's unquestioned ideal of the home. Evil does not exist because it died years ago in the woman's first pioneer experience with the wilderness. Evil when it appears (like Mr. Pryor) is only seeming evil, misguided good; it will dissipate before the forces of the hearth.

When we look at Mrs. Porter's own life, however, we realize that the author's supposedly autobiographical picture of an American family is really a sugar-coated adaptation of a problem-ridden family. Her parents had to sell their property and rent a farm, resulting in the collapse of all their dreams. The character of Laddie was based on her older brother Leander, worshipped by his sister, who indeed did decide to work on the farm. But he died, a drowning victim, at eighteen. The Stratton family took their misfortune, we are told, with Christian fortitude, but the fulfilled family of *Laddie* is not a reality. An ideal she perhaps wished had happened, *Laddie* was passed off as truth, and doubtless many readers believed her. An escape fantasy for her own life, it also gave solace and encouragement to a floundering middle class whose real experiences were more like Mrs. Porter's real life than that of Laddie. Nightmare vision became dream vision. So completely lacking in evil, *Laddie* becomes a narcotic, a false sensational high, a dream-like state, an Enchanted Land (to use the words of the romance). A romance in which all problems are solvable, it was an unadulterated cure-all for the confusion and anxiety of so many Americans. When the work was filmed, it was advertised in terms of utter escapism: "Now even the movies are filming *Laddie,* that bright and cheery tale. There's a wedding midway in the book and a double wedding at the close."

Mrs. Porter continued her success with *Michael O'Halloran* . . . , the story of an orphaned newsboy, but it was her last huge seller. She continued to write in the post-war years (for example, *The Keeper of the Bees* . . .) but her sales had fallen. Although one journalist remarked that her amassed wealth did not lure her from the beloved forest, the post-war attraction of Hollywood could not be ignored. She organized a film company in 1919, with her son-in-law as director, to make films of her works. But unlike her romances, her life did not move in easy, optimistic rhythms: on December 6, 1924, she was killed when her limousine was struck by a streetcar. The final irony perhaps: the automobile, so strongly the symbol of the despised new American society in the pages of popular fiction, now destroyed the author who had railed at the changes she saw taking place.

At the height of her power Mrs. Porter attracted an audience which revered her with an allegiance that bordered on a cult. Much of her public consisted of rural farm families, many walking the tight line of poverty; but she also was read in cities and towns by millions of others, all believing in the values of the middle-class imagination. Her call for a return to a childhood memory, her re-creation of a problem-less world, an America without tears, made her one of the most popular writers of all time. While some critics might despise her saccharine tales ("molasses fiction"), her readers adored her. Hers was an American identity they so desperately needed. "God has given you wonderful genius and the stamina to cultivate it," a woman wrote her. "Every right-minded American woman who reads is *proud* of you." For her vision was a patriotic one, consciously detected by her reviewers: "essentially Amer-

ican—as something which springs only from American soil and flourishes in it as it could nowhere else." Her romances of the home are documents in the provincial nationalism of the time.

She believed that the romancer must serve his nation, and such service could best be done by cheerful, buoyant pictures of the home. The leading of the good (conventional) life could contribute to American democracy. "Every one of us can do something for our government by being men and women of sound morals; this precludes bodily disease and the transmission of bad blood for generations." God comes first in our allegiance, but government is second; America is thus God's country. She fostered a reactionary political vision of America, remembering an old pioneer America where evil did not exist, an older America we must recapture if there is to be salvation. Modern America alarmed her: she was bothered by the movement of women out of the home, as well as the rise of socialism which wanted to plunge America "into chaos." So fearful was this evil specter that she advocates, in her reactionary fantasy, a fascistic scrutiny of American allegiance. In time of war, she says, the slogan is "show your colors," in which a house-to-house canvas is made, each family stating its stand on national policy. Mrs. Porter thought that we should have such canvassing at all times—"a capital idea in time of peace" so that malignant evil could be erased from America.

Her contribution to the American dilemma was to help people escape from it. She told Americans that if they were religious men and women (God is behind America), if they were honest, moral and upright, healthy of body and mind, then they would uphold the ideals of the past and infinitely superior America— and in the process they would insure the majesty of the land in the future. Here was an opiate that encompassed every consolatory gesture of the society—religion, love, patriotism, family—until the final picture assured man that America could resolve any problem. If the new philosophies and novelists suggested that man was not innately good (a conclusion which would shatter the American assumption of democracy perhaps) then she told her readers a different story. She was a stay against chaos: the complete immersion in goodness and wholesomeness. As her daughter recalled: "The keynote of it all is simplicity, in code, manner, and dress—so simple we fail to grasp it: just love, love of God, love of Nature, love of her fellow man." But Mrs. Porter said it best when she summarized the philosophy of her life and that of the genteel popular imagination of pre-World War I America, in the last moment of its innocence: "There is nothing to fear: think only of what is good and right and happy." But behind the optimistic words hovered the specter of growing fear. (pp. 757-65)

Edward Ifkovic, "The Garden of the Lord: Gene Stratton-Porter and the Death of Evil in Eden," in Journal of Popular Culture, *Vol. VIII, No. 4, Spring, 1975, pp. 757-66.*

MARY CADOGAN AND PATRICIA CRAIG (essay date 1976)

[*In the following excerpt from their survey of popular fiction written for girls, Cadogan and Craig discuss deficiencies in the plot and characterizations of* A Girl of the Limberlost.]

English fictional children at the beginning of the century tended to have their moral shortcomings ironed out in the course of a story; in America the process was inverted, with hardened adults gradually being humanized by contact with impossibly well-adjusted and sunny-dispositioned children, whose own characters appeared to need very little modification. The first of these catalytic small girls was *Rebecca of Sunnybrook Farm* by Kate Douglas Wiggin (1903); the most expertly realized was *Anne of Green Gables* by L. M. Montgomery (1908); and the most idiotic was *Pollyanna* by Eleanor H. Porter (1913). This group of stories was augmented with Gene Stratton Porter's emotionally deprived *Girl of the Limberlost*. . . . (p.89)

[If] *A Girl of the Limberlost* is on the whole a more solid piece of work than *Pollyanna*, its style is more lurid, more intense. It is still in print; but it is hopelessly out of date. It is full of archaisms, the most obvious of which are the chapter headings. "Wherein" savours of both the tome and the tombstone; "Wherein Elnora goes to high school and learns many lessons not found in her books" manages to sound at once heavily arch and lightly philosophical, and in this way sets the tone for the whole book.

The book follows the career of a Limberlost girl from adolescence to marriage. Its romantic theme functions on two levels: underlying the obvious inflation of the girl's sterling character and emotional difficulties is Gene Stratton Porter's glorification of Nature ("'We Limberlost people must not be selfish with the wonders God has given us. We must share with those poor cooped-up city people the best we can'"); and the "richness" of the countryside is expressed in practical terms when her heroine, Elnora Comstock, pays her way through high school by selling moths and other insects which she has gathered from the swamp.

Elnora suffers horribly from an intermittently demented mother, who sometimes goes out at night to implore the swamp to give her back her dead husband—for whose death she most unreasonably blames her daughter. He had drowned in the swamp while she—on the point of giving birth—was unable to help him; since this unfortunate incident she has subjected Elnora to the most blatant kind of mental cruelty. On page one she is jeering "'You are so plum daffy you are forgetting your dinner'"; before the end of the chapter, having refused to give Elnora a penny to pay for the books which she needs, and having gone out of her way to ensure that the girl makes a fool of herself on her first day at high school, she blusters, "'Of course I knew you would come home blubbering! But you don't get a penny! . . . Have your own way if you are determined, but I think you will find the road pretty rocky.'"

The culmination of the cruelty comes when Mrs Comstock, having undertaken to provide a graduation dress for Elnora, gives her at the last minute an old white dress which she simply has washed and ironed. The emotional build-up for this seemingly unimportant event is morbidly fostered, with the author thrumming for all she is worth on the exposed nerve-ends of Elnora, who ends up reliving the episode where her father was drowned, in a dream. "'I saw it last night just as he went down. And, oh, Aunt Margaret! I saw what she did, and I heard his cries. No matter what she does, I don't believe I can ever be angry with her again,'" she declares; but Mrs Comstock goes too far in the affair of the dress, and when, shortly afterwards, she wantonly destroys a rare moth which Elnora needs to complete a collection worth $300, her daughter's alienation from her seems assured.

But, "one of the Almighty's most delicate and beautiful creations was sacrificed without fulfilling the law, yet none of its species ever served so glorious a cause, for at last Mrs Comstock's inner vision had cleared". The clearing process is helped on by a nifty piece of amateur psychotherapy on the part of a neighbour, who stands up to Mrs Comstock and tells her the truth about the man whom she has idolized for twenty years.

"'I had an idea that it would kill you to know, but I guess you are tough enough to stand anything. Kill or cure, you get it now!'" The brutal truth is simply that Mr Comstock had been coming from another woman when he was drowned. The immediate effect of this revelation is highly melodramatic:

> Mrs Comstock gripped the hoe tighter, and turning she went down the walk and started across the woods to the home of Elvira Carney. . . .
>
> "Mercy!" gasped weak little Elvira Carney. "Have mercy! . . . If you knew what I've suffered. . . . All the neighbours have suspected and been down on me. I ain't had a friend. I've always felt guilty of his death. I've seen him go down a thousand times plain as ever you did. Many's the night I've stood on the other bank of that pool and listened to you, and I tried throw myself in to keep from hearing you, but I didn't dare. I knew God would send me to burn for ever, but I'd better done it; for now He has set the burning on my body, and every hour it is slowly eating the life out of me. The doctor says it's a cancer—"

The moral message is plain by this point, but Gene Stratton Porter cannot relinquish the hell-fire attitude which she has struck: "'Instead of doing a woman's work in life you chose the smile of invitation and the dress of unearned cloth. Now you tell me you are marked to burn to death with the unquenchable fire. And him! It was shorter with him, but let me tell you he got his share . . .'." Every last drop of retribution is extracted by Mrs Comstock from this sadistic confrontation; and then Elnora's delightful mother, with a complete change of face, returns home to lavish affection on the daughter whom she has persecuted and resented: "the girl was almost suffocated with tempestuous caresses and generous offerings".

At this point the second phase of the novel begins. Having had one intolerable emotional relationship smoothed over, Elnora is ripe for another: fatalistically, she falls in love with a man who is engaged to someone else. Of course he soon decides that he prefers Elnora—but both, with pigheadedness and inflexibility masquerading as chivalrousness, consider his engagement binding.

> "Elnora," he whispered, "will you kiss me goodbye?"
>
> Elnora drew back and stared at him with wide eyes. "I'd strike you sooner!" she said.

It can only be the repressive society in which such a nonsensical attitude is credible, even creditable, which is responsible for the misdirected sexuality with which the book seethes. Two images in particular stand out, and are at once ludicrous and horrifying. Two women racked with guilt and frustration (one suffering agonies for having, as she sees it, lured a man to his death, the other for having failed to save him) making fools of themselves in the dark at opposite sides of a pond, is one; the other is a night marauder, who, surreptitiously and salaciously, watches Elnora prepare for bed.

> Three steps out on the big limb the man shuddered. He was within a few feet of the girl.

He could see the throb of her breast under its thin covering and smell the fragrance of the tossing hair . . . nothing was worth a glance save the perfect face and form within reach by one spring through the rotten mosquito bar. He gripped the limb above that on which he stood, licked his lips and breathed through his throat to be sure he was making no sound.

This is the language of the shilling shocker: Mrs Porter's overwrought imagination veers, characteristically, from biblical ranting to erotic titillation, though no doubt she would have repudiated the charge of the latter. "Purity", here, is as much to be glorified as "Nature"—indeed the two are in some way implied to be interchangeable, however biologically paradoxical that may seem. Mrs Porter's high-minded young couple are impelled only by the purest of motives, and inhibited at every turn by airy-fairy scruples. Elnora gets her man, since the "children's book" context demands a happy ending; but not until both have indulged in a great deal of emotional masochism. To make the ending even more palatable to unrealists, a transformation is wrought in the empty-headed ex-fiancée, principally by contact with the ennobling Elnora.

Gene Stratton Porter's chief—indeed, her only—literary merit is an ability to convey to the reader her acute sense of place. The Limberlost, with its gnarled tree trunks, Indian relics and profuse vegetation, is as far removed from a clean New England village, or the pretty island where Anne grows up, as Elnora is unlike Rebecca and Anne. She is the least whimsical of heroines, and, in company with her creator, the most humourless. Mrs Porter's feeling for the swamp has determined the quality of her prose: both are lush, oppressive, unhealthy, and productive of noxious fumes. (pp. 101-05)

> *Mary Cadogan and Patricia Craig, "Orphans and Golden Girls," in their* You're a Brick, Angela! A New Look at Girls' Fiction from 1839 to 1975, *Victor Gollancz Ltd., 1976, pp. 89-110.*

BERTRAND F. RICHARDS   (essay date 1980)

[*In the following excerpt, Richards offers a balanced assessment of Porter's fiction and nonfiction.*]

The novels of Gene Stratton Porter are not as bad as those critics who deign to mention her at all in the history of American literature would lead one to believe. It cannot be denied that she mistook popularity for worth. She points in many instances to the statistics of the sales of her books as evidence of their greatness. She wrote, "I have done every one of my books from my heart's best impulse, made them as clean and decent as I know how, and as beautiful and as interesting." But she failed to recognize or to accept the fact that the appeal of her books lay not primarily in their cleanliness, their decency, or even in their beauty, but in the truth that they were interesting. For it is true that Porter possessed the rare quality of being able to arouse and sustain the interest of her readers through the most transparent of plots, the most obvious resolvement of situations, and the most advantageous workings of circumstance. The readers of her day were more willing to accept her "good" people leading their "good" lives (or suffering the consequences) than are the readers of today because her morality was somewhat closely attuned to the ideal morality of the time. But the modern reader who by some quirk of fortune picks up a Porter book for "idle reading on a summer's day" is likely to be gripped and carried along by the genuine interest of her story. Perhaps this fact accounts for the appeal that Porter novels still have for adolescent readers.

Porter made much of the fact that her stories were real; that her characters and incidents were drawn from life as she had lived it and knew it; that her stories were shared emotional experiences. She seemed unaware of Nietzsche's doctrine that no true artist tolerates reality. Yet, as Mrs. Porter builds scene on scene, her novels gain a certain intensity; they have a sense of the theatrical. It is no happenstance that Porter the photographer uses the photographic or scenic method in many passages of her novels. Even her descriptive passages are *composed* as if glimpsed through a view finder. It was this same quality which led to her ability to translate her novels into scenarios for the motion picture screen.

There are many minuses encountered in considering the works of Gene Stratton Porter, but there are also many pluses. Her works do lend themselves to criticism because of the limited depth of her characterizations; often cardboard characters lacking in scope people her stories. Her narratives are formula fixed, and her plots are self-evident. But it is not quite all true. The interest in the novels stems certainly not from curiosity; one knows unerringly what is going to happen, but one is intrigued by how it is going to happen. One element of this interest is that her characters are not as simply drawn as they seem; they behave in unexpected rather than expected ways. Many of Porter's women act quite unconventionally for women of her day. Jane Bakerman has drawn a comparison between Elnora of *A Girl of the Limberlost* and the Swamp Angel of *Freckles* and finds "a surprisingly refreshing dimension in her heroines," and, Bakerman continues, "Both young women, Elnora Comstock and the Angel are tough young women. This toughmindedness is used in a variety of ways, but each contributes to the sensationalism of the book—both intentionally and unwittingly."

Elnora's mother, Kate Comstock, is herself a study in contradictions, and it is these contradictions which make her an interesting character—perhaps the most finely drawn that Porter ever created. Her scathing denunciation of Elvira Carney (the woman with whom her husband had been unfaithful, and which infidelity led to his death) is followed immediately by her rejection of Elvira's cancer as retribution for her sin and by her suggestion of a remedy which Elvira could use to relieve her pain. The contradiction is heightened by the fact that Kate was obsessed in her grief to the point that she had grown habitually harsh in her treatment of Elnora and could only occasionally allow the deep love she actually felt for her daughter to express itself, at first gradually, but later increasingly.

Some characters in Porter books are as unpredictable as others are predictable. Often characters fail to react as they obviously should react in a given situation. The stubborn refusal of Ruth to accept all David Langston offers her seems unreal (*The Harvester*). Kate Bates seems almost blind in her inability to see the transparently right course of action she should take (*A Daughter of the Land*), Mickey's "adoption" of Lily Peaches is not the behavior one would expect from a tough, battling, city news urchin (*Michael O'Halloran*). Jamie MacFarlane must have been highly insensate not to see how he was being used by the Storm Girl (*The Keeper of the Bees*). And it is this uncertainty as to whether a character will react as the reader expects him to react that maintains the interest in a Porter book.

While a great deal of the imagery in the novels is admittedly shopworn by today's standards, it must be remembered that the writing is now well over a half century old; perhaps a degree of the triteness may be attributed to the passage of time and the use and reuse of what was somewhat more original when Porter wrote it. Even a cursory examination of newspapers, books, and periodicals of the time shows that such rather florid writing was highly popular.

Hamilton W. Mabie once congratulated William Dean Howells for his clean heart and genuine purity, but as Van Wyck Brooks noted, he ignored Howells's primly virtuous attitudes and ignored also the vast exclusions the possession of those traits in a novelist implied. But the novels of Gene Stratton Porter, in spite of her protestations as to their cleanliness and purity, are revealed, upon closer scrutiny, not to be so primly virtuous, after all.

The tantalization of sex is by no means absent from the novels of Gene Stratton Porter. On the contrary the suggestion is omnipresent; it is only the direct statement that is avoided. There is even the threat of rape in *A Girl of the Limberlost*, where Pete Corson watches Elnora in her bedroom with only rotten mosquito netting between them. The readers of Porter's day were titillated by the suggestion of sex, but they shrank— at least her readership shrank—from the bald treatment of it. Porter's heroines are creatures of flesh and blood—real living people. The Angel, Elnora, Mary Malone, Kate Bates, Mahala Spellman, Linda Strong; none of these is modeled on the simpering, swooning, depending heroine of post-Victorian romance. And they are women of action, they are sexually aggressive (in a genteel manner, of course) and they confront life and make it conform to their wishes and desires.

Porter was more successful in depicting the women in her novels than she was in dealing with her men. Her male characters are more like types than like individuals, and they are of a singleness of character. They are either all good or all bad; there is little or no admixture of those traits which make a man what he is—neither all good nor all bad, but human. The prime example is, of course, David Langston, the Harvester. He epitomizes all that is noble in man, even failing to succumb to normal jealousy when Ruth seems to prefer another.

The epitome of good *is* balanced by the epitome of evil, but the balance is achieved through the introduction of an opposing character, not by the commingling of traits in the same person. The Harvester is opposed by Henry Jameson, Ruth's grasping uncle; Freckles by Black Jack, the timber thief; Jason Peters by Junior Moreland (*The White Flag*); and Donald Whiting by Oka Sayye, the unscrupulous Oriental (*Her Father's Daughter*). There is even an instance in *A Girl of the Limberlost* where by indirection the evil of Pete Corson is contrasted with the good of Wesley Sinton. Pete Corson is also the one Porter male character who does display to a small extent a mingling of traits—he resists the temptation to rape Elnora and warns her of her danger from himself. Sometimes the contrast is between strength and weakness rather than between good and evil. Philip Ammon is paired with dilettante Hart Henderson (*A Girl of the Limberlost*), in much the same way that Elnora herself is opposed by Edith Carr, but these women are both strong, almost ruthless, while the men are passive, acquiescent.

The stuff of melodrama is not often to be found in the writing of Gene Stratton Porter. There is little hysteria. Even in her most sentimental passages, she does not attempt to force emotion; she quietly generates emotion by drawing an accurate picture of life during a tense moment. This is not always the case; for example, the overreaction of Elnora to Philip Ammon's asking for a kiss certainly approaches melodrama, as does the whole incident of Kate's giving birth to Elnora. But rather than melodrama these are the expected reactions of idealized characters in the moralistic world of the women's magazines.

Perhaps Porter failed to achieve the greatness she so desired as a novelist because her imagination was undernourished on inadequate experience. Her horizons were limited; she knew only the locale and the people of an extremely narrow and uncharacteristic area. For the swamplands and the swamp people were different from the farmland and farm people of closely neighboring areas of Northeast Indiana. Perhaps broader horizons and wider acquaintance are necessary for good fiction. But she knew her section of the land in minutest detail. She possessed keen powers of observation which enabled her to know her surroundings and the people of her particular milieu. Perhaps this keen observation and this faithful reproduction of a small segment of America could justify Gene Stratton Porter a place in the history of American letters as a local colorist.

It is only by definition that Gene Stratton Porter is not a local color writer. She wrote novels rather than short stories. But the two "Laddie" stories of the *Metropolitan* and other pieces she wrote for magazines and the short pieces in *After the Flood* and *Morning Face* are certainly examples of regionalism. Her handling of dialect was uneven to say the least. When she let her characters speak naturally in the vernacular of the Limberlost as she did in *Freckles*, her reproduction was faithful and not strained, but when she attempted to write Hoosier dialect in the manner of James Whitcomb Riley, she was to put it charitably unsuccessful. Nevertheless, her Indiana novels reproduce the differences between the world of which she wrote and that other world with compelling accuracy. She was a spokesman for an otherwise inarticulate portion of the population—she recreated a way of life, and it was a way of life closely akin to that which millions of people caught in the web of urbanization had only recently lost, and to which they longed to return, at least in the pages of romantic fiction.

Perhaps the stigma of having clothed nature in fiction kept Gene Stratton Porter from being recognized as the great nature authority she was. It is a rare reader indeed who displays an equal interest in sentimental romance and serious natural history. And while the vast numbers of Porter's reading public were not deterred by the background of woods and fields and swamps in which her characters acted out their little dramas, scientists were unwilling to sift out the nature from the fiction, no matter how accurate the observations of the former might be. It was only after the results of the reading of her faithful followers began to be revealed in an ever increasing interest in nature and the out of doors, and when nature study—not of course solely, but not negligibly either, due to the influence of Gene Stratton Porter—came to be an integral part of the curriculum in the public schools, that the natural historians began to take a closer look at the nature books of Porter.

Although today's ornithologists can point to errors in Gene Stratton Porter's knowledge of bird life, she combined artistry with skillful observation and somewhat proudly claimed that she was the first to present birds in a completely natural setting. Of course, Audubon and many others had attempted the same thing with some degree of success, but Porter wrote about the birds in the same manner as she depicted them. Her lifelong familiarity with birds and her keen observation of them enabled her to write of their habits and behaviors with the same perception she utilized in her photographing of them. The two went hand in hand. She was never a scientific naturalist; she was a nature lover. For her own taste and to bolster the perfect authenticity of her nature writing, she did study the scientific nature works relating to her own interests. But she was not interested in botany, entomology, or especially ornithology as fields of study. She wanted them as proof. She knew her accounts were true, that she was reporting what she actually had seen, but she wanted the verification of science—this is the attitude that is reflected in her writing.

Critics of writing concerning nature, perhaps influenced by the adverse criticism of the novels by litterateurs, passed over the writings of Porter in favor of those of John Burroughs, Enos Mills, John Muir, and Luther Burbank. Joseph Wood Krutch, anthologizing the ''great'' nature writing of America in 1950, failed to include Porter. John Kieran, who put out a collection not so selective as Krutch's and containing sixty pieces both by unknowns and by people like Roosevelt, Burroughs, and Peattie, also ignored Porter. And yet, a comparison of almost any passage from **Homing with the Birds** or **Tales You Won't Believe** with any of the writings selected by Krutch or Kieran discloses an equal or even superior accuracy of reporting plus a readability not often found in the writing of the naturalists included by these editors. It is true that the flourishing sentimentality which characterizes much of Porter's fiction does creep into her nature writing. It is true that at times the human/bird metaphor almost overpowers. But it is also true that there is as much of close and accurate observation and interpretation of nature as there is in almost any of the writing of Burroughs, Muir, or Seton. (pp. 134-40)

Most of Gene Stratton Porter's novels are now nearly forgotten, but interest in the nature books continues and, in fact, seems to be increasing. It can be maintained that she fell victim to changing times; the taste of the reading public altered greatly in the period of the Great Depression, when the affection for the old romantic quest was fading, to be replaced by an allegiance to the realism, naturalism, and satire which were to dominate the 1930s. Porter's death at the height of a rewarding and highly profitable career may have saved her the pain and disappointment of having to watch that career dwindle and fade.

Porter somehow failed to develop major powers of fiction, but then it must be remembered that she never intended her work to be judged solely as fiction but as *story* carrying a nature message. It was her undeniably fine portrayal of a region and her excellent discernment of the wonders of nature which sustained her through many successful years. If she neither knew nor cared how to construct a novel, she certainly possessed the power to weave a narrative and to tell a story. Considered as novels, the books had obvious faults which made literary critics scorn them. The plots were somewhat puerile, the characters had a tendency either to gush or to preach, and frequently the sentiment was too exuberant. But obviating these flaws—for most of her readers—were the facts that the people of whom she wrote were usually simple, honest, and good natured; that through their eyes one saw, and through their actions one experienced, the author's knowledge and love of outdoor things; and that, above all, here was a woman endowed with the real ability to tell a story.

As the years go by in the continuing reappraisal which is the history of American letters, what does the future hold for Gene Stratton Porter? For many years she has been relegated to the ranks of popular but inconsequential writers. This neglect is unjust in view of her actual range and versatility. In the reaction against the overromantic and sentimental novels and novelists of the early part of the century, the authors most properly attuned to their own and to past time were thrust farthest from the public gaze. In this sense, Porter belongs to a misunderstood past, a past which critics and historians of the last quarter of this century are willing to re-examine and to re-evaluate. It seems certain that no critic hereafter can refer to the popular culture of Porter's time and not feel the importance of her contribution to it. As the years go by it seems quite probable that Gene Stratton Porter will be elevated to a secure place among the minor American authors. (pp. 141-42)

> *Bertrand F. Richards, in his* Gene Stratton Porter, *Twayne Publishers, 1980, 165 p.*

ADDITIONAL BIBLIOGRAPHY

Cordell, Richard A. ''Limestone, Corn, and Literature: The Indiana Scene and Its Interpreters.'' *The Saturday Review of Literature* XIX, No. 8 (17 December 1938): 3-4, 14-15.*
    Survey of Indiana writers, including mention of Gene Stratton Porter.

Dahlke-Scott, Deborah, and Prewitt, Michael. ''A Writer's Crusade to Portray Spirit of the Limberlost.'' *Smithsonian* 7, No. 1 (April 1976): 64-8.
    Examines Porter's life and career, noting her early efforts in the areas of wildlife conservation and innovations in nature photography.

Hoekstra, Ellen. ''The Pedestal Myth Reinforced: Women's Magazine Fiction, 1900-1920.'' In *New Dimensions in Popular Culture*, edited by Russel B. Nye, pp. 43-58. Bowling Green, Ohio: Bowling Green University Popular Press, 1972.*
    Discusses the influence of women's magazines on fiction writers in the early twentieth century.

Meehan, Jeannette Porter. *The Lady of the Limberlost: The Life and Letters of Gene Stratton-Porter*. Garden City, N.Y.: Doubleday, Doran & Co., 1928, 369 p.
    Biographical portrait of Porter by her daughter including much of Porter's correspondence.

Mott, Frank Luther. ''The Family Novel in the New Century.'' In his *Golden Multitudes: The Story of Best Sellers in the United States*, pp. 215-23. New York: Macmillan, 1947.*
    Analyzes the formulaic nature of Porter's best-selling novels.

Overton, Grant. ''Naturalist vs. Novelist: Gene Stratton-Porter.'' In his *American Nights Entertainment*, pp. 270-92. New York: D. Appleton & Co., 1923.
    Review of Porter's novel *The White Flag* with largely favorable comment upon the overwhelming sincerity that is the chief characteristic of all that Porter wrote.

——. ''Gene Stratton-Porter.'' In his *The Women Who Make Our Novels*, pp. 312-24. New York: Dodd, Mead & Co., 1928.
    Briefly notes the ''freshness and vigor of feeling, unmistakable sincerity and a very limited sense of humor'' that ''were the qualities of Mrs. Porter's fiction.''

Pattee, Fred Lewis. "The Decade of the Strenuous Life: 1901-1909." In his *The New American Literature: 1890-1930*, pp. 103-20. New York: D. Appleton-Century Co., 1935.*

> Summarizes trends in early twentieth-century American literature. Pattee characterizes Porter's novels as examples of sentimentalized nature study, mentioning in particular *A Girl of the Limberlost* as "a skillful blend of extensive and exact knowledge with flattest sentimentality."

Witham, W. Tasker. "Literary and Cultural Background: Basic Novels of Adolescence before 1920." In his *The Adolescent in the American Novel: 1920-1960*, pp. 7-14. New York: Frederick Ungar, 1964.*

> Places Porter's novels within an American tradition of genteel and sentimentalized fiction about young protagonists that deals with themes of adolescence.

Premchand

1880-1936

(Also Prem Chand; pseudonym of Dhanpat Rai Srivastava; also wrote under pseudonym of Navab Rai) Indian novelist, short story writer, critic, essayist, dramatist, screenwriter, and translator.

A major figure in twentieth-century Indian literature, Premchand is credited with being the first author writing in the Hindi language to employ themes and techniques of literary realism earlier developed by modern European writers. Hindi prose narratives had hitherto been characterized by romance and fantasy; however, the novels and short stories of Premchand are predominantly devoted to realistic representations of Indian life of his time, which was a period of social and political upheaval. An adherent to the pacifist teachings of Mahatma Gandhi, who strove for India's complete independence from British rule, Premchand espoused nationwide social reform and in his fiction expressed a strong belief in the potential for good in all people. Premchand was also the translator of works by such European writers as Charles Dickens, Leo Tolstoy, and Guy de Maupassant, and he has been compared with these authors for the ethical concerns of his writing as well as for his sense of narrative realism.

The son of a post office clerk and his wife, Premchand was born in the village of Lamhi, near Benares. He was raised in a lower middle-class rural atmosphere and received his earliest education from a part-time tutor, later attending a mission school and Queen's College in Benares. In 1900, he became an educator in the government school system, a career that he pursued along with his literary ambitions for the next twenty years. He began publishing his work around 1901, and by 1904 his literary career was flourishing. At this time Premchand assumed the headmastership of a school in Kanpur and became a member of the literary circle in that city. He made friends with the editor of the respected journal *Zamana* and contributed fiction and essays to its pages as well as a regular column in which he voiced his opinions on current affairs. Over the next four years he also published the novels *Prema* and *Kishna* and the short story collection *Soz-e vatan,* which, like Premchand's other early works, were first written and published in the Urdu language. A mounting patriotic tenor and indictment of social corruption in Premchand's writings of this period led to a clash in 1910 with the British authorities, who ordered that *Soz-e vatan* (which can be translated as "Anguish of the Nation") be confiscated and burned. Afterward he abandoned his given name for the protective pseudonym he retained throughout the rest of his literary career.

With the publication of *Seva sadan* in 1918, Premchand secured his position as not only the leading Hindi novelist of the time but also as one of the most ardent defenders of the rights of India's lower classes. By then India's internal state of affairs was becoming increasingly turbulent as Gandhi and his followers gained popularity and began to represent a significant threat to British rule. The British, in turn, reacted to a native insurrection by instituting martial law in the Punjab region, thus greatly restricting the freedom of India's populace. Inspired by a Gandhi lecture he attended in 1921, Premchand abandoned his career in the government school system as a

protest against British authoritarianism. Two years later, needing a stable source of income and desiring to extend his influence among the Indian people, he started his own press and newspaper. This venture, though it continued until his death, proved a financial burden that required Premchand to take other jobs, including a position as a screenwriter for a Bombay film company. However, the deterioration of his health from a long-standing ailment and an unwillingness to compromise social and artistic responsibility to produce money-making films soon ended his screenwriting career. In the last decade of his life, Premchand edited and contributed to various periodicals, produced his most acclaimed works of fiction, and founded the literary and political monthly *Hans,* in which he commented perceptively on the political situation in India despite the very real danger of being imprisoned for his outspokenness. Shortly before his death in 1936, Premchand published the novel *Godan (The Giving of a Cow),* which is regarded as his masterpiece, and in that same year was elected president of the Progressive Writers' Association.

To Premchand, literature represented the opportunity to express ideas, beliefs, and moral questions relevant to Indian society. Critics agree that his importance as an author resides in his conscious incorporation of European novelistic practices for this purpose. In so doing, Premchand complemented the didacticism of his work with narrative methods new to Hindi writing. Although never fully versed in classical Indian literature, Premchand was knowledgeable in much English and European literature. Influenced by such writers as Dickens and Tolstoy, he not only emulated their styles and narrative techniques but also adapted and translated into Hindi a number of their works. Not surprisingly, a central tension in Premchand's fiction is created by his immersion in two disparate cultures: the progressive, democratic West and the traditional, socially stratified East. Critics find that this tension receives its most serious treatment in Premchand's later fiction, written when India's political crisis forced him to question both the morality of Western political and economic ideologies and the values of Indians who were resistant to social change. As a reflection of these concerns, Premchand's novels typically present a protagonist who must choose between self-aggrandizement and the humanist alternative, advocated by Premchand, of promoting the welfare and independence of the people.

Despite being faulted for the idealistic conclusions and simplistic conflicts of good and evil in much of his work, Premchand is considered a major Indian fiction writer. His masterpiece, *The Giving of a Cow*, is a realistic documentation of one of his enduring causes—the future of India's agricultural community—and is often cited as one of the greatest novels ever written about Indian life. According to Govind Narain, *The Giving of a Cow* "shows us a fragmented society which has a long way to go before it can become a nation, a society divided against itself, in which there is no sense of common purposes or goals and exploitation and injustice—social, economic, and political—are a way of life." Premchand's numerous short stories are also significant as artistic models of the realistic story and illuminating descriptions of the Indian people. As Narain has stated of Premchand: "To form a true estimate of his genius it is necessary to consider the totality of his output, which constitutes one of the most varied, rich, and comprehensive renderings of life ever achieved by a writer of fiction. The Premchand World in its richness and variety invites comparison with the Scott, Dickens, Hardy, and, with certain limitations, even the Tolstoy World."

(See also *Contemporary Authors*, Vol. 118.)

PRINCIPAL WORKS

Asrar-e mabid [as Navab Rai] (novel) 1903; published
     in newspaper *Avaz-e khalk*
Kishna [as Navab Rai] (novel) 1907
Prema [as Navab Rai] (novel) 1907
Soz-e vatan [as Navab Rai] (short stories) 1908
Jalva-e isar (novel) 1912; also published in Hindi
     version as *Vardan*
Prem pachisi I (short stories) 1915
Seva sadan (novel) 1918
Prem pachisi II (short stories) 1919
Premashram (novel) 1922
Rangabhumi (novel) 1925
Kayakalp (novel) 1926
Ghaban (novel) 1931
Karmabhumi (novel) 1932
Godan (novel) 1936
     [*Godan*, 1957; also published as *The Giving of a Cow*,
     1968]
Short Stories of Premchand (short stories) 1946
Mangal sutra (unfinished novel) 1948
A Handful of Wheat, and Other Stories (short stories)
     1955

The Secret of Culture, and Other Stories (short stories)
     1959
Manasarovar. 8 vols. (short stories) 1966-71
The Chess Players, and Other Stories (short stories) 1967
The World of Premchand (short stories) 1969
The Shroud, and Twenty Other Stories by Premchand
     (short stories) 1972
Twenty-Four Stories (short stories) 1980

*These works were first written and published in the Urdu language.

PREMCHAND (lecture date 1936)

[*In the following excerpt, Premchand discusses his view of the nature and purpose of literature.*]

Only that creation will be called literature which describes some truth, in a mature, refined, and graceful language and which has the quality to effect the head and the heart. And this quality is acquired by literature only when the truths and experiences of life are expressed in it. We might have been impressed by magic stories, by tales of fairies and ghosts, and by the narrations of lovers' separation at one time but now they possess very little interest for us. No doubt, a writer who is well versed with the essence of human nature can relate the truths of life even through love tales of princes, and magic stories, and create beauty. But this also strengthens the fact that to be effective, literature must be a mirror to the realities of life.

Literature has been defined in many ways, but in my opinion its best definition is "the criticism of life". Whether in the form of an essay, or a story, or a poem literature's chief function is to present an honest critical view of life.

The recent period, through which we have just passed, was not at all concerned with life. Our writers created a world of imagination and worked in it any magics they liked. Somewhere it was the fairy tales full of wonders, and somewhere the story about imaginary gardens, or books like Chander Kanta series. The sole purpose of these writings was to entertain and to satisfy our lust for the amazing. That literature had any link with life, was a mere delusion. A story is a story, and life is life; both were regarded as contradictory to each other. The poets were also infected with individualism. The ideal of love satisfied the lust, and that of beauty contented the eyes. The poets displayed the splendour of their brilliance and imagination in depicting these ornate feelings. To have, a new word—scheme or a new simile was enough to procure appreciation—how-so-ever remote it might be from reality. Imagery about a nest and a cage, lightning and granary and the narrations of different conditions of frustration and agony in separation used to be painted with such dexterity that the audience could not control their emotions. (pp. 166-67)

No doubt the purpose of poetry is to whet our emotions; but human life is not only the life of sexual love. Can that literature satisfy our needs related to thought, and feelings, the subject matter of which is confined only to ornamental emotions and its products,—the pangs of separation, frustration, and such others—and in which the success of life is regarded in escaping from the world and its difficulties? Embellished emotions are just a part of human life, and the literature which consists mainly of these cannot be a matter of pride either for its community or its age. Neither can it be a proof of its good taste.

Hindi and Urdu are both in the same condition as far as poetry goes. It was not easy to remain aloof from the influence of the contemporary tastes of the people for literature and poetry. Everyone has a desire for praise and appreciation. For poets their creations were the only means of livelihood. And who could appreciate poetry except the rich and the wealthy. Our poets either did not have the opportunities to come face to face with life and be influenced by its realities or such mental degeneration had set in, in everyone, that nothing had remained of the mental and intellectual life.

We cannot apportion the entire blame for this defect to the literary men of that time. The feelings and thoughts which stirred the people's hearts are reflected in literature too. In such a period of decline people either indulge in sexual love or lose themselves in spiritualism and renunciation. When literature is coloured by the inevitability of world's distinction, every word of it is steeped in frustration, is obsessed with the adversity of times, and is a reflection of ornate feelings, it should be understood that the nation has got into the grip of dullness and decline, and has lost its will to endeavour and struggle. It has shut its eyes to the high aims of life and has lost the capacity to discern and understand the world.

But our literary taste is changing very fast. Now literature is not merely an object of entertainment, but has in view some other purpose besides amusement. Now it does not merely relate the story of the separation or union of the hero and heroine; but it gives thought to the problems of life and tries to solve them. Now the writer does not run after amazing or astonishing incidents for his inspiration, and neither does he need to take the path of using words with similar sounds, but he is interested in those questions which influence the individual or the society. The present measure of his refinement is, the sharpness of impressions, with which he produces movement in our feelings and thoughts.

Ethics and literature have the same goal in view—the difference is only in the method of approach. Ethics endeavours to impress the brain and mind through logic and preaching, while literature has selected the field of ecstasy and feelings. Whatever we observe in life, or whatever we undergo, that experience, and these knocks, reaching our imagination inspire the creation of literature. To the extent the impressions of a poet or a writer are sharp to that very extent will his creations be attractive and exalted in quality. The literature which does not rouse our good taste, does not provide us a spiritual and mental satisfaction, does not produce in us activity, and strength, does not awaken our love for the aesthetic,—which does not produce in us resolution, and the determination to achieve victory over difficulties—is useless today; it does not deserve to be called literature. (pp. 167-69)

Premchand, "The Purpose of Literature," in Prem Chand: His Life and Work *by Hans Raj 'Rahbar', Atma Ram & Sons, 1957, pp. 165-82.*

INDAR NATH MADAN (essay date 1946)

[*In the following excerpt from a study of Premchand's novels and short stories, Madan assesses the value of Premchand's contribution to modern Indian literature and society.*]

Premchand, the thinker, cannot and should not be separated from Premchand, the artist. Any attempt to ignore the materialist conception of the base and its superstructure, any effort to present creative literature either as something completely self-motivated or as an immediate and direct expression of economic forces have nothing in common with the sociological approach to literature.

Premchand is great because he expressed very faithfully and vigorously the frame of mind of the peasantry and the outlook of the middle classes at the time of radical changes in India. The old foundations of the peasant economy and peasant life—foundations which had really existed for ages went crashing during this period of national struggle against foreign domination, against the advancing wave of capitalism, ruin and poverty of land. He reflected in his works the accumulated hatred and bitterness of the peasantry against economic exploitation and social oppression. He also embodied the protest and despair of the lower middle classes against the rising tide of capitalism or westernism which was spreading over the land during this period. (pp. 6-7)

Premchand correctly reflected this epoch. He saw and understood it with the eye of a sensitive artist and the mind of an earnest thinker. He correctly reflected the basic content of the age; but he did not understand the full implications of this age. He is great because he understood the way of life of the basic classes of his age; he also understood the way of life of the overwhelming majority of the population and reflected their ways in his creative work. He would have been greater if he had understood the paths of development. In his fiction he reflected the mood of the patriarchal peasant and the lower middle classes, their elemental hatred for the new order. It aroused both anger and fear against capitalism, against the city, against foreign domination, against all that was breaking down the old patriarchal order. Surdās [the blind beggar in **Rangabhūmi**] is a symbol of this order. **Rangabhūmi** embodies the author's protest against capitalism or industrialism which disrupted village economy based on co-operation. His warm, passionate and sharp protest against the government and its agents conveys the mind of the primitive peasant democracy. It is precisely his attitude to life or his world outlook that constitutes one of the most important links between his creative work and his social group, including his relation to various classes and the Indian National Congress. Tolstoy and Gandhi seem to have determined his world outlook and influenced his mind. The Gandhian ideology has shaped his attitude to life to such an extent that he finds himself completely under the influence of his master.

Premchand who has accepted this ideology approaches reality with already formed conceptions. Every writer, however eminent, is a product of his age. He studies and investigates nature and society with a pre-determined outlook on life and its problems. His attitude to the concrete material, his tendency to tone down or emphasise a particular set of characters are determined by his outlook on life. The artist's outlook has a direct effect on his creative work. Even if he does not directly express his own views, the objective significance of the events and characters he treats cannot but reveal the world outlook and motivating idea contained in his work. Premchand's wholly idealistic world-outlook is in the deepest sense of the word *utopian*; but there is much in him which is of positive value and significance. It is precisely the critical aspect of his work that has positive value. It is progressive in content. It has been of great benefit to the middle class population which was called upon to play a progressive role in that age. His works of art reflect the immediate past in all its variety and significance. He is at his greatest when he is dealing with the lower middle-class and the peasants. The background of his best novels is the life of the peasants. They are virtually a crusade against all forms of exploitation. The reprehensible practices of the Indian Barbasses, the inhuman oppression of the landlords, the vicious system of land revenue—all these have been mercilessly exposed by the author. The author feels the woes of the peasants so acutely that he seems to tremble at the injustices of the rich. He hates suffering and cruelty. He denounces injustice with all the forensic eloquence of a prophet. As he has seen the stark realities, the iron has entered his soul. He paints his exploiters in the darkest possible colours. The fact is that he is too good a propagandist to retain the rigidity and restraint of artistic treatment. (pp. 14-15)

The creative art of Premchand is of importance to us not because he wrote of the peasants and lower middle classes; but because he wrote against the reactionary tendencies of his age. It is great because he expressed the mood and ideas of millions of peasants during a period of crisis when capitalist civilisation was disrupting the old village economy, thereby strangling the peasant to a living death. At this historical period Premchand understood the basic social problems that were pressing for solution; he explored the relationship of these problems to all the social classes, and he made a concrete analysis of them in the form of novels and stories. (p. 18)

> *Indar Nath Madan, in his* Premchand [An Interpretation], *Minerva Book Shop, 1946, 177 p.*

HANS RAJ 'RAHBAR' (essay date 1957)

[*In the following excerpt, Rahbar examines the relationship between Premchand's fiction and his social and political ideals.*]

To know Prem Chand's life is to know his art. This is undoubtedly a great deal true of all writers, but in his case it is especially prominent. His three hundred stories and dozen novels survive because they capture, accurately, the zeitgeist of India of the 1930s; they are, in fact, a sort of historical record, expressed in literary terms, of that period. Roughly speaking, they cover the first thirty years of the twentieth century, listing nearly every political and social tendency of that crowded and tempestuous era.

But Prem Chand's art is not mere reflection of his age, on the other hand his pen-pictures of Indian life are so true and realistic that they help us to determine the future course of historical events. The writer is certainly not only to hold a mirror up to life; it is to try to fill up the gaps and deficiencies of life by creating life. And Prem Chand has done it well. After a thorough observation of the objective conditions he says with the sagacity of a sage in his novel *Karma-Bhumi:*

> In spite of all this our future is very bright. I have absolutely no doubt in it that soul of India is alive.

The changes always manifest themselves in individuals and events. If we look for the causes of the changes, they are not to be seen only in those particular events and individuals, but in the society to which they belong. It is the bounden duty of a writer to analyse these events and individuals and find out the root cause of them in society. The amount of success he attains in this respect, contributes to the affectiveness and utility of a writer's literature, and his failure makes his literature weak and unaffective.

In other words we can say that a writer picks up some salient events and characters and through them analyses the society as a whole.

> "There have been innumerable attempts to define literature," Prem Chand says [see excerpt dated 1936]. "I prefer the one that describes it as a criticism of life. Whether in the form of an essay or a poem or a short story, literature's chief function is to present an honest critical view of life."

We may doubt if literature can afford to stop at an "honest critical view of life." Writers like Dickens and Balzac have mercilessly explored the deplorable social conditions of their times. Their greatness lies in the criticism, but in our age the greatness of a writer should also be measured by the extent to which he influences society and effects changes in it. In a revolutionary epoch when a struggle is being waged to replace the old, decadent society by a more advanced new social structure, to remain merely critical may seem to remain divorced from the heart of life; the purpose of a writer in such times is to give added point and punch to the aspirations of the masses. At this time mere criticism is not enough, a writer has to give a clarion call to action. Prem Chand though confined his definition to criticism, he also exhorts people to action. A passage in *Karma-Bhumi* goes beyond his statement about literature being only a "criticism of life."

> "A social system built on iniquity," he says, "can be sustained only by more iniquity. It will fall sooner or later, and its gods trampled under foot like ordinary pebble and dust."

We might even add a third, and final, test for the writer—the most difficult of all. This test makes him compare new values with old, and to break away completely from the old if he finds the new better. A conventional system of society offers hundreds of attractions, small comforts, family bonds. Unless the breakaway is complete and the allegiance to the new cause absolute, a writer will at best be only a mildly sincere advocate of the new society, and must therefore be distrusted.

Prem Chand failed to reach the third step. Our perspective may help to explain why he clung to literature as simply a reflection of life coupled with honest criticism.

Prem Chand wrote with a definite purpose in mind. His chief aim was to further the cause of independence. In order to further this cause, he sacrificed his job. He frequently introduces characters into his stories who not only reflect about independence, but take an active part in the movement. But their actions do not go very much beyond the conventions of the old society. When they try to do so, Prem Chand interferes, and tries to satisfy their consciousness with what I believe is a false and out-dated philosophy. Sometimes even this philosophy, spoon-fed, fails to satisfy them, and they feel guilty about accepting it.

Take *Kaya-Kalpa.* Its hero is a truthful and bright young man called Chakradhar, who is sickened by social depredation and iniquity and hopes to create a free, happy new society. An upright young man, he will not even dream of doing evil for the sake of good, and he believes that man's spiritual life is rooted in his material condition.

> "There will come a time," he says, "when we will discover many of our spiritual yearnings

in our daily material life. The veil will then
have slipped from the great mystery.''

He works. He breaks convention. He challenges iniquity and
oppression through *satyagraha.* He sides with the suffering
peasantry. But he cannot take the final step. When the peasants
resolve to end the state of injustice and attack the forces of the
king, he backs out.

> He thought: murder is the limit. It never oc-
> curred to me to do a thing like this. . . But it's
> all my fault. I lack something. If I were clean
> of heart, they would never have dreamt of tak-
> ing the law in their own hands.

Evidently Chakradhar throwing away his belief in materialism
resorts to catch-phrases of idealism. Without looking into the
material causes of the spontaneous uprising of the peasants he
condemns it and finds in himself a neat metaphysical excuse
for the rebellion. But he is amazingly honest. The excuse is
after all an excuse. He finds he cannot deceive himself. ''What
is the point in joining hands,'' he reflects, ''if we don't do so
in order to fight injustice?''

The flash of light is however temporary; Chakradhar renounces
the world and enters the forest as a *sannyasi.* Giving up the
''material'' world, he begins to contemplate on the great mystery behind the veil which, earlier, he had thought, would
appear in everyday life without having to search for it. Prem
Chand's art in *Kaya-Kalpa* declines correspondingly with his
hero's conversion. ''There is fire and intimacy in the early
chapters of *Kaya-Kalpa,*'' even a non-marxist critic has said.
''But they gradually simmer, not into climax, but into smoke.''
We need not investigate the causes: the false and out-dated
philosophy has no appeal for the mind.

Amarkant in *Karma-Bhumi* is another instance. He is quicker-
witted and more vigorous than Chakradhar; he is also more
stubborn and pushing, more true to his ideals. His methods
are, consequently, more forceful, and his foresight longer. In
1930, the movement for independence had become firmly
grounded on economic foundations, whereas in 1922 it was
chiefly an emotional and semi-religious (witness the Khilafat)
striving.

> *''I am not interested in position and riches,''*
> Amarkant declares. ''These things are chains.
> I am not one of those who confuse life's chains
> with life. Life to me means struggle and as-
> piration.'' His revolution is actually a kind of
> purification by fire. ''He dreamt of a revolution
> that would wipe off all false ideals, crush un-
> truth and injustice, and establish a new order
> which removed dependence on the wealth of
> the rich and the power of callous authority.''

Amarkant starts rebelling against his father who has amassed
wealth by shady business deals. He goes to a village and begins
to organise the peasants. They take his advice with gusto, with
more gusto than he bargains for. So, when the time comes and
they prepare themselves for a showdown with the exploiting
class, Amarkant, viewing the situation through his old-social
values of justice and fair play, tries to dissuade them from their
dangerous undertaking.

Amarkant does not, like Chakradhar, regret his action. He has
no doubts, for he immolates himself in the all-purifying fire
of entering jail as a *satyagrahi.* Here the novel begins to flag.
Through a disturbingly corny coincidence, his father undergoes

a change of heart and enters the same jail. Both son and father
return home, reconciled.

A triumph for *satyagrahi,* but certainly a defeat of the revolutionary. We are entitled to ask: Why? What made Prem
Chand slip to such an embarrassing extent?

Most critics attribute it to the influence of Gandhian doctrine.
We must examine for ourselves what place Gandhian doctrine
then had in the structure of society.

All social changes reflect themselves in events and individuals,
and every philosophy born of this society reflects itself in
individuals. A social philosophy or outlook may take the name
of a particular person—Gandhism—but it is neither born with
him nor does it die with him. We must trace the growth of
Gandhism to its roots, and the roots we will find hidden in the
problems arising from the working of a class-ridden society.

Prem Chand went to Wardha in 1935 in connection with the
meeting of the Hindi Sahitya Parishad. In Wardha he met
Gandhiji for the first and last time in his life. He was tremendously impressed by Gandhiji's personality. [His wife] Shivrani Devi asked him:

> ''Does that mean that you intend to become his
> disciple?''
>
> ''Becoming a disciple doesn't mean worship-
> ping a man,'' Prem Chand replied. ''It means
> emulating his good points. I emulate them; I
> even made them the basis of *Premashram* in
> 1922.''
>
> ''You wrote that before Gandhiji was on the
> scene,'' she said.
>
> ''That's just what I mean,'' he said. ''From
> the literary point of view, I discovered Gan-
> dhiji's doctrine long before he expounded it.''
>
> ''That doesn't prove anything,'' his wife said.
>
> He smiled. ''I know it doesn't. All I meant
> was: Gandhiji is pulling up with the peasants
> in his own way. I'm doing it in mine—with
> my pen and a bottle of ink.''

It is so easy to deceive oneself, especially when deception is
in the daily atmosphere. Along with thousands of other Indians,
Prem Chand sincerely believed that Gandhiji's principles were
what he had followed all his life. But is the murder of Gous
Khan in *Premashram* a point of Gandhian principle? Manohar's
deed is described in detail and praised profusely. Gandhiji
could not have condoned such a deed. He came into the Congress leadership to put a stop to the revolutionary activities of
Manohar, the leader of the peasants.

Manohar is the representative of the exploited peasantry and
his action is their action. After Ghos Khan they would have
certainly attacked Gian Shankar, the Zamindar, his protectors
the English and the whole exploiting class. During the war the
toiling masses had imbibed a revolutionary spirit and they were
being drawn into the national struggle through it. The propertied classes were not unaware of this political change of the
masses and they feared them. So far the Congress movement
was confined to the middle class intelligentsia and its only aim
was to get concessions, to install Govind in place of John. Its
target was not at all the social structure which was based on
exploitation. To save this society it was necessary to check
these new forces.

Fear, cautiousness, and a go-slow policy are the pillars of Gandhism. Gandhism is meant to protect private property and the interests of the propertied class. We might profitably compare Gandhism to a tree whose roots are Ram Rajya and trusteeship, while 'satyagraha', 'ahimsa' and "change of heart" are its offshoots, leaves and branches.

The leftist movement was weak. The class-character of Gandhism was not analyzed and exposed. The freedom loving youth of the middle class easily adopted this outlook because they had no other programme to fight the aggression. Besides this, the middle class people by nature of their work are nearer to the workers, but socially they follow the traditions of the capitalists. In their heart of hearts a feeling to safeguard property and heritage remains hidden.

Prem Chand also belonged to the middle-class. He had inherited some land and house in the village and he, like the middle class folk, had a sentimental weakness for the "house". Due to this he always longed to settle in the village. He actually went to his village and built a new house of brick and mortar in place of old mud one of his forefathers. Though he wanted to participate actively in disobedience movement of 1930, yet Shivrani went to jail and he remained behind to look after the children.

Such was the nature of Satyagrah movement. It guaranteed the safety of house at the same time provided the pleasure of pilgrimage to jail. While the big people were in jail their business was running intact outside.

Prem Chand has very enthusiastically advocated the philosophy of sportsmanship. This philosophy is also an off-shoot of Gandhism. Mahatma had converted many a men to sportsmanship; but he tied their actions to the spinning-wheel. Prem Chand's Chakradhar and Amarkant were also sportsmen. They entered into politics with sincerity of purpose and noble aim. But as they never analyzed their deeds and never tried to understand the weaknesses of the movement, as being true satyagrahis they could take a defeat as a victory, consequently hypocrisy became a part and parcel of their life. If we today look out for them we shall find them among big congress leaders, high diplomats and ministers of states and centre and in their persons Gandhism is made the embodiment of hypocrisy.

The greatest sportsman in Prem Chand's characters is Surdas—the blind hero of *Rungbhoomi* who runs three miles at a stretch after a tonga simply to get a pice in charity, who fights alone and in an individualist manner to save his inherited land, ignoring the objective conditions and loses his life in this battle like a sportsman. Prem Chand depicts him with all the sincerity, partiality and devotion of an artist. He to him is an ideal man. But the irony of all this is that he himself has made him blind.

It is not easy to change one's class character. A man often shakes off the outworn traditions of his class, but they persistently come in his way in new garbs. Prem Chand in *Premashram* had gone a long way off from the old traditions. But they again overtook him in the garb of Gandhism and he without recognizing embraced them warmly.

But a conflict—a tug of war—was always raging within him. The tussel was between his realism and idealism. This internal conflict he has depicted through his characters. Amar Kant of *Karma-Bhumi* dreams of an all-out revolution and of a happy and glorious future in which husband and wife will live as comrades helping each other and the false gods will be trampled under foot. But as the novel ends his dreams come to nought and his idealism compromises with the old society which rears inequity and injustice.

Thus he was torn between realism and idealism. He depicted objective reality truly and faithfully but the conclusions he drew were idealistic. All the same he was a true son of the masses. He could not shut his eyes to the miserable lot of the toiling people. Gandhi-Irwin Pact served a severe blow to his idealistic inclinations. His belief in *Ahamsa, Satyagrah* and processions was shaken off. He realized that the freedom of the exploited cannot be attained through this type of a movement and the existing structure of society can provide them no relief. It was at this stage that reality won and his idealism lost. His story **"Kafan"** (**"Shroud"**) and his novel *Godan* are artistic embodiments of his new realization. These two works are regarded as his best by all critics howsoever they may differ idealogically. Hori in *Godan* is the embodiment of Prem Chand's idealism. He has got a noble soul. He represents the Indian peasantry as a whole. He is devoted to his family; he loves his land and oxen; he respects law and religion. In short, he is faithful to the old feudal society. But in this society he is exploited and oppressed even more. His family is broken; he loses his strip of land and his oxen; he is reduced to a mere wage-worker and through hard work comes to a miserable death.

This tragedy of Hori is the tragedy of millions and millions of poor peasants.

This is the process of disintegration of the existing society. To depict it in the literature is directly opposed to his old Gandhian faith. Prem Chand, by this time, had become fully conscious that the middle class cannot remain intact in the existing society of exploitation. This realization no doubt added new beauty to his artistic production and lent it new flavour and freshness. (pp. 147-56)

Hans Raj 'Rahbar', in his Prem Chand: His Life and Work, *Atma Ram & Sons, 1957, 188 p.*

USHA SAKSENA   (essay date 1962)

[*In the following excerpt, Saksena considers the influence that the novels of such writers as Charles Dickens, John Galsworthy, and Leo Tolstoy had on those of Premchand.*]

The intellectual and cultural climate in which modern Hindi literature has grown, largely conditioned by Western contacts, affected nearly all spheres of Indian life and literature. Though most of the Hindi writers preserved the individual flavor in their writings, they imbibed deeply the influences from abroad. The growth and the progress of the Hindi novel bears the unmistakable stamp of this influence. The works of Dhanpat Rai, best known as Premchand, provide an excellent example.

Premchand is an important figure in Hindi fiction, and it was he who brought a mature, literary, realistic social novel in Hindi. He lived at a significant time in the history of modern India. He grew up when the country was under the sway of nationalistic movements for independence, and Premchand got directly involved in it. (p. 129)

Before Premchand, the Hindi novel tended to cling closely to the Oriental romantic tradition. Dealing with kings and queens, lovesick maidens, and beggar boys in disguise, they very often transported the reader to the exotic world of the *Arabian Nights*. By contrast, Premchand stood out as a severe social critic. He attacked the decadent social, economic, and religious systems of India that failed to give any personal freedom to a man. Premchand was not alone in this feeling. A new system of education introduced in the nineteenth century by the British in India and the growth of the Press became the chief components which brought social and political awareness to the Indian people. Premchand, as a writer, made a conscious attempt to bring the literature close to the life of the people. A few attempts to achieve this had been made before him. The first novel in Hindi, *Pariksha Guru,* written by Sri Nivas Das in 1882, had been consciously patterned on *The Vicar of Wakefield,* but there was a big gap of time between *Pariksha Guru* and *Seva Sadan.*

In order to bring new ideas into a literature lacking in form, Premchand had not only to create his own atmosphere, but to introduce a new technique into the novel. For this purpose he drew heavily upon the sources available to him.

An Indian student between 1880 and 1910 had to know certain English writers. He shared the thrills of adventure with Daniel Defoe, enjoyed the drawing-room conversation of Jane Austen, sympathized with the characters of Dickens and plodded through Thackeray. Premchand's notes show that he went beyond this formal study and pursued those writers with whom he felt a kinship. Once he wrote to a friend of his: "I am deep in Tolstoy at the moment, and he seems to be influencing me a great deal. I know this is my weakness, but I cannot help it." (p. 130)

Premchand's familiarity with the Western literature made him try to bring some of the works to the Hindi reading public, and for this purpose he translated several works of Tolstoy, Anatole France, George Eliot, and Galsworthy into Hindi. He was trying to bring his readers to an appreciation of what the great masters in other languages had achieved, and at the same time he tried to establish certain standards into Hindi fiction by which his own works could be judged.

Even though he had these sources to draw upon, Premchand's writings were never just imitations. Various influences were absorbed and given a new direction by the nature of Premchand's genius. Still they could be grouped under two categories: first, the social and environmental influences, and second, influences concerning the style and technique of his novels.

From the English, Dickens and Galsworthy, and from the Russians, Tolstoy and Gorky were the main writers who enabled Premchand to deal with the problems faced by India in the same way as they had dealt with theirs. This social awareness made him take notice of his own environments. He was strongly drawn towards Realism and was trying to present an honest, critical view of life. He felt an affinity with these Western writers. The English Realists faced the crumbling order, the havoc caused by the displacement of labor, the shifting of population, the ugliness of town life, and Premchand's India was undergoing the same phase. Being born in the centre of the middle class, and feeling closer to the working people, he was conscious of a great upsurge in them, and he endeavored to portray these exploding classes.

This awareness was further intensified by Premchand's study of the Russian writers. The waves of national movement in Russia, the deep humanitarianism, sympathy with the poor— all these impressed Premchand, and he strove to bring the same sympathetic touch into his own writings. Premchand, born in a poor family, had not the aristocratic background of Tolstoy. But just as Tolstoy had sunk his roots into the masses of the Russian peasantry, Premchand stood for the suffering peasantry of India. Just as Tolstoy showed Russian soul and Russian

character at its greatest, deepest, and at its weakest, Premchand's novels revealed the core of the Indian people. His studies of Hori in *Godan* or Surdas in *Rangabhoomi* contain all that is noble, humane, and yet blind, superstitious, and caste-ridden in Indian character. Premchand possessed a power similar to that of Tolstoy to describe dispassionately what he saw during his struggle through life. He shared with Tolstoy the disgust for everything that was unreal, sham, and conventional. Premchand had suffered many hardships just because he was born in an Indian society, and he mercilessly attacked the priests and the pundits for their hypocrisy, and the evils inherent in Indian social system, like child-marriage, dowry, plight of the widows, prostitution, the tyranny of the family.

Like Tolstoy, Premchand tried to show people living out their lives on the margin of great events.

Gorky's influence on Premchand was not confined to his writings only. Premchand had great personal regard for his contemporary. The main theme of Gorky's life work is that men can no longer live the way they used to. Beginning his career as a spokesman for the underprivileged and oppressed, he later came to be the poet of general class reshuffle. Premchand's protagonists, like Gorky's, also are social rebels in full revolt against society. Premchand, too, succeeded in portraying the general awareness of India's millions. The long suffering, meek farmers and workmen suddenly unite in revolt against the oppressors in novels like *Kayakalpa, Karmabhoomi,* and *Rangabhoomi.* These characters are endowed with a consciousness to fight for their rights. Again, Premchand, like Gorky, was not a chronicler, but a fighting humanist, and his writings are full of a reformer's zeal. Premchand did not study his characters as a detached superior observer. He was one of them.

Both Premchand and Charles Dickens belonged to the people. Their early lives had acquainted them with the cruel conditions of society, and they shared a common sympathy for the helpless and the weak. Like Dickens, most of Premchand's unforgettable characters come from the lower strata of society.

Curiously enough, Premchand's novels show the same shortcomings as Dickens' do. It was the practice of Dickens to exploit the reader's sympathy by increasing his character's misfortunes. Premchand is guilty of the same thing. He also, like Dickens, developed the same fondness for many crowded events in the span of a novel, as also the over-crowding of characters. Premchand, though successfully portraying the lower classes, felt out of his depth when writing about the aristocracy.

Even though the major spheres of Galsworthy's and Premchand's writings were different, Premchand had a similar viewpoint towards the complacency and class consciousness of the rich in society. Premchand took up the idea of the *Silver Box* in one of his novels, *Karmabhoomi,* showing how justice is not imparted equally to the rich and the poor. (pp. 130-32)

[Premchand's] contacts with the West made him include new subject matters dealing with the problems of the day. His novels tell of the great social, political, and economic changes which were taking place in India.

This newness of the subject matter brought a whole range of different characters into his novels. The kings and queens and the lovesick maidens were banished from the scene forever. The illiterate farmers and the laborers, blind beggars and the rebellious skinners figured prominently in his novels. For the first time, the long-suffering, enchained Indian woman found a champion for her cause. Premchand portrayed her in all her

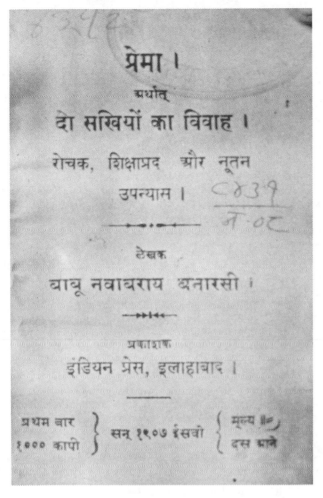

Title page of Prema.

helplessness and nobility, treating her, as he did his other characters, realistically, depicting the psychological processes very successfully.

Premchand experimented a great deal, consciously imitating the writers he liked, to find his own style. Once confident, he maintained simple and graphic and lucid language. He completely discarded the poetic language of his predecessors, and his characters talk in ordinary colloquial, everyday language.

Premchand's innate genius and clear grasp of human nature were supported by the sympathy and insight of Gorky, the realism of Tolstoy, the humanism of Dickens. All these traits, synthesized and coordinated, resulted in something entirely new and singularly Premchandian. (p. 132)

> *Usha Saksena, "Western Influence on Premchand,"* in Yearbook of Comparative and General Literature, *No. 11, 1962, pp. 129-32.*

DAVID RUBIN (essay date 1969)

[*Rubin is an American translator of the work of Premchand. In the following excerpt, he offers an introduction to Premchand's short stories.*]

To Premchand belongs the distinction of creating a genre of the serious short story—and the serious novel as well—in both

Hindi and Urdu. Virtually single-handed he lifted fiction in these languages from a quagmire of aimless romantic chronicles to a high level of realistic narrative comparable to European fiction of the time; and in both languages, he has, in addition, remained an unsurpassed master. . . .

From the early to the late fiction there is a steady and easily perceptible growth. The first stories, written often with a patriotic or nationalistic bias, tend towards romantic evocations of heroic exploits from Indian history or legend. In the early years Premchand also had a penchant for rather thin yarns about ghosts, lamias and the like. There is probably some influence of Maupassant in the occasional surprise or trick endings. (p. 13)

He very soon discovered the domain which was to remain the richest inspiration for his work—the life of the village. The villages of the eastern Uttar Pradesh, specifically the country districts around Allahabad and Banaras—apparently perfectly ordered according to mechanically exact social regulations that had functioned more or less unchanged for centuries—offered to Premchand an endlessly fascinating stage for the interplay of diverse personalities, at every stage of evolution, with a rigid, efficient, and often cruel social order. Caste snobbery—though it is more than snobbery, being a function of religion; the yearning for sons (a desire that overwhelms all others) to carry on the family and perform the rituals; the terror at the possibility of disgrace or loss of face; the shame of widowhood; the proverbial conservatism—and cunning—of the peasant: these are some of the recurring strands in the fabric of his portrayal of the village. In the early stories there is a tendency to editorialize, even sermonize, and to be redundant, which decreases gradually; the best stories of the late twenties and thirties are free of it entirely. But even in the early stories—**"The Power of a Curse,"** for example—Premchand's compassion, humour and psychological understanding of the villagers are apparent.

Influenced by Dickens, Tolstoy and Gandhi, among others, and strongly impressed by Marx, Premchand very early directed his fiction toward social reform. The inhumanity of caste hierarchies, the struggle for India's independence and the wretched plight of women are some of the problems that arouse his indignation most frequently. With his maturing as a writer his narration becomes increasingly dramatic and (at least, on the surface) objective, and the presentation of character immeasurably subtler than in the early works. The range of the later stories expands beyond the village to the world of those struck by what one of his characters calls 'the new light,' young intellectuals and emancipated women, people often further from happiness than uneducated villagers. Gandhian influence, perhaps, but more likely a matter of Premchand's own vision. Though the stories continue to be preoccupied with social problems their tone and technique become increasingly Chekhovian. Melodrama and moral thesis give way to tragi-comedy. In **"My Big Brother"** a potentially ludicrous situation is developed with pathos, although the touch remains light and the story is genuinely comic; in **"The Shroud"** the scarcely tolerable grimness of the characters' lives is developed in the mode of grotesque comedy.

Despite the changes in India since Independence, Premchand's world is still very much in evidence, particularly in the villages. Here and there the surface of daily life has changed but it would be premature to say that there has been any radical transformation. What may strike a Western reader as false, perhaps, or melodramatic in some of these stories is merely commonplace in India, as a perusal of today's Indian newspapers serves to confirm. No matter how much they are officially discouraged, in the countryside caste restrictions have weakened little; the mother-in-law still rules her sons' wives in the joint family; and above all, the swiftness, the unexpectedness of death—and the resignation with which it is accepted—can still be said to constitute a fundamental element of Indian life in both village and town.

Premchand's indignation and his very choice of subject matter tend somewhat to set him apart from contemporary Hindi fiction. Although he has had considerable influence, and there are still writers who deal with social problems and village life, the dominant trend at present seems to be more toward a psychological literature, more refined (and alas, more chic) in nuance and language and consequently less vigorous. The new Hindi writing is often heavily larded with Sanskrit, much of it gleaned from thesauri and lacking in any rich connotative power—indeed, denotative as well in some instances—and of course cleansed of Premchand's inexhaustible fund of humble metaphors and proverbs; similarly, the subject matter tends to be the restricted world and psyche of the writer himself, turned inward, away from the epic horizons of Premchand's multifarious world. Premchand makes many of the present generation of writers—to apply Katherine Mansfield's remark about the novelists who followed Dickens—look very small, 'and such pencil sharpeners!' (pp. 14-15)

David Rubin, in an introduction to The World of Premchand: Selected Stories of Premchand *by Munshi Premchand, translated by David Rubin, Indiana University Press, 1969, pp. 13-17.*

ROBERT O. SWAN   (essay date 1969)

[In the following excerpt from his highly regarded biographical and critical study Munshi Premchand of Lamhi Village, *Swan contrasts the ideology and narrative techniques of Premchand's early and later fiction.]*

During the greater part of Premchand's writing career he regarded himself as a writer with a message, a writer with a moral obligation to rid his society of many evils which he specifically pinpointed. The manner in which he could bring tears to the eyes of a stonehearted landlord or cause a prostitute to emerge as a spokesman for modesty placed the accent of his work upon his beliefs and ideals, and gave secondary importance to his literary skills. This has prompted critics to regard him primarily as a Gandhian or a Marxist or an idealistic realist or a nationalist.

The final period of Premchand's writing, however, shows clear evidence, both from his expressed views at this time on short story writing and from a number of the stories themselves, that he had become increasingly aware of the power which form and technique could exert upon the effectiveness of a short story. This period may be regarded as illustrating the struggle between the claims of moral purpose in his work and the claims of artistic expression. By the end of Premchand's life there was apparent a greater and more conscious technical scrutiny of his subject matter that released his characters from the burden of their creator's views or brought these views under the discipline of artistic tenets.

The nature of Premchand's final development may be described by an analysis of three major strands of criticism made of his work by his Hindi critics. While all critics admit to a new "realism" in his writing, this has not always been ascribed to his new mastery of technique. One group of critics finds that the content and treatment of these stories showed no fundamental change in Premchand. He remained what he had once called himself, an idealistic realist, or a Gandhian. When these critics speak of the new realism in Premchand's later stories, they suggest that the stories have more truth to life and more probability—for instance, a villain will not now become a hero without adequate and clever preparation. However, they stress the point that the villain will still usually become a hero, and that the ideal of social uplift is still clearly evident. The communist and Marxist critics, on the other hand, purport to see that the greater accent on realism in his later work, following the dominant idealism of his early work, revealed more than just technical maturity. They see in the change that Premchand had also altered his political, economic, and social views during the period. A third group of critics has recognized and placed importance upon varying technical aspects of his work, to which they ascribe much of the cause for his new excellence as a writer.

Although the critical views of Premchand's later work fall generally into the three classes listed above, many of the critics do not consistently fit into such rigid categories. There are seepages of opinion from one category to another: Marxists and idealists admit to technical improvements in the work, and critics of form concede evidence of communism or socialism or Gandhism. The three strands of criticism, thus, are generalized descriptions of Premchand's later work, and not of the detailed exceptions made by individual critics.

For the large number of critics who found unmistakable evidence of a Gandhian or reforming imprint in Premchand's earlier work, such new realism (as seen particularly in his late village stories) presented some difficulties for them in maintaining that Premchand remained essentially an idealist to the end. Occasionally, a critic expressed disappointment in some of his later work:

> I have read his last novel **Godan** with fitting respect, but my heart did not find in it that which I found in **Rangbhumi** [an earlier novel]. In **Rangbhumi** a blind beggar brought about a movement of unusual enlightment by his renunciation and power of spirit. It was an example of what soul force can do. In **Godan** [1936] we find no such noble character [Haribhav Upadhaya].

Nevertheless, the critics who found Premchand an idealist or a Gandhian or an idealistic realist contend that even though his economic views may have leaned toward socialism in the end, they were based on liberal and humanitarian views that came to him from Indian tradition, refurbished perhaps by Dayananda Saraswati, Vivekananda, Tolstoi, Gandhi, and others, but conforming to no doctrinaire position though representative of a strong desire to see abolished the great inequalities between man and man. (pp. 109-11)

These critics also claim that Premchand's denunciations of the evils in society were tempered by his "complete faith in the goodness and usefulness of the basic traditions of Indian life. . . . he did not wish to see spoiled the Indian system of marriage or the Indian view of love," for example. (p. 112)

In their analyses these critics draw forth arguments that cover a wide spectrum. Premchand was a "traditionalist," but he could also be a "progressive." He was a realist tempered by idealism. He was a Gandhian but with his own modifications. Their views depend primarily on an analysis of the subject matter of his works. They evade the question of the technical development of the author as perhaps being partially responsible for the quality of greater realism, or ''truth to life,'' in his later stories—a realism which they, however, generally acknowledge. (p. 113)

Premchand's final stories of village life, with their stark realism and the basic fight for survival unrelieved by explicit social cures, could perhaps lend themselves to the claim that he had become disillusioned with Gandhian prescriptions. However, when we move to the stories of middle-class life where the fight for survival is replaced by more subtle societal aims, the claims of Premchand's continued adherence to Gandhian or other social uplift and idealistic solutions find their strongest defense. The themes of these stories, enmeshed in some authorial purpose, often veer from what would normally be expected in life, and they illustrate perhaps best the continuing stress of social purpose that lingers even into his last years. In these stories, however, may be distinguished the early evidences, too, of Premchand's struggle to bring his subject matter under the discipline of conscious technical scrutiny.

The story **"Kayar"** (**"The Coward"** . . .) tells of the love of a brahman boy and a vaisya girl, classmates in college. The boy scorns old-fashioned ideas about inter-caste marriages. He loves the girl, Prema, and not her caste. The girl, however, hesitates: ''What right have I over my own body? That which my parents created with their own blood, which they nourished with their love—there can be no doubt that I can do nothing which will go against their wishes.''

Her parents arrange her marriage with a vaisya boy of her own caste, studying for the I.C.S. This rouses in her some rebellion. Now she thinks: ''This body belongs to my parents but whatever my spirit will have to endure, it will have to endure in this body . . . without dedicating one's spirit, can there be such a thing as love?'' She contrives to let her father know about her true love. The shock to him is great, but when he finds her grieving through the following months he begins to fear for her health and becomes resigned to the incredible. ''It is useless,'' he says to his wife, ''to hope that a bird having once opened its wings will decide to alight and live in your courtyard.'' He goes accordingly to see the brahman boy's father. The elder brahman, hearing his proposal, is furious and shouts: ''What are you saying? Don't you have any shame? I am a brahman and of the highest even among brahmans. No matter how low brahmans may have become they have not become such destroyers of tradition that they should go around marrying their sons to bania shopkeepers.' ''

The brahman father threatens to cut off his son without a penny if he marries Prema. Under this pressure the boy reconsiders his views and writes a letter to Prema, saying he has changed his mind about marrying her. Prema reads the letter carefully.

> She kept busy all day doing the housework, as if she had no worries or cares. At night she prepared dinner for everyone, then she ate her own dinner, and until late that night played on her harmonica and sang.
>
> But when morning came, her body lay dead in her room. The golden rays of the early morning sun gave to her face the appearance of shining life.

The story **"Kusum"** . . . is told mostly in the letters of a young married woman to her husband who is completely indifferent to her. She stays with her parents because he does not send for her nor answer her letters. There are five letters.

> My lord, have you thought against whom you are holding this anger? That helpless one who is prostrate at your feet, asking for the gift of your forgiveness, who through this and after births will remain your slave, can she endure this anger. . . . One ember from this fire of anger is enough to turn her to ashes.
>
> You are the sun, I am a small particle; you are fire, I am a blade of grass; you are a king, I am a beggar woman. You should be angry with equals, but I . . . how can I endure the blows of your anger?
>
> . . . . .
>
> Tell me, if I should die would you shed one tear over my corpse? For one whom you undertook a lifetime of responsibility . . . could you show that much kindness? . . . Everyone forgives those who are about to die. Will you also forgive? If you will come and wash my dead body with your own hands, and put on me the vermillion of a wife; if you will place on me a wife's bracelets, and with your own hand drop the Ganges water in my mouth and help carry my bier for a few yards, then my spirit will be satisfied and I will bless you.

The young husband who will not reply to these letters turns out to be angry because his father-in-law has not provided funds in the girl's dowry to send him to England for advanced education. When this becomes known to the girl, she finally renounces him. ''Any man who is so avaricious, so egotistic, so low—I will never live with him.''

In the stories **"Unmad"** (**"Madness"** . . .) and **"Miss Padma"** . . . , Premchand delineates his conception of the modern woman to throw into contrasting relief an ideal Hindu woman. In **"Unmad,"** an Indian, already married, goes to England for further study. (pp. 113-15)

> A year's contact with English society raised a tumult in Manhar's mind. Worldliness gained such an ascendancy in his nature that no place was left in it for gentler feelings. Vageswari [his Indian wife] could be a help to him in his education, but she could not help him to rise to higher positions of power. Her self-denial and service now became unimportant in Manhar's views . . . because in his materialistic view everything depended upon its value in getting him some benefit. . . . In comparison with a lively, cheerful, pleasure-loving English girl, Vageswari began to seem a light, useless thing. . . .

Manhar marries an English girl, obtains a high government position in India, avoids his family and first wife, and lives his life in high official circles in India, drinking, going to the hills, dancing. The English girl flirts outrageously with other men, and gradually she and Manhar grow apart and Manhar begins to remember his old life and his first wife. Finally, he leaves his English wife and returns to his village home. His great troubles also have affected his mind: he forgets everything about England and his English wife.

The English girl, not yet ready to give him up completely, follows him to the village.

> Suddenly Vageswari came outside. Seeing Jenny she sensed immediately that this was her English co-wife. With great courtesy she brought her inside. . . .
>
> Jenny sat on a dilapidated bed and said: "He must have mentioned me to you. We were married in London."
>
> Vageswari: "Yes, as soon as I saw you I realized you were the one."
>
> Jenny: "Hasn't he ever mentioned me?"
>
> Vageswari: "No. He doesn't remember anything."
>
> Jenny asked if they had taken Manhar to a doctor to be cured, and when Vageswari said "no," Jenny exclaimed: "Why . . . do you want to keep him sick forever?"
>
> Vageswari answered carelessly: "For me it's better for him to remain sick than well. Once he forgot his soul, now he has found it. . . . In my mind he was sick then and now he is well."
>
> Presently Jenny asked: "Are you his sister?"
>
> Vageswari smiled and said: "You are saying nasty things to me. He is my husband."
>
> It was as if a lightning bolt struck Jenny. The politeness fled from her face. The veins in her neck tightened, her fists became clenched. Angrily she said: "What a liar he is. How he has deceived me! He told me his wife had died. What a swine. He's not mad, this is just a pretense of insanity. I'll take him to court."
>
> She pulled out a pistol and would have shot someone, if Manhar coming into the room, had not disarmed her. . . .

In **"Miss Padma"** the heroine is a young, educated woman who has become a lawyer. She does not see the necessity for marriage. "When she could get all the pleasures by remaining free, why shouldn't she enjoy herself? She saw no barriers in the way of enjoyment. She regarded it as merely one of the hungers of the body. . . ." She meets a college professor, Mr. Prasad, and says to him with few preliminaries: "Why don't you come and live here in my bungalow?" Mr. Prasad is willing but he says: "I don't want to lose my freedom and you won't want to lose yours. Your lovers will come to see you and I'll get jealous, and when my sweethearts come, you'll get angry. There will be quarrels and hostility, and you'll turn me out of the house. . . ." After some discussion they agreed to regard themselves as belonging to each other and live together. Miss Padma finally gives birth to a baby, and while she is in the hospital, Mr. Prasad takes all her money out of the bank and goes on a tour of Europe with a young girl student of his.

If the stories summarized above are inquired into for their evidences of Premchand's advance toward a greater literary skill, the conclusion seems inevitable that his progress was uncertain. In most of his critical writing about the short story

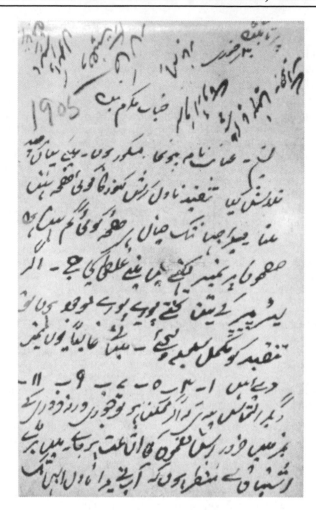

Holograph copy of one of Premchand's letters.

he admits the need to compel the interest of the reader, but at the same time he insists on the aim of moral uplift. To the reader this presents a vision of sugar in one spoon and castor oil in the other. The stories seem to reflect the struggle within him between achieving moral uplift and gaining the reader's interest, but the aim of conveying the author's message remains uppermost and the methods for achieving the illusion of reality in his creatures are overshadowed.

In **"Unmad"** and **"Miss Padma,"** Premchand's aim in writing was to teach the lesson that Indian culture stressed morality at its core, whereas the West had raised materialism and the love of pleasure to its central ideals. As long as a female character remained Western, she was no more than a dramatized prejudice. The events were carefully selected to stress the character's assigned role, and the free use of exposition tore any fictional veil from the author's purposes.

"Kusum," the story of the ignored letter-writing wife in her abasement, explored the depths of masochism to prove beyond doubt that she possessed all the forebearance of a traditional Hindu wife. Only after this was accomplished could she find a point beyond which she would not retreat. It might be suggested that Kusum's letters offer a psychological dimension which gives a richer suggestiveness to this story by analyzing the internal life of a young Indian woman with increased depth and subtlety. Certainly the device of the letter, by eliciting sympathy from the first-person misery of the character, was a technical improvement over the third-person author's descriptions so common to Premchand's earlier work. However, one is tempted to conclude that the psychological inferences themselves are deduced not so much from Kusum's own inner agony as from Premchand's conception of what a Hindu girl's agony should be.

The young girl Prema, in the story "**Kayar,**" is led to suicide, and the critic might conclude that reasonable probability has been overstepped. It is true that in India in 1933 ideas of inter-caste marriage and the free choice of a mate were well established in the minds of college students, even though these ideas were seldom put into practice. Premchand appears in this story to sympathize with the young girl, but the fact that the marriage could not take place accords with the realities in the world outside. However, Premchand, in his effort to show a middle-class girl who could give her heart but once to one man alone, could not end the story by leaving something to the reader's imagination, but had to prove his point beyond all chances of misinterpretation.

Concerning realism, which in its widest meaning implies the drawing up of a fictional world that appears believable and close to the world as the reader knows it, it is of interest to measure the believability of the female characters in these stories. In general, surface realism may be claimed in that the stories seem to reflect the changes that are taking place in society. Attempts are made at inter-caste marriage, women are becoming lawyers, dowries are being demanded to buy automobiles and for gaining advanced degrees in England, Indians are getting high positions and marrying English women. However, to Premchand these things are usually unwelcome. They offer him only new subject matter from which to hang an old attitude.

With regard to the heroines described, it might be asked: could this woman be a reality to Indian society? Even if she is only an ideal, is it so commonly accepted an idealization in Indian middle-class society as to inevitably attract Indian women to behave in a prescribed manner which then becomes their reality? On the other hand, is this ideal no more than a romantic pose that now is being exposed and questioned under the harsh lights of a new realistic age? Will the woman, hidden away in the home as some treasured dream to be kept from the touch of unclean reality, become with education, tight pajamas, and Italian hair-dos, a new creature? And will she leave behind Premchand's middle-class heroines as mere curios of a past age, outmoded because they had lived not private lives but prescribed ideals? Or will they live and show how "idealism" in America in 1930 could be "realism" in India, and that "realism" and "idealism" are things conditioned by place as well as time?

It is difficult to answer these questions without reference to Indian society itself. Perhaps the assumption can be made that middle-class Hindu society has been the bearer and conveyor of Hindu ideals such as those shown in the great classic epics, the Ramayana and Mahabharata. Storied women like Sita and Savitri have left a trail from the past, perfumed with an idealism that has influenced middle-class Hindu girls to the present.

If Premchand created women characters who broke or bent those ideals, they seem to have belonged to carefully chosen types. They could be low-caste women whose morals might belong to some "Little Tradition" of the anthropologists, which would cast no aspersions on a hallowed "Great Tradition."

They could be Western-educated, believing in women's rights and accepting all the cosmetics and behaviorisms of Hollywood. They might be Christian, or Parsi, or of another religious group (excluding Muslims) that was not Hindu. They might belong to families exclusively interested in making money, or be part of a profession whose ideals met with Premchand's hearty disagreement. Finally, they might occasionally be older women, aunts or mothers-in-law, who are needed to bully or intimidate or otherwise aid in accentuating the virtues of the heroine. Such older women in Premchand's idealistic realism genre of short stories seem to have the best chance of escaping fictional suffocation. They bring parts of many stories to life.

On the other hand, perhaps the only way Premchand may gain a distrustful Western critic's absolution for many of his middle-class heroines is that there first be found incontrovertible, extraliterary proof that middle-class Hindu women in real life are indeed as he depicts them. Of these young Hindu heroines however, one wonders if the traditional ideals set up for them were not still too strong for Premchand to break even if he had wanted to. To have created a heroine who, for whatever reason, ventured outside the prescribed codes of sexual morality, or who henpecked her husband, or who was too bold in public, would probably have made her seem quite unacceptable to the typical middle-class Hindu reader. However sharp tongued or quarrelsome his own wife might be, if the reader believed that he saw around him many women who represented the traditional Hindu heroine, it may not be surprising that the writer of Premchand's time, too, may have believed that in portraying her thus, he was representing the reality and not just dreaming dreams. Indeed, the question of reality and idealism, of dreams and objective fact, seem here so intertwined that a longer perspective of post-Premchand Hindi literature alone may decide whether Hindu heroines are going to remain different from their Western counterparts.

Writers of Marxist persuasion claim that Premchand's new realism came as a result of a disillusionment with Gandhian reformist thinking. They cited his affiliation with the Progressive Writers' Association, his several laudatory references to the Russian Revolution, and the rise to power of the middle classes as outward signs of his intellectual reorientation. A Marxist writer notes that within his last novel, *Godan,* contrary to habit in his earlier novels, Premchand has not created Gandhian heroes who go out into the villages, driven by the desire to create ideal villages through an appeal to the conscience of landlords and moneylenders. Premchand's villagers, he says, no longer have faith in such leaders. (pp. 115-21)

[Marxist writers argue] that Premchand had accepted a basic tenet of Marxism that the class of zamindar-moneylender-capitalist oppressors of his time must not remain. He was aware of a class struggle and described it in much of his writing. He accepted the fact that if the evil conditions continued they would inevitably lead to the destruction of the present organization of society. In his later years he appears not to have followed Gandhi's desire to create a village society. Finally, unlike Gandhi, at the end he had no belief in God or religion as agencies of human progress. Marxist writers point to these characteristics, not to claim that Premchand had come through a full cycle of change to suggest class warfare or violent overthrow of existing governments, but that he had come to lack faith in such methods of reform as the individual-by-individual conversion of thousands of zamindars and capitalists. His disillusionment strongly implied that he was groping toward more revolutionary solutions, and the only good recent example before him was the Russian Revolution.

The inferences drawn by Marxist critics from Premchand's private life, from his editorials, from what he said to his wife and to his friends, and from the individual and collected works themselves, find their rationale most nearly in the village stories of this period. The major theme of Premchand's village stories might state that a society based on the quest of personal material gain has bred class distinctions under which the powerful and wealthy oppress the weak and poor, the rich always getting richer and the poor, poorer. Much of his earlier work had sought in love, mercy, self-denial, non-violent soul force, a way out of a blighted reality. Only in his stories that were confined to characters who spent their whole lives in the village was the starkness of misery permitted to live itself out to tragedy. And these were few. Where there were landlords and outside officials coming into the villages, as happened frequently in the early periods, moral, Gandhian solutions had offered sweet endings to bitter beginnings. The stories written in the later period show the measure of Premchand's change of emphasis. In these village stories there lingers no afterglow of economic, social, or political hope. (pp. 121-22)

In these stories . . . no opportune event occurs to turn despair into hope or evil into righteousness. The heroes of the late village stories all come from the lowest classes of society, and the plots concentrate on the methods used in villages for crushing the poor. The stories show a different Premchand from the earlier one who had always preached that realism must be relieved by idealism, that literature must uplift and be useful in building a better, more moral society.

Marxist critics have found in [such stories as **"Kafan"** (**"The Shroud"**), **"Thakur-ka-Kua"** (**"The Thakur's Well"**), **"Pus-ki-Rat"** (**"A Night in the Winter's Month of Pus"**), and **"Dudh-ka Dam"** (**"The Price of Milk"**)] a picture that shows rejection of Gandhian reform. But in opposition to this point of view may be offered the argument of literary technique. Marxists, like Gandhians, had beliefs that promised a solution to India's rural misery. The fact that Premchand did not use Gandhian solutions in these late village stories would suggest that if he had accepted Marxist solutions, he would have used them in place of the Gandhian. But he used no economic or social reform lessons, which may well suggest that the awareness had come to him that art must differ from teaching, that whatever lesson might emerge from the misery of his villagers could only be delineated by the actions and thoughts and words of the villagers themselves, and that the intrusion of the author's abstract propositions of life would destroy the natural autonomy of the story's own life. (pp. 127-28)

The third group of critics, mentioned earlier . . . , took cognizance of the fact that the change toward greater realism in the content of Premchand's latest stories was brought about, not by a change in his political or social views, but by means of a new respect for technique. Whereas earlier he had disrupted the plausibility of a story's outcome by preaching through editorials or by unexpectedly converting villains into heroes, in this later period he began to find more artistic ways to solve his story problems.

Realism had long been a part of his work, and it remained for the artist to learn the detachment and control necessary to bring this realism to fruition. These critics point out that in the best of the late stories, along with better characterization, thought had been given to cause and effect, a new appropriateness had appeared between his "described situations and his expressed emotions," his description had become more psychological and true, and less artificial; the author's focus now was not on the union of outer activities and occupations but on basic influences that cause outward behavior. These critics also point out marked improvements in Premchand's plots, dialogue, language style, and other aspects of technique.

Certainly progress toward these claims can be seen in such stories as **"Naya Vivah"** (**"The New Marriage"** . . .). This is a story in two parts, the first a long, wasteful introduction to the second. It describes the marriage of a rich merchant, Lala Dangamal, and his first wife. He is forty-five years old and his wife about the same age, but while Lala is full of vigor and acts like a young man, his wife appears old. He has lost interest in her and treats her with indifference. When she dies Lala Dangamal decides to marry again.

The second part of the story, which should stand alone, describes the new marriage to a young girl. Lala's life changes completely. "Lalaji's old youth became younger than young youth. . . . I have always remained young," he says, "and will stay young. If old age comes here I'll blacken its face, put it on a donkey, and turn it out of the city. . . ." Lala gives many gifts to his young wife, he tries to take her out often to show her off, he spends money lavishly. But Asa, the young wife, remains quite indifferent. Instead she begins to find her only pleasure in talking to the cook's helper employed in the house, a simple but handsome young country boy. There are many subtly flirtatious conversations in the kitchen, interrupted only when Lala Dangamal comes home.

> The conversations became more pointed. "When your husband goes out with you he looks like your father or grandfather. . . . If I was married to some old woman of fifty, I'd leave home and run off. Either I'd take poison myself or give her poison. I suppose I'd be hung. . . ."
>
> Asa: "An old woman would love you more than a young girl, she'll serve you more. She'll keep you on a straight path."
>
> Cook's boy: "This is mother's work. The wife is for other work!"
>
> Asa: "O tell me, what is a wife's work then?"
>
> Cook's boy: "If you were not my boss I'd tell you what a wife's work is."
>
> Suddenly the sound of a car was heard. Somehow the top of Asa's sari had slipped from her head to her shoulders. Quickly she pulled it up over her head again, and running hurriedly toward her room she said: "Come back after Lala has had his meal and gone away."

In general Premchand shows change in this second part of the story by a new emphasis on the development of character and a lesser stress on event and plot structure. He reveals the attempt to bring about a concentration of effect, a quest for brevity, and the elimination of long descriptions.

In **"Naya Vivah"** the underlying message that "old men should not marry young girls" is implicit in the story rather than explicit through the author's commentary. The effects of dialogue are not dissipated by much accompanying explanation. Event is subordinated to character. Premchand did not impose the wifely code upon the young bride; rather he permitted her to be herself, to balance herself neatly between the prescriptions set for her as a Hindu wife and the wilful impulses of a young girl caught in an unpleasant situation. She achieves an individuality, frivolous and bold, and at the same time cautious, knowing when to pull her sari up over her head, but also letting it slip to her shoulders. And the moral of the story is left to fend for itself.

As has been seen in such village stories as **"Kafan"** and in city stories like **"Naya Vivah,"** the claims of critics who saw a sharpening of Premchand's techniques were justified in many respects. This type of story did not appear with any notable consistency, however, until 1934. Amrtrai, Premchand's biographer, takes note of this change in the following words:

> Munshi-ji wrote several stories of this new type, new subject matter, and new style, in which there is not the thick and strongly woven net of plot of his earlier stories. There is just some very small matter, some light point, some minor state of mind, his own way of looking at something, a flying glimpse of some beautiful truth which, without much thought for the plot, is unfolded in a measure of conversation.

The stories of the last three or four years of Premchand's life, even those not connected with the village, give final evidence that he had reached a new conception of the purpose of the short story. The characters appear to have taken over their own world; the creator has concealed himself. The objectives are no longer pointed at the specific problems of independence, social reform, or justification of East over West. Instead of themes such as "In order to get rid of the British we must be strong and brave," or "The landlord should be self-denying in order that the peasant may get a decent living," Premchand's new questions are such as: "How can an older brother maintain his pride and authority over a younger brother who is much smarter than he is? What happens to the principles of a young socialist when he goes for a weekend to a rich zamindar's house? What are the reactions of certain passersby at the sight of a girl sleeping on a bench in a public park in broad daylight?" The themes are personal questions. They evolve out of individual human situations and are not dictated by abstract propositions. (pp. 131-34)

In Premchand's earlier work it appears plausible to trace the influences upon him of Tolstoi, Vivekenanda, Gandhi, or Karl Marx, but in these last of his stories, influences become obscure as they are absorbed and reconstructed in his individual expression. The light from the candles that lighted his early way were forgotten when the central sun was established. The lessons of Tolstoi or Gandhi become untraceable ingredients of Premchand, the mature writer. To the end there may be pity and soul-force and self-denial or righteous indignation, but they have lost their specific sources and acquired the implicit intuitions of literature.

The political, moral, and economic lessons, which earlier Premchand had made so noticeable, had inhibited the effects of his art. In his later stories, such as **"Kafan"** and **"Prem-ki Holi"** (**"The Sacrifice of Love"**), published in his last collection, he appears to have adjusted his views to agree that "All fiction involves a certain theme, or idea, and emphasizes certain interpretations and values. . . . But . . . a piece of fiction ceases to be propaganda when the skill of the writer makes us feel the people as real and when he does not sacrifice their reality to prove a point."

It is with the collection *Kafan* in 1936 that Premchand's writing of short stories drew to its close. Premchand died in October, 1936, and since that time two generations of Indians have read

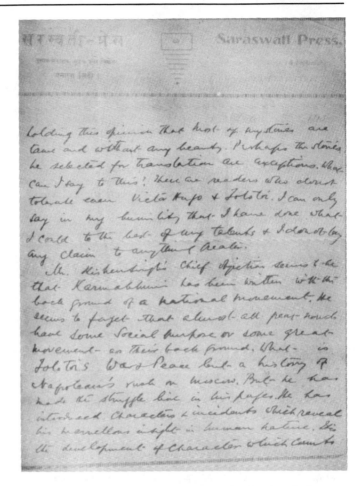

Holograph copy of a letter from Premchand written in English.

his stories in and out of school; many of his works have been translated into European and other Asian languages; his name is mentioned where modern Indian literature is mentioned. He wrote under great difficulties, pushed by economic necessity to write without adequate time for revision, impelled by his era to make his fiction serve national causes. These facts will not keep him from his place in the history of Hindi literature where his name will lie athwart a period called the Premchand Age. To live beyond the Premchand Age in more than textbooks and compulsory Hindi literature courses, however, his case may rest largely upon the stories he wrote in the last years of his life. (p. 138)

> *Robert O. Swan, in his* Munshi Premchand of Lamhi Village, *Duke University Press, 1969, 149 p.*

DANIEL CARNIE   (essay date 1974)

[*In the following excerpt, Carnie contrasts E. M. Forster's and Premchand's artistic treatments of India's middle class.*]

Godan and *A Passage To India* contain a striking, if superficial, similarity of construction. Both deal with the relationship between the educated bourgeoisie and another class—in Premchand's case, the peasants, in Forster's, the Anglo-Indians. Both are dramatically realistic, and both deal in psychological portraiture. These similarities however, belie an enormous, and very telling, difference in motive and conception. Forster might well be characterized as an effete English aesthete; such a description would be fully borne out by the man's works. *A Passage To India* is a book of form, of art—poetic and lyrical. Forster's concern is beauty, human and otherwise. Indians are approved or disapproved in so far as Forster finds them sensitive or aesthetic or intelligent, in so far as he finds them likeable. For instance, the Rajah of *The Hill Of Devi* is, from a Christian-social point of view, quite disgusting, but Forster finds him thoroughly charming, and therefore admirable.

Premchand on the other hand, is a crusader. His concern is social justice, and his works conform to that motive. Peasant misery, the strictures of caste, and the condition of women dominate *Godan* and the short stories. Characters are portrayed and manipulated around social themes, and exist almost entirely in relation to such themes. They exist to illustrate a morality and gain or lose favour accordingly.

Thus we find the professional of *Godan* wallowing in all the decadence, indolence, materialism and frivolity to which the educated middle classes are so prone. Premchand presents two powerful and very useful, if somewhat crude, character types. The first of these—the "butterflies"—would include Malti and Mirza. Mirza is the iconoclast of the group—perverse and irresponsible. A Robin Hood fighting his battles in capitalism's upper circles, he is "always up to some sort of crazy scheme to take money from the rich and give it to the poor." But we soon discover that this is the benevolence of a drunk and a dilettante, of one who finds it merely entertaining to dabble in the affairs of the poor and the underprivileged. With Mirza stands Malti. Educated in England, she is pretty, quite westernized and entirely frivolous. With no illusions about either her motives or her aims, Malti pursues a social career and amuses a jaded imagination. "In place of a conscience she had a glitter; in place of a heart, coquetry."

Our second category, that of the "hypocrites," would include practically everyone else. These are the educated liberals, devoted to that ethic, but burdened with overwhelming avarice, pretense and pomposity. There is Onkarnath—the self-seeking editor of a peasant-oriented socialist newspaper; Rai Sahib—the zamindar, simultaneously spouting liberal dogma and raising the land rent; and Khanna—dedicated businessman and lawyer, spicing his conversation with spiritualism and socialism. These three are so ridiculous in their pretension as to have almost come to believe it themselves.

Riding high above his fellows we find Mehta—the philosopher. Mehta is the virile and respected member of the group, the one with whom Premchand's sympathies obviously lie. Still, when first introduced, Mehta professes a kind of individualistic materialism. Out to cultivate his own garden, he might initially be classified with the "butterflies."

Premchand then, views this group of upward mobile young professionals in a scarcely favourable light. He finds them facile and selfish. While recognizing the prevailing liberal ethic, Premchand rages against the hypocrisy which lies behind it. This is a major theme in *Godan*. The group possesses all the wit, grace and noble morality which civilization has to offer. But their intelligence is impotent and their morality useless—it provides no meaningful service. The group is of no use to India and Premchand dismisses them. The poor are still poor, and the hungry still hungry, and that is Premchand's concern.

One may be sure that E. M. Forster would not have liked these Indians any better. Like Premchand, he would have found them materialistic, frivolous and especially insincere. And indeed Forster occasionally castigates his characters for very much the same reasons. The point however, is that Premchand chose to portray his characters in this socio-political light, while Forster did not. Morality is not a problem to that gentle Englishman.

But to Premchand of course, it is. Premchand's constant theme, when dealing with the educated middle class, is the conflict between traditional values and individual selfishness, and their generally liberal ideals. Over and over again liberalism falls prey to a stronger power. The short stories deal largely with the problems created by traditional structures. In **"The Price Of Milk"** we are mortified by the treatment a zamindar, "an educated man, and aware of the need for reform," inflicts on his dependent sweepers. In **"A Desperate Case"** the wife of a well-to-do and educated man cannot produce a son. We are informed that the husband knew it was not his wife's fault, but still he treats her with incredible cruelty. In the end the woman actually dies of despair. But perhaps the most powerful of these tales is **"A Servant Of The People."** An acclaimed leader and humanitarian professes equality for all, but is incapable of accepting it in his own home. His daughter asks to marry a man of low caste, and "the servant of the people looked at her with eyes of doom and turned away."

But such stories are usually narrated with some pathos. Premchand is far less kind when writing of hypocrisy and self-interest. In **"Intoxication"** and **"A Coward"** we witness the downfall of two ostensibly idealistic young men. "Like any young fellow he would argue his theories with a Passion and demonstrate his devotion with his tongue. But to suffer for them was beyond his capacity." Likewise, in *Godan* it is individual selfishness, rather than traditional strictures, that burdens the group. Caste rules are frequently broken, and even joked about. Rai Sahib served meat and alcohol at his dinner party, and untouchables were included on the guest list. The problem is personal, rather than cultural, immorality. "Like so many people, Khanna enjoyed—or suffered—a kind of double life. On the one hand he was devoted to sacrifice, and public service and benevolence, while on the other, to self-interest and indulgence and status . . . there was a constant conflict between the two parts, with the aggressiveness and persistence of the lower self usually overshadowing the gentility of the higher self."

So too Forster is not completely unaware of such things. In *The Hill Of Devi* Masood is accused of pomposity. There is not infrequent reference to religious discrimination in his works. Aziz, upon embracing Das, a Hindu, mutters: "I wish they did not remind me of cow-dung." And later: "We must try to appreciate these quaint Hindus." Forster also denigrates Aziz's attitude towards women, and there is a most pointed parallel drawn between Anglo-Indian prejudice and that which Aziz manages with Dr. Panna Lal. But although they appear, such incidents hold little emphasis in Forster's works. He seems completely ambivalent towards social concerns. The lower classes appear only as inefficient and faceless servants, or as symbols of the notoriously eternal East.

Not so for Premchand, for whom the peasantry form a constant backdrop against which to display ignoble liberals. The effect is startlingly similar to that of Zola's *Germinal*. Premchand presents a clear and intense contrast between the oppressed and the oppressors. Of major importance is Hori, and the people who surround him, but there are constant cameos of other simple peasant folk. Although crushed, starving and ignorant, to Premchand these people possess a wisdom far in excess of even Mehta, the philosopher's, learning. It is a wisdom of love and sacrifice, of devotion and service. The jungle girl which Mehta and Malti meet on their hunting expedition is a paragon of these practical virtues, this spirit of sacrifice.

In a less typical form, Premchand embodies the peasant virtues in Govinda, the wife of Khanna. It is from Govinda that Mehta learns the shallowness of his own ways, and the value of self-sacrifice. "Confronted by this devoted and selfless woman, he felt himself to be petty and small." Premchand here develops an attitude which Forster could never have divined. Premchand negates the value and wisdom of western liberal education, and puts in its place the simplicity of the peasant. "Even if you get an M.A. and a D. Litt. and even a Ph. D. Understanding doesn't come from reading books."

Yet that "Understanding", as Premchand certainly recognizes, is rather less than enough. One cannot dismiss the pathetic helplessness of Hori's condition. His peasant's wisdom is of little help when confronted by the wolf. I think it obvious that Premchand envisions our educated young liberals filling that gap. *Godan* possesses a sure and simple dialectic. The story opens with an expose of the materialism and frivolity of the rising middle class. Preying upon the peasantry, they pursue vain, meaningless and terribly chic lives. But there is a gradual realization of the beauty and nobility of that simple peasant wisdom. Mehta is overcome by Govinda's example, and soon leads the way for others. The story closes with Mehta and Malti, and perhaps a few more, engaging in meaningful, benevolent activity, devoting themselves towards service and self-sacrifice, towards humanitarian goals.

Premchand's attitude then, is an amalgamation of both approval and raging disapproval. He finds much to despise among the educated and westernized, most especially the shallowness of their character and the weakness of their ideals. But Premchand obviously approves of their liberalism, and many of the anti-traditional forces contained therein. He perhaps espouses a union of that "Understanding" peculiar to the peasant, and modern Western liberalism. The one would guarantee justice, the other, integrity.

E. M. Forster on the other hand, might have never seen a peasant. This single fact serves to indicate the prime difference between Forster and Premchand. Forster seems quite unaware of India's social problems, and if aware, then unconcerned. (pp. 25-30)

> *Daniel Carnie, "The Modern Middle Class: In Premchand and in Forster," in Indian Literature, Vol. XVII, Nos. 1 & 2, 1974, pp. 25-33.**

GOVIND NARAIN (essay date 1978)

[*Narain is an Indian-born critic and educator specializing in English and Indian literature. In the following excerpt, he discusses the importance of Premchand's contribution to Indian life and literature.*]

Of the various critical evaluations of Prem Chand's creative achievement Nagendra's is perhaps the most challenging. He feels that Prem Chand is not in the first rank of creative artists. Nagendra admires Prem Chand's natural, profound, and pervasive humanism, emphasizes the documentary value of his work, and doubts whether there is another Hindi writer who presents such a comprehensive picture of the sociopolitical, economic, and communal life during the first three phases of the Gandhian era. But he sees explicit limits to Prem Chand's

genius. His outlook is practical or utilitarian in the best sense of the word: he has no interest in truth or beauty for their own sake. Humanism is after all a materialistic philosophy: Prem Chand could only assimilate Gandhi's reformism but was unable to appreciate the spiritual side of Gandhism. He is not a creative writer of the first rank because his critical gaze is concentrated on contemporary problems; he has touched but rarely or not at all the perennial questions of life. There is a lack of intellectual solidity and firmness in him, qualities which can come only from deep philosophical thinking. Normality—the distinctive trait of Prem Chand's personality, according to Nagendra—can attain only the second rank; to be first-rate one must be exceptional.

Nagendra illustrates the sharp stratification of the reading public in our time between what may, for the sake of convenience, be called the high-brow and the middle-brow. To the high-brow critic Prem Chand is moralistic, didactic, reticent on the intimate aspects of life, earnest but blind to the possibilities of art and to the complexities of human nature. Ilā Chandra Joshī, for instance, regards his characters, particularly the female ones, as some sort of embodied abstractions, lacking in individuality and vitality. Prem Chand was a child of his age, and he has the strengths and weaknesses of his position. It is not simply that he is not interested in technical experimentation for its own sake or betrays a strange naiveté in matters of pure art: he would have considered preoccupation with concerns of this nature irrelevant and even irresponsible, as is clearly seen in his disapproval of the romantic school of Urdu poetry. Art for him is, unquestionably, the servant of life, and he would have answered his Art-for-Art's-sake critics with Samuel Butler's well-known sally: "Who is art that it should have a sake?" His best novels are, at bottom, the creation of a profoundly moral impulse. This does not mean that he did not have enough respect for the real, for fidelity to the surface as well as the depth of experience. Though he cannot match George Eliot's intellectual and analytical power, Dostoevski's piercing insight into the innermost recesses of the human soul, and Tolstoy's wide experience of the world, he has most of these qualities in ample measure to make him a writer of considerable stature. He has a rich and robust creative talent, a depth of understanding, insight, and moral passion to identify himself with a broad spectrum of humanity, specially the humble and the weak. He has the born creative artist's ability to render life in concrete detail, the sage's moral fervor to inspire and enthuse men to love decency and goodness. Though a master of humor and sarcasm, he is not a mere entertainer or chronicler of the social scene. He is really in the line of reformers and sages like Rām Mohan Roy, Vivekānand, and Tagore who strove to regenerate the Indian nation by arousing it from its millenial slumber. In the manner of the Victorian sages, the thinkers like Emerson, Thoreau, and Whitman, he points to his countrymen the dangers of an unthinking infatuation with modern materialism and reminds them of the moral and spiritual values enshrined in their own culture. In many of his earlier novels he seems to be retreating from the full and gloomy consequences of his own vision and taking refuge in a sentimental utopianism. Man's life, is, however, based on faith and hope: Prem Chand's utopian dreams are merely a manifestation of his strong faith in man. He was doing the same thing which *philosophes* like Condorcet and Godwin, Romantic poets like Blake and Shelley, and sages like Gandhi with his utopian ideal of *Rāma Rājya* ("The Reign of Rama") have done—using his creative imagination to project the vision of a perfect society in which men, transcending their selfishness and greed and forgetting the distinctions of caste and creed, could live like brothers and sisters. This does not mean that he is an armchair philosopher or an idle dreamer. Poverty and want were living realities to him because he was nurtured in their midst and had experienced them himself. But his faith in man led him to strive ceaselessly to impress on his upper-class countrymen the criminality of the economic and social system which they upheld. The degree of success attained by him is difficult to measure; maybe even scores of Prem Chands would not succeed in disturbing the self-serving slumber of the classes. But he did bring into existence the Hindi-Urdu social-political novel, molding the attitudes of younger writers who acknowledged their indebtedness to him and some of whom chose to call themselves "progressive." He helped widen the meaning of literature from the belletristic conception of Urdu writers and even those of the Bhārtendu school in Hindi. Literature for him implied a vigorous involvement with ideas and issues, rather than an escapist withdrawal into the realms of fantasy and romantic love. He evolved a style which is simple, lucid, sinewy, and supple, a finely tempered instrument which can with equal ease capture the raciness and vigor of the villager's idiom and the urbanity and elegance of that of the Persianized elite. Dr. Rāmvilās Shǎrmā is right to emphasize the magnitude of his achievement in this regard. . . .

The recurrent figure in Prem Chand's novels is the idealistic young man who is called upon to choose between his own self-advancement and the claims of the community and the nation. Some of these young men turn out to be lifeless and wooden like the "virtuous" heroes of even great novelists like Scott, George Eliot, and Tolstoy. Thus we have Amrit Rāi, Pratāp Chandra, Vinaya Singh, Prem Shankar, and Shankhdhar. But there are others who are living and real—Balrāj, Chakradhar, Amarkānt. So are heroes of another sort—Surdās and Horī—and the whole cast of other characters who enliven the novels in which they appear—Gyān Shankar, Totā Rām, Munshī Vajradhar, Lālā Samarkānt, Devīdīn, Gobar, Mātā Dīn. It is grossly unfair to describe, as Ilā Chandra Joshī does, the creator of Suman, Nirmalā, Manoramā, Jālpā, and Dhaniā as a painter of abstractions who had no understanding of women. They do not cease to be vital just because they symbolize something. Each of them is, in Henry James's terms, "a strikingly figured symbol," because each is also "a thoroughly pictured character." Moreover, stature as a writer cannot be assessed in isolation from the nature and amount of the output. Emily Brontë wrote one novel, but Dickens created a world. Prem Chand composed some outstanding works which are masterpieces in their own right—stories like "Boorī Kākī," "Qafan," and "Shatranj-ké-Khilāri"; novels like Sevā-Sadan, Rangabhumi and Godān. But to form a true estimate of his genius it is necessary to consider the totality of his output, which constitutes one of the most varied, rich, and comprehensive renderings of life ever achieved by a writer of fiction. The Prem Chand World in its richness and variety invites comparison with the Scott, Dickens, Hardy, and, with certain limitations, even the Tolstoy World.

Prem Chand was keenly aware of the indifferent status of the creative writer in Indian society. There was not likely to be much confusion about his place if he had composed works of piety and learning: if he were a Brahmin like Tulsīdās he would have been honored and revered, if a low-caste man like Kabīr he would have been unworldly and unconcerned about social status. The position would have been clear too if he were independently wealthy like Bhārtendu Harish Chandra and Tagore, or held an official position like Bankim Chandra. But if he did not belong to any of these categories, there was no option for him but to seek the patronage of the rich and powerful and adopt the servile attitude of the supplicant. Prem Chand is one of the first Indian writers who refused to follow this path, who was fiercely independent in his attitude and absolutely uncompromising in his principles. His resignation from government service was in its own way a step as momentous as Tagore's renunciation of the knighthood in 1919, his letter to the Mahārājā of Alwar as significant as Dr. Johnson's famous letter to Lord Chesterfield. How courageous these actions were can be realized when we compare Prem Chand with figures such as Sir Mohammad Iqbāl, who, with all their genius, could not resist the temptation of following the path of opportunism and alliance with the powers that were.

Thus great as Prem Chand is as a novelist, short-story writer, essayist, and moralist, he is equally great as a humanist, a humanitarian, and a man. An estimate of his worth as a creative writer which ignores his distinction as a human being runs the risk of being partial and inadequate. (pp. 153-56)

> *Govind Narain, in his* Munshi Prem Chand, *Twayne Publishers, 1978, 178 p.*

V. S. NARAVANE (essay date 1980)

[*In the following excerpt, Naravane discusses the shortcomings and strong points of Premchand's work.*]

Premchand created the tradition of the modern novel and short story in Hindi. In some other Indian languages, particularly Bengali, he had distinguished predecessors like Bankim Chandra Chatterji and Rabindranath Tagore. But the Hindi novelists and short story writers before Premchand were, generally speaking, caught up in out-of-date concepts of what this type of literature can offer. They were preoccupied with the mysterious, the strange, the romantic, the sensational. Even when social problems were raised, the treatment of these problems was artificial and unconvincing. The language was archaic or ornamental. The plots were loosely constructed, and sometimes the novel became merely a series of episodes strung together. When the author wanted to express certain ideals, he did so in a blatantly moralistic or didactic manner.

Some of Premchand's predecessors did try to remedy these defects. A few excellent and memorable stories were produced. But no one before Premchand dedicated himself to creative writing in this genre on such a scale and with such impressive results. Premchand was not only superior to his predecessors and contemporaries in this respect, but also influenced an entire generation of younger writers. This influence was many-sided. Many modern Hindi writers emulated Premchand's approach, his technique, even his language. It would not be correct to assume that Premchand rid himself entirely of the defects and limitations of Hindi fiction as he found it. Some of these limitations persisted. There were other defects which resulted from his own individual habits of expression and from the limitations of his equipment and training. Through a long process of trial and error, he succeeded in overcoming most of the limitations which he had inherited from the work of his predecessors. But some traces of these weaknesses remained even in his later work. A fair assessment of Premchand's total work is scarcely possible without pointing out the defects in his stories and novels. Indeed, when we consider the negative features of his work, the greatness that he achieved in spite of them appears all the more remarkable.

Coincidences, chance meetings, unexpected obstacles, and other elements of the fortuitous often mar the quality of Premchand's plots. I am not suggesting that a novelist should reject the role of chance in human life. There is a place for the unpredictable even in the most faithful and convincing delineation of life. But Premchand tends to make excessive use of coincidences, and thus gives the impression that he is seeking an easy solution to the problem of constructing his stories. Chance thus becomes a tool in the hands of the story-teller—a tool blunted by overuse. In the earlier novels one also detects a tendency to introduce dramatic situations. And dramatization brings in its wake exaggeration and overstatement.

Another device which Premchand uses, to the detriment of the aesthetic quality of his writing, is to get rid of his characters by making them commit suicide, or by subjecting them to accidental death. In almost every major novel there are a couple of suicides. In *Rangabhumi*, one of his two greatest novels, Sophia and Vinay commit suicide, Raja Mahendra Pratap is crushed to death under a statue, and some other characters meet violent deaths. The introduction of suicide and accident gives the reader the impression that once certain characters in the novel have served their purpose the author does not know what further role he should assign to them.

Premchand has, in fact, created very few characters which may be described as memorable and convincing. Most of the characters in the novel conform to 'types'. They do not stand forth in their own right as individuals. There is the social reformer, the 'good' aristocrat, the 'bad' aristocrat, the honest official, the dishonest official, the long suffering widow, the toiling peasant, the westernized woman, the self-sacrificing Indian woman, the struggling writer, the hypocritical priest, and so on. The author seems to have created, for each of his novels and most of his stories, characters that can be cast into one of these moulds. There are, of course, exceptions: Hori in *Godan*, Surdas in *Rangabhumi* and Premshankar in *Premashram* are drawn with a masterly hand. But the number of such figures, who really come alive with distinctive personalities of their own, is very small considering Premchand's vast output.

One of the greatest defects in Premchand's work—especially the novels—is that he has introduced long passages which sometimes try the readers' patience. The author evidently did not cultivate the virtue of brevity. "The greatest art is to omit," said Chesterton. Premchand rarely practises that art. These long passages are sometimes descriptive or narrative, sometimes they are monologues. These monologues are particularly inappropriate when they are introduced in short stories. As an example I will refer to a story of his middle period, "**Bank Ka Diwala**" ("**The Insolvent Bank**"). The main character in this story, Kunwar Jagdish Singh, indulges in heart-searching. He examines his own conduct, and the future course of his action. His musings occupy *five and a half pages* at one stretch in a story of twenty-three pages. Such long monologues or speeches occur in almost every novel.

What is even more regrettable, the author himself joins in as the narrator, and delivers long speeches or gives descriptive accounts in addition to those given by the characters themselves. This is a grave shortcoming. The personalities of the men and women in Premchand's novels are not given adequate opportunities to emerge from their own actions or utterances. The author takes over and adds to what his own fictional creation has already said. Sometimes, indeed, a dialogue becomes a trialogue. One of the characters makes a fairly long comment on some situation or event; the person to whom he is talking

gives an equally long reply; and the author steps in and expresses his own opinion. One gets the feeling that the author is always there, waiting in the wings, to supplement what is being said on the stage. This tendency of introducing long passages can be seen even in Premchand's last novel, *Godan*, acclaimed by many as his best work. Professor Mehta, the idealist philosopher, treats the elite of Lucknow to long and edifying discourses on a number of weighty issues.

Finally, in summing up the shortcomings in Premchand's work as a novelist and storyteller, it must be pointed out that his writings are deficient in poetic subtlety and philosophic depth. He writes with power, sincerity, directness. He probes the thoughts and actions of human beings in almost every conceivable practical situation. But he lacks the lyrical suggestiveness which we see in Rabindranath's *Shesher Kavita* or in some of the descriptions of the river at night in Sarat Chandra's *Shrikanta*. Premchand is completely engrossed in the affairs of actual, finite individuals in the dimensions of space and time. We do not get in his pages a feeling for the Infinite and the Timeless. We do not see the breath of man mingling with the breath of nature. We do not hear the music of cosmic melodies. There is no sense of wonder about the Unknown, no yearning to unravel the mystery of the Beyond. Ethical ideals are there, and they are expressed with great sincerity. But there is no journey from the empirical to the transcendental, no ascent from the ethical to the metaphysical. . . . [This] lack of lyrical subtlety and philosophical profundity can be ascribed to the limitations of his own early training, and the circumstances of his life, which prevented him from synthesising his experiences into a harmonious world-view.

In spite of all these shortcomings Premchand has earned his place as one of the most important figures in modern Indian culture. His contribution is unique, substantial and many-sided. His influence is likely to remain a major force in Hindi literature for a long time to come. And it would not be a rash prediction to assert that if his works are made available to non-Hindi readers through adequate translations, his influence can be an important factor in Indian literature as a whole in the foreseeable future. Premchand's significance, and the stature he has already acquired, can be understood if we take into consideration the main features of his work. These may be summarised as follows:

(*i*) Premchand was the first writer in Hindi to understand the potentialities of the novel. He realised that of all literary genres the novel alone was capable of reflecting the various aspects of Indian life in a broad sweep. He also realised the responsibility of the novelist. Precisely because of the tremendous scope of the novel, it was imperative that the writer who chose this medium of expression should be aware of the burden that he was taking upon himself. Having arrived at a true estimate of the scope of the novel, and having realised the novelist's responsibility, Premchand dedicated himself wholeheartedly to the task of carrying out that responsibility. Through sickness and health, and in the midst of uninterrupted personal difficulties, he threw himself into his work. Every paragraph that he wrote speaks of his sincerity and integrity. He carried his self-imposed burden with unremitting toil all his life.

(*ii*) In discharging his responsibility as a creative artist he displayed an acuteness of perception and a range of observation which remains unsurpassed in Hindi literature even today. He chose one particular part of India, with which he was thoroughly familiar, and depicted the life of this region with amazing wealth of detail. The mansion of a landed aristocrat; the hovel of a starving peasant; a *pan* shop at a street corner; a temple, mosque or church; factories, law courts, government offices—his gaze penetrated everywhere. Every facet of life, every type of work, people in every conceivable vocation, all the problems which engross the attention of men and women— social, economic, religious, political, professional, domestic— everything, in short, with which the fabric of human life is woven finds its reflection in the novels and stories of Premchand. Moreover, he sees human life in its interrelationships, and in the process of transformation. Premchand was a pioneer in depicting conditions of life in India in the light of the changes that had already come, and that were looming on the horizon.

(*iii*) Not only did he show a fine grasp of the human condition, in the midst of its changing pattern, but he also understood the trends of thought in contemporary India, and the social movements through which these trends were expressed. Specifically, we find in his works a vivid reflection of all the four major trends of his age: *first,* the nationalist movement, particularly in the phase which began with the emergence of Mahatma Gandhi; *second,* the new concept of social progress, and the reform movements to which they gave rise; *third,* a new religious consciousness based on the rejection of custom-ridden practices, empty ritual and superstition; and *fourthly,* the ideal of economic justice and equality, based broadly on the concept of a socialist society, and expressed through the struggles of peasants and workers against exploitation. The writings of Premchand provide a valuable record of all these trends of thought, and all these movements, as seen and understood by a gifted artist.

(*iv*) Unlike many other Indian writers, Premchand never expressed his love of India by an uncritical glorification of everything Indian. He did not hesitate to turn the floodlight on the darkest spots in Indian life. We are often asked to develop a pride in our national heritage. But how seldom are we asked to develop a sense of shame for all the cruelty, cunning and superstition that has been condoned in the name of tradition! Premchand was fearless in his exposure of the shams and evils that have darkened the record of India's evolution through the ages. This meant shattering many long-cherished illusions, offending many champions of orthodoxy. But he did not care. However, this criticism was born out of his profound love for India and her people, his great compassion for the victims of injustice and oppression.

Premchand, Sarat Chandra and Rabindranath roused India's conscience through their novels and stories. They showed the utter hypocrisy of sweeping all our evils under the rug and talking about spiritualism. But they did not dwell on the negative side of the Indian tradition without intense pain and deep compassion. We have to make a distinction between those who expose evils out of love and those who do so in a cynical spirit or to win the applause of western audiences. In every line that Premchand wrote we feel the agony he experienced when he saw the condition of the helpless widow, the insulted untouchable, the starving peasant. Do we feel that love and compassion, that concern and sorrow, when we read the writings of the Chaudharis, the Mehtas and the Naipauls who have received lavish praise for their "critical" approach? Premchand rebukes his compatriots with tears in his eyes, not with a sardonic smile on his lips.

(*v*) And this brings us to one of the strongest features in Premchand's writings: the faith in man and his future which they reveal. In spite of all the faults and failures that he sees in India, he never doubts the innate strength of India's spirit. Even when he depicts human actions at their worst, he does not lose faith in human nature. He does not write off humanity as beyond redemption. There is always scope for self-purification and self-uplifting, for nations as for individuals. In Premchand's novels and stories there are very few characters who can be described as wholly evil. In spite of all the inequity and tragedy which he depicts, he retains his optimism. I have seen only two stories in which the approach to life is wholly negative. These are "**Sadgati**" and "**Kafan**". . . . In "**Sadgati**" a heartless Brahmin makes a helpless untouchable work so hard that the poor wretch collapses and dies. Other untouchables refuse to remove the body, and of course no high caste Hindu would touch it. People cannot go to the well to fetch water from the well. The corpse begins to stink. At night the Brahmin ties the dead man's legs with a rope, drags the body out of the village and flings it in a farm where jackals and vultures devour it. This is a terrible picture, ferocious and frightening. In "**Kafan**" a father and his grown son chat outside a room in which the son's wife is dying. While shrieks of unbearable pain emerge from the room, the two men reminisce about the dainties on which they had once feasted. The woman dies, and they go out begging for money to buy a shroud for the corpse. When the money is obtained, they go to a tavern, get drunk, and begin to sing and dance. What's the use of a shroud, any way, they tell each other. After all, it would only be burnt along with the corpse. When the story ends, we see them completely drunk, lying unconscious.

I regard these stories as aberrations. Here men are shown as beasts. There are no extenuating circumstances for human brutality. These men are not victims of the "social system." In fact, in "**Kafan**" the author expressly tells us that Ghisu and Madhav—father and son—were poor simply because they were too lazy to earn a living and that there was plenty of work in the village if they wanted it. These are stories of pure misanthropy, totally out of keeping with Premchand's usual approach. Nowhere else, in all his fifteen novels and two hundred stories, have I seen man portrayed so black, so misshapen, so monstrous. The only explanation is that the author was, *for a brief period,* passing through a phase of unrelieved pessimism and gloom. He was ill, had very little money, was worried about the future of his wife and children. It is understandable that even a man with a basically well-balanced and optimistic temperament may, in the shadow of death and in the throes of difficulties, sink into a cynical mood for a temporary period. But it is difficult to understand why these stories should be selected by some critics for special praise. "**Kafan**" has been described by some as one of Premchand's greatest stories because of its "realism." Apparently, to show the best features of human nature is "idealism" and therefore not "modern"; to show man at his wickedest is to be realistic and progressive. I feel that such appraisals are utterly unfair to Premchand. These two stories should not be regarded as representative of his work but rather as unfortunate exceptions. (pp. 250-57)

What was Premchand's "philosophy of life?" Apart from his views on specific issues, did he involve a unified world-view or *weltanschaung*? Regrettably, the answer has to be in the negative. The more we admire Premchand's stand on the vital issues of man's practical life, the more disappointed we are that these views were not subsumed in a unified vision of reality. It is not difficult to understand, however, why his scattered responses should have failed to find their fulfilment in some kind of a synthesis. First of all, he was only fifty-six when he died. It is quite possible that a world-view would have emerged in his ripest years if he had been spared to develop his feelings and thoughts in a leisurely manner. Then again, his life had been one of constant struggle to solve the day-to-day problems which kept him on his toes. He toiled incessantly to fulfil his obligations to his students, his employers, his press, his journal. These obligations were in addition to his own creative work. He never had the time for calm, sustained reflection.

But there is an even more important factor to be considered. Premchand's ideas were formed as the result of wide but unplanned reading. He was a self-educated man, and read whatever he could lay his hands upon. He did not have a methodical grounding either in the Indian or in the western tradition. He once confessed that he had not read even Tulsidasa's *Ramacharitamanas* carefully. Being an extremely intelligent man, blessed with a fine memory, he picked up the basics of Indian religion and literature as he went along. Much of his reading was limited to fiction and, in later years, books on social and political subjects. He was a voracious reader, with an insatiable appetite for books. But he was not a discriminating reader. He was too easily impressed. He was never particularly fond of religious or philosophical literature. Even in Tolstoy's writings he saw only the reflection of social and political conditions. The deep spiritual significance of Tolstoy seems to have escaped him. Such being the sources upon which his mind was nourished, it is not surprising that he did not succeed in evolving a well-rounded world-view.

However, he did accept, in its broad features, the Gandhian way of looking at human problems. The most important single influence in his life was that of Mahatma Gandhi's personality and teachings. He accepted Mahatma Gandhi's concept of Satyagraha, his faith in "change of heart." Like many other outstanding Indians, he experienced something like a sudden conversion when he first saw the Mahatma and heard his voice. He placed Mahatma Gandhi in the same category as the Buddha, Jesus Christ and Prophet Muhammad. His conversion to the Mahatma's fold was not so much religious as ethical. Premchand was not a religious man by temperament, but he was deeply sensitive to ethical issues. He accepted all the major tenets of the Gandhian ethos: truth, non-violence, the cleansing power of suffering, the conscience as the final arbiter of righteousness. In all his novels written after he came under the Mahatma's influence, at least one major character is cast in the Gandhian mould. If at all we can speak of an abiding set of values which Premchand represented, it was derived from the Mahatma.

Some have asserted that Premchand, in the last phase of his life, "finally" rejected Gandhism and was moving on towards communism. Commenting on Premchand's unfinished novel, **Mangalsutra,** Madan Gopal says: "The Gandhi in him . . . had either gone to sleep or the image of the Mahatma had been dislodged from the inner temple of his heart" [*Munshi Premchand: A Literary Biography*]. Amrit Rai has also expressed the view that Premchand made a final break with the Gandhian concept of social change and came to look upon the class struggle as inevitable.

But is it really possible to ascribe finality to a position adopted by a man shortly before his death at the early age of fifty-six? After all, as early as 1919 Premchand had written to his friend Nigam: "I have now almost been converted to Bolshevik principles." Yet from 1920 to 1933 everything that he wrote was permeated by his reverence for Mahatma Gandhi. How can we say categorically that he would *never* have returned to the Gandhian way of life? Are we in a position to speculate what his reaction would have been if he had pondered over developments in the Soviet Union in the Stalin era and in China during the "cultural revolution"? I should like to emphasise that I am not asserting that Premchand would certainly have been disillusioned with some aspects of communism, as he had once become dissatisfied with some aspects of Gandhiji's teachings. I am merely pointing out that such a possibility cannot be ruled out.

If, therefore, we insist on speculating as to how Premchand would have felt about important issues if he had lived longer, let us at least refrain from asserting dogmatically that the views we ascribe to him would have become irreversible in his consciousness. Sometimes I wonder whether such speculation is warranted at all. After all, the dead are entitled to their privacy as much as the living. Even more, perhaps, since they are in no position to argue with us. (pp. 270-72)

> *V. S. Naravane, in his* Premchand: His Life and Work, *Vikas Publishing House Pvt. Ltd., 1980, 291 p.*

ADDITIONAL BIBLIOGRAPHY

Coppola, Carlo. "A Bibliography of English Sources for the Study of Prem Chand." *Mahfil* 1, No. 2 (1963): 21-4.
  Includes primary and secondary sources.

Gopal, Madan. *Munshi Premchand: A Literary Biography*. Bombay: Asia Publishing House, 1964, 462 p.
  Study of Premchand which "aims at projecting his personality and development as a writer who voiced the aspirations of the people of India in the early part of the century and during the Gandhi era."

Gowda, H. H. Anniah. "The World of Premchand: *Godaan* and Some Stories." *The Literary Half-Yearly* XII, No. 1 (January 1971): 15-22.
  Examines major themes in Premchand's fiction.

Jindal, K. B. "Prose." In his *A History of Hindi Literature*, pp. 204-70. Allahabad, India: Kitab Mahal, 1955.*
  Summary of Premchand's career and literary importance.

Lal, P. and Nopany, Nandini. Introduction to *Twenty-Four Stories by Premchand*, pp. 1-34. Translated by Nandini Nopany and P. Lal. New Delhi, India: Vikas Publishing House, 1980.
  Biographical and critical discussion, with a brief summary and evaluation of each of the stories in this collection.

Pande, Trilochan. "Aspects of Folk-life in the Writings of Premchand." *Folklore English Monthly* 21, No. 11 (November 1980): 259-65.
  Studies Premchand's selective inclusion of folk beliefs and customs in his fiction.

Prasad, Kashi. "Some Problems of Translation from Indian Languages: With Special Reference to Premchand." *Indian Literature* XXV, No. 5 (1982): 86-96.*
  Discussion of intricacies of translating Hindi into English.

Sadiq, Muhammad. "Prem Chand Novel and Short Story." In his *Twentieth Century Urdu Literature*, pp. 139-44. Karachi, Pakistan: Royal Book Co., 1983.
  Overview of Premchand's fiction, concluding that "Prem Chand began as a realist but his emotions and views are too strong for his sense of reality. Propaganda, sentimentalism, rhetoric—such are the forces that deflect the current of his observation into the stagy and the improbable."

Sahay, R. K. "Premchand and His Successors." *Indian Horizons* XXVI, No. 1 (1977): 16-22.*
  Overview of Hindi fiction dating from the works of Premchand, with special attention to Premchand's literary influence.

Vishnevskaya, Natalia. "Reading Premchand." *Soviet Literature*, No. 8 (August 1980): 165-70.
  Discusses the reception of Premchand's work in the Soviet Union.

(George) Bernard Shaw

1856-1950

(Also wrote under pseudonym of Corno di Bassetto) Irish dramatist, essayist, critic, novelist, short story writer, and poet.

The following entry presents criticism of Shaw's drama *Man and Superman: A Comedy and a Philosophy,* first published in 1903 and first performed in 1905. For a complete discussion of Shaw's career, see *TCLC,* Volumes 3 and 9.

Shaw is generally considered the greatest dramatist to write in the English language since Shakespeare. Following the example of Henrik Ibsen, he succeeded in revolutionizing the English stage, disposing of the romantic conventions and devices of the "well-made" play, and instituting a theater of ideas grounded in realism. During his lifetime, he was equally famous as an iconoclastic and outspoken public figure. Essentially a shy man, Shaw created the public persona of G.B.S.: showman, satirist, pundit, and intellectual jester, who challenged established political and social beliefs.

Shaw was born into genteel poverty in Dublin. His father was an alcoholic. His mother, a woman of some refinement and culture, introduced her son to music and art at an early age. In 1876 Shaw moved to London and was supported by his mother for nine years while he tended to his self-education. During this period, he wrote five unsuccessful novels and, through intensive reading, acquired a strong background in economics and politics. Shaw established himself as a persuasive orator during the 1880s, rising to prominence in the socialist Fabian Society. He also became well known as a literary critic, an art critic, a music critic, and, in 1895, the drama critic for the *Saturday Review.* G.B.S., as he now signed his work, began to be widely recognized for reviews that were witty, biting, and often brilliant.

Shaw had the unusual distinction of being a playwright whose works were successful in book form before appearing on the stage. His early plays aroused the interest of a small, enthusiastic audience, although several were rejected for performance because they were believed to be unactable or risqué. Nevertheless, six of his early dramas were collected in *Plays: Pleasant and Unpleasant* and were accompanied by lengthy explanatory prefaces that many critics consider as significant as the plays themselves. The critical and popular success of this endeavor, along with his marriage in 1898 to Charlotte Payne-Townshend, a rich Fabian, proved to be turning points in Shaw's life. From that time on, Shaw was closely associated with the intellectual revival of the English theater. *Man and Superman* was one of Shaw's greatest successes during the period from 1904 to 1907, when J. E. Vedrenne and actor-manager Harley Granville-Barker jointly produced, at the Royal Court Theatre, what are considered to have been definitive performances of some of Shaw's most highly regarded plays to great critical and popular acclaim. Shaw, always vitally interested in the staging of his dramas, worked closely with Vedrenne and Granville-Barker in casting, designing, rehearsing, and presenting the plays of this period, including *Man and Superman,* which was not performed for two years, despite the success of the published text, because Shaw found no actress suitable for the important role of Ann Whitefield.

In book form *Man and Superman* consists of three parts: the "Epistle Dedicatory to Arthur Bingham Walkley," in which Shaw credits his friend with having inspired the play; the play's four acts; and, as an appendix, "'The Revolutionist's Handbook and Pocket Companion,' by John Tanner, M.I.R.C. (Member of the Idle Rich Class)," a revolutionary tract and collection of aphorisms purported to be the work of a central character. Thus performances of *Man and Superman* necessarily omit large amounts of related material that Shaw originally presented with the published play. Furthermore, theater-going audiences rarely see the third act "hell scene" or dream sequence, as its inclusion results in a performance of impracticable length. Shaw invested this third act with the bulk of the "philosophy" of the subtitle; without Act Three *Man and Superman* is generally considered a sparkling, witty, and farcical comedy of manners. The work in its entirety is often held to represent a central and pivotal point in Shaw's career because it contains the fullest explication of Shaw's own ideas and beliefs to that time. *Man and Superman* is also the work in which Shaw began to explore his theories of the Life Force and Creative Evolution, ideas that were central to his personal and artistic philosophy and that he examined more fully in later works, particularly in the drama *Back to Methuselah.* Shaw conceived of the Life Force as an impersonal god of sorts, a natural force governing human affairs. Critics find that Shaw borrowed liberally from elements of many different philosophical, sociological, and scientific concepts in constructing his theory of the Life Force, most notably drawing on Friedrich Nietzsche's idea of the "Übermensch," the "overman" or "superman," the highest type to which humanity should strive; Henri Bergson's concept of *élan vital*, the creative tendency or impulse of nature toward continual adaptation and improvement; and Darwinian hypotheses of natural selection. Creative Evolution is simply the purpose and the result of the Life Force in action: the continual improvement of the race through eugenic breeding.

According to Homer Woodbridge, Shaw's subtitle for *Man and Superman*—"A Comedy and a Philosophy"—indicates his recognition of the dual nature of the play: a sparkling comedy, featuring skilled comic characterizations, intercut with a lengthy philosophic and religious discussion. The play's first, second, and fourth acts comprise the comedy, characterized by Shaw as "a trumpery story of modern London life, a life in which . . . the ordinary man's main business is to get means to keep up the position and habits of a gentleman, and the ordinary woman's business is to get married." Although *Man and Superman* is invested with more doctrine than any previous work of Shaw's, most of the discussion of ideas is relegated to the third act, which Shaw himself termed "wholly extraneous." The remainder of the play has proven to be an enormously successful, entertaining, and popular comedy. Shaw drew most of his characters from various treatments of the Don Juan legend, yet modified each with uniquely Shavian touches. Perhaps the most renowned of Shaw's changes was his reversal of traditionally sex-defined roles, so that in his play the woman is the ruthless pursuer of the hapless man. This inversion of the love chase is a stock comic device, occuring not only in Shakespeare but in much nineteenth-century comedy as well. Shaw, however, presented this inversion as an archetypal pattern. In assuming the universality of woman as aggressor, Shaw, according to such critics as G. K. Chesterton and Charles A. Berst, weakened the play's basic structure, since a large part of the action is predicated upon Shaw's assumption of this pattern as universal. The central figure of Ann Whitefield, Shaw claimed, was inspired by a viewing of the medieval morality play *Everyman*: "Every woman is not Ann, but Ann is Everywoman." Ann, like all women (according to Shaw) motivated primarily by the Life Force, instinctively knows that John Tanner will sire superior children and is therefore completely unscrupulous in pursuing and capturing him. The comic action derives from the obliviousness of the other characters—in particular Tanner himself—to Ann's intentions, and Tanner's horrified cross-continental flight when he realizes he is Ann's intended "victim."

A large part of the critical discussion surrounding *Man and Superman* focuses on the relationship between the hell scene in the third act and the rest of the play. In Act Three, the principal characters reappear as their actual or spiritual forebears from the Don Juan legend: John Tanner as Don Juan Tenorio, Ann Whitefield as Doña Ana de Ulloa; Roebuck Ramsden as Ana's father the Commendatore, slain by Don Juan in a duel over Ana's honor, and as the Devil, Mendoza, the brigand who briefly kidnaps Tanner during his flight from Ann. In an extension of the sex-role-reversal that Shaw established by presuming woman as the aggressor in human relationships, Shaw presented his Don Juan as the victim, and not the victimizer, of women, a man whose reputation as a philanderer was unfairly put upon him by the imploring women whom he fled. Louis Kronenberger has written of the hell scene

that "nowhere in English during the twentieth century has there been a more dazzlingly sustained discussion of ideas in dialogue form," although he questions whether the scene, consisting as it does of lengthy discourse and little action, ought technically even to be considered a part of the play. In analyzing the relationship between the play's two parts, Bernard F. Dukore has noted that "parallel snatches of dialogue" occur in both parts, and that the themes of "illusion and reality, the central images of the hell scene," are also the themes that most involve the actors and actions of Acts One, Two, and Four. Dukore also remarks upon some similarities between the predilections of the characters in the framing play and their alternate *personae* in the hell scene: for example, "Member of the Idle Rich Class" Tanner deplores his social milieu much as Don Juan Tenorio condemns the idleness of dwellers in hell. Both Ann and Ana profess to be conventional and dutiful, when in fact both are duplicitous and hypocritical. Dukore further notes that although "the philosophy [of the Life Force] underlies the action of the frame play, it is implicit only. The hell scene . . . makes the philosophy explicit. The Life Force is *mentioned* in the frame play; in the inner play, it is *explained*."

Many other critics have commented on the fact that the hell scene serves as explication of the Life Force theory, while the social comedy portion of the play demonstrates an instance of the Life Force at work. The exchange of ideas between the characters in the dream scene in some ways reinforces the relationships that already existed between them in the framing play. Ana, for example, is shown to be as dishonest and manipulative as Ann. Since the scene is Tanner's (and possibly also Mendoza's) dream, however, Tanner's forebear Tenorio comes off much more impressively than does Tanner in the rest of the play. In Acts One, Two, and Four, Tanner's heartfelt and impassioned speeches fall flat, fail to impress, or are summarily dismissed; in the hell scene, Don Juan Tenorio brilliantly outargues even the Devil. The equivocal ending of the dream scene—with Ana de Ulloa disappearing in search of "a father for the Superman!"—does not make clear if in fact she has fixed upon Don Juan as the intended father of her child, or if Tenorio, unlike Tanner, escapes this fate. It is often pointed out, however, that the dream scene in hell ends when Ann Whitefield triumphantly descends upon and "captures" Tanner. This is often taken by critics to mean that in hell, as on earth, the Life Force has won out and in both places Ana/Ann has successfully brought down her prey, to the eventual betterment of the race. The hell scene can be, and in fact often has been, performed successfully as a separate, one-act play. When the two parts of *Man and Superman* are performed together, however, most critics concur with Dukore that "the sum is greater than the mere addition of two parts."

Shaw's idea of the dramatic hero was one "whose passions are those which have produced the philosophy, the poetry, the art, and the stagecraft of the world, and not merely [the type] who have produced its weddings, coroners' inquests, and executions." Thus, Shaw's dramas invariably present characters who undergo a synthesis of outlook following a clash between other characters or with the moral and religious conventions of their time. The heroes are often reflections of Shaw himself: vivacious, sophisticated, and lucid. A frequent and central criticism directed at Shaw as a dramatist is that his characters are intellectual rather than human creations. From the time of Shaw's earliest plays, critics have claimed that he peopled his stage with cleverly disguised strawmen, only to have his favored protagonists knock them down with Shavian declamations by the final curtain. Many commentators, however, commonly consider *Man and Superman* the play in which Shaw "gave the devil his due": although clearly espousing a particular doctrine, Shaw did allow such characters as Doño Ana, and the Devil himself, in the hell scene, to muster convincing and persuasive arguments against the ideal life of the intellect propounded by the Shavian figure of Tanner/Tenorio. Even in the play's first act, the character of Roebuck Ramsden, intended as an archetype of outdated liberalism and superseded "advanced ideas," is granted an unexpectedly sympathetic stance when the assembled characters believe they are dealing with an unmarried pregnant woman. Even though the "trumpery story of modern London life" ends with Tanner defeated (that is, engaged to marry Ann), his counterpart in the hell scene, Don Juan, triumphs, expounding brilliantly on the Life Force, which he eventually summarizes in terms that critics note can be regarded as descriptive of nature or of God: "I tell you, as long as I can conceive something better than myself I cannot be easy unless I am striving to bring it into existence or clearing the way for it. This is the law of my life. This is the working within me of Life's incessant aspiration to higher organization, wider, deeper, intenser self-consciousness and clearer self-understanding." Further, some critics, such as A. M. Gibbs, hold that in "losing" to Ann and succumbing to the Life Force, Tanner in fact wins both that which will make him happiest and accomplish the greatest general good.

As Samuel Hynes has noted, Shaw was driven by *weltverbesserungswahn*—a rage to better the world. His vivid characters and clever dialogue only disguise his moral purpose, called Puritan by some: to expose the dilemmas, absurdities and injustices of society. Shaw turned away from the nineteenth-century concept of the English theater as a source of light entertainment, and made acceptable the drama of ideas. In this he altered the course of twentieth-century drama.

(See also *Contemporary Authors*, Vol. 104, and *Dictionary of Literary Biography*, Vol. 10: *Modern British Dramatists, 1910-1945*.)

BERNARD SHAW (essay date 1903)

[*In the following excerpt from his "Epistle Dedicatory to Arthur Bingham Walkley," composed in 1903, Shaw explains his theories on relations between the sexes and his reasons for inverting the traditions of the Don Juan myth in his play.*]

My dear Walkley

You once asked me why I did not write a Don Juan play. The levity with which you assumed this frightful responsibility has probably by this time enabled you to forget it; but the day of reckoning has arrived: here is your play! I say your play, because qui facit per alium per se ["He who does anything through another does it through himself"]. Its profits, like its labor, belong to me: its morals, its manners, its philosophy, its influence on the young, are for you to justify. You were of mature age when you made the suggestion; and you knew your man. It is hardly fifteen years since, as twin pioneers of the New Journalism of that time, we two, cradled in the same new sheets, made an epoch in the criticism of the theatre and the opera house by making it a pretext for a propaganda of our own views of life. So you cannot plead ignorance of the character of the force you set in motion. You meant me to épater

le bourgeois ["shock the middle class"]; and if he protests, I hereby refer him to you as the accountable party. (p. v)

The question is, will you not be disappointed with a Don Juan play in which not one of that hero's mille être adventures is brought upon the stage? To propitiate you, let me explain myself. You will retort that I never do anything else: it is your favorite jibe at me that what I call drama is nothing but explanation. But you must not expect me to adopt your inexplicable, fantastic, petulant, fastidious ways: you must take me as I am, a reasonable, patient, consistent, apologetic, laborious person, with the temperament of a schoolmaster and the pursuits of a vestryman. No doubt that literary knack of mine which happens to amuse the British public distracts attention from my character; but the character is there none the less, solid as bricks. I have a conscience; and conscience is always anxiously explanatory. You, on the contrary, feel that a man who discusses his conscience is much like a woman who discusses her modesty. . . . But my conscience is the genuine pulpit article: it annoys me to see people comfortable when they ought to be uncomfortable; and I insist on making them think in order to bring them to conviction of sin. If you dont like my preaching you must lump it. I really cannot help it.

In the preface to my *Plays for Puritans* I explained the predicament of our contemporary English drama, forced to deal almost exclusively with cases of sexual attraction, and yet forbidden to exhibit the incidents of that attraction or even to discuss its nature. Your suggestion that I should write a Don Juan play was virtually a challenge to me to treat this subject myself dramatically. The challenge was difficult enough to be worth accepting, because, when you come to think of it, though we have plenty of dramas with heroes and heroines who are in love and must accordingly marry or perish at the end of the play, or about people whose relations with one another have been complicated by the marriage laws, not to mention the looser sort of plays which trade on the tradition that illicit love affairs are at once vicious and delightful, we have no modern English plays in which the natural attraction of the sexes for one another is made the mainspring of the action. That is why we insist on beauty in our performers, differing herein from the countries our friend William Archer holds up as examples of seriousness to our childish theatres. There the Juliets and Isoldes, the Romeos and Tristans, might be our mothers and fathers. Not so the English actress. The heroine she impersonates is not allowed to discuss the elemental relations of men and women: all her romantic twaddle about novelet-made love, all her purely legal dilemmas as to whether she was married or "betrayed," quite miss our hearts and worry our minds. To console ourselves we must just look at her. We do so; and her beauty feeds our starving emotions. Sometimes we grumble ungallantly at the lady because she does not act as well as she looks. But in a drama which, with all its preoccupation with sex, is really void of sexual interest, good looks are more desired than histrionic skill.

Let me press this point on you, since you are too clever to raise the fool's cry of paradox whenever I take hold of a stick by the right instead of the wrong end. Why are our occasional attempts to deal with the sex problem on the stage so repulsive and dreary that even those who are most determined that sex questions shall be held open and their discussion kept free, cannot pretend to relish these joyless attempts at social sanitation? Is it not because at bottom they are utterly sexless? What is the usual formula for such plays? A woman has, on some past occasion, been brought into conflict with the law which regulates the relations of the sexes. A man, by falling in love with her, or marrying her, is brought into conflict with the social convention which discountenances the woman. Now the conflicts of individuals with law and convention can be dramatized like all other human conflicts; but they are purely judicial; and the fact that we are much more curious about the suppressed relations between the man and the woman than about the relations between both and our courts of law and private juries of matrons, produces that sensation of evasion, of dissatisfaction, of fundamental irrelevance, of shallowness, of useless disagreeableness, of total failure to edify and partial failure to interest, which is as familiar to you in the theatres as it was to me when I, too, frequented those uncomfortable buildings, and found our popular playwrights in the mind to (as they thought) emulate Ibsen.

I take it that when you asked me for a Don Juan play you did not want that sort of thing. Nobody does: the successes such plays sometimes obtain are due to the incidental conventional melodrama with which the experienced popular author instinctively saves himself from failure. But what did you want? Owing to your unfortunate habit—you now, I hope, feel its inconvenience—of not explaining yourself, I have had to discover this for myself. First, then, I have had to ask myself, what is a Don Juan? Vulgarly, a libertine. But your dislike of vulgarity is pushed to the length of a defect (universality of character is impossible without a share of vulgarity); and even if you could acquire the taste, you would find yourself overfed from ordinary sources without troubling me. So I took it that you demanded a Don Juan in the philosophic sense.

Philosophically, Don Juan is a man who, though gifted enough to be exceptionally capable of distinguishing between good and evil, follows his own instincts without regard to the common, statute, or canon law; and therefore, whilst gaining the ardent sympathy of our rebellious instincts (which are flattered by the brilliancies with which Don Juan associates them) finds himself in mortal conflict with existing institutions, and defends himself by fraud and force as unscrupulously as a farmer defends his crops by the same means against vermin. The prototypic Don Juan, invented early in the XVI century by a Spanish monk, was presented, according to the ideas of that time, as the enemy of God, the approach of whose vengeance is felt throughout the drama, growing in menace from minute to minute. No anxiety is caused on Don Juan's account by any minor antagonist: he easily eludes the police, temporal and spiritual; and when an indignant father seeks private redress with the sword, Don Juan kills him without an effort. Not until the slain father returns from heaven as the agent of God, in the form of his own statue, does he prevail against his slayer and cast him into hell. The moral is a monkish one: repent and reform now; for to-morrow it may be too late. (pp. vi-ix)

Molière's Don Juan casts back to the original in point of impenitence; but in piety he falls off greatly. . . . After Molière comes the artist-enchanter, the master of masters, Mozart, who reveals the hero's spirit in magical harmonies, elfin tones, and elate darting rhythms as of summer lightning made audible. (p. x)

After these completed works Byron's fragment does not count for much philosophically. Our vagabond libertines are no more interesting from that point of view than the sailor who has a wife in every port; and Byron's hero is, after all, only a vagabond libertine. And he is dumb: he does not discuss himself with a Sganarelle-Leporello or with the fathers or brothers of his mistresses: he does not even, like Casanova, tell his own story. In fact he is not a true Don Juan at all; for he is no more an enemy of God than any romantic and adventurous young sower of wild oats. . . . Let us, then, leave Byron's Don Juan out of account. Mozart's is the last of the true Don Juans; for by the time he was of age, his cousin Faust had, in the hands of Goethe, taken his place and carried both his warfare and his reconciliation with the gods far beyond mere lovemaking into politics, high art, schemes for reclaiming new continents from the ocean, and recognition of an eternal womanly principle in the universe. Goethe's Faust and Mozart's Don Juan were the last words of the XVIII century on the subject; and by the time the polite critics of the XIX century, ignoring William Blake as superficially as the XVIII had ignored Hogarth or the XVII Bunyan, had got past the Dickens-Macaulay Dumas-Guizot stage and the Stendhal-Meredith-Turgenieff stage, and were confronted with philosophic fiction by such pens as Ibsen's and Tolstoy's, Don Juan had changed his sex and become Doña Juana, breaking out of the Doll's House and asserting herself as an individual instead of a mere item in a moral pageant.

Now it is all very well for you at the beginning of the XX century to ask me for a Don Juan play; but . . . Don Juan is a full century out of date for you and for me; and if there are millions of less literate people who are still in the eighteenth century, have they not Molière and Mozart, upon whose art no human hand can improve? You would laugh at me if at this time of day I dealt in duels and ghosts and "womanly" women. . . . Even the more abstract parts of the Don Juan play are dilapidated past use: for instance, Don Juan's supernatural antagonist hurled those who refuse to repent into lakes of burning brimstone, there to be tormented by devils with horns and tails. Of that antagonist, and of that conception of repentance, how much is left that could be used in a play by me dedicated to you? On the other hand, those forces of middle class public opinion which hardly existed for a Spanish nobleman in the days of the first Don Juan, are now triumphant everywhere. Civilized society is one huge bourgeoisie: no nobleman dares now shock his greengrocer. The women, "marchesane, principesse, cameriere, cittadine" and all, are become equally dangerous: the sex is aggressive, powerful: when women are wronged they do not group themselves pathetically to sing "Protegga il giusto cielo"; they grasp formidable legal and social weapons, and retaliate. Political parties are wrecked and public careers undone by a single indiscretion. A man had better have all the statues in London to supper with him, ugly as they are, than be brought to the bar of the Nonconformist Conscience by Donna Elvira. Excommunication has become almost as serious a business as it was in the X century.

As a result, Man is no longer, like Don Juan, victor in the duel of sex. Whether he has ever really been may be doubted: at all events the enormous superiority of Woman's natural position in this matter is telling with greater and greater force. (pp. x-xii)

I have [thrust] . . . into my perfectly modern three-act play a totally extraneous act in which my hero, enchanted by the air of the Sierra, has a dream in which his Mozartian ancestor appears and philosophizes at great length in a Shavio-Socratic dialogue with the lady, the statue, and the devil.

But this pleasantry is not the essence of the play. Over this essence I have no control. You propound a certain social substance, sexual attraction, to wit, for dramatic distillation; and I distil it for you. I do not adulterate the product with aphrodisiacs nor dilute it with romance and water; for I am merely executing your commission, not producing a popular play for the market. You must therefore (unless, like most wise men, you read the play first and the preface afterwards) prepare yourself to face a trumpery story of modern London life, a life in which, as you know, the ordinary man's main business is to get means to keep up the position and habits of a gentleman, and the ordinary woman's business is to get married. In 9,999 cases out of 10,000, you can count on their doing nothing, whether noble or base, that conflicts with these ends; and that assurance is what you rely on as their religion, their morality, their principles, their patriotism, their reputation, their honor and so forth.

On the whole, this is a sensible and satisfactory foundation for society. Money means nourishment and marriage means children; and that men should put nourishment first and women children first is, broadly speaking, the law of Nature and not the dictate of personal ambition. The secret of the prosaic man's success, such as it is, is the simplicity with which he pursues these ends: the secret of the artistic man's failure, such as that is, is the versatility with which he strays in all directions after secondary ideals. The artist is either a poet or a scallawag: as poet, he cannot see, as the prosaic man does, that chivalry is at bottom only romantic suicide: as scallawag, he cannot see that it does not pay to spunge and beg and lie and brag and neglect his person. (pp. xiv-xv)

The Don Juan play . . . is to deal with sexual attraction, and not with nutrition, and to deal with it in a society in which the serious business of sex is left by men to women, as the serious business of nutrition is left by women to men. That the men, to protect themselves against a too aggressive prosecution of the women's business, have set up a feeble romantic convention that the initiative in sex business must always come from the man, is true; but the pretence is so shallow that even in the theatre, that last sanctuary of unreality, it imposes only on the inexperienced. In Shakespear's plays the woman always takes the initiative. In his problem plays and his popular plays alike the love interest is the interest of seeing the woman hunt the man down. She may do it by blandishment, like Rosalind, or by stratagem, like Mariana; but in every case the relation between the woman and the man is the same: she is the pursuer and contriver, he the pursued and disposed of. When she is baffled, like Ophelia, she goes mad and commits suicide; and the man goes straight from her funeral to a fencing match. . . . The one apparent exception, Petruchio, is not a real one: he is most carefully characterized as a purely commercial matrimonial adventurer. Once he is assured that Katharine has money, he undertakes to marry her before he has seen her. In real life we find not only Petruchios, but Mantalinis and Dobbins who pursue women with appeals to their pity or jealousy or vanity, or cling to them in a romantically infatuated way. . . . I find in my own plays that Woman, projecting herself dramatically by my hands (a process over which I assure you I have no more real control than I have over my wife), behaves just as Woman did in the plays of Shakespear.

And so your Don Juan has come to birth as a stage projection of the tragi-comic love chase of the man by the woman; and my Don Juan is the quarry instead of the huntsman. Yet he is a true Don Juan, with a sense of reality that disables convention, defying to the last the fate which finally overtakes him. The woman's need of him to enable her to carry on Nature's most urgent work, does not prevail against him until his resistance gathers her energy to a climax at which she dares to throw away her customary exploitations of the conventional affec-

tionate and dutiful poses, and claim him by natural right for a purpose that far transcends their mortal personal purposes.

Among the friends to whom I have read this play in manuscript are some of our own sex who are shocked at the "unscrupulousness," meaning the total disregard of masculine fastidiousness, with which the woman pursues her purpose. It does not occur to them that if women were as fastidious as men, morally or physically, there would be an end of the race. Is there anything meaner than to throw necessary work upon other people and then disparage it as unworthy and indelicate. We laugh at the haughty American nation because it makes the negro clean its boots and then proves the moral and physical inferiority of the negro by the fact that he is a shoeblack; but we ourselves throw the whole drudgery of creation on one sex, and then imply that no female of any womanliness or delicacy would initiate any effort in that direction. There are no limits to male hypocrisy in this matter. No doubt there are moments when man's sexual immunities are made acutely humiliating to him. When the terrible moment of birth arrives, its supreme importance and its superhuman effort and peril, in which the father has no part, dwarf him into the meanest insignificance: he slinks out of the way of the humblest petticoat, happy if he be poor enough to be pushed out of the house to outface his ignominy by drunken rejoicings. But when the crisis is over he takes his revenge, swaggering as the breadwinner, and speaking of Woman's "sphere" with condescension, even with chivalry, as if the kitchen and the nursery were less important than the office in the city. When his swagger is exhausted he drivels into erotic poetry or sentimental uxoriousness; and the Tennysonian King Arthur posing at Guinevere becomes Don Quixote grovelling before Dulcinea. You must admit that here Nature beats Comedy out of the field: the wildest hominist or feminist farce is insipid after the most commonplace "slice of life." The pretence that women do not take the initiative is part of the farce. Why, the whole world is strewn with snares, traps, gins and pitfalls for the capture of men by women. Give women the vote, and in five years there will be a crushing tax on bachelors. Men, on the other hand, attach penalties to marriage, depriving women of property, of the franchise, of the free use of their limbs, of that ancient symbol of immortality, the right to make oneself at home in the house of God by taking off the hat, of everything that he can force Woman to dispense with without compelling himself to dispense with her. All in vain. Woman must marry because the race must perish without her travail: if the risk of death and the certainty of pain, danger and unutterable discomforts cannot deter her, slavery and swaddled ankles will not. And yet we assume that the force that carries women through all these perils and hardships, stops abashed before the primnesses of our behavior for young ladies. It is assumed that the woman must wait, motionless, until she is wooed. Nay, she often does wait motionless. That is how the spider waits for the fly. But the spider spins her web. And if the fly, like my hero, shews a strength that promises to extricate him, how swiftly does she abandon her pretence of passiveness, and openly fling coil after coil about him until he is secured for ever!

If the really impressive books and other art-works of the world were produced by ordinary men, they would express more fear of women's pursuit than love of their illusory beauty. But ordinary men cannot produce really impressive art-works. Those who can are men of genius: that is, men selected by Nature to carry on the work of building up an intellectual consciousness of her own instinctive purpose. Accordingly, we observe in the man of genius all the unscrupulousness and all the "self-sacrifice'' (the two things are the same) of Woman. He will risk the stake and the cross; starve, when necessary, in a garret all his life; study women and live on their work and care as Darwin studied worms and lived upon sheep; work his nerves into rags without payment, a sublime altruist in his disregard of himself, an atrocious egotist in his disregard of others. Here Woman meets a purpose as impersonal, as irresistible as her own; and the clash is sometimes tragic. When it is complicated by the genius being a woman, then the game is one for a king of critics: your George Sand becomes a mother to gain experience for the novelist and to develop her, and gobbles up men of genius, Chopins, Mussets and the like, as mere hors d'oeuvres.

I state the extreme case, of course; but what is true of the great man who incarnates the philosophic consciousness of Life and the woman who incarnates its fecundity, is true in some degree of all geniuses and all women. Hence it is that the world's books get written, its pictures painted, its statues modelled, its symphonies composed, by people who are free of the otherwise universal dominion of the tyranny of sex. Which leads us to the conclusion, astonishing to the vulgar, that art, instead of being before all things the expression of the normal sexual situation, is really the only department in which sex is a superseded and secondary power, with its consciousness so confused and its purpose so perverted, that its ideas are mere fantasy to common men. Whether the artist becomes poet or philosopher, moralist or founder of a religion, his sexual doctrine is nothing but a barren special pleading for pleasure, excitement, and knowledge when he is young, and for contemplative tranquillity when he is old and satiated. Romance and Asceticism, Amorism and Puritanism are equally unreal in the great Philistine world. The world shewn us in books, whether the books be confessed epics or professed gospels, or in codes, or in political orations, or in philosophic systems, is not the main world at all: it is only the self-consciousness of certain abnormal people who have the specific artistic talent and temperament. A serious matter this for you and me, because the man whose consciousness does not correspond to that of the majority is a madman; and the old habit of worshipping madmen is giving way to the new habit of locking them up. And since what we call education and culture is for the most part nothing but the substitution of reading for experience, of literature for life, of the obsolete fictitious for the contemporary real, education, as you no doubt observed at Oxford, destroys, by supplantation, every mind that is not strong enough to see through the imposture and to use the great Masters of Arts as what they really are and no more: that is, patentees of highly questionable methods of thinking, and manufacturers of highly questionable, and for the majority but half valid representations of life. (pp. xvi-xxi)

There is a political aspect of this sex question which is too big for my comedy, and too momentous to be passed over without culpable frivolity. It is impossible to demonstrate that the initiative in sex transactions remains with Woman, and has been confirmed to her, so far, more and more by the suppression of rapine and discouragement of importunity, without being driven to very serious reflections on the fact that this initiative is politically the most important of all the initiatives, because our political experiment of democracy, the last refuge of cheap misgovernment, will ruin us if our citizens are ill bred. (pp. xxi-xxii)

I do not know whether you have any illusions left on the subject of education, progress, and so forth. I have none. Any pamphleteer can shew the way to better things; but when there is

no will there is no way. . . . Progress can do nothing but make the most of us all as we are, and that most would clearly not be enough even if those who are already raised out of the lowest abysses would allow the others a chance. The bubble of Heredity has been pricked: the certainty that acquirements are negligible as elements in practical heredity has demolished the hopes of the educationists as well as the terrors of the degeneracy mongers; and we know now that there is no hereditary ''governing class'' any more than a hereditary hooliganism. We must either breed political capacity or be ruined by Democracy, which was forced on us by the failure of the older alternatives. Yet if Despostism failed only for want of a capable benevolent despot, what chance has Democracy, which requires a whole population of capable voters: that is, of political critics who, if they cannot govern in person for lack of spare energy or specific talent for administration, can at least recognize and appreciate capacity and benevolence in others, and so govern through capably benevolent representatives? Where are such voters to be found to-day? Nowhere. Promiscuous breeding has produced a weakness of character that is too timid to face the full stringency of a thoroughly competitive struggle for existence and too lazy and petty to organize the commonwealth co-operatively. Being cowards, we defeat natural selection under cover of philanthropy: being sluggards, we neglect artificial selection under cover of delicacy and morality.

Yet we must get an electorate of capable critics or collapse as Rome and Egypt collapsed. (pp. xxiii-xxiv)

But I hear you asking me in alarm whether I have actually put all this tub thumping into a Don Juan comedy. I have not. I have only made my Don Juan a political pamphleteer, and given you his pamphlet in full by way of appendix. You will find it at the end of the book. I am sorry to say that it is a common practice with romancers to announce their hero as a man of extraordinary genius, and to leave his works entirely to the reader's imagination; so that at the end of the book you whisper to yourself ruefully that but for the author's solemn preliminary assurance you should hardly have given the gentleman credit for ordinary good sense. You cannot accuse me of this pitiable barrenness, this feeble evasion. I not only tell you that my hero wrote a revolutionists' handbook: I give you the handbook at full length for your edification if you care to read it. And in that handbook you will find the politics of the sex question as I conceive Don Juan's descendant to understand them. Not that I disclaim the fullest responsibility for his opinions and for those of all my characters, pleasant and unpleasant. They are all right from their several points of view; and their points of view are, for the dramatic moment, mine also. This may puzzle the people who believe that there is such a thing as an absolutely right point of view, usually their own. It may seem to them that nobody who doubts this can be in a state of grace. However that may be, it is certainly true that nobody who agrees with them can possibly be a dramatist, or indeed anything else that turns upon a knowledge of mankind. Hence it has been pointed out that Shakespear had no conscience. Neither have I, in that sense.

You may, however, remind me that this digression of mine into politics was preceded by a very convincing demonstration that the artist never catches the point of view of the common man on the question of sex, because he is not in the same predicament. I first prove that anything I write on the relation of the sexes is sure to be misleading; and then I proceed to write a Don Juan play. Well, if you insist on asking me why I behave in this absurd way, I can only reply that you asked me to, and that in any case my treatment of the subject may be valid for the artist, amusing to the amateur, and at least intelligible and therefore possibly suggestive to the Philistine. Every man who records his illusions is providing data for the genuinely scientific psychology which the world still waits for. I plank down my view of the existing relations of men to women in the most highly civilized society for what it is worth. It is a view like any other view and no more, neither true nor false, but, I hope, a way of looking at the subject which throws into the familiar order of cause and effect a sufficient body of fact and experience to be interesting to you, if not to the playgoing public of London. I have certainly shewn little consideration for that public in this enterprise; but I know that it has the friendliest disposition towards you and me as far as it has any consciousness of our existence, and quite understands that what I write for you must pass at a considerable height over its simple romantic head. It will take my books as read and my genius for granted, trusting me to put forth work of such quality as shall bear out its verdict. So we may disport ourselves on our own plane to the top of our bent; and if any gentleman points out that neither this epistle dedicatory nor the dream of Don Juan in the third act of the ensuing comedy is suitable for immediate production at a popular theatre we need not contradict him. (pp. xxv-xxvii)

I should make formal acknowledgement to the authors whom I have pillaged in the following pages if I could recollect them all. The theft of the brigand-poetaster from Sir Arthur Conan Doyle is deliberate; and the metamorphosis of Leporello into Enry Straker, motor engineer and New Man, is an intentional dramatic sketch for the contemporary embryo of Mr H. G. Wells's anticipation of the efficient engineering class which will, he hopes, finally sweep the jabberers out of the way of civilization. . . . Ann was suggested to me by the fifteenth century Dutch morality called Everyman. . . . As I sat watching Everyman at the Charterhouse, I said to myself Why not Everywoman? Ann was the result: every woman is not Ann; but Ann is Everywoman. (pp. xxvii-xxviii)

> *Bernard Shaw, "To Arthur Bingham Walkley," in his* Man and Superman: A Comedy and a Philosophy, *Brentano's, 1904, pp. v-xxviii.*

WILLIAM ARCHER (essay date 1903)

[*A Scottish dramatist and critic, Archer is best known as one of the earliest and most important translators of Henrik Ibsen's plays and as a drama critic of the London stage during the late nineteenth and early twentieth centuries. Archer valued drama as an intellectual product and not as simple entertainment. For that reason he did a great deal to promote the "new drama" of the 1890s, including the work of Ibsen and Bernard Shaw. Throughout his career he protested critical overvaluation of ancient drama, claiming that modern works were in many ways equal to or better than Elizabethan or Restoration drama. In the following excerpt, Archer reviews the published text of* Man and Superman, *disregarding the "Epistle Dedicatory" and the "Revolutionist's Handbook." Archer terms the play an allegorical farce and considers this a decline from the promise of skillful drama represented by earlier plays of Shaw.*]

Mr. Shaw's new volume [*Man and Superman*] falls into three sections: a long preface, disguised as an "Epistle Dedicatory" to Mr. A. B. Walkley; an allegory in dialogue labelled "Man and Superman"; and an appendix entitled "The Revolutionist's Handbook," and purporting to be written by the chief character in the allegory. These three books, or three pamphlets, would

not be Mr. Shaw's if they were not full of stimulating matter. There is said to be no sound in modern warfare so stimulating as that of the pom-pom—it keeps the most hardened veteran on the jump. Mr. Shaw's type-writer is the pom-pom of the literary battlefield. It is not (though it might be if he pleased) a weapon of great range or calibre; but for making people sit up it has no equal. Every page of these pamphlets crackles with wit and tingles with cerebral activity, if not always with thought. But it is impossible in a single article to respond to all, or one tithe, of the stimuli which Mr. Shaw here puts forth. I propose, then, to concentrate on the middle pamphlet of the three, and wholly to disregard the epistle to Mr. Walkley and the "Revolutionist's Handbook."

Man and Superman is Op. XII. of Mr. Shaw's "Theatre"; he ought, as a dramatist, to be approaching years of discretion. Perhaps he is, in a certain sense; for though he calls this play a comedy, he practically abandons all attempt at the representation of life, and gives us a frankly symbolic extravaganza— a "morality" in four acts and a dream. If this is all he is capable of, then it is clearly discretion on his part to attempt no more. To realize our limitations is the beginning of wisdom. Nevertheless, to those of us who thought we saw the makings of a dramatist in *Mrs. Warren's Profession, Candida,* and *The Devil's Disciple,* it is a great disappointment to find Mr. Shaw falling back upon allegoric farce. Apart from the easily detachable dream (of which more anon), there is nothing in the dimensions or the mechanism of the play to prevent its being put on the stage. Probably it will be, one of these days, and it will amuse us as did *The Admirable Bashville;* but, though written in prose, it is every bit as much of a travesty as that delightful piece of extravagance. Having in *Bashville* parodied Shakespeare, Mr. Shaw here flies at still higher game and parodies Shaw. If that was not his intention, all one can say is that the play shows a disquieting decline in inventive power. Like Ibsen in *When We Dead Awaken,* Mr. Shaw does little else than resuscitate characters and motives that have done duty in his earlier plays. The ineffably superior hero, witty, disillusioned, and equal to every emergency, we expect as a matter of course—he is Mr. Shaw's trade-mark. But the other characters, with scarcely an exception, are equally familiar. They are but colorable variations of Mr. Shaw's stock types.

As we read scene after scene, the sense of having gone through it all before, and knowing exactly what is coming next, becomes positively oppressive. The topics of his humor are jaded, and have to be flogged. The man who was "advanced" thirty years ago, and still considers himself a pioneer of thought, was far more amusing in *You Never Can Tell* (where, by the way, he was a woman) than he now is in the person of that exceedingly conventional "heavy father," Roebuck Ramsden. . . . [This play] is full of Shaw-stereotypes—tricks of manner so emphasized as to suggest the none too kindly parodist. I am genuinely uncertain how much of this Mr. Shaw may have intended. The piece, as we shall see, is a deliberate allegory; and having once renounced all effort at realism, Mr. Shaw is quite capable of consciously caricaturing himself. If that be so, he has indubitably succeeded, though not without a certain heaviness of touch.

The play, it will be noted, is described as "A Comedy and a Philosophy." That is Mr. Shaw's way of announcing his allegoric intention. And what is the philosophy? Simply that of Schopenhauer as transformed by Nietzsche from sullen pessimism into what may be called enthusiastic stoicism. Schopenhauer looked into Nature's laboratory, saw through her cajoleries and her anaesthetic pretexts, and vehemently denounced their hollowness. Nietzsche, accepting his reading of her motives and methods, held it the nobler part to fall in with them and to co-operate resolutely, consciously, gladly, in her stupendous series of experiments towards the production of the Overman, or, as Mr. Shaw prefers to say, the Superman. It was inevitable that such a doctrine, emphasizing as it does the sheer intellectual ecstasy of realizing and submitting to the purposes of the great Vivisector, should potently appeal to Mr. Shaw. But in this scheme of things, woman figures as Nature's blind and ruthless instrument, inexorably bent on fulfilling herself in motherhood, at the expense of the male, whom, in her heart of hearts, she despises as her puppet and dupe. We have in *Man and Superman,* accordingly, an allegory of woman as the eternal Wooer, adept in so hypnotizing the masculine will that it mistakes her suggestion for its own passionate impulse, and indefatigable in tracking down her victim, though he flee from her to the ends of the earth in an 80 h.-p. motor-car. The worst of treating this theme allegorically is that in making the protagonists typical instead of real one necessarily does injustice to the subtleties of Nature, or the Life-Force as she is called in Mr. Shaw's mythology. If the wiles of woman were no were no wilier than those of Miss Ann Whitefield, the Nirvana would be much nearer than the Overman. Nature has infinitely more complex and more delicate weapons in her armory than this shallow, mendacious minx. But no doubt the logic of allegory demanded that the case should be stated in its extremest form, and that the crudest feminity should, in the end, conquer the alertest and most open-eyed masculinity, by very much the same method employed by Mrs. Bardell for the capture of Mr. Pickwick. Simplification and exaggeration are the law of allegory; and though one may wish that Mr. Shaw would return to drama, one has no right to quarrel with his choice of a more primitive form.

The odd thing is that, setting forth to write a parable of Woman the Wooer, he should have had the quaint notion of describing his hero and her victim as a descendant of Don Juan. The traditional figure of Don Juan, no doubt, is perfectly reconcilable with the theory which represents that the essential initiative always comes from the female side. But, far from undertaking this reconcilement, Mr. Shaw makes his modern Don Juan the very antipodes of his great progenitor. The only motive one can discern for the whimsical genealogy is that it affords a peg upon which to hang a philosophic dialogue, in the form of a dream, which Mr. Shaw interpolates in his third act. Mr. John Tanner (pray observe the anglicized form of Juan Tenorio) being captured by a band of cockney brigands in Spain, falls asleep and dreams a conversation in hell between the Devil, Don Juan, Donna Anna, and the Statue of the Commander—fifty pages of humorous philosophy or philosophic humor, as you choose to look at it, in which Mr. Shaw dots the i's of his theory, and drives his moral home. In other words, it is a second preface, dropped into the middle of the play. Considered as a work of art, the dialogue is too long and too loosely constructed; but it is full of good things, and makes capital reading. (pp. 310-12)

The Don's studies of Nietzsche have even led him to accept that philosopher's hypothesis of the history of the universe as a series of perpetually recurring cycles of unthinkable magnitude. And yet, while he reduces man to the paltriest cypher in a stupendous repeating-decimal, he still gallantly praises and vindicates the Life Force.

It must not be supposed, however, that Mr. Shaw's philosophy gets the better of his humor. On the contrary, his humor fully holds its own against his philosophy, and too often gets the better of his art. The book swarms with quips and cranks in his best manner. Take, for instance, the first lines of the first stage-direction:

> Roebuck Ramsden is in his study, opening the morning's letters. The study, handsomely and solidly furnished, proclaims the man of means. Not a speck of dust is visible; it is clear that there are at least two housemaids and a parlor-maid downstairs, and a housekeeper upstairs who does not let them spare elbow-grease. Even the top of Roebuck's head is polished; on a sunshiny day he could heliograph his orders to distant camps by merely nodding. In no other respect, however, does he suggest the military man.

This is not by any means the only passage at which one lays down the book to laugh aloud. But, regarded as a play, *Man and Superman* is, I repeat, primitive in invention and second-rate in execution. The most disheartening thing about it is that it contains not one of those scenes of really tense dramatic quality which redeemed the squalor of *Mrs. Warren's Profession,* and made of *Candida* something very like a masterpiece. (p. 312)

> William Archer, ''Mr. Shaw's Pom-Pom,'' in The Critic, *New York, Vol. XLIII, No. 4, October, 1903, pp. 310-12.*

[ARTHUR BINGHAM WALKLEY]   (essay date 1905)

[*Walkley was an English drama critic for the London* Star, *the* Speaker, *and the* Times *from 1888 through 1902, and a major contributor to the* Times Literary Supplement *after it was founded in 1902. He has been noted for his disciplined, urbane literary tastes; in fact, his criticism is generally considered to have primarily a literary, and not a theatrical, basis. In the following excerpt from a review of* Man and Superman—*the play that Shaw dedicated to Walkley and claimed was inspired by his suggestion— Walkley regrets that while the play serves as an effective vehicle for ''the Shavian philosophy and the Shavian talent,'' it is imperfect as a theatrical work.*]

It has been lately bruited abroad that Mr. Bernard Shaw is a somewhat lukewarm admirer of Shakespeare. If this be so, it is only one more illustration of the familiar gnomic saying of Euripides that there is no enmity so fierce as that of brother against brother. For Mr. Shaw and Shakespeare have at least one conspicuous bond of fraternal relationship; they both use the same stage technique. To Mr. Shaw as to Shakespeare organic plot-development is a matter of indifference, as compared with the systematic exhibition of ideas. They both ignore the *liaison des scènes* with a splendid carelessness, and ruthlessly sacrifice imitation of external life to any passing velleity for propagandism. It is not the same propagandism, of course. Shakespeare's is the propagandism of current morality or beauty or sheer poetry; Mr. Shaw's is the propagandism of paradox or iconoclasm or sheer antinomianism. But the effect on the dramatic form is the same. Hamlet interrupts the action on the platform at Elsinore to expatiate on alcoholism, Gertrude keeps Ophelia's bier waiting in the wings while she gives a ''word picture'' of a river bank, John Tanner brings everybody and everything to a standstill (always ''talking,'' as Ann pithily puts it) in order to give forth so much of Nietzsche and Schopenhauer as Mr. Shaw has chanced to assimilate. Thus for the sake of something which may be very fine, but certainly is not

Poster advertising the Criterion Theatre's 1911 production of Man and Superman. *Mander & Mitchenson Theatre Collection (London).*

drama, both dramatists cheerfully let the quintessential drama go hang. Neither of them is, for stage purposes, a man "looking before and after"; they are both playhouse Cyrenaics, living in the moment for the moment's sake. This identical result has arisen from very different causes. For Shakespeare there were the limitations and the licence of the platform-stage, together with a tremendous energy of creation which was perpetually driving him outside the bounds of drama. For Mr. Shaw there are his own limitations; he is perpetually energizing outside the bounds of drama, and if for a moment he gets inside them it is by a mere fluke. It is piquant to find identity of form so absolute with such a world-wide difference of content. No need, is there, to account for that difference? On the one hand a born dramatist, and that the greatest; on the other a man who is no dramatist at all. We would not be misunderstood. When we say that Mr. Shaw is no dramatist we do not mean that he fails to interest and stimulate amuse us in the theatre. For our part we find him more entertaining than any other living writer for the stage. There are many things in his plays that give us far keener thrills of delight . . . than many things in Shakespeare's plays. But that is because he is bound to be an entertaining writer in any art-form—essay or novel or play. All we mean is that when he happens to choose the play as the form in which he shall entertain us there is a certain artistic

waste. There is waste, because Mr. Shaw neglects, or more probably is impotent to fulfil, what Pater calls the responsibility of the artist to his material. We forgive the waste for the sake of the pleasure. Nevertheless, in the interests of good drama it is our duty to be dissatisfied. We want a play that shall be a vehicle for the Shavian philosophy and the Shavian talent and, at the same time, a perfect play. Shall we ever get it? Probably not, in this imperfect world. We certainly do not get it in **Man and Superman.**

Had it not been for the typographical inconvenience of the arrangement we should have liked to draw up a balance-sheet of this play in two parallel columns. The left-hand column would display the action-plot. We use the term action, of course, in its widest sense, so as to cover not merely the external incident but the psychologic and, more particularly, the emotional movement and "counterpoint" of the play. The right-hand column would give the idea-plot—that is to say, the more or less logical *nexus* of concepts in the author's mind which form the stuff, the real *raison d'être* of the play. Only by that method of sharp visual contrast could we hope to bring to light the masked interdependence of the action-plot and idea-plot and the curious way in which the one is warped and maimed in being made to serve as the vehicle for the other. We should, we think, have been better able to show by the method of parallel columns that the action-plot is well-nigh meaningless without the key of the idea-plot; that regarded as an independent entity it is often trivial and sometimes null; and that it is because of this parasitic nature of the action-plot, because of its weakness, its haphazardness, its unnaturalness, considered as a "thing in itself," that we find the play as a play unsatisfying.

The idea-plot we are not called upon to criticize. In the play-house a dramatist's ideas are postulates not to be called in question. Theories of Schopenhauer about woman and the sex-instinct or of Nietzsche about a revised system of conduct are most assuredly open to discussion, but not by the dramatic critic. His business is, first and foremost, with the action-plot. For that is what we *see;* it is in fact the play itself, in the sense that it is what is being played under our noses; it is the sum of all the direct appeals to our sensation, before we start the secondary process of inferring and concluding. Now what do we see on the stage of the Court Theatre? What is it that we are asked to accept for an hour or two as part and parcel of our daily human life? We see, first of all, a smug bald-headed old gentleman who proceeds, *à propos de bottes,* to spout the respectable middleclass Mill-Spencer-Cobden Liberalism of the mid-Victorian age. Then we see him vivaciously "cheeked" by a youngish, excitable, voluble gentleman, who evidently stands for the latest intellectual "advance." He tells us, by-and-by, that he is a product of Eton and Oxford; but some of us who think we know that product will nourish a secret conviction that he is really, like his *chauffeur,* a product of the Board School and the Polytechnic. He has steeped himself in those fragments of the newest German philosophy which find their way into popular English translations, and he spends his time—mark, the *whole* of his time—in spouting these precious theories. He does this, as he admits, because he has no sense of shame; to put it more simply, he is a young person of rather bad manners. We note—for in the theatre the most trivial detail that we *see* outweighs the most important philosophy that we deduce—that he wears a beard which in a few years' time will resemble Mr. Shaw's; and he has already acquired Mr. Shaw's habit (an apparently deliberate piece of "business," and therefore we stand excused for mentioning it) of combing his beard with his fingers. It is not unfair to assume that there is as much of Mr. Shaw in Jack Tanner as there is of Shakespeare in Hamlet; and that (if Professor Bradley only knew it!) is saying a good deal. Casually, this young man lets fall the remark that he is descended from Don Juan. Why? What is Don Juan doing *dans cette galère*? That you soon discover when you are introduced to Miss Ann. For Miss Ann is the new Don Juan, the huntress of men—no, of one man (that is to say, no Don Juan at all, but for the moment let that pass), the one man being Jack Tanner. Miss Ann means to marry Jack, though he does not yet know it. What he does know (from the German) is that man is the helpless prey of the "mother woman" through the influence of the "life force." This Tanner expounds, in good set Schopenhauerian terms, to a sentimental young man, half-engaged to Ann, alleged to be a "poet." We say alleged, because this young man's profession of poet is, for stage purposes, a non-effective force. So far as the play is concerned the "poet" might just as well be a drysalter. And thus it is that, busied as in the theatre we must be with the action-plot, we are perpetually baffled and pulled up—wondering why Tanner is descended from Don Juan and why Octavius is alleged to be a poet. Also we wonder why Tanner lectures poor mild milksopish Octavius about the devastating egoism of the "artist man"—how the "artist man" is (apparently) the masculine of the "mother woman," how they are twin creators, she of children, he of mind, and how they live only for that act of creation, so that there is the devil to pay (examples from literary history) when they happen to become man and wife. This, we say to ourselves, may be all very true (for have we, too, not browsed in the Dictionary of National Biography?); but why does Tanner say it all, just at that moment, to the alleged poet but obvious barber's-block Octavius? While we are thus racking our brain we are interrupted by a new diversion. Octavius's sister (whom we have never seen or heard of) is suddenly reported to have "gone wrong." Agony of Octavius; glaring reprobation of the "respectable" types; and coruscation of Nietzschean fireworks from Tanner. Conventional morality, humbug! Is motherhood less holy—we beg pardon, less helpful—because it is motherhood without "marriage lines"? Etc., etc. (We say "etc., etc.," because the worst of Mr. Shaw's cheap German philosophic baggage is that when you see the first article you know all the rest of the set beforehand.) But stop; you may spare all trouble over the argument. For lo! it is a mistake, a false scent. Octavius's sister proves to be really and truly married. And the curtain of the first act descends upon a group cowering, as Tanner says, before the wedding ring.

Now this, the first section of the action-plot, is of course on the face of it a mere *pot-pourri*, a Caucus race, chaos come again. You have been immensely amused, cyrenaically enjoying the moment for the moment's sake, but looking before and after (as you cannot help looking in the theatre) you have been disconcerted and *dérouté*. What is the key to the mystery? The key is the idea-plot. Look at that for a moment and you will see why Octavius is alleged to be a poet and why his sister is falsely alleged to be no better than she should be. *(a)* Fundamental idea: the irresistible power of woman over man in carrying out the aim of nature (or the "life force") to make her a mother. *(b)* Development: partly in Ann's actions, mainly in Tanner's talk. And there, in that disproportion, at once we touch a dramatic weakness of the play. The properly dramatic development would have thrown all the onus upon Ann—we should have seen Ann energizing as the "mother woman," and nothing else—and would have kept Tanner's mouth shut. But Mr. Shaw cannot exhibit, or can only feebly exhibit, by character and action; his native preference is for exposition by

dialectic and ratiocination—*i.e.*, by abstract talk; which is one of the reasons why we say he is no dramatist. *(c)* Corollary of the fundamental idea: if motherhood is nature's aim, then marriage is a detail—our morality which brands motherhood *minus* a wedding ring is false. Hence the "false scent" about Octavius's sister's baby. *(d)* Antithetical question suggested by the fundamental idea: is there not a male counterpart to the "mother woman"? Mr. Shaw hunts about. Yes, no, yes—it must be, the "artist man." Hence the alleged poetic vocation of Octavius, in order that Tanner may have a cue for haranguing him about the "artist man" and the "mother woman." Not otherwise do they insert cues in "musical comedies" when the time has come for a song or dance. That is one reason why "musical comedies" are like Mr. Shaw's comedies—not comedies. If Mr. Shaw's play were a real play we should have no need to explain the action-plot by laborious reference to the idea-plot. The one would be the natural garment of the other; or rather the one would be the flesh of which the other was the bones. Octavius would be a real poet in the dramatic action (as is for instance the case with the poet in *Candida*); there would be no false alarm about Octavius's sister; Ann would exhibit Mr. Shaw's thesis "on her own," instead of by the help of Mr. Jack Tanner's lecture wand and gift of the gab. In that way we should miss many diverting moments; but only in some such way as that could we get a real play.

We have left ourselves little space for Acts II. and III. Fortunately little space is needed. For look again at the idea plot and you will see that it soon exhausts itself, so that the action-plot, being as we have said a mere parasite of the other, is bound very rapidly to give out. Tanner can only continue to Schopenhauerize, and the moment of his falling into the lady's arms will synchronize with that in which the author is tired of his game and brings down the curtain. The so-called poet peters out; indeed, never existed. His sister is provided with an American husband. Why? *Vide*, once more, idea-plot. The super-chivalric American view of woman, being a contrast to the Schopenhauerian, obviously calls for mention. Hence Mr. Hector Malone. Hence also, indirectly, Mr. Malone senior, American millionaire and ex-Irish emigrant (opportunity for short *bravura* episode about wrongs of Ireland)—a character which—rare mischance with Mr. Shaw!—hovers on the outer edge of the tiresome. All that is left to be done is to emphasize in Ann woman's talent for lying (type-example: Raina in *Arms and the Man*) at the same time getting it neatly hooked on to the Schopenhauerian "mother woman" theory. We must not forget two subordinate characters—Ann's mother, middle-aged, querulous, helpless in her daughter's hands, and the cockney *chauffeur*, the *fine fleur* of Board school education, Henry Straker. These two small parts, from the point of view of genuine and fresh observation, are among the best things in the play. In them Mr. Shaw has been content to reproduce, instead of deducing. We wish he would more often fall a victim to the same weakness. . . .

Mr. Shaw, as we have tried to show, has conceived Ann not as a character, but as a pure idea, a walking theory; [the actress Miss Lillah] McCarthy turns her almost into a genuine character, and entirely into an agreeable woman. How voluptuous she might have been, how credible a female Don Juan, if Mr. Shaw had only given her the chance! But examination of Mr. Shaw's *théâtre complet* has convinced us that it is not in him to "do" a voluptuary. His present play, *ex hypothesi*, was concerned with the World, the Flesh, and the Devil. The Devil (a delightfully prominent person in the printed version) has to our deep regret had to be omitted on the stage. As for the Flesh, it never began to be warm, but is merely an intellectual category. Mr. Shaw is no flesh-painter.

[*Arthur Bingham Walkley*], in a review of *"Man and Superman,"* in The Times Literary Supplement, *No. 176, May 26, 1905, p. 170.*

H. L. MENCKEN (essay date 1905)

[*From the era of World War I until the early years of the Great Depression, Mencken was one of the most influential figures in American letters. His strongly individualistic, irreverent outlook on life and his vigorous, invective-charged writing style helped establish the iconoclastic spirit of the Jazz Age and significantly shaped the direction of American literature. As a social and literary critic—the roles for which he is best known—Mencken was the scourge of evangelical Christianity, public service organizations, literary censorship, boosterism, provincialism, democracy, all advocates of personal or social improvement, and every other facet of American life that he perceived as humbug. In his literary criticism, Mencken encouraged American writers to shun the anglophilic, moralistic bent of the nineteenth century and to practice realism, an artistic call-to-arms that is most fully developed in his essay "Puritanism As a Literary Force," one of the seminal essays in modern literary criticism. In the following excerpt, Mencken characterizes* Man and Superman *as Shaw's "magnum opus," a "diverting farce" that Shaw overwhelmed by using it as a vehicle for "airing practically every radical doctrine in the modern repertoire."*]

Measured with rule, plumb-line or hay-scales, **Man and Superman** is easily Shaw's *magnum opus.* In bulk it is brobdignagian; in scope it is stupendous; in purpose it is one with the Odyssey. Like a full-rigged ship before a spanking breeze, it cleaves deep into the waves, sending ripples far to port and starboard, and its giant canvases rise half way to the clouds, with resplendent jibs, skysails, staysails and studdingsails standing out like quills upon the fretful porcupine. It has a preface as long as a campaign speech; an interlude in three scenes, with music and red fire; and a complete digest of the German philosophers as an appendix. With all its rings and satellites it fills a tome of 281 closely-printed pages. Its epigrams, quips, jests, and quirks are multitudinous; it preaches treason to all the schools; its hero has one speech of 350 words. No one but a circus press agent could rise to an adequate description of its innumerable marvels. It is a three-ring circus, with Ibsen doing running high jumps; Schopenhauer playing the calliope and Nietzsche selling peanuts in the reserved seats. And all the while it is the most entertaining play of its generation.

Maybe Shaw wrote it in a vain effort to rid himself at one fell swoop of all the disquieting doctrines that infested his innards. Into it he unloaded Kropotkin, Noyes, Bakounin, Wilde, Marx, Proudhon, Nietzsche, Netschajew, Wagner, Bunyan, Mozart, Shelley, Ibsen, Morris, Tolstoi, Goethe, Schopenhauer, Plato—seized them by the heels and heaved them in, with a sort of relieved "God help you!" The result is 281 pages of most diverting farce—farce that only half hides the tumultuous uproar of the two-and-seventy jarring sects beneath it. It is a tract cast in an encyclopedic and epic mold—a stupendous, magnificent colossal effort to make a dent in the cosmos with a slapstick. (pp. 70-1)

Shaw explains that he wrote the play in response to a suggestion by A. B. Walkley, the dramatic critic of the London *Times* that he should tackle the subject of Don Juan. In his 37-page preface he traces, at length, the process of reasoning which led him to the conclusion that Juan, as he was depicted by the

fathers, was a fraud and an impostor [see excerpt by Shaw dated 1903]. In the business of mating, he says (after Schopenhauer) it is not the man but the woman that does the pursuing. Man's function in life is that of food-getting. Woman's is that of perpetuating the race. Hence man's ordinary occupation is making money, and woman's is getting married. To protect himself against "a too aggressive prosecution of woman's business," he says, man has "set up a feeble romantic convention that the initiative in sex business must always come from him." But the pretense is so shallow "that even in the theater, that last sanctuary of unreality, it imposes only on the inexperienced. In Shakespeare's plays the woman always takes the initiative. In his problem plays and his popular plays alike the love interest is the interest of seeing the woman hunt the man down."

And so, the hero of this new play, John Tanner (our old friend Juan Tenorio) is the pursued, and Doña Ana (Miss Ann Whitefield) is the pursuer. John is a being of most advanced and startling ideas. He writes a volume called "The Revolutionist's Handbook and Pocket Companion," full of all sorts of strange doctrines, from praise of the Oneida Community to speculations regarding the probable characteristics of the Superman. He laughs at honor, titles, the law, property, marriage, liberty, democracy, the golden rule and everything else that God-fearing folks hold sacred; he has a good word for Czolgosz; he gives directions for beating children; he curls his lip at civilization; he ventures the view that "every man over forty is a scoundrel." And then, with all this cargo of nonconformity afloat in his hold, fate sends him sailing into a haven of staunch orthodoxy.

He and Roebuck Ramsden, a gentleman who hangs Herbert Spencer's portrait on his library wall as a sort of banner of his intellectual modernity, are appointed guardians for Ann, whose papa has just passed away, and John, to protect himself against being caught in ambush by the Life Force, as represented in his ward, endeavors to marry her off to Octavius Robinson, a harmless young man who has lived beneath her father's roof since his childhood. John is aware of the faults of Ann and has no yearning to be enmeshed in her web. He notices that she is a liar and politely calls her attention to the fact; he observes her pursuit of him and makes open preparations for flight. Finally, in full cry, he runs away in an automobile across Europe. But the Life Force is more powerful than gasoline, and Ann, yielding to its irresistible impulse, follows him—across the English channel, to Dover, and across France toward the Mediterranean. In the Sierra Nevada mountains she brings her game to bay and in old Grenada poor John receives his *coup de grace.* Thus he sinks to earth:

> TANNER. . . . The trap was laid from the beginning.
>
> ANN. (*Concentrating all her magic*) From the beginning—from our childhood—for both of us—by the Life Force.
>
> TANNER. I will not marry you. I will not marry you.
>
> ANN. Oh, you will, you will.
>
> TANNER. I tell you, no, no, no.
>
> ANN. I tell you, yes, yes, yes.
>
> TANNER. No.

ANN. (*Coaxing—imploring—almost exhausted*) Yes. Before it is too late for repentance. Yes.

TANNER. (*Struck by an echo from the past*) When did all this happen to me before? Are we two dreaming?

ANN. (*Suddenly losing her courage, with an anguish that she does not conceal*) No. We are awake and you have said no: that is all.

TANNER. (*Brutally*) Well?

ANN. Well, I made a mistake, you do not love me.

TANNER. (*Seizing her in his arms*) It is false: I love you. The Life Force enchants me: I have the whole world in my arms when I clasp you. . . .

And this is the story upon which Shaw hangs his 175 pages of play—it would take seven hours to perform it in its entirety—his thirty-seven pages of introduction, and his sixty-nine pages of appendix.

The conflict between Tanner and the ethics and traditions represented by Ramsden is riotously and irresistibly humorous. The first act of the play, indeed, is the most gorgeously grotesque in all Shaw. Better fun is scarcely imaginable. The famous Hell scene, which forms a sort of movable third act, is also a masterpiece of comedy. Tanner during his flight from Ann, is captured by a band of social-anarchist brigands, led by one Capt. Mendoza, a sentimental Anglo-Hebrew. Mendoza's story of his unrequited love for an English lass sends Tanner to dreamland, and he dreams that he is in Hell. And then an elaborately comic play within a play is performed. Mendoza appears as the Devil; Tanner as Don Juan; and Ann as Doña Ana de Ulloa. It is long, this episode, and beyond all hope of boiling down, but the persons who see *Man and Superman* without it miss two-thirds of the drama. An excellent exposition by the Devil of the superiority of Hell over Heaven forms part of it. During the rest of the action the characters discuss every imaginable subject, from love to the higher morality. (pp. 71-5)

The play is such a gigantic, ponderous thing that any effort to summarize it is difficult. The central idea—that, in mating, the man is pursued by the woman—is one that we have seen Shaw employ in *Arms and the Man, The Philanderer,* and other plays. As he himself says, it is not a new conception. Shakespeare had it, though maybe unconsciously, and its rudiments appear in the works of other men. Schopenhauer made it classical. In *Man and Superman* Shaw uses it as an excuse for airing practically every radical doctrine in the modern repertoire. . . . Shaw borrows part of the title from Nietzsche and makes sad sport of the mad German in many a scene, but that is no evidence that he is insincere when, in his introduction, he classes Nietzsche with those writers "whose peculiar sense of the world I recognize as more or less akin to my own." "The Revolutionist's Handbook and Pocket Companion" at the end of the play is given, he says, merely to prove that John Tanner, its author, is really the revolutionist and genius the drama makes him out to be. Too often, says Shaw, a playwright is content to say that his hero is a man of parts without offering any tangible evidence of the fact.

All in all, *Man and Superman* is a work worth the two years of effort the title page hints it cost the author. But it is a pity that Shaw didn't divide it into two plays, a volume of essays, two dozen magazine articles and a book of epigrams. The age of the epic is past. To-day we sacrifice Fortinbras to get "Hamlet" into two hours and a half. (pp. 76-7)

> *H. L. Mencken, in his* George Bernard Shaw: His Plays, *1905. Reprint by Edwin V. Glaser, 1969, 107 p.*

LEO TOLSTOY (letter date 1908)

[*Tolstoy is considered one of the greatest novelists in the history of world literature. His* Voina i mir *(1869;* War and Peace) *and* Anna Karenina *(1877) are almost universally regarded as all-encompassing documents of human existence and supreme examples of the realistic novel. Particularly esteemed are his insightful examinations of psychology and society, along with the religious and philosophical issues which occupied him later in his career. As a religious and ethical thinker Tolstoy has been criticized for the extremism, and sometimes the absurdity, of his ideas. However, he has also been admired for the gigantism of his ambition to discover absolute laws governing humanity's ethical and spiritual obligations amid the psychological and social complexities of the world. Tolstoy's doctrines were always founded on his expansive humanitarianism and based on one of the most intensive quests for wisdom in human history. Tolstoy ultimately believed that art should serve a religious and ethical code. In December, 1907, Shaw's publisher, Aylmer Maude, sent a copy of* Man and Superman *to Tolstoy. According to R. F. Christian, an editor and translator of Tolstoy's letters, Tolstoy's initial reading of the play was largely unfavorable; however, upon a second reading Tolstoy had some more favorable comments that he included in the following letter to Shaw, together with a general criticism of Shaw's light treatment of serious matters that was repeated in further correspondence (see Additional Bibliography).*]

Please excuse me for not having thanked you before this for the book you sent through Mr Maude.

Now on re-reading it and paying special attention to the passages you indicated, I particularly appreciate Don Juan's speeches in the Interlude (although I think that the subject would have gained greatly from a more serious approach to it, rather than its being a casual insertion in a comedy) and "The Revolutionist's Handbook."

In the first I could without any effort agree fully with Don Juan's words that a hero is "he who seeks in contemplation to discover the inner will of the world . . . [and] in action to do that will by the so-discovered means"—the very thing which is expressed in my language by the words: "to recognise the will of God in oneself and to fulfil it."

In the second I particularly liked your attitude to civilisation and progress, and the very true thought that however long both may continue, they cannot improve the state of mankind unless people themselves change.

The difference in our views only amounts to this that in your opinion the improvement of mankind will be accomplished when ordinary people become supermen or new supermen are born, while in my opinion it will come about when people divest true religions, including Christianity, of all the excrescences which deform them and when all people, uniting in that one understanding of life which lies at the base of all religions, establish a reasonable attitude of their own towards the world's infinite first principle, and follow the guidance for life which stems from it.

The practical advantage which my way of freeing people from evil has over yours is that one can easily imagine that very large masses of even poorly educated or quite uneducated people will be able to accept true religion and follow it, whereas to evolve supermen from the people who now exist or to give birth to new ones would need the sort of exceptional conditions which are as little capable of being attained as the improvement of mankind through progress and civilisation.

Dear Mr Shaw, life is a great and serious matter, and all of us generally, in this short interval of time granted to us, must try to find our appointed task and fulfil it as well as possible. This applies to all people, and especially to you with your great talents, your original powers of thought and your penetration into the essence of any question.

And so in the confident hope of not offending you, I will tell you what seem to me to be the defects of your book.

Its first defect is that you are not sufficiently serious. One should not speak jokingly about such a subject as the purpose of human life or the causes of its perversion and of the evil that fills the life of all of us mankind. I would prefer the speeches of Don Juan to be not the speeches of an apparition, but the speeches of Shaw, and similarly that "The Revolutionist's Handbook" should be attributed not to the non-existent Tanner but to the living Bernard Shaw, responsible for his own words.

A second reproach is that the questions you deal with are of such enormous importance that, for people with such a deep understanding of the evils of our life and such a brilliant aptitude for exposition as yourself, to make them only the object of satire may often harm rather than help the solution of these important problems.

I see in your book a desire to surprise and astonish the reader by your great erudition, talent and intelligence. And yet all this is not only not necessary for the solution of the problems you deal with, but very often distracts the reader's attention from the essence of the subject, attracting it by the brilliance of the exposition.

In any case I think that this book of yours expresses your views not in their full and clear development, but only in their embryonic state. I think that these views as they develop more and more will arrive at the one truth which we all seek and which we are all gradually approaching.

I hope you will forgive me if you find anything unpleasant in what I have said to you. I said what I did only because I recognise in you very great gifts, and have for you personally the most friendly feelings. . . . (pp. 677-79)

> *Leo Tolstoy, in a letter to George Bernard Shaw on August 17, 1908, in his* Tolstoy's Letters: 1880-1910, *Vol. II, edited and translated by R. F. Christian, Charles Scribner's Sons, 1978, pp. 677-79.*

G. K. CHESTERTON (essay date 1909)

[*Regarded as one of England's premier men of letters during the first half of the twentieth century, Chesterton is best known today as a colorful bon vivant, a witty essayist, and creator of the Father Brown mysteries and the fantasy* The Man Who Was Thursday (1908). *Much of Chesterton's work reveals his childlike joie de vivre and reflects his pronounced Anglican and, later, Roman Catholic beliefs. His essays are characterized by their humor, frequent use of paradox, and chatty, rambling style. In the following excerpt, Chesterton finds that* Man and Superman *repre-*

sents the first instance of Shaw's artistic maturity, the point at which his works took on their final character.]

In his latest work, especially in *Man and Superman,* Shaw has become a complete and colossal mystic. That mysticism does grow quite rationally out of his older arguments; but very few people ever troubled to trace the connection. (p. 173)

There are other places in which Shaw's argument is more fascinating or his wit more startling than in *Man and Superman;* there are other plays that he has made more brilliant. But I am sure that there is no other play that he wished to make more brilliant. (p. 212)

The outline of the play is, I suppose, by this time sufficiently well known. It has two main philosophic motives. The first is that what he calls the life-force (the old infidels called it Nature, which seems a neater word, and nobody knows the meaning of either of them) desires above all things to make suitable marriages, to produce a purer and prouder race, or eventually to produce a Superman. The second is that in this effecting of racial marriages the woman is a more conscious agent than the man. In short, that woman disposes a long time before man proposes. In this play, therefore, woman is made the pursuer and man the pursued. It cannot be denied, I think, that in this matter Shaw is handicapped by his habitual hardness of touch, by his lack of sympathy with the romance of which he writes, and to a certain extent even by his own integrity and right conscience. Whether the man hunts the woman or the woman the man, at least it should be a splendid pagan hunt; but Shaw is not a sporting man. Nor is he a pagan, but a Puritan. He cannot recover the impartiality of paganism which allowed Diana to propose to Endymion without thinking any the worse of her. The result is that while he makes Ann, the woman who marries his hero, a really powerful and convincing woman, he can only do it by making her a highly objectionable woman. She is a liar and a bully, not from sudden fear or excruciating dilemma; she is a liar and a bully in grain; she has no truth or magnanimity in her. The more we know that she is real, the more we know that she is vile. In short, Bernard Shaw is still haunted with his old impotence of the unromantic writer; he cannot imagine the main motives of human life from the inside. We are convinced successfully that Ann wishes to marry Tanner, but in the very process we lose all power of conceiving why Tanner should ever consent to marry Ann. A writer with a more romantic strain in him might have imagined a woman choosing her lover without shamelessness and magnetising him without fraud. Even if the first movement were feminine, it need hardly be a movement like this. In truth, of course, the two sexes have their two methods of attraction, and in some of the happiest cases they are almost simultaneous. But even on the most cynical showing they need not be mixed up. It is one thing to say that the mouse-trap is not there by accident. It is another to say (in the face of ocular experience) that the mouse-trap runs after the mouse.

But whenever Shaw shows the Puritan hardness or even the Puritan cheapness, he shows something also of the Puritan nobility, of the idea that sacrifice is really a frivolity in the face of a great purpose. The reasonableness of Calvin and his followers will by the mercy of heaven be at last washed away; but their unreasonableness will remain an eternal splendour. Long after we have let drop the fancy that Protestantism was rational it will be its glory that it was fanatical. So it is with Shaw. To make Ann a real woman, even a dangerous woman, he would need to be something stranger and softer than Bernard Shaw. But though I always argue with him whenever he argues,

I confess that he always conquers me in the one or two moments when he is emotional.

There is one really noble moment when Anne offers for all her cynical husband-hunting the only defence that is really great enough to cover it. "It will not be all happiness for me. Perhaps death." And the man rises also at that real crisis, saying, "Oh, that clutch holds and hurts. What have you grasped in me? Is there a father's heart as well as a mother's?" That seems to me actually great; I do not like either of the characters an atom more than formerly; but I can see shining and shaking through them at that instant the splendour of the God that made them and of the image of God who wrote their story.

A logician is like a liar in many respects, but chiefly in the fact that he should have a good memory. That cutting and inquisitive style which Bernard Shaw has always adopted carries with it an inevitable criticism. And it cannot be denied that this new theory of the supreme importance of sound sexual union, wrought by any means, is hard logically to reconcile with Shaw's old diatribes against sentimentalism and operatic romance. If Nature wishes primarily to entrap us into sexual union, then all the means of sexual attraction, even the most maudlin or theatrical, are justified at one stroke. . . . The justification of Ann, as the potential mother of Superman, is really the justification of all the humbugs and sentimentalists whom Shaw had been denouncing as a dramatic critic and as a dramatist since the beginning of his career. . . . To **Man and Superman,** as to all his plays, the author attaches a most fascinating preface at the beginning. But I really think that he ought also to attach a hearty apology at the end; an apology to all the minor dramatists or preposterous actors whom he had cursed for romanticism in his youth. . . . We have remarked the end of Shaw's campaign in favour of progress. This ought really to have been the end of his campaign against romance. All the tricks of love that he called artificial become natural, because they become Nature. All the lies of love become truths; indeed they become the Truth.

The minor things of the play contain some thunderbolts of good thinking. Throughout this brief study I have deliberately not dwelt upon mere wit, because in anything of Shaw's that may be taken for granted. It is enough to say that this play which is full of his most serious quality is as full as any of his minor sort of success. In a more solid sense two important facts stand out: the first is the character of the young American; the other is the character of Straker, the chauffeur. In these Shaw has realised and made vivid two most important facts. First, that America is not intellectually a go-ahead country, but both for good and evil an old-fashioned one. It is full of stale culture and ancestral simplicity, just as Shaw's young millionaire quotes Macaulay and piously worships his wife. Second, he has pointed out in the character of Straker that there has arisen in our midst a new class that has education without breeding. Straker is the man who has ousted the hansom-cabman, having neither his coarseness nor his kindliness. Great sociological credit is due to the man who has first clearly observed that Straker has appeared. How anybody can profess for a moment to be glad that he has appeared, I do not attempt to conjecture.

Appended to the play is an entertaining though somewhat mysterious document called "The Revolutionist's Handbook." It contains many very sound remarks; this, for example, which I cannot too much applaud: "If you hit your child, be sure that you hit him in anger." If that principle had been properly understood, we should have had less of Shaw's sociological friends and their meddling with the habits and instincts of the poor. But among the fragments of advice also occurs the following suggestive and even alluring remark: "Every man over forty is a scoundrel." On the first personal opportunity I asked the author of this remarkable axiom what it meant. I gathered that what it really meant was something like this: that every man over forty had been all the essential use that he was likely to be, and was therefore in a manner a parasite. It is gratifying to reflect that Bernard Shaw has sufficiently answered his own epigram by continuing to pour out treasures both of truth and folly long after this allotted time. But if the epigram might be interpreted in a rather looser style as meaning that past a certain point a man's work takes on its final character and does not greatly change the nature of its merits, it may certainly be said that with **Man and Superman,** Shaw reaches that stage. The two plays that have followed it, though of very great interest in themselves, do not require any revaluation of, or indeed any addition to, our summary of his genius and success. They are both in a sense casts back to his primary energies; the first in a controversial and the second in a technical sense. Neither need prevent our saying that the moment when John Tanner and Ann agree that it is doom for him and death for her and life only for the thing unborn, is the peak of his utterance as a prophet. (pp. 213-21)

> *G. K. Chesterton, in his* George Bernard Shaw, *1909.*
> *Reprint by John Lane Company, 1910, 257 p.*

DESMOND MacCARTHY (essay date 1946)

[*MacCarthy was one of the foremost English literary and dramatic critics of the twentieth century. He served for many years on the staff of the* New Statesman *and edited* Life and Letters. *Among his many essay collections,* The Court Theatre 1904-1907: A Commentary and a Criticism *(1907)—a detailed account of three seasons during which the Court Theatre was dominated by Harley Granville-Barker and Bernard Shaw—is especially valued. According to his critics, MacCarthy brought to his work a wide range of reading, serious and sensitive judgment, an interest in the works of new writers, and high critical standards. In the following excerpt from a 1946 radio broadcast, MacCarthy contends that* Man and Superman, *in its published three-part form, contains "a central exposition of Shaw's philosophy."*]

Man and Superman is one of the peaks in Bernard Shaw's dramatic work. (p. 32)

The play is a serio-comic love-chase of a man by a woman. But taken together with the preface, with the long dream interlude in Act III called "Don Juan in Hell," and with its appendix, "The Revolutionist's Handbook" (attributed to John Tanner), it remains a central exposition of Shaw's philosophy. This was the first time that his Evolutionary Religion, his conception of the Life Force as a Will striving through the minds and instincts of men to become conscious of itself, was set forth.

Yet in the play itself, with the exception of the dream interlude, there is nothing of this; and the theory which interprets sex attraction between men and women as one of the means the Life Force takes towards its end is a deduction from the play rather than a part of it. So also is the "practical" moral that selective breeding is more important than political reforms. What does, however, pervade the dialogue and action is Shaw's conception of sex and love. In **Man and Superman,** as he says in the preface, he set out to write a play in which sex attraction should be the main subject. This, he proclaimed, no dramatist had done before. The world's famous love-tragedies and love-comedies had only dramatised conflicts, either triumphant or unhappy, between lovers and marriage laws, or love and circumstance or love and moral obligations. No dramatist, he asserted, had attempted to reveal the underlying nature of a passionate mutual attraction between a particular man and a particular woman. That startling statement had some truth in it, though all it really meant was that no dramatist had yet interpreted on the stage "love" as the great German pessimist, Schopenhauer, had also interpreted it, namely as the Will of the Race expressing itself through the desires of the individual and often contrary to his or her happiness. Shaw also added that in love woman was really always the pursuer, and he pointed out that Shakespeare had unconsciously realised this in some of his plays. This theory, however, though it gains plausibility from the fact that women take love-likings as often as men, and in their own ways seek as often to win the object of their affections, cannot be accepted as sound. Still, if the case of Ann and Tanner is taken as a particular story, and not as illustrating a universal truth, this theory need not lessen our appreciation. The play is one of Shaw's most brilliant pieces of creative work.

Ann according to his philosophy is "Everywoman," though every woman is not Ann. As an individual she is excellently drawn. Instinct leads her to mark down Tanner as the father of her future children, but Tanner knows that for him marriage means loss of liberty, peace of mind, and what is far more serious, as likely as not the ruin of his revolutionary efforts.

Shaw and Harley Granville-Barker, 1901.

Jack Tanner, with his explosions of nervous energy, his wit, and vehement eloquence, is as vividly created as Ann.

The contrast to him is the poetical, chivalrous, romantical Octavius, the idealiser of women who is in love with Ann. "Ricky Ticky Tavy," as she half tenderly, half contemptuously calls him, instead of flying from her like his friend Jack Tanner, woos her humbly, but her deeper instincts—and through these, according to Shaw, the Life Force works—leads her to refuse him as a husband; the poetic temperament is barren—the Life Force passes it by.

But Tanner yields at last, because, as his previous incarnation Don Juan explains in the dream episode, he cannot help it. The Life Force which wills that the offspring of two particular people shall be born, is stronger even than his impulse to serve mankind in ways to which he had intended to dedicate himself. Tanner "loves" Ann in the sense of feeling this irresistible urge; at the same time he despises her. She is a bully and a liar and by "unscrupulously using her personal fascinations to make men give her what she wants," she is also "something for which there is no polite name." He knows that she will think his aspirations and efforts to reform society absurd and thwart him in so far as she dares in the interests of the family. Above all, Ann is a hypocrite, but from an ultimate point of view that was unimportant. Both Ann and Tanner, in submitting to their attraction for each other, become servants of the will of the world. They are instruments towards creating the superior race of the future—ultimately the Superman.

Now at the time Shaw wrote this play he was evidently in a state of impatient despair in regard to what political reform could achieve. In the preface he says: "There is no public enthusiast alive of twenty years' practical democratic experience who believes in the political adequacy of the electorate or the body it elects. The overthrow of the aristocrat has created the necessity of the Superman." Thus both are right to sacrifice; she, perhaps her life in child-bearing, he his happiness, aims and generous ambitions; for such things cannot compare in importance with bringing into the world a child born of their mutual attraction.

It follows, of course, that the institution of marriage which compels two people who have nothing in common save mutual sex-attraction to spend their lives together, is stupid, and that from the conception that the child is the sole end of marriage, it is absurd to make it binding. Moreover, the fact that marriage is binding makes men and women who know that they will have to spend the rest of their lives together, choose their mates for irrelevant reasons—affection, respect or self-interest. That is the moral of this serio-comedy, which keeps many people laughing who would not laugh perhaps if they really understood its drift. It is rather odd that the dramatist never again returned to the theme that in selective breeding or "eugenics," as that process is called, lay all hope of the future of mankind.

In the other characters, also, Shaw's skill in drawing types and making them speak out of themselves with arresting point is at its best. What an eye he has always had for types which were instantly recognisable and yet new to the stage or to fiction. Note here the appearance for the first time of the modern mechanician, 'Enry Straker, Tanner's chauffeur, and note too, how admirably the old-fashioned, free-thinking radical, Roebuck Ramsden, is presented, the man who can't believe that he is not still in the forefront of advanced thought, and yet is to Tanner the most ludicrous old stick-in-the-mud. The last moment of the first act, when Violet, that expertly drawn, empty-headed, possessive type of attractive girl, suddenly reveals that, instead of being the daring flaunter of conventions Tanner had hoped, she has all the time really been *married* to the man whose child she is about to bear, is one of the most amusing thunder-claps in modern comedy.

The scene at the end between Ann and Tanner, in which Ann at last gets her way, is also admirable. (pp. 32-5)

The dream-interlude, "Don Juan in Hell," is a marvellous example of Shaw's power of making the eloquence of ideas as riveting as action on the stage. Note, by the way, his contrast between Heaven and Hell.

The point which I wish to insist upon here is not that Shaw is not right in considering his Heaven superior to his Hell—it obviously is; but that his Heaven is not the contemplation of what is perfect, but of something that is struggling to become so. It is a condition in which there is still peril, where you "face things as they are"; in short, a "community of saints" which is really a community of reformers. Shaw describes them as filled with "a passion of the divine will"; but this passion is a desire to make the world better, and not a contemplation of perfection: in so far as it is a contemplative ecstasy at all, it is only rapture at the idea that perfection is possible.

What chills us, then, in his Heaven is the misgiving that the phrase "masters of reality" (so the heavenly inhabitants are described) is a euphemism for a society of people all devoted to making each other and everybody else more virtuous. Now we can imagine something better than that; and Shaw's Hell, if he had not been so unfair to it, where they value love, music and beauty for their own sakes, offers hints at any rate. (pp. 35-6)

> *Desmond MacCarthy, in his* Shaw, *MacGibbon & Kee, 1951, 217 p.*

JOHN MASON BROWN (essay date 1947)

[*Brown, an influential and popular American drama critic from the 1930s through the 1950s, wrote extensively on contemporary British and American drama. He had a thorough knowledge of dramatic history and his criticism often displays a scholarly erudition in addition to the qualities of popular reviewing. In the following excerpt from an October, 1947 review of a production of* Man and Superman, *Brown casts a retrospective look at the play forty-four years after it was written.*]

"Enough, then, of this goose-cackle about Progress: Man, as he is, never will nor can add a cubit to his stature by any of its quackeries, political, scientific, educational, religious, or artistic." Thus Mr. Shaw, alias John Tanner, in "The Revolutionist's Handbook" which serves *Man and Superman* as an appendix. (p. 121)

As a Nietzschean who had turned the dead, hence defenseless, Nietzsche into a Shavian, Shaw was championing the Superman. In him he saw our only hope. The Superman would belong to a new type, a new race. He would not, therefore, be condemned to repeat in each generation the errors and cruelties of his forefathers. Our chances of survival depended upon creating a world where the unaverage mortals would be the average ones. Man as we have known him, insisted Shaw, has proved himself incapable of net progress. Accordingly, he must be replaced by the Superman, a figure achievable only by the socialization of selective breeding.

Although Shaw admitted that during recorded history Man had added to his outward conveniences, his contention was that morally Man had not moved forward one iota. Shaw refused to believe that the chauffeur who drove a motorcar from Paris to Berlin was a more highly evolved creature than the charioteer of Achilles. Or that the modern prime minister was a more enlightened ruler than Caesar because he rode a tricycle, wrote his dispatches by electric light, and instructed his stockbroker through the telephone. Our notion of Progress, thundered Mr. Shaw, was only an illusion. It was civilization's most disastrous conceit.

Instead of actually happening, the forty-four years which have slipped by since *Man and Superman* was written must seem in many respects to have been invented by Mr. Shaw for the sole purpose of proving his argument. Anyone who in the contemporary world would serve Progress as its defense attorney faces a dismaying task. Although our doctors have learned to prolong individual life, the facts of peace no less than of war encourage many to ask why. For what kind of persons morally, for what sort of world internationally, has this private longevity been achieved? (pp. 121-22)

The Elderly Gentleman has not lived and thought and written and laughed entirely in vain. He remains far ahead of us all in sanity, brilliance, intellect, eloquence, wit, goodness, knowledge, and conscience. Yet there is some consolation to be had from the fact that a world shaken by Shaw's impact does not think (however it may act) as the globe did in its pre-Shavian days. The distance which separates *Man and Superman* from its audiences today is less great than it was at the century's turn.

The eternal iconoclast has become something of an icon himself. His plays are confronted with the awful fate of being received as classics. Classics usually are works accepted without protest because they are admired without thought. Shaw himself was conscious of this altered attitude and the hazards it presented when *Man and Superman* was first produced. "They used to laugh when I was serious," he wrote Forbes-Robertson, "but now the fashion has changed: they take their hats off when I joke, which is still more trying."

Another faint instance of progress comes from a surprising source—believe it or not, from today's dramatic critics. You may say that my being compelled to fall back on them is a measure of how desperate are the times. Nevertheless, the changed attitude toward what constitutes a good play, as shown in the recent reviews of *Man and Superman,* indicates that in some respects we have inched forward a little even in a troubled world. This advance is not limited to the reviewers alone. It includes the audiences for whom they speak.

There were real giants on the aisles of London's theatres when Mr. Shaw's comedy was new. Yet, distinguished as William Archer, A. B. Walkley, and Max Beerbohm were as critics, theirs was a far more dogmatic, therefore narrower, notion of playwriting than is nowadays prevalent. (p. 124)

Although they said their ideal was plays that were true to life, what they meant by this was plays which remain faithful to the stage—as it then was. Their passion for construction was such that they wanted dramatists to be engineers no less than architects. They could admire a playwright who, in the interest of thought, of freedom, or imagination, extended the stage's limited scope. If, however, he proved larger in spirit, mind, or practice than the form they prized, they refused to recognize him as a playwright. What all this amounted to was saying that a swimmer who had swum the Atlantic was no swimmer at all unless he wore a regulation bathing suit.

Beerbohm, for example, who was truly "incomparable," found *Man and Superman* "infinitely better, to my peculiar taste, than any play I have ever read or seen enacted." Yet even he was quick to add, "But a play it is not." In his confusion he was driven to compare it with Lucian and Landor; above all, with Plato. Although he admired it as a Platonic dialogue, Shaw's dramaturgy was too different from Pinero's for him to accept it as a play. Beerbohm was stubborn in his insistence that Shaw was "a critic, and not a creator at all."

The suave and charming Walkley was no less adamant. It is he, of course, in whose debt we stand for *Man and Superman*, since it was he who challenged Shaw to write a play on the Don Juan theme, even as Archer had once dared him, with *The Doctor's Dilemma* as the result, to write a play about death. In a coruscating review Walkley admitted he had been "immensely amused" (as who wouldn't be by Shaw's comedy?). Nonetheless, he was firm in his contention that its author was "no dramatist at all" [see excerpt dated 1905].

Whatever the lacks of contemporary playgoers or critics may be, we are freer now. We have at least shed those fetters of that earlier day. Mr. Shaw has been one of the major forces in the modern theatre to rid us of them. He has won his conspiracy against the stage of Sir Henry Irving. He is now universally revered, not only as a prophet, a preface writer, the world's foremost critic at large, a wit, and a Fabian, but also as a playwright. We find him funnier than Plato and thank God he is not Pinero. (pp. 125-26)

If we must have indefinable terms defined for us, we are willing to settle for Professor Baker's "A good play is an accurately conveyed emotion." Yet, having welcomed so all-inclusive a definition, we are delighted to find that *Man and Superman*, by being an accurately conveyed *lack* of emotion, fails to hold either water or Shaw.

We do not give a tinker's beldam at present whether Mr. Shaw's text has been built in the image of Pinero or Jones, Dumas or Augier, Ibsen or Hellman. We are happy because palpably it is Shaw's property and no one else's. We know only—and care only—that . . . *Man and Superman* is beyond question the gayest, the brightest, the most original and delectable comedy to be seen in New York just now.

A New York manager, when Robert Loraine was trying to get the play produced in 1905, may have been horrified by its plot idea of a woman chasing a man. He may have rejected the script because he feared its theme was "indullicate." No one finds it so today. To us Shaw's theme is at the core of his text's pleasure. In itself this may be a proof of progress—in the collapse of the romantic dream, the awakening to reality, or the spread of sad disillusionment.

My "old sobersides" approach to so diverting an entertainment may strike you as odd, if not utterly misplaced. I have my reasons. What we see and relish in the theatre ("that last sanctuary of unreality," as Shaw dubbed it) is no more the whole of *Man and Superman* than what glitters above the ocean's surface is the whole of an iceberg. . . . Not even people who would submit to being repeaters at *The Passion Play* or theatregoers accustomed to O'Neill's "mastodonic" dramas (courtesy of Richard Watts, Jr.) could be expected to absorb all of *Man and Superman* at a single sitting. For *Man and Superman* does not consist only of . . . three sprightly acts. . . . Taken by themselves, these acts are self-reliant and vastly entertaining. Yet, above and beyond them, and an integral part of the thesis Shaw is advancing with his glorious garrulity, there is, first of all and not unsurprisingly, the preface. This is a dazzling affair which, in the midst of its intellectual acrobatics on the subject of sex, marriage, woman in general, style, the purpose of life, its author's contempt for the pure artist, and Shaw only knows what else, explains what Shaw is doing with the Don Juan theme.

Then, there is the necessarily omitted third act. Beginning with the bandit Mendoza, and the mountain-pass meeting of the League of the Sierra, it reaches its climax in the famous "hell scene." This is long enough to make an evening in itself, and is one of the most eloquent and witty of all Shaw's dialectics. Finally, there comes, both as appendix and summation, "The Revolutionist's Handbook," which all too often is ignored. In it John Tanner sets down Shaw's philosophy unimpeded by plot; denies Progress; pleads for the Superman; and offers some maxims, some of which are brilliant but many of which find Shaw a nodding La Rochefoucauld.

Don't misunderstand me. None of this homework must be done in order to enjoy [a stage] production of *Man and Superman*. But all of it must be done (and the doing of it is as painless an operation as this world knows) to have a full understanding of what Shaw is up to. As usual he had more on his mind than he could squeeze into dramatic form. As usual, too, though he seemed to be laughing and makes us laugh, he was in deadly earnest.

When Tolstoi was confronted with a copy of *Man and Superman*, he complained at the gaiety with which Shaw dealt with a serious subject. "Why should humor and laughter be excommunicated?" replied Shaw. "Suppose the world were only one of God's jokes, would you work any the less to make it a good joke instead of a bad one?"

Being a Shavian jest, the comedy covers, even in its abbreviated form, a dizzying amount of territory. Art for art's sake it most decidedly is not. But talk for talk's sake it most certainly is. And what wonderful talk! A plot, which soon becomes the scenario for an extravaganza, leaves Shaw free to ventilate his unpredictable views on predatory and mendacious females, the inanities of respectability, the Life Force, the chauffeur as the prototype of the New Man, the American man's idealization of woman, and any number of other topics, all of which as treated betray the incredible agility of Shaw's mind. (pp. 126-28)

Although he may have pretended to hate Shakespeare's mind, Shaw has always doted on his music. Why not? As a word-musician, the author of *Man and Superman* is also capable of infinite magic. He, too, can strum the dictionary and fiddle the language. No one in the English-speaking theatre since the Bard's time has written speeches livelier in their melodies or lovelier in their cadences than has Shaw at his most eloquent. His great tirades, though in prose and filled with humor, have about them the aria quality of Shakespearean soliloquies.

When he was a dramatic critic, Shaw stated his contempt in no uncertain terms for actors who prided themselves on muffling the music in Shakespeare's lines by speaking them as if they were prose. We should be equally resentful of any players who, instead of luxuriating in Shaw's prose rhythms, seek to over-colloquialize them. The performer who would do justice to Shaw must keep up not only with Shaw's music but with his mind. (pp. 128-29)

We may sneer today at Shaw's notion of the Nietzschean Superman. No one, however, can deny in these imperiled times the urgency of Shaw's plea that for the sake of his survival Man must become better and wiser than he is. We have progressed, indeed rushed forward, to this tragic and decisive point. (p. 129)

John Mason Brown, "Progress and the Superman," in his Dramatis Personae: A Retrospective Show, *The Viking Press, 1963, pp. 121-29.*

MARTIN LAMM (essay date 1948)

[*In the following excerpt, originally published in 1948, Lamm characterizes* Man and Superman *as the work in which Shaw's philosophy of "mystical scientific materialism," becomes most evident, and finds that, like Voltaire, Shaw propounds a fundamentally serious point of view in a playful manner.*]

In 1899 came a break of four years in Shaw's dramatic work, and when he returned to the stage in 1903, with **Man and Superman,** something had changed. Hitherto Shaw had not pretended, any more than Ibsen, to present a philosophy in dramatic form. His ineradicable desire to explain himself caused him to write prefaces and notes for his plays, but the play is the important thing, and the explanations are only there to enable them to be enjoyed.

With **Man and Superman** a change has been effected. The play is preceded by an immense preface of no less than fifty pages, and is followed by "The Revolutionist's Handbook," a work by John Tanner which we hear spoken of in the play. The third act, which takes up about half the play and is only rarely performed, is a loosely attached exposition of Shaw's philosophy in dialogue form. (p. 271)

Shaw calls **Man and Superman** a comedy and a philosophy. That part of the play which earns it the name of comedy is really revue, the lightest form of comedy. It has all the right ingredients: a completely haphazard and incoherent plot, and changes of setting from place to place without reason or method.

The psychological moderation and observation of the unities with which Shaw was concerned in **Candida** have now been deliberately abandoned. The two chief characters, Tanner and Ann, are not primarily intended to be individuals, but types of Man and Woman. The artistic effect of **Man and Superman** is like that of Voltaire's satirical novels, such as *Candide,* where a fundamentally serious point of view is expressed in a playful and improbable tale. Exactly as in Voltaire, the characters, though treated by the author as puppets, are startlingly human.

Shaw has never before or since so ruthlessly created a puppet to his own purposes, as when he created John Tanner. It is not enough that he is made the author of Shaw's Revolutionist's Handbook, which, incidentally, appears on the stage before the author, and lands in the waste-paper-basket. When he falls asleep among the robbers in the Sierra Morena he dreams a hundred pages of Shavian philosophy. He is not intended to be a self-portrait, nor does he seem like one, but he is a concentrated expression of Shaw's philosophical and human ideals, both gently caricatured. From the literary point of view he has many predecessors. He is a mixture of the old raisonneur and the hero of the farce, always with a wisecrack or a piece of witty impertinence on his lips, always badly off but never dismayed, always equally cheerful and unconcerned in the way he meets misfortune.

He has also something in common with the clergyman Morell in **Candida.** Tanner is an extravert, a man entirely absorbed in his activities, which are ultimately less fruitful than those of Morell because they are less practical. Tanner is an intellectual to his finger-tips, and that is why in the end he becomes the helpless prey of Ann in her lust for marriage. Morell's weakness is that he does not know himself; Tanner's problem, like Shaw's, is that he knows himself far too well, and that, like Shaw, he cannot take himself seriously. With all his positiveness, there is something negative in the way he proclaims his ideals. He throws out bold truths, but with an undertone of scepticism. Despite his vitality, his brain has nothing to bite on. He is not naive, like Morell; indeed his weakness lies in his lack of naiveté. But to Shaw he is the true personification of modern man, man who has become pure intelligence, pure brain, and whose lot is therefore to be destroyed in the duel between the sexes.

This character is the most original conception in the play. Ann is to represent the sexual instinct; she is the female successor to Don Juan, the blind but certain Life Force that ensures the continuance of the human race. Occasionally this life instinct finds spontaneous expression, as when she replies to Tanner's question about whether she would really sell freedom and honour and self for happiness, with the moving words, "It will not be all happiness for me, perhaps death." But it is only exceptionally that she shows this side of her nature. Her trouble is that she knows her mind only too well. She is a masterpiece of feminine wiles and cunning, and when one sees how cleverly she has succeeded in trapping the highly intelligent Tanner in her net one gets the impression that she represents the blind sex-instinct that is working against him.

The problem is fundamentally the same as in Shaw's earlier plays, though on a rather different plane, wayward romance as against sturdy reality. Tanner, with his intelligence untouched by life, represents a sort of intellectual romanticism, while Ann represents another sort of reality in her determination to force him into at least one practical measure, getting married. This situation is made clear in the final scene. The engagement has been announced, and Tanner makes a long mocking speech in which he begins by stating that neither he nor Ann is happy, but that they have sold their freedom and happiness for a home and family. One of the ladies cries out in agitation that he is a brute, but Ann looks up at him with loving pride and strokes his hand, "Never mind her, dear, go on talking." This is an exposure of false sentiment as thorough as any in Shaw's dramas.

According to Shaw's own statement, the significance of **Man and Superman** lies in its philosophic content, and the third act is meant to be "a revelation of the modern religion of evolution."

It is suggested that Shaw developed the theories of Nietzsche and Darwin independently, and that he anticipated the pragmatism of James, as well as Bergson's doctrine of *l'élan vital.*

At first glance Shaw's philosophy appears to be a hotchpotch of all the ingredients of philosophical thought at the turn of the century. The most important result of this new approach to philosophy by Shaw is that it modified, if it did not entirely bring to an end, his terrifying rationalism. Both in his belief in the Life Force, and in his expectation of a Superman to come, he has developed a kind of mysticism which remains mystic even though it is based in scientific materialism. What matters in development is not the conscious will guided by reason; it is a blind force, the Life Force—Shaw even calls it stupid—which drives us on our way against our wills in order to create a Superman who will be as much an advance on man as we are above the apes. Everything which Shaw has hitherto condemned, romanticism, heroism, religious ecstasy and sexual passions—all these are now tools in the hand of the Life Force. Tanner would have left nothing more behind him than the Revolutionist's Handbook if the mystic Life Force had not lured him, against all the dictates of reason, to marry Ann in order to breed Superman. (pp. 272-74)

> *Martin Lamm, "George Bernard Shaw," in his* Modern Drama, *translated by Karin Elliott, 1953. Reprint by Norwood Editions, 1976, pp. 251-84.*

ALICK WEST (essay date 1950)

[*In the following excerpt, West charts the development of Shaw's socialist thought by examining changes in his approach to implicit and explicit socialist ideas in the novel* An Unsocial Socialist *and the play* Man and Superman, *written sixteen years later.*]

A comparison of **Man and Superman** (leaving aside for the moment "The Revolutionist's Handbook," which is not an integral part of the play) with **An Unsocial Socialist** shows the change in Shaw's [socialist] outlook during the intervening twenty years.

The attack on capitalism has been dropped. Tanner's speeches and the dramatic action only bring the charge that respectable society frustrates the sexual instinct by an obsolete moral code, and that the romantic sentimentality which hides the instinct is a lie.

But the more forceful and inspiring Tanner's eloquence on this subject, the more comic the effect it serves to prepare.

For example, Octavius's supposedly unmarried sister Violet is discovered to be going to have a child. Tanner says to Violet, thereby scandalizing (like the Devil's Disciple) the assembled family:

> . . . I know, and the whole world really knows, though it dare not say so, that you were right to follow your instinct.

But Violet is not going to have an illegitimate child. Flushing with indignation at being accused of sharing Tanner's "abominable opinions," she announces that she is married. Tanner is "in ruins."

His championship of the freedom of love offers a similarly comic defeat in the fourth act. A young American, Hector Malone, proclaims that he will woo Violet whether she is married or not. Tanner comes up to him with flashing eyes:

> "Well said, Malone! You also see that mere marriage laws are not morality!"

The next moment, Hector is discovered to be Violet's husband. Tanner "smites his brow and collapses."

And when Tanner, "working himself up into a sociological rage," makes a page-long speech of protest against the "vile abjection of youth to age," Ann, who has been watching him "with quiet curiosity," observes:

> I suppose you will go in seriously for politics some day, Jack.
>
> TANNER. (*Heavily let down*) Eh? What? Wh—?

The rebel being let down is the great joke of the comedy. Nobody takes him seriously, and they become more and more friendly as his surrender to Ann becomes more and more imminent; even Ramsden, that die-hard of the progressive Radicalism of the Dialectical Society, beams upon him benevolently.

The attack on capitalism has been dropped; so has socialism. There is a "poetic" socialist—Octavius, the bachelor darling of his landladies, but he remains dumb. Tanner neither is, nor professes himself, a socialist. True, he puts after his name the letters M.I.R.C., Member of the Idle Rich Class, and to Mendoza's dignified announcement, "I am a brigand: I live by robbing the rich," Tanner promptly replies, "I am a gentleman: I live by robbing the poor." But the fact does not disturb him, and the admission of it is not more than an amusing originality.

There is, however, in the play a caricature of socialism—Mendoza and his band of tramps and able-bodied paupers. In the stage directions they are portrayed as the counterpart to the middle-class artist, and as entitled to the same allowance as he for refusing to work against the grain. . . . What we are invited then to enjoy is a stupid, tasteless parody of the controversies in the socialist movement of the '80's, and of Marxism, in this style:

> MENDOZA. . . . Well, what is our business here in the Sierra Nevada, chosen by the Moors as the fairest spot in Spain? Is it to discuss abstruse questions of political economy? No: it is to hold up motor cars and secure a more equitable distribution of wealth.
>
> THE SULKY SOCIAL-DEMOCRAT. All made by labor, mind you.
>
> MENDOZA. (*Urbanely*) Undoubtedly.

And to complete the ridicule, this gang of social-democrats, one anarchist, and a majority who are "neither Anarchists nor Socialists, but gentlemen and Christians," is in reality a commercial syndicate, whose shares are quoted on the Stock Exchange and are bought up by an American billionaire, Hector Malone's father.

The other great change, as compared with **An Unsocial Socialist,** is in the hero's attitude to love.

In the novel, it will be remembered, the hero kept himself aloof from love by marrying off the woman who loved him, Gertrude Erskine, to Octavius's forerunner, the romantic poet; his own marriage was a means of wounding Gertrude's love and of displaying his individualistic superiority to the common feelings about marriage. Something of the hero's fear of love still remains: in the Dream of Don Juan in Hell, the ghost of Tanner who expounds the philosophy of the Life Force was in his earthly existence not married to Ann; she had again been married to the romantic, the Statue, who is Octavius's counterpart. In this way, Shaw is able to avoid the discussion of what Tanner's surrender to Ann means in terms of his philosophy: the Tanner who philosophizes in Hell did not marry on earth; the Tanner who marries on earth does not philosophize about it, because he had no intention of getting married until he is caught, and then the play stops. Shaw thus retains, in the figure of the unmarried Don Juan in Hell, the pleasure in his individualism and that early image of himself in his novels as untouched by emotion, while through the surrender of Tanner to the Life Force he satisfies his desire to yield to that "passion in us of which,'' as he said in *The Sanity of Art,* ''we can give no rational account whatever.''

These two changes, in regard to capitalism and love, are one. Shaw had by this time come to interpret society in terms of love, and love in terms of society. The same Godhead is at work everywhere: the woman seeking the father for her child, Humanity advancing from the age of reason to the age of the will, are driven by the same creative force. Society does not advance through the class struggle, but by the working of an inner power active among all classes, in every individual (at least, in theory). This urge it is that changes society and develops man; whether the individual opens his mind to it matters more than his views about capitalism or socialism. It matters more to him and more to society; for Humanity only discovers its purpose, and he only discovers his own, by his making himself the instrument of the will; and man unites himself with the will, not through sterile discussion on social democracy or anarchism, but through woman, and woman through man.

The subject of the play is not the actual relations between a man and a woman, but the abstract theme that the individual must identify himself with the metaphysical will embodied in woman. Ann is not a living woman, like Gertrude Erskine in *An Unsocial Socialist;* she is Woman. And that is the reason why Shaw's image can give himself to her. She has become a symbol of the principle which Shaw now assumes to be the creative power working in society, the consciousness of the actual character of capitalist society having been suppressed.

At the same time, just as Brassbound is sent off on some mysterious piratical voyage in order to maintain the fiction that he is still a rebel, Shaw maintains his individualism through the figure of the unmarried Don Juan in Hell, and through the fact that though the Life Force is theoretically at work in everybody, yet it spurns the Ramsdens, the poetic socialists, the tramps, and even the New Man, Straker, and chooses as its vehicles only Tanner and Ann; and Tanner alone knows himself to be its vehicle.

Without his will and against his purpose, Shaw's Life Force becomes part of something greater than itself: the attack on socialism and materialism. Among the ''masters of reality'' in Heaven (Nietzsche being the latest arrival) there are no socialists. The Life Force is served by the philosopher's brain, but not by the ploughman's. The Life Force says:

> I want to know myself and my destination, and
> choose my path; so I have made a special brain—
> to grasp this knowledge for me as the hus-
> bandman's hand grasps the plough for me.

The husbandman is only a hand, and the hand has nothing to do with the brain; and therefore according to this democratic philosophy the ploughman has no part in humanity's choosing of its path. (pp. 97-101)

Much of Shaw's comedy, as he himself has said, uses the oldest stock themes of comedy.... (p. 124)

There is a philosophy in the comedy which contradicts the plays' more explicit philosophy. Dramatically, Tanner's marriage to Ann is convincing, not because he is in the grip of the Life Force (which, without the scene in Hell, means not much more to the spectator, if he derives his knowledge only from the play, than it does to Ann, who says that it sounds like the Life Guards), but because he is a comic figure. He is the rebel who thinks himself a rebel, but is not; the clever man who understands nothing; and the more he works himself up,

the more he misfires. With pleased anticipation, the audience watch the woman stalk her prey, knowing in advance that the spider, the bee, the marked down victim may career all across Europe in his thousand-pound car, but he will not escape. In his final speech, Tanner may proclaim the cosmic purpose of his marriage and his bold determination to be married in a registry office and sell all the wedding presents to pay for the distribution of ''The Revolutionist's Handbook''; but he is let down once more.

> ANN. (*Looking at him with fond pride and ca-
> ressing his arm*) . . . Go on talking.
>
> TANNER. Talking!
>
> *Universal laughter.*

The dramatic action makes Tanner and his Life Force equally comic.

But it also makes *The Revolutionist's Handbook* comic, as well as the Life Force; and when one remembers what was in *The Revolutionist's Handbook,* the laughter turns sour. For it serves the purpose . . . of slurring over the class issue in the plays. . . . Consequently, there is a certain falseness in the ''good fellowship'' which Shaw said, in the introduction to his *Dramatic Opinions and Essays,* it was the function of comedy to create. His comedy also must serve his Fabianism; and therefore Shaw will not give full freedom to his comic vision, because he will not fully trust in the people. Just as the plays are haunted by voices which never speak out, so the popular comedy . . . never finds a voice or a character to say all that it means. What it does mean, is the opposite of that mysticism that places the energy of life outside people themselves; for the comedy springs entirely from the relations and the actions of the people themselves—both on the stage and in the audience, since the awakened pleasure of the audience contributes its momentum to the action. But Shaw, still holding to his Fabianism, suddenly becomes serious, and tells himself that power is not in the people, but in the individual and in the mystic principle by which the individual flatters himself he is possessed, in the realist and his Platonic-Bismarckian reality. (pp. 124-25)

> *Alick West, in his* George Bernard Shaw: ''A Good
> Man Fallen among Fabians,'' *International Publish-
> ers, 1950, 172 p.*

LOUIS KRONENBERGER   (essay date 1952)

[*A drama critic for* Time *from 1938 to 1961, Kronenberger was a distinguished historian, literary critic, and author highly regarded for his expertise in eighteenth-century English history and literature. In an assessment of Kronenberger's critical ability, Jacob Korg states: "He interprets, compares, and analyzes vigorously in a pleasingly epigrammatic style, often going to the essence of a matter in a phrase." A prolific and versatile writer, he also wrote plays and novels and edited anthologies of the works of others. In the following excerpt, Kronenberger discusses the importance of the third act hell scene to* Man and Superman, *comparing this scene with a Shavian preface, calling it ''dialog merely'' but finding it adds a sustained brilliance to what would otherwise be merely a traditional stage comedy.*]

Man and Superman is, of course, one of Shaw's major plays, though it perhaps achieves that rank from being, not one play, but two. Certainly without the long third-act dialogue in Hell, *Man and Superman*—for all that it dramatizes the best known of Shaw's theories—would diminish into one of his more tractable and traditional comedies. With the Hell scene, it expands into one of the most brilliant and Shavian of them.

Yet to speak of **Man and Superman** as two plays is not quite happy, either. The whole thing is more like a pleasant three-course comedy dinner, with an interruption—between meat course and dessert—in the form of a long dazzling dialectical floor show. The scene in Hell tremendously sharpens and complicates and enriches the rest of the story, but it is a dialogue merely, far more akin to several of Shaw's own prefaces than to *any* man's third act, and most akin of all to something like Diderot's equally brilliant dialogue, *Rameau's Nephew*. So that one is not merely metaphorical in treating Act III of **Man and Superman** as interpolated fireworks and Acts I, II and IV as ordinary comedy fare. The two things are related without being, really, interdependent: it is no offense against art to offer the play without the Hell scene, and it is all in all in the interests of art to offer the Hell scene without the play.

In any case Shaw deals here, in one of the most famous of his comedies, with one of the most famous of all theater courtships—a courtship that owes its fame to the fact that the woman is shown to do the courting. This has quite as much value as sheer entertainment as it could ever have as sexual biology; and the spectacle of demure Ann Whitefield plotting with all her strength to nab hardheaded, unconventional John Tanner is amusing enough, and has possibilities enough, simply as farce. She professes to be the most daughterly of girls, to want only to do what would please her dead father, were he alive. Actually she has seen to it that her father's will should have designated John Tanner one of her guardians—as the most practicable way of eventually making him her husband. Beyond that she tells the most barefaced lies, she goes in for the most flagrant hypocrisies—with her mother, with her guardian, with the man she *doesn't* want quite as much as with the man she does. And John recognizes the lies, and upbraids her. And sees through the hypocrisies, and denounces her. And, thanks to his chauffeur, perceives that she is pursuing him—and runs away from her. But she overtakes him in his flight, and he is once again face to face with her. And her sexual lure overwhelms not only him, but even all that he knows about her, and he marries her.

That is the story—which is to say, that is how any ordinarily competent light-comedy ironist would have viewed the situation, positing that no man is smart or strong-willed enough to escape a really determined woman whom he happens to find sexually attractive. And though Shaw has much to say on other subjects in **Man and Superman,** on *this* subject he hasn't, in the end, much more to say than the ordinary competent writer of light comedy. Shaw, to be sure, brings in the Life Force; and Shaw ultimately identifies the Life Force with humanity's upward striving rather than its intersexual strife. But in **Man and Superman** (the three-act play) Shaw's Life Force seems little more than what the old poets would have termed Nature, or at most the desire to carry on and improve the race. The Life Force is here, at least, something that can swamp the reason and defeat the will, something that can even rattle Shaw, and convert so great a champion of rationality to a kind of mysticism.

Philosophically, we may allow that Shaw's Life Force—if only because it *is* so instinctive a force, or metaphysical a process—might, for argument's sake, exist. But theatrically, in the case of **Man and Superman,** Shaw's Life Force, rather more than it is Bergson's *élan vital* or Shakespeare's plain nature or your mating instinct or my desire to carry on and improve the race—

theatrically, Shaw's Life Force here seems more than half our old friend, the god from the machine. It requires the Life Force at its most compelling to get Tanner to marry Ann. For the facts simply don't permit us to regard Tanner as the mere male who is no match for the scheming female. The whole basis of that theory is that the male isn't on to the female, or at least to *all* of her, that he interprets her aggressiveness as solicitude, that he supposes the ideas she plants in him to have grown there of themselves. Or he knows the worst about women, but finds his own woman an exception; or he is portrayed as an idealist, or an idiot, or ripe for plucking, or catchable on the rebound. Tanner, however, is not only in the general sense a very emancipated and extremely unsentimental man; he also knows exactly what Ann is up to: how deviously she conspires, how ruthlessly she pursues. He has every reason to dislike and distrust her, and Shaw—to make his point—has to make Ann somebody we dislike and distrust as well. Nor is Tanner presented as head over heels in love with the girl and powerless to resist her. For argument's sake, one may concede that she attracts him more than he will allow. But that is still not enough of an argument: the Life Force simply overpowers Tanner so that Shaw can make his point and have his joke, as some god from the machine appears in a more usual kind of play so that the author can round off his plot. The psychology behind Tanner would be more convincing if we treated him as ruefully resigned to marrying the determined Ann rather than unable to resist her; if he, quite as much as the audience, relished the irony of his situation; if, tied up with this transcendental mating instinct there were just a touch of a martyr complex.

Fortunately the Ann-Tanner relationship is not the only one that counts in **Man and Superman.** There are, in terms of subplot, Violet's marriage to Malone, and in terms of byplay, Tanner's relations with Straker. The matter of Violet Robinson, who we are led to believe is quite brazenly about to become a mother without having become a wife, is in Shaw's best prankish manner; for after milking the situation for all it is worth, and having all kinds of people react in all kinds of ways, Shaw lets Violet indignantly reveal that, of course, she's married. As for Tanner's relationship with Straker, though it seems more traditional than the joke about Violet seems pat, actually it has a good deal about it that is—or that once was—new. And what is new about the relationship is what is new about Straker, who is not just the resourceful, impertinent servant found in comedy of every age and nation, but the servant who has become educated and intellectually enlightened. A chauffeur or mechanic today, Straker will be an engineer or inventor tomorrow. In caste terms, he is of course still a cockney, and in cultural terms, which is more significant, he is still an outsider—for education does not quite mean culture, any more than birth means breeding. But that is by the way: the point is that Straker can not only, like a dozen Figaros, tell his master that Ann is set to have him; like no Figaro, when Tanner ascribes a quotation to Voltaire, he can say, oh no, it's from Beaumarchais. Intellectually Straker can talk Tanner's language, even though he still lacks his enunciation.

All this is good enough Shavian philosophy and Shavian fooling, but it operates at a different level, and for that matter in a literally quite different world, from the third-act scene in Hell. The Hell scene is only technically a part of the play. Indeed, it can only very doubtfully be regarded as playwriting; but that is of no importance, for nowhere in English during the twentieth century has there been a more dazzlingly sustained discussion of ideas in dialogue form. The Hell scene is a great blaze of fireworks and something more than fireworks,

The climactic final scene of Man and Superman *from a performance at the Criterion Theatre, 1911.*
BBC Hulton Picture Library/The Bettmann Archive.

even if of something less than clear intellectual light. The scene, which is a dream scene, contains four characters: Don Juan Tenorio, not only Mozart's and Molière's and Shadwell's and history's and legend's libertine, but John Tanner's ancestor; Doña Ana, whose descendant or double is Ann Whitefield; Doña Ana's father, the Commendatore whom Don Juan slew; and the Devil. None of these people is at all as we last met him elsewhere, nor is Hell or Heaven at all like what others have painted them. The Devil is not much of a surprise: as in his earthly appearances he is extremely eager to tempt, so in his own country he is exceedingly eager to please. He is rather like the owner of a resort hotel trying to dangle before the better type of guest the very best type of entertainment. He is much helped by the fact that, though Heaven has all the prestige of a Newport, it displays all the dullness of Old Point Comfort. Hell is indeed a home for the escapists, the pleasure-seekers, the reality-shunners, for those whose lives, conceived in frivolousness, have on earth gone unfulfilled. It is an ideal place for living an animal existence on a non-physical basis: where, that is to say, one can always be as young and look as young and act as young as one chooses, unmenaced by the ravages of Time. Shaw's Hell is a sort of vulgar idea of Heaven. There has been a great deal of switching over from the real Heaven; Ana's statue father, the Commendatore, a military man of wordly tastes and conservative values, has just come down from Heaven, leaving a forwarding address in Hell.

Ana, perhaps the most famous of the ladies whom Juan betrayed, has recently died and is incensed to find that she has been relegated to Hell. She is incensed even more to find that her father has turned his back on Heaven; indeed she is appalled in a great number of ways—as a wronged woman sent to the afterworld for wrongdoers; as a religious woman abandoned to the Devil; as a wifely and motherly woman thrust into a pit of courtesans and strumpets. She insists that Heaven be her reward, whether or not it turn out rewarding. Better to yawn in Heaven than whoop things up in Hell: though Doña Ana is quite sure that Heaven must be very agreeable.

It is Shaw's Don Juan who is most purely, most drastically Shavian. First of all, his reputation as a heartless rake and libertine is an ill-founded one: he kept running away from women because he found them getting possessive, not because, having possessed them, he found them getting dull. He ran away out of fear and in self-defense, exactly as John Tanner ran away from Ann Whitefield. He accordingly renounced the flesh, and he means now to reject the Devil. He believes in the brain, which alone distinguishes man from the brute, and by means of which man may, in time, evolve the superman. The Devil attempts to answer him:

> And is Man any the less destroying himself for all this boasted brain of his? Have you walked up and down upon the earth lately? I have; and I have examined Man's wonderful inventions. And I tell you that in the arts of life Man invents nothing; but in the arts of death he outdoes Nature herself, and produces by chemistry and machinery all the slaughter of plague, pestilence, and famine. The peasant I tempt today eats and drinks what was eaten and drunk by the peasants of ten thousand years ago. . . . But when he goes out to slay, he carries a marvel of mechanism that lets loose at the touch of his finger all the hidden molecular energies, and

leaves the javelin, the arrow, the blowpipe of his fathers far behind. In the arts of peace Man is a bungler. . . . I know his clumsy typewriters and bungling locomotives and tedious bicycles: they are toys compared to the Maxim gun, the submarine torpedo boat. . . . Man measures his strength by his destructiveness.

Don Juan has his answer for this:

Your weak side, my diabolic friend, is that you have always been a gull: you take Man at his own valuation. Nothing would flatter him more than your opinion of him. He loves to think of himself as bold and bad. . . . Call him tyrant, murderer, pirate, bully; and he will adore you. . . . Call him liar and thief; and he will only take an action against you for libel. But call him coward; and he will go mad with rage: he will face death to outface that stinging truth.

Don Juan is going to Heaven—the Exchange Plan works both ways—precisely because it is not for those who are forever seeking happiness, but because it is for those who will work and strive, who will face and become the masters of reality. Shaw's Heaven is a Puritan's Heaven where the Life Force can operate with benign efficiency (and in the Hell scene the Life Force approximates a kind of spiral movement upward, during which man sheds everything physical except his wings). It guides the one kind of man who, Don Juan says, "has ever been happy, has ever been universally respected"—the philosophic man. For Woman, Juan confesses, there was much to be said: through her he obtained not only amorous but much esthetic pleasure. What spoiled it all was that whenever he took happy leave of women, they murmured "When will you come again?" Since that meant falling into their clutches, it constituted the signal for running away, and he was asked the question so often, and ran away so often, that he became famous for running away—or, as Doña Ana puts it, infamous. The wrangling between Juan and Ana has its share of good things, as when Juan says to her: "I say nothing against your chastity, Señora, since it took the form of a husband and twelve children. What more could you have done had you been the most abandoned of women?"—and she answers, "I could have had twelve husbands and no children."

There is a good deal of point to the revision of ideas and reversal of values that go not only with Shaw's conception of Don Juan, but equally with Don Juan's conception of Hell and Heaven. Juan's Heaven is rather the headquarters of progress than the seat of perfection; a celestial workshop and meeting hall rather than a final abode of the blest. And the demonstration—or at any rate the dialectics—is brilliant. If Juan himself is more than a little windy, the general effect—as language, as wit, as paradox, as repartee, as intellectual gymnastics—is extraordinary. If there is a weakness, it is that Juan and Juan's Heaven and Hell can only be startlingly unorthodox at the cost of being uncommonly improbable. In turning accepted ideas inside out, the problem is always to provide something that seems challenging without seeming false. Sir Osbert Sitwell has recently told the story of Cinderella, in which Cinderella comes off a prig with a martyr fixation, whose stepsisters talk themselves blue in the face trying to get her to come out of the scullery. That idea is both amusing and conceivable, and so is Shaw's that Don Juan did not abandon women from boredom, but ran away from them out of fear. But even the fact that he ran away from so many of them does not acquit him of first approaching

them out of sexual desire: he may not have been the profligate of legend, but even less does he seem a Puritan like Shaw. Almost the reverse psychology would be sounder, I think: had Juan really been a libertine leading an altogether self-indulgent life of the flesh, he might so much have had his fill of sex on earth as to seek something almost immoderately spiritual in Heaven. And if the answer is that in that case he would have been a sinner and ineligible for Heaven, the counter-reply is that anyone is eligible for Shaw's Heaven—the point being that almost no one is eager for it. In strict logic, Heaven for Juan would be—among other things, at least—a place where beautiful and obliging ladies merely said "*Au revoir*" instead of "When will you come again?"

As for Heaven and Hell, though they need not be conventional abodes of bliss and suffering, it is hard to accept them on the terms offered by Shaw. I mean this less as a matter of morality than as a matter of taste. Shaw's Hell, though a place of pleasure rather than pain, remains morally sound because its inhabitants are shown to be second-rate—shoddy, spineless, pleasure-seeking. All the same, one is not much tempted by the spectacle of Shaw's Heaven, and for that matter, one is not much convinced. One could easily accept it as high-thinking and plain-living viewed as an end in itself—for the severity of that idea possesses real moral grandeur. But Juan's Heaven has a real odor of uplift and the social worker about it, a sense, in fact, of preparation for a still higher life to come. There aren't many things to insist on as basic requirements for Heaven, but surely one of them is that it should be more than a mere way station, a mere rung on a ladder. And the real reason for its not being is that Shaw's Life Force remains valid only as long as it remains evolutionary, as it continues to strive and progress; once it achieves its goal, not only has it no further reason to exist, but the Superman it has brought into existence would seem peculiarly lacking in personal—or even identifiable—qualities. Shaw's Superman would be at most a vibration in a void.

The brilliance of the Hell scene is thus a trifle self-defeating: the whole thing is a kind of triumph of Shaw over sense, and *any* triumph over sense must smack partly of failure. On a serious plane, Shaw is at once too doctrinaire about the Life Force and too vague about what it culminates in, just as when he isn't making sport of Heaven he is rather too solemn about it. But perhaps the main trouble with his brilliance here is that it is progressively at the expense of each of his characters and of all of their ideas: they kill one another off, they cancel one another out—which makes for very good comedy, but quite doubtful "constructive" thinking. One can only end as one began, by saying that the Hell scene is a very grand-scale and long-drawn-out display of fireworks. This whole dazzling side is, indeed, its magnificent merit; its doctrinaire side is its rather considerable weakness. Don Juan is jockeyed into being a mouthpiece for Shaw just as John Tanner is jockeyed into being a mate for Ann; they have no choice; the Life Force has about it more than a touch of *force majeure;* the superman, at several removes from Nietzsche's *Übermensch*, bears the stamp of Shaw himself. But the scene's defects of logic, its perversities of argument, can at worst only shrivel it to a mere triumph of wit. (pp. 239-47)

Louis Kronenberger, "Shaw," in his The Thread of Laughter: Chapters on English Stage Comedy from Jonson to Maugham, *Alfred A. Knopf, 1952, pp. 227-78.*

ARCHIBALD HENDERSON (essay date 1956)

[*Henderson was a noted American mathematician, literary biographer, critic, essayist, and historian who became known as the foremost American expert on the life and works of Bernard Shaw. He and Shaw met several times and corresponded extensively. Henderson's studies and biographies of Shaw include* George Bernard Shaw: His Life and Works (1911) *and* George Bernard Shaw: Man of the Century (1956). *In the following excerpt, Henderson contends that* Man and Superman *marked a new phase in Shaw's career as a writer and thinker in that he used the work to develop a conscious philosophy, that of Creative Evolution. Henderson finds, though, that the play is most often interpreted as social comedy because the "philosophical interlude" of the third act is rarely presented on the stage.*]

With **Man and Superman,** Shaw enters upon a new phase as writer and thinker. Up to this time, none of his plays reflects any conscious philosophy. The new play, with the subtitle *A Comedy and a Philosophy,* dramatizes the view of Creative Evolution reached by Shaw and Bergson after neo-Darwinism had been purged out of it by Butler. A brief study of this book shows that the comedy actually comprises only acts one, two and four; and is played as such. Act three, *Don Juan in Hell,* is a sort of philosophical interlude which is not at all necessary to the full comprehension of the society comedy, although it throws a flood of light upon Shaw's neo-Vitalist diathesis. The essence of his philosophy as embodied in this third act, together with "The Revolutionist's Handbook," a collection of aphorisms, is the most profound and impressive of any of his dramatic writings of the same compass. It is literature, philosophy and religion. Indeed, it is the first chapter in that book of modern religion which Shaw elaborated and completed in **Back to Methuselah.**

The book is dedicated to his friend and former colleague on the *Star,* then drama critic of the *Times,* the classical student and French scholar, Arthur Bingham Walkley. He was quite incapable of understanding Shaw in his higher philosophical flights and was constantly taking him to task, in a vein of witty, amusing banter, for his explanatory habit, his predilection for dialectic, and his disregard of the "rules of the game." Yet he always delighted in Shaw's plays and dealt with them at length, apparently never taking them seriously as drama but always recognizing Shaw as a "man who can give us a refined intellectual pleasure, or a pleasure of moral nature or of social sympathy, or else a pleasure which arises from being given an unexpected or wider outlook upon life." (p. 578)

Man and Superman is Shaw's fulfillment of Walkley's mischievous request of the Irish Puritan to write a Don Juan play. Shaw had repeatedly railed against plays which dealt with sex, but were devoid of sexual interest—"senseless evasions" of the real sex problem. Walkley's challenge was a poser; for Shaw was the avowed foe of romance with a profound distaste for the "mephitic atmosphere" of love and sex. The theme of Don Juan as literature had served the purposes of Molière, Mozart and Byron; and Goethe, with Don Juan's spiritual cousin, Faust, was almost a century out of date. There remained only to present Don Juan in the philosophic sense, imbued with all the advanced ideas of the age, "concerned for the future of the race instead of for the freedom of his own instincts." From this point on, in his career, Shaw appears as a race-futurist, a philosopher definitely engaged, in a manner cognate with that of his fellow Fabian and meliorist, H. G. Wells, with social and economic previsions and anticipations of a better race and a higher life. In **Man and Superman** Shaw for the first time reveals himself in prophetic, Messianic character.

At the time of the play's appearance, it was generally regarded as audaciously novel and original, for reversing the conventional idea expressed in the phrase: "Man is the hunter, woman the game." Yet it had often been employed as an effective theme in drama and fiction, from Shakespeare and Beaumont and Fletcher to Henry James and Anne Douglas Sedgwick. In the novels **Love Among the Artists** and **An Unsocial Socialist,** in the plays **Widowers' Houses** and **The Philanderer,** Shaw had already made effective use of the idea. "At no time," says Leonard Charteris [in **The Philanderer**], "have I taken the initiative and pursued women with my advances as women have persecuted me." In **Man and Superman,** Shaw denominates the driving power behind or of the universe—God, evolution, Vital Urge—the Life Force (after Bergson's *élan vital*). In woman he discerns the life force incarnate, the prime vital agency in the fulfillment of Nature's purposes and laws. He finds a superb motive for comedy in the doctrine that "woman is the pursuer and contriver, man the pursued and disposed of."

The society comedy was a mad success in the theater, with almost unbroken outbursts of merriment from the audience throughout. The epigrams and aphorisms, sallies and jests, hurtle at you like a continuous flight of arrows. Ann Whitefield, viewed by Shaw as Everywoman, makes of the comedy a modern "morality." Shaw has delineated her in strokes so bold as almost to seem crude. Ann is undoubtedly "an unscrupulous user of her personal fascination to make men give her what she wants"; but her methods are more virile than feline. The pursuit is not conducted with those obscure allurements and refined subtleties peculiar to woman; it is chiefly manifested through the comical loquacity of the pursued and fleeing man. Inability to portray sexual passion convincingly is a limitation of Shaw's art: he is no flesh painter. Yet we must not forget that, in an allegory, universal attributes require broad and sweeping treatment. Shaw himself attributes the play's popularity to its complete preoccupation with sex, and describes it as "the only play on the subject of sex ever written." (pp. 579-80)

The Dream in Hell—Act III—was largely ignored by the general public because it was almost always omitted in the stage production. The impact of Shaw's philosophy on the public was so slight as to be negligible; and there was no general understanding of his religion, which is briefly but clearly sketched in the Dream in Hell, until the appearance of **Back to Methuselah** eighteen years later.

In search for a religion, free from the Oriental legends and superstitions which inform the Christian religion, Shaw hit upon the idea which has influenced and possessed many modern thinkers: an imperfect God. He was driven to this belief by the effort to explain the problem of sin and suffering, unexplainable under Christianity. He is a confirmed mystic, rejecting entirely the notion of a personal God, but discerning a great force driving the universe. This Life Force drives steadily but experimentally towards the achievement of greater and greater power over circumstances and completer and completer intelligence; and to this end it creates organs of power and intelligence of which Man is only the last and most highly evolved in the long series of experiments which began with the amoeba and has progressed as far as Einstein. The last, be it noted, *as far:* Shaw has repeatedly warned us that we shall be scrapped for some new attempt if we persist in our present inadequacy. Thus the Life Force is God in the act of creating Himself; and we, as His instruments and helpers, can take heart and courage from this great opportunity and responsibility. It is humiliating, of course, to look in the glass, remember what you did last week, and realize that God has been able to produce nothing better! The thrust of the Life Force is onward and upward, striving ever to create higher and better forms. The crux of Shaw's philosophy is expressed in these words of Don Juan: "I tell you that as long as I can conceive something better than myself I cannot be easy unless I am striving to bring it into existence or clearing the way for it. This is the law of my life. That is the working within me of Life's incessant aspiration to higher organization, wider, deeper, intenser self-consciousness, and clearer self-understanding." Evolution, or the Life Force, may very well not stop at Man: it may go on to the Superman, the Super-Superman, the Angel, the Archangel, and finally omnipotent God. (pp. 580-81)

> *Archibald Henderson, in his* George Bernard Shaw: Man of the Century, *Appleton-Century-Crofts, Inc., 1956, 969 p.*

MORRIS FREEDMAN   (essay date 1967)

[*In the following excerpt, Freedman contends that the third act hell scene of* Man and Superman, *containing Shaw's assertion of the value and importance of truth, is integral to the play and not merely "an interlude" or "an appendage similar to a Shavian preface or sequel, stimulating but irrelevant."*]

One need hardly say that Shaw is a playwright of ideas, but the ideas gain their force precisely because they are embodied in the emotional and immediate. Consider *Man and Superman.* The play, except for the occasional outbursts about the Life Force and the references to one or another current issue, is really a straight enough Edwardian farce, legitimately classifiable in the company of Oscar Wilde's work. The scene in hell is rambling, discursive even for Shaw, highly abstract, and as high in genuine philosophic tone as the play is low in it. Are we to take the interlude as an appendage similar to a Shavian preface or sequel, stimulating but irrelevant, perhaps even to be dismissed as having no artistic justification? I think not. It is Don Juan, Jack Tanner's other incarnation, who carries the burden of the meaning of the hell scene.

We are asked to see Don Juan in his traditional image, a figure outside moral society, to be equated, one supposes, with such Shavian creations as Louis Dubedat, Dick Dudgeon, Caesar, Marchbanks, and Jack Tanner himself. All of the latter figures, however, are still mortal, on the way perhaps to the enlightenment of Don Juan, but in their various ways not nearly so complete, so perfect, as Don Juan. Only the man filled to brimming with realizing the mortal possibilities can know both the importance and unimportance of them. A Don Juan rejecting pleasure makes a more compelling case than an ascetic doing so. John Tanner has a long way to go to be Don Juan, for he is plainly identified as a man who is always putting words and ideas between himself and experience, sometimes indeed, as in the scene involving Violet's honor, simply baffled by the variety of possibilities in reality. For all that, it is Tanner who, Shaw indicates, will find his way to the height of Don Juan, for he does think, he does articulate, and presumably he can feel, he can be carried away by passion of a sort, as is plain from the scene in which Ann Whitefield finally pries him out of his thick shell of words. It is the thinking, feeling human being, then, who holds the future of the race, who can realize, as Don Juan says, that after all the pleasures are done with, when, indeed, it becomes pointless to pursue pleasures, as in

heaven, it is man's highest task which asserts itself, the need to use one's mind fully.

The devil and Don Juan do not disagree about man's worldly situation. Their opposition is to be found in the meaning of man's pettiness, foolishness, wickedness. The devil is sentimentally resigned about the possibility in man for improvement. He offers nothing but escape from horror. Don Juan relentlessly insists that the horror must be confronted and overcome, that overcoming evil in the world is a divine imperative. Man has a mind as well as a body and, while it may be difficult for mind to control or even understand body, it is the only way to salvation.

Shaw's heaven and hell, like the gulf between them, are parables for earthly states. Hell *is* a city much like Seville. Hell is also the mortal state of mind in which there are easy, loose, casual, self-indulgent pleasures, ideas, responses, with which one can smugly relax, lulled into a dangerous security, lulled into misconceiving such a state as heaven. "Heaven" is a hard place, offering no ready arrangements of things, insisting on an endless examination and reexamination of them, demanding an unflinching, unblinking viewing of truth, promising nothing but the reward of the effort itself, *yet all the time acknowledging the ultimate importance, the divinity, of man.*

Now, Don Juan's philosophy must be understood against the background of the play, with all its very human foolishness and brightness: life comes first and must come fully, but it must be succeeded by the thought, understanding, interpretation that comes after experience and with remoteness; on the other hand, the play must be understood as not final by any means in its handling of experience, for events, with thought, analysis, and time, will move toward the possibility of a Don Juan, who knows better than his partners in hell when to give up mortal urgings and accept the responsibility of immortality. Stripped of its topical allusions to evolution, the emancipation of women, the rise of the working class, etc., etc., *Man and Superman* seems to me Shaw's most triumphant assertion of the moral import of truth. (pp. 51-4)

> *Morris Freedman, "Shaw's Moral Seriousness," in his* The Moral Impulse: Modern Drama from Ibsen to the Present, *Southern Illinois University Press, 1967, pp. 45-62.*

BERNARD F. DUKORE   (essay date 1973)

[*In the following excerpt, Dukore examines the interrelationship between act three of* Man and Superman *and the rest of the play. Maintaining that the hell scene is not essential to a successful production of* Man and Superman, *and in fact can be performed on its own, the combination of the framing play and the hell scene result in an artistic whole that is greater than the individual parts.*]

In two of his plays Shaw expressly provided for the disengagement of [either the center of the play or the surrounding frame]—the third act from *Man and Superman,* the frame from *Fanny's First Play.* In one instance—*Caesar and Cleopatra*—he urged directors to cut the third act in order to save playing time, and in another—*The Apple Cart*—critics urged him to delete a scene from the play's center to preserve organic unity. Is there such unity . . . between the centerpieces and the frames that surround them?

Sanction for regarding the episode in the Sierras and the dream of Hell as detachable from *Man and Superman* comes from Shaw himself, who in his Preface calls the third act "totally extraneous.'' On numerous other occasions he reasserted this judgment and also indicated that a large chunk of the first act dialogue between Tanner and Ann is also detachable. Although most critics, following Shaw's suggestion, regard the play as bifurcated, they tend to be reluctant to leave it at that. To Louis Kronenberger, for instance, frame play and center play are ''not one play, but two.'' Then, in his very next paragraph, he adds:

> Yet to speak of *Man and Superman* as two plays is not quite happy, either. The whole thing is more like a pleasant three-course comedy dinner, with an interruption—between meat course and dessert—in the form of a long dazzling dialectical floor show. The scene in hell tremendously sharpens and complicates and enriches the rest of the story. . . . The two things are related without being, really, interdependent [see Kronenberger excerpt dated 1952].

Other critics reject the idea that the two ''plays'' are separable. . . . If the Hell scene is indeed crucial, however, why can it be—why has it been—(a) omitted in successful productions of the play, (b) successfully performed by itself? It seems to me that, of all commentators on this subject, St. John Ervine is most reasonable when he concludes that the third act can be detached but that the play is greater when performed in its entirety than when its parts are performed separately, for the shorter versions appear merely to be different plays on the same theme.

First, how are the two parts related? (pp. 166-67)

Though it contains such standard well-making ingredients as reversals, skillfully concealed and revealed secrets, and an intercepted letter, *Man and Superman* focuses on problems of character and conduct, self-knowledge, social assumptions and underpinnings, and so forth.

The play's two sections are related in part by parallel snatches of dialogue, for example: the romantic Statue and the romantic Octavius each states, with only a difference of tense, that at age eighty, one hair of the woman he loves will make him ''tremble more than the thickest gold tress from the most beautiful young head.'' Juan says of the married woman's neglect of such accomplishments as music that she ''throws away the bait when the bird is in the net,'' and Tanner even less chivalrously says of her decreasing care of her personal appearance that she ''[throws] away the bait the moment the trap snaps on the victim!''

Illusion and reality, the central images of the hell scene . . . , carry into the frame play. Ann tries to appear a dutiful daughter, but Jack knows the reality. It seems to Jack that Ann wants to marry Octavius, but the audience—and Straker too—know the reality. In the final scene Ann gives the illusion of having fainted, but Jack perceives the reality. When Ramsden at the end calls Jack a happy man, Jack explains that, whereas to a spectator he may appear to be happy, he as a participant knows the reality.

Also pertinent is Shaw's preparation for Ann's appearance in Tanner's dream. In the first act, Tanner associates her with Hell: He calls her ''Lady Mephistopheles,'' states she was ''diabolically clever'' and ''a devil of a child,'' and declares her to have ''a devilish charm.'' Does her appearance in *his* dream indicate his subconscious desire for her to catch him?

On the other hand, his departure for Heaven might signify his desire to escape her.

Especially important, to be sure, are the parallels between the characters of each section: Don Juan Tenorio and John Tanner, Ana and Ann, the Statue and Ramsden, the Devil and others. A member of the idle rich class, John Tanner condemns it and the society that supports it; a member of the idle world of Hell, Don Juan Tenorio condemns it. Both John and Juan denounce social indifference and conventional morality. Both applaud social conscience and philosophies subversive of received opinions and traditional conventions. Both renounce romantic love and art for the sake of art, flee women, embrace disinterested and unencumbered aspiration toward moral and social betterment.

Both Ann and Ana profess to be dutiful daughters obedient to their parents, both conform to the proprieties, and both are hypocrites. Each is an agent of the Life Force. ''I believe in the Life to Come,'' says Ana, who then ''[cries] to the universe,'' ''A father! a father for the Superman!'' The trap for Jack, affirms Ann, was laid ''from the beginning—from our childhood . . . by the Life Force.''

Octavius calls Ramsden ''the soul of honor,'' and the same description would serve for the Statue, who for honor's sake drew on his daughter's assailant and was killed. When Octavius proclaims that the man who seduced his sister will ''make reparation by marrying her . . . or he shall answer for it to me,'' Ramsden, statuelike, congratulates him and he calls the seducer what Ana's father might call Juan, ''a rascal . . . a libertine, a villain worse than a murderer.'' Both Ramsden and the Statue, observes McDowell, are pillars of respectability who have hypocritically pursued women.

Finally, there is the Devil, who parallels Mendoza. Each is an arch-romantic (Mendoza even refers to the subtitle of Dryden's *All for Love*, about Anthony and Cleopatra, when he says he counts ''the world well lost'' for his Louisa). Each has turned his back on the accepted society and has founded a rival establishment of which he is the leader. If the third act is detached from the rest of the play, however, the Sierra scene goes with it. No matter: parallels with the frame play also pertain. Octavius and Hector Malone, Jr., are both romantics, who enunciate ideals and attitudes congenial to the Shavian devil.

The foregoing suggests ways in which the Hell scene is related to the comedy surrounding it. What differences does its inclusion or omission make?

The Hell scene not only contains the play's philosophical substance, it sets forth its philosophical explanation as well. ''A Comedy and a Philosophy'' is Shaw's subtitle of *Man and Superman*. Generally speaking, the frame play is the comedy, the third act the philosophy. Although, to be sure, the philosophy underlies the action of the frame play, it is implicit only. The Hell scene—comic, though less comic than the frame play—makes the philosophy explicit. The Life Force is *mentioned* in the frame play; in the inner play, it is *explained*. And as Nethercot perceives, ''Without the third act the title has no meaning. It is not until the very end of Tanner's and Mendoza's mutual dream that the word Superman is mentioned; and it is used nowhere else in the play.''

Moreover, the Hell scene brings a different perspective and alternative solutions to the surrounding comedy, from which it differs in several key respects. The frame play is about love, which conquers. The inner play, despite the presence of Don

Juan, concerns not love but thought, which survives and surmounts the appeals of Hell, the home of romantic love. At the end of the frame play, John marries, thus subordinating his will to the woman's. In this respect, he resembles Hector Malone, Jr., his only counterpart in the play in regard to marriage, a man whose wife, like Ann, has a will more powerful than his own. At the end of the inner play, Juan escapes. Unlike John, he does not face a future as husband and possibly as member of Parliament (according to the Devil, whom Juan does not contradict on this occasion, a politician is "the catspaw of corrupt functionaries and the henchmen of ambitious humbugs"). Juan faces a future in Heaven.

In the frame play, John loses; in the inner play, Juan wins. Without the Hell scene, Tanner is merely a comic butt. . . . An object of satire, he is an ass to whom the bourgeois audience of Ramsdens can feel superior. With the Hell scene, and only with it, bourgeois audiences cannot feel superior to him. Without it, one wonders whether Tanner might become another Ramsden: an ineffectual, erstwhile advanced thinker already pompous and soon to become outmoded. Twentieth-century John Tanner represents a present that will become a past. Combined with his alter ego, the seventeenth-century Don Juan, he represents the future.

Put another way, the scene in Hell is a dream. Though a mutual dream of Tanner and Mendoza, it is—given the perspective of the entire play—essentially Tanner's, who dreams of himself as a success. In the frame play everyone disparages him; in the dream everyone makes much of him, even his chief opponent, the Devil. In the frame play he argues and is almost always demolished; in the dream he argues and always wins.

Jack loses his battle over the nicknames: "We're beaten—smashed—nonentitized." Reprimanded by Violet for having dared to suggest she holds his opinions, he apologizes, "(in ruins) I am utterly crushed." As if this were not sufficient, he says, "I shall know better in future than to take any woman's part." But he does not know better, for immediately—before anyone has a chance to say another word—he takes Ann's part: "We have all disgraced ourselves in your eyes, I am afraid, except Ann." Violet then replies that Ann knew the secret. In Act II, even after he catches Ann in the lie about Rhoda, and despite the fact that he knows she acts as she wishes while blaming a guardian or parent, Tanner believes her lie that her mother forced her to deceive Rhoda, and he launches into a diatribe against parental tyranny. Further, each time Tanner speechifies before Ann she demolishes him by ignoring the substance of his remarks. In Act I: "(placidly) I am so glad you understand politics, Jack: it will be most useful to you if you go into parliament (he collapses like a pricked bladder)." In Act II: "I suppose you will go in seriously for politics some day, Jack." He is "heavily let down" and after "collecting his scattered wits" she lets him down more heavily with "You talk so well." In the final act: "Go on talking." And in response to his exclamation, "Talking!" there is "universal laughter."

In the dream, all is different. There, Juan outargues everyone. Like Violet, Ana repudiates the immorality of his views on unwed mothers, but unlike John, Juan is not at all crushed. Calling virtue "the Trade Unionism of the married," he ridicules marriage as "the most licentious of human institutions," which is "the secret of its popularity." Whereas Ann Whitefield weasels out of arguments, Doña Ana is unable to do so. Ana defends chastity; Juan counters that her chastity took the form of a husband and a dozen children. That, she claims, is better than twelve husbands and no children; he counters that twelve children by twelve different husbands might have been better still. Juan defeats even the Devil at argument. The Devil mocks Juan's words—as Ann does Jack's—as "mere talk." Though Jack does not reply, Juan does, for he knows that his talk is mere rhetoric because moralistic concepts are "words which I or anyone else can turn inside out like a glove" and then proceeds to show his superiority to the Devil's "moralistic figments."

In Heaven, as Juan sees it, one faces things as they are. John does not. If he did, he would not misinterpret Ann's designs. If he did, he would not take at face value the apparent unconventionality of Violet, who he should realize is a conventional girl. If he did, he would hardly regard as an artist the sentimentalist Octavius, who conforms to none of Tanner's criteria for the artist. (pp. 167-71)

Quite simply, John is less advanced and more superficial than Juan. John talks of the birth of moral passion and his discovery of purpose in life. When Juan discusses the same subjects, he relates them to abstract principles and forces that govern life. John speaks out in favor of emancipation; Juan sings the philosophic man. John refers to the Life Force; Juan explains it. To a woman, "man is only a means to the end of getting children and rearing them. . . . Sexually, Woman is Nature's contrivance for perpetuating its highest achievement. Sexually, Man is Woman's contrivance for fulfilling Nature's behest in the most economical way." As Juan continues, he describes the evolutionary process and explains how woman feeds man on illusions that sustain him as he does her will. Compare Tanner's brevity on the same subject: "It is a woman's business to get married as soon as possible, and a man's to keep unmarried as long as he can."

Don Juan represents an advance over Tanner, who himself represents an advance over Roebuck Ramsden, Hector Malone, Jr., and Octavius. Considering the options open to Tanner, he does well, though not astonishingly well. A "political pamphleteer," as Shaw calls him in his Preface, he is not for that reason to be mocked, for his politics are in advance of those of the other characters in the frame play. Still, he is a talker rather than a talker-and-doer. Don Juan sings "the philosophic man: he who seeks in contemplation to discover the inner will of the world, in invention to discover the means of fulfilling that will, and in action to do that will by the so-discovered means." John fulfills the first two criteria, but he does not fulfill the third, except insofar as his composition of "The Revolutionist's Handbook" may qualify as action. Although he writes—or wrote—about revolution, he has stopped there, and if Shaw's comedy is any indication, he lives merely as a clever social gadfly in high circles. "I shatter creeds," says Tanner, "and demolish idols." No such thing, at least as presented on stage: His attempted destruction is exclusively verbal and usually ineffectual. With Juan, however, Shaw makes John suggest something more, for Juan projects what someone who starts from John's level might become, or at the least what he might aspire to. With Don Juan, Shaw also suggests that John Tanner might be effective. Regarding the frame play exclusively, Shaw has avoided the Scylla of a simplistic thesis play with an obvious raisonneur. He has, however, fallen into the Charybdis of reassuring the very audience he wants to disturb. By making his hero a fool—the learned fool of comic tradition, in fact—Shaw enables his audience to feel superior to him. Thus, he permits them to refuse to take seriously what the fool says and therefore waters down the revolutionary aspects of the play. [The critic adds in a footnote that: Shaw's socialist critics strongly object to this play, which they regard primarily as a portrayal of the taming and defeat of a revolutionist. They even object to the Hell scene, for according to them a Shavian revolutionist can win only in dreamland.]

From the point of view of the frame play minus the inner play, John Tanner suffers. From the viewpoint of the center play without the frame, Doña Ana does. At the end of the Hell scene, it is unclear whether Ana actually joins Juan in Heaven. The inclusion of the frame play ends the ambiguity. Directly following Ana's cry, ''a father for the Superman!'', Shaw transports us to the Sierras, where the search party, led by Ann, captures Tanner. The first of the search party to enter is Ann herself; she ''makes straight for Tanner,'' who cries, ''Caught!'' . . . Here, the resolution is unambiguous: Ana— who as Ann becomes Tanner's fiancée in Act IV—finds a father for the Superman. It must be pointed out to the reader of the play (the viewer would need no reminder) that the same actor plays John and Juan, the same actress Ann and Ana. From the viewpoint of the audience, the same woman captures the same man.

In brief, the Hell scene can be played separately from the frame play, as it frequently has been performed. When the two are played together, however, the sum is greater than the mere addition of two parts. (pp. 171-73)

> *Bernard F. Dukore, in his* Bernard Shaw, Playwright: Aspects of Shavian Drama, *University of Missouri Press, 1973, 311 p.*

MAURICE VALENCY (essay date 1973)

[*Valency is an American translator, dramatist, and critic. In the following excerpt, he provides an extensive and insightful discussion of all three parts of* Man and Superman. *Unexcerpted portions of the essay treat extensively the philosophies and sociological theories that, it is generally assumed, Shaw drew upon in conceiving and writing* Man and Superman.]

The first part of Shaw's career as a dramatist was a period of unbelievably intense activity. In the course of six years, in the intervals between his many chores—his journalistic duties, his work at the Fabian office, his research at the British Museum, his meetings and conferences with socialist colleagues, the workingmen's lectures to which he devoted his spare evenings, and the staggering load of correspondence he carried—he had somehow managed to write ten plays, jotted down piecemeal in shorthand in pocket notebooks, mostly while he was riding on trains and buses on the way to some engagement.

His labors brought him virtually to the edge of death. In 1901 nothing came from his pen but *The Admirable Bashville,* a dramatization of *Cashel Byron's Profession.* This play, written in blank verse of the utmost banality, was intended chiefly to preserve the stage copyright of the novel and has since served no useful purpose. But in 1903 Shaw finished *Man and Superman* and with this he entered upon his greatness.

In England the 1890's were a time of unusual spiritual fervor, evidenced, on the one hand, by a powerful renewal of Christian faith and, on the other, by a significant reawakening of interest in mysticism, magic, astrology, and the occult. (p. 200)

It is to this movement toward a revitalization of spiritual values that *Man and Superman* must be referred. Even before the composition of *The Devil's Disciple,* possibly as early as *The Philanderer,* Shaw had been working toward the formulation of a general idea of religious nature, something which would arrange his metaphysical notions in a meaningful pattern. In *Man and Superman* the design was for the first time unfolded in all its complexity, exemplified by a dramatic action, explained in a lengthy preface, symbolically extended through the philosophic dialogue interpolated in the third act, and supported by an appendix and a glossary of maxims in the style of La Rochefoucauld. Whatever may be thought of this performance as philosophy, it is certainly a very complete exposition of a dramatic idea, the most ambitious that anyone had so far put forth in the theater.

The action of *Man and Superman* is frankly exemplary. It involves a love story played in comic style, with episodes of melodramatic extravagance and a more or less conventional conclusion. The heart of the play is the dream sequence, a lens through which the love story is magnified to cosmic proportions, so that the characters are exhibited *sub specie aeternitatis,* or somewhere near it. The method marks a decisive change in Shaw's approach to comedy. With this play he departed from the type of realism he had learned from Ibsen, Becque, and Brieux. In *Candida* he had experimented with symbolism. *Man and Superman* was a full scale example of symbolist drama. (p. 201)

Shaw had seen several examples of symbolist drama when Lugné-Poë's Théâtre de l'Oeuvre came to London in March 1895, but he does not seem to have been aware at the time of the importance of the new movement. By this time both Walkley and Yeats were deeply concerned with symbolist ideas. Shaw, however, seems to have thought of this movement as an aspect of Pre-Raphaelitism unworthy of any special attention. In the lengthy preface with which he introduced *Man and Superman* he gave no evidence of being aware of the fact that with this play he was breaking new ground in English drama (p. 202)

Shaw was doubtless attracted briefly by the mystical aura of French symbolism, and he gave voice to this variety of religious experience through Father Keegan in *John Bull's Other Island;* but evidently he distrusted this poetic strain and ultimately rejected it in favor of a more energetic faith, the basis of which he found in the writings of Samuel Butler. It was through this heady blend of science and religion that ultimately he found his true vocation as a writer.

In the 1890's a sense of vocation was indispensable to a writer of serious leanings, and particularly to one who fancied himself a poet. Shelley had fixed the type of latter-day apostle in the popular imagination, and many a romantic young man believed himself to be marked, like the unknown poet in *Adonais,* with the sign of Cain or Christ. The problem of *l'homme engagé* had concerned Ibsen deeply. It was debated in his plays from *Brand* to *When We Dead Awaken.* In the circumstances a writer like Shaw could hardly avoid the need for a reliable cause to serve. In the absence of God, however, it was not easy to find an idea capable of sustaining a lifetime of dedication. There was, of course, the cause of humanity which Shaw early adopted, but the concept of humanity was vague, and at best provisional. It was in his search for God that Shaw at last came upon the Life Force, which henceforth monopolized his efforts.

The workings of the unconscious will, which Schopenhauer had so dramatically described in *Die Welt als Wille und Vorstellung* (1818) [*The World as Will and Idea*] furnished a basis considerably more interesting from a philosophic viewpoint than the vague imagery of the symbolists or the stark materialism of Marx. (p. 203)

Schopenhauer argued that reason could do no more than to arrange and classify the data of sensual perception. Science dealt only with phenomena; but behind the material world apprehended by the senses, it was possible to intuit the existence of an urge which was neither rational nor intelligible and which defied explanation. This was life itself, the vital principle. Schopenhauer called this urge the will to live. The resulting metaphysics seemed—in contrast to the idealism of his contemporaries—realistic. Its consequence in the latter part of the century was a mounting attack against rationalism and the supremacy of the scientific method which had so far dominated nineteenth-century thought. One aspect of this reaction was the symbolist movement.

It is unlikely that Shaw came directly to a knowledge of Schopenhauer's system, and even less likely that he thoroughly understood its implications, but the theory of love in **Man and Superman** seems to rest quite firmly on a Schopenhauerian basis, and it is evident that Shaw's thinking at the time of its composition was influenced by ideas that could have had no other source. (pp. 204-05)

Shaw began working on **Man and Superman** in 1901. It took him two years to finish it and obviously it represented an enormous investment of creative energy. The reward was not immediate. . . . The play was received with politeness, and the [first] production was praised, but though the play had been in print for a year, in England the importance of **Man and Superman** was not yet generally apparent.

Man and Superman is subtitled *A Comedy and a Philosophy*. Of the two the comedy is by far the less interesting component. The plot is a love story, in Shaw's words, "a trumpery story of modern London life, a life in which, as you know, the ordinary man's main business is to get means to keep up the position and habits of a gentleman, and the ordinary woman's business is to get married." The result is a well-made play of conventional shape, founded upon a *méprise*, centered upon a love chase, embellished with melodramatic incidents involving brigands and rescuers, and resolved, in accordance with the usual tenets of romantic comedy, in the happy union of young lovers.

It is chiefly in the dream sequence of the third act that its symbolism becomes apparent. This act was considered dispensable even by the author. Yet it is John Tanner's dream, and only this, that gives the play its extraordinary scope and grandeur. The rest is, as Shaw indicated in the introduction, simply the story of the conquest of an eligible, but reluctant young man by a girl who has set her cap for him. The dream makes it clear that the play, as a whole, is a conceit intended to suggest the nature of the attraction that draws the sexes together—in short, an attempt to define love in cosmic terms.

The pattern of the action is conventionally Scribean. There are four acts, and, as usual in plays of this sort, two plots which converge toward the climax and are simultaneously resolved in the final scenes. The main plot is of the A loves B loves C variety and has the itinerant quality of romantic sequences traceable to the sixteenth-century epic. As in *Candida,* the heroine has a choice of men, but the heroine of **Man and Superman** makes a choice different from Candida's. She chooses the man who needs her least. For the rest, the situation is not markedly different from that of the earlier play. The poet, Tavy, is a pale reflection of Marchbanks. Tanner is a younger version

of Morell. As between the two candidates for the hand of Ann it becomes evident that it is Tanner who is predestined to be the husband, while it is Tavy's lot to be the broken-hearted lover who creates poems instead of children. There is also Mendoza, his comic counterpart, the high quality of whose poetry it is possible to judge, since we are favored with a sample. He is evidently fated to be a brigand.

The *méprise* stems from the fact that, while Ann is supposedly in love with Tavy, who is solemnly warned against her wiles by Tanner, it is actually Tanner whom she is resolved to marry. This comes as a surprise to nobody except the men most nearly involved. When the situation is made clear to Tanner, however, he is terrified and makes off in his highpowered car, with Ann in hot pursuit. The chase takes them all halfway across Europe, to the Sierra Nevada in Spain. There Tanner is captured first by the brigand Mendoza, himself a hapless victim of love, and afterwards by Ann, who turns up with an armed escort and all the panoply of Eros, the police force and the Life Force.

The action could not be simpler. It is a love chase, the originality of which consists in the reversal of traditional roles. In this case, the lady is aggressive; the gentleman is coy; what gives the play its comic tone is that in this unconventional situation everyone tries to preserve appearances. The lady plays the coy maiden; and the gentleman, as the seemingly aggressive male, finds himself engaged in a rear-guard action against impossible odds.

In this play the main plot is concerned with courtship, the subplot with marriage; but there is little in it that can be called romantic. It is all extremely businesslike. Ann's sister Violet is supposedly bearing the child of an unknown lover, whose identity she refuses to disclose. In fact she is secretly married to Hector Malone, whose father opposes the match. It is the conquest of the father, and the father's millions, which principally occupies Violet; the conquest of Tanner is Ann's principal concern; and in the ruthless efficiency of the two young women in organizing their lives, the play makes its wry point: *amor omnia vincit* ["love conquers all"].

While **Man and Superman** is principally about love and marriage, it is also concerned with a closely related topic, the conflict of youth and age. The principal characters are all in their early twenties. "The Revolutionist's Handbook" appended to the play, as the work of John Tanner, is what one might expect from a bright young firebrand of the 1890's, and its radicalism inevitably conflicts with that of the still-smoking embers of an earlier age, such as Roebuck Ramsden. In the contrast beween the former radical, who will not grasp the fact that the times have passed him by, and the young enthusiast, who is still somewhat ahead of his day, Shaw is able not only to indicate the relativism of accepted beliefs at successive stages of social evolution, but also to prefigure in the pathetic figure of the older man the sad destiny of the younger. The inevitable transformation of the fiery radicalism of each age into the pompous conservatism of the next is the natural order of a developing society. The contrasts are comic in their effect, but the implications of this dialectic are not altogether funny.

The contrast of generations, in the case of the ladies, is less emphatic, but no less striking. The female character, it is intimated, is more stable than the male, if only because her function in life is more clearly defined. Mrs. Whitefield, having fulfilled her role as mother, is no longer an agent of the Life Force, but her vital energy has passed in full measure to her daughter, Ann, whose femininity she fears, dislikes, and serves.

The elderly Miss Ramsden, on the other hand, is the prototype of Violet, the supremely self-confident English gentlewoman, the backbone of the British Empire, the feminine principle upon which English manhood depends.

Shaw's purpose in juxtaposing the successive elements of a family history in this manner could not be more clear. In his view, the laws of heredity are irrefrangible. A chain of inexorable causation links each generation to the next. Just as the matrimonial choices of the generation that is departing has determined the shape of the generation that is taking its place, so the young people's love affairs of the moment are destined to shape the generation yet unborn. From the evolutionary viewpoint, love, the selective principle, is the essential biological determinant.

In the comedy of Tanner, Ann, and Tavy it is therefore possible to symbolize the eternal comedy of the husband, the lover, and the lady, and the triangle of romantic comedy is thus transformed into an exemplum of impressive magnitude. The situation in *Man and Superman* is assimilated to the myth of Don Juan, the legendary lover, in somewhat the same manner as James Joyce assimilated the itinerary of the peripatetic Mr. Bloom to the journeyings of Ulysses, the legendary wanderer. In the case of Shaw, also, the conceit is not especially apt, since the mythical Don Juan is an incorrigible philanderer, whereas John Tanner has no special interest in women, yet is fated for matrimony from the start. For Shaw's purposes, though, the analogy, however strained, was useful. John Tanner is what, in the course of evolution, Don Juan has become. The idea sprang, undoubtedly, from Shaw's experiences during the relatively brief period of his sexual flowering, the years from 1881 to 1898. Like *The Philanderer, Man and Superman* is both autobiographical and apologetic. (pp. 211-13)

Shaw cherished the belief all his life that he was interested in women primarily for literary purposes. The naïveté of this excuse for philandering need not obscure the ambiguity of Shaw's amatory proclivities, out of which he fashioned the doctrine of *Man and Superman.* (p. 215)

In Shaw's view Don Juan is not an exploiter of women. He is their victim.

The turn given to the Don Juan myth in *Man and Superman* developed the theme of a short story which Shaw had written a dozen years earlier, in 1887. In this story, entitled **"Don Juan Explains,"** the ghost of Don Giovanni appears to the narrator in a railway carriage in order, as he says, to correct through him the current misconception of his character and purposes. Don Giovanni begins by explaining that, while his friends considered him devoid of moral fiber, he was in truth an exceptionally evolved individual who, having come into existence long before his time, was not properly appreciated by his contemporaries. In fact, he was a preternaturally shy young man whose sexual maturity was deferred until at last a widowed lady threw herself into his arms and conquered his timidity so far as to permit him to possess her. Unhappily, after a month with this lady, he found the romantic side of the affair "tedious, unreasonable and even, except at rare moments, forced and insincere." This uncomfortable indoctrination into the mysteries of love rendered him immune to the attraction of sex. Neither Doña Ana nor Zerlina interested him in the least, and his passion for Elvira was simply a figment of her imagination. After his experience with the statue of the Commander, he was dragged off to a hell made up of well-intentioned nonentities who despised the saints in heaven as unfeeling snobs of frightfully boring character and disposition.

One needs no great acumen to locate the autobiographical elements in this story. The relation to the scene in hell in *Man and Superman* is equally clear. These identifications have a certain importance. They justify the inference that Don Juan in Hell essentially represents Shaw in hell, and that the dialogue with the Devil and the Statue is interpretable as a transcription of the author's inner debate with regard to issues of the deepest personal interest.

In Tanner's vision, hell is an eternity of pleasure. It is peopled by such souls as prefer to live in a state of perpetual illusion, bemused by such idle fancies as youth, beauty, love, and romance, together with the arts through which such fantasies are given a semblance of reality. This aesthetic dream world is fittingly presided over by the master illusionist, the Devil. To those who prefer reality, however, an eternity of pleasure is an eternity of boredom, the worst of all possible torments. For these elect, salvation is to be found only in the useful expenditure of energy, that is, in work. Heaven, accordingly, is a state of constant striving. (pp. 220-21)

The Epistle Dedicatory of *Man and Superman* begins with the remark that [Arthur Bingham] Walkley had once asked Shaw why he did not write a Don Juan play. After considering with some archness the various implications of this question, which he interprets as a request, Shaw decides that what Walkley required of him was "a Don Juan in the philosophic sense" [see Shaw excerpt dated 1903]. (pp. 222-23)

Shaw manages somehow to relate Don Juan's legendary exploits to his own relatively modest achievements as a philanderer and thus arrives at a conception of the arch-seducer as one more sinned against than sinning. In *The Philanderer* Shaw does not make out a very strong case for Charteris as a lover of women, nor does he do much better for Valentine, the sex duelist in *You Never Can Tell.* It is in *Man and Superman* that these characters are finally developed, and here, for the first time, the pursuer turns out to be the pursued. The difficulty with the characterization is, however, that while Charteris and Valentine are both depicted as woman-chasers, John Tanner gives no indication of being at all interested in the opposite sex.

The ingenious turn upon which *Man and Superman* depends was doubtless suggested by Shaw's own sense of being ruthlessly hounded by adoring females. It was a feeling—judging by his diaries—barely supported by the facts, but one which he evidently cherished and strove mightily to realize in his manifold flirtations with Fabian ladies. From Shaw's viewpoint, Don Juan is a man irresistible to women, who occasionally condescends to one or another while he keeps his mind resolutely fixed on the higher things of life.

Apart from the similarity of their names, it is difficult to see what John Tanner has to do with Don Juan Tenorio in Zorilla's play, or in Mozart's opera. It is with astonishment that we learn in Act One of *Man and Superman* that in some mysterious manner Tanner is descended from Don Juan, and even when we realize that their relationship is purely spiritual, the analogy seems strained. In fact, Don Juan, as he appears in hell, represents only the fugitive aspect of John Tanner; the rest of the similitude we must take on faith. In John Fletcher's comedy, *The Wild Goose Chase* (1621), it is the hero's elusiveness which makes him especially attractive to the ladies of the play. It is certainly not Tanner's recalcitrance which appeals to Ann

Whitefield. It is his forthright maleness that attracts her, while the soft romanticism of Tavy makes him, in her opinion, undesirable as a mate.

Tavy has only the vaguest relation to Don Ottavio in the Mozart opera. Like Marchbanks in *Candida,* he is not marriageable. He is the eternally frustrated lover, the poet who idealizes, but never possesses the lady, a vestige of the Petrarchan tradition. It is his destiny to create works of art, not children, and it is precisely because he never possesses the lady that he is able to idealize her in his fantasy. John Tanner, on the other hand, has no illusions about the lady in question. He sees through her wiles perfectly in everything save what concerns himself and, believing himself to be immune from her machinations, he thinks only of protecting his friend. This is not the cream of the jest. The practical joke, of which he is the victim, is of cosmic magnitude.

Tanner is not, like Hector Malone, *l'homme moyen sensuel* ["the average sensual man"], whose business in life is merely to perpetuate the species on its present cultural level. He is a superior being, intellectually advanced and physically apt above the other men in his circle, and he appeals to Ann for reasons more cogent than she knows. He attracts her precisely because, whether she is aware of it or not, it is his child she desires to create, one who will bring the species a step closer to its entelechy. Therefore she hastens to unite with him in obedience to high behests, which she heeds without in the least identifying them, and is willing to sacrifice everything to bring about this union—her modesty, her integrity, even, if need be, her life.

Tanner is the darling of the Life Force and for that reason destined for sacrifice. In the cut of his mind, and the cut of his clothes, he serves as a modern counterpart of that *kalokágathia* which the ancients prized in their young men. He is strong, but in the hands of the implacable power that pre-empts his energies, he is helpless. His position thus approximates that of the tragic hero of classic drama, and if we are disposed to laugh at his plight instead of feeling the appropriate measure of pity and terror, it is only partly because we lack imagination. In our social framework, marriage with a pretty woman cannot really be considered a fate worse than death, and the fact that Tanner sees the matter in this light gives a comic turn to a situation which on another scale might well fulfill the conditions of tragedy.

It is doubtless in order to suggest this higher level of interpretation that the Dialogue in Hell precedes the scene in the garden—one might say of Eden—in which the sacrifice of Tanner is celebrated. The upshot, as in *Candida,* is an interpretation of the age-old story of the wife, the lover, and the husband in a manner that seems original with Shaw. In his view, the cosmic Will asserts its biologic choices through the female, so that every woman knows instinctively the man best fitted by nature to serve her procreative function. The artist, the thinker, the poet—self-engrossed, meditative types primarily interested in creative activity along intellectual or aesthetic lines—are parthogenetic organisms not properly fitted for the task of bisexual procreation. The woman may find such men to her liking, but in her instinctive wisdom, she rejects them no matter how attractive they may seem. Nor is the ordinary man much to her liking, though she may have to settle for him, for she can do no more than to perpetuate his mediocrity. The truly desirable man is one who is developed beyond the generality, but not to the point where he is beyond the possibility of domestication. Such is John Tanner. In him, as Mrs. Whitefield remarks, Ann meets her match.

For Strindberg also, marriage was a form of martyrdom; but the purpose of marriage, as he saw it, was quite other than eugenic reproduction. In *To Damascus,* and *The Dream Play,* and in *The Dance of Death,* marriage is the refining flame through which the spirit is purified. Shaw takes another view of the matter. Tanner's martyrdom is real enough, but the dance into which Ann leads him is not the dance of death. It is the dance of life. His agony is measured by the extent to which the life to which marriage condemns him falls short of the ideal existence of which he dreams, but his sufferings are by no means unendurable. (pp. 223-25)

In Shaw's view, the good life is a constant labor and is consequently never a happy experience. Happiness implies stasis, which negates the vital principle. Heaven is a state of eternal dissatisfaction. Presumably the blissful moment which will lure Tanner into crying *"Verweile doch!"* ["Linger awhile!"] will thrust him instantly into hell. For the dedicated revolutionist in particular domestic happiness constitutes a mortal danger. Shaw's attitude in this regard was not especially original. "He that is unmarried," St. Paul admonishes, "careth for the things that belong to the Lord, how he may please the Lord, but he that is married careth for the things that are of this world, how he may please his wife."

In this manner Shaw, after a prolonged detour through the most advanced thought of his day, found a safe harbor in the traditional tenets of his youth. His aspiring geniuses, the Marchbanks, Dudgeons, and Brassbounds—to say nothing of the saints who already populate his heaven—are humanity's priests and, by reason of their vocation, are exempt from carnal involvements. They are, at most, philanderers, lovers for whom woman is a point of departure, never a stopping place. So it was with Don Juan also; and now, like the archetypal lover of the *Symposium,* he desires to relinquish the delights of hell.

The denizens of his hell are romantics, diligently torturing themselves in the endless pursuit of pleasure; but Don Juan has found no happiness in pleasure. Happiness, as Aristotle noted, "does not lie in amusement; it would, indeed, be strange if the end were amusement, and one were to take trouble and suffer hardship all one's life in order to amuse oneself." Don Juan's horror at the prospect of an eternity of pleasure corresponds to the misgivings of a highly evolved individual in this life who has nothing to do but to amuse himself as long as he lives. For such a man happiness is an impossible will-o'-the-wisp. The alternative is the quest for blessedness, the realistic substitute for happiness. It is this which Don Juan, like Marchbanks, hopes to find among those who are engaged in the eternal life of contemplation that is their heaven.

The Dialogue in Hell is obviously meant to be read metaphorically. It takes place in the mind of man, specifically in the mind of a certain man and is, in this sense, autobiographical. In the critical position in which Tanner is placed at the end of the second act, he finds himself torn by contrary impulses, doubts, and fears. It is this state of mental turmoil which the dream sequence represents. In the portion of *Man and Superman* which takes place on the plane of contemporary reality, this critical moment is effectively dramatized in terms of freedom and the loss of individuality. But in the aspect of eternity the problem of marriage is seen to center on much wider issues, on the nature of men and the purpose of life.

Practically the discussion in hell involves the choice between the carefree life of the senses, self-justified, and a life of intellectual labor, justified by an ideal. . . . In *Man and Superman* the Devil is a romantic. He speaks eloquently for the sensual life. Don Juan argues for the life of the intellect. Neither is the victor, for the issue is beyond resolution, and the conflict is never-ending.

In hell there are no hard facts, only agreeable enchantments. It is a *locus amoenus* of the order of the Bower of Bliss or the Garden of Armida, a pleasant place to be, but bad for the soul: one would imagine hell was Shaw's idea of a resort hotel on the Riviera. Heaven, on the contrary, is a never-ending contemplation of reality. Unlike the sensual life, which is aimless, the life of the mind has a goal. It aims at the extension of knowledge; it represents the desire of life to know itself. It is to the furtherance of this taste that Don Juan, having grown weary of pleasure, now resolves to devote his eternity. These activities, the Statue remarks, are not universally amusing. They require a special aptitude, which he no longer shares. He himself has decided, after a long sojourn in heaven, to spend some aeons in hell.

Between these two spirits who meet at the crossroads of the infinite—the Statue who is bored with heaven, and the sensualist who is weary of hell—the Devil plays an equivocal role. He is a suave and convincing personage, well-suited to manage the sort of luxury hotel which hell seems to be, and naturally anxious not to lose his clientele to the competition. Doña Ana is no match, intellectually speaking, for these gentlemen among whom her lot is cast, but she is impressively single-minded: she is eternally in search of fruition. Doña Ana belongs neither to heaven nor to hell. She embraces both. As the vehicle of life she is neutral and anonymous, but indispensable.

The Devil has no use for Doña Ana, but Don Juan sees clearly that squalling brats and household chores are the price humanity must pay for the perpetuation of the race. The Statue adds that a life without responsibility, while seemingly attractive, leads only to an endless demand for entertainment, and at last to the discomforts of old age and impotence. As an ancient hedonist, he himself has amply experienced the disadvantages of the sensual life. "I confess," he remarks, "that if I had nothing to do in the world but wallow in these delights I should have cut my throat." In these circumstances, his decision to settle in hell does not seem particularly logical. But the Devil understands it. Men tire of everything, he says, of heaven no less than hell. History is nothing but the record of the oscillations of the human spirit between these extremes. Under the aspect of eternity, Don Juan and the Statue continually change places, for Don Juan will weary of the life of reason just as surely as he has wearied of the life of pleasure. What appears to be progress is nothing but change, and all that can be said of this is *"vanitas vanitatum."* Life has neither aim, nor end.

It is at this point in the discussion that Don Juan loses patience, for the hit is shrewd. He has an answer. If life has no purpose, one will be found. The Life Force has devised consciousness in order to know itself. It is even now at work developing means for discovering its purpose and its destiny. The means is the philosophic mind. The philosopher is nature's pilot, "And there you have our difference," Juan tells the Devil, "To be in hell is to drift: to be in heaven is to steer." The Devil answers: "On the rocks, most likely." To which Don Juan answers: "Pooh! which ship goes oftenest on the rocks or to the bottom—the drifting ship or the ship with a pilot on board?" In the absence of precise statistics, the question remains unresolved; but the indication is that Don Juan means to take a course in navigation: he proposes to spend eternity in developing his mind.

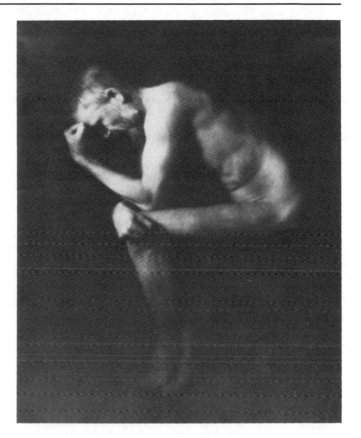

Shaw posed as Rodin's Thinker, *1906.*

The Devil sees no reason to develop the human mind any further. Man has shown himself, he points out, chiefly ingenious in devising means of destruction. What best captures his imagination is not life but death: "There is nothing in Man's industrial machinery but his greed and sloth: his heart is in his weapons. This marvellous force of Life of which you boast is a force of Death: Man measures his strength by his destructiveness." (pp. 225-28)

The argument, however, does not unsettle Don Juan. He answers that, while men seem to be bold and bad, they are really cowards and will undergo every humiliation in order to live. Man becomes heroic only in the service of an idea: "I tell you, gentlemen, if you can shew a man a piece of what he calls God's work to do, and what he will later on call by many new names, you can make him entirely reckless of the consequences to him personally." The task of the saints is, accordingly, the creation of ideas for men to live by, vital ideas. It is to this work that Don Juan proposes to devote his energies. The transition from hell is simple. When we think, we are in heaven. The Devil, for his part, wishes him joy of his undertaking. His reward will be, "in a word, the punishment of the fool who pursues the better before he has secured the good." Don Juan replies, "But at least I shall not be bored. The service of the Life Force has that advantage, at all events."

Thus Don Juan and the Devil part company . . . , and they leave Doña Ana to vanish herself in the void. She has just acquired an idea. She has overheard the Devil remark that to the superman—something conceived by a German-Polish madman named Nietzsche—the human race will seem an inferior species. Her mission suddenly becomes clear to her and, as she vanishes, she cries, apparently to the universe, "A father! a father for the Superman!"

On this note the dialogue ends. It is perhaps not entirely satisfactory from the viewpoint of philosophy, but it is beyond doubt a great masterpiece of English literature. It might seem that Don Juan's decision should hang on something more solid than the thought that an eternity of work is the only alternative to an eternity of boredom. But the *taedium vitae* he fears is a more potent threat to the Life Force than any other. Boredom is the one illness the will to live cannot survive. The final argument helps also to justify Shaw's position as a realist—and also Don Juan's—for his line of reasoning brings him very close to an idealistic conclusion, and he has no way of disproving historically the Devil's paraphrase of Ecclesiastes. To the observation that all is vanity an honest man can oppose nothing but the faith which perhaps in time moves mountains.

It is in "The Revolutionist's Handbook" that we most clearly sense the nature of Shaw's faith. He is, insofar as the present race of men is concerned, entirely pessimistic. His efforts are not directed to the immediate amelioration of the human lot. As humanity is presently constituted, he considers it hopeless. Socialism is therefore mainly an instrumentality intended to facilitate the creation of a new species which will be capable of leading a rational existence. The Third Kingdom which the sage Maximus describes in Ibsen's *Emperor and Galilean* is not, in Shaw's opinion, a kingdom of this world. The ideal anarchy of which Ibsen dreams is, for Shaw also, a castle in the air. The necessary basis of our future felicity is eugenic. In the world as it is, all is hopeless; save only hope. Tanner writes:

> . . .if you know the facts and are strong enough to look them in the face, you must admit that unless we are replaced by a more highly evolved animal—in short, by the Superman—the world must remain a den of dangerous animals among whom our few accidental supermen, our Shakespears, Goethes, Shelleys, and their like, must live as precariously as lion tamers do, taking the humor of their situation, and the dignity of their superiority, as a set-off to the horror of the one and the loneliness of the other.

The idea of comedy implied in this passage does not adequately suggest the source of Shaw's comic vein. It does not take into account Shaw's innate sense of fun which so often leads him into slapstick. But it indicates how close to the tragic his sense of comedy came. There is no doubt that Shaw felt himself to be one of the "accidental supermen" condemned to a precarious life among beasts who must be frightened into civility. He saw himself brandishing his thunderbolts from the height of his genius, saddened by the uncouth antics of his contemporaries, but more amused than saddened.

If the effect of *Man and Superman* is not quite that of classic comedy, it is because Shaw was both incurably romantic and essentially sentimental, and because also he was in some degree restricted by the comedic patterns of his time. In current practice, the sympathetic role, incidental to classic comedy, was indispensable. The result is that Tanner, whose role as raisonneur is comic, becomes pathetic as a principal in the action. Very likely that is what Shaw intended. At any rate, Tanner is caught in the trap of the Life Force very much as Oedipus is caught in Apollo's snare. It takes the Theban King some time before, at the very end of his life, he becomes aware of the injustice of his position. In the case of Tanner the irony of the situation is apparent to him at once, since he can hardly avert the sacrifice to which his own reasoning condemns him:

> Enough, then, of this goose-cackle about Progress: Man, as he is, never will nor can add a cubit to his stature by any of its quackeries, political, scientific, educational, or artistic. . . . Our only hope, then, is in evolution. We must replace the man by the superman.

The tragic element in Tanner's destiny was by no means something apparent only to Shaw. The sacrifice of the individual in the interests of the race is an idea common to all dramatic systems based upon an evolutionary concept. Tanner's sad fate is not precisely comparable to the destiny of the three sisters in Chekhov's play, but they too are sacrificed in the evolutionary process. *The Three Sisters* is perhaps a comedy, as Chekhov insisted; but the comic element in *Man and Superman* leaps to the eye, and the salt of the jest is that, in inviting personal annihilation, Tanner faithfully fulfills his own prescription for the survival of humanity:

> And so we arrive at the end of the Socialist's dream of "the socialization of the means of production and exchange," of the Positivist's dream of moralizing the capitalist. . . . The only fundamental and possible Socialism is the socialization of the selective breeding of Man: in other terms, of human evolution. We must eliminate the Yahoo, or his vote will wreck the commonwealth.

The implication is that the irresistible physical attraction which Ann concentrates upon Tanner, her charm and her youthful beauty, are, ultimately, nothing more than an expression of the racial need to eliminate the Yahoo. The mysterious power of love is a political force more potent than any man-made revolution, and, for reasons which at the moment escape him, Tanner is forced to unite in marriage with a woman he neither likes nor trusts, but merely loves. Schopenhauer had remarked, "in the case of difference of disposition, character and mental tendency, and the dislike, nay, enmity proceeding from this, sexual love may yet arise and exist; when it does, it blinds us to all that; and if it here leads to a marriage it will be a very unhappy one."

It would be a mistake to identify Shaw's theory of love too closely with this idea. In a play written from the strictly Schopenhauerian standpoint Tanner and Ann Whitefield would be drawn together by a mutual passion. In Shaw's plan, Ann tracks down her quarry with the implacability of a Javert in pursuit of Jean Valjean, while Tanner eludes her with comparable resolution. It is thus necessary for the success of the play that the *scène à faire* in the last act be played with extraordinary intensity. When the play was first performed at the Court Theatre, Shaw directed it so that Tanner—who was actually made up to resemble Shaw—seemed to be drawn little by little into a web over which Ann presided spiderlike, radiating chiefly animal magnetism until she darted in for the kill. Such an effect is not quite in accordance with what one might expect of the workings of the Will. Very likely Schopenhauer had something quite different in mind.

Man and Superman leaves Doña Ana in an equivocal position. In her maternal character she is the basis of the evolutionary process; but there is no doubt as to the intellectual superiority of Don Juan. Shaw's attitude toward Ann in *Man and Superman* seems hardly accordant with the feminist doctrine of *Mrs. Warren's Profession.* As socialist, Ibsenite, and Millite, Shaw was certainly committed to the movement for the equality of the sexes, but his advanced views were not always consistently applied, and it is by no means easy to say on which side of the woman's cause he actually stood. (pp. 228-32)

In *Man and Superman* the relation of the sexes is posed in terms that closely approximate the classic antithesis of form and matter. Man represents the spiritual principle; woman, the material component. Man is light; woman, darkness and mystery. In procreation man transmits form; woman receives it: she contributes only her warmth and her desire. Don Juan is self-sufficient. It is in the nature of spirit to be self-sufficient; but woman—judging by Doña Ana—represents the craving of matter for form in order to come into being. It is for this reason that woman is always the pursuer, and man the pursued.

In the last part of *Back to Methuselah* these distinctions have vanished, along with the other characteristics of sex which the race of the future relinquishes in infancy; therefore the views put forward in *Man and Superman* may be thought of as provisional. Save for their evolutionary aspect the sexual attitudes which Shaw developed in this play did not depart very far from the traditions which after the time of Gregory the Great were accepted by most clerical writers on the subject. The church approved—if with some reluctance—of cohabitation for utility, but never of cohabitation for pleasure, so that the love of woman was in every case suspect, since it distracted the soul from the proper object of its desire, which was God. (pp. 234-35)

Presumably in this play Shaw's attitude is realistic, and significantly post-Raphaelite. The difference between the woman who leads Dante upward through the spheres of heaven and the woman who runs John Tanner to earth in a rented garden in Granada in some sense measures the cultural abyss that separates the idealistic fantasies of the Middle Ages from those appropriate to the time of Shaw. The beauty of the unattainable Beatrice mirrors the splendor of Dante's God, an ineffable abstraction majestically enthroned beyond the bounds of human thought. The divine element in Ann Whitefield is not so clearly discernible, yet she too is fashioned in the image of the divinity she serves. Shaw's comedy is at the other pole from the *Comedy* of Dante; nevertheless there are some points of similarity in the conception. Don Juan needs no woman to show him the way to heaven. He knows the way by himself. But for John Tanner, his earthly counterpart, the way to God lies through woman, and—such is the implication—she leads him there through hell. (p. 236)

> *Maurice Valency, in his* The Cart and the Trumpet: The Plays of George Bernard Shaw, *1973. Reprint by Schocken Books, 1983, 467 p.*

A. M. GIBBS (essay date 1976)

[*In the following excerpt, Gibbs examines comedy and philosophy in* Man and Superman.]

Man and Superman is sub-titled "A Comedy and a Philosophy." Shaw himself, in his discussion of the play and its antecedents in the Epistle Dedicatory addressed to A. B. Walkley, tends to encourage the notion that the comedy and philosophy are largely unrelated entities in the work. He refers to the dream-sequence as something "totally extraneous" to the "perfectly modern three-act play." . . . But the dramatic artist

at work in *Man and Superman* brings the play and the philosophical Dream into a much more closely integrated relation than this comparison suggests. The play and the Dream are mutually modifying and mutually illuminating, and the "philosophy," that complex amalgam of views on politics, evolution, art, the relations of the sexes, and human nature in general which emerges from the work, is partly defined in its import and directions by the shape and development of the comic action.

This essay explores the relations between the philosophical themes expressed in the discussions in the play and Dream, and the meanings inherent in the action and in Shaw's manipulation of dramatic conventions. One of the main contentions is that although *Man and Superman* as a whole contains profoundly sceptical and pessimistic ingredients, the more affirmative and optimistic views which are voiced by Don Juan / Tanner in the Dream are, on the whole, aligned with the victorious forces in the action. In this account, Tanner's capitulation to Ann at the end of the play is seen as a defeat only in a very limited sense. In discussing the meanings inherent in the play's action, I have found it useful to compare the basic patterns of the main and sub-plots with an account of the classical New Comedy which Northrop Frye presented in his *Anatomy of Criticism* [1957]. (pp. 161-62)

In his chapter on comedy in *Anatomy of Criticism*, Northrop Frye provides us with the following description of the characteristic structure and import of plays which belong to the Greek and Roman New Comedy:

> What normally happens [in these plays] is that a young man wants a young woman, that his desire is resisted by some opposition, usually paternal, and that near the end of the play some twist in the plot enables the hero to have his will. In this simple pattern there are several complex elements. In the first place, the movement of comedy is usually a movement from one kind of society to another. At the beginning of the play the obstructing characters are in charge of the play's society, and the audience recognizes that they are usurpers. At the end of the play the device in the plot that brings hero and heroine together causes a new society to crystallize around the hero.

Elsewhere Frye summarises this by characterising the New Comedy as unfolding from "what may be described as a comic Oedipus situation." The pattern is of course recognizable as being widely pervasive in the comedy of later periods, and its relevance to the structure of *Man and Superman* is immediately obvious. The play abounds in paternalistic figures: the deceased Mr. Whitefield to whose authority Ann demurely and strategically appeals throughout Act I (Shaw's cue here is Doña Ana's overriding concern with the memory of her father in Mozart's opera); Ramsden; Malone Senior; and behind the characters on the stage in Act I, portraits, busts, and photographs of various father figures of Ramsden's political and social philosophy. It is this array which "Jack the Giant Killer" (to use Ann's nickname for Tanner in the play) must overcome, at least in effigy, for the comic resolution to be reached.

When the sub-plot is taken into account, the play presents us with two similar but contrasting patterns of the New Comedy type, the sub-plot being a negative and decadent version of the main plot. In both main plot and sub-plot we witness a complex and subtle manipulation of stock dramatic materials. In addition, in the main plot we also see a radical re-structuring of the action of the Don Juan story as it is found in the play's principal source, Mozart's *Don Giovanni*. The play begins with, if not a reading of a deceased relative's will (a device which Shaw himself refers to in the Preface to *Three Plays for Puritans* as a stock item in Victorian drama), a problematical situation brought about by the provisions of a will, namely the appointment of the conservative Ramsden and the radical Tanner as joint guardians of Ann. There are two potential marriage partners for the heroine, and the development of the plot brings about the rejection of one and capitulation to marriage of the other. Paternalistic opposition to the marriage of Ann and Tanner comes from Ramsden, who favours the possibility of a match between Octavius and Ann, as did the deceased Mr. Whitefield. In the sub-plot the two lovers, Hector Malone and Octavius's sister, Violet, have contracted a secret marriage in order to circumvent the opposition of Malone senior. In the course of the play Violet gains the approval and admiration of her father-in-law, and he becomes reconciled to the marriage.

In Shaw's treatment of these materials the conventional and relatively naturalistic surface of the social comedy is a veil through which we catch progressively clearer glimpses of the larger-than-life protagonists and universal conflicts which stand more fully revealed in the Dream. An early indication of Shaw's awareness of the way in which he is manipulating theatrical conventions is provided in the stage direction describing Octavius Robinson in Act I:

> *Mr Robinson is really an uncommonly nice looking young fellow. He must, one thinks, be the jeune premier; for it is not in reason to suppose that a second such attractive male figure should appear in one story. . . .*

The description which follows shows that Shaw wanted Octavius to appear as almost a parody of the pretty matinee idol, a comically obvious object of audience sympathy. . . . (pp. 162-64)

Only a few minutes after the entry of Octavius, John Tanner, a second strong contender for the position of jeune premier, whose "*Olympian*" appearances suggests "*Jupiter rather than Apollo,*" arrives on the scene and introduces a complicating factor in audience expectations. This unsettling appearance of a rival jeune premier forces us to attend closely to the comparison which is drawn between the two figures; and it is a comparison which lies close to the centre of the play's thematic concerns. In the larger allegory of the play, Octavius is associated with sentimentality, debased romanticism and the poetic idealisation of woman. In the play he is treated with good humoured comedy. But in the Dream the qualities he is associated with in the play are seen as forming part of the condition of hell. Heaven, in Tanner's account in the Dream, belongs to the "masters of reality." . . . It is a republic from which eventually the poets must be banished. Conversely, hell is partly defined in terms of certain literary forms and certain aspects of the literary sensibility:

> [In hell] there are no hard facts to contradict you, no ironic contrast of your needs with your pretensions, no human comedy, nothing but a perpetual romance, a universal melodrama. As our German friend put it in his poem, "the poetically nonsensical here is good sense; and the Eternal Feminine draws us ever upward and

onward and on"—without getting us a step farther.

Up to a point, Tanner's argument in the Dream can be seen as implying a defence of comedy as opposed to tragedy, melodrama and romance. The play itself, as distinct from the Dream, forms an analogy to Tanner's description of heaven in that in its human comedy the pretensions of the philosopher are indeed upset by the hard facts and ironies of experience. Perhaps the central point to be grasped about the Dream is that it refers us to the human comedy of the play as a typical arena in which the "heavenly" virtues can be realised and expressed. But in the final analysis no analogy to heaven can be invoked, and metaphor has to be discarded altogether: the heavenly condition is seen as a full, direct and courageous engagement with life:

> DON JUAN. In heaven, as I picture it . . . you live and work instead of playing and pretending. You face things as they are; you escape nothing but glamor; and your steadfastness and your peril are your glory. If the play still goes on here and on earth, and all the world is a stage, heaven is at least behind the scenes. But heaven cannot be described by metaphor. . . .

Man and Superman thus includes in its comic pattern a self-reflexive, critical contemplation of Art, which arises out of and is closely related to the dramatic action. In the conceptual hierarchy which is established in the play, Art, although it is seen as contributing to the contemplation of Reality, as offering a means of extending human understanding and self-consciousness, is subordinate to Reality. (pp. 164-65)

The death and the will which form the mainsprings of action in the play are also relevant to its thematic concerns. The fact that the action is initiated by a death is emphasised in the first few moments of the play. . . . The progression from this death to the announcement of a marriage at the end of the play relates the structural pattern to the primitive origins of comedy, in the rituals associated with fertility myths. But this pattern has a more particular significance in *Man and Superman* in that it is closely paralleled by the movement of the discussion in the Dream. The argument which precipitates Don Juan / Tanner's departure from Hell is the Devil's repudiation of the idea of a "continual ascent by Man on the stepping stones of his dead selves to higher things," . . . and his view of history as a cycle in which Man constantly regresses to degenerate and destructive behavioural patterns. (p. 165)

One of the obvious functions of the sub-plot is to extend the range of the play's critical and satirical reference. The young Hector Malone has a good deal in common with, and one suspects may have been partly modelled upon, the moralistic Hester Worsley in Wilde's *A Woman of No Importance*. He is described in a stage direction as a man of "*chivalrous manners to women, and . . . elevated moral sentiments,*" with a taste for improving rhetoric. He is an Eastern American, but, as Shaw facetiously informs us, "*English people of fashion . . . feel that he ought not to be made to suffer for what is clearly not his fault, and make a point of being specially kind to him.*" Not all of the stage direction description comes through in the play. One would scarcely gather from the dialogue, for instance, that "*Hector's culture is nothing but a state of saturation with our literary exports of thirty years ago.*" . . . But his speeches do indicate clearly enough the monotonously conventional character of Hector's high-minded outlook and his alliance with Octavius as a sentimental believer in the ennobling power of woman. Clearly the play holds out no hope of any profound social change being wrought by either the old or the new generation in America, and the action of the sub-plot underlines this humorously adopted but basically polemical stance. The reason for Malone Senior's opposition to the marriage of Hector and Violet is that he wants Hector to marry into the English aristocracy. But when this opposition is overcome by the calculating commonsense of Violet, what crystallizes around the hero is not a new society but, for all Hector's good intentions, a consolidation of the old. In generally genial, but unmistakable, terms, Malone and Violet are presented as embodiments of predatory, capitalistic forces. . . . In presenting the comedy of love overcoming parental opposition in the sub-plot, Shaw skilfully adjusts the convention to his purposes, principally through his treatment of Violet, who is the reverse of the sort of young innocent we might expect in her dramatic situation. Shaw attacks this convention through such speeches as her counsel to Hector in Act II in reply to his question about their secret marriage, "Why won't you let me own up?"

> We can't afford it. You can be as romantic as you please about love, Hector; but you mustn't be romantic about money. . . .

In contrast, the main plot presents a positive and vital comic rhythm. How this is achieved can best be seen by contrasting Shaw's treatment of the Don Juan story with that of Mozart in *Don Giovanni*. In the opera, the main pivot of the plot is Don Juan's slaying of Doña Ana's father. This is alluded to in the Dream scene in *Man and Superman* when, much to his surprise, Ramsden as Statue is introduced as not the Guardian but the father of Ann:

> THE STATUE. *(Puzzled)* My daughter? *(Recollecting)* Oh! the one you were taken with. Let me see: What was her name?
>
> DON JUAN. Ana.
>
> THE STATUE. To be sure: Ana. A good-looking girl if I recollect aright. Have you warned Whatshisname? her husband.
>
> DON JUAN. My friend Ottavio? No: I have not seen him since Ana arrived. *(Ana comes indignantly to light)*
>
> ANA. What does this mean? Ottavio here and your friend! And you, father, have forgotten my name. You are indeed turned to stone. . . .

The Dream thus temporarily restores the Mozartian relations between Tanner, Ann, Ramsden, and Octavius. *Don Giovanni* ends with the triumph, in a superficial sense, of conservative forces. The ghost of Doña Ana's father returns in the form of a statue, and after calling on Don Juan to repent and receiving his adamant refusal, takes him down to the fires of Hell. Ottavio is then assured, not altogether convincingly, that he will only have to wait another year for Ana to recover from the shock of all that has occurred and his hopes of blissful union will be fulfilled. (pp. 166-67)

Shaw's treatment of Tanner in the play is a natural extension of this comment. His most conspicuous alteration to the story is that of making the female the sexual pursuer instead of the male. But more significant in some ways is what happens to the Doña Ana, Ottavio and Don Juan triangle. In the marriage stakes of the play, as we have observed, Octavius is the candidate of the paternalistic characters Whitefield and Ramsden.

But by making Tanner a reluctant victor over this opposition, Shaw turns the Mozartian comic revenge plot into an entirely different structure and produces a comic pattern which endorses the new values associated with the hero. The marriage is a defeat in the sense that it undermines all Tanner's previously held resolves and convictions on the subject of marriage. But seen in relation to the play as a whole it is a qualified victory, symbolising as it does the planting of a revolutionary consciousness (however impaired this may be by Tanner's repeated failure of insight in practical matters) within the circle of the old society and the possible rescue of Ann from her Mozartian doom. Recognition, at the end of the play, of the strength of conservative forces does not negate the revolutionary thrust and critical energy of what has gone before.

In some respects, the comic methods of *Man and Superman* can be related to the political philosophies of Fabianism. (p. 168)

Certainly it would be a drastic oversimplification to interpret the play in its political aspects as simply an embodiment of Fabian principles. If by nothing else we should be warned against such a simplification by Tanner's Revolutionist's Handbook, where Fabianism is specifically referred to as one of the failed experiments in improving the human lot by political means. In this radically critical appendage to the Epistle Dedicatory (it contains some of Shaw's most acrimonious and pessimistic writing, and should strictly be called "The Evolutionist's Handbook"), revolutionary political activity, whether it be violent or non-violent in method, is seen as being ultimately incapable of bringing about profound social change. But despite this criticism there are in the play itself some clear analogies to Shaw's description of Fabian strategy in the 1892 Tract. In the opening stage direction Shaw is at particular pains to identify Ramsden precisely as a representative of old-fashioned nineteenth-century Liberalism. He is described as a Unitarian, a Free Trader and a Darwinian Evolutionist. The two busts and one of the portraits which adorn his study are of writers (Bright, Spencer, Cobden) who were major formative influences in the shaping of nineteenth-century Liberal philosophy. In the dialogue of Act I Ramsden boasts of his advanced, tolerant opinions, and of his stand for "equality and liberty of conscience" in social and religious matters. (p. 169)

The relation between Tanner and Ramsden at the beginning of the play is one of pure hostility. Their appointment as joint guardians of Ann is seen by both as a disastrous misalliance. Tanner sees the appointment as the unfortunate consequence of a piece of advice about politics which he gave to Whitefield before the latter's death: "I said the proper thing was to combine the experience of an old hand with the vitality of a young one. Hang me if he didn't take me at my word and alter his will . . . appointing me as joint guardian with you!" There is no indication of any substantial intellectual rapprochement between the two as the play develops, but their mutual hostility certainly declines. . . . By the end of Act I the two reach a point of close accord on the question of Violet's assumed disgrace. Early in Act IV Ramsden introduces Tanner to Malone Senior as "one of our circle"; and at the end of the play he steps forward to congratulate Tanner on his forthcoming marriage.

If we look at the end of the play for signs of a decisive and unequivocal victory of the new society over the old, we are, of course, disappointed. What we do see, however, is a significant realignment of social forces and a phase in the possible evolution of a new society.

The opposition, in political, philosophical and religious terms, between the old and new societies embraced by the comedy is most fully explored in the Dream. The debate in the Dream ranges over a wide variety of topics, but two central areas of conflict can be isolated. On the one hand, there is the fundamental opposition between the Devil and Don Juan / Tanner, an opposition between life-denying and life-affirming viewpoints. The Devil and Don Juan disagree not so much in their views of the facts about human history and civilisation as in the stances which they take towards them. The Devil is presented as both a sentimentalist and, at least in a shallow sense, a realist. He asserts that the power that governs the earth is not the power of Life but the power of Death, and that "Man measures his strength by his destructiveness." . . . Progress is "an infinite comedy of illusion." . . . He sees man as the most predatory and destructive expression of life. In the face of this recognition the diabolonian resources are the pursuit of happiness, the cultivation of good taste, connoisseurship and romantic idealisation of woman. What Shaw presents as Hell in fact is very close to the pleasures Mozart's Don Juan is enjoying before he goes to Hell. . . . The basis of the stance which Don Juan / Tanner presents in opposition is a belief in the possibility provided by man's creative and intellectual energies of achieving "higher . . . organisation and completer self-consciousness." . . . Like Milton, with whom he has a good deal in common, Shaw's Don Juan rejects the ethic of classical epic poetry: "I sing, not arms and the hero, but the philosophic man: he who seeks in contemplation to discover the inner will of the world." . . . (pp. 169-71)

In many respects the arguments of Don Juan and the Devil are closely aligned. Throughout the debate they vie with one another in presenting gloomy and unflattering descriptions of the human race. It is noteworthy that the Devil's comment on progress in the Dream is in fact an echo of one of the section headings in Tanner's "Revolutionist's Handbook," "Progress an Illusion." But in the face of these recognitions Don Juan rejects the Devil's retreat into bon viveurism and art. Music, in this Mozartian Dream, is described as "the brandy of the damned," and in one of his speeches Don Juan speaks of his discovery of romantic poetry as though it were the last phase in a spiritual Rake's Progress, because it led him to the worship of Woman. . . . (p. 171)

The second major conflict presented in the Dream is the struggle between the male and female spirits. In describing his relations with women Don Juan tells us that whereas the philosopher had told him to say "I think: therefore I am," woman had taught him to say "I am; therefore I think." . . . In other words, woman brings him to recognize the primacy of existence itself over rational contemplation of existence. Because of her more profound involvement in the creation of life, woman is seen, in this rather reductive account, as at once more powerful, more fully embodying primary energies than man, and therefore as less concerned with the contemplation of life. Her concern is not with higher states of consciousness but with possession of the male for her own creative purposes. (In the play itself, of course—it is one of the many points of ironic contrast between play and Dream—Ann is seen as being far from merely the embodiment of primary creative forces . . .). But Don Juan's quarrel is not with nature, with the procreative forces which drive woman in this role—he recognizes woman as being literally irresistible—but with the institutionalising of these forces in marriage, the idea of man being reduced to the role of a mere instrument of the Life Force in this narrower sense, rather than being enabled to pursue his own wider cre-

ative purpose of ennobling human life. Marriage, in the Dream, is described by Don Juan as a "mantrap baited with simulated accomplishments and delusive idealizations." . . . In short, Don Juan differentiates between masculine and feminine forms of creativity, and sees them as essentially hostile to one another. This is why Ann's final wooing of Tanner is presented as a Titanic struggle of wills. But here again, Tanner's capitulation is not strictly a defeat. The social comedy of the play perhaps suggests that the marriage between Tanner and Ann may turn out to be a relatively conventional affair, at least by the standards of the contemporary intelligentsia. But behind the final scene of the play looms the Dream, and in the cosmic framework which this provides the marriage can be seen as a union of contemplative and primary forms of creativity, as defined by Don Juan, and as an embodiment in the action of the play's positive affirmations.

Although the Dream is undoubtedly a daunting problem for producers, who, understandably enough, usually succumb to the temptation offered by Shaw of simply omitting it, it does nevertheless form an integral part of the whole and the play is the poorer without it. What the Dream does for the play is to brace its affirmative comedy with the profoundly sceptical diatribe against man with which Shaw arms the devil. What the play does for the Dream is to subject its lofty idealism and philosophising to the test of social realities, to place it in a context in which imposing concepts like the Life Force can be comically punctured (as by Ann's saying "it sounds like the Life Guards"); or in which a Quixotic defence of unmarried motherhood can be upset by the discovery that the mother in question is in fact married. In such ways the play's comedy and philosophy are brought into a dynamic and mutually modifying relation with one another.

The Dream is skilfully and imaginatively dovetailed into the main action, and is introduced by a scene which is one of the high points of the play's comedy. In his ambivalent position as advanced Socialist and wealthy Edwardian gentleman, Tanner leaves on his transcontinental flight for all the world like P. G. Wodehouse's Bertie Wooster, complete with car and chauffeur. The journey conveniently brings him to the Sierra Nevada, the home of the Don Juan legend, and it is here in the ensuing scene that the seeds of the Dream are sown. Preparing us for the universalising debate of the Dream, the brigands are presented less as individuals than as political and racial types who together form a comically impressionistic picture of political ferment on a world scale and of stultifying factious debate. With the marvellous freedom available to Shavian comedy the brigands are surprisingly discovered to be in their third day of debating the question "Have Anarchists or Social-Democrats the most personal courage?" With Tanner's arrival melodramatic possibilities are immediately cancelled by the exchange of introductions between him and Mendoza:

> MENDOZA. . . . (*Posing loftily*) I am a brigand:
> I live by robbing the rich.
>
> TANNER. (*Promptly*) I am a gentleman: I live
> by robbing the poor. Shake hands. . . .

As the scene develops, political discussion (during which Mendoza foreshadows his sceptical and ironic character as the Devil) gives way to romantic sentimentality with Mendoza's confession of his hopeless love for Louisa Straker. It is Mendoza's poem on this subject which finally sends everybody, including himself, to sleep.

With the eery Mozartian strains which are heard in the deep silence following Mendoza's recitation, the Dream commences. Don Juan appears in the half-light and then a new strain of music is heard which announces the approach of Doña Ana. This tune is part of the melody of the aria which Doña Ana sings to Ottavio just before the commencement of the Statue scene in *Don Giovanni*, "Crudele! Ah no! Mio bene," The stage direction says that the clarinet turns this tune into "*infinite sadness*." In the opera the aria is sung in response to Ottavio's bitter complaint at Ana's cruelty in delaying their union so long. Ana replies with magnificent indignation, "Cruel, ah no my love," and goes on to sing her beautiful consolatory aria which looks forward to the final union of the two lovers. Shaw's use of this music is highly effective dramatically. The "*infinite sadness*" clearly relates to the rather surprising introduction of Ana as an old and lonely woman. For a short while at the beginning of the Dream scene, the play takes a decidedly un-comic turn. . . . Shortly after the opening of the Dream Ana is rejuvenated and the play returns to its essentially comic path.

Shaw produced in *Man and Superman* a play which is at once deeply conventional—in one of his last comments on the so-called drama of ideas, Shaw remarked that for his part he had been "going back atavistically to Aristotle" in his dramatic methods—but which at the same time constantly turns conventions to his own account to produce a highly original and quite distinctive dramatic structure. No doubt the main reason for the extraordinarily long persistence of the comic form to which Frye draws attention is that it is rooted in forms of human experience which have remained essentially unaffected by social change: the struggle for the securing of sexual partners and the conflict between members of different generations which that struggle commonly involved. The salient point of Shaw's adaptation of the classic form to which *Man and Superman* is related, the centre of the play's comic philosophy, lies in the uniqueness of its principal male protagonist. Sexual attractiveness—and eventual dominance, in this oddly Darwinian comedy—is associated not with the sentimental and melancholy man of feeling in the Romantic tradition, nor with the rampant and insatiable seducer of the Don Juan legend, nor with the military hero, but with the politically alert, breezy, affable, vulnerable and humorous revolutionist. (pp. 171-74)

> *A. M. Gibbs, "Comedy and Philosophy in 'Man and Superman'," in* Modern Drama, *Vol. XIX, No. 2, June, 1976, pp. 161-75.*

WARREN SYLVESTER SMITH   (essay date 1982)

[*In the following excerpt, Smith explores some biographical reasons for Shaw's development of such concepts as the Superman and the Life Force as set forth in* Man and Superman.]

[When] Shaw was in his early forties, something happened—something of an inner spiritual nature. I do not wish to imply any specific "conversion" experience. There is nothing on the later side of this turning point that cannot be found in embryo on the earlier side. Still it is a perceptibly different Shaw who imposes himself on the new century, one who has gone beyond "the art of destroying ideals" to explore a personal cosmology—one might even say a theology. (p. 22)

But the appearance of *Man and Superman* in 1903 signaled more than a maturation of philosophical ideas hatched in the great Reading Room of the British Museum (his only alma mater, as he later said). [In *Bernard Shaw: Art and Socialism*

(1942)] E. Strauss finds him, at this time, writing on the edge of despair, "engaged in an attempt to save the remains of his crumbling hopes and beliefs by transferring them on to a new plane." It is true that there are such notes of urgency in "Don Juan in Hell," the dream scene that constitutes the third act of *Man and Superman*, but the spirit of the play is buoyant and vigorous, not in the least despairing. Shaw's biographer, St. John Ervine, may have been nearer the mark when [in *Bernard Shaw* (1956)] he attributed the new look to Shaw's "happy marriage" on 1 June 1898 to Charlotte Payne-Townshend. For the first time in his life, Ervine maintained, Shaw lived in a well-regulated house where decent meals were served on time. (pp. 22-3)

[Shaw had] struggled always to be free of sexual entanglement to devote himself to the higher moral passion. The parallel of this struggle to that of John Tanner in *Man and Superman* has often been noted. . . . But Shaw did not struggle against the union with Charlotte. Rather he was much relieved. Nor was Charlotte anything like the sexually provocative Ann Whitefield of the play. Their marriage, as their friends seemed to know and accept, was a companionate one in which sex had no place. (p. 24)

When the couple returned to London at the end of 1899 to settle in Charlotte's flat at Adelphi Terrace, Shaw was forty-three, Charlotte, forty-two. He had gained weight and was wearing good conservative clothes. Like the hero of the play he was about to write, his marriage had brought him into the establishment. Even after he had settled back into the London scene, the gestation period for *Man and Superman* was exceptionally long. In 1901 he wrote nothing but *The Admirable Bashville*, a blank-verse spoof of his early novel, *Cashel Byron's Profession*—hurriedly composed so that its copyright could forestall other dramatizations of the work. "*Man & Superman* no doubt sounds as if it came from the most exquisite atmosphere of art," he later wrote to his biographer, Archibald Henderson. "As a matter of fact, the mornings I gave to it were followed by afternoons & evenings spent in the committee rooms of a London Borough Council, fighting questions of drainage, paving, lighting, rates, clerk's salaries &c &c &c, and that is exactly why it is so different from the books that are conceived at musical at-homes."

Shaw later maintained that the first inkling of the play came to him as a scrap of dialogue: "I am a brigand: I live by robbing the rich. I am a gentleman: I live by robbing the poor," which found its place in the exchange between Tanner and Mendoza at the beginning of Act III. Despite these beginnings, it did not turn out to be another thesis play like *Mrs Warren's Profession*, but the culmination [as Alfred Turco, Jr., has pointed out in his *Shaw's Moral Vision: The Self and Salvation* (1976)] of everything since *Immaturity*, Shaw's appropriately titled first novel begun at age twenty. Turco has further pronounced it "the first play in which Shaw's belief in the possibility of an *effective* idealism is presented with real conviction."

The play, however, was not quite the new Evolutionary Bible that Shaw, in retrospect, claimed it was: "I think it well to affirm plainly that the third act, however, fantastic its legendary framework may be, is a careful attempt to write a new Book of Genesis for the Bible of the Evolutionists." . . . He later told a correspondent that "the 3rd Act of *Man and Superman* will remain on record as a statement of my creed." And in a 1910 letter to Count Leo Tolstoy accompanying a copy of *The Shewing-Up of Blanco Posnet*, he says again: "It is all in *Man and Superman*, but expressed in another way." All this might much better have been said of *Back to Methuselah*, which was still nearly twenty years in the future. As we shall see, *Man and Superman*, with all its crackling brilliance, is only a beginning of Shaw's exploration of the Life Force. In 1921 he recalled, more accurately, "... in 1901, I took the legend of Don Juan in its Mozartian form and made it a dramatic parable of Creative Evolution. But being then at the height of my invention and comedic talent, I decorated it too brilliantly and lavishly." ...

Man and Superman consists of what Shaw called a "trumpery story"—a sex-chase, really—surrounding an hour-and-a-half dream scene of Don Juan in Hell. As a practical man of the theatre Shaw realized that the complete play was not likely to achieve immediate production, even though it created considerable comment when it was published. Its first real stage run—minus the dream scene—replaced the successful *John Bull's Other Island* in 1905 at the Royal Court. It was immediately popular. The play, complete with dream scene, does make a unified whole, despite Shaw's prefatory apology that his play had "a totally extraneous act" and that you must "prepare yourself to face a trumpery story of modern London life, a life in which, as you know, the ordinary man's main business is to get means to keep up the position and habits of a gentleman, and the ordinary woman's business is to get married" [see Shaw excerpt dated 1903]. (pp. 25-7)

As to the comedy itself, it is all very well to call it "a Victorian farce in four neatly arranged acts," or to suggest that without the Hell scene the play is a bright sexual comedy not unlike those of Terence Rattigan. Even on these terms it outperforms all its models. In his merging of plot and counter-plot, in his use of triangles and reversals and the chase, in his elegant change of pace and character-contrast, and most of all in the subtleties that flow beneath the surface dialogue and inhabit the imagery—in all these ways Shaw, at the turn of the century, could give lessons to Eugene Scribe or any of the French farceurs, or to W. S. Gilbert or Oscar Wilde, or, for that matter, to the later Noel Coward or Terence Rattigan.

Samuel Butler, to whose thinking Shaw owed so much, made a happy figure of speech about the nature of evolution:

> As in the development of a fugue, where, when the subject and counter subject have been announced, there must henceforth be nothing new, and yet all must be new, so throughout organic life—which is a fugue developed to great length from a very simple subject—everything is linked on to and grows out of that which comes next to it in order—errors and omissions excepted.

Man and Superman, which deals with evolution, is also such a fugue, and its subject is simply: *The Life Force, acting through the will of woman, subdues man to its purpose, and thereby moves the race to its next higher level.* That is the subject that gives unity to the play, even though it proves somewhat limiting to its philosophical development.

It is a subject that calls for a sex play. And Shaw, himself a Victorian as far as his public manners were concerned, a man who could not bring himself to utter or write a vulgar four-letter word, and writing for an audience reared in an era of sexual repression, still managed to dramatize an obviously sexual pursuit, climaxing in a mutual orgasm played front and center. For there is no doubt that in the "obligatory scene" in Act IV, where Ann has finally caught up with Tanner and sheer feminine attraction keeps him from fleeing the garden in Gran-

ada, the act of mating virtually ceases to be symbolic and becomes all but actual. It is here that the term "Life Force" is first used in the play proper. (p. 27)

How is it ... that a society that only a few years before rejected *Mrs Warren's Profession* as scrofulous, accepted *Man and Superman* with such delight? There was in *Mrs Warren* no such provocative figure as Ann Whitefield, and no such physical encounter as the embrace of Jack and Ann. Louis Crompton has pointed out that emancipated Victorians—like Roebuck Ramsden in the play—had come to accept theological and political radicalism, but clung desperately to traditional sexual mores, despite such avant gardists as Havelock Ellis, Grant Allen, and H. G. Wells. Perhaps Shaw's most shocking heresy was to treat sentimental love, marriage, and child-bearing as though they were three unrelated phenomena, whereas in the Victorian-Edwardian code the three are, or at least ought to be, inseparable. (pp. 28-9)

Both women [in *Man and Superman*]—Violet and Ann—bring their quarries to earth. Violet has succeeded with rapacious ease and is already secretly married and pregnant when the play opens. Her struggle, the counter-subject of the fugue, is merely to win the consent of her Irish-American husband's father and to secure an income from him. But the real excitement of the play is the sex-chase: the subtle entrapment devised by Ann—even, as it turns out, before the play begins—and carefully laid out in Ramsden's drawing room; the discovery in the park by Tanner that the trap has been set for *him*, and not, as he imagined, for his friend Octavius; the flight across the channel and through Southern Europe with Straker racing Violet's husband's American steam car (the love affair of Straker with the automobile being another and prescient variation of the sex-chase); the capture by brigands in the Sierra Nevada and the Don Juan dream among the outlaws; the overtaking by the English and American party and the final capitulation of Tanner. ...

Shaw had a way of seeing things as a mirror-image—or perhaps since we are used to seeing ourselves reversed in the mirror, we should say a video-monitor-image—the shocking "reversal" of our own self-image, but as it is normally seen by others. A good paradox, in other words, is not merely a statement stood on its head regardless of the truth, but a surprising view from the other side. Such an inversion occurs when Don Juan Tenorio, the legendary pursuer of women, becomes John Tanner, the pursued. (p. 30)

But in the end Tanner, like any good character from any good writer of fiction, is essentially himself, despite any family resemblances he may have to others.

The inversions are not limited to the Don Juan-Tanner character. When we find ourselves in Hell, we are not so much in a place as in an atmosphere, a state of mind. And this we must assume to be a significant aspect of Shaw's "creed." Shaw no longer considered himself an atheist—as he had announced himself in his youth—but he had no belief in any kind of personal immortality. The "Hell" is recognizable only because it is introduced by Mozart's musical theme, because Don Juan assures the newcomer that that is where she is, and because it is supervised by a congenial Devil. These are Shaw's concessions to convention; but we are periodically reminded that both Heaven and Hell are constantly with us, that we continue to move from one state to the other, or that they are often mixed together. When Ana asks if she could go to Heaven if she wished, the Devil answers contemptuously, "Certainly, if your taste lies that way.'' And when she quotes Scripture: ''Surely there is a great gulf fixed,'' the Devil explains,

> Dear lady: A parable must not be taken literally. The gulf is the difference between the angelic and the diabolic temperament. What more impassable gulf could you have? . . . the gulf of dislike is impassable and eternal. And that is the only gulf that separates my friends here from those who are invidiously called the blest. . . .

The scene, then, is specifically Hell, but we are given views of Heaven by the Statue of the Commander, who comes to visit the Devil and decides to stay; by Don Juan, who is uncomfortable in Hell and at the end chooses Heaven; and by the Devil himself, who admits that he is prejudiced.

In Christian theology God is Love. The inversion here is that Love is Hell. Hell is the home of all the maudlin romantic emotions—joy, happiness, beauty—the mention of which tends to make Don Juan ill. In Hell you abandon all hope, that is, you abandon all moral responsibility. You have nothing to do but amuse yourself. That is the secret of its popularity. . . . It is notable that none of these attributes have anything to do with punishment. Hell is the natural condition of useless, selfish, pleasure-loving people.

But what then is Heaven? It is ''the home of the masters of reality,'' a place where ''you live and work instead of playing and pretending.'' . . . Most of all it is a place of contemplation. To the Devil and the Statue all this is pretty dull—''the most angelically dull place in all creation.'' The Hell-dwellers view it much as the youth in the final play of *Back to Methuselah* will view the elders who are becoming ''vortices of pure thought.'' ''Oh, it suits some people,'' the Devil admits. ''. . . it is a question of temperament. I dont admire the heavenly temperament. . . . but it takes all sorts to make a universe. There is no accounting for tastes.'' . . .

The Hell scene, despite the burden of its verbiage, has proved, on purely theatrical terms, to be eminently playable. But its substance remains in the vigor of its argument. Shaw must be on the side of Don Juan and the Life Force, but here as elsewhere he gives the Devil his due. (pp. 30-2)

At any rate his arguments are so forceful and so cogent that the result of the debate is left in doubt. As with Undershaft in *Major Barbara* and Cauchon in *Saint Joan,* the antagonist all but overpowers the cause which Shaw champions on the lecture platform. (p. 32)

The term [Life Force] itself is not mentioned until we are well into the dream scene, and its power does not become evident until the Ann-Tanner scene in Act IV. . . . Even in the celebrated Preface there is more about the need for a genuine sex play and about the development of a literary style than there is about the Life Force. Similarly, though there are a few highly illuminating sentences in ''The Revolutionist's Handbook,'' its basic theme is that improvement of the species can take place only through selective breeding. (pp. 32-3)

Still, one must not underestimate the significance of the breakthrough in Shaw's thinking that *Man and Superman* represents. At the core of that breakthrough is the much-quoted announcement of Don Juan:

> I sing not arms and the hero, but the philosophic man: he who seeks in contemplation to discover

the inner will of the world, in invention to discover the means of fulfilling that will, and in action to do that will by the so-discovered means. . . .

Now what Shaw had so far discovered about ''the inner will of the world'' was that a mysterious Life Force was at work in directing evolution. He had not yet thought this through, and it would be another twenty years before he did so. For the present he could perceive that this Force favored organization as opposed to chaos, and that it required brains—intellect: ''My brain is the organ by which Nature strives to understand itself.'' (p. 33)

The Life Force, however, has no brain of its own. Dependent as it is, for the moment, on human brains, its immediate task is to evolve a being superior to the present inadequate specimen. Since this can only be accomplished through the process of mating, the sex play is central in its exalted purpose.

It is to woman that Nature has given the responsibility for propagating the race, and she is therefore, whether she knows it or not, more in the service of the Life Force than man is. . . . But the male sex, once created, fulfilled its breeding purpose and had considerable energy left over. All of civilization is a sublimation of this energy, which has resulted in woman herself being dominated by man, and being forced to cooperate in ''a feeble romantic convention that the initiative in sex business must always come from the man.'' . . .

This notion . . . is something of a stumbling block to those who like to think of Shaw as a champion of women's equality, and seems to be in contradiction to his profession that ''I have always assumed that a woman is a person exactly like myself.'' . . .

There are cases—cases of genius—in which the creative flame burns as brightly in the man as in the woman. One gathers that the hope for the future lies with those who *know* they are in the service of the Life Force. . . .

This was about as far as Shaw had gone by 1903. There has been much scholarly speculation as to how he came by these ideas. (p. 34)

There were quite evidently many sources of such ideas available to Shaw by 1900. . . .

Shaw's idea of a Life Force was not original. But neither was it a copy. . . . Shaw had an unusual facility for absorbing all kinds of diverse material, refining and amalgamating it into something that could legitimately be called his own. It could hardly, at this point, be called a religious statement. He came closest to such a statement in ''The Revolutionist's Handbook'' when he pictured the political man as a failure, looking to the heavens for help and finding them empty. (p. 35)

But it is through Ann that the Life Force flows. . . . [Without] Ann's drive there would be no play at all—even though Tanner knows, perhaps subconsciously, that the childhood love-pact between them remains inviolate. Ann is the *efficient* organ of the Life Force.

It is important to point out that no ''superman'' appears in this play. Perhaps—but only perhaps—the Life Force is at work trying to create one, or at least move a step closer to one. At the end of the dream scene when Ana asks the Devil, ''Tell me: where can I find the Superman?'' his answer is unequivocal: ''He is not yet created, Señora.'' . . . As the scene fades, Ana, who has chosen neither Heaven nor Hell, decides that her work is not yet done, and cries out to the universe for "A father for the Superman!" . . . (p. 36)

In a later program note (1907) Shaw explained that "Though by her death she is done with the bearing of men to mortal fathers, she may yet, as Woman Immortal, bear the Superman to the Eternal Father." . . . When Octavius repeats to Ann a sentimental speech we have already heard in the dream scene, Ann has "a strange sudden sense of an echo from a former existence." . . . May we not also conjecture that Ana's final cry has a similar resonance in Ann's unconscious? (p. 37)

The idea of a Life Force, thus launched, continued to absorb more and more of Shaw's thoughts until, after the end of World War I, he returned to deal directly with it in the most extensive and probably the most misunderstood of all his works, **Back to Methuselah**. In the meantime there are no more plays specifically about the Life Force, but we can continue to sense its presence and discern some of its attributes by observing the characters who are most likely to be in its service. (pp. 37-8)

> *Warren Sylvester Smith, in his* Bishop of Everywhere: Bernard Shaw and the Life Force, *The Pennsylvania State University Press, University Park, 1982, 191 p.*

ADDITIONAL BIBLIOGRAPHY

Adams, Elsie B. *Bernard Shaw and the Aesthetes*. Columbus: Ohio State University Press, 1971, 193 p.
   An attempt to define Shaw's place in the fin-de-siècle aesthetic or art-for-art's-sake movement in arts and letters, comparing Shaw's treatment of such themes as the artist's relation to his society and Shaw's theory of morality in art with the traditional aesthete's approaches to these themes.

Bentley, Eric. "Bernard Shaw." In his *The Playwright as Thinker: A Study of Drama in Modern Times*, pp. 137-57. New York: Reynal & Hitchcock, 1946.
   Attempts "to set forth the theory and practice of Shavian drama as forthrightly as possible."

———. *Bernard Shaw*. New York: New Directions Publishing Corp., 1947, 242 p.
   A seminal analysis of Shaw's dramas which was highly regarded by Shaw himself.

Berst, Charles A. "*Man and Superman*: The Art of Spiritual Autobiography." In his *Bernard Shaw and the Art of Drama*, pp. 96-153. Urbana: University of Illinois Press, 1973.
   Extensive and insightful study of *Man and Superman*, exploring such areas as Shaw's intent in writing the work, his sources for the Life Force theory, and offering analysis of the comedy portion of the play.

Braybrooke, Patrick. "Man, Superman and a Woman." In his *The Subtlety of George Bernard Shaw*, pp. 97-117. Oxford: Cecil Palmer, 1930.
   Discussion of *Man and Superman* concluding that the play, Shaw's masterpiece, embodies Shaw's optimistic philosophy that humankind can create its own savior in the Superman.

Brower, R. H. "George Bernard Shaw: 1856-1950," and "*Man and Superman: A Comedy and a Philosophy*." In *Major British Writers*, rev. ed., edited by G. B. Harrison, pp. 681-94, 695-97. New York: Harcourt, Brace and Co., 1954.
   Chronologically arranged critical overview of Shaw's career. The second chapter cited, a prefatory essay discussing *Man and Superman*, notes especially Shaw's indebtedness to Mozart's opera *Don Giovanni*.

Carpenter, Charles A. "Notes on Some Obscurities in 'The Revolutionist's Handbook'." *Shaw Review* 13, No. 2 (May 1970): 59-64.
   Explains a number of topical references and obscure allusions in "The Revolutionist's Handbook."

Ervine, St. John. *Bernard Shaw*. New York: William Morrow and Co., 1956, 628 p.
   Biography of Shaw written by his intimate friend. Ervine's work contains many excerpts from Shaw's early diaries.

Irvine, William. "*Man and Superman*: A Step in Shavian Disillusionment." *The Huntington Library Quarterly* X, No. 2 (February 1947): 209-24.
   Interpretation of *Man and Superman* as "a complex satire of socialism," with which, the critic contends, Shaw had grown disillusioned.

Lewis, C. S. "What Lies behind the Law." In his *Mere Christianity*, pp. 31-5. New York: Macmillan Publishing Co., 1960.*
   Examines crucial problems in the philosophy of the Life-Force. "The wittiest expositions of it come in the works of Bernard Shaw," writes Lewis, "but the most profound ones in those of Bergson." Lewis denounces the Life Force as an insupportable hobby horse—"a sort of tame God. You can switch it on when you want, but it will not bother you. All the thrills of religion and none of the cost."

Masur, Gerhard. "The Confident Years." In his *Prophets of Yesterday: Studies in European Culture 1890-1914*, pp. 252-97. New York: Macmillan Co., 1961.*
   Examination of Shaw's many beliefs.

Meisel, Martin. *Shaw and the Nineteenth-Century Theater*. Princeton: Princeton University Press, 1963, 477 p.
   Explores Shaw's "new creation of a drama of ideas out of antecedent conventions and materials" from nineteenth-century drama. The book contains frequent scattered references to *Man and Superman*.

Mills, Carl Henry. "*Man and Superman* and the Don Juan Legend." *Comparative Literature* 19, No. 3 (Summer 1967): 216-25.*
   Interprets Shaw's treatment of the Don Juan legend not as a transformation of basic elements already existing in traditional myth but as a development of the story, bringing it up to date.

Morgan, Margery M. "*Man and Superman*: Verbal Heroics." In her *The Shavian Playground: An Exploration of the Art of George Bernard Shaw*, pp. 100-18. London: Methuen & Co., 1972.
   Examination of *Man and Superman* stressing the characterization of the play's central figures.

Nathan, George Jean. "Mr. Nathan Goes to the Play: *Don Juan in Hell*." *Theatre Arts* XXXVI, No. 1 (January 1952): 80.
   Favorably reviews the first production of the third act of *Man and Superman* as a solo work, calling it "Shaw's wise and witty exercise in paradox, with its sly and enormously cunning inquiry into the muddled philosophies of mankind in its search for self and happiness."

Nethercot, Arthur H. *Men and Superman: The Shavian Portrait Gallery*. Rev. ed. New York: Benjamin Blom, 1954, 327 p.
   Examines various of Shaw's dramatic character types with an eye to disproving the commonly accepted view, satirized by Shaw himself in *Fanny's First Play*, that "all Shaw's characters are himself: mere puppets stuck up to spout Shaw." An extensive study of Ann Whitefield is included in the chapter "The Female of the Species;" and of other *Man and Superman dramatis personae* in other chapters.

Roppen, Georg. "Two Evolutionary Utopias." In his *Evolution and Poetic Belief: A Study in Some Victorian and Modern Writers*, pp. 344-457. Oslo: Oslo University Press, 1956.*
   Comparison of evolutionary themes in the works of Shaw—in particular his concepts of the Life Force and Creative Evolution as set forth in *Man and Superman*—and some similar concepts explored in the work of H. G. Wells.

Stamm, Julian L. "Shaw's *Man and Superman:* His Struggle for Sublimation." *American Imago* 22, No. 4 (Winter 1965): 250-54.
Biographically oriented psychological study of *Man and Superman,* finding in the third act a thinly veiled portrayal of Shaw's ambivalence toward women stemming from his relationship with his own mother.

Stewart, J. I. M. "Shaw." In *Eight Modern Writers,* edited by F. P. Wilson and Bonamy Dobree, pp. 122-83. Clarendon: Oxford University Press, 1963.
Critical overview of Shaw's work.

Strauss, E. *Bernard Shaw: Art and Socialism.* London: Victor Gollancz, 1942, 126 p.
Socialist explication of Shaw's life and works, including scattered references to *Man and Superman* as the culmination of Shaw's development of his Socialist attitudes toward two problems: love and relationships between the sexes; and the place of the artist in society.

Tolstoy, Leo. Letter to Bernard Shaw. In *The Life of Tolstoy: Later Years,* Vol. II, by Aylmer Maude, pp. 642-43. New York: Dodd, Mead and Co., 1910.
Undated letter maintaining that "the problem about God and evil is too important to be spoken of in jest," which reiterates Tolstoy's criticism of *Man and Superman* made in an earlier letter to Shaw (see excerpt dated 1908).

Turco, Alfred, Jr. "Don Juan in Heaven." In his *Shaw's Moral Vision: The Self and Salvation,* pp. 145-71. Ithaca, N.Y.: Cornell University Press, 1976.
Employs internal evidence drawn from *Man and Superman* to counter two criticisms of the play: "that its characterization of women is both prejudiced and superficial; and that the brilliant hell scene is not organically related to the action proper."

Ward, A. C. *Bernard Shaw.* Harlow, England: British Council, 1970, 60 p.
Biography of Shaw tracing his career and illuminating his philosophies.

Weintraub, Rodelle, ed. *Fabian Feminist: Bernard Shaw and Woman.* University Park: Pennsylvania University Press, 1977, 274 p.
Collection of essays on Shaw's attitudes toward women as revealed in his essays and dramas. Included are essays on "Mill, Marx and Bebel: Early Influences on Shaw's Characterizations of Women," by Norbert Greiner, "The 'Unwomanly Woman' in Shaw's Drama," by Sonja Lorichs, and "Feminism and Female Stereotypes in Shaw," by Elsie Adams. Also included is a section of Shaw's own essays under the heading "Shaw on Feminist Issues."

Weintraub, Stanley. "Genesis of a Play: Two Early Approaches to *Man and Superman.*" In *Shaw: Seven Critical Essays,* edited by Norman Rosenblood, pp. 25-35. Toronto: University of Toronto Press, 1971.
Selection from a compendium of essays that were read at the Shaw Seminars held at Brock University in Ontario and at the Shaw Festival at Niagara-on-the-Lake during 1966, 1967, and 1968. In the cited essay, the critic relies almost exclusively on published material and biographical data to trace the development of the ideas that are expounded in *Man and Superman.*

Whitman, Robert F. *Shaw and the Play of Ideas.* Ithaca, N.Y.: Cornell University Press, 1977, 293 p.
Examination of the chief philosophic ideas espoused in Shaw's works.

Williamson, Audrey. "Success and the Court Theatre." In her *Bernard Shaw: Man and Writer,* pp. 129-52. New York: Crowell-Collier Press, 1963.
Biographical and critical account of the period of great theatrical success that Shaw enjoyed between 1904 and 1907 at the Royal Court Theatre while it operated under the partnership of Harley Granville-Barker and J. E. Vedrenne.

Woodbridge, Homer E. "*Man and Superman.*" In his *George Bernard Shaw: Creative Artist,* pp. 56-62. Carbondale: Southern Illinois University Press, 1963, 181 p.
Thorough and insightful examination of the two parts of *Man and Superman,* treating the comic play separately from the philosophic discussion of the third act hell scene.

(Johan) August Strindberg
1849-1912

(Also wrote under pseudonym of Härved Ulf) Swedish dramatist, novelist, short story writer, poet, essayist, and journalist.

Strindberg is considered one of the most important and influential dramatists in modern literature. With the plays *Fadren (The Father)* and *Fröken Julie (Miss Julie)*, he proved himself an innovative exponent of Naturalism, while the later *Ett drömspel (The Dream Play)* and the trilogy *Till Damaskus (To Damascus)* are now recognized as forerunners of Expressionism, Surrealism, and the Theater of the Absurd. While Strindberg's novels, short stories, and essays are highly esteemed, his dramatic achievements tend to overshadow his work in other genres.

The autobiographical nature of Strindberg's work has generated a number of popular misconceptions about his life. Recent biographers, however, have attempted with some success to construct a more accurate picture. In the novel *Tränstekvinnans son (The Son of a Servant)*, for example, Strindberg portrayed himself as the unwanted product of a union between an impoverished aristocrat and a servant, a situation that early biographers treated as fact. In reality, the circumstances of his birth were considerably more favorable. His father was involved in Stockholm's vigorous shipping trade, and although his mother had worked as a maid for a short time, she was the daughter of a tailor, and the disparity between her class and her husband's was not very great. Life in the Strindberg home was, by all objective accounts, rather comfortable, but Strindberg was an extremely shy and sensitive child who held an excessively negative perception of his own circumstances. Strindberg was educated first at the local primary school, then at the Stockholm Lyceum, a progressive private school. Though only an average student, he enrolled at the university of Uppsala in 1867. While still at the university, Strindberg wrote his first play; the endeavor afforded him such satisfaction that he resolved to make play writing his profession. During 1869, he wrote three more plays, two of which were accepted for production by the prestigious Royal Theater in Stockholm. However, these plays were not financially successful, and Strindberg was obliged to write stories and articles for periodicals in order to earn a living, a practice he considered degrading. It was not until the publication of his novel *Röda rummet (The Red Room)* in 1879 that Strindberg became a highly respected and nationally recognized author.

Essential material for Strindberg's subsequent works was provided by his three tempestuous marriages. The first and longest, to Sigrid von Essen, was the basis for one novel, *Le plaidoyer d'un fou (The Confession of a Fool)*, two collections of short stories, *Giftas (Married, Parts I and II)*, and several plays. Following the breakup of his second marriage in 1891, Strindberg experienced what are generally thought to have been psychotic episodes, a period of deep depression and hallucinations that he called his Inferno Crisis. While his behavior had always been slightly bizarre, a manifestation of his suspicious nature and feelings of persecution, during this period he is considered to have suffered a complete psychological break with reality. Described by biographers as severely paranoiac, he now moved

from lodging to lodging, convinced that his enemies were trying to murder him with electrical currents and lethal gases. Further manifestations of Strindberg's breakdown are observed in his abandonment of a literary career in order to devote himself to alchemical experiments and in the radical alteration of his religious thinking. In his youth, Strindberg had been agnostic and occasionally highly irreverent; *Married*, for example, contained passages which had caused Strindberg and his publisher to be charged with blasphemy. During the Inferno Crisis, however, Strindberg came to believe that his affliction had been decreed by God as a punishment for his sins, and he sought a reconciliation with the deity as a possible cure, becoming fascinated with the work of Emanuel Swedenborg, a Christian mystic who strongly believed in divine revelation.

Although Strindberg eventually recovered from his psychosis, the event did produce some lasting changes. His metaphysical perspective, which had been distinctly nihilistic, became traditionally Christian, while his work began to reflect his newly developed mysticism in its dreamlike, highly symbolic nature. His recovery was accompanied by a surge of creative activity. He returned to the theater to transform the horrors of the Inferno Crisis and his new-found religious mysticism into dramatic images. Although he wrote a number of dramas, several novels, and many essays and articles between 1898 and 1906, he devoted most of his energy to composing *En blå bok (Zones of the Spirit)*, a prodigious collection of essays expressing a variety of opinions and ideas. Strindberg's final years were relatively peaceful and productive. Although he was saddened by his failed marriages and the resulting separation from his children, he was revered by the Swedish people, who staged an enormous celebration in honor of his sixtieth birthday. He continued to write until he became incapacitated by illness. He died in 1912.

Critics divide Strindberg's work into two phases, citing the Inferno Crisis as the fulcrum of the dramatist's career. The satirical novel *The Red Room*, the historical drama *Mäster Olof (Master Olof)*, and the naturalistic plays *The Father* and *Miss Julie* are the most significant examples of his pre-Inferno writings. *The Red Room*, an episodic satire on Stockholm's bohemian circle, is based on the author's own experiences as a member of that coterie. His impressions of the artists, journalists, and intellectuals who comprised this circle have been praised, as has his vivid and picturesque prose style. *Master Olof*, Strindberg's first theatrical success, is also first in a cycle of twelve chronicle plays concerning Swedish rulers. As Shakespeare had done, Strindberg dramatized a series of historic events that embodied the social and political issues of the day.

While *Master Olof* had introduced Strindberg as an important Scandinavian playwright, *The Father* and *Miss Julie* established his reputation as a brilliant innovator of theatrical form. In these works Strindberg developed a new, intense form of naturalism. Influenced by Emile Zola, Strindberg depicted his characters and their lives with scientific objectivity. However, he furthered this concept by focusing solely on the "moment of struggle," the immediate conflict or crisis affecting his characters. Dialogue and incidents not pertaining to this "moment" were eliminated, removing all vestiges of the well-made play. *The Father, Miss Julie, Kamraterna (Comrades)*, and *Dödsdansen (The Dance of Death)* all have their thematic bases in Nietzsche's concept of life as a succession of contests between stronger and weaker wills. Strindberg applied this theory to his recurring subject of the conflict between the sexes for psychological supremacy. It was in his Naturalistic dramas, composed during the last, stormy years of his first marriage, that Strindberg demonstrated what has been called a distorted and misogynistic view of women. His female characters of this period are typically diabolic usurpers of the "naturally" dominant role of males in society: with infinite cunning and cruelty, they eventually shatter the male characters' "superior" psyches and drain their creative and intellectual powers. Critics contend that these alienated and abused male characters reflect the author's self-image, that of the perennial outcast and victim. Although critics have censured what they consider Strindberg's sexist views, their disapproval has not detracted from their estimation of the importance of these works.

The stylistic experiments of Strindberg's post-Inferno period proved a turning point in modern dramaturgy. From his studies, Strindberg concluded that earthly life is a hell which men and women are forced to endure, a nightmare in which they suffer for sins committed in a previous life. *To Damascus, The Dream Play*, and *Spöksonaten (The Ghost Sonata)* are based on this premise, presenting a fragmented and highly subjective view of reality that approximates the Inferno Crisis. To achieve this effect, Strindberg employed the symbolism and structure of dreams, creating a grotesque and ludicrous world that is both believable and frighteningly unreal: individuals appear and disappear at random, scenes and images change at the slightest provocation, and characters encounter their worst fears and

fantasies. With *To Damascus* and *The Dream Play*, Strindberg prefigured the major dramatic movements of the twentieth century, and his influence can be seen in the work of Samuel Beckett, Eugene O'Neill, and Eugène Ionesco.

Because Strindberg was an intensely autobiographical and self-analytical writer, a few critics, including Desmond MacCarthy, have dismissed his plays as "products of the unfortunate 'cathartic' type of creation, which purges no one but the creator." The majority of commentators, however, regard Strindberg as a major literary figure. O'Neill, for example, believed that Strindberg "was the precursor of all modernity in our present theater," and most critics agree that his work initiated, in both content and form, the dramatic methods of the modern theater.

(See also *TCLC*, Vols. 1 and 8, and *Contemporary Authors*, Vol. 104)

PRINCIPAL WORKS

Fritankaren [first publication] (drama) 1870
I Rom (drama) 1870
Fråan Fjärdingen och Svartbäcken (short stories) 1877
Röda rummet (novel) 1879
  [*The Red Room*, 1913]
Mäster Olof (drama) 1881
  [*Master Olof*, 1915]
Dikter på vers och prosa (poetry) 1883
Lycko-Pers resa (drama) 1883
  [*Lucky Pehr*, 1912; also published as *Lucky Peter's Travels* in *Lucky Peter's Travels, and Other Plays*, 1930]
Giftas. 2 vols. (short stories, essays, and aphorisms) 1884-86
  [*Married*, 1913; also published as *Getting Married, Parts I and II*, 1972]
Sömngångarnätter på vakna dagar (poetry) 1884
Tjänstekvinnans son (novel) 1886
  [*The Son of a Servant*, 1913]
Fadren (drama) 1887
  [*The Father*, 1899]
Hemsöborna (novel) 1887
  [*The People of Hemsö*, 1959]
Den starkare (drama) 1889
  [*The Stronger* published in *Plays by August Strindberg, second series*, 1913]
Fröken Julia (drama) 1889
  [*Countess Julia*, 1912; also published as *Miss Julia* in *Plays by August Strinberg, second series*,1913; and *Miss Julie* in *Miss Julie, and Other Plays*, 1918]
Le plaidoyer d'un fou (novel) 1895
  [*The Confession of a Fool*, 1912]
Inferno (novel) 1897
  [*The Inferno*, 1912]
Till Damaskus. 3 vols. [first publication] (drama) 1898-1904
  [*To Damascus*, 1913; also published as *The Road to Damascus*, 1939]
Folkungasagan (drama) 1899
  [*The Saga of the Folkungs* published in *The Saga of the Folkungs. Engelbrekt*, 1959]
Gustave Vasa (drama) 1899
  [*Gustavus Vasa* published in *Plays by August Strindberg, fourth series*, 1916]
Påsk (drama) 1901
  [*Easter* published in *Easter, and Stories*, 1912]

AUGUST STRINDBERG   (essay date 1888)

[*In the following excerpt from an essay originally published in
Sweden in 1888, Strindberg explains his perception of the function
and nature of drama.*]

Like almost all other art, that of the stage has long seemed to
me a sort of *Biblia Pauperum,* or a Bible in pictures for those
who cannot read what is written or printed. And in the same
way the playwright has seemed to me a lay preacher spreading
the thoughts of his time in a form so popular that the middle
classes, from which theatrical audiences are mainly drawn, can
know what is being talked about without troubling their brains
too much. For this reason the theatre has always served as a
grammar-school to young people, women, and those who have
acquired a little knowledge, all of whom retain the capacity
for deceiving themselves and being deceived—which means
again that they are susceptible to illusions produced by the
suggestions of the author. And for the same reason I have had
a feeling that, in our time, when the rudimentary, incomplete
thought processes operating through our fancy seem to be developing into reflection, research, and analysis, the theatre
might stand on the verge of being abandoned as a decaying
form, for the enjoyment of which we lack the requisite conditions. The prolonged theatrical crisis now prevailing throughout Europe speaks in favour of such a supposition, as well as
the fact that, in the civilised countries producing the greatest
thinkers of the age, namely, England and Germany, the drama
is as dead as are most of the other fine arts.

In some other countries it has, however, been thought possible
to create a new drama by filling the old forms with the contents
of a new time. But, for one thing, there has not been time for
the new thoughts to become so popularised that the public might
grasp the questions raised; secondly, minds have been so inflamed by party conflicts that pure and disinterested enjoyment
has been excluded from places where one's innermost feelings
are violated and the tyranny of an applauding or hissing majority is exercised with the openness for which the theatre gives
a chance; and, finally, there has been no new form devised for
the new contents, and the new wine has burst the old bottles.

In the following drama [*Miss Julie*] I have not tried to do
anything new—for that cannot be done—but I have tried to

modernise the form in accordance with the demands which I
thought the new men of a new time might be likely to make
on this art. And with such a purpose in view, I have chosen,
or surrendered myself to, a theme that might well be said to
lie outside the partisan strife of the day: for the problem of
social ascendancy or decline, of higher or lower, of better or
worse, of men or women, is, has been, and will be of lasting
interest. In selecting this theme from real life, as it was related
to me a number of years ago, when the incident impressed me
very deeply, I found it suited to a tragedy, because it can only
make us sad to see a fortunately placed individual perish, and
this must be the case in still higher degree when we see an
entire family die out. But perhaps a time will arrive when we
have become so developed, so enlightened, that we can remain
indifferent before the spectacle of life, which now seems so
brutal, so cynical, so heartless; when we have closed up those
lower, unreliable instruments of thought which we call feelings, and which have been rendered not only superfluous but
harmful by the final growth of our reflective organs.

The fact that the heroine arouses our pity depends only on our
weakness in not being able to resist the sense of fear that the
same fate could befall ourselves. And yet it is possible that a
very sensitive spectator might fail to find satisfaction in this
kind of pity, while the man believing in the future might demand some positive suggestion for the abolition of evil, or, in
other words, some kind of programme. But, first of all, there
is no absolute evil. That one family perishes is the fortune of
another family, which thereby gets a chance to rise. And the
alternation of ascent and descent constitutes one of life's main
charms, as fortune is solely determined by comparison. And
to the man with a programme, who wants to remedy the sad
circumstance that the hawk eats the dove, and the flea eats the
hawk, I have this question to put: why should it be remedied?
Life is not so mathematically idiotic that it lets only the big
eat the small, but it happens just as often that the bee kills the
lion, or drives it to madness at least.

That my tragedy makes a sad impression on many is their own
fault. When we grow strong as were the men of the first French
revolution, then we shall receive an unconditionally good and
joyful impression from seeing the national forests rid of rotting
and superannuated trees that have stood too long in the way
of others with equal right to a period of free growth—an impression good in the same way as that received from the death of
one incurably diseased.

Not long ago they reproached my tragedy **The Father** with
being too sad—just as if they wanted merry tragedies. Everybody is clamouring arrogantly for "the joy of life," and all
theatrical managers are giving orders for farces, as if the joy
of life consisted in being silly and picturing all human beings
as so many sufferers from St. Vitus' dance or idiocy. I find
the joy of life in its violent and cruel struggles, and my pleasure
lies in knowing something and learning something. And for
this reason I have selected an unusual but instructive case—
an exception, in a word—but a great exception, proving the
rule, which, of course, will provoke all lovers of the commonplace. And what also will offend simple brains is that my
action cannot be traced back to a single motive, that the viewpoint is not always the same. An event in real life—and this
discovery is quite recent—springs generally from a whole series
of more or less deep-lying motives, but of these the spectator
chooses as a rule the one his reason can master most easily,
or else the one reflecting most favourably on his power of
reasoning. A suicide is committed. Bad business, says the

merchant. Unrequited love, say the ladies. Sickness, says the sick man. Crushed hopes, says the shipwrecked. But now it may be that the motive lay in all or none of these directions. It is possible that the one who is dead may have hid the main motive by pushing forward another meant to place his memory in a better light.

In explanation of Miss Julie's sad fate I have suggested many factors: her mother's fundamental instincts; her father's mistaken upbringing of the girl; her own nature, and the suggestive influence of her fiancé on a weak and degenerate brain; furthermore, and more directly: the festive mood of the Midsummer Eve; the absence of her father; her physical condition; her preoccupation with the animals; the excitation of the dance; the dusk of the night; the strongly aphrodisiacal influence of the flowers; and lastly the chance forcing the two of them together in a secluded room, to which must be added the aggressiveness of the excited man.

Thus I have neither been one-sidedly physiological nor one-sidedly psychological in my procedure. Nor have I merely delivered a moral preachment. This multiplicity of motives I regard as praiseworthy because it is in keeping with the views of our own time. And if others have done the same thing before me, I may boast of not being the sole inventor of my paradoxes—as all discoveries are named.

In regard to the character-drawing I may say that I have tried to make my figures rather "characterless," and I have done so for reasons I shall now state.

In the course of the ages the word character has assumed many meanings. Originally it signified probably the dominant groundnote in the complex mass of the self, and as such it was confused with temperament. Afterward it became the middle-class term for an automaton, so that an individual whose nature had come to a stand-still, or who had adapted himself to a certain part in life—who had ceased to grow, in a word—was named a character; while one remaining in a state of development— a skilful navigator on life's river, who did not sail with closetied sheets, but knew when to fall off before the wind and when to luff again—was called lacking in character. And he was called so in a depreciatory sense, of course, because he was so hard to catch, to classify, and to keep track of. This middle-class notion about the immobility of the soul was transplanted to the stage, where the middle-class element has always held sway. There a character became synonymous with a gentleman fixed and finished once for all—one who invariably appeared drunk, jolly, sad. And for the purpose of characterisation nothing more was needed than some physical deformity like a clubfoot, a wooden leg, a red nose; or the person concerned was made to repeat some phrase like "That's capital!" or "Barkis is willin'," or something of that kind. This manner of regarding human beings as homogeneous is preserved even by the great Molière. . . . I do not believe . . . in simple characters on the stage. And the summary judgments of the author upon men—this one stupid, and that one brutal, this one jealous, and that one stingy—should be challenged by the naturalists, who know the fertility of the soul-complex, and who realise that "vice" has a reverse very much resembling virtue.

Because they are modern characters, living in a period of transition more hysterically hurried than its immediate predecessor at least, I have made my figures vacillating, out of joint, torn between the old and the new. And I do not think it unlikely that, through newspaper reading and overheard conversations,

modern ideas may have leaked down to the strata where domestic servants belong.

My souls (or characters) are conglomerates, made up of past and present stages of civilisation, scraps of humanity, torn-off pieces of Sunday clothing turned into rags—all patched together as is the human soul itself. And I have furthermore offered a touch of evolutionary history by letting the weaker repeat words stolen from the stronger, and by letting different souls accept "ideas"—or suggestions, as they are called— from each other. (pp. 96-101)

In regard to the dialogue, I want to point out that I have departed somewhat from prevailing traditions by not turning my figures into catechists who make stupid questions in order to call forth witty answers. I have avoided the symmetrical and mathematical construction of the French dialogue, and have instead permitted the minds to work irregularly as they do in reality, where, during conversation, the cogs of one mind seem more or less haphazardly to engage those of another one, and where no topic is fully exhausted. Naturally enough, therefore, the dialogue strays a good deal as, in the opening scenes, it acquires a material that later on is worked over, picked up again, repeated, expounded, and built up like the theme in a musical composition.

The plot is pregnant enough, and as, at bottom, it is concerned only with two persons, I have concentrated my attention on these, introducing only one subordinate figure, the cook, and keeping the unfortunate spirit of the father hovering above and beyond the action. I have done this because I believe I have noticed that the psychological processes are what interest the people of our own day more than anything else. Our souls, so eager for knowledge, cannot rest satisfied with seeing what happens, but must also learn how it comes to happen! What we want to see are just the wires, the machinery. We want to investigate the box with the false bottom, touch the magic ring in order to find the suture, and look into the cards to discover how they are marked.

In this I have taken for models the monographic novels of the brothers de Goncourt, which have appealed more to me than any other modern literature.

Turning to the technical side of the composition, I have tried to abolish the division into acts. And I have done so because I have come to fear that our decreasing capacity for illusion might be unfavourably affected by intermissions during which the spectator would have time to reflect and to get away from the suggestive influence of the author-hypnotist. My play will probably last an hour and a half, and as it is possible to listen that length of time, or longer, to a lecture, a sermon, or a debate, I have imagined that a theatrical performance could not become fatiguing in the same time. As early as 1872, in one of my first dramatic experiments, *The Outlaw,* I tried the same concentrated form, but with scant success. The play was written in five acts and wholly completed when I became aware of the restless, scattered effect it produced. Then I burned it, and out of the ashes rose a single, well-built act, covering fifty printed pages, and taking an hour for its performance. Thus the form of the present play is not new, but it seems to be my own, and changing aesthetical conventions may possibly make it timely.

My hope is still for a public educated to the point where it can sit through a whole-evening performance in a single act. But that point cannot be reached without a great deal of experimentation. In the meantime I have resorted to three art forms

A letter to Nietzsche written by Strindberg in 1889.

that are to provide resting-places for the public and the actors, without letting the public escape from the illusion induced. All these forms are subsidiary to the drama. They are the monologue, the pantomime, and the dance, all of them belonging originally to the tragedy of classical antiquity. For the monologue has sprung from the monody, and the chorus has developed into the ballet.

Our realists have excommunicated the monologue as improbable, but if I can lay a proper basis for it, I can also make it seem probable, and then I can use it to good advantage. It is probable, for instance, that a speaker may walk back and forth in his room practising his speech aloud; it is probable that an actor may read through his part aloud, that a servant-girl may talk to her cat, that a mother may prattle to her child, that an old spinster may chatter to her parrot, that a person may talk in his sleep. And in order that the actor for once may have a chance to work independently, and to be free for a moment from the author's pointer, it is better that the monologues be not written out, but just indicated. As it matters comparatively little what is said to the parrot or the cat, or in one's sleep—because it cannot influence the action—it is possible that a gifted actor, carried away by the situation and the mood of the occasion, may improvise such matters better than they could be written by the author, who cannot figure out in advance how much may be said, and how long the talk may last, without waking the public out of their illusions.

It is well known that, on certain stages, the Italian theatre has returned to improvisation and thereby produced creative actors—who, however, must follow the author's suggestions—and this may be counted a step forward, or even the beginning of a new art form that might well be called *productive.*

Where, on the other hand, the monologue would seem unreal, I have used the pantomime, and there I have left still greater scope for the actor's imagination—and for his desire to gain independent honours. But in order that the public may not be tried beyond endurance, I have permitted the music—which is amply warranted by the Midsummer Eve's dance—to exercise its illusory power while the dumb show lasts. And I ask the musical director to make careful selection of the music used for this purpose, so that incompatible moods are not induced by reminiscences from the last musical comedy or topical song, or by folk-tunes of too markedly ethnographical distinction.

The mere introduction of a scene with a lot of "people" could not have taken the place of the dance, for such scenes are poorly acted and tempt a number of grinning idiots into displaying their own smartness, whereby the illusion is disturbed. As the common people do not improvise their gibes, but use ready-made phrases in which stick some double meaning, I have not composed their lampooning song, but have appropriated a little known folk-dance which I personally noted down in a district near Stockholm. The words don't quite hit the point, but hint vaguely at it, and this is intentional, for the cunning (*i.e.,* weakness) of the slave keeps him from any direct attack. There must, then, be no chattering clowns in a serious action, and no coarse flouting at a situation that puts the lid on the coffin of a whole family.

As far as the scenery is concerned, I have borrowed from impressionistic painting its asymmetry, its quality of abruptness, and have thereby in my opinion strengthened the illusion. Because the whole room and all its contents are not shown, there is a chance to guess at things—that is, our imagination is stirred into complementing our vision. I have made a further gain in getting rid of those tiresome exits by means of doors, especially as stage doors are made of canvas and swing back and forth at the lightest touch. They are not even capable of expressing the anger of an irate *pater familias* who, on leaving his home after a poor dinner, slams the door behind him "so that it shakes the whole house." (On the stage the house sways.) I have also contented myself with a single setting, and for the double purpose of making the figures become parts of their surroundings, and of breaking with the tendency toward luxurious scenery. But having only a single setting, one may demand to have it real. Yet nothing is more difficult than to get a room that looks something like a room, although the painter can easily enough produce waterfalls and flaming volcanoes. Let it go at canvas for the walls, but we might be done with the painting of shelves and kitchen utensils on the canvas. We have so much else on the stage that is conventional, and in which we are asked to believe, that we might at least be spared the too great effort of believing in painted pans and kettles.

I have placed the rear wall and the table diagonally across the stage in order to make the actors show full face and half profile to the audience when they sit opposite each other at the table. (pp. 105-10)

Another novelty well needed would be the abolition of the footlights. The light from below is said to have for its purpose to make the faces of the actors look fatter. But I cannot help asking: why must all actors be fat in the face? Does not this light from below tend to wipe out the subtler lineaments in the lower part of the face, and especially around the jaws? Does it not give a false appearance to the nose and cast shadows upward over the eyes? If this be not so, another thing is certain: namely, that the eyes of the actors suffer from the light, so that the effective play of their glances is precluded. Coming from below, the light strikes the retina in places generally protected (except in sailors, who have to see the sun reflected in the water), and for this reason one observes hardly anything but a vulgar rolling of the eyes, either sideways or upwards, toward the galleries, so that nothing but the white of the eye shows. Perhaps the same cause may account for the tedious blinking of which especially the actresses are guilty. And when anybody on the stage wants to use his eyes to speak with, no other way is left him but the poor one of staring straight at the public, with whom he or she then gets into direct communication outside of the frame provided by the setting. . . . Would it not be possible by means of strong side-lights (obtained by the employment of reflectors, for instance) to add to the resources already possessed by the actor? Could not his mimicry be still further strengthened by use of the greatest asset possessed by the face: the play of the eyes?

Of course, I have no illusions about getting that actors to play *for* the public and not *at* it, although such a change would be highly desirable. I dare not even dream of beholding the actor's back throughout an important scene, but I wish with all my heart that crucial scenes might not be played in the centre of the proscenium, like ducts meant to bring forth applause. Instead, I should like to have them laid in the place indicated by the situation. Thus I ask for no revolutions, but only for a few minor modifications. To make a real room of the stage, with the fourth wall missing, and a part of the furniture placed back toward the audience, would probably produce a disturbing effect at present.

In wishing to speak of the facial make-up, I have no hope that the ladies will listen to me, as they would rather look beautiful than lifelike. But the actor might consider whether it be to his advantage to paint his face so that it shows some abstract type which covers it like a mask. (pp. 110-11)

In modern psychological dramas, where the subtlest movements of the soul are to be reflected on the face rather than by gestures and noise, it would probably be well to experiment with strong side-light on a small stage, and with unpainted faces, or at least with a minimum of make-up.

If, in addition, we might escape the visible orchestra, with its disturbing lamps and its faces turned toward the public; if we could have the seats on the main floor (the orchestra or the pit) raised so that the eyes of the spectators would be above the knees of the actors; if we could get rid of the boxes with their tittering parties of diners; if we could also have the auditorium completely darkened during the performance; and if, first and last, we could have a small stage and a small house: then a new dramatic art might rise, and the theatre might at least become an institution for the entertainment of people with culture. While waiting for this kind of theatre, I suppose we shall have to write for the "ice-box," and thus prepare the repertory that is to come.

I have made an attempt. If it prove a failure, there is plenty of time to try over again. (pp. 111-12)

> August Strindberg, *"Author's Preface,"* in his Plays, second series, *translated by Edwin Björkman, Charles Scribner's Sons, 1913, pp. 96-112.*

H. L. MENCKEN   (essay date 1912)

[*From the era of World War I until the early years of the Great Depression, Mencken was one of the most influential figures in American letters. His strongly individualistic, irreverent outlook on life and his vigorous, invective-charged writing style helped establish the iconoclastic spirit of the Jazz Age and significantly shaped the direction of American literature. As a social and literary critic—the roles for which he is best known—Mencken was the scourge of evangelical Christianity, public service organizations, literary censorship, boosterism, provincialism, democracy, all advocates of personal or social improvement, and every other facet of American life that he perceived as humbug. In his literary criticism, Mencken encouraged American writers to shun the anglophilic, moralistic bent of the nineteenth century and to practice realism, an artistic call-to-arms that is most fully developed in his essay "Puritanism As a Literary Force," one of the seminal essays in modern literary criticism. A man who was widely renowned or feared during his lifetime as a would-be destroyer of established American values, Mencken once wrote: "All of my work, barring a few obvious burlesques, is based upon three fundamental ideas: 1. That knowledge is better than ignorance; 2. That it is better to tell the truth than to lie; and 3. That it is better to be free than to be a slave." In the following excerpt, Mencken considers the origin of Strindberg's "appalling cynicism" in his discussion of the playwright's work.*]

[*Wer Ist's,* the German *Who's Who* notes] that Strindberg married Siri von Essen, an actress and the divorced wife of one Herr Wangel, in 1876; that he divorced Siri and married Frida Uhl, a lady author "out of Vienna," in 1893; that he divorced Frida and married Harriet Bosse, of the Stockholm theaters, in 1901; and that he has since divorced Harriet. And which, being revolved a bit in mind, and weighed, as it were, in the psychological scales, points to the origin, perhaps, of the two most salient characteristics of the man, as dramatist and as novelist; the one being his strong tendency to empty his personal experience, without effort at disguise, into his every fable, and the other being his liking for depicting the conjugal relation as a form of combat—not as a combat genial and romantic, of pretty love taps all compact, but as a combat savage and to the death, like that between two bull walruses or a pair of half-starved hyenas. Strindberg, indeed, has lived more stories than even Strindberg could invent, and they have been stories to bulge the eyeball and lift the lanugo on the baldest head. (p. 153)

Coming into the world to the wagging of tongues (for his father, a small shopkeeper, did not marry his mother until a few months before his birth) he moved, until well into middle age, in a fetid atmosphere of scandal. At twenty-six he was hero and villain of a peculiarly nasty divorce case; at thirty-five he faced a term in prison for a gross offense against Swedish prudery. And then came another divorce case, and then another, and then yet another. And in the intervals he more than once went hungry and half-clad, and more than once fled his country to escape his woes, and more than once meditated suicide as the one escape from despair. No wonder his own life bulks so large in his books and plays! And no wonder the dominant tone of those books and plays is a cynicism so appalling that it turns the virtuous liver to water!

Compared to Strindberg, old Ibsen seems an optimist, almost a sentimentalist. *Ghosts,* to be sure, gave us a shock in the naïve nineties, but that shock, as we all know, has since dissolved into a platitude. It would probably be difficult today to find a defender, not clerical or insane, for Mrs. Alving's disastrous fidelity to *mensa et thoro.* Even the flight of Nora Helmer, once so vile an infamy, is now admitted to have been excusable, if not actually ladylike. But who, so long as romance reigns and the family endures, will admit the essential truth, or even the ordinary sanity, of *The Dance of Death*, or *Motherlove*, or *The Bond*, or *Lady Julie*, or *The Father*? Here, indeed, is bitter, bitter stuff! Here is idol smashing with cobblestones! Here is the massacre of the gods! In the first play, husband and wife wallow in a morass of mutual hatred, wounding and besmirching each other at every roll; in the second a debauched mother, sniveling sentimentally, drags her young daughter down; in the third husband and wife tear their child to pieces between them; in the fourth a sort of extralascivious Hedda Gabler seduces her father's valet, and in the fifth a nagging wife drives her husband crazy. Certainly not plays for sucklings. Certainly not plays that make the slightest concession to the common assumptions and traditions of the theater. And yet, when all is said and done, plays of truly astounding mordancy, with living people in them and the rank smell of reality.

Not all of Strindberg's work, of course, is in that key. On the contrary, he has also tried his hand at the historical drama and even at the poetical drama. . . . But it is scarcely as a recreator of Swedish history and legend, whatever his talent in that field, nor as a heavy-handed imitator of Maeterlinck and the more romantic of the two Hauptmanns that he holds the attention of Europe today, but as a metaphysical realist who has carried the search for motives and causes to its uttermost limit. Not that he is a mere merchant of indecencies, a flabbergaster of the stalls. Far from it, indeed. It is always the psychological fact that interests him, and not the physical fact. What he tries to do is to find the genuine motive beneath the shells and trappings of conventional habit and morality. That husband and wife greet each other daily with certain words, that they engage in certain mummery before their children and the world, that they occasionally quarrel over this or that, that their union ends thus or so—all this is to Strindberg only the surface play of life. What he seeks to get at is what they actually *think* of each other deep down in their secret souls—what ideas and impulses lie at the bottom of their outward acts—what change and color of character each has derived from the other. Naturally enough, this quest involves the delineation of conflict, for it is only in the heat of conflict, when the primal emotions burst their bonds and the ceremony of civilization is forgotten, that self-revelation is ever genuine. And so, in his plays, one constantly encounters scenes like that famous one in the last act of *A Doll's House,* wherein Nora and Torvald Helmer face each other across the table, or that less famous but even more staggering one in *Friedensfest,* Hauptmann's "family catastrophe," wherein the skeletons of the Scholtz family come out to dance.

But whereas Hauptmann is a frank meliorist, with peace arising phoenix-like from his fires of combat, and even Ibsen, as a rule, hints humanely at a possible way out, Strindberg is ever impatient of compromises and happy endings. Seeing woman as a vampire, as the Nietzschean corruptor of the superman, as a parasite at war with masculine cleanliness and strength, he is unwilling to let her undergo any romantic metamorphosis, even for the sake of an affecting curtain. Not that he denies her a certain eleventh hour remorse, a temperamental incapacity for playing out her role to the bitter end, a tendency to be horrified, soon or late, by her own deviltry. That weakness, indeed, he actually insists upon, but only to show its unauthenticity and its moral futility. Thekla, in the last scene of *The Creditor,* appalled by her ruin of two men, babbles for a chance to make atonement; Lady Julie, caught in her own net, begs

Jean to assure her that she shall enter into grace; Laura, in *The Father,* like Alice, in *The Dance of Death,* mouths pious platitudes. But always to no purpose. The way of escape is ever closed. Responsibility is ever brought home. "Out with you, infernal woman!" shrieks Laura's victim. "And damnation on your sex!" "Atonement?" demands Thekla's. "One must atone by restitution—and you can't. You have not only taken, but you have destroyed what you have taken!" And the victim of Alice spits in her face, while Lady Julie's, her master at the end, puts the cold steel into her hand and—"There is no other way. Go!" Even in *The Bond,* though an armistice hangs vaguely in the air, if only because both antagonists are beaten, there is no escape for the woman. She talks sentimentally of peace at last, of sleeping near her child. "*You* hope to sleep tonight?" jeers her husband. *"You?"* (pp. 153-55)

H. L. Mencken, "The Terrible Swede," in The Smart Set, *Vol. XXXVII, No. 2, June, 1912, pp. 153-58.**

EDWIN BJÖRKMAN   (essay date 1913)

[*Björkman was a Swedish-American novelist and critic who, through his translations, introduced American readers to the works of such major Scandinavian authors as August Strindberg, Bjørnstjerne Bjørnson, and Georg Brandes. In the following excerpt, Björkman presents a discussion of Strindberg's major works, emphasizing the fact that while Strindberg's writings are biographical in nature, they are also comprehensible strictly in terms of art.*]

Regarding Strindberg primarily as an imaginatively creative writer, we find his career as such falling into three sharply defined periods. The first of these lasted from 1868 to 1885; the second, from 1886 to 1894; the third, from 1897 to his death. Between the second and the third periods occurred [an] interregnum of absolute unproductivity. . . . (p. 45)

For purposes of convenience, rather than with any claim at positive definition, those periods may be designated as: 1) the romantic; 2) the naturalistic; 3) the symbolistic. Of course, a tendency to naturalistic presentation of external facts characterized his work almost from the start, and it continued to assert itself even in the most mystical products of his final period. He was always a realist in the finest sense of that term— one insisting that art must cling closely to life as actually lived and stand firmly on this ground even when reaching most daringly into still unconquered realms of being. But on the other hand, there was always a touch of mysticism, of yearning idealism, of instinctive out-reaching for the life still to come, even in such characteristic works of the middle period as *The Father* and *Creditors*. It represented a strain of feeling and thought nearly inseparable from the Scandinavian temperament.

Of the first period, beginning with his initial gropings in the world of poetry, and coming to an end, in 1885, with the completion of the four short stories published collectively as *Real Utopias,* I have dared to speak as romantic chiefly because sentiment still holds almost equal sway with logic in the work belonging to it. (pp. 46-7)

The transition from the first to the second period caused no interruption in his creative activity. Evidence that some kind of border line was crossed about 1885 must be drawn from within the works then produced. But the moment we compare the preface of the first part of *Marriage,* dating from 1884, with that of the second part, written in 1886, we perceive that something of moment must have happened in the meantime. Of course, the real events took place in Strindberg's own mind.

Self-caricature by Strindberg, 1882.

But the principal external facts connected with those inner changes were the confiscation of the first part of *Marriage* and the beginnings of his marital unhappiness. (pp. 49-50)

His altered attitude toward womanhood is the first thing that makes itself felt. . . . But back of it we suspect the presence of changes reaching much farther down into the writer's conception of life. The man who wrote the first part of *Marriage* and *Real Utopias* was, on the whole, well content with his world. The author of the second part of *Marriage* and of *The Father* strikes us, on the other hand, as a man doubting the very possibility of happiness as a human state.

I deem it highly regrettable that for many years hardly any works by Strindberg except those dating from his middle period became known in the English-speaking countries. For in many respects I cannot but think that period abnormal—representing a deviation from his true line of development. During those years between 1885 and 1894, the nature of Strindberg, which was no whit less capable of love and faith than of hatred and doubt, became sadly warped. All the world lay wrapt in grey mist. Woman, once angelic, turned into a devil incarnate. Life was seen as war to the hilt—and love was the worst form this war could assume.

To me it seems quite logical that this period, and no other, should see Strindberg turn from his former social outlook to a temporary acceptance of Nietzsche's ultra-individualistic superman theories. It is the works from this period that have brought him the name of a misogynist and the reputation of being too grim and gloomy for races which are essentially wholesome and optimistic in their tendencies. Yet the same period gave the world a series of exquisite pictures from life among the peasant-fishermen on those islands between Stockholm and "the edge of the sea" where Strindberg had previously sought and won the inspiration for his *Master Olof.* (pp. 51-2)

The play *Master Olof* was at first named *The Renegade,* and under this title I hope it will become known to the English-speaking world. To Strindberg himself it was largely what *The Pretenders* was to Ibsen—at once a questioning and a formulation of his own genius. The greater modernity of the Swedish work is shown by the fact that its principal hero, who is one of three central figures, fails equally to reach a triumph like that of [Oehlenschläger's] *King Häkon,* the man divinely commissioned, and to suffer a disaster like that of the self-doubting *Earl Skule.* Instead he lives on to complete his work—in compromise. To win his way, or rather a way for his mission, he has to sacrifice a part of his vision—and so he is denounced as a renegade by him who sees too far ahead and will sacrifice nothing. This is life, of course; and thus Strindberg may be said to have, for all time, given the true symbolization of the everlasting struggle between the genius and the mass on one side, and between true and false genius on the other.

The Red Room is a satirical novel, embodying the conflict between bohemianism and philistinism at Stockholm in the seventies, and written in a vein that shows a rare combination of youthful vigor and merciless satire. But it gives also, as almost all of Strindberg's novels, a detailed study of social conditions in Sweden at that time. Hardly a phase of national existence is unrepresented, and each one of them is sketched in such manner that we also get an idea of the directional tendencies expressed through it. Strindberg's faculty for drawing lifelike pictures not only of individuals but of vast social groups and organisms is among the most striking of his gifts. And to the future historian his novels and autobiographical writings should prove exceedingly valuable. (pp. 54-6)

The first part of *Marriage* contains a dozen specimens of modern marital unions, presented in a far from unfriendly light. In the preface Strindberg laid out a programme concerning woman's position which vies in radicalism with that for which the women themselves are now fighting all over the world. Not only would he grant them the suffrage, but he insisted that normal social growth necessitated their having it. But in the second volume of stories issued under the same title, he made a frank attack on two principles generally accepted as essential to woman's complete emancipation, namely the right to hold property, and the right to work at anything for which they can qualify themselves. If their tendency be disregarded, the stories in both volumes will be found to possess high artistic value.

The Father was Strindberg's supreme effort to symbolize the life and death struggle between man and woman for such immortality as may be offered them by the child. The picture of that struggle is splendid but unfair. Man, as man, is given rational insight, while to woman is granted little more than low cunning. And as conscience is allied with reason, the victory falls to its unconscionable opponent. It may seem paradoxical to express a regret that the sex problem should enter at all into this play—a play designed wholly to exhaust that very problem. But there is a psychological side to the work that has nothing whatever to do with sex, and this side would hold our interest just as firmly if the conflict were raging between two men. The corrosive power of suggestion is here shown with diabolical skill. It is a duel of souls, with words for weapons, and by a seed of doubt sown in the right way at the right moment, one of those souls is shattered and scattered as fatally as a warship when its magazine explodes.

Miss Julie, perhaps the most widely known of Strindberg's works, was a frank experiment in new form. Not only are the stage arrangements unconventional, but intermissions have been dispensed with. Naturalism never came nearer to a conquest of the stage, and some of the innovations embodied in this drama are likely to form part of our future dramatic tradition. Again the plot seems to offer us nothing but a sex duel, with the man for winner. But back of Miss Julie and her valet-lover stand two contending strata of humanity—the so-called upper and lower classes. What Strindberg shows us is how a continued process of selective breeding may lead to over-refinement and a weakening of the vital instincts. The racial strain which has reached such a point can find salvation only in mixture with some strain less far removed from the general source of life. If class prejudices or other inhibitive tendencies prevent such a mixture, then the weakened strain will be sloughed off by the race, so that place will be made for other strains with unimpaired vitality and still dormant powers of refinement. (pp. 56-9)

It was during [his] middle period of embittered defiance that Strindberg first conceived the idea of a series of autobiographical novels, in which he would adhere closely to his own actual experience while the shock of such self-revelation was to be softened by a change of all proper names. The first volume of this series, issued in 1886 under the title of *The Son of a Servant* gives a picture of child life that is full of startling revelations and exquisite interpretations. Strindberg himself has said somewhere that all fiction must be autobiographical in order to obtain full documentary validity. Even if we hold this assertion too sweeping, we must at least grant him to have proved that the most intimate personal experience may be turned into legitimate fiction.

While at all times, to use his own expression, Strindberg "had three strings to his lyre," he appeared during the third period primarily as a dramatist, and it was as such that he preferred to be considered. There is hardly one play from his final period that would not warrant special notice on some account or another. In the eyes of his countrymen, his dramatic presentations of Swedish history have tended to take precedence. And on their account some have dared to call him the Shakespeare of Sweden. But the historical plays of Strindberg are widely different in mettle from that displayed in the "histories" of Shakespeare. No matter how much we find to admire in the latter, they must be held melodramatic in form and rhetorical in expression. The are, in a word, artificial in their portrayal of the past. What Strindberg strove to do—and succeeded in doing, I think—was to reconstruct the everyday aspect of by-gone days. In order to bring the true inwardness as well as lifelike appearance of those days within the ken of our own, he put on the stage not imagined creatures of supernatural size, but plain-speaking men and women of our own kind. But back of these men and women we catch lurid glimpses of big social forces at work. In other words, his works are symbolical in the very best sense of this much misused term—symbolical in the same manner as man's own thinking. . . . (pp. 60-2)

But for the present his main dramatic contributions to universal literature during this final period must be sought among the plays of modern life, and particularly among those that derived from a frankly acknowledged Maeterlinckian impetus. It was the early Maeterlinck of the puppet plays that set Strindberg once more seeking for a new form. The immediate result of this search was the fairy play *Swanwhite,* a very charming but not convincingly original production. Had he stopped there, the charge of imitation sometimes heard might have had some warrant. But to speak of the author of *The Dream Play* or *Toward Damascus* as the imitator of anybody becomes palpably ridiculous the moment you read these works. In both—but especially in the former—he strove to reproduce the kaleidoscopic flexibility and whimsical logic of the dream. And in this way he succeeded as perhaps no one before him to press all life into the narrow confines of a play.

At one time he described *The Dream Play* as a "Buddhistic and proto-Christian drama." Thereby he indicated its underlying philosophy of enlightened resignation and of almost Tolstoyan passivity in the face of violence and injustice and wrong. But we must not be misled by this effort of the matured poet to grasp and vitalize an ideal foreign to his own temperament. "I am a soldier," says the hunter in *The Great Highway,* speaking as the *alter ego* of the author; "I am always fighting—fighting to preserve my personal independence." To me the most potent element in *The Dream Play,* the one most likely to germinate and survive not only as art but as philosophy, is its tolerant acceptance of every human aspect as an integral part of life. Its main shortcoming lies in a tendency to consider all such aspects as established for all future. Viewing life statically, however, and not kinetically—from the realist's viewpoint rather than from the idealist's—it will prove difficult to find an artistic symbolization of it more subtle or more convincing than that given us in *The Dream Play.*

Although the trilogy *Toward Damascus* is autobiographical in source as well as purpose—a sort of gigantic private reckoning worked out by one deeming himself too seriously tried by life—its appeal is nevertheless universal. We may forget the fate of him who projected those mighty dramatic cloud-shapes, and read out of them nothing but a masterly record of the stumbling progress made by a human soul in its search for harmonious correlation of its own conflicting elements—its desires and aspirations, its selfish and unselfish tendencies. In the third part we find Father Melchior calling out to the Strindbergian protagonist, here named The Strangers: "You began life by affirming everything; you continued it by denying everything. End it now with a coordination. Therefore, cease to be exclusive! Say not 'either—or,' but say instead 'both—and!'" Here we have Strindberg's onward march through forty years of thinking and working outlined in a couple of sentences—and we cannot fail to recognize its identity with the general course of human progress, which runs from blind belief through arrogant denial to a reasoned balancing of faith and doubt.

Close as the trilogy must have stood to what was Strindberg's innermost self, there is a professedly objective work that seems to have come still closer, though in a different manner—a work where Strindberg's artistic aloofness makes us almost forget that, in spite of it, he was still dealing with his own spiritual experiences, and with nothing else. This work, the double play named *The Dance of Death,* I am often inclined to count the crowning climax of his production, the work in which his always remarkable art reached its highest potency of perfection. It is as closely knit as a Greek drama or a play by Ibsen at his

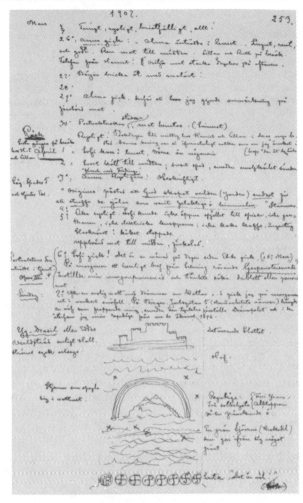

Holograph copy of the manuscript of the Occult Diary.

best. Only three characters figure in the first part, and five in the second. There are only two settings—one for each part. The dialogue has rarely, if ever, been surpassed for combined incisiveness and verisimilitude. Incident leads to incident with a fatality that vainly tries to mask its logic behind the leering face of chance. Some of the scenes are among the most tensely dramatic that may be found in modern literature, and yet the total impression is just what the author seems to have aimed at: a sense of the hopeless monotony underlying life's superficial disturbances.

A piece of the most delicate, and yet most deep-reaching symbolism (outwardly expressed by the round form of the room in which the action takes place) lies in the circular movement of the first part, whereby everything becomes reduced once more to the state of the opening scene. All the tumult of living is brought back to a pitiful striving at self-assertion on the part of the individual. Yet the suggestion is always present, that in all his seemingly futile striving the individual takes the place of a puppet in the hands of some higher power, working for great aims that he cannot perceive. Life and hell are rendered almost synonymous, but the Swedenborgian idea of hell as a state of mind is not for a moment left out of sight. The one possible agent of escape is the Hogarthian fiddler, always hovering on the horizon like a storm cloud before which all cower in panic. But when he comes at last and brings the dance to a close, he is seen to bring with him pardon and peace, mercy

and harmony. One of the figures in the play, Curt, might be called the superman of Strindberg's final period: a touching incarnation of the struggle between reasoned humility and instinctive pride that was always raging in the author's own breast. But the most striking figure of all is that of the Captain, the embodiment of ruthless self-concern, to whom nevertheless is given the pronouncement of Strindberg's ultimate philosophical creed: "Wipe out and pass on!" (pp. 63-8)

Inferno [was] his most original effort at autobiographical fiction. . . . In 1903 he wrote another volume in the same series, *Alone,* which might be called the antithesis of his previous record of wandering through a self-made hell. It is a piece of pure poetry—the autumnal reverie of a man who, at last, has made his peace with the world and paid the price for it. And in this volume Strindberg's marvellous power of word-painting stands revealed in all its glory.

I cannot end this all too brief characterization of Strindberg's main works without calling attention to an additional and somewhat confusing aspect of his passion for self-revelation. Not satisfied with giving us a detailed story of his life and artistic development, he wrote also stories of the story, revelations of how previous revelations had come to be made. In a number of pamphlets, and particularly in those quaint collections of notes, sketches, aphorisms and speculations which he named "Blue Books," material of this kind was piled up at a tremendous rate, until the image to be evoked became blurred by the superabundance of fact used to evoke it. I wonder, however, whether this condition may not alter as passing time places everything in proper perspective. For it would seem that concerning a mind so rich and so original, both in its coloring and in its tendencies, the amount of available data could hardly become too great. (pp. 70-2)

Edwin Björkman, "August Strindberg," in his Voices of To-morrow: Critical Studies of the New Spirit in Literature, *Mitchell Kennerley, 1913, pp. 11-120.*

LUDWIG LEWISOHN (essay date 1920)

[*A German-born American novelist and critic, Lewisohn was considered an authority on German literature, and his translations of Gerhart Hauptmann, Rainer Maria Rilke, and Jakob Wassermann are widely respected. In 1919 he became the drama critic for the* Nation, *serving as its associate editor until 1924, when he joined a group of expatriates in Paris. After his return to the United States in 1934, Lewisohn became a prominent sympathizer with the Zionist movement, and served as editor of the Jewish magazine* New Palestine *for five years. Many of his later works reflect his humanistic concern for the plight of the Jewish people. In the following excerpt, Lewisohn praises* The Dance of Death.]

What a play! Written in 1901 it leaps beyond its year and ours and establishes the dramaturgy of the future. Its method is as astonishing as it is simple. It deals with people, not with moral attributes. It does not let an abstract quality overshadow a man. (p. 774)

The Captain and his wife in *The Dance of Death* have seen each other so long and so closely that they no longer see each other at all. They try, like all people, to find moral tags in the name of which they can justify their mutual hatred. It is a profoundly true circumstance that Alice does this more continually than her husband, who yields quite unreflectively to his vindictive impulses. The woman is more passionate, yet more desirous of justifying her hatred. Hence she is eager to prove in him the qualities that explain it. She has, no doubt, chances enough. Again and again she convinces her friend and kinsman Curt. But in the end all hatred breaks down because all isolation of moral qualities becomes impossible. We know least those whom we know best, because we see them no longer analytically but concretely. We have no clues, because every clue becomes coarse and misleading when brought to the test of a reality so intricate and obscure. This husband and this wife feign, at times with passion and terror, to despise and hate each other. Yet they are unable to break their galling chains because, having passed beyond the perception of mere evil qualities in each other and seeing each other as concrete psychical organisms, they cannot hold either contempt or hatred long enough. They shift and waver and know too much to rise to the point of willing and they die in the inextricable bonds in which they are caught.

"There are disharmonies in life," Strindberg lets Gustav say in *Creditors,* "that cannot be resolved." The tragic outcome is that there is no tragic outcome. There is no liberating action and no appeasement of the heart. The years drag on and the shadows lengthen and then comes the dance of death. Children grow up and fall into the same entanglements and almost at once the familiar disharmonies begin to sound—as Alice hears them from Judith and Alan and the lieutenant. But the will to live and continue the race gilds all beginnings with romance, and the Captain and his wife in the tower-room are neither an example nor a warning. Nor is it only the young whom instinct robs of vision. Alice has but to make the immemorial gesture and Curt, the clear-minded and the disillusioned, is in flames.

Yet from this very play there arises a hope beyond the note of compassion with which, contrary to the custom of his more acrid years, Strindberg ends his action. It is no accident that the Captain and Alice live on an island. Most married couples do. They have the same friends and see the same scenes. People and the very trees and streets take on the blurred colors of that tense and monotonous and islanded existence. They cling to each other and restrict each other and seek to enforce agreements and concessions and harmonies of which the very nature must be the spontaneity of perfect freedom. They assume possession and practice force, and the island becomes a prison. The Captain and Alice stayed on the island as each other's keepers. Thus each became at once a tyrant and a slave. If only they had tried a little wandering and used their island as a place of peace and refuge, and renounced possession as the one hope of coming into their own at last! No, the disharmonies cannot be resolved. But they can be silenced. Where the hope of a rare and difficult happiness ends, peace and freedom may begin. (p. 775)

> Ludwig Lewisohn, "Jangled Lives," in The Nation, Vol. CX, No. 2866, June 5, 1920, pp. 774-75.

JOHN MACY (essay date 1922)

[*Macy was an American literary critic and an editor of the* Boston Herald *and the* Nation. *His most important work was* The Spirit of American Literature *(1913), which denounced the genteel tradition and called for realism and the use of native materials in American literature. In the following excerpt, Macy praises the verisimilitude of Strindberg's fiction.*]

Strindberg seems to have been continuously at war with Strindberg; and the peace that he found was but the death-bed repentance of a man whose forces were spent. He went through many phases. *The Growth of a Soul,* which is autobiographical, might better be called *The Conflicts of a Soul.* It seethes with

ideas, ends in a half-formed philosophy, and is only a section of Strindberg's intellectual adventures. He was ten men at ten different times, and he was ten men all the time. He expressed every aspect of himself. His manifold genius was master of all forms of literature. As Emerson said of Swedenborg, in whom Strindberg found all the light that his dark soul ever knew, he lies abroad on his times, leviathan-like. Undoubtedly to know him, one must know him entire, and I do not pretend to complete knowledge of his life and works.

Some fragments of his total artistic expression are not intelligible when they are read apart from his other books. *The Inferno* is a confused and murky nightmare which takes on form and purpose only when the light of biography is turned on it. Other works of Strindberg, read by themselves, are clear and shapely.

By the Open Sea is an intensely powerful study of an over-cultivated man and a primitively passionate woman. It is, moreover, the work of a poet who loves the sea. The passage in which the ichthyologist observes through his telescope the wonder-world beneath the surface of the water is rich with the essential poetry of natural fact. The translator, Ellie Schleussner, would probably say, as Strindberg's admirers all say, that his resonant poetic prose cannot be rendered in another language. Yet the things that he sees in nature and his interpretations of them are in their naked substance the imaginative stuff which is poetry. This Titan was not content to be poet, novelist, dramatist, essayist, philosopher. He was also a man of science, no mean rival, they say, of the professional student of biology and chemistry. The eye that looks through Borg's telescope has been trained in a laboratory and can also roll with a fine frenzy. . . . (pp. 135-37)

Strindberg has been called both misogamist and misogynist. Yet it is not possible to collect and compress within the bounds of such definite words a man whose ideas on any one subject fly far apart as the poles. If he sometimes, often, expresses virulent detestation of women and all their ways, he is not more tender toward men. He is not a caresser of life. He hangs the whole human race. But he analyzes; tries it before the twelve-minded jury in himself before he pronounces sentence. Point by point, detail for detail, he is just in perception of character and motive. His final view is simply not final, but contradictory as life itself. He thinks that woman is a snare to the feet of a man who would walk upright and accomplish something in the world. Yet he believes in the freedom of woman, would give her the vote, and emancipate her from economic bondage to the man. He even champions the liberty of the child, condemns "the family as a social institution which does not permit the child to become an individual at the proper time," and draws both parents as victims of "the same unfortunate conditions which are honored by the sacred name of law."

Marriage contains twenty short stories of married life, so many variations of Strindberg's thesis against the institution. So regarded, the book leaves one rather sore than enlightened. But these stories are stories, not tracts. Strindberg is a great, if rough and savage, artist. His opinions, whatever they are, do not devitalize his fiction. His short narratives are as skilful as Maupassant's in at least one respect, compression, sinewy economy. He can put in ten pages the domestic tragedy of a lifetime. He is a fine or, rather, a firm craftsman, and though the man rages, the artist has the artist's restraint and every other literary virtue short of ultimate beauty. He sets down terrible things with a cool succinctness. One story ends thus:

"The children had become burdens and the once beloved wife a secret enemy despised and despising him. And the cause of all this unhappiness? The want of bread! And yet the large storehouses of the new world were breaking down under the weight of an over-abundant supply of wheat. What a world of contradictions! The manner in which bread was distributed must be at fault. Science, which has replaced religion, has no answer to give; it merely states facts and allows the children to die of hunger and the parents of thirst."

The Red Room is a satire on life in Stockholm, on life everywhere. The pathetic struggle of the artistic and literary career, its follies and pretenses, the fatuity of politics, the dishonesty of journalism, the disillusion that awaits the aspiring actor, all these things run riot through the lively pages. Strindberg's satire is severe, it is sometimes hard, but it is not mean. He has a large if rather distant sympathy for the poor fellows whose aspirations, failures, dissipations, and friendships he portrays. Of two young critics he says: "And they wrote of human merit and human unworthiness and broke hearts as if they were breaking egg-shells." He writes of their unconscious inhumanity and blindness in a way that reveals his own clearness of vision and fundamental humanity. The laughter of a somber humorist has in it a tenderness unknown to merry natures.

The dramatic and literary critic may profitably read the chapter called "Checkmate," in which the young journalist is made to say: "The public does not want to have an opinion, it wants to satisfy its passions. If I praise your enemy you writhe like a worm and tell me that I have no judgment; if I praise your friend, you tell me that I have. Take that last piece of the Dramatic Theatre, Fatty, which has just been published in book form. . . . It's quite safe to say that there isn't enough action in it: that's a phrase the public knows well; laugh a little at the 'beautiful language'; that's good, old disparaging praise; then attack the management for having accepted such a play and point out that the moral teaching is doubtful—a very safe thing to say about most things."

Strindberg's imagination visualized and dramatized everything. He made plays of an astonishing variety of ideas ranging from wild poetic fantasy to grim realism—a range as great as Ibsen's and greater than Hauptmann's.

Glance at those in the third volume of Mr. Björkman's translations, not to analyze them but merely to note their diversity. *Swanwhite* is a fairy fantasy of love, confessedly inspired by Maeterlinck, yet in no sense an imitation of him. *Advent* is a Christmas miracle play, which embodies a gentle sermon on the forgiveness of sins—a strange sermon from the man who wrote the last chapter of *By the Open Sea! Debit and Credit* is a realistic sketch portraying the man who succeeds at the expense of other people. *The Thunderstorm* plays upon an old theme, one that Strindberg knew by experience, the failure of marriage between an elderly man and a young woman. It ends rather serenely for Strindberg, whose last years were not peaceful: "It's getting dark, but then comes reason to light us with its bull's-eyes, so that we don't go astray. . . . Close the windows and pull down the shades so that all memories can lie down and sleep in peace of old age."

In *After the Fire* the vanity and dishonesty of petty people are ruthlessly exposed. The Stranger who finds all reputations to have been based on sham and all pride founded on wind, is said to be Strindberg himself. "Vanity, vanity. . . . You tiny earth; you, the densest and heaviest of all planets—that's what makes everything on you so heavy—so heavy to breathe, so

heavy to carry. The cross is your symbol, but it might just as well have been a fool's cap or a strait-jacket—you world of delusions and deluded!" (pp. 138-42)

John Macy, "Strindberg," in his The Critical Game, Boni and Liveright, Publishers, 1922, pp. 135-42.

EUGENE O'NEILL   (essay date 1924)

[*O'Neill is generally considered America's foremost dramatist and is credited with creating the traditions of twentieth-century American drama. His plays consistently examine the implacability of an indifferent universe, the materialistic greed of humanity, and the problems of discovering one's true identity. Because O'Neill's plays are bleak portraits of a world without ultimate meaning, critics have come to regard him as the most pessimistic of American dramatists. O'Neill was greatly influenced by the work of Strindberg and in the following excerpt, originally used as a playbill for a performance of* The Ghost Sonata *in 1924, O'Neill discusses Strindberg's dramatic legacy.*]

In creating a modern theatre which we hope will liberate for significant expression a fresh elation and joy in experimental production, it is the most apt symbol of our good intentions that we start with a play by August Strindberg; for Strindberg was the precursor of all modernity in our present theatre, just as Ibsen, a lesser man as himself surmised, was the father of the modernity of twenty years or so ago when it was believed that *A Doll's House* wasn't—just that.

Strindberg still remains among the most modern of moderns, the greatest interpreter in the theatre of the characteristic spiritual conflicts which constitute the drama—the blood—of our lives today. He carried Naturalism to a logical attainment of such poignant intensity that, if the work of any other playwright is to be called "naturalism," we must classify a play like *The Dance of Death* as "super-naturalism," and place it in a class by itself, exclusively Strindberg's since no one before or after him has had the genius to qualify.

Yet it is only by means of some form of "super-naturalism" that we may express in the theatre what we comprehend intuitively of that self-defeating, self-obsession which is the discount we moderns have to pay for the loan of life. The old "naturalism"—or "realism" if you prefer (would to God some genius were gigantic enough to define clearly the separateness of these terms once and for all!) no longer applies. It represents our Fathers' daring aspirations toward self-recognition by holding the family kodak up to ill-nature. But to us their old audacity is blague; we have taken too many snap-shots of each other in every graceless position; we have endured too much from the banality of surfaces. We are ashamed of having peeked through so many keyholes, squinting always at heavy, uninspired bodies—the fat facts—with not a nude spirit among them; we have been sick with appearances and are convalescing; we "wipe out and pass on" to some as yet unrealized region where our souls, maddened by loneliness and the ignoble inarticulateness of flesh, are slowly evolving their new language of kinship.

Strindberg knew and suffered with our struggle years before many of us were born. He expressed it by intensifying the method of his time and by foreshadowing both in content and form the methods to come. All that is enduring in what we loosely call "Expressionism"—all that is artistically valid and sound theatre—can be clearly traced back through Wedekind to Strindberg's *The Dream Play, There Are Crimes and Crimes, The Ghost Sonata,* etc. (pp. 108-09)

Eugene O'Neill, "Strindberg and Our Theatre," in
O'Neill and His Plays: Four Decades of Criticism,
Oscar Cargill, N. Bryllion Fagin, William J. Fisher,
eds., New York University Press, 1961, pp. 108-09.

JOSEPH WOOD KRUTCH   (essay date 1926)

[*Krutch is widely regarded as one of America's most respected
literary and drama critics. A conservative and idealistic thinker,
he was a consistent proponent of human dignity and the preeminence of literary art. His literary criticism is characterized by
such concerns: in* The Modern Temper *(1929) he argued that
because scientific thought has denied human worth, tragedy had
become obsolete, and in* The Measure of Man *(1954) he attacked
modern culture for depriving humanity of the sense of individual
responsibility necessary for making important decisions in an
increasingly complex age. In the following excerpt, Krutch discusses the biographical factors involved in Strindberg's creation
of expressionistic dramas.*]

[*The Dream Play* illustrates] the difference between art and
sham as exemplified in what, for want of a better name, we
call expressionism. . . . [Whatever] else may be said of [Strind-
berg's] fantastic piece, it must be admitted that its chaos is at
least unforced and real. Born of a tardily legitimatized union
between a bankrupt shopkeeper and a bar maid, remembering
fear and hunger as his earliest sensations, and torn throughout
life by the conflict between the impulses of a perverse nature
and the judgments of a moralizing mind, gloom was not to
him a fashionable affectation nor formlessness a new form to
be assiduously cultivated. Heredity had given him a hopelessly
neurotic temperament, a lifetime of tortured maladjustment had
convinced him that suffering was the lot of all mankind, and
when, toward the end, he made *The Dream Play* a chaotic
compendium of human ills he was writing from his deepest
conviction. Perhaps his vision was awry and his reactions morbid; perhaps the confused but vivid scenes which he sketched
were the product of a mind on the point of dissolution; but to
him his vision was real and it bears the stamp of sincerity.

He had already, in a series of realistic plays, attempted to
illustrate some of the major discords of life, but his perceptions
had continually outrun his pen. Human misery seemed too vast
ever to be thus described, and its forms too manifold ever to
be set down one by one. The universe, as he contemplated it
in himself, lost its pattern and its logic; it became for him a
nightmare of suffering and injustice, and only as a nightmare
could it be reproduced. Into one play, if it were to be other
than ridiculously inadequate, must be crowded not one discord
or one tragedy but that endless succession of tragedies which
is the story of humanity and that cumulation of innumerable
discords which is existence. The whole catalogue of miseries,
from the pangs of despised love and the other ills which Hamlet
enumerated on through the results of economic injustice and
all the other sources of evil discovered by the sad experience
of mankind since his time, must be recited; and life must be
presented as the phantasmagoria of suffering which an epitome
shows it to be.

Thus expressionism was born, not out of conscious experiment
but out of a need for expression. Strindberg did not decide to
represent life in a free form with the logical illogic of a dream;
rather life suddenly came to be, for him, more like a nightmare
than like anything else, and as such he set it down. The scene,
like the scene of a dream, shifts without logical reason from
vaguely localized place to place, and the characters bob up,
often strangely transmogrified, in fantastic but curiously sig-

nificant situations; but, again as in a dream, the material from
which the fantasies are composed is the most poignant experience of the dreamer. Here, for example, is Strindberg himself
suffering under the tyranny of an absurd schoolmaster and,
though conscious that he has received his doctor's degree,
strangely unable to get away; there is the ugly girl at a dance
hiding her shame in a corner; and there in the midst of an
idyllic scene are suddenly observed two grimy workmen who
make possible the indulgences which they are forbidden to
share. All changes and all passes, but in the nightmare which
life has become for him no scene rises to his mind which has
not at its core some misery or some injustice simplified and
made typical. Strindberg is not exactly writing a dream play;
he is rather engaged in the process of dreaming, for as a result
of the gradual process by which his inward world became more
vivid and real than the outward one his work began to follow
the pattern of his fantasy instead of the pattern of objective
existence. He had ceased to live and to record; he merely tossed
in the nightmare which his life had generated. This is no place
to discuss the causes of this process or to undertake any final
evaluation of the work in question, but it ought at least to be
plain why it is that *The Dream Play* has all the vivid fascination
of a real dream, while some of the imitations which have been
laboriously made of it have, on the contrary, all the irritating
tediousness of the breakfast table liar who makes up tales out
of Freud. (pp. 122-23)

Joseph Wood Krutch, "Whips and Scorns," in The
Nation, *Vol. CXXII, No. 3161, February 3, 1926,
pp. 122-23.*

DESMOND MacCARTHY   (essay date 1931)

[*MacCarthy was one of the foremost English literary and dramatic
critics of the twentieth century. He served for many years on the
staff of the* New Statesman *and edited* Life and Letters. *Among
his many essay collections,* The Court Theatre 1904-1907: A Commentary and a Criticism *(1907)—a detailed account of three seasons during which the Court Theatre was dominated by Harley
Granville-Barker and Bernard Shaw—is especially valued. According to his critics, MacCarthy brought to his work a wide
range of reading, serious and sensitive judgment, an interest in
the works of new writers, and high critical standards. In the
following excerpt, MacCarthy assesses Strindberg's literary talent.*]

Undoubtedly Strindberg was what we call a "genius," and a
prodigiously prolific one. He wrote fifty-six plays, nine novels,
numerous autobiographical works, lyrical poems, newspaper
articles, historical and scientific treatises (the latter were apparently worthless); and although his work was often slapdash
and sometimes crazy, however poor he might have been at the
time of writing, there had never been a "pot-boiler" among
them. He could only write out of himself. As a young man,
though he had the intellectual energy of ten, he was repeatedly
ploughed in examinations, for he could not master, even in an
elementary fashion, a subject not vitally exciting to him at the
moment. And he could not write at all unless his passions were
engaged. Strindberg's intellect only functioned at the command
of his emotions. This is a characteristic common in writers, in
whom "genius" predominates over all their other faculties.
He possessed amazing insight without the power of weighing
evidence; an astoundingly vivid imagination without being a
great artist.

It is now commonly agreed that literary inspiration, at any rate
of the first order, draws upon the Subconscious; and the faculty

of tapping this source, combined with power, is what we usually mean when we use the word "genius." But it is a writer's gift for selecting from the contents of that "backward and abyss" of thought and passion in himself that makes him an "artist." The images, intuitions and ideas, which at the waving of his mysterious wand peer from those depths, are by no means necessarily of equal or indeed of any value. The spectacle of a poet emerging from a header into his subconsciousness, glistening and triumphant with an old boot or fruit-can in his hand is not infrequent to-day. Such objects come no doubt from the right place, but they are of small consequence. Strindberg's drama (his fiction is nearly all autobiography) is divers spoil. But if we compare the attitude of his conscious judgment towards such strange treasure to Ibsen's attitude (he also was an explorer of the Subconscious), we see the difference between a "genius" who is an "artist" and a "genius" who is not. (pp. 260-61)

Strindberg possessed in perfection that sincerity which lies in being loyal to every mood; but in the sincerity which allows for moods changing and seeks a stable point of view, and leads a literary craftsman to allow for changing moods and to temper them to artistic ends, he was abnormally deficient. His conceptions had the vigour of those of a man who flings himself whole into every emotion, every intuition, as though each was his first and each would be his last.

Imagine a man of profound excitability, violent passions, blazing temper, uncontrollable fastidiousness, seeing only one thing at a time as the emotional storm within him permitted, in whom a craving to enjoy a chivalrous worship of women, and an adoration of woman as a mother, struggled with an intense susceptibility to her as a mistress; imagine him planted in a society where many women were on strike against maternity, jealous of men, eager to emulate them, sick of being idealized yet perpetually on the defensive against criticism; remember, too, that this man is an imaginative creator and more than a little mad, perpetually overworked, frequently hallucinated by absinthe, and physically as nervous as a shying horse; and there you have the conditions out of which Strindberg's work springs. They are not those likely to produce perfect works of art, or even truthful pictures of life. Strindberg's works have not those virtues. But what he can give us are his torments, his madness, his struggles, shattered gleams of his ideals, guesses at the motives of others, half insane and half amazingly acute. It is not a *pleasant* experience thus to suffer with Strindberg, for he has the power to make his reader feel as though he himself were fighting for his own honour and his own sanity. But one can learn a good deal from him if one keeps judgment cool; and one has, at least, while thrusting at Hell's phantoms in the dark, the glow of identifying oneself for the time being with a man of undefeated courage.

The two most important psychological facts about him, apart from his genius, were his liability to violent attacks of suspicion-mania, and his inability to get on with or without women. He married wife after wife. He did not know how to live with women or how to quarrel with them, how to make it up or how to break with them. They threw him into a state of agonized bewilderment, shot with flashes of piercing hate-directed insight. Much of his work may be described as the torments of a henpecked Bluebeard. Possessing the lucidity of genius, he could also suddenly collect himself and see himself as mad or as impossibly exacting. He rightly named his longest account of such an intimacy *The Confessions of a Fool,* or to translate its title more accurately, *The Self-Justification of a Lunatic.*

Strindberg in 1891.

Being a poet, he could sometimes invest scenes with the tatters of a lurid beauty, making you feel, "O what a noble mind is here o'erthrown." But he could never keep the personal aspects of his subjects far enough off from his emotions; nor ever rid himself of resentment towards the creatures of his imagination on account of their resemblance to people who had made him suffer and served him as models. His intensely vivid recollection of all he had felt enabled him to fill his characters with vitality, but once on their feet, he could not allow them, as an artist should, liberty to live, however balefully, as independent beings.

This is discernible in even his best plays, and it degrades them from the category of the great to that of the remarkable. (I have not read or seen his historical dramas; perhaps they and his dream-dramas are different.) His art judged as a whole is of that kind which is euphemistically called "cathartic," and which tends to be unduly exalted in periods of literary experiment, like our own, when the most blatant literary egotism is admired, and a sense of the importance in art of qualities of intellect and feeling which we call by ethical names, magnanimity, nobility, disinterestedness, has become dim or confused. (pp. 262-64)

Desmond MacCarthy, "Strindberg," in his Portraits, *1931. Reprint by MacGibbon & Kee Ltd., 1949, pp. 259-65.*

HERMANN HESSE (essay date 1949)

[Recipient of the Nobel Prize in literature for 1946, Hesse is considered one of the most important German novelists of the twentieth century. Lyrical in style, his novels are concerned with a search on the part of their protagonists for self-knowledge and for insight into the relationship between physical and spiritual realms. Critics often look upon Hesse's works as falling into the tradition of German Romanticism, from the early bildungsroman Peter Camenzind *(1904) to the introspective* Steppenwolf *(1927) to the mystical* Das Glasperlenspiel *(1943;* Magister Ludi), *his last major work.* Magister Ludi *is generally held to epitomize Hesse's achievement, delineating a complex vision which intermingles art and religion to convey a sense of harmony unifying the diverse elements of existence. This work, along with such earlier novels as* Siddhartha, *established Hesse's reputation as an author who to many readers and critics approximates the role of a modern sage. In the following excerpt from an essay originally published in Germany in 1949, Hesse explains his affinity with the work of Strindberg.]*

When I became acquainted with August Strindberg's books, some forty years ago, he very soon took his place for me in that small group of martyr-poets, those lonely seers who not only critically recognized and intellectually explored the ambiguous, pathological, and perilous quality of their epoch, the apparently happy time of the long European peace and of liberalism and confidence in progress, but suffered it biologically, in their own bodies, these men to whom the still-unconscious problems of the times had become personal, physical and psychological distress and illness. I felt, just as I had with Nietzsche, reading him with an unforgettable shudder: here was one of the great sensitives and sufferers, a chosen one and at the same time a marked man, a most delicate seismograph for the coming convulsions, a northern brother to Nietzsche. It did not, to be sure, escape me that this suffering and quarreling, yes, quarrelsome, polemical, possessed, and embittered fanatic of true and of endangered mankind was in addition an important artist and, in many of his smaller compositions such as the one-act plays and the miniatures, a brilliant virtuoso.

But this was not the reason that for several years I repeatedly had to return to him and agonize over him, especially over his autobiographical and confessional books, among which for a time those dealing with the Parisian period were my favorites. No, it was not as an artist that he at that time moved and fascinated me but as the author of those terrifying, sad, almost monomaniacal books in which he brought the displaying of his own person and his own biography to a point of high-minded disregard of shame, in a way that somewhat later through psychoanalysis became familiar in many others but at that time was as single and challenging as a sinister darting flame and that brought a new macabre, threatening clangor into the elegant and weary atmosphere of the satiated prewar epoch. Out of his savage books in shrill tones arose much strife, much hatred, much bitterness, much harsh misunderstanding, now and again, too, spite and malice, but far stronger than all this I felt in him the deep, consuming suffering, not at all the lonely suffering of the psychopath in love with himself but rather a vicarious suffering: one that embraced us all. This won him my love. (pp. 315-16)

Hermann Hesse, "August Strindberg: In Memoriam," in his My Belief: Essays on Life and Art, *edited by Theodore Ziolkowski, translated by Denver Lindley, Farrar, Straus and Giroux, 1974, pp. 315-16.*

CARL E. W. L. DAHLSTRÖM (essay date 1955)

[In the following excerpt, Dahlström applies Aristotelian standards of tragedy to The Father, *noting also that Strindberg rejected the mechanistic perspective of his contemporaries.]*

[Martin] Lamm says that, thanks to his contact with Greek tragedy, Strindberg succeeded in making *The Father* a drama quite unlike those that he had earlier composed. In contrast to the latter, the former has a simple, definitive composition, a reduced list of dramatis personae, a plot which is concentrated on the catastrophic action, a condensed pathos, and a tragic sense of universal significance. Like most Greek tragedies, *The Father* has but one stage setting. Moreover, there is a clearly defined situational complex, based on the battle of the sexes, which takes on universal rather than particular significance. The plot which emerges from this situational complex is so tightly and narrowly woven that no room exists for more than one line of action. Because of the nature of the plot, the elapsed time is approximately twenty-four hours. Finally only eight dramatis personae are employed, and of these eight only two or three customarily appear on the stage at one time. Thus we may say that, superficially at least, *The Father* appears to be in harmony with classical patterns. To determine whether this is a sound or an unsound impression, we must proceed to examine the play more closely.

Will *The Father* respond to analysis according to the *Poetics* of Aristotle? The Greek philosopher defines tragedy as "an imitation of an action that is serious, complete, and of a certain magnitude; in language embellished with each kind of artistic ornament, the several kinds being found in separate parts of the play; in the form of action, not narrative; through pity and fear effecting the proper purgation of these emotions." Moreover, every tragedy must have six parts; namely, plot, character, diction, thought, spectacle, and song. To Aristotle, plot is of prime importance, and in eight different chapters he provides a detailed analysis of this element. Character is next in importance; then thought, diction, song, and spectacle. Of these elements, we shall consider the first three: plot, character, thought.

Most significant in the matter of plot is the completeness of the action, the proper magnitude, reversal of situation, recognition, the use of events that produce fear and pity, and the scene of suffering. In addition, "every tragedy falls into two parts—Complication and Unravelling or *Dénouement.*" An analysis of *The Father* reveals that Strindberg doubtless had an eye on the Aristotelian specifications for plot, or else on the Greek tragedies from which Aristotle derived the specifications. The focus of attention in *The Father* is clearly on an action, on the struggle for dominance between a man and a woman. In its immediate form, the action is not taken directly from the events of life but is created out of life by employing what Aristotle calls "the law of probability or necessity." (pp. 46-7)

In harmony with the Aristotelian dicta, the plot of the drama is marked by reversal of situation and by recognition. *The Father* opens with the Captain in favorable circumstances. He is a military man with a command, a scientist with a growing reputation, a husband, a father, the legal head of a household. The drama closes with the Captain shorn of his military command and cheated in his efforts to complete a scientific project of great significance. He does not know if he really is a father, and he is about to have a guardian appointed for him. Moreover, he is hovering between life and death. Even if he survives, his sanity will be in question. To all intents and purposes, the ruin is complete; the Captain has been destroyed. The events precipitating this reversal are not artificially created by the author, nor are they determined by preternatural interference; all are inherent in the situational complex of natural forces. Thus again *The Father* is in harmony with practices which met Aristotle's approval.

Recognition is defined in the *Poetics* as "a change from ignorance to knowledge, producing love or hate between the persons destined by the poet for good or bad fortune." Aristotle goes on to say that the "recognition which is most intimately connected with the plot and action is . . . the recognition of persons." Moreover, recognition, as well as reversal of situation, turns "upon surprises." In *The Father* the recognition is not of persons but of motives, intentions, and decisions of persons. Two people, husband and wife, are engaged in a struggle for controlling authority in the family. The husband at first scarcely realizes that he is engaged in a conflict, for he is convinced that his wife is legally, intellectually, and physically the weaker of the two. When, in the second act, Laura and the Captain engage in a verbal battle for supremacy and the latter complains bitterly about the brutal slavery of the man to the woman, Laura cries out, "Now you are completely insane!" The Captain replies that he realizes she hopes to drive him insane; he also declares that he has observed her tactics and has known what she has been about. But this is more like masculine bravado than recognition of Laura as the victor. Harassed as he is, the Captain still feels that he is actually the stronger of the two; yet his nerves are so frayed that he breaks down and weeps. The dramatist exploits this incident by portraying a specious approach to reconciliation, but this is quickly followed by a renewal of the verbal conflict. The Captain has asserted that might is what establishes right, and Laura declares that she has the right. She clinches the argument by announcing that she will have the might—full legal power—when, on the following day, the Captain is placed under guardianship. She convinces her husband that she is telling him the truth when she explains that she has the letter in which he wrote to a physician that he considered himself insane. Brutally she says, "You are no longer needed; so you will have to go." It is then that the Captain recognizes Laura for what she really is. The recognition produces such a powerful impact on his distraught nervous system that he loses control of himself and further plays into her hands by hurling a lighted lamp at her.

Before we consider the elements of pity and fear, we should briefly analyze the chief character. First of all, Strindberg explained to Axel Lundegård that the Captain was to be interpreted as a man of quality, a well-born gentleman. "Remember," he says, "that a cavalry officer is always a rich man's son; he is well bred and places high demands on himself as a member of society. He is cultured even in his relations with the soldiers. Thus no crude churl of the traditional type." . . . Aristotle says that the chief dramatis persona must "be one who is highly renowned and prosperous—a personage like Oedipus, Thyestes, or other illustrious men of such families." His character must be "that of a man who is not eminently good and just, yet whose misfortune is brought about not by vice or depravity, but by some error or frailty." Again, there are four desired qualities of character set forth in the Aristotelian specifications. First, the character must be that "which reveals moral purpose, showing what kind of things a man chooses or avoids." Second, the character must exhibit propriety. Third, the character must be true to life. "The fourth point is consistency: for though the subject of the imitation, who suggested the type, be inconsistent, still he must be consistently inconsistent." So too the poet should always aim at the "necessary or the probable." Strindberg's play responds quite well to the demands of the *Poetics*. The Captain is from the approved social class. As a royal officer he has a significant position, and as a scientist he has a reputation. He is "good" in his general life direction, but he is marked by a flaw in character, his inability to maintain mastery of himself in his relations with women. In this flaw he is like Hercules and Samson. His incapacity leads to successive experiences of frustration which in turn precipitate outbursts of anger that culminate in uncontrolled rage.

A crucial question arises: Does the Captain's fate arouse pity and fear in us? "Pity," says Aristotle, "is aroused by unmerited misfortune, fear by the misfortune of a man like ourselves." Surely the Captain's fate is one of unmerited misfortune. If we assume that Clytemnestra kills Agamemnon because the latter, contrary to the former's desire, has offered Iphigenia as a sacrifice, we may establish a parallel with *The Father* by stating that Laura destroys the Captain because the latter intends to sacrifice Bertha, that is, he will prescribe Bertha's education without regard for the mother's desires. Thus if Agamemnon merits pity, the Captain also merits it. We may also have a sense of fear, knowing that we too with our own personal flaws may fall victim to someone engaged in a psychological attack on us. Strindberg, of course, meant to arouse fear wholly within the limits of matrimony. Only women may be certain that children are their own; a man must accept fatherhood on faith. But if that faith is destroyed, a man's fatherhood is also destroyed. Anyone who has seen a performance of *The Father* will doubtless have developed so strong a reaction to Laura that he hates her as much as the Captain does. That a man should think that he himself might become intimately involved with so calculating and unscrupulous a female, and be destroyed by her, can readily fill him with a sense of horror. Indeed, when one has seen the play, he comes to the conclusion that close association with such a woman as Laura means serious trouble for any man, his self-control notwithstanding.

We may also consider briefly what Aristotle calls the thought of a tragedy. Thought, he says is "the faculty of saying what is possible and pertinent in given circumstances." "Under Thought is included every effect which has to be produced by speech, the subdivisions being,—proof and refutation; the excitation of the feelings, such as pity, fear, anger, and the like; the suggestions of importance or its opposite." "Thought is required wherever a statement is proved, or it may be a general truth enunciated." The thought in *The Father* is related to the domestic scene, particularly the relations of the mates. Not only are this man and this woman of the drama incompatible, but man and woman are incompatible. "Do you hate me?" the Captain asks Laura. "Yes, at times," she replies, "when you are man." "This is like racial hatred," says the Captain. "If it is true that we are descended from apes, then at least it must have been from two species. We are not like each other."

In *The Father* Strindberg has exploited an idea that has received treatment in many different ages and cultures: the conflict of interests arising through the intimate association of man and woman. He has thus struggled to give expression to something that has had universal recognition. Moreover, this thought provides the ideational focus of the drama. Out of it spring the situational complex, the plot, and the dramatis personae themselves.

This analysis should be sufficient to indicate that Strindberg could have been greatly influenced by classical ideas of tragedy. We need not insist that he struggled to make *The Father* a modern example of classical tragedy. But we must also not lose sight of the fact that if we go back to Aristotle rather than to neoclassical writers and critics, we find fairly generous provisions for the writing of tragedy. It is, then, not too difficult to fit many dramas into a general classical pattern. (pp. 49-54)

August Strindberg was writing in the latter half of the nineteenth century. For his hero, if such the Captain can be called, there is no destiny that overtakes each man; moreover, man is not an individual capable of modifying his own destiny and redeeming himself by his own acts. On the contrary, the Captain is caught in a mechanically ordered universe in which human life has no particular distinction. Human beings are thus simply aggregates of atomic stuff responding mechanically to the push and pull of other aggregates. The univese is without consciousness, apart from man's, and his consciousness is without significance because it brings with it no options. The universe and all within it, including *Homo sapiens,* operate like a vast machine, and the operations can be exactly described. These descriptions are the laws that govern all phenomena. In particular, there is the law that the stronger overcome the weaker. Exploiting this mechanistic view, Strindberg shows the Captain as the weaker party and hence the one that must give way.

The emotional suspense that lingers even after *The Father* has been brought to a close results in a sense of dissatisfaction. Something apparently is still not accounted for. From the standpoint of human values, the worse has not only triumphed over the better but will also surely capitalize on the triumph, and this is intolerable to teleologists. Yet, from the mechanistic point of view, nature has nothing to do with the so-called human values. Neither good nor evil obtains, for these are but subjective constructs which do not exist in nature. There are, in fact, only the stronger and the weaker. The Captain is caught in the midst of forces which he cannot meet and master. Since he must meet them—he has no option—he is destroyed.

Patently a sense of dissatisfaction could come only to one who has a perspective that is not mechanistic. From the latter point of view the Captain's defeat is simply a natural event, the inevitable effect of a given cause. If a part of a mountain falls away and empties a lake, it is a natural event but not tragic; if fire burns a thing or creature, it likewise is natural but not tragic; if a strong man kills a weak man, it is of the same class of events. For natural occurrences we require nothing more than factual reports wholly devoid of any feeling. We experience dissatisfaction with *The Father* because we cannot accept the Captain and his destruction merely as the play of senseless natural forces. For us, artists and those who appreciate art, life is not endurable if it has no moral significance, and it can have no moral significance unless men to some extent, no matter how limited, can choose how they shall live and how they shall die.

What kind of tragedy, then is *The Father?* What has Strindberg succeeded in doing or failed to do? We may say that the dramatist has done what every great artist has done at some time or other: he has come to grips with the world in which he found himself. Strindberg, a sensitive man of powerful feeling, reacted to the mechanistic perspective which was gaining wide acceptance among his contemporaries. Had he reacted positively, his sympathies would have been such that he would have become a scientist, for artist and mechanistic viewpoint are immiscible. But, regardless of superficial appearances,

Strindberg did not so react. Whether or not he was fully conscious of his position, Strindberg as artist showed himself to be a teleologist even in his very exploiting of mechanistic views. That *The Father* leaves a residue of painful experience is inescapable, for the artist's feelings about life have been qualified by an ingredient that cannot be absorbed or disposed of. The teleological view, without which art becomes mere decoration, and the mechanistic view cannot co-exist in harmony. As a consequence, in the very attempt to order the emotions, the artist intensifies them. A rhythmic objectification of feeling is obtained, but it does not bring with it a reconciliation to life. For the human being who is marked by feeling, the worse has triumphed over the better; thus in the artist's psyche and in the psyches of the spectators, an area of emotional chaos still exists.

In its very exploitation of the denial of moral order and purpose in the lives of men, *The Father,* perhaps in spite of the author's conscious intent, affirms such order. In its direct form it does not, and cannot, establish emotional equilibrium; and, if this is essential to our finest tragedies, *The Father,* is in this respect a failure. Indirectly, however, it is an artist's protest against a kind of life that is marked solely by the natural law of cause and effect, and as such it is a rejection of the mechanistic perspective. The drama is admittedly painful, but it is undeniably powerful. It may, in truth, be the only kind of tragedy possible when the raw materials of art are taken from a mechanically controlled universe. (pp. 61-3)

> *Carl E. W. L. Dahlström, ''Strindberg's 'The Father' as Tragedy,'' in* Scandinavian Studies, *Vol. 27, No. 2, May, 1955, pp. 45-63.*

WALTER JOHNSON (essay date 1960)

[*Johnson is an American critic and educator. In the following excerpt, he discusses Strindberg's transformation of medieval dramatic technique as exemplified in* The Dance of Death.]

While Strindberg remained as fascinated as ever by his own time after his Inferno years of 1894 to 1897, he became more intensely interested than ever before in the late Middle Ages as well. That two-fold interest helped lead to many developments, among them his creation of new dramatic techniques through (1) the extension of his superb realistic-naturalistic technical practices of the pre-Inferno period, (2) the transformation of medieval dramatic ideas and devices into techniques that became highly Strindbergian, and (3) the addition of modern technical elements that were essentially his own. All three matters, taken together, are frequently and loosely spoken of as expressionistic by most scholars and critics.

Strindberg's intensified post-Inferno interest in the Middle Ages stemmed both from his renewed interest in history and his so-called conversion. The latter led to increased attention to Biblical morality and religious faith and to a concern with the medieval mystery and morality plays throughout the post-Inferno years. It is significant that all the major historical plays except *Master Olof* were written after 1897; all of them are concerned in more ways than one with morality. It is equally significant that all his other post-Inferno plays are in technique or thought or both related in varying degrees to the medieval drama.

The three Damascus plays, for example, are to an appreciable extent, adaptations of the techniques of such morality plays as *Everyman.* *Advent* and *Easter,* to cite two more examples, are highly reminiscent of both the morality and mystery plays. Parallels to the medieval stress on life as a pilgrimage appear again and again in the post-Inferno plays, historical and non-historical. In all these plays there are, moreover, parallels to the Biblically-inspired medieval concern with human nature, the relationship between the individual and what Strindberg calls the Eternal One, and the moral problems implicit in both. There is in addition to all this sort of thing Strindberg's amazing psychological insight into the tragic tensions within modern man and his uncanny ability to bring those tensions into tangible expression for the stage.

The companion plays, *The Dance of Death I* and *The Dance of Death II* . . . , received a name that is ultimately medieval in its implications, and they have in them such elements as an emphasis on death, the vampire motive, and the repetition of the pattern of life generation after generation, which were of decided concern to the Middle Ages. Yet the two plays are as modern and contemporary as any plays could be. Strindberg had the genius for taking what he needed by way of inspiration and detail and transforming what he received into something peculiarly his own and always subtly different from anything he had done before. What he did in *The Dance of Death* plays illustrates all this.

The story that Strindberg tells in *The Dance of Death I* is the story of a modern marital hell created by a frustrated army captain stationed on an island called Little Hell and by his equally frustrated ex-actress wife. The story he tells in *The Dance of Death II* is of the same captain, now retired and for the first time really free to go to work as a vampire. What the late Middle Ages had for Strindberg by way of inspiration and detail for the dramatization of these stories can easily be demonstrated.

Medieval Europeans had good reasons for being aware of death as something ugly, horrible and gruesome. Plague, war, disease, disaster and want provided constant visible evidence that the priests were quite right in insisting that not only was Death taking neighbors, friends, and relatives but might at any moment take the individual himself. Both the morality and the mystery plays were used, moreover, by the church to warn medieval people about their frequently frantic attempts to conceal the macabre realities from themselves by escaping into worldly pleasures.

Recorded on thousands of paintings (murals, frescoes, oils, and water colors), engravings, and woodcuts and in many sculptures, poems, sermons, and plays was the so-called Dance of Death or *danse macabre*. On or in these medieval works of art are stressed such macabre matters as the omnipotence of death, its usually unexpected and undesired coming to everyone, its disregard for both rank and position, and the ugly and horrifying details of dying. Death, generally represented as a skeleton-like personified figure in many of these works of art, is presented as ready to lead everyman, everywoman, and everychild into a rough equivalent of the long dance, which ends for each individual in his final collapse as he holds the hand of Death. The medieval dances of death that survive place the emphasis squarely on the grotesque and the horrible; they apparently were deliberately designed to serve as warnings to everyone that he had better prepare for the next life by changing his way of living through acceptance of the moral code of the church and through trying to live up to it. The church understandably enough took advantage of the medieval fear of death and the agony of dying by emphasizing, too, the transitory nature of human life and the terrifying consequences of sin—

judgment day and eternal punishments in Hell. The priests did not mince words about the frailties of human nature and the presentation of both Purgatory and Hell as anything but figurative.

In the last of the Damascus plays, Strindberg promised never again to relate the story of his own suffering as he had been doing in surprisingly faithful fashion from the beginning of his literary career through the Damascus trilogy. He did not promise, however, not to direct his attention to other people's suffering or to the evil in other people's lives. In fact, with his newly reacquired faith in the moral nature of the universe, his suspicion that this life may be something like a dream state and not the *real* life, and his intensified interest in both good and evil, Strindberg naturally enough turned his attention to a family situation well known to him, found in it resemblances to the medieval dance of death, and composed in the companion plays two of the most effective dramas the modern theater possesses.

Strindberg's interpretation of the marriage is not primarily an objective case study in dramatic form; it is, instead, a deliberately distorted transformation of the source material to intensify the marital misery so that it will serve, figuratively, as a modern dance of death.

To understand what is at the core of the particular marital hell, one needs to recall that during the last fifteen years of his life Strindberg's plays deal to an appreciable degree with the problem of evil, its nature, its origins and causes, and its results. Perhaps no passage in all these plays throws more light on Strindberg's thinking about human nature and its potentials for evil than Indra's daughter's speech in *A Dream Play*. . . .

> All these are my children! Each one by himself
> is good, but they have only to get together to
> start quarreling and turn into demons.

That both Edgar and Alice in *The Dance of Death* have had potentials for personal and social good Strindberg suggests in abundant detail, but he makes it clear that they have become demons, whose inherent selfishness and egotism have never had real chances to be curbed or effectively controlled in an unhappy environment. Their whole marriage has been the nominal union of two constantly selfish and egotistic human animals. In their struggle for the freedom of their individual egos, they have become a devious vampire and a frustrated middle-aged coquette, whose only bond is an animal-like sexual attraction for each other, whose tactics are those of the jungle, and whose days are, to paraphrase the title of a Strindbergian disciple's play stemming not a little from these companion plays, a "long day's journey into night." In that journey, neither one has been willing to accept the smallest degree of personal responsibility: instead they blind themselves through rationalizing. Nor does Strindberg feel that Edgar and Alice are exceptional:

> ALICE. Is he a human being?
>
> KURT. When you asked that question first, I answered no. Now I believe him to be the commonest kind of human being—the kind that possesses the earth. Perhaps, we, too, are of the same kind—making use of other people and of favorable opportunities?

Strindberg applies what he says about evil universally, and, through what Kurt suggests, provides a remedy—submission, resignation, and humanity, all of them in striking agreement with the implications of the medieval dances of death. For the worldly life that Edgar and Alice lead is, figuratively speaking, a dance which usually turns their thoughts from death and the true sadness of their days. It is significant that so many theater critics down through the years have found Edgar's solo dancing of a Hungarian dance to the accompaniment of Alice's playing of Halvorsen's *Entry of the Boyars* one of the high points in the stage productions of the first *Dance of Death.* The lively, enthusiastic dance performed in grotesque contrast to the deadly and boring environment serves as an effective parallel to the medieval dance in which the living try to escape from thoughts of their own mortality. Just as the medieval dance ends in certain death, the captain's dance ends with his own collapse.

In a much broader and figurative sense, the twenty-five years have been a dance of death. The story Strindberg has to tell by way of illustration of his major theme in *Dance of Death I* may be said to be a repetition of basic steps which promise to lead to something that will break the ghastly pattern, but each time the promise fails and the pattern begins again. The lives of these two have tended to turn their thoughts from both death and the sad reality of their days.

Yet they never quite succeed in rationalizing away either thoughts of death or awareness of the sadness of the reality completely. Against the dismal and symbolic background of their prison-like home, these two have lived in "the most unreasoning hatred, without cause, without purpose . . . ," seemingly "without end." Except on rare occasions, they have tortured each other so effectively and thoroughly that Kurt can say with well-motivated justification:

> But tell me: what is going on in this house? What's happening here? There's a smell as of poisonous wall-paper, and one feels sick the moment one comes in. I'd prefer to get away from here, had I not promised Alice to stay. There are dead bodies beneath the floor, and the place is so filled with hatred that one can hardly breathe.

That the two are undergoing tortures similar to those depicted in a Swedenborgian hell—and, for that matter, any kind of hell—is clear to anyone who will read the play with a little care. That they are aware of the nature of their reality even though they usually try to conceal it from themselves is clear enough. As Edgar says, "But all life is horrible." But, only when Edgar has been struck down by his heart attack, can he even approach the idea of assuming his partial responsibility for having created this living death:

> Life seemed so peculiar—so contrary, so malignant—ever since my childhood—and people seemed so bad that I grew bad, too.

Strindberg's presentation of the reality of one marital hell is a macabre interpretation of tortured human beings, tortured not only by each other and others but by themselves.

In the midst of the nightmare that their life together is, they rarely succeed in eliminating thoughts of death. Alice is keenly aware of it, not as something that will strike her personally but as a two-fold thing: (1) her own release from the prison of her marriage to Edgar and (2) a weapon by means of which to torture Edgar. She is, for example, delighted by the signs of Edgar's aging—his failing eyesight, his increasing inability to enjoy his tobacco and whiskey, his illness. Edgar, on the other hand, tries to conceal as long as he can the significance of all

Lithograph of Strindberg by Edvard Munch, 1896.

these matters by insisting to Alice that he has never been seriously ill, that he will live for twenty years more, and that he will die like an old soldier—suddenly, painlessly. Yet his very insistence and occasional involuntary admissions reveal that he fears death and that he does not really believe that when it is over there is "Nothing left but what can be put on a wheelbarrow and spread on the garden beds." Strindberg traces with great but unobtrusive care Edgar's concern with death: the outward statements, the inner anguish, the heightened fears when it looks as if he is going to die, his grasping for straws then, and his renewed pretense when he recovers a little. There is, for Edgar, no resignation, no humility, no submission. He has become one of the living dead, figuratively, just as his marriage has been a living death.

But the first *Dance of Death* ends in a fashion decidedly parallel to another aspect of the medieval dance of death. Just as the *danse macabre* combines the gruesome and the grotesque with grim humor, Strindberg's first play ends with the grimly humorous scene of the two principals in the marital hell planning the celebration of their silver wedding. . . . (pp. 8-12)

The companion play takes place in a setting directly opposite to that of the first play. Instead of a home that is a prison, figuratively and literally, the setting is that of the beautiful quarters that Kurt has arranged for himself. They are cheerful, beautifully furnished, designed for pleasant living. The man who has provided himself with this home has achieved to a remarkable degree the submission, resignation and humanity needed for living in a world where other people, too, have their being. It is a promising setting, threatened, however, by the implications of Strindberg's well-motivated reversal of themes.

In the first *Dance of Death*, the dominant theme is that of the marital hell, but one other important theme—Edgar as vampire—is introduced and appreciably developed. A third important theme—the repetition of a pattern of life in one generation after the other—is suggested.

In the second *Dance of Death*, the importance of the themes is reversed. The dominant theme is that of Edgar as the vampire, that of the repetition of patterns in following generations is developed, and the marital hell is reduced to a secondary theme. All three are important, however, and Strindberg again treats them in counterpoint to each other.

It is the vampire theme, however, that in the second *Dance of Death* primarily supplies the macabre elements. In the first play Strindberg makes clear what he means by vampire:

> KURT.... for just now when he felt his life slipping away, he clung to mine, began to settle my affairs as if he wanted to creep into me and live my life.
>
> ALICE. That's his vampire nature exactly ... to seize hold of other people's lives, to suck interest out of other people's lives, to arrange and direct for others, when his own life has become absolutely without interest for him. And remember, Kurt, don't ever let him get hold of your family affairs, don't ever let him meet your friends, for he'll take them away from you and make them his own.... He's a magician at doing that! ... If he meets your children, you'd soon see them on intimate terms with him, he'd advise them and bring them up according to his own whims, and above all against your wishes.

The Edgar who in the first play was in constant danger of discharge has now been retired and on the basis of a pension that cannot be revoked, he is free to go to work as his egotism directs. The tragic mortal afraid both of life and death in *The Dance of Death I* has become one of the exceptionally active living dead in *The Dance of Death II*. It is to his activities in the destruction or selfish use and manipulation of the genuinely alive that the second play is primarily devoted. Edgar thrives and flourishes through the theft of ideas, things, and people. The illustrations are many; the point is clear: even those who have resigned themselves to earthly life and have accepted the ideal of humane living are in constant danger of losing in the uneven struggle with the vampires. The implications are macabre indeed.

Note, for example, the development of the secondary theme of the repetition of the pattern of life in a following generation. Edgar's daughter, Judith, lovely to look at, endowed with potentialities for becoming not only her father's image but also for becoming a woman who can love a well as hate, is a major pawn by which Edgar manipulates and uses the whole community—the aging colonel would like to marry her, and Edgar as the prospective father-in-law of the person in somewhat remote control of Little Hell can use the colonel's name most conveniently and effectively to gain his ends. It is egotistic Judith, humanized by love, that gives the vampire the death blow, however. When he is dealt that blow, Edgar in his self-

deception says, with ironic intention, "Forgive them for they know not what they do."

In Strindbergian terms, everything repeats itself, even the good repeats itself. In his development of the relationship between Judith and Allan, Strindberg has not only indicated clearly the possibilities for evil, but has shown just as clearly the possibilities for good in human beings in association with each other.

In the second play's continuing but somewhat subdued battle between husband and wife appears the use of a technique that Strindberg himself mentions in an unpublished note:

> What if all [the characters] should talk in asides? And in so doing blurt out their real thoughts, which they have to conceal in the masquerade of life, have to conceal for the sake of bread and butter and social acceptance, because of wife and children.

It is true, of course, that Edgar and Alice usually say what they believe will benefit themselves selfishly, but it is also true that they frequently do say exactly what they think about each other, relatives, acquaintances, and neighbors. It is one of the remarkable facts about Strindberg's dialogue that it frequently becomes the blunt expression of inner thought, and not the measured conventional exchange of primarily controlled ideas or patter.

In spite of the fact that Strindberg supplied unsurpassed psychological motivations for this macabre tragedy and detailed analysis of character which penetrates even to the unconscious and the subconscious, the major emphasis is not placed on either the dramatic motivation or the construction of plot but on the intensity of the atmosphere of horror and comfortless isolation. Concentrating on one point—symbolized by the dance of death, Strindberg presents a nightmare in which life becomes an evil dream. The plays suggest that actual death may be something great and even majestic in its release from the horror of a living death on Little Hell.

However distressing the companion plays may have been for the easily identified primary models for Edgar, Alice, and Judith at the time the plays first appeared and were presented, they are, dramatically and theatrically, among the very best plays in modern drama.... The plays as Strindberg wrote them can hardly fail to grip and to fascinate readers or theater audiences. (pp. 13-15)

> *Walter Johnson, 'Strindberg and the Danse Macabre,'' in* Modern Drama, *Vol. III, No. 1, May, 1960, pp. 8-15.*

RICHARD GILMAN   (essay date 1969)

[*Gilman is an American critic and educator. In the following excerpt, he contests the traditional view of Strindberg's early plays as examples of dramatic naturalism.*]

In November of 1887, when Henrik Ibsen was at the height of his fame, he received a copy of August Strindberg's new play, *The Father*. A few days later he wrote to the Swedish bookseller who had sent it to him that although the younger dramatist's "experiences and observations in the area of life" with which the play was concerned were not the same as his own, he found it impossible to deny or to resist the author's "violent force" in his new work. (p. 199)

That Ibsen was well aware of the Swedish playwright's originality and power is clear. . . . (p. 200)

Ibsen is linked forever to something that wasn't synonymous with the well-made play but that had assimilated its technical means. Naturalism is one of the terms we use to see to it that art remains within the realm of "culture," that is to say within the domain of pedagogy. For Ibsen's contemporaries—Zola, for example, or, provisionally as we shall see, Strindberg—the word naturalism meant a number of things, but a shared meaning was that it marked out the field of an exploration that was at the same time a repudiation of unseriousness and artificiality in literature and drama, an assault on them for having taken their eyes off what existence was really like. It was a word to describe a procedure and a morale that were felt to be necessary in art at the time, and *as a word*, it is useful in the history of changing attitudes and ambiences in art. But it was never a thing, a substance, or even a specific style, in the same way that "absurd" art or expressionism are not actualities but signs, climates, and terms we use for the sake of historical order and the exigencies of textbooks. (p. 204)

This is essential to remember in the case of August Strindberg. For Strindberg, almost a generation younger than Ibsen, naturalism as I have been describing it was already the prevailing serious attitude toward literary art when he came to artistic maturity, and his first important plays were written in its atmosphere and with its élan. Yet Strindberg's dramatic imagination, like that of Ibsen, was too far-reaching and original to have been content with the operation of a literary mode that understood itself largely as a principle of earnestness, a repudiation of spectacle and arid fantasy and a means of making the theater work for conscious, socially revelatory ends. Such things could not be much more than starting points, and in fact Strindberg early referred to himself as a *Nyanaturalist,* a "new" naturalist.

With less of a stake than Ibsen in maintaining a *plausible* theater, one in which a playwright worked to change things by indirection, withholdings and subtle departures, Strindberg was able to move more aggressively and quickly out of the well-madeness of naturalism as well as out of its area of social concerns, or at least socially oriented subject matter. For him, though he acknowledged Ibsen's contributions to the possibilities of a more open theater, the older writer remained essentially inside. Sharing in part what was then, as now, the reductive view of Ibsen, Strindberg saw his great fellow Scandinavian largely as an ideologue (on the wrong side of most issues; he thought *A Doll's House,* for example, was part of a feminist plot), a forensic dramatist and a man with whose spirit he felt no compelling impulse to link his own.

For all that his work plunged more deeply into psychic jungles than Ibsen's, was more "unconscious" and more taken up with extreme emotional states, Strindberg was a much more ready and voluble expositor of his own aesthetic ideas and attitudes. Ibsen's extreme reticence means that his imaginative starting points as well as his thinking about aesthetic problems have to be almost wholly inferred from the internal evidence of the plays, although there is some important help available from those scattered, lofty, understated pronouncements on process and those oblique essays in self-definition that we generally persist in ignoring: "I have been more the poet and less the social philosopher than people have generally been inclined to believe."

Strindberg has been more easily recognized as a poet, one reason being the closer coherence with our own concerns of

his inquest into aberration and of his ambiguous lyricism. He was extraordinarily conscious and clear-sighted about his art, knowing at all times that he was making something new and that these new compositions whose music was one of implication, internal logic, protean change, intuition and epiphany were not going to be easily understood by the public and not easily shrugged off by other playwrights. Out of his letters, his obiter dicta and, most important of all, his prefaces to his own plays there takes shape a history of a revolution in imagination, one that amounted to nothing less than the overthrow of a sanctified way of organizing experience into the formal patterns of drama, at the same time as it was an opening out to new kinds of experience. (And it is this simultaneity, the response to the claims of new and not-yet-identified experience and the necessity to find means for its disposition as art, that we so often lose sight of because of our habit of thinking of art as the *record* of experience and not as its transformation.)

The history begins with Strindberg's first plays in the mood or genre of what we call naturalism. To this moment he is nearly everywhere taught as having composed two distinct and even inimical kinds of plays, two major kinds, that is, in addition to the historical pieces with which he filled out his dramatic *oeuvre.* "Naturalistic" and "symbolic": the two species go on bearing their names in the textbooks like identification plates outside the cages in a zoo, with nothing to connect them as the work of a single imagination except a theory of psychological change or else one of cultural inevitability.

Strindberg, according to the first of these notions, went from the naturalistic to the symbolic in his writing when his psyche had passed through some similar process, something that is usually described (although never explained) as his deepening emotional instability and near madness. What this ignores is that during the last years of his life Strindberg wrote a kind of play that cannot be labeled either naturalistic or symbolic, that even at his maddest he was never less than lucid about his aesthetic procedures, and that in any case the word "symbolic" tells us almost nothing about the nature of his art at any time. The bias here in favor of the "real" over the "symbolic" is, however, striking; even when the later, so-called symbolic plays are preferred to the earlier ones, as by some commentators they are, the choice is usually made on the grounds of a governing notion of art as a form of pathology—interesting, important, but aberrant for all that—and a particular feeling for Strindberg as both a conscious and unconscious explicator of pathology's ways.

A related approach is through history: Strindberg's symbolic plays are seen as reflections of the general cultural breakup and ferment, as icons of the new "dissociated" sensibility and the onrushing movement of all art into abstraction. What both these theories do of course is throw on to psychology or intellectual history the burden of finding out why his art was as it was and why it showed itself as it had to. (pp. 204-07)

When in his late thirties Strindberg wrote his first plays in the atmosphere of what we call naturalism—*The Father* and *Miss Julie*—he had behind him a body of traditional and *acceptable* work, plays on historical themes such as the established Swedish theater was easily able to assimilate. But during the years immediately preceding the writing of *The Father* in 1887, he had done scarcely any writing for the theater at all. The stage, he wrote, was "mere pose, superficiality and calculation," something "reprehensible" when compared to poetry or fiction, for example, fixed in conventions, impermeable to new consciousness, lacking almost all means for the expression of thought. During this period he wrote mostly autobiographical books and engaged heavily in psychological and sociological research, some of it eccentric but most of it of an uncommonly advanced and radical kind. It was a period, too, of marital discord and sexual turmoil of the kind he was to experience even more violently later on.

When he went back again to writing plays, it was evidently with a new morale and ambition. Having engaged in an exploration of his own being during the creation of the autobiographies, he was prepared now for an expansion of the self into drama, an investiture of its events and scenes with the actualities of his own experience and nature. It was something that among his contemporaries Ibsen alone, in his oblique and scarcely visible way (scarcely visible, at any rate, since *Brand*), had done. But to accomplish this, to put dramatic form to the uses of the self, meant having to apply pressure to the reigning notions of characters in drama. Inhabitants of a world outside the specificities and exigencies of personal being, archetypes and stock figures of a protected universe of publicly maintained artifice, bound to the expected gesture and the categorical utterance, dramatic characters stood against personality, against private vision and all visions of private actuality.

In the *Biographia Literaria* Coleridge had written: "There have been men in all ages who have been impelled as by an instinct to propose their own nature as a problem, and who devote their attempts to its solution." Strindberg was such a man, and we mostly see his works as those kinds of attempts; what we don't so easily see is how the solution to himself lay in his being able to solve the problems of his art, to be able to create it.

In the preface to *Miss Julie* Strindberg composed a brilliant, elaborate justification for the dramatic practices of the play, for its aesthetic choices, and a manifesto for much future change on the stage. At the heart of his argument was the recognition of what "character" had come to mean on the stage and of how his own aesthetic urgencies could no longer be contained within that circumscribed meaning and use.... (pp. 208-09)

When we look at *Miss Julie* under the sign and governance of naturalism, it seems to be, like *The Father* before it, a work whose energies and apparatuses derive from life rather than from the stage, from an observed and inhabited world of social and psychic pathology into which acute insights have been made and a series of passionate incidents, a "plot," devised for their incarnation on the stage. A hard, violent, tightly constructed *equivalent* has been found for nature, in this case human nature in its extreme aspects of aggression, envy, fear, hatred, lust and so on. The naturalism of the play thus consists in its fidelity to these emotions as they show themselves in the world and not as abstract counters in a theatrical game, and the drama's revolutionary importance consists in its having gone beyond artifice and stock theatrical representation, in its having *told the truth*.

These are the assumptions on which the play is usually taught, and they are sophisticated assumptions for the most part. To hold them means, to begin with, to be open to the presence in art of emotion of a disturbing kind, not such an easy thing to be, and beyond that to be able to trace a kind of process, the aesthetic action itself, by which such emotion can make itself felt as significant. And yet the notion of equivalence—the idea that art making is the creation of counterparts to what exists already in other shapes—turns this way of contemplating plays and other works into a belief in art as surrogate history, as moral or social or psychological truth in a special form.

It leads finally, however much the pull of a sensuous appreciation holds out against it, to *Miss Julie's* being seen as a psychological or sociological document, or rather as both at once, its subject being changing class relations, the decadence of the Swedish aristocracy and the simultaneous rise of an aggressive, insensitive proletariat, along with the psychosexual manifestations and analogues of such a process. In the same way Chekhov's plays, so mysteriously and deceptively clear, full of arguments that make no points and of a reality that cannot have existed anywhere else, are nevertheless interpreted as "dramatized" accounts of the descent, through ennui, failure of nerve and irresistible social disqualification, of the Russian upper classes in the face of an ascending bourgeoisie.

The trouble with such interpretations (if it weren't trouble enough that for even their historical and sociological value to remain intact the most pointed and coerced analogies to our own experience have continually to be set out) is of course that they leave almost no space for the plays as art, which is to say for their existence as new, independent truths, new actualities. *Miss Julie* is indeed taken from "life," from experiences that have been gone through and not simply appropriated from the literary, the *invented*, past, and in its action a paradigm may indeed be traced for the new psychosocial actualities that have been the arena of those experiences. That, at the deepest level, was what naturalism was all about: a wheeling movement back to the sources in history of imagination, which had been feeding off itself, with more and more jejune results, for generations.

And yet that highest value of naturalism, that *truthfulness* (which art has again and again to recover), was something that had to be won aesthetically, achieved within the work and not simply applied there, as though through a transfer from one realm to another. Being so created, such truthfulness is no longer the equivalent or the recasting of data that has been obtained somewhere else, and it is no longer describable as a truth about "nature." Naturalism, like all such denotive terms, ceases to mean anything as soon as it is asked to account not for the staring point or the morale of a work of art but for the art itself.

Miss Julie is a social or psychological document only in so far as experiences have entered into it which it is possible to paraphrase into sociological or psychological information, such periphrasis being the responsibility of its perpetrator and not a true potentiality of the work. It is naturalistic only in so far as it begins with a repudiation of stage typologies and received artistic ideas, and as it wishes to be true, or rather—and most importantly—to *not be untrue* to what has been felt and observed. The poet is the man who sees, Ibsen had said, and Strindberg always had his eyes open. But what he saw was something more complex, fatal and unlocalized, above all more personal and unsystematic, than the changing class structure in Sweden or the armaments of a sexual combat, both of which served his purposes for the play as a kind of pretext, a necessary physical and histrionic ground. His preface tells us in part what he had *noticed:* how men and women have become "split" and "vacillating, a mixture of the old and new," how human souls are "fragments," "torn shreds . . . patched together."

To write a play is a problem in imagination, and just as Ibsen had had to struggle with the technical means available to him, to find means that would still be dramatic in a theater confined to only certain kinds of imaginative arrangements, so Strindberg had to devise a new kind of play, and not merely, as he remarked, "to create a new drama by pouring new ideas into the old forms." The play he needed to create was one that against all recent precedent would not simply incorporate what

Strindberg taking his last walk, April 1912.

he had discovered, or *seen*, but would exist as the discovery itself.

The form he was seeking, in other words, was one in which fragmentation, gaps in connections, discontinuity, self-division and vacillation would be the content itself, the true subject of the play. This was to constitute the real revolution, the alteration in experience that now had its aesthetic form, which in turn provided a new experience. Men lived, Strindberg had seen, in a new atmosphere, a changed medium, and against this interrupted and discontinuous air they went on trying to bring about continuity and wholeness by fiat, by *previous* forms of the imagination, in so far as they tried to do the thing through art. Plays had been images of wholeness, whether they were farces, melodramas or "naturalistic" and sober dramas; their very forms were in opposition to the way life was being most crucially known and felt.

At the center of Strindberg's changed dramaturgy for *Miss Julie* is the remarkable compression he achieves in making the events of a single night issue in a tragic denouement. In this era of the theater such compression would have been employed only for the purposes of a swift unfolding of melodramatic or farcical events, as in the rapid, circumstantially linked, "outer-directed" plays of Scribe or Sardou. In *Miss Julie* it is the effect of a substantial cutting away of integumentary material, of all that explanation and exposition that had burdened the "seri-

ous" theater and made bourgeois tragedy, where it existed, into something very like a sermon on the logic and coherence of human life, no matter how disastrous the action being portrayed might be. The connections in this play are inward for the most part, unstated, carried by implication in the gestures and utterances of the two main characters, whose conversation is mainly a series of instigations to internal activity rather than an exchange of information, a species of repartee or a means of advancing the "action" of the drama. (pp. 211-15)

The play's action advances, as it were, by fits and starts, by reversals, leaps and regroupings, although the dominant motif and impetus remains the movement toward Miss Julie's final loss of self-esteem and subsequent (implied) suicide. Yet there is no single motive for her action: "Another thing that will offend simple souls is that the motivation of my play is not simple and that life is seen from more than one viewpoint . . . This multiplicity of motive is, I like to think, typical of our times. And if others have done this before me, then I congratulate myself in not being alone in my belief in these 'paradoxes' (the word always used to describe new discoveries)."

Yet Strindberg was almost wholly alone in this "paradox" when it came to the stage. The crucial thing to notice about Julie's suicide is that it is not brought about by anything inexorable in the working of the plot; it is not even, properly speaking, a denouement at all, not an inevitable outcome of a logic of cause and effect. Jean has seduced her, as the drama's central event, but even the fact that the news will become known to everyone is clearly no sufficient reason for killing herself, and Strindberg makes no pretense (a conventional playwright would have made a mainstay out of it) of its being so. Nor is her shame a sufficient reason either, even if such a thing could have been, as it is not, "dramatized," made into an active force, a motive.

Julie has killed herself, in rather the same way that Ibsen's Hedda Gabler did, because she cannot live (we do not die from our deaths, Charles Peguy wrote, but from our whole lives), and she has discovered this truth—or rather the play is the process of such discovery—through what she has been made to feel and think and say. She doesn't hang together, she lacks a principle of coherence, which is what self-esteem ultimately depends on; she is "split" and "vacillating." The "plot" is the story of her self-division, the image of it, not a vehicle in which she travels to her destruction. And the play in its entirety is the very form of such being, the new aesthetic environment for what has up to now been only intuition and feeling.

Julie of course is only half the play, one of its duelists, and in being absorbed in her fate we tend to lose sight of that of her adversary, the servant Jean. Nothing demonstrates better that Strindberg was not engaged in writing history than that the latter character also "loses," is made aware of his own unfreedom, his riven and incoherent self. He prods Julie to suicide but he cannot really live either, being on one level still bound to his subservience, fear and unaccountable guilt—his psychology—and, more deeply, to his invented and therefore sterile persona. They have fought each other to a standstill: "You take all my strength from me, you make me a coward," he tells her at the end.

In the most subtle fashion Strindberg has arranged one of his "dances of death," in which elements and faculties of the soul (for that is what these characters are beneath their provisional and tactical incarnations) move to administer death blows that have been conceived in a fatality known and lived through before this—the death of the consistency and harmony of the self—and that are now fictions, strokes of the imagination which has erected their new environment, so that they may be delivered from chaos, dispersion and the fate of being mere nameless impressions or, worse, data.

This new environment, a realm of existence for characters who had been dislodged from their habitual function in drama as *summary judgments* or as metonymic actions, had been built up by Strindberg at certain public costs and with some incompletions. As he had anticipated, people were disturbed and distracted by the absence of a single point of view, for this, like Ibsen's spiriting away of Nora at the end of *A Doll's House,* was more truly revolutionary than the violent moral vision that the play was in one of its appearances offering. They were disturbed, too, by the drama's elisions and ellipses, the way it moved to invisible promptings and arrived suddenly at its climaxes with only the faintest sound of theatrical machinery being heard.

Yet for the most part, again like Ibsen, Strindberg had remained within the largest conventions of the stage. His characters, although complex, unprogrammatic and uncoerced—souls now and not automata—were still recognizable, unified in their essential presence within the drama, possible to "identify" with, no matter how difficult that might be. His plot, though subterranean and unmechanical, still moved in a linear fashion, and his narrative could be repeated, which is to say paraphrased. Ten years later, after a series of further new-naturalist plays and an interval of silence during which for six years he lived in his "inferno," Strindberg wrote a play, *To Damascus,* that broke wholly through the bounds of drama as they had existed until then. (pp. 215-18)

> *Richard Gilman, "Ibsen and Strindberg," in his* The Confusion of Realms, *Random House, 1969, pp. 172-218.**

MARY SANDBACH (essay date 1972)

[*Sandbach is an English critic and the translator of numerous works of Scandinavian literature, including those of August Strindberg and Per Olaf Sundman. In the following excerpt from the introduction to her translation of* Getting Married, *she contests the traditional view of Strindberg as a bitter misogynist.*]

In view of what he said about women in *Getting Married II,* particularly in the preface, and the portraits he drew of them in his plays, it is hardly surprising that Strindberg's contemporaries dubbed him a misogynist, but it is unfortunate that the misnomer has become so firmly attached. He only hated what he called 'Amazons,' 'tribades,' 'hermaphrodites,' that is women who ill-treated, abused, or tried to supersede men. Unfortunately when he sat down to write his plays these women dominated the stage, and the others were forgotten. But in his letters he remembers them, and constantly refers to his love for women and his inability to live without them. "You know that as a creative writer I mix make-believe and reality together, and the whole of my misogyny is theoretical, for I could not live without the company of a woman" he wrote to his brother Axel in February 1887. . . . Much later, in June 1892, he wrote to Charles de Casanove "J'aime les femmes et j'adore les enfants; quoique divorcé je recommande le mariage comme la seule forme du commerce entre les sexes" ['I love women and I adore children; although divorced I recommend marriage as the only form of intercourse between the sexes']. . . .

This is the spirit that imbues *Getting Married I.* Marriage itself is an admirable institution, the trouble is that people misuse it. What he himself loved and longed for above everything else was harmonious family life. (p. 21)

In *Getting Married* Strindberg set out to show why it was that people so often failed to achieve harmonious family life. Sometimes the causes of failure were social or economic, sometimes personal, but they often arose from woman's obstinate desire to be emancipated from the care of home and children. He claimed that the stories were based on situations he had observed. The book was to consist of "twenty self-contained pictures of twenty marriages or concubinage that I have seen with my own eyes," and added "I've had my models, of course, but I've taken them from remote places in the country, some of them are dead, and others are very obscure people! Ça ira!" . . . Unless his friends were 'very obscure people,' which seems unlikely, this does not accord well with his statement in *The Son of a Servant* . . . that "Johan wanted to describe as large a number as possible of the marriages he had seen; and he had seen a great many, for most of his friends of the same age were married."

The internal evidence of the stories themselves does not seem to bear out either of his statements. Many of them read much more like case histories invented to illustrate points he wanted to drive home.

It is true that early in his career Strindberg stated that "*An author is only a reporter of what he has experienced,*" . . . but his object then was to show Siri von Essen how easy it was to write. In a letter to his sister Elizabeth, written in June 1882, he presents the same idea in a much more complicated form. "To write," he says, "is not to invent, to make up something that has never existed. The man who narrates what he has experienced is an author, and he helps his fellow men by telling them about the things that may happen in life. But to narrate is not just to arrange events in a sequence. You must mean something by what you write, illumine one side of life. The art of the author consists in arranging many impressions, memories, and experiences, in leaving out subsidiary matter, and emphasizing the main points. If you see that your subject is too rich, take one episode by itself, and you will find your material easier to handle." . . . (pp. 22-3)

The question raised by this letter is what did Strindberg mean by 'experience'? He meant something wider than personal experience of other human beings. For Strindberg was hypersensitive to every kind of stimulus, and reacted as violently to what he heard and read as to what he experienced directly. Few writers have been more passionately involved with the ideas circulating in their own times.

Many of what we may call his 'literary' experiences were embodied in the stories of *Getting Married.* Take for instance "The Reward of Virtue," which is not a picture of marriage at all. "As you see," he wrote to Karl Otto Bonnier in June 1884, "'Alike and Unlike' and the upper classes haunt 'The Reward of Virtue' like anything. I nearly forgot all about the relations between the sexes." . . . (p. 23)

It is true that in "The Reward of Virtue" Strindberg adapted some of the circumstances and events of his own childhood and youth to suit his literary purposes, but in the main the story is concerned with two problems which he may have observed, but of which he had no direct experience. The first of these was the oppression of the lower classes by the upper classes, and the second the terrible effects of sexual abstinence.

His awareness of the first had probably been quickened by a book he obtained in February 1884, *A Final Settlement of Accounts with Swedish Law (Slutliqvid med Sveriges lag 1871-76)*, by N. H. Qviding. Many of the revolutionary changes in the Swedish social system proposed in this book were those that Strindberg put forward as desirable in *Getting Married I*, and it was from Qviding that he learnt the terms 'upper' and 'lower classes.' . . . Qviding believed among other things that women could not hope to achieve equality until men had been liberated, that government must be decentralized, that all examinations should be done away with, and that pupils should be taught sociology instead of dead languages, ideas that are all to be found in the pages of *Getting Married I*.

Strindberg's ideas about sex, and the effects of sexual abstinence, were also influenced by a book. This was *Elements of Social Science; or, Physical, Sexual, and Natural Religion* by a young English doctor and Neo-Malthusian, George Drysdale. Part II of this remarkable book deals in detail with almost every aspect of sexual life. Drysdale believed that you could not have a healthy mind unless you had a healthy body, and that a body could not be healthy if it was starved of sex. The best way to health was free love. . . . Strindberg believed in matrimony, not free love, but Drysdale's horror of sexual abstinence fitted in perfectly with his views. In **"The Reward of Virtue"** the hero's dreadful physical and moral decline follows the course mapped out by Drysdale in every particular. His influence is also evident in **"The Phoenix"** and **"Bread,"** while that of Qviding is particularly noticeable in **"Unnatural Selection"**.

Another writer whose ideas constantly crop up in *Getting Married* is the Jewish-Hungarian doctor and sociologist, Max Nordau. Like Drysdale, Nordau thought physical love was the only natural and healthy love, and that people needed sex more than they needed food. (pp. 23-4)

Because Strindberg insisted on introducing the bedroom into his stories, and suggested that sex was fun, and necessary, and important, the feminists and the moralists among his contemporaries were horrified. The only thing they grudgingly admired was his style, and even here they complained bitterly about his coarseness and his use of 'ugly' words.

This style is individual and surprising, even today. In this translation I have tried to follow it as closely as technical difficulties would allow. In *Getting Married* three of the most striking stylistic features are the crisp, matter-of-fact way in which the characters are introduced—e.g. "They had been married for ten years. Happily? As happily as circumstances allowed"—the sudden changes of tense, and the frequent use of emphatic indirect speech instead of dialogue, for instance:

> He was jealous, wasn't he?
>
> Yes, why not? He was afraid of something coming between them.
>
> For shame! He was jealous, what an insult! How infamous of him, how distrustful! What did he take her for?

This last feature contributes to the light-heartedness of Part I and is rarely used in Part II.

Another trick of style, most noticeable in **"Love and the Price of Grain,"** is the constant use of 'and,' intended to produce a breathless, fairy-story effect, as though challenging the reader to guess what would come next.

Strindberg's prose is also rich in simile and metaphor, and in the scope of his vocabulary. He had a great fondness for words that were modern in his day. Who else would have thought of comparing an amorous adolescent to an electrophore, or of talking about 'the sharp stones of life's macadam way'?

In a host of ways Strindberg imbued the Swedish language with new life, and for this if for nothing else the Swedes have reason to be grateful. Why is it that so many of them still dislike him so much? One answer is that when a thing takes firm root it is very difficult to eradicate. In the 1880s the idea that Strindberg was a moral danger, that he was coarse and licentious, was so deeply implanted in the Swedish mind that the roots are still there. The people responsible for this unfortunate state of affairs are vividly described by the Swedish author and critic Oscar Levertin when writing in July 1887 to the Danish author and critic Edvard Brandes. In this letter he says: "In this country practically every literary work reveals a fear of being boycotted by our anabaptist moralists. It is almost impossible to give you any idea of the lengths to which they go in their righteousness. A black death of castrating morality is sweeping over this country." . . . (pp. 25-6)

Perhaps the real reason for Strindberg's 'unparalleled unpopularity' was that he alone among contemporary Swedish writers refused to be castrated or muzzled. (p. 26)

> *Mary Sandbach, in an introduction to* Getting Married: Parts I and II *by August Strindberg, edited and translated by Mary Sandbach, Victor Gollancz Ltd, 1972, pp. 11-26.*

V. S. PRITCHETT (essay date 1973)

[*Pritchett is a highly esteemed English novelist, short story writer, and critic. Considered one of the modern masters of the short story, he is also one of the world's most respected and well-read literary critics. Pritchett writes in the conversational tone of the familiar essay, a method by which he approaches literature from the viewpoint of a lettered but not overly scholarly reader. A twentieth-century successor to such early nineteenth-century essayist-critics as William Hazlitt and Charles Lamb, Pritchett employs much the same critical method: his own experience, judgment, and sense of literary art are emphasized, rather than a codified critical doctrine derived from a school of psychological or philosophical speculation. His criticism is often described as fair, reliable, and insightful. In the following excerpt from a review originally published in the* New York Review of Books *in March, 1973, Pritchett praises the vitality of Strindberg's fiction.*]

Among the Ancient Mariners who arrive to stop guests from getting into the wedding feasts of the European middle classes in [the last half of the nineteenth century], Strindberg has the most frenzied and unrelenting grip. The calms that lie between the bouts of paranoia are themselves dangerous. We can easily "place" the sexual guilt in, say, *The Kreutzer Sonata*, for Tolstoy has immensely wider interests. But except, apparently, in his historical novels (which few people outside Sweden have read), Strindberg's personal obsession rarely ceases. He is the perpetual autobiographer who has at least three albatrosses—his three wives—hanging from his neck, and it is not long before he is telling us that the birds shot *him*. One of the surprising consolations of his life was that he liked going out into the country for a day's shooting, and it is a striking aspect of his lifelong paranoia in human relationships that he loved what he killed.

Strindberg's strange upbringing as the unwanted son of a successful businessman and a domestic servant, and as the victim of a stepmother; his poverty as a student; his quarrel with the Anabaptists and Pietists of a respectable society, who had him prosecuted for blasphemy because they hadn't the courage to bring him to court for his public campaign for sexual freedom; his flight from literature into experiments with sulphur that drifted into a half-insane obsession with something like alchemy; above all, his instability as a husband or lover—all these torments kept him at white heat. What astonishes is the lasting fertility—in his work—of these ingeniously exploited obsessions. I can think of no other writer with the possible exception of D. H. Lawrence who retold himself in so many impassioned ways.

One thought one had seen his case analyzed and dramatized for good in *The Father*—where he is the sea captain, in fact the Ancient Mariner in person, who was driven mad by the cunning calculations of a respectable bourgeois wife—or in *Miss Julie*. Yet, in 1903, much later, the whole personal story is retold as a legend, folk tale or saga for children, in the droll story called **"Jubal the Selfless."** This tale appears to be serene, but its playfulness and resignation are deceptive. The title itself is misleading. Jubal's selflessness is not that of the saints. It is the selflessness of an opera singer who, in old age, realizes that his ego or will has been systematically destroyed by a conspiracy between his father, his mother, and his wife (an actress who uses him in order to supersede him in his career). When he looks into his mirror—this is typical of Strindberg's brilliant theatrical imagination—he sees he is a body without a face. It is only when he finds his lost mother and puts his head in her lap that he recovers his ego—and, needless to say, dies!

The fable is a characteristic experiment with Strindberg's own history and it contains a truth about him as an artist and a person: the history and character are *disponible*. He is a model for the early nineteenth-century concept of Genius: the genius is free and without character but compelled to seek martyrdom. This is a matter for Strindberg's biographers. The work is far more important. Reading any story, particularly in the first section of *Getting Married*, one sees the link between the short story writer and the dramatist. He is a master in the use of overstatement; and one knows at once he is attacking a sententious and cliché-ridden society by the abrupt use of the offhand, natural voice:

> They had been married for ten years. Happily?
> As happily as circumstances allowed.
>
> (pp. 89-91)

This devilish, grinning abruptness gives his stories a swinging elation. In play writing and story, the cutting from outside to inside the people has to be drastic and fast. There is no doubt of Strindberg's enormous talent; so that, in these stories, when he moves from one marriage to the next, one finds that as a realist with a message Strindberg is at ease in his mixture of the pugnacious, the pitying and the revealing.

Mary Sandbach [see excerpt dated 1972] says that Strindberg's misogyny has been overstressed; that he is as much concerned with the false values of a powerful upper merchant class which produces the unbending man and the cunning, idle female. His attack on "Amazonian" women who wish to have careers or non-domestic interests is rooted in deep private jealousy of them—as in his first marriage—but he is talking of women who are "idle" only because they have a huge supply of working-class girls as servants.

The message in the first series of the stories is that men *and* women must be liberated. In the second series, the excellent little scenes of life in town and country, the delight in the sea journeys and outings which bring out his high quality as an imaginative writer give way to arid, harsher analysis and polemic. But in the first part of one tale, **"The Payment,"** one gets that compelling and shrewd power of social analysis which D. H. Lawrence was to take further. The story is a full statement of Strindberg's case: the stifling of the sexual instincts leads women to use sex as a weapon, so that the men become the slaves while the women grasp occupational power outside the home. It must be read in the context of nineteenth-century life, but it approaches the Lawrence of *St. Mawr*.

Helène, the young woman in the story, is the daughter of a general. In her home she sees the exaggerated artifices of respect paid to women and grows up to regard all males as inferiors.... One day she is out riding in the country alone—she in fact hates nature; it makes her "feel small"—and when she gets off her mare the animal bolts off to mate with a stallion before her eyes. She is shocked and disgusted. In the next phase she takes to the out-of-date library in her father's house and becomes infatuated with Mme de Staël's *Corinne*, and this leads her

> ... to live in an aristrocratic dream world in which souls live without bodies.... This brain-fever, which is called romanticism, is the gospel of the rich.

After the horse-riding episode, the analysis of the mind of a frigid, proud and ambitious girl as it grows degenerates into an essay, but it is nevertheless very thorough and alive.... In the end Helène marries in order to trade on her scholarly husband's political reputation and get herself into public life: she is a recognizable high-bourgeois female type. (pp. 91-3)

Strindberg's story fails not because it is false—emancipated groups, classes or individuals are often likely to be tyrannical and reactionary when they get power, as every revolution has shown—but simply because in the later part of this story the artist has been swallowed up by the crude polemical journalist. He has turned from life to the case book. Trust the tale, not the case history.

The original artist in Strindberg survives in his imaginative autobiographies, in the powerful and superbly objective and moving account of his breakdown in *Inferno;* in certain plays, and in the best of these stories. In many of these, a curious festive junketing, a love of good food and drink, a feeling for the small joys of Swedish life, and the spirit of northern carnival, break through. In **"Needs Must,"** the story of a bachelor schoolmaster who runs into a midsummer outing in the country and is eventually converted to a marriage which is very happy—"no part of this story," says Strindberg drily—Strindberg suddenly flings himself into the jollities of the trippers. The schoolmaster listens to the accordion and "it was as if his soul were seated in a swing that had been set in motion by his eyes and ears." It is a story that contains one of his happiest "Bangs":

> Then they began to play Forfeits, and they redeemed all their forfeits with kisses, real kisses bang on the mouth, so that he could hear the smack of them. And when the jolly bookkeeper had to "stand in the well" and was made to

kiss the big oak tree, he did so with comical
lunacy, putting his arm round the thick trunk
and patting it as one does a girl when no one
is looking, that they all laughed uncontrollably,
for they all knew what you do, though no one
would have wanted to be caught doing it.

If there is elation in the black Strindberg it springs like music
out of his sunny spells. One is always compelled by something
vibrant and vital in him. He is a bolting horse whatever direction he takes; and, as Mary Sandbach says, he brought new
life to Swedish prose by his natural voice and his lively images.
He was, as some have said, a cantankerous Pietist or Anabaptist
turned inside out. His lasting contribution was his liberation
of the language. The reader feels zest of that at once.

> *V. S. Pritchett, "August Strindberg: A Bolting Horse,"
> in his* The Myth Makers: Literary Essays, *Random
> House, 1979, pp. 89-94.*

ARTHUR MILLER   (essay date 1985)

*[Miller, an American playwright and critic, is the author of sev-
eral of this century's best-known dramas, including the classic*
Death of a Salesman *(1949). His works reflect his perception of
the tragedy in modern life, often using the plight of ordinary
individuals to explore themes of guilt, responsibility, and expia-
tion. Acutely aware of social, political, and moral issues, Miller
uses his plays to make philosophical statements and to denounce
evil and injustice, as in* The Crucible *(1953), which most critics
agree is a thinly veiled indictment of the McCarthy era. As a
result of Miller's conviction that art should reflect realistic concerns, his work has occasionally been criticized as overly didactic,
but he is most commonly ranked among the greatest playwrights
of the twentieth century. In the following excerpt, Miller comments
on the biographical elements of Strindberg's work and discusses
his influence on modern drama.]*

The impact of [Strindberg's] dramatic method, reflected in his
many plays, most notably [*The Father, Miss Julie,* and *The
Dance of Death*] . . . is probably greater and less acknowledged
than that of any other modern writer. If his plays are much
less frequently produced than Ibsen's, his playwriting personality, his way of approaching reality, is evidenced far more
deeply and more frequently in our contemporary theater.
Strindberg struck strongly into O'Neill, is quite directly mirrored in Beckett and Pinter, in Tennessee Williams and Edward
Albee. Writing before Freud was published, he wanted to offer,
in [biographer Olof] Lagercrantz's words, "the pure naked
truth." And this meant his entering into the world of the subconscious, where the sexual encounter especially was a fight
to the death, a world where the mother did not nurture but
suffocated and destroyed her offspring, a world where domination (usually female) was the key to life. And, of course, it
is this digging the unconscious for its terrors, its lawless desires
and its ultimately creative thrusts that has provided the fodder
of literature in this century. If Ibsen was the revolutionary,
seeking new, refurbished social institutions to order mankind,
Strindberg was the rebel for whom no order would ever be true
enough. (p. 1)

He was a triumphantly unhappy man, often unsure when he
was living in life or in one of his plays, and part of his modernism springs quite probably from his awareness that he was
dipping his pen directly into his unconscious where truth is of
a kind that is unarguable. His emotional nakedness is modern,
his blatantly confessional and autobiographical style, his having obviously witnessed what he was trying to express. Part

of the persuasiveness of his plays is that their truths seemed
to be driving him crazy.

Thus his dramatic method is obsessive, an endlessly repeated
drumming on a kind of monomanic and fearsome vision. If
O'Neill did not consciously imitate this feature he paralleled
it, but at far vaster length, Strindberg's major plays being quite
short and for many mercifully so. For even in his own time,
when the perverse news he brought was fresh and new, audiences often laughed in the wrong places because he was
carrying things much too far. Nor, with the possible exception
of *Miss Julie,* was he able to leaven the spectral unreality of
his dialogue with a depth of characterization. In any meaningful
sense there are no characters in his plays; there are lethal relationships, concatenations that illuminate the whole inside of
Strindberg's head, if nothing else, a head that was filled with
the fear and hatred of womankind.

In any other man without the physique of a horse and nerves
of piano wires, it would have been a fear that might have
perhaps left us with a play or two or a brilliant essay followed
by the mourning silence of a brain sick to death. But, as Mr.
Lagercrantz repeatedly demonstrates, the fecund Strindberg not
only suffered what by most definitions would be madness, but
managed it like a conductor managing an orchestra. It makes
his suffering no less real and painful to say that it was always
being turned over and over by the bloody fingers of his mind
unceasingly searching out the artistic possibilities inside his
explosions.

Inevitably, his social context having vastly changed with time,
he has come to seem a merely visceral playwright and a self-
confronter, but he thought of himself as a social prophet and
a healer, a brother to the Paris Commune of 1871. George
Bernard Shaw perceived him that way too, and until 1886
Strindberg thought of himself as a socialist. His later development, not unlike O'Neill's, was toward the occult, the Swedenborgian mysticism that would support work like *The Ghost
Sonata* and the other so-called Chamber Plays written for small
audiences of adventurers into the unknown. One wonders, indeed, whether Strindberg was not right in claiming himself as
the first of the modern writers if only because he came to
destroy the linear-thinking drama of cause and effect, the story
moving from point to provable point. His drama is the conflict
of essences not characters, and it lives where the sun hardly
rises and a perpetual twilight reigns. Indeed, his longing for
an ultimate, superhuman world of causation lends his work a
tragic grandeur at times, quite as though it were an effort to
scale human limits. . . .

[Strindberg's art] has endured, quite probably, because the
hallucinatory world Strindberg saw seems much closer now to
being real. We really walk the moon, and with the press of a
button can really crack the planet, and if we have mastered the
physics of this magical power, the morals of it all are, if
anything, farther from us than from Strindberg who, mad as
he was, believed that his labors were essentially moral and in
God's service. Or at least should be. He could be vile, hypocritical, opportunistic, violent, but one cannot avoid the hope-
fulness in him, of which his boundless creativity was the manifestation. . . . [Strindberg was] a maddeningly foolish, wrong
and presciently wise writer who was one of the prime inventors
of our theater and our time. (p. 30)

> *Arthur Miller, "The Mad Inventor of Modern Drama,"
> in* The New York Times Book Review, *January 6,
> 1985, pp. 1, 30.**

VERNON YOUNG   (essay date 1985)

[*Young is an English critic. In the following excerpt, he notes some characteristics of what he considers to be Strindberg's best works.*]

Strindberg, despite the reactionary nature of his manic irresolutions, was a modern man, much to his own astonishment. His best plays are distinguished by their internal consistency and their psychological persuasiveness. They are critical, and criticism—let us not avoid the charge—drives out tragedy. Their integrity is mirthless, yet for all that they are not inflexible. They are *playable:* the balance of their allegiances has been subtly weighed. The extent to which you sympathize with one or another antagonist depends very much on the acuity with which the director of the production you see has grasped the leeway that has been allowed him.

Even so, most of Strindberg's plays are hard to take. As Auden said, our grief is not Greek. It is not Swedish either! The morbid intensity of Strindberg's pious outlook is thoroughly Swedish and the social situation from which it was educed, resembling those of the Victorian period elsewhere, has nonetheless a cast of mind you can only appreciate by trying to live in Sweden today. If the order of relationships has been altered by time and social democracy, the *climate* of relationships has changed very little. You have not experienced Strindberg until, in Stockholm, you have emerged from a performance of, let us say, *The Father* or *The Ghost Sonata* or one of those never-ending pilgrimage pieces (e.g., *The Great Highway*) on a cold, dark winter's night when the streets are as devoid of promise as the play was devoid of charm: no café open, no one to talk to if there were, and the prospect of a midnight ride home to your deathly silent sleeping-suburb on the immaculate subway.

There is never a last word on any artist. There is always what seems to be the last word if we agree with whoever pronounced it. . . . Like D. H. Lawrence, who crucially resembled him— the splitting of the self, the identification with Christ, the unfailing spite and the breathtaking defamations—Strindberg commands attention. He resists affection. Among those writers who severally shaped what we call modernism for the first decade of our century (Freud, Hardy, James, Conrad, Ibsen, Chekhov), Strindberg surely was the most inflamed, the most intolerant and intolerable, the least ingratiating, the one among them whom we would have wanted least to know. (pp. 78-9)

> Vernon Young, "Strindberg's Ghosts," *in* The New Criterion, *Vol. III, No. 7, March, 1985, pp. 71-9.*

ADDITIONAL BIBLIOGRAPHY

Bradbrook, Muriel. "In Dreams Begin Responsibilities." In her *Women and Literature, 1779-1982: The Collected Papers of Muriel Bradbrook, Volume 2*, pp. 69-109. Totowa, N.J.: Barnes and Noble, 1982.*
  Discussion of Strindberg's dramatic treatment of women and marriage.

Brandell, Gunnar. *Strindberg in Inferno.* Translated by Barry Jacobs. Cambridge: Harvard University Press, 1974, 336 p.

Analysis of the Inferno Crisis. Brandell discusses the causes of Strindberg's breakdown, the crisis itself, and the literary style that emerged as a result.

Bulman, Joan. *Strindberg and Shakespeare: Shakespeare's Influence on Strindberg's Historical Drama.* New York: Haskell House, 1971, 219 p.*
  Examination of Shakespeare's influence on the conception, structure, and characters of Strindberg's historical dramas.

Carlson, Harry G. *Strindberg and the Poetry of Myth.* Berkeley: University of California Press, 1982, 240 p.
  Finds elements of traditional mythologies in Strindberg's major works.

Dahlström, Carl Enoch William Leonard. *Strindberg's Dramatic Expressionism.* New York: Benjamin Blom, 1930, 242 p.
  Discussion of non-naturalistic elements in Strindberg's plays.

Huneker, James. "August Strindberg." *The Lamp* XXIX, No. 6 (January 1905): 573-82.
  Biographical and critical comments.

Jarvi, Raymond. "Strindberg's *The Ghost Sonata* and Sonata Form." *Mosaic* V, No. 4 (Summer 1972): 69-84.
  Analysis of formal structural elements of *The Ghost Sonata.*

Johannesson, Eric O. "Strindberg's *Taklagsöl:* An Early Experiment in the Psychological Novel." *Scandinavian Studies* 35, No. 3 (August 1963): 223-38.
  Discussion of *Taklagsöl* as Strindberg's "most experimental, most modern work of fiction."

Lagercrantz, Olof. *August Strindberg.* London: Faber and Faber, 1984, 399 p.
  Comprehensive biography which dismisses earlier biographical assumptions drawn from Strindberg's fiction.

Lamm, Martin. *August Strindberg.* Edited and translated by Henry G. Carlson. New York: Benjamin Blom, 1971, 561 p.
  Biographical and critical study which treats the entire range of Strindberg's work from a biographical perspective.

Mays, Milton A. "Strindberg's *Ghost Sonata:* Parodied Fairy Tale on Original Sin." *Modern Drama* 10, No. 2 (September 1967): 189-94.
  Interpretation of *The Ghost Sonata* as a morality play in the structural form of the fairy tale.

McGill, V. J. *August Strindberg: The Bedeviled Viking.* 1930. Reprint. New York: Russell & Russell, 1965, 459 p.
  Biography focusing on the first half of Strindberg's life which quotes extensively from his autobiographical novels.

Meyer, Michael. *Strindberg.* London: Secker & Warburg, 1985, 651 p.
  Most comprehensive biography to date.

Nathan, George Jean. "Going Into Theatrical Details." *The Smart Set* XXXVII, No. 2 (June 1912): 149-50.*
  Negative review of *The Father.*

Robertson, J. G. "Strindberg's Position in European Literature." In his *Essays and Addresses on Literature*, pp. 255-71. Freeport, N.Y.: Books for Libraries Press, 1935.
  Discussion of Strindberg's life and his contribution to literature.

Smedmark, Carl Reinhold, ed. *Essays on Strindberg.* Stockholm: Beckman's, 1966, 175 p.
  Collection of essays on Strindberg's dramas and international reputation.

Spivack, C. K. "The Many Hells of August Strindberg." *Twentieth Century Literature* 9 (April 1963 - January 1964): 10-16.

Considers the evolution of Strindberg's concept of suffering and punishment.

Sprigge, Elizabeth. *The Strange Life of August Strindberg*. New York: MacMillan, 1949, 246 p.
Biography which relies heavily on information derived from the novels.

Valency, Maurice. "Strindberg." In his *The Flower and the Castle*, pp. 238-361. New York: Macmillan Co. 1963.
Thorough discussion of Strindberg's work and his influence on modern drama.

Williams, Raymond. "Torches for Superman." *London Review of Books* 7, No. 20 (21 November 1985): 17-18.
Reviews a new translation of *By the Open Sea* and the Meyer and Lagercrantz biographies.

Owen Wister

1860-1938

American novelist, short story writer, biographer, essayist, and dramatist.

Wister is credited with creating the archetypical American western novel and establishing the romantic folkmyth of the cowboy as a chivalrous hero. His novel *The Virginian* originated many of the patterns of western fiction, most notably that of the cowboy as a brave and honorable natural gentleman who upheld democratic values. Before Wister wrote *The Virginian*, novels about the West were generally sensationalistic fictions glorifying the violent world of western outlaws, and although a few authors, notably Bret Harte and Stephen Crane, attempted more authentic portraits of western life, their works had little impact on the popular imagination. A frequent visitor to the West who loved the culture of the region, Wister sought to portray a life that was quickly vanishing before the encroaching values of eastern American civilization. In *The Virginian*, Wister extolled western freedom and honesty and their adaptation to eastern law and education even as he attacked western lawlessness and eastern materialism and pretensions. Stylistically, the novel's synthesis of the literary conventions of the frontier novel and the novel of manners created thematic complexities unprecedented in the genre. The moral dilemmas and character types created by Wister were adopted by novelists and screenwriters and, through the dissemination of novels, movies, and television, had a profound effect on American popular culture.

Wister was born in Philadelphia where his father, a member of one of the city's oldest families, was a prominent physician. Wister's mother, the daughter of a famous English actress, played piano and contributed articles to the *Atlantic Monthly*. Beginning when Wister was ten years old, he was enrolled in boarding schools in Switzerland and England while his parents and grandmother travelled in Europe. There the family became friends with Henry James, who would later offer Wister literary advice. In 1873 Wister returned to the United States and attended St. Paul's preparatory school in Concord, New Hampshire, where he contributed to and edited the school literary magazine. Upon graduation he matriculated at Harvard University as a music major and subsequently composed music and lyrics for several school performances. The Harvard *Lampoon* printed his seven-part parody "The New Swiss Family Robinson" in his senior year, and the work was published in 1882. At Harvard Wister counted among his friends and acquaintances Henry Cabot Lodge, William Dean Howells, and Theodore Roosevelt; Howells and Roosevelt would later exert an influence upon Wister's career as mentors and critics.

In 1882 Wister graduated summa cum laude and left for Europe with letters of introduction from his grandmother to the pianist and composer Franz Liszt. Liszt was impressed with one of Wister's compositions, writing to Wister's grandmother that he had "un talent prononćé." Wister studied for a year at the Conservatoire in Paris until his father insisted that he return home to accept a job. Within a year of accepting a position compiling interest for a banking firm, Wister resigned and collaborated with a cousin on a novel, sending the manuscript to Howells, who advised against publication because he considered the work offensive to the tastes of genteel American

readers. Depressed over frustrated creative desires and mounting parental pressure to choose a career, Wister suffered an emotional collapse in 1885 and, upon the recommendation of a physician, went to Wyoming to recuperate. Such trips to the frontier West were not uncommon for young men during this era: similar ventures were undertaken by Roosevelt and the artist Frederic Remington, who illustrated Wister's early short story collections. During his trip Wister began a journal in which he recorded descriptions of the mountains and plains, reactions to the inhabitants of squalid towns, details of life among wealthy ranchers and their cow-hands, and the revitalizing effect of the environment upon his mental and physical well being. He travelled to the West each summer until 1900, but after his initial visit enrolled at Harvard Law School, from which he graduated in 1888. He then began a promising legal practice; however, he experienced a growing concern about the cowboy's need for a troubadour to preserve his era in literature before it vanished, and in 1891 began the short story "Hank's Woman." The following year this story and "How Lin McLean Went East" were published in *Harper's Weekly*, and in 1894 the magazine sent him on a research trip to the western states, ensuring a regular outlet for his work.

Wister's first short story collection, *Red Men and White*, appeared in 1896, followed over the next five years by *Lin McLean* and *The Jimmyjohn Boss*. However, Wister did not gain wide critical and popular success until the publication of *The Virginian* in 1902. Dedicated to Roosevelt, *The Virginian* remained an American best-seller for a year and a half, and by the time of Wister's death in 1938 had sold one and a half million hardcover copies, a level of popularity Wister's subsequent works never attained. Notable among these, however, are *Lady Baltimore,* a novel about a well-bred northerner awakened to the true meaning of aristocracy in the traditional South; *Roosevelt: The Story of a Friendship;* and a trilogy of book-length political essays published between 1915 and 1921: *The Pentecost of Calamity,* which urges U.S. participation in the first World War; *A Straight Deal or an Ancient Grudge,* which advocates postwar cooperation between America and England; and *Neighbors Henceforth,* which presents a sympathetic portrait of post-war France. A widower after 1913, Wister raised his six children and in later life dabbled in local politics and travelled in Europe and the eastern states. In 1938 he died of a cerebral hemorrhage.

Many modern critics consider Wister's early western stories apprentice works in which he developed his technical skills. *Red Men and White, Lin McLean,* and *The Jimmyjohn Boss* contain local color stories which are often narrated by a "tenderfoot" from the North or East whose naivete provides a device for familiarizing the reader with the landscape, customs, mores, laws, and stereotypical characters specific to the western plains states. These early works are concerned with the experiences of a variety of characters, although two, Specimen Jones, whom G. Edward White has called a "whimsical salute to the frivolity of the nomad," and Dean Drake, a more mature cowboy character, appear in several stories. However, in *Lin McLean,* which has been called both a collection of interrelated short stories and an episodic novel, the life of the title character is traced from his wild youth to his later years as a married man of property. McLean's honesty and independence typify Wister's conception of the vernacular western hero. For example, in "How Lin McLean Went East," McLean's naturalness is contrasted with the snobbery of his Bostonian brother, demonstrating McLean's symbolic function as a favorable antithesis to unnatural eastern pretensions. However, in later stories, as Wister acquired a more conciliatory attitude toward the value of eastern influences in the West, the character McLean, who he had once considered "the man whom among all cowpunchers I love most," degenerated into a comic foil of social ineptitude and perpetual adolescence. In the protagonist of *The Virginian,* Wister developed an alternative hero who adhered to what came to be known as the "Code of the West" and exhibited the natural gentleman's desire and ability to prosper in a developing community.

The Virginian was conceived as a historical romance concerned with the passing of a heroic American era. The novel's protagonist represents, according to Wister, America's "last heroic figure." Known only as the Virginian, he is endowed with the honesty, virility, bravery, and sense of humor that had characterized Lin McLean and others; however, from the Virginian's first appearance in the novel, he is portrayed as a man of native intelligence and decorum—traits recognized by the eastern tenderfoot narrator as signifiers of the born aristocrat. The antecedents of these noble traits are outlined in the essay "The Evolution of the Cow Puncher," in which Wister asserted that the cowboy is the "direct lineal offspring" of the medieval Anglo-Saxon knight, and that "the knight and the cowboy are nothing but the same Saxon of different environments." Noting among other similarities their mutual mastery of horses and weapons, he also contended that both adhered to codes of morality based on the chivalric defense of women and the protection of personal honor.

This implied "Code of the West" and the resulting vigilante justice depicted in *The Virginian* have received much attention, and critics are divided on the validity of the Virginian's arguments for violence in the protection of personal property and in defense of insulted honor. For example, when legal alternatives to a gunfight are accessible on the eve of his wedding, the Virginian chooses to face the villain Trampas in a shootout at the risk of losing his betrothed, insisting that "it is only the great mediocrity that goes to law in these matters." Yet, he will later tell his bride's grandmother that although he has killed, it has been neither for pleasure nor profit, "always preferring peace." Leslie A. Fiedler has argued that "behind the talk of honesty and chivalry, it is personal violence for which *The Virginian . . .* apologizes." Frederic Taber Cooper, however, contends that rather than "proclaiming the frontier code of Wyoming . . . superior to English common law," the novel is "simply insisting that if you or I are going to live in a community, we must accept the ethics cf that community if we wish to be respected." The use of the lynch mob and the duel are initially opposed by the Bishop of Wyoming and the New England school teacher Molly Wood, both of whom serve as harbingers of the arrival of eastern civilization in the West. However, the insufficient motivation provided for the easy conversion of Wood and the Bishop to the Virginian's point of view is regarded by Bernard DeVoto as the novel's major artistic flaw, for it simplistically dismisses a crucial moral question and thus prevents *The Virginian* from achieving its full potential as a work of literature.

Nevertheless, many critics consider *The Virginian* a serious literary work which gains thematic and moral complexity through its juxtaposition of western independence and coarseness with eastern tradition and gentility. John D. Nesbitt regards the novel as a synthesis of the "tradition of the frontier adventure with a more sophisticated and genteel Anglo-American literary tradition." Other critics have noted the influence of the novel of manners in the sections treating Molly Wood and her New England family, and in the pastoral love scenes between the hero and heroine. While some critics argue that this synthesis is proof of Wister's insight into the civilizing of the West and the importance of that process to the country at large, others regard the cowboy conflicts and the love interest as separate stories which are unsatisfactorily reconciled. James, for example, argued that the work would have maintained artistic integrity if it had remained the Virginian's story: "I thirst for his blood. . . . I should have made him perish in his flower & in some splendid and sombre way." However, Richard W. Etulain contends that the relationship between the Virginian and the teacher is important as an illustration of Wister's thesis that the cowboy lives "in a world that threatens to brush him aside unless he adapts to a rapidly changing society"; thus, the marriage of the Virginian and the school teacher is important as a symbol of the union of the best of eastern and western cultures.

While some critics consider this vision romantic wish-fulfillment, it nevertheless established the pattern for a large number of the western novels and screenplays that would follow, and Wister's Virginian and the novel's villain Trampas became the prototypes of western characters for the next half-century. It is estimated that over two million hardcover and innumerable paperback copies of *The Virginian* have been sold; this, along with Wister's influence upon other writers, is evidence of the profound effect his novel had upon American popular mythology. Although it is not considered a work in the first rank of American literature, like another such novel, *Gone With the Wind, The Virginian* has in many ways affected the vision Americans have of their nation's past and its popular legends.

(See also *Contemporary Authors*, Vol. 108, and *Dictionary of Literary Biography*, Vol. 9: *American Novelists, 1910-1945*.)

PRINCIPAL WORKS

The New Swiss Family Robinson: A Tale for Children of All Ages (short story) 1882
The Dragon of Wantley: His Rise, His Voracity, and His Downfall (novel) 1892
Red Men and White (short stories) 1896
Lin McLean (novel) 1898
The Jimmyjohn Boss, and Other Stories (short stories) 1900
Ulysses S. Grant (biography) 1900
The Virginian: A Horseman of the Plains (novel) 1902
Philosophy Four (novella) 1903
Lady Baltimore (novel) 1906
The Seven Ages of Washington (biography) 1907
Members of the Family (short stories) 1911
The Pentecost of Calamity (essay) 1915
A Straight Deal; or, The Ancient Grudge (essay) 1920
Neighbors Henceforth (essay) 1922
Watch Your Thirst (drama) 1923
When West Was West (short stories) 1928
The Writings of Owen Wister. 11 vols. (short stories, novels, essays, and biographies) 1928
Roosevelt: The Story of a Friendship (biography) 1930
Owen Wister Out West: His Journals and Letters (journals and letters) 1958

WILLIAM DEAN HOWELLS (essay date 1895)

[*Howells was the chief progenitor of American realism and the most influential American literary critic during the late nineteenth century. He was the author of nearly three dozen novels which, though neglected for decades, are today the subject of growing interest. He is recognized as one of the major literary figures of the nineteenth century: he successfully weaned American literature away from the sentimental romanticism of its infancy, earning the popular sobriquet "the Dean of American Letters." Through realism, a theory central to his fiction and criticism, Howells sought to disperse "the conventional acceptations by which men live on easy terms with themselves" that they might "examine the grounds of their social and moral opinions." To accomplish this, according to Howells, the writer must strive to record detailed impressions of everyday life, endowing characters with true-to-life motives and avoiding authorial comment in the narrative. Howells and Wister were college friends at Harvard University, and Howells later gave Wister literary advice, particularly about the degree of realism acceptable in a work of American fiction. In the following excerpt, Howells examines the strengths and weaknesses of the collection* Red Men and White.]

I begrudge the room given to the love-business of **"La Tinaja Bonita"** (though it is rather fresh and novel as love-businesses go) amidst the broad-shouldered, six-foot verities of Mr. Owen Wister's wild Western world [in *Red Men and White*]. Possibly it is all true enough, but it is comparatively unimportant, and

it does not impress itself as life, and the other things do. While I am about the disagreeable part of my affair, I will say also that I wish some one might get away from this most promising writer the blue-fire which he is fond of burning in some of his scenes. That belongs with the muted music and other devices of the theatre; and is not of the robust honesty of the rest of his art. Such a thing as the true homicide's killing himself, for instance, in **"Salvation Gap,"** to make it right with the wrong man whom they have hanged for his crime, does not commend itself as a thing that happened, and most things in Mr. Wister's stories bring the conviction that they happened. In fact the frontier, if we still can be said to have a frontier, lives in his pages, and is almost as sensible to the vision as Mr. Remington's most manful illustrations. The book is a man's book throughout, in text and picture, and perhaps it was well enough to subdue its intense masculinity with some guitar-tinkling, as in **"La Tinaja Bonita."** It is at any rate difficult to fancy a woman taking pleasure in such a potent bit of drama as **"The Second Missouri Compromise,"** though it is infinitely precious of its kind, and is the best thing in the book. Desperadoes, good and bad, have been done before; red savages and white semi-savages, gamblers, traders, miners, ranchmen, and the whole wicked world of the border have been done before, though never, I think, so well as Mr. Wister has done them. But the politicians of the far West, with their various origins North and South, remained for him, and he has made them immortal; or if not quite that, then he has made them what they really are, and that is perhaps more difficult. The whole situation in the sketch I mean, is deliciously humorous, while it is thrilling with repressed tragedy. It is masterly.

I do not know the military type so well, but Mr. Wister's soldiers, officers and men both, strike me as the real thing. He makes me see them as distinctly as Mr. Remington does, and with a satisfying suggestion which only the literary art can give. Their uniforms brighten immensely the picturesqueness of his scenes; and his Indians lend their savage splendor, their savage squalor to it with almost equal effect. They convince of their truth; you feel that it is quite so they would think, and that their motives for good and ill would be almost for the first time in literature those attributed to them.

I think Mr. Wister's humorous sense is keener than some other perceptions of his. It is at least native and unspoiled, and if I were very hypercritical I might accuse him of forcing the poetry of his material a bit, of coaxing its dramatic implications, of even over-painting his picturesqueness. In a word, I might grieve for some lingering traits of romanticism in his work. . . .

> William Dean Howells, in a review of "Red Men and White," in Harper's Weekly, *Vol. XXXIX, No. 2032, November 30, 1895, p. 1133.*

THEODORE ROOSEVELT (essay date 1895)

[*Roosevelt was the twenty-sixth president of the United States. Wister and Roosevelt became acquainted as students at Harvard University and maintained a close friendship until Roosevelt's death. As an easterner whose visits to the West had impressed him greatly, Roosevelt discussed with Wister the need for preserving the era of the cowboy in literature, and many critics contend that Roosevelt was the greatest influence upon Wister's decision to write western stories. In the following excerpt, Roosevelt praises the masculine style of* Red Men and White.]

Mr. Owen Wister's stories, some of which have now been gathered under the title of *Red Men and White,* turned a new page in our literature, and, indeed, may almost be said to have turned a new page in that form of contemporary historical writing which consists in the vivid portrayal, once for all, of types that should be commemorated. Many men before him have seen and felt the wonder of that phase of Western life which is now closing, but Mr. Wister makes us see what he has seen and interprets for us what he has heard. His short sketches are so many cantos in the great epic of life on the border of the vanishing wilderness. He shows us heroic figures and a heroic life; not heroes and the heroic life as they are conceived by the cloistered intellect, but rough and strong and native, the good and evil alike challenging the eye. To read his writings is like walking on the windy upland in fall, when the hard weather braces body and mind. There is a certain school of American writers that loves to deal, not with the great problems of American existence and with the infinite picturesqueness of our life as it has been and is being led here on our own continent, where we stumble and blunder, and still, on the whole, go forward, but with the life of those Americans who cannot swim in troubled waters, and go to live as idlers in Europe. What pale, anæmic figures they are, these creations of the émigré novelists, when put side by side with the men, the grim stalwart men, who stride through Mr. Wister's pages!

It is this note of manliness which is dominant through the writings of Mr. Wister. Beauty, refinement, grace, are excellent qualities in a man, as in a nation, but they come second, and very far second, to the great virile virtures, the virtues of courage, energy, and daring; the virtues which beseem a masterful race—a race fit to fell forests, to build roads, to found commonwealths, to conquer continents, to overthrow armed enemies! It is about the men who can do such deeds that Mr. Wister writes. So many of our writers are content to write merely with polish and daintiness, or are only capable of so writing; so many of them can give us nothing better than pretty poems or graceful little stories; that we welcome eagerly a man who deals with the elemental and basic qualities, a man who is free from any touch of valetudinarianism, and who has nothing morbid in his make-up. He tells of the strife of strong men, of their successes, of their failures, their high deeds, and their manifold shortcomings. He does not shrink from the blood and sweat of the conflict, nor yet does he grow unhealthy and think that in the conflict there is nothing else. At times he tells of lives that are dark and evil, and of the terrible deeds which such lives bring forth; but it would not be possible to imagine a book more opposed in every way to that criminal and monstrous literature which dwells only on the unclean and the abhorrent, and which portrays life as if it were one vast section of a sewer. . . .

No better work of the kind has ever been done than that which Mr. Wister is now doing. His style is excellent, his powers of observation remarkable; and he has that gift of gifts, the power to arouse and sustain interest, the power of the born storyteller. His tales are clean and fresh and strong, and healthy with an out-of-doors healthiness; they quicken our pulses, and our hearts beat quicker for having read them.

> Theodore Roosevelt, *"A Teller of Tales of Strong Men,"* in Harper's Weekly, *Vol. XXXIX, No. 2035, December 21, 1895, p. 1216.*

HENRY JAMES   (letter date 1902)

[*An American novelist, James is valued for his psychological acuity and complex sense of artistic form. Throughout his career,*

James also wrote literary criticism in which he developed his artistic ideals and applied them to the works of others. Among the numerous conceptualizations he formed to clarify the nature of fiction, he defined the novel as "a direct impression of life." The quality of this impression—the degree of moral and intellectual development—and the author's ability to communicate this impression in an effective and artistic manner were the two principal criteria by which James estimated the worth of a literary work. James became acquainted with Wister's mother and grandmother when Wister was twelve years old, and remained a family friend throughout his life. In the following letter to Wister, James praises The Virginian *and offers critical advice.*]

I have been reading **The Virginian** & I am moved to write to you. You didn't read him to me—you never send me nothing; as to which, heaven knows, you're not obliged, &, conscious of your probably multitudinous preoccupations, I mention the matter only from the sense of my having felt, as I read, how the sentiment of the thing would have deepened for me if I *had* had it from your hands. The point is that the sentiment of the thing so appealed to me, interested me, convinced me, that I thus unscrupulously yield to the pleasure of making an however ineffectual sign of the same to you across the waste of distance & darkness. Signs are, in this sort, poor things, & to talk with you would be the real delerium [*sic?*]; still, I want it to pass as dimly discernible to you that what I best like in your book deeply penetrates even my weather-beaten, my almost petrified old mind. What I best like in it is exactly the fact of the *subject* itself, so clearly & finely felt by you, I think, & so firmly carried out as the exhibition, to the last intimacy, of the man's character, the personal & moral complexion & evolution, in short, of your hero. On this I very heartily congratulate you; you have made him *live* [?], with a high, but lucid complexity, from head to foot & from beginning to end; you have not only intensely seen & conceived him, but you have reached with him an admirable objectivity, & I find the whole thing a rare & remarkable feat. If we *could* only palaver (ah, miserable fate!) & you were to give me leave, there are various other awfully interesting things I shld. like both to say & to sound you on; these same, & connected, questions, elements of the art we practice & adorn, being, to my judgment, the most thrilling that can occupy the human mind. I won't deny that I have my reserves,—perverse perhaps & merely personal—in respect to some sides of your performance; but in the first place they don't touch the Essence; in the second they would take space (tremble at what you escape!) & in the third you haven't asked me for them—an indispensable condition, I hold, of offering such observations. The Essence, as I call it, remains—the way the young man's inward & outward presence builds itself up, fills out the picture, holds the interest & charms the sympathy. Bravo, bravo. *I* find myself desiring all sorts of poetic justice to hang about him, & I am willing to throw out, even though you don't ask me, that nothing would have induced me to unite him to the little Vermont person, or to dedicate him in fact to achieved parentage, prosperity, maturity, at all—which is mere *prosaic* justice; & rather grim at that. I thirst for his blood. I wouldn't have let him live & be happy; I should have made him perish in his flower & in some splendid sombre way. . . . But I am letting myself loose among my [word] & I pull myself up. I only wanted to pat you officiously, & both violently & tenderly, on the admirably assiduous back. Bend this last possession again to—ah, not to the Virginian. *Don't* revive him again at your peril, or rather at his! I have an impertinent apprehension that you're promising yourself some such treat for his later developments. Damn his later developments—& yet I can't say Write me another Wild West novel all the same. For I believe the type you've studied & dismissed to be, essentially (isn't it?) ce qu'il y a de mieux [''what is best''] in the W. W. [Wild West]. But write me something equally American on this scale or with this seriousness—for it's a great pleasure to see you bringing off so the large & the sustained. How I envy you the personal knowledge of the W. W., the possession of the memories; that *The Virginian* must be built on, & the right to a competent [?] romantic feeling about them. (pp. 251-52)

Henry James, in a letter to Owen Wister on August 7, 1902, in American Literature, *Vol. 26, May, 1954, pp. 251-52.*

OWEN WISTER   (essay date 1902)

[*In the following excerpt from his note to the reader in* The Virginian, *Wister discusses the cowboy as a heroic figure and the realistic nature of his novel.*]

Certain of the newspapers, when this book was first announced, made a mistake most natural upon seeing the subtitle as it then stood. *A Tale of Sundry Adventures.* ''This sounds like a historical novel,'' said one of them, meaning (I take it) a colonial romance. As it now stands, the title will scarce lead to such interpretation; yet none the less is this book historical—quite as much so as any colonial romance. Indeed, when you look at the root of the matter, it is a colonial romance. For Wyoming between 1874 and 1890 was a colony as wild as was Virginia one hundred years earlier. As wild, with a scantier population, and the same primitive joys and dangers. There were, to be sure, not so many Chippendale settees.

We know quite well the common understanding of the term ''historical novel.'' *Hugh Wynne* exactly fits it. But *Silas Lapham* is a novel as perfectly historical as is *Hugh Wynne*, for it pictures an era and personifies a type. It matters not that in the one we find George Washington and in the other none save imaginary figures; else *The Scarlet Letter* were not historical. Nor does it matter that Dr. Mitchell did not live in the time of which he wrote, while Mr. Howells saw many Silas Laphams with his own eyes; else *Uncle Tom's Cabin* were not historical. Any narrative which presents faithfully a day and a generation is of necessity historical; and this one presents Wyoming between 1874 and 1890. (p. xiii)

What is become of the horseman, the cow-puncher, the last romantic figure upon our soil? For he was romantic. Whatever he did, he did with his might. The bread that he earned was earned hard, the wages that he squandered were squandered hard,—half a year's pay sometimes gone in a night,—''blown in,'' as he expressed it, or ''blowed in,'' to be perfectly accurate. Well, he will be here among us always, invisible, waiting his chance to live and play as he would like. His wild kind has been among us always, since the beginning: a young man with his temptations, a hero without wings.

The cow-puncher's ungoverned hours did not unman him. If he gave his word, he kept it; Wall Street would have found him behind the times. Nor did he talk lewdly to women; Newport would have thought him old-fashioned. He and his brief epoch make a complete picture, for in themselves they were as complete as the pioneers of the land or the explorers of the sea. A transition has followed the horseman of the plains; a shapeless state, a condition of men and manners as unlovely as is that moment in the year when winter is gone and spring not come, and the face of Nature is ugly. I shall not dwell upon it here. Those who have seen it know well what I mean.

Such transition was inevitable. Let us give thanks that it is but a transition, and not a finalty.

Sometimes readers inquire, Did I know the Virginian? As well, I hope, as a father should know his son. And sometimes it is asked, Was such and such a thing true? Now to this I have the best answer in the world. Once a cow-puncher listened patiently while I read him a manuscript. It concerned an event upon an Indian reservation. ''Was that the Crow reservation?'' he inquired at the finish. I told him that it was no real reservation and no real event; and his face expressed displeasure. ''Why,'' he demanded, ''do you waste your time writing what never happened, when you know so many things that did happen?''

And I could no more help telling him that this was the highest compliment ever paid me than I have been able to help telling you about it here! (pp. xiv-xv)

Owen Wister, ''To the Reader,'' in his The Virginian: A Horseman of the Plains, *1902. Reprint by Dodd, Mead & Company, 1968, pp. xiii-xv.*

WILLIAM MORTON PAYNE   (essay date 1902)

[*The longtime literary editor for several Chicago publications, Payne reviewed books for twenty-three years at the* Dial, *one of America's most influential journals of literature and opinion in the early twentieth century. In the following excerpt, Payne offers a laudatory review of* The Virginian.]

The Virginian is the story of a nameless hero. Throughout the book he is called ''the Virginian'' and nothing else. But although nameless, as far as we are informed, he is one of the most distinct personalities that have appeared in American fiction. A Wyoming cow-boy, representing a phase of our civilization that has almost completely vanished—although it was real enough a quarter of a century ago,—uneducated and unskilled in the amenities of artificial society, he conquers our sympathies by his innate refinement of character and the clean manliness of his living. He represents an ideal that was probably never realized, yet the separate touches by which he is drawn for us bear the visible stamp of truth. His story is a series of episodes that may be enjoyed independently of one another, although they are held in a sort of unity by his relations with the New England girl who comes to Wyoming to teach school, and who promptly develops into as satisfactory a heroine as one could wish for. She gives him books to read, and his frank comments upon them are both humorous and refreshing. There are other humorous features, notably that which describes the mixing up of a dozen babies by changing their clothes—a prank not quite in keeping with the Virginian's character, but nevertheless irresistibly amusing. In the course of his career he finds himself a member of a lynching party, and the author makes the usual sophistical defense of this wild form of justice. *The Virginian* is a man's book, with not one touch of sickly sentiment, and must be regarded as a valuable human document because of the author's intimate acquaintance with the scenes and types which it portrays.

William Morton Payne, in a review of ''The Virginian,'' in The Dial, *Vol. XXXIII, No. 392, October 16, 1902, p. 242.*

EDWARD CLARK MARSH   (essay date 1906)

[*In the following excerpt, Marsh praises the themes and construction of* Lady Baltimore, *noting its dissimilarity to* The Virginian.]

[The] art of the First Chapter has wellnigh perished; so there should be the heartier welcome for Mr. Wister's attempt to revive it. *Lady Baltimore* has both a preface and a first chapter. Let me not be understood as implying that they are inordinately clever, out of all proportion to the rest of the book. They are merely an admirable introduction to an entertaining story, pitched in just the right key and dangling a trail of tantalizing interest across the pages that follow. The spirit of them is right: the amused, indulgent spirit of true comedy. They have a leisurely, aristocratic quality that is too rare in these days of—to misquote a phrase of the author's—"yellow novelists." Mr. Wister writes like a gentleman; and while this would be damnatory enough of a dull book, it is high praise of an entertaining one. It is easy to guess that he enjoyed writing this novel. It is even possible to believe that he has ideals pertaining to his craft, that he considers writing an art worth studying and doing well for its own sake, that he is not ashamed nor afraid of conveying an idea now and then to his readers.

By all these characteristics Mr. Wister sets himself apart from the writing mob; by these, and some others. It will be remembered that Mr. Wister protested, with great justness, that *The Virginian* was a historical novel, though its period was the immediate, not the remote, past. So is *Lady Baltimore,* and the period too is not far different; but its setting is as different as if the author had set out deliberately to prove his versatility by as great a contrast as possible with his earlier work. Then it was the passing of the newest phase of American life that has had time to die out; now it is nearly the oldest society we have had, whose end he records. From the Wyoming cowboy to the Southern aristocracy of Kings Port is a long stride; but Mr. Wister takes it easily. In each case he has fixed the type of the life with delightful certainty; and there the resemblance ends, save for the humour which is intermittent in the first book and constant in the last. And for the reassurance of certain belittlers of *The Virginian,* let me at once record one noticeable difference. Three or four years ago Mr. Wister must have become heartily tired of hearing that his Western book was not a novel, but a mere collection of short stories artificially strung together; and the doubt was publicly expressed whether he could ever write a "real" novel. That feeble reproach must now be laid aside. Here at last he has given us a substantial book of four hundred pages, and it is absolutely organic. If it was "unity of design" that the carpers wanted, Mr. Wister has effectually closed their mouths.

But it is not merely for its adherence to an academic formula that *Lady Baltimore* is to be praised. It is good to read because of its characterisation, its geniality and its ideas. No more charming and delightful group has been brought together for many a day in the pages of a book than those fine Southern ladies, old and young, of Kings Port. Of the historical accuracy of the portraiture those must judge who know the South intimately; its truth in a larger sense is subject to a more general test. Undoubtedly these delightful ladies of an old aristocracy are witty and clever to a degree that raises them a trifle above crass realism; but to object to that would be both ungrateful and fallacious. Every novelist worthy the name makes his characters a little more articulate than actual life, and does it in accordance with some convention,—which, if it be pronounced, ill-disposed folk will call "mannerism." Mr. Wister's convention is to make his people talk wittily and toss off remarks that have the felicity and sententiousness of epigrams. That he is not a mere epigrammatist is shown by the fact that the best of these utterances lose something by quotation. Part of their effect is due to context and character. And if there is

a remote suggestion of Meredith in the elegant leisure of his beginning, there is a closer reference—a conscious indebtedness, indeed, I believe—to Henry James in his manner, the turn of his phrases, and even in the framework and articulation of his story. Mr. Wister's characters have, however, none of the mental complexity of Mr. James's richest creations; and by the same token his style has only a suggestion of the fine, high polish of the older man's. Indeed, the author of *Lady Baltimore* has shown himself capable of writing an occasional sentence that is positively bad, just as one scene in his story displays his taste as something less than impeccable. But to instance these lapses as faults implies on the whole a performance of high and sustained merit.

A more serious ground for criticism is the ideas, the fundamental "brain-stuff" that Mr. Wister has put into this book. He has not feared to make his creatures his spokesmen for the promulgation of reflections and opinions social, scientific and political. As a story-teller he has accomplished this remarkably well. The little drama never seems overweighted by the discussions and argumentative battles that are constantly waged by its characters. Success in this direction places the book in the class of great works in the comic *genre*. It is the quality of the ideas themselves that fixes its position in the class considerably below the greatest works. Mr. Wister's opinions are always readable, frequently amusing, sometimes stimulating; they are never profound, and they are, alas! occasionally callow. But this is criticism that cuts both ways. It will comfort many people to know that they may read *Lady Baltimore* without any fear that they will encounter something "deep." And if that negative assurance is not enough, they may know further that it is a capital story, fulfilling every fair expectation on behalf of one of the cleverest and most capable of our American novelists. (pp. 296-97)

Edward Clark Marsh, "Owen Wister's 'Lady Baltimore'," in The Bookman, *New York, Vol. XXIII, May, 1906, pp. 296-97.*

FREDERIC TABER COOPER (essay date 1911)

[*An American educator, biographer, and editor, Cooper served for many years as literary critic at the* Bookman, *a popular early twentieth-century literary magazine. In the following excerpt, Cooper discusses Wister as a natural storyteller whose works are successful despite poor craftsmanship.*]

No matter how willingly we may obey Candide's wise injunction to cultivate our garden, it is well to remember that not every writer can achieve an equal profusion and variety, nor an equal clearness of plan and purpose. Not to every one is it given to grow oranges and lemons, citrons and pistachios in oriental opulence.... But how, at first sight, is one to interpret a garden composed of much sagebrush, one towering redwood, a magnolia and a head of Boston lettuce? Yet this, in all courtesy be it said, is a fair inventory of the harvest which up to the present time has rewarded Mr. Wister's tillage in the fertile soil of his imagination. His short stories of Western ranch life, ranging from Arizona to Wyoming and comprising practically all his early work and an ample share of his later, are literally as redolent of the soil, as unmistakably indigenous, in color, form and atmosphere, as is the gray-green aromatic herbage that forms so conspicuous a feature of their setting. His one full-length novel, *The Virginian,* has a certain primal bigness about it that makes it seem to loom up, tree-like, in rugged dignity, a growth of nature rather than of art. *Lady*

Baltimore has by contrast a sort of hot-house charm; that southern softness of manners and of speech, as unmistakable and as delightful in their way as the form and fragrance of a magnolia bloom. And even Boston lettuce has not a flavor more local, a more unsuspected generosity of close-packed and succulent substance than that blithe little satire of college life, *Philosophy Four,* with its unpretentious outward showing, and the golden wisdom hidden at its heart.

Yet it is precisely the informality of Mr. Wister's garden, the absence of neat paths and close clipped hedge-rows, that gives the first important clue to his literary methods. The simple fact is that Mr. Wister has never attempted to pre-empt any special corner of the habitable world and make it his own, in any such sense as Mrs. Wilkins-Freeman pre-empted New England, Mr. Allen, Kentucky, or Mr. Cable, New Orleans. The fact that he has become identified in the popular mind with certain sections of the West is due less to his interest in the life of the plains as something curious and anomalous, something different from humanity as we ordinarily understand it, than to his recognition of the far more important fact that underneath the picturesque and striking surface differences, human nature west and east is at heart a fairly constant quantity. His obvious love for the characters of his own creating, Scipio Lemoyne and Steve and The Virginian, is not because they were cowboys, with a strange dialect and a still stranger moral code, but because, when one came to know them, one found them men, acting as the best of us might act if exposed to like conditions. In this connection, it is a significant fact that Mr. Wister almost always writes frankly as an outsider, bringing himself into the story after the method of Mr. Kipling's earlier tales, and writing in the first person as the one who has witnessed certain events or to whom certain others were repeated at first hand. The result of this method is that we are all the time forced to see and measure whatever is local and transitory through alien eyes, and that we think of such a book as *The Virginian,* not as the record of a phase of life that has already passed away, but as a vital and enduring presentment of types and characters that are most thoroughly, most widely, most delightfully American.

After conceding freely and gladly these merits to Mr. Wister, it will not be thought ungenerous to proceed to point out some of his shortcomings and to say at once frankly that he is one of those story tellers who have won fame not because of their craftsmanship, but in spite of their lack of it. To the fundamental doctrine of economy of means he shows a blithe indifference; in his long stories and his shorter ones alike, he refuses to trim his hedges or to prune back his vines, preferring to let them luxuriate, weed-like, in whatsoever direction they list. . . . [The] ability to digress with impunity Mr. Wister has to an unusual extent; even through the medium of the printed page, one is always conscious of a pleasing personality, and can almost see the indulgent smile or the amused twinkle of the eye that must accompany certain characteristic flashes of humor. For there can be no question that, besides being a story teller, the creator of "Emly" and the "Frawg's legs" episode must be numbered among our recognized American humorists,—and what is more, enrolled as one who has never, for the sake of scoring a point, degraded humor to the level of farce comedy.

Now, since an author is known by the company that he keeps upon his bookshelves, or at least by that smaller group which he considers worthy of emulation, it is worth while to pause for a moment over Mr. Wister's own confessions, in the preface to his latest published volume, *Members of the Family.* (pp. 265-69)

[His] own admissions prove him to be of widely catholic tastes, as free from attachment to any particular school as, let us say, was Marion Crawford. Howells, the veteran champion of realism; James, the subtlest of English psychologues; Stevenson, the belated romanticist, all find equal favor in his sight, not because of what they profess, but because he realizes that each of them achieves quite admirably the special thing that he has undertaken to do. In other words, Mr. Wister is an eclectic both in his theories and his practice of fiction. It is impossible to pronounce him realist or romanticist, symbolist or psychologue. His methods vary, not only from book to book, but from chapter to chapter in the same book. Maupassant, for instance, might have written more than one episode in *The Virginian,*—the lynching of the cattle-thieves, for instance, or that other even more cruel chapter in which a human fiend avenges himself upon a horse driven beyond its strength, by gouging out its eye. But none but a dreamer could have written the idyl of Molly's marriage to the Virginian, and the honeymoon on the sylvan island, the only fault of which is that it was all too beautiful to be quite true.

Having acquired this initial perspective of Mr. Wister's literary theory and practice, as a whole, we may now profitably take up the separate works. . . . And first of all . . . the stories of rather uneven merit, ranging all the way from mediocre to extremely good, that made up the contents of such early volumes as *Red Men and White* and *The Jimmyjohn Boss:*—well, to be quite candid, a detailed analysis of them would add nothing to a critical estimate of their author, because they are in a measure apprentice work. Had he never done anything better, "The Jimmyjohn Boss,"—the opening story in the volume of that name,—. . . this, and a dozen other tales, would have merited a certain amount of critical praise. But, as it happens, they were merely an earnest of something far better yet to come. And in due time that something better came in the form of *The Virginian,* which in its genesis is nothing more nor less than an accretion of short stories,—just as Maupassant's first novel, *Une Vie,* is an assemblage of short stories,— and with the additional point of resemblance, that in both cases a number of the stories have been published separately. . . . Mr. Wister belongs to that class of story tellers whose natural form is the short story rather than the long,—who see every story, in the first instance, as a single detached incident; and when they attempt a more sustained effort, find themselves simply stringing together a series of such incidents, upon just one rather slender narrative thread. As it happens, *The Virginian* proved itself, in defiance of mathematics, to be considerably bigger than the sum of its parts. But that, I think, was due less to a definite, carefully worked out plan than to a chance unity of ideas running through all the several segments. The West, as a broad, free, stupendous whole, had impressed Mr. Wister mightily, and in a way that could not be quickly formulated or easily put into words; but with each story, each episode, he came nearer to saying some part of what was struggling for utterance. And when all these separate parts were finally fitted together into a single volume, it would be interesting to know whether Mr. Wister himself was not just a trifle surprised to find how well he had succeeded in expressing a number of rather important truths.

If it were not for the danger of being misunderstood as praising *The Virginian* for qualities which it does not possess, the simplest way of defining its character and at the same time explaining why its very looseness of construction in some degree is a help rather than a hindrance, would be to say that it was of the epic type. . . . *The Virginian* is epic, in so far as it shows us certain individual lives struggling to reach a solution of problems equally vital to the length and breadth of the whole vast region in which they live; a small group of human beings trying to justify to themselves and the world at large the fundamental justice of the rude moral code that governs them. In a stricter sense of the word, *The Virginian* is not merely badly constructed,—it is almost without structure. There is not a chapter in it that we would willingly spare: but that does not alter the fact that, aside from a few crucial scenes, there is scarcely a chapter whose excision would destroy the book's essential unity. In other words, the book is so far of the *picaresco* type that its episodes are like so many pearls on a single thread,—undoubted gems of their kind, but so arranged that the removal of one or more would not leave a gap in the design. *The Virginian* has actually that lack of deliberate detail work for which so many critics wrongfully censure Mr. Kipling's *Kim.* Yet if we are willing to think for a moment of the West, that glorious, virgin West of earlier years, as a sort of anthropomorphized heroine, just as we think of India as the heroine of *Kim,*—then it becomes possible to forgive much of the looseness, the apparent irrelevancy, the digressions, because much that is either superfluous or beside the mark, so far as it is meant to help us understand the individual lives of Mollie or the Virginian, Steve or Trampas, becomes fraught with a new import when our interest is focused on the destiny of a community, almost on a nation. (pp. 271-76)

We find . . . I think, in the broad, general principle, expressed here and there in words, and throughout the book by implication, that in every community men must make such laws for themselves as the conditions under which they live demand. The trick of "getting the drop" on your adversary, the right to shoot an enemy at sight after a fair warning, the whole underlying theory of vigilance committees and of lynch law, are justified only by the exigencies of special conditions, the advantage of the crudest and most rudimentary form of justice over no justice at all. Mr. Wister has not the least intention of holding lawlessness up for our admiration, just because it comes in picturesque masquerade. When the Virginian co-operates in a murder, according to our Eastern standards, by helping to lynch his personal friend, Steve; and when again he puts himself upon a level with a skulking outlaw like Trampas, accepts his challenge to shoot at sight, and succeeds in shooting straighter, Mr. Wister is not proclaiming the frontier code of Wyoming to have been superior to the English common law. He is simply insisting that if you or I are going to live in a community, we must accept the ethics of that community if we wish to be respected. (p. 277)

Before proceeding to point out that *Lady Baltimore* . . . is in spite of all the obvious differences of subject, setting and workmanship, essentially the product of the same mind, the same philosophy, the same outlook upon life, it is necessary to clear up one or two possible misunderstandings regarding certain terms used in this chapter. There is, for instance, the statement that *The Virginian* is Mr. Wister's only sustained effort, his one full-length novel,—and to offset it is the indisputable fact that *Lady Baltimore* is issued in the conventional novel form, and contains upward of four hundred pages. . . . *The Virginian,* curtailed and compressed into fifty pages, would still be a novel, because of the serious purpose and the tremendous human truths behind it. *Lady Baltimore,* regardless of mathematical dimensions, can never be in spirit anything more than an amplified novelette,—exquisite in workmanship, perennially charming in its presentment of an exotic and evanescent civilization, yet containing little in the way of broad generalities

or of serious, practical philosophy. Nevertheless, there is the further important truth that technically *Lady Baltimore* is the most admirable artistry, the most nearly flawless piece of work that Mr. Wister has yet achieved.

Every conservative critic must deplore the rash extravagance of a certain type of reviewer who finds in the passing novel of to-day qualities worthy of comparison with Fielding and Thackeray, Balzac and Flaubert and Daudet. Even in Mr. Wister's case it is at least over-generous to pronounce him, within the limits of a single review, a worthy successor both of Meredith and of Henry James. Yet this is precisely what Mr. Edward Clark Marsh, a critic characterized equally by the modesty and the discernment of his judgment, has done, at least by implication, in a review of *Lady Baltimore* [see excerpt dated 1906]. A possible indebtedness to the author of *The Egoist* we may well let pass; considering how few novelists ever learn just where or how to begin or end a story, it is quite natural to attribute to the few who show intelligence in this respect a conscious imitation of one of the acknowledged masters. The influence of Henry James is a very different matter. In acknowledging his indebtedness to the author of *What Maisie Knew,* in the preface [to *Members of the Family*], Mr. Wister goes on to say that he once had the privilege of going over one of his own books with Mr. James, and of having the latter point out, page by page, his short-comings, his lost opportunities, his lack of that finished technique, without which no amount of native genius can reach artistic perfection. Mr. Wister does not state which of his volumes was thus criticised; but one does not feel much diffidence in venturing the conjecture that it was *The Virginian,* and that *Lady Baltimore* was Mr. Wister's prompt acknowledgment of his indebtedness, as well as a demonstration of his surprising aptness as a pupil. (pp. 285-87)

As all readers of *The Virginian* are aware, its author has always insisted that although its pages contain no famous characters, and its date is so recent as to be practically contemporary, it is nevertheless a historical novel, a record of a certain phase of American history caught and preserved during the actual making. In the same sense both *Philosophy Four* and *Lady Baltimore* are historical documents, representing eternal truths of human nature as reacted upon by transitory conditions. The setting of *Lady Baltimore* is a certain town of King's Port, a quiet backwater in the current of Southern social life, where old-time manners and customs still linger; and there is a fragrance of gentle dignity and bygone courtliness in the ordinary relations of life. Perhaps no story ever made claim to serious consideration while resting upon so fragile a foundation. *Lady Baltimore* is a local Southern name for a certain rare and glorified species of cake,—and the cake itself could not be of more airy and delicate consistence than the story it is here called upon to sustain. Imagine a Northerner plunged by certain whims of destiny,—the details are immaterial,—into this tranquil eddy of an alien civilization, of whose social code he is utterly ignorant; imagine him, while taking luncheon in the one available cake-and-tea room of the town, witnessing the purchase of a Lady Baltimore cake by a much embarrassed young man, who admits to the equally self-conscious young woman behind the counter that this cake, ordered for a day near at hand, is to serve at his wedding. In the embarrassment of the young man, the Northerner scents something unusual in the way of romance; and little by little he gleans the facts, and pieces them together. The young man, it seems, has committed an act which his family and friends choose to regard as suicidal,—he has engaged himself to a young woman of whose pedigree they know little or nothing; she may be a very worthy girl, but she is not one of them, she does not belong to the Southern aristocracy, she is not a part and parcel of King's Port. (pp. 288-90)

In *The Virginian*, Mr. Wister succeeded in giving us a thoroughly virile book without brutalizing it; in *Lady Baltimore*, he has achieved the harder task of producing a delightfully feminine book without stooping to effeminacy. Or, to put it in another way, he has juggled dexterously with soap-bubbles without breaking them in the process.

It remains to speak only of the technique of *Lady Baltimore*. It is no new thing to find Mr. Wister writing in the first person. But it is distinctly new to find him rigidly confining himself to that narrow segment of life that passes directly within the angle of vision of his spokesman, the Northerner. This is the Henry James trick, *par excellence*. Earlier novelists have sometimes done the same thing indifferently well, by instinct rather than intention; but Mr. James was the first to reduce this method to rules. And the admirable consistency with which Mr. Wister has followed out this principle of a single viewpoint not only proves him to be an apt pupil but makes *Lady Baltimore* one of those rare achievements in American fiction, a piece of technique that is almost without a flaw. (pp. 290-91)

> *Frederic Taber Cooper, "Owen Wister," in his* Some American Story Tellers, 1911. *Reprint by Books for Libraries Press, 1968; distributed by Arno Press, Inc., pp. 265-94.*

DOUGLAS BRANCH   (essay date 1926)

[*In the following excerpt, Branch contends that in* The Virginian *Wister created a romanticized and unrealistic portrait of the cowboy.*]

When Wister wrote those episodes later gathered into the volumes *The Virginian* and *Lin McLean*, he wrote with the fervor of a missionary. It was his part to bring the real West into American *belles-lettres*—in his own words, to "disperse the Alkali Ikes." (p. 193)

If Wister had done what he set out to do, the history of the Western scene in American literature would have been changed greatly for the better.

Wrote Wister of *The Virginian*, "Any novel which presents faithfully a day and a generation is of necessity historical; and this one presents Wyoming between 1874 and 1890." . . . [He] valued his own work too generously. *The Virginian* does present, in a pleasant and readable fashion—the Virginian.

> Lounging there against the wall was a slim young giant, more beautiful than pictures. His broad, soft hat was pushed back; a loose-knotted, dull-scarlet handkerchief sagged from his throat; and one casual thumb was hooked in the cartridge-belt that slanted across his hips. He had plainly come many miles from somewhere across the vast horizon, as the dust upon him showed. . . . The weather-beaten bloom of his face shone through it duskily, as the ripe peaches look upon their trees in a dry season. But no dinginess of travel or shabbiness of attire could tarnish the splendor that radiated from his youth and strength.

Such was the Virginian—Young Wild West groomed, his *naïveté* replaced by the quiet wisdom that comes with power, less of a crusader, but still a man among men. If *The Virginian* were "our last glimpse of the pioneer in the plainsman and cowboy types, then passing and now gone," as a critic has called it, then our last glimpse was of a cowboy hardly a type at all; for Wister has labored to make the Virginian distinctive, one actually revered by his fellow cowboys. Lin McLean, young, soft-hearted, much given to rough banter and practical jokes, "one of the boys," is much more a type, much more a cowboy, than the irresistible Virginian:

> As we drove by the eating-house, the shade of a side window was raised, and the landlady looked her last upon the Virginian. Her lips were faintly parted, and no woman's eyes ever said more plainly, "I am one of your possessions."

"A cowboy without cattle," writes Andy Adams, "is comparable to a lord without lands or a master without slaves." It is strange that Wister could have called his *Virginian* a historical novel of the cattle-country when there is not one scene set on the range among the cattle, when the cowboys seem throughout to spend their days in playful pranks, in love-making, in thief-hunting, in anything except work. Perhaps Wister believed that he had caught the spirit of the cattle-country, in the character of his hero and in the humorous by-play that enlivens the book, and could have gained nothing by introducing elements of life on the range at the expense of the love-interest. The great love of the Virginian for Molly Wood, the school-teacher from Vermont, is the unifying thread that binds the succession of incidents into a novel; and this great love is no more Western, no more related to "American faith," than the great loves of the fine young men in the drawing-room tales and desert-island romances of Louis Tracy, Morgan Robertson, and the Reverend Cyrus T. Brady.

Wister interrupts his narrative, in the approved fashion of the romancers of his day, to speculate on the mysterious thing called love, the grand passion so essential to his craft:

> Has any botanist set down what the seed of love is? Has it anywhere been set down in how many ways this seed may be sown? In what various vessels of gossamer it can float across wide spaces? Or upon what different soils it can fall, and live unknown, and bide its time for blooming?

And this is the essence of *The Virginian:* the tale of one seed in its particular vessel of gossamer alighting in a spot of the West, of the sprouting of that seed, of the hazards of its growth, of its maturity. It could as well have landed somewhere else than in the Northwestern cattle-country; *The Virginian* would still have been *The Virginian*. (pp. 196-99)

> *Douglas Branch, "'The Virginian' and Taisie," in his* The Cowboy and His Interpreters, *D. Appleton and Company, 1926, pp. 192-209.**

ALEXANDER WOOLLCOTT   (essay date 1930)

[*Woollcott is best known as one of America's most eccentric wits and raconteurs, as well as an influential pioneer of modern drama criticism. With his gossipy approach to reviewing—a style that focused on personalities, trivia, and general impressions of the plays—Woollcott attained and wielded the power of success or failure over Broadway's offerings. His reviews are characterized by the gushing admiration expressed for performers and performances Woollcott liked and by the cruel blasts he reserved for those he did not. Retiring from drama criticism in 1928, Woollcott turned to reviewing books as a much sought-after magazine columnist and radio personality. His popularity as a book reviewer, both on the air and in the pages of the* New Yorker, *soon rivalled that which he had earlier enjoyed as a theater critic. In the following excerpt from a review originally published in November, 1930, Woollcott attacks* Roosevelt: The Story of a Friendship *as prejudiced and sophomoric, comparing it with Wister's novella* Philosophy Four *and noting that Wister's work evidenced no intellectual development during the thirty years between the publications of the two works.*]

I had meant to reserve this space today for a nice, judgmatical review of Owen Wister's *Roosevelt: The Story of a Friendship.* But there is that about the flavor of this innocent exhibition of hero-worship and snobbery which induces a malaise in me and unfits me for dispassionate comment on this portrait of one Harvard man by another. Mr. Wister is the deep-dyed product of feudal Philadelphia. And seemingly, when the blue blood of Germantown is blended with the Harvard crimson, the result gives one a really oppressive sense of having been born in the deep purple. Any public manifestation of that sense provokes in members of the rabble an urchin impulse to shy a few such stones as this one.

You see—unjustly, I am afraid, perhaps even perversely—I keep thinking of this fond tome as a sequel to **"Philosophy 4,"** a Harvard short story which Mr. Wister published nigh on to thirty years ago. "Have just been reading '**Philosophy 4,**'" Roosevelt wrote him in 1916. "*You* may think it a skit. *I* regard it as containing a deep and subtle moral." Now that story had seemed to me about as subtle as a kick in the face. Indeed, it seemed to me when I first read it (and it still seems to me) one of the most smugly offensive bits of callow, unconscious Bourbonism I ever encountered.

"Philosophy 4," as you may recall, is the story of an ant and two grasshoppers, in which the grasshoppers triumph gloriously. They are two rosy, handsome, elegant Sophomores, scions of the Colonial aristocracy. Having improvidently cut all the philosophy lectures, they realize on the eve of examinations that they must hire a greasy grind to tutor them from his faithfully taken notes. And then, to Mr. Wister's undisguised delight, they pass with higher marks than he does. Oscar, the grind, is the butt of the story, a pale, cautious, bespectacled son of Jewish immigrants, who is painfully working his way through college, struggling for every penny and developing in the process such shifty, calculating eyes that Mr. Wister really cannot abide him. (pp. 319-20)

On the other hand, Bertie's and Billy's parents owned town and country houses in New York and were named Schuyler and things like that. Money filled the pockets of Bertie and Billy. "Therefore," says the stupefying Wister, "were their heads empty of money and full of less cramping thoughts." Bless the man, that sentence is sound Shavian doctrine. But a little later the story says: "Oscar felt meritorious when he considered Bertie and Billy; for, *like the socialists,* merit with him meant not being able to live as well as your neighbor." Indeed, there is a Let-them-eat-cake tone to the entire context which suggests that, after all, it will be some little time before we can hope to hail the author as Comrade Wister. To be sure, a little later in the narrative there seems to stir, even under the fine linen of the author's bosom, a faint sense of the story's mean and contemptuous insolence. He hastily makes the usual

and familiar disavowal. It seems that some of his best friends at Harvard were poor students. For one willing publicly to make so handsome an admission, Comrade Wister is scarcely adequate as a salutation. Let us call him Greatheart and be done with it.

Now even so leisurely a commentator as your correspondent, who usually discovers a book about a year after it has gone out of print, would scarcely be thrown into a pet over this 1903 yarn of Owen Wister's today if its tone were not continued right on into this monograph on Roosevelt. After all, **"Philosophy 4"** is a story about three Harvard Sophomores by a fourth—the fourth having remained a Harvard Sophomore for twenty years after graduation. It is interesting, therefore, chiefly as a phenomenon of arrested development. There may be some, to be sure, who might feel that Mr. Wister never does gain perspective with the recession of an event into the past, that his chapters on the war in this book, for instance, might have been written in 1918 for all the clarification of focus and readjustment of values acquired in the interim. It is then his fault, perhaps, if one gets a troubled impression that Roosevelt himself, during the war, knew no more what it was all about than the least of us did—that, indeed, the thwarted Colonel's attitude throughout was indistinguishable from that of the spinster who was having the time of her no longer young life dispensing sweet chocolate and arch smiles at Yaphank.

But it would be quite unwarranted for me to pretend that it is either the scantiness or the obtuseness of Mr. Wister's opus on Roosevelt which chiefly afflicts me. I am not even much disturbed by the hushed tones of the narrative, although toward his hero Mr. Wister did seemingly preserve, to the last, the manner of an awe-struck schoolgirl in the presence of her matinée idol. No, what irritates me almost to the point of intemperate statement, and even incivility, are the book's little patches of the aforesaid deep purple. They begin at the beginning when young Theodore Roosevelt, Harvard '80, is boxing in the gymnasium at Cambridge before a gallery full of Saltonstalls and pretty girls with nice furs. But the master patch of all—a tiny one, but how purple, how purple!—is that line at the end when the autumn of 1918 came to Sagamore Hill. The elder Roosevelts were watching the war from that manorial shelter. Poor Quentin lay dead in a French meadow. And the others? Mr. Wister accounts for them in the perfect Tory sentence of our time, a phrase that is an amalgamation of Harvard and Philadelphia combining the worst features of both. "Theodore, Kermit, and Archie," he says, "were with their soldiers." (pp. 320-22)

> *Alexander Woollcott, "Wisteria," in his* While Rome Burns, *The Viking Press, 1934, pp. 319-22.*

RALPH PHILIP BOAS AND KATHERINE BURTON   (essay date 1933)

[*In the following excerpt, Boas and Burton discuss the character the Virginian as an exemplar of Wister's conception of the democratic spirit.*]

It was Owen Wister who saw that to interest active men concerned with actual conditions one need not give up the historical or even the romantic. He saw clearly that the local-color stories were historical; that historical novels might happen to be first-hand studies. Howells's *The Rise of Silas Lapham* he calls an historical novel, saying that "any narrative which presents faithfully a day and a generation is of necessity historical." In *Lin McLean,* as later in *The Virginian,* he wrote of historical days he himself had known, "the old days, the happy days, when Wyoming was a Territory with a future instead of a State with a past," when "the unfenced cattle grazed upon her ranges by the prosperous thousands," and the foot-loose young cowpuncher, Lin, could lose seven hundred dollars—all he had—in a crooked card game, and ride about in freight trains, and, when he was ready, find a job in twenty-five minutes. One could take a train, now, to Cheyenne, Wister points out; but only a journey in the memory would bring one to the vanished, romantic world. . . . The books were thus historic, but they were also as romantic as the cowboys who were their heroes.

Lin McLean and the Virginian are cowboys as Easterners have always imagined them, as cowboys seem actually to have sometimes been: slim young giants, grave in manner, facetious in spirit, as dependable under responsibility as they were otherwise rollicking and apparently reckless; tender-hearted, sentimental; enemies to be dreaded, if one were crooked or a coward, but friends to be relied on utterly. Lin figures in separate stories which work out as the chapters of one whole. The Virginian, his occasional partner in mischief, gives in the later novel our best picture of the cowboy of the eighties—"one of thousands, but one in a thousand." In the land where the air was pure as water and strong as wine, he rode tall and loose in the saddle, playing pranks like a schoolboy, wooing with chivalry like the Southern gentleman he was—and doing his day's work withal.

It was the essence of democracy which Wister portrayed, a world in which there was no equality, where through competition everything was to be gained or lost. By the very Declaration of Independence, he pointed out, we Americans acknowledged the *eternal inequality* of men. "For by it we abolished a cut-and-dried aristocracy. We had seen little men artificially held up in high places, and great men artificially held down in low places, and our own justice loving hearts abhorred this violence to human nature. Therefore, we decreed that every man should thenceforth have equal liberty to find his own level. . . . Let the best man win! That is America's word. That is true democracy." Little is made of birth or of formal education. The Virginian was of good stock, but so was Nate Buckner, who went completely bad. The Virginian was not educated. His verdict on reading *Kenilworth*, lent him by the schoolmistress, was characteristic: "Right fine story. That Queen Elizabeth must cert'nly been a competent woman." What mattered was not his grammar, or his family, but that he was a man of action. He read *Kenilworth* on a trip to Chicago with two ten-car trains of cattle; he got the cattle safely there, and when Trampas lied to instigate mutiny, the Virginian lied with even greater abandon, intent only on bringing the crew safely back. The Virginian was always equal to the occasion—the only kind of equality Wister or the country at large, in actual practice, recognized. (pp. 191-93)

*Ralph Philip Boas and Katherine Burton, "Romance and 'The Strenuous Life' (1895-1914)," in their So-*cial Backgrounds of American Literature, *Little, Brown, and Company, 1933, pp. 179-217.**

MODY C. BOATRIGHT (essay date 1951)

[*Boatright was an American folklorist and critic whose works documented the folklore, history, and legends of America, particularly of Texas and the Southwest. In the following excerpt, Boatright discusses the artistic, personal, and political attitudes that contributed to Wister's depiction of the cowboy as an archetypal American hero.*]

One reason why the cowboy is a popular hero is that historically he possesses the qualities of which folk heroes are made. These qualities are two: prowess and cleverness. It is not necessary that both inhere in the same individual, but I know of no hero in any culture who has not exhibited at least one of them. Prowess, when accompanied by the virtues of bravery, skill, and loyalty, is a romantic ideal, aristocratic in its indifference to material gain, and, incidentally, accessible only to those who have economic security or are indifferent to it. An admiration for prowess thus qualified is an evidence of idealism. Cleverness is the defense of the weak against the strong, the practical against the ideal. It is the middle class's weapon against the aristocracy, the slave's weapon against his master. It is realistic and often cynical. In the folklore of the United States prowess is associated with the South, cleverness with the North.

The cowboy in the time of the open range and the overland drive exhibited both these traits. (p. 157)

But it was not until the heroic age of the cattle industry had closed that the cowboy emerged as a national folk hero. For qualities alone do not create folk heroes. Essential also is a troubadour, or perhaps a number of troubadours. Their function is not merely to publicize the hero. More importantly it is to develop myths about him and to assimilate these myths to the archetypical myths of the culture. A myth cannot flourish without a congenial climate of opinion. In contemporary civilization the troubadours are historians, biographers, journalists, novelists, script writers. (p. 158)

Owen Wister was not the first troubadour of the cowboy, but he was the first to get a national hearing and to make his heroes acceptable to gentility. When Wister's first western story appeared in 1891, Charlie Siringo's realistic biography was being ignored in literary circles. Several dime novelists had discovered the cowboy, but had referred him to a waning mythology. To some, because he was far away from the corrupting influences of civilization and close to nature, he was innocent and good. To some, he was the contemporary knight-errant, wandering through the cattle kingdom righting wrongs with no thought of material reward. Others believed that men removed from the refinements of urban life and the restraints of home life and religion necessarily degenerated. To them the cowboy was essentially a barbarian whose only recreations were physical violence and drunkenness.

Wister attempted a synthesis of all these concepts, throwing the chief emphasis upon chivalry. His cowboys are neither Arcadian innocents nor drunken rowdies. They are natural gentlemen. Looking on the scene of the Medicine Bow saloon, he is moved to write:

> Saving Trampas, there was scarce a face among them that had not in it something very likable. Here were lusty horsemen ridden from the heat of the sun, and the wet of the storm, to divert themselves awhile. Youth untamed sat here for an idle moment, spending easily its hard-earned wages. City saloons rose into my vision, and I instantly preferred this Rocky Mountain place. More of death it undoubtedly saw, but less of vice, than did its New York equivalents. And death is a thing much cleaner than vice. Moreover, it was by no means vice that was written upon these wild and manly faces. Even where baseness was visible, baseness was not upper-

Specimen Jones by Frederic Remington.

most. Daring, laughter, endurance—these were what I saw upon the countenances of the cowboys. . . . In their flesh our natural passions ran tumultuous; but often in their spirit sat hidden a true nobility, and often beneath its unexpected shining their figures took on heroic stature.

Even the weak-minded and weak-willed Shorty is not without a touch of nobility: he loves horses. Aside from Trampas, the only Wisterian cowboy without some such touch is Hank in **"Hank's Woman."** "The creature we call a *gentleman,*" Wister observes, "lies deep in the hearts of thousands that are born without the chance to master the outward graces of the type."

But the outward graces are important, and before Wister's cowboys can enter genteel society, they must acquire them. Even the Virginian must undergo a course in self-improvement—by reading Shakespeare and other literary classics—before he is a fit husband for Mollie Wood. And having observed the clothing of Judge Henry's eastern guests, he reaches Bennington properly attired.

The creature that we call a gentleman is above all chivalrous, and in Wister's cowboys is the chivalry of the aristocratic South modified by the West. Good women are not to be mentioned in levity. Public opinion supports the Virginian when he demands that Trampas rise up on his hind legs and admit that he

has lied about Mollie Wood. A gentleman does not boast of his exploits with women not so good. The Virginian's relations with the widow of Medicine Bow are to be inferred from circumstantial evidence, not from anything he has said.

But more than gallantry, Wister emphasized the code of honor. After Trampas had threatened to kill the Virginian if he did not leave town by sundown, the mayor offered to put Trampas in the calaboose until the Virginian married and left town, and Lin McLean and Honey Wiggin, feeling that the code might be suspended in view of the extraordinary circumstances, offered to "take this thing off your hands." But of course it could not be. "It had come to that point where there was no way out, save the ancient, eternal way between man and man. It is only the great mediocrity that goes to law in these personal matters."

In spite of a good number of shootings, stabbings, and lynchings, physical violence is not abundant in Wister's works. His cowboys triumph by cleverness more often than by force. The Virginian outwits Trampas at every turn until the final challenge to death. In a typical Wister short story, Scipio LeMoyne recovers the payroll by giving the robber misleading directions concerning a short route to the village. His cowboys are also tricksters for fun. The Virginian got the drummer's bed by pretending that he had fits, and he got rid of the Reverend MacBride by keeping him up all night on the pretense that he was about to be converted to the preacher's religion.

In Wister's cowboys, then, we have both prowess and cleverness. But more important, the Virginian exemplifies the American version of the myth of the faithful apprentice, the Horatio Alger story. Poor and obscurely born, he goes into the world—the West—to seek his fortune. He wanders from Texas to Montana and eventually settles down as a cowhand on the Sunk Creek Ranch in Wyoming. He serves his employer faithfully, never hesitating to risk life or limb, never complaining about injustices done him, but determined to make his master see his worth. He makes his own decisions and accepts the consequences of them. When duty demands, he can hang his own friend. There is no boss's daughter to reward him with; but Mollie Wood has all the qualifications except the fortune, and that is taken care of by a partnership in the firm, which under his management prospers when other ranches are going broke. But just in case drought or snows or adverse markets or cow thieves, or any act of God or man, should interfere with the profits of the ranch, a deposit of coal is found on the Virginian's land. This assures his ability to support Mollie in the style to which she would have been accustomed if the mills hadn't failed.

But Wister went much farther in making the cowboy a suitable hero for an industrial society.

Before Wister entered Harvard, the Great American Dream, the dream of a nation without great extremes of wealth and poverty, a nation in which all men might enjoy a comfortable living, had been shattered by sectionalism, civil war, and the rise of a socially irresponsible plutocracy. In the light of plain fact, the myths that had sustained unregulated business enterprise melted away. (pp. 158-60)

Clearly, a new mythology was needed. It came as soon as the leaders of American opinion had time to turn from war to peace. Its chief prophet was Herbert Spencer, who, even before the publication of *The Origin of Species*, made a travesty of Darwin's biology by applying it to society and arriving at the conclusion that the rich deserved to be rich and the poor deserved to be poor.... William Graham Sumner, Spencer's leading American disciple in the field of social theory, insisted that "poverty belongs to the struggle for existence" into which we are all born, and cannot be alleviated by social action. "Let every man be sober, industrious, prudent, and wise, and bring up his children to be so likewise, and poverty will be abolished in a few generations." It is not clear how the general diffusion of these qualities would lessen the intensity of the economic struggle or reduce the number of casualties, for Sumner could not conceive of a time when the contestants would be equal.... Theodore Roosevelt applied the theory of evolution to history in his *The Winning of the West;* Wister exemplified it in his western fiction. Indeed, a weighty element in his admiration for the culture of the cattle country was his belief that it permitted the law of natural selection to operate freely. The Virginian's comment on Shorty, who did not survive, is pertinent.

> Now back East you can be middling and get along. But if you go to try a thing on in this Western country, you've got to do it *well*. You've got to deal cyards *well;* you've got to steal *well;* and if you claim to be quick with your gun, you must be quick, for you're a public temptation, and some man will not resist trying to prove he is the quicker. You must break all the Commandments *well* in this Western country, and Shorty should have stayed in Brooklyn....

And in a passage that Spencer or Sumner might have written, Wister declares:

> All America is divided into two classes,—the quality and the equality. The latter will always recognize the former when mistaken for it. Both will be with us until our women bear nothing but kings.
>
> It was through the Declaration of Independence that we Americans acknowledged the *eternal inequality* of man. For by it we abolished a cut-and-dried aristocracy. We had seen little men artificially held up in high places, and great men artificially held down in low places, and our own justice-loving hearts abhorred this violence to human nature. Therefore, we decreed that every man would henceforth have equal liberty to find his own level. By this very decree we acknowledged and gave freedom to true aristocracy, saying, "Let the best man win, whoever he is." Let the best man win! That is America's word. That is true democracy. And true democracy and true aristocracy are one and the same thing. If anybody cannot see this, so much the worse for his eyesight.

In Wister's fiction the best man wins, but in fairness to him it should be said victory is not the only evidence of the winner's superiority: it is manifest also in his physical appearance, his bearing and manner, and in his native intelligence.

The businessmen who welcomed the new theory as a weapon against social legislation felt under no compulsion of consistency to refuse the bounty of a friendly government; and Wister apparently saw nothing wrong in the cattlemen's free use of the public domain, nor in the Virginian's homesteading known mineral land.

Wister shared the contempt for the masses inherent in the doctrine of social Darwinism. This contempt is implicit in the passage about the Declaration of Independence and in story after story. In **"Specimen Jones,"** for example, Adams has drawn a six-shooter and is making a young tenderfoot dance. "The fickle audience was with him, of course, for the moment, since he was the upper dog and it was a good show; but one in that room was distinctly against him." This one, Specimen Jones, befriends the youth and turns the crowd against Adams. Wister's exaltation of the hero at the expense of the other characters often interferes with the plausibility of his narrative. To cite one example, only the most naïve reader could believe that young Drake in **"The Jimmyjohn Boss"** actually intimidated the revolting cowhands and brought them to taw. This emphasis on leadership issues from something deeper than literary convention. In actual life, Wister's pathetic search for a leader brought him to the conclusion that Theodore Roosevelt was "the greatest benefactor we people have known since Lincoln."

Wister subscribed wholeheartedly to the myth of Anglo-Saxon racial superiority, which, like laissez faire economics, had found a new sanction in the theory of social evolution. White Americans had always proclaimed the racial inferiority of Indians and Negroes and, after the frontiers met, of Mexicans. Now the doctrine was extended to all races, vaguely confused with nationalities and other cultural groups; and it was boldly proclaimed by Josiah Strong, among others, that the Anglo-Saxon race, because of its innate superiority as manifest in its genius for politics and its moral purity, was destined, under God, to rule the world. Wister approved Jim Crow legislation, and in *Lady Baltimore* attempted to establish the inferiority of the Negro on the basis of physical anthropology. Contemplating three skulls, one of a Caucasian, one of a Negro, and one of an ape, Augustus exclaims,

> Why, in every respect that the African departed from the Caucasian, he departed in the direction of the ape! Here was zoölogy mutely but eloquently telling us why there had blossomed no Confucius, no Moses, no Napoleon, upon that black stem; why no Iliad, no Parthenon, no Sistine Madonna, had ever risen from that tropic mud.

Wister's admiration for Moses did not extend to contemporary Jews. His anti-Semitism is obvious in his treatment of the Jew drummers in *The Virginian* and of the Jewish student in *Philosophy Four*. And in comparing Justices Holmes and Brandeis, he wrote:

> I doubt if any gulf exists more impassable than the one which divides the fundamental processes of a Holmes from those of a Brandeis:— ''East is East and West is West, and never the twain shall meet.'' Holmes descends from the English Common Law, evolved by generations of people who have built themselves the greatest nation in a thousand years; Brandeis, from a noble and ancient race which has . . . failed in all centuries to make a stable nation of itself. *Liberty defined and assured by Law* is a principle as alien to the psychology of that race as it is native with Holmes and his ancestors.

There were Negro cowboys and Mexican cowboys, but they were few in the mountain states; and the appeal this region had for Wister was due in no small measure to the relative absence of foreigners, other than Britishers, there. . . . Wister admits that ''the Mexican was the original cowboy,'' but says that ''the American improved upon him.'' ''Soon he had taken what was good from this small, deceitful alien, including his name, *Vaquero* . . . translated into Cowboy.'' (pp. 160-63)

Wister made his first trip to Wyoming in the summer of 1885, when the cattle business was on the crest of a boom that broke the following winter. By the time Wister got around to writing his first western story six years later, the West he had first known was gone. He never pretended that his stories described the West of the time of their writing: he always maintained that his fiction was historical. While he was writing it, he was sorely beset by three principal fears: the fear of monopoly, the fear of labor unions, and the fear of immigration. Monopolies and unions interfered with the free operation of the law of survival, and immigration threatened the Anglo-Saxon race. . . .

But he had no program for checking them. Socialism, Populism, Free Silver, even the democratic liberalism of Woodrow Wilson, he hated. His social thinking was purely negative, and in his bafflement he turned to the golden age of the cattle West, an age he more created than perceived. It was not a perfect age, he admitted, but it was an uncomplicated one in which relationships were from man to man, and one in which the social myths of America might conceivably work.

There must be popular amusement—release from the tensions of modern life—and the cowboy is a hero with many faces, most of them innocent. But it is not altogether reassuring that in a time of greater complexity and greater insecurity than Wister lived to see, the cowboy with his six-shooter, his simple ethics, and his facility for direct action is our leading folk hero. (p. 163)

> Mody C. Boatright, '' 'The American Myth Rides the Range': Owen Wister's Man on Horseback,'' in Southwest Review, Vol. XXXVI, No. 3, Summer, 1951, pp. 157-63.

MARVIN LEWIS (essay date 1954)

[*Lewis is an American author who developed an interest in western Americana while living in Montana and subsequently did research on little-known writers of western literature. In the following excerpt, Lewis discusses the authoritarianism, puritanism, and belief in castes which inform Wister's cowboy stories and distort his portrayal of western life.*]

The problems raised by Western freedom had been studied by Charles Shinn, Josiah Royce, and Hubert Howe Bancroft in the decades before the publication of *The Virginian*. Charles Shinn enthusiastically wrote about those adventurers who came to California, mined for gold in places where there were no judges, lawyers or laws, and who forged instruments of self-government that settled disputes, maintained order and punished the criminal. For him freedom was realized by camp organization and self-government among the miners. Both Royce and Bancroft saw in the absence of sound political and judicial organization the cause for severe disorder.

Josiah Royce challenged the enthusiasm for a libertarian society, but it was Owen Wister who created in fiction the triumph of authoritarians over the rough libertarians of the West. Wister conceived of the average American in the West, at his best, as a mere boy, a prancing boy agog with mischief and roguishness, though an overwhelming number of portraits are devoted to delineating the character of the ignorant, crass and ignoble members of the canaille. Wister waxed enthusiastic over the moral profundities of a small circle of elect, who came to the West with their right feelings and reforming zeal, always resisting the primeval influence of the roughs, and often conquering and disciplining the canaille.

Wister created two types of persons: one of these types was the hero and heroine who were responsible and truthful representations of the American puritan; the other type was the rough and irresponsible child of the West who needed instruction and discipline. His best people are men of property or their loyal foremen. The way they demonstrate right action is the manner in which they handle menials. The great factor in creating lax discipline in the West, according to Wister, is the wrong notions that arise from the belief in liberty and democracy. The uncertainties engendered in the action of the individual when he is in a state of freedom was what formed his particular notion of democracy. The great traditions in Western America of loose class lines and demarcations, the ever-ready spirit of co-operation among the pioneers of the early days in Wyoming, Montana, Idaho, and Colorado, the idea of giving the next fellow a hand in making good, so often observed by even casual observers, had no significance for him when he thought of the harrowing experience of standing the caprices of the Westerner when he was not under thorough martial discipline. Men of property according to him had to expect trouble when the ''dangerous children'' decide to do as they please.

The difficulties created by the belief in liberty demand reformers who can handle rough and sentimental men. The Virginian and Lin McLean are won over to the side of reform. The Virginian separates himself from his former friends. He becomes the Judge's foreman; and he discovers that there are vast differences between himself and his former friends. No longer is he a mirthful and inattentive cowpuncher but a serious man of business. A complete reformation occurs in his character and he sets out to innovate a few reforms. When those under him think their interests are better served by leaving him, he is prepared to use force to keep the men in the employ of his boss since his boss has need of their services. The triumphs of a handful of autocratic reformers in a country that boasted of its manhood and of the resistance of its men to autocracy, injustice, and inroads on personal liberty and dignity, is one of Wister's recurrent and persistent themes.

A fundamental idea with him is that the objects of reform cannot be achieved unless men are made to yield to force and chicanery. It is true that a small group of men, men who have an instinct for the right, are amenable to peaceful reforms, but the others must be handled with a certain amount of roughness. Force is a real weapon, according to him, that can be effective. This means that reason and argument are ineffective to restore men to what you believe a proper view of things. It means that men must be deprived of their liberty, for they are simply too licentious to possess it. An authority must be established that is willing to assume responsibility for action, unhindered by the expressions and feelings of members of the community. Such an authoritarian is the Virginian. For no more reason than a mere expression of an intent to buy whiskey in a town the Virginian and his crew are leaving, the Virginian throws the man, who is under him, off the train. When the men under him decide to become gold diggers, the Virginian declares that the men must go with him because the Judge, his employer, has so decreed it. When one of his menials, Shorty, tells him that according to his way of thinking, he can make more money doing something else, his first impulse is to kick him out, but he restrains himself and treats the man kindly. Moreover, his employer encourages his progress in conceiving of himself as a knight-at-arms for a feudal baron, who can coerce his serfs whenever he desires. His employer tells the Virginian that when he puts a man in charge, he makes no reservations about the charges. "They're to be always his," he says.

When Owen Wister is preoccupied with discipline among the cowboys in *The Virginian,* "**The Jimmyjohn Boss,**" "**Lin McLean,**" and "**Little Old Scaffold,**" he is the supercharged autocrat. He devoted a story to depicting the maneuvers of a labor foreman in outwitting and disciplining the cowboys. In the story, "**The Jimmyjohn Boss,**" the men ask permission to go to town and their foreman refuses them permission by what Wister calls a "straight bluff." Christmas comes and the foreman gives them a special Christmas dinner. During the dinner a row breaks out and the men destroy the crockery and the furniture. The foreman decides to catch up with the malcontents who have fled and discipline the men because he is responsible for them. When he does find them, all the men prove to be contemptible cowards. They return to the ranch with him and he summarily deports several of the ringleaders to other camps. In his story, "**Little Old Scaffold,**" he reverses the sequence of action and character. The young cowhand becomes an agent for his boss. His boss teaches him the meaning of respect for an employer and what it means to be faithful to an employer's interest. It is necessary that the young hand spy on certain people. At first he refuses, but when his boss retorts that he

will do the spying himself, he blanches with shame and goes about the work of a spy. The methods of these autocrats in thought and action alternate from force to suggestion according to the personality of the victims.

In the story, "**A Pilgrim on the Gila,**" Wister declares: "The unthinking sons of the sagebrush ill-tolerate a thing which stands for discipline, good order, and obedience, and the man who lets another command him they despise." Imbued with an ardor for obedience and discipline, Wister exulted in fictional triumphs of authoritarians over the lawless herd. These fictional triumphs of authoritarians over members of the lawless herd do not tally with the reputation maintained by the Old West for defending justly conceived personal interests. In his story, "**The Jimmyjohn Boss,**" the hero says of the cowpuncher: "Weaken in the face of a straight-bluff, you see, unless they get whiskey courageous." Fancy won over fact in Wister's Western tales. The fact is, Wister admitted in the preface to the *Virginian,* that he valued fiction over fact. He repeated this personal predilection in the volume, *Roosevelt: The Story of a Friendship.* He asked: "But what was fiction doing, fiction, fiction, the only thing that has always outlived fact."

The reputation the Old West maintained for defending personal liberties inspired resistance to encroachments upon individual rights. Recollections of the early days emphasize the independence of the Westerner and his aversion to authority. Among others, Lincoln A. Lang, J. H. Cook, Granville Stuart, E. C. Abbott (Granville Stuart's son-in-law), John James Fox, and those participants whose stories appear in such characteristic collections as John K. Rollinson's *Wyoming Cattle Trails,* have recorded substantial comments on Western life and character. These reminiscences sketch a life that was not only adventurous and romantic but which also evinced traits that are to be found among spirited men. Granville Stuart could not conceive of a master and slave relation in those days. He says, for instance, that "the cowboys were reluctant to obey any law but their own and chafed under restraint." High-spirited men cannot be pushed around as contemptible cowards. E. C. Abbott, who was himself a cowboy, states quite definitely, that "there was never very much bossing done around a cow outfit, but any at all was too much to suit the average cowpuncher." (pp. 147-51)

What sometimes happened when a man overstepped the accustomed bounds of propriety in those days is related by E. C. Abbott. A ferocious frontiersman by the name of Pike had the habit of swearing at people when he became mad. "But after he got among cowpunchers and got to calling them son-of-a-bitch, he got his quietus because they wouldn't stand for being cussed like that. He was shot and killed by 'Kid' Curry in the town of Landusky, about 1895." If they wouldn't stand for an assault upon their personal dignity, what would they have done against an aggravated assault of the Owen Wister variety? Perhaps, Owen Wister exaggerated the triumphs of his authoritarians over the lawless herd.

The stories of Owen Wister are sustained by the idea of caste. Wister was carried away by his belief in caste. In his volume, *Roosevelt: The Story of a Friendship,* he reported the revulsion he felt as he campaigned for votes in "stinking halls amid rank tobacco to dirty niggers and dingy whites." Caste was for him the staff of life; it cropped out on every possible occasion. He concluded his discussion of the differences between Englishmen and Americans with a characteristic comment. "Recent people," he observed, "are apt to be thin-skinned and self-conscious and self-assertive, while those with a thousand years of tradition would have thicker hides and would never feel it necessary to assert themselves." In his earliest stories about the West he could not repress his bias for caste ideas. Lin McLean and the Virginian are caught in the web of caste. Lin is saved from low-caste women by a puritan heroine; the Virginian aspires to gain caste, after which he comes to feel the equal of Molly Wood.

He portrayed Lin McLean as a perfect cad toward women without caste. One of these women, Sabine, protests that she "ain't used to gentlemen taking me out and—well, treating me same as if I was a collie-dog." The author explained that McLean after winning the girl's easy favors, never thought of her again. His ideas about Miss Wood, the schoolmarm from an old Vermont family, are of a purer genera. In his mind she was a lady. The author reserved the deepest contempt for the Sabines and Miss Pecks; and whatever else derived from the great common herd. The physical description of Miss Peck is overwhelming in its lack of chivalrous sentiments toward the weaker sex. Miss Peck possessed "sluggish, inviting eyes," and a figure reminiscent of the larger specimens of California fruit. The effect of Miss Peck's "sluggish, inviting eyes" on McLean's amatory sensibilities, puts him in a mood to marry Miss Peck. When this piece of startling news is disclosed to the author, who is a party to the proceedings, he exclaims: "Marry her! I screeched in dismay. Marry her!" Wister's wrath waxes great as McLean is subdued by Miss Peck. "I felt a rising hate for the ruby-cheeked, large-eyed eating house lady, the biscuit shooter whose influence was dimming this jaunty, irrepressible spirit." After several misadventures with low-caste people, responsibility ripens McLean's spirit.

This ripeness of spirit reveals itself as disgust for the actions and character of his former low-caste companions. He beats Miss Peck when she suggests that he loved her once. He stands by impotently, filled with the greatest disgust, as one of his former companions accidentally falls into the grave dug to receive the coffin containing Miss Peck's remains. As the Virginian gains in caste, he lords it over his former companions. As Lin McLean gains in caste, he is seized by a feeling of revulsion for his former companions. Wister provided the happy opportunities for the Virginian and Lin McLean to gain caste, as he provided situations where the Virginian could act in an arbitrary manner.

Wister was carried away by his severe dislike for people without caste. He contemplated the average Westerner as a member of the great unwashed herd. In a story entitled **"Napoleon Shave-Tail,"** he observed that Augustus Albumblatt came from the Middle West, and what could be expected from a man who hails from a place "where they encounter education too suddenly, and it would take three generations of him to speak clean English."

The idea of equality that existed in the Old West piqued him. He observed that "one man has been as good as another in three places—Paradise before the Fall; the Rocky Mountains before the wire fence; and the Declaration of Independence." Drake, a young foreman set over some cowboys, remarks that they are a "half-breed lot." Wister described these same cowboys as "children," "primitive," and "pagan." In the story, **"Specimen Jones,"** he reported that among the men he met in Arizona, especially those who were bound for the mines, "no man trusted the next man." The "slipshod morals" of the frontier shocked him. The search of these adventurers for fortune he treated as fundamental greed. He related the sordid ambitions of the Westerners to enrich themselves amidst splen-

did opportunities for amassing wealth. He detected among the Westerners an incessant craving for money and an outrageous rapacity. In the tale **"Padre Ignazio,"** the Padre asserts that the American adventurer has no greater ideal than digging for gold.

While the charm of many a Western memoir is found in a zest for freedom and justice, the hand of Wister was engaged in writing fiction which paraded his most cherished caste superiorities. Charles Shinn, in his study of the early California mining camps, had called the legacy left by the California miners the "precious materials" out of which literature would provide "world-wide illumination." Shinn stood at an opposite pole from Wister. For him freedom did not breed licentiousness among the adventurers; he found that freedom was accompanied by justice; he demonstrated that equality demanded justice between man and man; he believed that the absence of caste gave new impetus to intelligence and enterprise.

Bayard Taylor and A. K. McClure, travelers who possessed ample opportunity to observe the miners of the Rocky Mountain West, felt that the free and unconventional life led by these adventurers did not make them bad citizens. (pp. 152-55)

What Bayard Taylor and A. K. McClure saw, during the early mining period in Montana and Colorado, was noted anew by many participants and commentators who arrived in Wyoming and Montana during the late 70's, 80's, and 90's. They agreed that the absence of caste was an important factor in cementing good fellowship and general harmony. Robert Vaughn, in a group of reminiscences of the pioneers of Montana, declared: "Those who settled in a new country, and located in a new settlement will agree with me, as a rule, that everyone was ready to assist another when in his power to do so; no class nor any of the faction element existed: all were happy and attended to their own affairs." John James Fox, another participant in the Wyoming range country of the 80's, declares that democracy was practiced "in its best and purest form," and that daily intercourse was "based on the golden rule, self-control and self-respect, by example."

Puritanism dominated Wister's approach to Western life. As a member of the elect, he disliked aggressiveness on the part of common men. Always aloof and critical, with no need to earn his own way in the world, he stood aside and caricatured the average Westerner from a distance. Even visitors from Britain, some of them with lineages that would have awed Wister, portrayed Western life and character with greater sympathy than did Wister.

The ideas of the early New England Puritan divines seemed to assume a new vigor and importance for Wister. He saw the elect and the damned wherever he went; he provided the opportunity by which ordinary mortals could enter the circle of the elect, and he determined the signs by which the elect and the damned could be known. He vibrated with thoughts of casteocracy and authoritarianism. From the common man he desired implicit obedience, but much indulgence could be shown to the elect when they departed from dictates of common decency.

Through Wister's smoked lenses, much of the spirit and even more of the meaning of the adventure that unfolded in the Old West is lost. In the Old West men and women broke away from all ideas of caste. If they were sometimes guilty of mob puritanism, they avoided creating sharp distinctions and barriers among themselves. As a class they accepted the pioneer spirit that promised equality and independence. Then they indulged in mob puritanism, ignoring the value of life, trampling on the rights of races and individuals weaker than they were, they demonstrated the difficulty involved in rising superior to the puritan complex even in a democratic society.

But Owen Wister had not come even that far. Caught up in the spirit of puritanism, the rights of ordinary folks and the value of life meant very little to him. As a vital part of his puritan outlook, he embraced enthusiastically the idea of rule by the elect. To realize the triumph of the elect in the Old West, he chose the realm of the imagination and feats of fiction to achieve his purpose. (pp. 155-56)

> Marvin Lewis, "Owen Wister: Caste Imprints in Western Letters," in Arizona Quarterly, Vol. 10, No. 2, Summer, 1954, pp. 147-56.

BERNARD DeVOTO (essay date 1955)

[*An editor of the* Saturday Review of Literature *and longtime contributor to* Harper's Magazine, *DeVoto was a highly controversial literary critic and historian. A man whose thought enraged much of America's literary establishment during the 1930s and 1940s, he was frequently motivated by anger at authors he considered ignorant of American life and history. As a critic, he admired mastery of form and psychological subtlety in literature. His own work is characterized by its scholarly thoroughness and vigorous, infectious style. DeVoto was "profoundly interested" in American history and authored several historical works, notably the Pulitzer Prize-winning* Across the Wide Missouri *(1947). In the following excerpt, DeVoto discusses elements of* The Virginian *which he argues make it an unrealistic horse opera rather than the serious portrayal of western life that Wister intended it to be.*]

The Cattle Kingdom, the era of large-scale cattle ranching on the unfenced public range, ended in the late 1880s with the collapse of inflationary financing, the increase of homesteading, the ferocious winter called the Big Freeze, and the enforced adoption of sensible ranch practices. Out in Wyoming a lot of wealthy Eastern, English, and Scottish ranch owners who had been living on capital without realizing it went broke and a lot more were going broke. But an afterglow of the exuberant era lingered on so pleasantly that the survivors could not understand that the world had changed. A portion of Wyoming, Johnson County, had slipped out of their personal control. It was filling up with small ranch owners and even farmers, who were homesteading the public range and sometimes stealing the Gentlemen's cows. Whereas the Gentlemen regarded the public range as theirs and had always had their foremen do the rustling. No convictions could be got in Johnson County, so it seemed a good idea to reverse a historical process with gunfire. A small army, composed of Gentlemen and hired Texas gunmen in about equal numbers, invaded Johnson County, to shoot it up. What got reversed was the army: Johnson County started shooting it up. It was saved in the last hundred feet of film by the U.S. Cavalry—just in time, the Gentlemen's Governor and their two Senators got the President of the United States and the Secretary of War out of bed to order the rescue. This small class conflict, whose surface is funnier than its roots and its sequel, is known in the texts as the Johnson County War. It occurred in 1892; almost every Hero of horse opera has had some connection with it.

Down to about 1880 the West in general and the cattle business in particular were realistically reported by the press. Fashions in journalism changed, however, and the roving correspondent began to find in cows and cowpokes a glamor which up to

then had escaped his attention. He filled *Harper's, Scribner's,* and the *Century* with reports that gallantry was roaming the high plains and that the narrow code of the East would not hold in horizon land. There had arisen a person in a big hat whose grammar would seem deplorable in the drawing-room but who could see right through the drawing-room's shams. This type loved horses, respected good women, and when working at his trade performed heroisms that must evoke powerful admiration in the Eastern breast. He was muscular, he was brave, he told the truth, he stuck to his pardner, he scorned to shoot an unarmed enemy, and if Miss Mary Eleanor Wilkins' New England nun would consent to come West he would make her fruitful, lawfully.

Five years of ecstatic journalism prepared the soil for Owen Wister and he went West in 1885. He gratefully discovered that Wyoming had one's own kind in quantity, Philadelphians, Bostonians, New Yorkers of good clubs, younger sons, and titles. He visited their ranches—one of his earliest hosts was to be the Gentlemen's commanding general in 1892—and frequented their Cheyenne Club. He returned for other summers, shot big game, and got about widely. He met lots of the magazine correspondents' indigenous noblemen and watched them working at their glamorous trade. He met "desperadoes" too and other quaint, startling, and stock characters of the Cattle Kingdom. He listened to their talk. He also listened to the ideas of the Gentlemen. (p. 8)

The Virginian is a novel published in 1902 but put together, with the joints left visible, from short stories he had published in *Harper's* during the 1890s. It was preceded in 1897 by a collection of short stories from the same period, but without the mythological Hero, called *Lin McLean,* which is important only as it shares the attributes of the later book. For in its earlier and its final form *The Virginian* created Western fiction—created the cowboy story, the horse-opera novel, the conventions, the clichés, the values, and the sun god. The cowboy story has seldom produced anything as good; apart from Gene Rhodes, it has not even tried to do anything different.

A fine comic sense informs much of the book. Also, I point out a surprising fact: the Virginian is permitted a casual and assured success in the seduction of women which the form has never since ventured to imitate. (The code holds that the cowboy reverences womanhood.) On the other hand, it is made clear that, though noble by virtue of his residence in Cibola, he has the humility to pattern his clothes, when not in costume, on the tailoring to be seen at the Cheyenne Club and to accept the literary taste of his schoolmarm, who is Miss Wilkins' New England nun. Finally, he has no name. Wister was unconsciously symbolizing the anonymity of the genre he was creating. (p. 9)

The Virginian is The Hero: a cowpoke righting wrongs, doing justice, avenging injury, triumphing over perils, eradicating evil, and shooting people. Shooting bad people. Shooting Johnson County "rustlers"; that is, quite uncultivated persons who have small land-holdings and small herds. He is one of those "good men in the humbler walks of life" who "make this world seem so little evil." But the Old West is fervently democratic and he can rise to equal status with the Gentlemen. As an employee of one of them, he adopts the values of the well-born and cultivates their manners. Miss Mary Stark Wood, of one of those gracious houses on Monument Avenue in Bennington, encourages him to read elevating books and he improves his spelling by himself. It is to be said further that the

Episcopal Bishop of Wyoming admires him—I believe that the see was then a mission and so the Bishop's acceptance of murder as a folkway may be regarded as a compromise necessary to the conversion of the heathen. Having patterned himself on the Gentlemen and executed their justice, the Virginian marries Miss Wood, becomes a ranch owner, acquires coal lands, makes a fortune, and so moves naturally among the Frewens, Gardiners, Careys, Teschemachers, and Warrens.

Till he went to work for Judge Henry the Virginian was a ramblin' cowboy and so, necessarily in the Old West, had shot an unspecified number of men. But he is able to tell Miss Wood's mother that he has "never killed for pleasure or profit" and is not "one of that kind, always preferring peace." Here is the bedrock reason why *The Virginian* and the genre it created were prohibited from being serious fiction. The declaration was true as Wister understood it. Before and during the Johnson County War, and after it too, the Gentlemen both killed and hired killing for profit, but murder in the interest of a master class is not unethical. The declaration sets forth another necessity: The Hero must be a goodie, he must conquer Evil. He acquires his Adversary, and the genre acquires its type villain, in Trampas, to whom in the second chapter he speaks the line that has become immortal, "When you call me that, smile." (pp. 12, 14)

Trampas is a rustler, so eventually The Hero must kill him; another necessity has been established. And the form acquires another device that is little less than universal when Miss Wood saves The Hero's life—after he has been shot by Indians, which is first-rate shooting for Wyoming in the 1890s.

Rustlers are preying on the Gentlemen's herds and must be killed. One of them is, or rather once was, The Hero's best friend, his partner. But The Hero has to help lynch him in protection of the Gentlemen's commercial hegemony. The failure of horse opera to become serious fiction pivots on this necessity and on Judge Henry's explanation of it to Miss Wood. I repeat that Wister tried hard, and he tried hardest here, confronting what is in artistic terms the problem of his novel. He tried honestly and conscientiously to solve it as an artist, but he could not make the grade.

It turns out that in one part of the Old West, or Cibola, small property owners have taken the mechanisms of government away from the Gentlemen. The Gentlemen have no choice but to replace them with murder. Judge Henry tells Miss Wood that murder is all right, it is in accordance with the strictest principles of our republican forms and with the evolution of law in society, when it is done—or in this instance hired—by Gentlemen of a certain economic station. Miss Wood has little difficulty believing him, for she might have been the heroine of "The Great Divide," but The Hero must grapple with an inner conflict. For obeying a major provision of the code requires him to violate a provision that had not previously been understood to be a lesser one. There was no getting away from the fact that Steve, the hanged baddie, had been his partner; it is a bitter thing that property must transcend not only law but friendship too. Still there is an alleviation: Steve dies game. (p. 14)

It was the Old West that supplied the Virginian as Hero with his past, stage properties, mannerisms, and code. It was the art of fiction that set up as the central action of the book—the pursuit and lynching of Steve. But it was the vanishing hegemony of the Gentlemen that provided the evasion and capitulation, Judge Henry's lecture on the place of law in society.

That did it. Wister would not be the West's Tolstoi nor even its unsuitable Thackeray, and the literary form called horse opera had been invented. He went on to give the form its supreme effect.

Having saved The Hero's life and accepted his employer's position on murder as an economic instrument, Miss Mary Stark Wood of the patrician East plights him her troth. . . . The two set off for town, where the Bishop of Wyoming will marry them, but on the way they see Trampas. The Hero must kill the baddie or the baddie will kill him. (The code will not permit him to have the baddie jailed.) A problem remains: what explanation shall he give his bride? As these contrivances are worked out, somewhere along the way motive as a component of human behavior, occasionally present up to now, makes it final exit from horse opera. It has never yet returned.

Meeting the Bishop of Wyoming, The Hero listens to the Christian's advice to run away for at least his wedding night, rejects it, and says good-by, the Bishop murmuring as he leaves, "God bless him! God bless him!" Though Miss Wood has divined what is to come, he tells her and will not yield when she falls on her knees and begs him "For my sake. For my sake." So, "'I have no right to kiss you any more,' he said. And then before his desire could break him down from this he was gone and she was alone."

The Hero's friends make sure that no minor baddie will do the job for Trampas. "Then he walked out into the open, watching." His friends follow at a proper distance, "because it was known that Shorty [an earlier victim of Trampas'] had been shot from behind." Presently, "A wind seemed to blow his sleeve off his arm and he replied to it, and saw Trampas pitch forward.

Wister as a young Philadelphia lawyer.

He saw Trampas raise his arm from the ground and fall again and lie there, this time still. A little smoke was rising from the pistol on the ground, and he looked at his own and saw the smoke flowing upward out of it. 'I expect that's all,' he said aloud.''

That is the first walkdown. In a moment The Hero steps into Miss Wood's arms. She thanks God that he has killed Trampas. And what you see disappearing over the horizon into the mirage of the Old West is an art form that might possibly have given us some true reports on and understanding of one segment of American experience but that is still looking for a serious novelist. And will never find one. (pp. 14, 16)

Bernard DeVoto, ''Birth of an Art,'' in Harper's Magazine, *Vol. 211, No. 1267, December, 1955, pp. 8-9, 12, 14, 16.*

G. EDWARD WHITE (essay date 1968)

[*In the following excerpt, White discusses Wister's perceptions of western life and the ways he distorted reality in* The Virginian *to present an archetypal westerner who embodied the strengths of both western and eastern culture.*]

On July 3, 1885, a tall, pale, dark-eyed young man and two middle-aged women stepped off the Pullman car of a Northern Pacific Railway train into the sun and dust of Omaha, Nebraska. The three were easily recognizable as Easterners: Owen Wister by his loose English flannel shirt, soft cloth hat, tailored coat, and close-fitting trousers; the Misses Maisie and Sophy Irwin by their white gloves, lace, and parasols. (p. 122)

Wister's first day and night in the West served to dramatize the two-pronged character of his eastern heritage, which was to loom large in his subsequent response to the sights and sounds of western America. The Misses Irwin suggested in their presence the teacupped, parasoled, drawing-room portions of the world of Philadelphia, with which, through the person of his mother, Wister was to remain in painfully close contact throughout the whole of his western travels. The Cheyenne Club symbolized the other side of that world—what one historian has called the ''stocks-and-bonds, havana-cigar, mahogany-and-leather side'' of the East that had emerged in Wyoming in the person of the Wyoming Stock Growers Association, a group of powerful cattle companies heavily financed by eastern capital and in some cases, such as that of Teschemacher and deBillier, owned and operated by upper-class Easterners. Wister's eastern background had identified him with both the Misses Irwin and the Cheyenne Club; and the implications of this dual identification were to condition his response to the West.

Wister's first recorded impressions of western life centered around the contrast he saw between the freedom of its nomadic cast and the regimentation of his Philadelphia existence. (pp. 122-23)

The specter of his family ties appears to have had a peculiar effect upon Wister's response to the expansiveness of his new environment. At times his western journals reflect a peevish denunciation of Proper Philadelphia, as in 1891, when he wrote from Yellowstone Park that he looked forward to a winter in the East ''with unmixed dislike . . . there are a few people I care to see and who care to see me, but Philadelphia is not the place I should choose either for my friends or myself if I could help it.'' But more characteristic was his sense that his eastern heritage rendered him somewhat apart from the life and men

he saw about him. No frantic attempts to acclimate himself to western manners and mores are apparent in his journals: far from being eager to obtain a buckskin shirt, as Roosevelt was, Wister, after nine years in the West, had to be persuaded by a cowboy friend to accept a pair of chaps as a gift, because he had ''always been shy of wearing or owning these garments, as being not enough of a frontiersman to be entitled to them.''

In virtually all of Wister's western fiction, which began after his fifth journey to Wyoming in 1891, a tenderfoot narrator serves as both a recounter of various anecdotes and an interpreter of them from a somewhat alien perspective. The use of this persona, who is as much a butt of his own jokes as a chorus to the action, gave Wister a mode of narration with which he felt comfortable, just as he took delight in his acknowledged success at being a ''brilliant listener'' who could remain ''passive in the clutches'' of his colorful native confidants. What authenticity exists in Wister's writings on the West is derived from his ability to observe and reproduce its sights and sounds, not from an immersion in the life itself, as in the case of Remington and, to a lesser degree, of Roosevelt. (p. 125)

Wister's disaffection for certain aspects of his eastern background, symbolized to some extent in his mother's presence, had led him to seek out the wildest and most uncivilized denizens of the West for his acquaintances. . . . To these friendships he had added his connection with their opposite numbers, the men of wealth, power, and prominence who ran the cattle industry and felt the political pulse of the territory. (p. 131)

The two-pronged nature of Wister's Wyoming experience manifested itself in his use of two radically different fictional modes, the ''picaresque'' and the ''heroic.'' Concomitant with the emphasis in his early writings on the picaresque qualities of his fictional protagonists is a fascination with the violent and rustic aspects of the West and a sneering at the false trappings of eastern civilization. In his work in the later 1890s and 1900s, by contrast, Wister tended to view the West not as anticivilized but as precivilized, and to portray his protagonists as precursors to more cultured times, even possessing some smatterings of culture themselves. This distinction is not absolute, nor is there a clear break between the two phases, but an indication of the direction in which Wister moved can be gathered from contrasting his statement to William Dean Howells in 1893 that ''he wanted to do a 'picaresque' novel of the West, as the life there was 'nomadic' and suited to the picaresque style,'' with his contention in the preface to the first edition of *The Virginian,* which appeared in 1902 and contained his most heroic western protagonist, that ''What has become of the horseman, the cowpuncher, the last romantic figure upon our soil. . . . He will never come again. He rides in his historic yesterday.''

Wister's journals of Wyoming provide examples of both these conceptions of the West. In 1885 he called the cowboys a ''queer episode in the history of the country,'' ''purely nomadic,'' and ''without any moral sense whatever,'' and in 1891 he described with fascination ''the mostly blackguards'' he had met, calling one ''a brilliant talker in his vagabond line''; but in 1885 he demonstrated an awareness of the historic qualities of the West by prophesying that ''Western life will slowly make room for Cheyennes, Chicagos, and ultimately inland New Yorks—everything reduced to the same flat prairie-like level of utilitarian civilization, and the ticket will replace the rifle.'' In 1891, on this same theme, he ''petitioned'' to be ''the hand that once and for all chronicled and laid bare the virtues . . . of this extraordinary phase of social progress.''

The fiction of Wister's early years in the West revolves around a combination of the landscape's "wildness" and the lives of a company of men "without any moral sense." Later his feeling that the older West had now become a phase in the history of American civilization was coupled with a rediscovery of some of the attractive features of his life in the East. The result was a curious return to the days of the Cheyenne Club and his cattle baron friends, now seen through the haze of years, and a romanticizing of the life they and their heroic ranch hands led.

The two leading protagonists of Wister's early western fiction are the picaros Specimen Jones and Lin McLean. The first is featured in a collection of stories Wister began for *Harper's* in 1893 and published as **Red Men and White** in 1895, and the second is the subject of an episodic novel which bears his name, written in 1895 and 1896 and published in 1897. Jones is a likable vagabond, "seasoned by the frontier," who has tried a little of everything: "town and country, ranches, saloons, stage-driving, marriage occasionally, and latterly mines." "He had," Wister notes, "exhausted all the important sensations, and did not care much for anything any more. Perfect health and strength kept him from discovering that he was a saddened, drifting man." After six years of wandering through Arizona, Jones and a friend enlisted in the army on an impulse, but Specimen's "frontier personality . . . was scarcely yet disciplined into the military machine of the regulation pattern." During his army tenure Jones manages, among other things, to mistake the general of his troop for a peddler and arrest the governor of his territory to save him from a particularly ticklish legislative struggle. He achieves certain small successes but primarily serves as a humorous foil to more respectable figures. Actually, the Specimen Jones stories are whimsical salutes to the frivolity of a nomad.

If Jones is a drifter, Lin McLean is a will-o'-the-wisp. Lin "came in the country about seventy-eight . . . and rode for the Bordeaux Outfit most a year, and quit." He then "blew in at Cheyenne till he was broke, and worked over on the Platte," "rode for Balaam awhile on Butte Creek," and later "drifted to Green River . . . and was around with a prospecting outfit on Galena Creek by Pitchstone Canyon." A contemporary of Lin's, aware of his habits, once predicted that "he'll wake about noon tomorrow in a dive, without a cent. . . . Then he'll come back on a freight and begin over again."

But although Lin is a perpetual adolescent, a fool for women, and a hopeless vagabond, he possesses qualities of honesty and frankness which serve to contrast him favorably in Wister's mind with certain members of the "city crowd." In **"How Lin McLean Went East,"** which appeared in *Harper's Monthly* in 1893 and was reprinted with slight changes as Chapter 3 of **Lin McLean**, Wister used his picaresque "son of the sagebrush" to expose flaws in the sham civilization of the East and to hold up the virtues of a frontier life.

In the midst of his wanderings Lin had an impulse to return to Swampscott, Massachusetts, his old home, to see his brother Frank and visit his parents' grave. (pp. 131-34)

When Lin inquired about Swampscott, Frank replied that it was a "dead little town"; and when Lin announced his plans to "take a look at the old house," Frank responded, "Oh, that's been pulled down since—I forgot the year they improved that block." Eventually Frank caught sight of one of the members of his club staring at Lin with "diverted amazement on his face," and the strain became too great. "Lin," he blurted out, "while you're running with our crowd, you don't want to wear that style of hat, you know":

> [Lin] stopped dead short, and his hand slid off his brother's shoulder. "You've made it plain," he said evenly, slanting his steady eyes down into Frank's . . . "Run along with your crowd, and I'll not bother yu' more with comin' round and caus' yu' to feel ashamed. . . . I guess there ain't no more to be said, only one thing. If yu' see me around on the street, don't yu' try and talk, for I'd be liable to close your jaw up, and maybe yu'd have more of a job explainin' that to your crowd than you've had makin' me see what kind of a man I've got for a brother."

The next morning Lin took a train for Swampscott, where he noticed that the grave of his parents had been left untended. From there he "blew in" to New York, hoping for some amusement, but left with nothing but "a deep hatred for the crowded, scrambling East." He bought a train ticket for Green River, Wyoming, and after four days, when "civilization was utterly emptied out of the world, and he saw a bunch of cattle, and, galloping among them, his spurred and booted kindred, his manner took on that alertness a horse shows on turning into the home road." (p. 134)

Frank McLean has become so caught up in the trappings of civilization that he has lost the qualities that in Wister's eyes made a man "civilized"—reverence for family ties, sense of tradition, and loyalty to kindred—but Lin exhibits these qualities and senses the selfishness that lies beneath Frank's superficial polish. In this gift for stripping away the veneer of civilization and catching the true gist of a man's nature, Lin, for Wister, is representative of his "spurred and booted kindred." "Celluloid good-fellowship passes for ivory with nine in ten of the city crowd," the erstwhile Philadelphian later wrote, "but not so with the sons of the sagebrush. They live nearer nature, and they know better."

It must have amused Wister to depict the great seriousness with which Frank McLean reacted to his club, the solemn ties he felt toward an association of clerks and bank tellers. To his delight in the unspoiled western wilderness Wister added a certain upper-class condescension toward men of commerce: he reserved some of his harshest prose for the "fetid commercial bores" he saw invading the West. "Every state in the Union seems to spawn them," he wrote in 1891, "and they infest every mile of railroad in operation. . . . The faces, the minds and the talk of these commercials in the Pullman cars are inferior to those in the conductor who takes the tickets and the brakeman who swings the lamp." This is reminiscent of Remington's remarks about the encroachments of industrial America upon the West, and indeed Wister noted after a conversation with Remington in 1893 that the illustrator "used almost the same words that have of late been in my head, that this continent does not hold a nation any longer but is merely a strip of land on which a crowd is struggling for riches."

"I am a thin and despondent man," Wister wrote after meeting Remington, "and every day compel myself to see the bright side of things because I know that the dark side impresses me unduly." If so, Wister was remarkably self-disciplined, for if Remington's "romantic" phase, as evidenced in such works as *John Ermine,* may be said to depict the dark, tragic side of the American West, Wister's writings in the same period emphasized those aspects of the western experience which were brightest for the future of the region and for America. This difference in tone between Remington and Wister can be seen by a comparison of Remington's *Men with the Bark On* with Wister's collection of stories *The Jimmyjohn Boss*, both of which were published in 1900. Though Dean Drake, the hero of *The Jimmyjohn Boss*, is a product of older, wilder times, he has the ability to adapt himself to the oncoming civilization from the East that Remington's protagonists lack. He suggests in his person a possible synthesis of the two regions and points in the direction of Wister's American colossus of Rhodes, the Virginian, who was meant to straddle the gulf between East and West. (pp. 135-36)

Drake has a vision of a more civilized way of life, which accompanies his darker thoughts. "Some day, when I'm old," he says at one point, "I mean to live respectable under my own cabin and vine. Wife and everything." He whistles light opera tunes, understands a smattering of Chinese, and develops a friendship with a New England schoolteacher named Bolles, whose presence symbolizes for Wister the more palatable aspects of eastern civilization, such as mildness, culture, and morality.

Dean Drake is a pivotal figure in the development of Wister's protagonists. More rogue than gentleman, he nevertheless demonstrates an ability to admire a man such as Bolles, who has never lived by his gun. This ability, which enabled Drake to transcend the level of a picaro, is spelled out by another Wister hero two years later: "I used to despise an Eastern man because his clothes were not Western. I was very young then. . . . A Western man is a good thing. And he generally knows that. But he has a heap to learn. And he generally don't know that." This is the Virginian, and the symbolic qualities of that renowned horseman of the plains, can best be seen in terms of the heroic phase of Wister's fiction, representing the resolution in his mind of the quarrels with his heritage that had led him West in the first place. (pp. 136-37)

In January of 1902 the Wisters, accompanied by their three young children, returned to Charleston, South Carolina, where they had honeymooned, and spent the winter and most of the spring there. Wister had most of *The Virginian* still to complete, including the crucial task of weaving previously published short stories into novel form. The effect of his surroundings was unmistakable. . . . Wister had found the "real America" in Wyoming; he now found the "true American tradition" in old Charleston. His task in *The Virginian* was to insure that the two were not incompatible.

In the "heroic" phase of Wister's response to the West his themes are historically oriented and his protagonists romantically portrayed. He departed radically from his previous vow to tell the truth about the West in *The Virginian*, which claimed to "present faithfully Wyoming between 1874 and 1890" but did nothing of the kind. One critic maintains that "it is strange that Wister could have called his *Virginian* an historical novel of the cattle-country when there is not one scene set on the range among the cattle, and when the cowboys seem throughout to spend their days in playful pranks, in love-making, in thief-hunting, in anything except work." Two others, in the course of their description of cowboy life in the Old West, have implied that *The Virginian* is not representative of Wyoming at any time [see the excerpt by Douglas Branch dated 1926].

The courtship of Molly Wood and the Virginian, around which most of Wister's novel revolves, is highly contrived. Few women at all lived in the Wild West, and cowboys on ranges almost never saw them. The social life of cowpunchers consisted for the most part of blowouts in saloons, not of quiet walks in peaceful valleys, but the Virginian (a ranch foreman) has uncommon amounts of free time and is able to court Molly in a slow and leisurely fashion. Although in 1895 Wister had said of cowboys, "War they made in plenty, but not love; for the woman they saw was not the woman a man can take into his heart," by 1902 "truth" had apparently become a secondary concern. The Wisters' return to Charleston, the scene of their honeymoon, had doubtless brought back a whole flood of romantic memories, and the Virginian's gentle initiation of Molly Wood (Mrs. Wister was also called Molly) into the rites of marriage was a reenactment of scenes dear to Wister's heart. The Victorian courtship of the cowpuncher and his sweetheart also awakened in Wister a sense of his own background: he wrote his mother that he thought it "essential that the hero should meet the Great Aunt."

Wister's most significant departure from "reality" was the deliberate idealization of his hero. In the first western story he wrote, **"Hank's Woman,"** published in *Harper's Monthly* in 1892, the Virginian is portrayed as a standard picaresque figure with a certain indefinable presence. He "indulges himself in several months' drifting" and states that he is not ready for "any such thing as a fam'ly yet. . . . Not till I can't help it." Although the Virginian "was unfathomable," little is made of the strong and silent aspects of his personality; in Wister's early stories he remains a picaro. By 1902, however, Wister had apparently lost all recollection of his earlier model, for the Virginian now advances resolutely toward his goals, has all the qualities of a gentleman, and eagerly learns Shakespeare, Jane Austen, Browning, and Thackeray from his sweetheart Molly Wood.

According to Mody Boatright [see excerpt dated 1951], the Virginian is a "folk hero," in that he possesses "prowess and cleverness," qualities which are deemed "universally heroic" in the American imagination. "Prowess, when accompanied by the virtues of bravery, skill and loyalty, is a romantic ideal, aristocratic in its indifference to material gain, and accessible only to those who have economic security or are indifferent to it." "Cleverness," on the other hand, "is the middle classes' weapon against the aristocracy, realistic and often cynical." These qualities can be seen in many American literary heroes of the nineteenth and twentieth centuries—Leatherstocking, Huck Finn, Jay Gatsby, and Holden Caulfield, for example—but a more illuminating discussion of heroism in *The Virginian*, for present purposes, would center on the cowboy protagonist's role as a cultural hero. The term "cultural" incorporates social change, whereas "folk" implies an idealized native consensus of a persistent nature. Americans have had different success models at different times in their history, and their cultural heroes are products of trends and changes in the social and economic structure of the nation. The interaction between the idealized traits of Wister's horseman of the plains and the aspirations of Americans at the close of the nineteenth century is particularly significant.

The Virginian's "manliness" is a quality to which a 1902 reader could warmly respond. It has been suggested that Roosevelt and Remington, as well as Wister, were attracted to the masculine aspects of the West for personal reasons, but the individual needs of each were strongly related to tensions within American culture at the last quarter of the nineteenth century. The triumph of industrial enterprise paradoxically produced a heightened consciousness of women as delicate flowers and men as their defenders against the evils of a strange new world, resulting in a nationwide assertion of masculinity. The Virginian's manliness is never in question: a shade over six feet, he is referred to as a "giant," and although he is gentle and polite to women, they are quick to sense his power. Molly Wood eventually abandons her civilized heritage in Vermont to marry the Virginian, because, as she confides to Grandmother Stark, "I wanted a man who was a man."

Wister's contemporaries must also have applauded the manner in which the Virginian rose from humble origins to become a captain of industry. Part of the success ethic of the post-Civil-War generation was self-help, and as a young man the Virginian "found out what he could do, and settled down and did it." He "put his savings in banks," because he "had to work right hard gathering them in," and he chose not to live off his earnings in the cattle bonanza but bought land as an insurance for the future. At the novel's close the ex-dirt farmer is "an important man, with a strong grip on many various enterprises." The Virginian's adaptability to industrialization, a far cry from Remington's feeling that cowboys and the industrial West are incompatible, is one indication of Wister's strong desire to integrate the Old West and the new order of the East in the person of his horseman of the plains. As the Virginian articulates the doctrines he practices, he extends his self-help philosophy to a larger view of life. "It may be," he reflects, "that them whose pleasure brings yu' into this world owes yu' a living. But that don't make the world responsible. The world did not beget you. I reckon man helps them that helps themselves." In a bet, in a card game, in "all horse transactions and other matters of similar business," the same rule applies: "a man must take care of himself." Competition is the essence, and the best man wins.

It might seem that the Virginian holds up a kind of inverse morality as the only expedient in a society where an honest man is all the law one can find for five hundred miles—he who lives best lives roughest, meanest, and trickiest—but in actuality another characteristic which must have endeared him to his readers was his combining of an acute awareness of blackguardism with a gentlemanly response to it. On one occasion he says to the outlaw Trampas, "We ain't a Christian outfit a little bit, and maybe we have most forgotten what decency feels like. But I reckon we haven't *plumb* forgot what it means," and he then forces Trampas to withdraw his off-color remarks about the character of Molly Wood ("Stand on your laigs, you pole-cat, and say you're a liar!"). In a rough world of rough men the hero is distinguished by his graciousness, civility, and reserve. The narrator of *The Virginian* finds that "here in flesh and blood was a truth which I had long believed in words, but never met before. The creature we call a *gentleman* lies deep in the hearts of thousands that are born without a chance to master the outward graces of the type."

Late nineteenth-century Americans revered the "rugged individualist," but matters of decorum were highly prized, even among the shadiest entrepreneurs. "The inner-directed business and banking entrepreneurs of this buccaneering age were only too eager to conform to the strict Victorian code of manners when they entered the drawing-rooms of society," notes one student of the business community. It was as if the world of manners formed a counterweight against the world of business, reassuring the businessman that virtue still existed.

Though he has come into contact with a good many of the "dark places in life," the Virginian is careful not to reveal them. Even in delirium, he addresses Molly as "Miss Wood,"

and "ma'am," and his ravings, Wister notes, "did not run into intimate, coarse matters." Unlike some of his cronies, he does not boast of his sexual exploits, and in matters of dress he is so careful that when Molly brings him to Vermont to meet her family, "Bennington was disappointed. To see get out of the train merely a tall man with a usual straw hat, a Scotch homespun suit of a rather better cut than most in Bennington—this was dull." "I have made one discovery," Molly says to her hero. "You are fonder of good clothes than I am."

Finally, the Virginian is a "good American." Impressed with their technological and financial triumphs yet annoyed by crowded conditions in their cities and an influx of immigrants from southern and eastern Europe, Americans in the nineties were aggressive patriots whose zeal sometimes surpassed their tolerance. The heredity and veterans' societies that grew by leaps and bounds in this period often marked their patriotism with an air of exclusiveness and nativism. The Virginian, for one, is not above an occasional nativist or racist salvo: he sings a song deriding the intelligence of Negroes ("I never went to college, but I'se come mighty nigh—I peeked through de door as I went by"); calls Germans "Dutchmen," Jews "Hebes," and doesn't consider Indians humans. For the most part, however, his Americanness is reflected in the breadth of his experience and the range of his background. Born in Virginia, at twenty-four he had seen Arkansas, Texas, New Mexico, Arizona, California, Oregon, Idaho, Montana, and Wyoming. By twenty-nine he has been East and confessed that a western man has a heap to learn, and his "various enterprises" will apparently increase his prestige and widen his scope. Wister must have especially cherished this quality, which symbolized his attempt to combine the best features of nature and civilization, rugged individualism and gentlemanliness, past and present, and West and East into a more perfect whole. He suggests in the marriage of Molly and the Virginian that the "true American" traditions of the eastern seaboard will constantly be revitalized as they pass westward, creating an even stronger and more unified nation. (pp. 135-43)

> *G. Edward White, "Wister's West: The Cowboy as Cultural Hero," in* The Eastern Establishment and the Western Experience: The West of Frederic Remington, Theodore Roosevelt, and Owen Wister, *Yale University Press, 1968, pp. 122-43.*

LESLIE A. FIEDLER (essay date 1968)

[*Fiedler is a controversial and provocative American critic. Emphasizing the psychological, sociological, and ethical context of works, he often views literature as the mirror of a society's consciousness. Similarly, he believes that the conventions and values of a society are powerful determinants of the direction taken by its authors' works. The most notable instance of Fiedler's critical stance is his reading of American literature, and therefore American society, as an infantile flight from "adult heterosexual love." This idea is developed in his most important work,* Love and Death in the American Novel *(1960), along with the theory that American literature is essentially an extension of the Gothic novel. Although Fiedler has been criticized for what are considered eccentric pronouncements on literature, he is also highly valued for his adventuresome and eclectic approach, which complements the predominantly academic tenor of contemporary criticism. In the following excerpt, Fiedler argues that Wister's romantic depiction of cowboys as western knights who lived by a "heroic" code of conduct is actually in the tradition of the racist, anti-intellectual, violent fiction of the post-Reconstruction South.*]

[Owen Wister's **The Virginian** was] once taught in high school classrooms side by side with its English prototype, *Ivanhoe*, since it asks to be accepted as *belles-lettres* rather than mere entertainment, like those shabby dime novels which fill the decades between it and the *Leatherstocking Tales*. But the very title of Wister's novel, completed appropriately enough in Charleston, South Carolina, in 1902, though set in Wyoming "between 1874 and 1890," declares the values of his hero—the so-called Code of the West—the very same which set in motion those other White Knights of the time, the Ku Klux Klan. And just as apologists for the latter present them as defending their women against the broken promises of politicians in the Northeast and the savage lust of Black Men at home, so Wister speaks of "the horseman, the cow-puncher, the last romantic figure upon our soil" as upholding standards of behavior long lapsed, not only for the renegade on the Western frontier, but for the overcivilized in the polite centers of the North and East. "If he gave his word, he kept it; Wall Street would have found him behind the times. Nor did he talk lewdly to women; Newport would have found him old-fashioned."

But behind the talk of honesty and chivalry, it is personal violence, taking the law into one's own hands, for which **The Virginian**—along with all of its recastings and imitations right down to *High Noon*—apologizes. The duel and the lynching represent its notions of honor and glory; and images of these have occupied the center of the genteel or *kitsch* Western ever since, in pulp magazines, in hardcover or paperback books, on radio, TV, or in the movies: the posse riding in a cloud of dust toward the moment of the kill, or the defender of the good tottering on his high heels down some dusty, abandoned street between false storefronts, his hand hovering just above the butt of his six-shooter. It hardly matters, band of vigilantes against band of outlaws or single champion against single villain—the meaning is the same: a plea for extra-legal violence as the sole bastion of true justice in a world where authority is corrupt and savagery ever ready to explode. And it is, perhaps, quite as much a product of the reaction against Reconstruction as those novels of Thomas Dixon, Jr., *The Leopard's Spots* and *The Clansman*, from which D. W. Griffith made *The Birth of a Nation*. Like Dixon, at any rate, Wister seems in retrospect only a preparation for films to follow—a storehouse of fantasies to be indulged in the communal loneliness of the darkened movie palace, after the Old West like the Old South was good and dead.

And just as Dixon's fictions were an imaginative, almost a mythological, justification for the oppression of the Negro, so those of Wister and his imitators were, though less explicitly, an analogous justification for the extermination of the Indian. The gunning down or mass pursuit of the man outside the law, the renegade, the White man turned "savage," is an analogue for genocide: the destruction of those savages to whom the West first belonged, and who insisted on remaining outside the White Man's law and order. (pp. 138-39)

[The] Redskins are present always by implication at least—even in the shootdown, traditionally reserved for WASPS only, when the paleface in a White Hat, beating the paleface in a Black Hat to the draw, symbolically kills the wild Indian in us all.

Such scenes aspire to the status of myth; but they are typically presented to us in a historic rather than mythic setting, taken out of the timeless archaic world which Fenimore Cooper was still able to imagine, and put into a just-vanished past, more appropriate to easy nostalgia than poetry. *When men were men and women liked it,* the customary regretful phrase goes, ambiguously suggesting that the wish-dream behind **The Virginian** could belong either to castrated man in an industrialized, urbanized world, or to the women who collaborated with the machines in their castration—and then lived to regret it. But such historicizing, sentimentalizing, and Southernizing, such a full-scale Sir Walter Scottification of the West, could not occur until the myth of the West had become a source of nostalgia rather than hope—a way of defining the Other Place rather than This Place, where we once were rather than where we go from here. (p. 140)

At that point, no one in the East seemed any longer to remember, and no one in the actual West (just beginning to contemplate tourism as a major industry) cared to remind them, that it was gunslingers and pimps, habitual failures and refugees from law and order, as well as certain dogged pursuers of a dream, who had actually made the West—not Ivanhoes in chaps, desexed and odorless, though still lethal to cross and quick on the draw. Careful men, if violent ones, real Westerners preferred to gun their enemies down with a shotgun from behind some convenient shelter; but in fantasy they walk toward each other forever, face to face, down sun-bright streets—ready for the showdown, which is to say, the last form of chivalric duel. No wonder the myth had to be immunized against reality, more and more narrowly localized in time and space—to keep anyone from making comparisons with a world he knew at first hand.

The decade just after the Civil War becomes the mythological time, the "Far West"—Montana, Wyoming, Texas, Nevada, etc.—the mythological place in which Indians are subdued, or Mormons (anti-Mormonism being the anti-Semitism of the West), or outlaws; though the essential war is against women who, sustained by misguided ministers or spineless dandies from the East, advocate not only charity and forgiveness, but also compliance with the Law, which to the writer of Westerns seems typically a mere camouflage for villainy. Or, perhaps, Christianity is the real, the final enemy; since in the fable first worked out in **The Virginian,** religious pacifism is invariably portrayed as capitulating to lynch law and the duel. And how could it be otherwise, since the spokesman for pacifism is always a woman; and readers, whatever their sex, of that transitional Western, which dominates the scene between the time of Cooper and the Dime Novel and that of the emergence of the New Western, would not have tolerated a defeat of the male. (p. 141)

> *Leslie A. Fiedler, "The Failure of the Waking Dream," in his* The Return of the Vanishing American, *Stein and Day, Publishers, 1968, pp. 120-49.**

NEAL LAMBERT (essay date 1969)

[*In the following excerpt, Lambert discusses the story "Hank's Woman" as an example of Wister's ambivalent portrayal of the conflict between genteel eastern civilization and the coarse, violent life of the West.*]

Owen Wister's avowed purpose for writing about the West was to save "the sagebrush and all that it signified" for future generations. (p. 39)

What Wister was trying for himself in . . . ["**Hank's Woman**"] was not just the preservation of the cowboy. Indeed had this been his motive, he might better have turned to history. Wister wanted to preserve something more than just the historical fact:

he wanted to save that human part of the Western experience which is the special province of literature.

Wister tried to explain as much to Henry Mills Alden when he sent **"Hank's Woman"** and **"How Lin McLean Went East"** to Harper's. In the draft of that initial cover letter, even the crossed out words become significant:

> This life I am trying to write about [doesn't] seem to me to have been treated in fiction so far—seriously at least. The cattle era in Wyoming is nearly over, and in the main unchronicled, though its brief existence created a life *permeated with eccentricity, brutality, and pathos* [sic] not only of most vivid local color, but of singular moral interest. Its influence upon the characters of all grades of men—from Harvard graduates to the vagrants from the slums has been potent [?] and very special. I should say the salient thing it did was to produce in educated and uneducated alike more moral volatility than was ever set loose before.

We can see from Wister's letter that "saving the sagebrush" did not mean a simple photographic catalogue of "the way the wild West really was," nor did it mean that adventure and romance would adequately render the Western experience. What Wister did sense was that only fiction could treat the subjective, yet fundamental human problems involved in man's situation in the West. History could not do it and remain, strictly speaking, history. Only fiction could permanently fix the West that Wister knew with all that it suggested about us as human beings. As Wister himself said of the West, "it is quite worthy of Tolstoi, or George Eliot, or Dickens. Thackeray wouldn't do."

But recognizing the possibilities for significant literature is one thing; actually writing that literature is something else. And the challenge that Wister accepted . . . was a difficult one. In the first place, he was working almost without literary precedent. The dime novels and pulp magazines were already popularizing the West, but in 1892 few writers had made any serious attempts to explore the real significance of the Western experience. No one yet had shown both the insight and the literary sophistication necessary to do the job. Indeed the problems Wister faced in writing about the horsemen of the plains were not unlike the problems James Fenimore Cooper faced in writing about the hunter and the forest. As Roy Harvey Pearce said of the Leatherstocking tales,

> The problem was to make the integral relationship between frontier and nonfrontier—a potentially tragic relationship between the known and the unknown, between the complex and the simple, between the heroic-savage and the civilized—artistically realizable. The problem was enormously difficult and its difficulty was increased because received literary forms and methods gave no direct indication of how it was to be solved. That solution required an originally creative artist—a pioneer, so to speak.

The first difficulty, then, was one of form and method. But, as Pearce suggests in this passage, this was only a further complication of a much more difficult and important artistic problem: the relationship between the frontier and the nonfrontier.

Owen Wister was an Easterner, a Philadelphian, the product of high Victorian society. And yet, he honestly loved much of the West. In short, he found himself attracted by two opposite ways of life. And whatever he wrote about the West had to take into account first of all this dual commitment. But the commitment itself was further complicated by elements in both Eastern society and Western life which repelled the sensitive writer. Thus, in trying to be the Tolstoi, Eliot or Dickens of the West, Wister tended to shape his materials around two opposite notions: the frontier and civilization. That is, the West and all it stood for in terms of freedom, simplicity, and spontaneity—grossness, cruelty, and violence was set next to the East and all it stood for in terms of gentility, veneer, and stereotype—refinement, taste, and tradition. As Wister says in that first cover letter, "This life of the Wilderness, brought into collision with the latest products of civilization, . . . is another eccentric shade in our Chameleon West." Those "latest products of civilization" were often men like Wister himself, thoroughly Eastern, civilized, refined, and genteel. Such "latest products" come into direct confrontation with a different, and in many ways an antithetical, culture—one in which life could be coarse and crude, but at the same time free, honest, and simple.

This is the formative principle of Wister's work. It is this antithesis in his material and his own ambivalence toward the values involved that led him to present the West as he did. In doing so, he wrote stories which are not only interesting examples of cultural conflict, but are also searching explorations of serious human problems, for the uncertainty about meanings and values reflected in these stories proved in the long run to be not merely a frontier uncertainty, but a human uncertainty.

All this can be better understood by seeing how Wister worked these problems out in that first story, **"Hank's Woman."** In the characters of Hank, the mean little miner; of Willomene, his genteel and gross bride; and especially of Lin McLean, the teller of this "traveler's tale," Wister sets up and begins to explore this antithesis in fiction.

The frame for the tale of **"Hank's Woman"** is an idyllic fishing scene in the Teton basin. The hunting, fishing, and camping are laced through with comment by the actual narrator (Wister himself) and the "traveler" who tells the tale proper, a cowboy by the name of Lin McLean. The topic of their conversation is the West's peculiar way of "bein' too quick." Or as Lin succinctly says, "as fer second thoughts, . . . animals in this country has em' more'n men do." Lin illustrates just how hasty people can be in the West by recounting the pathetic story of Willomene, a stranded lady's maid from Austria; and Hank, the frontiersman whom she married on one week's acquaintance.

Lin's own narrative gets under way as he tells how he, Hank, and Honey Wiggin "joined a prospectin' outfit when we was through seein' the Park, and Hank and me come into the Springs after grub from Galena Creek, where camp was." While "layin' around" a few days, Hank and Lin watch a "big wide-faced woman, thick all through . . . with lots of yaller hair," get cashiered and abandoned by her genteel mistress because of some lost luggage keys. The general scarcity of available women and the size of Willomene's last wages make her more than a little attractive to Hank, and in a short time, as Lin says, "he'd got stuck on her." After a couple of days of courting, Hank and Willomene go to Livingston and are married. "Hank was that pleased with himself," Lin says, "he gave Willomene a weddin'-present with the balance of his cash, spendin' his last nickel on buyin' her a red-tailed parrot.''

After a week's honeymoon on Willomene's money, Hank starts with her for the Galena camp. ''She'd never slep' out before,'' Lin reports, ''and she'd never been on a horse, neither, and near rolled off down into Little Death Canyon comin' up by the cut-off trail.'' By the time the newly-weds reach the mining camp, the conflict between Hank and Willomene is full blown:

> Yu'd ought to have seen them two pull into our camp. Yu'd sure never figured it were a weddin' trip. He was leadin', but skewed around in his saddle to jaw back at Willomene fer ridin' so poorly. . . . She was settin' straddeways like a mountain, and between him and her went the three pack animals, plumb played out, and the flour—they had two hundred pounds—tilted over downwards, with the red-tailed parrot a-hollerin' landslides in his cage tied on top.

In the days that follow, this conflict between Hank and his woman continues to grow until it finally focuses at the point of Willomene's crucifix, with Hank threatening violence if Willomene doesn't abandon her ''idol'' and her devotions.

Lin then tells how he and the rest of the camp go out for three days after meat, leaving Hank and his woman. When the hunters return, Hank and Willomene are gone. Searching for the missing pair, the hunters find a bullet hole in Willomene's crucifix, a bloody ax, and Willomene's trail ''heavy-like in the gravel.'' This leads Lin and his companions back to Little Death Canyon, where they find Hank. ''He was kind of leanin' queer over the edge of the canyon, and we run up to him. He was stiff and stark, and caught in the roots of a dead tree, and the one arm wheeled around like a scarecrow, pointin' and a big cut in his skull.'' And as they peer into the sulphurous depths of the canyon, they see the girl. As Lin says,

> Down there in the bottom, tumbled all in a heap, was Willomene. . . . When she was on that crumble stuff there she'd slipped. Hank got hooked in the tree root, and down she'd gone 'stead of him, with him stuck on top pointin' at her exactly like if he'd been sayin', ''I have yer' beat after all.''

Such, then, is the outline of Lin McLean's tale and the first story that Owen Wister wrote about the West.

That the essential conflict of the tale is between civilized and frontier culture would seem obvious. On the one hand the Westerners, Lin, Hank, Honey, and Chalkeye, represent a full gamut of frontier values both positive and negative. On the other hand, the Eastern dudes and Willomene either do not recognize or cannot adjust themselves to the basic differences between civilized and non-civilized cultures. The situation is, of course, full with both serious and comic possibilities. And Wister utilizes both, especially when he comes to the title character, Willomene. But while Wister could not resist the temptation of traditional Western comedy when it came to describing Hank's Woman through the sensibilities of Lin McLean, he obviously meant to make of her a character serious as well as comic. Her real significance finally arises from her songs, her prayers, and most important of all, her crucifix— in short from her attachment to tradition. Opposite her stands Hank: opposite in stature, in temperament, and in his system of values. If Willomene finally represents the positive values of cultured tradition, Hank represents the negative values of the vulgar West, a way of responding to experience that is unrefined, insensitive, boorish, coarse, and often cruel.

Significantly, Wister gives us nothing to dissociate Hank and what he represents from the West. Hank stands for a part of the frontier which Wister knew. Distasteful as such a character is, he was a legitimate part of the West. Indeed, Wister had seen and talked with many men who were not unlike Hank. Such men were a part of Wister's experience in the West; and they rightly became a part of his image of the frontier. Hence, this much of the story is based on the conflict between the negative aspects of the West and the positive values of civilization, a conflict in which those civilized values are destroyed by the very nature of the life with which they become involved. To Willomene, her final act of violence in the bludgeoning of her husband may seem a triumph of tradition, but the fact that she involves herself in the violence which characterizes the frontier already indicates that as the symbol of civilized culture, she has been destroyed by her environment, by the vulgar values of Western life. Hence, Lin's interpretation of the final canyon scene does, in effect, sum up the apparent theme of the story: ''she'd gone down 'stead of him, with him stuck on top pointin' at her exactly like if he'd been sayin', 'I have yu' beat after all.'''

If this conflict and resolution were the only element of this story, it might indicate an affirmation of Eastern culture and a corollary negation of Western life. But Wister's own attitude is not this clear cut. While he negates much of the Western system of values in the character of Hank, Wister shows a definite affirmative response to Western existence as well. We cannot forget, for example, that Lin's tale is framed by a positive, even a paradisiacal, image of the West that arises out of the opening fishing scene. A careful reading of the story shows a real ambivalence on Wister's part toward his subject. And while the confrontation of East and West in Willomene and Hank may result in clear-cut answers to some of the questions about relative values, there are other aspects of the confrontation for which the answers are less clear but finally much more significant.

Indeed, the most interesting figure in the whole story is neither the protagonist nor the antagonist. It is rather, the cowboy who tells the tale, Lin McLean. He is more complex as a character than either Hank or Willomene, and he is more significant as an embodiment of Wister's own commitment to the West.

Using Lin as the point of view from which to tell the story was a fortunate decision on Wister's part. But Wister did not come up with such an artistically satisfying narrator on his first attempt. Perhaps his most difficult technical problem in **''Hank's Woman''** was establishing and maintaining a satisfactory point of view. . . . Wister intended **''Hank's Woman''** to be told in something other than ''conventional English.'' . . . Wister's narrator will not only talk like a Westerner, he will tell the story from a basis of Western values as well. (pp. 39-46)

We need . . . to take careful note of the way that Wister's ambivalence about values has informed this story, particularly in the figure of Lin. For while Hank may represent a kind of negative, vulgar West, Lin represents a more positive system. Although Hank and Willomene may be a little overdrawn and oversimplified, the vernacular figure of Lin is significantly complex.

Lin's role in the story is that of the vernacular commentator. That is, he himself is thoroughly free from any stereotyped attitudes or responses. His way of life is simple, spontaneous, free, and based entirely on his own integrity as an individual. Thus, in the opening scenes of the story, that Wyoming fishing idyll, we meet a figure whose conversation is filled with allusions based on first-hand experience rather than current style, a man endowed with a kind of homely wisdom and rugged honesty, not a deep thinker, but a man full of common sense. (p. 47)

[His] insights and allusions are not profound, but they do have their basis in genuine human experience and for that reason have a certain positive value. Lin's attitude toward death and life is just as simple: "Anyway, what's a life?" he says. "Why, when yu' remember we're all no better than coyotes, yu' don't seem to set much story by it." . . .

But if Lin is significant for the Western vernacular values that he asserts, he is even more significant for the civilized values that he undermines. When Lin begins to describe the Eastern tourist whom he sees at "the Springs," his comedy is actually subversive to much that is important and significant to civilized gentility. It is the empty elegance and false refinement, the whole idea of traditional forms that have long since lost any relation to actual experience, that become subjects for Lin's sarcastic humor. (p. 48)

The almost vicious imagery with which Lin describes the Hotel people throwing up their false front of convention is very telling on the genteel tourists who are arriving: The initial "stampede" of the Hotel staff, the quickly arranged false front of the Syndicate manager, the cigar seller "a-clawin' his goods into shape," the musicians digging into their instruments and "raisin' railroad accidents"—all this represents a violent if not vicious preparation. And yet, the genteel visitors are entirely taken in by the performance. The "Raymonds" are perfectly willing, even anxious to believe the facade thrown up for them.

But Lin's vernacular views undercut more than just the genteel gullibility of the dudes. By his very nature he is potentially subversive to many of the positive cultured values of the non-frontier as well. The frontier Lin is, at bottom, antithetical to civilization. Thus, even though he has sympathy for Willomene, he still describes her posture before the crucifix as a "squat," and he admits, "I kind of laffed myself first time I seen Willomene at it." Of course, Lin is not consciously opposed to the tradition that Willomene represents in the same way that Hank is. Rather, Lin realizes, at least subconsciously, that cultured values and vernacular values are each a part of opposite ways of life and therefore irreconcilable—that Willomene would never fit in, and that "she was a good woman, but no account in a country like Galena Creek was." (p. 49)

It is this ambivalence toward both the East and the West that becomes increasingly important as Wister's career moved forward from that first attempt. Almost immediately after the publication of his first story, he began to feel not only the continuing urge to "save the sagebrush," to extract the central significance from the Western experience and give it continuing life in fiction, but he also felt the ever-mounting pressures of a host of genteel critics, friends, and relatives who would have his work as puerile as *Ramona* or as melodramatic as "The Outcasts of Poker Flat." It was under these pressures that his works took shape. But present as these critical pressures were, they were only slight compared to the central force that continued in Wister's imagination as he confronted the antithesis of East and West. (p. 50)

Neal Lambert, "Owen Wister's 'Hank's Woman': The Writer and His Comment," in Western American Literature, *Vol. IV, No. 1, Spring, 1969, pp. 39-50.*

EDWIN H. CADY (essay date 1971)

[*Cady is an American educator and prolific literary scholar who is the editor-in-chief of the distinguished periodical* American Literature. *He has written extensively on the works of William Dean Howells and other major American authors. In the following excerpt, Cady discusses* The Virginian *as an artistic failure that is nevertheless interesting for its embodiment of the social Darwinism that is a central element of American thought.*]

With all due respect to his learned opponents on the subject, Henry James was right about *The Virginian*. It remains, as he said, "a rare and remarkable feat," notwithstanding its flaws and shortcomings. Patiently read, the style of James's letter . . . to Owen Wister in praise of the cowboy novel [see excerpt dated 1902] conveys precisely the Master's registration of the book's strengths and failures. (p. 182)

James is right about the art of the Virginian's character. As presented to us by the narrative persona of the dude, the cowboy in personality, action, attitude and, above all, talk is superb—as James says. He is a creation, endlessly interesting, and he *lives*. But James, however sympathetic to a friend, is also dead right about the main flaw in Wister's novel. He should have drowned the schoolmarm at the ford in her first scene. To develop her and her part in the novel, Wister had to switch from that sensitive register's point of view which brought him all his success to a smeary and naive omniscient-narrator's point of view. And most of that part of the novel dominated by naive omniscience became artistic wreckage. To get Molly Stark Wood and all she represents into his book, Wister had to sacrifice its esthetic integrities: and he paid the price. For reasons of obvious parallel, Wister's predicament recalls Fenimore Cooper and the unforgettable comment in James Russell Lowell's "A Fable for Critics." With all Cooper's shortcomings, says Lowell's Apollo,

He has drawn you one character, though, that is new,
One wildflower he's plucked that is wet with the dew
Of this fresh Western world. . . . Natty Bumppo. . . .

But . . . the women he draws from one model don't
vary,
All sappy as maples and flat as a prairie.

The truth about Wister's case, however, is not that the women of *The Virginian* are stereotyped. Frontier ruggedness, humanity, democracy and good sense are apparent in Mrs. Taylor. Wister was at least a mite daring in sketching the selective sensuality of the beautiful railroader's wife who kept an eating-house, repelled the traveling salesmen, and slept with the handsome cowboy. The trouble is not nearly so much that the schoolmarm is badly done on her own ground as that Wister chose the wrong ground for her. Howells had called attention to the point in his 1895 review of *Red Men and White* [see excerpt above]. In spite of the authorial leanings toward melodrama, poesy, and "some guitar-tinkling," Howells said, the notable fact is the book's "intense masculinity"; it "is a man's book throughout." He admired Wister's humor, the skill with which he captured the veritable frontier, and especially the artfulness of his realism in presenting, uniquely well, a frontier politician, soldiers, and, above all else, Indians—"They convince of their truth: you feel that it is quite so they would think, and that their motives for good and ill would be almost for the first time in literature those attributed to them."

The right inference to draw from both James and Howells is that Wister could be extraordinarily good when he presented the West as he truly knew it. When he went wrong it was because he dealt in literary conventions or because he tried to reach for Significance—for the historical sense, the Meaning of the West.

As a whole, *The Virginian* simply cannot withstand critical analysis. There is no point in shattering cracked pots. The power of its masculinity and its wonderful matter give the book, and especially its hero, fine impetus and impact. But the lugged in significance exacts its price in bad art; Wister made a devil's bargain. Historically, his ill-wrought ideas were promptly displaced and forgotten. Popular and then mass-cult taste transformed his Great Western Novel into the Horse Opera of cinema and all its bastard progeny. If, as Upton Sinclair said, *The Jungle* was aimed at the heart of America but missed and hit its stomach, it might be said that Wister aimed at the historical imagination of America but struck the power-fantasy of modern man. (pp. 182-84)

For parts of Wister's motivation it is useful to look to his obvious American ancestor, Fenimore Cooper, and to his friend and half-rejected mentor, Howells. Worldwide, one of the archetypal themes of fiction has long been the motif of Dick Whittington, or the Young Man from the Provinces. Cooper, whose muse was Clio anyhow, saw that the epic matter of the American frontier flowed in a stream of the transit of culture from Europe down into the wilderness and thence back up to civilization again. He saw that the registry of movement (from wilderness to frontier to postfrontier to civilization in four stages) and of cultural contrast were essential to an art devoted to the matter of American history. He seems to have known intuitively what all serious observers would confirm: that fraud and confusion followed attempts to transport the frontier back East. To get at the truth, one had to reverse the Whittington motif and plunge civilized minds into the flowing process of the West. (p. 185)

Lacking as yet the awful intimation that the American doom was to be damnation by success, Cooper in his own middle phase distinguished his "epochs" as "pastoral," "equivocal," and "civilized." The Leatherstocking Tales he devoted to studying the transition from the wilderness period to the pastoral period. The Anti-Rent Trilogy, like *The Crater*, was given to a later Cooper's rage at intimations that perhaps his country could never make the final transit. But *Home As Found* confidently addressed to Cooper's countrymen his advice on how to make the best of their own advantages and of the resources of Europe, while avoiding the worst on both sides of the water, so as to triumph in fulfilling the destiny of the nation to create the best of all possible civilizations.

It would not, Cooper advised, be easy to make the transit. The "equivocal condition" is necessarily competitive, often mean and coarse, "perhaps the least inviting condition of society that belongs to any country that can claim to be free, and removed from barbarism." Like *Main-Travelled Roads, My Ántonia*, or *The Ox-Bow Incident*, Wister's novel deals with the matter of "the equivocal period." To make a long story short, *The Virginian* updates to the last frontier, on the fringe of industrialism, the whole of that theory of American history which Cooper developed for the Appalachian frontier on the fringe of agrarian civilization.

How much Wister's grasp of his intention coincided with Cooper's could be proved at once by paralleling the prefaces of *The Last of The Mohicans* and *The Deerslayer* with Wister's retrospective address "To the Reader" in *The Virginian* [see excerpt dated 1902]. Cooper and Wister both sought idealistically for an ultimate reality hidden behind the veiling actual; both appealed to the distancing perspectives of history as a means of seeing through the veil. Weir Mitchell's *Hugh Wynne*, and *The Scarlet Letter*, and *Uncle Tom's Cabin*, and *The Rise of Silas Lapham*, argued Wister, could all be said to be equally "historical." Why should he not share the privilege of snaring the past in art? . . . If the Leatherstocking was, Cooper wrote in 1823, "the foremost in that band of Pioneers, who are opening the way for the march of the nation across the continent," the Virginian Wister perceived, with a pain not merely romantic, to be the last. (pp. 186-88)

[The] triumph of Wister's natural gentleman smacks more of Cooper than of Howells. On the whole, Wister shared Frederic Remington's sense of irritation toward his old friend and advisor of St. Botolph's Club; and part of the great difference from Howells was motivated by Social Darwinism. The new scientism looked back over the heads of the realists and their faith in the common. The presidency of Theodore Roosevelt, Howells said, turned American life back to the age before Andrew Jackson when "the gentle man" ruled the "common man." And Wister's view of the civilizing process could have been expressed in Cooper's words: "Civilization" means "the division into castes that are more or less rigidly maintained, according to circumstances." It was over some such notion that Molly Stark Wood and her Vermont D.A.R. kinfolk agonized when they feared she had fallen in love with a frontier vulgarian.

The most interesting minor figure sketched in *The Virginian* is Shorty, the pitiful anticowboy from Brooklyn. Shorty is, at everything except affection for Pedro his horse, an incompetent. And Wister sees it to be the law of the West, the law of nature obeyed by man under the awful thumb of nature, that incompetence must die. Even worse, the doom of incompetence is contagious; strong men foolishly allied with it die too. The strong, and intelligence and integrity are strengths as much as hard muscles or fine coordination, live and win. The weak go down. Victorious, successful, the fittest, the Virginian was Shorty's polar opposite, nature's Darwinian gentleman of the West, and therefore worthy.

Though nobody seems to have studied the question adequately, there can be little doubt that the neoromantics, acting out Social Darwinism in life and art, helped to change American sexual mores around the turn of the century. Explicit in *The Virginian* is the notion of a real, essential masculine principle in the West and the cowboy confronting a sleepy feminine principle in Molly Stark Wood. In the Virginian himself a wild masculine principle, too easily isolated and antisocial, needs to be cultivated and made responsible: it must be civilized. But Molly needs to crack the shell of dead puritanism around her Vermont femininity. She must break out and leave behind the effete Easternism of a sexual genteel tradition. Within herself the feminine principle must be recognized, refreshed, and invigorated. To accept her cowboy lover is to confront and accept her own sexuality primitivized and set free. Conceivably because Wister did not dare, but more likely because he did not know how to treat of a lady in the same universe of sexual discourse with the mistress of the boarding house, he fell into an effetism for which there is a good old word, "mawkish."

The anticlimax which is the best Wister can bring to the eventual honeymoon in the Rockies really says everything:

> They made their camps in many places, delaying several days here, and one night there, exploring the high solitudes together, and sinking deep in their romance. Sometimes when he was at work with their horses, or intent on casting his brown hackle for a fish, she would watch him with eyes that were fuller of love than of understanding. Perhaps she never came wholly to understand him; but in her complete love for him she found enough. He loved her with his whole man's power. She had listened to him tell her in words of transport, 'I could enjoy dying'; yet she loved him more than that. He had come to her from a smoking pistol, able to bid her farewell—and she could not let him go. At the last white-hot edge of ordeal, it was she who renounced, and he who had his way. Nevertheless she found much more than enough, in spite of the sigh that now and again breathed through her happiness when she would watch him with eyes fuller of love than of understanding.

There was, finally, an esthetic Nemesis which pursued the faithlessness of the neoromantics.

And from the other "climax" of *The Virginian* one can see that an avenging justice camped on the trail of "the romanticistic" as well as "effectism." Wister was evidently self-compelled to bind all the other elements of his book with the sexual into one well-wrapped package of respectability. To avoid that, James told him, the master novelist would have let the Virginian "perish in his flower & in some splendid sombre way." As the novel stands, it supposes that all's well that ends well; and the cowboy ends as an entrepreneur. His success represents a standard neoromantic worship of the bitch-goddess on a Social Darwinian altar. In the perspectives of American cultural history, Wister ended by aligning his creation with the extractive-exploitative tradition of the Western rape of nature which, cubed, his brought us to the crisis of a technological culture on the edge of drowning in its own excreta. Wister's neo-Hamiltonian, Whiggish, "American Way" romanticization of the business mind was much like Cooper's, too, except that Wister substituted the tycoon for the Squire. (pp. 189-92)

Serious models of civilization failed Wister as they failed Cooper. But the doomed knight of the wilderness succeeds with the reader because he first succeeded with the imagination of the author. The Leatherstocking and the Virginian live on in their books. Is it their fault, or their authors', or ours that, essentialized to pure vulgarity, they have provided a grist, endlessly regrindable like the dust of the moon, for the mills of the entertainment industry? (p. 192)

> *Edwin H. Cady, "The Virginian," in his* The Light of Common Day: Realism in American Fiction, *Indiana University Press, 1971, pp. 182-92.*

RICHARD W. ETULAIN (essay date 1973)

[*Etulain is an American editor, bibliographer, and critic whose works are primarily concerned with the American West and western literature. In the following excerpt from his critical biography* Owen Wister, *Etulain discusses Wister's early western stories as apprentice works exploring the ideas he would develop more fully in* The Virginian.]

Wister's first Western stories are Janus-like: they illustrate what he learned about the West since his first trip to the West in 1885, and they also introduce themes, characters, and techniques that reappear in his later writings about the West. His first two Western yarns were "**Hank's Woman**" and "**How Lin McLean Went East**." Written in the fall of 1891, they were submitted—on the advice of S. Weir Mitchell—to Henry Alden at *Harper's*. Both stories were accepted in January 1892 . . . , and they appeared later that same year.

In "**Hank's Woman**" Wister utilizes the frame technique—a story within a story. "**Hank's Woman**" introduces a narrator and Lin McLean in the first section of the tale, and the second part is the tale of Hank and his woman that Lin shares with the first person narrator. Lin tells of a ne'er-do-well cowpoke who suddenly marries a muscular Austrian servant girl who has been fired from her position. Most of Lin's yarn centers on Hank's ill treatment of Willomene and on her attachment to her crucifix. Tension builds, and one day Lin and his cowpoke partner return to find their camp a scene of disarray. Willomene has murdered Hank, but while dragging his body along a narrow cliff she has fallen to her death.

Wister's story is artistically weak. As George Watkins has pointed out, Wister is telling two stories: the fight between Hank and "his woman," and the frame story of Lin and the narrator. The conflict between Hank and his wife is melodramatic and contrived; it is too full of "Gothic grotesqueries." The story could have been strengthened by emphasizing the narrator's initiation into new understanding of human nature, but Wister failed to take advantage of this opportunity.

Yet the tale is not, as Watkins argues, "virtually devoid of any significant meaning." . . . Throughout his career as a Western writer, Wister sought to find the meaning of the West. Frequently his search led him to compare and contrast the Western region with the East and sometimes with Europe. In "**Hank's Woman**" the conflict between the West and non-West is not yet very clear, but there are evidences of Wister's attempt to portray such conflicts. Lin and the narrator perceive the failures of Hank as a worthy Westerner, and they are sympathetic with Willomene's attachment to her church and to her past. The tension that could (and would) arise between the West and non-West is not well portrayed here because Wister was still uncertain what he thought about the West, how it differed from other regions, and what kind of values it might contribute to America.

In "**How Lin McLean Went East**" Wister seems more sure of what distinctions he wishes to make between the West and East. Lin has saved some money and decides to go East—to visit his Boston friends and family, particularly his brother Frank. Soon after he arrives, he realizes that the brother is embarrassed by Lin's ways. Lin returns to the West and tells the Bishop of Wyoming that his story is similar to that of the Biblical prodigal, except that he lacks a father. He too has squandered his funds in a far country, and now he has returned home—to the West. Wister makes clear that Lin's openness, his honesty and friendliness are Western attributes. Pitted against these positive values are Frank's pretentiousness and unfriendliness. When West and East meet in the confrontation between Lin and his brother, the West is superior. It breeds a better man, or, in the case of Lin, it pours new wine into an old wineskin.

This story is also important because it includes Wister's first extended comments about the cowboy. He is pictured as a breed apart. "He was a complete specimen of his lively and peculiar class. Cow-punchers are not a race. . . . They gallop over the face of the empty earth for a little while, and those whom rheumatism or gunpowder does not overtake, are blotted out by the course of empire, leaving no trace behind. A few wise ones return to their birthplaces, marry, and remain forever homesick for the desert sage-brush and the alkali they once cursed so heartily." Wister's picture of the cowboy is not entirely positive. As he showed earlier in his journals, the West produced noble men, but it also seemed to breed lazy, inferior men. Some of the cowboys, Wister says, "take a squaw to wife and supinely draw her rations with regularity." . . . Even Lin seems a mixture, for "beyond his tallness" were "eyes that seemed the property of a not highly conscientious wild animal." . . . Even though Wister sided with Westerners when comparing Lin with Easterners, he still wondered whether the Western experience was not a mixed blessing. (pp. 15-18)

The eight stories published as *Red Men and White* . . . were written under the pressure of deadlines. . . . If one expects Wister's best work in these short stories, he will be disappointed. They bear the brands of hurried composition.

Because *Harper's* was interested in fiction about Indians, Wister produced stories that centered on conflicts between the white and red races. **"Little Big Horn Medicine,"** the first of the series, deals with Cheschapah, a young Crow who convinces himself and his followers of his invincibility and his power over nature. Though his elderly father, Pounded Meat, tries to talk sense to his son, the young brave is determined to defeat the soldiers stationed nearby and to chase them from the lands of the Crows. At first, nature seems to follow Cheschapah's will, and other young Indians champion his cause. But in battle his shield of invincibility disappears, and his reputation vanishes as quickly as a smoke signal.

Wister's story is not freighted with meaning. It is a tale of youthful arrogance that leads to destruction. More interesting is his view of the Indian as ignorant and superstitious—as a child easily led astray. Cheschapah fails because of his own ego and because he is too naive to understand the treacherous promises of a wily white trader. Wister implies that the fall of Cheschapah is not atypical; it is more likely to happen to the Indian. The young brave is a synecdochic figure; for Wister he symbolizes the weakness of his race. Wister speaks of the Indians as "crafty rabbits" and of the young brave as "the child whose primitive brain . . . had been tampered with so easily." . . . (pp. 19-20)

Westerners like General Crook understand the nature of the Indians, but Easterners, "rancid with philanthropy and ignorance," comprehend little about the red man. Too often, Wister says, "the superannuated cattle of the War Department sat sipping their drink at the club in Washington and explained to each other how they would have done it." . . . In **"The General's Bluff"** Crook epitomizes the Western wisdom and bluff that are needed to survive in combat against the Indians—and against the stupidity of Eastern advisors.

Concurrent with his first attempts at picturing Indians is Wister's continued search for a Western hero. Here too Wister seems uncertain about what he wishes to say concerning the Western experience. Specimen Jones, a happy-go-lucky soldier, appears in three stories. In **"Specimen Jones"** he follows Jock Cumnor, a new recruit, through the desert and saves his life. Soon after they encounter the remains of an Apache ambush, they are confronted by the Indians. Specimen, realizing that their weapons are useless and drawing upon his understanding of red men's superstitions, begins to act as if he were crazy. He dances in drunken gyrations and pounds on an empty milk can. Specimen, who reminds one of some of the heroes of Eugene Manlove Rhodes, saves their lives because of his horse sense—a wisdom arising out of his Western experiences.

But Wister is not consistent in his portrayal of Specimen. In **"The General's Bluff"** he is the butt of several jokes and is more a good-natured and naive soldier than the wise, vernacular hero of **"Specimen Jones."** Then Wister changes again, and in **"The Second Missouri Compromise"** Specimen resumes his role as a Western wise man. He is portrayed as the shrewd but crude soldier who earns promotions because he knows what to do in times of crisis. Like Hemingway's heroes, he has a kind of "grace under pressure"; he knows *how* to act during crucial times. In this tale, Jones foreshadows the Virginian figure, for he has a folk wisdom that insures not only his own rise but also the safety of others. He drinks, carouses, and is a bit beyond polite society, but he has enough horse sense not to go to excess. He knows enough not to drink too much when he has responsibilities to carry out. As he says on one occasion, "If a man drinks much of that . . . he's liable to go home and steal his own pants." . . . In the character of Specimen, Wister portrays a man who may become a man among men, but one who lacks the graces to be a satisfactory partner for the Eastern schoolmarm, and one who still falls short of encompassing much of what Wister thought the West did in shaping human character. (pp. 20-1)

"The Second Missouri Compromise," "La Tinaja Bonita," and **"A Pilgrim on the Gila"** were the most ambitious tales that Wister had produced thus far. Previously his stories were ones centering on an incident or two. His stress on character development was minimal, and he seemed little interested in using any social criticism. But in these three stories, Wister aims at a higher mark.

"A Pilgrim on the Gila" illustrates some of Wister's enlarged goals, and thus it contributes significantly to an understanding of his developing career. The plot is easily summarized. The narrator visits Washington, D.C., and hears arguments pro and con for the statehood of Arizona. Then he travels to Arizona and sees the Territory first hand. While in the area he meets several of the Territory's leading men, becomes involved (innocently) in a robbery, and plays a role in a subsequent trial. Based on the well-known Wham robbery and on Wister's personal observations, **"A Pilgrim on the Gila"** closely approximates the mood, form, and content of Wister's Western journals of 1894-95. The narrator, who poses as an onlooker and Eastern tenderfoot, resembles the spokesman in the opening pages of *The Virginian*. Like Wister in his journals, the narrator sees through the corrupt façade of Arizona's political, religious, and economic life. Third-rate politicians, religious bigots, and thieves run the Territory. Honest men are more scarce than untarnished women, and Tucson is a blight upon the land. The narrator is considered a naive tourist, but ironically it is he who comprehends the worthlessness of the Territorial society.

This story illustrates again Wister's divided response to the West. Though the region encouraged new opportunities, it also seemed to spawn, at times, mobocracy—democracy gone sour. Here mob rule disregards law and order and denies the rights of citizens. When the story appeared in *Harper's*, residents of the Territory criticized Wister for his distorted picture. Perhaps

Arizona's being Democratic and Wister's being Republican made it easier for him to denigrate what he saw. His comments here are interesting prefigurations of the "Game and Nation" sections of *The Virginian*.

Concurrent with his work on the stories that were included in *Red Men and White,* Wister was struggling with what is his most significant short piece of prose. Soon after his first Western trips, he began thinking of writing a history of the West which he titled tentatively "Course of Empire." . . . This topic had intrigued Wister for some time, and in 1894 he began work on **"The Evolution of the Cow-Puncher,"** which was published in September of 1895.

In the opening paragraph of the essay, Wister describes two Anglo Saxons—an English peer and an American—eyeing one another while they travel on an English train. Soon thereafter the Englishman, who dresses immaculately and displays the best drawing room manners, comes to Texas. The change is immediate.

> Directly the English nobleman smelt Texas, the slumbering untamed Saxon awoke in him, and mindful of the tournament, mindful of the hunting-field, galloped howling after wild cattle, a born horseman, a perfect athlete, and spite of the peerage and gules and argent, fundamentally kin with the drifting vagabonds who swore and galloped by his side. The man's outcome typifies the way of his race from the beginning. . . .
>
> (pp. 21-3)

As Ben Vorpahl has pointed out in *My Dear Wister,* the essay is not about the evolution of a type but about its continuation. The Westerner is little more than the medieval knight stripped of his older trappings. . . . Wister discusses briefly the clothing, the life-style, and the lingo of the cowpuncher, but he seems most interested in their racial qualities. In short, Wister admires the cowboy, and his admiration is heightened when he sees strong symbols of continuity between Anglo Saxon heroes of the past and those who now punch cows in the American West.

The story of the cowboy ends tragically. Though like other Anglo Saxons he "cuts the way for the common law and self government, and new creeds, politics, and nations arise in his wake," he also sows the seeds of his own destruction. He moves around too much, he never marries, and so he does not reproduce his own kind. "War they make in plenty, but not love; for the women they saw was not the woman a man can take into his heart." . . . Progress—in the form of exhausted pastures, barbed-wire fences, and beef trusts—has pushed the cowboy aside. Wister laments his passing. Worst of all, as Wister notes, no poet has arisen yet to connect the man on horseback "with the eternal," and no skilled novelist has known the life of the cowboy sufficiently well "to lend him enchantment." . . . (pp. 23-4)

"The Evolution of the Cow-Puncher" summarizes Wister's ideas about race, reveals his view of the cowboy, and indicates his misgivings about the passing of the frontier and the coming of a new West. These three themes are central to an understanding of *The Virginian* and to an understanding of most of Wister's other Western fiction. And when he lamented that no writer had yet arisen to tell the story of the cowboy, he no doubt felt he was the man called out for that purpose. His friend Theodore Roosevelt thought so, and told Wister that the essay proved that he was now *the* writer of the cattle kingdom.

Wister's most important Western fiction after the appearance of the essay in 1895 dealt with the themes mentioned above: the Anglo Saxon cowboy in a world that threatens to brush him aside unless he adapts to a rapidly-changing society. (pp. 24-5)

By the end of 1895 he had written four stories in which Lin McLean appeared and several others in which the Virginian was either mentioned or played a major role. It was obvious, however, that not all the pieces would fit together. Wister realized he had two projects in the making, and he decided to add to the Lin McLean episodes in order to produce his first "novel." In 1897 the two remaining stories about Lin appeared, and the compilation of the six episodes was published as *Lin McLean* in late 1897.

Wister was disappointed—even disturbed—that reviewers of his novel stressed repeatedly its episodic nature. (p. 25)

Those who criticize the book's flimsy structure are correct. Several weaknesses are immediately perceptible. The first section was extensively revised before it appeared in the novel, and the revisions tightened an otherwise discursive narrative. But Wister failed to make other needed cuts. For example, **"Destiny at Drybone"** opens with a long conversation between Jessamine and Billy that brings readers up to date about hap-

Frank Campeau as Travis in the stage version of The Virginian. *Courtesy of American Heritage Center, University of Wyoming.*

penings in the previous episodes. For the magazine appearance this introduction was necessary, but unfortunately Wister allowed these pages to remain in the book, where they are superfluous. Indeed, throughout the book there is evidence that Wister was either a careless or lazy editor. Had he taken the time and interest, he could have strengthened the structure of his book.

A second major problem is that of point of view. Some sections utilize a first person narrator; others employ an omniscient spokesman. Transitions between the two points of view are rough, and this unevenness frequently disrupts the tone of the novel. In the first parts the tone is flippant, and Lin is pictured as carefree and something of a picaro. But the last sections are increasingly contrived and sentimental. Wister seems uncertain about his hero. At first Lin seems free of responsibility, but gradually he becomes entangled in the demands of society. Yet Wister is reluctant to allow Lin to become civilized. Lin marries and seems to mature, but even in the last story he is pictured as both a responsible man and a "six-foot innocent." These problems of uneven form and muddled point of view are immediately noticeable in the book.

To stress only these problems, however, is to undervalue the novel. While few readers will agree with Jack Schaefer that it is Wister's best book, it is Wister's best accomplishment before the publication of *The Virginian*. *Lin McLean* is another dividing point in Wister's literary career. It illustrates the ideas and techniques that he has developed thus far, but it also demonstrates that he is still an uncertain artist when dealing with certain themes and character types.

In "The Evolution of the Cow-Puncher" Wister spoke about the passing of the cowboy. Now he had the opportunity to develop this theme. The opening sentence of *Lin McLean* pictures the West as a frontier that is vanishing. The story is set in "the old days, the happy days, when Wyoming was a Territory with a future instead of a State with a past, and the unfenced cattle grazed upon her ranges by prosperous thousands." Lin's maturation is portrayed against a West that is also growing up. As Lin falls in love and marries and then goes through the process once again, he moves from a young, irresponsible cowboy working for someone else to a man who owns a ranch. Meanwhile, the West is in transition from a frontier to a settled community. As Lin prospers, the West is dotted with towns, and the railroads appear. The movement, however, is not always straight forward. After his unsuccessful first marriage, Lin withdraws from society until another symbol of civilization—Jessamine Buckner—draws him out of hibernation. So it is with the civilizing of the West. Sometimes the frontier seems to live on, and society is brushed aside. The railroad attempts to keep a ticket agent and a much-needed watertank in Separ, but the cowboys enjoy "educating" the agent and perforating the tank with pistol shots. (pp. 27-8)

One final point about *Lin McLean,* a point that too few readers have noted. The novel is a finger exercise for *The Virginian*. In the story of Lin, Wister shoots for several goals that he aimed at again in his later novel. Lin's tale is one of his being domesticated and civilized by his love for a woman. Though Jessamine is a faint resemblance of Molly Wood, she serves a purpose similar to that of the New England schoolmarm. And *Lin McLean* is a novel about the West as it moves from frontier to region, a theme that is at the center of *The Virginian*. Finally, Wister experimented with the perspectives of two narrators, as he would in his most important novel. *Lin McLean* was Wister's first Western novel, and in the writing of it he learned several

valuable lessons that he put to work in *The Virginian*. Seen in this perspective, the earlier novel is an important step forward in Wister's apprenticeship as a Western writer. (pp. 29-30)

Richard W. Etulain, in his Owen Wister, *Boise State College, 1973, 50 p.*

JOHN G. CAWELTI (essay date 1976)

[*Cawelti is an American author and essayist whose works are primarily concerned with American popular culture and mythology. In the following excerpt, Cawelti discusses the themes of* The Virginian, *contending that the work transformed the western from a form acceptable only for the sensational excesses of the dime novel into a suitable vehicle for serious literature.*]

More than any other book, [*The Virginian*] stands as the transition between the dime novel and the modern literary and cinematic western. Its characters and the chief incidents of its plot have been repeated in countless novels and films. Above all, Wister brought back to the tale of western adventure something of the thematic seriousness and complexity that had largely been absent since the works of [James Fenimore] Cooper. In short, Wister accomplished a major transformation of the western formula. (p. 215)

Undoubtedly, Wister's own sense of regeneration in the West was reflected in his portrayal of a young man who has left a decaying Virginia to find a new life in Wyoming and of a New England heroine who is transformed by her western experience. Wister's new treatment of the West depended on literary precedent as well as personal experience and need. Wister's version of the West caught on with the public because it synthesized a number of important cultural trends into the archetypal form of adventure. While Wister certainly knew Cooper and probably had some awareness of the dime novel tradition, another literary development had an important influence on his portrayal of the West. Along with the dime novel, there emerged in the later nineteenth century a new kind of western literature that, unlike most of the western adventure stories, was written by men with an actual experience of the area. The humorous, satirical, sometimes sentimental sketches written by Bret Harte, Mark Twain, and Stephen Crane, and their numerous imitators embodied an image of the West far different from Cooper's romantic wilderness. This new version of the frontier was social rather than natural, and it was of a society distinctively different from that of the East, to the point that a new kind of dialectic began to operate, replacing the opposition of nature and civilization by a cultural dialectic between the East and the West. (p. 216)

Though the cowboy had already become an American hero through the dime novel, through newspaper stories, books, and plays about western figures like Wild Bill Hickock, Wyatt Earp, and General Custer and, above all, through the enormously popular spectacle of the Wild West Show, Wister, in *The Virginian*, created a story that related the cowboy-hero to a number of important social and cultural themes. The novel begins with the relationship between the narrator and the Virginian, the first of a number of studies in cultural contrast between East and West. The narrator, a somewhat effete easterner on his first visit to friends in the West, encounters the Virginian at the railway station of Medicine Bow when he disembarks for the long overland journey to the ranch of his friend, Judge Henry. The Virginian, a cowboy on the Henry ranch, has been delegated to meet the "tenderfoot." Their first encounter immediately establishes the basic contrast between

401

East and West. The easterner is tired and confused. The railroad has somehow misplaced his trunk, and he feels utterly cast adrift in a savage wilderness. . . . In the midst of the narrator's despair, the Virginian politely introduces himself with a letter from Judge Henry. When the narrator adopts a condescending and familiar attitude toward this "slim young giant" who radiates an air of "splendor" despite his "shabbiness of attire," he is met by a sharp but civil wit that shakes him to the core and leads him to his first realization about the West: that this is not simply a savage wilderness but a land where the inner spirit of men counts more than the surface manners and attitudes of civilization. In such a setting a man must prove his worth by action and not by any assumed or inherited status. . . . (pp. 219-20)

After this realization, the narrator soon comes to a new view of the West. Despite the appearance of wildness or squalor, this landscape is a place where deep truths of human nature and life, hidden in the East by the artifices and traditions of civilization, are being known again. Soon he begins to see the apparent chaos and emptiness of Medicine Bow in very different terms. . . . Just as the purity of the landscape redeems the seeming squalor of the town, so the inner nobility of the cowboys illumines their apparent wildness. . . . (p. 220)

Wister's image of the West is dominated by the theme of moral regeneration. To some extent, his treatment of this theme reflects a primitivism not unlike Cooper's. Because civilization and its artificial traditions have not yet taken a firm hold in the West, the influence of nature is more strongly felt in that "pure and quiet light, such as the East never sees." But the influence of nature is less important for Wister than the code of the western community, a distinctive set of values and processes that is in many respects a result of the community's closeness to nature but also reflects certain basic social circumstances. Because institutional law and government have not yet fully developed in the West, the community has had to create its own methods of insuring order and achieving justice. As Judge Henry explains when the heroine is distressed by vigilante justice, the code of the west is not inimical to law. On the contrary, the vigilantes represent the community acting directly, instead of allowing its will to be distorted by complex and easily corrupted institutional machinery. Of course, Judge Henry insists this situation will change when civilization reaches the West, yet in his praise of the principle of vigilante justice, the judge intimates that the western type of direct action is not merely a necessary expedient, but a rebirth of moral vitality in the community. . . . (p. 221)

As presented by Wister, the code embodies the community's moral will but it also gives full weight to the importance of individual honor. Since the fundamental principles of honor and the will of the community transcend responsibility to the official agencies of government and the codified, written law, the Virginian finds it incumbent upon him to participate both in a lynching and a duel, illegal actions according to the written law, but recognized by all his fellow western males as inescapable obligations. The Virginian's difficulties do not come from the demands of the code. Though the actions it requires of him are dangerous, they cause him little inner conflict. His real problem is that he has fallen in love with the eastern schoolteacher, Molly Wood. Women pose a basic threat to the code, because they are the harbingers of law and order enforced by police and courts, and of the whole machinery of schools and peaceful town life. These institutions make masculine courage and strength a much less important social factor. The Vir-

ginian becomes increasingly aware of the danger his love poses to the code, and at one point his love makes him break with the code, by explaining to Molly the villainy of another man:

> Having read his sweetheart's mind very plainly, the lover now broke his dearest custom. It was his code never to speak ill of any man to any woman. Men's quarrels were not for women's ears. In his scheme, good women were to know only a fragment of men's lives. He had lived many outlaw years, and his wide knowledge of evil made innocence doubly precious to him. But to-day he must depart from his code, having read her mind well. He would speak evil of one man to one woman, because his reticence had hurt her.

But if the hero's romantic interest in the schoolmarm tends to draw him away from the code, his struggle with the villain Trampas reaffirms his dedication to it and ultimately demonstrates what seems to be Wister's main thesis: that the kind of individual moral courage and community responsibility embodied in the code is a vital part of the American tradition and needs to be reawakened in modern American society. Romance and the struggle against villainy are interspersed throughout the novel. At the very beginning of the novel, the Virginian confronts Trampas over a card game and puts him down with the immortal phrase, "When you call me that, *smile!*" This supremely cool challenge, which forces on Trampas the necessity of choosing either to draw his gun or back down, illustrates an important aspect of the code—one must never shy away from violence, but at the same time never bring it on by one's own actions. Honor cannot be compromised, but the true hero, as opposed to a lawless man like Trampas, always lives within distinct moral limits. He never fights out of anger or even from a desire for glory, but only when he must preserve his own honor or enact the community's just sentence. In this initial incident, the Virginian is supremely in control of himself and no inner conflict gives him any doubt about the proper course of action. But it is not long before the snake enters this garden of honorable masculinity. Careering across the countryside in a stagecoach driven by a drunken driver, Miss Molly Stark Wood of Bennington, Vermont, descendant of revolutionary heroes, is nearly tumbled into a dangerously high creek before a dashing man on horseback rides out of nowhere and deposits her safely on the other shore. After saving her life, a gallant gentleman can hardly avoid falling in love with the lady. When they meet again, some time later, the Virginian announces his determination to make Molly love him, even though she has just finished unmercifully roasting him for his part in some masculine high jinks. Thus begins the conflict between the masculine code of the West and the genteel ideas of civility that Molly carries with her from the East.

Wister develops the Virginian's courtship of Molly and his conflict with Trampas in counterpoint until the two lines of action intersect and the Virginian must choose between his two commitments. Molly is at first quite resistant to the Virginian's courtship. Her eastern manners and beliefs make her recoil at what seems to be the Virginian's crudity, childishness, and lack of civility. When she discovers that, despite his lack of formal education and social graces, the Virginian has an instinctive gentility as well as a strong native intelligence, she begins to become interested in him. We have already seen the narrator of the book go through a similar process. Molly's eastern prejudices against the West and her inability to conceive of the idea that a Wood of Bennington, Vermont, might marry a cowboy still defend her against the Virginian's love until a dramatic incident completely changes her attitude. On his way to a rendezvous with Molly, the Virginian is attacked and left for dead by a marauding band of Indians. (Note how in Wister, as in many later dime novels, the Indian has become a narrative convenience rather than a central element of the story.) When the Virginian does not appear at the rendezvous, Molly rides out along the trail and finds him seriously wounded. Wister represents this as a great moment of truth for Molly. Casting off her demure gentility, she summons up the courage and daring of her revolutionary ancestors, rescues the Virginian, and nurses him back to health in her cabin. This experience is the first real step in the westernizing of Molly, which Wister sees as a kind of atavistic return to the spirit of her ancestors. In this way, Wister suggests that the West is not entirely a new cultural experience, but a rebirth of the revolutionary generation's vigor.

Along with this awakening of the deeper instincts in her blood, Molly's love for the Virginian blossoms and she agrees to marry him. Now the story moves toward the final confrontation between Molly's eastern scheme of values and the code of the West. Trampas increasingly menaces the good community of the ranch. When he tries to persuade the ranch crew to go off hunting gold, he is outwitted by the Virginian. In response, he leaves the ranch and turns rustler, carrying along two of the Virginian's former friends to be members of his gang. The code of the West swings into action against the rustlers. Judge Henry, the ranch owner, makes the Virginian leader of a posse charged with the capture and execution of the rustlers. The Virginian must reluctantly join in the lynching of his former friend Steve, while Trampas escapes and succeeds in eluding further pursuit. Finally, Trampas returns to town and the Virginian prepares to meet his challenge to individual combat. Molly insists that the Virginian refuse to fight Trampas or she will break off their engagement and return to the East. Caught in this conflict of love, duty, and honor, the Virginian does not hesitate. He explains to Molly why the code of masculine honor must always take precedence over other obligations:

> "Can't yu' see how it must be about a man? It's not for their benefit, friends or enemies, that I have got this thing to do. If any man happened to say I was a thief and I heard about it, would I let him go on spreadin' such a thing of me? Don't I owe my own honesty something better than that? Would I sit down in a corner rubbin' my honesty and whisperin' to it. There! there! I know you ain't a thief'? No, seh; not a little bit! What men say about my nature is not just merely an outside thing. For the fact that I let 'em keep on sayin' it is a proof I don't value my nature enough to shield it from their slander and give them their punishment. And that's being a poor sort of a jay."

So the Virginian confronts Trampas, believing that his defense of his honor will lose him the woman he loves. But, of course, it doesn't work out that way. Once Molly sees her sweetheart in danger, she realizes that her love for him transcends all her moral compunctions. (pp. 221-24)

The fourth main plot line of *The Virginian* is the story of his success. Like some grown-up Alger hero, the Virginian, beginning as a poor cowboy, is soon appointed foreman of Judge Henry's ranch. In that post, he meets the challenge of lead-ership and demonstrates his aspiration to rise in life by investing his wages in land so that he can become a rancher himself. At the end of the novel, we are assured that the Virginian will continue to rise and in due course become one of Wyoming's leading citizens.

What Wister did with his story of the Virginian was to synthesize Cooper's opposition of nature and civilization with the gospel of success and progress, thus making his hero both an exponent of natural law and of the major ideals of American society. This shift is particularly evident in Wister's treatment of the code of the West, which, as we have seen, is based on both the individual's sense of personal honor and the moral will of the community. In the final conflict with Trampas, the hero not only maintains the purity of his individual image but acts in the true interest of the community. (p. 224)

For Wister, . . . the western hero possesses qualities that civilized society badly needs. It is not his lack of refinement that prevents the Virginian from assuming his rightful place as a social leader, but the shallow prejudices of an overrefined and effete society that has lost contact with its own most significant values. When the Virginian goes east to meet Molly's family, it is Molly's great aunt, the one closest to the family's revolutionary heritage, who understands and fully appreciates the Virginian's qualities. This representative of an earlier order sees the basic resemblance between the Virginian and General Stark, the founder of the family. Because of this she understands that the West is not a barbarous land, but a place where the original American traits of individual vigor, courage, and enterprise have been reborn: "'There he is,' she said, showing the family portrait. 'And a rough time he must have had of it now and then. New Hampshire was full of fine young men in those days. But nowadays most of them have gone away to seek their fortunes in the West.'"

Thus Wister resolved the old ambiguity between nature and civilization by presenting the West not as a set of natural values basically antithetical to civilization, but as a social environment in which the American dream could be born again. (p. 225)

> *John G. Cawelti, "The Western: A Look at the Evolution of a Formula," in his* Adventure, Mystery, and Romance: Formula Stories as Art and Popular Culture, The University of Chicago Press, 1976, pp. 192-259.*

ANNE ROWE (essay date 1978)

[*In the following excerpt, Rowe discusses* Lady Baltimore *as Wister's portrayal of the superiority of the elitist, racist, southern Anglo-Saxon society to the vulgar society of the mongrelized North.*]

Wister, as well as his friends and contemporaries Theodore Roosevelt and the illustrator, Frederic Remington, came to terms with the differences resulting from the polarities inherent in nineteenth-century America. These contrasts pitted urban life, big business, and the multi-ethnic backgrounds characteristic of the East against their opposites, the images of a rural, individualistic, and ethnically homogeneous West. [G. Edward] White sees the aim of these men as one of reasserting a "rural, egalitarian, Anglo-Saxon heritage"—of attempting to create an agrarian-based utopia to take the place of urban industrial society. He does not extend his "utopia" thesis to Wister's treatment of the South in his fiction, but a relationship can be established. (p. 97)

Although urged to write a sequel to *The Virginian*, Wister chose instead to follow it with a novel set in the South, and in *Lady Baltimore* he seems to have found the true counterpoint for the shortcomings of the northeastern establishment. Wister stated after the success of *The Virginian*, "Never again can I light on a character so engaging," but even though he did not wish to write a sequel, he did have the desire to write another book. He felt he needed another setting but would only write about something he knew well. By the time *Lady Baltimore* was written, he did indeed know a good deal about its setting, old Charleston.

Although a true product of the Northeast in background and education, Wister had strong family ties with South Carolina. . . . In addition to this direct family connection which allowed him access to some of the leading Charleston families, Wister learned much about the area during his several extended visits there. (pp. 109-10)

Few critics would disagree that *Lady Baltimore* contained many indictments of the North and was largely a prosouthern novel. The fact that this did not diminish its widespread appeal indicates the changes in attitude about the South which had come full circle by the first decade of the twentieth century. Reconstruction was generally viewed by southerners and most northerners to have been a failure, and only a minority in the North opposed the establishment of Jim Crow laws. Thus, when *Lady Baltimore* espoused the plight of white southerners and the general inferiority of the black man, few of Wister's contemporaries were offended.

Julian Mason has noted that the plot of *Lady Baltimore* seems secondary to other considerations, appearing "more as a thin frame to hold the canvas for a painting of that part of old Charleston still existing in the 20th century than for its own sake, except as the plot provides an opportunity for criticism of those who represent the opposite of old Charleston." Indeed, the predominant quality of the novel appears not in plot or characterization but in the author's explicit comparisons of North and South, in which Charleston (here called Kings Port) is held up as a model for all the positive values that the nation, specifically the Northeast, has forsaken. For in Kings Port the idea that it is blood, not skill in money-getting, that counts is sustained by the old aristocracy who have not yet been completely overrun by the rise of the industrial rich, as had happened in the North.

As in *The Virginian*, the narrator, Augustus, is a northerner (much like Wister himself) who is initiated into a section of the country to which he is a newcomer. In this way the reader is allowed to see the setting through curious and observant eyes. At the same time, the narrator, as a product of life in the North, can speak with authority when contrasting life there with his observations of life in Kings Port. (pp. 113-14)

The narrator repeatedly emphasizes that Kings Port has retained those virtues which the nation, as a whole, has lost. Stating that the genteel, ancient ladies of Kings Port "have made me homesick for a national and a social past which I never saw, but which my old people knew," . . . he concludes that in the past the United States constituted a family, but that all those qualities remaining in Kings Port have been ground into oblivion in the North. Wister stresses that an aristocrat is an aristocrat North or South, that these people have more in common with one another than either does with the sons of toil (except as peasantry) and the vulgar nouveau riche. Yet because the aristocracy of the North has been inundated with the "yellow

rich," only in the South are the aristocratic ideals still unadulterated. This is stated most succinctly when Augustus tells a Kings Port native that southern society retains "the manners we've lost, the decencies we've banished, the standards we've lowered, their light is still flickering in this passing generation of yours." . . . (pp. 114-15)

That the narrator sympathizes strongly with the southern attitude toward Reconstruction is evident in his conversation with the young heroine of the novel, Eliza La Heu. When he asks her why the South has not rebuilt the way the United States did after its battle with Britain, she replies, "Did England then set loose on us a pack of black savages and politicians to *help* us rebuild?" . . . And the narrator agrees with her sentiments.

It is in the narrator's comments on the southern black that Wister most directly reflected the period's characteristic acquiescence toward the Jim Crow attitude, an attitude that for Wister would be conducive to returning to the traditional class structure that sustained an aristocracy. In contrast to earlier northerners who wrote of the South, such as De Forest and Tourgée, Wister felt that the Negro could make only limited advances. Augustus makes this clear when he assures Eliza, "It was awful about the negro. It *is* awful. The young North thinks so just as much as you do. Oh, we shock our old people! We don't expect *them* to change, but they mustn't expect us *not* to. And even some of them have begun to whisper a little doubtfully. But never mind them—here's the negro. We can't kick him out. That plan is childish. So, it's like two men having to live in one house. The white man would keep the house in repair, the black would let it rot. Well, the black must take orders from the white. And it will end so." The condition of blacks, he concluded, must be "something between slavery and equality." . . . (pp. 115-16)

One of the best examples of Wister's attitudes is in his handling of the so-called Crum incident in *Lady Baltimore*. On December 31, 1902, President Roosevelt had appointed a respected black man, Dr. William D. Crum of Charleston, as port of custom's collector. In spite of the unimportance of this position, the same white Charlestonians who had earlier praised Crum were up in arms, appalled that a black should be placed in a position superior to that of white lady clerks. The fight between Senator "Pitchfork" Ben Tillman of South Carolina and the president over the appointment dragged on until 1904, with Tillman relying on filibustering until Roosevelt went out of office and Taft assured southerners that he would appoint no blacks to office in the South. In the novel Wister is sympathetic to the outrage of white Kings Port over the appointment of this black man. He pictures the young white hero of the novel, John Mayrant, as unfairly demeaned by having to "take orders from a Negro." The narrator, upon learning that Mayrant has engaged in a fight concerning the appointment, comments that Mayrant could not possibly have fought with his black superior—"as well might a nobleman cross swords with a peasant." . . . Wister's strongest indictment of the appointment comes, however, from Daddy Ben, an Uncle Tom creation whom the author presents as the "right" kind of Negro—a retainer, loyal to his white families, and indignant at the airs put on by "reconstructed niggers." Daddy Ben reassures John Mayrant, saying, "Mas' John, I speck de Presi*dent* he dun' know de culled people like we knows 'um, else he nebber bin 'pint dat ar boss in de Cussum House, no sah." . . . (pp. 116-17)

In his biography of Roosevelt he commented again on the Crum incident. Appointing Crum, he said, "finished him with those highly spirited, sorely bruised people. . . . It was the deep bruise; and the President, meaning well but not aware how sore it was still, had pressed it. It was not the Civil War . . . it was Reconstruction that was the real, lasting bruise."

In addition to the narrator's declaiming and the author's use of actual historical events, the more "fictional" aspects of *Lady Baltimore* also express Wister's favorable attitudes toward the South. The cast of characters—some based on real people, others fictional representatives of "types"—reflect the dichotomy of North and South. It is certainly no accident, I think, that the products of two towns—Newport and Kings Port—are juxtaposed. As the names imply, the visitors from Newport are largely, "new people," the nouveau riche whom Wister deplored as "the lower classes with dollars and no grandfathers, who live in palaces at Newport, and look forward to everything and back to nothing." . . . In contrast, the inhabitants of Kings Port are linked with aristocracy and the past. Indeed, two Kings Port aristocrats are described as analogous to their lovely old city. They are said to be "as narrow as those streets [yet] . . . as lovely as those serene gardens; and if I had smiled at their prejudices, I had loved their innocence, their deep innocence, of the poisoned age which has succeeded their own." . . . (pp. 117-18)

Wister calls Newport inhabitants the "yellow rich," and he directs not one generous remark toward them. They are loud, garish, tacky and, worst of all, are unaware of their vulgarity. They roar into Kings Port in loud, noisy motor cars, disturbing the placidness of the quiet city, and they are bored with the absence of fast life there. Wister describes the approach of these "northern invaders" in much the same way a nineteenth-century southerner might have described Sherman's army. (pp. 118-19)

The controlling element of the plot, the situation that has brought this Newport crowd to Kings Port, is a romance—the engagement of John Mayrant, of ancient Kings Port ancestry, to Hortense Rieppe, a southerner claiming to be from Kings Port, said by some to be "from Georgia" (a terrific indictment in the eyes of Kings Port), and presently the darling of Newport. Although the courtship is not technically a North-South one, for all intents and purposes it may be viewed as such. For Hortense has completely assimilated the manners of Newport, and her stature in Kings Port is decidedly that of an outsider. It is hinted further that although John Mayrant was dazzled by her, as would be any innocent young person on a visit into Newport society, upon returning to the South he has doubts about her but his southern code of ethics prevents him from breaking the engagement.

There is also a triangle aspect to the romance. As the story progresses, we see John increasingly attracted to Eliza La Heu, a young plantation girl of a poor but ancient South Carolina family. Eliza apparently shares John's feelings, but she too considers him bound by his pledge to Hortense, and, accordingly, the relationship seems permanently thwarted. (pp. 119-20)

The narrator, of course, favors Eliza over Hortense. Of Hortense he says, "She had at length betrayed something which her skill and the intricate enamel of her experience had hitherto, and with entire success, concealed—namely, the latent vulgarity of the woman." . . . Thus, the two women are dramatically different: "[Hortense] was wearing, for the sake of Kings Port, her best behavior, her most knowing form, and, indeed, it was a well-done imitation of the real thing; it would last through most occasions, and it would deceive most people.

But here was the trouble: she was *wearing* it; while, through the whole encounter, Eliza La Heu had worn nothing but her natural and perfect dignity." . . . (pp. 120-21)

The affair appears at an impasse, and the day of the wedding is approaching rapidly when Hortense unwittingly releases John from his bond. While they are spending a morning on Charley's yacht in Kings Port harbor, Hortense perversely jumps overboard to show herself a sport. John saves her and, in restoring her life to her, is released from further obligation.

Lady Baltimore draws to an end with two weddings. Hortense marries the wealthy Charley, and, to the narrator's delight, after a respectable waiting period Eliza and John are married. In describing the two weddings Wister puts the finishing touches on his theme, noting that if you did not happen to see the newspaper account of the first wedding, "just read the account of the next wedding that occurs among the New York yellow rich, and you will know how Charley and Hortense were married." In contrast, "The marriage of Eliza La Heu and John Mayrant was of a different quality; no paper pronounced it 'up to date'. . . . This marriage was *solemnized*." . . .

On this note Wister concludes, and the implication is that things have ended as they should. Kings Port has through this marriage withstood, for a while at least, contamination from the yellow rich, Newport, and the North in general, where "the soul of Uncle Sam has turned into a dollar inside his great, big strong, triumphant flesh." . . . (p. 121)

Anne Rowe, "Owen Wister and the Southern Rebuke," in her The Enchanted Country: Northern Writers in the South, 1865-1910, *Louisiana State University Press, 1978, pp. 96-122.*

JOHN D. NESBITT (essay date 1983)

[*In the following excerpt, Nesbitt explains how Wister created in* The Virginian *a unique synthesis of the conventions of popular western fiction and the novel of manners.*]

The works of Owen Wister, primarily *Lin McLean* . . . and *The Virginian* . . . , have earned him the generally conceded rank of father of the twentieth-century Western. These two novels, as is frequently pointed out, were composed of short stories that were cut, pasted, rewritten, and assembled into book form. In addition to these two books he published four other volumes of western short stories: [*Red Men and White, The Jimmyjohn Boss, and Other Stories, Members of the Family,* and *When West Was West*]. . . . Half a dozen of his short stories have been revived in *The West of Owen Wister* . . . ; and *Lin McLean,* though currently out of print, is still read by students of the Western. It is *The Virginian,* however, by virtue of its immediate success and perennial popularity, for which he is chiefly remembered and evaluated. And Wister's achievement as a western writer has been dubbed a great failure and a great success, depending on the interpreter. (p. 199)

In light of this varied response to Wister's work, it remains to assess what, specifically, he contributed to the western novel, and how successfully he worked with literary and cultural traditions.

To begin with, it is crucial to recognize that Wister did not merely revitalize the lifeless "ingredients" of popular literature that then existed in the watery versions of frontier and ranch adventure. The "ingredient" or "element" theory of literary history provides an inadequate account of how a literary milestone like *The Virginian* came into being. Richard Etulain's monograph on Wister provides a characteristic example of the "ingredient" theory of Wister's contributions to the western novel:

> *The Virginian* helped to establish the conventions of what has become known as the "formula Western." Wister's skillful blending of an idealized hero, the conflict between the hero and a villain, and the romance between the hero and heroine—all set against the romantic background of the frontier West—are important ingredients of the Western.

Historians and critics of western fiction, from Henry Nash Smith to Russel B. Nye, look upon conventions as so many ingredients for a recipe, and they assess a writer's contributions in terms of how well he combined or perpetuated the ingredients. This approach is limited because it does not account for the organic coherence of a novel like *The Virginian*, in which literary traditions and conventions are mutually reinforcing.

In order to dispense with this theory of direct line of descent and influence, it is imperative to observe that Wister was not simply working in the tradition of popular fiction and historical romance, nor was he "blending in" a few cups of local color and frontier humor. It took more than a felicitous reshuffling of "elements" to create *The Virginian*. While Wister was drawing from the above traditions he was also, simultaneously, revising his cultural assumptions about the western hero and drawing from the tradition of the novel of manners—or, more broadly, the novel of social realism.

The appeal generated by synthesizing the tradition of frontier adventure with a more sophisticated and genteel Anglo-American literary tradition was what brought *The Virginian* to be the nation's best-seller of 1902, and what gave the classic Western its twentieth-century boost. Moreover, the moral focus of the novel of manners brought thematic and moral complexity to the Western, and it brought the Western inside the pale of literary as well as social respectability.

Prior to *The Virginian,* however, Wister produced *Lin McLean,* and a brief consideration of this book will help illuminate Wister's full achievement. As most scholars are willing to agree, *Lin McLean* is not a highly successful novel in its own right as much as it is an episodic string of stories about its titular hero. This book is usually looked upon as a forerunner of *The Virginian*, a practice ground for narrative technique and character development. It is also preliminary to the later work in Wister's exercise of Anglo-American literary convention in the western story.

Although there are several high points of moral sensitivity in this volume, accompanied by occasional flourishes of fine writing, the book does not read smoothly as a story of the fall and rise of Lin McLean's fortunes. One source of discomfort is the narrative arrangement. In *Lin McLean* Wister experiments with what he seems to have appropriated as a personal convenience—shifting back and forth between third- and first-person narration. The first story, **"How Lin McLean Went East,"** is in third person; in the next two, **"The Winning of the Biscuit-Shooter"** and **"Lin McLean's Honey-Moon,"** Wister uses a first-person narrative persona he had introduced in his earlier stories and that he would put to use again in *The Virginian* and later works. The persona is presumably similar to Wister himself, a naive but morally conscious Easterner who gradually learns the ways of the new land, but who is always just a little bewildered by the rough-hewn existence in Wyoming.

In *Lin McLean* three of the stories are narrated by this persona and three by an omniscient narrator, and there are two plausible explanations for the alternation. One apparent design was to show by turns the western and eastern views of Wyoming life. The other reasonable explanation is that Wister was putting together six stories that were already composed, and three of them happened to be narrated in one style while three were already narrated in the other. Wister quite possibly saw in this inconsistency an aesthetic windfall: without revision, the narrative arrangement might give the effect of conscious comparison and contrast.

At any rate, Wister did not revise for consistency, and any attempts to make a great deal out of the narrative scheme must finally give way to an acknowledgment that the book is an uneven piece of patchwork. As Etulain points out, there is an inconsistent tone from one story to the next, shifting from comic to serious to sentimental, and there is not a gradual development in Lin's character to accompany the changes in tone [see excerpt dated 1973]. Neal Lambert also emphasizes Wister's failure to develop Lin's character satisfactorily [see excerpt dated 1969], and any reader must eventually feel as these two critics do—that the book is not successful as a novel, that it did not contribute much to the development of the *genre* Western, but that it was a valuable experiment in Wister's preparation for writing *The Virginian*. The experiment was successful insofar as Wister brought literary sophistication to western fiction, and pioneered in using the West as a serious subject for literary enterprise.

The transition from *Lin McLean* to *The Virginian* was accompanied by some ambitious changes, for Wister had expanded his conception of how he might depict the West. He changed from the local color or regional fiction mode to the historical romance, and this change was accompanied by a change in main character. As Neal Lambert demonstrates, Wister abandoned the vernacular or regional type in favor of the natural gentleman. Wister's conception of his new character can be illustrated by two other pieces of his writing. In his preface to *The Virginian,* wherein he refers to the novel as an historical romance, Wister tells how he changed the subtitle from *A Tale of Sundry Adventures* to *A Horseman of the Plains*. The chivalric emphasis to Wister's hero is illuminated at much greater length in **"The Evolution of the Cow-Puncher,"** a treatise he worked on extensively in the early 1890s. In this essay Wister compares the Anglo-Saxon knight with "his direct lineal offspring among our Western mountains," even unto their dress and gear. The strongest link between the two is significantly their horsemanship, "from the tournament at Camelot to the round-up at Abilene." It is not just equestrian status but dashing bravery that unites the two in Wister's image, for "in personal daring and in skill as to the horse, the knight and the cowboy are nothing but the same Saxon of different environments." . . . (pp. 201-04)

In his major novel Wister brought to western fiction an Anglo-American mythology, a combination of Cooper's natural nobleman and steward of the prairies and Scott's mounted Saxon. With that mythology he brought the Anglo-American literary tradition of historical romance, and a little more. When the Virginian rescues the damsel in distress (Miss Molly Wood of Vermont) from a stagecoach stuck in the river, the story becomes one of pride and prejudice as well as of chivalric adventure.

Much has been made of the similarities between this novel and the historical romance. There is the conflict between the lawless, western element (Trampas and Steve) and the ordered eastern element (the Judge and Molly). This conflict is mediated by the hero, the Virginian, who among other things rescues a damsel, gets wounded by Indians, kills the villain, and marries the heroine. But this does not account for the novel as a whole. Nor does the explanation that the novel poses a contrast between eastern and western values, a dialectic similar in structure to that of the historical romance. One important influence that is all too frequently omitted in discussions of *The Virginian* is evident in broad strokes and fine lines throughout the novel: the novel of social realism.

From her first introduction as the correspondent of Mrs. Balaam, Molly Wood is more than a walking concept or emblem of eastern values. She is not the stereotyped Easterner encountered, for example, in Rhodes' *Pasó Por Aquí*. She is witty in the fashion of Elizabeth Bennet or Isabel Archer. After her rescue at the hands of the Virginian, her attitude is reminiscent of the urbane novel of manners, with a hint of parodic irony that one finds in *Northanger Abbey:* "In a few miles Miss Wood entertained sentiments of maidenly resentment toward her rescuer, and of maidenly hope to see him again." In her subsequent meetings with the Virginian, especially in the chapter where she confronts him with his baby-switching prank, she holds up as archly as a James or Austen heroine, and she is as embarrassed and retrospective afterwards.

Wister's technique of characterization also invokes the techniques of earlier writers in the social realism tradition. He has Molly write home, "how delightful it is to ride, especially on a spirited horse," to which the response back home is, "I hope the horse is not too spirited.—Who does she go riding with?" One is reminded of similar subtlety in *Joseph Andrews*, in which Fielding's robust hero "rode the most spirited and vicious horses to water"; or perhaps of George Eliot's suggestion that Dorothea Brooke is emotionally healthy: "Riding was an indulgence which she allowed herself in spite of conscientious qualms; she felt that she enjoyed it in a pagan sensuous way, and always looked forward to renouncing it." To imply a direct influence would be stretching the point, perhaps, but it is evident that Wister uses characterization techniques—including the epistolary device—that were in the tradition of social realism.

Wister's narrative voice and prose style, in both first and third person, are similarly resonant of the manners mode, even when he is not describing his domestic heroine. The opening paragraph of the chapter entitled "Where Fancy Was Bred" is very much in the style of Trollope, who, by the way, also liked to depict a *fête champêtre*:

> Two camps in the open, and the Virginian's Monte horse, untired, brought him to the Swintons' in good time for the barbecue. The horse received good food at length, while his rider was welcomed with good whiskey. Good whiskey—for had not steers jumped to seventy-five? . . .

Again, the passage is more indicative of general similarity than specific influence. And even in the case of Henry James, whom Wister knew personally and whose novels had impressed him greatly, it is difficult to cite anything more specific than passages that strongly resemble James' style. . . . In the scene in which Judge Henry praises the Virginian for his leadership in the cattle drive and in managing the return of the men, Wister narrates the scene with Jamesian niceness. The Judge does not say everything at once, the Virginian does not understand everything at once—there are flashes of fine perception and comprehension, and there are patches of clouded communication. Nothing is blurted, and overall the Judge is "delighted" at his new foreman's "reticence."

This is not to say, however, that *The Virginian* is an unrecognized novel of manners. The center of the novel is occupied by the Virginian, who prefers Scott's *Kenilworth* to Molly's favorites, *Emma* and *Pride and Prejudice*. But the novel of manners influence is there, and it persists to the final chapter. After the Virginian has killed Trampas in their immortal showdown and has had the heroine swoon in his arms, there is one more chapter. The ordinary Western would end there (and invariably does), where the adventure and romance plot is resolved; but the manners plot needs another chapter. After a pastoral interlude for their honeymoon the couple go to Vermont to meet Molly's family. At this point comes the mutual testing of their manners and the final resolution and compromise of their points of view. The second to last chapter, not the last one, ends with her New England conscience capitulating to love. In the last chapter that surrender is recalled preparatory to their settling their respective prides and prejudices. First the remembrance, in a blend of romantic imagery and pregnant suggestion: "He had come to her from a smoking pistol, able to bid her farewell—and she could not let him go. At the last white-hot edge of ordeal, it was she who renounced, and he who had his way." . . . Then they journey to the East, where the compromise is completed and the Virginian passes muster with the great-aunt:

> And so she dismissed him to his wife, and to happiness greater than either of them had known since they had left the mountains and come to the East. "He'll do," she said to herself, nodding. . . .

This scene occurs on the last page, and with it the action of the novel is complete. There follows the summary narration of how the couple raised a family and how the Virginian became a prosperous man of affairs.

It is not surprising that the conventions of the novel of manners, which contributed so strongly to the novel's immediate success, did not endure in later western fiction. What did prevail, and what did remain memorable to generations of readers, were the romantic conventions that this novel of manners revived and set in a serious (though debated) moral context. There is the exceptional cowboy and his companion horse, the sinister villain bedecked in black . . . , and the heroine who is the harbinger of civilization. There are the preliminary encounters between the hero and the villain, each tenser than the previous meeting. And if there is a single line in the novel that approaches the immortality of "When you call me that, *smile*" . . . , it is the pronouncement of Trampas, who, "courageous with whiskey," tells the Virginian, "I'll give you till sundown to leave town." . . . (pp. 204-08)

Wister's most frequently cited contribution to the Western is the showdown, a formal and detached killing through which the hero resolves a culturally defined conflict. Outlawry, belligerence, affront to honor—all slump together in a dusky heap in the street. But Wister did not invent the showdown, for it is clearly the legacy of such historical romances as *Ivanhoe*, *The Yemassee*, and *The Last of the Mohicans;* and he did not invent the gunfight. He took this convention from the tawdry fiction that immediately preceded him, and he enshrined it along with the other romantic conventions in an enduring work of literary quality and ambition. What has made this convention enduring in Wister's novel has been the serious moral scrutiny of the novelist of manners. (p. 208)

> *John D. Nesbitt, "Owen Wister's Achievement in Literary Tradition," in* Western American Literature, *Vol. XVIII, No. 3, Fall, 1983, pp. 199-208.*

JOHN L. COBBS (essay date 1984)

[*In the following excerpt, Cobbs discusses the characterization of the Virginian, noting that he is the first fully realized hero in American western literature.*]

It should be clear from even . . . [a brief sketch of *The Virginian*] that integrity of plot is not its strength. Three main subplots thread hesitantly through the book, bumping each other casually in a sort of fictional Brownian movement. We can easily make out two of these: the courtship narrative and the heightening conflict between the Virginian and Trampas. Except for the final showdown chapter, when Molly begs her lover not to fight, these stories are almost totally unconnected. The novel flip-flops back and forth from violent confrontation to comic romance, and there are not even transitional passages to connect the world of Trampas with the world of Molly.

The courtship narrative divides itself tidily into four sections, symmetrically spaced throughout the novel: the arrival of Molly and the beginning of the battle of the sexes with the Virginian; the Virginian's deliberate "culturing" of himself to become worthy of her; the climax of the romantic action in which the Virginian recuperates under Molly's care and they plight their troth; and the last chapter describing the pastoral bliss of the wedding journey.

The struggle between hero and villain is also symmetrical. Trampas comes into the novel unequivocally damned: "There was in his countenance the same ugliness that his words conveyed." We are told this during his first episode, the famous card game, in which the Virginian earns his undying hatred. His second appearance is on the train back from Omaha, when he tries to incite the Virginian's men to desert and is bested in the telling of tall tales. A third section of the novel very much concerning Trampas, although he is physically absent, traces the rise of the rustler problem—we have no doubts that Trampas is the leader of the gang from which the luckless Steve is caught and hanged, and we also know that he is the murderer of Shorty on the Superstition Trail. His final appearance is as the antagonist and eventual corpse in his showdown with the Virginian, the only point in the book in which Molly's plot and Trampas's do not go their separate ways.

There is a third type of "action," which might be called "sketches of the Virginian." Much of the novel is really just a collection of anecdotes about the Virginian in particular and life in the West in general, interwoven with Wister's commentary on the significance of that character and life. In these sketches the hero appears in many guises: the masculine, spontaneous Virginian rollicking like a puppy in the streets of Medicine Bow; the whimsical, crackerbarrel philosopher Virginian commenting on the psychology of the hen Em'ly; the Peck's Bad Boy Virginian swapping babies at a ranch social; the crafty but sensible Virginian tricking the hellfire minister who tries to cow him with righteousness; the humane and righteous Virginian beating the bestial Balaam for blinding a horse; the authoritarian moralist Virginian upholding law and order as the leader of a lynch mob; and so on, through a hundred or more vignettes, some extended enough to claim status as full stories, others no more than a paragraph, but each illuminating the multifaceted character of this cowboy hero.

Perhaps the novel's greatest strength lies here. Incident by incident, Wister illuminates the various aspects of his hero until the final figure is more fully developed than any other in early Western fiction. Although he is a "character" in the Local Color tradition, he is less eccentric than most, except in his virtue, and far more substantial. Part of the stock-in-trade of Bret Harte, G. W. Cable, Joel Chandler Harris, Ambrose Bierce, and even Mark Twain in his weaker moments was the odd figure whose idiosyncrasies were often an exaggerated shorthand for the traits of the fictional region. Often, like some of Dickens's weaker caricatures, they were one-trick eccentrics—purely vicious like Simon Legree, insouciant like Harte's gambler Oakwood, rascally like Twain's duke and king. The Virginian's name, however, is Legion.

Preeminently, the Virginian is a substantial physical presence. This prototype for Gary Cooper and John Wayne literally stands tall, six-two. Much of his habitual understatement in speech is made possible by the effective overstatement of his physical appearance. Stature radiates from him, and the impact of his presence is attested to by every perceptive character in the novel. Men sense that he is not a man to be messed with. Women, like the boardinghouse keeper in Medicine Bow, breathe heavily and yield discreetly. The virginal Molly, before their marriage, stands trembling before his very picture. He is the epitome of that red-blooded health both Wister and Roosevelt found on fleeing the anemic East.

His substantiality in the present is accentuated by his lack of a past. From his beguiling namelessness to his lack of biography, he is the western "new man," asking to be taken for what he is and what he appears to be. He's not even really a Virginian, as Wister was well aware, for he wrote to his friend, the journalist Richard Harding Davis:

> There's nothing typically Virginian about him, save some accent, some bad grammar, and some apparent laziness; and he was meant by me to be just my whole American creed in flesh and blood. . . . It was by design he continued nameless because I desired to draw a sort of heroic circle about him, almost a legendary circle and thus if possible create an illusion of remoteness.

This very lack of roots detaches him from the corruption of the East and endows him with a mythic purity that might be less believable if the reader knew more of his past. His lover Molly, for all her virtue, shares some of the snobbish prejudices of her blue-blooded New England and must purge herself of them to form a more perfect union. He, though, is entirely a westerner because he is emphatically not anything else. Of his past, the narrator tells us only that he came from a big family, left home young, and has spent the intervening years wandering to and fro in the earth and up and down in it.

The correlative of the Virginian's overt physicality, his beauty, strength, and athletic grace, is the man's fundamental reserve. His obvious strength of body and character saves him from diffidence, but Wister repeatedly paints him as having an aristocratic introspection that sets him above the common run of cowboys. The hallmark of this reserve is his silence. He is not afraid of words, but he uses them deliberately and despises glibness. Several times Wister stresses his habit of falling into an almost morose silence after talk, as when he has bested Trampas with the tall tale of "frog ranching," and then, "the talking part of him deeply and unbrokenly slept." For him, both boasting and pleading betray weakness bordering on sin. He criticizes Browning's "Incident in the French Camp" because a brave and dying soldier says he's been killed, of which the Virginian comments, "Now a man who was man enough to act like he did, yu' see, would fall dead without mentioning it." Similarly, "he detested words of direct praise."

His silence and his modesty derive from a well of monumental self-confidence and self-respect. He always senses his worth and "felt himself to be a giant whom life had made 'broad gauge,' and denied opportunity." The novel is actually in large part about opportunity knocking in the form of Molly and the foremanship of Judge Henry's ranch, but even when he is a common cowpoke at the beginning, the Virginian knows that "the creature we call a *gentleman* lies deep in the hearts of thousands that are born without chance to master the outward graces of the type." The term *gentleman* subsumes for both the Virginian and his creator a panoply of virtues of which etiquette is the least important.

The most important is professionalism, the key to the character of the gentleman. In the case of the Virginian, it manifests itself in simple ability to outperform other men in virtually every phase of human activity. And not only is the man better than other men, but he knows it. Further, he makes that awareness a cardinal element in his moral code. Unlike some of Hemingway's more inarticulate heroes—the bullfighters, Ole Andreson, Harry Morgan—the Virginian does not exist simply in a world of pure sensory flow, behaving correctly by instinct but largely oblivious to the ethos of his behavior. He is as critic John Williams points out, both the Emersonian Natural Man who functions by instinct, and one of the Calvinistic Elect of God who function by reason and are well aware of their moral status vis-à-vis their fellowmen.

Casual readers of *The Virginian* may not notice how little of his superiority actually consists of mastery of the objective physical skills of the range—riding, roping, shooting—the skills of survival, both in terms of nature and of outlaws and Indians. No question, the Virginian is competent in these matters; from the opening scene taming the difficult horse to the final mano-à-mano defeat of Trampas, he bears out the book's opening comment on him—"That man knows his business." Still, the Virginian is a far cry from the simple men of James Fenimore Cooper's forest, or Vardis Fisher's mountain men. Natty Bumppo may be, to reverse Lowell's epithet, just an Indian daubed over with white, but the Virginian's skills far transcend primitive reflex. His real abilities, actually, are social. He is a master poker player, tall tale teller, bunkhouse lawyer. He can be the life of the party when he wants. He can outcon con men and outthink ministers in a religious talk. He has a flair for the dramatic, vanishing after rescuing Molly from the stage or ominously laying his pistol before him and commanding Trampas to "Smile!" He is an effective, but not ruthless, lover, knowing that the boardinghouse keeper can be won by a tip of the hat, but that for Molly he must learn Shakespeare. Naturally, he evidences the mind of a scholar and the memory of an actor when the occasion calls for it: at one point he recites from memory seven lines on *bees* from *Henry V*, when most people couldn't remember seven lines on kings.

The key to the Virginian's mastery of the puzzling manners and mores of western society is superior perception, an ability to see *through* appearances to the real meaning of things. Whether through moral, gentlemanly instincts, or through an almost animal cunning, Wister's westerner is able to penetrate to the truth underlying the apparent chaos of western life and to manipulate that life effectively by acting on his perception. The Virginian is not to be fooled or misled, for "the sons of the sage-brush . . . live nearer nature, and they know better." He does not scorn rational reason and, in its down-to-earth form, common sense, but rather welcomes it, although instinctive insight is more important. (pp. 80-4)

It is this superiority of insight that makes the Virginian not so much *of* his society as superior to it and which lends to the novel much of the mythic and epic quality that has fixed it in the American imagination. It has also made the book controversial, for Wister is saying that in the new world of the West the superior man must not only be better than others, he must act on that superiority. It is not so much that he is above the law as that he realizes that often there is no law for him to be above, and he must make his own. The lynching of Steve and the killing of Trampas have been repeatedly attacked by Wister's critics, who insist upon generalizing Wister's observations concerning justice and anarchy in a particular situation—one that Wister himself insistently points out is unique. Leslie Fiedler's diatribe in *The Return of the Vanishing American* [see excerpt dated 1968] is typical:

> But behind the talk of honesty and chivalry, it is personal violence, taking the law into one's own hands, for which *The Virginian*—along with all of its recastings and imitations right down to *High Noon*—apologizes. The duel and the lynching represent its notions of honor and glory; and the images of these have occupied the center of the genteel or *kitsch* Western ever since, in pulp magazines, in hardcover or paperback books, on radio, TV, or in the movies.

Fiedler, for all his brilliance as a psychological critic, shows his limitations as a social one, because he fails to take circumstances into account—the circumstances that Wister insists, and demonstrates through his painstaking delineation of subject, are at the very heart of his art. John K. Milton, a pedestrian writer, is closer to the mark when he points out that "when the Virginian changes from a soft-talking, gentle man into a brutal avenger, it is only because justice demands it. The Virginian is what he is—a killer—because of the world in which he lives, not in spite of it. His moral imperatives, borrowed by Wister from the prelegalistic medieval world, derive from an Augustinian conception of transcendent (or divine) law made manifest to a moral elect and through them imposed upon a society that has not yet generated law. The Virginian does not overthrow law and order; he creates it in a primitive form.

The obvious flaw in this interpretation of Wister's moral vision is that Trampas might just as well have won the famous gunfight. In fact, he had a better chance, since he shot first—once again incompetence is equated with immorality. It is exactly this point that moves the novel from the realm of realistic art to that of romantic wish fulfillment. Had the Virginian lost the shoot-out, or had Molly rejected him for fighting as she promised, or had he degenerated morally in a psychologically realistic fashion à la Hawthorne after killing a man, the novel might have gained enormously as a serious moral statement. But it would have never been one of the best-selling American novels of all time, reworked again and again to lead the reader to the same, masturbatory self-satisfying climax.

The ending of *The Virginian* was resolved to satisfy the reader and the author. Wister leads us with considerable skill to believe in a thoroughly established character and in the morally ambivalent and threatening world in which he lives. He convinces us that that world, the frontier West, is a different world with new rules and demanding a new kind of hero, equipped with special skills of reflex, insight, and survival. He places that hero at a moment of potentially tragic decision. The Virginian must opt for love, order and civilization, sacrificing honor and self-respect, or he must commit himself to either death or the loneliness of heroism. Wister gives him the best of both decisions, adding a "happily ever after" epilogue that explains that the Virginian becomes rich, founds a dynasty, and lives a long life.

Why did Wister, a serious artist and a conscientious craftsman, do this? Why did he bring his novel to a point at which, like Conrad, he could have delineated the genuine implications of moral decision, and then let his hero off the hook, telling the reader that morality has no painful price? The answer is the reason *The Virginian* sold and sold and sold: it was what the casual reader wanted to read. More important, it was what Wister wanted to write.

Even an armchair psychologist can see in the Virginian a synthesis of virtues that Wister found so disturbingly irreconcilable in his own life. Conscious from childhood of a lack of spontaneity in himself, resenting overrefinement yet yielding to it, Wister was a Philadelphia hothouse flower powerfully drawn to the natural, primitive life of Wyoming. There man was a more atavistic and instinctive animal than he could ever be on the Main Line. When it came to creating a hero, Wister wanted one with an animality of an almost naturalistic nature. This is one pole of the Virginian's nature—physical prowess, elemental personal magnetism, primal instincts, all producing not only survival but dominance in the jungle of the American frontier. The Virginian is an instinctive beast at home in his primitive environment.

His other face, though, is that of the Philadelphia society that Wister had fled—reserved, courtly, controlled, and most of all, discriminatory. The Virginian, like his creator, is compelled to weigh the moral consequences of every decision. Thus, the agony of choosing between Molly's love and honor. It was an agony that Wister was quite willing and able to work up. What he could not face was subjecting his beloved hero to the painful consequences of that decision, one way or the other. (pp. 84-6)

> *John L. Cobbs, in his* Owen Wister, *Twayne Publishers, 1984, 140 p.*

ADDITIONAL BIBLIOGRAPHY

Boynton, H. W. Review of *The Virginian,* by Owen Wister. *The Atlantic Monthly* XC, No. DXXXVIII (August 1902): 275-81.
Positive review centering around the novel's characterization of the protagonist.

Clark, Walter Van Tilburg. "Philadelphia Gentleman in Wyoming." *The New York Times Book Review* (30 March 1958): 1, 26.
Review of *Owen Wister Out West,* journals and letters written in Wyoming between 1885 and 1895. Clark argues that Wister's

observations—a mixture of awe and admiration for Wyoming's landscape and people, and contempt for the destructive behavior of many frontiersmen—reveal the author's paradoxical personality.

Davis, Robert Murray. "*The Virginian:* Social Darwinist Pastoral." *Acta Litteraria Academiae Scientiarum Hungaricae* 23, Nos. 3-4 (1981): 271-79.
Examines the novel's idyllic or pastoral elements. Davis considers the Virginian the perfect embodiment of bravery, youthful wildness, and physical strength and beauty—characteristics peculiar to the American pastoral hero.

Garland, Hamlin. Review of *Roosevelt: The Story of a Friendship,* by Owen Wister. *The Bookman,* New York LXXI, No. 5 (August 1930): 560-61.
Reviews Wister's account of his lifelong friendship with Theodore Roosevelt.

Heatherington, Madelon E. "Romance without Women: The Sterile Fiction of the American West." *The Georgia Review* XXXIII, No. 3 (Fall 1979): 643-56.*
Explores reasons behind the lack of serious critical and academic attention given western novels. Heatherington contends that even good western fiction such as *The Virginian* remains simplistic in part because of its failure to account for complexities in human behavior, particularly in the treatment of female characters.

Herron, Ima Honaker. "The Long Trail: The Far Western Town." In his *The Small Town in American Literature,* pp. 251-85. 1939. Reprint. New York: Pageant Books, 1959.*
Discusses depictions of western towns in American fiction. Wister's treatment of Medicine Bow, Wyoming, is included in descriptions of other works of American literature treating the frontier town.

———. "Owen Wister as Playwright." *Southwest Review* XLVII, No. 3 (Summer 1962): vi-vii, 265-66.
Contrasts the novel *The Virginian* with the comic drama based upon it.

Lambert, Neal. "Owen Wister's Lin McLean: The Failure of the Vernacular Hero." *Western American Literature* V, No. 3 (Fall 1970): 219-32.
Traces the development of Lin McLean, whom Wister once considered his "best fictional hero" and the reasons he was subsequently regarded by the author as an unsuitable symbol of the cowboy.

———. "Owen Wister's Virginian: The Genesis of a Cultural Hero." *Western American Literature* VI, No. 2 (Summer 1971): 99-107.
Analyzes Wister's adoption of the Virginian as a hero capable of representing the value systems of both the frontiersman and the gentleman.

Marovitz, Sanford E. "Treatment of a Patriot: The Virginian, the Tenderfoot, and Owen Wister." *Texas Studies in Literature and Language* XV, No. 3 (Fall 1973): 551-75.
Explores the significance of *The Virginian* as an expression of American patriotism and of the author's own new-found self-confidence.

Mason, Julian. "Owen Wister and World War I: Appeal for Pentecost." *The Pennsylvania Magazine of History and Biography* CI, No. I (January 1977): 89-102.
Examines Wister's concerns about U.S. involvement in the First World War, as expressed in his *Pentecost of Calamity.*

Matthews, Brander. "An Observant American in France." *The Literary Digest International Book Review* 1, No. 2 (January 1923): 12-13, 63.
Discussion of *Neighbors Henceforth,* Wister's impressions of post-war France.

Mulqueen, James E. "Three Heroes in American Fiction." *Illinois Quarterly* 36, No. 3 (February 1974): 44-50.*

Compares and contrasts respective characterizations of Natty Bumppo, the frontiersman in James Fenimore Cooper's *Leatherstocking* tales, the protagonist of Wister's *Virginian*, and Lew Archer, Ross MacDonald's Los Angeles detective, to illustrate the constants and variables in the perception and presentation of the American hero.

Payne, Darwin. *Owen Wister: Chronicler of the West, Gentleman of the East*. Dallas: Southern Methodist University Press, 1985, 377 p.
Biography, which Payne calls "the narrative of the life of an important American who happened to be a writer." Payne's study revolves around Wister's "association with his eastern acquaintances" and "his time on the trail with western companions."

Phillips, David Graham. "Owen Wister." *The Saturday Evening Post* 175, No. 27 (3 January 1903): 13-14.
Biographical sketch and interview.

Robinson, Forrest G. "The Virginian and Molly in Paradise: How Sweet Is It?" *Western American Literature* XXI, No. 1 (May 1986): 27-38.
Analyzes the Virginian's ambivalence toward marriage. Robinson concludes that there are "three competing dimensions to the Virginian's interior life. There is a strong pull toward a natural code; there is the promise of civilization; and, emergent from the fatigue and frustration that their incompatibility engenders, there is a tertium quid, a longing for a retreat to a condition imagined to antedate tension and discord and ambivalence."

Seelye, John. "When West Was Wister." *The New Republic* 167, No. 8 (2 September 1972): 28-33.
Review of *My Dear Wister: The Frederic Remington-Owen Wister Letters*, edited by Ben Merchant Vorpahl. Seelye argues that the Wister-Remington friendship parallels the earlier friendship of Nathaniel Hawthorne and Herman Melville, with Wister playing the role of mentor to Remington until the latter attained his artistic independence.

Stokes, Frances K. W. *My Father, Owen Wister*. Laramie: Privately printed, 1952, 54 p.
Wister's daughter provides biographical notes and reminiscences, along with ten previously undiscovered letters written by Wister to his mother while he was in Wyoming in 1885.

Topping, Gary. "The Rise of the Western." *Journal of the West* XIX, No. 1 (January 1980): 29-35.*
Evaluates the independent development of western writers at the end of the nineteenth century, their literary antecedents, and their subsequent influence on imitators.

Vorpahl, Ben M. "Henry James and Owen Wister." *The Pennsylvania Magazine* XCV, No. 3 (July 1971): 291-338.*
Discussion of "Jamesian" qualities in *The Virginian* and of the personal relationship between Henry James and Wister.

Ziff, Larzer. "Overcivilization: Harold Frederic, the Roosevelt-Adams Outlook, Owen Wister." In his *The American 1890s: Life and Times of a Lost Generation*, pp. 206-28. New York: Viking Press, 1966.*
Contrasts Wister's realistic Wyoming journal with the romantic western fiction based upon it. Ziff regards *The Virginian* as "the archetype of escape for the new century," which reflects the knightly warrior virtues espoused by Theodore Roosevelt and his proponents as those characteristic of the masculine democratic hero.

Emile Zola

1840-1902

French novelist, short story writer, critic, essayist, dramatist, poet, and journalist.

The following entry presents criticism of *L'assommoir, Nana,* and *Germinal,* which are considered Zola's three greatest novels. For further discussion of Zola's works, see *TCLC,* Volumes 1 and 6.

Zola was the founder and principal theorist of the Naturalist movement in nineteenth-century literature. His stated ambition was to write "the impersonal novel in which the novelist is nothing but a recorder of facts, who has no right to judge or form conclusions." With Zola, the realism of Honoré de Balzac, Gustave Flaubert, and Jules and Edmond de Goncourt lost some of its artistic qualities and gained features of the scientific and sociological document. In *Le roman experimental (The Experimental Novel),* Zola defined Naturalism as "a corner of nature seen through a temperament," and his series of twenty "Rougon-Macquart" novels, subtitled "The Natural and Social History of a Family under the Second Empire," were designed to dramatize the current theories of hereditary determinism as outlined in such works as Prosper Lucas's *Traité de l'hérédité naturelle.* Through depictions of successive generations of two families in the "Rougon-Macquart" novels, Zola demonstrated how various hereditary and environmental factors determine the psychology and behavior of his characters. The novels *L'assommoir, Nana,* and *Germinal,* generally regarded as Zola's most important works, are concerned with the misery and degradation of the French working class and have often been described as anatomies of disease, insanity, and perversion. While Zola did succeed in documenting a historical milieu with great detail and precision, commentators also find in the novels a highly personal vision expressed with emotion and intensity.

Born in Paris, Zola was raised in Aix-en-Provence, where his father was an engineer. When Zola was seven years old his father died and, without his financial support, the family was plunged into poverty. Zola began his education at the local College Bourbon where he became friends with Paul Cézanne. Considered a clever but indifferent student, Zola spent his leisure time wandering in the town and the countryside and reading and writing idyllic poetry. At eighteen he moved to Paris with his mother and attended the Lycée Saint-Louis; but, after twice failing his literature examinations, he left without a degree. For the next two years he lived under financially straitened conditions, until 1864 when he secured a position as a booksellers clerk. The same year he published *Contes à Ninon (Stories for Ninon),* which have more in common with medieval fables of fantasy than with the strict realism of his later works. He also began developing his journalistic skills as a critic of art and music, and with the publication of an article supporting the artists of the then controversial Impressionist school, to which his friend Cézanne belonged, Zola himself became a figure of controversy. His first novel, *La confession de Claude (Claude's Confession),* featured an unsentimentalized portrait of a prostitute, and when the book met with legal difficulties, Zola was accused of deliberately courting notoriety. With *Thérèse Raquin (The Devil's Compact)* and *Ma-*

deleine Férat (Magdalen Férat) he began to experiment with techniques that would lead to the naturalism of the "Rougon-Macquart" cycle.

In 1873 Zola joined Alphonse Daudet, Ivan Turgenev, Edmond de Goncourt, and others in a group of realist writers led by Gustave Flaubert. Zola himself was surrounded by disciples after *L'assommoir,* the seventh novel in the "Rougon-Macquart" series, brought him critical and financial success in 1877. Guy de Maupassant, Paul Alexis, Joris-Karl Huysmans, and others met at Zola's home in Paris and his villa in Médan on the Seine. Together they published *Les soirées de Médan,* to which Zola and the others each contributed one short story. The group broke up shortly after Huysmans split with Zola in 1884, the break resulting from Huysmans's desire to create works that were more personal and artistic than the Naturalist credo would allow. By then the analyses of depravity in the "Rougon-Macquart" novels had earned Zola a reputation among his contemporaries as a pessimistic determinist, if not a pornographer. In 1887, a group of young novelists writing in *Figaro* attacked *La terre (Earth)* as mercenary and pathogenic. Eventually Zola turned from the scientific analysis of the "Rougon-Macquart" cycle to the social pamphleteering of later novels such as *Fécondité (Fruitfulness).*

Zola's most famous example of social advocacy came in 1898 with his involvement in the notorious Dreyfus case. "J'accuse"

("The Dreyfus Case") is a vehement twenty-page open letter to the President of the Republic that appeared in *L'aurore*. The letter defended Alfred Dreyfus, a Jewish army captain accused of treason and sentenced to life on Devil's Island, and charged that army officials had perjured themselves during the Dreyfus trial. As a result of his role in the scandal, Zola was twice tried for libel, suspended from the Legion d'Honneur, and on the advice of legal counsel, fled to England. In 1899 the affair was reopened and Zola returned to Paris under a general amnesty. His actions in the case were considered instrumental in the eventual pardon of Dreyfus. In the next few years Zola published several more novels, including three volumes of the unfinished tetralogy "Les quatre évangiles." In 1902 he died during the night of asphyxiation caused by a faulty fireplace chimney.

In the "Rougon-Macquart" cycle Zola applied the methods of science to the novelist's art. F. W. J. Hemmings has remarked that "Zola reduced the craft of fiction to a mechanical technique," and this technique is visible in the author's *ébauches:* plot outlines, character sketches, and a general thesis to be worked out in each individual novel. An exhaustive researcher, Zola investigated the life of various social sub-groups for the background of his works: he compiled a dictionary of slang to lend verisimilitude to the dialogue of the lower classes in *L'assommoir;* he learned about the theater and horse racing during the preparatory stages of *Nana;* and he studied a coal mining district during a workers strike for *Germinal*. By his immersion in a particular milieu, Zola attempted to attain in his fiction the greatest possible fidelity to social fact. However, recent critics have questioned the extent to which Zola's novels actually reflect the guidelines of Naturalism. Ian Gregor and Brian Nicholas, for instance, have asserted that "the inclinations of the impressionist, the poet of humanity in the mass, presided at the conception of Zola's novels rather than any doctrinaire scientism." Three of the most notable "Rougon-Macquart" novels—*L'assommoir, Nana,* and *Germinal*—in fact have provided critics with evidence that Zola's work displays the concerns of both the scientist and the artist, as well as the conscience of the social reformer. *L'assommoir* traces the life of Gervaise, an industrious laundress with modest dreams whose kindness leads her into financial, moral, and physical destruction; *Nana* narrates the rise and fall of the precociously licentious daughter of Gervaise, who becomes the leading Parisian courtesan and symbolizes the ruin of Parisian society; *Germinal* features the son of Gervaise, Etienne, who becomes the socialist leader of an impoverished mining community. Despite scientific justifications for behavior in these works, modern critics have emphasized their artistry and point out that Zola's novels evolved from a desire for social change as much as a scientific urge to compile a social record. Such critics find that Zola's genius as both artist and propagandist are especially evident in his rendering of crowd scenes, most notably the comical wedding party in *L'assommoir* and the horrifying spectacle of rioting strikers in *Germinal*. Other aspects of Zola's novels that have been closely examined are his complex narrative techniques, his allusions to classical mythology, and the implied religious or philosophical basis of his works. Many critics now agree that Zola's works, once considered simple documentations of the surface of human life, can rewardingly be studied from various and far more sophisticated perspectives.

With Naturalism Zola articulated a theory that affected the course of literature throughout the world. His literary precepts can be seen as an influence on the naturalistic dramas of Henrik Ibsen and Gerhart Hauptmann, on the Italian *verismo* movement, and on such American realists as Theodore Dreiser and Ernest Hemingway. Although the strict scientific conception of literature is no longer popular, or even plausible, the best of the "Rougon-Macquart" novels are regarded as masterpieces that transcend the tenets of Naturalism.

(See also *Contemporary Authors,* Vol. 104.)

PRINCIPAL WORKS

Contes à Ninon   (short stories)   1864
   [*Stories for Ninon*, 1895]
La confession de Claude   (novel)   1865
   [*Claude's Confession*, 1882]
Thérèse Raquin   (novel)   1867
   [*The Devil's Compact*, 1892]
Madeleine Férat   (novel)   1868
   [*Magdalen Férat*, 1880]
La fortune des Rougon   (novel)   1871
   [*The Rougon-Macquart Family*, 1879]
La curée   (novel)   1872
   [*In the Whirlpool*, 1882]
Le ventre de Paris   (novel)   1873
   [*The Markets of Paris*, 1879]
La conquête de Plassans   (novel)   1874
   [*The Conquest of Plassans*, 1879; also published as *A Mad Love; or, The Abbé and His Court*, 1882]
La faute de l'abbé Mouret   (novel)   1875
   [*Albine; or, The Abbe's Temptation*, 1882]
Son excellence Eugène Rougon   (novel)   1876
   [*Eugene Rougon*, 1876]
L'assommoir   (novel)   1877
   [*Gervaise*, 1879; also published as *The "Assommoir,"* 1884]
Une page d'amour   (novel)   1878
   [*Hélène*, 1878]
Nana   (novel)   1880
   [*Nana*, 1880]
Le roman experimental   (criticism)   1880
   [*The Experimental Novel*, 1880]
Les romanciers naturalistes   (criticism)   1881
Pot-bouille   (novel)   1882
   [*Piping Hot*, 1889]
Au bonheur des dames   (novel)   1883
   [*The Bonheur des Dames; or, The Shop Girls of Paris*, 1883; published in England as *The Ladies' Paradise*, 1883]
La joie de vivre   (novel)   1884
   [*Life's Joys*, 1884]
Germinal   (novel)   1885
   [*Germinal*, 1885]
L'oeuvre   (novel)   1886
   [*His Masterpiece?*, 1886]
La terre   (novel)   1886
   [*The Soil*, 1886; also published as *Earth*, 1954]
La rêve   (novel)   1888
   [*The Dream*, 1888]
La bête humaine   (novel)   1890
   [*The Human Brutes*, 1890; also published as *The Human Animals*, 1890]
L'argent   (novel)   1891
   [*Money*, 1891]
La débâcle   (novel)   1892
   [*The Downfall*, 1892]

Le docteur Pascal   (novel)   1893
   [*Doctor Pascal,* 1893]
**Lourdes*   (novel)   1894
   [*Lourdes,* 1896]
**Rome*   (novel)   1896
   [*Rome,* 1896]
''J'accuse''   (letter)   1898
   [''The Dreyfus Case,'' 1898]
**Paris*   (novel)   1898
   [*Paris,* 1898]
***Fécondité*   (novel)   1899
   [*Fruitfulness,* 1900]
***Travail*   (novel)   1901
   [*Labor,* 1901]
***Vérité*   (novel)   1903
   [*Truth,* 1903]

*These volumes comprise the series ''Les Rougon-Macquart.''

**These volumes comprise the trilogy ''Les trois villes.''

***These volumes comprise the unfinished tetralogy ''Les quatre evan-
   giles.''

A. C. SWINBURNE   (essay date 1877)

[*Swinburne was an English poet renowned during his lifetime for
the skill and technical mastery of his lyric poetry, and he is
remembered today as a preeminent symbol of rebellion against
the Victorian age. The explicitly handled sensual themes in his*
Poems and Ballads *(1866) delighted some, shocked many, and
led Robert Buchanan to mention Swinburne in his 1866 condemnation of Charles Baudelaire and ''the fleshly school of poetry.''
To focus on what is sensational in Swinburne, however, is to miss
the assertion, implicit in his poetry and explicit in his critical
writings, that in a time when poets were expected to reflect and
uphold contemporary morality, Swinburne's only vocation was to
express beauty. In an explanation of his aestheticism, he stated:
''Art is not like fire or water, a good servant and a bad master;
rather the reverse. . . . Handmaid of religion, exponent of duty,
servant of fact, pioneer of morality, she cannot in any way become. . . . Her business is not to do good on other grounds, but
do good on her own: all is well with her while she sticks fast to
that.'' In the following excerpt, Swinburne describes the moral
repugnance he feels for* L'assommoir.]

For six months together—from July 9th, 1876, to January 7th,
1877—the pages of the magazine called *La Republique des
Lettres* were distinguished or disfigured by the weekly instal-
ments of a story or a study from life, called *L'Assommoir,* and
written by M. Emile Zola. During all those weeks my name
continued to appear on the cover of the magazine among the
names of its other contributors; a list on which I account it as
no small honour to have seen that name enrolled. But during
all those weeks not a line from my pen appeared on any one
of the pages inside that cover.

Between the first week of them and the last, a single number
of the magazine was made luminous and fragrant by the appearance of a poem on which I said my say some time since
in these columns—. . . . For that single week the publication
of *L'Assommoir* was suspended. It can surely be no impertinent
or unreasonable assumption if we infer—I know nothing personally on the subject—that for this momentary suspension
there can be but one of two reasons assignable. Either Victor
Hugo had distinctly stipulated that so it should be, as a per-

emptory condition of his contributing at all; or the conductors
of the magazine felt by instinct that to act otherwise would be
a gross and hideous outrage on the simplest and deepest instincts of human decency. In the one case they knew, in the
other case they felt, that on this matter the highest in station
among their contributors was or must be of one mind with the
humblest, and (probably in the one case, as assuredly in the
other) would as soon have flung any poem of his in the fire
as have permitted it to come before the world cheek by jowl
with a chapter of *L'Assommoir.*

This may seem a hard thing to say of a book which has found,
I believe, its champions (however few and far between) among
men of good repute; and which is, I know, the work of an
author whose public character as a man of high ability is un-
questionable, and whose private character—I am ready to take
his own printed and published word for it—is such as cannot
be refused to a man of simple and modest habits, of blameless
and unambitious life. Such is M. Zola's plea, put forward on
behalf of his book and of himself with the quiet force of unmistakable sincerity. But surely it needs not a tenth part of his
intelligence to anticipate the instant rejoinder which inevitably
must rise to any possible reader's lips. *Quid ad rem?* What in
the name of common sense, of human reason, is it to us,
whether the author's private life be or be not comparable only,
for majestic or for infantile purity, to that of such men as
Marcus Aurelius or St. Francis of Assisi, if his published work
be what beyond all possible question it is—comparable only
for physical and for moral abomination to such works as, by
all men's admission, it is impossible to call into such a court
as the present, and there bring them forward as the sole fit
subjects of comparison; for the simple and sufficient reason,
that the mention of their very names in print is generally, and
not unnaturally, considered to be of itself an obscene outrage
on all literary law and prescription of propriety?

To bring proof that I have said no harsh or unjustifiable word
on this subject is—unluckily for myself, and obviously to my
reader—a thing utterly out of the question. To transcribe the
necessary extracts would for me—I speak seriously, and within
bounds—would for me be physically impossible. But this much,
I think, it is but proper and necessary to say of them. They
are divisible into two equally horrible and loathsome classes.
Under the one head I rank such passages as deal with physical
matters which might almost have turned the stomach of Dean
Swift. The other class consists of those which contain such
details of brutality and atrocity practised on a little girl, as
would necessitate the interpolation of such a line as follows in
the police report of any and every newspaper in London:—
''The further details given in support of the charge of cruelty
were too revolting for publication in our columns.''

One question remains to ask: Whether anything can justify,
whether anything can excuse, the appearance of such a book
as this against which I have said the least that is possible to
say, in the mildest terms that are possible to use. To me it
seems, on the whole, that nothing imaginable can. To others
it may seem that one thing conceivable might. Considering the
book, so to speak, as a medical drug of the purgative or emetic
kind, they might hope or they might allege that it might remove,—that it might at least allay,—if duly administered or
applied, the malady described in it as eating out the vitals of
so many among the poorer class in Paris. And if we could
know or if we could believe that one family might thus be
saved from sinking into so horrible and foul a Malebolge as
slowly or swiftly swallows up the several families whose his-

tory is here set down,—if we could conceive of such a result as possible, I would not be slower than another to admit or to consider the force of this sole extenuating circumstance. But let us notice what is implied by such a plea. Nothing less is implied by it than this:—that such families as these are likely to take in such magazines as that which gave generous but incongruous shelter to the horrible homeless head of this wandering abomination—to a book which could find no other harbour, no port of refuge but this. . . .

One word before I close—one last egoistic word of irrepressible even if damnable iteration. It is perhaps possible that to some reader the substance of this note may suggest some suspiciously suggestive reminiscence of "the Puff Oblique." I can desire no heavier punishment for any one whose mind could give entrance to such a shameful and insulting thought than that he should act on it, and read *L'Assommoir* from the first page to the last; a thing which I confess I most certainly have not done, and most assuredly could not do. If he does not find this perusal a most heavy and most loathsome form of judicial retribution, a chastisement comparable to none in Dante's hell but that inflicted on the damned whose scalps were so densely overlaid with something I cannot here mention (as M. Zola would) by name—to borrow a bold phrase from Mr. Browning, so "immortally immerded"—that Dante could not see whether the crown were shorn or unshorn,—if he feels otherwise or less than this, he is not one for whose possible opinion or imputation I ever could greatly care. And herewith I thankfully wash my hands for ever of the subject, as I hopefully desire to cleanse my memory for ever from all recollection of the book; reiterating simply, on my own poor personal behalf, that whether it were or were not an accident which allowed not one line of this work to appear in that number of the magazine made sweet and splendid by the passing touch of Victor Hugo, it was by no manner of means an accident which during all the weeks and all the months of its long and loathsome progress kept out of the desecrated pages of *La Republique des Lettres* any line of verse, any message of prose, from the hand of

A. C. SWINBURNE.

A. C. Swinburne, "Note on a Question of the Hour,"
in The Athenaeum, *No. 2590, June 16, 1877, p. 768.*

HENRY JAMES   (essay date 1880)

[*As a novelist James is valued for his psychological acuity and complex sense of artistic form. Throughout his career, James also wrote literary criticism in which he developed his artistic ideals and applied them to the works of others. Among the numerous conceptualizations he formed to clarify the nature of fiction, he defined the novel as "a direct impression of life." The quality of this impression—the degree of moral and intellectual development—and the author's ability to communicate this impression in an effective and artistic manner were the two principal criteria by which James estimated the worth of a literary work. James admired the self-consciously formalistic approach of contemporary French writers, particularly Gustave Flaubert, whose approach contrasted with the loose, less formulated standards of English novelists. On the other hand, he favored the moral concerns of English writing over the often amoral and cynical vision which characterized much of French literature in the second half of the nineteenth century. After considering various fictional strategies, James arrived at what he thought the most desirable form for the novel to take. Basically objective in presentation—that is, without the intrusion of an authorial voice—the novel should be a well-integrated formal scheme of dialogue, description, and narrative action, all of which should be received from the viewpoint of a single consciousness, or "receptor." In James's novels*
this receptor is usually a principal character who is more an observer than a participant in the plot. Equal in importance to the artistic plan of a novel is the type of receptor a novelist chooses to use. The type demanded by James's theory possesses a consciousness that will convey a high moral vision, a humanistic worldview, and a generally uplifting sense of life. James's criteria were accepted as standards by a generation of novelists that included Ford Madox Ford, Joseph Conrad, and Virginia Woolf. In the following excerpt, James discusses the literary style and techniques employed in *Nana *and the degree to which the work reflects Zola's theory of Naturalism.]

M. Zola's new novel has been immensely talked about for the last six months; but we may doubt whether, now that we are in complete possession of it, its fame will further increase. It is a difficult book to read; we have to push our way through it very much as we did through *L'Assommoir,* with the difference that in *L'Assommoir* our perseverance, our patience, were constantly rewarded, and that in *Nana,* these qualities have to content themselves with the usual recompense of virtue, the simple sense of duty accomplished. I do not mean, indeed, by this allusion to duty that there is any moral obligation to read *Nana;* I simply mean that such an exertion may have been felt to be due to M. Zola by those who have been interested in his general attempt. His general attempt is highly interesting, and *Nana* is the latest illustration of it. It is far from being the most successful one; the obstacles to the reader's enjoyment are numerous and constant. It is true that, if we rightly understand him, enjoyment forms no part of the emotion to which M. Zola appeals; in the eyes of 'naturalism' enjoyment is a frivolous, a superficial, a contemptible sentiment. It is difficult, however, to express conveniently by any other term the reader's measure of the entertainment afforded by a work of art. If we talk of interest, instead of enjoyment, the thing does not better our case—as it certainly does not better M. Zola's. The obstacles to interest in *Nana* constitute a formidable body, and the most comprehensive way to express them is to say that the work is inconceivably and inordinately dull. M. Zola (if we again understand him) will probably say that it is a privilege, or even a duty, of naturalism to be dull, and to a certain extent this is doubtless a very lawful plea. It is not an absolutely fatal defect for a novel not to be amusing, as we may see by the example of several important works. *Wilhelm Meister* is not a sprightly composition, and yet *Wilhelm Meister* stands in the front rank of novels. *Romola* is a very easy book to lay down, and yet *Romola* is full of beauty and truth. *Clarissa Harlowe* discourages the most robust persistence, and yet, paradoxical as it seems, *Clarissa Harlowe* is deeply interesting. It is obvious, therefore, that there is something to be said for dullness; and this something is perhaps, primarily, that there is dullness and dullness. That of which *Nana* is so truly a specimen, is of a peculiarly unredeemed and unleavened quality; it lacks that human savour, that finer meaning which carries it off in the productions I just mentioned. What *Nana* means it will take a very ingenious apologist to set forth. I speak, of course, of the impression it produces on English readers; into the deep mystery of the French taste in such matters it would be presumptuous for one of these to attempt to penetrate. The other element that stops the English reader's way is that monstrous uncleanness to which—to the credit of human nature in whatever degree it may seem desirable to determine—it is probably not unjust to attribute a part of the facility with which the volume before us has reached, on the day of its being offered for sale by retail, a thirty-ninth edition. M. Zola's uncleanness is not a thing to linger upon, but it is a thing to speak of, for it strikes us as an extremely curious phenomenon. In this respect *Nana* has little to envy its predecessors. The book is, perhaps, not pervaded by that ferociously bad smell which blows through *L'Assommoir* like an emanation from an open drain and makes the perusal of the history of Gervaise and Coupeau very much such an ordeal as a crossing of the Channel in a November gale; but in these matters comparisons are as difficult as they are unprofitable, and *Nana* is, in all conscience, untidy enough. To say the book is indecent, is to make use of a term which (always, if we understand him,) M. Zola holds to mean nothing and to prove nothing. Decency and indecency, morality and immorality, beauty and ugliness, are conceptions with which 'naturalism' has nothing to do; in M. Zola's system these distinctions are void, these allusions are idle. The only business of naturalism is to be—natural, and therefore, instead of saying of *Nana* that it contains a great deal of filth, we should simply say of it that it contains a great deal of nature. Once upon a time a rather pretentious person, whose moral tone had been corrupted by evil communications, and who lived among a set of people equally pretentious, but regrettably low-minded, being in conversation with another person, a lady of great robustness of judgment and directness of utterance, made use constantly, in a somewhat cynical and pessimistic sense, of the expression, "the world—the world". At last the distinguished listener could bear it no longer, and abruptly made reply: "My poor lady, do you call that corner of a pig-sty in which you happen to live, *the world*?" Some such answer as this we are moved to make to M. Zola's naturalism. Does he call that vision of things of which *Nana* is a representation, *nature*? The mighty mother, in her blooming richness, seems to blush from brow to chin at the insult! On what authority does M. Zola represent nature to us as a combination of the cesspool and the house of prostitution? On what authority does he represent foulness rather than fairness as the sign that we are to know her by? On the authority of his predilections alone; and this is his great trouble and the weak point of his incontestably remarkable talent. This is the point that, as we said just now, makes the singular foulness of his imagination worth touching upon, and which, we should suppose, will do much towards preserving his works for the curious contemplation of the psychologist and the historian of literature. Never was such foulness so spontaneous and so complete, and never was it united with qualities so superior to itself and intrinsically so respectable. M. Zola is an artist, and this is supposed to be a safeguard; and, indeed, never surely was any other artist so dirty as M. Zola! Other performers may have been so, but they were not artists; other such exhibitions may have taken place, but they have not taken place between the covers of a book—and especially of a book containing so much of vigorous and estimable effort. We have no space to devote to a general consideration of M. Zola's theory of the business of a novelist, or to the question of naturalism at large—much further than to say that the system on which the series of *Les Rougons-Macquart* has been written, contains, to our sense, a great deal of very solid ground. M. Zola's attempt is an extremely fine one; it deserves a great deal of respect and deference, and though his theory is constantly at odds with itself, we could, at a pinch, go a long way with it without quarrelling. What we quarrel with is his application of it—is the fact that he presents us with his decoction of 'nature' in a vessel unfit for the purpose, a receptacle lamentably, fatally in need of scouring (though no scouring, apparently, would be really effective), and in which no article intended for intellectual consumption should ever be served up. Reality is the object of M. Zola's efforts, and it is because we agree with him in appreciating it highly that we protest against its being discredited. In a time when literary taste has

turned, to a regrettable degree, to the vulgar and the insipid, it is of high importance that realism should not be compromised. Nothing tends more to compromise it than to represent it as necessarily allied to the impure. That the pure and the impure are for M. Zola, as conditions of taste, vain words, and exploded ideas, only proves that his advocacy does more to injure an excellent cause than to serve it. It takes a very good cause to carry a *Nana* on its back, and if realism breaks down, and the conventional comes in again with a rush, we may know the reason why. The real has not a single shade more affinity with an unclean vessel than with a clean one, and M. Zola's system, carried to its utmost expression, can dispense as little with taste and tact as the floweriest mannerism of a less analytic age. . . . It is impossible to see why the question of application is less urgent in naturalism than at any other point of the scale, or why, if naturalism is, as M. Zola claims, a method of observation, it can be followed without delicacy or tact. There are all sorts of things to be said about it; it costs us no effort whatever to admit in the briefest terms that it is an admirable invention, and full of promise; but we stand aghast at the want of tact it has taken to make so unreadable a book as *Nana*. (pp. 274-79)

[There] are many different ways of being serious. That of the author of *L'Assommoir,* of *La Conquête de Plassans,* of *La Faute de l'Abbé Mouret* may, . . . with all its merits and defects taken together, suggest a great many things to English readers. They must admire the largeness of his attempt and the richness of his intention. They must admire, very often, the brilliancy of his execution. *L'Assommoir,* in spite of its fetid atmosphere, is full of magnificent passages and episodes, and the sustained power of the whole thing, the art of carrying a weight, is extraordinary. What will strike the English reader of M. Zola at large, however, and what will strike the English reader of *Nana,* if he have stoutness of stomach enough to advance in the book, is the extraordinary absence of humour, the dryness, the solemnity, the air of tension and effort. M. Zola disapproves greatly of wit; he thinks it is an impertinence in a novel, and he would probably disapprove of humour if he *knew* what it is. There is no indication in all his works that he has a suspicion of this; and what tricks the absence of a sense of it plays him! What a mess it has made of this admirable *Nana*! The presence of it, even in a limited degree, would have operated, to some extent, as a disinfectant, and if M. Zola had had a more genial fancy he would also have had a cleaner one. Is it not also owing to the absence of a sense of humour that this last and most violent expression of the realistic faith is extraordinarily wanting in reality? Anything less illusory than the pictures, the people, the indecencies of *Nana,* could not well be imagined. The falling-off from *L'Assommoir* in this respect can hardly be exaggerated. The human note is completely absent, the perception of character, of the way that people feel and think and act, is helplessly, hopelessly at fault; so that it becomes almost grotesque at last to see the writer trying to drive before him a herd of figures that never for an instant stand on their legs. This is what saves us in England . . .—this fact that we are by disposition better psychologists, that we have, as a general thing, a deeper, more delicate perception of the play of character and the state of the soul. This is what often gives an interest to works conceived on a much narrower programme than those of M. Zola—makes them more touching and more real, although the apparatus and the machinery of reality may, superficially, appear to be wanting. French novelists are at bottom, with all their extra freedom, a good deal more conventional than our own; and *Nana,* with the prodigious freedom that her author has taken, never, to my sense, leaves for a moment the region of the conventional. The figure of the brutal *fille,* without a conscience or a soul, with nothing but devouring appetites and impudences, has become the stalest of the stock properties of French fiction, and M. Zola's treatment has here imparted to her no touch of superior verity. He is welcome to draw as many figures of the same type as he finds necessary, if he will only make them human; this is as good a way of making a contribution to our knowledge of ourselves as another. It is not his choice of subject that has shocked us; it is the melancholy dryness of his execution, which gives us all the bad taste of a disagreeable dish and none of the nourishment. (pp. 279-80)

Henry James, "'Nana'," in his The House of Fiction: Essays on the Novel, *edited by Leon Edel, Rupert Hart-Davis, 1957, pp. 274-280.*

A. K. FISKE   (essay date 1880)

[*Fiske was an American journalist, essayist, and historian. In the following excerpt, he contends that* Nana *presents an unrealistic picture of the milieu it purports to represent, and also argues that the artistic virtues of the work do not excuse its unwholesome message.*]

Critics have had their say regarding the latest product of that genius of the muck-rake, Emile Zola. Many of them have endeavored to find a justification for his opening of the sewers of human society into the gardens of literature. Much ability is displayed in this offensive work of engineering skill, and people are asked to pardon the foul sights and odors because of the consummate art with which they are presented. But intellectual power and literary workmanship are neither to be admired nor commended of themselves. They are to be judged by their fruits, and are no more to be justified in producing that which is repulsive or unwholesome than a manufactory whose sole purpose is to create and disseminate bad smells and noxious vapors. Such an unsavory establishment might do its work with a wonderful display of skill and most potent results, but the health authorities of society would have ample occasion for taking measures against its obnoxious business, while those who encouraged the introduction of its products into their households would be guilty of inconceivable folly, besides exhibiting a morbid liking for filthy exhalations.

But it is not alone in M. Zola's literary talent that excuse is found for his work. It is said to lay bare a phase of human life whose existence is actual, and knowledge of which affords security and perhaps suggests remedies for its evils. The phase of life with which he deals in *Nana* is undoubtedly real, but is, unfortunately, not so far a realm of the unknown that an accurate exploration or a vivid portrayal of its characters and scenes is at all necessary or desirable. Those who are likely to make a salutary use of a knowledge of its secrets have no difficulty in obtaining it, and there is no reason for bringing its revelations into the family circle or the chamber of the schoolgirl. The life of the fallen among women is no deep mystery. It is well enough known in its glare and glitter, in its allurement and revelry, in its Circean fascinations and their besotting effects, in its coarse vulgarity and in its bestial pollutions. The whole Avernian descent from gay hilarity and defiance of doom to putridity and despair is a reality of the world's every-day experience. That can not be denied, and the fact is one not to be ignored. But so are the city sewers and cesspools a reality; yet their existence affords no reason for bringing them to the surface of the streets and exploring among their filthy contents in the light of day. It does not justify the introduction of their nastiness and their stenches into decent habitations.

But, though these things are real, M. Zola's delineations of them are not truthful. His work has been called "realistic," and that has been paraded as a merit; but what is meant by this word upon which a new meaning is thrust to serve the purposes of criticism? People averse to analyzing take it to mean that the work in question portrays life and character precisely as they exist, without the color or the glamour which fiction is supposed generally to throw over its descriptions. But as applied to Zola's work it means nothing of the kind. It means that he drags into literature what others would not touch because of its coarseness or its foulness. He displays no extraordinary power in painting scenes of actual life, in portraying human character or in fathoming the feelings or the motives of men. But, where another paints a garden of flowers, he depicts a dunghill; where others present to the imagination fields and trees and mountains or the charms of home-life, he conjures up the prospect behind the stables, the slough at the foot of the drain, and the disgusting bestiality of the slums. . . . To follow a debased drunkard through the career of a day and a night would fill us with disgust, and from a streetwalker's brazen solicitations we turn away with a sort of horror; and what better, more attractive, or more edifying are they if brought into our houses in a story?

But, if "realism" were an excuse for minutely depicting the vile phases of human society, it does not exist in *Nana.* M. Zola may know more of the life that he undertakes to portray than decent readers care to know, but men who go through the world with their eyes open, and are capable of making those inferences in regard to character and experience which surface indications suggest, know that this book is replete with exaggeration. It does not describe the real life of the class whose type is its central figure, with the sharp lines of truth. The picture is colossal in proportions and flaring in colors. It is no more in the tone of every-day reality than *King Lear* or *The Bride of Lammermoor.* This huge, fleshly Venus, with gross attractions of person and no touch of mental or moral charm, exercising a relentless dominion of lust over the rich and proud, the stupid and the brilliant, the unsophisticated and the experienced, is a daring figment of the imagination, as much so as the witch that lured the companions of Ulysses to their swinish fate. The favorite plea of justification in the dry reality of the scenes portrayed has no basis in this story. M. Zola has been writing on a theory, and, in following it out, he has left fact behind him with the ancestors of Nana. His drunkards and washer-women were real. It was a part of his theory that the ignorance, the poverty, the vice, the crime, and the brutality of their existence were somehow imposed upon them by the constitution of society, and made up a fate for which better or more fortunate people were responsible. In the course of generations, out of this compost at the bottom of society, reeking with pollution, sprang this "golden fly," to carry infection up to the ranks of the rich, the intelligent, and the favored, and work the vengeance of the slums. The theory has a certain delusive plausibility, but its Nemesis is a creature of the fancy. As poetry, as ingenious fiction, it might pass; but its pretensions to reality are a sham, and the poor excuse of "realism" for unveiling the retreats of infamy can not be allowed to the Parisian scavenger.

But real or fanciful, fact or fiction, does not this delineation of the fatal attractions of the "strange woman" and the consequences of yielding to her wiles find justification in the revelation of danger and the warning to the unwary? Does it not beget abhorrence of what it depicts with so much power? Perhaps the Spartan father did well to exhibit before his son the awful example of the drunken helot; but, if he had sent the boy to pass his time with drunken helots and become familiar with their ways and habits, the result would hardly have justified the wisdom of the experiment. We unconsciously take on the character of our social surroundings, and in the reading of fiction we subject our minds to the influences which its scenes are calculated to produce. The imagination works an inner experience whose effects upon tastes and sensibilities are not different in kind from those of the external experience of actual life. If there is any remedial influence in an acquaintance with lives of prostitution, how comes it that those who have cultivated that kind of acquaintance and obtained the knowledge which is so potent for defense are not the purest among men? Generally we find that the repulsiveness of vice loses its force upon those who come in close contact with it. The victims of Nana knew her character well enough; they knew her selfish prodigality, and the fatal consequence of dalliance with such as she; and they might even forecast her horrible fate and that of her victims. But this knowledge was no protection. Association with her did not beget repulsion; familiarity produced no warning, and those who cherished their ignorance of her world of tawdriness, of dissipation and excitement, were safest from its dangers. . . . This gilded realm with its sensuous attractions is opened to the mental ken, its characters are revealed, and its scenes laid bare with more or less of truth, and the familiarity which the reader acquires with its interior life seems to bring him into closer contact with it, and make an actual entrance an easy matter. Such a book, whatever its effect may be upon the thoughtful, is certainly not a warning to the unwary. It is no preacher of virtue, but a guide to debauchery.

On no ground, intellectual or moral, is the publication of this kind of literature to be justified, but it can not be prevented. Liberty has its penalties and its drawbacks, but it is too precious a boon to be easily placed in the power of official and officious meddlers. Zola's brain is at liberty to produce according to its nature, but the shame is, that thousands of decent people, people claiming the highest respectability and the purest taste, should take the foul brood of his incubation into their homes. To those for whom it has no novelty it is merely a new incitement to sensuality. To those for whom it brings a revelation it is contaminating, and opens to view a phase of life that had much better remain hid. (pp. 79-83)

A. K. Fiske, "Profligacy in Fiction," in The North American Review, Vol. CXXXI, No. 284, July, 1880, pp. 79-88.*

GEORGE MOORE   (essay date 1888)

[*Moore was an Irish novelist, autobiographer, and essayist who has been credited with introducing techniques characteristic of French Naturalism into English literature. His most acclaimed novel,* Esther Waters *(1894), gained notoriety for its depiction of human weakness and degradation, rendered with the kind of detailed objectivity that had been made popular in France by the novels of Zola. Moore, however, professed to be less interested in the human aspect of his works than in their artistic purity. In his critical writings he advocated the aesthetic doctrine of pure form, and in his fiction attempted to give precedence to artistic design over statements about the world or the lives of his characters. In the following excerpt from Moore's autobiographical novel* Confessions of a Young Man, *the narrator reveals his initial*

reaction to the literary school of Naturalism as represented by L'assommoir.]

One day . . . I took up the *Voltaire*. It contained an article by M. Zola. *Naturalisme, la vérité, la science*, were repeated some half-a-dozen times. Hardly able to believe my eyes, I read that you should write, with as little imagination as possible, that plot in a novel or in a play was illiterate and puerile, and that the art of M. Scribe was an art of strings and wires, etc. I rose up from breakfast, ordered my coffee, and stirred the sugar, a little dizzy, like one who has received a violent blow on the head. . . .

Naturalism, truth, the new art, above all the pharse, "the new art," impressed me as with a sudden sense of light. I was dazzled, and I vaguely understood that my *Roses of Midnight* [a collection of poems by the narrator of *Confessions of a Young Man*] were sterile eccentricities, dead flowers that could not be galvanised into any semblance of life, passionless in all their passion.

I had read a few chapters of the **Assommoir**, as it appeared in *La République des Lettres;* I had cried, "ridiculous, abominable," only because it is characteristic of me to instantly form an opinion and assume at once a violent attitude. But now I bought up the back numbers of the *Voltaire*, and I looked forward to the weekly exposition of the new faith with febrile eagerness. The great zeal with which the new master continued his propaganda, and the marvellous way in which subjects the most diverse, passing events, political, social, religious, were caught up and turned into arguments for, or proof of the truth of naturalism astonished me wholly. The idea of a new art based upon science, in opposition to the art of the old world that was based on imagination, an art that should explain all things and embrace modern life in its entirety, in its endless ramifications, be, as it were, a new creed in a new civilisation, filled me with wonder, and I stood dumb before the vastness of the conception, and the towering height of the ambition. In my fevered fancy I saw a new race of writers that would arise, and with the aid of the novel would continue to a more glorious and legitimate conclusion the work that the prophets had begun; and at each development of the theory of the new art and its universal applicability, my wonder increased and my admiration choked me. If any one should be tempted to turn to the books themselves to seek an explanation of this wild ecstacy, they would find nothing—as well drink the dregs of yesterday's champagne. One is lying before me now, and as I glance through the pages listlessly I say, "Only the simple crude statements of a man of powerful mind, but singularly narrow vision." (pp. 94-5)

But it was the idea of the new aestheticism—the new art corresponding to modern, as ancient art corresponded to ancient life—that captivated me, that led me away, and not a substantial knowledge of the work done by the naturalists. I had read the **Assommoir,** and had been much impressed by its pyramid size, strength, height, and decorative grandeur, and also by the immense harmonic development of the idea; and the fugal treatment of the different scenes had seemed to me astonishingly new—the washhouse, for example: the fight motive is indicated, then follows the development of side issues, then comes the fight motive explained; it is broken off short, it flutters through a web of progressive detail, the fight motive is again taken up, and now it is worked out in all its fulness; it is worked up to *crescendo*, another side issue is introduced, and again the theme is given forth. And I marvelled greatly at the lordly, river-like roll of the narrative, sometimes widening out into lakes and shallowing meres, but never stagnating in fen or marshlands. The language, too, which I did not then recognise as the weak point, being little more than a boiling down of a Chateaubriand and Flaubert, spiced with Goncourt, delighted me with its novelty, its richness, its force. Nor did I then even roughly suspect that the very qualities which set my admiration in a blaze wilder than wildfire, being precisely those that had won the victory for the romantic school forty years before, were very antagonistic to those claimed for the new art; I was deceived, as was all my generation, by a certain externality, an outer skin, a nearness, *un approchement;* in a word, by a substitution of Paris for the distant and exotic backgrounds so beloved of the romantic school. I did not know then, as I do now, that art is eternal, that it is only the artist that changes, and that the two great divisions—the only possible divisions—are: those who have talent, and those who have no talent. But I do not regret my errors, my follies; it is not well to know at once of the limitations of life and things. I should be less than nothing had it not been for my enthusiasms: they were the saving clause in my life. (pp. 96-7)

> George Moore, in a chapter in his Confessions of a
> Young Man, *edited by Susan Dick, McGill-Queen's*
> *University Press, 1972, pp. 93-108.* *

ARTHUR SYMONS (essay date 1893)

[*While Symons initially gained notoriety as a member of the English Decadent movement of the 1890s, he eventually established himself as one of the most important critics of the modern era. As a member of the iconoclastic generation of fin de siècle aesthetes that included Aubrey Beardsley and Oscar Wilde, Symons wholeheartedly assumed the role of the world-weary cosmopolite and sensation hunter, composing verses in which he attempted to depict the bohemian world of the modern artist. However, it was as a critic that Symons made his most important contribution to literature. His* The Symbolist Movement in Literature *(1899) provided his English contemporaries with an appropriate vocabulary with which to define their new aesthetic—one that communicated their concern with dreamlike states, imagination, and a reality that exists beyond the boundaries of the senses. Symons also discerned that the concept of the symbol as a vehicle by which a "hitherto unknown reality was suddenly revealed" could become the basis for the entire modern aesthetic. A proper use of the symbol "would flash upon you the soul of that which can be apprehended only by the soul—the finer sense of things unseen, the deeper meaning of things evident." This anticipated and influenced James Joyce's concept of an artistic "epiphany," T. S. Eliot's "moment in time," and laid the foundation for much of modern poetic theory. In the following excerpt, Symons examines the narrative techniques employed by Zola, unfavorably comparing* L'assommoir *to work of Edmond de Goncourt and Gustave Flaubert.*]

L'Assommoir [is] no doubt the most characteristic of Zola's novels, and probably the best; and, leaving out for the present the broader question of his general conception of humanity, let us look at Zola's manner of dealing with his material, noting by the way certain differences between his manner and that of Goncourt, of Flaubert, with both of whom he has so often been compared, and with whom he wishes to challenge comparison. Contrast *L'Assommoir* with *Germinie Lacerteux*, which, it must be remembered, was written thirteen years earlier. Goncourt, as he incessantly reminds us, was the first novelist in France to deliberately study the life of the people, after precise documents; and *Germinie Lacerteux* has this distinction, among others, that it was a new thing. And it is done with admirable skill; as a piece of writing, as a work of art, it is far superior

to Zola. But, certainly, Zola's work has a mass and bulk, a *fougue*, a *portée*, which Goncourt's lacks; and it has a savour of plebeian flesh which all the delicate art of Goncourt could not evoke. Zola sickens you with it; but there it is. As in all his books, but more than in most, there is something greasy, a smear of eating and drinking; the pages, to use his own phrase, *grasses des lichades du lundi*. In *Germinie Lacerteux* you never forget that Goncourt is an aristocrat; in *L'Assommoir* you never forget that Zola is a bourgeois. Whatever Goncourt touches becomes, by the mere magic of his touch, charming, a picture; Zola is totally destitute of charm. But how, in *L'Assommoir*, he drives home to you the horrid realities of these narrow, uncomfortable lives! Zola has made up his mind that he will say everything, without omitting a single item, whatever he has to say; thus, in *L'Assommoir*, there is a great feast which lasts for fifty pages, beginning with the picking of the goose, the day before, and going on to the picking of the goose's bones, by a stray marauding cat, the night after. And, in a sense, he does say everything; and there, certainly, is his novelty, his invention. He observes with immense persistence, but his observation, after all, is only that of the man in the street; it is simply carried into detail, deliberately. And, while Goncourt wanders away sometimes into arabesques, indulges in flourishes, so finely artistic is his sense of words and of the things they represent, so perfectly can he match a sensation or an impression by its figure in speech, Zola, on the contrary, never finds just the right word, and it is his persistent fumbling for it which produces these miles of description; four pages describing how two people went upstairs, from the ground floor to the sixth story, and then two pages afterwards to describe how they came downstairs again. Sometimes, by his prodigious diligence and minuteness, he succeeds in giving you the impression; often, indeed; but at the cost of what *ennui* to writer and reader alike! And so much of it all is purely unnecessary, has no interest in itself and no connection with the story: the precise details of Lorilleux's chain-making, bristling with technical terms: it was *la colonne* that he made, and only that particular kind of chain; Goujet's forge, and the machinery in the shed next door; and just how you cut out zinc with a large pair of scissors. When Goncourt gives you a long description of anything, even if you do not feel that it helps on the story very much, it is such a beautiful thing in itself, his mere way of writing it is so enchanting, that you find yourself wishing it longer, at its longest. But with Zola, there is no literary interest in the writing, apart from its clear and coherent expression of a given thing; and these interminable descriptions have no extraneous, or, if you will, implicit interest, to save them from the charge of irrelevancy; they sink by their own weight. Just as Zola's vision is the vision of the average man, so his vocabulary, with all its technicology, remains mediocre, incapable of expressing subtleties, incapable of a really artistic effect. To find out in a slang dictionary that a filthy idea can be expressed by an ingeniously filthy phrase in *argot*, and to use that phrase, is not a great feat, or, on purely artistic grounds, altogether desirable. To go to a chainmaker and learn the trade name of the various kinds of chain which he manufactures, and of the instruments with which he manufactures them, is not an elaborate process, or one which can be said to pay you for the little trouble which it no doubt takes. And it is not well to be too certain after all that Zola is always perfectly accurate in his use of all this manifold knowledge. The slang, for example; he went to books for it, in books he found it, and no one will ever find some of it but in books. However, my main contention is that Zola's general use of words is, to be quite frank, somewhat ineffectual. He tries to do what Flaubert did, without Flaubert's tools, and without the craftsman's hand at the back of the tools. His fingers are too thick; they leave a blurred line. If you want merely weight, a certain kind of force, you get it; but no more.

Where a large part of Zola's merit lies, in his persistent attention to detail, one finds also one of his chief defects. He cannot leave well alone; he cannot omit; he will not take the most obvious fact for granted.... He tells us particularly that a room is composed of four walls, that a table stands on its four legs. And he does not appear to see the difference between doing that and doing as Flaubert does, namely, selecting precisely the detail out of all others which renders or consorts with the scene in hand, and giving that detail with an ingenious exactness. (pp. 162-67)

And the language in which all this is written, apart from the consideration of language as a medium, is really not literature at all, in any strict sense. I am not, for the moment, complaining of the colloquialism and the slang. Zola has told us that he has, in *L'Assommoir,* used the language of the people in order to render the people with a closer truth. Whether he has done that or not is not the question. The question is, that he does not give one the sense of reading good literature, whether he speaks in Delvau's *langue verte*]''slang''], or according to the Academy's latest edition of classical French. His sentences have no rhythm; they give no pleasure to the ear; they carry

no sensation to the eye. You hear a sentence of Flaubert, and you see a sentence of Goncourt, like living things, with forms and voices. But a page of Zola lies dull and silent before you; it draws you by no charm, it has no meaning until you have read the page that goes before and the page that comes after. It is like cabinet-makers' work, solid, well fitted together, and essentially made to be used.

Yes, there is no doubt that Zola writes very badly, worse than any other French writer of eminence. It is true that Balzac, certainly one of the greatest, does, in a sense, write badly; but his way of writing badly is very different from Zola's, and leaves you with the sense of quite a different result. Balzac is too impatient with words; he cannot stay to get them all into proper order, to pick and choose among them. Night, the coffee, the wet towel, and the end of six hours' labour are often too much for him; and his manner of writing his novels on the proof-sheets, altering and expanding as fresh ideas came to him on each re-reading, was not a way of doing things which can possibly result in perfect writing. But Balzac sins from excess, from a feverish haste, the very extravagance of power; and, at all events, he "sins strongly." Zola sins meanly, he is penuriously careful, he does the best he possibly can; and he is not aware that his best does not answer all requirements. So long as writing is clear and not ungrammatical, it seems to him sufficient. He has not realised that without charm there

Illustration for L'assommoir *by Pierre Renoir.*

can be no fine literature, as there can be no perfect flower without fragrance.

And it is here that I would complain, not as a matter of morals, but as a matter of art, of Zola's obsession by what is grossly, uninterestingly filthy. There is a certain simile in *L'Assommoir,* used in the most innocent connection, in connection with a bonnet, which seems to me the most abjectly dirty phrase which I have ever read. It is one thing to use dirty words to describe dirty things: that may be necessary, and thus unexceptionable. It is another thing again, and this, too, may well be defended on artistic grounds, to be ingeniously and wittily indecent. But I do not think a real man of letters could possibly have used such an expression as the one I am alluding to, or could so meanly succumb to certain kinds of prurience which we find in Zola's work. Such a scene as the one in which Gervaise comes home with Lantier, and finds her husband lying drunk asleep in his own vomit, might certainly be explained and even excused, though few more disagreeable things were ever written, on the ground of the psychological importance which it undoubtedly has, and the overwhelming way in which it drives home the point which it is the writer's business to make. But the worrying way in which *le derrière* ["buttocks"] and *le ventre* ["stomach"] are constantly kept in view, without the slightest necessity, is quite another thing. I should not like to say how often the phrase "sa nudité de jolie fille" ["her pretty girl's nudity"] occurs in Zola. Zola's nudities always remind me of those which you can see in the *Foire au pain d'épice* at Vincennes, by paying a penny and looking through a peephole. In the laundry scenes, for instance in *L'Assommoir,* he is always reminding you that the laundresses have turned up their sleeves, or undone a button or two of their bodices. His eyes seem eternally fixed on the inch or two of bare flesh that can be seen, and he nudges your elbow at every moment, to make sure that you are looking too. Nothing may be more charming than a frankly sensuous description of things which appeal to the senses; but can one imagine anything less charming, less like art, than this prying eye glued to the peep-hole in the Gingerbread Fair? (pp. 162-72)

> Arthur Symons, "A Note on Zola's Method," in his The Symbolist Movement in Literature, *revised edition, E. P. Dutton & Company, 1919, pp. 162-79.*

ANDRÉ GIDE   (journal date 1934)

[*Many critics regard Gide as among France's most influential thinkers and writers of the twentieth century. In his fiction, as well as his criticism, Gide stressed autobiographical honesty, unity of subject and style, modern experimental techniques, and sincere confrontation of moral issues. In the following excerpt from his journal, Gide expresses his admiration for Zola's work.*]

Read *La Fortune des Rougon;* reread *L'Assommoir.*

I should like to write an article on Zola, in which to protest (but gently) against the present lack of appreciation of his value. I should like to bring out in it that my admiration for Zola is not recent and is in no wise inspired by my present "opinions" (simply those opinions allow me to gauge his importance better today); bring out that: barely out of school and in the midst of the Mallarmé circle, Pierre Louÿs used to recite to me, jumbled together with groups of lines from Hugo's *Le Satyre,* long passages from *La Faute de l'Abbé Mouret* (among others) and inculcated in me his youthful admiration. For several years I have reread each summer several volumes of *Les Rougon-Macquart* in order to convince myself anew that Zola deserves

to be placed very high—as an artist and without any concern for "tendency."

My predilection, immediately after *Germinal,* goes to *Pot-Bouille.* (pp. 314-15)

> *André Gide, in a journal entry of October 1, 1934, in his* The Journals of André Gide: 1928-1939, Vol. III, *translated by Justin O'Brien, Alfred A. Knopf, 1949, pp. 314-15.*

GEORG LUKÁCS   (essay date 1936)

[*Lukács, a Hungarian literary critic and philosopher, is acknowledged as one of the leading proponents of Marxist thought. His development of Marxist ideology was part of a broader system of thought which sought to further the values of rationalism (peace and progress), humanism (socialist politics), and traditionalism (Realist literature) over the counter-values of irrationalism (war), totalitarianism (reactionary politics), and modernism (post-Realist literature). The subjects of his literary criticism are primarily the nineteenth-century Realists—Balzac and Tolstoy—and their twentieth-century counterparts—Gorky and Mann. In major works such as* Studies in European Realism *(1950) and* The Historical Novel *(1955), Lukács explicated his belief that "unless art can be made creatively consonant with history and human needs, it will always offer a counterworld of escape and marvelous waste." In the following excerpt, originally published in Hungarian in 1936, Lukács compares and contrasts the artistic rendering and thematic significance of scenes treating similar situations in Zola's* Nana, *Leo Tolstoy's* Anna Karenina *(1887), Gustave Flaubert's* Madame Bovary *(1857), and Honoré de Balzac's* Illusions perdue *(1842-48; Lost Illusions).*]

In two famous modern novels, Zola's *Nana* and Tolstoy's *Anna Karenina,* horse races are depicted. How do the two writers approach their task?

The description of the race is a brilliant example of Zola's virtuosity. Every possible detail at a race is described precisely, colourfully and with sensuous vitality. Zola provides a small monograph on the modern turf; every phase from the saddling of the horses to the finish is investigated meticulously. The Parisian public is depicted in all the brilliance of a Second-Empire fashion show. The manoeuvring behind the scenes, too, is presented in detail. The race ends in an upset, and Zola describes not only the surprise outcome but also the betting fraud responsible for it. However, for all its virtuosity the description is mere filler in the novel. The events are loosely related to the plot and could easily be eliminated; the sole connection arises from the fact that one of Nana's many fleeting lovers is ruined in the swindle.

Another link to the main plot is even more tenuous, hardly an integral element in the action of the novel at all—and is thus even more representative of Zola's creative method: the victorious horse is named Nana. Surprisingly, Zola actually underlines this tenuous chance association. The victory of the coquette's namesake is symbolic of her own triumph in Parisian high society and demi-monde.

In *Anna Karenina* the race represents the crisis in a great drama. Vronsky's fall means an overturning in Anna's life. Just before the race she had realized that she was pregnant and, after painful hesitation, had informed Vronsky of her condition. Her shock at Vronsky's fall impels the decisive conversation with her husband. The relationships of the protagonists enter a new critical phase because of the race. The race is thus no mere tableau but rather a series of intensely dramatic scenes which provide a turning point in the plot.

The absolute divergence of intentions in the scenes in the two novels is further reflected in the creative approaches. In Zola the race is *desscribed* from the standpoint of an observer; in Tolstoy it is *narrated* from the standpoint of a participant.

Vronsky's ride is thoroughly integrated into the total action of the novel. Indeed, Tolstoy emphasizes that it is no mere incidental episode but an event of essential significance in Vronsky's life. The ambitious officer has been frustrated in advancing his military career by a set of circumstances, not the least of which is his relationship with Anna. For him a victory in the race in the presence of the court and of the aristocracy offers one of the few remaining opportunities for furthering his career. All the preparations for the race and all the events of the race itself are therefore integral to an important action, and they are recounted in all their dramatic significance. Vronsky's fall is the culmination of a phase in his personal drama. With it Tolstoy breaks off the description of the race. The fact that Vronsky's rival subsequently overtook him can be noted in passing later.

But the analysis of the epic concentration in this scene is not yet exhausted by any means. Tolstoy is not describing a "thing", a horse-race. He is recounting the vicissitudes of human beings. That is why the action is narrated twice, in true epic fashion, and not simply picturesquely described. In the first account, in which Vronsky was the central figure as a participant in the race, the author had to relate with precision and sophistication everything of significance in the preparations and in the race itself. But in the second account Anna and Karenin are the protagonists. Displaying his consummate epic artistry, Tolstoy does not introduce this account of the race immediately after the first. Instead he first recounts earlier events in Karenin's day and explores Karenin's attitude towards Anna. Thus he is able to present the race as the climax of the entire day. The race itself develops into an inner drama. Anna watches Vronsky alone, oblivious to all other events in the race and to the success and failure of all other participants. Karenin watches no one but Anna, following her reactions to what happens to Vronsky. This scene, almost devoid of dialogue, prepares for Anna's outburst on the way home, when she confesses her relations with Vronsky to Karenin. (pp. 110-12)

Linking Vronsky's ambition to his participation in the race provides quite another mode of artistic necessity than that which is possible with Zola's exhaustive description. Objectively, attendance at or participation in a race is only an incident in life. Tolstoy integrated such an incident into a critical dramatic context as tightly as it was possible to do. The race is, on the one hand, merely an occasion for the explosion of a conflict, but, on the other hand, through its relationship to Vronsky's social ambitions—an important factor in the subsequent tragedy—it is far more than a mere incident. (p. 112)

Compare the description of the theatre in the same Zola novel with that in Balzac's *Lost Illusions*. Superficially there is much similarity. The opening night, with which Zola's novel begins, decides Nana's career. The première in Balzac signifies a turning point in Lucien de Rubempré's life, his transition from unrecognized poet to successful but unscrupulous journalist.

In this chapter Zola, with characteristic and deliberate thoroughness, describes the theatre only from the point of view of the audience. Whatever happens in the auditorium, in the foyer or in the loges, as well as the appearance of the stage as seen from the hall, is described with impressive artistry. But Zola's obsession with monographic detail is not satisfied. He devotes

another chapter to the description of the theatre as seen from the stage. With no less descriptive power he depicts the scene changes, the dressing-rooms, etc., both during the performance and the intermissions. And to complete this picture, he describes in yet a third chapter a rehearsal, again with equal conscientiousness and virtuosity.

This meticulous detail is lacking in Balzac. For him the theatre and the performance serve as the setting for an inner drama of his characters: Lucien's success, Coralie's theatrical career, the passionate love between Lucien and Coralie, Lucien's subsequent conflict with his former friends in the D'Arthèz circle and his current protector Lousteau, and the beginning of his campaign of revenge against Mme. de Bargeton, etc.

But what is represented in these battles and conflicts—all directly or indirectly related to the theatre? the state of the theatre under capitalism: the absolute dependence of the theatre upon capital and upon the press (itself dependent upon capital); the relationship of the theatre to literature and of journalism to literature; the capitalistic basis for the connection between the life of an actress and open and covert prostitution.

These social problems are posed by Zola, too. But they are simply described as social facts, as results, as *caput mortuum* ["residue"] of a social process. Zola's theatre director continually repeats: "Don't say theatre, say bordello." Balzac, however, depicts *how* the theatre *becomes* prostituted under capitalism. The drama of his protagonists is simultaneously the drama of the institution in which they work, of the things with which they live, of the setting in which they fight their battles, of the objects through which they express themselves and through which their interrelationships are determined. (pp. 113-14)

The description of the agricultural fair and of the awarding of prizes to the farmers in Flaubert's *Madame Bovary* is among the most celebrated achievements of description in modern realism. But Flaubert presents only a "setting". For him the fair is merely background for the decisive love scene between Rudolf and Emma Bovary. The setting is incidental, merely "setting". Flaubert underscores its incidental character; by interweaving and counterposing official speeches with fragments of love dialogue, he offers an ironic juxtaposition of the public and private banality of the petty bourgeoisie, accomplishing this parallel with consistency and artistry.

But there remains an unresolved contradiction: this incidental setting, this accidental occasion for a love scene, is simultaneously an important event in the world of the novel; the minute description of this setting is absolutely essential to Flaubert's purpose, that is, to the comprehensive exposition of the social milieu. The ironic juxtaposition does not exhaust the significance of the description. (pp. 114-15)

Flaubert achieves his symbolic content through irony and consequently on a considerable level of artistry and to some extent with genuine artistic means. But when, as in the case of Zola, the symbol is supposed to embody social monumentality and is supposed to imbue episodes otherwise meaningless, with great social significance, true art is abandoned. The metaphor is over-inflated in the attempt to encompass reality. An arbitrary detail, a chance similarity, a fortuitous attitude, an accidental meeting—all are supposed to provide direct expression of important social relationships. There are innumerable possible examples in Zola's work, like the comparison of Nana with the golden fleece, which is supposed to symbolize her disastrous effect on the Paris of before 1870. Zola himself confessed to such intentions, declaring: "In my work there is a hypertrophy of real detail. From the springboard of exact observation it leaps to the stars. With a single beat of the wings, the truth is exalted to the symbol."

In . . . Balzac or Tolstoy we experience events which are inherently significant because of the direct involvement of the characters in the events and because of the general social significance emerging in the unfolding of the characters' lives. We are the audience to events in which the characters take active part. We ourselves experience these events.

In Flaubert and Zola the characters are merely spectators, more or less interested in the events. As a result, the events themselves become only a tableau for the reader, or, at best, a series of tableaux. We are merely observers. (pp. 115-16)

> *Georg Lukács, "Narrate or Describe?" in his* Writer and Critic and Other Essays, *edited and translated by Arthur Kahn, Merlin Press, 1970, pp. 110-48.**

WILLIAM TROY   (essay date 1937)

[*In the following review of a 1937 edition of* Germinal, *Troy discusses the novel as a triumph of narrative artistry over the abstract tenets of Naturalism.*]

Whatever the motive behind the re-issue of this particular novel of Zola's at the moment, it does force us to mark off more carefully the different stages in his career, to distinguish between Zola the salesman for Naturalism and Zola the Man of Action, between Zola the indefatigable charter of "forces" and Zola the artist into whom he now and then permitted himself to lapse. To put it rather naively, *Germinal,* which represents one of the more conspicuous of these lapses, is something better than one had remembered Zola even at his best capable of doing. Whether or not it is his most powerful novel, as Matthew Josephson maintains in the introduction, it is likely to be found the most successful of his novels that one has been able to get through. And one may improve on Mr. Josephson's compliment—that it can stand as a model of the *social* novel—simply by making certain claims for it as a novel: it is not, as a whole, in need of any such restrictive label. The point of this review, as a matter of fact, will be that it succeeds when it does succeed in spite of rather than because of Naturalism or the attempt to make of literary art the overworked drab of a mechanical philosophy. It will be seen as an example of quite another sort, a triumph of quality over quantity, of imagination over "forces," of mind over lumpy nineteenth-century matter. And in all these respects it will be seen as a particularly timely example.

From such a point of view its weaknesses, to consider these first, are easily demonstrable as effects of the inherent unsuitability of Naturalism, a system of causality based on quasi-scientic principles, to the practice of literature, a matter of grasping wholes of intelligible experience. Despite his determination to be "just" to the Hennebeaux, the Grégoires, and Dansaerts, the middle-class types required by the scheme, he never succeeds in making them as credible as his miners, putters, and others dwellers in the pit. Their conversations at dinner, their attitudes and sentiments, such an incident as the delivery of bakery goods at one of their doors immediately after a show of mob violence, all possess that sharpness of contour which means that they are more the products of an intellectual necessity than of a creative process. The will toward Justice dissolves before the greater will to apply the law of the primacy of economic forces. The single exception among these people is Deneulin, who is ruined by the marauding strikers, although he has always been a "good" employer. Up to a point Zola can ignore this man's role as member of the owning class; he can place him outside the diagram; but since he cannot make him too real without making him seem too sympathetic he is forced to line him up with the other "pawns" on the flat table of his doctrine. Irony is an uncomfortable mode for the doctrinaire; having blundered into it, Zola retraces his steps as quickly as possible. The greatest weakness in the novel, however, is the characterization, or rather lack of characterization, of the central figure of Etienne Lantier, through whom Zola reveals his own most profound embarassment. For to Etienne is given the impossible role of demonstrating the laws of heredity—a relative of the Macquarts, he is cursed with alcoholism and insanity—and of being an inspiration to the miners to exert their will sufficiently to throw off their chains. A dim phenomenon, arriving from nowhere and returning to the same place, moving like a somnabulist among the distraught miners but persuading them no more than the reader of his reality, he reflects the essential contradiction of his creator's career. That contradiction of course was how belief in any great creative movement, whether of literature or life, could be reconciled with a philosophy that gives to the individual so little control of the sources of creation.

It will be a transition to more positive aspects to suggest that in his practice Zola admirably transcends the theoretical recommendations of Naturalism in regard to the handling of crowds and the use of detail. Documentation was the name that the Naturalists gave to the concrete vehicle that literature had always had, and must always have, in order not to possess a body without substance. The peculiarity of Naturalism was not in its fondness for details but in its peculiarly inorganic use of them, which at times amounted to detail for detail's sake. Zola, a notorious offender, has here achieved such relevance because, as will be noted in a moment, most of his details are fused around a dominating symbol. As for his actual rendering of crowds, it is something different from the reference to vague "social masses" in his notes. A crowd is a notion, an abstraction, a language-symbol for an aggregate of separate realities. To become a symbol for art or literature it must take on the concretion that derives from its physical mass, as in the plastic arts, or from metaphor and partial individuation, as in literature. Otherwise it retains its abstract character, as in the Greek chorus, the anonymous and depersonalized voice of the collective code. Zola *realizes* the crowd that teems through the middle sections of the book through a wealth of metaphors that would repay close study. But what really makes it come alive is our previous familiarity with everything that need be known about the Maheus, Mouquettes, Pierrons, and others who make it up on the plane of intensive personal relationships.

Zola is probably so successful in treating these people because their experience approximated his own so closely that he could render them without the paralyzing interference of his system. There is also Mr. Josephson's point that he had spent some seven months in close contact with them in the mining region of the Loire valley. This desertion of the *longueurs* of the Medan villa was tantamount not only to an exchange of theory for experience but to a profound alteration of method. For the humbler characters in *Germinal* are not the "pawns" of anything but life itself; they are symbols of a deep and sympathetic intuition of the nature of human experience. This is true not only for individual creations, like old Maheu and the wanton Mouquette, but for the relationships between them and the whole structure of the work. The most moving of these relationships undoubtedly is the love affair between Etienne and the girl Catherine, in which the last scene, in the depths of the collapsed mine, brings us back to an atmosphere and a meaning at least as old as the story of Orpheus and Eurydice. For what is the mine itself but a re-integration of the Hades-Hell symbol? The immediate and particular social situation is contained within the larger pattern of a universal recrudescence—"the seeds of a new order sown underground." Etienne emerges from his journey underground to *la vita nuova* of his own and of social experience. Both the title and the heavily rhetorical final pages give support to the idea that in this work Zola was striving to integrate the theme of social revolution with the great tradition of literature which is, first and last, symbolical.

Chronologically, *Germinal* belongs late in his career, after that long cycle of novels in which he sought to compete with Matter, and at the moment when Huysmans and others were turning from Naturalism to the equally blind alley of Decadence. It came too late to stem the reaction which Zola's own earlier excesses had made inevitable. Symbolism came to mean the isolation of one of the several elements of the ancient pattern that he had attempted to revive in modern terms. But it may not be too late, in the light both of Naturalism and Symbolism, for the writer of today to profit from his effort.

This would seem to be the lesson: if literature is to be effective it had better be literature and not something else, and it is more effective when dealing with symbols than with theorems. To the reminder that "Symbolism" is a discredited movement the only answer can be that since literature cannot dispense with symbols the trouble must have been with the nature of the symbols and the particular use of them by the members of this movement. Zola has indicated the manner in which they might be recharged and reordered for our time. (pp. 64-5)

> William Troy, "The Symbolism of Zola," in Partisan Review, Vol. IV, No. 1, December, 1937, pp. 64-6.

F. W. J. HEMMINGS (essay date 1953)

[*Hemmings is an English literary scholar, biographer, and critic who regards himself as an "academic specialist in French literature." In the following excerpt from his study of Zola's life and works, Hemmings discusses theme and technique in* L'assommoir *and* Germinal.]

Zola's habitual use of symbolism to impose an artificial pattern on the meaninglessness of reality can be observed in *L'Assommoir,* but it is not disconcertingly obtrusive, as in some of the other novels. The colour of the waste water that runs from the dyer's workshop across the yard of the tenement house varies according to the state of Gervaise's fortunes; this is the pathetic fallacy, but in a minor degree, so that it enters into the artistic fabric of the book without standing out in a hard knot. Bazouge, the perpetually drunken undertaker's assistant, stands outside real life, a blear-eyed wizard casting a kind of malignant spell over Gervaise in her hour of contentment, and seeing it worked out at the end as he had prophesied; but if exception is to be taken to Bazouge, on the grounds that he conflicts with the uninspired banality of ordinary fact, the same objection would have to be brought against the blind beggar who haunts Emma Bovary in her decline, and the sinister moujik with his sack over his shoulder, of whom Anna Karenina dreams and who rides the train that crushes her to death. In *L'Assommoir* Zola did not strip his subject down to the "unvarnished truth"; but if he had done so, he could probably not have achieved a work

of great literature. Art is not photography, and bare realism is too constricted a formula. (pp. 97-8)

[We] can watch, in *L'Assommoir,* things of brick and metal starting into a species of independent sub-life and groping with deadly tentacles after the living whom they dwarf and devour. Again, it is symbolism, a transcending of reality by the artist who, outside his polemical works, was never a doctrinaire of realism. The distillery with its adjoining tavern has often been quoted as the materialization of the curse of drink; but in fact Zola gives it relatively little prominence, and only when Gervaise is tempted to drown her miseries in alcohol . . . does the still come to life, like "some witch with fire in her entrails." What has been less often pointed out is Zola's use of the huge apartment-house to symbolize the demoralizing promiscuity of slum life. The house impresses the reader as a giant sponge, alive itself and peopled by swarms of existences, right from the moment when Zola first shows it confronting Gervaise, who "slowly carried her gaze from the sixth storey to the pavement, and up again, surprised at this enormity, feeling she was in the midst of a living organism, in the very heart of a town; the house caught her interest, as if she had before her a gigantic person." Some years pass before she goes to live in the block, but when she does, "she had the impression of doing something very reckless, of throwing herself plumb in the middle of a toiling machine, as the hammers of the locksmith and the planes of the joiner banged and whistled at the back of the workshops on the ground floor."

These are elements in *L'Assommoir* which hint at a more significant universe than that visible to the mere observer; but the work remains realistic fiction none the less, not allegorical fantasy or a sombre rhapsody. The characters live in spite of their environment, which this time is not allowed to stifle them by its brooding presence. (pp. 98-9)

In particular, Gervaise is for Zola a unique achievement. She is not a type, which is why she has not broken loose and become self-subsistent like Becky Sharp or Sarah Gamp. But Zola gave her an imperishable local presence, and Gervaise is one of those figments of the imagination which for many book-lovers retain a more authentic existence than most of the people they have daily dealings with.

She was conceived under the sign of pathos, yet never was there a more discreet and purified pathos than this. She has what virtues she can and what ambitions she may; but her best virtue—simple good-heartedness—is the soft spot through which circumstance wounds her mortally, and her modest demands of life are cruelly rejected, one by one and one and all. (p. 99)

By moving us as deeply with his recital of Gervaise's disillusions as any tragic poet with the history of kings stricken by blindness and brought to beggary, Zola proved that, contrary to the classical doctrine, the aesthetic potentialities of a catastrophe do not vary directly with its magnitude. The fall of a sparrow is, in the artist's eyes, as pregnant with pity and terror as the fall of a conqueror. Balzac had invested the bankruptcy of a scent-manufacturer with the tragic pomp of the direst disasters. *L'Assommoir* was a further milestone, after *La Grandeur et la Décadence de César Birotteau,* along the path that led from the literature of feudalism to that of the age of the common man.

Only one or two of Zola's more discerning readers, among them Mallarmé [see *TCLC,* vol. 6], saw this overriding quality which is what ultimately confers greatness and permanence on *L'Assommoir.* (p. 100)

In the compositional technique adopted, *Germinal* differs altogether from *L'Assommoir* and, in fact, from all previous novels Zola had written. For the first time he employed a method of presentation which Balzac, notably, had favoured but which was not practised by Zola's other model, Flaubert. This method involves the use of an extremely lengthy prologue, filling at least a quarter of the novel, in order to develop the desired atmosphere for the subsequent dramatic action. The most frequently quoted instance, in Balzac, is *Eugénie Grandet,* a novel with probably no other analogies with *Germinal*. The description of the miser's house and family circle at Saumur, and the account of the disturbance set up by the arrival of Grandet's nephew from Paris, take up rather more than half the entire book. This prologue covers the events of a little less than twenty-four hours; the story proper that follows extends over some ten years or more. (p. 176)

Externally, there is no difference between the form of *Germinal* and that of a characteristic novel by Balzac; but each writer had a different purpose in adopting this form. Balzac needs time, in his exposition, in order to paint the back-cloth against which his drama is to evolve; without the rich and sombre colouring he uses, the plot (in the case of *Eugénie Grandet* particularly) would seem petty, a domestic tussle of no special account. But in *Germinal* the drama needed no such setting off; it was moving enough in its own right. The function of the first ten chapters is simply to accumulate the mass of impressions needed for the creation of a setting so far removed from the ordinary as to be almost otherworldly. Zola passes from one point to another in the grimy landscape and in the hot, damp galleries of the mines, registering wherever he goes brief visions of miners' cottages seen from outside and inside, introducing us into one where a family of nine is shown sleeping in one bedroom and on the landing outside, waking at four in the morning, dressing hastily and breakfasting meagrely; of other cottages emptying as men and girls, almost indistinguishable in their identical costume, tramp off to work; of the pithead in the half-light of dawn, a "hall vast as a cathedral nave, dimly lit and peopled by large, floating shadows," noisy with the rumble of trollies full of fresh-hewn coal; of cage-load after cage-load of workers dropping plumb into the depths of the earth under a continual patter of water oozing from an underground lake; of gangs of workers toiling at the seam in semi-darkness, stripped almost naked because of the heat—"spectral forms" lit by an occasional lamp, which shone on "the curve of an axe, a stringy arm, a fierce-looking head bedaubed as though for a crime"; of the soft hiss and cobwebby smell of fire-damp. Then, returning to the surface and to daylight, we are shown "the sky earth-coloured, the walls sticky with a greenish moisture, the roads covered with clammy mud, a mud peculiar to coal-mining areas, black with soot in suspension, thick and so sticky that clogs came off in it"; the bridle-path alongside a canal, "in the midst of plots of waste land, enclosed by moss-covered fences"; more roads with, on either side, "little brick houses, daubed with paint to brighten the scene" . . . ; and finally, in the evening, the "soup," the baths in the cottages, the miners gardening, chatting, or drinking, the children at play, the adolescents strolling in couples or mating in the waste ground round a disused mine.

When he has reached the end of this prologue, the reader has the impression of being completely enveloped by the atmosphere, of being himself a denizen of this narrow world. With a little imagination he finds himself breathing the air laden with coal-dust, feeling on his shins and shoulders the sore places rubbed by the jutting pieces of schist, experiencing the nausea of hard physical labour on inadequate rations. There is remarkably little plain description in all this: Zola has progressed since *Le Ventre de Paris* and *La Faute de l'Abbé Mouret*. Everything is shown as seen and felt by one character or another; dozens are introduced, though it is principally through Étienne's observations that the mosaic is built up—since he is new to the mines, his impressions are more acute and more varied. Descriptive writing gives place to the technique of accumulating scores of minor incidents which merge into a general picture of "a corner of nature." (pp. 177-78)

The form of *L'Assommoir* . . . could be illustrated by a curved line, rising to a zenith and then sinking again; but *Germinal* has more than one dimension: it has to be described in terms of cubic capacity, of the balance of weights and counterweights. In *Germinal* Zola constructs, where before he had simply painted. (p. 179)

Zola was quite honest, and even accurate, in declaring as he did that "*Germinal* is a work of compassion, not a revolutionary work." It escapes being revolutionary, however, only by a hair's breadth. (p. 182)

It was not in Zola to write a book preaching revolution: not altogether because he was temperamentally averse to revolutionary violence; nor even because, as a Marxist critic like Lukács will suggest, he was by the circumstances of his class origins opposed to revolutionary change; but chiefly because to admit the feasibility of progress through revolution would have meant repudiating his faith in the evolutionary interpretation of social growth borrowed from Darwinism. He preferred, as he would continue all his life to prefer, "a 'scientific' method in which society is conceived as a harmonious entity and the criticism applied to society formulated as a struggle against the diseases attacking its organic unity, a struggle against the 'undesirable features' of capitalism."

But the social injustice he recorded in *Germinal* was so monstrous, and seemed so immovably lodged in the social system, that it was only by omitting all discussion of causes and remedies that Zola succeeded in keeping up appearances as an impartial social chronicler. He could not dream of disguising the need for social reform: *Germinal* was an urgent warning to *laissez-faire* economists who blinked this need; but he was equally anxious not to seem to side with socialists of any description who proposed to substitute a new economic order which would be immune from the abuses of the old. His method was to remove the whole problem from the realm of economic argument and treat it in its human aspect alone.

The mining community he . . . depicted in *Germinal* is a race of men and women deformed in body and soul by the controlling conditions of their lives. (pp. 182-83)

It is a miracle that in such a fetid atmosphere some human virtues survive—that Maheu, for instance, on a rare occasion when his wife has been able to afford a piece of meat, scolds her for not giving the younger children their share, and sits them on his knees to feed them; that Chaval, the brutal and tyrannical lover of Catherine Maheu, comes to her rescue when she swoons in an overheated gallery, and finds kind words of sympathy to encourage her when she recovers; that Zéphyrin, never greatly attached to his sister, works like a demon to deliver her when she is trapped in the flooded pit, and is killed by an explosion of fire-damp brought about by his reckless haste. The miner is not flattered, and certainly he is no hero. He is the product, quite simply, of a degrading environment which smothers in him all except the most elementary social instincts.

But though not heroic in any moral sense, the miner is undeniably the true hero in the literary acceptance of the word. He is depicted in representative types—four or five of them have just been named, and there are a dozen more in the book—but above all he is presented in the mass. This method was an innovation, and one which Zola found so suited to his genius that he brought it into regular use in subsequent novels—notably in *La Débâcle, Lourdes, Paris, Travail,* and *Vérité.* (pp. 183-84)

> *F. W. J. Hemmings, in his* Émile Zola, *Oxford at the Clarendon Press, Oxford, 1953, 308 p.*

MARTIN TURNELL   (essay date 1959)

[*Turnell has written widely on French literature and has made significant translations of the works of Jean-Paul Sartre, Guy de Maupassant, Blaise Pascal, and Paul Valéry. In the following excerpt, Turnell discusses various structural and thematic aspects of* L'assommoir, Nana, *and* Germinal.]

L'Assommoir and *Germinal* are Zola's two finest achievements. They are also his two greatest feats of construction. Although it is a characteristic product of the nineteenth century, *L'Assommoir* possesses something of the economy and the linear simplicity of the French novels of the classic period. . . . Zola uses his principal character to give the book its artistic unity. In no other single work is the movement of the cycle so clearly reflected as in the story of the changing fortunes of Gervaise Macquart.

The novel is dominated to a remarkable degree by images of height and depth. They are directly derived from Gervaise's personal experience, but they become the symbols of the moral vicissitudes of the characters and they give the book its distinctive pattern. It opens with Gervaise waiting tearfully in her hotel bedroom for the return of her 'man' who is suspected of spending the night with another woman. She gazes *down* on the street from her window in the hope of seeing him and *up* at the Lariboisière hospital, which is in the process of construction and which is to play an important part in her story. The appalling fight in the wash-house with the sister of the man who has enticed Lantier away from her is a moral victory which starts Gervaise on her upward course. She meets Coupeau, a decent working man whose trade, significantly, keeps him perched on the roofs of buildings, decides to make a fresh start and marries him.

One of the earliest references to height occurs when Gervaise goes to the vast block of tenements to meet her fiancé's family. . . . (p. 147)

The tenements in the Rue de la Goutte-d'Or—the name is already an allusion to alcohol and to the distilling apparatus in the dram-shop—are to be the scene of Gervaise's triumph and disaster. From the first she has the impression that the building is not a mere inanimate thing of bricks and mortar, but a 'living organism', a 'gigantic person standing in front of her'. Her immediate reaction is one of 'surprise' and 'interest', but a moment later there is a change. . . .

The 'dead jaws yawning in the void' introduces a sinister note. The 'prison walls' betray that sense of claustrophobia from which nearly all the leading writers of the later nineteenth century suffered. 'The void' heightens the feeling of discomfort by placing the characters between the oppressive sense of being enclosed and the morbid fear of 'the void' outside the enclosure.

The exhausting climb to the sixth floor, where the Lorilleux live in their combined flat and workshop, looks forward to Gervaise's own painful but triumphant ascent:

> Alors, tout en haut, les jambes cassées, l'haleine courte, elle eut la curiosité de se pencher au-dessus de la rampe; maintenant, c'était le bec de gaz d'en bas qui semblait une étoile, au fond du puits étroit des six étages; et les odeurs, la vie énorme et grondante de la maison, lui arrivaient dans une seule haleine, battaient d'un coup de chaleur son visage inquiet, se hasardant là comme au fond d'un gouffre.
>
> (Then, right at the top, short of breath and with her legs feeling as though they would give way under her, she had the curiosity to lean out over the banister; now it was the gas jet down below which looked like a star at the bottom of the narrow well formed by the six storeys; and the smells, the enormous rumbling life of the house came up to her in a single gust, beat against her anxious face in a blast of hot air as she ventured there as though at the bottom of a gulf.)

The mysterious, repellent life of the building is emphasized by 'la vie enorme et grondante de la maison' and 'une seule haleine', while 'inquiet' and 'se hasardant' hint at the dangers to come. The downward glance and 'the star at the bottom of a well' are presages of Coupeau's fall and her own. (pp. 148-49)

The image of the prison, first mentioned ten pages earlier, is repeated, but this time the prison is seen from inside with the doors of the cells opening on to the dark, narrow, bewildering corridors. It is also a characteristic piece of nineteenth-century evocation. For Zola's novels are filled with descriptions of people passing through streets bordered by sinister buildings whose interiors are symbols of their own unexpressed and partly hidden fears. Fear is, indeed, the dominant sentiment. . . . (p. 149)

In nearly all these passages the images of height and depth are indissolubly linked. An upward movement is followed immediately by a downward movement bringing with it nameless fears and a gnawing sense of insecurity. Gervaise's marriage is the cause of her immediate prosperity and her ultimate fall. 'Ce furent quatre années de dur travail' ['There were four years of hard work'], runs the laconic opening sentence of the chapter which describes the early years of their married life. Gervaise and Coupeau are industrious and thrifty. In spite of her 'silly fears', Gervaise is determined to set up on her own as a laundress and saves hard in order to be able to lease a shop in the block in the Rue de la Goutte-d'Or. She is well on the way to succeeding when her hopes are dashed by Coupeau's accident. The *physical* fall from the roof is not merely the prelude to the *moral* fall of both of them; it is the direct cause. The accident destroys Coupeau's morale and brings out his hereditary alcoholism. This in the long run infects Gervaise who is also the child of a family of alcoholics.

Disaster does not come at once. In spite of the fact that her savings have been swallowed up by Coupeau's illness—she will not dream of allowing him to go to hospital—and by his

Zola's original Rougon-Macquart family tree.

disinclination to work when he recovers, Gervaise does not stop work herself or give up the idea of establishing herself. She manages to secure a shop on the ground floor of the block, but the foundation of her fortune is precarious; the money with which she starts is a loan from her friend Goujet. (p. 150)

We become increasingly aware of the theorist of Naturalism in the account of Gervaise's decline. There is no compelling reason for her downfall; the novelist is determined to prove that the combination of a certain milieu and a certain heredity will produce the moral *déchéance* which is the theme of the book. His laundress has many good qualities. She is industrious; she is courageous; and her natural decency prevents her from leaving her drunken husband and going away with Goujet which would, ironically, have been her salvation. Yet at bottom she is 'soft'—'molle' is another key-word—and it is this which causes her undoing. . . . (p. 151)

Gervaise's moral descent is marked by a physical ascent. When she saw the block for the first time, she reflected that 'if she had lived there, she would have liked a lodging at the end on the sunny side. . . . She had already begun to choose her window, a window in 'the corner on the left-hand side, where there was a little window-box, planted with Spanish beans whose thin stalks were beginning to twine themselves round a string cradle.' But her period of prosperity had been spent on the ground floor, and when she had to give up the shop she moved into one of the poorest flats on the top floor. . . .

The moment of hallucination in which the ageing ruined Gervaise thinks that she is looking down on the upturned face of the hopeful, courageous Gervaise of thirteen years ago is a very neat stroke of irony which anticipates a device that has been used extensively in the cinema. The sordid present is suddenly confronted by the brilliant past in a visual image. It brings home to us the skill of Zola's craftsmanship. The struc-

ture of the book is not a mere framework; it is organic. The central experience—a sense of hopeless waste and missed opportunities—is conveyed through the alternation of images of height and depth.

Coupeau's descent is both physical and moral. Gervaise, we remember, had first noticed him when he was working on the roof of the Lariboisière hospital, which was then in process of construction. . . . (p. 152)

She recalls the way in which Coupeau's career started 'up above', and is now coming to an end 'down below' in a padded cell in the hospital that he helped to build. For the irony is only fully apparent when we compare the memory of the 'playful amorous sparrow' with the raving, babbling madman whom she has just visited in his cell.

The wedding party and the great dinner that Gervaise gave in her shop on one of her birthdays have been warmly praised, and they are certainly among the highlights of the book. Less has been said of the distilling apparatus in the dram-shop which gave the novel its title. (p. 153)

In building up his picture of the distilling apparatus, Zola relies partly on the personal animism which was one of the most distinctive of his gifts, partly on the exteriorization of subjective fears, and partly on the technique of the nightmare. The animism is perceptible in Gervaise's uneasy sense of a presence behind her back, but . . . the novelist draws mainly on the technique of the nightmare. Gervaise is decidedly intoxicated and to her inflamed imagination the play of shadow suggests 'abominations', 'figures with tails' and 'copper claws'. . . . [The] emphasis shifts from the menacing thud of the machinery to the gurgling of the alcohol in the retort. The sound of it fills her with a blind drunken rage, a momentary desire to smash the enemy which is overwhelming her, the 'beast' which is about to rend her with its copper claws. The word 'brouillait' ['confused'] marks the point at which rage subsides and morale snaps. She has the impression that she has 'gone under', been drowned by the gurgling stream, as in a sense she has. (p. 154)

L'Assommoir was the first novel in which Zola adopted the neutral style. Ornate passages, which stand out from the rest of the book, have been rigorously suppressed. The images of the block of tenements and the distilling apparatus fall naturally into place, and the neutral tone of the background gives them precisely the right degree of relief without allowing them to become predominant. The texture of the book is more even. There is a graduated rise leading to the moments of hallucination which are followed by the relentless downward swoop. (p. 155)

The deepest thing in the book is a very real feeling of *compassion*. Gervaise has been rightly praised as being the most finely conceived and the most human of all Zola's characters. She is at once an individual and a symbol of the sufferings of the proletariat under nineteenth-century capitalism, the representative of the down-trodden masses whose aim in life was simply 'to work, to eat, to have a place of one's own, to bring up one's children, not to be beaten and to die in one's bed'. (p. 156)

Zola's attitude towards sexual relations was highly equivocal, and the emphasis on them in the novels verges on obsession. His personal views on sexual morality were conservative and there was a good deal of the puritan in him. (p. 157)

Zola disapproved strongly of sexual irregularities. He was never tired of insisting that procreation is not simply the aim, but the only justification for sexual intercourse. This view became more pronounced as he grew older. *Fécondité* is not a novel: it is a tract against contraception. Characters who try, for selfish reasons, to limit their families are savagely punished by the deaths of only children, or by themselves dying horribly in the abortionist's den. Women who have themselves sterilized in the hope of enjoying the fun without the responsibility of children lose their looks and their capacity for pleasure. Zola realized that promiscuity was unavoidable among the working classes, but considered that it was excusable so long as there was a child. He did not show the same indulgence towards the middle classes. Middle-class adultery was summarily condemned; extenuating circumstances were not admitted.

Zola regarded the act itself with horror, but also with fascination. He found ways of giving vent to his horror at the same time that he indulged his fascination. He was an adept at playing the dual role of moralist and *voyeur*. He reveals the puritan's delight in the contemplation of the rawest physical details and dwells gloatingly in one book after another on the conformation of women, the soiled sheets of lovers' beds, hands clutching savagely at pubic hair, or a *coitus interruptus* in the hay. (pp. 157-58)

The reasons which led to the writing of *Nana* were undoubtedly mixed. Zola could claim that there were strong artistic grounds, that a documentary on prostitution was essential to his picture of life under the Second Empire. He could also claim that his attitude was highly moral, and that he was demonstrating the part played by sexual disorder in the collapse of the Empire. The personal reasons seem to me to have been decisive. Zola had very conveniently provided himself with an excuse for writing a whole novel about sexual relations in their most lurid form, and for describing the intimate *dessous* ['underclothing'] in the greatest detail on the pretext that he was 'correcting' human nature.

The study of naked eroticism provided the *voyeur* with magnificent opportunities. The scene alternates between the sordid theatre, where Nana makes her début, and her gaudy town houses. In the theatre we go up and down tortuous, rickety staircases. Doors open and shut with tantalizing glimpses of shoulders, breasts and thighs. Actresses dodge coyly behind screens if a visitor arrives, only to emerge provocatively when the visitor turns out to be a wealthy old man or an English prince. Zola does not miss a single one of the sordid details from the smell of sweat mingling with cheap perfume to soiled water in cracked basins, which somehow heighten the erotic effect. At Nana's home the same details are lightly disguised by the luxury of the décors. 'A flock of men galloped through the alcove', we are told in one of the closing chapters. There is an inextricable confusion of clients and creditors. Men are hidden in the cupboards, in the kitchen, under the bed. A door opens and shuts, but the pious Comte Muffat has seen the scraggy legs of an aged rival emerging from Nana's bed—from the bed that had cost Muffat fifty thousand francs. The front staircase is blocked with creditors angrily demanding their dues. An elderly procuress arrives in the nick of time with the offer of a job. Nana slips out by the back door, keeps the date, returns with the proceeds and gets rid of the creditors.

It is said that Mme Zola was 'jealous of Nana'. If she was, her instinct was not at fault.

Nana makes her *entrée* in the novel when she appears on the stage of a small theatre as the protagonist in a play called *La Blonde Vénus*. (pp. 158-59)

The passage divides into two parts. In the first the appeal is directly to the reader. Zola tries to make us feel the immediate impact of Nana in the hope that we shall become susceptible to the contagious emotion of the second part. Her entry is signalled by the short, abrupt sentence: 'Un frisson remua la salle.' A shiver of expectation goes through the audience. The novelist then turns on the reader. The word *nue* ['naked'] is repeated in order to drive it home. It is followed by a catalogue of the most provocative parts of the body, which is heightened by the transparent gauze and by the hair under the arms gleaming in the footlights. The change of angle is marked by another short sentence: 'Il n'y eut pas d'applaudissements' ['There was no applause']. This gives the appearance of the Marine Venus a ritual quality. The reactions of the men are carefully particularized. We see the necks craning forward, the noses looking pinched in the dim light of the auditorium, almost feel the dry sour taste in our own mouths. (p. 160)

The exteriorization of collective emotion gives the scene its suffocating hallucinatory effect.

The choice of the role of the Marine Venus for Nana seems to have been deliberate. Whatever Venus may have signified for the Greeks, in modern times she is the symbol not of love but of promiscuous eroticism and disease. Zola's theme is Sexuality under the Second Empire: the refined, perverse, destructive sexuality which is incarnate in the expensive courtesan. In the Zola system it represents the stage of corruption of the primitive, brutal but healthy instinct described in *La Terre*. It does not stand for life: it is a prelude to death. And it kills the Empire. . . . (pp. 160-61)

The sight of the audience of fifteen hundred people swooning at the feet of the Marine Venus brings out the *ritual* element which is an essential component of the novel. They are clearly the worshippers of a new religion in which the music hall replaces church or temple, the stage with the naked courtesan the altar. The ritual element is apparent in the signature tune of the *Blonde Venus* which is also the signature tune of the novel. It is heard again at the wedding of the Muffats' daughter where it becomes the swan-song of a society which has sacrificed everything to Venus. The theme of the Marine Venus reappears in the ostentatious bed of gold and silver which is constructed for Nana at Muffat's expense. It was 'a throne which was sufficiently wide for Nana to stretch her naked limbs with royal ease, an altar of Byzantine richness which was worthy of the omnipotence of her sex and where, at that very moment, her sexual organ was exposed and displayed with the religious shamelessness that belongs to an idol feared by men'.

That Mlle Muffat's bridegroom—an old flame of Nana's—should have paid a hurried farewell visit to Venus in the bed which was part throne and part altar is a sign of the tightness of the novel's texture, and of much else besides. (p. 161)

Nana is one of Zola's most successful and ingenious novels. Its success depends on the skill with which he uses the ritual element to reveal the contrast between the real Nana and the image that she creates in the mind of the masses. There is only one Nana. She is the plump, well-favoured, lascivious daughter of the people who gives herself freely to friends and acquaintances, and who is never too proud to do a date for the Tricon when she is short of ready money and needs some cash to pay off importunate tradespeople. The other Nana, the Marine Venus, the 'force of nature', the goddess who reclines naked on the sumptuous bed of carved silver and gold, is the creation of the frenzied eroticism of the age, a projection of the collective neurosis in its sexual form. The process is gradual and cumulative. It begins with her appearance in the small theatre in the back streets, but once it has started it proceeds with a sort of inevitability. The clumsy, awkward girl who can't act or sing, who has nothing but her appearance to recommend her, is transformed by the power of mass emotion into an allegorical, a mythical figure who dominates and disrupts high society. (p. 162)

The scene on the race-course is a striking illustration of the peculiar ambivalence of Zola's creation. The infatuated Vandeuvres has named one of his race-horses after Nana. The horse wins the big race. Standing on the seat of her landau and listening to the crowd cheering on the winning horse, Nana imagines that it is she and not the horse whom they are acclaiming. There is an obvious contrast between this scene and the audiences swooning at the sight of the Marine Venus. Nana's world has become a theatre, a place of illusion. She herself has come to believe in the illusion at the moment when it is about to end—the mind of the crowd is fixed on horse flesh—and the myth is about to be exploded. For at this point the curve of the book dips sharply. Vandeuvres' win does not make his fortune; the horse is as much an instrument of disaster as the woman after whom it is named. He has been guilty of some particularly clumsy piece of sharp practice, is found out, ruined and disgraced. He shuts himself up in his stable with his race-horses, sets the stable on fire and perishes horribly with all his horses including 'Nana'. It is the beginning of the frenzy of ruin and destruction with which Zola's novels always end. (p. 163)

Nana, we are told in one place, was the child of four or five generations of drunkards whose excesses had led to 'un détraquement nerveux de son sexe de femme' ['a nervous disorder of her genitalia']. It is the phrase not the somewhat fanciful theory that matters here. *Nana* is a large-scale study of a nervous disturbance of the genital urge. What is impressive is the

Contemporary cartoon entitled "The Birth of Nana-Venus." Bibliotheque Nationale, Paris.

novelist's perception of the essentially destructive nature of eroticism, of the profound connection between the frenzied promiscuity of the age and the death-wish. La Faloise, 'who for some time past had insisted on the honour of being ruined by Nana', is the spokesmen of all the men who gallop through the alcove or who are 'piled up on top of one another' in Nana's house. They are all animated by a secret desire to bring the Empire down and themselves with it. The spectacle of the imperial chamberlain and the courtesan playing bears, of the courtesan kicking his backside and making him stamp or spit on his uniform is an ironical comment on the farcical ending of the gimcrack Empire.

The moralist takes good care to have the last word. There is a personal acrimony about the revolting description of the dead Nana as though the novelist were trying to excuse himself for such an orgy and to punish the reader for being his accomplice. Its full horror is only apparent when it is placed beside the account of Nana's entry in the role of the Marine Venus. Zola leaves nothing to chance. 'Vénus se décomposait' ['Venus rotted'], he observes savagely. Outside the populace are shouting: 'A Berlin.' It is the last illusion. A ruling class which had wasted its substance between 'the snowy thighs' of the strumpet was leading a people and a nation to their doom. (p. 164)

Zola's novels usually open in one of two ways. He either introduces the protagonist and works from character to situation, or he sets the scene and works from the setting to the characters. In *Germinal* he combines the two. The presentation of the protagonist and the setting is simultaneous. (pp. 164-65)

The atmosphere of desolation sets the tone of the novel. The mining community live in the middle of a treeless, windswept desert separated from the rest of the world. For generations the mine has swallowed its daily ration of undernourished ill-clad human beings who are constantly killed or maimed by it. Their destiny is regulated by mysterious anonymous figures who dwell far beyond the vast horizon. The novel is dominated by the colours black, white and red: the blackness of the pit, the coal, the skies, the soil, the figures of the men themselves; the pallor of undernourished bodies, anaemic lips and gums, the snow which covers the barren earth during the strike, the red of fire and lust. The sense of desolation is heightened by the monotony of the landscape. The biting March winds sweep across acres of 'marshland and barren earth'. The road runs 'dead straight' for ten kilometres.

The solitary figure walking along the straight road is Étienne Lantier. He has, as we know, just lost his job on the railways for striking the foreman in a characteristic fit of violence, and has come to look for work in the mines. He is the man of destiny, the outsider whose impact on the mining community is the theme of the novel. His arrival provokes the conflict between capital and labour which brings disaster and death to his friends.

His impact is twofold. He is accepted by the Maheuds as a friend and by the miners as a leader; but on his first day down the mine friction develops between him and Chaval who become rivals for the favours of Maheud's daughter, and when the strike occurs he is the agitator who arouses the special wrath of the mine-owners. This turns him into the disruptive element who operates in the spheres of both public and private relations. The balancing of public and private relations is an essential factor in the composition of the novel. The rivalry between Étienne and Chaval preserves the human interest in the novel, and it makes possible the welding of the human and the ideological conflicts.

The novelist's choice of an outsider as his principal character has another advantage. When he decided to write a novel about mining and visited a mining community in search of material, he was a newcomer to mining. It is through the eyes of the newcomer that we are introduced to life in a mining village. This enables Zola to impart all the information he wishes about the technical side of mining and to describe, with the freshness of someone seeing it for the first time, the very real horror of the life of the miner under nineteenth-century capitalism.

Germinal presented him with a much more difficult problem of construction than *L'Assommoir* because the issues are more complex and more varied. The skill with which he solved it deserves unstinted praise. The novel is divided into seven parts and possesses the solidity and tightness of a well-made stage play. Its seven parts all deal with a particular phase of the conflict between capital and labour; the chapters into which each part is divided—their number varies between five and seven—deal with the lesser developments and incidents which compose the phase. Each chapter makes an essential contribution to the part to which it belongs. It might, indeed, he said that the parts correspond to the acts, and the chapters to the scenes of a play. (pp. 165-66)

The division into seven parts, the careful welding of the chapters into the parts to which they belong, the gathering momentum which culminates in mob violence and its repression, give the novel its massive strength. It is no disparagement to say that this strength is a mechanical strength, that it depends on the careful arrangement of weights, on the nice balancing of the contending parties. We are shown the workers, switch

to the conservatives, return to the workers, then pass to the head-on collision between the two. The initial glimpse of the conservative party in Part II is completed by the picture of Hennebeau's private life in Part IV. There are sub-divisions within the parties. Lantier is matched against Rasseneur, and both are contrasted with Souvarine. In precisely the same way the Greégoires and the Hennebeaus are played off against Dneulin, the enlightened capitalist who tries to stand out against the big owners, has his mine wantonly damaged by the strikers and is forced to sell out to the common enemy. The weaknesses in the workers' ranks are balanced by weaknesses in the capitalist camp. Mob violence is met by military action; the first climax automatically produces the second.

It is sometimes said that the mine is the real protagonist of *Germinal*. It undoubtedly dominates the novel, and it is a much more complex image than . . . the distilling apparatus. It is essentially a symbol of Evil, is the embodiment of those evil forces which pervade Zola's world, and work actively for destruction in every sphere and at every level.

In order to heighten the impact of the mine on the reader Zola endows it with a personality. . . .

He knew that he could only establish the mine as a presence by showing it to us first through the eyes of one of his characters. He therefore exploited the animism which we have seen at work in *L'Assommoir*. Now animism belongs to the mental habits of primitive man. Zola was using a primitive device to express the reactions of a primitive individual, but he could also count to some extent on the survival of primitive habits in his readers. (p. 168)

The images of the mine are by no means identical. There is a judicious mixture of repetition and development. Zola preserves the illusion by striking a balance between direct description and subjective impressions. Étienne sees the mine; the novelist adds something to what he has seen; the next time Étienne also notices what the novelist has seen. (p. 169)

The pit appears in these passages as a modern Moloch swallowing up men and disgorging coal, reminding us that coal is paid for in human lives. 'Capable of absorbing a whole people' is a favourite expression. Zola had already used it, or something like it, in the descriptions of . . . the distilling apparatus, and it occurs several times in *Germinal*. Nor should we overlook the use of the word 'vorace'. 'Voreux' is a coined name. Zola cannot have been unaware that it suggests, as Lanoux points out, the words 'dévorant' ['devouring'], 'vorace' ['voracious'], 'dangereux' ['dangerous'], 'haineux' ['hating'] and so on. (pp. 169-70)

There can be no doubt that in Zola's personal mythology the mine stands for a secularized hell. The 'cité maudite' ['accursed city'] reintroduces the theme of destruction, punishment and purification by fire. It is curious to observe that . . . Zola like Dante reserves the deepest circle of his hell for those who are guilty of sexual perversion, but Zola's theology is coloured by his politics. His hell is primarily an earthly hell in which the innocent suffer. They are very conscious of their plight. They are continually seeking a momentary escape—complete escape is unthinkable—from the earthly hell in which they are prisoners through alcohol, sexual promiscuity or the extravagant dreams that Étienne weaves for them. . . . (pp. 170-71)

The sense of claustrophobia, the feeling that men are the victims of a malevolent power which condemns them to an appalling struggle to eke out a livelihood in their isolation in the middle of the open country, with 'the closed horizon' in front of them, 'the empty skies' above them—they are naturally unbelievers who 'make merry over the empty skies' and are superstitiously afraid of 'the Black Man'—and the hell beneath them, is the deepest thing in the book. . . .

The miners are not the only victims. Since the mine is the embodiment of Evil, the creator of the system which splits capital and labour, there can be no peace until the 'monster' is killed. The end of the mine symbolizes the end of the old order. . . . (p. 171)

The destruction of the mine in *Germinal* and the wreck of the express in *La Bête humaine* are two of the most striking examples in the whole cycle of Zola's highly individual mechanical imagery. They also illustrate the limitations of his prose-style. He excels in describing the moments which immediately precede or immediately follow disaster, but his style is too ponderous and slow-moving to make the moment of disaster entirely convincing. There is always a touch of science fiction about the actual moment of disaster which makes it grotesque instead of moving. That is why the end of the Voreux always reminds me of the collapse of the stage properties at the close of Fritz Lang's film *Metropolis.*

The sexual symbolism of the limp dangling cable, the falling chimney and the vanishing lightning conductor is unmistakable. The falling chimney looks back to the earlier image of it sticking up into the air like the 'threatening horn' of an animal, the limp dangling cable to the hideous spectacle of the old crone carrying Maigrat's severed member on a pole. The mob castrate the dead Maigrat because he had abused their daughters. It is not sufficient to kill the mine; it too must be castrated because it had abused the miners.

Zola is concerned all through the cycle with the conflict between the forces of life and death. The destruction of the mine is repeated by the human drama which is going on below ground. About the same time that the mine is destroyed Étienne kills Chaval in a moment of homicidal fury, then possesses Catherine a few minutes before she dies of exhaustion and hunger. . . . (p. 172)

The crucial words are 'de faire de la vie une dernière fois' ['to experience life for the last time']. In the unending conflict between the forces of life and death the sexual instinct stands for life. It is man's principal weapon in the struggle against inevitable death because it creates new life to replace the ravages of death and ensures the continuance of the human race. The almost ceaseless fornication of the miners is not merely a temporary escape from the earthly hell; it is a sign of the unrelaxing battle against death. It is because the sexual instinct is equated with life that castration is the final act in the death of the mine. It is, as in the case of Maigrat, the appropriate punishment for the misuse of virility.

The spectacle of the earth opening to swallow the mine, which is accompanied by another reference to the 'villes maudites', is a prelude to the necessary Disaster which will swallow the nation; the 'rosy dawn' which breaks at the close of the novel is, as I have already suggested, the symbolic dawn of the new age which is supposed to follow the Disaster. Zola and Lantier step into the novel together on the first page. Although a rift develops when Lantier becomes a demagogue who brings about the death of his friends, the rift is healed and the pair walk out of the novel on the last page, Lantier to continue the struggle against capitalism as a full-time worker in the International, the novelist to continue the fight on paper in the fond belief that he is co-operating with Science in the redemption of man. (p. 173)

Martin Turnell, "Five Novels," in his The Art of French Fiction: Prévost, Stendhal, Zola, Maupassant, Gide, Mauriac, Proust, *Hamish Hamilton, 1959, pp. 140-79.*

ELLIOTT M. GRANT   (essay date 1962)

[*Grant was an American literary critic, essayist, and scholar of French literature. His contributions to literary journals were primarily concerned with the lives and works of Zola and Victor Hugo. In the following excerpt from his book-length study of* Germinal, *Grant praises the poetic vision and mastery of imagery, tone, and characterization which Zola employed to transform a limited, commonplace subject into something epic and grandiose.*]

[In *Germinal,* Zola] managed to transform a subject which at first glimpse seems limited, drab, and dismal into something grandiose and, on occasion, even poetic. For Zola was a poet. Not a lyric poet, to be sure, but an epic poet. Writing in 1885 to Henry Céard, the novelist declared that his work was "une grande fresque" ["a great fresco"], and that he himself possessed a poetic temperament. . . . [We wish] to take certain portions of *Germinal* and subject them to a fairly close scrutiny for the purpose of observing the artistic devices which permitted Zola to paint a convincing picture of commonplace reality or enabled him to bestow on that reality grandeur and epic force. (p. 104)

The opening chapter of *Germinal,* in which nothing much happens, is nevertheless a masterly introduction. An unemployed worker, Étienne Lantier, comes to Montsou, meets an old wagoner named Bonnemort, and talks to him about the possibility of employment. That constitutes all the action of the chapter. Its richness lies in everything surrounding that action. A man walking alone in a pitch-black, starless night, whipped by the March wind "blowing in great gusts like a storm at sea," a wind made icy "from sweeping over miles of marshes and bare earth," surrounded by a flat, treeless, unending plain, advancing on a road that runs "with the straightness of a jetty through the blinding, swirling sea of darkness,"—such is the initial picture painted by Zola. It contains already some of the essential elements of the book: the hero (if there be one), the suggestion of storm and struggle, the grim bareness of the landscape, the emphasis on darkness which introduces the most important tone of the novel,—a tone which comes naturally enough to Zola's mind in view of the subject and which carries with it a presentiment, a foreboding, perhaps even a prediction of disaster. The only break in this almost infinite blackness comes when the traveller perceives pools of red, "three braziers apparently burning in mid-air." They seem to him like "smoky moons," and they hover over a "solid black mass, . . . dimly outlined by five or six dreary lanterns hanging on blackened timber-work which stands like a row of gigantic trestles." From this "fantastic, smoke-black apparition arises the heavy, laboured panting of escaping steam." Here again, the picture is prophetic, with hints of something monstrous and fearful. M. Girard has said that the predominant colours of *Germinal* are black and white, the latter being defined as "le blanc terne" ["dull white"]. He is correct, though we persist in thinking that he is more correct when he says that Zola uses them through "fidélité au réel" ["faithfulness to the real"] than when he attributes to these colours any profound philosophical significance. In any case, in this opening chapter white is absent. Red is chosen in its stead. The flames playing on the black background are suggestive of Hell,—the hell which Zola stated in his *Ébauche* he intended to expose.

Throughout the chapter these basic elements of darkness, cold, bareness, and storm are recalled. (p. 105)

The something monstrous and fearful suggested by the first object emerging from the blackness of the night takes on identifiable shape and form as the traveller recognizes a mining pit with its surface machinery. But the frightening and fantastic aspect of the apparition is carefully maintained. The first distinguishable workers are pictured as "living shadows." The old wagoner is stunted and his spittle black. The mine itself, Le Voreux, with its suggestive name, "its chimney sticking up like a menacing horn," appears like an "evil, voracious beast, crouching ready to devour the world." The escaping steam of the pump with its long, heavy, monotonous panting" is like "the snorting breath of a monster." And the chapter ends on the same note. On this "naked plain deep in darkness" Le Voreux inspires fear. "Huddled in its lair like some evil beast," it "crouched ever lower and its breath came in longer and deeper gasps, as though it were struggling to digest its ration of human flesh." There is more than realism, there is a form of poetry in this evocation of the mining scene.

Atmosphere is not all. The chapter informs us that the traveller's name is Étienne Lantier, that he is about twenty-one years old, dark, good-looking, strong in spite of his slight build. We learn something of his past, his dismissal from his railroad job after striking his boss, his week-long endeavour to find work, his total destitution. We realize that as an outsider, coming into the mining area, he can observe the scene more effectively than one long familiar with it. . . . The person of [an] old man reveals the effect of forty-five years spent underground. His short stature, big head, powerful neck, square hands, simian arms, his flat, livid features blotched with blue, his game legs, his dreadful cough and black spittle, all testify to the unhealthy life he has led. Bonnemort represents the worker who has been brutalized and stupefied by a lifetime in the mines. He deserves retirement and a little ease, but here he is, clinging to a surface job which he is barely able to accomplish in order to get a few more francs pension. His family history, related before the leaping flames, sums up a hundred and six years of hard, dangerous labour in which five members of the family had "left their skins."

We also learn in this chapter something about the Montsou Company. While not as wealthy as its neighbour, the Compagnie d'Anzin, it is still rich and powerful with nineteen active pits and several others for drainage and ventilation. Its general manager, we are told, is a M. Hennebeau, a paid employee. And when Étienne Lantier asks who owns the mine, the old man can only make a kind of impotent gesture and say: "God knows . . . People . . ." "And he pointed to some vague unknown distant spot. . . . His voice had taken on a kind of religious awe, as though he were speaking of some inaccessible tabernacle, where dwelt unseen the gorged and crouching deity whom they all appeased with their flesh but whom no one had ever beheld." Like the mine itself this remote god is voracious.

At the end of the first chapter, the exposition is not, of course, complete. But the atmosphere has been created, two of the human protagonists introduced and others mentioned, the non-human protagonists—the insatiable, devouring mine and the distant capitalistic ogre—have been evoked, the storm image presented. An epic struggle of men against forces more powerful than they lies just ahead.

These colours and images seem to us naturally suggested by the subject which Zola has chosen to treat. To compare the mine with hell is an obvious comparison. To personify capitalism as an ogre or to present it as a remote deity to which men are sacrificed was not in 1885, thirty odd years after the *Communist Manifesto*, particularly startling. But natural as they may be, the colours and images of this opening chapter are appropriate and effective, and they continue throughout the book, both in its action and its descriptive passages. Much of the action takes place underground where black is, logically, the surrounding colour. White, except when the miners are seeking to escape from their subterranean condition, rarely is synonymous with the pleasant or the brilliant, but rather with the sickly, the wan, or the weak. The storm theme, as Mr. Walker has eloquently stated, reappears in the imagery of the "human flood thundering across the plain in Part V" and the "catastrophic, apocalyptic descriptions of the inundated mines in Part VII." The voracious monster evoked in the first chapter swallows its daily ration of men as Étienne later watches them disappear into its gluttonous jaws and is in turn absorbed. The remote deity, against whom the workers are pitted, never ceases to be all-present though invisible. The hell conjured up in the opening chapter is confirmed by the underground scene where the gallery being exploited by Maheu's squad is explicitly stated . . . as being "in hell." The concept recurs with greater force in the first chapter of Part V. Here the proximity to the Jean-Bart mine of Le Tartaret creates hellish conditions indeed, and the name itself is, of course, suggestive of the classical lower-world region, Tartarus, as far below Hades as Heaven is above the earth. The classical comparison is doubtless commonplace. Indeed, the resemblance of a mining region to phenomena of ancient mythology had already been indicated in one of Zola's principal source-books: Simonin's *La Vie souterraine*. . . . [The] images of storm and struggle strewn throughout the book, sometimes classical, sometimes not, help markedly to lift the text above the drab and dreary scene which Zola chose to depict and to give the subject greater distinction. The images are not incompatible with his concept of the naturalistic novel. As a naturalist, he lets reality carry its own meaning, and uses imagery, not to explain action, but to confer greater stature on reality. His images are, therefore, appropriate and effective. It is not necessary to clothe them with supernatural significance.

The fourth chapter of Part I is devoted to an account of Étienne's first day in the mine. Here we see the men at work. The chapter . . . is skilfully constructed from Zola's personal observation at Anzin and from his reading. . . . We find in this chapter of *Germinal* a thoroughly naturalistic description of coal mining under similarly difficult conditions. "In order to get at the coal," says Zola, "they had to lie on one side with twisted neck, arms above their heads, and wield their short-handled picks slantways." In the French original, the correct technical word, *rivelaine*, is used . . . for the type of pick in question. In this cramped posture, in the midst of intolerable heat, these men hacked away without exchanging a word. "All that could be heard," writes Zola, now utilizing his imagination together with his information, "was their irregular tapping, which sounded distant and muffled, for in this dead air sounds raised no echo but took on a harsh sonority. The darkness was mysterious in its blackness (il semblait que les ténèbres fussent d'un noir inconnu). . . . Ghostly forms moved about and an occasional gleam let one glimpse the curve of a man's hip, a sinewy arm, a fierce looking face daubed with dirt as if for a crime. . . . . The scene is interpreted as well as described,—a good example of naturalistic art.

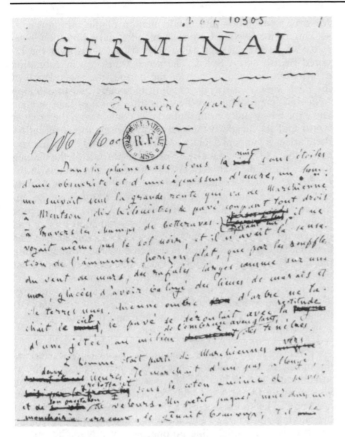

First page of the manuscript of Germinal.

Further details on the terrible task of getting out the coal follow on these initial passages. But a considerable part of the chapter is devoted to Étienne and Catherine,—to their work which requires less experience and skill than demanded of the hewers *(les haveurs)* but arduous indeed, and to their personalities, of which Zola gives us various traits during the luncheon break. Here it is that he links the novel with the Rougon-Macquart series when Étienne tells of his mother, a laundress in the *rue de la Goutte d'or*, and admits the effect alcohol has on him. Here it is, too, that after first finding the girl unattractive, Étienne begins to perceive her charm. And here, too, Zola gives important details on Catherine: her frank friendliness, her fundamental decency, her intellectual limitations. In the last moments of this scene we have also the beginning of the rivalry between Étienne and Chaval over the girl when this brutish miner, seizing her by the shoulders, plants a kiss on her mouth, just before Étienne can do so. The whole scene is an effective one, adding to the reader's knowledge and understanding of this pair, and laying the groundwork for later action.

But at the end Zola returns to the collective scene, and the final, eloquent paragraph renews in us a strong impression of the incredible labour required of these men and girls to earn a modest day's wage.... The vocabulary, the whole arrangement is not only calculated to tell the truth, to reproduce reality, but also to arouse compassion, to inspire pity, and to win the reader's sympathy. It succeeds.

Another chapter worthy of analysis is the last one of Part VI relating the clash between the miners and the soldiers summoned to guard the pits. In contrast to the opening pages of

the book, these are full of action, announced by an ominous paragraph at the end of the preceding chapter where a bugle-call orders the soldiers to take up their arms and "in the growing daylight a band of men and women could be seen coming down from the village *(le coron)*, their anger apparent in every gesture."

Logical, clear construction with the narrative marching implacably to its inevitable conclusion of death is an important method used by Zola in this chapter which is also particularly notable for its skilful mixture of truth and invention. The first device is dramatic. The events unfold with chronological exactitude, creating automatically their formidable impact. The second relies on a technique which Zola uses here with special skill: the weaving of fact and fiction into a single, integral pattern.

The novelist assembles gradually most of the miners and mining women whom we have met, and gives to each a rôle consonant with his or her character. La Maheude, for example, is there and her mood of angry exaltation which has been growing throughout the strike reaches its foreordained climax when she urges her husband to violence. Catherine plays a somewhat unexpected rôle which Zola takes pains to motivate. But La Mouquette and her brother arrive and act as we might predict. Zacharie exhibits his usual indifference, Souvarine his customary aloofness. And so it goes.

The assembled strikers are increased by Zola in a rapid build-up from thirty-five to four hundred, then more than five hundred, with new waves still arriving to swell the flood. Against them stand but sixty soldiers. Only their guns keep the mob at bay.

The action falls into several fairly distinct parts. There is a kind of prologue in which the corpse of Trompette is brought to the surface while the author, with his habitual love of animals, relates the creature's friendship with Bataille and the latter's despair when his younger friend sickened and died. The episode creates a grim, lugubrious note. Meanwhile the original thirty-five miners have been joined by others, and soon the platoon of soldiers is confronted by a mob far outnumbering them. During this first stage, Étienne typically tries to win over the captain in charge. Zola is here utilizing an idea that he had found in Laveleye's *Le Socialisme contemporain:* that the supreme peril for the established order would be the conversion of the army to socialism. Failing in this attempt, Étienne ceases to hold back his comrades, who rush ever closer to the troop, shouting insults and threats. Some of the actual words and gestures were found by Zola in the newspaper accounts of the violence that occurred during the strikes at La Ricamarie and Aubin in 1869.... But, with his good sense of novelistic needs and of dramatic composition, Zola does not rely exclusively on source material. When one hears the shrill voice of Lydie say: "En voilà des andouilles de lignards" ("Just look at those silly old sausages of soldiers"), the cry is doubtless in the spirit of La Ricamarie, but the vocabulary is Zola's own. The intervention of Richomme is also original. It introduces a moment of hope, quickly dashed by the tactless, if courageous, appearance of Négrel. The rôle of La Brûlé, while suggested in part by the newspaper accounts all of which emphasized the wrath of the mining women, is explained even more by the traits of character that Zola attributed to her.

A new part of the action now begins. Before the growing and ever threatening mob, the captain, like his prototype at La Ricamarie, orders the guns to be loaded in the hope of cowing the crowd. Here again, while employing some of the actual words and gestures from the 1869 strikes—such as the reference to the Crimean campaign—, Zola has used his own imagination, for La Mouquette's famous gesture had no counterpart at La Ricamarie or Aubin. It brings this section of the narrative to a colourful climax.

The final section begins with the captain's decision to take a few prisoners. It leads to what Zola—again utilizing details from the strikes of 1869—calls the "bataille à coups de pierre" ["battle of stone-throwing"], appropriately begun (as was seen in an earlier section of this study) by La Brûlé, and this battle in turn culminates in the spontaneous discharge of the guns by the exasperated soldiers. Here, Zola skilfully combines fact and fiction. At La Ricamarie the soldiers had likewise fired spontaneously, before the captain could utter the command. At Aubin the clash had resulted in fourteen dead and twenty-odd wounded. In *Germinal* the number is the same. But, of course, the persons killed are of Zola's choice and invention. He selects Maheu to be the victim of the last shot, which in the Aubin strike killed one of the company's guards, a man greatly esteemed, as Maheu is highly regarded by his comrades and, before the strike, by the company's officials. He introduces the noble act of La Mouquette who saves Catherine at the cost of her own life. At the end, he reminds us of the corpse of Trompette lying in eloquent juxtaposition to the human corpses, and he brings to this lugubrious scene abbé Ranvier, the socialist priest, who calls down God's wrath on the assassins and the fire of heaven on the bourgeois guilty of massacring the wretched workers of the earth.

The chapter is notable as well for its skilful manipulation of the crowd.... In these pages, as elsewhere in the book, Zola displays great powers of epic narration and description. The dramatic night meeting of three thousand men and women in the nearby forest with its admirable chiaroscuro effects under the rising moon (in Part IV), the march of the miners and their women singing the Marseillaise and demanding bread (in Part V), and now this conflict between the strikers and the troops,—these are unforgettable scenes in which Zola has proved his genius. Dr. Hemmings explains his success by his intuitive recognition of the truth that "people in the aggregate are more ferocious, and yet more cowardly, than each separate component of the group." Without the contagion of mass emotion would Maigrat in that earlier scene have received his extraordinary treatment? Without the circumstance of mass action would a man like Toussaint Maheu have pressed his bared breast against the fixed bayonets of the soldiers?

The chapter is very different from the opening pages of the novel. It is narrative rather than expository. It utilizes specific, documentary data in combination with invented material. The former, which Zola could conceivably have imagined but which he was doubtless glad to find, lends authenticity to the total composition, for it has the ring of truth. The struggle forecast in the initial chapter comes to a great climax here. With it come compassion and pity for these human beings caught in a conflict which they seem powerless to avoid. (pp. 106-15)

Elliott M. Grant, in his Zola's "Germinal": A Critical and Historical Study, *Leicester University Press, 1962, 224 p.*

FRANCES McNEELY LEONARD (essay date 1963)

[*In the following excerpt, Leonard examines structure and symbolism in* Nana.]

Nana is a revelation and condemnation of the immoral self-seeking of the Second Empire, which is typified by the *Grand Prix,* where the chestnut filly Nana (flesh) wins over the favored British entry, Spirit. The novel is also an investigation of a particular phenomenon of the period, the ascendancy of the *demi-monde,* a society existing in society and threatening to devour its progenitor. When this little world of kept women and expensive gaiety comes into direct contact with the broader world and its façade of sobriety and conscientious morality, there arises a pungent social comedy illuminating the hypocrisy and foibles of both. Finally, *Nana* is a portrait of the French theatre, for Nana is an actress first introduced to society at the *théâtre des Variétés,* and she moves from the stage into society just as the emanation of sexuality moves throughout the audience when she appears as the "Blonde Venus." The scope of the novel, then, is a series of stages graduated in size and influencing each other: recognized society is imitated by the *demi-monde,* which, in turn, is depicted by the dramas within the novel, in each of which Nana is the featured star. Conversely, Nana, as she moves from the stage into society, sets up a new direction of influence until at last she, the theatre, and the *demi-monde* remold society in their own image. Ultimately it is the symbol of the theatre and the motif of play-acting which gives the novel its form.

As a representative of the Macquarts, Nana is characterized through a series of animal images which indicate that she is something less than human. She is a great animal of a woman with a heavy blond mane and a covering of downy hair over her body. She roasts herself before the fire like a goose. At the running of the *Grand Prix* the identification of Nana woman and filly is so complete that no one, not even Nana herself, is sure whether the cheering is for the one or the other. In her moral decadence she insists on playing as an animal with Count Muffat: she is a woolly bear or he is a dog. Nana and all the Macquarts are essentially animals sent to avenge themselves upon society for the very fact of their existence. This vengeance she achieves through turning all whom she meets into animals—Zola says, a pack of dogs chasing after a bitch not in heat, who turns and mocks them. In this role Nana functions like Circe; she makes evident the bestiality just beneath the surface of society. Playing a fallen Odysseus is her principal lover, Count Muffat. He wanders through the rain-splashed streets of Paris to attend her, all the while suffering from the unfounded belief that his Penelope, Countess Sabine (a literary ancestor of Molly Bloom) patiently awaits him at home.

The animal images which are spread throughout the first half of the novel are brought to a focal point in the center before they are again dispersed. This pattern of imagery parallels and reinforces Nana's first introduction to society, her withdrawal, and her return to be queen of the *demi-monde.* At the focal point Zola explains both the family character and the social function of his heroine. Fauchery, one of Nana's acquaintances, writes of her in *Le Figaro:*

> ... the "Golden Fly" was the story of a girl born from four or five generations of drunkards, her blood tainted by a long succession of misery and drink, which, in her, had transformed itself into a nervous decay of her sex. She had sprouted on the pavement of one of the Paris suburbs; and, tall, handsome, of superb flesh, the same as a plant growing on a dunghill, she avenged the rogues and vagabonds from whom she sprang. With her, the putrefaction that was left

to ferment among the people, rose and polluted the aristocracy. She became, without herself wishing it, one of nature's instruments, a ferment of destruction, corrupting and disorganizing Paris. It was at the end of the article that the comparison with the fly occurred—a fly of the colour of the sun, which had flown from out some filth—a fly that gathered death on the carrion left by the roadside, and that, buzzing and dancing, and emitting a sparkle of precious stones, poisoned men by merely touching them in their palaces which it entered by the windows.

Nana is so much an animal that she does not detect the condemnation of herself, although her lover squirms uncomfortably before the prophecy of his own doom. Yet he does not heed the warning, settling instead to become the most pathetic of Circe's brutes and the clearest testimony of her polluting power.

The novel is, however, more than a history of Nana and the Rougon-Macquart family. It is an analysis of the moral corruption lying at the very heart of the Second Empire. Society itself is merely a façade over the putrefaction. Countess Sabine's evening at home is a drama of cold morality and polite conversation undergirded by feverish arrangements to attend Nana's party on the following evening. Fauchery at once perceives the emptiness of Sabine's morality; he senses an affinity between her and the actress, and he soon succeeds in becoming her lover. When the countess reappears, it is at her party honoring the engagement of her daughter to Daguenet, one of Nana's lovers. The mask is now stripped away, and the countess stands calmly between her husband and her lover while the chorus of the "Blonde Venus" swells through the rooms. Madame Hugon, on the other hand, is genuinely moral, but she is stupid in her morality. She believes that she can force her sons to goodness by denying them money. Instead, she loses one son to dishonor and the other to death. Zola's comment here is that her type of morality while genuine is not functional: it exists for its own sake rather than for preservation of the individual in the presence of evil.

Existing within the social fabric are other conventions revealed as both atrocious and immoral. There is the proudly foolish display of patriotism, appearing first at the countess' home, recurring at Nana's party, and last shown in the discussion of the coming war while the women sit around Nana's decomposing corpse. There is also the immoderate love of nobility—the anticipation of the Prince of Scotland's visit, the recurrent conversations of Count Bismarck and the Shah of Persia. That the prince falls victim to Nana's sensuality reveals the putrescence in even the highest representatives of the social and political order. Moreover, the society is one which exists upon money and destroys those who have no money. When he fails to recover his fortunes at the *Grand Prix*, Count Vandeuvres can see no alternative to locking himself in his stable and setting it afire. The financier Steiner makes and loses fortunes with comparative ease, but he does so at the expense of common humanity. When he devotes himself to Nana, she consumes not only his money but also the life of the working class. "There were there, in a corner of the country, workmen black with coal dust, bathed with perspiration, who, night and day, tightened their muscles and heard their bones crack, to supply the means for Nana's pleasures." . . . There is no moral objective in society; it, like Nana, is a carnivore which feeds upon any victim or, in the absence of a victim, upon itself.

Functioning as a foil against which the evils of society are revealed is the equally contemptible *demi-monde*. Zola intends by his juxtaposition of the two that this stratum be seen as a direct reflection of all the foolish mores and sentiments of the higher level. Nana frequently indulges in sententious pronouncements of her fine morals, a parallel to the moral display of Countess Sabine. The polite conversation of the coming Exposition which prevails at Countess Sabine's home is repeated in the succeeding chapter at Nana's party. The pretension to morality and manners at Mme. Hugon's house party is set off against the courtesan's anger that her paramours appear not to recognize her when she passes by. At the running of the *Grand Prix*, recognized society occupies the pavilion immediately opposite the open area where the *demi-monde* is gathered, and the two vie in their determined oblivion and covert inspection of each other. Throughout the first half of the novel Zola establishes the exact relationship of the two worlds and defines Nana's function as scourge by moving in a consistent pattern from the one to the other. In the second half where Nana's triumph is universal, the structure of recognized society crumbles away and the *demi-monde* emerges as the standard.

It is from the theatre, however, that *Nana* derives its controlling form and its motifs of decadent mythology, social comedy, and moral perversion. The figure of the stage is recurrent in the novel as a symbol of the revelation of personal and social truths. Nana first appears on the stage. Count Muffat, suspicious of his wife's fidelity, watches a shadow drama in which two figures pass back and forth across the shade of Fauchery's window. When he returns to Nana, she angrily opens her bedroom door and reveals the goat-like actor Fontan sprawled on her bed. Nana later orders a gold and silver bed on which to display herself to her lovers; Count Muffat comes unannounced and discovers her with his father-in-law. Each time the stage symbol appears, Nana functions as either stage manager or actress, controlling her constant audience, Muffat, by means of her brute sensuality.

In a sense, all the action of the novel as well as the controlling images arise from the burlesque drama of Chapter One, the "Blonde Venus." The Olympians, especially gamin-like Rose Mignon as Diana, are but a mockery of the mythical gods in their bickering, their descent to the Shrove Tuesday feast, and their final discovery of Venus ensnarled with Mars in Vulcan's net. Rose-Diana is married to a panderer who arranges all her amours and happily instructs their two sons in the ways of the world. Just as she informs Vulcan of his wife's infidelity, so does she turn informer in real life, sending to Muffat a love letter the countess has written to Fauchery. And as the goddess of chastity must ever be at war with the goddess of love, so she and Nana contend bitterly for lovers, theatrical roles, and leading positions in their society. Time and again she loses her lovers, Steiner, Muffat, and Fauchery, to Nana; but her revenge takes an ironical twist by being directed against the lover rather than the blond goddess. (pp. 149-53)

Another significant action coming from the drama is Nana's infatuation for Fontan, who portrays Vulcan. First she forces his recognition by society when she insists that the Prince of Scotland drink a toast to him on his saint's day. Then she takes him as her lover. After her expulsion of Muffat and Steiner, the two elope to a love nest which actually becomes a foul stithy, for Fontan is merely a selfish brute and Nana's adoration of him is manifested as an eager masochism. This relationship is a wry fulfillment of her childhood dream of living in a pasture as a goatherd; Fontan is goat-like in appearance and action.

Again the myth provides an ironical comment upon life: Nana is devotedly true to Fontan, sleeping with others only to earn enough money to support him; it is he who takes another mistress and finally turns her out from their home.

The ultimate contribution of the burlesque to the novel is the character of Venus herself. Nana becomes the high priestess of the cult of love, and men rush to sacrifice their fortunes and their lives for her pleasure. She is the personification of sensuality, from her first appearance on the stage to her departure into death.... Nana is not the ancient Venus, however, but the modern decadent, homosexual as well as heterosexual. She takes George Hugon as lover when he is dressed in her clothes. When she tires of the adulation of men, she turns to her old companion in street walking, Satin. At times she dresses as a man and visits the brothels of Paris. With both men and women, however, her love is merely an extension of self-love, so that she is Narcissus as well as Venus. (pp. 153-54)

A final impact of the ''Blonde Venus'' is the birth of a new religion to replace the effete church of society. Count Muffat deserts the ineffectual unfrocked priest, M. Venot, to worship at the shrine of Queen Venus. When he later goes to church to pray, he can only sit helpless in the hushed darkness realizing, ''God had not yet arrived.'' Nana is the priestess and the divinity of the decadent mythology to which society now turns, and the theatre is the cathedral in which she first manifests herself to mankind: ''. . . the emptiness of the house, the dim light that pervaded the whole, the opening and shutting of doors, and the hushed voices [were] suggestive of a church.'' . . . When Nana leaves the stage, the theatre is emptied. Upon her return, it is a dismantled church: ''The rest of the stage, full of a kind of fine dust similar to that which hangs about houses in the course of demolition, resembled a gigantic nave undergoing repair . . . whilst a ray of sunshine, which had penetrated through some window intersected the darkness above like a bar of gold.'' . . . (p. 155)

The first drama in which Nana appears prefigures much of the action and form of the novel. Her second role is that of a duchess in a comedy of manners. Nana's failure as the respectable, naive duchess represents the foolishness of all her pretensions to morality. The function of this drama is to objectify the social comedy of the novel, centralizing those scenes which precede it and pointing to those which follow. Nana's assumption of the role alone involves several ironic twists. The drama is Fauchery's portrait of one mistress, Countess Sabine Muffat, who is to be played by his other mistress, Rose Mignon, who is also mistress to Muffat. Nana, however, resumes Muffat as lover, takes the role, and succeeds in supplanting Rose and the countess both on the stage and in life.

On one level the novel is a *déclassé* comedy of manners attacking the artificiality and vices of the Second Empire. Much of the action is typical of the genre, including the exchanges of wit, which are essentially mere exchanges of innuendo; the pretence of innocence, which occurs on both levels of society; and the repeated performance of ''dramas'' meant to dupe the observer into a belief in the actor's sincerity and integrity. (pp. 155-56)

Also drawn from the comedy of manners are certain stock characters, choric figures in the novel. There is the old woman, both sentimental and ridiculously sensual. Mme. Lerat, Nana's aunt, believes in the sanctity of Nana's obsession for Fontan and attempts to seduce old Bosc at the Twelfth Night dinner in the love nest. The Marquis de Chouard is the vilely lecherous

old man who publicly disdains his son-in-law for setting up Nana in her mansion but privately attends her himself. Zoé and Francis are the traditional servants who give advice to their mistress, professing great fondness for her at the same time that they batten upon her excesses. There are the husbands who serve as procurers, whether intentionally or ignorantly, and there are the ''stage managers'' of little plots and schemes, eminently Labordette, who directs the *demi-monde* much as Bordenave directs the actors in the theatre. Finally, there is the fop, here a country boy who comes to the city to be a wit and a man-about-town. (p. 156)

Like the mythology, the comedy of manners has its basis in the first drama and extends from there into society. From the second drama it returns again to society, with a mercurial interchanging of roles among the representatives of both worlds. The comedy is, like the myth, *déclassé;* for while Zola presents the follies of society, he shows no golden mean. Nature, however, may choose to allow none, and the nature of the Second Empire is his guide.

The final drama in which Nana appears is a fairy piece called *Mélusine.* Here she appears in three silent poses, displaying her sensual power once again for the benefit of Paris. This, her last appearance alive, is a restatement, a final symbol of what she is and has been—an ikon that Paris has adored and worshiped. Thus Nana's career as an actress provides a frame introducing, restating, and concluding both her social existence and the character of society.

Drawing from the theatrical tradition of his day, Zola provides a total structural pattern for the novel which is admirable mechanically if not always consonant with the action of the novel. Structurally it is a well-made drama, like the dramas of Scribe, each part having a perfect correspondence to another part. The novel breaks almost evenly into two books, each containing seven chapters. The first half contains Nana's career as actress, her introduction to Parisian society, and her disappearance to the love nest with Fontan. The second half presents her reappearance, her rise to supremacy of the *demi-monde,* and concludes with her final disappearance, into death. Midway in each half Nana rises to her greatest triumphs. In part one (Chapter Four), she is recognized as the celebrity of the theatre when all the gentlemen of society either come invited to or crash her dinner party. In part two (Chapter Eleven), she is apotheosized as Queen Venus before all society, the triumph of the *demi-monde.*

Furthermore, each of the first seven chapters is balanced against a mathematical opposite in the second seven, as if Zola had inverted his outline in constructing the two parts of the novel. Chapter Seven, in which Nana sends the cuckold Muffat to walk the streets, has as its companion Chapter Eight, in which Fontan and his new mistress expel Nana, once again a streetwalker, from the love nest. Chapter Six, where Nana, after upsetting the demeanor of Mme. Hugon's house party, finally takes Muffat as lover, is balanced against Chapter Nine, where Nana in her foolish desire to play a ''respectable woman'' usurps Rose Mignon's role and resumes Muffat as lover. Chapters Three and Twelve, each two from the beginning and end of the novel, concern parties at the home of Countess Sabine. And certainly Chapter Fourteen is a repetition of Chapter One. As Paris awaited the revelation of Nana at the *théâtre des Variétés,* so do the *demi-monde* and the reader await the final unveiling of Nana destroyed by smallpox. When she first comes onstage, Nana is hailed by the cry of George Hugon, ''She is divine.'' Immediately before the final revelation, Rose Mignon murmurs, "She is altered." The novel begins with the cry from the crowd, "Nana, Nana!" and it ends with the cry from the crowds in the streets, "To Berlin! To Berlin! To Berlin!" Then the curtains open and Nana is revealed. (pp. 157-58)

For all this mathematical and architectural precision, however, the novel lacks the *essence* of unity and organization, a fundamental weakness of Zola's art. The two-book division normally calls for a climax at the junction; but insofar as the novel is a history of Nana, it is a rather negative climax, the center of attention being not Nana but Muffat. Insofar as the novel is a history of society, the shift of emphasis to Muffat can be justified. However, his absence from the scenes of Chapter Eight is conspicuous enough to deny full satisfaction in selecting Society as the major actor in the novel. There is, then, a separation of the content and the architecture of the novel.

Further, one must acknowledge that the imagery and symbolism of the novel are somewhat labored. This is especially true of the animal imagery which is interpreted in Chapter Eight, and of the Venus symbol and water imagery, which Zola openly announces at the onset: "It was Venus rising from the sea." The religious connotations are slightly less defined, yet even they are obvious in the texture of the novel.

Despite these transparencies, the novel remains admirable for its plan and execution and for the vitality which survives even the smother of details. Nana has a life of her own which transcends the limits of a careful definition; so too, the novel. There is an integration of constructive elements which springs from and returns to the center of the novel—the actress and the theatre as symbol and source of the disease of society. (p. 158)

Frances McNeely Leonard, "'Nana': Symbol and Action," in Modern Fiction Studies, *Vol. IX, No. 2, Summer, 1963, pp. 149-58.*

JOHN PORTER HOUSTON (essay date 1972)

[*An American essayist and critic, Houston has written extensively on French literature. In the following excerpt, he discusses Zola's narrative technique in* L'assommoir.]

One of the problems Flaubert faced in writing *Madame Bovary* was the disparity between the author's highly literary voice and a style for indirect discourse which would seem suitable for Emma's banal emotions. He found a kind of shifting compromise: here and there Emma thinks in the style of books she has read; elsewhere her words are quoted directly. This is all very well when dealing with a young woman who "reads too much," but these ambiguities are impossible with a very literate author treating the character of an almost illiterate washerwoman, such as Gervaise in *L'Assommoir*. Zola took the plunge and devised a narrative tone which one still encounters today. His notion was to blend together description, indirect discourse, and dialogue into a stylistic continuum where the grammar and vocabulary must fuse so that the reader feels no disparity among them. This stylistic formula completely shocked Flaubert: he called it "inverted preciosity," because the narrator's voice is discreetly colored with slang and lower-class usage. There is consequently a good deal of ambiguity; at times it is difficult to distinguish between the narrator and free indirect discourse on the part of the characters. Here are Copeau's plans for the wedding: "In the meantime Copeau didn't have a dime. Without trying to show off, he intended to do things right. . . . Sure, he didn't like the skirts, it killed him to pay

his six bucks to those fat pigs who didn't need it to wet their whistles. But a wedding without a mass, whatever you say, it's just not a wedding. He went himself to the church to bargain and for an hour hassled with a dirty old crow who would have sold his own grandmother." Zola can occasionally, with some attention to transition, rise to a more formal tone, but this tends to be reserved for solemn moments.

L'Assommoir was Zola's first great success, and, with his usual foxy sense of publicity, he planned his subsequent novels (a general scheme for them already existed) so that, rather than following any strict chronological order in the history of the Rougon-Macquarts, they varied in genre and tone. This arrangement had the advantage of regularly surprising the reading public, and avoiding the monotonous character of a true *roman-fleuve* ["saga in several volumes"]. . . . The use of symbolism also changes greatly from book to book. Aside from Zola's unfortunate tendency to crudely personify machines, we find that certain works have elaborate patterns of imagery which are not to be found in others. Nor does the taste for symbolism exclude highly committed social themes and attitudes, despite the silly antithesis so commonly made between realist and symbolist modes. Both currents reach perhaps their highest point in *Germinal* . . . , which, in addition, offers us the most elaborate example of Zola's devising new and significant handlings of the correlation of time and point of view.

The first two of the seven parts of *Germinal* recount the events of one long day, but not at all in the manner of Balzac. Zola created a curious and subtle shifting back and forth between hours and characters. The novel begins with Etienne's arrival before dawn at the mine in search of work. The second chapter describes the awakening and departure of the working members of the Maheu family. From Chapter 3 on, we are again following Etienne's consciousness as he sees the Maheus arrive at the mine, is employed, learns through the day the routine of his job, and leaves in the afternoon with Maheu, who finds him lodgings. Part II now returns us to eight o'clock in the morning and the awakening of the Grégoire family. We see their typical preoccupations until the moment when la Maheude arrives to ask for help. This conclusion of the first chapter serves as a liaison to the next one, which moves us again back in time to the hours between the working Maheus' departure and la Maheude's getting herself together and setting off for the Grégoires'. We now move through the whole scene of la Maheude at the Grégoires' and follow her day through to five o'clock in the afternoon: we meet her neighbors, Maheu comes home, having left Etienne at the end of Part I, and they busily eat, bathe, make love, and garden. Part II concludes with Etienne's activities from twilight to nine o'clock.

All this elaborate backtracking in time and shifting from one consciousness to another demonstrates a stage of virtuosity well beyond anything Flaubert ever dreamed of and anticipates certain devices in *Ulysses*. What is particularly skillful is the way in which chapters do not necessarily regress to the point in time which another has begun; they tend more to overlap partially, with the exact moment of the day often suggested rather than precisely indicated. It sometimes happens with this technique that a scene occurs twice or more in the narrative, as point of view shifts from chapter to chapter. In Part IV, for example, we first hear at the luncheon party that a delegation of miners has arrived to present their grievances. In the following chapter we see the miners going to press their case. A far more dramatic example occurs in Part V, where in Chapter 2 those in the Jean-Bart mine learn that the cables of the elevator have been cut; in the next chapter, Zola redoes it all as seen by the hostile mob on the surface. And finally, in Chapter 5 of the same part, Zola actually indicates the hour—five o'clock—three times as the scene and point of view shift from one group of characters to another. The high sophistication by which the chpaters and parts of *Germinal* are interwoven introduces a new kind of illusionism into realist fiction: once the simple, smooth line of chronology is broken, it is possible to imagine all manner of peculiar effects, including some of more recent invention.

Equally striking in *Germinal* is the cosmology of the novel, with its numerous allusions to myth. Of all Zola's novels this is the one in which symbol prevails most over conventional notions of realism or, more accurately, is blended with them. I do not think that cosmology is too pretentious a word for Zola's representations of the mooon, the sun, the surface of the earth and its bowels, and, finally, the cycle of the ages.

At first we see the plain alternately sterile and fecund; the idea of a crop, present in the title *Germinal,* is supported by many references to harvest, but the harvest will be one of men: the agricultural cycle is primarily symbolic of social change, and the sun figuratively presides over this, both the mild April sun, as at the end of the book, and the red winter sun bathing the landscape in blood, as the mob of striking miners rushes over the plain: "And what they [the bourgeois] saw was a red vision of the revolution that would inevitably carry them all off one bloody evening at the end of this epoch. . . . Fires would blaze . . . not a single stone would be left standing in the cities, and men would return to primitive life in the woods after the great orgy."

The red sun, of course, suggests another complex of myth and color symbolism: during Etienne's first day in the mine, red and black, the colors of hell, are constantly mentioned, although Zola, with his description of water pouring into the pit, is preparing us for the ultimate symbol of the mine—the uncharted subterranean sea, which the sabotaged mine will become. Another form of infernal symbolism is Le Tartaret (from a Greek word for Hell), the mine which has been burning for years and so warms the ground that there is vegetation all year round. It is interesting that Mme Hennebeau and her party, on the day violence breaks forth, go to see this as a curiosity: they admire it without remembering the loss of life which it caused. For Catherine, working in the nearby Jean-Bart, Le Tartaret is a punishment visited on the mine crew for their sins. Various other elements of the supernatural are associated with the Voreux mine: the Black Man who comes to punish loose female mine workers, the yellow horses Etienne sees as he first approaches the mine (horses are never yellow in French or English: this is a fantastic beast), and the red cat who leaps from the mine just before it collapses (needless to say, cats are never red). The collapse of the superstructure of the mine again brings in a myth: it is compared to a giant, that is, to one of the Titans whom Zeus hurled into Hades.

A special group of associations if found in passages dealing with the Grégoire family. Their colors are white, pink, and blue, their estate a garden of Eden, a protected orchard in the dismal plain. But the enjoyment of all this is only possible by their worship of the "hidden god," who manifests himself through stock in a corporation—felicitously called in French an Anonymous Society. The Grégoires constitute the perfect antithesis to the miners, which is why their house and attitudes are so carefully portrayed. (pp. 87-91)

John Porter Houston, "Flaubert, His Disciples, and Impersonal Narration," in his *Fictional Technique in France, 1802-1927: An Introduction, Louisiana State University Press, 1972, pp. 62-94.**

RICHARD A. ZAKARIAN   (essay date 1972)

[*In the following excerpt from his book-length study of the sources for* Germinal, *Zakarian analyzes Zola's use of factual documents and historical events in writing the novel.*]

Germinal's documentation is the result of a logical and carefully planned selectivity in which Zola's thematic and artistic aims are always in play. To discern how Zola utilized the truth and in what manner he modified it is, in a sense, a means to understanding not only a novel but a novelist. Zola is motivated by an imperious need to begin the creative process with fact, for "la vérité enfante la vie" ["truth begets life"] (*Le Figaro,* June 6, 1896) and truth serves as a point of departure for Zola's artistry. At a particular moment, Zola chooses a relevant fact which he wishes to incorporate into the novel. He reproduces it in its minutest detail remaining objectively faithful to the document. For a moment, Zola is dominated and restrained by an inherent scrupulousness. But the very choice of this detail, the psychological and chronological moment of its selection, its place and frequency of use in the novel are contingent upon the artist, not on the compiler of fact. The documents, in *Germinal,* owe their transformation to the dramatic, epic and thematic aims of Zola and to the unique nature of Zola's poetic eye. (p. 187)

The author used his customary documentary procedure—an on-the-spot investigation of an environment, historical and technical works, personal oral and written communications. . . . Zola amassed documents, the substance of which may be classified according to three types of information: data relating to the mining industry and the sociology and psychology of the miner and the mining community; information concerned with social, political and economic problems and philosophies in France after 1871; historical accounts of strikes in France from 1869-1884. Most of Zola's technical and scientific information [J. F. Blanc, *Encyclopédie Roret: Nouveau manuel complet pour l'exploitation des mines;* Louis-Laurent Simon, *La vie souterraine, ou les mines et les mineurs;* Emile Dormoy, *Topographie souterrain du bassin hoviller de Valenciennes*] and his most significant medical source were published in the sixties and coincide with the actual dates of the action in *Germinal* (1866-1867). The major socialist, economic and political theories of the novel were based on material published after 1870, particularly in 1883-1884. All of these data were tempered and supplemented by Zola's [visit to the Anzin mine] . . . and the resulting detailed notes. Whenever the documentation is sketchy or the facts questionable, Zola calls upon his infallible intuition, his logic and his artistic temperament to fill in the gaps. A study of the vast quantity of raw materials underlines the extreme need for organization and order on the part of the novelist. Zola's highly developed method of preparatory creative documents—First Plan, *Ebauche, Personnages,* the two sets of Detailed Plan—was indispensable to his whole artistic creation of the novel. Only such a sensitive and, at the same time, methodical and pragmatic technique, closely allied to certain architectural procedures, could produce the unified and superb fiction which all critics maintain that *Germinal* is. A work like *Germinal* which is a fusion of fact and fiction (impossible to determine to an exact degree the percentage of each) could not have been put together in the two and one half months alloted to preliminary research and to the composition of the imaginative documents, without the habitual methodology. This study permits certain generalisations which pertain not alone to the elaboration of *Germinal* but also to the novelistic techniques and procedures of the author.

A study of Zola's preliminary notes, creative and documentary, proves conclusively that the artist and researcher are at work concurrently. The document does not always precede the creative development and imagination is always present to guide the research. A documentary notation will often contain an indication of where, by whom, and at what precise moment, the information is to be used in the part and chapter scheme of the novel. All of the creative and documentary notes are interdependent and are developed progressively. No imaginative document is definitive until its incorporation into the finished text of the novel. Zola's research is guided by the central philosophical theme and the narrative thread (both developed in the early paragraphs of the *Ebauche*); the creative elements are influenced by the inspiration of the document. In short, imagination and documentation are closely allied and interrelated and Zola tends to move from the general philosophical principle expounded in the initial paragraph of the *Ebauche* to its particularization in his fiction.

Zola's documentation in certain highly specialized areas tends to overlap and be duplicated. This is particularly true with data alien to the author's habitual way of life. Zola blends skillfully several accounts of the same technical, sociological, medical and political phenomena and he usually tempers the final product with what he learned at Anzin (verbal and graphic accounts) or through personal contact with specialists in this field. His intuitive, artistic and logical sense helps him arrive at the right alloy of elements.

The techniques of assimilation, synthesis, transformation and adaptation of the factual documents seem to fall into a general pattern. First, although most of the notes find their way into the novel, Zola excludes the irrevelant and the inappropriate. For example, Zola omits incidents in the violent strike scenes (thievery, wanton destruction, acts of anticlericalism) which would tend to lessen the reader's sympathy for the oppressed miner. Facts amassed with specific uses in mind had to be discarded sometimes for lack of space or sometimes because a last minute change in narrative thread rendered the fact unnecessary. Secondly, the author may take one factual or historical incident and modify it to soften or exaggerate the event. This is particularly exemplified in Zola's poetization of Simonin's description of Tartaret and Côte Verte. Other examples of the same technique may be seen in his adaptation of the history of the Anzin Mining Company (Dormoy) to Montsou or, in general, in his allegorical treatment of the miner's moral and spiritual traits as related in [H. Boëns-Boissau's *Traité pratique des maladies, des accidents et des difformités des hovilleurs* and Georges Stell's *Les cahiers de doléances des mineurs français*] and attributed to la Mouquette and Jeanlin. Thirdly, Zola frequently takes several historical events and compresses them into one or two outstanding fictional scenes, for example, the destruction of the Voreux mining shaft, the rescue operation, and the experiences of the emprisoned miners are taken from several unrelated accounts in Simonin; the hunger march and military skirmish are an outright composite of the strike outbreaks of Ricamerie and Aubin (1869), of Fourchambault (1870) and of Anzin (1884). Finally, its converse, the expansion of one historical incident or fact into several fictional events or ideas, is more evident in the area of political,

social and economic theory adapted to *Germinal* from [Paul Leroy-Beaulieu's *La question ouvrière au XIX siècle*, Emile Victor Louis de Laveley's *Le socialism contemporain*, and Oscar Testut's *L'internationale: son origine, son but, son caractère*].

A study of the documents seems to attest to Zola's use of material contemporary not with the dates of *Germinal*'s action (1866-1867) but rather with the period following the fall of the Second Empire (1870-1884). Most of Zola's socialist, economic and political documents, the information on the Anzin strike of 1884, and his highly utilitarian and significant Anzin notes, are works of the eighties and reflections of the Third Republic. Almost any discussion of the International [an international labor union] and the inclusion of a prototypical anarchist in a novel, the action of which takes place in the middle of the sixties, are outright anachronisms. Zola has been criticized frequently for his tendency to adapt contemporary incidents of the Third Republic to the "Rougon-Macquart" series. Working within a framework of about eighteen years (1852-1870)—the Second Empire—Zola was often forced to pile event upon event to fit them into a tightly circumscribed predetermined chronological sequence; more often than not, he used events contemporary with the inception and development of the novel, making little, if any, attempt to camouflage the fact. He would date his work, as he does in *Germinal,* by the inclusion of one or two historical events of importance (the Emperor's Mexican venture), and then with no further concern for chronology he would include whatever material his artistic or thematic requirements would dictate. Zola's deliberate or careless falsification of the true dates of *Germinal* ("Or mon roman se passe de 1866 à 1869" ["My novel takes place between 1866 and 1869"]—*Correspondance* . . . in a public letter to Francis Magnard, editor of *Le Figaro*, dated April 4, 1885, may indicate his concern to justify his inclusion of the International, to justify in turn his use of the Ricamerie and Aubin strikes of 1869 as historical models for his strike action, and may underline his sensitivity to the problem of Etienne's phenomenal development into a strike leader of stature and influence within an incredibly short period of time. Zola has openly admitted that he "use sans remords de l'erreur volontaire quand elle s'impose, par une nécessité de construction" ["uses without remorse an intentional error when it becomes indispensible through a necessity of structure"] (*Le Figaro,* June 6, 1896) and an analysis of *Germinal*'s documents reaffirms this truth. Poetic licence is the right and prerogative of all novelists, even those using a scientific methodology.

Philip Walker, in his structural study of the creative documents which went into the preliminary development of *Germinal* and whose study resulted in a revealing analysis of certain artistic principles, has compared Zola's research techniques in *Germinal* to those of an editor or movie research department, since both Zola and the film editor are concerned principally with creating an illusion of truth rather than truth itself. We can agree with Walker's conclusions as far as he has gone. However, his study was confined to the manuscript notes and to Zola's catalogue of them in the Detailed Plans. The problem for Zola in the Plans was essentially one of organization, sequence and continuity, and here Zola is one with the film maker. But this is only part of the story and does not carry the discussion through to its logical conclusion. A detailed study of the factual materials . . . emphasizes one paramount idea, the fidelity of Zola not alone to the substance and spirit of his primary sources but occasionally even to the language. Modification occurred to facilitate a more efficient, economical and effective assimilation of these facts into the novel. Changes in the facts take place for obvious thematic or artistic reasons or both. He excludes tedious technical explanations and translates the phenomenon into a readily comprehensible idiom which he chooses to dramatize or narrate. If he commits an anachronism, it is obvious that Zola believes that more will be lost by the omission of the fact or deed than by the criticism which it was certain to provoke. All of the documents put to use are attuned to the central philosophical theme, to the immediate artistic exigencies of the fiction, and, for the most part, to Zola's personal editorial policy or *parti pris*. A comparison of the primary sources with the relevant paragraphs in the novel will attest to the conclusion that Zola, whenever possible, reproduced his documents without change in idea and with the usual literary and stylistic considerations of the novelist. *Germinal,* a happy fusion of fact and fiction, is, in the main, a credible and for the most part truthful recreation of the letter and spirit of a mining community in the 1860s. Here I am one with Ida-Marie Frandon (*Autour de "Germinal"*) and Henriette Psichari (*Antomie d'un chef-d'oeuvre*) both of whom find Zola's depiction of the miner and the mining community historically accurate notwithstanding the fact that Zola is first and foremost a novelist and only incidentally an historian. It should also be underlined here that the twenty year gap that bridges the time of the action in *Germinal* (1866-1867) from the date of its composition (1884-1885) changes little in the actuality and essential truth of the mining scene as portrayed by the author in *Germinal.*

Zola, like Flaubert, had little interest in, and almost a deep scorn for, his documents, or at least so he maintains, once they fulfilled their function; their function was to inspire Zola to greater feats of creativity. Zola was so constituted that truth for him, amassed in his documentation, was the springboard from which his imagination took off. Zola's aim was to create life, or, a sense of life, to formulate tomorrow's hypotheses and thus to anticipate or announce the future by using all of the documents liberally collected and plundered.... If Zola's feelings towards his documentation were those of complete indifference as he pretends, then why the deliberate effort to assure for posterity the preservation of these creative and factual manuscript notes? Whatever Zola's announced policy towards his documents, this study reveals one all-pervasive finding: Zola's strict adherence to the information found in his vast documentation, any modification or anachronism being instrumental to a more efficacious and direct presentation of the novel's central theme. The result is a novel which is an amalgam of fact and fiction and a highly representative, truthful and credible picture of the human environment which it set in motion. Future historians are certain to find in Zola's depiction of a mining community in the second half of the nineteenth century a most enduring, intimate, complete and revealing account of a vanished era. (pp. 187-91)

Richard H. Zakarian, in his Zola's "Germinal": A Critical Study of Its Primary Sources, *Librairie Droz, 1972, 198 p.*

COLIN SMETHURST   (essay date 1974)

[*In the following excerpt from his book-length study of* Germinal, *Smethurst examines the allusions, imagery, and other rhetorical devices which contribute a dimension of myth to the naturalistic events depicted in the novel.*]

Zola conceived *Germinal* as a drama of violent contrasts. One of them is the scandal of the misery of the present put against the dream of a shining world that might be. Zola has infinite faith in the idea that humanity will progress from the one to the other. In spite of his suggestions towards a political solution, he is not clear how this change can be brought about and creates the myth of the seed planted in the soil of the present, flourishing and being harvested in the future. The conflict between the reality and the dream is thus resolved in poetic myth.

Before this germination, however, the mine, a monster in itself, has been the scene of cosmic conflict where all the elements, earth, air, fire and water, have been exploited by Zola. The various forms of physical death or mental torture are represented by presences and monsters. For these latter Zola draws on the resources provided by Greek, biblical and Celtic mythology for many of his figures of speech. One of the keys to his use of these mythologies is in his assimilation of the life underground to a life in the underworld, the miners becoming damned creatures in hell. All the associations of hell and hell-fire are called upon. Their influence covers the specific burning hell of Le Tartaret underground. The name evokes the Greek Tartarus, the abyss in which the Titans were confined. Zola does not pursue these associations, however, preferring the biblical connotations of the destruction of the city of Sodom and the eternal torments of hell-fire.... These notions of fire invade even the world above ground, starting with simple denomination as in the case of *Le Volcan,* the name of a bar, or la Roussie ..., the name of a female miner of long ago, and being elaborated in la Brûlé, a wild figure scorched into revolt by the mine, who becomes a witch in the attack on Jean-Bart, shrieking 'Faut renverser les feux! aux chaudières!' ['Knock down the chimneys! to the boilers!'] egging on the women

> toutes sanglantes dans le reflet d'incendie,
> suantes et échevelées de cette cuisine de sabbat

> ['all bloody in the firelight, sweating and dishevelled from this witches' kitchen'].....

(pp. 57-8)

The damned souls are pursued not only by fire but also by flood. The sabotage of the mine-shaft at the level of an underground lake and consequent flooding of the workings is transformed by Zola into an immense cataclysmic scene. References are made to drowned cities. In spite of the miners trapped below, the scene is represented in terms of a spectacle. The watching miners are fascinated by the cosmic forces at work and end by fleeing in terror. In the actual description of the collapse of the pit ..., Zola has eliminated any direct feeling of pity for the trapped miners or sense of revenge on the mining company, concentrating all his effects instead on the animate natural forces at play. In such a scheme human beings are irrelevant, for the enormity of the spectacle witnessed is but one drama contained within a vaster one yet:

> Jusqu'où devait-on fuir, pour être à l'abri, dans cette fin de jour abominable, sous cette nuée de plomb, qui elle aussi semblait vouloir écraser le monde?

> ['To where should one flee, to find shelter, in this abominable day's end, under this leaden sky, which also seemed to want to crush the world?'].....

A whole chain of images of the earth squeezing, squashing, flattening the miners below ground is here repeated above ground level. Even in the open air the miners are subject to these huge commotions, being squeezed below the weight of the sky and with the earth splitting, cracking and being engulfed below them. The terror of humanity becomes then the basic fear of no longer existing, and the gnawing worry that human existence or non-existence seen in this cosmic perspective is perhaps almost of no import anyhow. The result is a sense of pity at human fate. The image of Maheu at the coalface:

> entre les deux roches, ainsi qu'un puceron pris entre deux feuillets d'un livre, sous la menace d'un aplatissement complet

> ['between the two rocks, as though he were an insect caught between the pages of a book, threatened with being completely crushed'] . . .

can stand as a typical statement of this situation. At this level Zola is writing an evolutionary epic, in which the role of humanity is negligible. This sort of conclusion throws doubt on the validity of the optimistic ending to the novel, and indeed on the whole theme of germination and *Germinal* as a political novel. Zola plays on the ambiguity and tensions between these two conclusions, the one pessimistic, the other optimistic, and succeeds in transforming the former into the latter by reversing the connotations of images. For example, while the earth is shown normally as digesting its regular ration of human flesh in its belly, these images of the various stages of digestion are transformed into notions of germination or gestation. The belly of the earth turns in the end from a stomach into a womb, the word 'ventre' covering both meanings. Similar are the connotations of mud and filth (as opposed to the simple images of blackness and whiteness in the earlier parts of the novel) which dominate the opening of Part VI, ch. 4, symbolizing at this stage misery and desolation. This picture is continued at the moment of the collapse of Le Voreux, one of the final statements being 'un lac d'eau boueuse occupa la place où était naguère le Voreux . . .' ['a muddy lake occupied the place where le Voreux had just stood . . .'] . . . . Out of this drama of filth and degradation, we have reached a point where the disgust has drained away, leaving a sense of moral punishment, which in its turn gives way at the end of the last chapter to images of the rich and fertile earth, where the liquid element is now sap, and life. Such transformations are not specific to *Germinal*. In *La Terre*, too, Zola shows human and animal excrement being transformed from disgusting faecal muck to solemn and richly fertile manure.

This mythology of cosmic struggle and renewal contains within it the similar human struggle of misery, death and promise of renewal. It is at this level that the political and psychological dramas take place, each producing its own mythology. . . . [In the key scenes of the raging mass of miners] Zola draws on a simplified mythology of the French Revolution to underline his meaning, with mouths (not whole people) singing the *Marseillaise*, an axe-blade transformed into the blade of the guillotine, repeated cries for bread and a blood-red light bathing the whole spectacle. . . . This particular scene, drawing on what is virtually a folk-memory of the Revolution, illuminates that other aspect of the title of the novel which refers to the day of 12 Germinal in the third year of the Republican era (1 April 1795) when, in protest at reactionary measures taken since the fall of Robespierre, the Convention was invaded by Parisians demanding bread and a return to the more revolutionary constitution of 1793. The title thus refers not only to the idea of springtime but also to the French Revolution and gives full weight to both of the terms used by Zola when he described his novel as representing 'un avril révolutionnaire' ['a revolutionary April']. This revolutionary theme is linked by Zola to that of instinctual behaviour. At the same time as he is appealing to revolutionary mythology he is also describing a progressive invasion of animal-like instincts which displace individual behaviour in the scenes of riot. The masses gallop over the countryside. The frequent repetition of the word gallop in *Germinal* signifies most often the idea of a wild, natural, virile but blind force driving the miners on. At the same time, under extreme pressure human beings are not only physically dislocated by Zola, becoming limbs, eyes, feet, and so on, indistinguishable except as a mass, but also revert to a primitive, prehuman shape, essentially wolf-like. The substance of such a deformation is treated most fully in *La Bête humaine*, but is already outlined in *Germinal*, where the 'faces placides des houilleurs de Montsou' ['placid faces of the Montsou coalminers'] become 'mâchoires de bêtes fauves' ['jaws of wild beasts']. . . . Come the revolution, the men 'auraient ces mâchoires de loups, ouverts pour mordre' ['would have those wolves' jaws ready to bite']. . . . The moral ambiguity of such a mythological anthropology is evident. For how can one approve an event which, while supposedly liberating, implies a regression to the caveman or earlier species? It seems that Zola is in fact again mediating the bourgeois 'frisson d'horreur' ['thrill of horror'] in such images, while stressing the inevitability of such a process. This inevitability links with another series of images where the mass of miners becomes a river bursting its banks, swelling and overflowing the countryside, an unstoppable torrent in full flood.

This relative dehumanizing of human beings, particularly at moments of high tension or when seen in the mass, is paralleled by the relative humanizing of inanimate objects, such as the mine and pithead machinery. Both the sexual symbolism apparent in the description of the machine and the fascination and terror in the face of the instincts and appetite of the mine, are figures of a prevailing spirit moving the universe as a whole which includes the procreative urge as well as the urge to kill, but which turns in *Germinal* on the nodal image of appetite. The mine is repeatedly described as voracious, swallowing its daily ration of miners. . . . The revolutionary cries for bread represent 'le cri du ventre' ['the cry of the belly']. . . , and the revolution may be brought about 'en se mangeant les uns les autres' ['in devouring one another']. . . . (pp. 58-61)

[For] Zola it is clear that the life force is essentially an appetite, a voracious hunger. Death is not eating. Such imagery is not merely the manifestation of Zola's notions of 'physiological' man, but expresses the way in which human biology links with the evolution of nature as a whole. While this evolution is progressive and leads in the end to happiness, Zola nevertheless remains as creative novelist much more in the realm of the hell-fire preacher playing on fears, terror, disgust, the plagues and afflictions of the world. It is this which gives such extraordinary power to his oppressive evocations of cold, hunger, sickness, death, collapse and catastrophe.

At the time of the publication of *Germinal* Zola was widely known, notorious some would say; his literary influence, though hotly contested, was enormous, and was for many inseparable from his long history as a journalist and especially as a fighting journalist. His novels were not regarded simply as artefacts interesting mainly to the literary world, but increasingly as public statements by a polemicist. Thus, for many readers

Germinal is an example of committed literature, in spite of Zola's efforts at impartiality and the attitudes we have shown to be often ambiguous. The picture of miners' delegations at Zola's funeral crying 'Germinal! Germinal!', the recent account by Jean-Pierre Chabrol of *Germinal* forming, with Hugo's *Les Misérables* and the Bible, part of the folk-lore of the mining and peasant communities of the Cévennes, demonstrate clearly how far this work has overflowed the boundaries of readership and influence granted normally to works of art. However much we may wish to modify this popular appreciation, such a framework must necessarily form a part of the understanding of the novel.

Zola himself would not automatically have refused the suggestion that *Germinal* is a piece of committed literature, but would have limited it to the idea of provoking a reaction to a social problem and its implications rather than to providing specific solutions. His aesthetic stance as a naturalist novelist expounding the facts of a given situation with an attempt at what he conceived to be scientific impartiality, while not necessarily excluding the drawing of conclusions, does at least inhibit him from turning the work into a propaganda exercise.

While it is clear that the explicit subject of the novel is the struggle between capital and labour placed in the stylized battle situation of a strike, it is equally clear that the resulting composition is far from being simply that. The recurrence of a good number of scenes and themes found in Zola's other works shows the permanence of certain traits, certain situations repeated obsessively, so that the exposition of a strike in the pits becomes also the occasion for a personal drama in Zola's mind. The resulting tensions and ambiguities between the 'public' and the 'private' dramas go a long way to giving this novel its particular tone.

Ultimately, however, both these aspects of the novel are subsumed into a cosmic drama of life and death, shot through with passion. At this level, while not denying the importance of either the individual or the group, Zola sees his subject in mythological terms, in which all nature is animate and human struggles are but one factor in the continuation of the life-force. The evolution and, it may be, the progress of humanity is a by-product. Teeming and swarming may simply be instinctive reactions by humans to these huge stresses, and pity at such a fate the most dignified emotional response after the initial terror of realization. Thus we have a novel moving freely from the day-to-day to a time-scale suggesting millennia, from the picture of the Maheu family's clogs lined up under the sideboard to the eternal forces of nature. (pp. 61-3)

> *Colin Smethurst, in his* Emile Zola: Germinal, *Edward Arnold, 1974, 64 p.*

DAVID BAGULEY (essay date 1975)

[*In the following excerpt, Baguley discusses the importance of theme and structure to the plot of* L'assommoir.]

In his preliminary notes for the *Rougon-Macquart* series Zola resolved to pay particular attention to the wholeness and construction of his novels. . . . As several monographs on Zola novels have demonstrated, it is invariably the overall scheme outlined in the *ébauche* that directs the elaboration of his works. Indeed, the novelist's usual method could be summarized as the *expansive* accumulation of empirical detail rigorously controlled by the *restrictive* reinforcement of an initial design. (p. 823)

Not until he had discovered the organizing principle of [*L'Assommoir*] (the return of Lantier) did the author proceed to fill out the detail of the work by direct observation and documentation. Furthermore, in the interest of organic unity, he ruthlessly reduced to a few passing references the political considerations that he had intended to depict. With less ease he abandoned the melodramatic ending of vitriol and violence that he had first imagined, but the traditional requirements of probability and necessity finally prevailed. . . . Moreover, Zola was constantly intent, while preparing his novel, on carefully measuring his effects. *"Bien graduer la chute de Gervaise"* ["Graduate well the fall of Gervaise"], he notes and underlines in the summary plan. "Graduer L'ivresse de Coupeau" ["Graduate Coupeau's drunkenness"], he frequently enjoins in his chapter plans. Each stage of Gervaise's decline is plotted as "un degré nouveau dans la chute" ["a new degree in the fall"] and an appropriate dosage of illusion and foreboding is prepared for the early chapters. . . . The whole fabric of *L'Assommoir* is made up of the interplay of such effects presented in a uniform pattern of measured gradation. By the constant application of such concerns at a time when the novel in general was undergoing formal changes, there resulted a work with a distinct unity of design.

The formal qualities of *L'Assommoir* have not gone unnoticed, but critics have generally concerned themselves exclusively with the innovative features of the work. Contemporary reviewers shrank before Zola's extensive use of argot and many a critic, like one of the characters of the novel, Madame Lerat, "se blessait seulement des mots crus; pourvu qu'on n'employât pas les mots crus, on pouvait tout dire" ["took offence only at coarse language; provided that one avoided coarse language, one could say anything"]. . . . Others deplored the absence of an uplifting moral example or overt message. Significantly, it was certain of Zola's fellow novelists who were most responsive to the powerful total effect of the work, like George Moore who later recorded his admiration for the novel's "pyramid size, strength, height, and decorative grandeur" and for the "immense harmonic development of the idea" [see excerpt dated 1888]. Since then, critics have tended to single out for study certain features of the novel such as its sources, social and moral implications, or, in particular, its narrative technique, and thus the shaping principles of the plot have gone largely unexplored. (pp. 823-24)

The following analysis of *L'Assommoir* is an attempt to take into account both perspectives and to demonstrate their interrelation. It begins by defining, in abstract terms, certain fundamental aspects of theme and structure—equivalent and contrasting features of character, event, and description—that a close reading of the text reveals to be prevalent in the work. Second, in an extended analysis of the plot of *L'Assommoir*, these elements are shown functioning together in the novel's evolving action, even structuring its successive phases.

Thus the aim of this study is primarily to lay bare the internal organization of the novel by performing the rudimentary kind of structural analysis of a work that René Girard summarizes in the following way: "Dégager les structures serait dégager l'armature de l'analyse thématique, en souligner les lignes de force, en accentuer les arêtes" ["To lay bare the structures would be to lay bare the thematic construction, emphasizing the lines of strength, accentuating the intersections"]. Consequently, no attempt is made to relate such structural features to psychological, sociopolitical, or ideological structures external to *L'Assommoir*, or to relate the work to any typology of the novel. The forms of expression of the work, Zola's use of image and symbol, and the rich and vivid popular style that he chose as his primary mode of narration are all largely incidental to this analysis whose point of focus is resolutely that of the development of the plot. Such an approach, though limited in its purview, is particularly appropriate to the study of a novel like *L'Assommoir,* which deals essentially with a process of gradual development and which unfolds, through the devised succession of its elements, in a total harmonious order. The reader of *L'Assommoir* is thereby engaged in a double response: an emotional involvement in distressing events combined with an esthetic reaction to structure and form.

The distinguishing structural features of *L'Assommoir* may be represented best by three oppositions: work/idleness, cleanliness/filth, and abstention/indulgence (drink, food, and sex), which could appear on a simple chart, as follows, with + and − signs corresponding to the *values* and the *anti-values* of the novel:

+		−
work	→	idleness
cleanliness	→	filth
abstention	→	indulgence (drink, food, and sex)

The arrows indicate that the essential development of each action in the novel involves the passage from one side to the other of this chart (or the imminence of such a movement in the first half of the work).

Each of the foreground characters of the novel can be said to illustrate one or more of these features. Lantier, for example, is firmly established on the negative side of the scheme. Idleness is his profession, combined with a talent for exploiting others. He is characteristically in league with "une fameuse fainéante" ["a notorious do-nothing"], . . . Virginie, and from his return in Chapter vi onward he never does a day's work. . . . Furthermore, the dashing figure that he cuts disguises less appealing characteristics; his trunk of clothes emits "une odeur d'homme malpropre, qui soigne seulement le dessus, ce qu'on voit de sa personne" ["the odor of an unclean man, who took care only of his surface appearance, what one saw of his person"]. . . . Finally, Zola constantly emphasizes his literal and metaphorical appetites until the philandering Lantier becomes a kind of ogre eating his way through the shops of the whole quarter. . . . (pp. 824-25)

In significant contrast Goujet exemplifies all the positive qualities of our scheme. He is an exemplary worker, skillful and assiduous. . . . Zola never fails to describe the cleanliness of the home that Goujet shares with his mother each time the admiring Gervaise pays them a visit. . . . Needless to say, Goujet abstains from drinking, hurries past the Assommoir, and lives a chaste existence in his mother's protective care. To a lesser degree other characters exhibit one or more of the same virtues or failings. Mes Bottes, for example, with his gargantuan appetite, is pure indulgence, idle and sordid, too, until an ironic stroke of fortune leads him to marry a rich lady and display his fine linen. . . . The pitiable Lalie Bijard has an equally undeserved fate, worn by her drunkard father's brutal treatment, but, with her dying words, faithful to her essential task of keeping clean the little room that she shares with her wretched family: "C'est assez propre, n'est-ce pas? . . . Et je voulais nettoyer les vitres, mais les jambes m'ont manqué" ["It's pretty clean, isn't it? . . . And I wanted to wash the windows, but my legs gave out"]. . . . (p. 825)

Together with elements of the environment like the still in père Colombe's Assommoir or the huge apartment building in the rue de la Goutte-d'Or, which Zola, in typical fashion, animates and transforms into active forces in the novel, the function of these static characters is first to arrest or to further in some degree the moral development of the two characters who do evolve, Gervaise and Coupeau. This development involves a total transition from the values of one side of our chart to the anti-values of the other. Coupeau follows a more precipitous course when his accident transforms the neat, industrious, and abstemious roofer into an idle drunkard, whose subsequent decline is but a documented representation of the stages of a chronic case of alcoholism down to the well-known delirius tremens. It is especially Gervaise's abandonment of the values of the novel that shapes the plot of *L'Assommoir* as this zealous and principled laundress, whose very mission in life is to clean, comes to renounce her trade and wallow in the filth and immorality that her progressive degradation entails. These values are clearly evident in what Zola frequently refers to in the novel as Gervaise's "ideal," the modest ambitions that she recalls with bitterness in her debasement at the end of the novel: "Elle se souvenait de son idéal, anciennement: travailler tranquille, manger toujours du pain, avoir un trou un peu propre pour dormir, bien élever ses enfants, ne pas être battue, mourir dans son lit" ["She remembered her former ideal: to work peacefully, to always have bread, to have a clean place to sleep, to raise her children well, to not be beaten, to die in her bed"]. . . . (pp. 825-26)

L'Assommoir thus presents a series of actions in which Gervaise either attempts to assert these values (mainly in the first half of the novel) or is shown submitting to the opposite tendencies until such time as her archenemies, the Lorilleux, can be reported to observe, neatly reviving our tripartite scheme: "Non, jamais ils n'espéraient la voir si bas, le nez à ce point dans la crotte. . . . Au rancart les gourmandes, les paresseuses et les dévergondées!" ["No, never had they wished to see her this low, her nose at this point in the filth. . . . Away with gourmands, layabouts, and profligates!"]. . . .

A secondary function of characters and situations in *L'Assommoir* is to anticipate, to reflect, and ironically to recall (successively as the novel evolves) the stages of Gervaise's decline rather than to contribute to it, thereby determining in the principal character and reader alike the appropriate emotional response of expectation or lamentation and further integrating the phases of the narrative. Generally a different group of characters fulfills this function. There is, for example, the destitute old house painter père Bru whose "demi-siècle passé à peindre des portes et à blanchir des plafonds aux quatre coins de Paris" ["half-century spent painting doors and whitewashing floors in the four corners of Paris"] . . . has left him wizened and spent like Flaubert's Catherine Leroux. This character, whose occupation is not unlike Gervaise's, becomes the mirror of her misfortune and anticipates her end in the filthy niche under the stairs where Gervaise is destined to die.

In the other direction Virginie Poisson, having played her part in contributing to Gervaise's downfall, comes to follow the exact course of her rival's ruin. . . . Finally there is the macabre undertaker, . . . whose fatidical role and grotesque gaiety remind one of the blind beggar in *Madame Bovary*. He is the living parody of Gervaise's "ideal," the repository of her despair, and the absolute expression of the anti-values of the novel. The very presence of "ce sacré soûlard" ["this accursed sot"] in his filthy garb, "pantalon noir taché de boue" ["black

Four paperback covers for the novel L'assommoir.

the rhythmic beating of the paddles and to the continual whir of the steam engine, all clouded in the billows of white steam that are pierced by reddish rays of sunlight. Indeed, the whole chapter is like a ritual cleansing. Despite her despair at losing Lantier and certain disquieting signs like the stream of filthy water in the hotel alley that greets her on her return and, more strikingly, the dirty stain from Lantier's hands in the washbasin, Gervaise asserts her prowess as a washerwoman, rids herself of much of the squalor of her surroundings, and gains a ceremonial victory over adversity when she wins the respect of the whole neighborhood in her famous battle with Virginie. In short, she liquidates her past, however temporarily, and dominates the agencies that will eventually bring her down. Chapter i is therefore like the rest of the novel in reverse.

The exposition proper occupies the next two chapters, in which Zola narrates the courtship of Gervaise and Coupeau . . . and dramatizes the celebrations on their wedding day. . . . The main purport of these chapters is clearly to build up the couple morally as industrious, clean, and sober. (pp. 826-27)

But telling signs of imminent misfortune are carefully introduced to countervail the character's illusions, like the sudden storm that threatens to ruin the wedding day. More important, in these pages are introduced the material agents of her ruin, the "assommoirs." Gervaise recoils in fear before the still in père Colombe's establishment and already feels the oppressive presence of the apartment building where she will end her days. In a less explicit manner, there are the bodeful images of filth, like the grimy interior of the Assommoir itself, the reek and squalor of the apartment house, the greasy stains and smells in the restaurant, and especially the "mare de boue écoulante" ["sea of flowing mud"] in the streets that comes with the storm, all foreshadowing a world of putrescent materiality against which Gervaise must measure her principles and her resolve. Even as she accepts Coupeau's marriage proposal, a drunkard ominously weeps outside her window and a violin is heard playing "un quadrille canaille à quelque noce attardée" ["a vulgar quadrille to some belated nuptual"]. . . . Appropriately, to close this section of the novel, the sibylline figure of Bazouge makes his first appearance, lumbering drunkenly into the wedding party and mumbling about death. The exposition, then, presents in neat array the conflicting values and forces in Gervaise's character and environment which, in the following chapters, will provide the dramatic conflict of the novel, for as yet the heroine has maintained a guarded but precarious distance from the forces and temptations that threaten to undermine her values, and her misfortunes are still at the level of forebodings.

Neatly separating the exposition from the beginning of the dramatic action proper are "quatre années de dur travail" ["four years of hard work"], years that include the events recounted in Chapter iv that precede Coupeau's fall (the move to the rue Neuve de la Goutte-d'Or, the birth and baptism of Nana), years of good fortune and prosperity that are measured at the outset on the triple scale of values of the novel. . . . The success of the household is reflected in the company that it keeps, namely the clean, industrious, and virtuous Goujets, but especially in the position that it occupies on the rue Neuve de la Goutte-d'Or "à l'endroit où les constructions . . . laissaient descendre l'air et le soleil" ["in the section where the buildings . . . let in the air and the sun"], halfway between the clean and gay stores at the Paris end of the street and the unwholesome area of the rue de la Goutte-d'Or with its "boutiques sombres, aux carreaux sales" ["gloomy shops with dirty windows"]. . . .

trousers spattered with mud"], "cuir encrassé par la poussière des enterrements" ["leather encrusted with the soil of burials"], is a constant invitation to Gervaise to seek the supreme renunciation of her struggle in the enforced idleness of death.

The plot of *L'Assommoir,* viewed in this way as more than its mere sequence of events, is constituted by a total system of such interrelated features of character, description, and occurrence, which are shown to determine, anticipate, reflect, and ironically recall the stages through which Coupeau and especially Gervaise pass in their vain attempt to impose their fragile resolves on a world that is unbendingly impervious to their attempts. (p. 826)

At the start Gervaise conveniently surveys from her hotel window the theater of action of the novel with the ominous landmarks that Zola frequently mentions, the stinking abattoirs and the Lariboisière hospital, between which Gervaise's destiny will be played out. Conveniently, too, Gervaise recounts her past and present circumstances to the inquisitive Madame Boche. But the particular significance of this chapter is due to the presence of the essential components of the novel. Working is the dominant theme of the chapter. There is a typically Zolaesque description of the troops of laborers and *employés* descending upon Paris to start their day, bathed in a sunlight that is invariably associated with work in this novel. There is also the scene of gay and frenzied activity in the washhouse, set to

But, lured by the prospect of running her own laundry, "une boutique très propre" ["a very clean shop"] on the rue de la Goutte-d'Or, Gervaise makes the fatal error of moving into this area, into the dismal territory of the "assommoirs," and daring thus to take on the dirty linen of the whole neighborhood exposes herself to the debilitating forces that will prompt her decline.

In each of the chapters belonging to the central, dramatic phase of the novel . . . , the chapters of Gervaise's struggle, there is a single critical occurrence that marks a stage in this decline and relegates Coupeau and Gervaise to the negative side of our scheme. In Chapter iv, just as the sun of work symbolically goes down, the roofer has a fall which leaves in him "une sourde rancune contre le travail" ["a silent rancour against work"], "une lente conquête de la paresse, qui profitait de sa convalescence pour entrer dans sa peau et l'engourdir, en le chatouillant" ["a slow conquest by laziness, which took advantage of his convalescence to enter into his skin and numb him"]. In Chapter v, Gervaise makes her first concession to the devitalizing effects of her trade. As if intoxicated by the malodorous linen, asphyxiated by the "vieux linges empoisonnant l'air autour d'elle" ["old linens poisoning the air around her"], she weakly submits to her drunken husband's attentions. . . . When, in the following chapter, Coupeau takes to serious drinking in the Assommoir, another stage is complete. Indeed, Coupeau is now a spent force, no more than a burden to Gervaise in her struggle to uphold her values.

Essentially, in the first half of the novel, Gervaise succeeds in preserving her integrity. There are, it is true, disturbing symptoms of inconstancy: a growing propensity to idleness and neglect, above all the emergence of her darling vice gluttony. When Virginie reappears with news of Lantier (who, signifi cantly, is now living "dans une sale rue ou il y a toujours de la boue jusqu'aux genoux") ["in a dirty street where the mud is always knee-deep"] and reinstates Gervaise's past, a crisis is clearly imminent. . . . (p. 828)

But counteracting her fatal "physiological" attraction to Lantier is the elevating romance with Goujet who now forms with Gervaise's former lover, in view of the virtual eclipse of Coupeau, the real triangle of "affections" on which Gervaise's future will henceforth largely depend. Chapter vi, which precedes the central birthday scene, recounts Goujet's victory, just as the corresponding chapter after the feast . . . will recount his defeat in favor of Lantier. Here Goujet's fire purges Gervaise of her evil appetites as she watches him working at his forge. . . . At his forge, in the spring-long idyll that they enjoy, Goujet's iron and fire temporarily dispel the gradual erosion of Gervaise's being that her perpetual contact with rotten matter and filthy water entail. . . . But this is Gervaise's last reprieve and her last taste of spring, for the following chapter, the pivotal birthday feast, ushers in the winter of her degradation.

The central chapter of *L'Assommoir* has been widely appreciated mainly as a masterpiece of realistic representation, but also for its very centrality in the work. In both respects it has been compared to the famous "comices agricoles" scene in *Madame Bovary*. At the anecdotal level the bacchanalia scene involves not only most of the characters of the novel, including Lantier who here makes his opportune appearance, but also the whole Goutte-d'Or district. Thematically, however, it is above all an orgy of gluttony performed in the very place where Gervaise plies her trade and involves even the sober Goujet in the uninhibited indulgence. It represents therefore a total renunciation of the values of the novel and marks the moment

of transition to the advantage of the negative principles of our scheme. What Gervaise intends as a defiant display of her wealth and achievements to her hostile environment, in a desire to "crush" the Lorilleux and the other gossips, proves to be a fatal error of judgment on her part, a kind of alimentary hubris that seals the character's downfall and binds her to her destiny.

Thus, in strict accordance with the traditional prescription for the "complex" plot, the heroine's hamartia is inseparably related to the "reversal" of the action, to the "peripety," which, in Humphry House's words, can be described as "the boomerang or recoil effect of one's own actions, of being hoist with one's own petard." Or, to use an expression more appropriate to the context, Gervaise "cooks her goose," for Zola leaves no doubt that it is the heroine's indulgence that leads her weakly to admit her former lover to the feast. . . . And, for the first of many times, she vindicates her conduct by reference, not to her moral principles, but to the easy moral relativism and indifference of her milieu: "Mon Dieu! à quoi bon se faire de la bile, lorsque les autres ne s'en font pas, et que les histoires paraissent s'arranger d'elles-mêmes, à la satisfaction générale?" ["Good Heavens! What good would it do to worry, when others never did so, and when things always seemed to work themselves out satisfactorily anyway?"]. . . . Thus the magnificent goose, which is curiously described in terms similar to the very descriptive traits of Gervaise . . . , will prove in reality to be, not a monument to her success, but a kind of sacrificial offering in a cannibalistic orgy of which the heroine herself is the unwitting victim.

After this scene of Gervaise's ritual entry into the imbroglio of her fate there follow three chapters in a narrative and analytical mode (what Zola calls in his notes "récit"), recounting three gradated phases of her decline and equivalent to the three chapters that preceded the "feast." First of all, Gervaise is drawn to Lantier's bed . . . , ironically in the same quest for cleanliness that led her to take on the laundry. . . . Then, in Chapter ix, she comes to accept, even to enjoy, the idleness and filth of her new condition, which is the very travesty of her lost "ideal." . . . Finally she too goes drinking in the Assommoir. . . . In these pages Lantier gains the upper hand, subverting Goujet's influence on Gervaise and engaging her with his enormous appetites on a ruinous prolongation of the feast. . . . (pp. 828-29)

Thus Gervaise becomes firmly entrenched in the anti-values of the work, wallowing in the dirt, idleness, and indulgences that she previously contemned. . . . As before, her whole surroundings take on the character of her moral state, for now the sunlit and busy scenes have given way to descriptions of dark, bleak, rain-drenched, muddy streets. . . . The last chapter in this development (Ch. x) is the clear antithesis of Chapter iv. The Coupeaus' dingy and sunless room is a sad reminder of their bright apartment. . . . By means of a series of retrospective references to the time of her early hopes and ambitions Zola binds his plot, replacing the technique of foreboding of the first half of the novel by a technique of bitter recall. In the final scene where Gervaise is driven by the rain to seek refuge in the Assommoir, the imagery of dirt, darkness, and devouring converges in a macabre and graphic representation of the victim's doom. . . . Gervaise emerges, a finished woman, and staggers drunkenly into the filthy water of the gutter, into the very matter of her downfall. Zola adds a bitter twist: "Elle se crut au lavoir" ["She thought she was in the laundry shop"]. . . . (p. 829)

[The] function of Chapter xi (insofar as it deals with Gervaise) and Chapter xii is to illustrate and reaffirm the terms and extent of Gervaise's degradation rather than to show the development of her decline as do the previous seven chapters. This section of the work (Chs. xi and xii) is therefore exactly equivalent and in an inverse relation to the exposition of the novel (Chs. ii and iii). The latter establishes what have been called the values of the novel and implied (in anticipation) its anti-values; the former establishes the anti-values of the work and implies (in retrospect) its values. Now Gervaise's incapacity for work and the sordidness of her person and of her surroundings are the dominant themes. (p. 830)

The final chapter of *L'Assommoir* in its concision is like an "épilogue retraçant brièvement la fin des Coupeau" ["epilogue briefly retracing the end of the Coupeaus" (Jacques Dubois, *L'Assommoir de Zola*)]. It deals mainly with the husband's end, obviously delayed until now for effect. But in the brief final section that deals exclusively with Gervaise, the chapter is significantly antithetical to the prologue (Ch. i) of the work. There the heroine confidently asserted her separateness from the environment in which she found herself and purified herself of its contamination. Here she is totally integrated into the most sordid features of her surroundings. She is now imbecile, sleeps in the filthy niche that belonged to père Bru and, bereft of any remnants of her pride, has become the stooge of the whole quarter. . . .

The plot of Gervaise's fortunes, therefore, not only follows a rigorous line of development, but, as a study of the main equivalent and graduated episodes and phases shows, comprises a complex pattern of dynamically related elements in a tightly structured framework. It forms as "integrated" an "organism" as any traditional theorist could require of a fictional work and closely adheres to those Aristotelian exigences that Lafcadio Hearn for one found wanting, as we have seen, in French novels of his time: a clearly defined beginning, middle, and end, an ordered succession of events of a proper "magnitude" and "arrangement," even the symmetrically regulated rising and falling action with its pivotal reversal scene that are traditionally required of the "complex" plot. (p. 831)

The particular esthetic effect that *L'Assommoir* achieves can be said to derive from this thorough integration of contingent, contemporaneous realities, portrayed with a vividness characteristic of the naturalist writer's concern for "human documents" and unadulterated facts, into a determinate poetic form, which, as we have seen, approaches the mythos of tragic drama. (p. 832)

> David Baguley, "Events and Structure: The Plot of
> Zola's 'L'assommoir'," in PMLA, 90, Vol. 90, No.
> 5, October, 1975, pp. 823-33.

DIANA FESTA-McCORMICK (essay date 1979)

[*In the following excerpt, McCormick discusses the hardships of Gervaise in* L'assommoir *and their relationship to the city of Paris.*]

L'Assommoir . . . stands as one of Zola's masterpieces and among the important novels of all times. Compact in characterization and development, visual, compelling, it depicts the uneventful life of an uncomplicated being, a washerwoman named Gervaise. What is relevant here is not so much the curve of Gervaise's fortune—mildly ascending before starting on the downslope, to end in a gradual plunge toward dissipation and,

finally, death—but the forces that brought about the collapse of her simple dreams and of her obstinate efforts to hold on to a modicum of dignity. Those forces are all embedded in the city; for, although it was important for Zola to trace the hereditary factors driving Gervaise and her family toward the fatality of alcoholism, those factors are not crucial or distinctly manifest in the development of the story. What is conspicuous is the complexity of exterior forces at work, the dusky streets in which Gervaise comes to live and where the main attraction is the corner bar, the cramped tenement that is her home early in the novel and in which people swarm antlike, her life held in the throes of lingering poverty and in contact with dissolution in a remote section of the indifferent city. Readers are aware that, withdrawn but always present, Paris is the mold here, expanding and contracting, where resides a forgotten humanity of which Gervaise is a simple heroine and a victim.

The story, with the exception of the wedding-party exploration of Paris all the way to Place Vendôme and to the Louvre, takes place mostly in the same section of town and, for the greater part, in the same street and the same building. Yet there is a marked sense of movement and physical displacement, the impression of motion and change. What does change, in effect, is the perspective, which assimilates the characters' inner workings and their spiritual-moral oscillations with the objects around them. Streets and houses are thus seen in turn as images with color and shape, shadows, light, and also as receptacles, the holding grounds of people's lives, swaying with their presence and their fortunes. Each street, the apartment building, the rooms in which Gervaise lives, become themselves living mechanisms with hidden contrivances dictating motion and direction, and working in unison, fusing, with the rhythm and actions of the people they hold. It is in this blending of purpose and resolve, of people and objects, that Paris takes shape and assumes a reality greater than both people and objects while removed from both.

L'Assommoir contains, of course, a variety of personages: Gervaise's lover, Lantier; her husband, Coupeau; her sisters-in-law; acquaintances; and friends. Yet the novel essentially explores only her character, and it is only she who comes alive fully and fully reveals the inner workings of her mind and soul. The others are simply her world, quantities with various degrees of importance in the unfolding of her life and of the events that lead her to her brief triumph and final defeat. But the presentation of a single character does not limit the story either in horizons or in applicability, for each person embodies a whole class of beings, and Gervaise leads the way in conferring upon them depth and understanding. The narrow circle of her acquaintances, noticeable above all for its greed and vindictiveness, for weakness in temptation and ostentatiousness in celebrations, suggests a whole mass of other people from the same class, men and women who spend their days shaping metal and bricks, washing clothes or painting walls, all the unrecorded years of their uneventful lives. What emerges is the picture of a society, a segment of Paris that is not Paris but is shaped by it. It has only peripheral contacts with the rest of the city, yet it is a fundamental and visceral part of its existence.

The novel opens in a cheap hotel facing what is now the corner of Boulevard Barbès and Boulevard Rochechouart, but overlooking at the time the outer gates (Barrière Poissonnière) that led from the poorer sections of La Chapelle and Montmartre to the center of Paris. Gervaise, shivering, has been waiting through the night for the return of her lover, Lantier. The room is barren, the window opens onto a cold street, spectral at night and gradually coming alive with the bustling of workpeople going to their appointed tasks.

> She looked to the right towards the Boulevard de Rochechouart, where butchers in blood-stained aprons were standing about in groups in front of the slaughterhouses, and now and again the fresh breeze wafted an acrid stench of slaughtered animals. To the left her eyes ran along a stretch of avenue and stopped almost opposite at the white mass of the Lariboisière hospital, then being built. She let her gaze travel slowly along the octroi wall from one horizon to the other; behind that wall she sometimes heard in the night the scream of men being done to death. And now she stared into secluded angles and dark corners, black with damp and refuse, terrified of discovering Lantier's body lying there dead with its belly stabbed through and through. When she looked up and beyond the unending grey wall which girdled the city like a belt of desolation, she saw a great light, the golden dust of sunrise filled already with the morning roar of Paris.

Weaving in and out of Gervaise's apprehensions and anguished wait, Paris is introduced, drenched in the smell of blood, with cries suspended in the air, and dark recesses where fear and death stand watch. The lurid wall by the city is a barrier against sunshine and hope; there is only the "acrid stench of slaughtered animals" there, and "the scream of men being done to death." The suggestive quality of this often-quoted passage fuses the reality of both man and animal through sensory perception—those of hearing and of smelling, to be sure, but also that of seeing. It is Gervaise's eyes—and the reader's—that behold the vast boulevards, the butchers' splattered aprons, the forbidding wall, and the luminous rays behind it. The inner reality of dread finds a monster at every step; it is in turn echoed and nourished through the bitter smells in the air and the gloomy images all around. Objectivity does not mean removal from emotions here, nor does it mean the presentation of scientific reality divorced from man's passions and his thoughts. It is rather the blending of the two, and from this blending man and beast are joined in the powerful presence of poverty in a distant corner of the city.

With Paris, this first chapter introduces one day in the life of Gervaise. It is a day that begins when dusk has long receded into night and morning is still engulfed in darkness, a day arisen in tears and ending in dismay, bringing a renewed sense of loneliness in the face of betrayal, but also a certain determination and the shadow, at least, of a passing victory. Its importance is real and symbolic at the same time, for it brings change without suggesting renewal, and the act of chastising a rival is devoid both of triumph and of joy. The reader notices also that it is in this chapter, when the city is not yet in control of Gervaise's life, that occurs the scene at the washing house; the cleansing water—and the beating of Virginie's bare bottom, fiercer even than that administered to the soiled clothes—have a quality of redress, the enjoyment of order and propriety, in a place that tramples virtue and rewards expediency. Gradually, as the story advances and Gervaise settles more and more in the slums of Paris, cleanliness will give way to slovenliness, rectitude to impurity and profligacy. Hell lies in wait outside along the sidewalks, biding time but assured of victory....

The "blazing heat" of the street has a smoldering quality, through which energy and courage will gradually diminish, along with the will to survive; the city-hell watches, symbolically, "between a slaughterhouse and a hospital," exuding the smell of illness and death, while Gervaise fearfully leans by the window in unconscious contemplation of her last days of innocence.

What follows is predictable. After a respite and a brief period of contentment, the downward movement begins unremittingly, and Gervaise's short-lived peace is shattered. Financial difficulties become the visible reason for the relaxing of moral fiber, but the causes for the eventual downfall are complex and lie much deeper than in the mere arithmetic of money. Gervaise is on her ascending curve when the reader first meets her; she is endowed with courage and the determination to be a responsible mother to her children; when Lantier abandons her with the two young sons to her charge in the miserable room of the Hotel Boncoeur, she is of course dismayed. Yet she soon pulls herself together and brings order to her life; she remains, for a time, pleasant, serene, hard-working, and painfully aware of the dangers of giving in to the temptations the city offers and of losing control over her life. Coupeau convinces her that he is just as well-intentioned, and she accepts him as a husband. The hard-working couple that embarks on a fruitful and peaceful bourgeois existence, which only serves, however, to lull them into false security, a kind of sleep where dangers are ill-defined and seem remote. After four years during which dreams almost become reality, Coupeau suddenly falls and breaks his leg; the forced idleness gradually veers him toward Papa Colombe's corner bar and a distaste for work. Here is the tragedy in a nutshell; but Coupeau's accident and the disappearance of their savings are only catalysts in the ruin that ensues, one that had already been present in the first images that the city had offered.

The fact that the heroine of the story is not a Parisian is surely by design. Had Gervaise been brought up in the city slums and been accustomed to the tenacious fever for gain all around, and the games of spite and dominance, presumably she might have been a less likable person but one endowed with greater resistance against the stifling atmosphere and against the temptation of compassion for those who are less privileged. Her models would have been all the Lorilleux and the Boche who inhabit the crowded sections of town, those who have vile smiles in times of abundance but who refuse to open their doors to their old mothers in need; she might have been less tempted to keep her husband home when he broke his leg, and she would not have administered him such loving care as to sacrifice, with hardly a word of complaint, her hard-earned money. Coupeau would have gone to the hospital to try to get well, and he might even have benefited from this and remained, perhaps, unspoiled. But Gervaise is from Plassans, in the South of France, where life is less harried and inimical, where "it smelt better than it does here" . . . and where even greedy Lantier "used to be quite all right" to her. . . . Her life had been fully exposed to her share of suffering in the hands of a drunken father and a brutalized mother, but not to the dehumanizing effects of a mechanized world that leaves no room for sentiment. (pp. 36-40)

Central to the story stands the large tenement building in Rue de la Goutte d'Or; this building is not merely the physical but also the moral "theater" of the story. It stands by itself for all the sins of the city and for the city itself, for the visible ills of crowd and for dirt, with the rivulets of water and puddles in the courtyard, and the viscous stairways saturated with rancid odors. The hidden ills are only revealed when, after fermenting in the infectious atmosphere, they erupt in plagues, when proximity becomes promiscuity and unemployment drowns it sorrows in alcohol and indifference. The tenement building is, finally, the symbol of all those forces in city slums which conspire to assuage desire and kill the will.

It is important to notice that Gervaise's brief and relative affluence, and her contentment as mother and wife in the city of Paris, coincide with her residence in a quiet, small, and countrylike house in Rue Neuve de la Goutte d'Or. . . . It is here, away from the absorbing noises of crowded city quarters, that all the joys of a simple bourgeois existence unfold like flowers, the repeated marvel each morning of transforming the bedroom into a diningroom, the fluffy white curtains at the window and the religiously dusted furniture; here live the memories of Plassans, not those relating to a drunken father, but the days in the sun, by the river, and in the peace of country life. Work is nearby, and while ironing she can keep an eye on her house, with the uninterrupted sense of possession and naive pride that breed loyalty and continuity. It is in this small house that Gervaise meets the only friends she will ever have in Paris—the Goujets across the hall, the only other tenants on her floor and the only people that offer her the example of an orderly life in which sentiment and duty are not separable. Had Zola really wanted to emphasize the dynastic foibles in Gervaise, he might at least have exposed her to some destructive temptation while she lived still in the Rue Neuve; she is, instead, gracefully assimilated in the serenity of the atmosphere there, reinforcing with her presence the advantages of an intimacy that respects privacy, and of discretion that nurtures amity.

It is true that Coupeau's accident happens while they are still living in the small house next to the Goujets and that the young husband is already forgetting old aims and purposes; it is also true that residence in the big building is taken up with the inauspicious beginnings of debts and illness. Yet it cannot be seen as sheer coincidence that while in the Rue Neuve Gervaise's dream remains unchanged, even if now it appears as "an unclean thought" . . . , in defiance of the stark reality and as an indirect reproach to her husband's helplessness. She still wants a shop of her own, where she could exercise freedom of movement through a certain independence of means. Goujet advances her the money and she accepts, confident in her own reliability.

Where small size with a sense of space had dominated in the Rue Neuve apartment, the building where Gervaise now moves with her family offers the reverse image. Truer to the spirit of the city, its large size conveys a sense of restriction, and the multitude of people within increases the feeling of loneliness. . . . The building that arrogantly dominates the neighborhood contains no echo of Plassans, and the puddles of dyewater at the entrance suggest no vision of river banks. It is in itself all of a small city with a mechanism of its own dictating functions and directions for the people inside; it stands as a miniature and deformed vision of the city itself, contemplated through an imaginary and magnifying lens that broadens all ills while conferring the illusion of triumph to minute victories. Here, in this microcosmic Parisian world, Gervaise is condemned to perish.

It is then in Rue de la Goutte d'Or that appear the first signs of change in Gervaise, in the tenement building that symbolizes size, squalor, and all the other ills of the city. She is the proud owner of a laundry, well liked by all, and, at twenty-eight, still beautiful. But she is beginning to "put on a bit of flesh." Complacency replaces scrupulous behavior, and a kind of relaxed contentment abates the solicitude of older days.

> Her fine features were taking on a certain chubbiness and her movements the slowness of contentment. Nowadays she would sometimes dawdle on the edge of a chair while waiting for an iron to heat, with a vague smile on her round, jolly face, for she was getting fond of food, everyone agreed; but it wasn't a bad fault, quite the reverse. When you can earn enough to treat yourself to little luxuries you would be silly to live on potato-peelings, wouldn't you?
> . . .

Her hypothetical musing here is presented in the form of general considerations, as if they really applied to most people and were universally held truths; yet these are merely her own rationalization and self-indulging thoughts meant to soothe an uneasy conscience and put guilt to rest. The future no longer exists when Gervaise begins to betray her past.

Gervaise's first signs of deterioration within the gray walls of the tenement building take the form of gluttony and a quiet indulgence for candies and cakes. As the placid owner lulls herself in a false sense of ease, the laundry shop, symbol until now of cleanliness and order, begins gradually to exhale a bad odor. ("In the heat all this dirty linen being raked over gave off a sickening stench" . . .). Rather than a harsh rubbing of dirt from the clothes, so that these may regain their original whiteness, there is lazy chatter in the shop, with the girls giggling in the heat of long-drawn afternoons instead of applying themselves seriously to their tasks. There are salacious remarks and obscene gestures made, which are meekly condoned by Gervaise.

> She begged Clémence to get a move on, but the girl went on with her remarks, stuck her fingers into the holes, with allusions about the articles which she waved about like the flags of Filth Triumphant. And still the heaps went on piling up round Gervaise until, perched on the edge of her stool, she almost vanished from sight between the skirts and the petticoats. . . .

Gervaise's "begging" of Clémence not only lacks the voice of authority but that of conviction, for she is herself submerged in the "Filth Triumphant" waved around her. Her laundry shop, which had been intended to be a heaven within the hellish city, no longer gives her asylum. Far from representing a private struggle against dirt and from upholding purity, the laundry is itself gradually drawn into the corrupting dynamism of the city, until it is so pervaded by it that it becomes indistinguishable from the most depraved elements around it. Like the building in which it is located and the streets that it seems to dominate with its height, it loses both identity and vigor, as it is absorbed in the "Filth Triumphant" of Parisian life. Its door is merely a transparent barrier that, far from keeping the city odors away, shuts in the rancid smells that have intruded within and permeated the air. Mesmerized by this filth, Gervaise begins slowly to sink, and, "feeling a bit giddy with the mountain of washing" . . . , she abandons herself to the smell of decay and the fascination, eventually, of her own failure. The symbolic value of her trade will then have followed faithfully the graph of her physical and spiritual health: stable and mounting at the outset, as Gervaise administers energetic slaps to remove dirt from clothes; wavering, when work is sloppy and the laundress undemanding; and degenerating at the end, as the shop is liquidated, with the decline of its owner's fortune and the disintegration of her life.

A very important aspect in this novel, and the one that lends it particular interest within the large frame of reference of Zola's work, is the inadvertent suspension—or so it seems—of hereditary factors in the shaping of Gervaise's destiny, and the encroachment instead of the city's diabolical forces. The poor woman's "immorality," or at least her lack of adherence to her own principles, is merely a surrender to something larger than she had been able to envisage; if it is true that she is partially aware of her betrayal of both frugality and probity, it is also true that her very gentleness and generosity have deprived her of the necessary strength to uphold old virtues in the face of the city's evils. The fatality would then seem to reside outside of her, and not within, even if she does acknowledge her share of responsibility. "Yes, it was their own fault if things went from bad to worse each season," she recognizes; "But you never admit things like that to yourself, especially when you are in the soup. They put it down to misfortune, God had something against them." . . . Yet "misfortune" it is—the corroding elements of the tenement building in which the Coupeaus have come to live and the vindictive city that allows for no redemption and wields the worst punishment against those who are trusting and defenseless. Gervaise has come to know this by now, but she can only watch helplessly, unable to arrest the ravages against all that she had ever cherished.

Not everybody perishes in Zola's Paris; the Lorilleux, the Boches, all those who can compensate and accommodate, bend and sway with situations, do "make it." And there are also the Goujets, whose candor and single-mindedness preserve them from evil. Gervaise and Coupeau, on the other hand, lack the stamina to oppose their will to that of the city. For Coupeau, whose interest to the reader is limited to the impact he has on his wife's life, one cannot properly speak of tragedy; his is merely the failure to rise above the contaminating elements in which he was bred, of casually falling in Bibi-la-Grillade's footsteps. Coupeau, bred from infancy in seedy Parisian sections, betrays nothing and hardly anybody; had his wife been able to continue facing the city undaunted, in fact, had she not so meekly abandoned her original distrust of alcohol, he might even have been spared, perhaps, from passively following his friends to the corner bar. But Gervaise's defeat is a tragedy comparable, in its very modest way, to a new Theseus bravely entering a labyrinth but being slaughtered by an invisible Minotaur—a Theseus without magic—human, weak, and perishable.

One might argue here that Gervaise, conscious at least to a degree of the forces she set out to fight at the beginning, should have measured her own strength accordingly instead of relaxing in false security. But this would be to ignore the malevolent will of the city, the monster Zola has created that preys upon innocence and generosity; for Paris is, in *L'Assommoir,* the sum total of collective ills, each in itself negligible perhaps—the poverty, the crowded quarters, the lack of roots, or the dominant dirt and prevailing disorder—but Cyclopean when viewed together and overwhelming for the defenseless individual. There is little resemblance between the Paris in Zola's *Love Story,* with its feline appearance and the seductiveness of a siren ensnaring the passerby, and the decaying forces at work

in Gervaise's world, other perhaps than in both cases (as in *Nana* or *Savage Paris—Le Ventre de Paris* in its original title) the means of corruption are invidious and surreptitious. By showing itself for what it is from the beginning, lying in wait "between the hospital and the slaughter-house," Paris hides the strength of her weapons in the very act of revealing them; she thus dictates the false measures through which Gervaise will inevitably perish—for the poverty that, alone, had been feared is a mere manifestation of the city's pervasive ills. (pp. 41-6)

In this carefully built novel where Gervaise is the principal character but Paris the dominant force, the movement is concentric and, to a considerable extent, symbolic. The story is introduced from an outer layer of Parisian life, with Gervaise in the Hotel Boncoeur at one of the peripheral boulevards, a stranger, unaccustomed to the vagaries and the impersonality of the city. She then moves first into a little un-Parisian house, in what turns out to be a temporizing measure, a protracted lull necessary before the eventual immersion into a more typical city tenement. The four years in the Rue Neuve appear on the one hand as the realization of a promise, the just reward for serious endeavor; but on the other, they represent the surreptitious movement deeper into the hellish circles of the city, a stealthy, satanic brew intended to dull the senses and to weaken resistance. The move to the Goutte d'Or is thus anticipated in passive acceptance through tantalizing promises of well-being and ownership; Gervaise is, at this point, already defeated without suspecting it. Pushed by the demon of "her shop," she borrows money that she will never be able to return, and she plunges in this manner, at an early stage of the story, into the mesmerizing city dealings she had sought to avoid. Unsuspectingly, she has surrendered to the threatening forces of disorder and decay that had appeared menacing at the very beginning—one endless night of wait at the Hotel Boncoeur. (pp. 47-8)

What prevails in [Zola's] novel is a parade of "truths," visible, discernible to the naked eye, as scene after scene unfolds in tides of life in motion, irrepressible and uncontrollable. But life itself has a shape here, a dimension, a color, and depth, and, as the story progresses, what emerges beyond the crowd, the buildings, the streets, beyond Gervaise, Coupeau, and Lantier, is the mold that contains them all, the "body" of which people are merely a digestive apparatus, the city of Paris. (p. 48)

Diana Festa-McCormick, "Zola's 'L'assommoir': Paris's Stranglehold on the Lives of the Poor," in her The City as Catalyst: A Study of Ten Novels, *Fairleigh Dickinson University Press, 1979, pp. 33-48.*

PHILLIP A. DUNCAN　(essay date 1980)

[*In the following excerpt, Duncan posits that in* L'assommoir, *the presentation of the differing environments, cultural traits, and geneologies of Goujet and the Lorilleaux family introduces a mythic aspect into the novel.*]

In Emile Zola's equation of human destiny, one force is equal to genetic predestination: the effect of the physical and cultural milieu. In his vast novel of the urban working classes, *L'Assommoir,* this influence is expressed first of all in terms of the aggression of the material environment or its repulse. Good and Evil, Salvation and Damnation contend along with the axes of expanding and contracting living space.

At the beginning of *L'Assommoir,* Zola crowds Gervaise Macquart, her lover, Lantier, and their two sons into a small room at the Hôtel Boncœur. He catalogues each item in the room including an additional bed for the children that fills two-thirds of the interior. Gervaise senses that Lantier is about to abandon her, and the objects about her appear to fill the void of his anticipated absence. They are excrescences of a worker's ghetto that extends appropriately from the Lariboisière Hospital to a slaughterhouse.

The environment of *L'Assommoir* in its every expression is, by Zola's definition, malevolent; but its threat can be deflected, its deadly embrace eluded. With strength of will and untiring labor, Gervaise can and does create living space. She prospers, opens her own laundry, and from it her joy and her influence spill out to purge the implicit malignancy from the neighborhood. Early in the novel, water is her instrument as she purifies her dependency. But in her workroom the stove, reminiscent of the blacksmith's forge, where the irons for pressing the linen heat, becomes the focus of the work place. With this Promethean gesture of the capture of fire, Zola symbolizes her hubris. She has dared to pass from her assigned condition as worker to that of proprietor. Her happiness is great; her pride excessive. The gods punish the transgressor who has overstepped her natural boundary. Her happiness and pride lead to complacency, self-indulgence, and sloth, which erode the disciplined existence that had insured her success. Her weakened resistance to the assault of the social and economic environment is manifested once again in the encroachment of matter. After losing the laundry, she and Coupeau are obliged to move to meaner quarters—a single room "large comme la main" ["wide as a hand"]. Their daughter's bed, like that of her sons earlier at the Hôtel Boncœur, will barely fit the space. Not only are her quarters cluttered with material things, but the substance of the surrounding architectural mass seems to infiltrate her own body. She has become a glutton, and as the narrative progresses, she becomes almost monstrously fat. She dies, finally, squeezed into a kind of closet or upright coffin, under the stairs. The malevolence brooding over the city's poor is metasthesized in the somber, heavy forms and the stifling spaces that converge and ultimately crush out her life.

While the hospital and the slaughterhouse, parallel emblems, delimit the visual landscape, two symbolic antagonists define the cultural topography. Goujet, the idealized blacksmith, gentle and diligent, offers the heroine a positive example, while the Lorilleux, her sinister in-laws, are a pernicious influence. Although animating conflicting values, the Lorilleux couple and Goujet are linked on the same allegorical plane by duplicate features of their situations. The work place of both, for example, must be reached by a difficult, even frightening journey through a maze-like landscape that objectifies once again the antagonism of the milieu. To reach the Lorilleux, Gervaise must pass through the unnaturally massive and forbidding apartment building—an enormous block "se pourrissant et s'émiettant sous la pluie" ["decaying and crumbling under the rain"]. . . . When she looks up the stairwell on her first visit, a lamp in the upper reaches appears to be a distant star in a black sky and the steps of the spiral stair "interminable" and "strangely" illuminated. She mounts along an endlessly curving wall past a microcosm of the city's misery: corridors of identical dormitory doors open on scenes of pieceworkers at ceaseless labor, family quarrels, and drudging domestic activities. She enters a corridor, dilapidated and barely lit, that winds, divides, and narrows. Even when Coupeau announces that they have arrived, the gauntlet has not yet been run. Fi-

nally, as Coupeau opens the door, there is a sudden flash of light, a dazzling instant of entrance to another dimension. . . .

Within, two spiteful gnomes husband a wealth of gold and grub out a mediocre existence in a tunnel-like apartment almost lost under the rafters of the vast structure. This attic corner of the "enfer des pauvres" ["hell of paupers"] Zola appropriately represents as a shadowy den of the Underworld where chthonian creatures "spin" fine gold wire from their treasure into chains for jewelers and spin webs of calumny from their store of pettiness and jealousy. The chromatic tonality of this devil's aerie reflects its evil. Black is pervasive—the color of filth everywhere visible, the color of life exiled from the sun, the color of even the unburnished gold. The only relief is that center of false light: the small forge used to heat the metal that pulsates an angry red dying in a gangrenous glow. (pp. 52-4)

What makes Gervaise especially anxious on her first visit, says Zola, is "la petitesse de l'atelier [et] . . . toute la saleté noire . . ." ["the shabbiness of the workshop (and) . . . all the black filth"]. . . . The lodgers are equal to the place, with their small, dirty souls that surface in Lorilleux's "minces lèvres méchantes" ["thin, menacing lips"]. . . . And the suffocating heat warns the reader that Gervaise has entered a satanic space.

Gervaise's first sortie to Goujet's foundry is a similar adventure. She loses her way before she is very far along the Rue Marcadet. The sooty street is lined with graying sheds and workshops that seem unfinished and skeletal—a jumble of queer and senile structures. She is assailed by violent factory sounds—bursts of steam through thin pipes, a power saw that makes a noise like the tearing of cloth, a button factory that shakes the ground with the rumble and tic-tac of its machines. The Rue Marcadet has become another dark and menacing gauntlet, an industrial labyrinth. After a sudden suffocating gust of wind, Gervaise opens her eyes to find that she is miraculously before Goujet's foundry. She hesitates but finally discovers an awkward passage through the yard of a demolition company and then is lost in a strange forest of old overturned carts with their shafts upright and ruined sheds whose denuded frames still stand. She enters the foundry guided by a red glow and approaches the work area. The dormant forge, like the pale gleam of a star, exaggerates distance in the dark building. She calls for Goujet. Suddenly a brilliant light fills the chamber as the bellows brings the flame to life—the dazzling instant of another entrance to a latent dimension. . . .

Darkness is easily routed from Goujet's hanger. Here light creates protective space in contrast with the pinched interior of the chain makers. (pp. 54-5)

Both Goujet and the Lorilleux work with fire to shape metal, but certain details of their respective crafts clarify their opposing roles. Goujet's work is paced by an aggressive, rhythmic pulse as the strokes of his hammer model the rivets. A powerful will and ceaseless, regular effort are the secret of his victory over the stubborn metal and by extension over a hostile environment. There is no comparable tempo in the Lorilleux *atelier* where predators gnaw at the diameter of the wire and twist the remaining filament around a shaft to be cut—sinuous movements and grating sounds in a torture chamber beyond time.

Goujet, the superhuman worker, is Zola's enhancement of the order that Gervaise has already brought into her own enterprise and that guaranteed her temporary success. When she began to save for the laundry that she coveted, she bought a clock under which she kept her savings passbook. The clock's periodic ticking and chiming encodes the even, constructive pace of her life, just as the repeated sound of metal on metal transposes that of Goujet. Gervaise's eventual sale of the clock signals a final disorder in her tragic decline.

The universe of *L'Assommoir* and the destiny of Gervaise are governed by the contest of Manichean forces. The colossus, Goujet, is a benevolent deity who, says Zola, "faisait de la clarté autour de lui, il devenait beau, tout-puissant, comme un bon Dieu" ["created light all around him, became beautiful, omnipotent, like a benevolent God"].... He is like Zeus of the golden rain. His "mistress," Gervaise, receives the golden sparks from his hammer and, on another occasion, the golden dandelions that he tosses into her basket. Goujet is more epic than divine, however. Zola refers to him as Herculean, and like the Greek hero whose labors reflect the seasons and temporal order, Goujet's hammer regulates his world.... Hercules' exploits revealed strength and cunning, and he exemplified man's role as worker fused with the role of the sun as source of life and as temporal regulator. The immolation of the hero who is wrapped in a cloak of fire and then physically extinguished on a funeral pyre can be read as the death of the sun at the close of the day's work.

The hero's martyrdom and his defeat of unnatural monsters signifying death have suggested the Hercules myth as an antecedent to the example of Christ. Goujet, too, will suffer immolation. The day of the smith, the artisan of the foundry, is coming to an end. He guides Gervaise, on her first visit, into a wing of the building where the mass production of rivets by machines has already begun. The noise is deafening. Gervaise senses rather than hears above her head a great rubbing of wings.... Goujet-Hercules confronts a power like the black harpies of the Stymphalean marshes, but he is helpless and faces defeat: "Il regarda celle-là trois bonnes minutes sans rien dire; ses sourcils se fronçaient, sa belle barbe jaune avait un hérissement de menace. Puis, un air de douceur et de résignation amollit peu à peu ses traits" ["He looked at it for a good three minutes without saying anything; his brows were knit, his beautiful yellow beard bristled menacingly. Then, an air of docility and resignation softened his features little by little"].... Soon the machine will displace the craftsman. Already the smoke is "peuplée d'êtres vagues, des hommes noirs affairés, des machines agitant leurs bras, qu'elle [Gervaise] ne distinguait pas les uns des autres" ["peopled with vague beings, busy, black men, machines moving their arms, that she (Gervaise) could not distinguish one from another"].... Human robots move among bestial machines such as the power chisels "croquant un bout [des barres de fer] à chaque coup de dents, crachant les bouts par derrière, un à un ..." ["crunching one end (of iron bars) with each bite, spitting the ends out behind, one by one"].... (pp. 55-6)

Among the rivet-making machines, Gervaise feels threatened by the spiderweb of belts; elsewhere she perceives the Lorilleux as "araignées maigres" ["scrawny spiders"]. Man and machine are indistinguishable in the factory; in the lair of the Lorilleux, Gervaise watches the husband working "continuellement, mécaniquement" ["continually, mechanically"].... Later, she sees the pair as possessing the mindless insensitivity of old tools in their simple, machine-like labor.... The Lorilleux are subterranean creatures who seem the mythic progenitors of the new race of blackened, dehumanized workers, of an antihuman spirit that Goujet-Hercules cannot overcome.

In addition to their labor function, both Goujet and the Lorilleux couple have a social and moral function with a mythic dimension. The smith exemplifies the Christian ethic. In the narrative he is the ideal by which all others are measured. The Lorilleux are, by contrast, evil. They represent that "mauvaise société" Gervaise had always feared and whose influence, she says, is as deadly as a blow from a club.... The Lorilleux resent the marriage of Coupeau to Gervaise and envy the success of her laundry. They attempt to undermine her position.... They provoke Coupeau's resentment of her two sons fathered by Lantier.... Later, Mme Lorilleux claims that Gervaise earned the money for her business from Goujet, that she had surprised them one evening on a bench on the outer boulevards.... Then when Gervaise begins again her adulterous affair with Lantier, the Lorilleux "vomirent d'abord mille horreurs" ["at first disgorged a thousand curses"] ... against her. In time, feigning concern for her brother, Coupeau, Mme Lorilleux incites indignation among the neighbors over the adultery of his wife, and finally, in the words of Zola, "le quartier tomba sur Gervaise" ["the whole neighborhood fell upon Gervaise"].... Victim of her own weakness and the ill-will of the neighbors, Gervaise is obliged to consider abandoning the laundry. It is the Lorilleux who, with skillful insinuation, encourage her to surrender her lease. These "scrawny spiders" are malicious, envious, and artful in demeaning their enemies. Among Gervaise's neighbors they are the arbiters of her destiny. At one point we find Gervaise replying to them in monosyllables "comme devant des juges" ["as if before judges"].... (pp. 56-7)

It can be no accident that Zola has given the Lorilleux the work of drawing wire so like the task of spinning, then measuring and severing the skein. They are the Parcae of the city's lower depths. They gauge the course of the heroine's travail and mark her fated time. In the end, Gervaise, virtually abandoned by Coupeau and starving, makes a final, desperate entrance into the ominous passage that seemed to be "bâti pour une anguille" ["constructed for an eel"] ... to beg the Lorilleux for food. With complacent scorn they cut the strand and send Gervaise into the streets to consummate her tragic destiny. Famished, she is soliciting passers-by when she meets Goujet. Goujet sees that she is losing the will to survive. He feeds her, consoles her, forgives her in a Christ-like gesture, but must despairingly release her to her fate.

Gervaise's expeditions into the supra-natural worlds of Goujet and the Lorilleux introduce a mythic dimension into the realistic statement of the Naturalist novel. The way to Goujet leads to possible salvation; the way to the Lorilleux leads into the mesh of a predatory environment and the grave. To escape the hellish and corrosive fire of the Lorilleux, Gervaise must receive the solar fire of Goujet. But she rejects union with the solar Hercules-Christ and pursues independently a happiness and self-fulfillment unsanctioned by the gods. The punishment for her ambition is degradation and death immured between the hospital and the slaughterhouse. After the final, painful shuttle from one charnel house to the other through the lowering streets in search of food, Gervaise is drawn through the dark maw of the giant apartment building and into the hands of the last of the three Fates, neighbor of the Lorilleux—Bazouge, the undertaker. (p. 57)

Phillip A. Duncan, "Symbols of the Benign and the Malevolent in Zola's 'L'assommoir'," in The French Review, *Vol. LIV, No. 1, October, 1980, pp. 52-7.*

SUSANNA BARROWS (essay date 1981)

[*In the following excerpt, Barrows discusses Zola's ideas about alcoholism implied in* L'assommoir *and his depiction of crowds in* Germinal.]

In 1877 [Zola] published the devastating portrait of Parisian working-class culture, *l'Assommoir.* The novel brought notoriety to the problem of drink and to Zola. In less than a year, thirty-eight printings of *l'Assommoir* had been issued, and by 1882 over 100,000 copies had been sold.

Alcohol blackens the existence of nearly all the characters in Zola's novel. Liquor propels Coupeau into insanity, the asylum of Sainte-Anne, and a graphically described dance of death. His neighbor, the perpetually inebriated Bijard, murders his own daughter. Under the spell of alcohol, the heroine Gervaise abandons her livelihood, sinks to prostitution, and ultimately dies like a dog on a bed of straw. Moreover, she and her children carry the inherited stigmata of alcoholism. Because Gervaise was conceived in a drunken, violent sexual encounter, she is born with a humiliating limp, and although she scarcely drinks during her childbearing years, her children inherit other alcoholic defects. Her daughter Nana becomes a notorious, insatiable prostitute, and her son Etienne—the strike leader of *Germinal*—is transformed into a homicidal monster under the influence of liquor. In later novels of the Rougon-Macquart series, Zola depicts the two other sons of Gervaise as a psychopath and a talented but emotionally unstable artist.

From reading *l'Assommoir,* thousands of Frenchmen discovered the fatal legacy of drink. In translating contemporary scientific theory into fictional form, Zola had constructed a labyrinth of alcoholism and poverty from which few could ever escape. His gloomy portrayal owed much to science, yet he, far more than his scientific contemporaries, viewed alcoholics compassionately. Unlike most French scientists, Zola stressed the crucial factor of the environment that shaped the quality and destiny of working-class existence.

In the closing chapters of *l'Assommoir,* Zola provided a key to the difference between his own view of alcoholism and that of most French doctors. Once she discovers that Coupeau has been admitted to Sainte-Anne, Gervaise travels twice to see her dying husband. As she approaches his cell for the first time, she is terrified by Coupeau's savage screams. Observing her husband is a young, "pink" physician, tapping his fingers while he takes notes. As Gervaise draws near, he admonishes her to be silent, as her husband is an "interesting case." Overwhelmed by the sight of Coupeau, Gervaise leaves. The following day, she returns to the hospital where she finds Coupeau being scrutinized by two physicians—the pink man and an "elderly doctor wearing a ribbon of the Legionn of Honor." When the decorated doctor finally addresses Gervaise, he inquires only about Coupeau's parents; "Did this man's father drink?" "Did the mother drink?" "And you drink too?" As Gervaise stammers, he cuts her off with a sharp prediction: "One of these days you'll die in the same way!"

The doctor was right, but for the wrong reasons. So convinced were French physicians of alcohol's hereditary effects that they for the most part ignored the debilitating role of squalor, miserable housing, and sheer penury as causal factors of working-class alcoholism. In their enthusiasm to blame distilled liquor for all of France's social problems, they cast alcohol as the invariable cause rather than the result of poverty.

Although Zola had subtly intertwined the strands of alcoholism and environment, very often his readers saw alcohol as the sole villain. From *l'Assommoir* and from medical treatises, literate Frenchmen formulated an image of alcoholism unparalleled in its ferocity. On the basis of current research, they concluded that alcohol drove human beings to savagery, murder, insanity, and ultimately to the pollution of the race.

Seldom has any disease been invested with an emotional resonance as terrifying and well publicized as was alcoholism in late nineteenth-century France. Alcoholism was not merely an illness; it emerged as the nexus of France's social ills. Crowd psychologists soon exploited the associations to violence, insanity, and hereditary disability that reference to alcoholism entailed. The crowd . . . was a ferocious and unpredictable being comparable to the wildest of French drunkards. Such a metaphor, which appears unwarranted to twentieth-century readers, embodied for fin de siècle France a lengthy catalogue of national pathology, both social and psychological. It suggested, too, that crowds, like alcoholics, could be studied by science, but not cured.

Much like the decorated doctor in *l'Assommoir,* French crowd psychologists had isolated the pathology of the crowd and described its many symptoms and complications. Yet they, like him, were powerless to stem the course of the disease. The crowd, like the drunkard and the emancipated woman, would destroy France. By equating crowds with these "irrational" and "threatening" groups—all supposed agents of decadence, insanity, and race suicide—[Hippolyte] Taine and his contemporaries summarized the fears of a generation in a single stark phrase. (pp. 69-72)

After the publication of *l'Assommoir* in 1878, Zola could command the entire literate public of France as his audience, and he was revered as an authority on the poor. Only Victor Hugo outstripped Zola for the title of France's Prince of Letters. Both men were endowed with powerful imaginations, strong wills, and prolific pens. Like Hugo, Zola demonstrated that he was a sturdy, even vociferous republican, whose social criticism was both artful and acerbic. (pp. 95-6)

In January 1885 *Germinal* was published, and Zola's devotees rushed to purchase the thirteenth novel in the Rougon-Macquart series. Within the six hundred pages of the novel, they found much that was familiar; the Lantier family, the interlocking determinants of heredity and the environment, frank exposition, and skilled narration. Yet in spite of all the elements so characteristic of Zola's earlier works, a number of critics viewed *Germinal* as a new departure. In *Germinal,* Zola had shifted his attention from the individual to the crowd, and the result was a tale of singular violence.

The central drama of *Germinal* revolves around mass activity, a strike of miners in the prefecture of Lille. The leader of the strike belongs to the Rougon-Macquart family tree; he is Etienne Lantier, Gervaise's son, who slips into Montsou in search of work. Shortly after he joins the miners, a strike erupts in the village, and Etienne becomes its leader. (pp. 97-8)

Etienne is undoubtedly the hero of *Germinal,* yet even he is overshadowed by the crowd. It is the mass of workers which informs most of the dramatic moments of the novel, the public meetings which presage its violent climax, the mobs which destroy and are destroyed. Even the peaceful aspects of working-class existence focus largely on the group—the swarming descent into the mines, the cortege following injured workers, the public stroll, the congested and raucous dance of leisure.

In *Germinal,* Zola carefully documented the crowd in all its guises, but he placed the most striking emphasis upon the politically agitated and potentially violent mob.

Four of the most compelling scenes in the novel are centered upon the crowd of miners on strike. Two of these are political assemblies: the meeting led by the organizer Pluchart to encourage the men to join the International and the subsequent mass meeting of 3,000 workers in the Plan-des-Dames. Two other haunting scenes describe the crowd in action: the violent day of rioting and pillage in the mines, beginning with the destruction of the Jean-Bart mine and ending with the castration of Maigrat; and the massacre of fourteen workers by the occupying troops. In these four scenes, Zola had encapsulated his vision of crowd behavior into a portrait remarkably similar to that of his old mentor Taine.

Although Zola deplored Taine's emphasis [in *Les Origines de la France contemporaine*] upon the atrocities committed by crowds, he most dramatically stressed the violence unleashed by men and women in groups. As early in the novel as the meeting at the Plan-des-Dames, the crowd, won over by the religious fervor of Etienne's socialism, becomes enraged at his rival Chaval. Infuriated by his unwillingness to strike, the crowd hounds him with clenched fists, threats and cries of "Kill him." Chaval artfully diverts the "murderous instinct" with a promise to strike the following day.

The next morning five hundred strikers descend upon the Jean-Bart mines, where they discover that some miners have indeed gone down into the pits. Etienne, who has lost control of the mob, can no longer restrain them from violent retribution. The owner of the mine narrowly escapes death, his mining operations are wrecked, and his workers are nearly stranded in the mines. When the strikebreakers finally scramble to the surface, they are manhandled by the crowd.

Once the crowd has whetted its lust for destruction, a crescendo of rioting begins. From mine to mine, the swelling crowd pillages all buildings in sight and assaults their colleagues who dare to work. The first victims are merely insulted and flailed, but as the day wears on, the blacklegs are stoned, stripped naked, and ridiculed before the mob. At sundown the crowd, which now numbers nearly 3,000, attacks the village of Montsou. Screaming for bread, for socialism, and for death to the bourgeois, the "horde" threatens the persons and property of the rich. The grocery is stormed, and in an effort to save his establishment, the grocer Maigrat falls to his death. His body is mutilated and quickly castrated by bands of "stampeding furies."

The arrival of the police and of occupying troops postpones the final encounter for several weeks. When the miners learn that Belgians have been imported to work the local mines, they descend upon the pits of Montsou, where they confront sixty soldiers. The strikers first insult, then stone the military, who eventually retaliate with bullets. Fourteen of the demonstrators die (including women and children); twenty-five are wounded.

In Zola's eyes, this carnage was inevitable, since crowds reduce men and women to the brutal state of nature. Any member of a crowd reverts to mankind's primal state of instinct, violence, and irrationality. Crowds, as Zola describes them, are units capable of only the most primitive levels of reasoning and prone to emotional excitation. They represent the perfect medium for instinctive catharsis; once aroused, they clamor for revenge, murder, and destruction.

The true leader of the crowd, then, is instinct. Any individual who attempts to direct and control the energies of his followers will be frustrated. Zola sharply delineated the ingratitude, even perfidy, of the mob when the miners flatly reject their old idol Rasseneur in the early stages of the strike. With a prophecy few readers could disregard, Rasseneur shouts to Etienne, the new hero of the workers: "You think it's amusing. . . . Well, I hope it happens to you. . . . And mark my words, it will happen."

But Etienne is too intoxicated with his own success to appreciate the truth of his rival's statement. That evening the crowd is his to seduce and to win. His power over the crowd, however, is short-lived. The moonlight resolution he has extracted from three thousand workers fades within twelve hours to the determinatiion of a mere five hundred. The crowd's will is not his to influence; vainly he struggles to control their lust for murder and the frenzy of destruction.

In *Germinal,* the leader acts as a mere spark in the conflagration of a strike. He can ignite, but never control, the explosion he has engendered. With "simple and energetic images," Etienne—or any other leader—can exite the passions of his followers; he can exploit their messianic fervor to the point of delirium, but no leader can restrain the instincts of an aroused crowd. Of Etienne, Zola writes, "reason tottered . . . and left only the idée fixe of a fanatic. His scruples and good sense were gone, and nothing seemed easier than the realization of this new world." And under the power of Etienne's idée fixe, the crowd is transformed into a herd of sexually excited beasts:

> And here, in this glacial night, a fury of faces
> emerged . . . their eyes shining, their mouths
> open, a band of people in heat.

Even at the moment of his triumph, Etienne's ultimate failure is presaged by Zola; no leader can restrain the instincts of an aroused crowd. Not until the final section of the novel is Etienne actually stoned by the mob, but his alienation from the workers, as well as his impotence in controlling them, have been interwoven throughout the novel.

As if to underscore the rising wave of irrationality in crowds, Zola stressed the alcoholic thirst of mobs. Under ordinary circumstances the coal miners drink beer and gin. Although they are virtually surrounded by cafés, the miners drink little during the early stages of the strike. The march on Jean-Bart, however, is accompanied by a thirst for liquor. While pillaging the canteen of La Victoire, the crowd discovers fifty bottles of gin, which disappear "like a drop of water in the sand." Symbolically, Etienne succumbs that day to the ineradicable compulsion for drink he has inherited from his alcoholic parents. Drunkenness, as Zola has already warned, unleashes the "lust for murder." Sober, Etienne has at least the possibility of restraining the base instincts of the mob; inebriated, he nearly murders his rival Chaval and loses whatever slender restraining influence he might have had upon his "Flemish" followers.

As Zola suggests, Etienne's loss of control has particularly dire consequences, since the miners of Montsou come from Flemish stock. Unlike the impetuous but relatively innocuous crowds of the Midi, Flemish crowds are slow to anger and singularly violent once they are aroused: "All the old Flemish blood was there, heavy and placid, taking months to warm up, but then giving in to abominable savageries . . . until the beast in them was drunk with atrocities."

As the crowd storms through the villages around Montsou, Etienne—and Zola—are most terrified by the atrocities of women. Throughout *Germinal,* women act as the agents of destruction. When first admitted to the mass deliberations, they stand as quiet, as solemn "as if in church." But their initial decorum rapidly crumbles as they are intoxicated by Etienne's rhetoric and by the contagious atmosphere of the crowd. As they visualize the socialist "cathedral" of the future pictured by their leader, the men become resolute and inspired, the women, "delirious."

Because of their excitability, women are the first to threaten violence, the first to gratify their savage instincts. During the day of general pillage, the females push, scream, and exhort the men to lynch the bourgeois, and in a scene reminiscent of a "witches' sabbath," they gleefully destroy machines and flog the strikebreakers. In the ultimate confrontation between workers and soldiers, it is the women who precipitate the shooting by heaving stones at the military. Throughout *Germinal,* Zola positioned women at the forefront of the crowd. They precede the men, he explained, for strategic reasons, because neither soldier nor policeman would dare to attach the "gentle sex." Yet, in another sense, their primacy has a symbolic value as well, since women—as Zola described them—are the instigators and the most merciless perpetrators of violence.

The women's acts of stoning and machine-breaking serve as vivid proofs of female irascibility, but Zola pushed the image to an even more dramatic and threatening level. Five instances of sexual assault occur in *Germinal;* all five are enacted by women. As a mark of provocative disdain for the bourgeoisie and for the military, La Mouquette twice bares her buttocks, a gesture which Zola interpreted as "fierce" and certainly not amusing. In two other scenes, the band of "savage furies" pounces upon a female strikebreaker and the charitable young Cécile with the express purpose of sexual humiliation. The working-class girl is stripped of her clothes, her nakedness exposed to the laughing crowd. The assault upon the middle-class Cécile is less successful, since she is rescued before her pantaloons are removed. Had she not been snatched from the wild women, Cécile would surely have lost more than her veil.

Such sexual attacks were shocking to nineteenth-century readers, but none could compare with the horrifying castration of the grocer Maigrat. Again, it is the women who perform the mutilation, an act so bestial that it stuns even the male members of the mob. Like "she-wolves," the women dance around the dead body of the grocer, hurling insults and seeking revenge for the decades of sexual abuse he has heaped upon them. With their "claws and teeth bared," they maul his body, stuff his mouth with dirt, castrate him, and parade about the crowd with the "abominable trophy." Thus Zola drew his vision of female aggressive "hysteria" to its dramatic and psychological climax. (pp. 98-104)

In writing *Germinal,* Zola entertained at least three ambitions: to explore, as he put it, "the most painful and burning subject of our epoch," to unravel the causes of violent uprisings, and to create an epic poem of rebellion. Even before he sifted through the accounts of miners' strikes, Zola had determined to push the violence in *Germinal* to the "last possible degree." For Zola as for Taine, the imaginative blueprint preceded research, and as he wrote, he decided that castration represented the ultimate act of violence, the most apt symbol of revolution.

Such a nightmare of female sexual frenzy fit into Zola's dark world of eros, a world that stretched far beyond the mining towns of northern France. Its contours were shaped in part by the official wisdom of late nineteenth-century science but greatly amplified by the private universe of Zola's own fantasies and fears. Both Zola the artist and Zola the man were haunted by the vast subterranean world of instinct and primal passions. Freely confessing his terror in the presence of crowds or in the dark and enclosed spaces of tunnels or mines, Zola repeatedly projected upon women the most destructive image of sexuality. Throughout the Rougon-Macquart series, Zola depicted women with sexual feelings as femmes fatales, destroyers of family fortunes, individual reputations, even of artistic creativity. In the mid-eighties, Zola, much like the frustrated engineer Hennebeau, was both envious and fearful of the relatively free expression of sexuality among miners. Interpreting their mores as sex in its raw and uninhibited state, Zola used the castration scene to dramatize in extremis his own persistent association of violence and sexual passion.

Although the private sources of their anxiety differed, Zola, like Taine, came to couple revolution with the spectre of castration. (pp. 105-06)

But although Zola's vision of the crowd and his artful science owed much to Taine, it would be misleading to view *Germinal* as the direct fictional transposition of the *Origines.* In the act of composing *Germinal,* Zola moved closer to a sympathetic understanding of his workers and the crowd; Taine's research, however, only redoubled his horror and disdain for his "bestial" subjects. At the beginning of 1884, Zola had told Edmond de Goncourt that his next "social novel" would feature the strangulation of a bourgeois on its first page. As he immersed himself in the documents, however, and as he came to know the miners of Anzin, Zola substantially modified his outline and humanized his protagonists. Bonnemort's strangulation of Cécile occurs not on the first page but toward the end of the novel and under "extenuating circumstances": the senile old man has lost control of his senses. Similarly, the castration is not, in any legal sense, a crime. Maigrat, after all, is mauled only after he has fallen to his death, and both before and during that graphic scene, Zola underscored the "justice" of the horrible act. Those hysterical "furies" were avenging long years of sexual abuse in kind. Unlike the mobs in the *Origines,* Zola's crowd was almost wholly composed of local residents, who, under all but the most extraordinary circumstances, were lawful and resigned to their lot. Even the prostitute, La Mouquette, was depicted as a decent human being, vital, generous, and humane. Zola's crowds, in short, were not the faceless *canaille* ["rabble"]; their desperate acts of violence were, in Zola's eyes, a savage but comprehensible reaction to a dehumanizing, indeed immoral, system. Reducing men to beasts, he warned, made bestial retaliation inevitable.

Beyond Zola's empathy, both the ending and the grandiose title of his novel set it apart from the tradition of the *Origines.* The Montsou strike had clearly failed, yet rebellion, successful rebellion, would soon spring up throughout the "decadent nations." In his final sentence, Zola summarized his faith in that cause: "Men were springing up, a black avenging army was slowly germinating in the furrows, thrusting upwards for the harvest of the next century. And very soon their germination would crack the earth asunder."

The very title of the novel, taken from the seventh month of the republican calendar, strengthened the image of the revolutionary rejuvenation. Despite his initial misgivings about its "mystical" overtones, Zola adopted the title because it was a "patch of sunlight which illuminates the entire work.... It represents a revolutionary April, the flight of a decrepit society toward springtime.''

That ''patch of sunlight'' illuminates even more clearly differences between Taine and Zola. Both men saw their epoch as the battleground of egalitarianism; Taine detested the movement, and Zola hoped that the worst of social inequities would be banished. For the vision of an ideal society, Taine looked back, somewhat inaccurately, to the Middle Ages; Zola looked to the future. . . . In writing *Germinal*, Zola assumed that his audience was blind, rather than callously insensitive, to the ugliness and inhumanity which had accompanied the industrial revolution. It was the system, not the individual *rentiers* [''stockholders''] or the managers themselves, which had produced such degradation; it was the system which ruined both workers and small businessmen. In *Germinal* Zola struggled to make affluent contemporaries see what had theretofore been invisible: the squalid life of industrial workers. ''Look beneath the earth,'' he pleaded; ''see those miserable creatures who work and suffer . . . but bring justice quickly . . . otherwise the danger is that the earth will open up and nations will sink in the most horrifying cataclysms in history. By appealing to the eyes and the hearts of his readers, and simultaneously playing upon their worst fears of revolution, Zola tried to force men to ''see'' and to act upon their knowledge. There was still time to avoid the apocalypse. (pp. 107-110)

In writing *Germinal*, Zola had stepped from genealogy to violence; his contemporaries were quick to observe how timely and incisive that shift was. For the critic and naturalist Henry Céard, *Germinal*'s sharp portraits captured ''our epoch, where the social question is posed with an explosive violence.'' *Germinal* reflected the explosiveness of French society in the eighties; it anticipated, too, the escalation of violence in the early nineties.

Zola, circa 1888.

As even Zola's political adversaries would concede, the beauty and dramatic focus of *Germinal* lay in its rendering of the crowd. Céard hailed Zola's crowds as ''the source of the incontestable grandeur of *Germinal*.'' Jules Lemaître, the noted critic and Academician, eloquently concurred. *Germinal,* he proposed, was not the history of an individual or an isolated strike; it represented the epic poem of all workers, all strikes, all crowds. M. Zola, he argued, ''has magnificently rendered the fatal, blind, impersonal, irresistible nature of a drama of this sort; the contagion of assembled anger, the collective soul of crowds—violently and easily infuriated.'' Even after his death in 1902, writers both conservative and socialist praised Zola as the epic poet of crowds.

Of all the examples of late nineteenth-century crowd psychology, Zola's *Germinal* was undoubtedly the most widely read. . . . So intensely did Zola believe in the social message of his novel that he allowed any newspaper or periodical to reproduce *Germinal* without charge. No other French tract on crowds reached so large and politically so diverse an audience. Such a broad public could read *Germinal* in a variety of ways: as an artistic triumph, as the epic poem of crowds, as a rare affirmation, as a cry for reform, as the prologue to revolution. (pp. 111-12)

> Susanna Barrows, ''Metaphors of Fear: Women and Alcoholics'' and ''The Crowd and the Literary Imagination: Emile Zola's 'Germinal','' in her Distorting Mirrors: Visions of the Crowd in Late Nineteenth-Century France, *Yale University Press, 1981, pp. 43-72, 93-113.**

PHILIP WALKER   (essay date 1984)

[*Walker is an American critic who has written extensively on Zola and his works. In the following excerpt from his* ''Germinal'' *and* Zola's Philosophical and Religious Thought, *Walker contends that throughout* Germinal *Zola expressed his pantheistic view of life.*]

Over and over again in Zola's works we find evidence of a persistent struggle to meet . . . [the] needs for, on the one hand, escapist reveries, and, on the other hand, a serious new faith: a large stock of heterogeneous ideas that possessed spiritual value for him and—fashioned out of them—a whole array of more or less different daydreams, visions, professions of faith, idealistic philosophies, ''new religions'' leaping far beyond the restrictions imposed by his positivism and strongly contrasting with his pessimism. (p. 23)

Of course, a secular faith does not necessarily have to be religious in any of the narrower senses of the term, and it is true that many of the ideas Zola invested with religious or quasi-religious worth may not seem to most readers particularly religious. Like many other nineteenth-century thinkers, he seemed at times to use such words as *religion, religious, sacred,* and *holy* loosely. Yet we cannot study this side of his character without being impressed by its authentically religious dimensions. An atheist only in the sense that he had rejected the Christian deity, he never denied the existence of some kind of supreme being. On the contrary, he was always, to borrow Tillich's terminology, vitally concerned with that ultimate reality to which we give the symbolical name of God. . . . Moreover, it would seem that Zola was subject at certain privileged moments to genuinely religious experiences: overwhelming urges to worship, Kierkegaardian leaps of faith, divine revelations, beatific visions, mystical union with the supreme forces of reality. Anything short of a true religion was incapable of permanently satisfying him, and this was one of the reasons, we may gather, why he was always moving restlessly from one of his new personal "religions" or religious-substitutes to another.

His persistent tendency to sacralize his central values—nature, love, life, force, work, science, progress, humanity, France, etc.—or even at times, as we shall see, to deify one or another of them is also indicative of the essentially religious orientation and thrust of his thought. So also is his compulsion to employ traditional religious models. He had a penchant for basing characters on biblical figures—e.g., Adam and Eve, Jacob, Lazarus, or Christ—or for introducing into his fiction variations on biblical events (e.g., the Flood) or parts of the Christian cosmos (e.g., Paradise or Hell). Commencing with the still partly Christian profession of faith in his letter of August 10, 1860, to Baille . . . , he more than once cast his beliefs of this or that moment in forms reminiscent of Christian creeds, the best known being Pascal's Creed, in *Le Docteur Pascal.* Not only in such early works as **"Paolo," "Doute," "Religion,"** and the Prologue to *La Genèse,* but here and there throughout his writings, we discover him composing prayers for himself or his fictional alter egos. . . . Zola also created rites reminiscent of Christian rites like the elaborate public religious ceremony modeled on the Eucharist in *Travail.* In *Vérité,* his last novel, posthumously published in 1903, he imagined a "scientific catechism" meant to replace the Catholic catechism. If he included in his last fictional series four "Gospels" instead of three, as originally planned, it was in order to match the four Gospels of the New Testament, Matthew, Mark, Luke, and John. Not surprisingly, the heroes of the three "Gospels" that he completed are Mathieu, Marc, and Luc, and the hero of the fourth, "Justice," would have been named Jean.

The degree of seriousness with which Zola may have embraced any of the visions, creeds, and whole new faiths that he created or associated himself with over the years is debatable. Some he may never have thought of as more than purely escapist dreams. Each of the credos he inserts in his writings has an air of conviction about it; yet we cannot help but notice that he never repeats the same credo twice. (pp. 24-6)

Yet whether he ever absolutely believed in any of these visions, creeds, and whole new faiths, there can be no question as to their importance to him both as a man and as an artist—or as to the urgency of his desire for an acceptable secular faith or the sincerity of his commitment to his prophetic vocation. Like Michelet, one of the principle sources of his thought, he accepted the Viconian thesis that religion is the central feature of any civilization—or of any individual personality, for that matter. "It is impossible to know a people," he had once observed, we recall, "without a complete knowledge of its religious beliefs. . . . I am convinced that an archeologist and a scientist, an historian and an artist must know the gods before they can know men. Tell me whom you worship, and I will tell you who you are." . . . For such a man, it was essential that a civilization which, like his own, was in the process (or so he believed) of losing its traditional faith should have a new one to replace it. At issue was nothing less than an existential *sine qua non.* More than one of his earliest works are already "gospels" in the same sense as his last series of novels, that is to say, works conceived of as means of promulgating ideas of religious value, if not the rudiments of a new faith. (p. 26)

[The] Zola whom we are discussing here was indeed a true pantheist at heart, and there is much in *Germinal* which can be construed as reflective of the pantheism, or, more precisely,

several forms of pantheism, he associated himself with at one time or another.

Pantheism, as we know, can be defined as the tendency to view the world as a single whole of closely interrelated parts, with nothing beyond it, and either to regard this whole as divine and the proper object of worship or to assume that it contains some divine indwelling principle.

The tendency to conceive of the world as a single whole of closely interrelated parts, with nothing beyond it, was undoubtedly one of Zola's most persistent traits. Following in the footsteps of Hugo and the other romantics, he took part in the modern endeavor to break down traditional distinctions between subject and object, the self and the world, the material and the spiritual, the conscious and the unconscious, the divine and the profane, the world and its creator. (p. 27)

This monistic bent, an essential element of his pantheism, may also be seen in his attachment to a number of traditional concepts presupposing the unity, or close-knit coherence, of nature. (p. 27)

This tendency to conceive of the world as a single whole can be seen also in Zola's rejection of the old dualism between body and soul, matter and spirit. (p. 28)

Inspired by the same monistic vision, Zola also emphasizes just as frequently the numerous affinities that he perceived between the animal and vegetable kingdoms. (p. 29)

Throughout Zola's writings, images suggesting resemblances between human beings and seeds, human lives and the life cycles of plants, point in the same metaphysical direction. (p. 30)

Driven by his longing for immortality and abhorrence of death, he habitually emphasized, moreover, the irrepressible persistence of life. In writing **"Printemps: Journal d'un convalescent,"** he had thought in terms of "the great battle, the eternal battle, of life against death" . . . , but as he grew older and his fear of death more obsessive, he was tempted more and more to regard death as not so much the foe of life as an essential part of the life process and therefore good and acceptable, always preparing the way for new life, fertilizing the ground. He also liked to think that, since life is universal, therefore omnipresent, it must be present even in death—that death is not annihilation as he sometimes assumed, but, like birth, just another phase of life. "Birth, death, these are only states, words; she [Earth] creates only life. (p. 33)

Zola's exaltation of fecundity—women, children, potent males, the acts of procreation and giving birth—and his concomitant obsession with seminal imagery (including the equation of sap with semen) are also deeply rooted in his cult of life. He always regarded as of great worth everything that contributes to the life process: rivers irrigating the land, for example, or the warm springtime sun. At those moments when exaltation of life dominated his thinking, he tended to assume, whatever he might maintain at other moments, that the supreme task of every man, woman, and other being is to reproduce, that the unique purpose of life must forever be to bring forth ever more abundant life. . . .

A stubborn, instinctive (or so it has seemed to such critics as Anatole France) confidence in life and tendency to revere, worship, deify life were indeed among Zola's most persistent traits. In moments of despondency, he turned to his faith in life for succor. (p. 34)

However, alongside Zola's pantheistic cult of life, we can also discern in many of his works a veritable cult of love.

This cult, too, had strong pantheistic characteristics. Love, as Zola defined it, was first and foremost passionate love, love between the sexes. But he defined the word very broadly, denoting by it not only passionate love, maternal love, filial love, fraternal love, friendship, love for God, the sense of solidarity binding human groups together, the affection that we feel for animals—an affection which, he insisted, was a distinct form of love, not to be confounded with any other . . .—but also every kind of attraction. Love, in Zola's opinion, included "the great fraternity of the trees and the waters" . . . , the "loves of a flower" . . . , and "the tranquil, universal love of the earth, which gives nourishing juices to every seed." . . . Love, in Zola's opinion, even included universal gravitation. He liked to think of all the celestial bodies held in place "by a law of love." . . . (p. 35)

Moreover, just as, at certain moments, Zola liked to suppose that life is the chief principle of all being, at other moments, he conceived of love (which, it must be admitted, he often treated as synonymous with life) as fulfilling the same cosmic function. This idea, which was probably as deeply rooted in his childhood Christianity as in his classical education and adolescent romanticism, is implicitly or explicitly expressed in many of his writings, including writings from every major period of his career. (pp. 35-6)

Can we not quite legitimately discern reflections of one or more of these same interrelated yet somewhat divergent pantheistic visions in *Germinal*? Can we not regard this novel as in part a product of the same tendency, first of all, to conceive of the world, nature, reality, as a single whole of closely interrelated parts with nothing beyond it and, secondly, to look upon either this Great Whole or one or another of its three leading indwelling principles—life, love, and work—as identical with God?

Certainly, even those critics who may question whether *Germinal* can be absolutely proven to be a pantheistic work strictly speaking must admit that it expresses quite as unmistakably as most of Zola's other major novels the same monism which in many of his writings does assume an unmistakably pantheistic form. Indeed, in no other major novel does he employ more intensively most of the poetic procedures that he uses elsewhere to suggest the tight kinship, the strong affinities, the common destiny uniting everything with everything else.

The epically vast cast of characters includes numerous animals—Bonnemort's yellow horse, the chaffinches competing in the singing contest, the red cat that startles us as it leaps out of the shadows just before the collapse of Le Voreux, the dog howling during the same disaster, Souvarine's pet rabbit, Pologne, and the two mine horses Bataille and Trompette. Zola, true to his monistic vision of reality (and the immense sense of solidarity with animals that went along with this vision), gives these dumb creatures an important place in the narrative, thoroughly integrating them, as he would have said, into "the great ark." As if to drive home the point of our common nature, he shows them, like all his other fictional animals, suffering and loving along with his human characters, sharing with themm some of the same sentiments and dreams, completing them, confounded with them, caught up in the same life, subject to the same fate. The same bitterly cold March wind that makes Etienne's hands bleed in the opening scene blows up on end the hair of Bonnemort's long-suffering horse's coat. Both the old man and the horse move with the same sommnambulistic motions. The hundred and eighty finches, blinded, each in its darkened cage, egged on to sing in such furious rivalry that some collapse and die, are victims of the same exploitative system as their owners, the Marchiennes nailworkers, and the Montsou miners cheering them on. Bataille and Trompette labor along with the human workers in the endless subterranean night, and their friendship with each other has something nobly human about it. They share with the human workers the same longings for deliverance, the same obsessive dreams of sunlight and green fields. Bataille's and Catherine's death scenes complement each other, reinforce each other. Each is as memorable as the other. Pologne's suffering as Jeanlin drags her along with a piece of string tied round her neck, "on her belly or her back, just like a pull-toy" . . . , is as excruciating to watch as any human martyrdom, and when Souvarine pales at the thought that he has just, without knowing it, devoured his pet, cooked up in Madame Rasseneur's stew, there is nothing funny about it. We sympathize with his shock and grief.

But the cast of *Germinal* not only contains animals; it also includes, quite as much as any other Zola novel, representatives of the vegetable and mineral kingdoms: the beets and wheat, the thick vegetation around the abandoned Réquillart mine shaft . . . , the giant beeches and frozen moss of the Forest of Vandame, the mines, the wind, fire, and rain, the Torrent, the clouds, moon, sun, and stars. And here, too, Zola, undoubtedly spurred by the same monism, poetically erases the distinctions separating the different categories of reality, decompartmentalizing creation, endowing plants and so-called inanimate objects with attributes we normally ascribe to man or beast. . . . [The] giant beeches, the moon, the sky, are capable of feeling, if nothing else, at least a vast indifference to human woes. Marcel Girard is probably right in intimating that the thick vegetation, full of copulating couples, around the rim of the Réquillart shaft represents in Zola's imagination the mine monster's pubic hair. . . . The engine of Le Voreux squatting solidly on its masonry base becomes in Part VII, Chapter iii, a reclining giant. Nor must we forget the train of carts and the black flood water that turn into reptiles, or how, toward the end of the novel, the vision of the mines as hell gives way to that of the earth as a giant womb, still another biological image. (pp. 38-40)

[Plants] and objects in *Germinal* are caught up in the same drama as man and beast. In this hungry novel, we recall, even the winds in Part I, Chapter i, cry famine. In the mob scenes in Part V, even the sun shares in the carnage, soaking the rampaging strikers in the blood of its dying light. At the sight of the murdered soldier Jules, the clouds flee in horror. . . . Just before Le Voreux goes down, watched by the aghast crowd, the weathercock on the headframe creaks in the wind "with a tiny shrill cry—the single, sad voice of these huge buildings destined to die." . . . Then the square tower housing the "gasping" drainage pump falls over "on its face like a man cut down by a cannonball." The engine, torn from its masonry base, its limbs outspread, struggles against death. "It moved," Zola tells us, "it stretched its connecting rod, its giant knee, as though to rise, but then it died—was shattered and engulfed." . . . The Montsou strike is not just an isolated human event, but a universal disturbance, a giant storm involving all nature as well as man, foreshadowed in the sea-tempest imagery of the overturelike first chapter—the wind coming in "mid-sea bursts," the "blinding darkness of the shadows" buffeting Etienne on the jetty-straight road . . .—and reaching two climaxes in the human flood thundering across the plain in Part V and the cosmic deluge evoked in Part VII.

Furthermore, Zola not only brings out the animality of man . . . , but also transforms human characters into vegetables and minerals. In Part IV, Chapter viii, the crowd of strikers is poetically turned into a wave, a flood, a stormy sea. Elsewhere, Bonnemort becomes "an old tree twisted by the wind and the rain." . . . La Brûlé, her breast torn open by a soldier's bullet, falls forward, "crackling like dry firewood." . . . Just after Le Voreux drops into the abyss, members of the fleeing, shrieking crowd are swept along by horror "like piles of dry leaves." . . . Chaval's corpse looks like "the black hump of a pile of slack." . . . Along with endowing beasts, plants, and so-called inanimate things with qualities of beings higher up on the scale of creation, Zola obviously felt obliged to do the reverse. Here, too, we are justified in perceiving possible evidence of his monism—with its attendant compulsion to emphasize with metaphor and simile and every other poetic device at his disposal the essential oneness of all being. In *Germinal,* just as much as in many of Zola's other writings, we are introduced, it would seem, into a monistic reality, a reality in which everything is related, everything shares in the attributes and destiny of everything else, everything is part of the same unity.

Along with Zola's monism—and monism, as I have noted, is an essential part of any pantheistic conception of the world— *Germinal* also very probably expresses Zola's pantheistic worship of nature.

On a certain level, the chief protagonist of the novel is not, as some would say, Etienne or, as others have maintained, the embattled colliers of Montsou (or, more precisely, the whole modern industrial proletariat, for which they stand), but Nature, Earth, the Great Whole. The mass lovemaking that constantly goes on around the abandoned Réquillart mine shaft is, Zola explains, Nature's own doing:

> They would settle down, elbow to elbow, without paying any attention to their neighbors, and it was as though all around this lifeless machine, next to this shaft weary of spewing forth coal, the powers of creation were taking their revenge—unbridled love, under the lash of instinct, planting babies in the bellies of girls scarcely more than children themselves. . . .

Reviving forgotten beliefs, the miners entrapped by the inundation of Le Voreux invoke the earth, "for," as Zola goes on to say, "it was the earth that was avenging itself, making the blood flow from the vein because one of the arteries had been severed." . . . Twice in the text, the proletariat is referred to as "a force of nature." . . . Earth, Zola's symbol par excellence of Nature, the Great Whole, also dominates the concluding vision of the novel, with its evocation of men and plants surging forth from earth's womb. Since Zola seems, as we know, to have chosen very carefully the last word of each of his novels, it is also significant that *Germinal,* like *La Terre,* that great canticle to Goddess Earth, ends with the word *earth.*

But as we study *Germinal* in the light of Zola's pantheism, which, as he possibly would have been the first to admit, was not at all systematic, we would also seem to find him exalting the three major indwelling principles of his monistic universe, life, love, and work, each of which, as we have observed, he tended to sacralize and even in turn to deify.

To say that *Germinal* expresses Zola's rejection of the traditional Western belief in numerous individual lives, individual souls, in favor of the concept of a single, universal life, a single, universal soul, simply because he himself as much as says so in his letter of March 14, 1885, to Jules Lemaitre would be to succumb to what has rightly been called the intentional fallacy. Obviously, works of art do not always do exactly what their creators want them to do. Yet we do not have to know of this letter to come away from a reading of *Germinal* with the impression that it is indeed a unanimistic novel, a novel portraying the world as endowed with a single all-pervasive life, a single all-pervasive soul—Sandoz' "immense ark, where everything is animated by the breath of every being." . . . (pp. 40-2)

> *Philip Walker, in his "Germinal" and Zola's Philosophical and Religious Thought, John Benjamins Publishing Company, 1984, 157 p.*

ELIZABETH LANGLAND   (essay date 1984)

[In the following excerpt, Langland discusses Zola's view of society in Germinal.*]*

Germinal explores the relationship of workers and masters at Le Voreux mine during a crisis provoked by a disguised wage cut. Although society is focused in a particular place, that place is seen as paradigmatic of the larger world. This society is characterized by class divisions, which are represented as economic in nature; that is, *Germinal,* like other sociological novels, depicts society as a set of class relationships determined almost exclusively by wealth. Political systems reflect the economic structure. There exist rich and poor, workers and masters, the governors and the governed. The action of the novel revolves around class conflicts. The novel, in its structure and action, argues for social determinism and for the economic base of human relationships. This is the "reality" Zola wanted to stress, not an historical reality but a scientific one. He claims not to be writing a story about people who really existed but to be deriving true, general hypotheses about the behavior of human beings under certain conditions. By stressing the interdependence of individuals and environment, he is making social change a prerequisite to individual development.

Characters thus act by determinable laws. In characterization, then, the promptings of human hearts and souls are not represented. . . . Although most novelists do trace behavior at least partly to heredity and environment, they often assume there exists some larger motive or cause. Indeed, in many cases, characters ennoble themselves by transcending their heredity and environment. D. H. Lawrence tried to give this larger motive a name—"inhuman will"—and although his articulation of this concept was new, the belief in it was not. There is something more to character than inherited nature and nurture. . . . The naturalistic novelist, in contrast, concentrates on determinism by heredity and environment in order to make social reform an issue, in order to harry the social conscience. Since an individual cannot transcend his inherited nature, then it becomes imperative to alter his social environment. Only through social change can individuals grow.

In this logic, of course, morality is relative and must be seen as socially or hereditarily determined, rather than as an absolute expression of individuality and personal integrity. Moral absolutes interfere with a full revelation of the compulsion that social environment exerts on individuals. Moral behavior, rather than being a matter of social conscience, becomes a matter of social status, largely determined by material well-being. For example, in *Germinal*, La Mouquette is described as "an eighteen-year-old haulage girl. She was a strapping wench, with a bosom and buttocks that almost split her vest and breeches." A free and easy sexuality accompanies this physical endowment, but we, as readers, are not encouraged to judge or blame her for her promiscuity. In fact, her generous sexual nature is complemented by a very likable generosity in all other matters, both are simply an expression of heredity that is manifest physically. She even dies cheerfully, having shielded Catherine from bullets, but we do not see this act as a moral choice or as a complex psychological decision, a perception that would lend her character dignity. Her behavior is physiologically and socially determined.

Class and economic status also determine morality. No individual moral norms are absolute; they can shift as rapidly as social conditions shift. Until the strike at Le Voreux mine and the subsequent starvation, La Maheude violently opposes begging. Suddenly we learn that "neither Lénore nor Henri had come back from tramping the streets with Jeanlin, begging for coppers." . . . Étienne Lantier, the novel's protagonist, learns of this behavior "with aching heart. She used to threaten to kill them if they begged in the street. Now it was she who sent them out." . . . People will adopt whatever morality a situation demands. A great objection lodged against social or naturalistic novels is that they make character into mere mechanism. . . . The social novelist faces the difficult task of coupling stature and significance for his protagonists with social determinism. Zola's characters gain stature through their resentment; their moral flexibility does not prevent their bitterly resenting their subjugation and degradation. Individuals are aware of moral alternatives largely by contrast with a more dignified past. They are, after all, reflective beings, and their acute sense of degradation redeems in part their swift, amoral adjustment to new social conditions and their debasement within those conditions.

Because Zola is interested in art as well as social reform, he uses the resources of novelistic art to enhance his novel's examination of social process. In *Germinal*, Zola found the means to shape his work artistically—to create its beginning, middle, and end—without falsifying social reality. To do so, he conceived character and scene both metaphorically and objectively, and he conceived the action both in personal and in social/political terms. The novel thus has two complementary narratives.

We turn first to Zola's metaphoric conception of character. Although Zola binds most of his characters by heredity, environment, and the probabilities of the two, he also introduces various symbolic characters whose personalities and fates express the logic of his represented society. In this light, La Maheude and Maheu, with their larger concerns for justice and morality, are the matriarch and patriarch of the society. Their individual degradation charts for readers the larger degradation of society. Writers have difficulty in making readers identify with such an abstraction as society. When a fiction asks us to identify with individuals, its writer usually illustrates society's values in minor characters. Since the naturalistic novel's principal purpose is to reveal the nature of a particular society, even major characters are subsumed to that purpose. Personal development is subordinated to a desire to reveal flaws and limitations in society. For example, the patriarch Maheu—kind, considerate, and judicious—wins our sympathy through his concerned interest in Étienne and his unselfish desire to share what little meat he has with his children. As the strike

progresses, Maheu fades further and further into the background. Suddenly he is shot down by the soldiers. We know little of his motives for being in the front lines except that La Maheude has goaded him on. When Maheu is killed, it is hard to feel the sympathy one would expect for such a likable character. It seems that the traits characterizing him neither explain why he is where he is nor do they provide sufficient psychological insight into his emotions at the moment. Zola distances us from his deliberately so that Maheu's experience can represent something outside himself. The system of symbolic structures—the use of red, of anger, of violence—suggests that Maheu, from a metaphorical standpoint, is consumed just as the society is consuming itself. We focus not on the loss of one sympathetic character but on a didactic point: society structured in this way will lead to senseless bloodshed and so destroy itself. (pp. 127-30)

Maheu, then, dramatizes one immediate end of social process. Zola employs other characters—Jeanlin, Bonnemort, and Cécile—to dramatize the ultimate end of this process. Bonnemort and Cécile, although very much products of heredity and environment, also represent a final confrontation between an overfed bourgeoisie and a starved working class: "They gazed at each other in fascination, she, buxom, plump, and pink from the days of well-fed idleness of her race, he blown out with dropsy, hideous and pathetic like some broken-down animal, ravaged by a century of toil and hunger passed down from father to son." . . . Bonnemort, a figure out of the past, the paradigmatic victim of social injustice, wreaks his vengeance on the flower of the bourgeoisie, Cécile.

Jeanlin, the other symbolic character, is first described as possessing a "face, like a small, frizzy-haired monkey's, with its green eyes and big ears." . . . The evolutionary implications of this description follow later: "Unhealthily precocious, he seemed to have the mysterious intelligence and bodily skill of a human foetus reverting to its animal origins," . . . and later: "[Étienne] contemplated this child, who, with his pointed muzzle, green eyes, long ears, resembled some degenerate with the instinctive intelligence and craftiness of a savage, gradually reverting to man's animal origins. The pit had made him what he was, and the pit had finished the job by breaking his legs." . . . In the last sentence Jeanlin's character is attributed to the pit, but he represents the end of a process that has been going on, a reduction of man to his animal instincts, a reversion back to his animal origins. We are to conclude that the ultimate effect of social determinism here is the dehumanization of man. Society, which is intended to humanize, becomes an agent to destroy him. Zola makes a powerful didactic point through this character; if society does not destroy itself, in perpetuating itself in its present form, it will destroy humanity.

Zola's strongest social criticism and his only social optimism—his vision of a new society—emerge through the structure of his novel: a paralleling of metaphor with fact, of personal experience with social experience. The novel opens at night when Étienne Lantier arrives at Le Voreux mine. The narrator describes the mine both as an evil beast and as an objective thing. . . . The first sentence personifies the mine. A literal description of the works follows, and the last sentences once again personify the mine, now as an evil beast. This metaphor makes us expect and fear certain events and desire alternative ones; it makes us feel the inevitability of destruction at this point. It allows us to anticipate the developing conflict. In short, it shapes Zola's objective presentation of society in novelistic ways. More important, in this juxtaposition of metaphor and fact, Zola remains faithful to the objective reality of the world he depicts. Part of the naturalistic novelist's effect depends on persuading readers to accept the fidelity of his vision of society. Implicit in Zola's theory of the novel lies a desire *not* to be seen as tampering with social conditions and represented society in the effort to suit larger artistic ends. Hence Zola insists that the novelist sets up his experiment and lets it run by itself; he does not prejudge the results. Zola's talent as artist, however, enabled him to discover means to shape events without falsifying social reality.

In addition to conceiving character and scene both metaphorically and objectively, Zola also conceives the action in two dimensions. *Germinal* entwines complementary narratives: a personal one, which focuses on the relationship between Étienne and Catherine and is resolved in their sexual consummation, and a social one, which depicts the larger class struggle and cannot realistically be resolved since that resolution would dictate the dawn of a new era based on general equality. Unlike Thackeray's *Vanity Fair*, whose two narratives create conflicting social realities and therefore prevent the reader from arriving at a coherent set of social expectations, Zola's *Germinal* makes its two narratives share a social reality so that the expectations that shape one narrative can, by analogy, suggest a shaping to the other. The effect, then, of this intermingling of stories is that Étienne and Catherine's relationship shapes our expectations for society and ultimately allows us to anticipate another, better social reality that has its seeds in the destruction of the present one, although, in fact and realistically, society cannot change so quickly and dramatically, and our optimism is unwarranted.

Germinal begins with Étienne's arrival at Montsou. He almost decides to leave after one day in the mines, but two things detain him: "Suddenly Étienne made up his mind. Maybe he thought he saw Catherine's pale eyes up yonder, where the village began. Or perhaps it was some wind of revolt blowing from Le Voreux. He could not tell. But he wanted to go down the mine again to suffer and to fight." . . . He is attracted by a woman and a social situation. First he pursues Catherine, but, losing her to Chaval, he becomes interested in the political situation at the mines. He comes closer to Catherine for a while when he moves in with the Maheus, but she moves out to join Chaval, and her rupture with her family is mirrored by the miners' strike. Étienne becomes wholly involved in the strike, but love is also a factor in his political ambition. At the meeting in the woods, Étienne is spurred on by the thought of Catherine: "He had recognized Chaval among his friends in the front row, and the thought that Catherine must be there too had put new fire into him, and a desire to be applauded in front of her." . . . By this parallel structure, Zola has identified the romantic situation with the political one, a very important identification in the final effect of the novel.

The parallels continue. The miners seek violent retribution for injustice; Chaval and Étienne immediately thereafter come to blows over Catherine. The miners protest the importation of workers from Belgium and are shot. Catherine, too, is bloodied, but "it was the pent-up flood of her puberty released at last by the shock of that dreadful day." . . . Catherine's physical maturation suggests a maturity in the consciousness of the workers. The seeds now planted will grow to fruition. Finally, Étienne decides to return to the mine with Catherine. His love is at least a partial motive. Souvarine speculates, "When a man's heart was tied up with a woman he was finished and might as well die." . . . Étienne and Catherine have their con-

summation: he plants his seed in her womb in the bowels of the earth, a larger womb.

Although the workers return to work with seemingly no gains, we do not feel that *Germinal* is a pessimistic novel. The seed has been planted and will burst through the earth: "Men were springing up, a black avenging host was slowly germinating in the furrows, thrusting upwards for the harvests of future ages. And very soon their germination would crack the earth asunder." . . . Étienne's hopeful lyrical speculations on society would be unwarranted without the parallel love situation and its powerful consummation. In other words, our reaction to the novel has been precisely determined by the complex interrelationship between a personal situation and a social one.

Zola lays a social situation before us in great complexity, and he refuses to resolve it except by means of this parallel relationship between Étienne and Catherine described above. In a sense there are two resolutions in *Germinal:* a personal one and a social one. The personal one is resolved in the bowels of the earth; the social is actually never resolved. The workers return to work. We would like them, after all their suffering, to win their demands, but they do not, and to this extent we feel that we are in touch with the way things happen in the real world. Zola has, in short, enhanced his didactic ends; he affirms social determinism; he illuminates the inevitable consequences of class divisions in a capitalist society. Yet, at the same time, he has used parallel structures to achieve the power of resolution in anticipated social change without warping the social reality he wants to depict. As a result, Zola has created no simple social document but a novel with a strong element of reality that propounds a social theory and urges social change and that does so by engaging us with characters for whom we deeply care. (pp. 130-34)

> Elizabeth Langland, "The Art of Sociological Naturalism in Zola and Dreiser," in her Society in the Novel, *The University of North Carolina Press, 1984, pp. 124-46.*

ADDITIONAL BIBLIOGRAPHY

Auerbach, Erich. *"Germinie Lacerteux."* In his *Mimesis: The Representation of Reality in Western Literature,* translated by Willard R. Trask, pp. 493-524. Princeton, N.J.: Princeton University Press, 1953.*
    Discusses the influence of Jules and Edmond de Goncourt's novel *Germinie Lacerteux* on the novels of Gustave Flaubert, Charles Baudelaire, Zola, and others. Auerbach asserts that Zola "stands out boldly from among the group of the aesthetic realists," adding that errors and limitations found in Zola's works do not "impair his artistic, ethical, or especially his historical importance."

Baguley, David. "The Function of Zola's Souvarine." *Modern Language Review* LXVI, No. 4 (October 1971): 786-97.
    Contrasts the characterization and function of Souvarine and Etienne in *Germinal*.

Bellos, David. "From the Bowels of the Earth: An Essay on *Germinal.*" *Forum for Modern Language Studies* XV, No. 1 (January 1979): 35-45.
    Psychoanalytical interpretation of *Germinal,* which Bellos regards as a "social and political novel of a past age . . . that is also an involuntary and efficient exercise in mass psychotherapy."

Berg, William. "A Note on Imagery as Ideology in Zola's *Germinal*." *Clio* 2, No. 1 (October 1972): 43-5.
　　Examines Zola's use of imagery in the novel to convey his views on capitalism and the working class, as well as his understanding of their roles in history.

Bethke, Frederick J. "Realism in Zola: The Miners of Montsou." *The North Dakota Quarterly* 32, No. 3 (Summer 1964): 64-5.
　　Discusses isolated passages in *Germinal* and *L'assommoir* which the critic considers unrealistic, tasteless, and grotesque. While Bethke considers Zola's artistic flaws minor, he concludes that one "wishes that Zola would be either sufficiently gauche to let us toss his books in the trash . . . or sufficiently polished so we could enjoy them undisturbed.

Brady, Patrick. "Phenomenon, Imitation, Epiphany: Gates of Ivory within Gates of Horn." *L'Esprit Createur* XVIII, No. 2 (Summer 1978): 76-81.*
　　Identifies manifestations of the occult in novels by Abbé Prévost (*Manon Lescaut*), Michel Butor (*La modification*), and Zola (*Germinal*) as proof that "even the most naturalistic novel may rely heavily on the subliminal effect of concealed myth structures."

————. "Lukács, Zola, and the Principle of Contradiction." *L'Esprit Createur* XXI, No. 3 (Fall 1981): 60-8.*
　　Defense of Zola, whom Grant calls "a great socialist writer I believe to have been grievously maligned by Georg Lukács."

Caute, David. "Realism and Reality." In his *The Illusion: An Essay on Politics, Theatre, and the Novel*, pp. 88-108. London: Andre Deutsch, 1971.*
　　Compares *Germinal* and Maxim Gorky's *The Mother*, a novel representing the school of socialist realism. Although Caute notes the differences in the two works' presentation and aim, he defends Zola's work against attacks by such Marxist critics as Georg Lukács on the grounds that the "positivistic naturalist school and the Marxist realists . . . share in common the assumption that literature can and should reflect social and political reality."

Cirillo, N. R. "Marxism as Myth in Zola's *Germinal*." *Comparative Literature Studies* XIV, No. 3 (Sepember 1977): 244-55.
　　Analyzes Zola's Marxian conception of class struggle in *Germinal*. Stating that *Germinal* is the "only major proletarian novel of the nineteenth century," Cirillo argues that Zola's use of Marxist theory in the novel "is purely literary: he transforms historic dialectic into historic myth and resolves . . . major western literary archetypes by means of it."

De Amicis, Edmondo. "Emile Zola." In his *Studies in Paris*, translated by W. W. Cady, pp. 178-242. New York and London: G. P. Putnam's Sons, 1887.
　　Criticism and reminiscences.

Goldberg, M. A. "Zola and Social Revolution: A Study of *Germinal*." *The Antioch Review* XXVIII, No. 4 (Winter 1967-68): 491-507.
　　Focuses upon instincts—hunger, sex, power—which motivate actions of the characters in *Germinal*. Goldberg commends Zola for giving primacy to instincts over introspection and analysis in his novel about the poor, arguing that as a result of generations of deprivation which deny "the life of the soul, the inner life," instincts replace reflection among the impoverished.

Grant, Elliott M. "Marriage or Murder: Zola's Hesitations Concerning Cecile Gregoire." *French Studies* XV, No. 1 (January 1961): 41-6.
　　Recounts Zola's artistic struggle in deciding the fate of this innocent bourgeois character. Aided by Zola's copious notes, Grant follows the author's changing view of the fate of Cecile Gregoire, and applauds his realization that in social conflicts of the type depicted in *Germinal*, "there is fortune and happiness for none, misfortune and tragedy for all."

Gregor, Ian, and Nicholas, Brian. "The Novel as Social Document: *L'assommoir* (1877)." In their *The Moral and the Story*, pp. 63-97. London: Faber and Faber, 1962.

Asserts that despite Zola's stated aims as dramatic reporter and investigator of scientific fact, his works display a "strong sense of artistic expediency," revealing that "the inclinations of the impressionist, the poet of humanity in the mass, presided at the conception of novels rather than any doctrinaire scientism."

Herbert, Eugenia W. "Naturalists and Realists." In her *The Artist and Social Reform: France and Belgium, 1885-1898*, pp. 144-79. New Haven: Yale University Press, 1961.*
　　Examines thematic and stylistic changes in the French novel of the period, considering *Germinal* and Camille Lemonnier's *Happe-Chair* "not the first novels in French to deal with the working class, but . . . the first of any importance to make the conflict of the classes their dominant motif."

Knight, Everett. "Balzac, Flaubert, Zola, Stendhal." In his *A Theory of the Classical Novel*, pp. 68-105. New York: Barnes & Noble, 1970.*
　　Includes discussions of the downfall of Gervaise in *L'assommoir* and of the conclusion of *Germinal* to illustrate that Zola's fiction disproves his theoretical assertion that poverty is a consequence of society rather than of individual identity.

Matthews, J. H. "The Art of Description in Zola's *Germinal*." *Symposium* XVI, No. 4 (Winter 1962): 267-74.
　　Analyzes the double significance of descriptive passages in Zola's novel, which Matthews states "bring his narrative to life, and at the same time exploit the latent content of the things he evokes."

Moore, George. "My Impressions of Zola." In his *Impressions and Opinions*, pp. 66-84. New York: Brentano's, 1891.
　　Reminiscence revealing Moore's changing perceptions of Zola and his works.

Niess, Robert J. "Remarks on the *style indirect libre* in *L'assommoir*." *Nineteenth Century French Studies* III, Nos. 1 & 2 (Fall-Winter 1974-75): 124-35.
　　Assesses the effectiveness of Zola's exaggerated use of the *style indirect libre* in presenting "emotions and the other pre-logical or non-logical elements that constitute our personal existence."

————. "Some Notes on Authenticity: *L'assommoir*." *Kentucky Romance Quarterly* XXVI, No. 4 (1979): 509-21.
　　Challenges the accuracy of Zola's portrait of the proletariat in *L'assommoir*, noting that Zola's preliminary work on the novel includes information that was omitted in the final work, an omission which Niess finds contributed to flaws in the depiction of the working class.

Orr, John. "Zola: *Germinal* and Tragic *Praxis*." In his *Tragic Realism and Modern Society: Studies in the Sociology of the Modern Novel*, pp. 87-98. Pittsburgh: University of Pittsburgh Press, 1977.
　　Dismisses labels applied to Zola's works (Marxist, journalistic, scientific, sentimental) as misleading. Orr considers *Germinal* Zola's greatest work because it "violates naturalist convention in practically every aspect" and is not restrained by the "shackles of heredity and physiological" theories, but rather is dominated by the conflict between capitalism and labor in a closed community.

Pasco, Allan H. "Myth, Metaphor, and Meaning in *Germinal*." *The French Review* XLVI, No. 4 (March 1973): 739-49.
　　Discusses various interpretations of *Germinal*'s ending. Pasco contends that Zola's use of traditional metaphors in the text support interpretations of the novel both as one of hope and one of despair, with the outcome of each prophecy contingent upon the course of future human action.

Peck, Harry Thurston. "Emile Zola." In his *Studies in Several Literatures*, pp. 201-23. New York: Dodd, Mead and Co., 1909.
　　Defense of Zola and his work, with a biographical sketch and information about his social and literary milieu.

Perry, Thomas Sargeant. "Zola's Last Novel." *The Atlantic Monthly* XLV, No. cclcci (May 1880): 693-99.

Review of *Nana*, which Perry regards as "shameless and disgusting."

Petrey, Sandy. "Goujet as God and Worker in *L'assommoir*." *French Forum* 1, No. 3 (September 1976): 239-50.

Questions whether the existence of the exemplary Goujet contradicts Zola's sociological explanation of the degrading effect of brutal working-class life. Petrey notes that since his hard work, long hours, and self-denying industry earn him less than a living wage, "the figure of Goujet is *L'assommoir*'s most compelling statement that society as structured mercilessly condemns workers to a bestial existence."

Place, David. "Zola and the Working Class: The Meaning of *L'assommoir*." *French Studies* XXVIII, No. 1 (January 1974): 39-49.

Examines the working notes and final text of *L'assommoir* for evidence of Zola's changing, sometimes contradictory conception of the working class. Place contends that the novel presents both a moral tale (the life of Goujet) and a social document (the life of Gervaise).

Richards, Sylvie L. F. "*The Communist Manifesto* and Idealistic Mystification in Emile Zola's *Germinal*." *French Literature Series* VII (1980): 46-53.

Discussion based on the concept that "there is a movement in the novel, away from the reality of the worker's struggle as contained in the *Communist Manifesto* (which acts as an intertext to the novel), and towards a new kind of idealistic mystification of the worker-miner."

Rosenberg, Rachelle A. "The Slaying of the Dragon: An Archetypal Study of Zola's *Germinal*." *Symposium* XXXI, No. 4 (Winter 1972): 349-62.

Examines *Germinal* as an example of an archetypal tale ending with "the defeat of the Terrible Mother," in which Zola's "extensive use of vessel symbolism and his obsessive preoccupation with the activity of devouring . . . speak forcefully of that experience."

Schor, Naomi. *Zola's Crowds*. Baltimore and London: The Johns Hopkins University Press, 1978, 221 p.

Study of crowds in the Rougon-Macquart novels as "the royal way to an understanding of some of the fundamental questions which obsessed Zola. . . . And these are the anxieties of origin and difference."

Walker, Philip D. *Emile Zola*. New York: Humanities Press, 1969, 117 p.

Provides an account of Zola's work "through a series of carefully chosen extracts" which are "accompanied by commentary and analysis, drawing attention to particular features of the style and treatment."

Wenger, Jared. "The Art of the Flashlight: Violent Techniques in *Les Rougon-Macquart*." *PMLA* LVII, No. 4, part 1 (December 1942): 1137-59.

Examines types and recurrence of violence in the series of novels.

Appendix

The following is a listing of all sources used in Volume 21 of *Twentieth-Century Literary Criticism*. Included in this list are all copyright and reprint rights and acknowledgments for those essays for which permission was obtained. Every effort has been made to trace copyright, but if omissions have been made, please let us know.

THE EXCERPTS IN TCLC, VOLUME 21, WERE REPRINTED FROM THE FOLLOWING PERIODICALS:

The Adelphi, v. II, March, 1925.

American Literature, v. 26, May, 1954. Copyright 1954, renewed 1982, by Duke University Press, Durham, NC. Reprinted by permission.

The American Review of Reviews, v. XLIII, February, 1911.

Arizona Quarterly, v. 10, Summer, 1954 for "Owen Wister: Caste Imprints in Western Letters" by Marvin Lewis. Copyright 1954, renewed 1982, by the *Arizona Quarterly*. Reprinted by permission of the publisher and the Literary Estate of Marvin Lewis.

The Athenaeum, n. 2590, June 16, 1877.

The Bookman, London, v. XLIV, April, 1913; v. XLIX, February, 1916; v. LXXXVI, July, 1934.

The Bookman, New York, v. XXIII, May, 1906; v. XXV, August, 1907; v. XLI, August, 1915; v. LIV, December, 1921; v. LVI, September, 1922.

The Canadian Bookman, v. IV, June, 1922.

The Canadian Forum, v. XIII, June, 1933.

The Canadian Magazine of Politics, Science, Art and Literature, v. LX, January, 1923.

Chicago Sunday Tribune, October 10, 1943.

The Christian Science Monitor, June 23, 1937.

Costerus, v. 7, 1973. © Editions Rodopi NV, 1973. Reprinted by permission of Humanities Press International, Inc.

The Criterion, v. II, April, 1924.

Ahmad, Jalal Al-e. From "The Hedayat of 'The Blind Owl'," translated by Ali A. Eftekhary, in *Hedayat's "The Blind Owl" Forty Years After*. Edited by Michael C. Hillmann. Center for Middle Eastern Studies, University of Texas at Austin, 1978. Copyright © 1978 by the Center for Middle Eastern Studies. All rights reserved. Reprinted by permission.

Apter, T. E. From *Thomas Mann: The Devil's Advocate*. New York University Press, 1979. © T. E. Apter 1978. Reprinted by permission of New York University Press.

Barrows, Susanna. From *Distorting Mirrors: Visions of the Crowd in Late Nineteenth-Century France*. Yale University Press, 1981. Copyright © 1981 by Yale University. All rights reserved. Reprinted by permission.

Bate, Walter Jackson. From *Criticism: The Major Texts*. Edited by Walter Jackson Bate. Harcourt Brace Jovanovich, 1952. Copyright 1952 by Harcourt Brace Jovanovich, Inc. Renewed 1980 by Walter Jackson Bate. Reprinted by permission of the publisher.

Bithell, Jethro. From *Modern German Literature: 1880-1950*. Revised edition. Methuen, 1959. Copyright © 1959 Jethro Bithell. Reprinted by permission of Methuen & Co. Ltd.

Björkman, Edwin. From *Voices of To-morrow: Critical Studies of the New Spirit in Literature*. Mitchell Kennerley, 1913.

Bleiler, E. F. From an introduction to *The Golem* [and] *The Man Who Was Born Again: Two Supernatural Novels*. By Gustav Meyrink [and] Paul Busson, edited by E. F. Bleiler, translated by Madge Pemberton [and] Prince Mirski and Thomas Moult. Dover, 1976. Copyright © 1976 by Dover Publications, Inc. All rights reserved. Reprinted by permission.

Boas, Ralph Philip and Katherine Burton. From *Social Backgrounds of American Literature*. Little, Brown, and Company, 1933.

Bogle, Leonard. From "The Khayyamic Influence in 'The Blind Owl'," in *Hedayat's "The Blind Owl" Forty Years After*. Edited by Michael C. Hillmann. Center for Middle Eastern Studies, University of Texas at Austin, 1978. Copyright © 1978 by the Center for Middle Eastern Studies. All rights reserved. Reprinted by permission.

Branch, Douglas. From *The Cowboy and His Interpreters*. D. Appleton and Company, 1926.

Brown, E. K. From *On Canadian Poetry*. Revised edition. Ryerson Press, 1944.

Browne, Douglas G. and Alan Brock. From *Fingerprints: Fifty Years of Scientific Crime Detection*. George G. Harrap & Co. Ltd., 1953.

Cadogan, Mary, and Patricia Craig. From *You're a Brick, Angela! A New Look at Girls' Fiction from 1839 to 1975*. Victor Gollancz Ltd., 1976. © Mary Cadogan and Patricia Craig 1976. Reprinted by permission of the authors.

Cady, Edwin H. From *The Light of Common Day: Realism in American Fiction*. Indiana University Press, 1971. Copyright © 1971 by Indiana University Press. All rights reserved. Reprinted by permission of the author.

Cawelti, John G. From *Adventure, Mystery, and Romance: Formula Stories as Art and Popular Culture*. University of Chicago Press, 1976. © 1976 by The University of Chicago. All rights reserved. Reprinted by permission of The University of Chicago Press and the author.

Chandler, Raymond. From *Raymond Chandler Speaking*. Edited by Dorothy Gardiner and Kathrine Sorley Walker. Houghton Mifflin, 1962. Copyright © 1962 by the Helga Greene Literary Agency. All rights reserved. Reprinted by permission of Houghton Mifflin Company.

Chandler, Raymond. From *Selected Letters of Raymond Chandler*. Edited by Frank MacShane. Columbia University Press, 1981. Letters of Raymond Chandler copyright © 1981 College Trustees Ltd. All rights reserved. Reprinted by permission of Columbia University Press.

Chesterton, Gilbert K. From *George Bernard Shaw*. John Lane Company, 1909.

Cobbs, John L. From *Owen Wister*. Twayne, 1984. Copyright 1984 by Twayne Publishers. All rights reserved. Reprinted with the permission of Twayne Publishers, a division of G. K. Hall & Co., Boston.

Collin, W. E. From *The White Savannahs*. The Macmillan Company of Canada Limited, 1936.

Cooper, Frederic Taber. From *Some American Story Tellers*. Henry Holt and Company, 1911.

Dale, Jonathan. From "Drieu la Rochelle: The War as 'Comedy'," in *The First World War in Fiction: A Collection of Critical Essays*. Edited by Holger Klein. Macmillan, 1976. © The Macmillan Press Ltd. 1976. All rights reserved. Reprinted by permission of Jonathan Dale.

Donaldson, Norman. From *In Search of Dr. Thorndyke: The Story of R. Austin Freeman's Great Scientific Investigator and His Creator*. Bowling Green University Popular Press, 1971. Copyright © 1971 by the Bowling Green University Popular Press. Reprinted by permission.

Dukore, Bernard F. From *Bernard Shaw, Playwright: Aspects of Shavian Drama*. University of Missouri Press, 1973. Copyright © 1973 by The Curators of the University of Missouri. All rights reserved. Reprinted by permission of the University of Missouri Press.

Ellis, Havelock. From an introduction to *Social Decay and Regeneration*. By R. Austin Freeman. Houghton Mifflin Co., 1921.

Etulain, Richard W. From *Owen Wister*. Boise State College, 1973. Copyright 1973 by the Boise State College Western Writers Series. All rights reserved. Reprinted by permission of the publisher and the author.

Festa-McCormick, Diana. From *The City as Catalyst: A Study of Ten Novels*. Fairleigh Dickinson University Press, 1979. © 1979 by Associated University Presses, Inc. Reprinted by permission.

Fiedler, Leslie A. From *The Return of the Vanishing American*. Stein and Day, 1968. Copyright © 1968 by Leslie A. Fiedler. All rights reserved. Reprinted with permission of Stein and Day Publishers.

Francke, Kuno. From *German After-War Problems*. Cambridge, Mass.: Harvard University Press, 1927.

Freedman, Morris. From *The Moral Impulse: Modern Drama from Ibsen to the Present*. Southern Illinois University Press, 1967. Copyright © 1967 by Southern Illinois University Press. All rights reserved. Reprinted by permission of Southern Illinois University Press.

Friedberg, Maurice. From an introduction to *The Twelve Chairs*. By Ilya Ilf and Eugene Petrov, translated by John H. C. Richardson. Vintage Books, 1961. Copyright © 1961 by Random House, Inc. All rights reserved. Reprinted by permission of the publisher.

Gallagher, Douglas. From an introduction to *The Comedy of Charleroi and Other Stories*. By Pierre Drieu La Rochelle, translated by Douglas Gallagher. Rivers Press, 1973. Introduction copyright © 1973 Rivers Press Ltd.

Gide, André. From *The Journals of André Gide: 1928-1939, Vol. III*. Translated by Justin O'Brien. Alfred A. Knopf, 1949.

Gilman, Richard. From *The Confusion of Realms*. Random House, 1969. Copyright © 1969 by Richard Gilman. All rights reserved. Reprinted by permission of Random House, Inc.

Grant, Elliott M. From *Zola's "Germinal": A Critical and Historical Study*. Leicester University Press, 1962. © Elliott M. Grant 1962. Reprinted by permission.

Gray, Ronald. From *The German Tradition in Literature: 1871-1945*. Cambridge at the University Press, 1965. © Cambridge University Press 1965. Reprinted by permission of Cambridge University Press.

Gronicka, André von. From *Thomas Mann: Profile and Perspectives*. Random House, 1970. Copyright © 1970 by Random House, Inc. All rights reserved. Reprinted by permission of the publisher.

Grover, Frédéric J. From *Drieu La Rochelle and the Fiction of Testimony*. University of California Press, 1958. Copyright © 1958 by The Regents of the University of California. Reprinted by permission of the University of California Press.

Hall, Florence Howe. From *Julia Ward Howe and the Woman Suffrage Movement*. By Julia Ward Howe, edited by Florence Howe Hall. Dana Estes & Company Publishers, 1913.

Hall, Florence Howe. From *The Story of the Battle Hymn of the Republic*. Harper & Brothers, 1916.

Haycraft, Howard. From *Murder for Pleasure: The Life and Times of the Detective Story*. Appleton-Century, 1941. Copyright 1941 by D. Appleton-Century Co., Inc. Renewed 1968 by Howard Haycraft. All rights reserved. Reprinted by permission of E. P. Dutton, a division of New American Library.

Hemmings, F. W. J. From *Émile Zola*. Oxford at the Clarendon Press, Oxford, 1953.

Henderson, Archibald. From *George Bernard Shaw: Man of the Century*. Appleton-Century-Crofts, Inc., 1956. Copyright, 1932, by D. Appleton and Company. Renewed 1960 by Archibald Henderson. Copyright, © 1956, renewed 1984, by Archibald Henderson. All rights reserved. Reprinted by permission of E. P. Dutton, a division of New American Library.

Hesse, Hermann. From *My Belief: Essays on Life and Art*. Edited by Theodore Ziolkowski, translated by Denver Lindley. Farrar, Straus and Giroux, 1974. Translation copyright © 1974 by Farrar, Straus and Giroux, Inc. All rights reserved. Reprinted by permission of Farrar, Straus and Giroux, Inc.

Hines, Thomas M. From an introduction to *The Man On Horseback*. By Pierre Drieu la Rochelle, translated by Thomas M. Hines. French Literature Publications, 1978. Copyright 1978 French Literature Publications Company. Reprinted by permission of Summa Publications, P.O. Box 20725, Birmingham, AL 35216.

Hirschman, Jack. From an afterword to *The Golem*. By Gustav Meyrink, translated by Madge Pemberton. Mudra, 1972. Copyright © 1972 by Mudra. Reprinted by permission of Jack Hirschman.

Hough, Graham. From *Image and Experience: Studies in a Literary Revolution*. Gerald Duckworth & Co. Ltd., 1960. © Graham Hough, 1960. Reprinted by permission.

Houston, John Porter. From *Fictional Technique in France, 1802-1927: An Introduction*. Louisiana State University Press, 1972. Copyright © 1972 by Louisiana State University Press. All rights reserved. Reprinted by permission of Louisiana State University Press.

Howe, Julia Ward. From *Reminiscences: 1819-1899*. Houghton, Mifflin and Company, 1899.

Howe, Julia Ward. From a poem in *Carlyle's Laugh and Other Surprises*. By Thomas Wentworth Higginson. Houghton Mifflin Company, 1909.

Hynes, Samuel. From *Edwardian Occasions: Essays on English Writing in the Early Twentieth Century*. Oxford University Press, 1972, Routledge & Kegan Paul, 1972. Copyright © 1972 by Samuel Hynes. Reprinted by permission of Oxford University Press, Inc. In Canada by Routledge & Kegan Paul Ltd.

Irwin, Robert. From "Gustav Meyrink and His Golem," in *The Golem*. By Gustav Meyrink, translated by M. Pemberton. Dedalus, 1985. Introduction copyright © Robert Irwin 1985. Reprinted by permission.

Jennings, Lee B. From "Meyrink's 'Der Golem': The Self as the Other," in *Aspects of Fantasy: Selected Essays from the Second International Conference on the Fantastic in Literature and Film*. Edited by William Coyle. Greenwood Press, 1986. Copyright © 1986 by The Thomas Burnett Swann Fund. All rights reserved. Reprinted by permission of Greenwood Press, Inc., Westport, CT.

Jones, Alun R. From *The Life and Opinions of T. E. Hulme*. Victor Gollancz Ltd., 1960. © 1960 by Alun R. Jones. Reprinted by permission.

Kamshad, H. From *Modern Persian Prose Literature*. Cambridge at the University Press, 1966. © Cambridge University Press 1966. Reprinted by permission of Cambridge University Press.

Kermode, Frank. From *Romantic Image*. Routledge & Kegan Paul, 1957. © 1957 by Routledge & Kegan Paul Ltd. Reprinted by permission.

Krieger, Murray. From *The New Apologists for Poetry*. The University of Minnesota Press, 1956.

Kronenberger, Louis. From *The Thread of Laughter: Chapters on English Stage Comedy from Jonson to Maugham*. Knopf, 1952. Copyright 1952 and renewed 1980 by Louis Kronenberger. Reprinted by permission of Alfred A. Knopf, Inc.

Lamm, Martin. From *Modern Drama*. Translated by Karin Elliott. Philosophical Library, 1953.

Langland, Elizabeth. From *Society in the Novel*. University of North Carolina Press, 1984. © 1984 The University of North Carolina Press. All rights reserved. Reprinted by permission of The University of North Carolina Press.

Leal, Robert Barry. From *Drieu la Rochelle*. Twayne, 1982. Copyright 1982 by Twayne Publishers. All rights reserved. Reprinted with the permission of Twayne Publishers, a division of G. K. Hall & Co., Boston.

Levenson, Michael H. From *A Genealogy of Modernism: A Study of English Literary Doctrine 1908-1922*. Cambridge University Press, 1984. © Cambridge University Press 1984. Reprinted by permission of Cambridge University Press.

Logan, J. D. From *Marjorie Pickthall, Her Poetic Genius and Art: An Appreciation and an Analysis of Aesthetic Paradox*. T. C. Allen & Co., 1922.

Lukács, Georg. From *Writer and Critic and Other Essays*. Edited and translated by Arthur Kahn. Merlin Press, 1970. © The Merlin Press Ltd. 1970. Reprinted by permission.

MacCarthy, Desmond. From *Portraits*. Putnam & Co. Ltd., 1931.

MacCarthy, Desmond. From *Shaw*. MacGibbon & Kee, 1951.

ISBN 0-8103-2403-2